THE SOVIET POLITY IN THE MODERN ERA

D0792567

CONTRIBUTORS TO THIS VOLUME

Jeremy R. Azrael
U.S. Department of State
Joseph S. Berliner
Brandeis University
Seweryn Bialer
Columbia University
Cyril E. Black
Princeton University
George W. Breslauer
*University of California at
Berkeley*
Zbigniew Brzezinski
Columbia University
Paul Cocks
U.S. Central Intelligence Agency
Stephen F. Cohen
Princeton University
Timothy J. Colton
University of Toronto
Murray Feshbach
Georgetown University
Thane Gustafson
The Rand Corporation
Darrell P. Hammer
Indiana University
John N. Hazard
Columbia University
Erik P. Hoffmann
*State University of New York at
Albany*
David Holloway
University of Edinburgh
Jerry F. Hough
Duke University
Amy W. Knight
U.S. Library of Congress
Robbin F. Laird
Center for Naval Analyses

David Lane
University of Birmingham
Gail Warshofsky Lapidus
*University of California at
Berkeley*
Richard Lowenthal
Free University of West Berlin
Alfred G. Meyer
University of Michigan
James R. Millar
The University of Illinois
Alec Nove
University of Glasgow
William E. Odom
U.S. Department of the Army
Henry Rowen
U.S. Central Intelligence Agency
Blair A. Ruble
*Kennan Institute for Advanced
Russian Studies*
Robert Sharlet
Union College
Alexander Shtromas
University of Salford
Konstantin M. Simis
Virginia, USA
Hedrick Smith
The New York Times
Aleksandr I. Solzhenitsyn
Vermont, USA
Ned Temko
The Christian Science Monitor
Rolf H. W. Theen
Purdue University
Robert C. Tucker
Princeton University
Stephen White
University of Glasgow

THE SOVIET POLITY
IN THE MODERN ERA

Edited by

ERIK P. HOFFMANN
State University of New York at Albany

ROBBIN F. LAIRD
Institute for Defense Analyses

Aldine Publishing Company
New York

About the Editors

Erik P. Hoffmann is Professor of Political Science, The Nelson A. Rockefeller College of Public Affairs and Policy, State University of New York at Albany, and Senior Associate, Research Institute on International Change, Columbia University. He is coauthor of *Technocratic Socialism: The Soviet Union in the Advanced Industrial Era; The Politics of Economic Modernization in the Soviet Union;* and *"The Scientific-Technological Revolution" and Soviet Foreign Policy;* editor of *The Soviet Union in the 1980s;* and coeditor of *The Conduct of Soviet Foreign Policy* and *Soviet Foreign Policy in a Changing World.*

Robbin F. Laird is Senior Researcher, Strategy, Forces, and Resources Division, Institute for Defense Analyses, Alexandria, Virginia. He is author of *France, the Soviet Union, and the Nuclear Weapons Issue;* coauthor of *Technocratic Socialism: The Soviet Union in the Advanced Industrial Era; The Soviet Union and Strategic Arms; The Politics of Economic Modernization in the Soviet Union;* and *"The Scientific-Technological Revolution" and Soviet Foreign Policy;* and coeditor of *Soviet Foreign Policy in a Changing World.*

Copyright © 1984 Erik P. Hoffmann and Robbin F. Laird.

Aldine Publishing Company
200 Saw Mill River Road
Hawthorne, New York 10532

Library of Congress Cataloging in Publication Data
The Soviet polity in the modern era.
  1. Soviet Union—Social conditions—1945–   —Addresses, essays, lectures. 2. Soviet Union—Politics and government—1953–   —Addresses, essays, lectures.
I. Hoffmann, Erik P., 1939–   . II. Laird, Robbin F. (Robbin Frederick), 1946–
HN523.5.S659 1984   306'.0947   84-3078
ISBN 0-202-24164-5
ISBN 0-202-24165-3 (pbk.)

Printed in the United States of America
10 9 8 7 6 5 4 3

To Caroline Ann Laird
and the memory of
Adrian S. Mann

CONTENTS

Introduction

I. THE HISTORICAL ROOTS

II.   LEADERSHIP AND ADMINISTRATION

III.   THE ECONOMY AND SOCIETY

IV.   CONTINUITY AND CHANGE

INTRODUCTION

Erik P. Hoffmann
Robbin F. Laird

Our purpose in compiling this anthology is ambitious. We have attempted to produce a comprehensive, integrated, and stimulating collection of major Western writings on the most important elements of contemporary Soviet politics and society. The volume focuses on political, economic, and social change and stability and their influences upon one another. We present diverse ideas and abundant information about the historical antecedents, fundamental characteristics, performance, and prospects of the present-day Soviet polity. We devote attention both to the shaping and implementation of public policies in the Soviet Union *and* to the impact of these policies on the lives of average Soviet citizens. In a word, we seek to understand the political behavior of the rulers and of the ruled.

We concentrate on the internal or domestic politics of the USSR. This anthology was designed to serve as a companion volume to *The Conduct of Soviet Foreign Policy*, 2nd edition, edited by Erik P. Hoffmann and Frederic J. Fleron, Jr. (Hawthorne, N.Y.: Aldine Publishing Company, 1980). Because the present editors consider Soviet domestic and foreign policies to be increasingly intertwined, we urge that readers consult both anthologies for an overarching analysis of the contemporary Soviet system.

Our view of the Soviet polity, then, is far-ranging. We think it is crucial to understand the historical legacies that affect the structure and functioning of the Soviet political system; the policymaking and administrative processes and the substance of national policies; the economic and social contexts within which political power is exercised; and the ways in which the Soviet polity influences and is influenced by socioeconomic and scientific-technical developments at home and abroad.

The organization of our volume reflects these concerns. Part I examines the historical roots of the current Soviet system, while Part II discusses leadership and administration. Part III investigates the economy and society, and Part IV explores the issue of continuity and change, especially as it pertains to Soviet politics in the 1980s. We juxtapose alternative interpretations of similar key themes primarily in Parts I and IV, and we present authoritative analyses of different key themes primarily in Parts II and III. However, the essays in this anthology cannot be neatly compartmentalized. Essays devoted chiefly to one topic often contain important insights and information on other topics. The reason for this lies in the nature of the Soviet polity.

The official Soviet conception of politics is much broader than Western conceptions, and the activities of the Soviet party-state are much more extensive than the combined activities of Western executive, legislative, and judicial institutions. No governmental body in the West assumes responsibility for making all major foreign and domestic political and economic decisions at the national, regional, and local levels; for "guiding" the organizations that must implement these decisions; for recruiting and deploying personnel in all leadership and administrative positions in all major bureaucracies in the country; and for designing and conducting political education programs for all citizens, both adults and children. However, these are precisely the responsibilities that the post-Stalin Communist Party of the Soviet Union (CPSU) has assumed, in accordance with the theory and practice of Leninism, and the responsibilities that the Politburo and Secretariat of the CPSU have been carrying out to the extent that they possess the knowledge and power to do so. Hence, it is fruitful—indeed, often essential—to analyze the interconnections among Russian historical traditions, Marxist-Leninist ideology, institutional relationships, policymaking, policy outputs and outcomes, public responses to policies, socioeconomic trends, scientific and technological advances, and international relations.

It is worth recalling that two of the earliest post-World War II studies of the Soviet Union stressed the reciprocal influences of the Soviet polity and its socioeconomic environment, namely, Barrington Moore, Jr.'s, *Soviet Politics—The Dilemma of Power* and Merle Fainsod's *How Russia Is Ruled.*[1]

Moore's work has a significant central theme—the impact of political ideas on social change, and vice versa. Moore carefully examines the ways in which the aims and accomplishments of Soviet leaders influenced one another in different time periods. He also judiciously emphasizes the situational constraints on Soviet policymakers, the responsiveness of party officials to rapidly changing conditions and unexpected events, and the evolving functions performed by the values, attitudes, and beliefs of political elites. For example, Moore forcefully argues that the Bolshevik "ideology of means," exemplified in the words and actions of Lenin and in the Russian revolutionary tradition, exerted a tremendous influence on the development of the Soviet political system in its formative years. This instrumental ideology, according to Moore, had a substantially greater effect on the behavior of CPSU officials than did the much less authoritarian and less clearly reasoned goals and ideals of classical and Russian Marxism.

Fainsod, too, presents a distinctive and prodigiously documented theoretical analysis and interpretation of the Soviet system. His emphasis on the concept of "totalitarianism" helps to produce an even more macrotheoretical study than Moore's, and one that profoundly influenced the questions posed by a generation of Western scholars. Rereading Fainsod, one is likely to appreciate, even more highly than before, his abilities as a social scientist, especially in the spheres of organization, communication, and modernization theories. Fainsod is not usually thought of as a "conflict" theorist because of his stress on the dictatorial nature of Soviet policymaking, but he is acutely aware of the importance of inter- and intraorganizational conflict in the implementation of national policies, and of the top leaders' continuous efforts to prevent "the pluralization of authority." Also, Fainsod fully understands that Stalin relied heavily on terror to spur socioeconomic and political transformation, and that Stalin adroitly altered career incentives and the legal system to stabilize and institutionalize many of the new socioeconomic and political relationships.

To be sure, Moore's book devotes insufficient attention to Stalinist coercion, which he subsequently analyzed in *Terror and Progress— USSR.*[2] Also, Fainsod deemphasizes organizational inputs into the policymaking process, and he tends (in the 1965 edition) to overstress the similarities between the purposes and powers of Stalin and Khrushchev. Nonetheless, the sophistication and scholarship of these early broad-gauged studies are of a high order indeed.

A generation later, students of Soviet politics are finding it even more important to take multidisciplinary and theoretically informed approaches to their subject. Scholars and policy analysts are having an increasingly difficult time distinguishing between ends and means, processes and outputs, and intent and effect in the Soviet polity. One cannot be certain that Stalin's successors pursued specific objectives primarily as ends in themselves or as means to achieve more highly valued goals. Also, policymaking procedures and substantive policies strongly influenced one another, especially under the more consensual but still oligarchical "collective leadership" of the Brezhnev period. Furthermore, the Brezhnev administration found itself increasingly locked into its own and traditional political, economic, social, military, and international commitments. The dwindling energies of the aging CPSU leaders helped to circumscribe policy alternatives and to postpone hard choices. In addition, major and minor decisions became more numerous, complex, and interrelated (with one another and with the decisions and fortunes of other socialist, capitalist, and Third World countries).

Such developments stem largely from the extraordinary scope of

Soviet politics, and from the predominance of the politics of details over the politics of principles in highly industrialized and structurally differentiated societies. To be sure, Brezhnev and his colleagues tried to formulate and implement well-informed, widely supported, feasible, and coordinated domestic and foreign policies. Brezhnev's integrated policy objectives of the early 1970s were allegedly based on "rational" or "scientifically substantiated" assessments of priorities, resources, costs, and benefits—political, economic, and social. But this set of policies, and particularly the subsequent Soviet responses to its many disappointing results, were shaped and reshaped by uneasy compromises and trade-offs among shifting bureaucratic coalitions. Also significant were Soviet officials' ongoing pursuit of personal and organizational rather than national goals, the inefficient use of pertinent information and other scarce resources, and the difficulties of coping with an awesome array of self-imposed responsibilities, mounting socioeconomic problems, and unanticipated political and economic circumstances in the international arena. Hence, incremental and reactive policies became a hallmark of the Brezhnev administration. Indeed, they became an integral part of the emerging official interpretation of "developed socialism."

Party leaders have characterized the USSR as a "Soviet but not a socialist society" from 1917 to 1936, a "socialist society" from 1936 to 1967, and a "developed socialist society" from 1967 to the present. The concept of developed socialism focuses primarily upon the structural adaptations of the Soviet polity to social, economic, scientific-technical, and international change. A balance is to be struck between traditional socialist values and behavior, on the one hand, and the modernization of the Soviet Union, spurred by the worldwide "scientific-technological revolution" (STR), on the other. Stated differently, the fundamental political, economic, and social characteristics and institutions of the USSR are to be preserved under the "radically" new conditions generated by the STR. To do so, and to increase the scientific, technical, commercial, military, and other capabilities of the Soviet system, some of its basic features are to be periodically adjusted and many of its secondary features are to be substantially altered to meet the continuous challenges posed by the STR.

In contrast to Khrushchev's conception of a rapid surge toward communism, Brezhnev's collective leadership focused upon a prolonged transitional or intermediate stage between the establishment of socialism and the attainment of communism. The ultimate goal—a classless society of material abundance and personal fulfillment—remained, but this idea was projected so far into the future that it was of little significance in shaping the specific policies and policymaking procedures of the transition period. Precisely because the utopian goals of development have become more distant, Soviet perspectives on the processes and structures of the transition have become increasingly important.

Briefly stated, the Brezhnev administration conceptualized developed socialism more and more in *procedural* rather than *substantive* terms, and the distinction between ends and means, or between what Western observers have called communist "goal culture" and "transfer culture," was increasingly blurred in Soviet theory and practice.[3] The distinction between successful and unsuccessful national policies, and the responsibility for initiating and implementing specific policies, were likewise blurred. Indeed, the establishment or maintenance of certain policymaking practices and institutional relationships, rather than the attainment of particular policy outcomes, may have been a chief aim of many party and state officials during the Brezhnev years. If policies were formulated in regularized and agreed-upon ways, the results were, by definition, feasible, legitimate, and "progressive."

The contributors to the present volume offer many insights into the reciprocal influences of the Soviet polity and its changing domestic and international environments. The authors are distinguished journalists, government officials, and scholars specializing chiefly in politics, economics, sociology, and history. All are Westerners or former Soviet citizens currently living in the West. Many of their essays are seminal, some have been revised and updated specifically for this collection, and one (Cyril Black's) is published here for the first time. The editors' contribution has been to identify the key elements of contemporary Soviet politics and society, to construct a mosaic of thought-provoking, succinct, and well-documented studies, and to make them available to a wide audience. The reader new to the subject can learn much in a short amount of time from these selections, and the reader knowledgeable about certain (even many) aspects of the Soviet system can add to his or her knowledge of other topics and the linkages among topics.

One of our contributors, Aleksandr Solzhenitsyn, raises key methodological as well as substantive issues, and seriously questions the capacity of Western analysts to understand the nature of the Soviet political system. Solzhenitsyn contends that Western scholars often ape the conceptual orientation of official Soviet spokesmen, and that Westerners consequently ignore or distort the realities of Soviet political and social life. Robert C. Tucker, directly,[4] and the other contributors to this volume, indirectly, respond to Solzhenitsyn. All would affirm that they have judiciously and independent-mindedly used the best available approaches and data to add to Western knowledge about important aspects of Soviet politics. The reader must judge for himself or herself the significance of the topics chosen by Western researchers, the appropriateness of their methodologies, and the persuasiveness of their argumentation and evidence.

We have designed this volume for undergraduate and graduate courses in comparative politics and in all of the disciplines that comprise Soviet area studies; for scholars and journalists concentrating on Soviet politics, economics, society, culture, and history; for United States and foreign government officials; for professionals in fields such as business, law, science, technology, and military affairs; and for the general reader with the time to study or peruse only one book on the Soviet Union.

We hope that this anthology will contribute to Western understanding of the Soviet polity in the contemporary era. We believe that policymakers, professionals, and informed citizens should be exposed to diverse ideas and approaches and to pertinent information from a wide variety of disciplines. Also, we seek to foster greater awareness of what is not and perhaps cannot be known about certain issues, and keener sensitivity to the various degrees of speculation inherent in different interpretations, arguments, and evidence. Furthermore, we wish to elucidate some of the values and assumptions that have undergirded Western analyses of the nature and performance of the Soviet system. Thus, we are not grinding a methodological, ideological, or any other kind of axe. Our chief objectives are to encourage Westerners to think more critically, judiciously, and imaginatively about the contemporary Soviet polity; to comprehend better its origins, basic characteristics, socioeconomic setting, and likely future development; and to appreciate more fully the fascination and frustrations of scholarly and policy-relevant research in a most significant field.

Notes

[1]Barrington Moore, Jr., *Soviet Politics—The Dilemma of Power* (New York: Harper & Row, 2nd ed., 1965); Merle Fainsod, *How Russia Is Ruled* (Cambridge, Mass.: Harvard University Press, 2nd ed., 1965). Our discussion of these two works draws from Erik P. Hoffmann's examination of various general studies on Soviet politics, "The Soviet Union: Consensus or Debate?" *Studies in Comparative Communism*, 8 (Autumn, 1975), pp. 231–244. For an extensively revised and enlarged edition of *How Russia Is Ruled*, see Jerry Hough and Merle Fainsod, *How the Soviet Union Is Governed* (Cambridge, Mass.: Harvard University Press, 1979).

[2]Barrington Moore, Jr., *Terror and Progress—USSR* (New York: Harper & Row, 2nd ed., 1966).

[3]See, for example, Chalmers Johnson, ed., *Change in Communist Systems* (Stanford: Stanford University Press, 1970), especially the introduction by the editor; and Frederic J. Fleron, Jr., ed., *Technology and Communist Culture: The Socio-Cultural Impact of Technology Transfer under Socialism* (New York: Praeger, 1977), especially the introduction and conclusion by the editor.

[4]Solzhenitsyn first published his essay in *Foreign Affairs*, 58, 4 (Spring, 1980); criticisms by Tucker and other writers appeared in *Foreign Affairs*, 58, 5 (Summer, 1980) and 59, 1 (Fall, 1980). Solzhenitsyn responded to his critics in *Foreign Affairs*, 59, 1 (Fall, 1980). The original article and entire debate have been reprinted in Aleksandr Solzhenitsyn, *The Mortal Danger: How Misperceptions about Russia Imperil America*, 2nd ed. (New York: Harper & Row, 1981). See especially the Solzhenitsyn-Tucker exchange regarding Tucker's article, "Stalin, the Last Bolshevik" (*The New York Times*, December 21, 1979). Tucker's essay in the present volume is a much longer rejoinder to Solzhenitsyn.

I

The Historical Roots

What is the relative importance of tsarist, Leninist, and Stalinist legacies, and how and why have they influenced the contemporary Soviet polity? These are political as well as intellectual questions that have often been debated by Western students of the USSR, Soviet dissidents, and Communist party leaders. Some emphasize that Stalinism was a natural or "necessary" outgrowth of Leninism; others emphasize that Stalin perverted or discarded key aims and achievements of Lenin. Some stress that Stalin emulated the forceful and effective "state-building" tsars, such as Ivan the Terrible and Peter the Great; others stress that Stalin's violent collectivization of the countryside, establishment of centralized planning and management, all-out commitment to heavy industry, blood purges of party and state officials, creation of a personal dictatorship, and imposition of tight controls on intellectual, artistic, and religious expression were flagrant attacks on the basically positive legacy of the tsars. Some affirm that substantial changes have taken place in Soviet policymaking and policies since Stalin's death in 1953, and that Khrushchev and Brezhnev made considerable efforts to apply Leninist principles (e.g., the primacy of the party) to dramatically new socioeconomic and scientific–technical conditions in the USSR and abroad; others affirm that Stalin laid the basic political, economic, and social foundations of the current Soviet system during the rapid collectivization and industrialization drives of the early 1930s and that the essential elements of Stalinism remain intact and continue to dominate the thinking and behavior of Soviet leaders and citizens today. And some underscore the similar autocratic traditions of the tsarist and Soviet polities; others underscore the ongoing competition between conservative and reformist tendencies in nineteenth-century Russia and throughout the Soviet era, especially during the New Economic Policy (1921–1928) and post-Stalin periods and even during "the third revolution" (1929–1934) and Stalin's one-man rule (1935–1953).

These are among the major issues discussed in the four significant chapters that follow. All of the authors emphasize the importance of historical legacies on successive stages in the development of the Soviet polity. But each author emphasizes the importance of different legacies or attributes different importance to a similar legacy. Hence, diverse interpretations of contemporary Soviet politics are presented.

3

1 ALEKSANDR I. SOLZHENITSYN

The Mortal Danger*

Two Fallacies about Communism   Anyone not hopelessly blinded by his own illusions must recognize that the West today finds itself in a crisis, perhaps even in mortal danger. One could point to numerous particular causes or trace the specific stages over the last sixty years that have led to the present state of affairs. But the ultimate cause clearly lies in sixty years of obstinate blindness to the true nature of communism.

I am not concerned here with those who cherish, glorify, and defend communism to this day. To such people, I have nothing to say. Yet there are many others who are aware that communism is an evil and a menace to the world, but who have nevertheless failed to grasp its implacable nature. And such individuals, in their capacities as policy advisers and political leaders, are even now committing fresh blunders which will inevitably have lethal repercussions in the future.

Two mistakes are especially common. One is the failure to understand the radical hostility of communism to mankind as a whole—the failure to realize that communism is irredeemable, that there exist no "better" variants of communism; that it is incapable of growing "kinder," that it cannot survive as an ideology without using terror, and that, consequently, to coexist with communism on the same planet is impossible. Either it will spread, cancer-like, to destroy mankind, or else mankind will have to rid itself of communism (and even then face lengthy treatment for secondary tumors).

*Reprinted by permission of the author and Claude Durand from *The Mortal Danger: How Misperceptions about Russia Imperil America*, 2d ed. (New York: Harper & Row, 1981), pp. 1–71. Copyright 1980 by Aleksandr I. Solzhenitsyn. Translated from the Russian by Michael Nicholson and Alexis Klimoff.

The second and equally prevalent mistake is to assume an indissoluble link between the universal disease of communism and the country where it first seized control—Russia. This error skews one's perception of the threat and cripples all attempts to respond sensibly to it, thus leaving the West disarmed. This misinterpretation is fraught with tragic consequences; it is imperiling every nation, Americans no less than Russians. One will not have to await the coming of future generations to hear curses flung at those who have implanted this misapprehension in the public awareness.

I have written and spoken at length about the first of these errors, and in so doing have aroused considerable skepticism in the West, but agreement seems to be increasing with the passage of time and as the lessons of history are assimilated.

The present essay is mainly devoted to the second fallacy.

Russia and the USSR

To begin with, there is the careless and inaccurate use of the words *Russia* and *Russian* in place of *USSR* and *Soviet*. (There is even a persistent emotional bias against the former: "Russian tanks have entered Prague," "Russian imperialism," "Never trust the Russians," as against "Soviet achievements in space" and "the triumphs of the Soviet ballet.") Yet it ought to be clear that these concepts are not only opposites, but are *inimical*. *Russia* is to the Soviet Union as a man is to the disease afflicting him. We do not, after all, confuse a man with his illness; we do not refer to him by the name of that illness or curse him for it. After 1917, the state as a functioning whole—the country with its government, policies, and armed forces—can no longer be referred to as Russia. It is inappropriate to apply the word *Russian* to the present authorities in the USSR, to its army, or to its future military successes and regimes of occupation throughout the world, even though the official language in each case might be Russian. (This is equally true of both China and Vietnam, only in their case no equivalent of the word *Soviet* is available.) A certain American diplomat recently exclaimed: "Let Brezhnev's Russian heart be run by an American pacemaker!" Quite wrong! He should have said "Soviet heart." Nationality is determined not by one's origins alone but also by the direction of one's loyalties and affections. A Brezhnev who has connived at the ruin of his own people in the interests of foreign adventures has no Russian heart. All that his ilk have done—to destroy the national way of life and to pollute nature, to desecrate national shrines and monuments, and to keep the people in hunger and poverty for the last sixty years—shows that the communist leaders are alien to the people and indifferent to its suffering. (This is equally true of the ferocious Khmer Rouge, the Polish functionary who may have been reared by a Catholic mother, the young communist activist, taskmaster over a group of starving coolies, or the stolid Georges Marchais with his Kremlin-like exterior; each has turned his back on his own nationality and has embraced inhumanity.)

For present-day purposes, the word *Russia* can serve only to designate an oppressed people denied the possibility of acting as one entity or to denote its suppressed national consciousness, religion, and culture. Or else it can point to a future nation liberated from communism.

There was no such confusion in the 1920s when progressive Western opinion exulted over bolshevism: the object of its enthusiasm was then named *Soviet* outright. During the tragic years of the Second World War, the concepts *Russian* and *Soviet* seem to have merged in the eyes of the world (a cruel error, which is discussed below). And with the coming of the cold war, the animosities generated were then directed principally toward the word *Russian*. The effects are being felt to this day; in fact, new and bitter accusations have in recent years been leveled against all things Russian.

Ignorance through Scholarship

The American reader receives his information about and forms his understanding of Russian history and the present-day Soviet Union chiefly from the following sources: American scholars (historians and Slavists), American diplomats, American correspondents in Moscow, and recent émigrés from the USSR. (I am not including Soviet propaganda publications, to which less credence is given lately, or the impressions of tourists, which, thanks to the skillful efforts of Intourist, remain altogether superficial.)

When American historical scholarship is confronted with the paucity of Soviet sources and with their Marxist distortion, then, for all its apparently unlimited scope and freedom from prejudice, it often unwittingly adopts the Procrustean framework provided by official Soviet historiography and, under the illusion of conducting independent research, involuntarily duplicates the approach and sometimes even the methodology of Soviet scholarship, in imitation of which it then duly skirts certain hidden and carefully hushed-up topics. It is sufficient to recall that until the most recent times, the very existence of the Gulag Archipelago, its inhuman cruelty, its scope, its duration, and the sheer volume of death it generated, were not acknowledged by Western scholarship. To take a further example, the mighty outbreaks of spontaneous popular resistance to communism in our country between 1918 and 1922 have been quite disregarded by scholars in the West, and where they have been noted, they are termed *banditry*, in line with Soviet parlance (e.g., by Moshe Lewin).[1] In overall evaluations of Soviet history, we still encounter the raptures with which "progressive" public opinion in Europe greeted the "dawning of a new life," even as the terrorism and destruction of 1917–1921 were at their height in our country. And to this day, many American academics seriously refer to "the ideals of the revolution," when in fact these "ideals" manifested themselves from the very first in the murder of millions of people. Nor has Russia's distant past been spared the distorting effects of fervent radical thought in the West. In recent years, American scholarship has been noticeably dominated by a most facile, one-dimensional approach, which consists in explaining the unique events of the twentieth century, first in Russia and then in other lands, not as something peculiar to communism, not as a phenomenon new to human history, but as if they derived from primordial Russian national characteristics established in some distant century. This is nothing less than a racist view. The events of the twentieth century are explained by flimsy and superficial analogies drawn from the past. While communism was still the object of Western infatuation, it was hailed as the indisputable dawning of a new era. But ever since communism has had to be condemned, it has been ingeniously ascribed to the age-old Russian slave mentality.

This interpretation currently enjoys wide support, since it is so advantageous to many people: if the crimes and vices of communism are not inherent to it, but can be attributed entirely to the traditions of old Russia, then it follows that there exists no fundamental threat to the Western world; the rosy vistas of détente are preserved, together with trade and even friendship with communist countries, thereby ensuring continued comfort and security for the West; Western communists are freed from incrimination and suspicion ("they'll do a better job; theirs will be a really good communism"); and a burden falls from the conscience of those liberals and radicals who lent so much of their fervor and their assistance to this bloody regime in the past.

Scholars of this persuasion treat the history of the old Russia in a correspondingly peremptory manner. They permit themsleves the most arbitrary selection of phenomena, facts, and persons and accept unreliable or simply false versions of events. Even more striking is their almost total disregard for the spiritual history of a country that has been in existence for 1000 years, as though (as Marxists argue) this has had no bearing upon the course of its material history. It is regarded as essential when studying the history and culture of China or Thailand, or any African country, to feel some respect for the distinctive features of that culture. But when it comes to the 1000 years of Eastern Christianity in Russia, Western researchers by and large feel only astonishment and contempt: why ever did this strange world, an entire continent, persistently reject the Western view of things? Why did it refuse to follow the manifestly superior path of Western society? Russia is categorically condemned for every feature which distinguishes her from the West.

Richard Pipes's book, *Russia under the Old Regime*,[2] may stand as typical of a long series of pronouncements that distort the image of

Russia. Pipes shows a complete disregard for the spiritual life of the Russian people and its view of the world—Christianity. He examines entire centuries of Russian history without reference to Russian Orthodoxy and its leading proponents (suffice it to say that St. Sergius of Radonezh, whose influence upon centuries of Russian spiritual and public life was incomparably great, is not once mentioned in the book, while Nil Sorsky is presented in an anecdotal role).[3] Thus, instead of being shown the living being of a nation, we witness the dissection of a corpse. Pipes does devote one chapter to the church itself, which he sees only as a civil institution and treats in the spirit of Soviet atheistic propaganda. This people and this country are presented as spiritually underdeveloped and motivated, from peasant to tsar, exclusively by crude material interests. Even within the sections devoted to individual topics, there is no convincing, logical portrayal of history but only a chaotic jumble of epochs and events from various centuries, often without so much as a date. The author willfully ignores those events, persons, or aspects of Russian life which would not prove conducive to his thesis, which is that the entire history of Russia has had but a single purpose—the creation of a police state. He selects only that which contributes to his derisive and openly hostile description of Russian history and the Russian people. The book allows only one possible conclusion to be drawn: that the Russian nation is antihuman in its essence, that it has been good for nothing throughout its thousand years of history, and that as far as any future is concerned, it is obviously a hopeless case. Pipes even bestows upon Emperor Nicholas I the distinction of having invented totalitarianism. Leaving aside the fact that it was not until Lenin that totalitarianism was ever actually implemented, Mr. Pipes, with all his erudition, should have been able to indicate that the idea of the totalitarian state was first proposed by Hobbes in his *Leviathan* (the head of the state is here said to have dominion not only over the citizens' lives and property, but also over their *conscience*). Rousseau, too, had leanings in this direction when he declared the democratic state to be "unlimited sovereign" not only over the possessions of its citizens, but over their *person* as well.

As a writer who has spent his whole life immersed in the Russian language and Russian folklore, I am particularly pained by one of Pipes's "scholarly" techniques. From among some forty thousand Russian proverbs, which in their unity and their inner contradictions make up a dazzling literary and philosophical edifice, Pipes wrests those half dozen (in Maxim Gorky's tendentious selection) that suit his needs and uses them to "prove" the cruel and cynical nature of the Russian peasantry. This method affects me in much the same way as I imagine Rostropovich would feel if he had to listen to a wolf playing the cello.

There are two names that are repeated from book to book and article to article with a mindless persistence by all the scholars and essayists of this tendency: Ivan the Terrible and Peter the Great, to whom—implicitly or explicitly—they reduce the whole sense of Russian history. But one could just as easily find two or three kings no whit less cruel in the histories of England, France, or Spain, or indeed of any country, and yet no one thinks of reducing the complexity of historical meaning to such figures alone. And in any case, no two monarchs can determine the history of a 1000-year-old nation. But the refrain continues. Some scholars use this technique to show that communism is possible only in countries with a "morally defective" history, others in order to remove the stigma from communism itself, laying the blame for its incorrect implementation upon Russian national characteristics. Such a view was voiced in a number of recent articles devoted to the centenary of Stalin's birth, for instance in a piece by Professor Robert C. Tucker (*The New York Times*, 21 December 1979).

Tucker's short but vigorous article is astounding: surely this must have been written 25 years ago! How can a scholar and student of politics persist to this day in misunderstanding so fundamentally the phenomenon of communism? We are confronted yet again with those familiar, never-fading ideals of the revolution, which the despicable Stalin ruined by ignoring Marx in favor of the abominable lessons of Russian history. Professor Tucker hastens to salvage socialism by suggesting that Stalin was not, after all, a *genuine* socialist! He did not act in accordance with Marxist theories but trod in the footsteps of that wearisome pair, Ivan the Terrible from the sixteenth century and Peter the Great from the eighteenth. The whole Stalin era, we are to believe, is a *radical reversion* to the former tsarist era and in no wise represents a consistent application of Marxism to contemporary realities; indeed, far from carrying on the Bolshevik cause, Stalin contributed to its destruction. Modesty prevents me from asking Professor Tucker to read at least the first volume of *The Gulag Archipelago* and better still all three. But perhaps that would refresh his memory of how the communist police apparatus, which would eventually grind up some sixty million victims, was set up by Lenin, Trotsky, and Dzerzhinsky, first in the form of the Cheka, which had unlimited authority to execute unlimited numbers of people without trial; how Lenin drew up in his own hand the future Article 58 of the Criminal Code, on which the whole of Stalin's Gulag was founded;[4] and how the entire Red Terror and the repression of millions of peasants were formulated by Lenin and Trotsky. *These* instructions, at least, Stalin carried out conscientiously, albeit only to the extent of his limited intellectual abilities. The only respect in which he ventured to depart from Lenin was his destruction of the Communist Party leadership for the purpose of strengthening his own power. But even here he was merely enacting a universal law of vast and bloody revolutions, which invariably devour their own creators. In the Soviet Union it used to be said with good reason that "Stalin is Lenin today," and indeed the entire Stalin period is a direct continuation of the Lenin era, only more mature in terms of its results and its long, uninterrupted development. No "Stalinism" has ever existed, either in theory or in practice; there was never any such phenomenon or any such era. This concept was invented after 1956 by intellectuals of the European Left as a way of salvaging the "ideals" of communism. And only by some evil figment of the imagination could Stalin be called a "Russian nationalist"—this of the man who exterminated fifteen million of the best Russian peasants, who broke the back of the Russian peasantry, and thereby of Russia herself, and who sacrificed the lives of more than thirty million people in the Second World War, which he waged without regard for less profligate means of warfare, without grudging the lives of the people.

Just what "model" could Stalin have seen in the former, tsarist Russia, as Tucker has it? Camps there were none; the very concept was unknown. Long-stay prisons were very few in number, and hence political prisoners—with the exception of terrorist extremists, but including all the Bolsheviks—were sent off to exile, where they were well fed and cared for at the expense of the state, where no one forced them to work, and whence any who so wished could flee abroad without difficulty. But even if we consider the number of nonpolitical prisoners at forced labor in those days, we find that it amounted to less than one ten-thousandth of the population of Gulag. All criminal investigations were conducted in strict compliance with established law, all trials were open and defendants were legally represented. The total number of secret police operatives in the whole country was less than that presently available to the KGB of the Ryazan district alone; secret police departments were located only in the three major cities and even there surveillance was weak, and anyone leaving the city limits immediately escaped observation. In the army there was no secret intelligence or surveillance whatsoever (a fact which greatly facilitated the February Revolution), since Nicholas II considered any activity of this type an insult to his army. To this we may add the absence of special border troops and fortified frontiers and the complete freedom to emigrate.

In their presentation of prerevolutionary Russia, many Western historians succumb to a persistent but fallacious tradition, thereby to some extent echoing the arguments of Soviet propaganda. Before the outbreak of war in 1914, Russia could boast of a flourishing manufacturing industry, rapid growth, and a flexible, decentralized economy; its inhabitants were not constrained in their choice of economic activities, distinct progress was being made in the field of workers' legislation, and the material well-being of the peasants was at a level that has never been reached under the Soviet regime. Newspapers were free from preliminary political censorship (even during the war), there was complete cultural freedom, the intelligentsia was not restricted in its activity, religious and philosophical views of every shade were tolerated, and institutions of higher education enjoyed inviolable autonomy. Russia, with her many nationalities, knew no deportations of entire peoples and no armed separatist movements. This picture is not merely dissimilar to that of the communist era, but is in every respect its direct antithesis. Alexander I had even entered Paris with his army, but he did not annex an inch of European soil. Soviet conquerors never withdraw from any lands on which they once have set foot—and yet these are viewed as cognate phenomena! The "bad" Russia of old never loomed ominously over Europe, still less over America and Africa. She exported grain and butter, not arms and instructors in terrorism. And she collapsed out of loyalty to her Western allies, when Nicholas II prolonged the senseless war with Wilhelm instead of saving his country by concluding a separate peace (like Sadat today). Western animosity toward the former Russia was aroused by Russian revolutionaries in emigration, who propounded crude and simplistic views inspired by their political passions; these were never counterbalanced by responses or explanations from Russia, since no one there had any conception of the role of "agitation and propaganda." When, for example, on 9 January 1905, tragic events culminated in the death of about a hundred people during a St. Petersburg demonstration (no one was arrested), this came to be regarded as an inerasable stigma, a shameful episode which amply characterizes Russia. Yet the Soviet Union is not constantly reproached for the 17 June 1953, when 600 demonstrators in Berlin were killed in cold blood and 50,000 more arrested. Indeed, such episodes seem to inspire respect for Soviet strength: "We must seek a common language."

Somehow, over the years, the friendship that existed between Russia and the young, newly formed United States in the eighteenth century has been forgotten. Hostility toward Russia gained ground from the early twentieth century on. We are still witnessing its consequences today. But today, these are much more than just remote sentiments; they threaten to lead the entire Western world into a fatal error.

Misinformation by Informants

With American scholars demonstrating such a fundamental misunderstanding of Russia and the USSR, the blunders perpetrated by politicians come as less of a surprise. Although they are ostensibly men of action, their heads are ever under the sway of current theories and their hands shackled by the exigencies of the moment.

Only the combined effect of these factors can account for the notorious resolution on the "captive nations" (Public Law 86–90), passed by the U.S. Congress on 17 July 1959 and subsequently renewed: the manifest culprit, the USSR, is nowhere identified by name; world communism is referred to as "Russian"; Russia is charged with the subjugation of mainland China and Tibet, and the Russians are denied a place on the roll of oppressed nations (which includes the nonexistent "Idel–Ural" and "Cossackia").

Ignorance and misunderstanding have clearly spread far beyond this one resolution.

Many present and former United States diplomats have also used their office and authority to help enshroud Soviet communism in a dangerous, explosive cloud of vaporous arguments and illusions. Much of this legacy stems from such diplomats of the Roosevelt school as Averell Harriman, who to this day assures gullible Americans that the Kremlin rulers are peace-loving men who just happen to be moved by heartfelt compassion for the wartime suffering of their Soviet people. (One need only recall the plight of the Crimean Tatars, who are still barred from returning to the Crimea for the sole reason that this would encroach upon Brezhnev's hunting estates.) In reality, the Kremlin leadership is immeasurably indifferent to and remote from the Russian people, a people whom they have exploited to the point of total exhaustion and near extinction, and whom, when the need arises, they will mercilessly drive to destruction in their millions.

By means of his essays, public statements, and words of advice, all of which are supposedly rooted in a profound understanding of Soviet life, George Kennan has for years had a major detrimental influence upon the shape and direction of American foreign policy. He is one of the more persistent architects of the myth of the "moderates" in the Polit-buro, despite the fact that no such moderates have ever revealed themselves by so much as a hint. He is forever urging us to pay greater heed to the Soviet leaders' pronouncements and even today finds it inconceivable that anyone should mistrust Brezhnev's vigorous denials of aggressive intent. He prefers to ascribe the seizure of Afghanistan to the "defensive impulses" of the Soviet leadership. Many Western diplomats have abandoned painstaking analysis in favor of incurable self-delusion, as we can see in such a veteran of the political arena as Willy Brandt, whose *Ostpolitik* is suicidal for Germany. Yet these ruinous ventures are the very ones honored with Nobel Prizes for Peace.[5]

I would note here a tendency which might be called the "Kissinger syndrome," although it is by no means peculiar to him alone. Such individuals, while holding high office, pursue a policy of appeasement and capitulation, which sooner or later will cost the West many years and many lives, but immediately upon retirement, the scales fall from their eyes and they begin to advocate firmness and resolution. How can this be? What caused the change? Enlightenment just does not come that suddenly! Might we not assume that they were well aware of the real state of affairs all along but simply drifted with the political tide, clinging to their posts?

Long years of appeasement have invariably entailed the surrender of the West's positions and the bolstering of its adversary. Today, we can assess on a global scale the achievement of the West's leading diplomats after 35 years of concerted effort: they have succeeded in strengthening the USSR and Communist China in so many ways that only the ideological rift between those two regimes (for which the West can take no credit) still preserves the Western world from disaster. In other words, the survival of the West already depends on factors which are effectively beyond its control.

These diplomats still fall back on their precarious assumptions about an imaginary split within the Soviet Politburo between nonexistent "conservatives" and "liberals," "hawks" and "doves," "Right" and "Left," between old and young, bad and good—an exercise of surpassing futility. Never has the Politburo numbered a humane or peace-loving man among its members. The communist bureaucracy is not constituted to allow men of that caliber to rise to the top—they would instantly suffocate there.

Despite all this, America continues to be fed a soothing diet of fond hopes and illusions. Hopes have been expressed of a split in the Politburo, with one particular version claiming that it was not in fact Brezhnev who occupied Afghanistan! Or else leading experts have offered the fancy that "the USSR will meet its Vietnam," be it in Angola, Ethiopia, or Afghanistan. (These experts and their readers may rest assured that the USSR is at present quite capable of gobbling up five more such countries, swiftly and without choking.) And again and again we are asked to set our hopes on détente despite the trampling of yet another country. (There is indeed no cause for alarm here, for even after Afghanistan the Soviet leaders will be only too happy to restore détente to the *status quo ante*—an opportunity for them to purchase all that they require in between acts of aggression.)

It goes without saying that America will never understand the USSR or fully grasp the danger it poses by relying on information from diplomats such as these.

But politicians of that ilk have lately been reinforced by recent émigrés from the Soviet Union, who have set about actively promoting their own spurious "explanation" of Russia and USSR. There are no outstanding names among them, yet they earn prompt recognition as professors and Russian specialists thanks to their sure sense of the kind of evidence that will find favor. They are persistent, outspoken, and repetitious contributors to the press of many countries, and the more or less concerted line which they take in their articles, interviews, and even books may be briefly summed up as follows: "collaboration with the communist government of the USSR, and war on Russian national consciousness." While these individuals were still in the USSR, they generally served the communist cause in various institutes, or were even actively employed for a number of years in the mendacious communist press, without ever voicing opposition. Then they emigrated from the Soviet Union on Israeli visas without actually going to Israel (the Israelis term them "dropouts"). Having reached their destinations in the West, they immediately proclaimed themselves experts on Russia, on her history and national spirit, and on the life of the Russian people today—something they could not so much as observe from their privileged positions in Moscow. The most energetic of these new informants do not even blame the Soviet system for the sixty million lives it destroyed or reproach it for its militant atheism. They condone its wholesale repression while proclaiming Brezhnev a "peacemaker" and openly urging that the communist regime in the USSR be given maximum support as the "lesser evil," the best alternative open to the West. Yet they simultaneously accuse the Russian national movement of this same kind of collaboration. The significance of the current spiritual processes in Russia is seriously misrepresented to the West. Western public opinion is being encouraged to respond with fear and even hatred to any revival in Russian national awareness, a sentiment that has been crushed almost to extinction by 60 years of communist power. In particular, contrived and disingenuous attempts have been made to link that revival with the government's calculated encouragement of anti-Semitism. For this purpose, Soviet people are portrayed as nothing but a herd of sheep, utterly incapable of forming their own conclusions about their fate over the last 60 years or of understanding the cause of their poverty and suffering, entirely dependent upon official explanations from the communist leaders, and hence quite content to accept the anti-Semitic excuses which the government foists upon them. (In actual fact, the average Soviet citizen has a far shrewder understanding of the inhuman nature of communism than has many a Western essayist and politician.)

Several of these émigrés also indulge in rather uninformed digressions into earlier periods of Russian history, in close conformity with the above-mentioned myopic school of American historiography. Of the many members of this group, we could here mention Dimitri Simes or Alexander Yanov.[6] For 17 years on end, Yanov was a loyal communist journalist, who never spoke out against the regime, but now he glibly regales his credulous American readers with distorted pictures of Soviet life or else skips lightly over the surface of Russian history, studiously avoiding its fundamental principles and blowing out one soap bubble after another. Simultaneously, and on almost consecutive pages, Yanov imputes to Russian national awareness two mutually exclusive tendencies: messianism (a bizarre fabrication) and isolationism, which for no apparent reason he regards as a threat to the rest of the world.

Given that a hostile and distorted portrayal of old Russia has been a tradition in American historical scholarship, seeds such as these are capable of bearing poisonous fruit.

The efforts of these tendentious informants have been supplemented and reinforced over the last year by a number of articles written by American journalists and in particular by Moscow correspondents of American newspapers. The gist of these articles is more of the same: the grave threat which any rebirth of Russian national consciousness is said to pose to the West; an unabashed blurring of distinctions between Russian Orthodoxy and anti-Semitism (when it is not explicitly claimed that the two are identical, they are obtrusively juxtaposed in consecutive phrases and paragraphs); finally there is the extraordinary theory according to which the rising forces of national and religious consciousness and the declining, cynical communist leaders have but a single dream—to merge together into some sort of "New Right." The only puzzling question is what has been stopping them from doing just that for all these years? Who is there to forbid it? The truth of the matter is that religious and national circles in the USSR have been systematically persecuted with the full force of the criminal code.

At first glance one is struck by how closely accounts by émigré informants and by free American correspondents coincide: if two independent sources report one and the same thing, then there must surely be something to it. But one must take into account the circumstances under which all Western correspondents have to operate in the Soviet Union: authentic Soviet life, especially life in the provinces and in the rural districts, is hidden from their view by an impenetrable wall; any trips they make out of the city are purely cosmetic, and are carefully stage-managed by the KGB; moreover, it is extremely hazardous for ordinary Soviet people in the provinces to engage in conversation with a foreigner other than at the KGB's behest. Typical is Robert Kaiser's admission that in the 4 years he spent as Moscow correspondent of the *Washington Post*, he had heard no mention whatever of the massive Novocherkassk uprising of 1962![7] The Western correspondent relies for his information upon the following: a careful screening of the vacuous and sterile official Soviet press; off-the-record comments and speculations gleaned from Western diplomats (the sources coincide!); and chance encounters with middle-level representatives of the Soviet elite (but as human material this is too shoddy and unreliable to merit serious attention). Their chief source, however, is the conversations they have with those few Muscovites who have already irrevocably violated the ban on fraternizing with foreigners; usually these are representatives of the same Moscow circles to which the aforementioned émigré informants once belonged. They are the chief source of information used in strident, doom-laden articles about the worldwide menace of Russian nationalism. And this is how some anonymous anti-Semitic leaflet in a Moscow gateway is taken up by the Western press and invested with universal significance. But it also explains why the sources so often agree: an image of the world is formed in accordance with its reflection in a single splinter of glass. In physics this is known as systematic instrument error.

But when some information happens to point in a different direction, when it fails to tally with what the Western press is presently looking for in Moscow, then it is simply suppressed. A case in point is the extremely important interview that Igor Shafarevich gave to Christopher Wren of *The New York Times*, but that was not published in the Western press. In the same way Western scholars and the Western press have been ignoring the *Herald of the Russian Christian Movement* [*Vestnik Russkogo Khristianskogo Dvizheniia*], a Paris-based journal that has been appearing for half a century; yet the journal enjoys great popularity in cultivated circles and is in fact published with their direct participation. Acquaintance with this journal would give Western commentators quite a different picture, far removed from the horrors they are wont to describe.

Only this absence of informed opinion can account for the warped view that the main problem in the USSR today is that of emigration. How can the problems of any major country be reduced to the issue of who is allowed to depart from it? Here and there in the Russian provinces (Perm was a recent example) strikes involving many thousands of starving workers have been dispersed by force of arms (paratroops have even had to be dropped onto the factory roof)—but is the West alert enough to note all this and to react to it? And what of the far-reaching process that is now under way in Russia and is scheduled for completion in ten to fifteen years, a process threatening the very survival of the Russian people? It aims at nothing less than the final destruction of the Russian peasantry: huts and villages are being razed, peasants are being herded together in multistoried settlements on the industrial model, links with the soil are being severed; national traditions, the national way of life, even apparently the Russian landscape and the national character—all are disappearing forever. And the reaction of the meager Western news media to this murderous communist onslaught on the very soul of our people? *They have not so much as noticed it!* In the first revolution (1917–1920), Lenin's curved dagger slashed at the throat of Russia. Yet Russia survived. In the second revolution (1929–1931), Stalin's sledgehammer strove to pound Russia to dust. Yet Russia survived. The third and final revolution is irrevocably under way, with Brezhnev's bulldozer bent on scraping Russia from the face of the earth. And at this moment, when Russian nationhood is being destroyed without pity, the Western media raise a hue and cry about the foremost threat to the world today—Russian national consciousness . . . .

Russia Prostrate

Moscow is not the Soviet Union. Ever since the early 1930s, general living standards in the capital have been artificially boosted above the national level—by plundering the rest of the populace, particularly in rural areas. (The same is partially true of Leningrad and of certain restricted scientific settlements.) Thus for more than half a century, the population of Moscow has had its diet artificially augmented and has been artificially maintained at a psychological level quite unlike that of the pillaged country at large. (The Bolsheviks learned the lesson of 1917, when the February Revolution broke out in hungry Petrograd.) As a result, Moscow has to come to be a special little world, poised somewhere between the USSR and the West: in terms of material comfort, it is almost as superior to the rest of the Soviet Union as the West is superior to Moscow. However, this also means that any judgments based on Moscow experiences must be significantly corrected before they may be applied to Soviet experience in general. Authentic Soviet life is to be seen only in provincial towns, in rural areas, in the labor camps, and in the harsh conditions of the peacetime army.

For my part, I spent the entire 55 years of my Soviet life in the remoter areas of the USSR, never enjoying the privileges of residence in the capital. I can thus draw upon my experiences without having to make any such correction, and my comments will consequently pertain not to Moscow but to the country as a whole.

To begin with, the West's vision has been obscured by the false cliché according to which the Russians are the "ruling nationality" of the USSR. They are no such thing and never have been at any time since 1917. For the first 15 years of Soviet power, it fell to the Russians, Ukrainians, and Byelorussians to bear the crippling, devastating blow of communism (the declining birth rates of recent years have their roots in that period), and in the process, their upper classes, clergy, cultural tradition, and intelligentsia, as well as the main food-producing section of the peasantry, were wiped out almost without trace. The finest names of the Russian past were outlawed and reviled, the country's history was systematically vilified, churches were obliterated in their tens of thousands, towns and streets were renamed in honor of executioners—a practice to be expected only of armies of occupation. But as the communists felt more firmly in control, they dealt similar blows to each of the remaining national republics in turn, acting on a principle equally dear to Lenin, Hitler, and the common thug: always crush your enemies one by one. Thus in the USSR there simply was no "ruling nationality":

the communist internationalists never had need of one. The decision to retain Russian as the official language was purely mechanical; one language after all had to serve in this capacity. The sole effect of this use of Russian has been to defile the language; it has not encouraged Russians to think of themselves as masters: just because a rapist addresses his victim in her own language, this does not make it any less of a rape. And the fact that from the end of the 1930s, the communist leadership came to be increasingly composed of men of Russian and Ukrainian origin did absolutely nothing to raise those nations to hegemony. The same law operates throughout the world (in China, too, and in Korea): to cast in one's lot with the communist leadership is to repudiate not only one's own nation but humankind itself.

But the bigger sheep yields more fleece, and so throughout the Soviet period it has been the RSFSR[8] that has borne the main brunt of economic oppression. Fearing an outbreak of national resistance, the authorities were a little more cautious in applying economic measures to the other national republics. The inhuman *kolkhoz* system was installed everywhere; nevertheless, the profit margin on a hundredweight of oranges in Georgia was incomparably more favorable than that on a hundredweight of Russian potatoes harvested with greater expenditure of labor. Each of the republics was exploited without mercy, but the ultimate degree of exploitation was reached in the RSFSR, and today the most poverty-stricken rural areas of the USSR are the Russian villages. The same is true of Russian provincial towns, which have not seen meat, butter, or eggs for decades and which can only dream of even such simple fare as macaroni and margarine.

Subsistence at such an abysmally low level—for half a century!—is leading to a biological degeneration of the people, to a decline in its physical and spiritual powers, a process that is intensified by mind-numbing political propaganda, by the violent eradication of religion, by the suppression of every sign of culture, by a situation where drunkenness is the only form of freedom, where women are doubly exhausted (by working for the state on an equal footing with men and also in the home, without the aid of domestic appliances), and where the minds of its children are systematically deprived. Public morality has declined drastically, not due to any inherent failing in the people, but because the communists have denied it sustenance, both physical and spiritual, and have disposed of all those who could provide spiritual relief, above all the priesthood.

Russian national consciousness today has been suppressed and humiliated to an extraordinary degree by all that it has endured and continues to endure. It is the consciousness of a man whose long illness has brought him to the point of death and who can dream only of rest and recuperation. The thoughts and aspirations of a family in the depths of Russia are immeasurably more modest and timid than the Western correspondent can possibly gather from his leisurely Moscow chats. This is how their thoughts run: if only the petty local communist despot would somehow quit his uncontrolled tyranny; if only they could get enough to eat for once, and buy shoes for the children, and lay in enough fuel for the winter; if only they could have sufficient space to live even two to a room; if only a church would be opened within a hundred miles of where they live; if only they were not forbidden to baptize their children and bring them up knowing right from wrong; and if only they could get father away from the bottle.

And it is *this* yearning on the part of the Russian hinterland to rise and live like men, not beasts, to regain some portion of its religious and national consciousness, which the West's glib and garrulous informants today label "Russian chauvinism" and the supreme threat to contemporary mankind, a menace greater by far than the well-fed dragon of communism, whose paw is already raised, bristling with tanks and rockets, over what remains of our planet. It is *these* unfortunates, this mortally ill people, helpless to save itself from ruin, who are credited with fanatical messianism and militant nationalism!

This is just a phantom to scare the gullible. The simple love of one's mother country, an inborn feeling of patriotism, is today branded "Russian nationalism." But no one can possibly incite to militant nationalism a country that for fifty years has not even had enough bread to eat. It is not the average Russian who feels compelled to hold other nations captive, to keep Eastern Europe encaged, to seize and arm far-off lands; this answers only the malignant needs of the Politburo. As for "historical Russian messianism," this is contrived nonsense: it has been several centuries since any section of the government or intelligentsia influential in the spiritual life of the country has suffered from the disease of messianism. Indeed, it seems inconceivable to me that in our sordid age, any people on earth would have the gall to deem itself "chosen."

All the peoples of the Soviet Union need a long period of convalescence after the ravages of communism, and for the Russian people, which endured the most violent and protracted onslaught of all, it will take perhaps 150 or 200 years of peace and national integrity to effect a recovery. But a Russia of peace and national integrity is inimical to the communist madness. A Russian national reawakening and liberation would mark the downfall of Soviet, and with it, world communism. And Soviet communism is well aware that it is being abrogated by the Russian national consciousness. For those who genuinely love Russia, no reconciliation with communism has ever been possible or ever will be. That is why communism has always been most ruthless of all in its treatment of Christians and advocates of national rebirth. In the early years, this meant wholesale execution; later, the victims were left to rot in the camps. But to this very day, the persecution continues inexorably:

Vladimir Shelkov was done to death by 25 years in the camps,[9] Ogurt-sov has already served 13 years, and Osipov twelve;[10] this winter, the completely apolitical "Christian Committee for the Defense of Believers' Rights in the USSR" was smashed;[11] the independent priests, Father Gleb Yakunin and Father Dimitri Dudko, have been arrested,[12] and the members of Ogorodnikov's Christian seminar have been hauled off to prison.[13] The authorities make no attempt to hide the fact that they are crushing the Christian faith with the full force of their machinery of terror. And at this moment, when religious circles in the USSR are being persecuted with such unmitigated ferocity, how fine and edifying it is to hear Russian Orthodoxy reviled by the Western press!

The present anti-Russian campaign by those who provide the West with its information is beginning to flourish even in the foremost American newspapers and journals, and it is of the greatest value and comfort to Soviet communism (although I do not wish to insist that the whole campaign is necessarily Soviet-inspired).

For the West, on the other hand, this campaign stands the facts on their head, inducing it to fear its natural ally—the oppressed Russian people—and to trust its mortal foe, the communist regime. The West is persuaded to send this regime lavish aid, which it so badly needs after half a century of economic bankruptcy.

When Is Communism in the Saddle?

But even a humbled, defeated, and despoiled nation continues to exist physically, and the aim of the communist authorities (whether in the USSR, in China, or in Cuba) is to force the people to serve them unfailingly as a work force or, if need be, as a fighting force. However, when it comes to war, communist ideology has long since lost all its drawing power in the USSR; it inspires no one. The regime's intention is thus obvious: to take that same Russian national sentiment that they themselves have been persecuting and to exploit it once more for their new war, for their brutal imperialistic ambitions; indeed, to do so with ever greater frenzy and desperation as communism grows ideologically moribund, in a bid to derive from national sentiments the strength and fortitude they lack. This is certainly a real danger.

The informants discussed earlier see this danger, indeed they recognize nothing *but* this danger (rather than the true aspirations of the national spirit). Hence, at their bluntest, they abuse us in advance as chauvinists and fascists, while, at their most circumspect, they argue as follows: Since you can see that any religious and national renascence of the Russian people may be exploited by the Soviet authorities for their own vile purposes, you must renounce not only this renascence but any national aspirations whatever.

But then the Soviet authorities also try to exploit the Jewish emigration from the USSR in order to fan the flames of anti-Semitism and not without success ("See that? They're the only ones allowed to escape from this hell, and the West sends goods to pay for it!"). Does it follow that we are entitled to advise Jews to forgo the quest for their spiritual and national origins? Of course not. Are we not all entitled to live our natural life on the earth and to strive toward our individual goals, without heed for what others may think or what the papers may write, and without worrying about the dark forces that may attempt to exploit those goals for their own ends?

And why should we speak only about the future? We have our recent past to draw on. In 1918–1922 throughout Russia, throngs of peasants with pitchforks (and even in some recorded cases bearing only icons) marched in their thousands against the machine guns of the Red Army; in bolshevism, they saw a force inimical to their very existence as a nation. And in their thousands, they were slaughtered.

And what of 1941–1945? It was then that communism first succeeded in saddling and bridling Russian nationalism: millions of lives were affected, and it took place in full view of the rest of the world; the murderer saddled his half-dead victim, but in America or Britain no one was appalled; the whole Western world responded with unanimous enthusiasm, and "Russia" was forgiven for all the unpleasant associations her name aroused and for all past sins and omissions. For the first time, she became the object of infatuation and applause (paradoxically, even as she ceased being herself), because this saddle horse was then saving the Western world from Hitler. Nor did we hear any reproaches about this being the "supreme danger," although that is in fact precisely what it was. At the time, the West refused even to entertain the thought that the Russians might have any feelings other than communist ones.

But what were the real feelings of the people under Soviet dominion? Here is how it was. June 22, 1941 had just reverberated into history, Old Man Stalin had sobbed out his bewildered speech,[14] and the entire working population of adult age and of whatever nationality (not the younger generation, cretinized by Marxism) held its breath in anticipation: Our bloodsuckers have had it! We'll soon be free now. This damned communism is done for! Lithuania, Latvia, and Estonia gave the Germans a jubilant welcome. Byelorussia, the Western Ukraine, and the first occupied Russian territories followed suit. But the mood of the people was demonstrated most graphically of all by the Red Army: Before the eyes of the whole world, it retreated along a 2000-kilometer front, on foot, but every bit as fast as motorized units. Nothing could possibly be more convincing than the way these men, soldiers in their prime, voted with their feet. Numerical superiority was entirely with the Red Army, they had excellent artillery and a strong tank force, yet back they rolled, a rout without compare, unprecedented in the annals of Russian and world history. In the first few months, some three million officers and men had fallen into enemy hands!

That is what the popular mood was like—the mood of peoples some of whom had lived through 24 years of communism and others but a single year.[15] For them, the whole point of this latest war was to cast off the scourge of communism. Naturally enough, each people was primarily bent not on resolving any European problem but on its own national task—liberation from communism.

Did the West see this catastrophic retreat? It could not do otherwise. But did it learn any lessons from it? No. Blinded by its own pains and anxieties, it has failed to grasp the point to this very day. Yet if it had been unflinchingly committed to the principle of *universal* liberty, it should not have used Lend–Lease to buy the murderous Stalin's help and should not have strengthened his dominion over nations which were seeking their own freedom. The West should have opened an independent front against Hitler and crushed him by *its own* efforts. The democratic countries had the strength to achieve this, but they grudged it, preferring to shield themselves with the unfortunate peoples of the USSR.

After 24 years of terror, no amount of persuasion could have enabled communism to save its skin by saddling Russian nationalism. But as it turned out (deprived of outside information in the hermetically sealed communist world, we had no way of anticipating this), another, similar scourge was bearing down on us from the West, one, moreover, with its own special antinational mission: to annihilate the Russian people in part and to enslave the survivors. And the first thing the Germans did was to restore the collective farms (whose members had scattered in all directions) in order to exploit the peasantry more efficiently. Thus, the Russian people were caught between hammer and anvil; faced with two ferocious adversaries, they were bound to favor the one who spoke their own language. Thus was our nationalism forced to don the saddle and bridle of communism. At a stroke, communism seemed to forget its own slogans and doctrines, remaining deaf to them for several years to come; it forgot Marxism, whereas phrases about "glorious Russia" never left its lips; it even went so far as to restore the Church—but all this lasted only until the end of the war. And so our victory in this ill-starred war served only to tighten the yoke about our necks.

But there was also a Russian movement which sought a third path: attempting to take advantage of this war and in spite of the odds, to liberate Russia from communism. Such men were in no sense supporters of Hitler; their integration into his empire was involuntary, and in their hearts, they regarded only the Western countries as their allies (moreover, they felt this sincerely, with none of the duplicity of the communists). For the West, however, anyone who wanted to liberate himself from communism in that war was regarded as a traitor to the cause of the West. Every nation in the USSR could be wiped out for all the West cared, and any number of millions could die in Soviet concentration camps, just as long as it could get out of this war successfully and as quickly as possible. And so hundreds of thousands of these Russians and Cossacks, Tatars and Caucasian nationals were sacrificed; they were not even allowed to surrender to the Americans, but were turned over to the Soviet Union, there to face reprisals and execution.

Even more shocking is the way the British and American armies surrendered into the vengeful hands of the communists hundreds of thousands of peaceful civilians, convoys of old men, women, and children, as well as ordinary Soviet POWs and forced laborers used by the Germans—surrendered them against their will, and even after witnessing the suicide of some of them. And British units shot, bayoneted, and clubbed these people who for some reason did not wish to return to their homeland. More amazing still is the fact that not only were none of these British and American officers ever punished or reprimanded, but for almost thirty years, the free, proud, and un-fettered press of these two countries unanimously and with studied innocence kept its silence about their governments' act of treachery. For thirty years not a single honest pen presented itself! Surely this is the most astonishing fact of all! In this single instance the West's unbroken tradition of publicity suddenly failed. Why?

At the time, it seemed more advantageous to buy off the communists with a couple of million foolish people and in this way to purchase perpetual peace.

In the same way—and without any real need—the whole of Eastern Europe was sacrificed to Stalin.

Now, 35 years later, we can sum up the cost of this wisdom: the security of the West today is solely dependent upon the unforeseen Sino–Soviet rift.

A Succession of Errors   The selfish and ruinous mistake that the West com-mitted during World War II has since been repeated time and time again, always in the fervent hope of avoiding a confrontation with communism. The West has done its utmost to ignore communist mass murder and aggression. It promptly forgave East Berlin (1953) as well as Budapest and Prague. It hastened to believe in the peaceful intentions of North Korea (which will yet show its true worth) and in the nobility of North Vietnam. It has allowed itself to be shamefully duped over the Helsinki agreement (for which it paid by recognizing forever all the communist takeovers in Europe). It seized on the myth of a progressive Cuba (even Angola, Ethiopia, and South Yemen have not sufficed to disenchant Senator McGovern), and put its faith in the alleged key to salvation represented by Eurocommunism. It solemnly participated in the interminable sessions of the sham Vienna Conference on European Disarmament. And after April 1978, it tried for almost 2 years not to notice the seizure of Afghanistan. Historians and future observers will be amazed and at a loss to explain such cowardly blindness. Only the appalling Cambodian genocide has exposed to the West the depth of the lethal abyss (familiar to us, who have lived there for 60 years), but even here, it seems, the Western conscience is already becoming inured and distracted.

It is high time for all starry-eyed dreamers to realize that the nature of communism is one and the same the whole world over, that it is everywhere inimical to the national welfare, invariably striving to destroy the national organism in which it is developing, before moving on to destroy adjacent organisms. No matter what the illusions of détente, no one will ever achieve a stable peace with communism, which is capable only of voracious expansion. Whatever the latest act in the charade of détente, communism continues to wage an incessant ideological war in which the West is unfailingly referred to as the enemy. Communism will never desist from its efforts to seize the world, be it through direct military conquest, through subversion and terrorism, or by subtly undermining society from within. Italy and France are still free, but they have already allowed themselves to be corroded by powerful communist parties. Every human being and any society (especially a democracy) tries to hope for the best; this is only natural. But in the case of communism, there is simply nothing to hope for: No reconciliation with communist doctrine is possible. The alternatives are either its complete triumph throughout the world or else its total collapse everywhere. The only salvation for Russia, for China, and for the entire world lies in a renunciation of this doctrine. Otherwise, the world will face inexorable ruin. The communist occupation of Eastern Europe and East Asia will not come to an end; indeed, there is an imminent danger of a takeover in Western Europe and many other parts of the world. The prospects for communism in Latin America and Africa have already been clearly demonstrated; in fact, any country that is not careful can be seized. There is of course the hope that things will turn out differently: that the communist aggressors will ultimately fail, like all aggressors in the past. They themselves believe that their hour of world conquest has arrived, and scenting victory, they unwittingly hasten—to their doom. But to achieve such an outcome in a future war would cost mankind billions of casualties.

In view of this mortal danger, one might have thought that American diplomatic efforts would be directed above all toward reducing the threatening might of these imperialistic "horsemen," to ensuring that they will never again succeed in bridling the national feelings of any country and drawing upon the vitality of its people. Yet, this path has not been followed; in fact, the opposite course of action has been pursued.

American diplomacy over the last 35 years presents a spectacle of sorry bumbling. The United States, only recently the dominant world power, the victor in World War II, and the leader in the United Nations, has seen a steady, rapid, and often humiliating erosion of its position at the United Nations and in the world at large, a process even its Western European allies have come to condone. It has continually declined vis-à-vis the USSR: things have reached the point where American senators make apologetic visits to Moscow in order to ensure that the debates in the Senate are not taken amiss in the Kremlin. The whole thrust of American diplomacy has been directed to postponing any conflict, even at the cost of progressively diminishing American strength.

The lesson of World War II is that only desperate, pitiless circumstances can bring about any cooperation between communism and the nation it has enslaved. The United States has not learned this lesson: the Soviet and Eastern European governments have been treated as the genuine spokesmen of the national aspirations of the peoples they have subjugated, and the false representatives of these regimes have been dealt with respectfully. This amounts to a rejection—in advance, and in a form most detrimental to American interests—of any future alliance with the oppressed peoples, who are thereby driven firmly into the clutches of communism. This policy leaves the Russian and the Chinese people in bitter and desperate isolation—something the Russians already tasted in 1941.

In the 1950s, an eminent representative of the postwar Russian emigration submitted to the U.S. Administration a project for coordinating the efforts of Russian anticommunist forces. The response was formulated by a high-ranking American official: "We have no need of any kind of Russia, whether future or past." A conceited, mindless, and suicidal answer as far as American interests are concerned. The world has now come to the point where, without the rebirth of a healthy, national-minded Russia, America itself will not survive, since all would be annihilated in the bloody clash. In that struggle it would be ruinous for America to fail to distinguish, in theory and in practice, between the communist aggressors and the peoples of the USSR so tragically drawn into the conflict. It would be disastrous to fight "the Russians" instead of communism and thereby force a repetition of 1941, when the Russians will again grasp at freedom and find no helping hand.

The day-to-day implementation of current American foreign policy has served to support this perverse and pernicious surrender of the Russian national consciousness to its communist taskmaster. And now, after 35 years of failure, American diplomacy has gambled on another short-sighted, unwise—indeed mad—policy: to use China as a shield, which means, in effect, abandoning the national forces of China as well and driving them completely under the communist yoke. (In the interests of this policy, it was even deemed acceptable to contribute Taiwan as a down payment.)

This act of betrayal is a blow to the national feelings of both Chinese *and* Russians. ("America is openly supporting our totalitarian oppressors and equipping them against us!")

I hardly dare ask where that leaves the principles of democracy. Where is the vaunted respect for the freedom of all nations? But even in purely strategic terms, this is a short-sighted policy: a fateful reconciliation of the two communist regimes could occur overnight, at which point they could unite in turning against the West. But even without such a reconciliation, a China armed by America would be more than a match for America.

The strategic error of not realizing that the oppressed peoples are allies of the West has led Western governments to commit a number of irreparable blunders. For many years, they could have had free access to the oppressed people via the airwaves. But this means was either not used at all or else used incompetently. It would have been an easy matter for America to relay television broadcasts to the Soviet Union via satellite, but it was easier still to abandon this project after angry protests from the Soviet regime (which knows what to fear). It goes without saying that this medium would require a proper appreciation for the needs and intellectual concerns of the suffering people to whom it is addressed. And it also goes without saying that offensive commercial broadcasts are not what is needed—this would merely be an affront to the hungry viewers and would be worse than nothing.

The defective information about the USSR that reaches America brings about a mutual lack of communication, and as a result Americans, too, find it difficult to understand what they look like from the other side. A case in point is the Russian section of the Voice of America (VOA), which seems to go out of its way to repel the thoughtful Russian listener from any understanding of America, to alienate his sympathies, and even to shock and distress him.

The West is incapable of creating balanced and effective broadcasts to the Soviet Union precisely because information about the USSR is received in the West in skewed and distorted form. The Russian section of the VOA, with its large staff and considerable budget, serves American interests poorly, in fact frequently does them great disservice. Apart from news and topical political commentary, hours of the daily program are filled with trite and inconsequential drivel that can do nothing but irritate the hungry and oppressed millions of listeners whose paramount need is to be told the truth about their own history. Instead of transmitting this history to them (with frequent repetition to compensate for the difficulties of radio reception), together with readings from those books the very possession of which is punishable by imprisonment in the USSR, instead of bolstering the anticommunist spirit of these potential allies of the United States, hours of radio time are filled with frivolous reports on enthusiastic collectors of beer bottles and on the delights of ocean cruises (the fine food, the casinos and discotheques are described with particular relish), with biographical details about American pop singers, any amount of sports news, which the citizens of the USSR are not prevented from knowing anyway, and jazz, which they can pick up without difficulty from any of the other foreign stations. (Hardly more felicitous is the policy of broadcasting accounts by recent Jewish immigrants to the United States, who tell in great detail about their life, their new jobs, and about how happy they are here. Since it is common knowledge in the USSR that only Jews have the right to emigrate, these programs serve no purpose except to further the growth of anti-Semitism.) It is clear that the directors of the VOA are constantly trying not to arouse the anger of the Soviet leadership. In their zeal to serve détente, they remove from their programs everything that might irritate the communists in power. There are plenty of examples of such political kowtowing to the Central Committee of the CPSU, but I will cite two instances from my own experience simply because they are easier for me to document. My statement concerning the arrest of Alexander Ginzburg on 4 February 1977 consisted of only three sentences of which the following two were cut by the censors at VOA:

> This reprisal affects people in the West far more than it might seem at first sight. It is a significant step in the unremitting and all-inclusive policy of securing the Soviet rear in order to facilitate the offensive operation which it has been conducting so successfully over the last few years and which can only be intensified in the future: an assault on the strength, spirit, and the very existence of the West.

My statement to the 1977 Sakharov Hearings in Rome was completely rejected by VOA because of the following passage:

> . . . [I would like] to hope that the spine-chilling accounts heard from your rostrum might pierce the deafness of material well-being which will respond only to the trumpet of doom but heeds no lesser sound. May they penetrate the awareness of those short-sighted individuals who are content to relax and to bask in the venomous melodies of Eurocommunism.

The chaste guardians of the VOA could not permit such words to reach the ears of its listeners in the East, or, for that matter, in the West. But this is not the worst of it: at times, the VOA dances to the tune called by the communist regime or indeed becomes indistinguishable from a Moscow radio station. A recent broadcast apropos of Tito's illness announced that there was also "joyful news" to report from Yugoslavia:

in the days of their leader's illness, thousands of citizens are eagerly joining the Party! Is this really any different from the insulting Leninist–Stalinist drivel that blares forth every day from Soviet loudspeakers? Such a broadcast can only cause Soviet listeners to doubt the mental competence of those who transmit it. And the religious program almost completely excludes Orthodox services, which are what Russian listeners most need, deprived as they are of churches. In the meager time slot available to religion as a whole, Orthodoxy is curtailed (as it is curtailed in the USSR) because it is "a religion uncharacteristic of the U.S.A." This may be so, but it is surely characteristic of Russia! And the broadcast *is* conducted in Russian.

If we add to this the fact that the broadcasts are presented in a language difficult to acknowledge as Russian (replete with crude grammatical errors, poor syntax, inadequate enunciation, and misplaced stress), then it is fair to conclude that every reasonable effort has been made to turn away Russian listeners from this radio station.

This is an inept utilization of the mightiest weapon that the United States possesses to create mutual understanding (or even an alliance) between America and the oppressed Russian people.

It is true that other Western Russian-language radio stations have similar defects. The BBC, too, shows a marked eagerness not to offend communist sensibilities and a superficial understanding of the Russian people of today; this leads to an inability to select what is genuinely important for its listeners, and many valuable hours of broadcasting time are taken up with worthless and irrelevant twaddle.

What My Letter to the Soviet Leaders Attempted To Do

For the multinational human mass confined today within the boundaries of the Soviet Union, there are only two possibilities: either a brutally imperialistic development of communism, with the subjugation of countries in many parts of the globe, or else a renunciation of communist ideology and a shift to a path of reconciliation, recovery, love of one's country, and care for one's people.

As a Russian, I find little consolation in the thought that Soviet communism might, after all, suffer defeat in the pursuit of the first alternative and that a certain number of today's bosses (those who fail to make a getaway) will face a military tribunal on the Nuremberg model. There is no comfort in this thought because the human cost of achieving this outcome would fall most heavily on the deceived and afflicted Russian people.

But how to make the second alternative attainable? It is extraordinarily difficult to achieve such an outcome with indigenous strength alone in the conditions of a communist dictatorship, especially because the rest of the world, in its blindness, shows little sympathy for our attempts to free ourselves from communism and, at best, washes its hands of us.

When I came to understand this problem, I decided 7 years ago to undertake an action which it was within my limited powers to accomplish: I wrote my *Letter to the Soviet Leaders,* in which I call on them to shake off the communist delirium and to minister to their own devastated country.[16] The chances of success were naturally almost nil, but my aim was at least to pose the question loudly and publicly. If not the current leaders, then perhaps one of their successors might take note of my proposals. In the *Letter,* I attempted to formulate the minimum national policy that could be implemented without wresting power from the incumbent communist rulers. (It would surely have been entirely unrealistic to expect them to relinquish their personal power.) I proposed that they should discard communist ideology, at least for the time being. (But how painful it would be to renounce this weapon, insomuch as it is precisely to communist ideas that the West yields most readily! . . .)

In the sphere of foreign policy, my proposal foresaw the following consequences: We were not to "concern ourselves with the fortunes of other hemispheres," we were to "renounce unattainable and irrelevant missions of world domination," to "give up our Mediterranean aspirations," and to "abandon the financing of South American revolutionaries." Africa should be left in peace; Soviet troops should be withdrawn from Eastern Europe (so that these puppet regimes would be left to face their own people without the support of Soviet divisions); no peripheral nation should be forcibly kept within the bounds of our country; the youth of Russia should be liberated from universal, compulsory military service. As I wrote: "The demands of internal growth are incomparably more important to us, as a people, than the need for any external expansion of our power."

The reaction of the addressees to my proposal was hardly surprising: they did not bat an eye. But the reaction of the Western and, in particular, the American press simply astonished me. My program was construed as conservative, retrograde, isolationist, and as a tremendous threat to the world! It would seem that the consciousness of the West has been so debilitated by decades of capitulation that when the Soviet Union, after seizing half of Europe, ventures into Asia and Africa, this evokes respect: we must not anger them, we must try to find a common language with these progressive forces (no doubt a confusion with "aggressive" here). Yet when I called for an immediate halt to all aggression, and to any thought of aggression, when I proposed that all those peoples who so wished should be free to secede, and that the Soviet Union should look to its domestic problems, this was interpreted as, and even noisily proclaimed to be, reactionary and dangerous isolationism.

But at the very least, one should be able to draw a distinction between the isolationism of the world's chief defender (the United States) and the isolationism of the world's major assailant (the Soviet Union). The former withdrawal is certainly a grave danger to the world and to peace in general, while the latter would be highly beneficial. If Soviet (and today also Cuban and Vietnamese, tomorrow Chinese) troops would cease taking over the world and would go home, whom would this endanger? Could someone explain this to me? I cannot understand to this day.

Furthermore, I never proposed any kind of total isolationism (involving cultural and economic withdrawal, for instance), nor did I call for Russia to sequester herself as if there were no one else on the globe. To my nation—an organism gravely ill after 60 years of communism and after sixty million human victims (not counting war casualties)—I offered the only advice that can be offered to someone so seriously afflicted: Stop wasting your valuable strength on fighting and pushing around healthy people; concentrate on your own recovery, conserving to this end every grain of the nation's strength. "Let us find strength, sense and courage to put our own house in order before we busy ourselves with the cares of the entire planet"; "the physical and spiritual health of the people must be the goal." I envisaged an ascent from the material and moral abyss in which the people find themselves today. Children were to be preserved from having their heads stuffed with ideology, women were to be shielded from backbreaking physical labor, men saved from alcohol, and nature protected from poison; the shattered family upbringing was to be restored; schools were to be improved, and the Russian language itself saved before it could be destroyed by the communist system. To achieve all this would require some 150 to 200 years of external peace and patient concentration on internal problems. Whom could this possibly endanger?

But this letter was a genuine address to very real rulers possessed of immeasurable power, and it was plain that the very most one could hope for would be concessions on their side, certainly not capitulation: neither free general elections nor a complete (or even partial) change of leadership could be expected. The most I called for was a renunciation of communist ideology and of its most cruel consequences so as to allow at least a little more breathing space for the national spirit; for throughout history, only national-minded individuals have been able to make constructive contributions to society. And the only path down from the icy cliff of totalitarianism that I could propose was the slow and smooth descent via an authoritarian system. (If an unprepared people were to jump off that cliff directly into democracy, it would be crushed to an anarchical pulp.) This "authoritarianism" of mine also drew immediate fire in the Western press.

But in the *Letter* I qualified this concept then and there: "an authoritarian order founded on love of one's fellow man"; "an authoritarianism with a firm basis in laws that reflect the will of the people"; "a calm and stable system" which does not "degenerate into arbitrariness and tyranny"; a renunciation, "once and for all, of psychiatric violence and secret trials, and of that brutal, immoral trap which the camps represent"; the toleration of all religions; "free art and literature, the untrammeled publication of books." I doubt that anyone can offer any temporary measures more beneficial than these to take effect after we emerge from our prison.

As concerns the theoretical question whether Russia should choose or reject authoritarianism in the future, I have no final opinion and have not offered any. My criticism of certain aspects of democracy is well known. I do not think that the will of the English people was implemented when England was for years sapped of its strength by a Labor government—elected by only 40% of the voters. Nor was the will of the German people served when the Left bloc had a majority of one seat in the Bundestag. Nor is any nation served when half the electorate is so disillusioned that it stays away from the polling booths. I cannot count among the virtues of democracy its impotence vis-à-vis small groups of terrorists, its inability to prevent the growth of organized crime, or to check unrestrained profiteering at the expense of public morality. And I would note that the terrifying phenomenon of totalitarianism, which has been born into our world perhaps four times, did not issue from authoritarian systems but, in each case, from a weak democracy: the one created by the February Revolution in Russia, the Weimar and the Italian republics, and Chiang Kai-shek's China. The majority of governments in human history have been authoritarian, but they have yet to give birth to a totalitarian regime.

I have never attempted to analyze this whole question in theoretical terms, nor do I intend to do so now, for I am neither a political scientist nor a politician. I am simply an artist who is distressed by the painfully clear events and crises of today. And in any case, the problem cannot, I think, be settled by any journalistic debate or any hasty advice, even if it be buttressed by scholarship. The answer can only emerge through an organic development of accumulated national experience, and it must be free of any external coercion.

Here I would like to point once more to the respectful consideration which scholarship has always accorded the various unique features in the cultural development of even the smallest nations of Africa or Asia. And I would simply ask that the Russian people not be denied the same kind of treatment and that we not be dictated to, just as Africa is not. The Russian people have a 1100-year-long history—longer than that of many of Russia's impatient teachers. Over this long period, the Russians have created a large store of their own traditional social concepts, which outside observers should not dismiss with a sneer. Here are a few examples. The traditional medieval Russian concept of justice (*pravda*)[17] was understood as justice in the ultimate sense. It was an ontological rather than a juridical concept, something granted by God. The social ideal was to live justly (*pravedno*), that is, live on a higher moral plane than any possible legal requirement. (This of course does not mean that everyone lived up to such precepts, but the ideal was accepted by all.) A number of Russian proverbs reflect this concern:

- The world itself weighs less than one just word (*odno slovo pravdy*).
- The Lord resides in justice (*v pravde*), not in strength.
- If all men lived justly (*po pravde*), no laws would be needed.

According to another traditional Russian concept, the truth cannot be determined by voting since the majority does not necessarily have any deeper insight into the truth. (And what we know of mass psychology would suggest that the reverse is often true.) When representatives of the entire country gathered for important decisions (the so-called Assemblies of the Land), there was no voting. Truth was sought by a lengthy process of mutual persuasion, and it was determined when final accord was reached. While the decision of the Assembly was not legally binding on the tsar, it was morally incontestable. From this perspective, the creation of *parties,* that is, of segments or parts which fight for their *partial interests* at the expense of the other segments of the people, seems an absurdity. (Indeed this is less than worthy of mankind, at least of mankind in its potential.)

It is no accident that the powerful regime before which the free world trembles (including the free Western leaders, legislators, and journalists) has made no effort more concentrated and ferocious in 60 years than its attempt to eradicate Christianity—the world view of its subjugated country. And yet they have proved incapable of destroying it!

And at this time, the latest informants hasten to persuade the West that this ever-vital Christianity is in fact the greatest danger.

Some Words of Explanation   Any public statement with social or political overtones always elicits a great deal of comment, much of it sober and scrupulous, but the distorted reactions are invariably the loudest, they acquire hysterical headlines and attempt to imprint themselves on the memory, not without occasional success. My way of life, my work habits, and principles of behavior usually preclude any response on my part to all this cacophony. But now that I have touched upon some issues of consequence, I would like very briefly to comment on a number of distortions.

Apropos of my *Letter to the Soviet Leaders* and on other occasions since then, I have been repeatedly charged with being an advocate of a theocratic state, a system in which the government would be under the direct control of religious leaders. This is a flagrant misrepresentation; I have never said or written anything of the sort. The day-to-day activity of governing in no sense belongs to the sphere of religion. What I do believe is that the state should not persecute religion, and that, furthermore, religion should make an appropriate contribution to the spiritual life of the nation. Such a situation obtains in Poland and Israel and no one condemns it; I cannot understand why the same thing should be forbidden to Russia—a land that has carried its faith through ten centuries and earned the right to it by sixty years of suffering and the blood of millions of laymen and tens of thousands of clergy.

At the same time, I was accused of propounding some kind of "way back"; one must think a man a fool to ascribe to him the desire to move against the flow of time. It was alleged that I am asking the future Russia "to renounce modern technology," albeit "on a small, non-gigantic scale."

The path that I do propose is set forth in the conclusion of my Harvard speech, and I can repeat it here: there is no other way left but—*upward*. I believe that the lavishly materialistic twentieth century has all too long kept us in a subhuman state—some of us through superabundance, others through hunger.

The Harvard speech rewarded me with an outpouring of favorable responses from the American public at large (some of these found their way into newspapers). For that reason, I was not perturbed by the outburst of reproaches that an angry press rained down upon me. I had not expected it to be so unreceptive to criticism: I was called a fanatic, a man possessed, a mind split apart, a cynic, a vindictive warmonger; I was even simply told to "get out of the country" (a fine way of applying the principle of free speech but hardly distinguishable from Soviet practice). There were indignant questions about how I dare use the phrase "our country" in reference to the one that banished me. (The point of course is that the communist government, not Russia, had deported me.) Richard Pipes brought up the "freedom of speech which so annoys Solzhenitsyn." In fact, it was stated plainly enough for all who can read that I had in mind not freedom of speech, but only the irresponsible and amoral abuse of this freedom.

But the most widespread allegation was that I "call upon the West" to liberate our people from the communists. This could not have been said by anyone who had made a conscientious effort to read and comprehend the text. I have never made any such appeal either in my Harvard address or at any time before that, indeed never once in all my public statements over the years have I appealed for help to a single Western government or parliament. I have always maintained that we shall liberate *ourselves*, that it is *our own* task, difficult as it may be. To the West, I have made but one request and offered but one word of advice.

First, the request: please do not force us into the grip of dictatorship, do not betray millions of our countrymen as you did in 1945, and do not use your technological resources to further strengthen our oppressors. And the advice: take care lest your headlong retreat lead you into a pit from which there is no climbing out.

After the Harvard speech, some members of the press asked with feigned surprise how I could defend the "right not to know." As a rule, they cut the quotation short, omitting: "not to have their divine souls stuffed with gossip, nonsense, vain talk." My answer is already expressed in that omitted passage. They pointed out reproachfully that this is the same Solzhenitsyn who, when in the USSR, struggled for the right *to know.* Yes, I did struggle for the right of the whole world to know—about the Gulag Archipelago, about the popular resistance to communism, about the millions of dead, about the famine of 1933, and the treachery of 1945. But we who have lived through these grim years are pained when the press offers us gratuitous details about a former British Prime Minister who has undergone surgery on one testicle, about the kind of blanket Jacqueline Kennedy uses, or about the favorite drink of some female pop star.

A more serious misunderstanding arose from the passage where I said that the deadly crush of life in the East has developed greater depth of character than the well-ordered life of the West. Some bewildered commentators interpreted this as praise for the virtues of communism and an assertion of the spiritual superiority of the Soviet system. Of course, I meant no such thing. This is no more than the ancient truth that strength of character comes from suffering and adversity. Oppressed and driven as they are by constant poverty, it is inevitable that many of our people are crushed, debased, warped, or dehumanized. But evil that bears down openly upon men corrupts less insidiously than does the furtive, seductive variety of evil. Direct oppression can give birth to a contrary process too—a process of spiritual ascent, even of soaring flight. Russian faces seldom, if ever, wear a token smile, but we are more generous in our support of one another. This is all done voluntarily and informally, and such sacrifices are in no sense tax deductible; indeed no such system even exists in our country. Taking risks for the sake of others is part of the moral climate in which we live, and I have more than once had occasion to witness the transformation which people from the West have undergone after living and working for a long period in Soviet conditions. It was reported that one American reader had offered his daughters one hundred dollars each to read the second volume of *The Gulag Archipelago*—but that the girls had refused. In our country, on the other hand, people read it even under threat of imprisonment. Or compare two young people—one a cowardly terrorist in Western Europe turning his bombs against peaceful citizens and a democratic government, the other a dissident in Eastern Europe stepping forth with bare hands against the dragon of communism. Compare, too, young Americans anxious to avoid the draft with the young Soviet soldiers who refused to fire upon insurgents—in Berlin, in Budapest, or in Afghanistan—and who were summarily executed (as they knew they would be!).

I can envision no salvation for mankind other than through the universal exercise of self-limitation by individuals and peoples alike. That is the spirit which imbues the religious and national renascence currently under way in Russia. It is something that I put forward as my fundamental belief in an essay entitled "Repentance and Self-Limitation in the Life of Nations," published 5 years ago in America.[18] For some reason, my opponents avoid mentioning this essay or quoting from it.

Not long ago, *The New York Review of Books* carried a prominent and ominous headline: "The Dangers of Solzhenitsyn's Nationalism." But neither the journal nor its informants had the wit to indicate in the essay thus advertised where exactly these dangers lay. Well, then, I shall help them out with some quotations from my published writings.

From my *Letter to the Soviet Leaders:*[19]

- "I wish all people well, and the closer they are to us and the more dependent upon us, the more fervent is my wish [p. 7]."
- "One aches with sympathy for the ordinary Chinese too, because it is they who will be the most helpless victims of the war [p. 16]."

From my essay on "Repentance and Self-Limitation" in *From under the Rubble:*

- We shall have to find in ourselves the resolve . . . to acknowledge our *external* sins, those against other peoples [p. 128]."
- "With regard to all the peoples in and beyond our borders forcibly drawn into our orbit, we can fully purge our guilt [only] by giving them genuine freedom to decide their future for themselves [p. 135]."
- "Just as it is impossible to build a good society when relations between people are bad, there will never be a good world while nations are on bad terms and secretly cherish the desire for revenge. . . . Among states too the moral rule for individuals will be adopted—do not unto others as you would not have done unto you [pp. 134, 137]."

So there you have the danger of "Solzhenitsyn's nationalism." This is the threat of the Russian religious and national revival.

**One Step
from the Brink** Today, Afghanistan, yesterday, Czechoslovakia and Angola, tomorrow, some other Soviet takeover—yet even after all this, how good it would be to go on believing in détente! Could it really be over? "But the Soviet leaders haven't repudiated it at all! Brezhnev was quite clear about that: it was in *Pravda!*" (Thus Marshall Shulman and other, like-minded experts.)

Yes indeed, the Soviet leaders are quite prepared to carry on détente; why shouldn't they be? This is the same détente that the West basked in so contentedly while millions were being exterminated in the jungles of Cambodia. The same détente that so gladdened Western hearts at a time when 1000 men, including 12-year-old boys, were being executed in one Afghan village. (And this was surely not a unique case!) We Russians immediately recognize an episode like this. That's the Soviet way of doing things! That's the way they slaughtered us, too, from 1918 on! Détente will continue to stand Soviet communism in very good stead: for the purpose of stifling the last flicker of dissidence in the Soviet Union and buying up whatever electronic equipment is necessary.

The West simply does not want to believe that the time for sacrifices has arrived; it is simply unprepared for sacrifices. Men who go on trading right until the first salvo is fired are incapable of sacrificing so much as their commercial profits: they have not the wit to realize that their children will never enjoy these gains, that today's illusory profits will return as tomorrow's devastation. The Western allies are maneuvering to see who can sacrifice the least. Behind all this lies that sleek god of affluence, now proclaimed as the goal of life, replacing the high-minded view of the world which the West has lost.

Communism will never be halted by negotiations or through the machinations of détente. It can be halted only by force from without or by disintegration from within. The smooth and effortless course of the West's long retreat could not go on forever, and it is now coming to an end; the brink may not have been reached, but it is already the merest step away. Since the outlying borders were never defended, the nearer ones will have to be held. Today, the Western world faces a greater danger than that which threatened it in 1939.

It would be disastrous for the world if America were to look upon the Peking leadership as an ally while regarding the Russian people as no less a foe than communism: by so doing, she would drive both these great nations into the maw of communism and plunge in after them. She would deprive both great peoples of their last hope of liberation. The indefatigable denigrators of Russia and all things Russian are forgetting to check their watches: All of America's mistakes and misconceptions about Russia might have been purely academic in the past but not in the swift-moving world of today. On the eve of the global battle between world communism and world humanity, would that the West at least distinguished the enemies of humanity from its friends, and that it sought an alliance not of foes but of friends. So much has been ceded, surrendered, and traded away that today even a fully united Western world can no longer prevail except by allying itself with the captive peoples of the communist world.

Notes

[1]The reference is to Lewin's review of a book by Oliver H. Radkey, *The Unknown Civil War in Soviet Russia: A Study of the Green Movement in the Tambov Region, 1920–1921,* in *Slavic Review* 36, no. 4 (December 1977), pp. 682–683. [Tr. note]

[2]New York: Charles Scribner's Sons, 1974.

[3]Sergius of Radonezh (1314–1392), perhaps the best-loved Russian saint, combined mystical spirituality with a practical concern for the Russian nation. In 1380, he gave his blessing to Dmitri, Prince of Moscow, to fight in a battle that proved to be the first decisive Russian victory over the Mongol occupiers.

St. Nil Sorsky (Nilus of Sora, 1433–1508) represents the mystical and contemplative tradition of Eastern monasticism. He argued that the church and the state should be independent of each other. [Tr. note]

[4]On Lenin's contribution to the drafting of the Criminal Code, see *The Gulag Archipelago,* vol. I, pp. 325–354. [Tr. note]

[5]The Nobel Peace Prize of 1971 was bestowed upon Willy Brandt, then the Chancellor of West Germany, for "concrete initiatives leading to the relaxation of tension" between East and West. [Tr. note]

[6]Dimitri K. Simes was, until 1972, a staff member of the Institute of World Economy and International Relations in Moscow. He emigrated soon thereafter and is presently Director of Soviet Studies at Georgetown University's Center for Strategic and International Studies in Washington, D.C. He has written extensively on détente.

Alexander L. Yanov emigrated in 1974 and has been associated with the Institute of International Studies, University of California at Berkeley. He is the author of *Détente after Brezhnev* (1977) and *The Russian New Right* (1978). [Tr. note]

[7]On the Novocherkassk uprising, see *The Gulag Archipelago,* vol. 3, pp. 507–514. [Tr. note]

[8]RSFSR is the official designation of that portion of the country that remains when the 14 outlying "national republics" are excluded.

[9]Vladimir Shelkov, head of the independent branch of the Adventist Church in the Soviet Union, died in a strict-regime camp in January 1980. He was 84 years old. [Tr. note]

[10]Igor Ogurtsov headed an organization that advocated the rebuilding of Russia on Christian principles. Arrested in 1967, he was sentenced to twenty years of imprisonment and exile.

Vladimir Osipov, editor of *Veche,* a *samizdat* journal dedicated to religious and nationalist themes, was sentenced to 8 years in 1975. He had also served an earlier term for dissident activities. [Tr. note]

[11]The "Christian Committee" was formed in 1976. [Tr. note]

[12]Fr. Gleb Yakunin, a founding member of the "Christian Committee" and an outspoken critic of the compliant policies of the Moscow Patriarchate, was arrested in November 1979.

Fr. Dimitri Dudko brought hundreds of persons, including many students and intellectuals, into the Russian Orthodox Church, largely through his remarkable sermons. He was arrested in January 1980. [Tr. note]

[13]In 1974, Aleksandr Ogorodnikov launched a study group in Moscow for the discussion of religious and philosophical issues. The idea caught on in university circles, and soon similar Christian seminars were organized in Leningrad, Smolensk, and other cities. Ogorodnikov was arrested in 1978, several other leading figures in 1979. [Tr. note]

[14]On July 3, 1941, almost 2 weeks after Germany's attack on the USSR, Stalin made his first wartime radio address to the nation. In a voice heavy with emotion, he addressed his listeners as "brothers and sisters" and "friends." [Tr. note]

[15]A number of countries and territories were annexed by the USSR in 1939–1940. These included Western Ukraine and Western Byelorussia (detached from Poland in 1939), Estonia, Latvia, Lithuania, Northern Bukovina, and Bessarabia. [Tr. note]

[16]The *Letter* was sent to its addressees in September 1973. The Russian text and its English translation were published in 1974. [Tr. note]

[17]In modern Russian, this word means *truth*. In medieval Russia, this term signified *justice, right,* as well as *law* in the broad sense. The first Russian code of laws (eleventh century) was called *Pravda Russkaya.* [Tr. note]

[18]In *From under the Rubble* (Boston-Toronto: Little, Brown, 1975).

[19]Aleksandr Solzhenitsyn, *Letter to the Soviet Leaders* (New York: Harper & Row, 1974).

2 ROBERT C. TUCKER

Swollen State, Spent Society: Stalin's Legacy to Brezhnev's Russia[*]

I Russia today is a mighty world power with the largest territory of any state, a population of 260 million, great mineral resources in a resource-hungry world, and a geopolitical position that gives it a large role in both European and Asian affairs. It is a military superpower with intercontinental and intermediate-range nuclear missiles in large numbers, supersonic airplanes, a huge standing army based on universal military service, and fleets in all oceans. It controls an East and Central European empire extending deep into Germany and the Balkans. Its power and influence radiate into Asia, the Middle East, the Mediterranean, Africa, and Latin America.

This formidable global presence is serviced and maintained by an internal state system centered in Great Russia's capital city, Moscow; the formal autonomy of the outlying, non-Russian Soviet republics is constitutional fiction. Staffed by an army of party, government, and other officials (it has been estimated that full-time party officials alone number close to half a million), the party–state edifice comes to a peak in the 23 departments of the party's Central Committee, whose Politburo is the focal point of decision-making authority. Under this supreme directorate, about 60 government ministries provide centralized administration of the Soviet realm. Two of these bureaucracies, the police and the military, have roles and prerogatives of special importance. Their chiefs, along with the chairman of the Council of Ministers and his first deputy, the minister for foreign affairs, the principal Central Committee secretaries, the first secretaries of the Moscow, Leningrad, and one or two republic party organizations, sit with General Secretary Brezhnev on the Politburo and take part in policymaking.

*Reprinted by permission of the author from *Foreign Affairs* 60, no. 2 (Winter, 1981–1982), pp. 414–435. Copyright 1981 by Robert C. Tucker.

This system lays official claim to the title "developed socialism." A source inside the Soviet establishment, writing under the name of Fedor Zniakov, more aptly calls it "supermonopoly capitalism." Ownership, he explains, is concentrated in a single center, the "supermonopoly," which possesses the plenitude of economic and political power.[1] The economic system may be likened to a single gigantic conglomerate incorporating industries and other state-controlled activity, including state and collective farm agriculture, under unified management at the Politburo level.

The Politburo's control is ensured by a hierarchically organized ruling class that represents and defends the supermonopoly's interests in all spheres of social life. The fundamental aim is the preservation, strengthening, and extension of the supermonopoly's power. The ruling class starts at lower levels with plant directors, collective farm chairmen, and heads of local party and governmental bodies and extends to Central Committee secretaries and members of the Soviet government at the top.[2] It is sometimes informally called the "nomenclature class" because of the system of nomenclature (*nomenklatura*) or lists of posts, appointment to which requires the approval of a given higher or lower party body. The nomenclature class comprises those cleared for assignment to responsible positions in the party–state.

Its members and their families live in a relatively closed world of privilege, which so sharply differentiates their life experience from that of ordinary citizens that they could almost be living in different countries. People of the nomenclature class have comfortable apartments, cars, and, in many cases, country houses. They are served by a network of so-called closed distributors, inconspicuous special shops where food and other products, including foreign goods, are available at subsidized prices. They have opportunities for foreign travel, adequate health care, and can enjoy the facilities of desirable Soviet resorts at desirable times of the year. Through informal channels of influence, their children can make their way into the restricted number of openings for higher education and thence into careers in the official world.

Perquisites in that world are carefully differentiated according to gradations of rank. Thus, in the Science Settlement at Novosibirsk, according to an ex-Soviet science journalist, "a full member of the Academy lives in a villa, a corresponding member has half a villa; a senior research officer has an apartment with three-meter ceiling height, while a junior has one with a two and a quarter meter ceiling, on a higher floor with a communal bathroom."[3]

II   Was this rigid, centralized, and highly stratified sociopolitical structure an inevitable outgrowth of the single-party dictatorship established by Lenin and his fellow Bolsheviks after the October Revolution? Or did it evolve as *one* possible sequel to the Revolution, the result of historical decisions that might have been taken differently and that reflected, in some measure, the unique political personality and outlook of Lenin's successor, Josef Stalin?

I believe the latter is the case. Although Brezhnev's Russia differs from Stalin's in the absence of an all-powerful dictator ruling by terror and in other ways that will be discussed, in the fundamental aspects already mentioned, it is indeed an inheritance from the Stalin era. It took shape in the course of what can best be called a state-building process that was launched around 1929 when Stalin finally achieved ascendancy in the Soviet political leadership. Taking advantage of the ability that this gave him to manipulate the regime's policy (he was not yet the personal dictator that he became in the mid-1930s), Stalin steered a course in internal affairs predicated upon the imperative need to build an industrially and militarily powerful Soviet Russian state within 10 years in preparation for what he considered an inevitably oncoming great new war—a war that, with assistance from his own diplomacy, did break out about 10 years later, in 1939.

The state-building process started with Stalin's policy of collectiviza- tion of the peasantry. Looking back proudly in later years, he spoke of collectivization, whereby about 25 million private peasant farms were abolished and the peasants organized into some 200,000 state- supervised collective farms, as a state-initiated and state-directed "revo- lution from above" that matched or surpassed in historical significance the October Revolution of 1917 by which Lenin and the Bolsheviks acquired power.[4] His phrase is applicable to the entire statist transformation of Soviet Russia during the 1930s.

In using it, Stalin forebore to mention a fact of which he was well aware, that coercive revolution from above in a long-range state- building process was no new phenomenon in Russia's history. A previous such process had its background and origin in national adver- sity: the conquest in 1240 and 200-year subjugation of the Russian lands by the Tatars. The tsarist state, centered in Muscovy, developed from the fourteenth to the seventeenth centuries in a protracted struggle for the reconstitution of the national territory, a "gathering of Russian lands," in a hostile international environment that was composed of not only the declining but still strong Tatar khanates but also powerful neighbors on three sides: Ottoman Turkey in the southwest, Poland– Lithuania, in the west, and Sweden in the northwest. Through war and diplomacy, Muscovy expanded from an area of about 15,000 square miles in 1462 to that of the transcontinental Eurasian state that it finally became.

The expansionist drive placed a great premium upon military strength. Because of the country's economic backwardness and tech- nological inferiority to its Western neighbors, the government sought to mobilize the resources for war by enlisting the population directly in its service. The exploitative relation of the state to the society brought an extension of coercive controls and the growth of the centralized governmental system. This took place largely through a series of revolutions from above. Claiming ownership of the land, the state destroyed the land-owning boyars as a class and created a controlled nobility of serving men whose landed estates were allotted on condition of military service to the state. This was the foundation for the later growth of an "aristocracy of rank" under which bureaucratic distinction rather than birth became, in principle, the highroad of entry into the nobility. The fastening down of serfdom upon the peasants in the seventeenth century was another aspect of what older Russian historians called the "binding of all classes" in compulsory service to the state.

Under Peter the Great in the early eighteenth century, the state underwent coercive remodeling from above through a Europeanization that connoted the borrowing of advanced technology from the West and the forced development of Russian industry under governmental auspices for military power in the continuing process of external aggrandizement. Thus the primacy of foreign policy and the need for military strength for external defense and expansion were the mainsprings of the internal state-building process. In his summation of this process, the pre-1917 historian V. O. Kliuchevsky wrote that "the expansion of the state territory, straining beyond measure and exhausting the resources of the people, only bolstered the power of the state without elevating the self-confidence of the people. . . . The state swelled up; the people grew lean."[5]

The pressure of external upon internal policy relaxed with tsarist Russia's achievement of its commanding world position by the close of the eighteenth century, making it possible for the government to give more attention to the needs of internal welfare rather than territorial expansion. The earlier binding of all classes in compulsory state service gave way to a partial unbinding of classes with the release of the nobility from its compulsory service obligations in the late eighteenth century.[6]

The "unbinding" proceeded in slow uneven steps. Not until 1861 was the peasantry released from serfdom by imperial decree. That action inaugurated a time of transforming change (from above) known as the epoch of Great Reforms. Although it witnessed a considerable liberalization of Russian life, the autocratic, authoritarian, centralized, bureaucratic state structure that evolved in the state-building process was too well entrenched, its repressive powers too formidable, and the history-bred submissiveness of the people too enduring, for the processes of change to work their way to fruition peacefully. What had developed as a dynamically active autocratic state authority in the earlier state-building process proved so strong as a static force later on that it could successfully block its own thorough transformation, as shown by its capacity to withstand the nationwide insurrectionary movement of 1905.

Only under the unbearable strains of the third year of the World War did the structure finally buckle and collapse in 1917.

III The Bolshevik party–state that emerged in control of what remained of the Russian Empire after the ensuing time of troubles was not initially oriented toward a renewed state-building process in the Russian national tradition. The Marxist ruling party's programmatic commitment was not to the restoration of a militarily powerful bureaucratic Russian state under a new tsar–autocrat, but to "socialist construction," meaning the building over time (a generation, at least, Lenin said) of a socialist or communist society characterized by cooperative forms of production in a setting of economic and technological advance, by material abundance for the entire populace, and by a steady growth of popular self-administration in place of rule by a governmental bureaucracy. By the seizure and monopolizing of power and the establishment of a party dictatorship, Lenin and the Bolsheviks had, however, created a medium in which a dynamic resurgence of statism could occur. Moreover, by virtue of the losses of territory in the revolutionary period and the new state's isolation in an unfriendly international environment, now called "hostile capitalist encirclement," the country's situation in the 1920s showed a certain parallel to that of the early Muscovite period.

Among the leading Bolshevik contenders for power after Lenin died, Stalin alone was disposed by personal politico–ideological orientation to take that historical parallel seriously. His orientation is best described as "Russian national bolshevism," an amalgam of Bolshevik revolutionary theory and practice with Great Russian nationalism. When he expressed it in moderate terms in the platform of "socialism in one country" that he advocated against the party Left in the debates of the mid-1920s, it had strong persuasive appeal to large elements of the ruling party, particularly the younger party members. But linked as it was with his special perception of a parallel between Muscovite Russia's situation in earlier times and Soviet Russia's now,[7] Stalin's actual position was far more radical in its political implications than his followers suspected—until he began acting upon it in 1929.

Such basic elements of the Bolshevik program as the construction of a socialist society in Soviet Russia and the international communist revolution were preserved but at the same time transformed by Stalin's Russian national bolshevism. Communist revolution abroad was reconceived as a process spreading out from a base in the USSR to neighboring countries, hence as, in part, a revived "gathering of Russian lands," such as those lost to Poland and to the independent Baltic states during the revolutionary period.

In Stalin's Russian national bolshevism, further growth of the international communist revolution and Soviet Russian expansion, territorially or in terms of spheres of influence, were fused into one process. Since a focal area for expansion was Eastern Europe and the Balkans, a diplomacy of accord with Germany, looking (among other things) to a new partition of Poland, was a fixture of Stalin's foreign policy conception from early on. While encouraging Foreign Commissar Maxim Litvinov to pursue, in the mid-1930s, an open diplomacy of collective security and popular fronts against fascism, Stalin made his way by secret diplomacy toward the Nazi–Soviet pact that he concluded in 1939.

Thus, Russian national bolshevism resurrected the historic Russian primacy of foreign policy and with it the necessity—to Stalin's history-oriented mind—of a renewed, but this time *Soviet*, Russian state-building process centering on forced-draft industrialization with emphasis upon heavy industry and military–industrial power. Collectivization was designed to undergird the industrialization drive by organizing the peasantry into collective and state farms. This ensured government control of the great bulk of agricultural produce, including large amounts for export abroad to finance the importation of technology. That aim required lightning collectivization rather than the long-range "cooperating" of the peasantry by persuasion that Lenin had envisaged. Lightning collectivization was, and could only be, accomplished by terrorist methods, whose utilization on Stalin's orders backfired because the mass of peasants, seeing in the collectives a revived form of Russian serfdom (which they were), slaughtered a huge proportion of their livestock before entering them. Although the state got control of the produce by the draconian means Stalin employed, it did so at the cost of an estimated 10 to 15 million lives lost in the ensuing great famine, whose effects are still felt in Russia's agricultural economy 50 years later.

Restoring as it did something comparable to old Russia's serfdom, collectivization was not only a coercive revolution from above but a first phase of a renewed state-building process. Stalin moved to bring every element of society under regimentation and control. He reenacted the "binding" of all strata in compulsory service to the state authority. He pursued a policy of direct exploitation of the human resources of the economically backward country for amassing military power through industrialization. One major expression of this was the expansion of the vast "Gulag" forced-labor empire in Siberia, the Far North, and elsewhere, much of it initially recruited from the rural *kulaks* whose violent dispossession and deportation into the interior in 1929–33 was the means used to terrorize the peasantry as a whole into joining the collectives. Another was the binding of the industrial worker to his place of work by the reintroduction of an internal passport system, like the one that existed before 1917, and by legislation of the later 1930s, prohibiting voluntary changes of jobs. Total exploitation of the populace meant totalitarian control. Since a large bureaucratic apparatus of police and other governmental regulation was needed for this, a leviathan of a state resulted. Not only was a powerful, highly centralized, bureaucratic state revived, its control of people's lives extended well beyond the limits reached by tsarist rulers.

Russia's history in Stalin's time retraced, therefore, the course epitomized by Kliuchevsky in his phrase cited earlier: "The state swelled up; the people grew lean." The people "grew lean" in the shrinkage of the unregimented parts of their lives, and in the simple sense of being hungry, living on rations, going without desperately needed housing, and enduring other hardship. Nevertheless, Stalin publicly proclaimed in 1936, when promulgating a new Stalinist version of the Soviet constitution, that the foundations of a socialist society had now been built. This claim contradicted Leninist assumptions that socialism connoted richer lives rather than poorer, more equitable distribution rather than less, less bureaucratic regimentation rather than more, more meaningful public involvement in administration rather than less. But it was consistent with Stalin's Russian national bolshevism, in which socialism-building and state-building were fused, so that the construction of a mighty Soviet Russian military–national state in which all strata were bound in compulsory service to the state power became the fundamental meaning of "socialism." Such a view required that Stalin revise the long established Marxist and Leninist tenet that it was the destiny of the state as an institution to wither away with the advent of a socialist society. As Stalin reformulated the dogma, in 1939, the Soviet socialist state had to grow great and strong in order to defend itself within a hostile capitalist encirclement.

Much of this was alien to the thinking of the great majority of surviving Old Bolsheviks, as well as to many of their juniors in the new party generation that had matured during the early years of the Soviet regime and was heavily influenced by the Old Bolsheviks in its way of thought. Even many who had been "Stalinists" in supporting Stalin's platform of building socialism in one country were unprepared for what his Russian national bolshevism meant in practice—a replication under Soviet conditions of the patterns of revolution from above that had found earlier expression in the tsarist state-building process. They were appalled by the ghastly tragedy of collectivization by terror and the resulting hushed-up famine of the early 1930s. They were, many of them, repelled by the new, stratified society of privilege that they saw emerging in those years of privation, and by the swelling of a bureaucratic state that, to minds conditioned by Marxism and Leninism, should have been beginning to atrophy if socialism were really being built in Russia.

Their disenchantment with the new statist society over whose construction Stalin was presiding was expressed in negative attitudes, even in opposition, to him. Some Old Bolsheviks made an abortive attempt during the Seventeenth Party Congress in 1934 to carry out, belatedly, Lenin's parting confidential advice to the party elders that Stalin be removed from his position of power. His lethal response was the Great Terror, which began with the assassination of the Leningrad party leader, Sergei Kirov, in December 1934 and is estimated to have cost the lives of about 2 million Communists and previously expelled party members, plus large numbers of their non-party relatives and associates.[8]

The Terror, by opening careers en masse to replacements for the victims, brought into being a new, state-created, as well as Stalin-oriented Soviet elite. It lived far better than ordinary citizens but was just as securely bound in service to the state as were the peasants and the worker. Hence, the Great Purge was another revolution from above or another phase in the larger revolution from above of the 1930s. It recapitulated, in a highly magnified twentieth-century way, the binding of the landed aristocracy in compulsory state service. Like the boyars of old, the Old Bolshevik ruling elite was exterminated in large part and, for the rest, submerged in a new Soviet service nobility. The purge as a revolution from above was, moreover, the crucible of the reemergence of Russian absolutism in a Soviet setting, the rule of a new tsar–autocrat in whose dictatorial system the still ostensibly dominant political party was, like all other institutions of Stalin's state, a transmission belt for implementing his policies.

This interpretation of the Stalinist 1930s conflicts with a view that has enjoyed wide credence in the West. That view sees Stalin's revolution from above as a harsh and cruel way of bringing backward Russia into the modern world; a revolution of "modernization."[9] There is no question but that Russia underwent considerable industrialization and urbanization in the Stalinist 1930s, accompanied by growth in literacy, in the availability of education, chiefly technical, and in other indices. Yet all this took place in a state-building process similar in a fundamental way to one seen earlier in history.

The upshot is that what happened in Russia in the 1930s is not only superficially described but actually obscured by the use of a term like *modernization*. In fact, the nation underwent a reversion to the Russian past in its developmental mode. Without a clear comprehension of this, it is not possible truly to understand either the legacy of Stalin and Stalinism to the Russian present or the depth of the problems confronted by Stalin's successors. In particular, no accurate diagnosis can be made of the present situation of Soviet society.

IV   "Russ is where the true belief is," a noted émigré interpreter of Russian thought and society has written.[10] His point was that *Rus'* developed in history as a community of right believers, meaning those of the Russian Orthodox faith. In what we may call its sustaining myth, Russian society was a political community of the faithful, an Orthodox tsardom. So persistent was this pattern that as late as the early twentieth century, a peasant—and the vast majority of Russians were peasants then—would speak of himself not as "Russian" but as "Orthodox" (*pravoslavny*).[11] Russian was his language; Orthodoxy, his identity. Since the Tsar was a centerpiece of the mythos, waning faith in the Tsar was a sign of the coming end of the tsardom. Bloody Sunday in January 1905 has been mentioned in this context. On that day, a priest-led, icon-bearing procession of common people was met with murderous gunfire on its walk to the Winter Palace in Petersburg to ask the Tsar for redress of grievances. The priest, Father Gapon, is said to have declared in the midst of the carnage, "There is no Tsar anymore."

The revolutionary reconstitution of a society always sees the rise of a new conception of the meaning of membership in that society. Bolshevism's revolutionary republic, which Lenin called *Rus'* in an article of 1918, soon generated its own sustaining myth in the concept of Soviet *Rus'* as a community of "builders of socialism." The Bolsheviks' militant atheism, their unremitting effort through antireligious propaganda to dislodge Orthodoxy from Russian minds, was the other side of their project of instilling in those same minds a new set of right beliefs, a new transnational orthodoxy. The society was envisioned as a collective of citizens united in believing in future socialism and eventual full communism as a transcendently worthy life goal. As Lenin formulated the idea in his speech of 1920 to a congress of representatives of the Young Communist League:

> The generation of people who are now at the age of fifty cannot expect to see a communist society. This generation will be gone before then. But the generation of those who are now fifteen will see a communist society and will itself build this society. This generation should know that the entire purpose of their lives is to build a communist society.[12]

Though not in Lenin's audience on that occasion, one of the youths whom Lenin meant to address was a Leonid Brezhnev. Born in 1906, he was just turning fifteen. He must have been among the many in the growing generation in whom the mythos of building a socialist *Rus'* was deeply implanted.

During the brief remainder of his active life, Lenin tried to formulate guidelines for building what must initially be a socialist rather than a fully communist new society. It would entail the creation of a machine industry based especially on electric power, overcoming persisting class differences, the growth of general prosperity, and the "cooperating of Russia," that is, the enlistment of the whole population, peasantry included, into cooperative societies and cooperative forms of work. The coming socialist *Rus'* would likewise be to a great extent popularly administered, free of the "bureaucratism" bequeathed by history. The construction of socialism was not envisaged as a state-building process of the kind that subsequently occurred, although Stalin, in part by selective quotation of earlier Lenin texts, sought to obscure the gulf between Lenin's guidelines and his policies.

Under Stalin, the meaning of Soviet citizenship continued to be defined as belief in socialism and communism, but the contents of the belief system changed. As of about 1936, a Soviet citizen was supposed to believe that Stalin's Russia of the 5-year plans had basically made the transition to socialism and was now on the way to an indefinitely deferred communist future which must serve as the nation's goal. Furthermore, the belief system was personalized in a new way. It had already been personalized upon Lenin's death because the deceased founder of Bolshevism was made into a cult figure, a venerated supreme authority whose writings figured as sacred texts on, above all, the society's goal and the way to achieve it. Then, in the early and middle 1930s, the Lenin cult became overlaid and overshadowed by official glorification of Stalin as the "Builder of Socialism." Soviet citizens were expected to believe not only in socialism as a fait accompli and in communism as the further objective, but also in Stalin as the party's genius–leader to whom credit was due for the society's history-making breakthrough to the socialist stage of development foretold by Marx, Engels, and Lenin but not realized in their lifetimes.

The Old Bolsheviks, as already indicated, were mostly Old Believers as well (to borrow another term from Russian history) and so were many of their younger contemporaries who had come into the party during the Civil War and the 1920s. Most of them had been willing followers of Stalin when he spoke in the mid-1920s of socialism in one country. But not being Russian national Bolsheviks of his peculiar stripe, few could accept the unprosperous, deeply stratified, bureaucracy-ridden society of the mid-1930s, with its reimposed state of virtual serfdom and its increasingly bound working class, with its more and more strident Great Russian nationalism, as a "socialist" society. Nor could they believe in Stalin, the colossal bungler of collectivization, as the leader of genius portrayed in his personality cult. Those generations of Leninist Old Believers were mowed down wholesale in the terrorist purges of the later 1930s.

We should beware, however, of assuming that the people who took their places in leading positions, or in lesser ones with higher status in store, were cynical opportunistic nonbelievers. Some, perhaps many, were, to be sure, just that. But Stalin, however vicious, was not stupid in this phase of his state-building policy. He consciously brought along a new generation of state servitors who could be and in very many cases would be believers of a new kind. These people accepted the society he was building as the socialist one he proclaimed it to be. They admiringly looked upon him as indeed the Builder of Socialism.

Risen from simple, often peasant origins, these New Believers were culturally disposed to think of Russia as a new Orthodox tsardom of Marxist–Leninist–Stalinist persuasion, naturally with a new tsar, albeit an uncrowned one, at its head. They could accept the equation of a socialist Soviet Russia with an industrially developed and militarily strong one, take satisfaction in their participation in the state-building effort, and be proud of the country's emergence as a great power. They, or many of them, could uncritically accept the results of the devious foreign policy that made a deal with Hitler that turned his aggression westward and meanwhile opened the way for Russia's and communism's expansion into Eastern Europe.

V   When, after confounding Stalin's calculation on a long debilitating war in the West, Hitler "perfidiously" (as the Soviet version goes) hurled the full force of the Wehrmacht against his ally of 1939–1941, the New Believers were a rock of support for the defense effort. As for the common people, they were wary as the war began, not knowing what to expect from the Germans, who were European and hence (as Russians had always supposed) a "cultured" nation. When they discovered that the invaders were behaving like savages rather than liberators, they were ready to respond to the Stalin regime's call to arms. It did not say, "Rise in defense of Soviet socialism," but, "Mother Russia calls you." The symbols invoked, such as General Kutuzov, who commanded Russia's defense in the war against Napoleon, were Russian national symbols.

Having no one to defend it but the people, whose material conditions of life had to grow worse rather than better in wartime, the regime made the one concession possible: it lifted the terror-tinged atmosphere of the prewar years and allowed the warring nation a relaxed sense of more-freedom-to-come. During those awful years of death and privation, commitments were quietly made to the population. Not by open proclamation, but by spreading the word through the grapevine that serves the country's real communication needs, the regime encouraged the people to believe that victory would be a great turning point toward materially better as well as freer conditions, that peasants would be allowed to leave the collectives, that intellectuals would enjoy a respite from cultural regimentation, that there would be opportunities for foreign travel and study in a no longer hostile world, and even that the Americans would be invited to open department stores in Soviet cities.

So, at a cost of 20 or more million casualties and with critically important aid from the Western allies, Russia prevailed. The war itself became a popular one in the sense that the great bulk of the population was behind it. Stalin himself became, for the first time, a popular hero as beleaguered Russia's rugged war leader. The fact that he had panicked and had a temporary nervous breakdown at the beginning was not known outside a tiny circle at the top. Nor did the people know about his grievous faults as supreme commander of the fighting forces. Many had but a hazy realization, if that, of the fact that his terrorist collectivation and methodical destruction of seasoned cadres in all fields in the fury of the Great Purge had done far more to wreck the war effort in advance than to prepare for it.

It was an article of faith in the Soviet public mind that the end of the war would bring the beginning of a new period in the country's life, a time of peace, liberalization, and growing plenty. I heard a Red Army officer cry, "Now it is time to live!," during the joyous victory celebration in Red Square on May 9, 1945. But the anticipated and longed-for new period of economic betterment and liberalization did not come with the victory for which the people had paid so dear a price.

Instead, Stalin, now a supremely glorified hero as well as absolute ruler, defined the postwar period as a new prewar period. That was the underlying message of his postwar address of February 9, 1946, in which he spoke of the necessity of three or four more heavy industry-oriented 5-year plans in order to prepare the country for "all contingencies" in a world where the continued existence of imperialism made new wars inevitable. Although Russia was no longer isolated and threatened as before, Stalin was decreeing a new round of the state-building process for what was already then becoming, in his foreign policy, an era of cold war and near total isolation of the nation from the outside world. That meant a new round of strain, sacrifice, and austerity internally. A Russian of the older generation in whose Moscow apartment I sat as Stalin's words were transmitted to the people by radio, placed his head on his folded arms when he heard them. All over Russia, people figuratively were doing the same. In a society founded on the presumption of belief, that signified the beginnings of a crisis.

Aware of the mass disenchantment, Stalin prescribed as antidote what has been called the *Zhdanovshchina*, the campaign, initiated in 1946 by his party lieutenant Andrei Zhdanov and others to revitalize political consciousness and belief. They castigated what was called "apoliticality" and "non-ideologism." The phenomena so designated were real, whereas the means employed to counteract them, including propaganda of Russian chauvinism and, increasingly, anti-Semitism, were impotent to reinstill active commitment in a generally dispirited people that had lost hope for a better life in their time. Fear became the main stimulus, and the security police lorded it over all other organs of power, including the theoretically ruling party. By Stalin's death in 1953, the society was in the grip of something close to paralysis.

VI   Stalin's successors were bound to pursue a politics of change, although they were divided over how far and fast it should proceed, in what directions, and who should preside over it. Some staunch Stalinist conservatives, such as Lazar Kaganovich and Viacheslav Molotov, appear to have wanted only limited change hypercautiously administered, whereas younger leaders like Georgi Malenkov and Nikita Khrushchev stood for substantial reform but differed over the course it should take and who should implement it. Having achieved a sort of supremacy in a 2-year struggle, Khrushchev embarked in 1955 upon a reform course and made the Twentieth Party Congress in February 1956 his forum for it. His reform course was aimed at making the Soviet system work by restoring it to a condition of economic and sociopolitical health.

A peculiar blend of Old and New Believer in his makeup, Khrushchev was a tirelessly itinerant politican who went around Russia and the world preaching the superiority of the Soviet way. But his faith in the Soviet system did not stand in the way of a realistic appreciation of its failings. This believing Communist could be astonishingly frank in exposing the actualities, whether it was the grim state of Soviet agriculture in 1953, or the ills of the Moscow-centered bureaucratic management of the economy, or Stalin's criminality in the terrorist purge of the party. It took a deep believer in the fundamental underlying rightness of the Soviet order to be such a scourge of past tragedies and present malfunctioning.

The watchword of Khrushchev's special brand of reformism was "Back to the path of Lenin," connoting, above all, revival of the system of single-party rule that had been eclipsed for 20 years by Stalin's police-based personal depotism. Accordingly, the grand theme of his secret report to the Twentieth Congress in 1956 was Stalin's violation of the "Leninist norms" of rule by the Communist party as a collectivity. His chilling exposé of tyranny was not published in Russia, but its contents soon became known through the grapevine after the speech was read at closed meetings of party cells all over the country. Hence, the whole of politically literate Russia became aware, if it had not been before, of the Stalinist heritage of anti-party terror, and millions of its still surving victims began returning to Soviet society from concentration camps.

Khrushchev was acutely aware that a widespread failure of belief was both a part of and a cause of the crisis bequeathed by Stalin to Soviet society and, hence, that the system could not be made to work well, even under reformed party auspices, unless belief was rekindled in the minds of Soviet citizens. He realized that this would not be possible unless people could anticipate concrete benefits in the not far-off future. After decades of privation accompanied by promises of future bliss, the people must be shown that the system, meaning first of all the economic system, could be made to work for their welfare, and soon. In a literal sense, it was time to deliver the goods. Khrushchev made plain his awareness of this by sponsoring the slogan: "The present generation of Soviet people will live under Communism!" It appeared on signboards everywhere, along with a still more concrete message that a visitor could see even along dusty Siberian roads in the summer of 1958, "We shall overtake and outstrip the U.S.A. in per capita production of meat, milk and butter!"

This was to be accomplished in a few short years. The new program adopted by the Twenty-Second Party Congress in 1961 formalized the theme: during the 1960s, the USSR would outstrip the United States in per capita output, make agriculture flourish, provide a sufficiency of material goods, basically meet the country's housing needs, and become the land with the shortest working day. In the 1970s, it would establish the material base for full communism, secure material and cultural abundance, make a start on distribution according to need (e.g., rent-free housing and free public transit). *"Fundamentally a communist society will be constructed in the USSR,"* the Program declared in italics, leaving the construction to be "fully completed" in 1981–1990.

Many new departures in domestic policy were aimed, if not at achieving communism by 1980, then at raising depressed Soviet living standards very sharply in the near future. They included the large-scale cultivation of virgin lands in southern Siberia and northern Kazakhstan for grain production, the effort to solve the fodder problem by the cultivation of corn, the sale of the farm machinery of the state-owned machine–tractor stations to the collectives, and various changes in the structure of economic administration. The great Stalinist ministerial bureaucracies were dissolved and their officials scattered across the country into regional economic councils in an effort to decentralize the economy.

When this failed to produce the desired results, Khrushchev resorted to another organizational panacea: the party apparatus was split into industrial and agricultural divisions locally so as to compel party official-dom to concentrate upon problems of production. Under the banner of democratization, certain reforms were adopted that chipped away somewhat at the privileged status of higher officials. Ministerial salaries were reduced from extremely high Stalinist levels. The new Party Rules adopted in 1961 mandated rotation of membership in party committees, the Central Committee included. A reform affecting children of persons from the privileged class, along with others, made vocational experience mandatory between school and higher education.

Inherent in Khrushchev's reform orientation was a shift in the relationship between domestic and foreign policy that had been fundamental to the Stalinist state-building process. The latter had harnessed the nation's energies to war preparation before 1941, warmaking during the Second World War, and the cold war after 1945. Now, under Khrushchev, the cold war gave way to competitive coexistence in Soviet foreign policy, and domestic needs, including consumer needs, took high priority as part of the effort to make the system work. To divert resources from the military to the civilian economy, as Khrushchev tried with some success to do (for instance, by restricting the growth of the Soviet navy), it was imperative to seek relief from the relentless demands of the arms race; for this, a changed relationship with Russia's chief adversary, the United States, was essential. Hence, the theme of coexistence as a complex process of competition *and* cooperation appeared in Soviet official thinking, and détente with the West became an intermittently pursued goal.

Ironically, the effort to economize on war preparation did not always lead to reduced tensions. Thus, Khrushchev's missiles gamble in Cuba in 1962—a move to offset U.S. strategic superiority cheaply so as to allocate to civilian needs resources that would otherwise have to be invested (and were later invested) in a costly program of intercontinental ballistic missiles—temporarily halted the search for a modus vivendi with the United States. But the nuclear test ban agreement of the following year found Khrushchev back on the road to an understanding with Washington.

Impetuous in style, given to organizational solutions, Khrushchev lacked a coherent longer range reform program that would have liberated middle- and low-level management and people at large to unleash initiative untrammeled by the party overseers. His economic decentralization only transferred power over the economy to regional party bosses, and the party as such could not serve as the reform instrument that he thought it could be. So, his optimistic faith in the capacity of reforms within the frame of the restored single-party system to make the economy perform productively for the benefit of the populace proved largely misplaced.

There were some successes, especially in housing construction, and the virgin-lands scheme paid off temporarily. But the promises of overtaking America in per capita food production and of giant strides toward full communism in the near future were not borne out. Sino–

Soviet relations deteriorated drastically during Khrushchev's tenure, while relations with the West showed no corresponding improvement. The Cuban missiles gambit backfired in a manner that was politically damaging to him at home. The military leadership undoubtedly chafed at his effort to hold back on military expenditures. Conservative hackles were raised by the liberalizing ferment that the de-Stalinization campaign aroused in the creative intelligentsia. Meanwhile, his shake-up of the party and state bureaucracy intensified the opposition in high places to his leadership and prepared the ground for the palace revolution that swept him out of power in 1964.

Before this final defeat, however, he made a last-ditch attempt to mobilize support against the conservative pro-Stalinist opposition by bringing his anti-Stalin campaign into the open at the Twenty-Second Party Congress in 1961. Here, he and his party lieutenants repeated in public many of the sensational revelations that had been made behind closed doors in 1956, and the congress ended with a dramatic decision to remove Stalin's remains from the mausoleum on Red Square and erect a monument to the victims of his bloody crimes.

It is not clear whether this bluff man, not given to psychological subtleties, realized what impact the revelations about Stalin would have upon the minds and spirit of very many people in Russia. We have noted previously, with the rise of Stalin's personality cult in the 1930s, the entire official Soviet belief system became personalized in a special way: to believe in socialism and communism as the goals of Soviet society meant believing in Stalin as the Builder of Socialism and the inspired leader who was guiding Russia on its path to the ultimate goal. Now this leader stood condemned before the people as a man guilty of criminal abuse of power on an appalling scale.

Many in the generation of New Believers who had come up during the heyday of Stalin's rule in the 1930s and the war years were deeply shocked and disoriented. Some resisted the blow to their beliefs; others ceased to believe in anything. To still others, albeit a small minority composed of intellectuals, the revelations about Stalin meant a welcome break with the Stalinist past and a promise of more far-reaching reforms pointing the way to a humane socialism in Russia. That point of view found expression in Roy A. Medvedev's *samizdat* work, *Let History Judge: The Origin and Consequences of Stalinism*. On the whole, however, Khrushchev's politics of de-Stalinization worked against his effort to revitalize the communist faith in Soviet minds. By the time of his removal from power, the crisis of belief was in some ways more serious than it had been when he assumed the leadership and embarked upon his reform course.

VII   Taking over from the willful, erratic, yet believing and reform-minded Khrushchev, Brezhnev and his associates changed the course and pace of policy. To them, Khrushchev's administrative reorganizations were (to use their words) "harebrained scheming" and fraught with a potential to destabilize the system. Taken together, his reform efforts had been worse than a failure. Not only was the slowed growth of the Soviet state's military machine undesirable. Not only was the promised high economic performance not forthcoming. Unreal hopes had been aroused among the people for early economic betterment and among intellectuals for more liberalization. This, too, was potentially a source of trouble. So, the new group's coming to power spelled conservative and, in some ways, reactionary government. To be sure, a modest managerial reform was promulgated in 1965 under Premier Alexei Kosygin's auspices, but its effect was negligible. If Khrushchev had the reform impulse without a coherent overall design, his successors lacked the impulse. Their central concern has been to keep the great centralized state system that Stalin built in being. They have given Russia a regime of stabilization.

Structurally, they restored the system to something close to the form it possessed in Stalin's time, minus the autocracy at the top and police supremacy over the party hierarchy. They undid Khrushchev's organizational innovations and reestablished the centralized economic ministries, enabling the ministries' official families to return from the provinces to Moscow. Khrushchev's emphasis upon vocational education for the younger generation was discarded. The nomenclature class was given to understand that it could, finally, breathe easily in the knowledge that the new masters of the state would be protective of its interests. Such was the deeper meaning of the slogan, "Trust in cadres," which Brezhnev introduced early in his period in power.

Higher officialdom was released not simply from the perpetual fear endured under Stalin's terroristic despotism—Khrushchev had seen to that—but also from the career uncertainties, the insecurity of tenure and privilege that Khrushchev's zigzag reform course had entailed. But only the privileged section of society was so emancipated. This development bears some comparison with the "unbinding of the nobility" in the Russia of the late eighteenth century. It affected particularly the men at top levels of political life. In place of the strong personal leadership that Khrushchev sought to furnish with the aim of change, Brezhnev offered consensual leadership for order and stability. He has been content with, and may owe his longevity in power to, his willingness to be first among equals in a truly oligarchical regime in which the various power blocs, including the military and the police, wield a heavy influence on policy.

This shift in the character and orientation of the regime led to a resumption of the steady buildup of military power. The Soviet military–industrial complex was accorded resources that it had, for a time, been denied. The unsuccessful effort to overtake America in per capita production of meat, milk, and butter gave way to an eventually successful one to rival her in missiles and other components of strategic military power. The formidable Soviet blue-water navy of today is largely a product of this change in policy and an intensified search for bases in distant places has been one of the accompaniments. The focus on military strength that characterized Stalinist policy has been restored in Brezhnev's time.

This has meant less effort to redirect resources into expanding the civilian economy and less hope of improved conditions for the mass of nonprivileged Soviet citizens. True, in the aftermath of Poland's food-price riots of late 1970 and amid portents of unrest at home, Brezhnev came before the Twenty-Fourth Party Congress in March 1971 with a program for raising depressed Soviet living standards. But it was not made meaningful by a concomitant decision to hold back on military outlays. One possible way out was the vigorous attempt made by the Soviet government in the early 1970s to obtain Western and Japanese economic aid on a large scale through technology transfer, enlistment of Western firms in developmental work for the Soviet civilian economy, and farm imports. This called for a policy of limited détente, which was formalized in the U.S.–Soviet Moscow summit meeting of 1972.

If Khrushchev intermittently sought accommodation with the West in order to economize on military expenditures, Brezhnev seems to have done so for the opposite reason: to enable the Soviet government to provide more for the population *without* skimping on military expenditures and without making fundamental changes in the Soviet system. Above all, he needed—and needs—a relationship with the United States that ensures the regular flow of American grain to a Russia whose agricultural economy is chronically ill because of the present regime's refusal to relinquish those hopelessly failed institutions, the state and collective farm.

The regime of stabilization very quickly put an end to Khrushchev's periodic exposés of Stalin's tyranny and imposed restraints on efforts by writers and scholars to testify in writing what Stalinism meant. Stalin himself was restored to posthumous official respectability, especially in his role as Russia's war leader in 1941–1945, and futher attempts to excavate the political history of his time and lay bare the facts about it were driven underground. While no real revival of the cult of Stalin occurred, a regime determined to preserve so much of his institutional and political legacy had to enforce a fictional history of his reign. For Khrushchev, the raking over of the Stalinist past appears to have served as personal penance as well as a political expedient. His successors, on the contrary, seem to reason the way the character of Glebov does in the play based on the late Yuri Trifonov's novel *House on the Embankment:* "The past is what we remember. If we stop remembering, the past will have ceased to exist, and we'll be all right."

A post-Khrushchev crackdown on the creative intelligentsia began in earnest in 1966 with the political trial of two prominent writers, Andrei Sinyavsky and Juli Daniel, and the campaign of protest against their conviction by numbers of intellectuals inaugurated the unofficial Russian human rights movement whose leadership was subsequently assumed by Academician Andrei Sakharov. Speaking more broadly, the contemporary dissident movement in Russia can be traced in large measure to the abandonment of regime-initiated reform under Brezhnev. So long as Russians could pin their hopes for change on the party–state's leadership, many were willing to try to work within the system and to envisage change in the system's own terms. The disappointment of those hopes after the passing of the Khrushchev era encouraged a further quest for new directions in national life.

As the dissident movement grew, especially after the Soviet military suppression of Czechoslovak communism's reform movement in 1968, the Soviet leaders have pursued an increasingly repressive policy toward people of unorthodox views. Its forms range from exile and imprisonment to punishment by psychiatric confinement to the hounding of individuals of talent and spirit into emigration.

The military takeover of Czechoslovakia made manifest a determination to preserve one other large part of Stalin's legacy: imperial rule in the communist sphere, and, in particular, single-party rule on the Soviet model in Eastern and Central Europe. Unlike 1956, when the Hungarian uprising confronted Moscow with a direct prospect of the departure of a Communist-ruled nation from the Soviet sphere, the Czech reform movement presented a case of a communist regime's internal transformation through democratization. As the Czech reformers saw it, socialism was not being abandoned; it was being realized. When the Czechoslovak and Soviet leadership groups met at the border town of Cierna not long before the Soviet invasion, Alexander Dubček offered assurances to Brezhnev that socialism was not going to be given up in Czechoslovakia. Brezhnev made his regime's philosophy brutally plain by replying, "Don't talk to me about 'socialism.' What we have we hold."[13]

Is the Brezhnev period to be described, then, as one of Stalinism's revival? Despite its reactionary tendencies, such a characterization would be wide of the mark. The renewed military buildup and associated economic priorities are far from resurrecting the Stalinist state-building process in its pattern of revolution from above. Intense Soviet competition for political influence in the Third World is a different phenomenon from the cold war as waged by Stalin. Severe as it is, the present regime's repressiveness is not a replica of what went on in Stalin's terror state. The country is not isolated from the world as under Stalin. There is no freedom of emigration, yet many thousands of Jews and others have been allowed to leave in recent years. There are no freedoms of speech, press, and assembly, yet an unpublished and unpublishable literature of *samizdat* has its shadowy existence, and there is freedom of table talk among friends in their homes. The nation is not reduced, as in Stalin's time, to communicating in frightened whispers. This list of differences could be extended.

"Not Stalin's heirs but his heritage," Josip Broz Tito of Yugoslavia is said to have remarked about the men who succeeded Stalin in power. Just so, their regime is not one of Stalinism resurgent but of attempted custodianship of much of its legacy: the swollen centralized state with superpower status in the world enforced by military might, the hierarchical system of power, the economic supermonopoly, the state and collective farm setup in the countryside, the foreign communist empire, the closed world of privilege for the nomenclature class. There is, however, another great part of Stalinism's legacy that the custodians would like to eliminate or alleviate but cannot: the crisis of Soviet society.

VIII
Economically as well as politically, the state swelled up during the Stalin era and has continued doing so in the recent past so far as basic industries and military production are concerned. Second only to the United States in gross national product, Russia is first in the world in steel, pig iron, and cement, second in aluminum and gold. Its aerospace establishment is America's sole competitor. It produces ample arms for its own and subject states' needs and for export far and wide. It is self-sufficient in oil production and exports oil and gas to countries of its empire and beyond.

Yet, the people in their great majority remain "lean"[14] This great industrial power does not and, within the frame of the system of supermonopolistic capitalism inherited from the Stalin period, cannot provide the bulk of its population with a decent standard of living. The transfusions of foreign technology during the Brezhnev détente have only somewhat eased the situation without seriously altering it. Above all, agriculture is in bad shape. It does not feed the country adequately, and the food situation has grown worse during the later 1970s and start of the 1980s, save for the privileged minority. Bread alone remains cheap and plentiful, at least in urban centers.

Moscow food stores have been closed on Sundays to stem the flow of people who travel for considerable distances from the surrounding countryside on their day off in search of locally unobtainable produce that can be bought in the country's best supplied city—its capital. A resident of Russia's second city, Leningrad, when asked not so long ago when the food situation there had been worse than it is now, answered: "During the [World War II] blockade." The food shortage seems to be worst in small provincial towns in central areas of the country and even on some of the state-run farms themselves. Thus, children living on a large state farm (*sovkhoz*) whose produce is taken for Moscow have been observed with stomachs distended from malnutrition. The reintroduction of a limited form of food rationing, not practiced since World War II, is reportedly under consideration. There is no one cause of the deteriorated food situation, but the fundamental fact is that Soviet state-run agriculture, a legacy of Stalin's reenserfment of the peasantry by brute terror, is an unmitigated disaster.

The shortage of factory-produced goods is not comparably acute, but neither are they, with few exceptions, in plentiful supply. Many goods are of shoddy quality, and some construction projects go for years uncompleted. An entire "second economy" has come into being to provide goods and services not obtainable from the first. Moreover, graft and corruption abound in the official economy itself, for example, in the common practices of bribery and the temporary hiring under flimsy arrangements of so-called *shabashniki* (people who work privately for cash payment) by state managers who cannot get a job done properly by their unmotivated state-employed workers. In sum, the Soviet people, in its great majority, is under-fed, under-housed, and under-almost-everything except under-ruled, under-policed, and under-propagandized.

Since the limited targets for higher living standards, adopted by the Twenty-Fourth Party Congress in 1971, not to mention Khrushchev's glowing promises in 1961 of communism by the 1980s, have not been fulfilled, the leadership has had to radically revise (downward) its timetable for the society's advance toward communism. Brezhnev went before the Twenty-Sixth Party Congress in February 1981 and declared that it was necessary to rewrite the party program adopted in 1961, eliminating its vision of the complete construction of a communist society during the 1980s. It was inappropriate, he explained, for the program to stipulate specifics. Yet, the idea of the party's and society's commitment to the goal of full communism is indispensable to the regime. Upon it rested and rests the Communist party's claim to a rightful monopoly of all power and an authoritative guiding role in all governmental and nongovernmental organizations in Russia. The legitimacy of the system turns on the concept of the *one party* as the possessor of a true teaching, Marxism–Leninism, which holds the key to the society's (and every society's) ultimate goal of communism. If there were no such goal and no authoritative knowledge of the way to it, the party could not present itself to the people as their "conscious vanguard" in the long march to what its propaganda has called the "glittering heights" of communism.

Here is the context for understanding the crisis of society in contemporary Russia. Every society has its real existence in the minds of its members, their sense of constituting together an association with historical significance, of common participation in a worthwhile collective enterprise. This is what the society's sustaining myth signifies. In the Soviet case, as a consequence of all the shocks that the history reviewed here has administered, the myth no longer sustains more than a small minority, if that. People en masse have stopped believing in the transcendent importance of a future collective condition called "communism." They have stopped believing in the likelihood of the society arriving at that condition and the desirability of trying to achieve it through the leading role of the Communist party or through themselves as "builders of communism," which is how the official party program defines Soviet citizens. In a society with an official culture founded on just those beliefs, this spells a deep crisis.

The evidence for this comes in many forms: first of all, the testimony of knowledgeable people. Andrei Sakharov has said in a message from his apartment–prison in Gorky: "There are few people who react seriously anymore to slogans about building Communism, although there was a time when, perhaps as a result of a certain misunderstanding, Communist slogans reflected a wish for justice and happiness for all in the world."[15] A Moscow intellectual, himself a party member, estimated recently that no more than 1 or 2% of party members are true believers and said: "Most of them would not belong if they could get away with it. But they are afraid."[16] The popular mind, as expressed in anecdotes, suspects that the leaders themselves no longer believe the slogans they repeat. According to an anecdote I heard in Russia in 1977, the country is a train headed for a destination called "communism," with Stalin, Khrushchev, and Brezhnev in charge. When, after a time, the train grinds to a halt, Stalin orders the engineer shot and the fireman sent to a concentration camp. The train moves on and then stops again. Now it is Khrushchev's turn to give orders. He posthumously rehabilitates the executed engineer and frees the fireman from camp to drive the train. When that happens, the train moves on, then comes to a halt again. Now it is Brezhnev's turn to solve the problem, and he says: "Let us draw the curtain and pretend the train is moving."

The widespread failure of belief is at least one of the main causes of a variety of other more overt phenomena indicative of a profoundly troubled society: the desire of many people, and not just Jews, to start new lives elsewhere, despite the risks and difficulties entailed; the defections of prominent cultural figures who enjoyed every advantage that high position in Soviet society could bring, such as the orchestra conductors Kirill Kondrashin and Maksim Shostakovich; the veritable epidemic of chronic alcoholism that afflicts Russia nowadays; the already mentioned shoddy work that so many perform on the job; and the near universal indifference toward what is written in the official press. These facts must be balanced, however, against the realization that Russians still have patriotic feelings and that many doubtless take a certain pride in, and are defensive about, the military might of their state and its superpower status in the world. But even this pride is intermixed with a haunting fear of another great destructive war in a society where the memory of the horrors of World War II is still alive and the authorities consciously play upon war fears in order to solidify popular support.

The failure of belief in the official myth of Soviet communism among the many has been accompanied by a recovery of belief in new forms among some—those known in the West as the "dissidents." Indeed, the dissident movement may more accurately be described as *a belief movement*. For those who have joined it, whatever the divisions between them in the content of their beliefs, are united in the discovery, one way or another, of a *Rus'* that they *can* believe in as distinct from the official Russia of their daily lives. As one of them, Lev Kopelev, said on his departure from Moscow airport in December 1980, in parting words to his friends: "I believe in Russia." If the movement had a motto, that could be it.

The *Rus'* that Aleksandr Solzhenitsyn and his followers believe in is a resurrected pre-Bolshevik Orthodox Russia. Andrei Sakharov and some others believe in a *Rus'* convergent with open societies, one in which human rights are secured, and whose government cooperates with others in addressing the great problems of conflict, population growth, resource depletion, pollution, and the like on the darkening globe of the late twentieth century. Roy A. Medvedev and his fellow reformers envisage a movement from the closed Soviet system to a democratized Marxist Russia. Many people have reverted to some form of religious belief, and many in the non-Russian republics have found meaning in their own forms of nationalism.

The belief movement should not be written off as of little significance because of the relatively small numbers actively involved and the fact that most of the activists have by now been imprisoned or intimidated into silence or expelled from the country. Its roots lie in the very failure of belief that characterizes contemporary Soviet society. The recovery and profession of belief in new forms is a response by those individuals for whom the frequently found combination of inner unbelief and outer conformism is not a tolerable way of living. If this is so, the movement can be temporarily repressed but not stamped out. As Georgi Vadimov, a distinguished writer and president of the Moscow chapter of Amnesty International, said some time ago (when the chapter was down to six members), "The movement is shattered. But it will rise again, in a new form, with new people, It is the only way for Russia to get out of this mess."

We have credible indications that there are in the middle rungs of the Soviet establishment itself some people who have come to feel that the supermonopolistic economy has reached an impasse and that fundamental changes are essential. They are linked with the present regime by the circumstances of their lives and careers—most are members of the Communist party. They are not visionaries with recipes for Russia's salvation but simply patriotic functionaries with training and experience in the management of an industrial society and concern over the critical condition of their society. Fedor Zniakov, in the already cited memorandum, describes them as an emergent "middle class" of factory directors and others who desire liberation from "supermonopolistic totalitarianism" so that their production units may function autonomously according to economic criteria.[17]

Alexander Yanov, writing from his extensive experience as a journalist who interviewed industrial executives before his emigration from the USSR, cites as typical the views of one important Leningrad industrialist. He and other managers, engineers, economists, and the like, who have learned to think independently would like, the industrialist said, to be able to *work* independently. He went on:

> They are ashamed of Soviet backwardness, its dependence on foreign technology, its humiliation. They believe that one reason for this backwardness is that their hands are tied—and tied tightly. Give them free rein, and tomorrow they will fire half the workers in their shops and pay the rest two, three, or five times more, depending on their skills (this assures them of sympathy and support from the skilled segment of the working class); they will introduce innovative, fundamentally new modes of work organization; they will be ready to experiment day and night. [The only obstacle is] the party administration's total domination of the economy.[18]

How widespread such views and feelings are in the ranks of middle and higher management is a matter on which we can only speculate. What can be said for certain is that those views and feelings exist. The people who harbor them have the mental freedom to think critically because, despite their linkages with the supermonopoly, their personal futures are not necessarily bound up with its perpetuation or its continuation in the present form; their talents and energies would be as needed in a postsupermonopolistic Russia as in the present one and would, indeed, have far more useful outlet. They are a potential constituency for change. The kind of change they envisage, however, is peaceful evolutionary change, not an upheaval. Given the country's historical traditions and political culture, the sine qua non of liberalizing change of the sort envisaged would be strong political leadership from above.

A fact that must be faced is that the one part of the Soviet system that truly works efficiently is the police and military establishment, which cannot make the system perform well but can keep it from being changed. As in tsarist Russia, what developed as a dynamic autocratic state authority in the state-building process remains so strong now as a force for the preservation of the system that the state can successfully block its own thorough transformation—unless leadership for change appears from above. Such leadership is out of the question so long as the present aging oligarchy remains in control. Whether it will emerge when new leaders take over in the not distant future is hardly likely, but we should not rule it out as unthinkable.

IX   Writing in European exile in the second half of the nineteenth century, the expatriate Russian, Alexander Herzen, said of the contemporary tsarist state that "It wields power in order to wield power." It had lost whatever spiritual raison d'être it had earlier possessed. By force of the whole circular movement of Russia's history in the twentieth century, that judgment once again applies. Stalin's protégés in power are men in control of a spent society. As a system of power expressed in military and police institutions, Soviet communism remains strong, very strong. But as a culture, it is historically played out because the belief system on which it was founded has lost its meaning. The rulers wield power in order to wield power.

This, despite everything, puts change on Russia's agenda, although no one can say how and when it will start and what direction it will take. The great problem is how to overcome the legacy of the past, to bring about a Russian renewal peaceably and evolutionarily. That would mean a change in the relationship between state and society—not something unprecedented in the country's history. The tsar-initiated reforms of the 1860s inaugurated the gradual emancipation of Russian society from the all-encompassing tutelage of the bureaucratic state. Official Russia contracted somewhat under its own leadership, and Russia's society emerged into the open from behind the "shroud" with which, as Herzen put it, the state had covered it up previously. Social forces acquired some scope for self-expression. As noted earlier, this process stopped short of its natural culmination in the transormation of the state system itself.

Can such a process of society's emancipation develop in the Soviet Russia of our time? There is reason for pessimism when one considers the weight of the legacy, its deleterious effects on the popular consciousness and ethos, the strength of the repressive agencies, and the material interest of a dominant minority as a group in the system's preservation more or less as is. On the other hand, there is ground for hope when we consider the critical condition of the country as just described previously and the fact that there are people among the intelligentsia, among the working classes, and in the bureaucracy itself who are conscious of and troubled by the situation and see the urgent need for some kind of change in the state–society relationship. They have no better spokesman than the recently exiled Soviet writer, Vladimir Voinovich, who says:

> Democracy is the natural state of society, as a live organism that can stumble, be mistaken, get burned. But society has its nerve endings that register pain and force the whole organism to learn its lesson from those mistakes. . . . No problems in the Soviet Union, economic, political, national, or religious, can be decided without democratization of the whole society. Is that possible? I don't know.[19]

The matter had best be left on that sensible note of uncertainty.

The rest of the world has a vital stake in the Russian renewal in question here. But does the West, the United States in particular, have any meaningful part to play in facilitating it? Only in an indirect way, it seems, but this indirect way is an important one. The West can, first, continue, as it has done in the recent time of détente, to accord Soviet Russia the status that it claims as a great power with worldwide interests and responsibilities. But, beyond this, it can seek incessantly to engage the Soviet Union in cooperative efforts toward constructive solutions for increasingly menacing world problems. At the same time, it can and should do everything possible to create a less tense international atmosphere in which it will be easier for Russian minds to concentrate attention, as they need to do, upon their difficult internal and imperial situation and find a way out of it.

Notes

[1] Fedor Zniakov, "Pamiatnaia zapiska" ("Memorandum"), *Arkhiv samizdata,* document no. 374, (May 1966), p. 3. Fedor Zniakov is believed to be a pseudonym.

[2] Fedor Zniakov, "Pamiatnaia zapiska" ("Memorandum"), *Arkhiv samizdata,* document no. 374, (May 1966), p. 3.

[3] Mark Popovsky, *Manipulated Science: The Crisis of Science and Scientists in the Soviet Union Today;* trans. Paul S. Falla (Garden City, New York: Doubleday, 1979), p. 179.

[4] *History of the Communist Party of the Soviet Union/Bolsheviks/Short Course* (Moscow, 1945), p. 305. First published in 1938, this book was written by a commission under Stalin's personal direction. In his *Marxism and Linguistics,* (New York: International Publishers, 1951), p. 28, he reverted to the theme of the Soviet "revolution from above" as one that "did not take place by means of an explosion. . . ."

[5] V. O. Kliuchevsky, *Kurs russkoi istorii (Course in Russian History),* vol. III (Moscow, 1937), p. 11. First published in 1911.

[6]Alexander Kornilov, *Modern Russian History from the Age of Catherine the Great to the End of the 19th Century;* trans. by Alexander S. Kaun (New York: Knopf, 1943), pp. 18–19. First published in 1917.

[7]See, for example, his speech of 4 February 1931, J. V. Stalin, "The Tasks of Business Executives," *Works* 13 (Moscow, 1955), pp. 40–41.

[8]Roy A. Medvedev, *On Stalin and Stalinism* (New York: Oxford, 1979), p. 214. Based on evidence now available, Stalin's responsibility for arranging the Kirov murder as a pretext for the Great Purge is beyond reasonable doubt.

[9]Thus Isaac Deutscher writes that Stalin undertook "to drive barbarism out of Russia by barbarous means," and Deutscher adds

> The nation has, nevertheless, advanced far in most fields of its existence. Its material apparatus of production, which about 1930 was that of any medium-sized European nation, has so greatly and so rapidly expanded that Russia is now the first industrial power in Europe and the second in the world. Within little more than one decade the number of her cities and towns doubled; and her urban population grew by thirty millions. The number of schools of all grades has very impressively multiplied. The whole nation has been sent to school.

Stalin: A Political Biography, 2d ed. (New York: Oxford, 1967), p. 568.

[10]Nicholas Berdyaev, *The Russian Idea* (London: Macmillan, 1947), p. 9. "Russ" (*Rus'*) is the ancient Russian word for Russia.

[11]Leonard E. Hubbard, *Soviet Labour and Industry* (London: Macmillan, 1942), p. 10.

[12]Robert C. Tucker, ed., *The Lenin Anthology* (New York: W. W. Norton, 1975), p. 674.

[13]I have this on the authority of a person who was present and overheard Brezhnev's words.

[14]In "The Harsh Decade: Soviet Policies in the 1980s," *Foreign Affairs* (Summer 1981), p. 1008 (see Chapter 31), Professor Seweryn Bialer has written: "The last 15 years have seen a growth in the standard of living of the Soviet people that was rapid by any—but especially by the Soviet—measure, particularly in the area of durable consumer goods. . . . The Soviet citizen—worker, peasant and professional—has become accustomed in the Brezhnev period to an un-interrupted upward trend in his well-being and more demanding in what he expects from the government in terms of goods and services." I beg to differ with the idea that the overall standard of living of the Soviet common man has improved in the Brezhnev period. Any improvement in supply of some durable goods has been greatly counterbalanced by the serious deterioration in the central element of Soviet living standards—food supply.

[15]"Sakharov: A Letter from Exile," *The New York Times Magazine,* June 8, 1980.

[16]Craig R. Whitney, "Crisis in Ideology in Soviet Turns Rulers to Old Values," *The New York Times,* October 12, 1980.

[17]Fedor Zniakov, "Pamiatnaia zapiska" ("Memorandum"), *Arkhiv samizdata,* document no. 374 (May 1966), p. 9.

[18]Alexander Yanov, *Détente after Brezhnev: The Domestic Roots of Soviet Foreign Policy* (Berkeley: University of California Institute of International Studies, 1977), p. 29.

[19]Vladimir Voinovich, "I Am Not a Dissident." *The New York Times,* May 23, 1981.

3   ZBIGNIEW BRZEZINSKI

Soviet Politics:
From the Future to the Past?[*]

Soviet politics cannot be separated from Russian history. This history has shaped a political tradition and a political culture that have deeply influenced the manner in which Marxism was assimilated to the Russian tradition, the way in which Lenin adapted that doctrine to the political circumstances of the moment, and the means which Stalin employed to reshape society to fulfill certain political and ideological purposes. Revolutionary doctrine and a revolutionary elite, to be sure, produced a new political style, but with the passage of time, the elements of historical discontinuity in the Soviet political experience have become less dominant, while more enduring patterns of Russian political culture have begun to surface with growing clarity and have been impinging more directly on the Soviet future.

The central and significant reality of Russian politics has been its predominantly autocratic character. Unlike its western European neighbors, Russia had not experienced a prolonged feudal phase. The overthrow of the Tartar yoke gave rise to an increasingly assertive and dominant autocracy. Property and people were the possesions of the state, personalized by the Autocrat (designated as such explicitly and proudly). The obligation of well-nigh complete subordination of any individual to the personalized symbol of the state was expressly asserted.[1] Control over society—including the church by the state— among other means, through a census mechanism adopted centuries ahead of any corresponding European device, was reminiscent of Oriental despotisms and, in fact, was derived directly from that historical

*Reprinted by permission of the author from *The Dynamics of Soviet Politics*, ed. Paul Cocks, Robert V. Daniels, and Nancy Whittier Heer (Cambridge, Mass.: Harvard University Press, 1976), pp. 337–351, 414–415. Copyright 1976 by Zbigniew Brzezinski.

experience.[2] The result has been to establish a relationship of state supremacy over society, of politics over social affairs, of the functionary over the citizen (or subject), to a degree not matched in Europe; and differences of degree do become differences of kind.

This historical tradition can be neither ignored nor underestimated. It has been a living one, reinforced through time by legal codes, thereby solidifying that relationship of supremacy. Indeed, some of the expressly assertive codification of that relationship of domination of the society by the state took place during the nineteenth century, when the rest of Europe was moving toward more liberal conceptions of social order and more pluralistic concepts of political organization. Revisions in the Russian criminal code, undertaken in 1846, and then again extended in 1881, gave the government unprecedented powers of arrest, not only for acts against the state, but even for alleged intentions to commit such acts. Moreover, the right to exile a citizen as "untrustworthy" became the prerogative of local police, a situation which has endured beyond the tsarist era.

The autocratic character of the Russian political tradition has gone hand in hand with a somewhat ambivalent attitude toward the West—an attitude that oscillated between periods of fascination and imitation, on the one hand, and conservative rejection and mystical superiority, on the other, with the two sometimes combining. This self-consciousness has tended to express itself periodically through phases of sustained competitive imitation of the more tangible aspects of the Western way of life, be it through Peter's reforms or Stalin's social engineering or recently through the obsessive competition with America. The effect has been to give Russian history a repetitive pattern of "fits and starts," as E. H. Carr has noted, with the state periodically initiating "revolutions from above," thereby reasserting its dominant relationship over society. This process has also had the effect of transforming "institutions and social groups deriving directly from imitation of Western models into something alien to the West and distinctively national."[3]

The adaptation of Marxism to Russia accordingly took place in a context that was bound to emphasize the authoritarian and dogmatic aspects of Marxism. That it took place at a time of accelerating social change in Russia, of the first pangs of the industrial revolution, and of increased political suppression, which came in the wake of unsuccessful populist terrorism, further tended to prompt more Manichaean, simplistic, and autocratic expressions among those who dedicated themselves to destroy the old for the sake of the new.[4]

The Meaning of Revolution

Leninism in its political style and organizational form thus became—for all of its sincere revolutionary content and obvious revolutionary social significance—a continuation of the dominant tradition rather than its termination. In terms of political tradition, the Duma-based Provisional Government was *more revolutionary* than Lenin's—though, to repeat, on the plane of social relations, property relations, and the role of classes, Leninism obviously meant a more profound and significant change. But on the level of politics, the Provisional Government, because of its democratic character, involved a sharper break with the past, a deeper discontinuity, than did Leninism.

Moreover, Lenin and Leninism set in motion an organizational dynamic that tipped the internal balances within the ruling class in favor of a leadership that concentrated effectively on maintaining political supremacy over societal affairs, without becoming diverted prematurely into external or domestic adventures. Awareness of the centrality of the power factor—so instinctively appreciated by Lenin and so deliberately inculcated by him among his supporters—worked to Stalin's advantage in the struggle for power.[5] Capitalizing on the instinctive desire for consolidation of power and yet also for some ideological fulfillment, Stalin gave the new elite satisfaction on both the level of self-interest and self-esteem. (This appeal of Stalinism to the young and relatively ideologically crude *apparatchiki* emerges extremely well from Khrushchev's memoirs.) Leninism thus loaded the historical dice in Stalin's favor and made Stalinism an extension—rather than an aberration—of what immediately preceded.

Stalin further revitalized the autocratic tradition—though he gave it a qualitatively new character. Through acts not only of unprecedented terror but of unprecedented social engineering, he undertook yet another revolution from above. Its political effect was to reassert, to an extreme degree, the domination of the political system over society—but with the added features of ideological motivation and technologically more advanced coercion. It is because of this experience, and its institutional and procedural legacies that have continued to this day, that one is justified in asserting that on the plane of politics, the Bolshevik seizure of power marked not the end but the renewal and extension of a tradition deeply rooted in the Russian past.

That tradition has been marked by:

1. Concentration of power in the political organism as distinct from the social organism;
2. Concentration of power in an extremely narrow circle of decision makers, frequently a single individual;
3. Insistence on the primacy of the official truth over any other version or interpretation of reality;
4. Identification of the state with divinity or history;
5. Subordination of other groups—be they boyars or managers and / or intellectuals—to the state;
6. Domination by the state of property relationships and particularly of the rural masses;

7. Periodic phases of social engineering or "revolutions from above";
8. Insistence that political opposition equals treason and, hence, the subordination of civil rights to political interests.

With only extraordinarily brief periods of time as exceptions, these eight points have been true of the pre-, as well as the post-, Revolutionary Russian experience.

That, in turn, justifies perhaps an even more radical assertion: the Bolshevik revolution not only was not a break from the predominant political tradition, but was, in historical perspective, an act of revitalized restoration. The late Romanov period was a period of decay, of the gradual weakening of the hold of the state over society. This was produced by the combined influence of social change (urbanization and industrialization, which also prompted the appearance of a more assertive bourgeoisie and intelligentsia and finally working masses) and of internal loss of vitality within the top elite, not to speak of the autocrat's own personal weaknesses. The overthrow of that ruling elite brought to power a new group, much more vital, much more assertive, and imbued with a new sense of historical mission. The political result of the Bolshevik revolution was thus revitalized restoration of long dominant patterns.[6]

The Question of Labels or Concepts

To postulate the above is not to slight the depth and the extent of the social revolution that communism brought to Russia. That revolution was a revolution. It created a new society based on new structures and new social patterns. That society, however, does not have as yet a qualitatively new relationship with the political system, and the future, as will be shortly argued, may thus involve again some familiar dilemmas.

It is important to remind ourselves, in the context of this argument, that the relationship between the political system and society, even when falling within a certain general and established pattern, tends to be changing and dynamic. This change also creates problems of definition and confusion about labels, including more recently about the term *totalitarianism*.

To debate anew the relevance or utility of that political term might not be productive, but some observations are pertinent to the case developed here. The appearance of movements committed to a comprehensive social reconstruction, and the availability to these movements of means of social control commensurate to the monumental tasks undertaken, is a new phenomenon. This does not mean that totalitarianism comes into being and persists from the moment that power is taken by such a movement. Rather, the term—or some other term, if the word *totalitarianism* evokes too much passion[7]—is meant to define a particular phase in the system / society relationship in which that society is in almost complete subordination to the state. That phase may or may not persist for too long, depending on circumstances, but in itself it does involve significant expansion in the dimension of politics, and it, therefore, commands analytical recognition as a qualitatively distinct phenomenon.

Speaking more specifically of the Soviet experience, the above might be clarified if the following stages are differentiated:

1. The appearance and formation of a movement, dedicated to a radical and extensive social reconstruction, 1902–1917;
2. Seizure of power by that movement in the context of political disintegration and social inertia, 1917–1920;
3. Consolidation of power by that movement and the beginnings of social mobilization, 1921–1928;
4. Transformation of society from above by political means, including very heavy reliance on violence, 1929–1939;
5. Following the end of the war (which prompted social mobilization reinforced by political means and by patriotism), consolidation of coercive social control by the political system, 1945–1956;
6. Limited retraction of political control over society and the surfacing of some societal pressures from below, since 1956.

What has at times been called totalitarianism thus emerged in the Soviet setting in stage 4 and it was consolidated in stage 5. (For other systems, some of these stages may be shorter or longer or simply telescoped.) It does not matter how these stages are labeled, but if one is concerned with understanding the scope of politics and the essence of politics in a given historical moment, then one should not ignore the specific character of the system / society relationship and not obscure it by use of concepts that apply to other phases as well or that are meant to embrace at once several different kinds of authoritarian regimes.

Stalinism involved creating a system. In contrast, the historical essence of the Khrushchev era was perceived by his opponents as representing "objectively" an effort, mounted from within the political system, to weaken or even to break down its Leninist–Stalinist character. (Khrushchev, to be sure, thought he was revitalizing it and making it more "Leninist.") But that system, institutionally entrenched, proved resilient, especially since the relationship between the political system and society under Stalin already had become less revolutionary and more dominant (i.e., the difference between phase 4 and phase 5).

As a result, by the mid-1970s, the Soviet system had become in some respects more akin to traditional authoritarian regimes but with an enormous and increasingly dysfunctional totalitarian residue, inherent in the doctrinal and political system of controls still bureaucratically, ritualistically, and occasionally coercively imposed on society. The contemporary Soviet system thus combines residual elements of revolutionary totalitarianism with features reminiscent of the more traditional autocracy.[8]

Given that context, the recently debated issue of pluralism and degeneration takes on a somewhat different meaning.[9] Institutional pluralism ceases to be an alternative view of what is, since a condition of Stalinist total control no longer prevails; rather, it is an elaboration of what one aspect of the political reality has become, namely, a condition akin to the more familiar traditional authoritarian pattern within which limited institutional pluralism, coordinated from above on the basis of a shared and essentially conservative orthodoxy, is tolerable and normal. That being the case, the concept of institutional pluralism represents neither a definitional challenge nor a political prognosis. It does not challenge the overall interpretation but reinforces it. And by itself, it does not tell us a great deal about the future, for an institutionally pluralistic authoritarianism may still revert to a more centralized form (a new revitalized revolution from above?) or, in time prompt—through more overt policy and power conflicts—a new and more fundamental challenge to the autocratic pattern as a whole.

The Question of Social Change

Perhaps a better guide to the future can be provided by analysis of social change in the Soviet Union. It can be argued, and it has been argued, that urbanization and industrialization produce a much more complex society, and that in time, such evolution tends to be reflected also in changes within the political system.

The argument is certainly a potent one, and on the social level, evidence for it is overwhelming. Soviet society has changed dramatically. A new relationship among the classes has emerged after 50 years of Soviet rule and the substance of class structure and class identity has similarly been dramatically altered. There is a new pattern of differentiation in Soviet society, the urban element has become increasingly dominant, and industrial values have been superimposed over the older rural tradition. The enormous extension of the educational system has similarly introduced profound changes in the subjective consciousness of the Soviet population, and that necessarily affects the system / society relationship.

This social change has led some of the more optimistic observers of the Soviet scene—especially Marxists like Roy Medvedev—to argue that change in the Soviet Union has already allowed a variety of groups to contest the ideological influence and authority both of Marxism–Leninism and of the party. In Medvedev's words:

In the last few years these various moods among the masses have provided the ground for the appearance of several explicit political trends and groups, in what is now a continuing process. As a general rule, they proceed from a socialist viewpoint but try to interpret socialism and communism in their own way. For the most part they exist and are evolving *outside* the party, though they have their supporters inside it as well. Their development is largely independent of Marxism-Leninism, although some of them do not reject many of its most important propositions. Nearly all of them are oppositional in character, but on the whole it is a question of loyal opposition involving only ideas and convictions.[10]

A central question, however, is whether such social change is capable of altering, or has in fact already altered in a significant fashion, the underlying character of Soviet politics. That character, as I have argued, has been shaped largely by political traditions derived from the specifics of Russian / Soviet history, and it is deeply embedded in the operational style and institutions of the existing Soviet system. The ability of that system to resist de-Stalinization seems to indicate a considerable degree of resilience on the part of the dominant mode of politics in the Soviet context. It suggests, at the very least, that political changes are produced very slowly through social change, and that one must wait for at least several generations before social change begins to be significantly reflected in the political sphere.

This argument is reinforced by the contemporary experience of Eastern Europe. Eastern Europe has undergone social change in many ways similar to that of the Soviet Union. The make-up of social classes and the nature of class relations have been altered on the basis of a pattern derived largely from the Soviet experience, in the context of political systems that were initially almost carbon copies of the Soviet. However, the last decade and a half has seen the emergence of remarkably diverse patterns of political behavior in the various East European countries. The character of their political systems seems to be quite different *in spite of* the similarity of social change within them. The spread in the political style and procedures among East Germany, Rumania, Poland, Hungary, and Yugoslavia is quite remarkable, and it does point to the conclusion that similarity in social change does not dictate identity of political behavior. It suggests, on the contrary, that political processes have a viability of their own. If not independent, they are at least not rapidly affected by the patterns of social change.

A more fertile approach to the political consequences of social change might involve analysis based on generational change. But that itself implies that change will be slow, with politically significant effects felt only gradually after a prolonged passage of time. Moreover, even here one must be careful not to assume that a generational change means automatically political change. Transfer of values and of procedures from one generation to another is likely to be more effective in a closed and highly bureaucratized system than in more open pluralistic conditions. In any case, it is unlikely that the effects of the entrance into the upper levels of the Soviet political leadership of the first genuinely post-Stalinist generation would be felt before the late 1970s, and even then, the generation immediately to follow may be more conservative or restorative.[11]

All this is not to deny the argument that alterations in social structure create conditions that affect the scope of the political process and that can moderate the extremes of politics, but it does appear that the process is an extremely tenuous and slow one. Here, too, the contrasting experience of Poland and East Germany in the last two decades is suggestive, since in one case it has involved a relatively stable modus vivendi between the ruling party, a powerful Catholic church, and a relatively free and large agricultural sector, and in the other, the further consolidation of what has emerged as the most successful modern and centrally controlled communist state.

The foregoing would indicate, in turn, that economic change is not the decisive variable in inducing political change as occasionally has been argued. Varying political systems may coexist with similar economic systems and vice versa; they have done so in the past, and they are likely to do so in the future. That being the case, increased economic sophistication in the Soviet Union need not dictate any particular political form, for it can be adjusted to a more centralized or to a more decentralized political framework. Thus, in evaluating the prospects of change, the ability of the Russian political tradition to continue itself through the institutions and procedures of Soviet politics should not be underestimated.

In this connection, one must also take into account the coercive capabilities of the state. That state does have at its disposal extensive means of controls and coercion—and these means are not restrained by legal checks. The following list is a mere summary of the means already available now to the Soviet elite for the enforcement of political compliance:

1. Wiretapping of conversations;
2. Mail surveillance;
3. Informer networks;
4. Control on movement and residence;
5. Personal registration;
6. Computerized data banks;
7. Electronic surveillance, voiceprint detection devices, and so forth;
8. Exile (internal or abroad);
9. Imprisonment in labor camps;
10. Confinement in an insane asylum;

11. Chemical and psychological treatment;
12. Imposition of the death penalty.

With increasing technological, especially electronic, sophistication, the ability of the state to control its citizens will grow—unless legal restraints are deliberately adopted. Since the means of coercion are designed to protect that elite's power and privilege, it seems prudent not to expect too soon the Soviet KGB or MVD to find themselves checked by legal restraints or mass media exposure. These considerations tend to reinforce Medvedev's rather pessimistic conclusion—reached despite his Marxist–Leninist optimism about the effects of social change—that "We see that the movement toward 'tightening of the screws' still seems a more likely prospect than a systematic development of social democracy."[12]

The Question of Degeneration

If it can be argued that social change by itself is not a reliable indicator of the future, then what may be said concerning the future evolution of the Soviet system?[13] Present trends are certainly ambiguous enough. It is here that it may be useful to consider again the argument for degeneration. The tsarist system, given its own historical patterns (the standards for degeneration for a Western type of social–political system would necessarily differ), was degenerating as a political system because—to put it in rather broad terms:

1. It was losing control over social change, and that social change was acquiring external political manifestations contradictory to the values and effective operations of the system.
2. The ability of the political system to make basic policy choices was becoming narrowed by an internal paralysis stemming from increased institutional pluralism.
3. Its elite was beginning to question its own values and was becoming increasingly susceptible to values hitherto perceived as inimical to its interests.
4. The routinization and bureaucratization of elite recruitment was prompting the supremacy of mediocrity over talent, with the latter increasingly forced outside of politics.
5. The authority of the system was becoming questionable both on the grounds of legitimacy and efficiency.

The present Soviet system manifests to a degree some of the symptoms listed—perhaps least so with regard to the third and the last. Admittedly, to assert this is not the same thing as to prove it. Alas, in political science, what is more easily "proven" tends to be also more trivial.[14] More significant propositions concerning the historical processes or even the quality of decision makers necessarily tend to be elusive of the reassuring precision of the statistical method and require somewhat impressionistic and, therefore, also controversial judgments. Since controversy is also a tool of thought, let us run this risk, in the knowledge that what follows cannot be fully "proven" but also in the hope that argument will help us see more clearly the larger picture.

Insofar as the first aspect of degeneration is concerned, recent years have seen relatively little social experimentation from above. The Soviet government has introduced policies designed to narrow somewhat the income gaps, but it has not undertaken to promote any far-reaching social change. Khrushchev's agricultural reforms as well as his administrative reform schemes were perhaps the only recent, but abortive, efforts involving significant change from above. Scholars have been debating the question of whether social differentiation is or is not widening in Soviet society, but there is in any case evidence of considerable inegalitarianism in access to higher education[15] and in lifestyles. Aspirations for more consumption and for more leisure do clash with official values, but these contradictions generally would appear to be less acute than in the later Romanov days.

To the extent that Soviet political institutions and some social ones have now acquired institutional cohesion of the kind lacking under Stalin, it would follow that the ability of the top rulers to make grand choices tends to be narrowed. Incremental decision making becomes more the rule, with bureaucratic bargaining more the normal process. This condition interacts with the first, by gradually increasing the narrow scope for more autonomous social change.

With regard to the morale and motivation of the ruling elite, it does appear that cynicism is widespread—if the testimony of recent emigrés is to be credited. This cynicism evokes lip-service to the official ideology and much passion in the pursuit of privilege and in the preservation of official positions. In that sense, the erosion of revolutionary and ideological fervor is a symptom of degeneration. Moreover, but on a very narrow front, there have been known cases of actual rejection of orthodoxy and of official ideology and its replacement by alternative views. The histories of Sakharov and Medvedev—precisely because both claim to be still Marxists and both have been members of the elite—are in that sense more relevant here than dissidents like Solzhenitsyn. Given the political tradition, given the official and unofficial pressures on behalf of general social orthodoxy, it is a safe—but again unprovable—assumption that cases like Sakharov's stand out not as isolated exceptions but more likely as tips of an iceberg.

To be sure, Sakharov is primarily a scholar. Accordingly, one should also note the larger ideological significance of the remarkable case of Khrushchev. Apart from what his memoirs reveal about the evolution of his own thinking, the fact that he ultimately dictated portions of his memoirs in the knowledge that they would appear in the West—published by the ideological enemy—does signal a degree of ideological revisionism that is objectively inimical to the interests of the established orthodoxy. Shelest's apparent susceptibility to some form of Ukrainian nationalism, which he combined with high ideological orthodoxy, provides another example of ideological vulnerability even at the highest elite level.

That Soviet elite recruitment has become highly routinized and bureaucratized cannot be disputed. That it attracts less talent to the top cannot be conclusively demonstrated. The top Soviet leadership is doubtless better educated and trained than its predecessors and, given its key role in running the system (probably without parallel elsewhere), this is presumably an improvement. The Central Committee, similarly, has a higher quotient of degrees in technology and has a more widely experienced membership than used to be the case. It has also been co-opting the better trained and more successful individuals outside of the Party system, though this could have the effect of diluting the values of the political elite. Moreover, technical or professional expertise does not in itself mean the same thing as political creativity, imagination, responsiveness to change and to new ideas—all of which the Soviet bureaucratic context tends to confine.

It is pertinent to note here that the offspring of the top Soviet elite, young people in a better position than most of their contemporaries to make a free choice of the most fulfilling occupation, tend on the whole not to choose politics, thus telling us something about the attractiveness of Soviet politics.[16] Reports of American students who have studied in Soviet universities—confirmed again by recent emigrés—indicate that generally the Komsomol attracts the less creative, the more careerist, and the rather opportunistic elements in schools of higher learning. With subsequent advancement dependent on—and shaped entirely by—a rigid bureaucratic process, one is justified in hypothesizing that conformity and collusion, rather than creativity and initiative, provide the keys to political elevation.

Finally, with regard to the legitimacy and efficiency of this system, the social situation appears to be somewhat mixed. The efficiency of the system in satisfying daily needs probably is not gaining in public esteem, especially given increasing opportunity of comparison with Eastern Europe and even with the West. But, with the periodic exception of the harvest, neither has it dropped dramatically. The legitimacy of the system also does not appear to be widely questioned, especially among the urban masses, though there are indicators suggesting that increasing (but difficult to estimate) numbers of non-Russians are beginning to press more overtly for national rights—a development that in time could make less legitimate the system for a significant proportion of the Soviet population.

The Past in   Cumulatively, the preceding discussion suggests the
the Future?   conclusion that a process of degeneration has set in, but
                   also that it has not reached critical proportions. That
other political systems, for similar or different reasons depending on
circumstances, may be undergoing a similar process (an argument
sometimes raised in rejoinder to such a proposition) is neither here nor
there, especially since the above by itself casts no light on the adaptability to change of various political systems. In the Soviet case, adaptability
appears to be narrowly circumscribed by the institutional weight and
vested interests of the existing system, by its ideological legacies, and by
the cumulative effects of political tradition on behavior and thought.
Recent efforts to promote a deliberate break with the autocratic past, as
Khrushchev's anti-Stalinism campaign has shown, were effectively resisted and defeated. That experience as well as earlier tsarist cases of
aborted liberalizations suggest that obstacles to a true liberalizing evolution may be difficult to overcome without some dramatic internal or
external catalyst. Perhaps such a catalyst may come to the Soviet Union
from the cultural crisis of the urban-technological society that is likely to
reach it by the end of this decade from the West, but it does not follow
that internal turbulence, *which is to be expected*, will necessarily promote a
liberal–pluralistic evolution.

Rather, we may witness a period of confusion, even of some political
breakdown, made all the more severe by the rapid injection into the
political arena of internal national tensions. The national question inherently complicates any prognosis based on a straight-line projection of
Soviet domestic liberalization. The experience of the last several decades
has shown that communism intensifies nationalism by stimulating mass
popular political awareness. The East European countries and China are
today more nationalistically self-conscious—in depth of feeling and in
scope of social–class–national awareness—than at any point in their
histories. This is also true of the Great Russians in the Soviet Union.
And if that is the case, then it is also likely that the non-Russians of the
Soviet Union will become steadily more and more nationally self-aware.
In fact, there is considerable evidence that this is the case already.

This national self-awareness of the non-Russian nations of the Soviet
Union—denigrated deliberately to the level of Soviet nationalities (a
Soviet term which Western scholars need not adopt)—is still often
Soviet in content; but increasingly, non-Russians wonder why their
nations should not have more autonomy or even formally independent
status—like communist-ruled Hungary or even Mongolia—rather than
be ruled from Moscow by a largely Great Russian elite. These sentiments, if tolerated and accommodated, are likely to grow; if suppressed,
they are likely to grow, too, unless the suppression becomes massive

and sustained (which then would have systemic consequences as a whole).

In either case, the national problem in the Soviet Union bears directly on the problem of change in the Soviet Union. The Great Russian elite knows that an adaptive evolutionary pattern, leading to a more pluralistic system, inevitably means more autonomy and freedom for the non-Russians. This, for nationalistic, big-nation reasons, reinforced by the territorial imperative (especially in regard to the riches of Siberia), they will not tolerate. The national question, therefore, creates a major block to gradual evolution. More than that, it could prove itself to be the fatal contradiction in Soviet political evolution.

The national question also has the effect of strengthening the importance of the party as the coordinating organ, or if the party should weaken, of the military. Some keen observers have already noted the intensifying "militarization of the Soviet social ethos" (in Seweryn Bialer's apt phrase), and that process has obvious political implications. It is noteworthy that Soviet military publications have been taking a noticeably harder line against tendencies that could imply a liberal evolution, and it is reasonable to assume that in internal bureaucratic conflicts, the top Soviet military have been backing the more nationalistic, centralizing, and ideologically orthodox elements.[17] The shift in national goals from a world revolution to world military preeminence also inherently enhances the domestic importance of the military. The military is thus increasingly becoming the major repository of the state tradition and an alternative unifying symbol.

If political change in the Soviet Union should gradually begin to threaten the autocratic tradition, either through an evolution toward a significantly more pluralistic system, or if such change should involve a dangerous decay in the party's ability to integrate the system as a whole or to cope effectively with the social turbulence that might even by the end of this decade spread from the West to the more advanced portions of the Soviet Union, then the military would become the force most likely to respond—with new vigor—in keeping with the imperatives defined by long-enduring traditions. It is certainly no exaggeration to say that today the military are in a more symbiotic relationship with the ruling party, and are thus more directly influential on policy matters, than at any point in Soviet political history.

A dictatorship fusing some of the party and some of the more politicized top military hence becomes a scenario for the future to be taken quite seriously. There is no other elite group in the Soviet Union capable either of supporting the party in the event of a major crisis or of replacing the party in the event the crisis should get out of hand. The managerial elite has neither the coherence nor the ethos. However, even if a Soviet marshal in full uniform were at some future party congress to mount the podium as the party's new Secretary General, his appearance should not be hailed as indicating a sharp discontinuity nor even as marking the end of the period ushered in by 1917. Rather, it would again signal the shaping of the Russian future by the living past.

Notes

[1] On this, see A. M. Kleimola, "The Duty to Denounce in Muscovite Russia," *Slavic Review* (December 1972) especially pp. 777–779.

[2] On use of the census, see Karl A. Wittfogel, "Russia and the East: A Comparison and Contrast," *Slavic Review* (December 1963) especially pp. 638–640.

[3] E. H. Carr, *Socialism in One Country*, vol. 1 (Baltimore: Penguin Books, 1970), p. 25.

[4] Another aspect of the problem pertains to what Samuel P. Huntington has defined as the "bifurcated society." He has argued that "A one-party system is, in effect, the product of the efforts of a political elite to organize and to legitimate rule by one social force over another in a bifurcated society. . . . One-party systems, in short, arise from pronounced bifurcations that cannot be resolved by secession and territorial separation" (*Authoritarian Politics in Modern Society: The Dynamics of Established One-Party Systems* [New York: Basic Books, 1970], pp. 11–12).

[5] This emerged extremely well from I. Deutscher's *The Prophet Unarmed* (London: Oxford University Press, 1959).

[6] Indeed, it may be intriguing to examine other revolutions from this standpoint. To what extent have most revolutions involved revitalization of the dominant social–political patterns and traditions in a slightly new guise, and to what extent do they really mark a fundamental break? More generally, continuity tends to be the rule in political systems, as suggested recently by Ted Robert Gurr, "Persistence and Change in Political Systems, 1800–1971," *American Political Science Review* 63 (December 1974), pp. 1482–1504.

[7] However, the argument that the word *totalitarianism* is a Cold War invention is not really an intellectual argument; those who allege this open themselves to the charge that they themselves may be politically motivated in rejecting it, and hence the argument becomes futile.

[8] I have argued elsewhere that *"This has made for a relationship between the political system and society which is ideologically ritualistic, defensive in character, and—very important—increasingly dysfunctional to the requirements of scientific and intellectual innovation in a relatively developed industrial society.* The political system itself is still totalitarian in its organizational and ideological modes in the sense that it monopolizes effective power and programmatic thinking, and suppresses information of alternative political groupings and programs. But with the political system no longer exacting from society total obedience on behalf of doctrinally defined goals, the relationship between the political system and society is becoming gradually more interacting, more instrumental and less

ideological." Z. Brzezinski, "Dysfunctional Totalitarianism," in *Theory and Politics*, ed. Klaus von Beyme (The Hague, 1972), p. 379.

[9]Jerry F. Hough, "The Soviet System: Petrification or Pluralism?" *Problems of Communism* 21 (March–April 1972):

[10]Roy Medvedev, *On Socialist Democracy* (New York: Alfred A. Knopf, 1975), pp. 67–68. Medvedev develops in his book a much more detailed analysis of the outlook of various oppositionist groups and concludes with a lengthy statement of the desirable evolution toward socialist democracy in the Soviet Union.

[11]In a discussion of Soviet political generations presented by Professor Seweryn Bialer to my seminar at Columbia University, the following scheme for political generations was developed: (1) the conspiratorial:1902–1917; (2) the civil war:1917–1927; (3) the revolution from above / Stalinist:1929–1939; (4) the wartime:1941–1945; (5) the latter-day Stalinist:1945–1953; (6) the post-Stalin turbulence:1956–1964; (7) the bureaucratic restoration:1965–1975.

[12]Roy Medvedev, *On Socialist Democracy* (New York: Alfred A. Knopf, 1975) p. 107.

[13]For an earlier attempt to discuss it, see my *Between Two Ages*, Chapter 4, in which different futures for the Soviet system are discussed. For a perceptive critique, including of my own views, see William Taubman, "The Change to Change in Communist Systems: Modernization. Postmodernization, and Soviet Politics," in *Soviet Politics and Society in the 1970's*, ed. Henry W. Morton and Rudolf W. Tokes (New York: The Free Press, 1974).

[14]I am sympathetic to the arguments developed by Joseph Ben-David, "How to Organize Research in the Social Sciences," *Daedalus* (Spring 1973):

[15]Vladimir Shubkin, " 'Bank Grez' i Balans Sudeb," *Literaturnaia Gazeta*, no. 2 (January 8, 1975), p. 11.

[16]In some East European countries, notably Poland and Czechoslovakia, initial "depoliticization" of the offspring of the upper political elite led rapidly to a "counterpoliticization," which expressed itself both in the Prague "spring" and in the Polish events of March 1968. However, in the Soviet case, there has so far been less evidence of such rapid progression from "depoliticization" to "counterpoliticization."

[17]Roy Medvedev, *On Socialist Democracy* (New York: Alfred A. Knopf, 1975), p. 90.

| 4 | STEPHEN F. COHEN |

The Friends and Foes of Change: Reformism and Conservatism in the Soviet Union*

> The combination of conservative institutions with revolutionary ideas meant that the Republic was the first successful attempt to reconcile the conservative and revolutionary traditions in France. But it also meant that in the twentieth century the forces of change were resisted and obstructed to the point of frustration.
>
> DAVID THOMSON,
> *Democracy in France*

> The theme of the meeting, "Tradition and Innovation," offers an occasion to talk about serious things.
> MIKHAIL ROMM (1962)

Change in the Stalinist system and stubborn resistance to change have been the central features of Soviet political life since Stalin's death in 1953. The rival forces of "innovation and tradition," to use the language

*This chapter grows out of a larger project supported at different times by the John Simon Guggenheim Memorial Foundation and the Center of International Studies at Princeton University. I wish to express my gratitude to these institutions. I wish to point out also that though I speak here of "the Soviet Union," my discussion really applies to the Russian nation within that multinational union.

of the official press, have become "two poles" in Soviet politics and society, which are expressed through "sharp clashes between people standing on both sides of the psychological barrier."[1]

Western students of Soviet affairs were slow to perceive this deep-rooted conflict. Accustomed to seeing only one political tradition and thus only continuity in Soviet history and to imagining the Soviet Union as a frozen "totalitarian" system, most scholars began to think seriously about change and the large controversies it has engendered only in the mid-1960s.[2] Although a valuable scholarship on the subject now exists,[3] it remains inadequate in important respects. Conflict over change is often treated narrowly—either in terms of high Soviet politics and thus apart from society itself, or, at another extreme, in terms of avowed dissidents and thus outside the official political system. No less important, many treatments of the subject lack historical dimensions; and quite a few are couched in a jargon-ridden or value-laden language that obscures more than it reveals.

I propose to argue that the fundamental division between these "two poles" in Soviet life is best understood as a social and political confrontation betweeen *reformism* and *conservatism* in the sense that these terms convey in other countries. In generalizing about different aspects of this great conflict during the 30 years since 1953, I shall raise some questions that I cannot answer. My overview of the post-Stalin era should therefore be read also as a proposed agenda for further discussion.

Reformism and Conservatism

The terms *reformist* and *conservative* do not embrace the full diversity of political outlook, ranging from far left to far right, that has emerged so dramatically in the Soviet Union since the 1950s. As in other societies, these terms designate only mainstream, not extremist, attitudes toward the status quo and toward change. Even a spectrum of political outlook inside the Soviet Communist party, for example, would require at least four categories: authentic democrats, reformers, conservatives, and neo-Stalinist reactionaries.[4] But while full-fledged democrats and neo-Stalinists may, respectively, share many reformist and conservative attitudes, the policies of either would mean radicalism in the Soviet context today, not reform or conservatism. In times of profound crisis, reformism and conservatism everywhere usually give rise to extremist trends and may even grow into their most extreme manifestations—revolution and counterrevolution.[5] But apart from extraordinary historical moments, reformers and conservatives represent the majority of mainstream antagonists—the friends and foes of change—in the Soviet Union as well as in other countries.

Though most scholars use other words to characterize these antagonists in the Soviet Union,[6] the terms reformer and conservative are preferable in important ways. Unlike *functional technocratic modernizer* and similar contrivances, they are not jargonistic or exotic. Unlike liberal and dogmatist or revisionist and orthodox, they do not prejudge or simplify the nature of Soviet reformism and conservatism, which are complex amalgams of opinion and attitudes requiring further analysis rather than restrictive labels. (It is a serious analytical mistake, for example, to insist that real change or reform in the Soviet Union must mean *liberalization* or *democratization* in our sense of these words.) The terms anti-Stalinist and neo-Stalinist are very important, but they identify components within the larger conflict. Above all, archetypical reformers and conservatives are, as even the reticent Soviet press makes clear, "two popular types" in Soviet life, and the universal meaning of reformism and conservatism corresponds fully to the "partisans of the two directions" in the conflicts of the past 25 years. Or as the conservative Molotov put it, "There are . . . reforming Communists, and then there are the real Communists."[7]

Reformism and conservatism, therefore, are concepts that require no special definition in the Soviet context. Both tendencies take on certain national characteristics in different countries because they are expressed in the different idioms of those political cultures. (Soviet conservatives today often speak, for example, in a neo-Stalinist or nineteenth-century Slavophile idiom.) Moreover, the full nature of reformism and conservatism everywhere is always historical, changing from one period to another. (Liberalism and conservatism in England, France, and the United States are not the same today as they were earlier in the twentieth century.) But despite these cultural and historical variations, the basic antagonism between reformers and conservatives is similar in different countries, including the Soviet Union.

Reformism is that outlook, and those policies, which seek through measured change to improve the existing order without fundamentally transforming existing social, political, and economic foundations or going beyond prevailing ideological values. Reformism finds both its discontent and its program, and seeks its political legitimacy and success, within the parameters of the existing order. This distinguishes it from radicalism. The essential reformist argument is that the potential of the existing system and the promise of the established ideology—for example, Marxist socialism in the Soviet Union or liberal democracy in the United States—have not been realized, and that they can and must be fulfilled. The reformist premise is that change is progress. Unlike the conservative, the reformer everywhere, therefore, tends to be agnostic about history and cults of the past. He is opposed to "prejudices inherited from the yesterday of our life," to the "tendency to accept as generally valid many propositions that were appropriate for only one period of our history."[8]

The pivot of conservatism is, on the other hand, a deep reverence for the past, a sentimental defense of existing institutions, routines, and orthodoxies which live on from the past, and an abiding fear of change as the harbinger of disorder and of a future that will be worse than the present as well as a sacrilege of the past. Conservatism is often little more than the sum total of inertia, habit, and vested interests. But it can also be a cogent philosophical justification of the status quo as the culmination of everything good in the historical past and thus the only sturdy bridge to the future.[9] Many conservatives can distinguish between stability and immobilism, and they do not flatly reject all change. But the conservative insistence that any change be slow and tightly controlled by established authority, based on law and order, and conform to prevailing orthodoxies is usually prohibitive. In the end, conservatives usually prefer cults of the past and those authorities (notably, the armed forces and the political police) which guard order against change, native tradition against "alien" corruption, the present against the future.[10]

Authentic reformism and conservatism are always social and political. Both trends are expressed below, in society, in popular sentiments and attitudes, and above, in the middle and higher reaches of the political system, in groups, factions, and parties. And still higher, so to speak, they take the more exalted form of ideological and philosophical propositions.

Both reformism and conservatism have been apparent as antagonists on all three of these levels in the Soviet Union since the 1950s. Although we lack the kind of polling and other survey information available for other countries, we know, for example, from firsthand accounts, that profoundly conservative attitudes are widespread among ordinary citizens and officials alike.[11] Detailed scholarly studies point out the sustained struggles between reformist and conservative groups inside the high political establishment, including the party itself.[12] And, as we shall see, the ideological and even philosophical dimensions of this quarrel have become particularly evident in recent years.

What we do not know, and indeed barely perceive, is the relationship between these trends in society below and in the political apparatus above. Though this is partly a problem of inadequate information, it derives also from the untenable but persistent notion that Soviet party–state officialdom is somehow insulated from society itself. This conception makes no empirical sense in a country where the state employs almost every citizen and the party has 18 million members. All of the trends in society, even those expressed by dissidents, also exist, however subterraneanly, inside political officialdom. There is, at best, as one Western scholar argues, a "soft boundary" between the two.[13] Once we abandon the commonplace image of a gulf separating political officialdom and society, and see them instead, in the imagery of a Soviet dissident, as "upstairs" and "downstairs,"[14] the fuller social dimensions of the political conflict between Soviet reformism and conservatism will at least come into view.

At the level of politics and policy, the conflict between reformism and conservatism derives its scope and intensity from the fact that it is simultaneously a quarrel about the past, the present, and the future. The historical agnosticism of the reformer and the historicism of the conservative are, therefore, especially antagonistic in a country such as the Soviet Union, where what its citizens call "living history" has been unusually traumatic. Not only the immediate Stalinist past but also the remote tsarist past are subjects of fierce controversy. Conservatives bitterly protest the reformist "deheroization" of the past and the view in which "the past, present, and future . . . turn out to be isolated, shut off from each other." The conservative extols the "continuity of generations"; the reformer replies, "If the children do not criticize the fathers, mankind does not move ahead." For conservatives, reformist perspectives "distort the past"; for reformers, conservatives "idealize the past" and try "to save the past from the present."[15]

These historical controversies have been an essential part of almost all policy disputes throughout the post-Stalin era. They reflect the political struggle between the forces of reform and conservatism inside Soviet officialdom from 1953 to the present—from an official reformation to a far-reaching conservative reaction.

From Reformism to Conservatism

Because of the unusually despotic nature of his long rule, Stalin's death unleashed a decade-long triumph of Soviet reformism which was disproportionate to its actual strength in society or officialdom. Virtually every area of Soviet life was affected (and improved). Though bitterly opposed, often contradictory, and ultimately limited, the changes of the 1950s and early 1960s constituted a reformation—within the limits of the authoritarian system—in Soviet politics and society, as indicated by a brief recitation of the most important reforms.

The kind of personal dictatorship exercised by Stalin for more than 20 years ended, and the Communist party was restored as the ruling political institution. Twenty-five years of mass terror came to an end, and the political police, the main agency of Stalin's dictatorship, was brought under control. Millions of prison camp survivors were freed, and many who had perished in the terror were legally exonerated, thereby enabling survivors and relatives to regain full citizenship. Many administrative abuses and bureaucratic privileges were curtailed. Educated society began to participate more fully in political and intellectual life. A wide array of economic and welfare reforms were carried out. Major revisions were made in Soviet censorship practices, in the official ideology of Marxism–Leninism, and in foreign policy.

Insofar as this was official reformism, or reform from above, Nikita Khrushchev was its leader, and his overthrow in 1964 marked the beginning of its political defeat.[16] Khrushchev himself was a contradictory figure. His background and career made him the representative of the old as well as the new; and some of his policies, as in certain areas of science, favored conservative forces. But in terms of his over-all administration, Khrushchev was, as Russians say, a great reformer (*velikii reformator*).

Nonetheless, Khrushchev and his faction at the top were only part of a much broader reformist movement inside Soviet officialdom. During the decade after 1953, the struggle between the friends and foes of change spread to all areas of policymaking—to the areas of administration and planning, industry and agriculture, science, history, culture, law, family matters, welfare, ideology, and foreign affairs.[17] In each of these areas, reform found notable spokesmen and important allies.[18] Like conservatism, whose adherents ranged from old-line Stalinists to Tory-style moderates, Soviet reformism must be understood as an amalgam of diverse types and motives. It included technocrats in search only of limited change in their special areas as well as authentic democrats; it derived from self-interest as well as idealism. But in relation to the overarching question of change, something akin to two distinct parties—reformist and conservative—emerged inside Soviet officialdom, and within the Communist party itself, counterposing rival interests, policies, and ideas over a wide range of issues in all political quarters.[19]

Conservatism, as a defense of the inherited Stalinist order, was more fully formed as an ideological and policy movement in the years immediately following Stalin's death. By the early 1960s, however, reformers had developed a characteristic cluster of reformist policies, historical perspectives, and ideological propositions. Most of these were developed, both as critique and program, in opposition to conservative ones, which still drew heavily upon the Stalinist past. There were many of these reformist ideas by the early 1960s, and they cannot easily be summarized. A few examples must suffice.

While conservatives eulogized the tsarist and Stalinist pasts, and particularly the 1930s, when many existing Soviet institutions took shape, reformers rehabilitated the radical intelligentsia of the nineteenth century, the Soviet 1920s, and a generation of Old Bolsheviks purged by Stalin. While conservatives accented the authoritarian stands in Marxism–Leninism, the Stalin cult, and the dangers of revisionism, reformers stressed socialist democracy, Lenin himself, the criminality of Stalin, and the dangers of dogmatism. Against the conservative themes of Russian nationalism, Soviet hegemony in the communist world, and xenophobia, reformers emphasized internationalism, different roads to socialism, and an opening to the West. In contrast to the conservative preference for heavy-handed censorship, reformers promoted varying degrees of cultural and intellectual liberalism. As opposed to the overly centralized Stalinist system of economic planning and administration, with its decades of heavy industrialism, agricultural retardation, waste, and austerity, reformers advocated the market, decentralized initiative, efficiency, consumer goods, and innovations in order to encourage private initiative in the collective system. Against the Stalinist tradition of terror, reformers called for rule of law and due process.[20]

Soviet reformers won many victories during the Khrushchev years. But reform from above everywhere is always limited in substance and duration, and it is usually followed by a conservative backlash. This circumstance is partly a result of the nature of reformism, which struggles against the natural inertia of people and institutions on behalf of limited goals. Many adherents of reform are quickly satisfied, many allies are easily unnerved, and many who only tolerated reform are soon driven to oppose further change. All become part of a neoconservative consensus, defenders of the new, reformed status quo, and critics of reformist "excesses." Indeed, this reformist–conservative rhythm is thought to be axiomatic in American and British politics, where Republicans and Tories are expected to follow Democrats and Labourites.

The overthrow of Khrushchev in October 1964 reflected this swing of the pendulum in Soviet officialdom and possibly in society as well. His fall ushered in, after an interlude of uncertain direction in 1964–1965, a far-reaching conservative reaction, which brought an end to major reform and even some counterreform in most areas of Soviet society, from economics and law, to historiography, culture, and ideology. After 1966, and especially after the Soviet overthrow of the reform communist government in Czechoslovakia in 1968, the Brezhnev administration was a regime of conservatism. It revived many of the conservative practices just noted as well as the preeminent symbol of the past, Stalin himself. Its antireformist spirit and policies were expressed in a galaxy of refurbished conservative catch phrases and campaigns—"stability in cadres," "law and order," "the strengthening of organization, discipline, and responsibility in all spheres," "military–heroic patriotism," "developed socialism," "vigilance against bourgeois influences," and more.[21] In short, it reasserted conservative views on the past, the present, and the future.

The conservative reaction since 1964, though far-reaching, has not meant a restoration of, or return to, Stalinist policies. With society and politics themselves, conservative attitudes and policies change. Stalinism no longer defines Soviet realities, and therefore mainstream Soviet conservatism, as it did in the early 1950s. The Brezhnev government reversed some reforms of the Khrushchev years; but, for the most part, it tempered and administered already accomplished reforms as part of the new status quo while deploring earlier "excesses" and setting itself against further change. (Republicans and Tories did the same upon returning to office in the United States and England in the 1950s.)

Some ideas and policies once associated with Soviet reformers—consumerism, higher investment in agriculture, welfarism, scientific management, legal proceduralism, detente, repudiation of Stalin's "excesses" were even incorporated into the new conservatism. This did not demonstrate, as some Western observers thought, the reformist spirit of the Brezhnev government because these once reformist ideas were infused with deeply conservative meaning. "Economic reform," for example, has been an official idea intermittently since 1964; but the original reforms were stripped of their essentials—the role of the market and decentralization—so that, in the words of one reformer, they became "purely superficial, partial changes which do not affect the essence of the prereform system."[22] The official repudiation of reform since the mid-1960s was clearly understood by people inside the Soviet Union: "We are ruled not by a Communist or a fascist party and not by a Stalinist party, but by a status quo party."[23]

By the late 1960s, the increasingly censorious conservatism of the Brezhnev government had muted reformist voices, and thus explicit conflict, in many policy areas. At the same time, however, and possibly for this reason, the conflict between reformers and conservatives broke out dramatically in a different way in the official press: in an often abstract controversy about the nature of Russia as a historical society. Focusing on philosophical, cultural, and even religious themes, the two rival outlooks have now been openly at odds for more than a decade.[24] This controversy echoes the split between Westerners and Slavophiles in nineteenth-century Russia, but its real importance is contemporary and intensely political. It is a confrontation, couched in a philosophical and older Russian idiom, between present-day Soviet reformism and conservatism. The traditional idiom of the conservatives, with their advocacy of Russia's "eternal values," has become particularly forthright, leading reformers to protest that their ideas are "borrowed, transcribed, taken on hire from the storehouse of conservative literature of the past century."[25]

This neoconservative philosophy, which was, in many respects, congruent with the policy spirit and Russian nationalism of the Brezhnev government, has spread throughout the Soviet press (and *samizdat*) and demonstrated remarkable appeal to many segments of the population. Its popularity tends to confirm firsthand evidence that official conservatism is not a regime-made artifice but a reflection of broad and deep currents in Soviet officialdom and society.[26] It has become clear that the great reforms of the Khrushchev years derived more from unusual historical circumstances than from the actual political and social strength of reformism in the Soviet Union. For a fuller perspective on the post-Stalin era and on the future, we need, then, at least a brief look at the historical origins of contemporary reformism and conservatism in the Stalinist past.

The Stalinist	The first great reform in Soviet history was the
Roots of	introduction of the New Economic Policy (NEP) in
Reformism	1921. Intended to replace the extremist practices of
and	the civil war years, NEP quickly grew into a whole
	series of policies and ideas which Lenin, the father
Conservatism	of NEP, called "a reformist approach."[27] For 4 years

after Lenin's death in 1924, NEP remained official
Soviet policy, with Nikolai Bukharin as its interpreter and great defender. Thus, when Stalin forcibly abolished NEP in 1929, he inadvertently created a historical model for future generations of communist reformers. Since that time, and especially after 1953, NEP—with its dual economy, concepts of market and plan, cultural diversity, more liberal politics, and Leninist legitimacy—has exercised a powerful appeal to anti-Stalinist party reformers everywhere, from Moscow to Eastern and Western Europe. Soviet reformers have revived many NEP economic ideas; reformist historians have studied NEP admiringly; cultural liberals have cited its tolerant censorship; and reform politicians have sought legitimacy in it.[28]

With the defeat of the Bukharinist opposition (or "right deviation"), the end of NEP, and the onset of Stalin's revolution from above in 1929, party reformism became the special enemy and victim of Stalinism. There were at least two serious attempts by high officials to initiate reform from above during the Stalin years. The first involved the so-called Kirov group in the Politburo in 1933–1934, which proposed to ameliorate the terrible hardships of forcible collectivization and heavy industrialization. The second was in 1947–1948; it apparently involved similar proposals, by the Politburo member Nikolai Voznesensky and others, for change in economic policy. Both attempts to reform Stalinism ended horribly—in the great terror of 1936–1939 and in the Leningrad purge of 1949 and Voznesensky's execution.[29]

Nonetheless, this melancholy history of failed reform shows that even during the worst Stalin years, there was a reformist impulse among high party and state officials. These early strivings toward a "Moscow Spring" (as an insider termed them in 1936) were the official antecedents of Khrushchev's reformism, as he tacitly acknowledged by associating his de-Stalinization campaign with the Kirov affair and by rehabilitating Voznesensky. But it also shows that reform from above stood no chance in the conditions of Stalin's terroristic autocracy and in the face of his personal hostility, which remained adamant to the end.[30]

And yet while Stalin martyred reform at every turn, his system and policies were creating the future political and social base of reformism. The historical Stalinism of 1929–1953 was an extraordinary composite of dualities. Stalinism began as a radical act of revolution from above and ended as a rigidly conservative social and political system. It combined revolutionary traditions with tsarist ones; humanitarian ideas of social justice with terror; radical ideology with traditional social policies; the myths of socialist democracy and party rule with the reality of personal

dictatorship; modernization with archaic practices; a routinized bureaucracy with administrative caprice.

Reformism and conservatism grew out of these dualities after Stalin
in two general ways. First, the values and ideas of both post-Stalin
reformers and conservatives has been perpetuated in Stalinism. Russian
nationalism, terror, and privilege came to dominate, for example, but
their opposites remained part of the official ideology. They were maintained in an uneasy state of latent conflict, as a kind of dual Soviet
political culture, by the Stalin cult and the terror.[31] After Stalin's death,
these currents went separate political ways into the conflict of the last 30
years, especially into the conflict between anti-Stalinism and neo-
Stalinism, which in the 1950s and early 1960s played a special role in the
confrontation between reformers and conservatives.

The second way in which the Stalinist system prepared its own
reformation was, as Marxists say, dialectical. Stalinism created within
itself an alternative model of political rule.[32] The agent of this potential
change was not, as Marxist critics of Stalinism had hoped for so long, an
activist working class, but Stalin's own political–administrative bureaucracy. Having grown large and powerful under his rule since the 1930s,
the leading strata (nachal'stvo) of the party–state bureaucracy gained
almost everything—income, privilege, status, power over those below.
But what they lacked was no less important: security of position and,
even more, of life. Stalin's terror inflicted one demographic trauma after
another. And no one was more vulnerable after 1934 than the party–
state nachal'stvo.

The history and ethos of Stalinism made this bureaucracy profoundly
conservative in most political and social ways.[33] It yearned, however,
for one great reform that would free it from the capricious terroristic
regime at the top and allow it to become a real bureaucracy—that is, a
conservative force based on stability, personal security, and predictability. While Stalin lived, even the highest officials felt themselves to be
"temporary people" and sought protection against the abnormality of
the terror in various legalisms.[34] But normality in this sense could come
only with the end of the autocrat.

Both reformism and conservatism were thus already in place when
Stalin's death finally came in March 1953. The first words of his heirs,
imploring the population to avoid "panic and disarray," revealed them
as fearful conservatives (who always imagine disorder below) in important respects. Fear of retribution from below and another terror from
above led them quickly to major reforms, from which others followed:
the dismantling and curtailment of Stalin's primary institutions (his
secretariat, the terror system, and the cult) and the restoration of party
dictatorship and collective leadership.[35] Restoring the party to political
primacy was in itself a major change that had far-reaching ramifications.
It proved to be remarkably easy, reformist rather than revolutionary,

partly because it promised at last protection from terror to high officials throughout the system. Indeed, this was the essential reformist meaning of Khrushchev's "secret" speech against Stalin in 1956. For most high officials, this may have been not only popular but also sufficient.

These circumstances help to explain the success of Khrushchev's initial reforms, even though reformism probably was, and remains, a minority outlook in Soviet officialdom. His rise to power and policy successes in 1953–1958 were based on a kind of reformism, or de-Stalinization, which had broader appeal in these special historical circumstances. The majority of Soviet officials and elites wanted, it seems clear, an end to terror, a diminishing of the police system, some historical revisionism, relaxation of international tensions, and certain welfare reforms (in pensions, for example) which benefited them as well. They wanted, and got, a thaw—but not a spring.

After 1958, Khrushchev's reformism and renewed de-Stalinization campaign began to mean something different. They came to include quasi-populist policies, or ideas, that impinged directly upon the nature of the central party–state bureaucracy and its relations with society, rather than with the regime above.[36] The quiescent conservative majority emerged and began to resist. Khrushchev became an embattled leader. That he managed to achieve as much as he did after 1958, despite the opposition, his many ill-conceived policies, and his personal inadequacies as a reform leader, is probably explained partly by the momentum and political appeal of anti-Stalinism.[37] When this cause was spent in the early 1960s, so, too, were Khrushchev's great reforms.

Soviet Conservatism and the Future of Reform

The real obstacle to future reform in the Soviet Union is not this or that institution, group, faction, or leader but the profound conservatism that seems to dominate them all, from the ordinary family to the Politburo, from local authorities to the state *nachal'stvo*. It can be argued that the Soviet Union has become, both downstairs and upstairs, one of the most conservative countries in the world.[38] Real discussion of the prospects for further change, therefore, must await fuller scholarly study of this political and social conservatism, which manifests itself daily, in all areas of life, as a preference for tradition and order and a fear of innovation and disorder.

It may be argued that a system born in revolution and still professing revolutionary ideas cannot be called conservative, but history has witnessed other such transformations as well as the inner deradicalization of revolutionary ideologies.[39] Indeed, the conservative aftermath of a great social revolution may be a kind of historical law.[40] If so, we might expect this to have been doubly the case in Russia, where revolution from below in 1917 was followed by Stalin's revolution from above in 1929–1933. Early Bolsheviks worried that even their own party might end in this way. One warned: "History is full of examples of the transformation of parties of revolution into parties of order. Sometimes the only mementos of a revolutionary party are the watchwords which it has inscribed on public buildings."[41]

There are, in addition, many specific, and mutually reinforcing, sources of Soviet conservatism. Although specialists disagree as to the most important factors in Soviet political life, almost all of these factors have contributed to its conservatism. There is the legacy of tsarist Russia, with its own bureaucratic and conservative traditions. There is the subsequent bureaucratization of Soviet life in the 1930s, which proliferated conservative norms and created a *nomenklatura* class of zealous defenders of position and privilege.[42] There is, in this connection, the persistent scarcity of goods and services, which redoubles the resistance of vested interests. There is the increasing age of Soviet ruling elites. And there is even the official ideology, whose domestic thrust turned many years ago from creating a new order to extolling the existing one.

Underlying all of these factors is the Soviet historical experience with its particular combination of monumental achievements and mountainous disasters. Man-made catastrophes have repeatedly victimized millions of ordinary citizens and officials alike—the first European war, revolution, civil war, two great famines, forcible collectivization, Stalin's great terror, World War II, and more. Out of this experience, which is still autobiographical for many people, have come the joint pillars of today's Soviet conservatism: a towering pride in the nation's modernizing and Great-Power achievements, together with an abiding anxiety that the next disaster forever looms and that change is "some sinister Beethovean knock of fate at the door."[43] This is a conservatism at once prideful and fearful, and thus powerful. It appears to influence most segments of the population, even many dissidents, to be a real bond between upstairs and downstairs, and, therefore, the main obstacle to change.

Much would seem to favor, then, only conservatism in Soviet politics. And yet, as we have seen, this has not been the entire story of the post-Stalin years; nor is it now. Advocates of change, however weak their position and however diverse their reformist aspirations, continue to exist in most policy areas and even to hold responsible positions in lower and middle levels of the party–state officialdom.[44] Indeed, one enduring reform of the post-Stalin years has been a broadening of the political system sufficient to tolerate such people even during a conservative regime. Therefore, some of the general factors favoring a resurgence of official reformism must also be taken into account. Leaving aside the possibility of serious domestic crises and assuming that Soviet reformers stand a chance only in an international environment of diminishing tensions, three weaknesses in Soviet conservatism should be emphasized because they point to permanent sources of reformism in the Soviet system.

Like conservatives everywhere, Soviet opponents of change need a usable past in order to justify and defend the status quo. The relevant past includes, however, the criminal history of Stalinism. Soviet conservatives have coped with this problem in two ways since the fall of Khrushchev. They have selectively rehabilitated the Stalinist past, largely in terms of the great Soviet victory over Germany in World War II, and without fully rehabilitating Stalin himself.[45] And they have groped toward a surrogate past in tsarist history. Neither seems to be a durable solution. Historical de-Stalinization, which is a powerful source of political reformism, retains its appeal not only because tens of millions died, but because millions of wartime casualties can be blamed directly on the Stalinism government. As for the tsarist past, though partially rehabilitated under Stalin and of considerable appeal today, its traditions are nonetheless contrary to the ideas of the Russian revolution, which official conservatives still embrace as the main source of their legitimacy. These two traditions cannot be durably reconciled. Ultimately, they inspire rival currents, conflict not harmony in political life, as was the case in postrevolutionary France.[46]

The second conservative weakness and source of reformism is the plain discrepancy between the official ideology and everyday Soviet realities. Except for a small segment of the population, this is not foremost a discrepancy between democratic ideas and dictatorial practices but something more fundamental. As an official ideology, Soviet communism has come increasingly to mean, in addition to Russian nationalism and national security, consumer goods plus the welfare state. These latter commitments are exceedingly important to ordinary citizens, to middle-class officials, and to the government. They were the main domestic pledges of the conservative Brezhnev government after the mid-1960s as well as its most glaring failures.[47] Though elementary welfare provisions were achieved much earlier, low standards of living, chronic shortages of basic foodstuffs and housing, and the scarcity of other consumer goods remain widespread and intractable problems of everyday Soviet life.

As repeatedly expressed ideological commitments, to officialdom as well as to society-at-large, these consumer-welfare promises cannot be easily withdrawn or forever deferred. They are a relentless threat to Soviet conservatives because they attract constant attention to the inadequacies of the centralized economic system and thus keep meaningful economic reform permanently on the agenda. And, as both reformers and conservatives understand, this kind of economic reform, involving decentralization and the market, must have reformist implications in political life as well.[48]

The third factor favoring reform also involves official ideology. The role of Marxism–Leninism, or communism, may have declined in recent years, but it remains the essential framework for discourse and conflict throughout official Soviet politics. No reformist or conservative movement anywhere can be successful if it is estranged from established political norms and culture. Soviet conservatives and reformers must have a Soviet face; they must find inspiration and legitimacy somewhere within historical Marxism–Leninsim. Conservatives are trying, as reformers complain, to fill "Marxist formulas" with their own meanings.[49] But Marxism–Leninism is an unreliable conservative vehicle because it is an ideology, even in its dogmatized version, based upon the very idea, desirability, and inexorability of change. Soviet reformers miss no opportunity to make this point: "Any apologetics for things as they are is alien to the materialistic dialectic. . . . This applies to any particular form society may have assumed at any stage in its development. To search constantly for new and imaginative ways to transform reality— that is the motto of the dialectic."[50]

In this respect, Soviet reformers have an important advantage over their nineteenth-century counterparts in tsarist officialdom, whose experience may be highly relevant.[51] Struggling against a conservative majority of Russian officials in the decades leading up to the major reforms from above in the 1860s, tsarist reformers were seriously hampered by an official ideology thoroughly hostile to the idea of real change. They had to seek ideological inspiration and legitimacy elsewhere, in suspect "foreign" cultures. Official Soviet reformers do not have this problem, or at least not as acutely. Moreover, they can, and regularly do, point to existing models of communist reform in Eastern Europe as examples which are Marxist–Leninist and thus fraternal rather than "foreign."[52]

The experience of official reformers under tsarism suggests another important perspective. The growth of reformist sentiments and "enlightened" officials was a slow, cumulative process. It extended over decades and included many setbacks. During the long winter of reform, such ideas could openly circulate only outside the bureaucracy, in circles of nineteenth-century nonconformists, before percolating into the bureaucracy to influence policy. The role of today's Soviet dissidents and their *samizdat* discussions is pertinent to this process. Incapable of effecting reform themselves, since it can come only from above, their real function must be to contribute to the growth of reformist ideas and thus to the "enlightenment" of future officials.[53] Viewed in this way, it could be argued that the sudden, escalating reforms of the Khrushchev years were premature, that the "enlightenment" process was just beginning in officialdom, and that the conservative reaction of the Brezhnev years was not the end but only a stage in the history of post-Stalin reform.

This perspective raises a final question. Successful reform is always a result of political coalitions, a fact of special importance to Soviet reformers, who apparently represent a distinct minority of officials. Unable to draw strength directly from protest movements below, as reformers in other societies have done, and advocating economic policies that threaten many petty administrators and even workers,[54] Soviet reformers can find allies only among the conservative majority of officials, who have seemed more attracted by neo-Stalinism in recent years. Is this a real possibility?

"The boundary between progressive and conservative runs through each of us," remarked a Czech official during the Prague Spring.[55] Soviet reformers must appeal to this "progressive" element in moderate conservatives. Historians tell us that conservatives are uncomfortable reformers, but that many become reformers to save what they believe is most important in the existing order of things.[56] There is some evidence that in the 1960s and 1970s, a consensus for change was forming between moderate reformers and moderate conservatives, at least among the party intelligentsia. It seemed to center on commonly perceived problems such as the degradation of country life, declining labor productivity, drunkenness, the Stalinist past, and the heavy-handed censorship that frustrated conservatives as well as reformers.[57] The emergence of such a consensus may not yet be in the making, but it is the best, and probably only, hope for reform.

Notes

[1] A. M. Rumiantsev, "Vstupaiushchemu v mir nauki," *Pravda*, June 8, 1967; "Kogda otstaiut ot vremeni," *Pravda* (editorial) (January 27, 1967); and O. Latsis, "Novoe nado otstaivat," *Novyi mir*, no. 10 (1965), p. 255. The theme of innovation versus tradition has been the subject of endless polemics since 1953. It also runs persistently through Soviet fiction, from Vladimir Dudintsev's *Ne khlebom edinym*, published in 1956, to Aleksandr Zinov'ev's *Svetloe budushchee* (Lausanne, 1978).

[2] For critical discussion of these habits in Soviet studies, see Stephen F. Cohen, "Bolshevism and Stalinism," in *Stalinism: Essays in Historical Interpretation*, ed. Robert C. Tucker (New York, 1977), pp. 3–29; Carl A. Linden, *Khrushchev and the Soviet Leadership* (Baltimore, 1966), pp. 1–9; and William Taubman, "The Change to Change in Communist Systems," in *Soviet Politics and Society in the 1970's*, ed. Henry W. Morton and Rudolf L. Tökés (New York, 1974), pp. 369–394.

[3] Among the most interesting studies are Zbigniew Brzezinski, "The Soviet Political System: Transformation or Degeneration?," in *Dilemmas of Change in Soviet Politics*, ed. Zbigniew Brzezinski (New York, 1969), pp. 1–34; Jerry F. Hough, *The Soviet Union and Social Science Theory* (Cambridge, Mass., 1977), chap. 1; George W. Breslauer, "Khrushchev Reconsidered," *Problems of Communism* (September-October, 1976), pp. 18–33; and George W. Breslauer, *Five Images of the Soviet Future: A Critical Review and Synthesis* (Berkeley, 1978).

[4] My categories derive from, though they do not fully correspond to, the following firsthand accounts: Roy A. Medvedev, *On Socialist Democracy* (New

York, 1975), chap. 3 and *passim*; Alexander Yanov, *Detente After Brezhnev: The Domestic Roots of Soviet Foreign Policy* (Berkeley, 1977); and Igor Glagolev, "Sovetskoe rukovodstvo: Segodnia i zavtra," *Russkaia mysl'* (August 31, 1978). Considerable information on trends in the party is available in *Politicheskii dnevnik*, 2 vols. (Amsterdam, 1972 and 1975).

[5]Arno J. Mayer, *Dynamics of Counterrevolution in Europe, 1870–1956: An Analytic Framework* (New York, 1971), chap. 2.

[6]There are important exceptions. See Sidney I. Ploss, *Conflict and Decision-Making in Soviet Russia: A Case Study of Agricultural Policy, 1953–63* (Princeton, 1965); Linden, *Khrushchev and the Soviet Leadership*, which includes an excellent discussion of this spectrum (pp. 18–21); and Moshe Lewin, *Political Undercurrents in Soviet Economic Debates: From Bukharin to the Modern Reformers* (Princeton, 1974).

[7]Alexander Yanov, "Essays on Soviet Society," *International Journal of Sociology* 6, no. 2–3 (Summer–Fall, 1976), esp. pp. 75–175; G. Kozlov and M. Rumer, "Tol'ko nachalo (Zametki o khoziaistvennoi reforme)," *Novyi mir*, no. 11 (1966), p. 182; F. Chapchakhov, "Pod vidom gipotezy," *Literaturnaia gazeta* (August 16, 1972), which is an attack on, and an inadvertent confirmation of, Yanov's two "types"; and Molotov, quoted in Giuseppe Boffa, *Inside the Khrushchev Era* (New York, 1959), p. 108. The word *conservative* (*konservator*) is commonly used in the Soviet Union. Various words or expressions are used to express "reformer," though the English word (*reformist*) is coming into use. See Valentin Turchin, *Inertsiia strakha* (New York, 1977), p. 5. Soviet writers often use these concepts, with obvious implications for the reader, in analyzing other political societies. See, for example, M. P. Mchedlov, *Evoliutsiia sovremennogo katolitsizma* (Moscow, 1966).

[8]V. Lakshin, "Ivan Denisovich, ego druz'ia i nedrugi," *Novyi mir*, no. 1 (1964), p. 230; Medvedev, *On Socialist Democracy*, p. 41.

[9]For the range of factors (fear, self-interest, philosophy) that animate conservative opposition to economic reform in the Soviet Union, for example, see the series of articles by A. Birman in *Novyi mir* between 1965 and 1968, and especially his "Sut' reformy," in no. 12, 1968, pp. 185–204.

[10]For a summary of the extensive literature on modern conservatism, see Clinton Rossiter, "Conservatism," *International Encyclopedia of the Social Sciences*, vol. 3 (New York, 1968), pp. 290–295.

[11]See, for example, Turchin, *Inertsiia strakha*; Medvedev, *On Socialist Democracy*; Yanov, *Essays on Soviet Society*; Andrei Amalrik, *Will the Soviet Union Survive until 1984?* (New York, 1970); and Note 9.

[12]In addition to the titles cited in Note 6, see Michel Tatu, *Power in the Kremlin: From Khrushchev to Kosygin* (New York, 1969); H. Gordon Skilling and Franklyn Griffiths, eds., *Interest Groups in Soviet Politics* (Princeton, 1971); Seweryn Bialer, *Stalin's Successors* (New York, 1980); and George W. Breslauer, *Khrushchev and Brezhnev as Leaders* (New York, 1982).

[13]See Lewin, *Political Undercurrents in Soviet Economic Debates*, pp. 262, 298.

[14]Alexander Yanov, *The Russian New Right: Right-Wing Ideologies in the Contemporary USSR* (Berkeley, 1978), p. 15.

[15]*Politicheskii dnevnik*, I, p. 123; F. Chapchakhov, "Pod vidom gipotezy," *Literaturnaia gazeta* (August 16, 1972); *Politicheskii dnevnik*, no. 66 (*samizdat*;

Moscow, March 1970), p. 36; A. Iakovlev, "Protiv antiistorizma," *Literaturnaia gazeta* (November 15, 1975).

[16]See Linden, *Khrushchev and the Soviet Leadership*; and Breslauer, "Khrushchev Reconsidered."

[17]In addition to the titles cited in Notes 6 and 12 see the sections on the 1950s and 1960s in the following works: Nancy Whittier Heer, *Politics and History in the Soviet Union* (Cambridge, Mass., 1971); Peter H. Juviler and Henry W. Morton, eds., *Soviet Policy-Making: Studies of Communism in Transition* (New York, 1967); Peter H. Juviler, *Revolutionary Law and Order: Politics and Social Change in the USSR* (New York, 1976); Gail Warshofsky Lapidus, *Women in Soviet Society: Equality, Development and Social Change* (Berkeley, 1978); Aron Katsenelinboigen, *Studies in Soviet Economic Planning* (White Plains, N.Y., 1978); Timothy McClure, "The Politics of Soviet Culture, 1964–1967," *Problems of Communism*, (March–April, 1967), pp. 26–43.

[18]Individuals such as Aleksandr Tvardovskii in literature; A. Birman, V. G. Venzher, and G. S. Lisichkin in economics; A. M. Rumiantsev and F. M. Burlatskii in the social sciences; M. D. Shargorodskii in law; V. P. Danilov and M. Ia. Gefter in history; and so on. One *samizdat* writer has suggested that "it would be truer to call the epoch of Khrushchev, the epoch of Tvardovskii," because of his editorship of the reformist journal *Novyi mir*.

[19]*Pravda* (January 27, 1967) discussed the reformist journal *Novyi mir* and the conservative journal *Oktiabr'* in terms of the "two poles" in Soviet politics. Soviet intellectuals sometimes spoke of them privately in the 1960s as the "organs of our two parties."

[20]To give a few more cryptic examples of code words in the conflict, reformers and conservatives emphasized, respectively, the following: bureaucratism as the main danger—anarchy as the main danger; the Lenin of 1921–1923—the Lenin of 1918–1920; the importance of the intelligentsia—the importance of the worker and the soldier; the Twentieth and Twenty-second Party Congresses—the Twenty-third, Twenty-fourth, and Twenty-fifth Congresses; modernism in art—traditionalism in art; internal problems—external threats; women's rights—the stability of the family; innovation—discipline; renewal of cadres—stability of cadres; social interests—the organic unity of society.

[21]See, for example, *Razvitoe sotsialisticheskoe obshchestvo: Sushchnost', kriterii zrelosti, kritika revizionistskikh kontseptsii* (Moscow, 1973); P. M. Rogachev and M. A. Sverklin, *Patriotizm i obshchestvennyi progress* (Moscow, 1974); and the editorials in *Pravda*, February 5 and 24, and October 17, 1978. For discussion of important aspects of these conservative policies, see T. H. Rigby, "The Soviet Leadership: Towards a Self-Stabilizing Oligarchy?," *Soviet Studies* (October 1970), pp. 167–191; his "The Soviet Regional Leadership: The Brezhnev Generation," *Slavic Review* 37, no. 1 (March 1978), pp. 1–24; and Breslauer, "Khrushchev Reconsidered."

[22]Quoted in Iu. Subotskii, "Upravlenie, khozraschet, samostoiatel'nost'," *Novyi mir*, no. 7 (1969), p. 265.

[23]Lev Kopelev, quoted in *The New York Times*, December 3, 1978, p. 14.

[24]The controversy began with the rival journals *Novyi mir* and *Molodaia gvardiia*, but it has since spread to many publications. For an excellent survey and analysis, see Frederick C. Barghoorn, "The Political Significance of Great

Russian Nationalism in Brezhnev's USSR with Particular Reference to the 'Pseudo-Slavophiles'" (Paper delivered at the AAASS Conference, Washington, D.C., October 1977).

[25]Yanov, *Essays on Soviet Society*, p. 124. For similar protests, see A. Dement'ev, "O traditsiiakh i narodnosti," *Noyvi mir*, no. 4 (1969), pp. 215–235; Iakovlev, "Protiv antiistorizma," *Literaturnaia gazeta* (November 15, 1975); and the running objections in the *samizdat* journal *Politicheskii dnevnik*. Though the idiom is plainly Russian, it is sometimes universally conservative, even Burkean. See, for example, the eulogy of "social authority" and the "continuity of generations" in S. Semanov, *Serdtse rodina* (Moscow, 1977), pp. 92–93.

[26]See Note 11 above.

[27]See Stephen F. Cohen, *Bukharin and the Bolshevik Revolution: A Political Biography, 1888–1938* (New York, 1973), pp. 132–138. Soviet reformers have been eager to identify NEP as "the first reform." See, for example, A. Birman, "Mysli posle plenuma," *Novyi mir*, no. 12 (1965), p. 194.

[28]See, for example, Lewin, *Political Undercurrents in Soviet Economic Debates*, chap. 12 and *passim*; G. S. Lisichkin, *Plan i rynok* (Moscow, 1966); M. P. Kim, ed., *Novaia ekonomicheskaia politika: Voprosy teorii i istorii* (Moscow, 1974); and A. Rumiantsev, "Partiia i intelligentsia," *Pravda*, February 21, 1965).

[29]Cohen, *Bukharin and the Bolshevik Revolution*, pp. 341–347; Ploss, *Conflict and Decision-Making in Soviet Russia*, pp. 28–58.

[30]This was also the case in foreign policy. See Robert C. Tucker, *The Soviet Political Mind*, rev. ed. (New York, 1971), chap. 4.

[31]For a cultural approach to Stalinism, see Robert C. Tucker, "Stalinism as Revolution from Above," in *Stalinism*, ed. Robert C. Tucker, pp. 77–108. For the conservative aspects of Stalinism, see Note 33.

[32]As Moshe Lewin has argued in "The Social Background of Stalinism," in *Stalinism*, ed. Robert C. Tucker, pp. 133–135.

[33]See Vera S. Dunham, *In Stalin's Time: Middleclass Values in Soviet Fiction* (Cambridge, England, 1976); Leon Trotsky, *The Revolution Betrayed* (New York, 1945); Nicholas S. Timasheff, *The Great Retreat* (New York, 1946); and Frederick C. Barghoorn, *Soviet Russian Nationalism* (New York, 1956).

[34]Lewin, "The Social Background of Stalinism," pp. 133–135; and Robert H. McNeal, "The Decisions of the CPSU and the Great Purge," *Soviet Studies* 23, no. 2 (October 1971), pp. 177–185. The quote is from *Khrushchev Remembers* (Boston, 1970), p. 307.

[35]For the fearful atmosphere surrounding these decisions, see *Khrushchev Remembers*, pp. 315–353.

[36]See Breslauer, "Khrushchev Reconsidered."

[37]For a critical discussion of Khrushchev's inadequacies by two dissident reformers, see Roy A. Medvedev and Zhores A. Medvedev, *Khrushchev: The Years in Power* (New York, 1978). For the Stalin issue, see Stephen F. Cohen, "The Stalin Question Since Stalin," in *An End to Silence: Uncensored Opinion in the Soviet Union*, ed. Stephen F. Cohen (New York, 1982), pp. 22–50.

[38]This does not mean that there are not special bastions of Soviet conservatism such as the elites of the KGB, the Komsomol, the Trade Unions, and the Political Sector of the Army. It does mean, however, that we should not assume that the division between reformers and conservatives is a function of generations. Older people played a major, even leading, role, for example, in the struggles for

economic and cultural reform in the 1950s and 1960s. More generally, there is evidence that Soviet youth is no less conservative than its elders. For a discussion of this question, see Walter D. Connor, "Generations and Politics in the USSR," *Problems of Communism* (September–October 1975) pp. 20–31.

[39]See Robert C. Tucker, *The Marxian Revolutionary Idea* (New York, 1969), chap. 6.

[40]This does not mean that the revolution must be repudiated. Often, it is simply reinterpreted in a conservative fashion, as has happened in the Soviet Union and the United States. See Michael Kammen, *A Season of Youth: The American Revolution and the Historical Imagination* (New York, 1978).

[41]Cohen, *Bukharin and the Bolshevik Revolution*, p. 186.

[42]See Bohdan Harasymiw, "*Nomenklatura*: The Communist Party's Leadership Recruitment System," *Canadian Journal of Political Science* 2, no. 4 (December 1969), p. 512; and Mervyn Matthews, *Privilege in the Soviet Union: A Study of Elite Life-Styles under Communism* (London, 1978).

[43]The phrase is Yanov's, used in another context. *Essays on Soviet Society*, p. 85. The Soviet press sometimes asks, "Where do the conservatives come from?" (R. Bakhtamov and P. Volin, "Otkuda berutsia konservatory?," *Literaturnaia gazeta* [September 6, 1967].) Although this historical explanation may not be sufficient, it is essential.

[44]The sources cited in Note 4 relate to the post-Khrushchev period. See also Abraham Brumberg, "A Conversation with Andrei Amalrik," *Encounter* (June 1977), p. 30. Reform proposals, though of a lesser sort, continue to be expressed by responsible officials in the Soviet press.

[45]See, for example, G. A. Deborin and B. S. Tel'pukhovskii, *Itogi i uroki velikoi otechestvennoi voiny*, 2nd ed. (Moscow, 1975).

[46]David Thomson, *Democracy in France* (London, 1960). For historical de-Stalinization, see Cohen, "The Stalin Question Since Stalin," in An End to Silence: Uncensored Opinion in the Soviet Union, ed. Stephen F. Cohen (New York, 1982), pp. 22–50.

[47]For the importance of this "contract," see George W. Breslauer, "On the Adaptability of Welfare-State Authoritarianism in the USSR," in *Soviet Society and The Communist Party*, ed. Karl Ryavec (Amherst, Mass., 1979), pp. 3–25. Interviews with Soviet emigrés over a thirty-year period suggest the great importance citizens place on the welfare provisions of the Soviet state. See Alex Inkeles and Raymond A. Bauer, *The Soviet Citizen* (Cambridge, Mass, 1959), esp. chap. 10; and Zvi Gitelman, "Soviet Political Culture: Insights From Jewish Emigres," *Soviet Studies* 29, no. 4 (October 1977), p. 562.

[48]Lewin, *Political Undercurrents in Soviet Economic Debates*, chaps. 6–9.

[49]Iakovlev, "Protiv antiistorizma," *Literaturnaia gazeta* (November 15, 1975).

[50]P. Kopnin quoted in Yanov, *Essays on Soviet Society*, p. 76. Similarly, see A. M. Rumiantsev, "Vstupaiushchemu v mir nauki," *Pravda* (June 8, 1967); and A. Bovin, "Istina protiv dogmy," *Novyi mir*, no. 10 (1963), pp. 180–187.

[51]My comments here are based on a reading of S. Frederick Starr, *Decentralization and Self-Government in Russia, 1830–1870* (Princeton, 1972); Richard S. Wortman, *The Development of a Russian Legal Consciousness* (Chicago, 1976); and W. Bruce Lincoln, "The Genesis of an 'Enlightened' Bureaucracy in Russia, 1825–1856," *Jahrbucher für Geschichte Osteuropas*, 2, no. 3 (June 1972), pp. 321–330.

[52]The connection between East European and Soviet reformers has been very

important since 1953. Since the Soviet overthrow of the reform communist government in Czechoslovakia in 1968, Soviet conservative literature on the dangers of "right-wing revisionism" has grown into a virtual industry aimed implicitly at domestic reformers as well. Nonetheless, reformers continue to make the point. See, for example, P. Volin, "Liudi i ekonomika," *Novyi mir*, no. 3 (1969), pp. 154–168. For the reform movement in Eastern Europe, see Vladimir V. Kusin, "An Overview of East European Reformism," *Soviet Studies* (July 1976), pp. 338–361. Soviet conservatives have insisted that East European reforms are not relevant to the USSR because those countries are small. Economic reforms underway in China in the early 1980s may diminish the force of that conservative argument.

[53]This perspective has been adopted by some dissidents. See, for example, Medvedev, *On Socialist Democracy*; and, for a more systematic statement, L. Okunev, "Slovo–tozhe delo," *Politicheskii dnevnik*, no. 68 (Moscow: Samizdat, May 1970) (translated in *An End to Silence*, ed. Stephen F. Cohen pp. 299–310). But many dissidents have lost all hope of reform in recent years and now address their activities and thoughts not to Soviet officialdom but to Western governments.

[54]See Karl W. Ryavec, *Implementation of Soviet Economic Reforms* (New York, 1975), pp. 299–300.

[55]Quoted in H. Gordon Skilling, *Czechoslovakia's Interrupted Revolution* (Princeton, 1976), p. 495.

[56]Rossiter, "Conservatism," pp. 292, 294.

[57]For example, journals with different outlooks began to emphasize the same social problems. *Novyi mir* is of particular interest in this connection. Well-known as a kind of reformist community, the journal published, or favorably reviewed, conservative writers such as Efim Dorosh and Vladimir Soloukhin. It also published many newer fiction writers who identified with conservative rural values but whose writings depicted a postcollectivization countryside in need of reform. The *samizdat* publications *Pamiat'* and *Poiski*, which include authors of different political outlooks, may be a sign of a similar development in dissident circles.

II

Leadership and Administration

According to Zdenek Mlynar, a former Czech Politburo member now living in the West:

> the thing that is so extraordinary about the [post-Stalin] Soviet system is the fact that the individual segments of the power elite, which include the economic bureaucracy, the army officer corps, the police, and the political–administrative bureaucracy, are all united in one single organization—the Communist party. Consequently, each group surrenders some of its independence to the party, but they gain a share in the absolute monopoly power of the party. This constitutes the basis of the systemic strength of the party. . . . The conflict between various groups in this system amounts to a conflict for influence *within* the party, but not a conflict *with* the party.[1]

The chapters in this section focus on the exercise of power and authority in the Soviet Union. Although we offer considerable information about the content of policies, we are primarily concerned with the formulation and implementation of policies. Particularly significant are the relationships among the Politburo, Secretariat, some 24 departments of the Central Committee, and the Central Committee itself. Also very important is the interaction of these top party bodies with the highest organs of the state, the Council of Ministers and the bicameral Supreme Soviet, and with the two most powerful state bureaucracies, the army and the secret police (KGB). The activities of regional, as well as national, political institutions are examined. The functions of Soviet law, especially the Constitution of 1977, are assessed. Corruption in the party and state apparatuses is illuminated by a former Soviet lawyer, and the politics of administrative reform are analyzed.

Policymaking and administration are highly secretive in the USSR, and Soviet leaders have maintained a facade of "monolithic unity" since the time of Lenin, in accordance with a key party rule (I/3/b) that forbids free discussion of policy alternatives in CPSU meetings and in the press *after* a party organization has reached a decision. But Soviet officials continuously attempt to influence one another through public, as well as private, communications. Writing in newspapers or journals or speaking on radio or television, a top party leader may be striving to mobilize bureaucratic support for policy changes under consideration in the Politburo, Secretariat, or a Central Committee department. Or, commenting in the national or regional media, a ministerial or production executive may be prodding superiors, colleagues, or subordinates to take concerted action to further a specific program.

Hence, the Western analyst can infer the motivations behind some political–administrative initiatives and responses and can obtain information about organizational behavior and socioeconomic conditions in the USSR. Especially when one corroborates one's inferences and evidence with personal observations and interviews with Soviet officials, one is rewarded with pertinent, although often very tentative and incomplete, information on important themes. Such themes include current political issues, the legitimation of power and policies, bureaucratic coalition-building, patron–client relationships, administrative rights and responsibilities, and the everyday operations of Soviet institutions. Western research on these and other elements of Soviet leadership and administration are presented in the following chapters.

Note

[1]Zdenek Mlynar, Stenographic report of presentation to the University Seminar on Communism of Columbia University, New York, April 14, 1982, pp. 8–9 (emphasis in original).

5   ERIK P. HOFFMANN

Soviet Perspectives on Leadership and Administration*

Stalin's Views on Leadership   Stalin's view of the ideal political organization of society has been characterized as "monolithic" in the Soviet Union and as "totalitarian" in the West.[1] Western analysts stress that its essential features were the assumption of an extraordinary range of responsibilities by the national government and the extension of state power into virtually all areas of human life. Soviet commentators emphasize that Stalin's basic aim was to unify the civic values, attitudes, and beliefs of the entire population and to mobilize all material resources and human energies for the task of rapidly creating a "socialist" society and eventually transforming it into a "communist" one. The impressive buildup of heavy industry, the brutal but thorough collectivization of agriculture, and the waves of mass terror against the Soviet people are the best known of Stalin's policies in the 1930s. Also important were his efforts to enhance the national defense capabilities of the USSR throughout the decade and to consolidate the mature Stalinist system of the late 1930s by strengthening Soviet law and the Soviet family, by promoting scientific–technical and vocational education, and by recentralizing and expanding the political indoctrination programs.

The political order Stalin created to accomplish these goals was itself a vital product of "the third revolution" that swept away the economic, social, and political systems Lenin had launched in 1917. Lenin's New Economic Policy (NEP) of 1921 legitimized a mixed capitalist and socialist economy and a society that was relatively tolerant of intellectual,

*Reprinted in revised form by permission of the author and publisher from *The Soviet Union since Stalin*, ed. Stephen F. Cohen, Alexander Rabinowitch, and Robert Sharlet (Bloomington, Ind.: Indiana University Press, 1980), pp. 71–92. Copyright 1980 by Indiana University Press.

artistic, and cultural diversity. Significantly, a one-party polity was consolidated in this period, and measures were taken that concentrated power in the very highest Communist party bodies, especially the Central Committee and its key subcommittee, the Politburo. By 1937, however, Stalin had replaced the previous oligarchic dictatorship of the party with a personal dictatorship or one-man rule. The CPSU was in no sense a ruling or sovereign party. Its highest organs met with increasing infrequency in the years 1934–1953, and over a million of its members (almost half of them) were arrested or perished in the mid- and late 1930s.[2]

In the fully developed Stalinist system that emerged after the Great Purges, the party was reduced to more or less equal status with the other major bureaucracies—the secret police, army, and state apparatus (councils of ministers and soviets). Stalin, through loyal agencies, dominated all of these institutions, using them as instruments of his policy and personnel preferences and inner needs for power and adulation. Stalin deliberately pitted officials of these institutions against one another and established overlapping and imprecise spheres of bureaucratic jurisdiction. He did so to ensure that major (and many minor) political decisions and disputes would be resolved by him, personally, and to increase the likelihood of obtaining accurate information from various organizational sources and speedy compliance with his commands. To ensure further that his dictates would be followed—and that lower-level officials would pursue national goals in the absence of precise and consistent directives and adequate resources—Stalin created an elaborate system of rewards and sanctions, which included extraordinary opportunities for career advancement as well as life-and-death power over all officials (and citizens).

Stalin's most important goals were few and clear-cut, and the polity he molded emphasized heavily the unquestioning support of the leader and the effective fulfillment of policies and targets, not the efficient use of resources or cooperation among organizations and groups. For instance, planning was focused on ends, not on means, and generous bonuses were given only for complete fulfillment (or overfulfillment) of assigned tasks and for immediate, rather than long-term, benefits. Hence, the political–administrative system was designed to allow institutions and individual officials considerable flexibility both in choosing the methods of achieving centrally prescribed aims and in competing with one another for political power and material and human resources to do so. As Merle Fainsod points out, "The bureaucratic hierarchies . . . operated as centers of influence in their own right. . . . Behind the monolithic facade of Stalinist totalitarianism, the plural pressures of professional bureaucratic interests found expression."[3] But group participation in the formulation and reformulation of public policies was not a part of the theory or practice of Stalinism. The power to determine and choose among policy alternatives was highly concentrated in Stalin's personal secretariat (not in the party Politburo) and, above all, in the hands of Stalin himself.

During World War II, Stalin was compelled to enter into a political, economic, and military alliance with the major Western democracies and to allow greater institutional and ideological diversity within the USSR. Collaboration with the United States, "different roads to socialism" in the world communist movement, and relaxation of controls at home— all were paths that former Soviet leaders had advocated unsuccessfully in the 1920s but that had to be explored in a time of crisis.

After World War II, however, Stalin reestablished the Soviet political system of the late 1930s. In a time of peace and of "cold war," Stalin reaffirmed his commitment to the prewar resource allocation priorities and institutional relationships. Despite the leader's caution and possible willingness to consider alternative policies, despite the intensified jockeying for power among the major bureaucracies, and despite considerable public yearning for a less coercive polity, Stalinism was reimposed and the industrial output of the USSR was revived with remarkable rapidity in the time-tested ways (e.g., autarkic economic development, forced labor, tight supervision over the scientific and cultural intelligentsia). Stalin's chief effort abroad, the forging of a totalitarian interstate system that included Eastern Europe and eventually China, was primarily intended to meet internal economic and national security needs; and, at least in the short run, this effort was successful.

The shortcomings of Stalin's policies and policymaking procedures became increasingly evident to Soviet officials and foreign observers in the new domestic and international conditions of the postwar period. As Alfred Meyer observes:

> This crude, primitive, but effective Stalinist system . . . became obsolete because of its success. Having built an industrial society, it was poorly equipped by its own structure and operating methods [e.g., terror, command, centralized control] to maintain, manage, and improve this [more complex, heterogeneous, and interdependent] society.[4]

That is, Stalin had achieved absolute power to issue commands; he did not have to persuade or reason with anyone to gain compliance with his specific directives. But the political system he had created did not have the capacity to provide its leader and highest officials with the information they needed to make large numbers of feasible, timely, and integrated policies and commands in the increasingly complex political-administrative, socioeconomic, and scientific–technological environments of the postwar era. Nor did Stalin have the capability, or in some cases the will, to utilize the policy-relevant information he received. The

Stalinist political order repressed creativity and initiative in most fields, and it lacked the flexibility to adjust plans and decisions to rapidly changing domestic and international conditions and to unanticipated opportunities and problems. Robert C. Tucker succinctly states that when Stalin died, the question was not, "Who shall replace him?" but "What shall take the place of Stalinism as a mode of rule and pattern of policy and ideas?"[5]

Khrushchev's Views on Leadership

The response of Stalin's successors, as is well known, was to revitalize the Communist party and to reassert its predominant role in Soviet society. The CPSU's power vis-à-vis the other major bureaucracies increased, its involvement in industrial management and operations in the countryside expanded, and its membership grew. Less recognized is that Khrushchev, like Stalin, conceived of the party as primarily an administrative organ for implementing policies formulated by the top leader. By the late 1950s, Khrushchev had gradually put together a "grand design": a coordinated set of new domestic and international goals and policies that included peaceful coexistence with the West; serious efforts to upgrade agriculture, light industry, and consumer goods; systematic application of scientific discoveries and technological innovations to production problems and national defense; and social and economic egalitarianism. He then tried to develop various reform programs to implement these basic ideas. Such programs included decentralization of economic decision making; major changes in Soviet law; a campaign to improve mass and elite political indoctrination; and a proposed substantial reduction of Soviet ground troops.

Khrushchev was not very successful in attaining his objectives. His lack of accomplishment was in part the result of poor planning, formidable bureaucratic resistance and inertia, unfavorable external developments, and the intractability of human nature. The first secretary's inability to mobilize institutional support for his policies was especially frustrating, and it promoted his increasingly persistent, even frenetic, search for public acclaim and new administrative measures to fulfill his cherished (and often unchanging) aims. Khrushchev, by almost any yardstick, was less effective and efficient in achieving his chief goals than Stalin was in achieving his. Carl Linden notes that "Khrushchev's power and prestige were, to a far greater extent than Stalin's, dependent on the success of his policies."[6] Whereas Stalin could govern either *through* or *over* the party,[7] Khrushchev found it more and more difficult to do either.

The difficulties of being Stalin's successor may well have been enhanced by residual elements of Stalinism in Khrushchev's conceptions of authority. Khrushchev apparently believed that all party and state officials should actively help to administer national policies that they had little or no part in shaping, and that they could be made to carry out their responsibilities by means of job insecurity and a peculiar mix of performance and moral incentives. The new CPSU leader most assuredly did not conceive of himself as an arbiter of competing "interests" or claims from the major institutions and social strata, or from scientists, technical specialists, or economic executives, to whom power to shape national policy was devolving or should devolve.

Khrushchev did seek, as George Breslauer observes, "to expand the boundaries of decision-making arenas," and his "ideal conception of decision-making processes envisaged cooperative problem solving among talented actors."[8] But increased elite and popular participation in administration do not necessarily lead to greater democratization of the policy-making process, and Khrushchev almost surely did not intend them to do so. The first secretary had a highly instrumental view of scientific, technical, economic, and managerial expertise. He vigorously strove to use the contributions of the specialized elites and the masses to implement *his* vision of the national interest and to refine *operational*, not strategic, decisions. Khrushchev sought competence and initiative wherever he could find them, in order to help translate his general goals into reformist policies and to carry out workable programs expeditiously within the spirit, if not always the letter, of the party statutes and the law.

The grand design advocated by Khrushchev consisted primarily of substantive goals; he was less clear about the means by which these goals were to be achieved. Khrushchev does not seem to have given extensive thought to the interrelationships between ends and means, or perhaps he simply lacked the political-administrative skills to link them. To be sure, Khrushchev made an enormous contribution to Soviet politics by foreswearing terror as a means of resolving political disputes. But this decision eliminated any possibility of his ruling *over* the major bureaucracies and having them compete with one another to realize his objectives. Also, Khrushchev probably assumed (incorrectly) that the elimination of physical coercion against party and state officials would increase bureaucratic support for his policy preferences. He apparently failed to recognize that new decision-making procedures and institutional reorganizations are not likely to be very effective if important groups of bureaucrats perceive them to be illegitimate or threatening. For example, the first secretary insisted on disbanding the economic ministries in 1957 and on bifurcating the regional party apparatus in 1962—administrative changes that were quite unpopular with state and party officials, respectively.

For Khrushchev, appropriate political processes were, by definition, those which augmented the prestige and supported the policies of the top leader and not the goals of other officials, organizations, and social groups. Political power and the policy-making system were not perceived as ends in themselves but as means to promote centrally prescribed objectives. Khrushchev frequently refused to accede to his Presidium colleagues when his policies and programs faltered. When he was increasingly forced to do so, Khrushchev responded by trying to break away from the bonds of oligarchic party rule—for example, by appealing for the support of public opinion and of "his" regional CPSU officials and scientific–technical experts. In the process, Khrushchev alienated, one by one, the leaders and many of the lesser officials of all the major Soviet bureaucracies, including the party.

Khrushchev's ouster in 1964 stemmed mainly from his quite authoritarian ideas about the preponderant power of the party's first secretary over even the highest party bodies;[9] his cavalier treatment of party and state bureaucrats; his penchant for grandiose but insufficiently planned projects; and his demanding, unpredictable, disruptive, and impatient political style. Important, but probably secondary, factors were his often farsighted and idealistic policies and priorities. Khrushchev's colleagues objected in varying degrees to the content of his grand design, but especially to his methods of advocating and implementing it.

Brezhnev's View's on Leadership

Khrushchev's policy-making procedures had a major impact on his successors' conceptions of power and authority. The Brezhnev administration, primarily between 1964 and 1969, devoted considerable effort to establishing stable and clearly defined institutional relationships. Notable were the immediate decisions to recentralize the ministerial system and to reunite the regional party committees. The bifurcation of the latter in 1962 had produced considerable administrative confusion as well as anxiety and resentment among the CPSU's apparatus workers, especially the ideological specialists, who fit into neither the new industrial nor agricultural organs and whom Khrushchev frequently castigated for their lack of practical knowledge. Moreover, the new collective leadership gradually worked out decision-making methods to promote cooperative problem solving and institutional checks and balances to ensure the "mutual control" of top officials.[10] For example, two men were given the chief positions that Khrushchev had simultaneously held (Brezhnev became General Secretary of the CPSU, and Kosygin became Chairman of the Council of Ministers). For another example, the highly sensitive job of head of the hierarchy of organizational-party work departments, which are responsible for hiring, firing, and reassigning all CPSU, government, and other major officials from the national to the local levels, was awarded to a rather independent figure. I. V. Kapitonov, a long-time Central Committee member who apparently had no strong ties to *any* Politburo member or party grouping, held this position through the Brezhnev years and beyond.

Relatively few substantive policies were formulated or programs launched in the first 4–5 years of the Brezhnev-Kosygin leadership, prompting some Western critics to discern "degeneration" or "immobilism" in the Soviet political system. But the Kosygin economic reforms of 1965 and the heightened repression of dissidents in 1966 were major decisions. The most portentous and difficult decision—the military intervention by the USSR and other Warsaw Pact nations in Czechoslovakia in 1968—was largely a response to powerful external influences, such as the prospects of disintegrating party control and of mounting political, economic, and cultural demands, fanned by anti-Sovietism, throughout Eastern Europe. The harsh Soviet response in Czechoslovakia energized the collective leadership, which then proceeded to put together the comprehensive and integrated domestic and foreign policies elaborated at the Twenty-fourth Party Congress in 1971.

The content of Brezhnev's grand design was quite similar to Khrushchev's: it included detente with the United States; the rapid modernization of defense capabilities; the use of advanced Western technology to spur Soviet economic development; a strong commitment to improve agricultural production; and wage increases for the lowest paid workers. Whereas Khrushchev's grand design had consisted largely of substantive policies, Brezhnev's incorporated significant policy-making practices in addition to domestic and international goals. Brezhnev's program, adopted at the Twenty-fourth Congress, was not imposed from above; rather, it was the product of extensive consultation, controlled debate, and bargaining among the top leaders, the major bureaucracies, the scientific, technical, managerial, and educational elites, and, to a much lesser extent, the rank-and-file Communists.

Key elements of the emerging new policies on how to make policy were the following: broader and deeper participation by specialists at different stages and levels of decision making; group decision making in party committees and departments; major compromises *before* innovative programs were launched; prior consolidation of bureaucratic support for policy implementation; "trust in cadres" (i.e., the presumption that managers are competent and diligent); clearer and more stable spheres of responsibility; a strong preference for incremental change; and expanded opportunities for party and state executives to assess the consequences of decisions before *and* after they were made, especially at official CPSU meetings. Also, political–administrative, socioeconomic, and scientific–technological information were to be actively solicited throughout the party hierarchy and at various stages and levels of decision making and implementation. Particularly encouraged were the evaluation of data on the effects of prior decisions as well as practical suggestions for formulating more feasible social, economic, and research and development programs, and for improving the planning and organizational work needed to realize general party goals.

Today's Soviet leaders and management theorists view goal setting and decision making as a complex and ongoing process, requiring large amounts of diverse information, technical and administrative skills, coordination and control, institutional stability, and bureaucratic perquisites. "Problem situations" can be managed but rarely eliminated. Policy outcomes must be continuously monitored, and decisions and decision-making procedures must be periodically adjusted to take into account unanticipated consequences, changing conditions, and new management techniques and organizational technology. CPSU and government officials view the political–administrative system as increasingly permeable to internal and external influences, and many cadres consider these growing interdependencies a source of economic and social progress, not of systemic weakness or vulnerability.

Leading Soviet officials and theorists consider one of their prime challenges to be the enhancement of the directive, responsive, and "learning" capacities of the central political organs. Particularly important is the adaptation of traditional principles, such as integrated economic and social planning and "democratic centralism," to dramatically changing scientific–technological and socioeconomic conditions.[11] Other perceived challenges are to avert the possibility of an increasingly unfavorable competitive position vis-à-vis the industrialized nations of the West and to utilize advanced Western techniques and technology without promoting the "technocratization" of the Soviet intelligentsia or the "embourgeoisement" of Soviet society.[12]

Brezhnev and Aleksei Kosygin, much more pragmatic than their predecessor but different from one another, recognized the significance of establishing uncontested and regularized methods of governing to meet these challenges. Specifically, they saw numerous benefits in creating more permanent institutional relationships and more consensual, responsive, and routinized policy-making and administrative procedures. For example, the collective leadership's reunification of the regional party committees, which Khrushchev had recently divided into industrial and agricultural units, and the reconstituting of strong, centralized ministries were organizational changes of major importance. Above all, the highest Soviet leaders hoped that these and other adjustments in the policy-making process would generate greater support and contributions from the officials and specialists whose cooperation and skills were essential in formulating, as well as in carrying out, realistic and farsighted national programs.

Khrushchev had been unable to accomplish his central aims in the face of bureaucratic obstructionism at home and a frequently unresponsive, even hostile, political environment abroad. Khrushchev possessed a distinctive vision of the national interest and found it very difficult to compromise with his domestic political opponents, except in response to overwhelming opposition or the obvious failure of his policies. Somehow, he never lost the power to initiate programs, such as the expansion of the chemical rather than the steel industry in 1958, the reduction of ground troops in 1960, and the development of chemical fertilizers for agriculture and the rapprochement with the West in 1963. But when accomplishments fell short of his clearly stated aims, responsibility rested squarely with the first secretary. And when entrenched bureaucratic interests undermined the implementation of Khrushchev's dramatic proposals, the credibility and bargaining power of the CPSU's top leader were diminished. Indeed, some Soviet officials might have formally supported Khrushchev's decisions in the expectation that they would fail and thereby reduce his influence.

From Khrushchev's experience, Brezhnev and his colleagues developed a keener understanding of the close connections between the effectiveness and legitimacy of policies and the ways in which they are formulated. Khrushchev's problems sensitized his successors to the inseparability of ends and means, of politics and administration, of domestic and foreign policy, of domestic and foreign policy-making practices, and of the substantive and procedural aspects of leadership. Significantly, Brezhnev believed that the processes by which policies are made, as well as the content and effectiveness of these policies, determine their legitimacy. In contrast to Khrushchev's authority, Brezhnev's was much less dependent on the success of his policies. The power to determine purposes and to define success was exercised by a collective leadership composed of representatives of all the chief party and state bodies. Hence, initiative and responsibility were widely diffused among many individuals and organizations.

Initially, the Brezhnev Politburo and Secretariat assumed or hoped that more legitimate policymaking procedures would produce more effective policies. The leadership's efforts to increase bureaucratic acceptance of the policy process were quite successful. Indeed, the political system under Brezhnev enjoyed a considerable degree of legitimacy among virtually all of the bureaucratic elites. Many administrators liked the prevailing decision-making and recruitment practices, which usually assigned responsibility for specific segments or phases of a task, did not impose inordinate pressures to learn new skills, and provided considerable professional and personal security to competent and/or loyal bureaucrats, especially at the highest levels. Even when an administrative unit or grouping did not get much or most of what it sought, it had very likely had an opportunity to make its view heard, and it felt—and top party officials communicated expectations and incentives to make it feel—an obligation to carry out the probably incremental policy changes agreed upon at the center. It is not surprising, then, that the predominant majority of party bureaucrats and state administrators were willing to abide by the Brezhnev administration's decision-making rules. The highest Soviet officials benefited most of all, because they securely held the positions to which many capable but increasingly restless middle- and lower-level officials aspired.

Stalin and Khrushchev had a much greater distrust of professional bureaucrats than did Brezhnev. Stalin developed powerful rewards and sanctions to motivate officials, whereas Khrushchev, by choice and circumstance, placed considerably more reliance on public supervision over their activities. Stalin, in hopes of improving administrative performance, fostered in cadres the fear of losing life and job; Khrushchev proscribed terror but tried to manipulate the official's fear of losing his job; Brezhnev, until 1969–1970, did neither. Brezhnev's approach to administrative productivity and motivation was reminiscent of the executive who assures his subordinates of career security and ample material and psychological rewards and then tells them "Now get to work!" In contrast to Khrushchev's personnel policies, Brezhnev's were characterized by a low turnover of executives and reduced shifting of officials from one assignment to another. Brezhnev assumed that greater administrative stability and clearer delineation of rights and responsibilities would markedly improve the quality of work in many fields. Only from the early 1970s did Brezhnev begin to lose patience with the concept of *trust in cadres* and periodically link job performance with job security in his public pronouncements.[13]

Brezhnev increasingly questioned his belief that legitimate policy-making practices are necessary *and* sufficient to produce effective policies. The Soviet elites' widespread acceptance of the political system was not accompanied by a significant rise in bureaucratic accountability or responsiveness to national goals and initiatives. Though more and more technical and administrative contributions were forthcoming to implement the top leadership's conception of the public interest, organizational and departmental interests were still quite powerful. If anything, they were becoming increasingly formidable because of the greater direct representation of the major bureaucracies in the Politburo and Central Committee (e.g., the heads of the secret police [KGB] and of the Ministries of Defense and Foreign Affairs became full members of the Politburo in 1973); the diverse policy preferences of key leaders (especially after the difficulties encountered by the Twenty-fourth Party Congress program); and the growing ties between Soviet and foreign economic institutions.

According to two Western specialists writing in 1971, "the [Soviet] leadership has recognized that its own authority can best be maintained if various groups are given more leeway to pursue independently the general interest of society."[14] But thereafter the Brezhnev leadership increasingly sought to enhance the center's capacity to plan, budget, and "manage by objectives," to elicit organizational contributions in support of *national* goals, and to control the chief bureaucracies.[15] This trend does not necessarily represent a return to a more authoritarian form of government. Rather, it may be a kind of holding action to prevent what Jerry Hough calls "the devolution of power to the major institutional centers" and the transformation of the leadership's role to that of "a broker mediating the competing claims of powerful interests."[16]

Special interests are well entrenched in the myriad party and state organizations in Moscow, as well as in the localities. Politburo officials themselves have different views and continuously debate the merits of current objectives, priorities, and programs. However, a national and rational perspective, together with a widely supported set of comprehensive and feasible domestic and foreign policies, are the officially stated and probably the operative goals of most Politburo members. The Politburo is the only organ in the Soviet polity committed to formulating a long- and short-term conception of the common good and to making it prevail over group and individual interests and immediate pressures. After all, the capacity to plan and manage the economy and society in the interests of the entire population, not just of the wealthy, highly skilled, or politically powerful, is allegedly a fundamental advantage of the Soviet-type socialist system.

The Role of the Party in "Developed Socialism"

Soviet leaders and theorists stress the growing significance of the Communist party in "developed socialist society," the official name for the socioeconomic order achieved by 1967. The traditional functions of the party—to provide political, organizational, and ideological leadership—are to remain the same. But these activities will become more important as their content and interrelationships change. The reasons given include the following: the need to formulate the large-scale, complex and interconnected tasks of "communist construction"; the need to mobilize the specialized elites and citizenry to help fulfill these tasks; the need to develop integrated social and economic forecasting; the need to nurture "socialist democracy" through more effective political education work; and the need to direct the USSR's international relations in the era of the worldwide "scientific and technological revolution" (STR).[17] In a word, the Soviet polity and the CPSU are both viewed as "dynamic" organisms whose purposes, activities, and structure are constantly evolving. To quote an official Soviet interpretation, "Developed socialism is at the same time developing socialism, the functioning mechanism of which is inseparable from the mechanism of its development."[18]

The enhancement of "the leading role of the party" is nonetheless an ambiguous idea which is in need of considerable theoretical elaboration and is the subject of ongoing competition and debate among CPSU and state leaders. For example, does the "growing" importance of the party refer to its accumulation of power relative to that of other institutions in Soviet society? Prominent officials and theorists deny this, suggesting instead that there is a trend toward a more equal distribution of power among Soviet institutions. This trend, coupled with the greater scope and complexity of the problems to be managed, increases the significance of the party's "coordinating" and "unifying" activities. V. S. Shevtsov comments that "The growth in the party's role does not, and cannot, imply any increase in its rights vis-à-vis other organizations of the working people. What it really means is a growth in the party's obligations, in the significance of its ideological and political guidance, and in the scale of its activities."[19]

Theorists of developed socialism and of "the scientific management of society" stress the traditional Leninist idea that a "conscious" party leadership must impose its view of the national interest on the "spontaneity" of the masses. But the present emphasis is on improving the CPSU's capacity to elicit contributions from all strata of society and from all state and public organizations in order to help formulate and implement decisions in a collaborative manner for the benefit of all. The party's role is to be the "decisive coordinator," "integrator," "regulator," "synthesizer," "adjuster," "mobilizer," and "energizer" of the activities of an increasingly well-educated and politically sophisticated general population. As a Soviet text affirms, "The party is a unique political organization because it is not connected with any private, departmental, or similar kinds of interests, but embodies and expresses to the fullest extent the interests of the working class, of all the toilers. Precisely because of this, the party can correctly aggregate the interests of all classes and social groups in socialist society and of all its nationalities and peoples, can induce these strata to serve the national interest, and can lead them along the charted course—toward communism."[20]

The policy-making procedures and policy outcomes of the Brezhnev administration, however, proved to be less successful than its leaders anticipated. The power of the Politburo and Central Committee to *make* decisions was greater than their power to *implement* these decisions, and this gap appears to have widened. The problem was not as serious as it was under Khrushchev, but top party leaders were clearly concerned about it. A senior political analyst asserted: "It must be especially emphasized that real collective leadership is not only freedom of discussion and debate, but also the active struggle for putting into practice the collectively reached decisions."[21] Brezhnev himself noted at the 25th

Party Congress in 1976 that the Politburo and Secretariat had "devoted far more attention than in the past to control over and verification of the fulfillment of adopted decisions." He felt constrained to deny that "any alarming situation has developed in the party" with respect to "decisions [that] are not fulfilled or are fulfilled imprecisely or incompletely," and he implied that the leadership's perception of and impatience with the problem had increased, not the problem itself. Brezhnev added: "At times, after some decision or other is not fulfilled, a second, occasionally even a third, decision is adopted on the same question. In terms of content, they may seem rather good. But the point is that something should have already been done. The question automatically arises: Isn't a new decision on an old subject something like a concession, isn't it a manifestation of liberalism? Isn't the result a lowering of exactingness? We must put an end to this practice!"[22]

Although Brezhnev did not offer reasons why party decisions were sometimes inadequately carried out, the beginnings of a most interesting official explanation can be pieced together from various sources. The key idea is that the CPSU, as the "nucleus" of the polity and of all state and public institutions, "is not connected with any private, departmental, or similar kinds of interests."[23] The state organs, in contrast, *are* reportedly developing stronger occupational and organizational interests. And the source of the accompanying "technocratic and bureaucratic manifestations [*tekhnokraticheskie i biurokraticheskie proiavleniia*]" is the STR.[24]

This situation is characterized as a "nonantagonistic contradiction." The growing use of scientific and technical advances in management and production calls for greater specialized training and professionalization, which simultaneously create opportunities and problems for Soviet political authorities. Although "negative tendencies" in the ministries, scientific-technical research institutes, and economic production units are not "fatally inevitable," their "neutralization" is not an "easy or automatic matter." According to Iu. E. Volkov, "the more the STR adversely affects the sphere of management, the stronger and more effective must be party and social control, ensuring the timely removal of possible elements of *a technocratic and bureaucratic approach to the leadership of social life.*"[25] The party, despite its extraordinary size and differentiation,[26] is allegedly "monolithic," or free from such divisive and harmful tendencies.

P. N. Fedoseev links this interpretation to larger questions concerning the nature and development of socialist democracy. He maintains that the use of scientific and technological advances in management and production necessitates greater specialized training and professionalism in both socialist and capitalist societies. In Western democracies this leads to "the intensification of technocratic tendencies . . . and to the actual concentration of all power in the hands of executive bodies." But in the USSR

> the professionalization of the executive bodies of management is combined with enhancing the role of the representative bodies—the soviets at all levels and the social and political mass organizations: party, trade union, and youth organizations, production conferences, and so on. In the socialist countries systematic work is conducted to develop the activity and effectiveness of all democratic bodies in every possible way, *to ensure their control over the activity of the executive organs of government* and to draw the masses, on an increasingly larger scale, into the administration of state affairs. This is facilitated by raising the general and the political education of the population, their cultural and professional level and their growing social consciousness and maturity.[27]

Note the sharp distinction Fedoseev and Volkov make between the party and government of the USSR (i.e., between the "democratic bodies" and "the executive organs of government"). Note, too, their implication that the STR is having similar negative effects on capitalist states and on the ministries and committees of the *Soviet* state.

Fedoseev suggests that the STR is contributing to the decline of legislatures in the West, and that the rising power of the executive branches of government, which are subservient to monopoly capital, are subverting more and more the interests of the citizenry. Were it not for the persistent and skillful efforts of the party and other "social and political mass organizations" and "representative bodies," the same trend might well develop in the USSR, Fedoseev and Volkov imply. Undergirding this portentous conclusion is the idea that the STR produces "spontaneous," even harmful, tendencies in the Soviet state, which "conscious" party leadership at all levels must surmount or offset.

Both Fedoseev and Volkov depict the CPSU as united, selfless, and unaffected by the onerous consequences of the global STR, and the state as fragmented, parochial, and vulnerable to the STR's "negative" side effects. Only through the combined efforts of "democratic" and "representative" bodies, especially the party and the soviets, can the technocratic tendencies within "the executive organs" be curbed, and can "the unity of scientific, technological, social, and moral progress" be ensured.[28]

What is implied, but never stated, in contemporary Soviet writings is that the CPSU is the sole centripetal force in a society consisting of increasingly powerful centrifugal forces. Among the centrifugal factors are major socioeconomic developments such as manpower shortages and strong ethnic loyalties, and amorphous forms of "spontaneity" such as alcoholism, juvenile delinquency, and "indifference to politics." Also, the centrifugal elements now include a very large number of administrative and production units. Only the party's "great authority . . . enables it to accommodate the interests of different organizations and departments, to coordinate their work, and unify and direct it. In so doing, the party gives the whole political organization of Soviet society a purposefulness that multiplies its strength many times."[29]

CPSU leaders were attracted to Western "systems analysis" in the 1960s precisely because of its *lack* of emphasis on purposes and motivations other than those prescribed by the central political authorities. Systems analysis helps to explain and justify increased party supervision over state organs and reduced subsystem autonomy (or parochialism) in the major bureaucracies and society. That is, comprehensive approaches to policy making subordinate departmental and local interests to national party policy, within the framework of greater elite and mass participation in the formulation and implementation of various decisions. Also, some top Soviet officials considered systems approaches to be useful means of increasing the consistency and clarity of central directives, and of promoting unified national support for *their* policy preferences.

The party, however, was not able to perform these integrating and motivational functions to the satisfaction of the Khrushchev and Brezhnev leaderships. Members of the Politburo and Secretariat bemoaned the declining influence of the CPSU in industrial management, for example.[30] Brezhnev underscored the decision-making and administrative responsibilities of scientific and technical specialists, and he increasingly stressed the need to improve their political education. Despite such efforts, the manageability of the major Soviet bureaucracies was an article of faith, not an accomplished fact. Growing problems were caused by the multitude of administrative units, the extensive fragmentation and overlapping of responsibilities, and the lack of sufficient interorganizational coordination in the planning and management of the economy—a phenomenon aptly described as "centralized pluralism."[31]

Hence, the chief constraint on centralized socioeconomic planning and societal guidance, and on the effective use of information in decision making and administration, is *not* technological. Rather, it lies in the highly differentiated and bureaucratized nature of the myriad party and state political-administrative bodies and alliances, whose members are reluctant to relinquish their group or organizational power to anything but a strongly unified Politburo interpretation of the national interest.[32] The Manichaean pronouncements regarding the positive influences of the STR on the party and the STR's negative effects on the state (discussed above) signaled high-level concern about the difficulties of providing effective leadership in a complex bureaucratized society. These statements were part of an effort by the Brezhnev leadership to delegate still greater responsibility to the major bureaucracies, while at the same time guarding against the possible dissipation of national initiative and control over the policy process.

Brezhnev's Politburo and Secretariat were well aware that the broadening and deepening of specialized elite participation in decision making in some ways enhances, but in other ways reduces, the central party bodies' capacity to lead. This "nonantagonistic contradiction," which has been and will continue to be exacerbated by the contemporary STR, produces ongoing tensions in party-state relations. At issue are the CPSU's role in public policy making and its recruitment and deployment of party and state officials. Such vital choices necessitate continuous reassessment of risks and costs by all of the Soviet bureaucratic elites. For example, shifts of power are quite likely to occur within administrative units when new cadres, organization technology, or management techniques are introduced. Party and state executives have always had to gauge the relative importance of the personal loyalty and professional competence of their subordinates. But contemporary Soviet officials must calculate with heightened technical knowledge and political acumen the advantages and disadvantages of numerous technological and organizational innovations.

Moreover, Soviet commentators on developed socialism began to grapple with the fact that many policy alternatives are formulated within and between the major bureaucracies, and that the highest party officials must continuously strive to ensure that the final aggregation of interests occurs in the Politburo. In other words, major decisions can be significantly shaped by, and for all practical purposes actually made by bodies other than the Politburo and Secretariat (e.g., the armed forces, KGB, and industrial ministries). Some Soviet leaders might privately agree with David Lane, one of the few Western observers who refuses to view the present-day CPSU as a "ruling" party, and who stresses instead "the real powers of social forces and institutions outside it."[33]

Soviet theorists are beginning to catch up with practicing administrators in their understanding of the capacity of politicians, politician/experts, and experts to influence one another, and of the political and economic implications of their cooperation and noncooperation. Soviet analysts contend that the scientific and technical intelligentsia must put its expertise at the disposal of the party committees and the soviets, thereby expanding elite and popular participation in decision making and administration.[34] Soviet scientists, engineers, and agronomists are exhorted to contribute their skills and knowledge to the solution of centrally prescribed political-administrative, socioeconomic, and scientific-technological tasks. In return, such specialists, many of whom hold responsible positions in the party and in other major bureaucracies,

are given increased, but carefully circumscribed, power to help determine the purposes and nature of their tasks, as well as the criteria and
standards used to evaluate their performance.

In short, Soviet analysts imply that the inherently competitive nature
of the relationship between political leaders and experts, and the
obvious potential benefits of their close collaboration in formulating and
implementing feasible national policies, *enhance* the responsibilities of
the party in the era of the STR. This "contradiction" and its uncertain
political and administrative implications help to explain why key aspects
of Soviet leadership theory, such as "democratic centralism" and party
guidance of state and public institutions, lie so heavily in the normative
realm, and why there are still many ambiguities regarding the evolving
"leading" role of the CPSU in a mature socialist society.

Conclusion

The Brezhnev administration made sustained
efforts to improve the central party organs' capac-
ity to lead and manage society in the era of the scientific and technological revolution. To do so, the collective leadership experimented
with various ways to rationalize policy making and implementation. The
Soviet interpretation of rationality includes many elements. As David
Holloway observes, "It stresses the hierarchical nature of administrative
structures; it points to the possibility of optimal decision making; it
emphasizes the role of information flows in administration . . . and the
uses of the new data processing technology; and it assumes that the
self-regulation of Soviet society is to be achieved through the interaction
of two subsystems: the controlling and the controlled."[35] The emerging
Soviet views on societal guidance are founded on a modified cybernetic
or "steering" model of government and place heavy emphasis on
improving the efficiency or "technocratic rationality" of administrative
processes.[36]

Whether these evolving Soviet perspectives were elements of continuity or change since Stalin is a highly subjective question. Did
Khrushchev and Brezhnev alter the essence of Stalinism or merely adapt
fundamental characteristics of the Stalinist system to new conditions?
One's answer depends heavily on one's view of the basic features of
Stalinism and of the importance of certain undeniable post-Stalin
changes in policy making and administration.[37]

On the one hand, it is difficult to conceive of Stalin agreeing with the
contemporary Soviet analysts who acknowledge "the impossibility of
decision making from the center on many, let alone all, questions,"[38] or
who assert: "One of the basic criteria of the democratic nature of any
political organization is its capacity for critical analysis of its own activity
in order to bring to light its own mistakes and take effective measures to
prevent them recurring in the future."[39] On the other hand, one must

give considerable weight to the elements of secrecy, orthodoxy, arbitrariness, coercion, insularity, inefficiency, mendacity, corruption, careerism, status consciousness, and lack of initiative from below—in short, the Stalinist legacy—in present-day Soviet politics. To be sure, Brezhnev and his colleagues encouraged the bureaucratic, scientific–technical, and educational elites to contribute their expertise on policy-relevant questions, and some specialists actively supported the introduction of modern managerial techniques and information technology. But the top Soviet leaders continue to suppress criticism of Stalinism and its consequences, which greatly reduces the effectiveness of their renewed emphasis on political and administrative rationality and on the "democratic" side of democratic centralism in party and state activities. Traditional, although not necessarily Stalinist, bureaucratic patterns, such as resistance to pressures from the center, and communication pathologies, such as reluctance to transmit accurate information about shortcomings to one's superiors, also persist.[40]

Generally speaking, the top Soviet leaders' *perspectives* on policy making have undergone greater changes since Stalin than the *styles* of leadership and administration. As we have seen, the Politburo functioned in very different ways under Stalin, Khrushchev, and Brezhnev. But Khrushchev and Brezhnev, using quite different methods, were both frustrated by their inability to alter Stalinist attitudes and behavior in the major bureaucracies and economic production units. For example, Soviet factory managers strongly opposed the Kosygin economic reforms of 1965 and succeeded in emasculating them.[41] What this reveals is a persistent tension between national and local and between national and departmental perspectives in the post-Stalin polity and society. It also suggests that Brezhnev's successors must seriously consider major changes in institutional relationships and bureaucratic incentives and to maintain highly unified positions on public policies.

The Stalin, Khrushchev, and Brezhnev "cults of personality" must be seen in this light. The glorification of the top leader is an element of continuity in the style of Soviet politics after Lenin. But the content and functions of the Stalin, Khrushchev, and Brezhnev cults differ in important respects. Stalin sought to create the impression that he was an omniscient and omnipotent leader who possessed a deep understanding of the "laws" of historical development and of the contemporary relevance of the authoritarian politico–religious relationship between the tsars and the masses. Khrushchev portrayed himself as a man of the people who was eager to support practical initiatives and to meet individual citizens' material, social, and psychological needs rather than to promote conservative bureaucratic interests. Brezhnev cultivated the image of an effective, responsible, businesslike executive who knew how to manage complex organizations and dynamic forces, domestic and foreign.

Correspondingly, Stalin's cult served as a means of strengthening personal dictatorship and of mobilizing institutional and public support for the radical transformation of society "from above." Khrushchev's efforts to enhance his popularity among the masses were an attempt to circumvent collective leadership in the Presidium and to pressure party and state bureaucrats who opposed his reformist policies and his unsettling policy-making and administrative practices. The growing official adulation of Brezhnev was a collectively agreed-upon method of increasing the power of the Politburo vis-à-vis the major bureaucracies, of improving the effectiveness of group decision making by establishing the general secretary as "first among equals," and of producing a prestigious chief-of-state to further Soviet interests in contemporary international relations. The Brezhnev cult might have been a partisan effort to strengthen the hand of one faction within the collective leadership. But the chief function of the public praise of Brezhnev was to promote controlled change and to help manage powerful socioeconomic and scientific–technological forces "from below" and from abroad. Hence, Stalin, Khrushchev, and Brezhnev all developed distinctive cults and used them to pursue rather different goals, each deliberately enhancing the cult of Lenin and seeking to identify current aims and methods with Lenin's.

The sine qua non of developed socialism is the "scientific management" of Soviet society, of which the key element is "scientific leadership." Under Brezhnev there were at least three competing Soviet perspectives on scientific guidance—one that sought to rationalize centralized party leadership through the use of new techniques, technology, and incentives; another which advocated reducing CPSU supervision over the major nonparty bureaucracies; and a third which called for greater regional planning and decision making by party and state organs. The first was the dominant perspective in the Brezhnev years. But the Soviet scientific–technological and educational elites increasingly supported the second and third alternatives. And future national party officials may well feel compelled to experiment with institutional decentralization—greater autonomy to the production associations and more effective economic development, at the very least—in order to formulate and administer more feasible *centrally prescribed* goals and policies.

In summary, the Brezhnev collective leadership clearly recognized that the "revolutionary" socioeconomic and scientific–technological changes since World War II were increasing the volume and interconnections of political decisions of one-party systems at a rate faster than Stalinist or Khrushchevian methods could handle. Top CPSU officials acknowledged that the extraordinary complexity of modern production increased the interdependence of Soviet institutions and society with one another and with those of other nations, and had made the Soviet polity more sensitive or permeable to powerful domestic and international economic forces. Furthermore, party leaders perceived the need to be responsive to, but not to be dominated by, the rapid advances of modern science and technology, whose sociopolitical and ecological consequences are often difficult to anticipate and control. According to Soviet analysts, the STR makes necessary the closer "correlation" of domestic and foreign policy, "dynamic" and "comprehensive approaches" to planning and decision making, and more "creativity," "flexibility," and "integration" of specialist and public contributions to society. Thus, Brezhnev and his colleagues cautiously encouraged social theorists and politician–administrators to do some fresh thinking about the theory and practice of leadership and about the many questions concerning the present era "which have only been touched upon and await profound analysis."[42]

Notes

[1]For example, Carl Friedrich and Zbigniew Brzezinski, *Totalitarian Dictatorship and Autocracy* (Cambridge, Mass.: Harvard University Press, 1956), especially pp. 9–10. Cf. Gregory Grossman, "The Solidary Society," in *Essays in Socialism and Planning in Honor of Carl Landauer*, ed. Gregory Grossman (Englewood Cliffs, N.J.: Prentice-Hall, 1970), pp. 184–211; T. H. Rigby, "Stalinism and the Mono-Organizational Society," in *Stalinism: Essays in Historical Interpretation*, ed. Robert C. Tucker (New York: W. W. Norton, 1977), pp. 53–76.

[2]Andrei Sakharov, *Progress, Coexistence, and Intellectual Freedom* (New York: W. W. Norton, 1968), p. 55.

[3]Merle Fainsod, *How Russia is Ruled*, 2nd ed. (Cambridge, Mass.: Harvard University Press, 1963), p. 579. See also Jerry Hough and Merle Fainsod, *How the Soviet Union Is Governed* (Cambridge, Mass.: Harvard University Press, 1979), pp. 184–191.

[4]Alfred Meyer, "The Soviet Political System," in *The USSR after 50 years: Promise and Reality*, ed. Samuel Hendel and Randolph Braham (New York: Alfred A. Knopf, 1967), p. 51. See also Alfred Meyer, "Authority in Communist Political Systems," in *Political Leadership in Industrialized Societies*, ed. Lewis Edinger (Huntington, N.Y.: Krieger Publishing Co., 1976), pp. 84–107.

[5]Robert C. Tucker, *The Soviet Political Mind: Stalinism and Post-Stalin Change* (New York: W. W. Norton, 1971), p. 173 (emphasis in original).

[6]Carl Linden, *Khrushchev and the Soviet Leadership, 1957–1964* (Baltimore: Johns Hopkins Press, 1966), p. 15.

[7]See Leonard Schapiro, *The Communist Party of the Soviet Union*, 2nd ed. (New York: Vintage, 1971), pp. 556 and *passim*.

[8]George Breslauer, "Khrushchev Reconsidered," *Problems of Communism* 25, no. 5 (September–October 1976), pp. 21–22. This essay contains a thoughtful discussion of Khrushchev's "populist" or non-Stalinist views on authority.

[9]Richard Lowenthal, "The Revolution Withers Away," *Problems of Communism* 14, no. 1 (January–February 1965), p. 11.

[10]See, for example, T. H. Rigby, "The Soviet Leadership: Towards a Self-Stabilizing Oligarchy?" *Soviet Studies* 22, no. 2 (October 1970), pp. 167–191.

[11]See, for example, A. S. Akhiezer, *Nauchno-tekhnicheskaia revoliutsiia i nekotorye problemy proizvodstva i upravleniia* (Moscow: Nauka, 1974).

[12]See, for example, D. M. Gvishiani, *Organizatsiia i upravlenie*, 2nd ed. (Moscow: Nauka, 1972).

[13]This last point is developed in George Breslauer, "On the Adaptability of Soviet Welfare-State Authoritarianism," in *Soviet Society and the Communist Party*, ed. Karl Ryavec (Amherst, Mass.: University of Massachusetts Press, 1978), pp. 7–8, 16–17.

[14]Donald Barry and Harold Berman, "The Jurists," in *Interest Groups in Soviet Politics*, ed. H. Gordon Skilling and Franklyn Griffiths (Princeton: Princeton University Press, 1971), p. 293.

[15]Paul Cocks, "The Policy Process and Bureaucratic Politics," in *The Dynamics of Soviet Politics*, ed. Paul Cocks, Robert Daniels, and Nancy Heer (Cambridge, Mass.: Harvard University Press, 1977), pp. 156–178; Paul Cocks, "Retooling the Directed Society: Administrative Modernization and Developed Socialism," in *Political Development in Eastern Europe*, ed. Jan Triska and Paul Cocks (New York: Praeger, 1977), pp. 53–92.

[16]Jerry Hough, "The Soviet System: Petrification of Pluralism?" *Problems of Communism* 21, no. 2 (March-April 1972), pp. 32, 33, 37ff. See also Jerry Hough, *The Soviet Union and Social Science Theory* (Cambridge, Mass.: Harvard University Press, 1977); and Hough and Fainsod, *How the Soviet Union Is Governed*, especially pp. 518–555.

[17]For example, G. Kh. Shakhnazarov, *Sotsialisticheskaia demokratiia: nekotorye voprosy teorii*, 2nd ed. (Moscow: Politizdat, 1974), pp. 112ff.; *Razvitoe sotsialisticheskoe obshchestvo: sushchnost', kriterii zrelosti, kritika revizionistskikh kontseptsii*, 2nd ed. (Moscow: Mysl', 1975), pp. 272ff.; V. I. Kas'ianenko, *Razvitoi sotsializm: istoriografia i metodologiia problemy* (Moscow: Mysl', 1976), pp. 173ff. On the STR, see Erik P. Hoffmann and Robbin F. Laird, *In Quest of Progress: Soviet Perspectives on Politics, Society, and Technology under Brezhnev* (forthcoming); T. H. Rigby and R. F. Miller, *Political and Administrative Aspects of the Scientific and Technical Revolution in the USSR* (Canberra: Australian National University, Occasional Paper No. 11, 1976).

[18]*Sotsialisticheskoe obshchestvo* (Moscow: Politizdat, 1975), p. 6.

[19]V. S. Shevtsov, *The CPSU and the Soviet State in Developed Socialist Society* (Moscow: Progress, 1978), p. 65.

[20]*Razvitoe sotsialisticheskoe obshchestvo*, pp. 163–164.

[21]P. A. Rodionov, "Leninskii stil'—vazhnoe uslovie uspekha partiinogo rukovodstva," in *Partiia v period razvitogo sotsialisticheskogo obshchestva* (Moscow: Politizdat, 1977), p. 74.

[22]Leonid Brezhnev, "Central Committee Report," in *Current Soviet Policies VII* (Columbus, Ohio: American Association for the Advancement of Slavic Studies, 1976), pp. 24–25.

[23]*Razvitoe sotsialisticheskoe obshchestvo*, p. 164.

[24]Iu. Volkov, "Vlianie nauchno-tekhnicheskoi revoliutsii na sistemu vlasti i

demokraticheskie uchrezhdeniia," in *Sotsiologiia i sovremmenost'*, vol. 1 (Moscow: Nauka, 1977), p. 89.

[25]*Ibid.*

[26]In the early 1980s the party consisted of a central apparatus of about 24 departments, regional and local secretariats, a national and 14 union republic central committees, 156 territory and province party committees, 10 regional party committees, 4388 city and district party committees, and 414,000 primary party organizations, and over one million shop party units and party groups.

[27]P. N. Fedoseev, "Social Significance of the Scientific and Technological Revolution," in *Scientific–Technological Revolution: Social Aspects*, ed. Ralf Dahrendorf *et al.* (Beverly Hills, Calif.: Sage Publications, 1977), p. 103 (emphasis added).

[28]*Ibid.*, pp. 103–105.

[29]Shevtsov, *The CPSU and the Soviet State in Developed Socialist Society*, pp. 63–64.

[30]See Darrell Hammer, "Brezhnev and the Communist Party," *Soviet Union* 2, no. 1 (1975), especially pp. 8–12.

[31]Alec Nove, *The Soviet Economic System* (London: Allen and Unwin, 1977), pp. 60–84ff.

[32]For detailed information on the character and difficulties of altering the highly bureaucratized Soviet political system, see Roy Medvedev, *On Socialist Democracy* (New York: W. W. Norton, 1975).

[33]David Lane, *Politics and Society in the USSR* (New York: New York University Press, 1978), p. 230.

[34]E. M. Babosev, "Scientific and Technological Revolution: The Growing Role of Scientific and Technological Intelligentsia" (Paper presented at the Eighth World Congress of Sociology, Toronto, 17–24 August 1974, pp. 15–16.

[35]David Holloway, "The Political Use of Scientific Models: The Cybernetic Model of Government in Soviet Social Science," in *The Use of Models in the Social Sciences*, ed. Lyndhurst Collins (London: Tavistock, 1976), pp. 116, 121.

[36]*Ibid.*, pp. 116–117ff. See also, for example, Donald Schwartz, "Recent Soviet Adaptations of Systems Theory to Administrative Theory," *Journal of Comparative Administration* 5, no. 2 (August 1973), pp. 233–264.

[37]On the most essential or fundamental elements of the Soviet system, see especially John Hazard, *The Soviet System of Government*, 5th ed. (Chicago: University of Chicago Press, 1980), pp. 228–243.

[38]V. G. Afanas'ev, *Pravda* (May 2, 1976), p. 2.

[39]Shakhnazarov, *Sotsialisticheskaia demokratiia: nekotorye voprosy teorii*, pp. 72–73.

[40]See Erik P. Hoffmann, "Technology, Values, and Political Power in the Soviet Union: Do Computers Matter?" in *Technology and Communist Culture: The Socio-Cultural Impact of Technology under Socialism*, ed. Frederic Fleron (New York: Praeger, 1977), pp. 397-436; Erik P. Hoffmann, "Information Processing in the Communist Party of the Soviet Union: Recent Theory and Experience," in *Soviet Society and the Communist Party*, pp. 63–87. Cf., for example, Viktor Afanas'ev, *Sotsial'naia informatsiia i upravlenie obshchestvom* (Moscow: Politizdat, 1975).

[41]See Karl Ryavec, *Implementation of Soviet Economic Reforms: Political, Organizational, and Social Processes* (New York: Praeger, 1975).

[42]*Razvitoe sotsialisticheskoe obshchestvo*, p. 275.

6

ROLF H. W. THEEN

*Party and Bureaucracy**

> A (good) bureaucracy exists to serve politics; but it is not the purpose of politics to serve a (good) bureaucracy.
>
> —Lenin (1921)

> Cadres decide everything. . . . If we had not created the apparatus, we would have been lost.
>
> —Stalin (1935)

> The decisive question of the revolution, now as before, is the question of power.
>
> —Brezhnev (1977)

Franz Borkenau, some 40 years ago, reflecting on the fate of the Paris Commune, the Spanish Civil War, and the Russian Revolution, proclaimed what he called the "law of the twofold development of revolutions." According to this law, "[revolutions] begin as anarchist movements against the bureaucratic state organization, which they inevitably destroy; they continue by setting in its place another, in most cases, stronger bureaucratic organization, which suppresses all free mass movements."[1]

The evolution of the Soviet political system since 1917 in many respects would seem to bear out the validity of Borkenau's observation regarding the course and consequences of revolution. The Bolshevik Revolution succeeded in bringing about many fundamental changes in Russian society. However, its record in regard to the abolition of the

*Reprinted in revised form by permission of the author and publisher from Gordon Smith, ed., *Public Policy and Administration in the Soviet Union* (New York: Praeger Publishers, 1980), pp. 18–52. Copyright 1980 by American Society for Public Administration.

institution of bureaucracy—one of the professed goals of the October Revolution—must be judged a dismal failure. We have every reason to believe that nothing was quite so demoralizing to Lenin, the founder of the Soviet state, as the realization, toward the end of his life, that the institution of bureaucracy had not only survived but was in fact flourishing under Soviet rule.[2] With Stalin came the full-blown second phase of the development of revolution that Borkenau had spoken about in 1937. Stalinism, *inter alia*, involved the glorification of the state and the growing acceptance and respectability of the bureaucracy. A modern equivalent of the famous Table of Ranks, the elaborate grading of bureaucratic ranks instituted by Peter the Great, was introduced under Stalin in the civil service, the military, and the diplomatic corps. Within two decades after the Revolution, which had set out to destroy and smash bureaucracy once and for all, elaborate uniforms were being designed in Soviet Russia for the new generation of Stalinist bureaucrats. A few years later, Georgi Malenkov, one of Stalin's most faithful lieutenants and his short-lived successor, found it possible to say in public: "We are all servants of the state"[3]—a profoundly Stalinist, but equally profoundly un-Leninist, statement. So much for how closely the second phase of the Russian Revolution followed Borkenau's 1937 script.

The bureaucratic nature of communist regimes, in general, and the Soviet regime, in particular, have never been a secret to the communist leadership or to outside observers. Of the more than 200 passages in Lenin's *Collected Works* dealing with, sometimes *in extenso*, the subject of bureaucracy and red tape (*volokita*), more than half are devoted to a discussion of the "rebirth" (*vozrozhdenie*) of bureaucratism in Soviet Russia. Lenin's caustic critique of the Soviet system in 1922–1923 focused on the institution and phenomenon of bureaucracy;[4] so did Trotsky's scathing indictment of Stalin's regime in *The Revolution Betrayed*.[5] The bureaucracy figured prominently in Milovan Djilas's famous argument that a "new class" had come into being in the Soviet Union.[6] Even in the post-Stalin period, the bureaucracy has been such a pervasive feature of the Soviet political system that a prominent Western scholar, Alfred Meyer, has felt impelled to conceptualize the entire Soviet polity as a "bureaucracy writ large."[7]

The concept of *bureaucracy*, as a number of scholars have pointed out, poses serious problems for the analyst of politics in general and the student of Soviet politics in particular—problems that arise, on the one hand, from the historical evolution of the concept itself and, on the other, from the lack of consensus among scholars concerning its meaning.[8] Moreover, one suspects that all too often the concept of bureaucracy has been seized upon by Western writers as a convenient analytical construct that meets minimal standards of scholarly rigor and at the same time, because of its strong and firmly established pejorative connotations, serves as an acceptable basis for a negative assessment and/or condemnation of the Soviet system.[9] Even in more serious recent efforts to employ the concept of bureaucracy within a comparative framework, the Soviets, it seems, always end up drawing the short end of the ticket: their bureaucracy is either not as "rational" as Western bureaucracy, "less efficient," or not as far along in its development in the direction of "postbureaucratic administration" such as is said to exist already in the West.[10]

At the same time, the historical record clearly shows that the institution of bureaucracy, although "new" and "Soviet" more in name than in spirit and character, has served the Soviet regime very well indeed. That regime, now more than 65 years old, has weathered no less than four major changes in political leadership, a number of bitter factional fights within the CPSU, a radical industrial and agricultural revolution, a devastating purge, and a war of unprecedented destructiveness. Both inside and outside the apparatus of the CPSU, the institution of bureaucracy has been a major factor in consolidating, maintaining, and extending the power of the Soviet regime.

Rather than employing the concept of bureaucracy in ways which, explicitly or implicitly, entail an a priori qualitative assessment of the Soviet system as a whole, it seems appropriate and expedient for our purposes here to follow the example of Boris Meissner and use the concept of bureaucracy in a more limited way to describe certain groups of people in key positions in the Soviet system. This will allow us to view the bureaucracy as one of several important groups and institutions in Soviet society and to approach its evaluation more from the standpoint of its utility to the Soviet regime. Meissner has argued that there are two politically significant groups in the USSR, viz., the bureaucracy and the intelligentsia, the latter group being further distinguishable into the technical–economic intelligentsia and the scientific–cultural intelligentsia.[11] Our primary concern will be the bureaucracy, in particular its nexus with the party structure; we will deal with the intelligentsia only insofar as this is necessary for an understanding of the nature and role of the bureaucracy.

The most important group attribute of the bureaucracy is the fact that it monopolizes not only organizational functions in Soviet society but also economic and political power. While not exclusively composed of technical specialists, the bureaucracy, especially in recent years, has recruited the majority of its members from the technical–economic intelligentsia, whose upper stratum is made up of the economic managers. Consequently, the overlap in membership between the bureaucracy and the scientific–cultural intelligentsia is not nearly so great. Unlike the intelligentsia, whose authority, prestige, and relative influence in Soviet society are in the final analysis a function of specialized types of knowledge indispensable to the operation of a modern industrialized society, the power of the bureaucrats is derived from the control of key positions throughout the Soviet system. The upper stratum of the bureaucratic structure constitutes, as it were, a kind of high or "super-bureaucracy" (Meissner employs the term *Hochbürokratie*)—perhaps more felicitously conceptualized as the "central political bureaucracy" or monopolistic bureaucracy (*Monopolbürokratie*)[12]—to which the lower echelons of the bureaucracy, or the petty bureaucracy, and the majority of members of the intelligentsia find themselves in a relationship of distinct social and political subordination. This relationship reflects the hierarchical structure of the Soviet political system and Soviet society—a structure which is fostered politically by an extreme form of one-party rule and economically by the pursuit of state socialism and the administration of a centrally planned economy.

How large are the two key groups in the USSR? According to Soviet data, the intelligentsia (including in this category only specialists actually performing functions commensurate with their training) numbered 18.2 million in 1973; white collar workers in nonspecialist positions numbered 11.3 million in the same year.[13] Among the specialists, graduates in engineering, agronomy, and economics clearly predominate, with engineers and technicians accounting for 40.5% of all specialists in 1970. Another important group, in numerical terms, is the teachers and cultural experts, including scientists as well as doctors. However, they share with the economists and jurists a distinctly subordinate and inferior role in Soviet administration, which is heavily dominated by certified engineers and agronomists.[14] Turning to the bureaucracy now, Meissner, using 1970 Soviet data, estimates this group at over 6 million, with the leadership personnel in politics and the economy accounting for approximately 2.6 million and the "leading cadres," the so-called *rukovodiashchie kadry*, for about 3.1 million.[15] Focusing on those bureaucrats who serve in government positions at the various levels of the territorial–administrative structure of the USSR, we can refine this estimate one step farther and also update it. According to recently published Soviet data, the CPSU members serving in leadership positions at the district (*raion*), city (*gorod*), national area (*okrug*), regional (*oblast*), territorial (*krai*), and republic level, as well as in the central institutions and their structural subdivisions, on 1 January 1977 accounted for 5.5% of the total CPSU membership, that is, 879,696.[16] If the same percentage is used as the basis for calculation, this category included 961,442 in February 1981—at the time of the Twenty-Sixth CPSU Congress.

Western estimates of the central political bureaucracy range from 100,000 to 500,000.[17] In his 1960 work, Leonard Schapiro estimated the number of *apparatchiki* (i.e., full-time paid party officials at 230,000.[18] According to Boris Meissner, the officials belonging to the *Hochbürokratie* (i.e., the top bureaucracy) in 1959 numbered nearly 400,000.[19] In a recent study published by the foremost research institute on the USSR in West Germany, the number of party functionaries in leading organs of the party was estimated at 500,000 or more.[20]

In many important respects, the Soviet bureaucracy has become increasingly similar to its Western counterparts. If the perceptions of European bureaucrats who have had extensive contacts with their opposite numbers in the USSR are reliable, there is evidence to suggest that Soviet administrative elites share a good many behavioral characteristics with their counterparts in Western Europe.[21] Perhaps even more striking are the growing similarities emerging with regard to educational qualifications and professional backgrounds. Educational qualifications, for example, have risen sharply among party bureaucrats, economic managers, and other members of the Soviet political and administrative elite. During the 1950s and 1960s, the percentage of Politburo members and regional party secretaries with a technical higher education rose dramatically from 45 to 80%.[22] By 1967, fully 97.6% of the party secretaries at the republic, regional, and territorial levels had a completed higher education and an additional 1.4% had an incomplete higher education. Even among the secretaries of the CPSU at the national, city, and district levels, 91.1% had completed a course of higher education, and 6.3% had an unfinished higher education.[23] By 1977, 10 years later, party secretaries with a completed higher education in the two categories had increased to 99.5 and 99.3%, and in 1981 to 99.9 and 99.7%, respectively.[24]

In other important respects, however, the Soviet bureaucracy differs significantly from its counterparts in Western industrialized societies. These differences reflect the political fact of authoritarian one-party rule and the sociological reality of a society which, in spite of the October Revolution and its aftermath, has thus far achieved full modernization only in certain selected areas and limited modernization in others and is a society which is under the sway of a political doctrine that in many ways has proved to be counterproductive to the objectives of the Soviet leadership. Within the framework of an increasingly performance-oriented industrial society, the Soviet bureaucracy, therefore, constitutes an anachronism, as it were, which has already resulted in the creation of substantial "fetters"—to use Marx's terminology—on the socioeconomic development of Soviet society by setting rather narrow limits on its ability to assimilate and institutionalize values reflecting a greater degree of economic rationality. It comes as no surprise that the "anachronistic" nature of the Soviet bureaucracy is most pronounced in its upper stratum, composed of the central political elite, that is, those individuals who, because of their absolute power monopoly and control over the reward system in Soviet society, derive the greatest personal benefit from the political status quo and thus have the highest stake in its preservation, who act as the self-appointed guardians of the doctrine, and who are most interested in setting limits to the adoption of more rational, performance-oriented norms in Soviet society. It is this group which is most directly and intimately involved in the policy making process and in the elaborate machinery set up for the purpose of *proverka* (i.e., checking on and verifying the implementation of policy).[25]

The Role of   According to Article 6 of the new Constitution of the
the Party   USSR, adopted on October 7, 1977:

> The Communist Party of the Soviet Union is the leading and guiding force of Soviet society, the nucleus of its political system and of [all] state and public organizations. The CPSU exists for the people and serves the people.
>
> Armed with the Marxist–Leninist teaching, the Communist Party determines general prospects for the development of society and the lines of the USSR's domestic and foreign policy, directs the great creative activity of the Soviet people, and gives their struggle for the victory of communism a planned, scientifically substantiated nature.[26]

In Western scholarly literature on Soviet politics, too, common wisdom has it that the Soviet political system is one in which the party reigns supreme. One writer has even conceptualized the entire Soviet elite as a *partocracy* (*partokratiia*), that is, a system entirely ruled and dominated by a new type of party, a system which ex definitione precludes any kind of dualism in power between party and state, a system which centers around the ever-present and permanent cult of the party—a polity, in short, in which government, state, and people exist of, by, and for the party.[27]

There are many persuasive reasons for such a perspective on the Soviet system. During most of the history of the Soviet regime, the CPSU certainly has occupied the center stage among all the institutional hierarchies in the USSR. Its central place in the Soviet scheme of things was dramatically illustrated when the CPSU apparatus, under the skillful leadership of Khrushchev, emerged victoriously from the 5-year-long succession struggle following Stalin's death in March 1953. At the same time, conceptualizing the Soviet political system as a *partocracy* ignores the fact that during the Stalin period, the CPSU was both decimated in the purges, especially at the leadership level, and politically eclipsed by the government bureaucracy, with which Stalin increasingly identified himself—to the point that even members of the top political elite, like Malenkov, became persuaded that power had effectively (and, presumably, permanently) shifted from the Politburo and the Secretariat of the CPSU Central Committee to the USSR Council of Ministers. If we conceptualize the Soviet political system as a *partocracy*, it becomes more difficult to recognize and to deal with the seemingly inherent tendency of that system to become qualitatively transformed from one that is based on the cult of the party into one that centers around the cult of the leader. While most conspicuous during the Stalin period, this transformation also manifested itself under Khrushchev and Brezhnev; and in every instance, it has brought with it important changes in the structure of institutions and the process of Soviet politics.

Furthermore, such conceptualization inhibits our understanding of the relationship between the top political leadership and the party. It is most doubtful, to say the least, that any of Lenin's successors ever considered the party as much of an end in itself or as indispensable an instrument as did Lenin. For Stalin, the party became merely another organization whose membership had to be, and was, terrorized into total and abject submission. In his history of the CPSU Schapiro correctly speaks of "Stalin's victory *over* the party."[28] For Khrushchev, to cite another example, the party *apparat* initially was a useful, needed, and, therefore, welcome ally in his struggle for power. However, once he had succeeded, with the aid of the party *apparatchiki* in defeating his political rivals, whose designation as the "anti-party group" entailed both historical fame of sorts and personal oblivion, once he had managed to side-line the military (his erstwhile allies in his struggle with the "anti-party group") through the ouster of Marshal Zhukov and the dismissal from active duty of many of Zhukov's supporters in the military, and once he had contrived emasculation of the secret police and the dismantling of most of the centralized state ministries, Khrushchev clearly sought to reduce his dependence on the party and to develop a more balanced institutional base for his power.

After he assumed the chairmanship of the USSR Council of Ministers in addition to his post as First Secretary of the CPSU, he moved gradually but with determination toward the reestablishment of a more highly centralized system of economic management and state administration. Khrushchev's proposal for "democratizing" the CPSU by applying (retroactively) "the principle of systematic turnover" to all members of the party, including even leading *apparatchiki* and excepting only those with extraordinary "authority and high political, organizational, and other abilities"—a move, in effect, which was tantamount to a permanent bloodless purge—clearly was motivated less by his concern for greater party democracy than by political considerations. Similarly, one suspects that his radical reorganization of the entire party machine in 1962 into two separate hierarchies, one for agriculture and one for industry, had less to do with considerations of economic rationality than with his desire to make the party apparatus a more pliable subject for manipulation from above. The creation of a separate Bureau for the RSFSR within the Central Committee apparatus was another move calculated to increase Khrushchev's independence from the party.[29]

Thus, while the early Khrushchev period was characterized by Khrushchev's drive to revive the party and to reestablish its primacy, the years after the ouster of the "anti-party group" were increasingly marked by his efforts to acquire a wider and more diversified base of power, more specifically by his attempt to establish once again a system of parallel and competing bureaucratic hierarchies, whose internal and external conflicts, in Stalin-like fashion, could be exploited and manipulated from the very apex of the Soviet political structure for the transparent purpose of maximizing his independence from the party apparatus and his power vis-à-vis his political rivals. The point is that the party apparatus has not always been in a position of clear supremacy; at times, there has been a shift of power or a more balanced distribution of power among the institutional hierarchies in the Soviet Union. Conceptualizing the Soviet political system as one in which the party reigns supreme, as a *partocracy*, tends to inhibit rather than increase our ability to perceive such developments—developments that are clearly of signal importance for an understanding of Soviet politics. Ceteris paribus, the best and most reliable single indicator of such developments has been the changing composition of the Politburo and its interrelationship with the other elements of the central political bureaucratic elite.

While it is true that to date no counterelite has emerged in the Soviet Union capable of mounting an effective challenge to the CPSU and the principle of one-party rule, the place of the CPSU within the network of power relationships in the USSR does not seem to justify drawing too sharp a distinction between party *apparatchiki*, even at the top leadership level, and leading cadres in various other bureaucratic hierarchies. As we shall see, party membership and position tend to go hand in hand with advancement in a bureaucratic hierarchy. The professional backgrounds, educational qualifications, social attributes (and probably values as well) of the party *apparatchiki* and state (ministerial) bureaucrats, economic managers, etc., tend to be remarkably similar. What is important is the existence of a central political bureaucracy, a power elite whose membership cuts across all of the institutional hierarchies in the Soviet Union. The members of this elite, as Hough has pointed out,[30] are men with extensive bureaucratic experience, almost classical "Weberian" career patterns, men who have spent most of their lives learning how to survive, operate, and advance within a centralized hierarchy. Even those individuals in the USSR whom we tend to regard as "politicians" by virtue of the fact that they are presumably most intimately involved in the process of policy formation and constitute, as it were, the opposite numbers of our politicians, it must be recognized, differ from many, if not all, of their Western counterparts in that they are, in the best sense of the word, bureaucrats. Their perspectives, expertise, and values, therefore, are likely to be different from those of elected or appointed officials in a Western political system who have not come up through the ranks, who perhaps have pursued a career in business, practiced law, held an academic position, are newcomers to the world of politics and bureaucracy, and maybe have no intention of making politics a lifetime career.

By comparison with political elites in the West, the central political bureaucracy in the USSR not only possesses a much greater range and scope of power, but it also constitutes a largely self-perpetuating ruling group which is more highly politicized and integrated, consensual, and relatively homogeneous. Modern elite theory associates these characteristics not only with political stability and effectiveness but also with the development of oligarchic tendencies. Another important attribute of the central political bureaucracy in the Soviet Union is the fact that this group is in more or less firm control of a vast network of key posts or "responsible posts" (*dolzhnostnye litsa*) which, in truly totalitarian fashion, extend to and permeate all significant spheres and segments of Soviet society. We shall turn our attention to this network later in an attempt to elucidate how the central political bureaucracy in the USSR controls the policy formulation process and the vast machinery set up to check on the execution of policy.

When, on the eve of the October Revolution, Lenin addressed himself to the question: "Can the Bolsheviks retain state power?", he not only answered in the affirmative and reiterated his party's willingness to assume the burden of power alone, but also explained in rather detailed terms how it would be done. He pointed out that the proletariat already "enjoys the sympathy of the majority of the people"[31] and would thus be able to generate widespread support among the masses. Second, he argued that the Bolsheviks would, indeed, be able to "master the state apparatus in technical terms."[32] The existing state apparatus—more specifically, the standing army, the police, and the bureaucracy—would be smashed and a new apparatus, such as history had never seen before, would be substituted in its place. Lenin pointed to the Soviets of Workers', Soldiers', and Peasants' Deputies as constituting the new state apparatus and suggested that the Bolsheviks would be able to staff it with technically competent and politically reliable cadres. He went on to say that the admittedly difficult task of the Bolsheviks would be facilitated by the fact that not all parts of the old state apparatus would be smashed. "Within the modern state," he wrote, "there exists an apparatus which has extremely close connections with the banks and syndicates, an apparatus which performs an enormous amount of accounting and registration work. . . . This apparatus must not, and should not, be smashed." On the contrary, after wresting it away from the control of the capitalists, this apparatus "must be expanded, made more comprehensive, more nationwide." In more specific terms, Lenin indicated, "the big banks *are* the 'state apparatus' which we *need* to bring about socialism, and which we *take ready-made* from capitalism. . . ." As a matter of fact, Lenin concluded, *"without big banks socialism would be impossible."* He then developed the vision of "a single state bank, the biggest of the big, with branches in every rural district, every factory," accounting for "as much as nine-tenths of the *socialist* apparatus" and constituting, so to speak, the *"skeleton* of socialist society."[33] In the administration of the state in the spirit of revolutionary democracy, Lenin confidently asserted, the Bolsheviks could "at once set in motion a state apparatus consisting of ten, if not twenty, million people, an apparatus such as no capitalist state has ever known."[34] Thus the idea that the postrevolutionary order would include a huge state apparatus, a far-flung network of responsible posts, goes back to Lenin himself.

Within the context of the conditions prevailing in Russia in 1917, it was clear that popular support for the Bolsheviks hinged on the fulfillment, at least in the short run, of certain programmatic commitments, including such revisionist programs as "Bread, Land, and Peace"—a fact acknowledged by Lenin himself. And, as subsequent history was to show, Lenin possessed the requisite doctrinal and programmatic flexibility to ensure a sufficient level of popular support for his party. But Lenin realized that in the long run, the survival of the Bolshevik regime and the successful construction of socialism also, and in fact more crucially, depended on tactical flexibility. Such flexibility, as Lenin had learned in his long years of revolutionary politics and underground existence, could be guaranteed only by a reliable organization, in this case a reliable party and state apparatus.[35] It was the creation of precisely such an apparatus, "a gigantic machine, the like of which mankind has not seen in any era of its existence"—to use the apt words of Bukharin,[36] which, more than anything else, enabled the Bolsheviks not only to retain state power but to expand it vastly, to return to some of their original programmatic commitments, to abandon others, and in the process, to "overturn the whole of Russia," as Lenin had promised to do in 1902.

Quite apart from Lenin's vision of the postrevolutionary order, however, there were other, objective reasons for the development of the "gigantic machine." The vast size of the country, its relative socioeconomic and cultural backwardness, its own long-established habit and tradition of bureaucracy—all of these combined to propel the development of the "new" Russia in the direction of another kind of bureaucratic empire. Perhaps most important, the ambitious nature and scope of the goals pursued by Lenin and his Bolshevik party, as well as the means advocated to attain them against the background of the impatience so characteristic of revolutionaries, logically led to the development of an enormous state apparatus, especially in a country with a largely apathetic population, an "Oblomov republic," as Lenin in moments of despair caustically described the Soviet Union. The implementation of the "nationalization of the means of production" alone, coupled with the administration of a central economic plan, made the creation of a vast network of bureaucratic agencies and hierarchies a foregone conclusion. Thus, the vision of "government over persons" being replaced by "the administration of things and the direction of production processes," the utopian idea of a postrevolutionary state power that would gradually become more superfluous and ultimately "wither away" as predicted by F. Engels, the intellectual comrade-in-arms of Karl Marx,[37] was destined from the very outset to remain an idle dream. What instead has come into being is a party and state apparatus of unprecedented size and scope, an apparatus which not only directs production processes but also, more than any other modern industrial state, is involved in "government over persons."

The "gigantic machine" consists essentially of two main types of organizations: public or mass organizations (obshchestvennye organizatsii) and state organizations. The CPSU, the trade unions, and the governing bodies of the soviets, all of which are, at least in a formal sense, elected, are examples of public organizations. State organizations—whose personnel, by contrast, is appointed and, within certain limits defined by law and endowed with legal authority—include such bodies as the ministries and the state committees attached to the Council of Ministers structure. Both the public and the state organizations are organized into two formally separate but related power hierarchies and operate on four main territorial levels:

1. The national level, with headquarters in each of the 15 constituent union republics[38]
2. The regional (oblast) and territorial (krai) levels
3. The city (gorod) level, frequently subdivided into a number of urban districts (gorodskie raiony)
4. The rural district (raion) level

The CPSU, in addition to these territorial levels, also operates on a still lower level of organization, viz., that of the primary party organization, reflecting the "production principle" or a functional basis of party organization. Primary party organizations exist in factories, schools, state and collective farms, as well as various governmental, cultural, scientific and educational institutions.

Complex and bewildering though this picture of the Soviet territorial-administrative system may seem, it is actually an oversimplification since Soviet administrative units are organized on the basis of two different, and in some ways conflicting, principles: First, there are divisions and subdivisions that are purely territorial or geographical in nature; and second, there are divisions based on distinct nationality, ethnic, and linguistic groups. Suffice it for our purposes here to say that in 1967, for example, there existed, in addition to the 15 union republics, a total of nearly 48,900 administrative units in the USSR.[39] Between 1967 and 1977, approximately 2000 new units were added. Thus in 1977, there were 15 union republics, 6 territories (*kraia*), 120 regions (*oblasti*), 10 national areas (*okruga*), 3117 districts (*raiony*), 2040 cities (*goroda*), 572 urban districts (*gorodskie raiony*), 3784 urban-type settlements (*poselki gorodskogo tipa*), and 41,249 rural soviets (*sel'soviety*)—a total of 50,913 units.[40] The RSFSR, the largest of the 15 union republics, alone accounted for 27,933 of these administrative units.[41]

In contrast to the formal government structure of the USSR, which seeks to project the facade and decorum of a federal system and thus provides for a certain amount of decentralization of authority, the CPSU does not claim to be federal in character. As a matter of fact, it has never made even theoretical pretenses in this regard. Article 19 of the Rules of the Communist Party of the Soviet Union declares that the basic principle of the organizational structure of the party is "democratic centralism"—a principle of organization, we might add, which in practice has involved a heavy emphasis on the word *centralism*. Democratic centralism, according to the Rules of the CPSU, means:

1. Election of all leading party bodies, from the lowest to the highest
2. Periodic reports of party bodies to their party organization and to higher bodies
3. Strict party discipline and subordination of the minority to the majority
4. The decisions of higher organs are unconditionally binding on lower ones[42]

In practice, this has meant that the Leninist legacy of extreme centralization in the party has been fully preserved to this day—even though the conditions on the basis of which Lenin had originally justified the highly centralized nature of his party (which at the time led a precarious existence as an underground organization of revolutionaries) have long since ceased to exist.

The principle of democratic centralism was confirmed as the basic principle of Soviet political organization in Article 3 of the new Constitution and extended to include all state organs as well. "Democratic centralism," in the language of the new Constitution, "combines single leadership with local initiative and creative activeness, with the responsibility of every state agency and official for the assigned task." The concept of *democratic centralism* also forms part of the basis for the Soviet claim that the USSR today represents a new kind of state, a "state of all the people." The Preamble of the new Soviet Constitution is quite candid in acknowledging that it is a state in which "the leading role of the Communist Party—the vanguard of all the people—has grown."

The Party Congress — Theoretically, the apex of the CPSU is the All-Union Party Congress, an institution, which during the initial years of Soviet power, was, indeed, an important decision-making organ and constituted a bona fide forum for the discussion of policy issues. At that time, it met on an annual basis and had a relatively small number of delegates—a number that, however, grew from 104 in 1918 to 825 in 1923. Since then, a substantial increase in the number of delegates (5002 at the Twenty-Sixth CPSU Congress in 1981) and a decrease in the frequency of its meetings (once every 5 years, according to the Rules of the CPSU, as amended at the Twenty-Fourth CPSU Congress) have combined to bring about the progressive decline in its actual political significance and authority. Moreover, the delegates to the Party Congress do not represent individual party organizations: indirectly elected and hand-picked as they are by the higher party organs, they constitute a captive audience for the top party leadership. Of the 5002 delegates to the most recent Party Congress in 1981, members of the central political bureaucracy alone accounted for 42.3% (47.2% in 1976), including: party functionaries—21.5% (24.8% in 1976); state functionaries and leading officials of public organizations—13.8% (15.4% in 1976); and the military—an estimated 7%, as in 1976. The economic managers made up 12.2% (14.6% in 1976), and the members of prestige elites (scientists, writers, and artists), finally, accounted for 5.4% (6% in 1976). This left only 40.1% (32.2% in 1976) of the delegates to represent the workers and peasants, who together constitute more than 70% of the population. Bearing in mind the classification problems inherent in Soviet statistics, there seemingly has been a slow trend toward improving the representation of workers and peasants at party congresses. Compared to 1961, for example, the delegate share of workers has increased from 22.3 to 27.4% and the delegate share of peasants from 10.6 to 12.7%.[43]

Despite this possible trend toward increased representation of the workers and peasants among delegates to the party congresses, however, it is clear that this institution is not broadly representative of the Soviet population. Nor can the delegates be said to be representative of the party membership. I. V. Kapitonov, the CPSU Secretary who directs the Central Committee Department for Organizational-Party Work, revealed at the Twenty-Fifth Party Congress in 1976 that nearly 90% of the delegates had a complete or incomplete higher education or a secondary education. The corresponding figure for the membership of the CPSU on January 1, 1977, that is, 9 months after the Congress, was 49.5%. The educational level of the Twenty-Sixth Party Congress in 1981 was even higher: 94% of the delegates had a complete or incomplete higher education or secondary education—a figure which compares to 72.1% for the party as a whole on January 1, 1981 and illustrates the degree to which the members of the CPSU, and especially its leaders at the various levels, have achieved elite status based on education.[44]

In terms of the age structure, too, the delegates to the party congresses are hardly representative. There has been a continuing shift in favor of the old, established generation of party members. Only 12.5% of the delegates to the Twenty-Fifth Party Congress in 1976 were under 35 years of age, compared to 17.9% of the delegates to the Twenty-Fourth Party Congress in 1971. The "aging" of the CPSU leadership is reflected by the fact that the share of delegates aged 51–60 increased from 19.7% in 1976 to 25.7% in 1981, and the share of delegates over 60 years of age increased from 9.8 to 11.7%, whereas the share of delegates in the 35–50 age group decreased from 58% in 1976 to 50.4% in 1981 and the age group under 35 from 12.5 to 12.2%. These figures are significant, inter alia, because they indicate the continued presence of CPSU members from the Stalin era in the higher echelons of the CPSU. Like the CPSU Central Committee elected at the 1981 Party Congress, in which the central political bureaucracy accounts for no less than 83.7% of the full or voting members (86.1% in 1976), the party congress has become an institution in which, above all, the central political bureaucracy at the various levels of the Soviet system is represented.[45]

The Central Committee   Of greater importance in the policy-making process than the party congress is the CPSU Central Committee, an organization which, according to the Rules of the CPSU, "shall hold not less than one plenary meeting every six months" (Article 37). As of March 3, 1981, the Central Committee consisted of 317 full, that is, voting, members and 151 candidate, that is, nonvoting, members—by far the largest Central Committee ever elected. In many respects, the Central Committee may be regarded as an index of membership in the Soviet elite or a kind of Who's Who in the USSR, since it consists of representatives of all walks of life, party and government officials, economic managers, military officers, scientists, writers, artists, educators, members of the diplomatic corps, etc., and includes only a token contingent of workers and peasants. If, however, Central Committee membership is indicative of elite status in the Soviet Union, this is true, above all, with respect to the *political* or *power* elite. As the figure just cited indicates, the Central Committee is primarily composed of members of the central political bureaucracy. In other words, Central Committee membership seems to be largely a function of certain key positions in the Soviet political system and Soviet society. Thus, for example, all members of the CPSU Politburo and the Secretariat of the CPSU Central Committee, that is, the central party leadership, are always members of the Central Committee, as are the first secretaries of the republic and important *oblast* party organizations, most members of the USSR Council of Ministers, as well as certain key ambassadors, military officers, etc.

The Central Committee manages the affairs of the party between sessions of the party congress according to the Rules of the CPSU. But in practice, this is, of course, impossible since the Central Committee only meets for relatively short periods of time approximately twice a year. Actually, the enormous task of day-to-day management of party affairs is handled by the Secretariat in the name of the Central Committee, as we shall see.

The Central Committee also pays an important role in the Soviet legislative process through the issuing of decrees (*postanovleniia*) which—although they do not constitute laws in the technical sense—are, in fact, binding on those in authority to enact laws. The Central Committee also serves an important legitimizing function for the top political leadership, since Politburo decrees are usually issued in the name of the Central Committee. The close nexus between party and state in the legislative process is illustrated by the fact that frequently decrees are issued jointly by the Central Committee and the USSR Council of Ministers.

The growth in membership of the Central Committee from 21 full members and 4 candidates at the time of the Revolution to its present size of 317 full members and 151 candidates suggests not only the increase that has taken place in the overall size of the Soviet political elite during more than half a century of communist rule, but, more importantly, it is indicative of the expansion of the pool from which members of the central political leadership may be selected. While there is no requirement in the Rules of the CPSU that members of the Politburo and the CPSU Secretariat must be selected from the membership of the Central Committee, political practice has followed an unwritten law to that effect. At the same time, the expansion in the size of the Central Committee ipso facto has not meant greater consultation. On the contrary, frequently the involvement of the Central Committee in the decision-making process is only pro forma; at times, important political decisions are made without any consultation of the Central Committee. On the other hand, in recent years, the Central Committee has occasionally functioned as the arbiter of conflicts within the Politburo (e.g., in the case of the unsuccessful challenge of Khrushchev by the "anti-party group" in June 1957 and the ouster of Khrushchev in October 1964). From this point of view, the revival of the political significance of the Central Committee and the subsequent occasional transformation of its plenary meetings into a kind of mini-party congress, as well as its increased ceremonial role in the legitimation of important political decisions, constitute one of the most interesting and important developments in Soviet politics in the post-Stalin period.

The Politburo   Throughout much of the history of the USSR, effective political power has been concentrated in the Politburo (called Presidium of the Central Committee from 1952–1966). Considering the formal structure of the Soviet government, that of a parliamentary system, one is tempted to argue that the Politburo comes closest to being an equivalent to the "cabinet" in a Western parliamentary system—at least with respect to the decision-making process. Unlike the cabinet members in a Western parliamentary democracy, however, the members of the Politburo, as a rule, do not have specific governmental responsibilities in terms of being identified with a particular portfolio.[46] Moreover, their tenure of office is not subject to the precarious support of a majority in parliament, frequently made even more precarious by the formation of a coalition government involving several political parties. Ex definitione, in the Soviet political system, there is no loyal opposition nor, given the ideological postulates on which the system is based, can there be one. Consequently, the members of the Politburo are not subject to votes of confidence or interpellations in the USSR Supreme Soviet, that is, the Soviet "parliament." Generally speaking, their position can be effectively challenged only from within their own ranks. Not only the famous formal Resolution on Party Unity, adopted at the Tenth Party Congress in 1921 on the urging of Lenin himself, but also nearly six decades of tradition militate against open disagreement with the Politburo. Differences of opinion among Politburo members are concealed from public view (and the rank and file of the CPSU as well) by the observance of an unwritten rule of solidarity; this much the Politburo does have in common with the British Cabinet.

Since 1952, the size of the Politburo has ranged from 36 (25 full, i.e., voting, members and 11 candidate, i.e., nonvoting, members) to 13 (10 full and 3 candidate members). At present, there are 12 full and 7 candidate members. The variation in the size of the Politburo suggests, inter alia, a fairly flexible division of labor at the very apex of the party leadership. In more recent years, the size of the voting membership of the Politburo has tended to stabilize somewhat: during the past decade, it has ranged between 11 and 16; during the decade prior to 1968, it ranged from 10 to 15; since April 27, 1973, when the last large influx of new members occurred, it ranged from 16 to 12.[47]

The majority of Politburo members, even some of those who now hold government positions, have spent a large part of their professional careers in the party apparatus. By far the most common avenue to membership in the Politburo is through the territorial party apparatus, more specifically through the office of first party secretary of an important party organization at the republic or regional (*oblast*) level. Another important group in the Politburo in terms of professional background are the economic managers. However, it would probably be misleading to make too much of these differences in professional training and career background. The career patterns, activities, and values of high Soviet officials in both party and government tend to converge to a considerable extent.

As a group, the Soviet top leadership is quite old. At the time of Brezhnev's death on November 10, 1982, the collective age of the 13-member Politburo came to 909 years, that is, the average age was 69.9 years, the median age 71 years. The oldest member of the Politburo, A. Y. Pel'she, Chairman of the Party Control Commission, is 83; the youngest, M. S. Gorbachev, Central Committee Secretary, is 51 years old. Brezhnev, the General Secretary of the CPSU for 18 years and, since June 1977, President of the USSR, died in office at the age of 75, barely more than a month before his seventy-sixth birthday. The situation is virtually the same with regard to the candidate members of the Politburo: the average age is 66.7, the median age 65. The age range in this group goes from 81 to 54. In short, the top echelon of the Soviet political leadership is well beyond the norms of retirement commonly accepted in the developed world and, today, constitutes a veritable "gerontocracy."

Not a great deal is known about the procedures of the Politburo. It reportedly meets once a week and makes decisions on a collegial basis. In formal terms, there is no chairman.[48] But clearly the General Secretary (or First Secretary) at times has virtually dominated the Politburo (e.g., Stalin—if Khrushchev is a reliable witness[49]) or has been able to act as *primus inter pares* (e.g., Khrushchev after 1957 and Brezhnev in recent years). While the top leader of the party is very powerful, indeed, it is well to remember that Khrushchev was challenged by a Politburo majority in 1957 and ousted by his colleagues in 1964. Whether Stalin was reluctant to move openly against the Politburo as a group and institution, or whether he found its continued nominal existence useful, is difficult to say. In any case, instead of abolishing it outright, he chose to undermine its authority indirectly by effectively bypassing it, by not convening it, and by isolating its members through a system of committees.

From a historical perspective, it is probably correct to say that no comparable leadership group anywhere has been surrounded by so much secrecy or has had in its ranks such a high percentage of alleged "traitors," "spies," and "foreign agents." Of the 72 individuals who have been full members of the Politburo and its predecessors since 1917,[50] relatively few have died a natural death in office, and very few have been able to retire in honor and dignity. By contrast, especially if one discounts those who were newly "elected" as part of the enlarged Presidium of the Central Committee in 1952 in Stalin's transparent attempt to prepare yet another purge of the Soviet leadership, as well as those who for various reasons served only briefly on the Politburo, the number of Politburo members who ended up being executed in the purges, died under mysterious circumstances, committed suicide, were assassinated, or ended their careers in political disgrace, becoming—in truly Orwellian fashion—"unpersons" overnight, is simply stupendous and probably unprecedented.[51] With the sole exception of Lenin, the Soviet Union has not been kind to its political heroes.

The Secretariat and the Central Party Apparatus

One of the reasons for the powerful position of the Politburo vis-à-vis the government is the fact that the top party leaders do not have to rely on the government for information and policy proposals. In dealing with a wide range of issues—from labor productivity in industry, investment priorities in agriculture, relations with ruling and nonruling communist parties, the challenge of Red China, the 1980 Olympics in Moscow, and internal party matters to the improvement of education and the determination of the ideological merits of a work of art or literature—they have at their disposal an enormous staff agency, the so-called central party apparatus under the direction of the Secretariat.

The central party apparatus consists of at least 24 different departments. The following 11, together with the appropriate government ministries or state committees, are involved in the management of the Soviet economy.

Agricultural Machine-Building Department
Agriculture Department
Chemical Industry Department
Construction Department
Defense Industry Department
Heavy Industry Department
Light and Food Industry Department
Machine Building Department
Planning and Finance Organs Department
Trade and Domestic Services Department
Transport and Communications Department

While the actual operation of industries and economic enterprises falls within the jurisdiction of the ministries, the central party apparatus exercises important functions in regard to information gathering and processing, control and supervision. In addition, the central party apparatus enjoys the all-important power of appointment (*nomenklatura*)—to be discussed in more detail—with respect to key positions in the various economic ministries.

Three departments of the central party apparatus—the Culture Department, the Propaganda Department (formerly called Agitation and Propaganda or Agitprop Department), and the Science and Educational Institutions Department—are in charge of supervising literature and the arts, scientific research and education, and orchestrating the party's far-flung internal propaganda campaign.

The international operations of the CPSU are conducted by the International Information Department; the International Department (in charge of relations with the noncommunist world, i.e., primarily relations with nonruling communist or procommunist parties); the Department for Liaison with Communist and Workers' Parties of Socialist Countries, responsible for relations between the CPSU and other communist parties in power; and the Department for Cadres Abroad, which supervises foreign travel by Soviet citizens.

Housekeeping operations for the CPSU are managed by the Administration of Affairs Department, which, among other things, has charge of the rent-free and tax-free properties (apartments, dachas, sanatoria) maintained in and around Moscow, the Northern Caucasus, the Black Sea, etc., for the use of party leaders and other high-ranking officials. This department also provides all kinds of special services for the Soviet elite, maintains a library for the Central Committee, and runs the Party Publishing House.[52]

Internal security, secret communications, and general coordination among all the departments of the central party apparatus are the responsibility of the General Department, headed by K. U. Chernenko, a Central Committee Secretary and full member of the Politburo since November 1978. The Main Political Directorate of the Soviet Army and Navy, though a part of the Ministry of Defense, is also a department in the central party apparatus and constitutes an important instrument of party control over the military. Such important agencies of the government as the regular police, the secret police, and the courts are under the control of the Administrative Organs Department, which exercises *nomenklatura* powers over these agencies.

By far the most powerful structure within the central party apparatus is the Organizational-Party Work Department. Headed by I. V. Kapitonov, a Central Committee Secretary since December 1965 and a full member of the Central Committee since 1952, this department is responsible for the party's personnel and cadre policy both inside and outside the CPSU. More specifically, it is this department which exercises the all-important power of appointment over the parts of the CPSU apparatus, the Komsomol, the trade unions, etc., both at the territorial and national levels. It maintains personnel files on all CPSU members, develops statistical information on the membership of the party, and may be assumed to play an important role in the determination of the party's overall recruitment policy.

On April 26, 1979, the existence of another Central Committee department was finally revealed: the Department of Letters (*Otdel pisem*), headed by B. P. Iakovlev.[53] This department was added to handle correspondence from the population.

Before proceeding to a more detailed discussion of the mechanism through which the central political leadership in the USSR controls the entire party apparatus and, through it, the government, the mass organizations, and all significant institutions in Soviet life, let us briefly add here that, next to the Politburo, the Secretariat is clearly the most powerful body within the CPSU. While the Rules of the CPSU (Article 38) limit the function of the Secretariat to the direction of "current work, chiefly the selection of personnel and the verification of the fulfillment of party decisions,"[54] there is little doubt that the Secretariat also plays an important role in the formulation of policy. At least there is no a priori reason for assuming that the Soviet policy-making process is immune to the bureaucratic impact so frequently observed and widely acknowledged with respect to Western political systems. As a matter of fact, an exceptionally strong bureaucratic impact on policy formulation in the Soviet Union is quite likely, considering (A) the multitude and wide range of issues handled by the top political leadership; (B) the personnel overlap between Politburo members and the Central Committee Secretaries;[55] and (C) the fact that, in an important sense, all Soviet leaders have a bureaucratic background, that is, have themselves advanced through various bureaucratic hierarchies, have learned to rely on various bureaucracies, and have, to a certain extent, become dependent on them.

The number of Central Committee Secretaries has ranged from a low of 3 to a high of 14 (in 1963), suggesting a fairly flexible division of labor at the highest level of the Secretariat. At the present time, there are 9 Secretaries. Six of them are fairly recent appointments: Iu. V. Andropov (1982); M. S. Gorbachev (1978); N. Ryzhkov (1982), the only Secretary thus far appointed after Brezhnev's death; K. V. Rusakov (1977); and M. V. Zimyanin (1976). The others, however, have many years of experience in the Secretariat. Prior to his death in January 1982, veteran Politburo member M. A. Suslov, whose responsibilities in the Secretariat included ideological and foreign affairs, had been a Central Committee Secretary since 1947, that is, for more than a generation. Andropov, the current General Secretary, served as Central Committee Secretary from 1962–1967, prior to assuming the direction of the KGB. Brezhnev, the former General Secretary, served as Central Committee Secretary during 1952–1953, 1956–1960, and 1963–1982—the last 18 years as General Secretary.

Unlike the Politburo, the Secretariat of the Central Committee is almost exclusively composed of Russians. One can speak of an established pattern in this regard, for very few representatives of minority nationalities have ever served as Secretaries of the Central Committee. As in the case of the Politburo, the most common path to membership in the Secretariat is through the territorial party apparatus—in particular through the office of first secretary of an *oblast* or republic party organization. The position of Central Committee Secretary has frequently served as a springboard to membership in the Politburo: for example, of the 12 current Politburo members, 3 are now Secretaries of the Central Committee. In the 13-member Politburo under Brezhnev, 6 were or had been Central Committee Secretaries.

In many important respects, the Secretariat represents the pinnacle of the CPSU, supervising and controlling at the base (*osnova*) of the party some 414,048 primary party organizations and a party hierarchy consisting of 2887 rural district party committies (*sel'skii raikom*), 631 urban district party committees (*gorodskii raikom*), 864 city party committees (*gorkom*), 10 national area party committees (*okruzhkom*), 2 city party committees given the same standing as regional committees (Moscow and Kiev), 150 regional or *oblast* party committees (*obkom*), 6 territorial or *krai* party committees (*kraikom*), and 14 central committees in the non-Russian union republics—all with *buros* (presidium in the Ukraine) and secretariats.[56] More clearly than any other structure within the CPSU or the political system in general, therefore, the central party apparatus in relation to the territorial party machine and all other centers of power embodies a vertical integration and control function which, together with the horizontal interlacing of key posts with the party apparatus (involving the "elected" leading party organs), assures the CPSU effective control of the leadership positions throughout the USSR and enables its leadership to aspire to the more or less total control of Soviet society.

The power of the central political bureaucracy derives from its control and manipulation of the elected party and government organs at all levels of the territorial–administrative structure and its monopolization of the selection, assignment, and education of leading cadres both inside and outside the CPSU. The central political bureaucracy's control over the recruitment and promotion of CPSU members assures its effective independence from the base; its power over the appointment of personnel to all key positions outside the CPSU, on the other hand, forms the basis of its enormous societal control.

Nomenklatura and *Rekomendatsiia*	One of the important characteristics of the central political bureaucracy in the USSR has to do with the degree to which it is politicized and self-selected. We shall now turn our attention to the mechanisms

used in this process of self-selection—a process which is of great interest to the political scientist because it illustrates how a complex but essentially monocratic political system copes with the problem of elite selection.

The control over the selection of cadres in all areas of Soviet life and at all levels of the Soviet system is an integral part of what is called "party leadership" (*partiinoe rukovodstvo*) in the Soviet Union. This fact is openly acknowledged by Soviet writers:

> . . . in our country the principle of party leadership of all state and public organizations is quite openly proclaimed and realized in practice.[57]

> The CPSU proceeds from the fact that the increase in the role of the party and the strengthening of its influence on all areas of social life, though an objective requirement of our development, by no means happen automatically, but as the result of conscious, purposeful actions by the party itself. . . .
> Cadre policy was and remains the key link of party leadership and the powerful lever through which the party influences all affairs in society.[58]

> The most important component of the political leadership of the soviets is the active influence of the party on the selection and placement of cadres in the soviets.[59]

> It is precisely in the realm of cadre policy that the *commanding* function [*vlastnaia funktsiia*] of the Communist Party as the leading force of socialist society manifests itself.[60]

While acknowledging the principle and fact of party control over key appointments throughout Soviet society, the Soviet press is much less candid about the mechanisms involved in this process. From time to time, however, specialized studies have appeared which have thrown some light on this very secretive aspect of Soviet politics.[61] Occasionally, the direct and decisive role of the CPSU in the selection of important officials has even been openly described in the Soviet press. Thus, for example, A. B. Aristov, at the time the deputy head of the Central Committee Bureau for the RSFSR, told the 1959 session of the RSFSR Supreme Soviet that the Central Committee of the CPSU considered it necessary that the Presidium of the RSFSR Supreme Soviet be headed by one of the leading members of the Presidium of the CPSU Central Committee, as the Politbureau was then called. He specifically recommended the election of N. G. Ignatov, a full member of the Politbureau and CPSU Secretary since 1957.[62] A recently published book dealing with the relations between the CPSU and the soviets states that the regional, *krai*, city, and district committees of the party discuss *ahead of time* the personnel composition of the executive committees of the local soviets, as well as the candidates for the posts of department heads and chief administrators of the executive committees; it also indicates that similar discussions take place at the Central Committee level in regard to the candidates for the USSR Supreme Soviet.[63]

The role of the CPSU in cadre selection, however, is not limited to the recommendation (*rekomendatsiia*) of candidates for public office. On the contrary! As has already been mentioned, *all* important positions in the Soviet Union—whether in the party, the government, the military, the trade unions, the press, agriculture, science, education, or the world of arts—are subject to the so-called *nomenklatura* system. The term *nomenklatura* refers to a list of key positions, the appointments to which are directly or indirectly controlled by the secretariats of the CPSU at the various levels of the political and territorial–administrative structure of the Soviet system. It is the officials in the personnel departments of these secretariats who, together with the relevant political leaders, especially the party secretaries, at a given level serve as the ultimate selectors of the members of the Soviet political elite.[64]

More specifically, there are three different types of *nomenklatura* positions and name lists:

1. The so-called basic *nomenklatura* (*osnovnaia nomenklatura*), which covers the positions over which the CPSU, in the form of one of its organs at a given level, holds the exclusive power of appointment.
2. The registration and control *nomenklatura* (*uchetno-kontrol'naia nomenklatura*) covers the positions that can be filled only with the consultation and approval of the CPSU.
3. The reserve *nomenklatura* (*reserv na vydvizhenie*), whose basic purpose, as the name suggests, is to identify potential candidates for various positions of interest to the party. The reserve *nomenklatura* can be traced back to at least 1922 but seems to have been largely nonexistent until the end of the 1960s. Today, the reserve *nomenklatura*, it is estimated, may encompass up to twice as many names as the number of *nomenklatura* posts at a given level; it exists at all levels from the *oblast* down to the enterprise. For the higher level positions included in the basic *nomenklatura* at any level, the second category, that is, the registration and control *nomenklatura*, evidently functions as a "reserve."

Through its exclusive or joint control over the personnel appointed to all key positions in Soviet society via the basic and the registration and control *nomenklatura*, the CPSU has gained a preponderant institutional advantage. The potential extent of this advantage and its political import become apparent if one examines the scope of the *nomenklatura* system at the various levels at which it is operated.

Nomenklatura
of the CPSU
Central
Committee

At the highest level, that of the Central Committee of the CPSU, the *nomenklatura* includes the entire membership of the Central Committee, the Politburo, Secretariat, and full-time personnel in the central party apparatus. The Central Committee also appoints the first party secretaries and other full-time officials of the regional committees and their auditing commissions.

Outside the CPSU, the direct reach of the Central Committee extends to all top positions in the government, the military, the KGB, the mass media and the public organizations, such as the Komsomol and the trade unions, etc. Members of the USSR Supreme Court, the diplomatic corps, and ministers and members of the presidia of the Supreme Soviets down to the level of the union republics fall under the *nomenklatura* of the Central Committee, as do the chairmen of the executive committees of the soviets at the *oblast* and *krai* level in the RSFSR, that is, the most important local administrators. The police chief of Leningrad, the members of the General Staff, the top officials in the Main Political Directorate of the Soviet Army and Navy, political officers (*zampolit*) down to the corps, division, and squadron level, and the directors of certain especially important enterprises complete the list. It is characteristic of the sweep of the Central Committee *nomenklatura* that during the Virgin Lands campaign, Khrushchev even suggested the inclusion of the directors of the larger state farms (*sovkhozy*) in the *nomenklatura* of the Central Committee.[65] Similarly, the chairmen of the regional economic councils (*sovnarkhozy*), established in the course of Khrushchev's economic reforms in 1957, initially were included in the basic *nomenklatura* of the Central Committee.[66]

Unfortunately, no reliable data are available concerning the numerical size of the *nomenklatura* at this level. We can, therefore, only estimate indirectly the approximate number of key positions whose personnel is assigned by the Central Committee or with its approval. If at times even *sovkhoz* directors were suggested for inclusion in the Central Committee *nomenklatura*, it stands to reason that, a minimum, all members of the central political bureaucracy, that is, the top echelon of the bureaucracy, are included at this level. The existence of an elaborate hierarchical order in the appointment process *within* the Central Committee *nomenklatura* system supports this supposition.[67]

As we have seen, estimates of the central political bureaucracy by Western scholars range from 100,000 to 500,000. According to recent Soviet data, the "leaders (*rukovoditeli*) of *raion*, city, *okrug*, *oblast*, *krai*, republic, and central institutions, organizations, and their structural subdivisions" on January 1, 1977, accounted for 5.5% of the total party membership, which translates into an absolute figure of 879,696.[68] While not all of these officials fall under the *nomenklatura* of the Central

Committee, it is highly probable that a substantial number of them, probably one-third to one-half, are included. Thus, on the basis of the best available Western estimates and the scanty data from Soviet sources, it seems reasonable to conclude that the highest level of the *nomenklatura* system encompasses 300,000 or more positions.

Nomenklatura of the Central Committees of the Union Republics   The *nomenklatura* system at this level presumably includes regional party secretaries (with the exception of the first secretaries, who are included in the *nomenklatura* of the Central Committee of the CPSU), the secretaries and department chiefs of city (except the capital) and district party committees, and the full-time functionaries in the party apparatus of all central committees at the republic level. According to available data, the *nomenklatura* of the Central Committee of the Kirghiz Republic, one of the smaller republics in terms of population, included 2700 positions in 1952, 1707 in 1971, and 1680 in 1974. Nationwide, the *nomenklatura* of the 14 central Committees at the republic level is estimated to have included 190,000–260,000 positions in 1976.[69]

Nomenklatura of the Regional (Oblast) Party Committees   Positions of tertiary importance fall under the *nomenklatura* powers of the regional or *oblast* party committees (*obkomy*). Keeping in mind that the most important positions in any *oblast* are preempted by the *nomenklatura* prerogatives of the CPSU Central Committee and the republic central committees in the case of the 14 non-Russian union republics, the *nomenklatura* system at this level includes such positions as:

1. Leading party, soviet, trade union, and Komsomol officials of the region, its cities, and districts
2. Secretaries of the primary party organizations of large industrial enterprises and construction sites
3. Executives, managers of industrial conglomerates, and directors of enterprises, chief engineers, chief economists, as well as other "responsible workers"
4. Instructors of the regional party committees
5. First secretaries of city party committees (*gorkomy*), secretaries and department chiefs of city and district party committees (*raikomy*), the chairmen of the executive committees of the soviets at the city and district levels, secretaries of the district Komsomol committee, etc.

Our knowledge about the kinds of positions included (and not included) in the *nomenklatura* at the *oblast* level as well as about the general operation of the system at this level was greatly enhanced by the fortuitous seizure of the archives of the CPSU in Smolensk by the German army during World War II. These archives, which eventually found their way to the United States, constitute a most important source of information about the *nomenklatura* system, giving us an "inside" view, as it were, by a party organization which was an integral part of that system.[70] Unfortunately, we have no comparable documentary information about more recent years. However, the available evidence suggests that the *nomenklatura* jurisdiction of the typical *oblast* party committee has remained essentially the same, and much of the information in the Smolensk Archive is relevant to the situation today.

Observing that the ratio of *nomenklatura* posts to the number of primary party organizations or to the total number of party members at a given level of the territorial–administrative structure tends to be fairly constant throughout the USSR, it is possible to arrive at reasonably meaningful estimates of the numerical scope of the *nomenklatura* at the *oblast* level. Using this technique, the number of *nomenklatura* posts at the oblast level has been estimated as 88,000 in 1969 and 76,000 in 1973.[71]

To trace the *nomenklatura* system fully in all its ramifications through the district and city levels down to the level of the primary party organization is beyond the scope of this investigation. Suffice it to say that the principle is the same: important officials at a given level of organization are appointed only with the approval of the next higher level of political authority. At the lower levels of the *nomenklatura* system, the process is somewhat more transparent. Article 49 of the Rules of the CPSU, for example, states the principle clearly and openly: The party secretaries at the local level must be "confirmed by the respective regional or territorial committee, or by the Central Committee of the Communist Party of the union republic."[72]

The party *nomenklatura* of an average city typically includes several hundred positions: Tula—700 in 1968; Kalinin—930 in 1969; Novosibirsk—800 in 1971.[73] In the case of Moscow and Leningrad, as might be expected, the figures are considerably higher: Moscow—22,000 in 1956, 17,000 in 1958; in 1965 the *nomenklatura* of the Leningrad party committee and the Leningrad *oblast* party committee together included approximately 5000 positions.[74] In general, the size of the *nomenklatura* at the city level seems to be a function of its administrative importance rather than its size in terms of population. The positions encompassed in the *nomenklatura* at the district level may range from leaders of district organizations and secretaries of primary party organizations to directors of kindergartens and leaders of *kolkhoz* brigades. To illustrate the reach and tendency of the party *nomenklatura* system further: When in 1962–

1963 the subject of social studies was introduced in public schools in the Ukraine and Belorussia, the teachers responsible for the new subject were included in the *nomenklatura* of the city and district party committees.[75]

Finally, in recent years, the primary party organizations in large industries and agricultural enterprises have begun to maintain their own *nomenklatura* lists—including secretaries of primary party organizations and party groups, trade union, and Komsomol personnel, technicians, inspectors, etc. In the case of a very large enterprise, the *nomenklatura* of a primary party organization may include up to 400 positions.

The *Nomenklatura* System outside the Party

To complete the picture, we must add that the *nomenklatura* system is not limited to the CPSU. While, as we have seen, the most important positions in all areas of life in the Soviet Union are preempted by the *nomenklatura* of the CPSU at various levels, other public organizations and the state organs from the national to the local level exercise *nomenklatura* powers over "responsible personnel" (i.e., cadres in decision-making positions). To realize the full scope of the *nomenklatura* system and its importance as an instrument in the recruitment of cadres and mechanism of political control, we must be aware that the appointment, advancement, transfer, and dismissal of key personnel in the apparatuses of the trade unions, the Komsomol, the central and local soviets, the administrative organs (police, courts, procuracy), the vast ministerial structure, as well as all economic and cultural organizations, are subject to a *nomenklatura* process controlled by the leading officials in those institutions (i.e., almost invariably members of the CPSU or non-party individuals who are considered politically trustworthy).

The dimensions of the *nomenklatura* system outside the CPSU may be illustrated by a few pertinent facts and examples. In the case of the far-flung structure of the soviets alone, more than 50,600 different organizations are involved at the present time.[76] In the early 1970s, the executive committee of the Leningrad City Soviet employed 656,695 people and exercised basic *nomenklatura* power over 1600 top positions in the administration of the city. Each department in the city administration, in turn, maintained its own *nomenklatura* lists. According to data published in a 1974 Soviet work, the executive committee of the Moscow City Soviet has *nomenklatura* power (both basic and registration and control) over 1851 top positions; its departmental *nomenklatura* includes 10,825 positions. Since the city of Moscow is divided into 30 districts (*raiony*), each with its own district soviet, the positions controlled by these soviets must be added—another 8043—for a total of 20,719 *nomenklatura* posts.[77] For a city of over 7 million inhabitants, this may seem like a relatively small number, until we consider the fact that (*a*) the really important and sensitive positions are included in the party *nomenklatura*; (*b*) many of the city's organizations and enterprises are directly subordinated to the appropriate ministries (with their own *nomenklatura!*); and (*c*) Moscow (and Leningrad), if anything, are exceptional in that they illustrate the subordinate position of local administration in the Soviet scheme of things to an extraordinary extent.

Viewing the *nomenklatura* system in its entirety, we find that it is not limited to political decision makers at the various levels of the Soviet system as is frequently assumed in the literature on Soviet politics. The kinds of positions encompassed in the basic *nomenklatura*, the registration and control *nomenklatura*, and the reserve *nomenklatura* cover a smooth and uninterrupted range of positions from the top political decision makers at the national level through positions with purely executive and administrative functions to relatively low-level personnel, which clearly does not fall into the category of "responsible" or "leading" posts.

How effective is the *nomenklatura* system and how well does it serve the interests of the central political bureaucracy?

There is little doubt that it is very cumbersome system. The elaborate personnel records and the complex process of consultation with organizations and officials at various levels required by the system alone contribute a great deal of weight to the massive Soviet bureaucratic structure. The overlap in the various *nomenklatura* jurisdictions and *nomenklatura* types—that is, the fact that the basic *nomenklatura* and the registration and control *nomenklatura* do not always constitute discrete categories, thus making it possible for a position to be included both in the registration and control *nomenklatura* at a given level and in the basic *nomenklatura* of a different organization or at a different level—probably causes many conflicts and serious problems of coordination. One only has to read the party press in order to become convinced that not all is well in the realm of cadre policy, and this despite the fact that cadre policy has been of paramount concern to the CPSU for more than six decades.

Since 1966, there has been a tendency to reduce the *nomenklatura* lists at the regional, district, and city levels by approximately one-third. The net result has been a certain decentralization of the *nomenklatura* process and a shift in the burden of selecting and evaluating personnel downward, more specifically to the primary party organizations. Whether this will actually improve the selection and evaluation of cadres significantly, or at all, is questionable. On the other hand, it seems reasonable to conclude that, despite all of the existing mechanisms for consultation at the various levels, the new, more decentralized approach will further complicate the realization of a uniform personnel and cadre policy.

Clearly, the elaborate *nomenklatura* system in the USSR has brought with it the institutionalization of an elitism that is totally at variance with the professed egalitarian goals of the CPSU for Soviet society. The dream of a society in which the state would be administered by all, a society in which "everybody would become a 'bureaucrat' for a time so that, therefore, nobody could become a 'bureaucrat'," a society in which those who administer the state would be paid the same wage as a worker, would be elected, and would be subject to recall at any time, a society, finally, in which the state would be needed only "temporarily" by the proletariat and ultimately "wither away," as Engels had predicted—that dream, so vividly depicted by Lenin in *The State and Revolution*,[78] today seems more remote than ever before. As a matter of fact, considering the unprecedented scope of the state in Soviet society, one is tempted to argue that the USSR today represents, in many respects, the very obverse of Lenin's dream.

At the same time, the evidence is compelling that the *nomenklatura* system effectively militates against the party's objective to create an efficient system of public administration within the framework of a society which, ideological claims notwithstanding, has granted de facto recognition to the state as a viable and permanent institution. In order for any bureaucratic organization to maximize its potential in terms of technical rationality, it must develop a certain autonomy; its jurisdiction and competence must be clearly defined, recognized, and respected. However, as is evident from the preceding discussion of the all-embracing nature of the *nomenklatura* system, such a development, with the exception to some extent of certain pockets (e.g., the military, the armaments industry, and the space program) has not yet taken place in the Soviet Union. And for good reason! As Max Weber pointed out long ago, the general spread of rational bureaucratic administration would destroy nonrational structures of political rule.

Apart from its obvious value as a political control mechanism, the great utility of the *nomenklatura* system from the perspective of the Soviet political leadership lies in the fact that it sets limits to the bureaucratization (in Weber's sense) of the Soviet Union and makes possible a cadre policy which combines nonrational and rational criteria (i.e., political reliability and professional competence). "The leader of today," Brezhnev said in his report to the Twenty-Fifth Party Congress in 1976, "must organically combine dedication to the party (*partiinost'*) with great competence, discipline with initiative and a creative approach to the business at hand."[79]

Whether this kind of cadre policy will prove to be viable in the long run, given the growing complexity of Soviet society, remains to be seen. The party leadership, for the time being at any rate, seems determined to pursue the development and training of the "dual executive" (i.e., the politically reliable individual with extensive experience in the party apparatus who also possesses a high degree of professional competence). That its past success in this endeavor has not been altogether satisfactory even at the highest level of the *nomenklatura* system is indicated by the recent creation of a new center for the training of specialized staff for central, republic, *krai*, and *oblast* party and state bodies, institutions concerned with ideology, and other organizations.[80]

It would appear, however, that the real problem with the CPSU's cadre policy lies not so much in the inadequate training of cadres as in the very conception of that policy as centering around the *nomenklatura* system—a system which in many respects has become obsolete and today constitutes an anachronism in an increasingly modern society. For it is, above all, the *nomenklatura* system which prevents the influx of young, highly qualified personnel into leadership positions in the Soviet Union today.[81] It is the *nomenklatura* system which bears a large share of responsibility for the gerontocratic structure of the Soviet leadership. It is the *nomenklatura* which constitutes an important obstacle to upward social mobility in the USSR. It is the *nomenklatura*, in short, which today inhibits the rationalization of the recruitment process not only in the party and state apparatus but throughout Soviet society.[82]

In his preparatory materials for the Tenth Party Congress in 1921, Lenin noted that the *raison d'être* of the party apparatus is politics, which he then went on to define as "the revision and correction of the relations among classes, not politics for the sake of the apparatus!"[83] Looking at the party apparatus in the Soviet Union more than half a century later, one can only conclude that its *raison d'être* has fundamentally changed. Indeed, one is tempted to perceive a prophetic dimension in Lenin's reaction to the 1922 census of the RKP(b), as the CPSU was then called, in a letter to V. M. Molotov: "The power of the Central Committee," Lenin wrote, "is immense. The possibilities gigantic. We are assigning 200,000 to 400,000 party workers, and through them thousands upon thousands of workers without party affiliation. And this gigantic communist undertaking is being spoiled to the core by stupid bureaucratism."[84]

The magnitudes involved in describing the power of the CPSU apparatus today, needless to say, are of a very different order. The possibilities, to use Lenin's words, are even more gigantic—not only because of the vastly enlarged apparatus and the trained manpower available to the Soviet leadership but also because of developments in science and technology that Lenin could not even anticipate. Yet the results achieved thus far, when measured against the original objectives, fall short of the goal. Were Lenin to conduct a "*proverka*" of the activities and the modus operandi of his successors today, he would most likely not only recommend that court proceedings be instituted against them and that they be made an example of in a public trial attended by a great deal of publicity; he would probably also conclude that they have been making progress at the rate of "one step forward, two steps back."

Notes

¹F. Borkenau, "State and Revolution in the Paris Commune, the Russian Revolution, and the Spanish Civil War," *The Sociological Review* 29 (1937), p. 67.

²See, for example, Lenin's last essays and his correspondence with A. D. Tsiurupa, Deputy Chairman of the Council of People's Commissars, in V. I. Lenin, *Polnoe sobranie sochinenii*, 5th ed. (Moscow, 1974–1975), vol. 44, pp. 364–370; vol. 45, pp. 343 ff. [Hereinafter cited as *PSS*]. For an English translation of Lenin's last essays and selected pertinent passages from his correspondence, see Robert C. Tucker, *The Lenin Anthology* (New York, 1975), pp. 715–718, 729–746.

³Georgi M. Malenkov, *O Zadachakh partiinykh organizatsii v oblasti pro-myshlennosti i transporta* (1941), p. 39, cited in Robert C. Tucker, *The Soviet Political Mind* (New York, 1963), p. 82.

⁴Rolf H. W. Theen, *Lenin: Genesis and Development of a Revolutionary* (Philadelphia and New York, 1973), pp. 150 ff.

⁵L. Trotsky, *The Revolution Betrayed* (1936), various editions.

⁶Milovan Djilas, *The New Class* (New York, 1957).

⁷Alfred G. Meyer, *The Soviet Political System* (New York, 1965), p. 472.

⁸Cf. S. N. Eisenstadt and Klaus von Beyme, "Bürokratie," in *Sowjetsystem und demokratische Gesellschaft: Eine vergleichende Enzyklopädie* I (Freiburg, 1966), pp. 954 ff., and Horst Herlemann, "Zum Problem der Bürokratie in der Sowjetunion," *Osteuropa* 12 (December 1976), pp. 1064–1078.

⁹Cf., for example, the interesting "dual" use of the concept of bureaucracy by C. J. Friedrich in *Constitutional Government and Democracy* (Boston, 1941) and his later work, coauthored with Z. K. Brzezinski, *Totalitarian Dictatorship and Autocracy* (Cambridge, 1956), pp. 178 ff.

¹⁰For example, Jerry F. Hough, "The Bureaucratic Model and the Nature of the Soviet System," *Journal of Comparative Administration* 5, no. 2 (August 1973), pp. 134–167.

¹¹Boris Meissner, "Der Entscheidungsprozess in der Kreml-Führung und die Rolle der Parteibürokratie (II)," *Osteuropa*, no. 3 (March 1975), pp. 174 ff., and, by the same author, "Der Wandel in der sozialen Struktur der Sowjetunion," *Osteuropa*, no. 10 (October 1976), pp. 906 ff.

¹²Jacek Kurón and Karol Modzelewski, *Monopolsozialismus* (Hamburg, 1969), p. 13.

¹³M. N. Rutkevich, "Tendentsii izmeneniia sotsial'noi struktury sovetskogo obshchestva. Stat'ia pervaia," *Sotsiologicheskie issledovaniia*, no. 1 (1975), p. 72.

¹⁴On January 1, 1977, engineers, technicians, and agricultural specialists accounted for no less than 44.0% of the total CPSU membership. See "KPSS v tsifrakh," *Partiinaia zhizn'*, no. 21 (November 1977), p. 28. During 1965–1981 the number of the CPSU members falling into the category of "employees" (*sluzhateli*) increased by approximately 2 million—with engineers, agronomists, teachers, physicians, scientific personnel, and workers in literature and art accounting for almost 75% of the entire membership in this category (see "KPSS v tsifrakh," *Partiinaia zhizn'*, no. 14 [July 1981], p. 17). After the Twenty-Fifth CPSU Congress in 1976 the number of specialists in industrial and agricultural production increased from 60 to 65%. In 1981, it was reported that 76% of the secretaries of *obkoms*, *kraikoms*, and the central committees of the union republics

were engineers, technicians, economists, and specialists in agriculture (Ibid., p. 25).

[15]Meissner, "Der Wandel in der sozialen Struktur der Sowjetunion," p. 906.

[16]"KPSS v tsifrakh" (1977), pp. 21, 28.

[17]Günter Wagenlehner, "Ideologie und Macht in der Sowjetunion," *Osteuropa*, no. 9 (September 1978), p. 790.

[18]Leonard Shapiro, *The Communist Party of the Soviet Union* (New York, 1960), p. 525.

[19]Boris Meissner, ed., *Social Change in the Soviet Union: Russia's Path toward an Industrial Society* (Notre Dame, 1972), p. 121, Table 19 (pp. 108–109). This estimate is somewhat incongruent with Meissner's more recent calculations, according to which the *Hochbürokratie* accounted for 1.5% of the total CPSU membership. If one translates this percentage into absolute numbers, one arrives at the figure of 197,703 (i.e., 1.5% of the CPSU membership in 1968). See Meissner, "Der Entscheidungsprozess in der Kreml-Führung und die Rolle der Parteibürokratie (II)," p. 177.

[20]Gylula Józsa, *Die Herrschaftsfunktion des Parteiapparats der KPdSU*. Bericht des Bundesinstituts für ostwissenschaftliche und internationale Studien (Cologne), no. 5 (1975), p. 18.

[21]J. A. Armstrong, "Sources of Administrative Behavior: Some Soviet and Western European Comparisons," *American Political Science Review* 59, no. 3 (September 1965), pp. 643–655. See also R. D. Putnam, *The Comparative Study of Political Elites* (Englewood Cliffs, 1976), *passim*.

[22]T. H. Rigby, "The Soviet Politburo: A Comparative Profile 1951–1971," *Soviet Studies* 24 (July 1972), p. 11; Robert E. Blackwell, Jr., "Elite Recruitment and Functional Change: An Analysis of the Soviet Obkom Elite 1950–1968," *Journal of Politics* 34 (February 1972), pp. 135–137.

[23]See Ellen Mickiewicz, *Handbook of Soviet Social Science Data* (New York, 1973), p. 167.

[24]"KPSS v tsifrakh" (1977), p. 40; "KPSS v tsifrakh" (1981), p. 25.

[25]The concept of *proverka* figured importantly in Lenin's thinking concerning the best and most effective ways of combating the rising tide of bureaucracy in Soviet Russia. See Lenin, *PSS* 44, pp. 367–370.

[26]Robert Sharlet, *The New Soviet Constitution of 1977: Analysis and Text* (Brunswick, 1978), p. 78.

[27]Abdurakhman Avtorkhanov, *The Communist Party Apparatus* (Chicago, 1966), especially pp. 371 ff.

[28]Leonard Schapiro, *The Communist Party of the Soviet Union* (New York, 1960), pp. 399 ff.

[29]On Khrushchev's political maneuvering, see Carl Linden, *Khrushchev and the Soviet Leadership, 1957–1964* (Baltimore, 1966).

[30]Hough, "The Bureaucratic Model and the Nature of the Soviet System," pp. 138 ff.

[31]Lenin, *PSS* 34, p. 300.

[32]*Ibid.*, pp. 302 ff.

[33]*Ibid.*, p. 307 (emphasis added).

[34]*Ibid.*, p. 316.

[35]Later on, Lenin explicitly associated flexibility in politics with the "firmness" (*tverdost'*) of the *apparat*. See Lenin, *PSS* 43, p. 373.

[36]*Izvestiia*, March 30, 1934.

[37]Friedrich Engels, "Anti-Dühring," in Karl Marx and Friedrich Engels, eds, *Werke* 20 (Berlin, 1968), p. 262.

[38]The CPSU has central committee organizations in the 14 non-Russian union republics. Party affairs of the largest republic, the RSFSR, are administered directly by the central, all-Union party apparatus in Moscow.

[39]*SSSR: Administrativno-territorial'noe delenie soiuznykh respublik na l iiulia 1967 goda* (Moscow, 1967), p. xxiv. More specifically: 20 autonomous republics (*avtonomnye respubliki*), 16 of these in the RSFSR; 8 autonomous regions (*avtonomnye oblasti*), 5 of these in the RSFSR; 10 national areas (*natsional'nye okruga*), all in the RSFSR; 6 territories (*kraia*), all in the RSFSR; 105 regions (*oblasti*), 49 of these in the RSFSR; 2559 districts (*raiony*), 1720 of these in the RSFSR; 415 urban districts (*gorodskie raiony*), 253 of these in the RSFSR; 1888 cities (*goroda*), 955 of these in the RSFSR; 825 cities of republic, *krai, oblast,* or national area subordination, 510 of these in the RSFSR; 1063 cities of district subordination, 445 of these in the RSFSR; 3460 urban-type villages (*poselki gorodskogo tipa*), 1819 of these in the RSFSR; and 40,229 rural soviets (*sel'sovety*), 22,322 of these in the RSFSR.

[40]*SSSR: Administrativno-territorial'noe delenie soiuznykh respublik na l ianvaria 1977 goda* (Moscow, 1977), p. 12.

[41]*RSFSR: Administrativno-territorial'noe delenie na l ianvaria 1977 goda* (Moscow, 1977), pp. 8–11.

[42]For the Rules of the CPSU or the Party Statutes, see *Resolutions and Decisions of the Communist Party of the Soviet Union. Vol. 4: The Khrushchev Years 1953–1964* (Toronto, 1974), pp. 264–281, and John N. Hazard, *The Soviet System of Government*, 4th rev. ed. (Chicago, 1968), pp. 242–257.

[43]See Boris Meissner, "Parteiführung, Parteiorganisation und soziale Struktur der KPdSU," *Osteuropa*, no. 8–9 (August–September 1976), p. 646; no. 9–10 (September–October 1981), 767–768.

[44]"KPSS v tsifrakh" (1977), p. 29; Meissner, "Parteiführung" (1981), p. 767; "KPSS v tsifrakh" (1981), p. 17.

[45]Meissner, "Parteiführung" (1976), pp. 602, 649, and (1981), p. 768.

[46]Occasionally senior ministers have been members of the Politburo (e.g., during World War II and the immediate postwar period, as well as following Stalin's death). Since April 1973, the Ministries of Foreign Affairs and Defense, as well as the State Committee for Security (KGB), which may be regarded as a de facto ministry, have been represented in the Politburo by a full member: A. Gromyko, D. F. Ustinov (who replaced A. A. Grechko in March 1976), and Iu. V. Andropov (until May 1982), respectively. In addition, P. N. Demichev, the Minister of Culture, has been a candidate member of the Politburo since 1964. The new head of the KGB, V. V. Fedorchuk, holds the military rank of Colonel General but is not a member of the Politburo; as a matter of fact, he has yet to attain Central Committee membership.

[47]See Herwig Kraus, comp., *The Composition of Leading Organs of the CPSU (1952–1976)* (n. p., n. d.), Supplement to the Radio Liberty Research Bulletin and Central Intelligence Agency, National Foreign Assessment Center, *Directory of Soviet Officials, Volume I: National Organizations* ([Washington, D.C.], 1978), pp. 3–4.

[48]In an interview with American journalists on June 15, 1973, Brezhnev indicated that the Politburo meets every Thursday afternoon for 3–4 hour

sessions chaired by himself in his capacity as General Secretary or by Suslov or Kirilenko. According to Brezhnev, voting is relatively rare, since extensive discussion of the issues usually leads to a consensus (United Press International, June 15, 1973).

[49]In Khrushchev's words: "A 'proposal' from Stalin was a God-given command, and you don't haggle about what God tells you to do—you just offer thanks and obey." See *Khrushchev Remembers* (Boston, 1970), p. 279.

[50]The Politburo was made a permanent organ of the CPSU only at the Eighth Party Congress in March 1919. However, there were some earlier predecessors. See G. K. Schueller, *The Politburo* (Stanford, 1951), p. 1, and Schapiro, *The Communist Party of the Soviet Union*, pp. 173, 606.

[51]See *ibid.*, pp. 399 ff. and Zbigniew K. Brzezinski, *The Permanent Purge* (Cambridge, 1956), pp. 98 ff.

[52]For an illuminating discussion of the special privileges of high-ranking party and government officials in the USSR, see Hedrick Smith, *The Russians* (New York, 1976), pp. 25 ff.

[53]See *Pravda*, April 26, 1979.

[54]Hazard, *op. cit.*, p. 250.

[55]At the present time, 3 of the 12 full members and 3 of the 7 candidate members of the Politburo (i.e., 31.6% overall) are CPSU Secretaries. In the past, the Secretariat has been even more strongly represented in the Politburo—at times to the extent of 100% (e.g., in 1962 under Khrushchev). As recently as 1974, 7 out of 10 CPSU Secretaries were Politburo members.

[56]"KPSS v tsifrakh" (1981), pp. 20, 22.

[57]*Voprosy istorii KPSS*, no. 7 (1977), p. 86.

[58]I. Kapitonov, "Rukovodiashchaia napravliaiushchaia sila sovetskogo obshchestva," *Partiinaia zhizn'*, no. 23 (December 1977), pp. 25, 27.

[59]N. Vikulin and A. Davydov, "Partiia i Sovety," *Partiinaia zhizn'*, no. 4 (February 1978), p. 32.

[60]P. P. Ukrainets, *Partiinoe rukovodstvo i gosudarstvennoe upravlenie* (Minsk, 1976), p. 65. For two recent Soviet discussions of the role of party leadership in Soviet society, see E. Z. Razumov, *Partiinye komitety—organy politicheskogo rukovodstva* (Moscow, 1978) and *Rukovodiashchaia rol' KPSS v usloviiakh razvitogo sotsializma* (Moscow, 1979).

[61]See, for example, *Pytannia partiinoi raboty* (Kiev, 1956); P. D. Morozov, *Leninskie printsipy podbora, rasstanovki i vospitaniia kadrov* (Moscow, VPSh, 1959); and D. G. Strel'tsov, "Leninskie printsipy podbora i vospitaniia kadrov mestnykh Sovetov deputatov trudiashchikhsia—v deistvii (na materialakh Moskvy)," in *Iz istorii bor'by KPSS za pobedu sotsialisticheskoi revoliutsii i postroenie kommunisticheskogo obshchestva*, vyp. V, ed. G. M. Alekseev *et al.*, (Moscow, 1974).

[62]*Pravda*, April 17, 1959, cited in Frederick C. Barghoorn, *Politics in the USSR* (Boston, 1972), p. 180.

[63]G. V. Barabashev and K. F. Sheremet, *KPSS i Sovety narodynykh deputatov* (Moscow, 1978), p. 39.

[64]On the *nomenklatura* system, cf. Boris Lewytzkyj, "Die Nomenklatur: Ein wichtiges Instrument sowjetischer Kaderpolitik," *Osteuropa*, no. 6 (June, 1961), pp. 408–12; Bohdan Harasymiw, "Nomenklatura: The Soviet Communist Party's Leadership Recruitment System," *Canadian Journal of Political Science*, no. 4

(December 1969), pp. 493–512; by the same author, "Die sowjetische Nomenklatur: I. Organisation und Mechanismen," *Osteuropa*, no. 7 (July 1977), pp. 583–598; by the same author, "Nomenklatur: II. Soziale Determinanten der Kaderpolitik," *Osteuropa*, no. 8 (August 1977), pp. 665–681; Barghoorn, *Politics in the USSR*, pp. 180 ff.

[65]*Kazakhstanskaia Pravda*, March 19, 1961, cited in Lewytzkyj, "Die Nomenklatur: Ein wichtiges Instrument sowjetischer Kaderpolitik," p. 409.

[66]*Ibid.*

[67]Apparently there are three categories of appointments within the Central Committee *nomenklatura* system: In declining order of importance, they are (1) those made by the Central Committee Plenum (presumably on the recommendation of the Politburo and the CPSU Secretariat); (2) those made by the Secretariat; and (3) those made by the relevant departments within the Central Committee apparatus. See Ghita Ionescu, *The Politics of the European Communist States* (New York, 1967), pp. 61–63.

[68]"KPSS v tsifrakh," (1977), pp. 20, 28.

[69]Harasymiw, "Die sowjetische Nomenklatur: I. Organisation und Mechanismen" (1977), p. 585.

[70]See Merle Fainsod, *Smolensk under Soviet Rule* (Cambridge, 1958), pp. 64–66, and *passim.*

[71]Harasymiw, "Die sowjetische Nomenklatur: I. Organisation und Mechanismen" (1977), p. 586.

[72]Hazard, *op. cit.*, p. 253.

[73]Harasymiw, "Die sowjetische Nomenklatur: I. Organisation und Mechanismen" (1977), p. 587.

[74]Harasymiw, "Nomenklatura," p. 500.

[75]Harasymiw, "Die sowjetische Nomenklatur: I," p. 588.

[76]N. Vikulin and A. Davydov, "Partiia i Sovety," p. 27.

[77]D. G. Strel'tsov, *op. cit.*, cited in Harasymiw, "Die sowjetische Nomenklatur: I," p. 592.

[78]Lenin, *PSS* 33, pp. 101–102, 109, 60.

[79]*Pravda*, February 25, 1976.

[80]This center was created through the amalgamation of the Academy of Social Sciences attached to the CPSU Central Committee (in existence since 1946), the Higher Party School, and the Higher Party Correspondence School. The new center is headed by V. A. Medvedev, former secretary of the Leningrad City Party Committee and deputy head of the Propaganda Department of the CPSU Central Committee since February 1971. Like one of its constituent predecessors, it is called the Academy of Social Sciences attached to the CPSU Central Committee. See *Pravda*, September 2, 1978.

[81]For a fascinating discussion of the social determinants of *nomenklatura* status in the USSR, including interesting particulars on the age structure of those who hold *nomenklatura* positions, see Bohdan Harasymiw, "Die sowjetische Nomenklatur: Soziale Determinanten," pp. 669–670, and Meissner, "Parteiführung" (1976), pp. 648 ff.

[82]Wolfgang Leonhard, *Am Vorabend einer neuen Revolution? Die Zukunft des Sowjetkommunismus* (Munich, 1975), pp. 109–110.

[83]Lenin, *PSS* 43, p. 373.

[84]Lenin, *PSS* 44, p. 329.

7

NED TEMKO

*Soviet Insiders: How Power Flows in Moscow**

Clark Gable, in a deservedly forgotten 1940 film, plays a spy posing as a journalist in Moscow. Along the way, our hero adds one bit of wisdom to Western man's understanding of the Kremlin: "Face the facts, baby, there ain't no news in Russia!"

Comrade Gable remains largely right about one key area of "reporting" on the Soviet Union—the emptiness of many of the political stories to which we in Moscow devote most of our time and energy. Such dispatches should carry some kind of consumer warning, like packs of cigarettes.

For instance, on the Polish crisis: "The following article, however knowledgeable it may sound, is based on what the Soviet news media say—not necessarily what Soviet officials think—about Poland. The author can claim no insight into such thinking, much less into Soviet intentions. The 'diplomatic sources' are in the same fix."

(One example of the potential discrepancies: For weeks now the Soviet media have reported a gradual "normalization" in Poland. One Soviet official, when interviewed recently, shrugged this off— "Normalization? Yes, in about five years, maybe. . . .")

The current Monitor series, if written from anywhere but Moscow, would be in a Monitor wastebasket. The first article is about reporters and reporting, something reporters are not supposed to write about for the excellent reason that the subject puts most people to sleep.

The rest is about Soviet politics, policy, and power at the tail end of the 17-year-old Leonid Brezhnev era.

*Reprinted by permission of the author and publisher from *The Christian Science Monitor*, February 22–25, 1982. Copyright 1982 by The Christian Science Publishing Society.

The subject is not at all new. The approach, however, is a bit unorthodox: based both on the Western reporter's normal fare of news media and diplomatic sources—and on 32 lengthy interviews over the past year with ranking Soviet officials.

The plan was simple, and, to at least some Soviet offficials, clearly crazy. I wanted a firsthand account of how the Soviet system works, how power and paper flow, of who matters and who does not: What kind of men are at, or at least near, the top? And on specific policy issues, like Poland, do they really think in the stark blacks and whites of *Pravda* commentary? (All evidence on this last question was, incidentally, "no.")

A little like the Soviet bureaucracy, I quickly found planning far easier than results.

"I'm calling about a possible interview with Mr. Mikhail Suslov," began one phone call early last year to the Communist party Central Committee. (Mr. Suslov, who passed on last month, was a member of the central Soviet leadership for some 35 years.)

After a moment of stunned silence, the voice on the other end of the line erupted into hearty laughter. "I suppose the next thing you'll tell me is that you want to see Comrade Brezhnev!" (It was. Neither interview materialized.)

Or, there was the head of the Central Committee's "Letters Department," which handles the swelling thousands of requests and complaints the committee has been encouraging, and receiving, from ordinary citizens. His office's initial response (with no discernible trace of irony) was: "Write a letter" (to the Foreign Ministry).

Word of my shenanigans evidently spread. A few months back, I met Yuri Chernyakov, the tall, stately chief of the Foreign Ministry press department. "Ah, so you're the Mr. Temko who has been trying to see our senior officials," he said, not at all unkindly. "Well, I think you should keep at it. There are still unfortunate tendencies—mostly, I would say, from earlier days—that make this difficult. But really, do keep at it."

My eyes lit up. I suggested he might help me in my longtime quest for an interview with his boss, Foreign Minister Andrei Gromyko. Mr. Chernyakov smiled and, in several wonderfully crafted sentences, delivered a polite, but unmistakable, "no."

Yet ultimately, 18 high-ranking Soviets agreed to lengthy interviews and, in some cases, to four or five interviews. Fifteen of the officials were members of the Communist party's Central Committee. The rest sat on the Central Auditing Commission, theoretically a troubleshooter for party finances and bureaucracy and often a way station to a place on the Central Committee.

Two men interviewed turned out to be, in effect, unlisted members of the Central Committee's Secretariat—next to the party Politburo, the country's most powerful political body. At least one-third of the officials had attended both Politburo and Secretariat meetings. Boris Pastukhov, leader of the party's youth wing, said he did so quite often.

Another official attended Secretariat sessions less frequently but gets what were described as thorough briefings on top-level discussions and decisions.

Within the government (as opposed to party) hierarchy, one man held the rank of minister. Another, though without formal rank, said he attended all meetings of the Council of Ministers.

Perhaps inevitably, some of the officials open to the idea of an interview were foreign policy specialists with some experience in dealing with Western diplomats or reporters. These included men like Georgi Arbatov from Moscow's Institute of the United States and Canada, and political commentators like Alexander Bovin of *Izvestia* and Yuri Zhukov of *Pravda*.

But much of the material in the articles that follow came from others: people like Mr. Pastukhov; the editors-in-chief of *Pravda* and *Sovietskaya Rossiya* (the equivalent of *Pravda* for the Russian Republic); the two Council of Ministers men; and the chief of the Communist party's official ideological journal, *Kommunist*.

A few of the interviews were a bit frustrating. Arranging them in the first place sometimes involved a fair amount of verbal acrobatics. On one occasion, this plainly backfired.

In seeking an interview with a Ukrainian novelist, who happened to be a member of the Central Committee, I professed a not entirely genuine adoration for his writing. So when we met in the lobby of a Moscow hotel, Alexander Gonchar afforded an encyclopedic briefing on the subject. I then slipped in a question about the workings of the Central Committee, to which he promptly replied: "I won't say anything on that subject. Let's talk about literature. . . ." We did.

Yet even the more reticent or formal of those interviewed often provided insights into the way the system works or the way its protagonists think and act. Most went much further, addressing with what I sometimes found remarkable frankness issues of politics, policy, and power.

What emerged was not a perfectly precise picture of the workings of a nation Churchill called "a riddle wrapped in a mystery inside an enigma." But the officials did uncover some parts of the puzzle and, in other areas, at least suggest which pieces went where.

The sections that follow may present merely the picture Soviet officials want to offer. But I have sought to skirt, or at least minimize, the possibility by cross-checking information and by speaking with various senior officials more than once. Information that seemed suspect has been explicitly hedged or omitted.

Without overstating the value of this series, there is another sense in which the interviews were worth doing. From the start, the idea had been—regardless of what facts and insights ranking Soviet officials might or might not provide—to go beyond the generally passive approach that marks our everyday reporting on the Kremlin.

When reporting on other subjects—like the way Russians live, or joke, or dissent—we work harder and write better. To be fair, this is probably natural. Ordinary Russians and dissident Russians talk more openly than official Russians.

Leonid Brezhnev's latest utterances on the perfidy of world imperialism tend to be somewhat less riveting than the jokes Muscovites tell about him.

But will Soviet tanks rumble into Poland? Or out of Afghanistan? Here, we rely almost exclusively on "sources" that cannot possibly, by themselves, answer such questions. We absorb the enormous daily word-spew of *Pravda*, *Izvestia*, Tass, Soviet television, and the like.

Then we talk to diplomats who rely largely on the same "sources." Official or not, even the most sophisticated of Soviet media commentaries tell us only what the Kremlin thinks, perhaps even only what the author thinks. Often, we cannot be sure which. As for what the Kremlin will "do," we are left to make an educated guess.

Worse, in a town where journalists routinely collaborate with diplomats and with one another, we are often satisfied with a single, consensus guess. Worse still, our dispatches, no matter how carefully peppered with stock Moscow adverbs like "apparently" and "reportedly," often suggest a far greater certainty about Kremlin workings and intentions than any of us can honestly claim.

One example: Intermittently over the past year, Moscow dispatches have noted parallels between Soviet media commentary on the upheaval in Poland and official coverage of Czechoslovakia before the tanks rolled into Prague some 14 years ago. The implication was that the Kremlin might be revving up its tanks once again.

Yet just as conceivably, the media rumblings could have meant the Kremlin wanted the outside world, particularly the Poles, to *think* the tanks were about to roll. Ultimately, we could not know.

Sometimes, we admitted this problem, starkly and explicitly. Yet at other times, we finessed it with a quotation or two from a Moscow diplomat no more clued in to Kremlin thinking on Poland than we were. Depending on the diplomat chosen, Soviet intervention was portrayed as more, or less, likely.

Almost never did we track down a Soviet official for at least a hint of what the men in the Kremlin were planning. In most places outside the Soviet Union, this would be a Western reporter's automatic impulse.

Clark Gable is right. Things are different here. A few days after I arrived in Moscow, a European colleague told how he had tried to chase down rumors of an impending Warsaw Pact summit meeting. With pristine logic, he phoned the information department of the Central Committee.

"Why are you calling us?" he was asked.

"You are, I was told, the information department," he rebutted dryly.

"Yes, said the voice, polite and patient. "But we don't *give* information. We *get* it."

It Is Not "Democracy," but Many Soviets Have a Say	"Things were, well, *different* before Brezhnev," the Soviet official began. He paused, took a sip of tea, and smiled: "I remember once Khrushchev, all of a sudden, decided a certain man must be named deputy premier. . . . Well, it was done. Then Khrushchev said, no, this wasn't the man he wanted. . . .

"The first man, who of course couldn't figure out from the start why he was suddenly becoming deputy premier, was given a nice job somewhere else. . . ."

The moral, various senior officials suggested, is this: Under Leonid Brezhnev, there is greater stability, logic, "professionalism," in the business of making decisions and policy. More people—better-trained, more-specialized people—have a say: individuals and institutions well outside the "interlocking directorate" of Politburo and Secretariat.

But in practice, some of these "individuals and institutions" matter much more, or differently, than others. There *is* often an enormous amount of input in the formulation of domestic or foreign policy. Yet the extent to which input equals influence depends on the particular people and issues involved. Ultimate policymaking power remains the province of a very few. Below them trails an intricate, if not always perfectly decipherable, hierarchy of influence . . . and of access.

For some, access is more indirect, influence less powerful, than for others. But the story begins with nonmembers:

Down a nondescript alleyway almost literally within shouting distance of the Kremlin sits a lobby that, with its public writing tables, looks a little like a post office. A sign outside says it is an official "reception" area. There you will typically find a small gathering of quite ordinary Russians (or Byelorussians, or Ukrainians)—bundled old women and war veterans and younger working people.

Most are hunched over tables, scribbling requests or complaints to the Central Committee of the Communist party of the Soviet Union. By official figures, there are some 600,000 "Dear Central Committee" notes a year. Yet if the small percentage penned at the reception room is any guide, most seem to seek no real "policy" input.

On my latest visit, I found a huddle of people, including a young woman from Byelorussia and a war veteran from south Moscow, framing requests for more apartment space. An older woman wanted to get back at a prosecutor for wrongfully hauling one of her relatives into court.

"I don't know if the letters work," said a third woman. "Some people say they do. . . ."

The letters do get read—by a recently created Central Committee department attached to the Secretariat. Thus the voices of these people, and of many other Soviet citizens without high official rank—whether workers or shoppers, or local government and party officials—do get heard near the top. They undoubtedly matter. *How much* is impossible for a foreign reporter to say with any certainty.

But senior Soviet officials made one thing clear: The major role in policymaking belongs to people and institutions that do not have to write the Secretariat (or to those explicitly asked to do so).

The cast of characters tends to be largest, their individual roles most predictable, for set pieces like the framing of the yearly economic plan or of a long-anticipated Brezhnev foreign policy address.

Yet occasionally, most often in foreign relations, the Politburo and Secretariat cannot set their own agendas. Dissident physicist Andrei Sakharov, for instance, may go on hunger strike. A Soviet submarine may run aground off Sweden. Ronald Reagan may give the green light for production of a neutron weapon—or announce economic sanctions over the Polish crisis. Then, the cast of characters is apt to narrow.

One group, officials said, has virtually automatic input: the Secretariat's own departments and apparatus. (If one is not a member, it helps at least to move in the same circles.) Beyond this? One official said eloquently, "It depends. . . ."

In August 1981, Ronald Reagan decided to go ahead with production of a neutron weapon. (Leonid Brezhnev was vacationing in the Crimea.) The Soviet response came a week later: an acridly worded official statement ending with a nicely vague hint that Moscow may build a neutron warhead of its own.

The cast of characters, officials suggested, had been small: principally Mikhail Zimyanin (a member of the Secretariat and former editor of *Pravda*) and Leonid Zamyatin (head of the Central Committee's international information department and former director of Tass).

The task required relatively little consultation, one official said. After all, Jimmy Carter had moved, then retreated, on the neutron weapon issue during his term in the White House.

"Our position was already formed, in large part," the official said. What remained, he suggested, was to refine the script a bit— "Reaganize" it.

A few months later came a trickier challenge: A Soviet submarine faltered in a restricted area of Swedish coastal waters. That was bad enough. But the Swedes said the vessel appeared to be carrying nuclear weapons—a particularly unwelcome charge at a time when Moscow was pushing for a "nuclear-free zone" in northern Europe.

Officials here would give no details on how the Soviet policy machine handled the sub's mishap but did outline the pattern of response to similar foreign policy problems. Other actors come into play:

In addition to virtually automatic participants like Foreign Minister Andrei Gromyko and various other Politburo and Secretariat-level figures, one official said, "The response [to more urgent questions] typically involves reports from the relevant embassy, from the [Soviet] press there, maybe from the KGB, and, if there is a military aspect, from military intelligence. . . . Also there may be a meeting of the Defense Council." (The existence of this senior military group was first revealed in 1976, when the Soviet press offhandedly mentioned Mr. Brezhnev as its chairman.)

Conspicuously absent from this blueprint are what Western analysts often call the Soviets' "foreign policy specialists": academics or writers like Georgi Arbatov, head of Moscow's Institute of the United States and Canada, or *Izvestia* commentator Alexander Bovin. Their influence began in the late Khrushchev years and widened after Mr. Brezhnev took over.

One official recounts that "various" specialists, "Bovin and Arbatov among them, began to work, at first somewhat informally, later formally" with the Secretariat and its apparatus. Through the 1970s, the role of such specialists has continued to matter, officials suggest, but its nature has gradually changed.

Mr. Bovin's own (good-natured) characterization of the change— "Back then, I gave my opinion even when no one asked, now I give it when they ask me"—is exaggerated, other officials say.

He, Mr. Arbatov, and various fellow "specialists" are said to retain frequent enough contact with men of at least Secretariat level to make an important contribution to the policy machine, asked or unasked. Besides, officials say, they *are* asked. The distinction is that more of their contribution is now apt to be "of a longer range nature," as one official put it, "not necessarily, for instance, on how to answer such-and-such diplomatic note."

The issues may range from arms talks to Mideast policy. Both Arbatov and Bovin said that, typically, they are asked for their written assessment—often by the Secretariat, sometimes by the Foreign Ministry. In some instances, other officials said, the foreign policy specialists are invited to Secretariat or Politburo sessions or are called on by individual members of either group.

Men like Arbatov and Bovin also participate in preparation of some foreign policy statements by Soviet leaders, officials said. Such specialists were among those who helped prepare the foreign affairs portion of Brezhnev's keynote address to last year's Communist party congress.

When Reagan announced economic sanctions against the Soviets late last year, Arbatov wrote a commentary for *Pravda*. Bovin wrote a piece in *Izvestia*. Neither seems to have been summoned for urgent policy consultation. Bovin, at least, says he was not. Arbatov, who had been scheduled to go on vacation at the time, did so.

On the domestic front—at least on the economic front—policymaking typically moves more slowly. Both the economic crisis and the pattern for dealing with it have become something very close to institutions in recent years.

Policy "input" is enormous, almost constant. Policy output, officials say, is in large part a function of bargaining among actors like Gosplan (the gargantuan state planning organization), government ministries, and party officials; or among competing regions and economic sectors.

The scientific community plays an increasingly important role, the officials said. So do other, not strictly economic, groups: for example, the youth organization of the Communist party, whose say stems largely from the importance of young work brigades in key economic projects.

Much more rarely on the domestic front than in foreign policy does the Soviet decision-making machine have to cope with the equivalent of an errant submarine.

(Perhaps partly from lack of practice, the machine seems to have flubbed a recent exception: Dr. Sakharov's hunger strike in appeal for an exit visa for his daughter-in-law. The initial decision, as officials tell it, was to stand tough. Yet, as Dr. Sakharov kept fasting, as the Western press kept writing about him, and as Western scientists began shouting at Moscow, the men at the top rethought things. One official said Anatoli Alexandrov, head of the Academy of Sciences, was a key voice for compromise. "He and others did not want the death of Sakharov on the Soviet Union's shoulders." Moscow, in the end, gave in.)

More typical of domestic policymaking was Mr. Brezhnev's late 1980 call for a novel "food program" to deal with a not-so-novel problem: a growing shortage of meat and dairy products on Soviet store counters. The groundwork and bargaining quickly got into full swing.

By the time of the party congress in early 1981 (they are held every 5 years), Alexei Smirnov, head of a nationwide system of food cooperatives and a man with ministerial rank in the Soviet government, says that his group "had already calculated we would provide an increase of 15% [in food supplies] in the current 5-year plan."

By July, he had done some new figuring: "After working this out with our regional contacts, we decided we could provide an increase of 25%—assuming we get some help from the state in increasing equipment and transport capacity for some farming enterprises. . . ."

"The food program will surely be announced at the fall [1981] plenum of the Central Committee, in conjunction with next year's economic plan," Mr. Smirnov said.

It was not. Mr. Brezhnev told the plenum, in effect, that work on drawing up the program was continuing and that the full package would be offered at a later committee session. (Meanwhile, officials said, some aspects of the program—like a shift of agricultural resources from wheat to more appropriate livestock feedgrains—were being carried out piecemeal.)

The bargaining may, in any case, continue even after a food program is announced. Last year, the Secretariat and the Soviet government published guidelines for shoring up another problem area: coal mining. Shortly afterward, a follow-up meeting (organized by the Secretariat, one senior official said) was held in Moscow. Among the participants listed in *Pravda* were senior government ministers, two members of the Secretariat, and various regional and local representatives. Boris Pastukhov, head of the party youth organization, was not mentioned in *Pravda*, but he was at the meeting:

"Various speakers were exclaiming, 'The youth will do this, the youth will do that.' I said, 'The living conditions [for young miners] are still far from good. There is no [activities] club, for instance. . . . Until you meet these demands on our part, you will not get young workers.'"

Yet whether the issue is coal or neutron weapons, whether you are Boris Pastukhov or Leonid Zamyatin, not all those with input and influence in the Soviet system are created equal.

For a foreign reporter, charting an individual's precise place in the policy hierarchy can be roughly akin to counting angels on a pin. Still, hints of the intricate dividing lines do come across in interviews with various officials:

Pastukhov, for instance, said he quite often attended Politburo and Secretariat sessions. But when asked why "Komsomol [the party youth wing], or you, don't have a formal place on the Politburo," he did suggest the distinction mattered.

He first, chuckling reply was: "Well, maybe if you put in a good word for us. . . ." Then, more seriously, he said "this highest echelon" of leadership required vast experience. He in effect said he saw Mikhail Gorbachev, the youngest Politburo member and a one-time regional leader in Komsomol, as speaking for the group at "the highest echelon."

Mikhail Nenashev, editor of the newspaper, *Sovietskaya Rossiya*, regularly attends Secretariat sessions, although he is not formally a member. He participates in discussions which, with protocol minimal and formal votes rare, constitute much of the Secretariat's work. Yet in some functions, he suggested, he had less influence than official members of the group: either when "things are rejected from the start, or [it is decided to have them] moved to the Politburo for further discussion."

Or, there is Leonid Zamyatin, the department chief said to have helped frame the Soviet statement on the neutron weapon. Alexander Bovin lists Mr. Zamyatin, who also acts as press spokesman on President Brezhnev's trips abroad, as one of those who "can give advice even when not asked."

Yet when I asked a senior official whether Zamyatin may therefore be called the coordinator of foreign policy input for the Secretariat, the man replied: "No, not really. Remember, he is not a member of the Secretariat. . . ."

(A glimpse of the hierarchy was offered in talks last year between the visiting Canadian agriculture minister and Soviet officials. At one session, Mikhail Gorbachev, an agricultural specialist who is a member of both Politburo and Secretariat, was joined by the Soviet agriculture minister and the head of the Central Committee's agriculture department. Gorbachev is said to have done "literally" all the talking for the Soviet side.)

Here, as elsewhere, access to men at the top cannot help but influence policy for those further down the hierarchy. Given the degree of power vested in the Politburo and Secretariat, access is especially important.

Though it is sometimes hard to confirm officials' portrayal of their own access or lack of it, two interviews did provide a hint of the intricate pecking order: Yuri Zhukov, a veteran *Pravda* commentator, remarked shortly after last year's meeting between Foreign Minister Gromyko and U.S. Secretary of State Alexander M. Haig, Jr.: "Well, I haven't seen Gromyko yet. He is still in the U.S. . . ."

Later, Alexander Chakovsky, editor of the newspaper, *Literaturnaya Gazeta*, offered me help in arranging interviews with other officials: "I can't help with the Gromyko level, of course. . . . But on the Zamyatin level, I'd be glad to."

Another editor, Vasily Golubev of the newspaper; *Sotsialisticheskaya Industria* (*Socialist Industry*), showed me a roughly 20-page report he had sent the Secretariat summarizing comments from various workers, executives, engineers, and scientists on the current economic plan. This, he said, was one form of policy input. But as if to say the real requisite was "access," he added: "I know Dolgikh," referring to the member of the Secretariat specializing in industrial issues.

At times, the drop-off between those with "access" and those without it can be abrupt: After Mr. Reagan's neutron weapon decision, I talked with Nikolai Novikov, a deputy chief editor of *Izvestia*. (His boss, like the editors of *Pravda* and *Sovietskaya Rossiya*, attends regular Secretariat meetings. The *Pravda* editor, in an interview, had earlier demonstrated rather detailed familiarity with another military question, which led me to believe Mr. Novikov might conceivably be helpful.) Mr. Novikov, indeed, addressed the neutron issue—hinting ominously at Soviet plans to build a similar weapon.

Later, I asked a Central Committee member about this. He replied, not unkindly: "Well, Novikov wouldn't be in a position to know anyway. That's for sure."

Who Pulls the Levers of Power in the Soviet Machine?

Mikhail Fedorovich Nenashev is something of a Soviet socialist Clark Kent/Superman.

He is a softspoken newspaper editor few Russians, and fewer Westerners, have heard of. Yet for about 90 minutes each week, he lays aside his red pencil and helps run the Soviet Union.

His name is not on any official leadership list. Still, the slight, bespectacled Mr. Nenashev takes part in the meetings of a group second in policymaking power only to the Soviet Politburo: the Secretariat of the Communist party's Central Committee.

There is another strange thing about Mr. Nenashev (who edits *Sovietskaya Rossiya*, the official organ of the Russian Republic). Within the full, 468-member Central Committee, he is only a "candidate," or nonvoting, member. That means, officials suggest, a little less prestige but not necessarily any less influence.

Mr. Nenashev, at 55, is young by Soviet political standards. He has not been editor of *Sovietskaya Rossiya* and an "unlisted" participant in Secretariat meetings for all that long.

Meanwhile, behind the traditionally closed doors of the committee's twice-yearly sessions, it may not matter much, in practical terms, whether you have a vote or not. . . .

There was, for instance, the "Nixon question." The time was 1972, back when U.S. officials spoke of detente in the present tense. Richard Nixon had joltingly broken stride in his run-up to a Moscow summit: to announce the mining of North Vietnamese ports. The Soviets, it was thought, might cancel the summit. Just three days before Mr. Nixon was due here, the full Central Committee met in special session:

"The decision to receive Nixon had already been taken," relates one senior official. "The Politburo called the meeting, for another reason: to explain why the decision had been made. Comrade Brezhnev did this. Then he announced he would protest the American action, in the committee's name, to Nixon. . . . No one spoke against the decision."

What follows is an attempt to assemble an insiders' guide to the policy-making machine Leonid Brezhnev, now in his mid-70s, will hand over to whomever comes after. It is an effort to unravel the present, not predict the future.

It is largely the story of three senior Communist party bodies that work, for all practical purposes, in secret: the Politburo, the Secretariat, and the full Central Committee. Other individuals, other institutions, influence decisions—a subject for the next section in this chapter.

Yet by Soviet law and party rules, these three groups direct the nation's policy. And they do, senior officials say . . . only not quite as advertised.

On paper, it should all be quite simple. The party Central Committee (318 full members and 150 "candidates") determines basic policy lines between infrequently held national congresses. It then "elects" two other bodies to do the day-to-day work. The Politburo (13 full members and 8 candidates) is top dog. The committee Secretariat (9 members) ensures that what the Politburo decides gets done.

Yet then come the disconcerting puzzle pieces offered, sometimes almost offhandedly, by officials who have participated in the work of the three party bodies:

• The Politburo, though genuinely the top power, is not always the most important actor in policy decisions.

• The Secretariat does much more than dispose what the Politburo proposes. It is a more powerful policy body than its official brief suggests. On occasion, the two top groups meet as one. (The party rules do suggest substantial autonomy for the Secretariat in one very important area: appointment of "cadres." Officials confirm this role and note it applies to positions both inside and beyond party organizations.)

• The official membership lists of both groups can be a chancy guide to whom actually attends their regular, generally weekly, sessions. (This applies not only to men like Mikhail Nenashev, but also to men like Leonid Brezhnev.)

• The Brezhnev Central Committee can sometimes influence, as opposed to *make*, policy, but not all policy equally. The full committee does not, as a rule, meddle in questions of foreign relations.

"The day-to-day [power] relationships," began one Central Committee member who has attended Politburo and Secretariat meetings, "are not perfectly predictable . . . even though some of us like to explain how it is all wonderfully logical."

But the model this and other officials tended to settle on involved an "interlocking" policy directorate of sorts. The Politburo and Secretariat do the interlocking. "Don't forget," said one official, "five men are members of both." (They include Mr. Brezhnev, the two men most often tipped by diplomats as likely successors, and the youngest man on either body, agricultural specialist, Mikhail Gorbachev.)

The easiest place to start a search for how the Soviet policy machine works is, officials suggested, in the Secretariat.

It generally meets once a week, officials said. (They said the same went, as a rule, for the Politburo, but it occasionally meets less frequently.) Sometimes the session is at Central Committee headquarters, other times it is in the Kremlin. Wallet photographs of the group's nine official members are not likely to help the uninvited interloper identify the players.

Leonid Brezhnev, party general secretary, is the official chairman. But he is "not necessarily" there. Several officials suggested he was often absent and said Politburo ideological authority, Mikhail Suslov, then ran the show before he passed on in January, 1982.

When neither he nor Mr. Brezhnev attended, officials said, the chair went to Andrei Kirilenko or Konstantin Chernenko, the two men Western analysts consider frontrunners to succeed Brezhnev as party chief. *Sovietskaya Rossiya* editor, Nenashev, *Pravda* chief, Victor Afanasyev; and *Izvestia* editor, Pyotr Alexeyev, are invited to the weekly sessions. Mr. Afanasyev says Sergei Lapin, head of the state broadcasting authority, also attends.

"They do not only attend, but participate in the discussions," a colleague said. (Since discussion takes up much of the Secretariat's work, men like Afanasyev and Nenashev amount to something very close to full members—but not quite, as the next section in this chapter suggests.)

Directors of various of the Central Committee's roughly 20 specialized policy "departments"—really Secretariat departments—also attend regularly. "And other people from outside are called in according to the particular issue or issues being discussed. . . ."

Some end up at Secretariat sessions almost as frequently as Afanasyev and Nenashev. Two, in particular, were mentioned: party youth leader, Boris Pastukhov, and the head of the Soviet Academy of Sciences, Anatoli Alexandrov.

Six other officials, among those interviewed, said they had taken part in Secretariat meetings: U.S. affairs expert, Georgi Arbatov, *Izvestia* commentator, Alexander Bovin, *Socialist Industry* editor, Vasily Bolubev, *Kommunist* editor, Richard Kosolapov, consumer cooperative director, Alexei Smirnov, and publishing committee chief, Boris Stukalin.

Protocol, in the Soviet system, is inversely proportional to power. And protocol, in Secretariat sessions, is at a minimum. (Politburo meetings tend to be smaller and even less formal.) "No one [at the Secretariat] really asks for the floor, in any formal manner," said one official. "Suslov or Brezhnev, or whoever, just looks around. You raise your hand and you can speak." The pace is brisk.

The agenda is crowded, often with matters of everyday policy direction that would seem, to the outsider, less than momentous. "Some decisions can be made at lower levels," one official complains. "But there is a reluctance to take responsibility. . . ." Still, the meetings generally last only about 90 minutes, according to Mr. Nenashev. "Most of the work is done outside these meetings, within the [specialized departments and] apparatus."

And "most of the work" for the Politburo can, in many cases, be done in the Secretariat. It is here that the business of "interlocking" gets more complex and the role of individual actors and groups more unpredictable.

In the end, the Politburo takes precedence. This is particularly true, officials said, in two areas: foreign policy and "major departures, or new policies," on the home front. As it happens, there have been precious few issues of the second variety in the more recent years of the Brezhnev era. Soviet officials did not say this. But the phenomenon may help explain something they did say: In practice, the dividing line between the provinces of Politburo and Secretariat can often be blurry.

"The Secretariat *frames* policy decisions," is how one senior official put it. "By the time an issue reaches the Politburo, the framework for the decision is usually already there."

This can apply even to foreign policy issues, where the Secretariat is said to "coordinate" and "organize" information and analysis from various sources. Yet it is particularly true for domestic questions. On a good number of such questions, especially those involving nuts-and-bolts direction for running the country, the Secretariat was said to make the decisions itself.

One official who has attended Secretariat and Politburo sessions pointed out that, theoretically, "The Secretariat does not have competence in areas of state, as opposed to party, fundings, and expenditure. Moreover, in the party hierarchy, the Secretariat cannot give directives to the government, while the Politburo can. . . ."

"Thus, a number of economic questions must technically be decided by the Politburo, he said. But he added: "Even on some decisions that fall in this category, the Secretariat will, in effect, work everything out and pass it up to the Politburo just to be looked at."

This the Politburo does—at a large table in a room next to Mr. Brezhnev's Kremlin office. Here, the ultimate decision-making prerogative rests. And here, again, an official score card will not necessarily do the interloper much good.

Mr. Brezhnev, officials say, is "generally" at Politburo sessions when in Moscow. So are others in the group who are based in the capital. But seven members are prominent party men from outside. They do not necessarily attend unless an issue relating to their areas is being discussed.

This, said one senior official, even applied to the Leningrad party leader, Grigori Romanov, whom diplomats sometimes mention as a dark-horse contender to succeed Mr. Brezhnev.

"The opinions of those who do not attend are often sought by phone," said another official.

Like the Secretariat, the Politburo sometimes invites outsiders to its meetings. (Again, Pastukhov and Alexandrov are frequent visitors. And again, various other officials among those interviewed had attended Politburo sessions.) But more often than the Secretariat, the senior body will get its outside input in written form.

"Candidate" members talk but cannot vote. As it happens, there often is not a formal vote anyway. "Usually when I've been there," remarked one official, "the chairman will say, 'OK, my understanding is that the proposal is to do such-and-such. Any objections?' And that's that." (Officials suggested the full members do, as a rule, carry more weight than the candidates, but the equation is imperfect. They indicated that a man like Boris Ponomaryov—a candidate member of the Politburo but also part of the Secretariat—wielded greater practical policy influence than some full Politburo members from outside Moscow.)

More often in the Politburo than at Secretariat meetings, the focus is on foreign policy issues. Foreign Minister Andrei Gromyko, a member of the Politburo but not of the Secretariat, "reports periodically," said one Soviet foreign policy analyst. "Naturally, the Politburo thoroughly considers his assessment of all initiatives."

And "sometimes," another official adds, "the Politburo may decide to raise an issue before the full Central Committee." This third component in the policy machine has, in theory, considerable power—if only because it "elects" the Politburo and Secretariat. (In the late 1950s, Nikita Khrushchev once marshalled support on the committee to foil a bid by Politburo colleagues to oust him.) Yet in specific policy decisions, the Central Committee has clearly come to play a junior role.

The Central Committee membership list reads like a *Who's Who* of prominent communists, yet it generally meets only twice a year. In addition to the topmost political and military figures, it includes people like filmmaker, Lev Kulidzhanov, and former cosmonaut, Valentina Nikolayeva-Tereshkova. Unsurprisingly, interviews with 15 committee members made clear, the group debates more than decides policy issues.

There is protocol. At the end of discussion, an issue is either deferred for further study or put to a vote. In recent years, members say, all votes have been unanimous.

"I don't see a lot of difference between my position as a candidate member and a full member," remarked an official who has been both, "except for prestige."

Yet the debate can sometimes be sharp. And members say the committee does exert a measure of influence in at least one policy area: economic planning. The committee includes, after all, effective representatives of various regions, interest groups, sectors of the economy, professions.

"There is some hot discussion," a committee member said. "For instance, if you try to get a certain republic, or ministry, or plant to increase or change its contribution, . . . it is a bargaining process from beginning to end."

Beyond this, the group can play another policy, as opposed to "policy-making," role: a kind of sounding board for various decisions. This, members suggested, explains the 1972 session on the "Nixon question."

Similarly, Mr. Brezhnev said recently that the committee would devote a coming session to a "food program" that has been laboriously, and still incompletely, pieced together over the past 15 months. As on the state's yearly economic plan, members suggest, some hot "bargaining" is conceivable.

On foreign policy issues—whether Richard Nixon or Poland or Afghanistan—the committee is much less apt to bargain. One reason is straightforward: "Many of the people," one member said, "are not from the foreign policy side, so they can't speak with great authority." Individual committee members can and do influence foreign policy moves but generally by virtue of their roles outside committee sessions.

No full committee meeting was called, members said, before Soviet troops intervened in Afghanistan at the end of 1979. Nor, they said, was the committee convened for dispatch of an angry letter last June (in the committee's name) to Poland's beleaguered communist leadership.

The initiative came from the top. (One senior official said flatly it originated in the Secretariat; another said it should be "assumed" it came from the Politburo.) The Secretariat, various officials agreed, handled the task of drafting the note. It was, the officials said, "shown" to all committee members.

The Next Kremlin Generation: Crisis Managers as Much as Communists

In central Moscow, if you take Marx-and-Engels Street to the end, you will find a dimly lit office distinguished by lofty ceilings and an enormous bust of Karl Marx.

The room belongs to Richard Kosolapov, the quiet, articulate editor of *Kommunist*, the Soviet Communist party's ideological journal. Asked about Poland (two days after the imposition of marital law), he replies:

"It is not possible for Polish leaders to bypass Solidarity. . . . Undoubtedly, there will have to be a dialogue, an intensive, effective dialogue. . . ."

Younger men—like *Kommunist's* Richard Kosolapov, *Pravda* editor Viktor Afanasyev, or Mikhail Nenashev of *Sovietskaya Rossiya*—have moved into positions of "access" and influence within the policy machine. ("Younger," by Soviet political standards, means men between 50 and 60 years old—some 15–25 years less than men like Mr. Brezhnev.)

The older men might have changed a bit, too. They did not roll tanks into Poland when many in the West said they would. A few weeks back, I asked a younger Central Committee member why.

"Everyone on the Politburo," he said, "knew there were some problems tanks wouldn't solve. . . . They realized such a step should be avoided under any—*almost* any, I should say—circumstances."

A few days later, I asked another of the younger men, foreign policy analyst Alexander Bovin, about the "gradual normalization" the official Soviet news media were detecting in Poland:

"Normalization? Yes, in about 5 years, maybe. . . . We cannot speak of normalization. The issue, in the shorter run, is canceling martial law. It will gradually change in color. Some aspects will remain, others will be changed. . . . At least, this is how I see things."

Only a fool would venture precise predictions on the men who will lead the Soviet Union when Leonid Brezhnev is gone. Only a greater fool would presume they will necessarily be men like Alexander Bovin or Richard Kosolapov—strikingly (to the outsider) more articulate, so-phisticated, open, and self-confident than the typical older official. With others of roughly the same age group (Mr. Afanasyev, for instance, or party youth leader Boris Pastukhov) the impression comes over less strongly.

And whether such officials who are now in the younger generation will rule differently when they eventually reach the top remains to be seen. Yet they do often seem to think—or at least talk and act—differently, with two marked exceptions:

They seem in most cases to share with much older officials a sense of national, as opposed to personal, insecurity. It is the sense that their nation remains an acutely vulnerable superpower, not fully accepted by the United States as a member of the club, and beset by problems at home and abroad. The economy is not working right. And beyond Soviet borders lie real or potential sources of trouble: Poland . . . and upheaval in Iran . . . and Afghanistan . . . and China . . . and (in the longer run, suggested one official interviewed) Japan.

Officials of both generations projected a starkly bipolar vision of the way the world should be: Two superpowers, Soviet and American, should in effect run things. That, after all, is the *point* of being a superpower. They should help each other out, respect each other.

This arrangement, in Soviet eyes, presupposes that what Moscow does to its dissidents, for instance, is Moscow's business. (Older officials interviewed were much more likely to address this subject, yet the younger ones who mentioned it plainly shared their view.) On in-ternational issues, "respect" would cover a Soviet sphere of influence, or legitimate concern, deemed to embrace Afghanistan as surely as Poland. Also, Iran and other bits of the Mideast.

But can the world really run this way? Does it? And what can the Soviet Union do about all this?

Yuri Zhukov, *Pravda* political commentator and party Central Com-mittee member, has written newspaper copy of equal distinction under Joseph Stalin, Nikita Khrushchev, and Leonid Brezhnev. ("Stalin . . . I mean Brezhnev," he began one sentence in the second of our in-terviews.) He is an incisively articulate man, a file cabinet on the ups and downs of superpower relations, yet he prefers speechfying to conversation. Still, he did open up considerably as time went on. So I asked about Afghanistan:

"Suffice it for Reagan to tell [Pakistani leader] Zia to sit down with Babrak Karmal," was the sharp, unhesitating response.

Izvestia foreign policy analyst, Alexander Bovin—a man who offers analysis not only to his readers, but also at times to the men who rule the Soviet Union—speaks with more nuance. When Israeli jets struck an Iraqi nuclear reactor last year, the Soviet media held Washington responsible.

Mr. Bovin, too, said United States support for the Israelis had "created the conditions" for such an attack. But he added: "Personally, I can conceive that Reagan or Haig might have been against the attack . . . or against the [earlier] Israeli strike on populated sectors of Beirut. I think Israel is really starting to get out of control, presenting the U.S. with a problem."

No official interviewed suggested it was time to shelve superpower "détente"—that would constitute a departure from unwritten rules of behavior that would be somewhat akin to calling Brezhnev a tired old man. Yet there were occasional hints, nonetheless, of a difference in outlook between old and younger.

I asked everyone, for instance, whether Soviet policy may be affected by the fact that younger people had not endured the horrors of world war. The typical reply from younger officials was: No, hatred of war is an irrevocable part of our national psyche.

Septuagenarian Alexei Romanov took the question differently, replying: "If the nation faces any danger, it will unite the people. All of them . . . I am confident youth today is very patriotic . . . strong, and tough."

Alexander Chakovsky, editor of the newspaper, *Literaturnaya Gazeta*, literally read a typewritten text at me during our "interview." He alternated condemnation of the United States with a call for negotiation and "détente," then digressed near the end.

Obviously, he said, Ronald Reagan was trying to force Moscow to spend money on guns and not butter. "But we are not afraid of any difficulties. We know how to overcome them. If need be, we can subsist on brown bread and potatoes, but we will never compromise our security." He added: "We will never put up with any imbalance in the sphere of armaments. What we stand for is full equality in this respect."

Another of the older men interviewed ventured that Soviet soldiers could do better in tougher conditions than American soldiers.

(He was among those who quite happily took on the issue of Soviet dissidence. He mentioned an official Soviet committee on compliance with the Helsinki Accords. This group, he said, monitored compliance only in the Soviet Union. "But the Americans are concerned with compliance in *our* country." The man chuckled, as if to emphasize the audacity, the very ludicrousness of such a scheme, and then added, more seriously: "We regard this as a violation of our sovereignty.")

Interestingly, it is the younger men among the ranking officials interviewed who have come to play a more direct role in the policymaking process. (Perhaps less surprisingly, it is younger men—as opposed to younger women—who matter most. I interviewed the highest-ranking women in the country. If any of them play a major policy role, they hid this fact expertly.)

These "younger men" are not a single group. Background matters. Boris Pastukhov, the party youth leader, has spent his entire career in that group's ranks, picking up an engineering degree (1958) along the way. He talks a lot more like his elders than do men like Alexander Bovin.

Mr. Bovin's background—and those of Mr. Kosolapov and United States affairs analyst Georgi Arbatov—are different. These men got a nontechnical education, then were seconded as experts or consultants to the Central Committee Secretariat. They speak, in some cases, more like crisis managers than communists. (Oddly, it is ideology that often seems to puzzle Soviet officials most about Ronald Reagan. . . .)

Alexander Bovin is intelligent, irreverent, irrepressibly good-natured. Sitting in his seventh-floor office, his corpulent frame imperfectly restrained by suspenders, he looks vaguely like the late Zero Mostel. "Diplomacy is something of a game," he says in one of five lengthy conversations. On one wall of his office is a poster from the U.S. Military Academy at West Point. ("An American gave it to me.") On another is a poster from Israel. ("I got it when I was in Tel Aviv.")

"There is something in common between Reagan's policy and [Ayatollah Ruhollah] Khomeini's," he said at one point last year. "Reagan is looking for answers in the nineteenth century. Khomeini is looking in the seventh century. . . . Both want to escape from our epoch. . . ."

"You have your game," he said 3 weeks ago—after the latest dip in the roller coaster of superpower relations. "We understand the reasons, . . . and on some specific issues, like Poland, we tell you to go to hell. . . ."

The Soviet strategy now, he says, is to "wait."

Echoing, indeed outdoing, public remarks from Mr. Brezhnev, the *Izvestia* analyst dismisses as "stupid" a Reagan administration proposal for mutual cuts in European-based nuclear missiles. (The Soviet line is that Mr. Reagan is demanding "unilateral" Soviet disarmament.) Yet Mr. Bovin quickly adds that the U.S. proposal could provide a starting point for agreement. "There should be a compromise" somewhere between the current U.S. and Soviet stands, he says.

He terms it "without doubt encouraging" that, even after the imposition of marital law in Poland, U.S. Secretary of State Alexander Haig has not altogether stopped talking about the possibility of strategic-arms talks.

"I am positive there will be further [Soviet–American] meetings" on various issues—"a lot of them."

Mr. Bovin argues there can be no other way. "The first place must be taken by Soviet–American relations." This can be a guide for other regions, like the Middle East: "Of course, the U.S. has vital interests there. I will acknowledge this." But "the region is much closer to Soviet borders." So if, for instance, Israel and Syria go to war, Moscow could not "stay behind a screen." The idea, he says, is to avoid war. "The U.S. should persuade Israel. . . . We can talk to the Syrians. This is a good area for compromise."

Meanwhile, Bovin says, the Soviet Union would welcome better relations with more pro-Western Mideast parties, like Saudi Arabia or Egypt. He says progress on both these fronts will likely take time—precisely how much depending on Egypt and Saudi Arabia. With the Saudis, "There are, of course, some ideological considerations . . . like Islam, or the Saudis' ties with America.

"But that is their business. We consider that normal. Fundamentally, between the national interests of the Soviet Union and Saudi Arabia, we see no contradiction."

These "national interests," he maintains, involve a comprehensive Mideast settlement that is "impossible without the Soviet Union."

I asked in one conversation what he thought of United States suggestions that the Soviet Union may intervene in a nearer swath of Mideast soil—Iran—when Ayatollah Khomeini goes. "Such fears are premature," he said. "Until now, all conflict situations in Iran are because of the American presence [under the Shah], not a Soviet one." Then he added: "It is very important for us to have on our borders a strong, stable state . . . supporting good relations with us."

Viktor Afanasyev of *Pravda* has a somewhat more direct role in the policy machine. He attends regular meetings of the Secretariat.

At first glance, seated in a penthouse office in *Pravda's* new headquarters, he seems more like a Brooks Brothers model than a Soviet socialist politician. He is sun-tanned, looks younger than he is, and wears an immaculately tailored sky-blue suit. He smokes imported cigarettes, with an anti-tar filter ("it's American"). And he begins with an assault on Ronald Reagan's administration. Like Bovin, one of his sharpest immediate concerns is the Middle East.

Yet the line is harder, the nuances fewer. (Perhaps only as speculation is it worth noting that he, unlike Bovin, is not a trained foreign-policy man.) "With U.S. support and connivance," says the *Pravda* chief, "Israel flouts international law. . . . The [U.S.] Rapid Deployment Force is purely aggressive, directed at the Soviet Union.

"Or take Afghanistan. The U.S. and the West don't want a solution. At one point Pakistan agreed to talks but, under U.S. pressure, withdrew." Then, he comes to what appears the major source of his anger: the somewhat ham-handed search by U.S. customs agents last year of diplomatic cargo on an outgoing Aeroflot jet.

"Reagan seems to have forgotten with whom he is dealing," snaps Afanasyev. "We are not El Salvador or Panama. We are a superpower, with the self-respect of a superpower."

With this out of the way, he becomes more circumspect. "We assess very positively," he says, Reagan's lifting of a Carter-era grain embargo. And about U.S. fears in the Mideast: "If the Americans help us with our oil deposits, why should we go to the Mideast for oil?" On grain purchases from the United States (this was shortly before Moscow contracted for more American grain): "I think we will buy from the U.S.. . . . To be honest, it is much more convenient for us."

Then, unprompted, the national sense of insecurity exhibited by older officials emerged: "The time may not come soon. But eventually I think we will become even a grain exporter."

Finally I asked about Poland: "We hope the Poles themselves will decide their own problems. [The crisis manager emerges.] They have to. Nobody else will feed 36 million people."

Afanasyev's mere willingness to discuss the issue sets him apart from an earlier generation of officials. Older officials are much less likely to tell an American reporter that American grain is a help. Still the *Pravda* man seemed somewhat less comfortable in the give-and-take of an interview than others of the younger officials interviewed.

A few weeks later, I had just completed an interview with Yuri Zhukov down the hall from Afanasyev's office. The chief editor happened to be near the elevator when I emerged. He turned, not quite quickly enough, to avoid recognition. I said hello. A little like a guilty schoolboy, he replied: "I was just out for a minute smoking a cigarette. . . ."

This sense came across much more strongly in an interview with party youth leader Pastukhov. Of all the younger men, he was the only one visibly ill at ease. He seemed to approach an interview with a Western reporter in the same way as officials much older.

He was demonstratively friendly, his taut boxer's face frequently creasing into a smile. Yet it was somehow the friendliness of a headwaiter, rehearsed and performed. When he did open up, the catalyst was, as often with Soviet officials, the question of the world war:

"My father was killed in the war," he said quietly. "Yes, in some ways, kids are different nowadays. They don't feel as acutely the hardships of the war years. But that will change: "I am sure young people will do everything asked of them by party and country. . . ."

Three other younger officials interviewed—Kosolapov, Arbatov, and, to a slightly lesser degree, *Sovietskaya Rossiya* editor, Nenashev—were more at ease, often less strident, particularly on issues of foreign relations.

Nenashev began with a comment frequently heard from a variety of Soviet officials: Americans, with their election lurches every 4 years, challenge the crucial imperative of "continuity" in superpower relations.

"What," I asked, "should the Soviets do about this?" He replied that one imperative was "not to act in haste."

Nenashev, like the *Pravda* editor, attends Secretariat meetings. I saw him shortly before the Polish Communist party's extraordinary congress last year, amid a distinct lull in Soviet media commentary on events in Poland. Why the lull, I asked.

His reply: "There is no need to pump up the [tense] situation. . . . Also our press must be careful not to interfere . . . on the eve of the congress." He said this was because Polish "opposition" elements "are standing somewhat expectantly" to use such a move to their political advantage.

Georgi Arbatov, like *Izvestia's* Alexander Bovin, is a foreign policy specialist. His is the vocabulary of *Realpolitik*, Soviet style. Its underlying assumption: Superpowers (read: the United States) should act like superpowers, not like outmoded crusaders (read: Ronald Reagan) who presume they can dictate terms to another superpower (the Soviet Union).

Take Poland, for instance. "Nobody knows how it will end. The Poles have a lot of problems, economic, . . . internal. . . ." Before martial law some extremists "wanted a showdown, even would have welcomed Soviet intervention."

Public statements in Poland indicate a measure of continued reform is possible and suggest "this is not a move backward," he says. In this context, martial law is "by far not the worst of things that could have happened," Mr. Arbatov concludes. "No one has really serious reasons to complain."

Richard Kosolapov stands between the world of foreign policy specialists like Georgi Arbatov and Alexander Bovin and the more direct domestic policy involvement of men like *Pravda's* Viktor Afanasyev.

Mr. Kosolapov is a smallish man typically outfitted in a somber three-piece suit. He was once deputy head of the Secretariat's (domestic) propaganda department, then the No. 2 man at *Pravda*. Now he is the top man in the party's official journal of politics and ideology. He sometimes attends Secretariat sessions. When he does not, officials say, he is among those fully briefed on top-level discussions and decisions.

Last June, he was one of a group of Soviet editors and journalists on a fact-finding visit to Poland. He is a hard man to pigeonhole: He is equally articulate and open on foreign and domestic issues, with a vocabulary that suggests both the crisis manager and the devoted, if not didactic, communist.

Détente? "I don't even need to harp on such things as the 'mystical Russian soul,'" he says with a half smile. "The imperative is social tasks at home." Later, he says that a system of "incentives" for Soviet workers would seem another obvious prerequisite for shoring up the economy. ("In a free market, prices really do provide for efficiency. Our system is more humane, but more difficult.") The challenge: find similar economic "stimuli," not just money, but "higher-quality goods" for Soviet workers to buy with their money.

General international relations? "We see much potentially in common in the [geopolitical] interests of our country and the U.S., also in use of natural resources." Meanwhile, "consider the danger if a man like Idi Amin, let's say, or Pakistan, got the bomb."

On Libya's Muammar Qaddafi: "One must not forget he is a fanatic Muslim, with all that implies."

Poland: Yes, there must be "intensive, effective" dialogue with Solidarity even after martial law, a search for some kind of entente. The union group "is an organization of millions of people. . . ."

"Even if the crowd is wrong, someone has to talk to it."

"Quite a lot of [Polish Communist] party members are in Solidarity," the editor of *Kommunist* had said in a conversation some 6 months earlier.

"One cannot say, at this point, whether that is necessarily a good or bad thing. . . . A process of discussion continues, within the party and within Solidarity, too."

"The system has failed in Poland," he said a little later. Then, he added: "Much is said in the West about the fact that the Soviet system failed there. . . . This is not quite true. It is the Polish system that failed."

In a further interview, Kosolapov turned again to Poland: "One mistake [by the leadership] was not paying enough attention to the Catholic Church. The Poles are religious people. The church is important. . . ." And, a few months later: Yes, the situation is becoming more tense. It is almost as if some "extremists are sort of having fun, a kind of national masochism. . . ."

Was he referring to Solidarity as a whole? No, Solidarity, "I think, includes mostly ordinary people. . . ."

"You know," he went on, smiling slightly, "there's a joke I heard not too long ago: There are two dogs running, and they collide at the Czechoslovak–Polish border. . . . The one coming from Poland says: 'I am running in order to get something to eat.' The one from Czechoslovakia, who is a little puzzled at this, replies: 'I was running in order to bark freely.'

"Solidarity is scared of taking economic, and other, responsibility, scared of being discredited. . . . They only destabilize, and damage, and demand. . . ."

Yet above all, Kosolapov stressed in five lengthy conservations, there must be an understanding on the part of the United States that Poland is not "the kind of issue that should be allowed to strain our relations. . . ." Ronald Reagan, he argues, must learn "the talent, the art even, of speaking with people as equals." By "people," Mr. Kosolapov clearly meant the Soviet Union. The "Reagan approach . . . well, this is not the century for such things. Distances have become so small, . . . peoples so interrelated. . . ."

On Afghanistan, the sense of superpower vulnerability surfaces anew. Had Soviet troops not intervened, he says, "the situation in Iran would be very different" for Moscow. "Our southern border would be encircled with unfriendly neighbors."

The concept, he suggests, applies much farther afield. The Soviets, for instance, have occupied since World War II a small group of islands claimed by Japan, the Kuriles. Could Moscow give in?

"No," says Kosolapov. "First, this water has become in effect an internal Soviet sea. . . . The Americans wouldn't compromise, either, in our place. Second, there is the problem of creating a precedent:

"It is like acupuncture. You have an ache in your ear and get a pin in your heel. . . . It could mean reopening [territorial] issues like Poland . . . or areas of Soviet Asia. . . ."

Soviet Officials Interviewed for This Chapter

Central Committee Members

Afanasyev, Viktor Grigorevich: Editor-in-chief, *Pravda*. Board chairman of USSR Union of Journalists. Born 1922.

Arbatov, Georgi Arkadyevich: Director, Institute of the U.S. and Canada. Member USSR Academy of Sciences. 1923.

Biryukova, Mrs. Alexandra Pavlovna: Secretary, All-Union Central Council of Trade Unions. 1929.

Chakovsky, Alexander Borisovich: Novelist. Editor-in-chief of newspaper, *Literaturnaya Gazeta*. Board secretary, USSR Union of Writers. 1913.

Gonchar, Alexander Zerentevich: Novelist. Board secretary of USSR Union of Writers. Chairman, Ukrainian Republic Committee for Defense of Peace. 1918.

Kosolapov, Richard Ivanovich: Editor-in-chief of *Kommunist*. 1930.

Kruglova, Mrs. Zinaida Mikhailovna: Chairman of Presidium of Union of Soviet Societies for Friendship and Cultural Relations with Foreign Countries. 1923.

Kulidzhanov, Lev Alexandrovich: First secretary, USSR Union of Cinematographers. Producer at the M. Gorky Central Cinema Studio for Children's Films. 1924.

Nenashev, Mikhail Fedorovich: Editor-in-chief of *Sovietskaya Rossiya*. 1929.

Nikolayeva-Tereshkova, Mrs. Valentina Vladimirovna: Former cosmonaut. Chairman, Soviet Women's Committee. Member of Presidium of USSR Supreme Soviet. 1937.

Pastukhov, Boris Nikolayevich: First secretary, Central Committee of Komsomol. Member of Presidium of USSR Supreme Soviet. 1933.

Romanov, Alexei Vladimirovich: Editor-in-chief of Party Central Committee newspaper, *Sovietskaya Kultura*. 1908.

Smirnov, Alexei Alexeyevich: Board chairman, USSR Central Union of Consumer Cooperatives. 1921.

Stukalin, Boris Ivanovich: Chairman, USSR State Committee for Publishing Houses, Printing Plants, and the Book Trade. Member USSR Council of Ministers. 1923.

Zhukov, Georgi Alexandrovich: Political commentator, *Pravda*. 1908.

Central Auditing Commission

Bovin, Alexander Yevgenevich: Political commentator, *Izvestia*. 1930.

Fedulova, Mrs. Alevtina Vasilevna: Secretary, Central Committee Komsomol. Chairman, Central Council of Pioneer Organization. 1940.

Golubev, Vasily Nikolayevich: Editor-in-chief of Party Central Committee newspaper, *Sotsialisticheskaya Industria*. 1913.

8   DARRELL P. HAMMER

*Brezhnev and the Communist Party**

Nikita Khrushchev was removed from office because of his management, or mismanagement, of the internal affairs of the Communist party. Of course, many events converged to create the crisis of October 1964: Khrushchev's handling of the Soviet economy and especially his radical proposals to shift investment priorities toward consumer goods; the gradual erosion of his prestige after the Cuba fiasco and his other foreign policy failures, as in Berlin; and his flamboyant personal style, the "phrase-mongering" and "empty-headed scheming" which were so widely criticized later on. But it was an urgent concern over the party and its future which forced the other members of the Presidium into a coalition against the first secretary. As the Georgian party leader remarked a few months later, the leadership had put up with a great deal from Khrushchev, and kept silent. But there was one thing that they would not stand for, and that was an effort to tamper with the party itself.[1]

The new leadership under Leonid Brezhnev had much to complain about because Khrushchev's internal reforms and organizational projects had left the Communist Party of the Soviet Union (CPSU) in serious disarray. Khrushchev had tried to make the party a more effective instrument of political decision making and social control. In particular, he had tried to give the party bureaucracy a greater voice in economic affairs. Throughout his career as national leader, he had tried to refocus the thinking of the professional party functionaries, the *apparatchiki*, and to direct their attention to new problems.[2] It was this effort to turn the apparatus around which gradually alienated Khrushchev's natural base

*Reprinted by permission of the author and publisher from *Soviet Union* 2, no. 1 (1975), pp. 1–21. Copyright 1975 by Charles Schlacks, Jr. and University Center for International Studies, University of Pittsburgh. All rights reserved.

of support, the middle-level party officials, and led to his downfall. Most of the organizational reforms were scrapped after his departure from the leadership. But the spirit of Khrushchevism was not wiped out entirely. It seems to survive in scattered pockets within the party, and particularly, in the city of Leningrad. Some writers in the party press have addressed themselves to the continuing problem of reform—usually in the guise of learned discussions about the impact of the "scientific and technological revolution" on Soviet society. One official of the central apparatus has been bold enough to ask whether the "scientific and technological revolution" would leave the party behind.[3]

A few Western observers have argued that the older generation of *apparatchiki*, the men who survived Khrushchev and are now the mainstay of the Brezhnev regime, is now giving way to a new generation of "technocrats." Ideology, in this view, is giving way to a more pragmatic outlook and especially to a more rational economic policy. By the logic of this argument, carried to its extreme conclusion, the party must eventually give way to new and more rational forces within Soviet society.

The trouble with this interpretation is that it overlooks the forces working toward reform which can be perceived within the party itself. What is going on in the USSR is not a conflict between the party and society, but a conflict over policy. A careful scrutiny of the party press (especially if one is willing to read between the lines) suggests a series of disagreements between reform elements in the party and those who represent a more orthodox point of view. These are disputes about recruitment policy, about the relationship between party and society, and particularly about the party's role in the economy.

Brezhnev's own position on these issues is not clear. But certainly Brezhnev has not perceived himself as a reformer or innovator, as Khrushchev was. He seems to have played the role of power broker among the great bureaucracies which manage the USSR; the essence of his internal policy has been to maintain a balance of power among potentially conflicting groups. In staffing the national party leadership, Brezhnev has tended to call on old established cadres rather than on younger men. He has, to be sure, "coopted" some experienced engineers and industrial managers into the national leadership. But this is hardly innovative—Stalin did the same thing when he brought young managers like Pervukhin, Saburov, and Kosygin into his inner circle.

This chapter is not concerned, except indirectly, with the better known institutions of the CPSU such as the Politburo or the Central Committee. It will focus instead on the concerns of the party professionals in the territorial and central apparatus and thus will deal with such matters as membership recruitment and job security for party officials. These are not the global issues with which Brezhnev must deal in his role as national leader. But it should not be forgotten that Brezhnev's official job is that of chief executive of the party, and so the party's affairs must always be among his principal concerns. He cannot afford to repeat Khrushchev's mistake of taking the party for granted.

The Heritage of Khrushchevism

From the point of view of the ordinary party functionary, the most disruptive of Khrushchev's reforms was the rule which called for systematic "renovation" (*obnovlenie*) of the elected bodies of the party. The rule was in effect from 1961 until 1966, and it was an obvious effort to infuse new blood into the apparatus, especially at the lower levels. Higher levels of the party bureaucracy were also subject to periodic "renovation." There was even provision for systematic turnover in the Central Committee leadership.

Obnovlenie had a deleterious effect on the morale of the middle- and lower-level apparatus. The lower ranking party secretaries were slowly being squeezed out, unless they could find new positions in different organizations. Indeed, there is some indication that many secretaries escaped from the operation of the rule in just this way. They were simply shuffled around in a form of *krugovaia poruka* that defied Khrushchev's schemes. Still, every party secretary could see that his career was in jeopardy, and there can be no doubt that Khrushchev became an unpopular figure. Shortly after his resignation, criticism of *obnovlenie* came into the open. M. S. Solomentsev, who was then head of the Rostov regional organization, told the Central Committee in 1965 that the rule was only "false democracy" and should be abandoned. More recognition should be given, he said, to the importance of *experience* and *maturity* within the apparatus.[4]

In addition to *obnovlenie*, Khrushchev had sponsored a variety of organizational changes that upset the traditional balance of forces within the party bureaucracy. The apparatus, and especially the territorial secretaries, served as Khrushchev's power base in the internal struggles of 1953–1957. Khrushchev was able to appeal to the apparatus against other elite interests. On the other hand, it should not be assumed that Khrushchev became the absolute master of the apparatus. He was able to control the central secretariat, and by means of strategic appointments, he could try to install his own men in strategic positions. But Khrushchev never succeeded in bringing the apparatus under his personal control. The best evidence for this conclusion is the fact that he was constantly tinkering with the organizational machinery of the party, trying to make it more responsive to his own will and more effective in carrying out his programs. The widespread criticism of his *donkikhotstvo* was directed at the unsettling effect which his leadership had on the party machinery, as much as at Khrushchev's foreign and domestic policies.

The creation of the "Bureau of the Central Committee for the RSFSR" is an illustration of this point. Apparently when this bureau was set up in 1956, the purpose was to create an alternate decision-making organ to the Presidium and one where Khrushchev would have greater influence. The bureau was created just after the adjournment of the Twentieth Congress—a congress which had significantly failed to make any change in the full members of the Presidium, although some new candidate members had been promoted.[5] Khrushchev probably fell back on this particular "empty-headed scheme" when he found that he could not accomplish any substantive change within the top leadership.

The reorganizations of 1962 are further evidence that Khrushchev was not having his own way within the apparatus and was trying to find ways to get around the existing machinery of decision-making and control. The "bifurcation" of the national party organization has attracted most of the attention of Western analysts, and this particular scheme certainly had a disruptive effect. The speed and publicity with which this plan was abandoned (in the month following Khrushchev's dismissal) make it clear that bifurcation had little support.

At the same time that bifurcation was forced on the party, Khrushchev had produced another scheme for restructuring the central apparatus. This plan also had the signs of a makeshift project. It called for the creation of a rather complicated superstructure of special "boards" and "commissions" which would watch over the work of the various departments of the central apparatus. The published decree on the reorganization provided for only two such boards—new "bureaus" of the Central Committee for agriculture and industry, which corresponded to the division of the whole party into two sectors. In fact several such special boards were set up in November 1962:[6]

1. Central Committee Bureau for Industry and Construction—Chairman, A. P. Rudakov.
2. Central Committee Bureau for Agriculture—Chairman, V. I. Poliakov.
3. Commission for Organizational and Party Questions—Chairman, V. N. Titov.
4. Central Committee Bureau for Chemical and Light Industry—Chairman, P. N. Demichev.
5. Ideological Commission of the Central Committee—Chairman, L. F. Il'ichev.
6. Party–State Control Committee—Chairman, A. N. Shelepin.

All these chairmen were to serve as secretaries of the Central Committee and thus would be subordinate to Khrushchev as first secretary. None of them belonged to the top level leadership. Indeed, until the November 1962 plenum, Poliakov and Rudakov were not even full members of the

Central Committee; they were promoted to full membership at the same time that they were elected to the secretariat, and this is rather rapid advancement in the USSR. Most of them seemed to be Khrushchev's proteges. Poliakov, who was a journalist by profession, had for some time been Khrushchev's unofficial chief adviser on agricultural matters and had no previous experience in the apparatus. Il'ichev was a propaganda specialist who had thrown his lot in with Khrushchev. Apparently, he was Khrushchev's nominee for the office of chief ideological specialist and a possible counterweight to Suslov. The precise functions of the new boards were not made public. Only the ideological commission and the party–state control committee were given much publicity.

As Downs has pointed out in his study of bureaucracy, the establishment of separate monitoring agencies like the 1962 boards is generally a symptom of rigidity and unresponsiveness within the original organization.[7] Undoubtedly, there was conflict and tension between the boards and the operating agencies which they were to supervise. Khrushchev thus left the apparatus of the party in a state of confusion, with the lines of authority fuzzy and uncertain. The heads of the traditional departments of the Central Committee were watched over by Khrushchev's proteges. In this, and in other ways, Khrushchev undermined the morale of the *apparatchiki* by the way he treated them as a group. He is said to have been particularly abusive of the ideological officials, those who "neither reap nor sow, but only eat."[8]

In 1965, a regional secretary reported that he had chosen some of his best younger men to be sent to study at the Higher Party School in Moscow. But once in the capital, they had decided to transfer out to other educational institutions because they found party work unrewarding and lacking in prestige.[9] An attitude such as this among the younger officials of the apparatus would certainly cause grave concern within the leadership. In 1964, one of the immediate aims of the new regime must have been to make party careers more attractive to younger men and also to eliminate the confusion and tangled lines of authority which were the outcome of Khrushchev's continual tinkering with the organization.

The Brezhnev Regime: First Steps

The first 18 months of the Brezhnev regime were devoted to a rapid dismantling of most of Khrushchev's organizational experiments. The reorganization of industrial management took place amid much publicity (and with considerable attention from outside observers) in September 1965; the system which Khrushchev created in 1957 was effectively abandoned in favor of an organizational structure much like that of the Stalin era. But the CPSU was being reorganized at the same time, and although this refurbishing of the party has attracted much less attention than the economic reform, it is not without interest.

The new leadership was quite careful to observe party legality in undoing Khrushchev's work. (This fact alone marked a change from Khrushchev's habits.) The bifurcation of the party had been ordered by a plenary decree of November 1962; it was revoked by a plenary decree 2 years later.[10] On the other hand, the creation of the RSFSR Bureau and the rule calling for systematic "renovation" of elected bodies had been affirmed by the Twenty-Second Congress and written into the party statute, which only a new congress could change. So the Bureau was not officially abolished until the Twenty-Third Congress, which also repealed *obnovlenie* and so saved the national leadership from its effects.

The decree abolishing the special boards and commissions was never made public. The boards just quietly withered away. Of the six chairman, it would appear that Poliakov was the weakest and most dependent on Khrushchev, and he was also the first to go. In November 1964, he was dismissed from the secretariat and vanished from public view; no more was heard about him or his board. Il'ichev was released from the secretariat in March and transferred to the foreign office. Rudakov remained in the apparatus until his death in 1966, but his bureau, too, was abolished. The case of Titov is of special interest and will be examined later.

Demichev and Shelepin, unlike the other chairmen, advanced in the leadership after Khrushchev's dismissal. In November 1964, Demichev became a candidate member of the Presidium, and Shelepin was elected directly to full membership. Moreover, Shelepin's party–state control committee, unlike the other creations of 1962, survived and continued to function until a year later.

Nothing is known of Brezhnev's personal attitude toward the various Khrushchev schemes, as distinct from the attitude of the leadership as a whole, which was certainly hostile. There is some evidence, however, that Brezhnev tried to salvage what he could for his own purposes. The survival of the Shelepin committee would suggest this. Brezhnev had succeeded to only one of Khrushchev's jobs, according to the public announcement—that of first secretary of the Central Committee. Moreover, a Central Committee decision (made public later) resolved that the offices of first secretary and premier would now be kept separate.[11] Brezhnev thus did not have the formal authority within the government bureaucracy that Khrushchev had enjoyed. The party–state control committee might have appeared to him as a useful channel of communication and control between the first secretary and the machinery of government. In the circumstances of 1964, Brezhnev probably welcomed the support of Shelepin, who was then both a deputy premier (under Kosygin) and a party secretary (subordinate to Brezhnev). Second, Brezhnev also succeeded to Khrushchev's position as chairman of the RSFSR Bureau, although no public announcement was made of this fact at the time of the change of regime.[12] The Central Committee departments which operated under the Bureau survived until 1966. Probably Brezhnev, like his predecessor, looked upon the RSFSR Bureau as a useful device for getting around the other leaders and reinforcing the personal power of the first secretary. But if that conclusion is correct, then the decision to abolish the Bureau (taken by the Twenty-Third Congress) can be viewed as a defeat for Brezhnev at the hands of his colleagues in the new Politburo.

Recruitment Policy and the Composition of the Party

The decision to slow down the recruitment of new members was full of portent for the future of the party. Under Khrushchev, the membership had been growing at a rapid rate. Furthermore, the rate of increase itself was tending to increase. This was not merely a matter of size, because the social and ethnic composition of the party was also changing. The party had admitted classes of people who had been underrepresented in the past: workers and peasants and members of minority nationalities.[13] Toward the end of the Khrushchev regime, the question of recruitment policy was becoming a serious political issue. In 1963, Khrushchev himself confessed that he had some concern about the composition of the party. He told the Central Committee at its June plenum that for some members, *partiinost'* had become an empty formality; it meant little more than carrying a party card. Khrushchev went on to say that there were some nonmembers of the CPSU who were actually "better Communists" than those who carried the card in their pocket.[14] The implication of these remarks was that recruitment policy should be studied and recruitment perhaps slowed down. But Khrushchev had left office before this change took effect.

The new regime took several measures to reduce the admission of members, and the formal rules on recruitment were tightened up by the Twenty-Third Congress. In 2 years, the party's annual rate of growth was reduced from 6.7 (for 1964) to 2.6% (1966).

One of the themes of the Twenty-Third Congress, and of later statements on party policy, was an emphasis on "quality, not quantity," so far as the membership was concerned. The party, it was said, was raising its standards for the admission of new candidates, with a view to improving the quality (*kachestvennyi sostav*) of the membership.[15] The clear implication was that the party had been too lax in the past, and perhaps undesirable elements had been admitted. In 1971, the leadership took the next step and announced plans for an administrative purge of the party by means of calling in all membership cards for exchange.

"The exchange of party cards is not a purge."[16] This has been the theme of numerous speeches and statements since 1971, as if to quiet the inevitable concern within the rank-and-file membership. It has been said that the social conditions which led to the great purges of the 1930s are now completely changed, so that the party is "united" and "monolithic" as never before. On the other hand, various authoritative statements about the exchange procedure make it clear that "individual violators" of party discipline are to be removed from the CPSU rolls.

Preparations for the exchange were given great publicity, probably in hope of reducing rank-and-file concern while still emphasizing the importance of the process.[17] But the regime has moved with characteristic deliberation. Throughout the long preparatory period, the party continued to accept new members but at a declining rate of recruitment. In the 2-year period following the Twenty-Fourth Congress, it can be estimated that the membership of the party grew at an annual rate of less than 1.5%.[18]

According to the rather sparse published statistics, the Brezhnev regime has continued the policy, initiated by Khrushchev, of encouraging the recruitment of working-class members. As of 1971, workers accounted for more than one-half of all new members (56.9%) as compared with 45.4% in 1966. During this 5-year period, the overall number of new members recruited each year fell by more than 20%. What this means is that the reduction in party recruitment has been accomplished by cutting down on the number of "specialists" (i.e., educated persons), white-collar workers, and peasants—not by cutting down on the recruitment of workers. On the contrary, more workers are entering the party now than under Khrushchev.[19]

The cutback in peasant recruitment is hardly surprising. Peasants had been a prime target of Khrushchev's recruitment efforts so that their number within the party had greatly increased—and at a time when the proportion of "peasants" in the Soviet population was rapidly declining. The membership level among the peasantry must have reached the saturation point some time ago.

But the apparent decision to cut back on the recruitment of specialists and white-collar workers is another matter. The party press has been filled, in recent years, with references to the "scientific and technological revolution" and to the implications of this revolution for the party. It may be assumed that in order to meet the challenge of the new era, the party would seek to recruit more people with advanced skills and higher education. But the membership statistics tell a different story.

The Party
and the
"Scientific and
Technological
Revolution"

One of the recurrent themes in Western analyses of communist-ruled societies is a distinction between *apparatchiki* and "technocrats." In this perception, the *apparatchik* is the old-line party official, typically poorly educated or else trained in the party's own schools. The "technocrat" is the younger and better-educated official. The *apparatchik* is supposed to be concerned with ideological work and mass-agitational activities, which are his traditional specialties. The technocrat has been trained in an engineering school and usually has first-hand experience in management and planning. The technocrat is supposed to take a more pragmatic and less ideological view of society's problems. Although different terminology is used, this basic dichotomy has influenced much of the recent research on the Soviet elite.[20]

But this distinction, it seems to me, really misses the point of much of the present controversy in Soviet politics. There is indeed a sharp conflict over the role of the party, over recruitment policy, and in particular over the relationship between the "technocrats" and *apparatchiki*. Such an analysis is based on the erroneous notion that policy is determined primarily by the career experiences of policymakers. A simple comparison of the most recent party leaders should be enough to cast doubt on this general proposition. It was Khrushchev, the old-line *apparatchik*, who tried to modernize the party and recruit more members with higher education. It was Brezhnev, the graduate engineer, who presided over the reversal of Khrushchev's policies.[21]

If the present controversies can be narrowed down to two points of view, they could more accurately be described as the views of the "engineers" versus the "managers." The engineer is one whose main concern is the traditional goal of a high level of output for heavy industry; he tends to regard raising output as primarily a technical problem—one calling for the skills of the engineer. The manager, on the other hand, is more concerned with raising productivity and improving the quality of output. He is not unmindful of the need for better technology, but he is also concerned with problems of management, accounting, and control. The manager believes that improved economic performance requires not more engineers but more and better-trained accountants, systems analysts—and perhaps even marketing specialists.

In the political context, the "engineer" is a traditionalist who has something in common with both the "technocrat" and the *apparatchiki*. The "manager" is a reformer. But these terms represent attitudes and not career groups. A professional engineer may very well belong to the reformers, and an industrial manager may be very orthodox in his outlook.

The engineers (as thus defined) and the *apparatchiki* are not enemies but natural allies. Nothing could be more misleading than the notion that "technocrats" represent the wave of the future in the USSR. On the contrary, the traditional Soviet approach to industrial management was technocratic. Stalin's procedure was to leave operational control over industry in the hands of technical specialists who usually had been trained as engineers. In Stalin's Russia, there was a straightforward division of labor between the industrialists who ran the factories and the party officials who ran the *agitprop* campaigns to stimulate production and encourage the workers to keep on the job: Both the plant director and the *apparatchiki* who represented the party had a common interest in plan fulfillment—which meant maximizing output, sometimes in disregard of cost. This traditional way of doing things, however, was upset by Khrushchev, who forced through a complete reorganization of industrial management and encouraged more direct interference, by party officials, in the day-to-day affairs of the industrial plant.

The success of the economy can no longer be measured by gross output. As G. V. Romanov has remarked, the time is now past when the aim of the party should be to "push through the plan at any cost" (*vykolachivat' plan liuboi tsenoi*).[22] Continuation of economic growth requires *optimizing*, rather than *maximizing* behavior. Effective party control over economic decision making requires a new outlook within the party, and perhaps new men within the apparatus.

The views of Romanov on this point are worth special attention, because he is a party official with extensive experience in industry, first secretary of the Leningrad regional party organization, and since 1973 a candidate member of the Politburo. As is always the case with junior members, Romanov has had little so say in public since his elevation to the national leadership. But before 1973, he was emerging as the chief spokesman for younger party officials who were calling for better training for industrial managers and also for a greater voice for the party in industrial affairs. Romanov's views are linked to a series of reforms in the organization of industry, carried out under his sponsorship in Leningrad over the past 10 years. Thus, Romanov's ideas can be summed up as the "Leningrad plan"—though this is simply a convenient label for several different ideas that are associated with the city.

Romanov has expressed open concern about the diminished authority of the party within industry. In 1966 he reported on a sociological study in Leningrad in which factory workers had been asked the following question: Does plant management pay attention to the views of the party organization? About one-third said "Not always," and 7% said "Never." This offered some measure of the party's loss of authority.[23]

In his published writings on matters of industrial organization, Romanov has taken the role of defender of the factory manager against the "center"; he has criticized the ministries for sending too many instructions and too many detailed orders without leaving the manager sufficient flexibility. He has talked about giving more planning authority to the local level. But at the same time, he has called on the local party authorities to take a more activist role in economic affairs. There is a certain element of Khrushchevism in Romanov's concept of the proper role of the party official.

In order that the party functionary can take a more active role, Romanov has called for better economic training. In 1972, he published a frank plea to make room for younger, more vigorous, and better-trained men in both the economic and the political bureaucracies. This was after he had become first secretary, when he probably had inherited a large number of old-line *apparatchiki* whose best years were behind them. He called for a more rapid turnover of personnel, especially in the lower ranks: ". . . [T]oo long a term of service in the party apparatus in one job frequently leads to losing interest in the work. If a man has served for ten years as an official of the district committee [*raikom*], then the time has come to think where he might be better used in the future."[24] Clearly Khrushchevism is not dead.

There has been considerable opposition to Romanov's conception of the role of the party. The opposition takes the form of an emphasis on the *political* (rather than economic) functions of the party and on the importance of "ideological work."[25] The opposition points, in a none-too-subtle way, at the dangers of "right opportunism." In particular, his opponents reject the idea that Soviet managers have anything to learn from their Western counterparts. Instead, the emphasis is on the "intensification of the ideological struggle [*obostrenie ideologicheskoi bor'by*] between capitalism and socialism in the international arena."[26] This formulation carries a strong echo of the Stalinist theory of the "intensification of the class struggle" (*obostrenie klassovoi bor'by*)—one of the few elements of Stalinist theory that was specifically repudiated under Khrushchev.[27]

The main issue, however, is the relative weight which should be given to managerial and technical expertise as against political experience in the selection of the party's leading cadres.[28] Romanov has called for more economic training—but it should be emphasized that he is concerned with the economics of management and not with engineering skills. More than one writer, in opposition to the Leningrad plan, has argued that the party is recruiting too many economic specialists. The idea that the party should take a more activist role in economic management is often heard (it is said) among the younger officials of the apparatus but this is a "mistaken view." "Party organs have been and must remain organs of political leadership."[29] One writer has argued that the very nature of the "scientific and technological revolution" will prevent the party from playing an operational role in economic affairs. The revolution, according to this line of reasoning, is moving so fast that executives—and especially industrial administrators—will have to be retrained every 3 or 4 years.[30] Presumably this would be out of the question for party officials.

But Romanov is not without supporters. The party has been warned, by an official of the central apparatus, that it must not allow the "scientific and technological revolution" to pass it by.[31] N. N. Rodionov, also a product of the Leningrad organization, has taken a position similar to Romanov's. It is well-established doctrine, tirelessly repeated, that the party's function is to guide and direct the national economy and Soviet state but not to take the place of economic and government authorities. Rodionov, however, has warned that this doctrine must not be taken too literally. "Party organs are not supposed to replace economic organs, or interfere in their operational functions. But this should not be taken in a simple-minded way. While avoiding petty tutelage over economic, soviet, and other organs, party committees do not in any sense reduce their expectations of these organs. They do not loosen their control or keep aloof from giving direction to the economy."[32]

The "managers" or reformers thus are not necessarily opposed to direct party participation in economic decision making. The central issue is not the question of who influences the decisions but rather how the decisions are made. Some of those who are identified with the issue of economic reform believe that in order to carry through a successful reform, the party bureaucracy must take a more active role in economic affairs. Romanov, who epitomizes the point of view of the "manager," would have the party oversee the training of economic specialists and the recruitment of officials in industry. This point of view, however, seems to be much more prevalent among the local and regional secretaries than among officials of the central apparatus.

The Central Party Apparatus

The function of the central apparatus of the CPSU is to serve as a control mechanism with respect to the other great bureaucracies which run the Soviet Union. The apparatus is a centralized "monitoring agency" which provides a constant flow of information to the Politburo and thus reduces the leaders' dependence on the army, the industrial bureaucracy, or the other agencies of government. But as Downs has pointed out, there is a fundamental conflict of interest between monitoring agencies and the bureaucracies which they are supposed to control.[33] This is a conflict which arises out of the situation and not out of the career experiences of officials within different bureaucracies. There is no reason to suppose that the recruitment of more technically trained personnel into the central apparatus would reduce the potential for conflict of interest with other bureaucracies.

It is also characteristic of monitoring agencies that they tend to grow into bureaucracies in their own right. Because it is a bureaucratic organization, we can look for certain basic operating characteristics in the apparatus's behavior. For example, a bureaucratic organization will ordinarily have a rather well-defined division of labor, with the tasks of the organization assigned to men with specialized skills. Within the party apparatus, certain jobs appear to be set aside for political appointees—who usually turn out to be men who have come up from the territorial apparatus. The cadres operation (presently the "department of organizational and party work") is the most purely political department within the central apparatus, and it has consistently been headed by a "political" appointee in this sense of the word. In addition, the agricultural department has usually been entrusted to a "political" type of official. The reasons for this pattern are fairly obvious. The agricultural department has economic responsibilities and certainly needs specialists on its staff. But, on the other hand, the success of the party's agricultural program has always depended on the work of the territorial secretaries. Under both Khrushchev and Brezhnev, the regional party leader has been more intimately involved in agricultural problems than in problems of industry; the ideal party secretary is depicted as a man who spends a large part of his working day in the fields, encouraging hard work, overcoming bottlenecks, and urging the peasants on. The management of agriculture is a more *political* operation than the management of industry. The director of the Central Committee's agricultural department will necessarily work with the regional secretaries—and will usually come from this group himself.

The other economic departments of the apparatus have, almost without exception, been assigned to specialists with technical training and usually extensive working experience in their area of responsibility—experience acquired outside the party career line. But this does not necessarily mean that the economic directors in the apparatus represent a point of view different from that of the Politburo, most of whose members typically have come from the party bureaucracy. In the first place, as already suggested, the line between "technocrats" and *apparatchiki* is neither as sharp nor as divisive as is usually supposed. Second, it seems quite probable that new men brought into the apparatus are subject to some process of socialization. Most of the apparatus directors, including many of the economic specialists, have served enough time in the lower operating level to have acquired a shared attitude toward the organization. For those who have been brought into executive positions without previous experience in the apparatus, there is doubtless some cross-pressure between the ingrained habits of the industrial bureaucracy (the industrial manager, for example) and the attitudes of the professional *apparatchiki*. But the tendency has been toward promotion from within the apparatus. This tendency, moreover, has grown much stronger under Brezhnev. Such a pattern of internal recruitment should promote continuity of behavior, stability, and a certain sense of organizational autonomy.

The apparatus is a powerful organizational weapon in the hands of the party leadership. It is directly subordinate to the central secretariat, and so it is under the overall supervision of the General Secretary.[34] But the central apparatus is certainly not Brezhnev's personal fiefdom—a fact which will be demonstrated in the discussion which follows.

The apparatus is also a potential constraint on the leadership's power. Simple logic would suggest that the apparatus enjoys greater autonomy and wields greater power under a regime of collective leadership than under personal rule. Before 1964, the consolidation of personal power (or the attempt at consolidation) by Stalin and Khrushchev was accompanied by a weakening of the authority of the central apparatus. The Brezhnev regime thus is dependent for information and organizational support on a political bureaucracy which has a vested interest in the oligarchical status quo.

Certainly we could expect that if Brezhnev's aim were to seek personal power at the expense of the other members of the Politburo, the first signs of this would be changes in the central apparatus. The recent history of the apparatus provides some confirmation that this has not, in fact, been Brezhnev's goal.

The apparatus was Stalin's creation. It grew up in the 1920s in the midst of the political struggles of that era, and its authority was consolidated during the period of the 5-year plans. The most important function of the apparatus was "work with cadres" (i.e., the assignment of personnel). Originally, the apparatus was concerned with checking on the political reliability of those who worked in the party or government, placing Stalin's protégés in strategic posts while neutralizing anyone thought to be an enemy. Later, when the Stalinist autocracy was established and the opposition scattered, "work with cadres" meant finding competent and technically trained men to manage Soviet industry. The most important function of the economic departments was to find managers and engineers who were technically competent and politically reliable. In the 5-year plan era, the apparatus acquired the additional function of carrying on the party's "ideological work"— managing the vast program of internal propaganda and indoctrination as well as policing the media to assure adherence to the general line of the party.

In the last years of the Stalinist autocracy, the central apparatus became less important and less powerful. Partly, this was the result of the rise of Stalin's personal apparatus (the "secretariat of Comrade Stalin"), which operated independently of the apparatus of the Central Committee and took on more sensitive functions, such as watching over the political police. Another important reason was the growth of Soviet industry and the ministerial bureaucracy which served it. Increasingly, the ministries took over the responsibility for "work with cadres." The ministries gradually developed their own pool of technically trained men, often the product of the ministries' own special schools. Finally, there was a tendency during the war and also in the postwar period for government authority to grow at the expense of the party. Stalin became premier in 1941 and generalissimo at the end of the war, and these titles overshadowed the office of "general secretary." The apparatus continued to exercise important ideological functions. But in other respects, the central apparatus was no longer a powerful bureaucracy in 1953.

From the beginning, it was Khrushchev's policy to revitalize the party and in particular to strengthen the authority of the apparatus. Until 1958, Khrushchev held no official position in the government; thus building up the party's authority was an obvious strategy to bolster his own position within the national leadership. He relied heavily on his former Ukrainian associates to staff the major bureaucracies in Moscow: beginning in 1953, we can see an influx of former Ukrainian officials into the party apparatus, the procuracy, and the police. By 1960, these former Ukrainians seemed to be well entrenched. The cadres department played an important role in this operation, and it is certainly not an accident that beginning in 1954, and perhaps earlier, the cadres department was under the control of men who had come from the Ukraine. (This was first V. M. Churaev and after 1961, Titov.)

Still, as has been pointed out, Khrushchev did not succeed in bringing the apparatus under his total control. He was responsible for the revitalization of the apparatus, but he was not able to reap all the benefits of his accomplishment. Like all complex organizations, the central apparatus acquired a certain life of its own. Theoretically, the first secretary was head of the apparatus, and yet the organization was not the pliant tool of an autocratic ruler that it had been in the past. Certainly Khrushchev was the dominant figure in the regime, and on those issues where he could give full attention to the details of execution, he could usually have his own way. But he found, apparently, that he could not make a decision and then rely on the apparatus to carry it out. For the apparatus was becoming, in a degree, independent of the person of the first secretary. Doubtless, the directors of the apparatus saw themselves in a role in which they served the party, or at least the party leadership as a whole—and not the interests of a single ruler. The apparatus seemed to be developing a sense of group loyalty rather than loyalty to a leader.

It is possible that Brezhnev wanted to do what Khrushchev had done earlier. He did reorganize and restaff the central apparatus of the party. But when we examine the details of this process, it is clear that there have been decisive limits on Brezhnev's power.

Like Khrushchev, Brezhnev has reached into his own past to find clients and loyal protégés. Just as there was an influx of "Ukrainians" into Moscow in the 1950s, after 1964 a number of obscure men who had served in Dnepropetrovsk or Moldavia suddenly appeared in positions of power. But Brezhnev has been far less successful than Khrushchev in inserting his own protégés into strategic posts. Some Brezhnev men have joined the central apparatus. But with the significant exception of the police organization, Brezhnev has not been overly successful in putting his own clients into the government. Perhaps most important of all, Brezhnev and his group have not taken control over the cadres department.

After Khrushchev's departure, Titov was very quickly removed from this sensitive job. Indeed, nothing shows the importance of the cadres operation more than the speed with which the new regime disposed of Titov. (Officially, he remained in good graces, and early in 1965, he was sent to Kazakhstan as second secretary. But he was then removed from the national secretariat, even though he remains a member of the Central Committee.) Shortly after the October coup, I. V. Kapitonov was recalled to Moscow, the cadres operation was reorganized, and he took charge.

Apparently, the most important thing that would have recommended Kapitonov for this role is that he had no visible connections with any of the possible contenders for power. There is nothing in his record to link him to Brezhnev, or Podgornyi, or Suslov. Furthermore, Kapitonov had been rusticated by Khrushchev under somewhat mysterious circumstances.[35] Kapitonov was an experienced *apparatchik* who had good reason to dislike Khrushchev, and seems to have been appointed as an agent of the collective leadership. The fact that he is still in office 10 years later suggests that the collective leadership has survived.

Within the central apparatus the "Brezhnev group" includes S. P. Trapeznikov, director of the department of science and education; K. U. Chernenko, head of the department of security and secret communications; and G. S. Pavlov, administrative director (*upravliaiushchii delami*) for the Central Committee. They can be identified as "Brezhnev men" from their earlier careers. Pavlov, for example, finished engineering school in Dneproderzhinsk in 1936, a year behind Brezhnev, so the acquaintance of these two dates back almost 40 years.

But it must be said that these positions are not the most important jobs within the gift of the party leadership. Except for Trapeznikov, the Brezhnev men within the apparatus are not involved in substantive policy or sensitive political matters. Trapeznikov has become a kind of lighting rod for political dissenters; they have attacked him as the leading representative of "Stalinism" within the Brezhnev regime.[36]

Brezhnev did preside over a general shake-up of the apparatus beginning in 1964. But for the most part, the men who took control of the departments within the apparatus were promoted from within the apparatus itself and not brought from the outside. Moreover, the newcomers did not always come from the "Brezhnev group." For example F. D. Kulakov, who became head of the agricultural department (succeeding Poliakov) had been a regional secretary. M. S. Solomentsev, who has already been mentioned as a spokesman for apparatus interests, succeeded Rudakov in the heavy industry department. When Solomentsev was promoted to the post of RSFSR premier, he was apparently succeeded by V. I. Dolgikh, a leading Soviet industrialist who had had a brief career as a territorial party secretary. If we look at the apparatus today, studying the background of the department directors and their principal deputies, this is the pattern:

- 5 are holdovers from the Khrushchev era (i.e., they hold the same position as in 1964)
- 15 are men who have been promoted from within the central apparatus.
- 8 have been brought in from the outside, usually from the territorial apparatus (and of these outsiders, only three are "Brezhnev men")

A few of Khrushchev's directors were quickly dismissed; the cases of Il'ichev, Titov, and Poliakov have been mentioned already. But there was no general "purge" of Khrushchev men. I. A. Grishmanov, who had been director of the Central Committee's construction department, entered the government as minister of the construction materials industry. V. A. Kirillin, who was replaced by Trapeznikov in the department of science and education, became chairman of the State Committee for Science and Technology and later was promoted to the post of deputy premier.

The Territorial Apparatus

If we turn from the central apparatus in Moscow to the territorial secretaries—that is, the heads of the regional and republic organizations of the CPSU— we find a similar pattern. The republic secretaries have shown a high degree of stability during the Brezhnev period. There have, of course, been many changes in republic posts during this 10-year period, but much of the change can be attributed to normal turnover within the party hierarchy. Certainly there is little evidence that Brezhnev has used appointments within the territorial apparatus in order to build up a personal following. When changes have been made in the position of republic first secretary, the new leadership has in every case come from within the republic itself and usually from within the republic party organization. Brezhnev has never forced a republic party to accept a new leader brought in from the outside—as Khrushchev did with Mzhavanadze in Georgia in 1953 or as Stalin did with both Khrushchev (Ukraine) and Brezhnev (Moldavia). The changes that have taken place in the republics have usually come about when a leader retired (as Mzhavanadze did in 1972), or died in office (Snechkus in 1974), or else left the republic for a higher post (as Mazurov and Pel'she did). At the present writing, 6 of the 14 republic first secretaries are holdovers from the Khrushchev regime (7, if we consider the special case of Kunaev[37]).

The important fact, however, is the continuity of leadership within each republic party organization. Typically, the new republic first secretary has held office as second secretary, or premier, or as first secretary in the republic capital. The same general pattern can be seen in the apparatus at the regional level. The turnover rate has not been high, and usually when the post of first secretary falls vacant, it is filled by an appointment from within the regional secretariat. As if to publicize this fact, the Soviet press has adopted a new practice in announcing the appointments of regional first secretaries; the central press usually identifies the former position of the new secretary, and it always turns out to be a post within the region.

Political Alliances and Countervailing Power

Appointments to high position within the apparatus apparently require direct approval of the Politburo. Under Brezhnev, important posts within the central apparatus have sometimes been left vacant for rather long periods of time—a fact which suggests that these appointments are the outcome of bargaining with the leadership.[38] At least within the central apparatus, there seems to have been some effort to balance off different interests. Rigby has described this as an effort to maintain "countervailing power" among the top-ranking leaders.[39] Consequently, no single leader—Brezhnev included—has been able to build up a "network of patronage" within the party or the government. In particular, the fact that Brezhnev has not been able to put his own protégés within the cadres department must be considered a major limitation on his power.

The directors of the central apparatus have traditionally had a "passion for anonymity," although under Brezhnev, they have become somewhat more visible than they were in the past. Still, their activities receive little publicity. As a general rule, appointments and dismissals within the apparatus are not made public so that the composition of the organization must be reconstructed from fugitive information that appears in the press.[40] Thus it is not easy to weigh the effects of "countervailing power" within the central apparatus, and our analysis must be partly conjectural.

Under Brezhnev's leadership, the apparatus has for the most part been staffed by experienced and well-educated men who are familiar with their areas of responsibility. The directors who are concerned with industry and economic affairs have had considerable experience. I. N. Dmitriev is typical of this group. He spent 16 years in the construction industry before he began his party career. In 1964, he became a secretary of the Gor'kii city organization and 5 years later was brought into the central apparatus as director of the department of construction. Similarly, K. S. Simonov worked for more than 20 years in the Soviet railroad system before he became director of the department of transportation and communications.

Brezhnev thus has continued a pattern set by Khrushchev of sometimes coopting into the central apparatus men with practical experience in engineering and industry. But the ideological specialists in the apparatus represent a quite different background. Their educational pattern is surprisingly uniform: first, study at a pedagogical institute (sometimes as an external student); second, an advanced degree from the Higher Party School or the party's Academy of Social Sciences. In the hierarchy of Soviet educational institutions, pedagogical institutes are near the bottom—especially those in the provinces. In the eyes of the intellectual community, party schools rank even lower. The economic directors, on the other hand, represent some of the most prestigious institutions in the country, such as the Bauman Higher Technical School.

In their day-to-day work, the economic directors will be dealing with men in the industrial bureaucracy who have much the same educational background and career experience as the directors themselves. A meeting between the minister of the chemical industry, L. A. Kostandov (graduate of the Moscow Institute of Chemical Engineering, 1940) and the Central Committee's director of the chemical industry, V. M. Brezhnev (graduate of the Moscow Institute of Chemical Engineering, 1941) is hardly a confrontation between an ideologically motivated *apparatchik* and a pragmatic "technocrat." It is a conference of engineers, called together to deal with common problems but from a different perspective.

This kind of relationship does not appear to exist in the ideological sphere. The present director of the Central Committee's cultural department, V. F. Shauro, was graduated as an external student from the Mogilev pedagogical institute and subsequently received a degree from the Higher Party School. It is his responsibility to represent the party's interests in dealing with the artists, the musicians, and the writers. Of course, it is possible that a man who took a teacher-training course in a third-rate school and then had a career in the provincial apparatus of the party can have the sophistication to manage cultural affairs in a sensible way. But surely the odds are against this. It is certainly true that Brezhnev has not looked to the intellectual community to take the leadership in cultural policy. There are men with impeccable party credentials, such as A. B. Chakovskii or T. N. Khrennikov, who could deal with the creative artist as intellectual equals. But the party has not coopted such men into the central apparatus as it has done with the industrialists.

It has already been noted that most of the present directors were promoted from the apparatus itself. These men can be classified as "old *apparatchiki*" (i.e., men who had some career experience at the working level within the apparatus before becoming director or deputy director of a department). On the basis of this classification, there are presently 17 "old *apparatchiki*" among the directors, while 8 are newcomers. It is not so easy to get precise information on the Khrushchev apparatus, especially during the 1950s, but it appears to be the case that Khrushchev was much more likely to go to the outside to find directors—going back to the Ukrainian organization, or to other branches of the territorial apparatus, or else coopting men from other career fields. There has been less coopting under Brezhnev because the central apparatus itself is more experienced and better educated. It is much easier now, by comparison with the 1950s, to find old *apparatchiki* who are competent to take on specialized responsibilities.

This is one reason why the number of obvious "Brezhnev men" within the central apparatus is so limited. Some of the other apparatus directors have career backgrounds that suggest links to other members of the Politburo. Two of the present directors have a history of service in the Belorussian apparatus and could, conceivably, be allies of Mazurov, the first deputy premier.[41] Ia. I. Kabkov spent his early career in the Ukrainian food processing industry, which suggests a possible link with Podgornyi. But on the basis of available information, there is no indication that the other directors are protégés of individual members of the Politburo or the central secretariat.

The timing of some appointments within the apparatus suggests a deliberate effort to strike a balance. In 1965, Podgornyi left the secretariat to become chief of state—certainly not a "promotion," even though Brezhnev's career demonstrates that the Soviet presidency is no longer a dead-end position. At the same time, Kabkov came into the apparatus, resuming a position which he had held earlier (1958–1962). It was also in 1965 that Mazurov gave up the leadership post in Belorussia to become first deputy premier. In the Soviet system, this was not necessarily a promotion in rank. A nice political balance was assured when Shauro also came to Moscow to enter the party's central apparatus. Early in 1973, Polianskii was demoted from first deputy premier to the post of USSR minister of agriculture. This left Mazurov the only first deputy premier and a logical candidate to succeed Kosygin. At about the same time, Abrasimov, a possible ally of Mazurov, left the diplomatic service to become a director of the central apparatus. Such inferences contain a considerable amount of speculation, but they do lend weight to Rigby's hypothesis about the power structure of the Soviet oligarchy.

Conclusion

From the preceding discussion, it should be clear that the familiar image of the party as a band of narrow-minded ideologues, uniformly opposed to all progress, is quite misleading. There are certainly powerful conservative forces within the party. But there are voices for reform within the party's own bureaucracy as well.

The conservative trend of the present leadership is manifest in the emphasis on "ideological work." From the point of view of the tradition-minded *apparatchik*, it must seem that the outbreak of political dissidence since 1965 is the result of laxity in the Khrushchev years. That is, it is the result of an overemphasis on "practical" problems, of the fact that Khrushchev diverted the party's attention from its primary responsibilities and downgraded the work of ideological specialists. The Brezhnev regime has paid much more attention to the need for proper political education—especially of the scientific and technical elite. At the same time, as discussed, the regime has drastically reduced the recruitment of party members from this part of Soviet society. An article published in 1968 puts stress on the need for ideological training of technical specialists: "We must be pleased with the fact that Soviet scientists and specialists in all fields of knowledge stand in the vanguard of world science. But at the same time the party and the people want their scientific workers not only to be creators and organizers of scientific and technological progress—but *political* leaders too, active in the struggle for the Communist cause."[42] The important thing, in this view of the world, is not to lose one's "political orientation." Even the best educated specialists can become "morally obsolescent" (*mogut moral'no ustaret'*) if they do not keep up with their ideological training.[43]

In the face of this trend toward a more rigid emphasis on ideology, it is of particular interest to find that some writers based in Leningrad have called for greater freedom for scientific research. A group of Leningrad scientists has asked for more autonomy in planning their work and selecting their own problems for study. They have reportedly circulated a draft of a "statute on the socialist scientific institute" which would set down the basic rights of research organizations. Romanov has suggested that this statute be tried out on an experimental basis. He also has argued for the use of "economic methods" in organizing the work of research institutes. The idea is that a research institute would operate like a Soviet firm. Much of its work would be done by contract with industry—an approach which would presumably reduce the amount of research that is not of economic value. The "scientific firm"—if that is the correct name—would have a great deal of autonomy in planning its work, recruiting personnel, and setting pay scales. Romanov also suggests that party organizations would not interfere in the work of these scientific firms.[44]

Another writer, in *Kommunist*, has taken an even stronger stand. The scientist, he argues, has a basic right to scientific independence, including the right to select his own themes for research. The party should encourage the organization of research along the lines suggested by the Leningrad group on the basis of contractual relations with firms. This would enable enterprises to buy new technology as they need it, and it would permit rational "planning" of science on a sound economic basis.[45]

This is precisely the kind of social or economic experimentation that the present leadership has been reluctant to try out. Khrushchev was overthrown in the name of cautious leadership and opposition to "empty-headed scheming," and the men who forced him out still dominate the leadership. The groups that suffered the most under Khrushchev have seen their former authority restored and their most serious grievances taken care of. This applies in particular to the industrial managers, who have now seen some of their own number serving in the central apparatus and even in the national secretariat of the party. It applies as well to the ideological specialists, who had so much to complain about under Khrushchev. But the increasing prominence of experienced industrialists, as has been argued in this chapter, is not a sign that a new generation of "technocrats" is coming to power. On the contrary, the restored prestige of engineers and ideological specialists may be a step backward. For these two groups had an implicit alliance in the past, a mutual understanding that (1) the *apparatchiki* would not interfere in the operation of industry and (2) the industrial leaders would accept the ultimate authority of the party.

However, while Brezhnev and his colleagues managed to dispose of Khrushchev, they have not cleansed the party of his ideas or his approach. The proposals coming out of Leningrad are a kind of neo-Khrushchevism which could someday upset the political balance which Brezhnev has tried so hard to achieve. This is not to suggest that Brezhnev is going to be overthrown in the name of "Khrushchevism without Khrushchev." But sooner or later, the succession question must arise again. When that happens, so will some of the issues which have been raised in this chapter.

Notes

[1]Speech by V. P. Mzhavanadze, *Plenum Tsentral'nogo komiteta Kommunisticheskoi partii Sovetskogo Soiuza 24–26 marta 1965 g.: stenograficheskii otchet* (Moscow, 1965), p. 89.

[2]Sidney I. Ploss, *Conflict and Decision-Making in Soviet Russia* (Princeton, 1965), esp. pp. 61, 185; Howard R. Swearer, "Changing Roles of the CPSU under First Secretary Khrushchev," *World Politics* 15 (1962), pp. 20–43.

[3]B. Moralev, "Podgotovka i perepodgotovka rukovodiashchikh kadrov," *Partiinaia zhizn'* [hereafter *PZh*], no. 1 (1971), p. 31.

[4]*Plenum TsK KPSS 24–26 marta 1965 g.*, p. 120.

[5]Creation of the Bureau was announced in a rather offhand way (*Pravda*, February 29, 1956). The Twentieth Congress had rewritten the party Statute but made no provision for this new organ. The Bureau was not given a legal basis in the Statute until 1961 (*XXII s"ezd KPSS* [Moscow, 1962], III, 347).

[6]*Pravda*, November 19, 1962.

[7]Anthony Downs, *Inside Bureaucracy* (Boston, 1967), p. 148.

[8]Speech by F. S. Goriachev, *Plenum TsK KPSS 24–26 marta 1965 g.*, p. 83.

[9]Speech by N. F. Ignatov, *Plenum TsK KPSS 24–26 marta 1965 g.*, p. 188.

[10]*Pravda*, November 17, 1964.

[11]P. A. Rodionov, *Kollektivnost'—vysshii printsip partiinogo rukovodstva* (Moscow, 1967), p. 219.

[12]See the biography of Brezhnev in *Ezhegodnik bol'shoi sovetskoi entsiklopedii*, 1967.

[13]Darrell P. Hammer, "The Dilemma of Party Growth," *Problems of Communism* 20, no. 4 (July–August 1971), p. 16.

[14]*Plenum TsK KPSS 18–21 iiunia 1963 g.* (Moscow, 1963), p. 258.

[15]L. Slepov, "Nadezhnaia osnova vnutrennei zhizni leninskoi partii," *Kommunist*, no. 4 (1968), p. 27.

[16]*PZh*, no. 5, (1973), p. 5.

[17]A. Silin, "Chlenstvo v KPSS," *PZh*, no. 2 (1973), pp. 22–29.

[18]From the data given in *Kommunist*, no. 13 (1973), p. 21, the size of the party for 1973 can be estimated at 14,859,282. This works out to a percentage rate of growth of 1.39 per year for the period 1971–1973. It is the lowest rate of growth since 1955 when the party was recovering from the post-Stalin purge. This estimate is consistent with data provided by Kapitonov in 1972. (I. V. Kapitonov, "Nekotorye voprosy partiinogo stroitel'stva v svete reshenii XXIV s"ezda KPSS," *Kommunist*, no. 3 [1972], p. 27.)

[19]During the period preceding the Twenty-Third Congress, the CPSU admitted 760,000 new members a year, as an average. For the period from then until the Twenty-Fourth Congress, the average number of new members was only 600,000. From these figures, it can be estimated that the number of workers admitted in 1971 actually had increased as compared with 1966, despite the great drop in total admissions.

[20]Fischer makes a distinction between the "official" who is a political functionary and the "technician" who has no significant political experience. (George Fischer, *The Soviet Union and Modern Society* [New York, 1981], p. 39.) Robert Blackwell concluded that the party leadership "needs technocrats and at the same time fears them." ("Elite Recruitment and Functional Change: The Soviet Obkom Elite 1950–1968," *Journal of Politics* [February 1972], p. 143.) "Technocrat" here seems to mean "one with technical expertise." Milton Lodge drew a similar distinction between *apparatchiki* and "specialist elites." (*Soviet Elite Attitudes since Stalin* [Columbus, Ohio, 1969].)

Of course, different writers drew quite different inferences from this same dichotomy. Z. K. Brzezinski has argued that there is a need for "adaptation" of the regime through cooptation of industrial managers and economists—but he appears to be skeptical of the regime's ability to adapt and thus prevent its own "degeneration." ("The Soviet Political System: Transformation or Degeneration?" in *Dilemmas of Progress in Soviet Politics* [New York, 1969], p. 33.) On the other hand, Fischer sees a clear trend toward adaptation through recruitment of top-level officials who have technical training or managerial experience.

[21]In Fischer's analysis, Brezhnev is classified as a "technician," while Khrushchev is classified as an "official." *The Soviet Union and Modern Society*, pp. 186, 191.

[22]G. Romanov, "Partiinaia zabota o povyshenii effektivnosti obshchestvennogo proizvodstva," *Kommunist*, no. 3 (1970), pp. 80–91.

[23]On his economic views, see *Sotsialisticheskaia industriia*, January 7, 1971, p. 2;

G. Romanov, "Sovershenstvovanie proizvodstva i upravleniia—delo partiinoe," *PZh*, no. 6 (1971), pp. 9–17; G. V. Romanov, "Tsel'—povyshenie effektivnosti proizvodstva," *Ekonomicheskaia gazeta*, no. 34 (August 1970), pp. 4–5. See also, G. Romanov, "Proveriat' fakticheskoe ispolnenie dela, ukrepliat' partiinuiu i gosudarstvennuiu distsiplinu," *PZh*, no. 5 (1967), pp. 46–60.

[24]G. Romanov, "Novye usloviia—novye trebovaniia k kadram," *Kommunist*, no. 5 (1972), p. 57.

[25]See, for example, I. Bondarenko, "Edinstvo politicheskoi i organizatorskoi raboty partiinykh komitetov," *Kommunist*, no. 11 (1970), pp. 28–38. Bondarenko is first secretary of the Rostov regional party organization.

[26]See Bondarenko, *Kommunist*, pp. 28–38, and also N. Konovalov, "Partiinye komitety—organy politicheskogo rukovodstva," *Kommunist*, no. 12 (1970), p. 43. Konovalov is first secretary of the Kaliningrad regional Party organization.

[27]"O preodolenii kul'ta lichnosti i ego posledstvii (Postanovlenie TsK KPSS 30 iiunia 1956 g.)." *KPSS v rezoliutsiiakh . . .* , 7th ed. (Moscow, 1960), IV, 229.

[28]G. Krivoshein, "Partiinyi rabotnik: eruditsiia i opyt," *Kommunist*, no. 12 (1970), pp. 27–37.

[29]G. Krivoshein, "Partiinyi rabotnik: prizvanie i dolg," *Kommunist*, no. 5 (1968), p. 53 (italics added—DPH).

[30]A. Pershin, "Avtoritet rukovoditelia," *Kommunist*, no. 11 (1971), p. 78.

[31]Moralev, "Podgotovka i perepodgotovka rukovodiashchikh kadrov," p. 31. Moralev is a deputy director of the department of organizational and party work of the Central Committee.

[32]N. Rodionov, "Ob effektivnosti partiinoi raboty," *Kommunist*, no. 9 (1967) p. 57. Rodionov served for several years in the Leningrad party organization and in 1962–1965 was deputy chairman of the Leningrad economic council (*sovnarkhoz*). This would have put him in intimate contact with Romanov, who was then a regional secretary with basic responsibilities in the area of industrial management.

[33]Downs, *Inside Bureaucracy*, p. 149.

[34]*Partiinoe stroitel'stvo* (Moscow, 1970), p. 158.

[35]Until 1959, Kapitonov was first secretary of the Moscow regional organization—a post of national importance. In that year, he was rather suddenly shunted off to the regional capital of Ivanovo.

[36]See A. D. Sakharov, *Progress, Coexistence, and Intellectual Freedom* (New York, 1970), p. 56: Roy A. Medvedev, *Let History Judge* (New York, 1971), p. 89.

[37]D. A. Kunaev held office as first secretary in the Kazakh republic but was purged by Khrushchev in 1962. He returned to office only a few weeks after Brezhnev took Khrushchev's place.

[38]N. R. Mironov died in 1964. The regime waited until February 1968 to appoint his deputy, N. I. Savinkin, as director of the administrative organs department. Andropov left the department of liaison with other ruling parties in May 1967, when he became chairman of the KGB. His deputy, K. V. Rusakov, was not appointed to the directorship of this department until May 1968.

[39]T. H. Rigby, "The Soviet Leadership: Towards a Self-Stabilizing Oligarchy?" *Soviet Studies* 22, no. 2 (October 1970), p. 167.

[40]The appointments of Solomentsev (*Pravda*, November 17, 1966) and P. A. Abrasimov (*Pravda*, April 10, 1973) were made public. These two announcements were unusual.

[41]Shauro was first secretary in Minsk during the period when Mazurov was first secretary in the Belorussian republic, an obvious career link. Abrasimov also served under Mazurov as first deputy premier when Mazurov was republic premier.

[42]N. Sviridov, "Partiinaia zabota o vospitanii nauchno-tekhnicheskoi intelligentsii," *Kommunist*, no. 18 (1968), p. 37.

[43]N. Roban, "KPSS—Partiia nauchnogo kommunizma," *Kommunist*, no. 18 (1971), p. 45.

[44]G. Romanov, "Nauchnym issledovaniiam—vysokuiu effektivnost'," *Kommunist*, no. 3 (1967), pp. 58–67.

[45]F. Ovcharenko, "Partiia i nauchno-tekhnicheskaia revoliutsiia," *Kommunist*, no. 14 (1970), pp. 28–41.

9 GEORGE W. BRESLAUER

On the Adaptability of Soviet Welfare-State Authoritarianism*

Specialists on the USSR have for decades searched for organizing concepts that would best characterize the nature of the Soviet system or the direction in which it has been moving. For many years, the totalitarian model provided such a concept. With the field's increasing dissatisfaction with the totalitarian label, has come a series of efforts to find substitutes. Terms such as *mobilization system, mono-organizational society*, and *institutional pluralism* have been offered. Other terms suggested capture not the nature of the current system but the extent of deviation from the totalitarian syndrome; in this context, such terms as *change* and *adaptation* have been offered to characterize the direction of metamorphoses since Stalin.[1]

Some scholars undoubtedly experience frustration with the proliferation of concepts and must wonder about the pay-off. Why not simply abandon the search for organizing concepts and get on with the task of empirical research? Such a reaction is understandable but somewhat shortsighted; it ignores the fact that we all employ organizing concepts in our work, implicitly or explicitly, articulated or unarticulated. The concepts we choose guide the types of questions we raise and the components of the political order to which we direct our attention. The problem with the totalitarian model, for example, was that it directed our attention almost exclusively toward the political control network

*Reprinted by permission of the author and publisher from Karl W. Ryavec, ed., *Soviet Society and the Communist Party* (Amherst, Mass.: University of Massachusetts Press, 1978), pp. 3–32, 178–182. Copyright 1978 by The University of Massachusetts Press.

and thereby blinded us to sources of political and social support for the regime. The problem with such concepts as *adaptation* and *change* is somewhat different: they are so broad as to be almost meaningless. Adaptation of what to what? Change of what, in which directions, and with what consequences?

This last question implies the need for standards by which to judge the performance of a system—lest the mere documentation of changes or adaptations become an end in itself. It also implies the need for a definition of *system*, identifying political, social, and ideological bases, that will then allow us to specify when systemic or within-system change has taken place. Such useful labels as *institutional pluralism* deal with only one dimension of change since Stalin: the political process. The concept of a *postrevolutionary oligarchy*[2] focuses upon both the political process and changed political goals but ignores the socioeconomic base that buttresses the regime. An alternative to the totalitarian label is needed, lest we ignore the fundamental character of change since Stalin, but it should broaden our perspectives to incorporate both the character of regime politics and the direction of its social policies. Let me characterize the Soviet regime under Brezhnev, therefore, as *welfare-state authoritarianism*.[3]

Although this concept has obvious shortcomings for use in the comparative analysis of one-party systems, it can be useful for Soviet specialists in clearly differentiating the Brezhnev regime from the Stalinist, as indicated by their respective approaches to political participation, social transformation, and material standard of living. Accordingly, I view the contemporary regime as authoritarian rather than totalitarian for a number of reasons. First, it has moved far in the direction of a form of "corporate pluralism" within the political elite.[4] Second, it has expanded and regularized opportunities for specialist input into decision-making processes on social and economic issues. Third, it has abandoned the use of mass terror as an instrument of policy, has depoliticized many realms of social life, and allows a considerable measure of physical security and privatism for the politically conformist. Thus, whereas the regime has retained its mobilizational character, it no longer engages in totalitarian forms of mass mobilization.

I label the regime a *welfare-state* because its policy includes a basic commitment to minimal and rising levels of material and social security, public health, and education. Equally important, its commitment to welfare includes an egalitarian commitment to job security and subsidized prices for basic commodities—even at the cost of considerable economic inefficiency and failure to develop entrepreneurial initiative. The level of material welfare, or the quality of public health, might not accord with many Western definitions of a *welfare-state*, but the term strikes me as useful in differentiating the social policies of the Brezhnev era from both Stalinism and alternative approaches currently under discussion within the Soviet establishment.

Hereafter, I shall refer to the approach to political participation, social transformation, and material welfare just outlined as the basic social and political "contract" of welfare-state authoritarianism. It is not a contract in the liberal–democratic sense of an authoritative agreement between equals; what it represents is the pattern of political, social, and material benefits offered by the ruling authorities since Khrushchev's dismissal, both to regulate relationships among themselves and to elicit compliance and initiative from groups in society. This package of benefits and constraints differs from that offered by Stalin and Khrushchev and may not survive the Brezhnev succession. However, it does define the boundaries within which policy changes have taken place during the Brezhnev era. Thinking of a contract helps us to avoid the inordinate ambiguities associated with defining the "nature" of the Soviet "system." Those seeking to evaluate the adaptability of the Soviet "system" would be better advised to explore the durability of this contract and the realistic alternatives to it.

Three alternatives come to mind as responses to the tensions inherent in this contract: (1) varying types or degrees of public disorder ("instability") resulting from economic shocks of centrifugal ethnic pressures; (2) pressures from within the political elite for the constitutionalization of political relationships among the corporate groups comprising that elite (but without mass democratization), coupled with a social policy that allows massive material differentiation and managerial autonomy for the sake of economic efficiency (an alternative I have labeled *elitist liberalism*); (3) pressures from within the political elite for a right-wing reaction against the compromise, secularization, and lack, of "discipline" that characterize welfare-state authoritarianism in the eyes of many a neo-Stalinist. This third, fundamentalist alternative would return to a "contract" based upon autocratic rule—or highly exclusive committee rule—and economic austerity, mobilizing the masses through such nonmaterial values as Russian chauvinism and anti-intellectualism.

Any of the three alternatives would constitute *systemic change*, if *system* is defined as the social and political contract of welfare-state authoritarianism. We who are concerned to explore the prospects for "within-system" change in the USSR must examine the range of policy alternatives possible within the bounds of the contract. We must investigate the trade-offs possible among the conflicting goals of efficiency and equity, scientific expertise and the political docility of scientists, material incentives and party activism, military–industrial might and consumer satisfaction, and managerial discretion and political intervention. Moreover, we must delve into the *political* feasibility of different combinations of values. Can the political elite build coalitions that will maintain a stable bargaining structure supportive of the continuation of this contract in one form or another? Evaluating the durability of the contract requires an appreciation of its adaptability; and this assessment, in turn, requires an investigation of the levels and types of polarization within the political elite, of the ways in which elite groups define their interests, and of the compatibility of the decision premises advanced by different interests. The more compatible these premises, the greater the prospects for shifting coalitions and alliances within the context of the basic contract of welfare-state authoritarianism.

These are the big questions for students of the Soviet present and future, and although they cannot be answered definitively at this time, the cause of cumulative research requires that we gather evidence with an eye to addressing them. The purpose of this chapter will be, therefore, twofold: (1) to explore the character of regime policies during the Brezhnev era in order to justify the characterization I have proposed; and (2) to explore the character of policy *changes* within the Brezhnev era in order to illuminate the linkages among issues and the trade-offs possible within the contract of welfare-state authoritarianism. What makes the exercise all the more interesting is that the Brezhnev era, today, may fruitfully be divided into two phases (1965–1969 and 1970–1978), which differ importantly in the mix of approaches and the character of policies.[5] The two phases may be distinguished by analyzing the regime's approaches to issues of political participation, social transformation, and economic achievement, as these have affected the treatment of workers and peasants, members of the intelligentsia, and party and state officials. Phase One constituted a mix of policy premises weighted in the direction of a left-wing version of welfare-state authoritarianism. Phase Two was characterized by a backlash against that particular direction of movement, a shift in the mix of premises, and a selective retrenchment to the political right.

The Brezhnev Era, Phase One: Political Participation

The dismissal of Nikita Khrushchev in October 1964 brought in its wake a cluster of policy changes. Khrushchev was no welfare-state authoritarian, though he was also not a Stalinist. On the one hand, he shared and sponsored post-Stalin emphases on consumer welfare, an expanded amount of consultation with empirically oriented scientists, the abandonment of mass terror, and collective leadership. On the other hand, his commitment to radical and rapid social transformation, his efforts to circumvent the constraints of collective leadership, his attempts to redefine the terms of political participation by combining a personality cult with populist efforts to mobilize the masses against their hierarchical superiors, his erratic economic and administrative policies—all combined to shape a regime quite different from welfare-state authoritarianism. These tendencies alienated Soviet officials by threatening their personal security and political prerogatives, alienated many members of the scientific intelligentsia by failing to regularize specialist impact on policy, and alienated many workers and peasants by threatening their hopes for privatism and material security.[6]

After Khrushchev's overthrow, his successors moved quickly to redefine the terms of political participation, social transformation, and economic achievement. In the realm of political participation, the new regime immediately took measures to reassert the political autonomy of Soviet officialdom from personalistic rule and public, unregulated, mass criticism. The bifurcation of the party apparatus was immediately revoked; the rotation of officeholders was suspended; the Party–State Control Commission was transformed into an organization that would leave the party apparatus to check up on the behavior of its own; the practice of expanded plenary sessions attended by non-party specialists was dropped, and, after the March 1965 session on agriculture, stenographic transcripts of the proceedings of the sessions were no longer published. In addition, most of the "diploma specialists" recruited into the apparat during 1962–1964 were purged shortly after Khrushchev's overthrow, and the importance of training in a party school before advancement into, and within, the party *apparat* was restored. Further still, the role of the non-party population in the adult political education program was rapidly reversed. In sum, Khrushchev's tendency to "go public" and to circumvent normal channels in legitimizing and implementing policy was rejected, as were his attempts to diminish or close the gap in relative political status between the *aktiv* and the *apparatchiki*.

Political participation in the uppermost, ruling circles was also placed on a new basis. Criticisms of Khrushchev's "subjectivism," "voluntarism," and "hare-brained schemes" implied, among other things, a commitment to *proceduralism* in the conduct of collective leadership and a determination that stable norms for political interaction among the members of the Politburo would be developed and respected. Although much discussion must have occurred behind the scenes in defining these norms, the most important example of this commitment of which we have gained knowledge is the Central Committee resolution of October 1964 declaring that henceforth the posts of party first secretary and chairman of the Council of Ministers would not be combined in the same person. Moreover, informal understandings were apparently also reached, limiting the ability of the first secretary to dominate the allocation of patronage and establishing a norm against disproportionate Politburo representation by either the party Secretariat or the Council of Ministers.[7]

The combination of restored political status for Soviet officials and collective leadership at the top made clear that Khrushchev's successors would cater to the most basic yearnings and interests of Soviet officialdom. Indeed, the new leaders were quite explicit in signaling to the

Soviet political elite that Soviet officials would be the beneficiaries of a retreat from "unremitting pressure as a principle of rule."[8] Thus, numerous statements during 1965–1966 indicated formal rejection of Khrushchev's contention that policy failures were a consequence of the administrators' lack of will or competence. At the Twenty-Third Party Congress, Brezhnev gave such assurance to party cadres, when he declared that "the development of the principle of democratic centralism has found expression in . . . the manifestation of *complete trust* in cadres. . . ."[9] Similarly, Kosygin, in his presentation of the economic reforms of 1965, described the regime's changing posture toward its managerial executives by reassuring them that "the party and the people value the country's experts and executives *whom they fully trust and support in their difficult work* for the good of society."[10] The two critical words in this statement are, of course, *trust* and *difficult*. The conception of *trust* indicated a formal rejection of the earlier notion that mistakes by officials would be taken as indications of their lack of social consciousness. Moreover, the recognition that their work is difficult accorded cadres the assurance that some mistakes are acknowledged to be in the nature of the task and that these will not be interpreted simply as gross incompetence.

Although the regime avoided ideological redefinition during 1964–1966, it did diminish the salience in public literature of ideological conceptions with antiofficial, Khrushchevian overtones. By 1967, however, there began to appear in *Pravda* and *Kommunist* articles and official statements indicating a redefinition of the "State of All the People." These statements still spoke of *self-regulation* as the ideal and even as the best way of describing the current reality. But this concept was no longer viewed as in any way contradictory to the notion of "strengthening" the state, using it as the "organizational principle in solving problems of communist construction," or using it as an instrument of "discipline."[11] This change was part of a larger effort to reaffirm both the professionalized character and political status of state officials: "There functions in a socialist state a specialized apparatus, consisting of officials who are professionally concerned with questions of administering public affairs."[12] This perspective stood in marked contrast to previous doctrine, as expressed in the 1961 Party Program's contention that work in the state bureaucracy could "cease to constitute a special vocation."[13] Thus, the terms of mass political participation were being redefined, a tendency that complemented the policy changes listed above and reinforced both a reduction in opportunities for mass criticism of the terms of political participation and a crackdown on cultural dissidence.

Yet within the context of reasserting the political autonomy of Soviet officialdom, the regime also sought to upgrade the quality of specialist input into decision-making processes by changing both the channels of access and the ethos of the regime. Scientific commissions were attached to party committees, and bureaus for "concrete sociological investigations" were established throughout the country. A resolution calling for expanded public opinion polling had already been passed at the October 1964 plenum. The state and party bureaucracies also moved to rationalize information flows between the Academy of Sciences and the political authorities at the top.[14]

At the same time, both the policy premises and the ethos of the regime were altered in order to create conditions under which expanded specialist input might be processed and find its way into policy outputs. Accordingly, the new regime immediately rejected Khrushchev's overly optimistic and arbitrary approach to planning, criticizing him for "actions based on wishful thinking, boasting and empty words."[15] More to the point, speeches by Soviet leaders suddenly included a ceaseless repetition of the need for "realism" in planning. Target setting was no longer to be a process of anticipating the unprecedented so much as a process of judging possibilities on the basis of past performance. Or, as Brezhnev put it in September 1965: "In brief, everything must be done to put an end to voluntarism and subjectivism in planning. Workers in the planning agencies must be guided in their work exclusively by objective economic calculations, and they must have the possibilities for this."[16] These perspectives, in fact, found expression in the targets for the Eighth Five-Year Plan (1966–1970), which, compared with the Seven-Year Plan (1959–1965) and the Party Program of 1961, reduced the gap between aspirations and capacities to a very great extent.

A corollary to the need for "realism" was the persistent call for "scientific decision making." It is true that party leaders had always claimed special, scientific insight into the laws of historical development, based upon their ideological legacy in Marx's "scientific socialism." Used in that way, however, the term was basically a cover for the definitional function and political autonomy of party officials, who would provide the direction and basic goals for the nation. What was occurring after Khrushchev was something different: a redefinition of the meaning of "scientific decision making" in the direction of a more open-ended, empirical approach that did not excessively prejudge conclusions.[17] The task of communicating this redefinition to Soviet officials fell to Pyotr Demichev, CPSU Central Committee Secretary for Ideological Affairs:

> Lenin saw a truly scientific approach to lie in a precise evaluation of the facts of life, of the existing situation, of the correlation of class forces. . . . He often repeated that a concrete analysis of a concrete situation is the soul of Marxism. . . . It ill becomes a scientist to forego the truth under the influence of the political situation or other attendant circumstances. In their struggle to discover and know the truth, to put the fruits of scientific work

at the service of the interests of the people, the interests of peace and
progress, Soviet scientists will always have the complete support of the
party and the government.[18]

These words (and others like them) should not be dismissed as mere
rhetoric: not only were they consistent with policy changes at the time,
but they also had behavioral consequences in serving to assure specialists that their efforts to conduct empirical research, and to gain access to
officials, would receive political support at the top. It would be remarkable indeed if many specialists were not emboldened by such assurances. They now had further ammunition to bring to ongoing political
conflicts: they could cite the authorities' stress on realism, scientific
decision making, the "scientific–technological revolution," and the ever-
increasing "complexity" of problems to support the cause of expanded
empirical input into decision-making processes.[19]

The Brezhnev Era, Phase One: Social Transformation and Economic Achievement

The political contract of the first phase of the
Brezhnev administration, then, entailed a dual
commitment to institutionalizing the privileged
political status of Soviet officialdom and expanding
specialist input on social and economic issues. The
social contract, in turn, entailed a repudiation of
Khrushchevian efforts to use campaignist pressure
against yearnings for privatism and security. The
premises for these changes, in fact, were reflected
in Soviet leaders' speeches almost from the time of Khrushchev's
overthrow. In November 1964, for example, Brezhnev declared that
"Now more than ever the necessity is evident for the wide application in
our country of economic stimuli in the development of production."[20]
One month later, Kosygin amended the Party Program's earlier emphasis on the role of collective rewards: "Despite the growing role of public
consumption funds, the principal source for satisfying the people's
needs in the conditions of socialism remains payment according to
labor, which derives from the principles of socialism."[21] In April 1965,
Demichev chimed in, pointing out that "the augmentation of the wealth
of the collective farms and the growth on this basis of the personal
incomes of the collective farmers do not contradict the interests of
socialist society."[22] And at the Twenty-Third Party Congress (April
1966), Kosygin noted that *"the main thing in our labor-payments policy* is a
steady rise in the stimulating role of wages in solving the major production tasks of the five-year plan."[23] Although there must certainly have
been conflict within the political elite, and the Politburo itself, over the
extent and the *structure* of material incentives and individual rewards, it

did not prevent a distinct shift in perspective and emphasis in the direction of each.

Indeed, major policy changes at the time reflected these premises. A comprehensive program for improving agricultural production, unveiled in March 1965, represented a clear break with Khrushchev's commitment to optimism and pressure.[24] Production norms were reduced and made more uniform, and promises were extended that they would remain stable from year to year. Khrushchev's restrictions on the private sector were lifted, and the peasant was given financial incentives to raise productivity in this sphere. Procurement prices were raised dramatically, and a vast program of state investments was announced. Most significantly, increases in procurement prices for most products reflected the regime's attempt, much more serious than in the past, to adjust prices to previous years' *costs*. Indeed, after outlining these measures, Brezhnev gave a principled justification to the new approach: "We proceed on the premise that (these measures) will allow us to place the grain economy on a firm basis, and to put an end to the low profitability of grain production on the collective and state farms in a number of the country's zones."[25]

The industrial reforms announced in September 1965 had a similar emphasis on economic rationalization through appeals to personal material gain and stable expectations. Accordingly, the role of profits was to increase substantially and "to constitute the principal source of managers' and workers' bonuses."[26] Moreover, these bonuses were henceforth to constitute a greater percentage of total earnings, as larger and more varied bonus funds were introduced. Decision rules were changed so as to lead managers to pursue profitability and salability as their primary success indicators. The number of success indicators was reduced drastically, and the amount of discretion formally accorded the manager in manipulating resources within his enterprise was increased. In contrast to the traditional Stalinist emphasis on detailed directives and unremitting pressure, the reforms of 1965 were based upon a greater faith in "automatic levers," through which managers would be induced to exercise entrepreneurial initiative. In contrast to the Khrushchevian penchant for frequent administrative reshuffling, these reforms promised officials a more stable and predictable task environment in which to work. The doctrine of "trust in cadres" was thus supplemented by a doctrine of administrative stability: frequent reorganizations, Brezhnev declared, "created an atmosphere of nervousness and bustle, deprived managers of a long-range perspective and undermined their faith in their abilities."[27]

The expanded emphasis on individual material rewards, instead of political pressure, as a means of spurring initiative among workers, peasants, and administrators was accompanied by other changes that further sacrificed Khrushchevian social values. The regime moved quickly to remove many restrictions on private housing construction and to make a commitment to vastly expanded production of private automobiles, at the same time abolishing, as noted, many restrictions on the private sector in agriculture.

The regime further sacrificed goals of radical social transformation to those of immediate economic achievement in its approach to educational access. The educational reforms of 1958, which had called for polytechnical education for all and work in the factories for almost all who aspired to a university education, were formally revoked, allowing a return to relative elitism in the universities.[28] Children of the intelligentsia would henceforth increase their proportions at the universities, since their generally superior preparation and motivation tended to give them a competitive advantage on entrance examinations. The achievement-based needs of the scientific–technological revolution, it seems, were at the time perceived to be more important than the egalitarian pay-offs resulting from rapid social mobility for the underprivileged.

Indeed, all these changes in the political, social, and economic realms were accompanied by interesting trends in the philosophical literature related to the concept of *social interest*. According to the traditional Soviet monolithic image of society, "there is no room for particular purposes that diverge from those of society."[29] By this interpretation, the interests of one were the interests of all. Harmony between state and society reigned supreme. The individual's "interests" were defined by his class affiliation and were therefore considered to be objective characteristics, interpreted for him by the state. Unremitting pressure on factory managers was justified by the demand that they place "state interests" over "personal" or "enterprise" interests. The goal of radical social transformation legitimized a simplified view of society that did not accord recognition to the "interests" of social groups within classes. The independence of the political elite from unregulated social forces was legitimized by the party and state's exclusive right to define the public interest, a task that was not viewed as problematic.

After Khrushchev's dismissal, however, all these assumptions became open to question. The sociological and philosophical literature introduced a significant revision of the traditional, *solidary* conception by acknowledging the existence of differentiated interests in society. Society began to be viewed as being composed not simply of *classes* but of *groups* and *strata* with interests of their own.[30] Similarly, and in line with the thrust of the economic reform, factories and other organizational units were viewed as having distinct interests, with the role of the state being to coordinate and harmonize those diverse interests.[31] The philosophical literature also moved toward a revision of traditional doctrine, and many theoreticians embraced a movement away from the notion that interests are "essentially" objective phenomena to a definition of interests as "the unity of the objective and subjective." Because the notion of *unity* was vague, it began to be equated with *correlation*, which led to calls for using concrete sociological research to determine the correlation in Soviet society between the objective positions of certain groups and their subjective definitions of their group or class interests.[32] The implication was that the regime recognized the profoundly problematic nature of the task of defining and enforcing the "public interest." The regime acknowledged that it could not manipulate society effectively without taking into account the existing level of consciousness among various groups of society, a process that required learning more about how people themselves define their interests. In a sense, there was a temporary victory of "system management" over "revolution from above."[33]

These philosophical changes had many practical policy consequences. After Khrushchev's overthrow, social scientists were given greater latitude to explore the distinctive characteristics and "interests" of groups and strata in society, in part through the public opinion polling noted previously. Sociologists expanded their inquiries into the character of intraclass mobility and intraclass differentiation. Jurists expanded their discussions of ways to define the rights and responsibilities of Soviet citizenship, while economists delved more deeply into the role of material incentives and administrative rationalization in spurring economic efficiency. At the same time, the authorities expanded their efforts to revise methods of mobilization in line with their more complex appreciation of societal differentiation. The role of *politinformator* was developed to supplement the traditional agitator in political education.[34] *Politinformatory* would be more educated and specialized mobilizers, whose sophistication would make them more effective in relating to the more highly skilled and educated strata of the population. In a similar vein, the regime sought to revise public lecture programs to infuse them with a more "differentiated" approach to their audiences. In short, Khrushchev's successors combined a reemphasis on statism with a diminished emphasis on radical transformation but tried to upgrade the capacity of welfare-state authoritarianism for social engineering.

The
Elitist–Liberal
Illusion

The cluster of policies and premises that followed quickly on the heels of Khrushchev's removal pointed in the direction of a left-wing version of welfare-state authoritarianism.[35] By upgrading the importance of political institutionalization and proceduralism, specialist input, managerial autonomy, material incentives, privatism, and social differentiation, these measures raised questions in the minds of Western observers of whether the Soviet leadership had abandoned its traditional values to become pragmatic or technocratic in orientation.[36] At the same time, these changes initially raised the hopes of many members of the Soviet intelligentsia that further movement to the left might be forthcoming. Some hoped for further political institutionalization—or even constitutionalization; others looked forward to further development of the spirit of the economic reforms, allowing for substantial managerial autonomy in industry and agriculture, coupled with massive income differentiation designed to spur worker and managerial initiative. "Libermanism," the Shchekino experiment, and the link system in agriculture provided their rallying cry. In sum, to many liberalizers within the Soviet establishment, the changes immediately following Khrushchev's dismissal provided hope of further development toward elitist liberalism.[37]

Yet the hope turned out to be an illusion and not only because a backlash later set in—as we shall see below. The mistake came from an overestimation of the strength of these new premises and a view of them, in many cases, as potential *substitutes* for earlier orientations. If we reexamine what was happening at the time, we find that what took place was a shifting of the weights within a mix of premises. The industrial reforms, for example, were severely limited by the continued commitment to political intervention and an egalitarian social policy. Administrative forces within the system continued to prescribe managerial behavior in great detail, and the size of bonuses allowed managers engaging in successful innovation was deliberately circumscribed. Unwilling to create a system in which managers would be free of political intervention and pressure or in which managers' incomes would exceed still more greatly those of the workers in their factories, the regime created conditions under which "automatic levers" would be stifled or undermined, even as they were being extolled as harbingers of technological innovation.

Most of the other changes noted were also constrained or supplemented by competing premises. Material incentives and the possibilities of private accumulation for workers and peasants were increased but remained far from sufficient to elicit a significant rise in labor enthusiasm or individual responsibility. Regime aspirations in the Eighth Five-Year Plan (1966–1970) were considerably lower than the targets of the 1961 Party Program, but they remained, nonetheless, ambitious enough to require mobilization and pressure for their attainment. The ability of specialists to ensure or anticipate responsiveness to their input was constrained by the simultaneous reinforcement of the political status of party officials, apparent efforts to rehabilitate Stalin, and the prosecution of an antirevisionism campaign after the trial of Sinyavsky and Daniel in February 1966. The economic reform challenged the traditional conception of party activism in the factory, but the regime simultaneously worked to *extend* party agitation in residential areas,[38] and primary party organizations began, already in 1966, to seek ways of recovering their traditional mobilizational role in the factory. Achievement criteria were stressed in university admissions, but some "affirmative action" programs remained, and the regime continued to expand construction of specialized secondary educational establishments as a means of encouraging mobility out of the less-skilled, blue-collar strata. The material privileges of top officials, which had been challenged by Khrushchev, were restored, but measures were taken to strengthen the overall post-Stalin trend toward income equalization among the classes.

Thus, the post-Khrushchev adjustments represented a shifting of weights among the premises that comprise the basic contract of welfare-state authoritarianism but *within the context of* an ongoing commitment to political intervention in cultural, economic, and social affairs, resocialization of the populace, and a relatively egalitarian social policy. The more realistic question under these circumstances would have been not whether post-Khrushchev changes presaged a breakthrough into elitist liberalism but whether the changes could survive a backlash. Indeed, during 1966–1968, the pressures of mobilizational, anti-revisionist, and egalitarian premises expanded. By 1969, they crystallized and a backlash set in, ushering in still another selective shifting of weights.

The Brezhnev Era, Phase Two: Political Participation   After 1969, changes initiating a selective retrenchment and movement to the right could be observed in each of the dimensions of political participation under review in this chapter. At the top, the delicate balance within the collective leadership appeared to shift. Brezhnev visibly expanded his role, acquiring primary supervision over foreign policy.[39] By most Kremlinological evidence, the general secretary became the most visible and central figure in the collective leadership, with levels of adulation rising steadily through the 1970s. Indeed, by 1976, one could speak of a genuine personality cult, expressed in paeans of praise in newspapers, journals, and speeches of other leaders. By 1977, the general secretary had gone still farther, acquiring the titles of marshal of the Soviet Union, supreme commander of the armed forces, and chairman of the Defense Council of the USSR. Also in 1977, Brezhnev crowned the expansion of his political base by dropping Nikolai Podgorny from the Politburo and himself stepping into Podgorny's post as chairman of the Presidium of the Supreme Soviet.

Paralleling Brezhnev's rise has been the steady expansion of both the ideological status and the administrative role of party organs in relation to state administrators.[40] Ideologically, the concept *Party of All the People* has been effectively dropped from the doctrine, being replaced by a formulation that emphasizes the Communist party's privileged political status. The party is therefore now routinely declared to be "the political leader of the working class, of the working people, and of the entire Soviet people."[41] Similarly, the new Soviet Constitution, finally completed and ratified in 1977, placed exceptional emphasis on the leading role of the party in all spheres of Soviet life, a feature that distinguished this constitution from that of 1936.[42] Augmented status has also been accompanied during the 1970s by an expanded role: since 1971, primary party organizations within ministries, scientific research institutes, and certain other state institutions have for the first time been given the formal right to exercise supervision over state officials within their domain; in like manner, there has been expanded penetration of central ministerial decision-making processes by representatives of the Central Committee apparatus and an expanded role for December plenary sessions of the Central Committee in supervising ministerial affairs.[43]

All these developments have been accompanied by the formal rejection of the major premises underlying the Kosygin reforms of 1965. Brezhnev sounded the death-knell of those premises at the December 1969 plenum, where he seized the initiative on economic and administrative reform. Referring to the Kosygin reforms, he exclaimed: "These measures have yielded good results. But naturally they still have been unable to solve the problem of increasing the efficiency of the economy as a whole."[44] From this time forward, the entire ethos of regime articulations about the responsibilities of cadres began to change, reflecting a repudiation of the earlier emphasis on "automatic levers." The literature on "scientific management of society," for example, now emphasizes systems analysis and selective application of pressure from above and below as the means of introducing new technologies, while criticizing earlier approaches as fostering "spontaneity."[45] In practice, the authorities have returned to a centralist–prescriptive form of public administration, supplemented by campaigns to overcome human and bureaucratic inertia.

Under these circumstances, the "contract" between the political authorities and the administrators has also been redefined. Since the December 1969 plenum, speeches by leaders have been filled with criticisms of "bad management," "wastefulness," and "lack of discipline." Enterprise directors and ministers alike have been criticized for behavior arising from causes that "cannot be considered objective."[46] The earlier emphasis on "trust in cadres" is now almost always supplemented by the caveat that such trust must be combined with "principled exactingness toward them," indicating that such trust is contingent on adequate performance and that none of them have the right to keep their positions indefinitely.[47] Under these conditions of expanded use of pressure to induce administrative responsibility, the regime has made a concerted effort to recruit young, technically competent individuals into the *apparat*, while vastly expanding the enrollment of party and state officials in courses devoted to both practical skills and ideology. The stress on technical competence for party officials is meant to ensure upgrading of their abilities to supervise technical administrative affairs. The stress on ideology for state officials is meant to expand their awareness of their responsibilities and thereby to increase their responsiveness to pressure. Indeed, an additional measure taken during the early 1970s was an exchange of party cards, a step ostensibly designed to weed out party members who had been defaulting on their social responsibilities.

The redefinition of the political contract of welfare-state authoritarianism was extended to the regime's relationship with the intelligentsia as well, and at about the same time. A Central Committee resolution of 1970 was the signal for an intensified antirevisionism campaign in scientific research institutes.[48] Since 1971, scientists have been required to take part in larger numbers of ideological seminars as a means of countering any narrowly pragmatic tendencies. Also in 1971, the regime announced that primary party organizations in scientific research institutes would be given a greater role and augmented authority to approve the lists of research topics and to demand displays of political conformity from scientific personnel. In 1972, party officials purged the Institute for Concrete Sociological Research, scattering the liberal-minded sociologists who had worked there among various institutes. Since then, Soviet sociology has been developed "intensively" rather than "extensively," with a narrower range of topics and conclusions gaining access to publications of wide circulation. Moreover, through the 1970s, there has been an escalating crackdown on overt political defiance ("dissent"), which has resulted in a Constitution placing extraordinary emphasis on "the interests of the state," the "interests of society," and the obligation of the citizen to subordinate personal interests to state interests. Finally, one can detect in Soviet leaders' speeches during the 1970s a much increased use of the term *scientific decision making* in its traditional normative meaning and a diminished use of the term in its newer, more empirical meaning.[49]

The Brezhnev Era, Phase Two: Social Transformation and Economic Achievement
During this period, the regime has also expanded the use of pressure on workers and peasants as a means of increasing labor productivity. Soviet leaders' speeches since the December 1969 plenum have had a persistent refrain: "automatic levers" are not the only means of increasing labor productivity; a crucial factor is the attitude of the individual toward his job and his social obligations. Typical of the messages was Suslov's warning that "our party has never believed and does not now believe that the action of economic

incentives is the only action that produces results. . . . Disregard for moral factors is capable of causing just as much national-economic and political damage as ignoring the principles of material interest."[50] The stress has not been simply upon moral incentives, however, for in leaders' speeches there has been an even greater concern for "discipline," "organization," and "responsibility."

Buttressing this change of ethos has been a series of policy changes pointing in the same direction:

1. Continuing campaigns for mobilizing reserves, socialist competition, Stakhanovism, and a "regime of savings"

2. Administrative measures designed to reduce labor turnover and increase the penalties for lax performance

3. A resurgent role for the agitator in pressuring workers on the job

4. Increased pressure on the party *aktiv* to adopt "social assignments" and to exercise "iron discipline"

5. The spread of an industrial tutelary movement (*nastavnichestvo*) geared toward increasing the benevolent supervision of younger workers by older ones

6. Personal productivity plans for workers, specifying their responsibilities and expanding the regime's capacity to monitor poor performance

All these changes, we should bear in mind, have taken place since 1969–1970.

The resurgent emphasis on pressure has also led to the demise (however temporary) of such administrative experiments as the Shchekino innovation and the link system.[51] The legitimacy of each has been undermined by resistance to the wide material differentiation they would require and the threat to lower-class job security they would entail. In addition, in the case of the link system, such a reform would threaten the political prerogatives of the rural party *raikom*. In a period during which pressure has been gaining ascendancy over "automatic levers" in the mix of policy premises and in which the political status of party organs has been reinforced, it should not come as a surprise that these experiments have been undercut.

Egalitarian premises also experienced a comeback in 1969 on questions of social mobility. In September of that year, the regime passed new laws facilitating entrance to universities for children of peasant background, demobilized soldiers, and the working class. "Preparatory sections" were established for people from these categories, and those who successfully completed the course of study were promised admission to the university without entrance competition. As one Western scholar observed, "The post-Khrushchev leadership evidently found that active intervention in this important social process was needed in order to counteract the marked elitism which Soviet institutions of higher education [that is, universities], like those of many other lands, seem to engender."[52]

The Fundamentalist Illusion

Indeed, the cluster of changes in policy and premises represented something of a right-wing reaction against the leftist form of welfare-state authoritarianism that was taking shape in 1965. It would be a grave mistake, however, to overstate the extent and character of this backlash through the indiscriminate use of such labels as "neo-Stalinism." Just as we saw that the orientations of the mid-1960s represented a subtle mix of premises weighted at first in the leftist direction, so we now find that the backlash since 1969 constitutes a selective retrenchment through a shifting of weights within a cluster of premises. The shift did *not* violate the basic contract of welfare-state authoritarianism, for it did not entail a return to austerity, terror, or arbitrary, personalistic rule. It *did*, however, reinforce those forces opposed to further movement in the direction of elitist liberalism, which would have constitutionalized collective leadership,[53] ensured managerial autonomy, and encouraged much wider social and material differentiation and social insecurity for the sake of economic performance. It behooves us, therefore, to reexamine this backlash in order to define its character more precisely.

Let me begin with realms of policy relating to political participation. At the top of the policy-making pyramid, Brezhnev's role expansion should not be overstated. There is no evidence to indicate that he has acquired widespread purge powers or even the ability to push through far-reaching policy changes challenging the prerogatives of major institutions. In fact, his domestic policy program for budgetary reallocation and administrative reform has been resisted by the political and administrative elite.[54] Moreover, after assuming Podgorny's post, Brezhnev felt constrained to reassure the political elite that he would not engage in arbitrary behavior or personalistic rule,[55] and his behavior as general secretary during the 1970s has conformed to the image of a leader who respects (willingly or unwillingly) stable procedural norms in the conduct of policy making. I conclude, therefore, that Brezhnev's accumulated power has been largely self-protective and defensive in character, allowing him perhaps to weather political storms that others might not survive, but not allowing him to violate the political contract of corporate pluralism within the ruling elite.

Party intervention in administrative affairs has also been selective, in no way approaching the degree of interventionism practiced under Khrushchev. To the contrary, mobilization premises have been accompanied by an ongoing effort to define more clearly the rights, responsibilities, and jurisdictions of administrative presonnel as a means of fostering administrative responsibility.[56] As Brezhnev put it at the Twenty-Fourth Party Congress in 1971:

At all levels of management . . . extensive rights with little responsibility create opportunities for administrative arbitrariness, subjectivism, and ill-considered decisions. But extensive responsibilities with few rights [that is, the Khrushchevian pattern] is no better. In such a situation, even the most diligent official often finds himself powerless, and it is difficult to hold him fully responsible for the job assigned.

And at the Twenty-Fifth Party Congress, Brezhnev reiterated this concern and upgraded its importance still further, dubbing it "the essence of organizational questions" and the "foundation of foundations of the science and practice of administration." At the same Party Congress, he continued to call for rationalization of administrative success indicators, indicating the problematic character of establishing administrative responsibility in the absence of such rationalization. Success indicators, he averred, "must harmonize the interests of the worker with the interests of the enterprise, and the interests of the enterprise with the interests of the state."[57]

This admission that augmented pressure cannot solve the problems of administrative control in an irrationally planned command economy has had an important political corollary. Unlike Stalin or Khrushchev, the current regime, in its criticisms of managerial behavior, has not gone so far as to equate "bad management" with "antistate" behavior. It is not questioning the *loyalty* of its personnel, or does it feel the need to devolve all responsibility for economic difficulties. At the Twenty-Fourth Party Congress, for instance, Brezhnev rejected a return to earlier definitions of "discipline" and called instead for "discipline that is not based on fear or on methods of ruthless administrative fiat, which deprive people of confidence and initiative and give rise to overcautiousness and dishonesty. What is involved here is discipline that is based on a high level of people's consciousness and responsibility."[58]

This subtle shift in premises should not be written off as political rhetoric, for it has been accompanied by policies consistent with its thrust. Thus, the authorities have not engaged in a purge of the administrative elite. Indeed, the exchange of party cards during 1973–1975 resulted in expulsion of only about 1% of the party membership.[59] Moreover, the selective reemphasis on pressure has not prevented a rather steady effort to diminish the imbalances in the 5-year plans. The Tenth Five-Year Plan (1976–1980), in fact, is especially noteworthy for its unprecedented degree of congruence between aspirations and capacities (though it is ambitious nonetheless).[60] The expanded emphasis on "de-mandingness" toward cadres, therefore, does not imply either a purge or a "great leap forward" mentality.

The retrenchment has also been selective and ambiguous with respect to specialist input and the status of the intelligentsia. The normative definition of "scientific decision making" has acquired increased prom-inence, but it has coexisted with continued deference to the empirical definition. Moreover, since the early 1970s, the regime has simul-taneously upgraded the ideological status of science. Science is no longer just *becoming* a direct product force, as was declared in the Party Program of 1961; it now has become such a force, according to official Soviet doctrine.[61] Then too, officially articulated deference to the "potential" and "complexity" of the "scientific–technological revolu-tion" continues unabated. All these items reflect an ongoing commit-ment to the development of a knowledge industry relatively un-encumbered by dogmatic preconceptions.

But there are strict limits as well. Scientific empiricism is called upon to play a distinctively instrumental role, helping the authorities to better understand the environments they are trying to manipulate. Scientists will be accorded official status only in return for political docility. Thus, whereas scientists have had to attend more philosophical seminars and their research projects have been subjected to closer scrutiny, the priorities of economic progress have not been sacrificed. Rather, the current message appears to be that in return for a certain latitude in research and regularized access to officials within their fields of specialization, the scientific community has a reciprocal obligation to: (1) focus its research on problems related to the priorities defined by the regime, and (2) compartmentalize its critical faculties, exercising them within scientific fields of inquiry but not extending them to critical questions of political authority. In short, the regime has committed itself to creating conditions under which scientists can be experts, but it expects them not to become public intellectuals.

The backlash on questions of social transformation and economic efficiency has also been a limited one. The renewed emphasis on regimentation, exhortation, and obligation has not constituted a return to the philosophy of deferred gratification or economic austerity, notwithstanding ideological criticism of the "cult of things and the standards of the notorious consumer society."[62] There has been no cutback in the material reward that one can earn for hard work; if anything, material incentives have been continually expanded in an effort to spur productivity. In addition, the regime has expanded its investments in agricultural development to massive dimensions (now investing more in agriculture than do the United States and Western Europe combined). In a similar vein, the authorities have committed scarce foreign currency to the importation of varying types of consumer goods and have expanded very greatly the availability of consumer goods other than food. Then, too, in 1971, when the campaigns for "moral incentives" were gaining momentum, Leonid Brezhnev proposed to the Twenty-Fourth Party Congress a program for inducing heavy industrial enterprises to expand their production of consumer-oriented products.[63] In the light of these trends, the conclusion is unmistakable that the backlash entails a subtle redefinition of the social contract: The regime attempts to increase the availability of consumer goods at measured rates and maintains its commitment to meeting consumer expectations; in return, however, the authorities demand that consumers keep these expectations within strict bounds and respond with labor contributions to the current levels of material incentives. Political and social pressure, in turn, are counted on to supplement material incentives and make them effective. Indeed, such pressures are directed against the attitudes vividly expressed by the Moscow workers' saying of the 1970s: "As long as the bosses pretend to be paying us a decent wage, we'll pretend we're working."[64]

Nor has the regime taken actions reminiscent of Khrushchevian campaigns of social transformation. The backlash since 1969 has hardly— if at all—affected the post-Khrushchev commitment to privatism. Pressure on the agricultural private sector has not been notably increased. Housing and automobile production have proceeded at levels sufficient to give many urban dwellers the hope of some day having a single-family apartment and a private automobile. As for social mobility, the educational reform of 1969 was significant, but although it may be further developed in the future, it has thus far not been as detrimental to the aspirations of children of the intelligentsia as were the reforms of 1958. Young scientists are not being asked to work in the factories before entering the university. Preparatory sections do not appear to have caused a major shift in the social composition of student bodies.[65] The current approach, then, is clearly a compromise between the meritocratic demands of the "scientific–technological revolution" and the more egalitarian, mass-oriented basis of early Soviet political culture.

Finally, the resurgent emphasis on both regimentation and the privileged political status of official organs should not be interpreted as a return to Stalinist methods of control. Contemporary calls for "discipline" lack the paranoid component of the Stalinist era. Today, "discipline" usually means that the masses are expected to be politically conformist and to remain sober, arrive at work on time, labor hard and conscientiously, upgrade their skills, and participate in such occasional rituals as *subbotniki* (donation of off-work time to state projects) and political lectures. Moreover, while the political prerogatives of official organs have been restored since Khrushchev and enhanced since 1969, there has been no systematic return to the commandist and heavy-handed leadership orientation of earler years. Quite the contrary: the right of trade unions to protect workers against being fired has been reinforced and reaffirmed. Moreover, the new Constitution contains an extraordinary article to the effect that citizens who feel they have been subjected to arbitrary official behavior may appeal for redress of their grievances beyond the bureaucracy in question to the courts. It remains to be seen how this system will work in practice, but this feature of the Constitution, combined with a pervasive emphasis on "legality" in the document and contrasted with the Constitution's simultaneous emphasis on the "interests of the state," provides an important clue to the strategy of the authorities for maintaining political stability. They appear to be attempting to isolate the mass of politically conformist workers from the dissenters by providing a less austere and repressive daily life for the masses, while cracking down on the dissenters. As Brezhnev put it in his closing words to the Twenty-Fourth Party Congress, his regime was creating an atmosphere in which people who do not become dissenters can "breathe freely, work well, and live quietly."[66]

Policy Clusters And Political Support

Ambiguity remains, however, about the precise reason for the shifting mix of premises since 1969. If we accept conflict as a universal feature of oligarchic rule but nonetheless view the Soviet Politburo as a *relatively* unified elite possessing multiple goals (efficiency *and* equity; expertise *and* political docility on the part of scientists; political autonomy *and* expanded input; military–industrial might *and* consumer satisfaction; material incentives *and* party activism), then we explain the changes as resulting from a learning experience: in response to the Khrushchevian experience, the actor pays considerable attention to one set of premises during 1964–1968, finds that his actions have unanticipated consequences violating his other goals, and takes corrective measures. Interpretations that point to environmental changes as mediating factors also employ this unitary image. Thus, a scarcity of resources in the late 1960s could have triggered regime attention to the need for cheaper, mobilizational approaches to productivity. Similarly, the Dubček movement in Czechoslovakia could be viewed as an impulse leading to greater distrust of Soviet intellectuals and expanded emphasis on the political status of party organs, and worker riots in Poland might have alerted the regime to the desirability of increasing attention to consumer welfare.

On the other hand, one might argue that the changes resulted from a shift in political alignments, with those forces favoring the leftist movement of the mid-1960s suddenly finding themselves on the defensive. Environmental factors, such as events in Czechoslovakia and Poland or domestic problems, would then be viewed as triggering a shift in *political coalitions*. If the changes at the turn of the decade reflect a political change, then the current mix of premises (as well as the mix of 1965–1966) might be interpreted as a *resultant* of bargaining and compromise rather than a result of rational calculation by a more or less unified Politburo.

To decide the issue would require evidence of a different sort from that collected in this chapter. Content analysis of leaders' speeches or careful examination of discussions among academics and officials might help us to evaluate the extent to which occupants of different positions view the premises under discussion here as incompatible or antithetical. This analysis would move us beyond two of the gravest weaknesses in Soviet studies to date: (1) the tendency to impute the interests of different groups and deduce their political postures, thereby largely ignoring the possibilities for coalition-building across institutions; and (2) the failure to differentiate among types and degrees of political conflict within the political elite, assuming instead that all observable conflict must necessarily be severe and potentially destabilizing.[67]

The Brezhnev era provides an especially intriguing case for investigation along these lines. The backlash of 1969, however selective and measured, was nonetheless real, and it occurred across such a broad range of issue-areas as to suggest a high degree of linkage among policy premises within the Soviet political elite. At the same time, the very selectivity of the backlash suggests that the linkages are not fixed and that trade-offs among the premises are possible.[68] Also intriguing is the remarkable stability, despite the shift, of the composition of the Politburo. From April 1966 to April 1973, no individual was removed from full membership in the Politburo. And between December 1965 and May 1977, the inner core of that body (Brezhnev, Kosygin, Podgorny, Suslov, and Kirilenko) did not change. Those positing an unusually high level of overt conflict, or perceived *incompatibility* among policy premises in the eyes of the decision makers, cannot explain these trends.

And what of the future? It is undeniable that within the broader Soviet attentive public there exists support for both elitist liberalism and for a fundamentalist reaction.[69] How broad that support might be and how much of an echo it finds within the political elite, however, remain open questions. The record of the Brezhnev era suggests considerable support for the social and political contract of welfare-state authoritarianism, with conflict focusing largely upon differences along a left–right continuum within welfare-state authoritarianism. I have argued elsewhere that a rightist version of this regime-type would have little chance of mitigating social and political tensions within society-at-large and that it would probably result in increasing polarization within the elite.[70] A centrist or leftist version, however, would perhaps be viable. Whether changes during the Brezhnev succession will be marked by another within-system shift in the mix of premises, or whether they will result in disorder, elitist liberalism, or a fundamentalist reaction cannot be predicted. Much will depend on circumstances, accidents, and personalities. But much will also depend upon the extent to which different groups find the social and political contract of welfare-state authoritarianism to be tolerable and the extent to which policy premises within that contract are viewed as compatible. Then, too, much will hinge on the lessons drawn by members of the political elite from 14 years of experimenting with a constrained set of policy options.[71] Insofar as the present and past can be a guide to the future, the evidence adduced in this chapter constitutes a first step toward a research strategy for evaluating the adaptability of welfare-state authoritarianism.

Notes

[1]See Chalmers Johnson, ed., *Change in Communist Systems* (Stanford: Stanford University Press, 1970); T. H. Rigby, "Politics in the Mono-Organizational Society," in *Authoritarian Politics in Communist Europe*, ed. Andrew C. Janos (Berkeley: Institute of International Studies, 1976); Jerry F. Hough, "The Soviet System: Petrifaction or Pluralism?" *Problems of Communism* (March–April 1972); Jane P. Shapiro and Peter J. Potichnyj, eds, *Change and Adaptation in Soviet and East European Politics* (New York: Praeger, 1976).

[2]This term was coined in Richard Lowenthal, "The Soviet Union in the Post-Revolutionary Era: An Overview," in *Soviet Politics since Khrushchev*, ed. Alexander Dallin and Thomas B. Larson (Englewood Cliffs, N.J.: Prentice-Hall, 1968).

[3]What follows immediately is based upon George Breslauer, *Five Images of the Soviet Future: A Critical Review and Synthesis* (Berkeley: Institute of International Studies, 1978), in which I identify, label, and criticize the assumptions underlying five images (and five additional subimages) of the Soviet future that are implicit in Western and Soviet-dissident literature.

[4]Samuel Huntington finds the notion of *corporate pluralism* useful for capturing the character of Soviet pluralism since Khrushchev. See his "Social and Institutional Dynamics of One-Party Systems," in *Authoritarian Politics in Modern Society*, ed. Samuel P. Huntington and Clement H. Moore (New York: Basic Books, 1970), p. 35.

[5]I first identified and interpreted the differences between these two phases in "Leadership and Adaptation in the Soviet Union since Stalin" (Paper presented at conference on CPSU Adaptation, New Hampshire, May 1974).

[6]For a fuller discussion of my interpretation of the Khrushchev administration, see George Breslauer, "Khrushchev Reconsidered," *Problems of Communism* (September–October 1976).

[7]See T. H. Rigby, "The Soviet Leadership: Towards a Self-Stabilizing Oligarchy?" *Soviet Studies* (October 1970).

[8]This term was first coined by Reinhard Bendix to characterize Stalinism in East Germany. See his *Work and Authority in Industry* (New York: Harper and Row, 1956), p. 390.

[9]Leonid Brezhnev, *Leninskim kursom*, 5 vols. (Moscow: Politizdat, 1970–1976), 1: 347; italics added.

[10]*Pravda*, September 28, 1965; italics added.

[11]See, for example, D. Chesnokov, in *Pravda*, February 27, 1967; the same author's "Leninskoe uchenie o sotsialisticheskom gosudarstve," *Kommunist* 13 (1967); and V. Chkhikvadze and N. Farberov, "V. I. Lenin o sotsialisticheskom gosudarstve," *Kommunist* 5 (1967). That this redefinition reflected official policy was confirmed by the Central Committee Theses on the Fiftieth Anniversary of the Revolution (*Pravda*, June 25, 1967) and by Brezhnev's major anniversary day address (*Pravda*, November 7, 1967).

[12]Chkhikvadze and Farberov, "V. I. Lenin o sotsialisticheskom gosudarstve," p. 20. For an almost identical formulation by official sociologists, see *Klassy, sotsialnye sloi i gruppy v SSSR*, ed. Ts. A. Stepanyan and V. S. Semenov (Moscow: Nauka, 1968), pp. 16–17.

[13]In *Current Soviet Policies IV: The Documentary Record of the 22nd Party Congress of the Communist Party of the Soviet Union*, ed. Charlotte Saikowski and Leo Gruliow (New York: Columbia University Press, 1962), p. 24.

[14]Ellen Mickiewicz, "Policy Applications of Public Opinion Research in the USSR," in *Public Opinion Quarterly* (Winter 1972–73), pp. 566–578; Linda Lubrano Greenberg, "Soviet Science Policy and the Scientific Establishment," *Survey* (Autumn 1971).

[15]*Pravda* (editorial), October 17, 1964.

[16]Brezhnev, *Leninskim kursom*, 1: 215.

[17]Contrast the discussion of "scientific decision making" in Jerry Hough, "The Brezhnev Era: The Man and the System," *Problems of Communism* (March–April 1976), pp. 15–16.

[18]*Pravda*, April 23, 1965 (Lenin Anniversary speech).

[19]Generalized statements in this chapter about the content of "leaders' speeches" are based upon a reading of all published speeches by Brezhnev and Kosygin between October 1964 and November 1977, as well as annual Lenin Day (April 22) and Revolution anniversary (November 7) speeches by representatives of the leadership. These are statements of trends that may not be reflected in *every* speech, however.

[20]Brezhnev, *Leninskim kursom*, 1: 20.

[21]*Pravda*, December 10, 1964 (*Current Digest of the Soviet Press* 26, no. 49, p. 8).

[22]*Pravda*, April 23, 1965.

[23]*XXIII syezd Kommunisticheskoi Partii Sovetskogo Soyuza: stenografichesky otchyot*, 2 vols. (Moscow: Politizdat, 1966), 2: 46.

[24]See *Pravda*, March 27, 1965, for Brezhnev's report on the new agricultural program.

[25]Brezhnev, *Leninskim kursom*, 1: 74.

[26]Alec Nove, "Economic Policy and Economic Trends," in Dallin and Larson, *Soviet Politics since Khrushchev*, p. 90. See also Kosygin's report on the reforms in *Pravda*, September 28, 1965.

[27]Brezhnev, *Leninskim kursom*, 1: 69.

[28]Mervyn Matthews, *Class and Society in Soviet Russia* (London: Allen Lane, 1972), pp. 270 ff.

[29]Gregory Grossman, "The Solidary Society: A Philosophical Issue in Communist Economic Reforms," in *Essays in Socialism and Planning in Honor of Carl*

Landauer, ed. Gregory Grossman (Englewood Cliffs, N.J.: Prentice-Hall, 1970), p. 186.

[30]See Murray Yanowitch and Wesley A. Fisher, eds., *Social Stratification and Mobility in the USSR* (White Plains, N.Y.: International Arts and Sciences Press, 1973), pp. xviii–xxiv; Stepanyan and Semenov, *Klassy, sotsialnye sloi i gruppy v SSSR*, passim; and G. Glezerman, "Sotsialnaya struktura sotsialisticheskogo obshchestva," *Kommunist* 13 (1968): 28–39.

[31]The first elaboration by an official spokesman for dominant forces within the regime came before Khrushchev's overthrow; see G. Glezerman in *Kommunist* 12 (1964): 44–54.

[32]For a summary of this literature, see A. S. Aizikovich, "Vazhnaya sotsiologicheskaya problema," *Voprosy filosofi*, 11 (1965).

[33]The concept *system-management* was first introduced into Soviet studies in Alfred Meyer's highly original "Authority in Communist Political Systems," in *Political Leadership in Industrialized Societies*, ed. Lewis J. Edinger (New York: John Wiley and Sons, 1967), pp. 84–107.

[34]Aryeh L. Unger, "Politinformator or Agitator: A Decision Blocked," in *Problems of Communism* (September–October 1970). See also the very perceptive discussion of the "relational" role of the party in post-Stalinist Marxist-Leninist states, with specific reference to the agitator's role, in Kenneth T. Jowitt, "Inclusion and Mobilization in European Leninist Regimes," *World Politics* (October 1975). Jowitt has also initiated important ways of reconceptualizing the role of the *aktiv* in these systems; see his "State, National, and Civic Development in European Leninist Regimes" (Paper presented at the annual meeting of the American Political Science Association, San Francisco, September 1975).

[35]I outline the difference in policies between a "right-wing" and a "left-wing" version of welfare-state authoritarianism, though without gainsaying the possibility of numerous centrist versions, in *Five Images of the Soviet Future*.

[36]See, for example, Lowenthal, "The Soviet Union in the Post-Revolutionary Era," p. 7.

[37]On the hopes for further development of the political contract, see A. I. Lepeshkin, in *Sovsetkoye gosudarstvo i pravo* (February 1965), pp. 5–15; F. Burlatsky in *Pravda*, January 10, 1965; and A. Rumyantsev in *Pravda*, February 21, 1965 and September 9, 1965. On hopes for further development of the social contract as well, see Alexander Yanov, *Detente after Brezhnev* (Berkeley: Institute of International Studies, 1977). It does not follow that all these individuals, and others, were in agreement on the desirability of *both* the political and social contract of elitist liberalism.

[38]On residential agitation, see Aryeh Unger, *The Totalitarian Party* (London: Cambridge University Press, 1974), pp. 128 ff.

[39]The useful concept *role expansion* was first suggested to characterize this phenomenon by Grey Hodnett in "Succession Contingencies in the Soviet Union," *Problems of Communism* (March–April, 1975).

[40]Jowitt ("Inclusion and Mobilization") has introduced into Soviet studies the important Weberian distinction between "status" and "role."

[41]See, for example, Brezhnev's speech at the Twenty-Fifth Party Congress (*Pravda*, February 25, 1976).

[42]For the new Soviet Constitution as amended and ratified, see *Pravda*, October 8, 1977.

[43]For discussion of the changing administrative and political relationships between party and state, see T. H. Rigby and R. F. Miller, *Political and Administrative Aspects of the Scientific and Technical Revolution in the USSR*, Occasional Paper no. 11, Department of Political Science, Research School of Social Sciences, Australian National University (Canberra, 1976).

[44]L. I. Brezhnev, *Ob osnovnykh voprosakh ekonomicheskoi politiki KPSS na sovremennom etape*, 2 vols. (Moscow, 1975), 1: 417–418. The speech was not published in the Soviet Union at the time, but Brezhnev repeated the same message, verbatim, in a publicized speech of April 13, 1970 (*Pravda*, April 14, 1970).

[45]Rigby and Miller, *Political and Administrative Aspects*, p. 82.

[46]For the initial change in line, see Brezhnev in *Pravda*, April 14, 1970 (echoing the message of the December 1969 plenum), and Kosygin in *XXIV s"ezd.*, 2: 14.

[47]Typical was the formulation of Brezhnev at the Twenty-Fifth Party Congress, "Trust and respect for people must be combined with strict demandingness for the assigned task . . ." (*Pravda*, February 25, 1976).

[48]See "On the Work of the Party Committee of the USSR Academy of Sciences' P. N. Lebedev Physics Institute," *Partynaya zhizn* 21 (1970): 8–10.

[49]This generalization applies to Brezhnev's speeches; Kosygin has largely avoided use of the terminology of scientific decision making. For an additional revealing comparison, contrast Demichev in *Pravda* (April 23, 1965) with Demichev in *Kommunist* 15 (1971).

[50]*Pravda*, November 7, 1970.

[51]See Yanov, *Detente after Brezhnev*.

[52]Matthews, *Class and Society*, p. 305.

[53]For a very useful discussion of the distinction between "institutionalization" and "constitutionalization," see Grey Hodnett, "The Pattern of Leadership Politics" (mimeo, September 1977).

[54]See George Breslauer, "The Twenty-Fifth Party Congress: Domestic Issues," in *The Twenty-Fifth Congress of the CPSU*, ed. Alexander Dallin (Stanford: Hoover Institution Press, 1977).

[55]*Pravda*, June 5, 1977, June 18, 1977.

[56]See Erik Hoffmann, "The 'Scientific Management' of Soviet Society," in *Problems of Communism* (May–June 1977).

[57]*XXIV s"ezd*, 1: 93; *Pravda*, February 25, 1976.

[58]*XXIV s"ezd*, 1: 126.

[59]These figures are tentative but the best guess available; see Rigby and Miller, *Political and Administrative Aspects*, p. 31.

[60]See Gregory Grossmann, "The Brezhnev Era: An Economy at Middle Age," *Problems of Communism* (March–April 1976).

[61]This doctrinal change was emphasized by Leonid Brezhnev in a speech in Kiev on July 26, 1973 (*Leninskim kursom*, 4: 218).

[62]*Sovetskaia Belorussiya*, 1 June 1971, as noted in Werner Hahn, *The Politics of Soviet Agriculture, 1960–1970* (Baltimore: Johns Hopkins University Press, 1972), p. 250.

[63]*XXIV s"ezd*, 1: 69–71, 75–77.

[64]Quoted in Hedrick Smith, *The Russians* (New York: Quadrangle, 1976), p. 215.

[65]See the discussion in Stanley Rothman and George Breslauer, *Soviet Politics and Society* (St. Paul: West Publishing Company, 1978), pp. 120–121.

[66]*XXIV s"ezd*, 2: 216. Moreover, in 1977 Brezhnev claimed "that some 10,000 administrators are fired annually because of citizens' complaints" (*San Francisco Sunday Examiner and Chronicle*, January 29, 1978). This figure is surely inflated, and we are told nothing about the fates of those managers (are they demoted or simply moved to a comparable job elsewhere?). But even if the claim is only partially true, the phenomenon would be consistent with the strategy just described.

[67]For a Kremlinological analysis that attempts to avoid this problem, see Breslauer, "The Twenty-Fifth Party Congress."

[68]An additional, important finding is the high correlation between changes in articulated policy premises and changes in actual policy. Once we control for the symbolic rhetoric, a careful analysis of Soviet leaders' speeches can be an important guide to their political behavior.

[69]See Yanov, *Detente after Brezhnev*.

[70]Breslauer, *Five Images of the Soviet Future*. A fuller evaluation of the viability of different political coalitions would require investigation of foreign policy premises as well, and of their compatibility with clusters of domestic policy premises.

[71]Thus, in "The Twenty-Fifth Congress" I have documented Brezhnev's apparent dissatisfaction with the pace of administrative reform.

10   ROBERT SHARLET

The New Soviet Constitution of 1977[*]

In 1977—after nearly 20 years in the making—the Soviet Union finally promulgated its long-awaited new Constitution. With little advance warning, impending publication of the draft document was announced at a Central Committee plenary session in late May. But the significance of this event was at once overshadowed by the simultaneously announced ouster of Nikolay Podgorny from the CPSU Politburo. Podgorny's dramatic exit from the party leadership and his "request" for retirement from chairmanship of the Presidium of the USSR Supreme Soviet paved the way for General Secretary Leonid Brezhnev to be elected to the Soviet "presidency" at the regular Supreme Soviet session in mid-June.[1]

Thus, in the space of a few weeks, Brezhnev reached the summit of his political career. Having successfully engineered the fall of a reputedly major Politburo rival, he became the first CPSU leader to serve as not only de facto but also de jure head of state. In this new capacity, he immediately embarked on a major and well-publicized state visit to France, where his reception was marked by considerable ceremony. Yet while the General Secretary's new office attracted the most attention abroad, the proposed Constitution quickly occupied center stage at home. Indeed, the nationwide "public" discussion of the Draft during the summer and early fall followed by revision and ratification of the 1977 Constitution in October, took on the central role in the activities leading up to the celebration on November 7 of the sixtieth anniversary of the Bolshevik Revolution.[2]

*Reprinted by permission of the author and publisher from *The New Soviet Constitution of 1977: Analysis and Text* (Brunswick, Ohio: King's Court Communications, Inc., 1978). Copyright 1978 by King's Court Communications, Inc.

The process of drafting a new Constitution was not a smooth one. The published Draft surfaced after nearly two decades of discussion and uncertainty—not just about its contents but about whether it would even appear at all. Entangled in the politics of destalinization, the passage of the new Soviet Constitution through the more open, factionalized, and conflict-ridden policy-making process of the post-Stalin era proved a complex undertaking, requiring numerous changes and compromises to accommodate the diverse interests involved in such a broad, overarching document.

The Path of Constitutional Reform

These circumstances contrast considerably with those surrounding the appearance of the "Stalin Constitution" some four decades before. A constitutional commission was appointed in 1935 and charged with replacing the constitution of 1924, which, after nearly a decade of social upheavals, no longer reflected the structure and content of the rapidly changing Soviet system. The commission produced a draft by mid-1936 and submitted it for nationwide discussion during the summer and fall. After mainly stylistic and semantic changes, it was ratified in late 1936, and December 5 has since been celebrated as "Constitution Day," invariably calling forth paeans of praise in the nation's media.[3]

The times then, of course, were very different. By the mid-1930s, Stalin had completed his "revolution from above," radically transforming the socioeconomic configuration of Soviet society in the process and, at the same time, ensuring his personal ascendancy over party and state. With collectivization behind him and heavy industrialization well under way, Stalin chose to consolidate these changes and stabilize the resulting status quo. Among other things, this entailed reconstructing the legal system as a means of providing a formal framework for the planned, public economy and of affording a larger measure of predictability to the individual citizen, who had just lived through a time of extraordinarily disruptive, indeed violent, social change. Toward this end, Soviet civil law, which had been rapidly "withering away" under the impact of radical Marxist jurisprudence, was gradually revived. A collective farm statute, legislating the peasant's rights to a personal garden plot, was enacted in 1935; and new, more conservative family legislation, designed to stabilize the family as a social unit, was passed in mid-1936. The new Constitution which followed served as Stalin's most public "signal" that the "revolution from above" was over and that "stabilization" was the new political and legal order of the day.[4]

The "Stalin Constitution" proclaimed that the Soviet Union had become "a socialist state of workers and peasants." It implied that the class war had ended, secured the peasant's garden plot in basic law, and constitutionally mandated the citizen's right to personal property. Although the "great purge" was reaching its crescendo at the same time, and while the new constitutional guarantees of personal security were being honored in the breach for millions of Soviet citizens, the personal economic rights granted under the "Stalin Constitution" did extend to the individual some greater degree of certainty in his daily life.[5]

After the dictator's death and the onset of destalinization, the rapid pace of reform and developmental change soon surpassed the Constitution's structural capacity to reflect it through the usual piecemeal process of amendment and revision. Efforts to draft a new Soviet Constitution formally began in 1962, but the removal of Nikita Khrushchev 2 years later understandably interrupted the process.[6] Brezhnev was elected Chairman of the Constitutional Commission in place of the deposed Khrushchev; thus, the project was not abandoned. Yet, while the post-Khrushchev leadership thereby maintained a commitment to replace the supposedly long-outdated "Stalin Constitution," progress on a new draft slowed appreciably.[7] Nor was this surprising, since previous Soviet constitutions had reflected each succeeding phase of Soviet political development and since the Brezhnev regime in the latter half of the 1960s set about counterreforming many of Khrushchev's innovations while advancing new policies of its own. Another plausible reason for the delay in constitutional change was that the project presumably did not have the same priority for the pragmatic Brezhnev that it had for his more ideological predecessor. The 1936 Constitution was easily amendable; the more serious gaps could be filled by additional statutory legislation and the major anachronisms superseded by new legislative principles and codes. Thus, the long established practice of incremental constitutional change could be continued while the post-Khrushchev leadership addressed itself to the more urgent problems of agriculture, the economy, and foreign policy.

In the late 1960s and early 1970s, however, several Western scholars learned in private talks with Soviet colleagues that the drafting process was under way once again.[8] The prospects for imminent constitutional change gradually gathered a modest momentum in the Soviet legal press and were stimulated from time to time by authoritative political hints. Speculation over the timing of the new Constitution was rife among Western specialists, although anticipation from all quarters mounted as the Twenty-Fifth CPSU Congress approached. The most popular scenario making the rounds among Western journalists and scholars at the time predicted that Brezhnev would crown his career with a new Constitution, to be presented at the Congress, which, presumably, would be Brezhnev's last in view of his age and deteriorating health. But the expected announcement failed to materialize, and Brezhnev confined himself to fresh promises on the subject in a few brief remarks at the end of his long opening-day Report. His statement that work on the constitution was going forward, although "without haste," was echoed subsequently in the legal press but without elaboration or indication of any deadline for completion.[9] Then, without the usual advance clues, there came the abrupt announcement in May 1977 that the new Draft Constitution would soon be published for nationwide discussion.[10]

Continuity and Change

In keeping with Brezhnev's political style, the Constitution is a moderate, middle-of-the-road document, neither anti-Stalinist nor neo-Stalinist in its thrust but rather a generally pragmatic statement of already existing practice and principle. Despite its association with the General Secretary's concurrent political triumphs, however, this document should not be regarded simply as a "Brezhnev Constitution." In the first place, as stressed in its Preamble, the 1977 Constitution displays much "continuity of ideas and principles" with the three previous constitutions.[11] For example, most of the articles dealing with property and the economy (Chapter 2 of the Constitution) and with the ordinary citizen's economic rights and duties (Chapter 7) date from the 1936 Constitution, in which they helped institutionalize and consolidate Stalin's "revolution from above." Moreover, Brezhnev himself made constitutional "continuity" a keynote in his plenum Report.[12]

Second, and of much greater importance, the 1977 Constitution codifies major social and political changes which extend beyond the scope of Brezhnev's leadership alone. In the most general sense, this is demonstrated by the fact that Soviet authorities describe it as the constitution of an advanced industrial society, one which, in Soviet parlance, has reached the stage of "developed socialism" (*razvitoy sotsializm*). In contrast, earlier constitutions were designed to serve a Soviet society at very different stages of revolutionary development or postrevolutionary consolidation.

More specifically, the new Constitution takes full account of the great volume of post-Stalin legislation that has affected nearly every branch and area of Soviet law. In fact, there are few points in the Constitution that have not been raised or institutionalized already in code law, statutory legislation, or the scholarly juridical commentary explicating the extensive post-Stalin legal reforms. For example, the environmental protection clauses (Articles 18 and 67), the foreign policy section (Articles 28–30), and the constitutional prescription (and pun) of a 41-hour maximum work week in Article 41 are all novel in comparison with the 1936 Constitution. But they break no new ground in terms of post-Stalin policy, practice, and legal development.[13]

In broader terms, the Constitution serves as a useful register of both the accomplishments and the limits of destalinization. In retrospect, it is clear that Khrushchev himself set out the boundaries of destalinzation in his famous "secret speech" to the Twentieth Party Congress in 1956. Although he indicted Stalin for the "cult of personality" and its egregious consequences for the party and "socialist legality," Khrushchev also explicitly praised his predecessor for the latter's "great services to the party" in forging the socioeconomic foundations of the Soviet system, laid out in the course of the first Five-Year Plan.[14]

One major aspect of destalinization affirmed in the new document is the constitutionally enhanced status of the individual in relation to the state, especially in criminal proceedings (Articles 151 and 160) but in civil matters as well (Article 58).[15] No less important is the formally institutionalized "leading" role of the party (Article 6), a change in constitutional form that culminates the party's renaissance following the end of Stalin's personal dictatorship. At the same time, the moderate tone and obvious compromises in the Constitution illustrate the consequences of post-Stalin leadership change, political factionalism, and interest group conflict.

The limits to change, however, are no less significant. Most important, the party has constructed in the new Constitution a political instrument for routinizing the governance process, but it has done so in such a manner as to leave sufficient ambiguity for a jurisprudence of political expediency to circumvent the system of "legality" (zakonnost') when necessary. In fact, the party has merely "constitutionalized" the traditional dualism of law and extralegal coercion.[16] In this fundamental sense, the 1977 Constitution represents codification of the post-Stalin system as a party-led constitutional bureaucracy.

Still, a potentially important qualification should be added. During the course of the lengthy constitutional drafting process, a lively theoretical debate developed among Soviet legal scholars over the concept of constitution in Soviet jurisprudence. In essence, two schools of thought vied in the legal press over the seemingly "academic" question of whether to call Soviet public law "state law" (gosudarstvennoye pravo) or "constitutional law" (konstitutsionnoye pravo).[17] In fact, this debate held significant implications for the 1977 Constitution's draftsmen. "State law" refers to the traditional view that argues that the Soviet Constitution basically is intended to reflect the structure of state power prevailing in Soviet society. From this perspective, the Constitution, through the continuous process of amendment, performs little more than a codification function, recording and legitimating the changes in state structure as they occur.

The "constitutional law" school, which for years was in a decided minority within the Soviet legal profession, asserts that the traditional approach tends to reduce the Constitution to a mere sociopolitical mirror while neglecting its normative potential. In contrast, this side proposes that the Constitution be conceptualized as both a reflective *and* a programmatic instrument. The latter function would incorporate the Communist party's ideological and policy goals into a more open-ended, future-oriented document. The "constitutionalists" also insist that their perspective would better facilitate the constitutional elaboration of the citizen's increased rights and duties, which have found legislative expression in the context of the changing post-Stalin relationship between state and individual.

The "constitutional" school seems to have prevailed[18]—at least to the extent that the 1977 Constitution includes greater programmatic content in comparison with the 1936 version. A further "constitutionalist" contribution may be the Constitution's greater emphasis on the sociopolitical, economic, and legal status of the Soviet citizen and the explicit correlation of the state's powers with its corresponding obligations to the citizen and vice versa.

To be sure, the party leadership intends to use the post-Stalin Constitution as a stable and orderly framework through which to govern the increasingly differentiated and specialized socioeconomic system, while at the same time reserving for itself the inherent power of dictatorship to bypass the "legal state" by resorting to *ad hoc*, extralegal action when it thinks appropriate. Yet, in addition to providing a general legal policy that fixes the boundaries and functions of the social regulation process in higher law, the new Soviet Constitution itself contains the seeds of a major party metapolicy—that is, a set of goals and rules of behavior given normative value and with system-wide, and not merely legal, ramifications.[19]

A Soviet "Systems" Approach
As expressed by Soviet political and legal commentators, a major purpose of the new Soviet Constitution is to reflect the infrastructure of the Soviet system now, after 60 years of development. In particular, this means recording in constitutional language the most important and enduring political, legal, socioeconomic, and doctrinal changes since promulgation of the 1936 Constitution and especially following Stalin's death. In this connection, the more dynamic, "systems" approach to sociopolitical structure that is contained in Part I of the Constitution (Articles 1–32) stands in decided contrast to the static, state-society formula of its predecessor.

Western-style "systems analysis" has come into vogue in the Soviet social sciences in recent years, although its reception in jurisprudence is still in its formative stage. In its legal context, the "systems" approach stems from post-Khrushchevian recognition of the distinction between the state (*gosudarstvo*) and the political system (*politicheskaya organizatsiya sovetskogo obshchestvo*).[20]

The Constitution's description of the whole Soviet system, therefore, delineates a dominant political system (Chapter 1), together with economic and social subsystems (Chapters 2 and 3). This framework implies a possible concession of at least some developmental autonomy for social and economic patterns in Soviet society. And it may suggest a perceptible change in stress, from a political system which is essentially transformist to one that is more explicitly regulative.[21] The introduction of a new article that appears to advance the notion of "political culture" (Article 9) stands in support of this interpretation.[22] Moreover, Chapter 4, which describes the functions of the Soviet system in the international environment (foreign policy), and Chapter 5, which describes the functions of defending the Soviet system from possible threats in the international environment, suggest extension of the "systems" model to a global scale.

One particularly notable feature of the post-Stalin "political system" is the doctrinal evolution from the "dictatorship of the proletariat" to "the state of all the people." Although Soviet jurists have failed to conceptualize this notion clearly since it first emerged under Khrushchev, the "state of the whole people," to a large extent, remains today—as earlier—a political metaphor signaling the leadership's interest in greater participation in the implementation of the party's policies by both mass organizations (Article 7) and the public in general (Article 5).[23] These participatory declamations are in turn operationalized in Articles 113 and 114, which provide, respectively, for legislative initiative by mass organizations and for general discussion of draft legislation by the public as a whole. With regard to both, however, the new Constitution merely confirms existing practice.

Chapter 1 also includes a clause on the legal subsystem, a reference that points to another of the major changes in the post-Stalin period. The 1936 Constitution included a statement of the citizen's duty to obey the law,[24] but the present document requires both the citizen (Aritcles 59 and 65) and the state (Articles 4 and 57) to observe the requirements of "socialist legality." Of course, the state's obligation to observe the law gives first priority to its function of protecting "law and order," a key slogan of the Brezhnev period.[25]

Finally, Article 6 in Chapter 1 makes explicit a party-dominant political system. The Communist party, which was mentioned twice in the 1936 Constitution and only in connection with the rights of mass organizations,[26] has been institutionalized in the new Constitution as "the leading and directing force of Soviet society, the nucleus of its political system"—finally in accord with its actual role during the past decades of Soviet history. Since the Preamble declares that the Soviet system will strive to build communism in the future, the party's role is described in the more functional terms of serving as the guiding source for the domestic and foreign policy of the USSR.

The chapter on the economy describes the same infrastructure of public and personal economy set forth in the 1936 Constitution but also consolidates those structural changes associated with post-Stalin economic development.[27] Thus, Article 9 of the 1936 Constitution permitted the "small-scale private economy" of individual peasants and handicraftsmen; the corresponding Article 17 of the 1977 Constitution allows "individual labor activity" (*individualnaya trudovaya deyatel'nost'*) in the delivery of "consumer services for the population."[28] Trade union property has been added as a type of "socialist property" (Article 10). This, of course, had been its de facto status for many years, a situation recognized formally in the 1961 Fundamental Principles of Civil Legislation. The planning clause (Article 16) incorporates some of the features of "Libermanism" and the 1965 economic reforms with its reference to the "economic independence and initiative of enterprises, associations, and other organizations" and its explicit bow to the importance of profits, costs, and *khozraschët* (economic accountability). Article 18 declares the state's commitment to the protection and rational utilization of the environment, an injunction of both reflective and programmatic dimensions.

More purely programmatic is the consumption and labor productivity clause (Article 15), which earmarks social production (*obshchestvennoye proizvodstvo*) for the satisfaction of people's wants and needs and charges the state with the task of raising labor productivity in order to fulfill this commitment. The prominence accorded consumer needs in Articles 14 and 15 of the Constitution constitutes a marked departure from the corresponding passage in the "Stalin Constitution," which placed relatively greater stress on economic growth.[29] Both the socialist emulation or competition technique, "inspired" by Stakhanov in the 1930s, and the more recently launched "scientific–technological revolution" are invoked in quest of higher labor productivity. In view of the questionable effectiveness of the former technique and widespread doubts regarding Soviet capacity to stimulate and manage innovation, Article 15 is likely to remain more programmatic than "reflective" for some time.[30]

Finally, the 1936 exhortation to work has been softened somewhat in the new Constitution (Article 14) but nonetheless ends on a phrase that maintains the spirit of the antiparasite legislation: "*socially useful* labor and its results shall determine the status of a person in society" (italics added).[31] This impression is strengthened in the more exhortative "rights and duties" section (Article 60), in which "conscientious labor in one's chosen field of socially useful activity" is described as both a duty and a "matter of honor."

The chapter on the social subsystem consists largely of a set of programmatic directional signs on the road to communism, as Brezhnev acknowledged in his plenum Report. Included are commitments to the enhancement of social homogeneity (Article 19), the eventual abolition of manual labor through mechanization (Article 21), and the development of consumer services (Article 24)—all in connection with the long-standing commitment to encourage development of the "new man" (Article 20). These social articles in the 1977 Constitution give rise to a sense of déjà vu—the rhetoric is reminiscent of Khrushchev's 1961 Party Program, minus the detail and accompanying timetable for the realization of specified goals.[32]

The short chapters on foreign policy and defense contain a mix of reflective and programmatic elements but basically proceed from recognition of the fact that the Soviet Union has emerged as a superpower. There is here, too, a degree of continuity with the 1961 Party Program, particularly in the clauses on peaceful coexistence (Article 28) and socialist (read "proletarian") internationalism (Article 30).[33] Absent, in comparison with the earlier documents, are the repeated references to world capitalism and imperialism and the spirit of competition with the West. Article 29 essentially incorporates the Helsinki principles. At the same time, the socialist internationalism clause has been written broadly enough to accommodate both the Brezhnev doctrine and Soviet leadership of the Council for Mutual Economic Assistance (CMEA).[34] The defense clauses offer a straightforward elaboration of the State's defense function that was described in the 1936 Constitution.[35] In addition, the state's defense functions and foreign policy objectives have been supplemented by the citizen's military obligation (Article 63), the more diffuse duty "to safeguard the interests of the Soviet state and to help strengthen its might and prestige" (Article 62), and a still vaguer "internationalist duty" (Article 69).

The Citizen and the State The second main purpose of the new Constitution is to define the relationship between the state and the individual. This relationship can be divided, for analytic purposes, into the citizen's economic, civil, and participation rights and duties.

Economic Rights. The economic rights need only brief review, since they are the same rights as those of the 1936 Constitution, albeit with a few additions and amplifications.[36] A constitutional guarantee of housing (Article 44) and the right to use the achievements of culture (Article 46) have been added, while the 1936 Article on economic security has been expanded and divided in the 1977 Constitution into two articles on health protection (Article 42) and old age maintenance (Article 43). The right to work also has been enlarged to include the freedom to choose one's profession, occupation, or employment, provided the choice is consistent with society's needs (Article 40), a constitutional "right" made possible by the higher level of economic development and general affluence of Soviet society today as compared with life in the mid-1930s. Indeed, while many of the economic rights were programmatic when first included in the "Stalin Constitution," they are now, for the most part, simply reflective of a highly developed welfare state.[37]

At the same time, the economic rights of the Soviet citizen are balanced by a basic economic "duty," also carried over from the 1936 Constitution. In this connection, the citizen's obligation to protect socialist property has been reaffirmed, although in destalinized form— that is, public property is no longer described as "sacred and inviolable," and persons who commit property crimes are no longer castigated as "enemies of the people." The property protection clause is already amply supported in the criminal codes of the various union republics. Yet, in view of the extent of economic crime and the scale of the "second economy" or "parallel market," it would seem fair to predict that countless Soviet citizens, from factory workers to enterprise directors, will continue to disregard this constitutional injunction.[38]

Civil Liberties. The civil rights clauses of the new Constitution, which should be judged together with the sections on the courts (Chapter 20) and the Procuracy or prosecutor's office (Chapter 21), reveal much more about the citizen's status vis-à-vis state and provide further evidence for assessing the current scope and limits of destalinization. Most important, the basic civil rights continue to be limited by the standard caveat that the rights of speech, press, association, assembly, public meetings, and demonstration are guaranteed to the citizen only in conformity with "the people's interests and for the purpose of strengthening" and developing the socialist system (Articles 50–51).[39] The same preference for the social over the individual interest also limits the new civil right of "freedom of scientific, technical, and artistic creation" (Article 47). In fact, the new Constitution has two additional paragraphs that further emphasize the social limits on the citizen's right to exercise his economic rights and his civil liberties. In the article introducing Chapter 7, on the "Basic Rights, Liberties, and Duties of USSR Citizens," Soviet citizens first are granted the "whole range of social, economic, political and personal rights and liberties" which follow—but under the condition of the closing injunction, which points out that the "exercise of rights and liberties by citizens must not injure the interests of society and the state or the rights of other citizens" (Article 39). The predominence of the prevailing social interests is reinforced in the "duty to obey" clause (Article 59). The spirit and some of the language of this clause incorporate most of the antecedent article from the 1936 Constitution,[40] although with an added phrase stressing the nexus between citizens' rights and their social obligations: "The exercise of rights and liberties is inseparable from the performance by citizens of their duties." Again, as with much of the Constitution's content, this concept of *linkage* does not represent an innovation in Soviet law. Moreover, it is relevant to all of the citizen's rights and obligations and is not addressed exclusively to the criminal justice process.[41]

Turning now to the position of the individual in the criminal justice system, we find that the most significant aspects of post-Stalin legislation on criminal law and procedure also have been incorporated into the new Constitution. From arrest through appeal, the position of the individual in the Soviet criminal justice process has been considerably strengthened since enactment of the all-union Fundamental Principles of Criminal Procedural Legislation in 1958.[42] A Soviet "due process" in *ordinary* (nonpolitical) criminal cases has developed and survived leadership turnover and the vicissitudes of Soviet politics.[43] For the vast majority of individual citizens, this may have been the most important and durable accomplishment of destalinization.

Much of this change, of course, arose from post-Stalin reaction to the conditions of official lawlessness and terror that prevailed at the time of the adoption of the 1936 Constitution and that continued, though significantly reduced in scale, up to and even after Stalin's death in 1953. Although the current personal inviolability clause (Article 54) resembles its 1936 antecedent, the injunction against arrests without either court order or approval of a procurator is now grounded in the operative legislation and codes on criminal procedure as well as in actual post-Stalin Soviet practice.[44] After the arrest, contemporary Soviet justice is, in fact, "administered solely by the courts" (Article 151). The judiciary clause in the new Constitution is far more explicit in this respect than its predecessor and is firmly based on the Fundamental Principles of Legislation on the Court System of 1958. At the same time, neither the current clause nor the Fundamentals mention the existence of "special courts" which were acknowledged in the 1936 Constitution and which still exist.[45]

Once in court, the contemporary Soviet defendant, in theory and for the most part in practice, enjoys equality "before the law and the court" (Article 156). In practical terms, the class approach to justice, characteristic of revolutionary Marxist legal theory, was generally abandoned in the late 1930s.[46] Still, it is doubtful that all Soviet citizens do, in fact, enjoy equal standing before the court "regardless of their social" or "official status," for in most legal systems, there often is an unacknowledged differential of treatment based on status, however it may be measured in a particular society.

The citizen's right to defense has also been strengthened in the new Constitution in accordance with previous legislative development. The 1936 Constitution contained a "right to defense" clause, the language of which is nearly the same as that of the current clause (Article 158). But the right to defense is now supported by constitutional recognition of the collegia of defense attorneys and by the right of mass organizations to assign a "social defender" to a case in support of one of its members (Articles 161 and 162).[47] To be sure, the defense bar has existed for a long time, and the institution of citizen defenders is rooted in the earliest days of Soviet legal history.[48] At the same time, the regime evidently has chosen to install these well-known institutions in the new Constitution as reaffirmation of the post-Stalin commitment to the Soviet version of due process. In this context, the "open court" clause (Article 157), a carry-over from the Stalin Constitution, is now more meaningful and less frequently violated.[49]

The judiciary's constitutional monopoly over the administration of justice is explicitly reinforced in a clause that reflects post-Stalin dissolution of the notorious "special boards."[50] The constitutional declaration that "no one can be adjudged guilty of committing a crime and subjected to criminal punishment other than by the verdict of a court" and in accordance with law (Article 160) is both a reminder of and a response to the extralegal traditions of Stalinism as well as one of several "signals" in the current document that there will be no return to what Brezhnev himself called in his May 1977 plenum Report "the illegal repressions" that "darkened" the years following ratification of the 1936 Constitution.[51] Although the clause assuring judicial independence (Article 155) still is liable to the party's contravention, there have been some indications, if difficult to document, that direct party interference in the work of the judiciary has abated since the Stalin years.[52] On the other hand, the individual's relationship to the state also has been at least somewhat clarified following destalinization of the Procuracy in 1955. Article 164 reflects in constitutional law the Procuracy's fully restored responsibility for overseeing compliance with the law—by institutions, organizations, officials, and ordinary citizens—and thus underscores the leadership's concern for administrative legality as part of a long-range effort to raise the public's legal consciousness and build a viable "legal culture" through which the party can insure that both the state and the individual observe the laws that express the party's policies.[53]

Collectively, these constitutional clauses appear to codify a significant stabilization in contemporary legislation and legal practice of the relationship between the individual and the state in Soviet society, particularly in the criminal justice process. Although many of Khrushchev's reforms have been repealed by the Brezhnev leadership, the policy and legislative commitment to "due process" for the criminal defendant has been maintained and even strengthened to some extent through the development of a body of "case law."[54]

With respect to the tiny minority of activist dissidents, however, both the personal security clauses and the formal rights accorded criminal defendants have been sorely abused by the regime, especially since the Sinyavsky–Daniel' trial in early 1966.[55] In the endless stream of dissident cases reported in *samizdat*, there have been numerous recorded violations of the inviolability of the home (Article 55) and of the confidentiality of correspondence and telephone conversations (Article 56). In recent years, incidents of intimidation, mugging, physical assault, and, in a few instances, death under mysterious circumstances—all believed to have been provoked or even perpetrated by KGB personnel in mufti—indicate that for dissidents, the right to legal protection against threats against life and health, property and personal freedom and "honor and dignity" (Article 57) is, for all practical purposes, a dead letter. If, as is often the case, the bureaucratic harassment and administrative actions directed against dissidents have led to criminal prosecution for either a political offense or an ordinary crime, the dissident defendant routinely finds his due process rights violated both in the preliminary investigation and during the subsequent trial. In fact, the constitutional due process clauses in the present document are frequently inverted to the disadvantage of the dissenter. Instead of executing his responsibility to legally prevent the official capriciousness experienced by dissidents (Article 164), the procurator usually shares complicity. Rather than benefit from a strengthened right to defense (Articles 158 and 161), the dissident's right to choose a defense counsel generally is subject to KGB interference and is frequently abridged. Finally, instead of enjoying equality before the law and the court (Article 156), the dissident is classified as a "political case" and subjected systematically to a pattern of discrimination by the legal personnel formally involved and by the party and KGB officials who may discreetly direct the administration of political justice from behind the scenes. In effect, as Harold Berman has aptly pointed out, in political cases, "socialist legality" breaks down into its constituent parts—socialism versus legality.[56]

The dissidents' response to the regime's political justice has been to put up a "legalist" defense, confronting the judges and prosecutors in an orderly fashion with a detailed and documented account of the violations of their due process rights.[57] In their "pretrial motions," their traditional "final word" to the court, and in the postincarceration protests, dissidents caught up in criminal process and their supporters "replay" the law to their persecutors, citing the appropriate code articles, fundamental principles, and even constitutional clauses which the legal cadres and their mentors have violated. The legalist defense has not won any cases for dissenters. But, in using it, political defendants have succeeded repeatedly in indicting the regime and putting it "on trial" in the court of Western public opinion.

It is doubtful that the new Constitution's strengthened emphasis on the "public interest" will discourage significantly the "legalist" defense.

The injunction against injuring one's fellow citizens and the society in the exercise of one's rights (Article 39) and the "rights and duties" clause (Article 59) are neither specially designed for dissidents nor exclusively relevant to criminal law. At best, these additional caveats merely reinforce the constitutional legitimacy of bringing political prosecutions against dissidents who have chosen to exercise their civil rights in contradiction to the officially defined social and political interests (Articles 50 and 51). Still, assuming that the dissident or even an ordinary Soviet citizen failed to perform his duties and damaged the social interest (Articles 59 and 39), there is nevertheless no constitutional mandate in either clause for denying that person the rights of personal security and due process that are incorporated into existing Soviet law on criminal procedure. That is, commission of a political offense does not waive an individual's right to due process as provided under the new Soviet Constitution. Yet what the regime does, in practice in such cases, is another matter. The legalist defense, focusing as it does on procedural violations, may be expected to continue in the future with similar outcomes for both the dissidents and the regime's image abroad.

Participatory Rights. The Soviet citizen's economic rights and civil liberties have been supplemented in the new Constitution by an increased emphasis on his participatory rights. In theory, this is a result of the transition from a proletarian dictatorship to a "state of all the people" (Art. 1). In structural terms, a greater scope and opportunity for citizen involvement in public life is outlined in the political and economic chapters of the Constitution just reviewed. The individual's specific participatory rights may be viewed as giving practical meaning to this enlargement of participatory space in the Soviet system. In general, the participatory rights are to be exercised mainly in the broad process of *policy implementation,* while the opportunity for greater citizen input into the *policy-making* process, as presented in the new Constitution, is confined at most to the arena of local government.

Thus, the new Constitution guarantees to the citizen the general right of public participation (Art. 48); the right to submit proposals and to criticize with impunity the performance of governmental agencies (Art. 49); the right to lodge complaints against public officials and, in some cases, to seek judicial remedy (Art. 58); and the right to sue government agencies and public officials for tort liability incurred by illegal actions causing the citizen–plaintiff damage (Art. 58).[58] In regard to the citizens' slightly increased opportunities for participating in local policymaking, Chapters 14 and 19 of the Constitution codify those post-Stalin changes in state law (*gosudarstvennoye pravo*) associated with the growth of the responsibilities of local soviets and of the powers of their deputies. In the spirit of the "all-people's state," the soviets of "working people's deputies" have been renamed soviets of "people's deputies" (Art. 89).

And, consistent with the increased interest in citizen participation which began under Khrushchev and continues under Brezhnev, the new Draft Constitution was published in June 1977 for nationwide public discussion, as stipulated in its discussion clauses (Arts. 5 and 114).

Participation and Public Discussion   At midpoint in the nationwide public discussion, it was clear that the Draft Constitution was headed for ratification. Before the Draft had even been published, Brezhnev in his address to the May plenum referred to the document several times in a way that seemed to forecast ratification sometime in the fall of 1977. He considered in detail some of the problems involved in "implementation of the new Constitution," and he ended his Report on the reassuring note that "the adoption of the new USSR Constitution will be an important milestone in the country's political history."[59] Brezhnev's confidence about the prospects for ratification soon was echoed in lead editorials and the speeches of senior party leaders at meetings of major party organizations and at sessions of the union republic supreme soviets.[60] In a published interview with a Japanese correspondent several days after the public discussion began, Brezhnev again stressed the importance he attached to ratification, remarking that the "adoption of the new Constitution" would have great significance not only at home but abroad as well.[61]

With ratification thus a foregone conclusion, Brezhnev and the party leadership set the stage for a carefully planned, well-orchestrated public "discussion" of the Draft during the summer and early fall of 1977. Enjoined by Brezhnev to take the lead in drawing "the mass of the working people and representatives of all strata of the population" into discussion and to use the occasion for "the further invigoration of all social life in the country,"[62] subordinate party leaders returned to their constituencies and made organization and leadership of the discussion a matter of highest priority for all party cadres under their jurisdiction.[63] Shortly after the Draft was published, a *Pravda* editorial appropriately characterized the discussion as an "exchange of opinion on the basic questions of the development of our society and state."[64] According to well-informed sources, special arrangements were made at every level of the Soviet system for recording the subsequent comments and suggestions and for forwarding them to the Constitutional Commission for consideration.[65]

Specifically, every party organization, state institution, social organization, etc., was expected to discuss the Draft Constitution and forward its statement and/or proposals for amendment through the appropriate channels to the newly established Secretariat of the USSR Constitutional Commission (the Institute of State and Law of the USSR Academy of Sciences reportedly played a key role in the work of the Secretariat). This

Commission, together with its Editorial Subcommittee, was assigned the tasks of evaluating the amendments proposed in the course of the nationwide discussion and finalizing the Draft for the fall ratification session of the USSR Supreme Soviet.

In addition, prominent scholars, including several jurists, published in the leading newspapers lengthy individual articles presenting what appeared to be their personal views on the Draft Constitution. Evidently, many of those articles, especially those which appeared in June and July, had been written earlier, their authors having received advance copies of the Draft Constitution for this express purpose in the spring prior to the document's publication.

All commentary, both internal and published, was evaluated in generalized form by the Constitutional Commission in the process of revising the published Draft for final ratification in the fall of 1977. Toward this end, the Presidium of the USSR Supreme Soviet renewed the Commission in April 1977 by adding 21 new members to replace the 43 members who had "left" the Commission since its last reorganization in 1966 as a result of death, demotion, retirement, or failure to gain reelection as a Supreme Soviet Deputy. The April additions increased the size of the Commission to its 1966 strength of 75 members, among them various Politburo members, Central Committee secretaries, republic party first secretaries and premiers, officials of all-union state and public organizations, prominent individuals, and the leading legal officials (including Procurator-General R. A. Rudenko, Chairman of the USSR Supreme Court, Judge L. N. Smirnov, and USSR Minister of Justice, V. I. Terebilov).[66] Each member apparently was expected to represent his particular regional or institutional interests in the politics of revision and ratification.

While an analogous "public" discussion preceded ratification of the 1936 Constitution, extensive public "commentary" on various legislative proposals has become, since Stalin's death, a much more common method of involving the average citizen in public affairs. In general, this involvement is circumstantial and very limited—usually to no more than suggesting changes in tone, wording, or emphasis in a given piece of legislation, for which the basic framework already has been set by party authorities. Public discussion has thus become an oft-used leadership technique for mobilizing the population and encouraging citizen participation in policy *implementation*, while the party uses the occasion for a mass political socialization campaign at the same time.[67]

The 1977 constitutional discussion stood apart from previous discussions of legal reform, at least in terms of its scope and duration. But it marks no obvious watershed in either the extent of public political participation or in the quality of regime–society relations. It was extremely doubtful that the public discussion would result in significant changes in the Constitution before its ratification. At most, a number of

major and minor semantic revisions and shifts in stress were anticipated, although attempting to link such changes with the public
discussion was problematic at best in many instances. It is useful to keep
in mind that the proposals or criticisms that appeared in the Soviet
media passed through several cautious and purposive "filters" and,
therefore, reflected the inclinations and political sensitivities of editors,
censors, and various party authorities in addition to those of the given
authors.

At the same time, it was almost surely the case that within general
guidelines laid down by the central party leadership, editors and local
government and party officials exercised a substantial amount of discretion in deciding which views were to be published. It also seems clear
that the scope of what is considered permissible for public discussion in
the Soviet press has grown enormously since Stalin's death, a development to which the 1977 constitutional discussion gave eloquent testimony. To be sure, commentary on certain issues remained proscribed.
Thus, even passing remarks on the Draft articles concerning either the
party's role or Soviet foreign policy were exceedingly rare in the discussion published in the general press. On the other hand, the discussion
brought forth a remarkable variety of proposals on a wide range of
concerns. In a narrow sense, the discussion afforded to individuals and
groups an opportunity for self-advertisement and the promotion of
group or institutional interests that might be advantaged by some
constitutional modification. The discussion also served, however, as a
forum for individuals who were more interested in the Constitution
itself and certain of its provisions. This second category of commentators seemed to take rather seriously the normative potential of the
Constitution, increasingly emphasized by Soviet legal scholars.

In general, then, the discussion of the 1977 Constitution represented
an important indicator, in two major respects. First, the whole of the
discussion for the most part delineated the boundaries of what the party
leadership regards as legitimate for public consumption and consideration. Second, those particular issues that were raised indicate in which
aspects of Soviet social, economic, and political life the party hopes to
stimulate the public's interest, as well as those issues on which the party
is willing to tolerate the public's comments and suggestions. This is the
overarching context in the light of which the published discussion
should be appraised.

In its opening weeks, this discussion was largely ceremonial in nature
and produced little of substance. Major party organizations contributed
laudatory statements to the pages of *Pravda* set aside for the discussion;
Izvestiya's special page was used to accommodate the enthusiastic declarations of different union republic supreme soviets and their presidia.
In the same vein, lengthy articles by major party and government
figures appeared in both newspapers during June, primarily offering a

recitation of various social and economic achievements within their signatories' jurisdictions.[68] At this stage of the discussion, numerous photos displaying the public's "enthusiasm" for the new document appeared throughout the press. And daily the major newspapers carried a page reserved for the nationwide discussion, which typically contained survey articles by correspondents reporting first impressions of ordinary citizens, a supportive statement by a worker and deputy to a local soviet, and often a more lengthy, obviously prepared essay by a scholar on a general theme of the Constitution. Occasionally, brief letters from average citizens were also included.

By the end of June, the discussion had mushroomed into a great volume of citizen activity. *Izvestiya*, for example, reported that it had received over 2.5 million letters on the Draft, while the municipal party organization in Kiev announced that exactly 41,787 groups were discussing the Constitution in that city alone.[69] Meanwhile, below the surface of published comment, more substantive consideration of the Draft already was taking place in every institution and organization throughout the nation. These aggregated comments, suggestions, and recommendations on different constitutional articles began to flow upward through the various hierarchies and, via specially established channels, to the Constitutional Commission in Moscow. Since only a small fraction of such statements could possibly be published or broadcast, the greater part of both the ceremonial and substantive discussions inevitably took place behind the scenes and out of the public's view.

Beginning in July, however, the published commentary took on a decidedly more substantive tone. A recurring pattern of issues, reflecting themes of the leadership, group interests, and individual concerns, began to emerge in the national and regional press. Basically, the nationwide discussion of the Draft seems to have revolved around three sets of issues—what I will call sociopolitical, socialist legality, and "motherhood" issues. Of course, this did not prevent publication of a diverse range of individual concerns: the citizen from Sverdlovsk who suggested adding to the personal property clause (Art. 13) explicit mention of an individual's right to own a car; or the pro-women's liberation letter that advocated that a phrase promising "equal pay for equal work" be given a place in the document (Art. 35).[70] One "old-timer," a member of the party since 1919 and a veteran of the discussion of the 1936 Constitution, simply expressed his pleasure at again having the opportunity to take part in such a great undertaking.[71] But for the most part, these were isolated comments, tangential to the main lines of the discussion.

Worker discipline and productivity and socioeconomic and political participation were the "sociopolitical" issues that generated the greatest volume of attention—from party organizations, government agencies, managers, workers, and the average citizen. Two "socialist legality" issues—"law and order" and civil liberties—stimulated somewhat less voluminous but much sharper, more intense comment. Finally, numerous letters in support of environmental protection and the promotion of science appeared. No one, of course, explicitly opposed either of these, hence the label "motherhood issues."[72] Although these particular communications were marked by greater spontaneity, they were also notably less intense. If, in fact, there were ad hoc "lobbies" operating from below in the course of any part of the discussion, they would appear to have been the diffuse coalitions of specialists and concerned citizens that mobilized in response to these two concerns.

Some of the issues, both within and between categories, seemed to be complementary. A stress on "law and order" dovetailed nicely with support for public participation in peer justice institutions. Between other issues, however, there was natural, and not merely implicit, conflict. Such appeared to be the relationship between the numerous and aggressive "law and order" proposals and the fewer, though more articulate, propositions for strengthened civil liberties. Finally, some of the pro-science suggestions were relevant to production questions. In contrast, advocates of environmentalism seemed to stand alone, neither antagonistic to nor supportive of the other, basic issues in the discussion.

Sociopolitical Issues

At the heart of the "work issue" was the across-the-board concern over the need for improved labor discipline. Focused primarily on the labor discipline clause (Art. 60) and, to a lesser extent, on related ones (Arts. 14 and 40), numerous articles and letters called for recasting this theme with stronger language, greater emphasis, and, sometimes, the assistance of coercive remedies. Brezhnev touched on the general problem at the May plenum, and both *Pravda* and *Komsomol'skaya pravda* cued the issue in lead editorials specifically on Article 60.[73] While the public commentary included advice such as a factory *kollektiv's* suggestion of awarding more medals for good work and the woman engineer's argument that the Constitution must emphasize the correlation between marriage and a positive attitude toward work,[74] the mainstream of the discussion divided between those who recommended writing more moral stimuli into the pertinent articles (usually Art. 60) and those who favored adding more practical language—for example, the Lithuanian engineer who stressed the importance of mechanization and increased worker education "in the struggle to raise the effectiveness of production and the quality of work."[75] In general, most workers' comments inclined toward the moral approach, whereas management personnel seemed more likely to agree with the engineer's emphasis.

At the same time, a number of letter writers proposed a more coercive approach to the problem. One Moscow factory worker favored holding those who violate labor or production discipline "morally and materially responsible before society." In more specific terms, various engineers and skilled workers advocated adding to Article 60 the language of legal sanction. And several writers from the Ukrainian, Lithuanian, Kazakh, and Kirgiz Republics explicitly recommended including the letter and spirit of the extant antiparasite legislation.[76]

In comparison with the "work" issue, the theme of socioeconomic and political participation evoked a much broader spectrum of interests. Concerns ranged from enhancing the individual's participatory rights of making suggestions (Art. 49) and filing complaints (Art. 58) to expanding institutional discretion in correspondence with responsibilities—of enterprises in economic decision-making (Art. 16) and of local soviets with respect to local socioeconomic development (Art. 146).

Institutional participation attracted the attention of middle-level elite members in particular. Both the Irkutsk Regional Party Committee and a Moscow factory manager, for example, offered nearly identical recommendations that supplementary wording be added to Article 16 to ensure that ministries be held accountable for their economic decisions and that they comply with existing legislation permitting greater initiative on the part of the enterprise.[77] (In somewhat related fashion, several letters from workers indicated interest in strengthening the section on worker participation in enterprise management [Article 16 in the Draft, which was moved forward to become Article 8 in the 1977 Constitution], although actual suggestions consisted of minor semantic revisions which seemingly would expand the scope of such participation only slightly.[78])

The status of local soviets—especially their position vis-à-vis higher state organs—drew comment from local party and soviet officials and from prominent jurists as well. Thus, the chairman of the executive committee of a village soviet in the Kirgiz Republic recommended strengthening the language of the clause which empowers deputies to address inquiries to higher-ranking officials or institutions (Art. 105). The official wanted to ensure that the deputy receives a reply which is "clear and timely." The deputies of the Moscow City Soviet, advised by a leading legal scientist, proposed enlarging the scope of the clause that defines the basic jurisdiction of a local soviet (Art. 146). In the same spirit, a party secretary from Tomsk Oblast suggested giving the standing committees of the local soviets a basis in constitutional law.[79]

At the same time, and with the apparent aim of increasing the accessibility of both the local soviets and individual deputies, a number of letters from ordinary citizens "below" concentrated on buttressing the provision of a deputy's accountability to constituents, contained in the basic clause that defines the role of "people's deputy" (Art. 103). For example, a citizen from Odessa proposed writing into the clause a stipulation that deputies be required to appear in person before their constituents and answer questions. Another set of proposals was aimed at ensuring the responsiveness of the executive committees of local soviets by reinforcing the requirements that they report to the local soviet as a body and, in the words of one writer, "before the population and before workers' collectives," too (Art. 149). In a related sense, still another citizen proposed extending the concept of accountability to the people's courts as well, by incorporating specific and demanding terminology in the last paragraph of the judicial election clause (Art. 152), which was largely pro forma as written in the Draft.[80]

Another aspect of the broad issue of participation relates to the citizen's right of criticism (Art. 49). A prominent legal scholar emphasized the importance of this right in a major article published in *Izvestiya*, and the Chairman of the Lithuanian State Committee on Television and Radio Broadcasting proposed before the Lithuanian Supreme Soviet that Article 49 be supplemented to include a requirement that officials also shall be obliged to examine and reply to citizens' proposals and requests which have been "published in the press and broadcast over television and radio."[81] The citizen's right of complaint (Art. 58) likewise received considerable attention. Two citizens wanted Article 58 to specify that "bureaucratism and red tape in the consideration of complaints" were not permitted, while an engineer from Moscow suggested making far more explicit the paragraph outlining the citizen's right to judicial remedy.[82]

Finally, there was some interest in the press in those peer justice institutions that have persisted, if on a reduced scale, since the Khrushchev period. Two writers, one a juridical scholar and the other a factory foreman, recommended that the comrades' court be mentioned specifically in the Constitution. In addition, a lead editorial in *Pravda Ukrainy* elaborately praised the people's voluntary patrols (*druzhinniki*) and suggested politely that they, too, should be included in the new Constitution. Neither institution had been mentioned in the Draft.[83]

"Socialist Legality" Issues   Since he assumed office in 1964, Brezhnev and his associates in the party leadership have consistently stressed the need for "law and order." Not surprisingly, this issue became a popular one in the nationwide discussion of the Draft, with the "rights and duties" and property protection clauses (Arts. 39, 59, 61) serving as special foci of attention. Several jurists and many more workers, including political activists, contributed their thoughts on both the general theme of maintaining "socialist legality" and the more specific problem of reducing economic crime. Even a few veiled, critical references to Soviet dissidents appeared. A. F. Shebanov, a distinguished legal scholar and editor of the leading Soviet law journal, *Sovetskoye gosudarstvo i pravo*, set the tone for this part of the discussion in an article in *Pravda* by characterizing "socialist law and order" as an "organic part of the Soviet way of life." One borough procurator in Moscow proposed amending Article 59 so that the citizen would be obliged "to know" as well as to observe (*soblyudat'*) the Constitution and the laws. In addition, another Moscow lawyer suggested that the citizen should be obliged to "observe" (*soblyudat'*) rather than merely "respect" (*uvazhat'*) the norms of "socialist morality" as well. This apparently was a frequent suggestion, for *Izvestiya* noted that similar recommendations had been received "from many others."[84]

Typical of the more sharply worded letters concerning economic crime was the one which suggested that Article 59 ought to include a requirement that the citizen adopt an implacable attitude toward "the psychology of private property." A number of individuals offered similar revisions of the public property protection clause (Art. 61). Thus, an army officer proposed adding a constitutional prohibition against the use of public housing for "the acquisition of unearned income." In fact, numerous letters addressed to *Izvestiya* from various parts of the Soviet Union recommended that even the personal property clause be revised to include a general prohibition against using such property for "private gain" (Art. 13).[85] Other letters concentrated on the problem of economic crime in the factories, the prime focus of the property protection clause, with suggestions that ranged from the addition of more inspirational language to reworking into a more intimidating form the phrase that threatens legal sanctions against violators of the law.[86]

The polemics between General Secretary Brezhnev and President Carter over human rights and détente during the summer of 1977[87] offered several lower party and government officials the opportunity to publicly rebut Western criticism of Soviet human rights policy, while scoring points on the "law and order" issue at the same time. In a prominent article in *Pravda*, the secretary of a party organization in the Academy of Sciences in Moscow asserted that the new Constitution exposed the "noisy campaign in defense of the rights and freedoms of citizens of the socialist states" as mere "demagogic speculation." Moreover, he recommended greatly strengthening the linkage between rights and duties in Article 59 in language that had some clearly antidissident overtones. A week after this was published, *Pravda* printed a small box on its discussion page that indicated that the party secretary's article had evoked considerable interest from other readers. Two of these responses were published. One, from a metal worker in Khabarovsk, referred to the dissidents as "renegades" and strongly supported the proposal to strengthen the linkage between rights and duties. In the other, a local party secretary from the Armenian SSR observed that it was "no secret that there are still citizens who opposed their personal interest to the interests of society as a whole." He, too, supported his party comrade's recommendation that "it is necessary to strengthen Article 59." Finally, a rather singular communication from Lithuania managed to touch obliquely on all aspects of the "law and order" issue. The writer, a worker and a member of the People's Voluntary Patrol, urged that the latter organization be given the authority and power to deal with "not only violations of the social order" but "antistate acts" as well.[88]

Treatment of the "civil liberties" issue differed from the "law and order" discussion in two respects. First, civil rights was a theme of both the public discussion in the press and the "underground" discussion in *samizdat*, while "law and order" had been a topic only in the approved public forums. Second, the civil rights issue appeared to draw its support primarily from two identifiable "interest groups," one official and institutional in nature, the other decidedly unofficial and associational. In contrast, the supporters of "law and order" seemed far more diffuse.

The public discussion of civil rights had already produced a well-articulated, interrelated set of proposals by the time the "underground" discussion was just beginning to surface midway in the nationwide discussion, although in the long run the scope and depth of the latter undoubtedly will eclipse the former. The jurists as a group dominated the media discussion of civil rights, while various dissidents dealt with the issue in *samizdat*. After only 2 months of constitutional discussion, the combined if independent efforts of jurists, ordinary citizens, and a handful of dissidents had produced commentary on 22 constitutional clauses and had raised more than two dozen specific proposals, questions, and criticisms concerning the status of civil liberties in the new Constitution. This commentary covered a wide spectrum of questions concerning both substantive and procedural due process, and several prominent jurists reopened old debates from the criminal and civil legal reforms of the late 1950s and early 1960s.

The tone of the public discussion of civil rights was set early in the summer by V. M. Savitskiy, the head of the Criminal Procedure Section of the prestigious Institute of State and Law of the USSR Academy of Sciences. He proposed emulating the East European constitutions by adding a new clause on the purpose of Soviet justice, which should be protection of the "Soviet social and state system, the rights and legal interests of citizens, as well as the rights and legal interests of state institutions and enterprises and of social organizations." More substantive concerns over due process centered first on the general socialist legality clause (Art. 4). Savitskiy pointed out that its placement at the beginning of the Constitution emphasized the significance now attached to "socialist legality." A lower-court judge in the Ukraine stressed the positive implications of the article for local soviets in regard to their maintenance of law and order and observance of socialist legality.

Nevertheless, a Moscow "shock worker" argued that the draft clause was inadequate as worded and offered a substitute version that rendered the obligation of the state and its agents to obey the Constitution and the laws in far more explicit terms.[89]

The public discussants refrained from criticizing the clauses on the substantive rights of speech, press, association, and religion (Arts. 50, 51, 52); but dissidents did not. On June 2, 1977, 2 days before the Draft Constitution was published, Andrey Sakharov and a group of dissidents openly appealed to the Soviet government for a "general amnesty of political prisoners" on the occasion of ratification of the forthcoming new Constitution. Implicit was criticism of the regime's practice of prosecuting dissidents for exercising their civil rights in contradiction to the officially construed caveats of the main "bill of rights" clauses (Arts. 50 and 51). The day after the Draft appeared, Sakharov announced that a "strong new wave of repression was under way" in Moscow and in the provinces.[90] On June 8, the "Christian Committee for the Defense of the Rights of Believers of the USSR" issued an appeal to Brezhnev as Chairman of the Constitutional Commission, proposing a three point resolution of the "legal crisis" for Christians that seemed implicit in the restricted "freedom of religion" clause (Art. 52).[91] First, the committee urged deleting from *party* rules the section requiring a party member to oppose "religious survivals." Next, it suggested incorporating a new statement into the party charter that would merely underscore, in principle, the incompatibility of communism and religion. Having thus proscribed religious activities and beliefs for party members, the petition continued, the party leadership should then be in a position to introduce into the text of the new Constitution a provision that allowed "the possibility in principle of religion under communism."[92]

In the published discussion, suggestions for improving operationalization of the substantive aspects of due process dominated. A pensioner and old party veteran from Azerbaidzhan, for example, believed the "right of criticism" clause (Art. 49) was too weak. Remarking that administrative suppression of criticism was dangerous for society and could lead to serious abuses, he argued that it should be not merely "prohibited" but classified as a punishable criminal offense. The well-known reform jurist, Academician M. S. Strogovich, rather eloquently elaborated the merits of the "right of complaint" article (Art. 58) but also proposed additional language for further protecting the citizen's exercise of this right. He pointed out that, under provisions of the Draft, not only did the citizen enjoy the constitutional right to make complaints, but that the state and its officials were constitutionally obligated to respond as well. Most important, he added, the judicial remedy phrase now made it possible for a citizen to turn to the courts not only in criminal and civil matters but also to remedy purely administrative abuses by government officials. Yet, to be quite certain that this important right would not be undermined, Strogovich advised adding to the clause the stipulation that "all state and social organizations shall be categorically prohibited from referring complaints for rectification to those individuals whose actions are the objects of the complaint."[93]

Certain proposals were made, too, to ensure that the structure of the legal system is compatible with the full realization by citizens of their rights. For instance, G. Z. Anashkin, a former judge of the USSR Supreme Court, suggested clarifying the judicial supervision clause (Art. 153) to better ensure that the highest court would exercise effective supervision over the work of subordinate courts. Savitskiy, the criminal procedure specialist and a colleague of Strogovich, advocated substitution of a new text for the collegial decision clause (Art. 154). The revised article would include "complaints against the actions of administrative organs" within the jurisdiction of the courts. In addition, both this jurist and a "cadre inspector" from Sverdlovsk separately argued for the inclusion of more specific language in the "judicial independence" clause (Art. 155).[94] The inspector proposed increasing the responsibility of the judge and the assessors, while Savitskiy offered phrasing that would subject to prosecution anyone trying to pressure the court on a decision. Finally, former Judge Anashkin advocated decentralization of the power of pardon. This power, vested in the Presidium of the USSR Supreme Soviet by the Draft Constitution, should be extended, he argued, to the presidia of the union republic supreme soviets as well (Art. 121). But more interestingly, this jurist also urged that the clause specifying the citizen's right of complaint (Art. 58) be broadened so that individuals in custody could turn to the courts when administratively deprived of their rights by investigators and procurators in the course of the preliminary investigation.[95]

There apparently was great interest in questions of procedural due process. In fact, *Pravda* found itself the target of so many questions from readers that it decided to interview the Deputy Procurator General of the USSR, S. I. Gusev, to obtain the appropriate answers.[96] For example, a number of citizens in various parts of the Soviet Union had written asking for clarification of the right of inviolability of the home (Art. 55). The Procurator replied that, in comparison with the corresponding article in the 1936 Constitution, this right now had been clarified and strengthened, and he added that the appropriate guarantees could be found in the criminal procedure codes of the union republics. Another letterwriter's question on the privacy clause (Art. 56) received a similar response. The most interesting question, however, came from a citizen who noted that the personal inviolability clause (Art. 54) essentially was identical with the same clause in the "Stalin Constitution" and, therefore, wanted to know what guarantees today existed that this provision would not be violated. In reply, Gusev assured the readers that such guarantees were now well established in the criminal codes of the union republics.[97]

In contrast, Anashkin suggested a few days later that the personal inviolability clause needed to be supplemented so that not only arrest but also "detention" could only be carried out subject to the law (Art. 54). On a somewhat different point, Savitskiy strongly recommended combining and greatly strengthening the two clauses which reserved the administration of justice for the courts alone (Arts. 151 and 160). He advised inserting this synthesized statement at the beginning of Chapter 20 on "The Courts and Arbitration" in place of the currently worded Article 151. Finally, the clause providing "open" sessions for all court proceedings, except when exempted by law (Art. 157), elicited the criticism of a dissident who implied that this "right" had been made a mockery of in a recent Ukrainian case and in many other cases where the trials have actually taken place *in camera*.[98]

Possibly the most important point of procedural due process was raised by Savitskiy, the prominent Moscow criminal proceduralist. He ended his aforementioned article in *Izvestiya* with a strong appeal to include an explicit presumption of innocence in the right of defense clause (Art. 158), thereby reopening, no doubt, an old debate between "reformers" and "conservatives" within the Soviet legal profession. In effect, he suggested that this addition would institutionalize a meaningful right of defense in both Soviet criminal process and constitutional law. Furthermore, two letters written by jurists working as defense lawyers argued for strengthening that part of the same article that declares a defendant's right to counsel. The second letter writer, also the secretary of the party organization in a local defenders' collegium in a provincial city, proposed extending the right of defense beyond that presently provided for in Soviet criminal procedure law. He believed that the Constitution should include a citizen's right to defense counsel during the "preliminary investigation" rather than at its conclusion, thereby recalling another major issue in the earlier debates on criminal procedure reform.[99]

"Motherhood" Issues   While the civil rights issue was, for the most part, the province of lawyers and dissidents—two relatively cohesive if diametrically opposed "groups"—the "motherhood" issues seemed to stimulate the interest of ad hoc "lobbies." Nearly everyone, especially those specialists working in the fields, was *for* science or environmentalism. Each issue attracted an extraordinary number of letters from every part of the country and at every level of the media.

Article 26 in the Draft committed the state to ensuring the "planned development of science and the training of scientific cadres" as well as the application of the results to the economy. Scientists and technicians from every field and discipline, from research laboratories, and from teaching departments wrote to endorse this clause and propose an additional phrase or two that would tighten the "link with production," increase funding for basic research, or produce still more cadres.[100] Academicians, university presidents, and lab chiefs flooded the press with their enthusiasm for science, each one taking a few paragraphs to promote a particular specialized interest within the science community. Occasionally, a communication from a nonspecialist appeared but, even in these instances, from someone with an indirect connection with science and technology—for example, letters from a retired colonel and from a journalist polar explorer. Most of the letters, however, were written by highly educated and well-affiliated scientists.[101]

Similarly, concern for the environment proved to be an extremely popular topic in the public discussion. Specialists put forth proposals on this issue, too, but a considerable number of concerned citizens took strong environmentalist positions as well. Letters supporting the protection of nature clustered around elaborating the state's commitment (Art. 18) or strengthening the citizen's obligation (Art. 67). Many letters, such as the one from an official of the "All-Russian Society for the Protection of Nature," suggested relatively mild changes in language, although a few from average citizens advocated the inclusion of legal sanctions. While most writers promoted a general interest in environmentalism, a few seem to have had more special interests in mind, such as the forester who wanted a prohibition against poaching written into the Constitution.[102]

Constitutional Revision and Ratification

Beginning in September 1977, the public discussion of the Draft Constitution began to wind down and gradually resumed the ceremonial character of its opening weeks in June. The quieter, more formal tone was in keeping with the then approaching ratification process, and beyond, the sixtieth anniversary of the Bolshevik Revolution on 7 November. The final communiqué of the USSR Constitutional Commission appeared in the press on 28 September, signalling the official end of the nationwide discussion, both in its public and its internal nonpublic forms. The brief communiqué indicated that the Commission's Secretariat, having coopted numerous specialists from the ranks of government and the universities, had managed to sift through the great volume of communications and that on the basis of its study the Commission was recommending a number of amendments to the Draft Constitution. Speaking as Chairman of the Constitutional Commission, the communiqué reported that Brezhnev had outlined the major amendments that concerned such issues as "the role of labor under socialism, a solicitous attitude toward socialist property, and the further development of socialist democracy."[103]

Just as he had dominated the process of bringing forth the Draft in the spring, Brezhnev presided over every phase of the ratification process in the fall. In sequence, he delivered the Report on the proposed revisions of the Draft before the Presidium of the USSR Supreme Soviet (30 September), a plenary session of the Central Committee (3 October), and finally before the Extraordinary Seventh Session of the Ninth USSR Supreme Soviet, which convened on 4 October, 4 months after the appearance of the Draft and on the twentieth anniversary of *Sputnik*, which inaugurated the space age.

In the Report published the following day throughout the USSR, Brezhnev first recited the statistics of the discussion, then outlined the major proposed amendments to the Draft, and finally, before turning to the foreign reaction to the document, discussed briefly the rejected proposals. Statistically, the whole undertaking was overwhelming: 140 million people had discussed the Draft in several million meetings, all of which had produced approximately 400,000 proposals for amendments to the various articles of the Draft Constitution. Aside from purely stylistic changes, the Constitutional Commission recommended to the Supreme Soviet 150 amendments to, and textual clarifications in, 110 individual articles plus the addition of one new constitutional article. In outlining the major amendments, it was clear that Brezhnev and the leadership were responding to the sociopolitical issue of participation in the nationwide discussion as well as to the more amorphous theme of strengthening social discipline that tended to cut across the sociopolitical, "socialist legality," and, to a lesser degree, even the "motherhood" issues of the public discussion.

Finally, Brezhnev in his Report dealt swiftly with the proposals found to be "incorrect" and therefore rejected, including proposals for egalitarianism in wages and pensions, for eliminating or sharply curbing the use of the garden plot, for the abolition of the federal system and creation of a unitary state, and the "profoundly erroneous" proposals advocating the withering away of the state and the assumption by the party of its functions. Most of the offending proposals must have reached the Constitutional Commission through internal channels because few such proposals had been permitted to pass through the press "filters" and surface in the public phase of the discussion. After a prefunctory and pro-forma 3-day discussion of Brezhnev's Report and the revised Draft, the Supreme Soviet ratified the new Soviet Constitution on October 7, 1977, which henceforth became "Constitution Day," and the final text of the document was published in the major newspapers throughout the country the next day.[104]

The final text revealed the dozens of changes, stylistic and substantive, from the Preamble throughout all 9 parts and 21 chapters of the document. Although few of the amendments substantially altered the Draft, the numerous changes nonetheless provided further insight into the state of Soviet "public opinion" and the points of its congruence with the party's priorities. Of the major issues that arose during the public discussion, only the reform-minded jurists' proposals on civil liberties were generally ignored by the party and the constitutional draftsmen in the revision process. At the same time, while a number of the changes were indirectly responsive to the pro-discipline impetus behind the countervailing "law and order" issue, the many illiberal proposals for strengthening the nexus between "rights and duties" were disregarded and the "linkage" clauses remained unchanged (Arts. 39 and 59).

Nearly all of the changes contributed to the further perfecting of the constitutional "housing" designed by the party to encompass the Soviet system, but generally speaking, they fell into two broad categories. One set of changes tended to enlarge the interior political space or the participatory domain within the system for both individuals and institutions; while the other set of changes tended to further strengthen and reinforce the external, binding structure of the system by sealing off cracks and filling in gaps in the control and regulatory processes. The two tendencies complemented each other, the latter effecting greater system-closure, while the former pointed in the direction of "opening" up to a greater degree certain intrasystem relationships and interactions.

Although some of these changes bore no observable relationship to the issue patterns discernible in the public discussion, they were apparently responsive to the internal phase of the constitutional discussion. For instance, there was little or no public commentary to foreshadow the amendments to the party hegemony clause (Art. 6), the peaceful coexistence clause (Art. 28), or the clause on state arbitration (Art. 163). In perhaps the most startling change, the party hegemony clause was supplemented by the amendment—"*All party organizations operate within the framework of the USSR Constitution*"—raising the spectre of "limited government" in the Soviet Union (Art. 6). The full construal of the intended meaning of this interesting change will necessarily have to await the process of constitutional implementation. Less surprising and far less mysterious was the inclusion in the peaceful coexistence clause of the propaganda ploy of committing the USSR to "*general and complete disarmament*" (Art. 28). This is a familiar Soviet phrase that raises the question of why it was left out of the Draft in the first place.

While these two revisions probably came about as the result of intraelite discussion of the Draft, the third example tended to reflect Soviet-style group politics. The state arbitrators, seeing themselves primarily as specialists in settling intrasystem economic disputes, apparently preferred to be in the economic rather than the legal chapter of the Draft. Lobbying as a group through internal channels, they achieved at best a compromise. The arbitration clause remained where it was originally in the Draft, but was amended to stipulate that the basic operation of the arbitration system would be defined by an all-union statute (Art. 163). This, in turn, opened up new vistas for future lobbying efforts by the arbitrators to amend their governing statute in the direction of changing their de facto status in the constitutional order.

However, more often than expected, changes in the final text of the Constitution of 1977 were traceable to the general themes that shaped the public portion of the discussion of the Draft. Basically, the constitutional draftsmen revised and amended the Draft in response to the very widely expressed desire for broader and more dependable opportunities for both individual and institutional participation in the process of implementing party policy and state legislation, as well as to the intensely felt demands for more and stricter discipline throughout the society. This twofold response to public opinion can be seen initially in the changes and emendations to the Preamble. The advocates of increased participation undoubtedly appreciated the addition of the open-ended concept of *communist social self-government*, a holdover from Khrushchev's days, which carries with it the implication of comrades' courts, people's voluntary patrols, people's control commissions, and other vehicles of mass participation. Similarly, the social disciplinarians were no doubt pleased with the *strengthened linkage* concept by which citizens' "rights and liberties" were interconnected not merely with the performance of their "civic responsibility" as in the Draft Preamble but with *"their duties and responsibility to society"* in the final text. To drive the point home, the *linkage* concept was also inserted in the revised conclusion of the Preamble that *"proclaim*[s]" the linkage of rights and duties among other ideas as the core of the new Constitution.[105]

The Participation Amendments

Most of the participation-oriented amendments to the Draft Constitution appear to have been designed to have an effect on both mass and elite participatory structures and processes, as well as on the accountability procedures by which constituent groups at different levels in the system obtain knowledge of their elected representatives' actions. Essentially, these changes were addressed more to the quantitative aspects of participation (how much can occur) rather than the qualitative side of the issue (how effective it may be). The increased participatory emphasis was dramatically keynoted in the opening articles of the final document as the expanded worker's participation clause was moved up from the economic chapter (Art. 16 of the Draft) to the political chapter (Art. 8 of the Constitution). The theoretical increase of mass participation in lower-level economic decision making was paralleled by the one new article added to the Draft that constitutionally legitimated the citizen's right of indirect participation in local policymaking by elevating to full constitutional status the concept of the *"voters' mandates"* (Art. 102). In addition, the clause on the citizen's general right of participation in national policymaking was recast and strengthened, particularly with reference to the increased emphasis on the mass public's right to participate *"in the discussion and adoption of laws and decisions of nationwide and local importance"* (Art. 48). This tendency was complemented by the increased attention to the concept of the nation-wide *"referendum"* (Arts. 108, 115, and 137), and the empowering of the USSR Supreme Soviet to submit for nationwide discussion not just "draft laws" but also *"other very important questions of state life"* (Art. 114).

Governmental bodies, as well as voters and workers, also received enhanced constitutional attention to their participatory status. The pow-ers of local soviets, autonomous republics, and union republics were all enlarged to include ensuring *"comprehensive economic and social develop-ment"* on their territories (Arts. 147, 83, and 77). In addition, each governmental strata, respectively, gained greater supervisory authority over enterprises and other institutions of higher subordination on its territory, all of which represented a commitment by the Soviet leader-ship to a slightly greater degree of decentralization by means of creating considerably more decision-making space for subordinate governmental levels within the system (Arts. 147, 83, 77, and 142).

Making the various representational strata of the government more accessible and accountable to their respective constituencies, at least in terms of periodic information about their activities, was the other aspect of the intensified stress on the participatory motif. As a result, a people's deputy is now obliged to report on his work not just to his constituents but *"also to the collectives and public organizations that nominated him as a candidate for Deputy"* (Art. 107). In turn, the executive committees of the local soviets must not only report to their soviets at least once a year but *"to meetings of labor collectives and of citizens at their places of residence"* as well (Art. 149). Another amendment enjoins the *"Soviets of People's Deputies and the agencies created by them [to] systematically inform the population about their work and the decisions they adopt"* (Art. 94). Even judges and people's assessors or cojudges have now been explicitly required to *"report"* on their work from time to time to "the voters or the agencies that elected them" (Art. 152).

Ascending the bureaucratic hierarchy, the higher administrative bod-ies as well were made, theoretically at least, more accountable to the legislative branch of government. This was accomplished by amending the clause on standing committees of the USSR Supreme Soviet to read:

> *The committee's recommendations are subject to mandatory consideration by state and public agencies, institutions and organizations. Reports are to be made to the committees, within established time periods, on the results of such consideration or on the measures taken* (Art. 125).

Last, but hardly least, the right of criticism clause (Art. 49) was significantly amended in a way that bridged both the themes of participation and discipline in the discussion of the Draft Constitution. To better facilitate and protect citizen participation and to help ensure official adherence to the requirements of administrative legality, the existing prohibition against officials persecuting their critics was noticeably strengthened to read: *"Persons who persecute others for criticism will be called to account"* (Art. 49). If faithfully executed, this amendment alone could well prove to be the most important revision of the Draft in terms of making the Soviet system somewhat more responsive to the concerns of the individual citizen. Most likely, however, the "criticism" clause probably contains an implied "catch" to the effect that only "constructive" criticism will be afforded constitutional protection from retaliatory persecution. Under the best of circumstances, reasonable men will differ over what constitutes "constructive" criticism in a given situation; therefore, a safe conjecture would be that generally neither dissidents nor even persistent "whistleblowers" should expect too much from the amended safeguards in this clause.

New Constitutional Duties

Considerably less ambiguous are the additional constitutional directives addressed to the Soviet citizen in his various roles. On top of the maze of overlapping obligations imposed on the citizen in the Draft Constitution, amendments provided for nine new or reinforced duties. These can be grouped together as the party's and the draftsmen's response to the strongly articulated and widespread demands for more discipline of all kinds cutting across the three sets of issues that had dominated the nationwide public discussion. Although largely rhetorical and frequently unenforceable, these new constitutional burdens qualify the Soviet citizen as one of the most constitutionally bound individuals of modern times.

In the final, official text of the 1977 Constitution, children are enjoined to *"help"* their parents (Art. 66), residents to *"take good care"* of their housing (Art. 44), and all able-bodied persons are expected to engage in *"socially useful labor"* (Art. 60). Individuals may now only use their personal property (Art. 13) or engage in "individual labor activity" in the *"interests of society"* (Art. 17), and those people assigned garden plots are directed *"to make rational use"* of them (Art. 13). All adults are cautioned against using socialist property for *"selfish purposes"* (Art. 10), while collective farmers *"are obliged to use land effectively"* (Art. 12), and workers are instructed *"to take good care of the people's property"* (Art. 61). In addition, everyone's civic duty to help save historical monuments has been semantically reinforced and enshrined in a separate article in the final text of the new Constitution (Art. 68). Finally, all citizens are put on notice that their exercise of the civil liberties of speech, press, and assembly must now not only contribute to the "strengthening" but also to the "*developing*" of the socialist system as well (Art. 50).

Aside from the new constitutional strictures on land use, the "motherhood" issues of science (Art. 26) and environmentalism (Arts. 18 and 67) received only nominal attention in the constitutional revision process, despite the avalanche of proposals on these issues. "*Water resources*" were brought under the umbrella of environmental protection (Art. 18), the citizen's "protective" duties became the sole focus of a single constitutional article (Art. 67), and the state's vast legislative and executive powers were marginally amended to include environmental and science legislation among its myriad other responsibilities (Art. 73, Sec. 5; and Art. 131, Sec. 7).

Succinctly summarizing the process of revising the Draft into the new Soviet Constitution of 1977, the party has skillfully exploited the existing illiberal currents of public opinion to justify the near completion of its theoretical closure of the Soviet system while constitutionally acknowledging the participatory impulse "from below" through incremental adjustments and marginal changes, the realization of which awaits implementation.

The Constitution as "Magic Wall"

The number of individuals who participated in the discussion and the nature of many of their suggestions indicated that many Soviet citizens are attentive to—and may even take seriously—the potentially prescriptive aspects of their new Constitution. While their perceptions may prove to be unjustified, they do serve, implicitly, as "public support" for the more normative Constitution envisioned by the "constitutionalist" scholars. More important, the extent to which the 1977 Constitution does function as a prescriptive document will provide a benchmark for measuring the scope and limits of change in the Soviet polity.

In a more fundamental sense, however, the new Constitution still represents the sedimentation of six decades of Soviet rule. This Constitution is a distillation of that cumulative experience, although it also serves to codify the shifting emphasis from rule by force to rule by law that has emerged since Josef Stalin's death a quarter of a century ago. The result is a Soviet-style *Rechtsstaat*, a legal framework through which the party can govern its vast domain without irrevocably limiting its ultimate power of action. In essence, the Brezhnev regime has created in constitutional form a "magic wall" that conceals the "close cohabitation between wide stretches of certainty for mass man's daily living conditions and unheard of areas of oppression [and] lawlessness."[106]

Notes

[1]*Pravda* (Moscow), May 25, 1977, p. 1; and *ibid,* June 17, 1977, p. 1 For the Constitutional Commission's brief communiqué, see *ibid.,* May 24, 1977, p. 1. The Draft was subsequently published on 4 June throughout the national and regional press. See the translation in *Current Digest of the Soviet Press* (hereafter *CDSP*), June 29, 1977, pp. 1–11, 22.

Podgorny did not appear in person before the Supreme Soviet; his "resignation" was made in his behalf. In addition, the May plenum also relieved Konstantin Katushev from his post as Central Committee Secretary supervising relations with ruling Communist parties. He was replaced by K. V. Rusakov, in a change apparently unrelated to the decision to publish the new Constitution.

[2]The growing constitutional discussion in short order subsumed both the campaign preceding the local soviet elections, scheduled for 19 June, and the socialist competitions in honor of the then forthcoming sixtieth anniversary celebration. See *Pravda,* June 20, 1977, for coverage of the elections. For a typical "socialist emulation" pledge by a factory in response to the constitutional discussion, see *Ekonomicheskaya gazeta* (Moscow), no. 28, 1977, p. 4. On the constitutional revision and ratification process, see *Pravda* and *Izvestiya* (Moscow), September 28–October 8, 1977. The final text of the new Constitution appeared in the issues for October 8, 1977.

For a translation of the final, official text of the new Soviet Constitution of 1977, see *CDSP,* November 9, 1977, pp. 1–13. In order to assist the reader, the translator's italics and brackets have been retained to indicate where, respectively, additions to and deletions from the earlier Draft text were made in the final document.

[3]On the drafting, discussion, and ratification of the 1936 Constitution see S. I. Rusinova and V. A. Ryanzhin, eds., *Sovetskoye konstitutsionnoye pravo* (Soviet Constitutional Law) (Leningrad: Izdatel'stvo Leningradskogo Universiteta, 1975), pp. 75–79. Since December 5, 1965, "Constitution Day" has also been the occasion for an annual silent-protest demonstration by human rights dissidents in Moscow's Pushkin Square. See *A Chronicle of Human Rights in the USSR,* no. 23–24 (October–December 1976), p. 10.

[4]See Robert C. Tucker, "Stalinism as Revolution from Above," and Moshe Lewin, "The Social Background of Stalinism," both in *Stalinism: Essays in Historical Interpretation,* ed. Robert C. Tucker (New York: Norton, 1977), pp. 77–108 and 111–136, respectively.

[5]See the 1936 Constitution, Articles 1, 2, 7, 9, and 10. For an English translation see Harold J. Berman and John B. Quigley, Jr., eds., *Basic Laws on the Structure of the Soviet State* (Cambridge: Harvard University Press, 1969), pp. 3–28.

[6]For a summary of the constitutional revision process from World War II through 1970, see John N. Hazard, "Soviet Law and Justice," in *The Soviet Union under Brezhnev and Kosygin,* ed. John W. Strong (New York: Van Nostrand, 1971), esp. pp. 109–114. For an authoritative account by a leading Soviet legal scholar of the constitutional proposals under discussion prior to the creation of Khrushchev's constitutional commission, see P. S. Romashkin, "New Stage in the Development of the Soviet State," *Sovetskoye gosudarstvo i pravo* (Moscow)

(October 1960), pp. 31–40. A *CDSP* translation of this important article is reprinted in Jan F. Triska, ed., *Constitutions of the Communist Party–States* (Stanford: Hoover Institution, 1968), pp. 77–87. Several of the major ideas outlined by Romashkin in 1960 are included in the Constitution ratified 17 years later. For a Western analysis of the various proposals for constitutional revision before the creation of Khrushchev's commission in 1962, see George Ginsburgs, "A Khrushchev Constitution: Projects and Prospects," *Osteuropa Recht* (Cologne) (August 1962), pp. 191–214.

[7]See Jerome S. Gilison, "Khrushchev, Brezhnev, and Constitutional Reform," *Problems of Communism* (September–October 1972), esp. pp. 75–78.

[8]See Hazard, "Soviet Law and Justice," in Strong, *op. cit.*, p. 111.

[9]L. I. Brezhnev, "Report of the CPSU Central Committee and the Immediate Tasks of the Party in Home and Foreign Policy," *XXVth Congress of the CPSU* (Moscow: Novosti, 1976), pp. 101–102. For the "echo" in the legal press, see for example, the unsigned lead article, "The 25th Congress of the CPSU: Further Development of the Soviet State, Democracy, and Law," *Sovetskoye gosudarstvo i pravo*, no. 5 (May 1976), esp. pp. 7–8.

[10]Shortly after publication of the Draft Constitution, Politburo member G. V. Romanov, First Secretary of the Leningrad Obkom and a member of the Constitutional Commission, reported that the Draft had been discussed "repeatedly" in the Politburo, Central Committee Secretariat, Constitutional Commission, and various state institutions. To some extent, he attributed the length of the drafting process to the thoroughness with which the constitutional principles were discussed in these different forums. He noted that many well-known Soviet scholars were consulted during the drafting process, including historians, jurists, philosophers, and sociologists, as well as representatives of the mass social organizations. At the same time, he also made specific reference to Brezhnev's "initiative [in the decision] to approve (*prinyat'*) this historic document in the year of the 60th anniversary of the Great October. . . ." See *Leningradskaya pravda* (Leningrad), June 9, 1977, p. 2.

[11]For translations of the 1918 and 1924 Constitutions, see Triska, *op. cit.*, pp. 2–36.

[12]*Pravda*, June 5, 1977, pp. 1–2. Brezhnev's Report was published verbatim in the national and regional press on June 5, one day after publication of the Draft Constitution. For a translation, see *CDSP*, July 6, 1977, pp. 6–10.

[13]For environmental legislation, see, for example, *Fundamentals of Legislation of the USSR and the Union Republics* (Moscow: Progress Publishers, 1974), pp. 15–16 and 39–40. Also, see Zigurds L. Zile, "Soviet Struggle for Environmental Quality: The Limits of Environmental Law Under Central Planning," in *Contemporary Soviet Law: Essays in Honor of John N. Hazard*, ed. Donald D. Barry *et al.* (The Hague: Martinus Nijhoff, 1974), pp. 124–157.

For recent Soviet perspectives on international law, see G. I. Tunkin, *Theory of International Law*, trans. William E. Butler (Cambridge: Harvard University Press, 1974), especially Chapters 2 and 3. Tunkin is a former diplomat and the leading Soviet scholar on international law.

On labor legislation, see the Fundamental Principles of Labor Legislation, in *Fundamentals of Legislation of the USSR*, p. 91. On the labor law reforms generally, see A. K. R. Kiralfy, "Soviet Labor Law Reform Since Stalin," in *Contemporary Soviet Law*, pp. 158–74.

[14]Nikita S. Khrushchev, "The Crimes of the Stalin Era—Special Report to the 20th Congress of the Communist Party of the Soviet Union," *The New Leader*, supplement, July 16, 1956, p. s63.

[15]Although, as we shall see, this is not the case with respect to the Soviet Union's political, religious, ethnic, and cultural dissidents. See M. S. Strogovich, "On the Rights of the Individual in Soviet Criminal Procedure," *Sovetskoye gosudarstvo i pravo*, no. 10 (October 1976), pp. 73–81, and translated in *Soviet Review* 18, no. 2 (Summer 1977), pp. 3–17. On civil process, see Donald D. Barry, "The Specialist in Soviet Policy-Making: The Adoption of a Law," *Soviet Studies* (October 1964), pp. 152–165; and Whitmore Gray, "Soviet Tort Law: The New Principles Annotated," *University of Illinois Law Forum* (Spring 1964), pp. 180–211.

[16]On the duality of legality and extralegality, see Robert Sharlet, "Stalinsim and Soviet Legal Culture," in *Stalinism*, pp. 155–179.

[17]The "state law" school continues to be heavily represented in the Soviet academic legal establishment, although the late Professor A. I. Lepeshkin was probably its most influential spokesman. His *Kurs Sovetskogo gosudarstvennogo prava* (A Treatise on Soviet State Law), vol. 1 (Moscow: Yuridicheskaya literatura 1961), was a basic reference in the debate that emerged in the early 1960s. The early leader of the "constitutionalists" was the late V. F. Kotok, who broke new ground in contemporary Soviet jurisprudence with his introductory essay to the book he edited with N. P. Farberov, *Konstitutsionnoye pravo sotsialisticheskikh stran* (Constitutional Law of the Socialist States) (Moscow: Akademiya Nauk SSSR, 1963). Kotok's article was sharply criticized in the legal press and at a special meeting of the faculty and graduate students of the Department of State Law and Soviet Construction at Moscow University Law School during the academic year 1963–1964. The next major position statement of the "constitutional law" school was I. E. Farber and V. A. Rzhevskiy's *Voprosy teorii Sovetskogo konstitutsionnogo prava* (Theoretical Questions of Soviet Constitutional Law), no. 1 (Saratov: Saratovskiy yuridicheskiy institut, 1967). For a subsequent statement of the orthodox position, see B. V. Shchetinin, *Problemy teorii Sovetskogo gosudarstvennogo prava* (Theoretical Problems of Soviet State Law), part I (Moscow: Yuridicheskaya literatura, 1969), and part II, published in 1974. Compare this to the latest and most authoritative statement of the "constitutionalists," Rusinova and Ryanzhin, *Sovetskoye konstitutsionnoye pravo, op. cit.* For an account of the unfavorable reception that this last study received at a special meeting of legal scholars, held under the auspices of the Department of State Law and Soviet Construction at Moscow University Law School in February 1976, see N. A. Mikhaleva, "The Discussion of the Book *Soviet Constitutional Law*," *Vestnik Moskovskogo Universiteta: Pravo* (Moscow) (July–August 1976), pp. 86–90. The rapporteur is a member of the "state law" school. For a Western article which points out the Rusinova and Ryanzhin volume's implications for the process of Soviet constitutional reform, see Christopher Osakwe's review essay in *Tulane Law Review* 51 (1977), pp. 411–22.

[18]In spite of the already noted hostile reaction to the constitutionalists' latest statement, the author was told by a reliable source that even before publication of the new Draft Constitution, several leading representatives of the "old guard" had conceded privately, albeit reluctantly, that the concept of *constitutional law* had won the day in Soviet jurisprudence. If this in fact is the case, the "victory"

should soon be consolidated by changes in law school curricula, and, eventually, the disciplinary/departmental name "state law" should be at least supplemented with the phrase "constitutional law."

[19]For a conceptual analysis of metapolicy and ad hoc action as legal policy, see Robert Sharlet, "Soviet Legal Policymaking: A Preliminary Classification," in a special issue edited by Harry M. Johnson, "Social System and Legal Process," *Sociological Inquiry* 47, nos. 3–4 (1977), esp. pp. 212–214 and 218–219.

[20]See, for example, V. M. Chkhikvadze *et al.*, eds., *Politicheskaya organizatsiya Sovetskogo obschchestva* (The Political Organization of Soviet Society) (Moscow: Nauka, 1967); and M. N. Marchenko, *Demokraticheskiye osnovy politicheskoy organizatsii Sovetskogo obshchestva* (The Democratic Principles of the Political Organization of Soviet Society) (Moscow: Izdatel'stvo Moskovskogo Universiteta, 1977).

[21]In a seminal essay written nearly a decade ago, Richard Lowenthal argued that advancing socioeconomic modernization seems to make this shift inevitable. See his "Development versus Utopia in Communist Policy," in *Change in Communist Systems*, ed. Chalmers Johnson (Stanford: Stanford University Press, 1970), pp. 33–116. For his recent analysis of the dilemmas that modernization creates for one-party systems, see "The Ruling Party in a Mature Society," in *Social Consequences of Modernization in Communist Socieities*, ed. Mark Field (Baltimore: The Johns Hopkins University Press, 1976), pp. 81–118.

[22]Article 9 reads: "Further development of socialist democracy constitutes the basic direction in the evolution of the political system of Soviet society: [that is] the ever wider participation of working people in the management of the affairs of society and government; the improvement of the state apparatus; a heightening of the activeness of public organizations; the strengthening of the people's control; the reinforcement of the legal foundations of state and public life; the expansion of publicity; [and] the continual regard for public opinion." (Author's translation.)

[23]See Roger E. Kanet, "The Rise and Fall of the 'All-People's State': Recent Changes in the Soviet Theory of the State," *Soviet Studies* (July 1968), pp. 81–93. Years of doctrinal paring have stripped the Khrushchevian concept of its emphasis on the "withering away" of the state through the transfer of selected state functions to mass organizations of "social self-government." The contemporary concept merely envisions limited democratization of the Soviet political system through a somewhat greater participation of mass social organizations as collective entities. See, for example, B. N. Topornin, "The All-People's State and Socialist Democracy," *Pravovedeniye* (Leningrad) (March–April 1975), pp. 7–17.

[24]See Stalin Constitution, Art. 130.

[25]See Peter H. Juviler, *Revolutionary Law and Order: Politics and Social Change in the USSR* (New York: Free Press, 1976), pp. 85–116.

[26]See Stalin Constitution, Arts. 126 and 141.

[27]Cf. *ibid.*, Arts. 4–12.

[28]I am indebted to Professor John Hazard of Columbia Law School for alerting me to this change of wording as well as for several other helpful suggestions in connection with this article. For a complementary analysis of the new Soviet Constitution, see his "A Constitution for 'Developed Socialism,' " in *Social Engineering Through Law in the Soviet Union*, George Ginsburgs, Peter B. Maggs, and Donald D. Barry, eds.(Leiden: A. W. Sijthoff, forthcoming).

[29]Cf. Stalin Constitution, Art. 11.

[30]See *Sotsialisticheskoye sorevnovaniye v SSSR 1918–1964* (Socialist Competition in the USSR, 1918–1964) (Moscow: Profizdat, 1965), pp. 127–140 and Part Three. Also see Erik P. Hoffmann, "The 'Scientific Management' of Soviet Society," *Problems of Communism* (May–June 1977), pp. 59–67; and Robert F. Miller, "The Scientific–Technical Revolution and the Soviet Administrative Debate," in *The Dynamics of Soviet Politics,* eds. Paul Cocks, Robert V. Daniels, and Nancy Whittier Heer (Cambridge: Harvard University Press, 1976), pp. 137–55.

[31]Cf. Stalin Constitution, Art. 12. See also R. Beermann, "The Parasite Law in the Soviet Union," *British Journal of Criminology* 3 (1962), pp. 71–80.

[32]See "The 1961 Programme of the Communist Party of the Soviet Union," in *Soviet Communism: Programs and Rules,* ed. Jan F. Triska (San Francisco: Chandler, 1962), esp. Part Two, pp. 68–122.

[33]*Ibid.,* pp. 35–39 and 63–67.

[34]Article 29 includes "Basket Three," or the human rights principles, of the Helsinki document. Cf. "Conference on Security and Cooperation in Europe: Final Act," *The Department of State Bulletin* (Washington, D.C.: Government Printing Office, September 1, 1975), pp. 323–350. From the Soviet perspective, these principles must be looked at within the context of Part II of the Constitution, on "The State and the Individual." The "Brezhnev doctrine" is covered in Article 30 in the guise of "comradely mutual assistance."

[35]Cf. Stalin Constitution, Art. 14.

[36]Cf. *ibid.,* Arts. 118–122.

[37]In a June 1977 session at the Kennan Institute (Washington, D.C.) devoted to a discussion of the Draft Constitution, Professor Moshe Lewin characterized the cluster of economic and other rights as descriptive of a "super welfare state," based on an obligation to work. For the details of Soviet health care legislation, see the Fundamental Principles of Health Legislation of 1969 in *Fundamentals of Legislation of the USSR,* pp. 62–88. The new article on old age maintenance has been elaborated in practice by a developing body of pension law. See, for example, M. L. Zakharov, ed., *Sovetskoye pensionnoye pravo* (Soviet Pension Law) (Moscow: Yuridicheskaya literatura, 1974).

[38]See Stalin Constitution, Art. 131. On the contemporary problem of economic crime, see, for example, Gregory Grossman, "The 'Second Economy' of the USSR," *Problems of Communism* (September–October 1977), pp. 25–40; and Valery Chalidze, *Criminal Russia: Essays on Crime in the Soviet Union* (New York: Random House, 1977), Chs. 8–10.

[39]Cf. Stalin Constitution, Arts. 125–126.

[40]Cf. *ibid.,* Art. 130.

[41]I believe it is misleading to describe the "linkage" of rights and duties as the regime's "answer" to the dissidents. For an argument in this direction, see "New USSR Draft Constitution," *International Commission of Jurists Review* (Geneva) (June 1977), p. 30. Rather, the nexus of rights and duties is a general principle in contemporary Soviet legislation. See, for example, the Land Fundamentals, Art. 11, and the Civil Fundamentals, Art. 5, in *Fundamentals of Legislation of the USSR,* pp. 15–16 and 153–154, respectively.

[42]*Fundamentals of Legislation of the USSR,* pp. 271–99. See also John Gorgone, "Soviet Jurists in the Legislative Arena: The Reform of Criminal Procedure, 1956–1958," *Soviet Union,* vol. 3, part 1 (1976), pp. 1–35; and Harold J. Berman's

Introduction to Berman and James W. Spindler, eds., *Soviet Criminal Law and Procedure: The RSFSR Codes*, 2nd ed. (Cambridge: Harvard University Press, 1972), esp. pp. 47–70 and 84–89.

[43]See Christopher Osakwe, "Due Process of Law Under Contemporary Soviet Criminal Procedure," *Tulane Law Review* 50, pp. 266–317. Nine such "cases" were translated by Harold Berman in *Soviet Statutes and Decisions* (Summer 1965), pp. 5–41. Numerous others are translated in John N. Hazard, William E. Butler, and Peter B. Maggs, eds., *The Soviet Legal System: Fundamental Principles and Historical Commentary*, 3rd ed. (Dobbs Ferry, N.Y.: Oceana, 1977), Ch. 7.

[44]Cf. Stalin Constitution, Art. 127. See also the Criminal Procedural Fundamentals, Art. 6, in *Fundamentals of Legislation of the USSR*, p. 274; the RSFSR Criminal Procedure Code, Art. 11, in Berman, *Soviet Criminal Law and Procedure*, p. 209; Berman's analysis of the personal inviolability articles in *ibid.*, pp. 48–50; and the Bortkevich case in Hazard *et al.*, *The Soviet Legal System*, pp. 112–113.

[45]See Stalin Constitution, Art. 102. The "special courts" were transportation courts with jurisdiction over criminal offenses that took place on the railway and water transport system. They were abolished in the post-Stalin era and are not mentioned in the Fundamental Principles of Legislation on the Court System. See *Fundamentals of Legislation of the USSR*, Art. 1, p. 137. On contemporary "special courts" which have special legal personnel and jurisdiction over individuals engaged in classified work, see Yury Luryi, "The Admittance of the Defence Counsel to Common Criminal (Non-Political) Cases in Soviet Criminal Procedure as the Most Essential Part of the Right of the Defendant for Defence" (Paper read at the annual meeting of the American Association for the Advancement of Slavic Studies [AAASS], St. Louis, Missouri, October 7, 1976).

[46]On the class approach to justice and its abandonment, see John N. Hazard, "Reforming Soviet Criminal Law," *Journal of Criminal Law and Criminology* (July–August 1938), pp. 157–169.

[47]Cf. Stalin Constitution, Art. 111. For analysis of the changing status of the Soviet defense counsel, see Jean C. Love, "The Role of Defense Counsel in Soviet Criminal Proceedings," *Wisconsin Law Review*, no. 3 (1968), pp. 806–900; and Lawrence M. Friedman and Zigurds L. Zile, "Soviet Legal Profession: Recent Developments in Law and Practice," *ibid.*, no. 1 (1964), pp. 32–77. The mass organizations may also assign a "social accuser" to assist a procurator in a criminal case. For a brief analysis of both social accusers and defenders, see Berman, *Soviet Criminal Law and Procedure*, pp. 69–70.

[48]See John N. Hazard, *Settling Disputes in Soviet Society: The Formative Years of Legal Institutions* (New York: Columbia University Press, 1960), pp. 34–35, 47–49, 159–162.

[49]The "open court" clause specifies: "The examination of cases in all courts is open. The hearing of cases in closed court is permitted only in instances provided for by law, and then with the observance of all the rules of judicial procedure." (Author's translation.)

[50]Harold J. Berman, *Justice in the USSR*, rev. ed. (Cambridge: Harvard University Press, 1963), p. 70.

[51]*Pravda*, June 5, 1977, p. 1.

[52]Except for "political" cases, in which *partiynost'* (party-mindedness) routinely supersedes *zakonnost'* (legality), the following statement by a Soviet university lecturer seems to characterize the administration of justice in the

post-Stalin period: "The party organs oversee the selection, placement, and ideological education of juridical cadres. But, at the same time, any kind of interference in the administration of justice in specific cases is absolutely ruled out." *Pravda*, August 19, 1977, p. 3. See also the author's review of Samuel Kucherov's *The Organs of Soviet Administration of Justice* in *Columbia Law Review* 71, no. 7 (November 1971), esp. pp. 1346–1348.

[53]See Stalin Constitution, Art. 113. The corresponding passage in the 1977 Constitution is more specific and emphatic and appears at the beginning of a separate chapter on the Procuracy (Ch. 21). For a history of the Procuracy's functions under Stalin, see Glen G. Morgan, *Soviet Administrative Legality: The Role of the Attorney General's Office* (Stanford: Stanford University Press, 1962), pp. 76–126.

[54]See the 13 cases analyzed in Christopher Osakwe, "Due Process of Law and Civil Rights Cases in the Soviet Union," in *Law Reform under Khrushchev and Brezhnev*, ed. Donald D. Barry, George Ginsburgs, and Peter B. Maggs (Leiden: A. W. Sijthoff, 1978). Even in ordinary (nonpolitical) cases, however, a "major retreat of the due process function in favor of the crime control function" has taken place at least temporarily during the various anticrime campaigns under Khrushchev and Brezhnev. See Stanislaw Pomorski, "Criminal Law Protection of Socialist Property in the USSR," in *ibid*.

[55]See Max Hayward, ed., *On Trial: The Soviet State versus 'Abram Tertz' and 'Nikolai Arzhak,'* rev. and enlarged ed. (New York: Harper and Row, 1967). See also Robert Sharlet, "Dissent and Repression in the Soviet Union," *Current History* (October 1977), pp. 112–117 and 130.

[56]Harold J. Berman, "The Educational Role of Soviet Criminal Law and Civil Procedure," in *Contemporary Soviet Law*, pp. 14–16. The literature on violations of dissidents' rights is voluminous. See, for example, Christopher Osakwe, "Due Process of Law, and Civil Rights Cases in the Soviet Union," *loc. cit.*, for a detailed and systematic analysis of the due process violations reported in political cases; and *A Chronicle of Human Rights in the USSR*, for continuing unofficial documentation of Soviet political "justice."

[57]For recent examples of the "legalist" strategy see Valery Chalidze, *To Defend These Rights: Human Rights and the Soviet Union* (New York: Random House, 1974); and the "legalist" analyses of Soviet constitutional law, prior to publication of the Draft Constitution, by Henn-Juri Uibopuu and Alexander Volpin in *Papers on Soviet Law*, eds. Leon Lipson and Valery Chalidze (New York: Institute on Socialist Law, 1977), pp. 14–51 and 52–107, respectively. For a "legalist" analysis of the Draft Constitution, see Sofia Kallistratova, "Comments on the Draft Constitution," *A Chronicle of Human Rights in the USSR*, no. 27 (July–September 1977), pp. 56–64. This critique appeared in the West via *samizdat* just after the 1977 Constitution was ratified.

[58]For the pertinent post-Stalin legislation on tort liability, see the Civil Fundamentals, Ch. 12, in *Fundamentals of Legislation in the USSR*, pp. 188–190; enactment of the Civil Fundamentals in the RSFSR Civil Code of 1964, Ch. 40, in Whitmore Gray and Raymond Stults, eds., *Civil Code of the Russian Soviet Federal Socialist Republic* (Ann Arbor: University of Michigan Law School, 1965), pp. 117–124; and the analysis of the Principles, code law, and selected cases in Donald D. Barry, "The Soviet Union," in *Governmental Tort Liability in the Soviet Union, Bulgaria . . . and Yugoslavia*, ed. Donald D. Barry (Leiden: A. W. Sijthoff, 1970), pp. 54–70.

[59]*Pravda,* June 5, 1977, p. 2. The following account of the constitutional discussion was based on a survey of articles and letters about the Draft Constitution published from 4 June through mid-September 1977, in the following newspapers: *Pravda, Izvestiya, Vechernyaya Moskva* (Moscow), *Literaturnaya gazeta* (Moscow), and *Ekonomicheskaya gazeta.* In addition, six other national and republican newspapers were surveyed intermittently during the same period: *Komsomol'skaya pravda* (Moscow), *Krasnaya zvezda* (Moscow), *Sovetskaya Litva* (Vilnius), *Pravda Ukrainy* (Kiev), *Bakinskiy rabochiy* (Baku), and *Leningradskaya pravda.*

[60]See, for example, G. V. Romanov's report to the *aktiv* of the Leningrad Party organization, *Leningradskaya pravda,* June 9, 1977, p. 2; *Pravda's* lead editorial, June 9, 1977, p. 1; and P. P. Grishkyavichus' report to the Lithuanian Supreme Soviet, in *Sovetskaya Litva,* July 3, 1977, p. 1. Grishkyavichus is First Secretary of the Central Committee of the Lithuanian Communist party and, like Romanov, was elected a member of the Constitutional Commission in April 1977.

[61]*Pravda,* June 7, 1977, p. 1.

[62]*Ibid.,* June 5, 1977, p. 2.

[63]See, for example, *Pravda's* lead editorial, June 6, 1977, p. 1; Romanov's remarks of June 9, 1977, *loc. cit.;* and Sh. R. Rashidov's report to the *aktiv* of the Uzbek republic party organization, *Pravda,* June 10, 1977, p. 3. Rashidov is First Secretary of the Central Committee of the Uzbek Communist party and a member of the CPSU Politburo.

[64]June 9, 1977, p. 1. This theme was reiterated in *Pravda's* lead editorial of June 29, 1977, p. 1.

[65]The following description is based in part on several conversations the author had with well-informed persons.

[66]See Christian Duevel, "A Secretive Reorganization of the Constitutional Commission," *Radio Liberty Research,* RL 141/77, June 7, 1977, especially pp. 2, 4, and 6–8; and *Vedomosti Verkhovnogo Soveta SSSR* (Moscow), no. 18 (1884), May 4, 1977, Item 274.

[67]See Robert Sharlet, "Concept Formation in Political Science and Communist Studies: Conceptualizing Political Participation," in *Communist Studies and the Social Sciences,* ed. Frederic J. Fleron, Jr. (Chicago: Rand McNally, 1969), pp. 244–253.

[68]See, for example, *Pravda,* June 11, 1977, p. 3; *Ibid.,* June 13, p. 3; and V. V. Grishin's article in *ibid.,* June 14, pp. 2–3. Grishin is First Secretary of the Moscow City Party Committee and a member of the Poltiburo. See also the article by the Chairman of the Presidium of the Ukrainian Supreme Soviet in *Izvestiya,* June 14, 1977, p. 2.

[69]*Izvestiya,* July 8, 1977, p. 2; and *Pravda Ukrainy,* July 3, 1977, p. 2. Subsequently, the Constitutional Commission reported that through July 20, 1977, more than 650,000 meetings of working collectives had been held, involving 57,000,000 people. See *Izvestiya,* July 30, 1977, p. 1.

[70]See *Izvestiya,* July 10, 1977, p. 2; and *ibid.,* July 15, 1977, p. 2.

[71]*Pravda,* July 9, 1977, p. 3.

[72]In the context of electoral politics, these have been called "valence-issues." See Donald E. Stokes, "Spatial Models of Party Competition," in *Elections and the Political Order,* ed. Angus Campbell *et al.,* (New York: Wiley, 1966), pp. 161–179.

[73]*Pravda,* July 13, 1977, p. 1; and *Komsomol'skaya pravda,* July 14, 1977, p. 1.

[74]*Pravda,* July 18, 1977, p. 3; *Izvestiya,* July 19, 1977, p. 2.

[75]*Sovetskaya Litva*, June 29, 1977, p. 1. For other letters agreeing with the engineer's emphasis, see also *Bakinskiy Rabochiy*, June 28, 1977, p. 2; *Izvestiya*, July 7, 1977, p. 2; and *Pravda*, July 17, 1977, p. 3. For letters advocating increased "moral" incentives, see, for example, *Sovetskaya Litva*, June 28, 1977, p. 2; *Izvestiya*, July 12, 1977, p. 2; *Vechernyaya Moskva*, July 30, 1977, p. 2; and *Krasnaya zvezda*, August 16, 1977, p. 2.

[76]For the comment of the Moscow factory worker, see *Vechernyaya Moskva*, July 16, 1977, p. 2. For letters proposing legal sanctions, see, for example, *Literaturnaya gazeta*, no. 27, July 6, 1977, p. 2; *Komsomol'skaya pravda*, July 23, 1977, p. 2; and *Pravda*, August 1, 1977, p. 3. See the proposal on antiparasitism by Deputy A. V. Ivanov at the first session of the newly elected Leningrad City Soviet, *Izvestiya*, June 25, 1977, p. 3. See also *Pravda Ukrainy*, July 1, 1977, p. 2; *Sovetskaya Litva*, July 7, 1977, p. 2; *Pravda*, July 12, 1977, p. 3; *ibid.*, July 13, 1977, p. 3; *ibid.*, August 3, 1977, p. 3; *Vechernyaya Moskva*, August 10, 1977, p. 2; and *Pravda*, September 9, 1977, p. 3.

[77]*Pravda*, July 8, 1977, p. 3; and *Vechernyaya Moskva*, July 9, 1977, p. 2. See also, *Pravda*, September 8, 1977, p. 3.

[78]*Vechernyaya Moskva*, July 7, 1977, p. 2; *Izvestiya*, July 9, 1977, p. 2; and *Komsomol'skaya pravda*, July 22, 1977, p. 1. See also, *Vechernyaya Moskva*, August 17, 1977, p. 2; and *Pravda*, August 21, 1977, p. 3.

[79]*Izvestiya*, July 7, 1977, p. 2; *ibid.*, June 30, 1977, p. 2; and *ibid.*, July 2, 1977, p. 2. See also, *Pravda*, September 14, 1977, p. 3.

[80]*Izvestiya*, June 28, 1977, p. 2; *ibid.*, July 9, 1977, p. 2; and *Pravda*, July 9, 1977, p. 3. See also, *Izvestiya*, July 14, 1977, p. 2; *Pravda*, August 14, 1977, p. 3; and *ibid.*, September 9, 1977, p. 3. A related participatory clause, Art. 96, which conferred the "right . . . to be elected" Deputies on 18-year-olds, stirred considerable discussion pro and con. See, for example, *Pravda*, September 18, 1977, p. 3. The result in the final, amended text was a compromise.

[81]*Izvestiya*, July 15, 1977, p. 2; *Sovetskaya Litva*, July 3, 1977, p. 2.

[82]*Izvestiya*, July 16, 1977, p. 2; *Komsomol'skaya pravda*, July 22, 1977, p. 1; and *Vechernyaya Moskva*, July 22, 1977, p. 2. See also *Pravda Ukrainy*, July 3, 1977, p. 2; and *Pravda*, August 1, 1977, p. 3.

[83]*Izvestiya*, July 7, 1977, p. 2; *Pravda*, July 3, 1977, p. 3; *Pravda Ukrainy*, June 29, 1977, p. 1. See also *Pravda*, June 27, 1977, p. 3; *Pravda's* lead editorial, July 3, 1977, p. 1; *Izvestiya*, August 6, 1977, p. 2; *Pravda*, August 23, 1977, p. 3; and *Izvestiya*, September 9, 1977, p. 2. The absence of reference to these two institutions in the Draft Constitution was apparently not meant to signal their gradual "withering away." In a May 1977 speech, USSR Minister of Justice V. I. Terebilov indicated that both institutions have been given increased authority and responsibility in order to fulfill their assigned roles in the implementation of the new legislation on juvenile delinquency, enacted in February 1977. See *Pravda*, May 20, 1977, p. 3, as translated in *CDSP*, June 15, 1977, pp. 1–2. For basic studies on these institutions, see Harold J. Berman and James Spindler, "Soviet Comrades' Courts," *Washington Law Review* 38 (1963), pp. 842–910; and Dennis M. O'Connor, "Soviet People's Guards: An Experiment with Civic Police," *New York University Law Review* 39 (1964), pp. 579–614.

[84]*Pravda*, July 15, 1977, pp. 2–3; *Vechernyaya Moskva*, June 28, 1977, p. 2; and *Izvestiya*, July 13, 1977, p. 2. See also *ibid.*, August 6, 1977, p. 2; and *Vechernyaya Moskva*, August 10, 1977, p. 2.

[85]*Pravda*, July 8, 1977, p. 3; *Krasnaya zvezda*, July 23, 1977, p. 2; and *Izvestiya*,

July 24, 1977, p. 2. See also *Pravda*, July 28, 1977, p. 3. For a readers' "debate" on the personal property clause (Art. 13), see *ibid.*, July 30, 1977, p. 3.

[86]*Vechernyaya Moskva*, June 21, 1977, p. 2; *ibid.*, July 11, 1977, p. 2 (two letters); *ibid.*, August 22, 1977, p. 2; *Komsomol'skaya pravda*, July 31, 1977, p. 1; and *Izvestiya*, August 6, 1977, p. 2.

[87]See, for example, the attacks on Zbigniew Brzezinski in *Komsomol'skaya pravda*, May 25, 1977, p. 3, as translated in *CDSP*, June 22, 1977, pp. 6–7, and on President Carter in *Izvestiya*, June 9, 1977, p. 5. Later in the summer, the polemics shifted from personalities and policies to the U.S. system as a whole. See, for example, the extended comparative critique of the U.S. Constitution in *Literaturnaya gazeta*, no. 35, August 31, 1977, p. 13.

[88]*Pravda*, July 8, 1977, p. 3; *ibid.*, July 16, 1977, p. 3; and *Sovetskaya Litva*, July 8, 1977, p. 2. See also *Pravda Ukrainy*, July 1, 1977, p. 2. Brezhnev had given some emphasis in his Report to the linkage of rights and duties, and the press cued the public on this issue rather heavily in lead editorials. See *Vechernyaya Moskva*, June 6, 1977, p. 1; *Izvestiya*, June 8, 1977, p. 1; and *Krasnaya zvezda*, June 21, 1977, p. 1.

[89]*Izvestiya*, July 3, 1977, p. 2; *Pravda Ukrainy*, July 8, 1977, p. 2; and *Pravda*, July 14, 1977, p. 3. See also *Izvestiya*, August 18, 1977, p. 2.

[90]On Sakharov's appeal, see *Le Monde* (Paris), June 4, 1977, p. 5. For his subsequent statement, see *The New York Times*, June 6, 1977, p. 4. See also G. Snigerev's "Open Letter to the Soviet Government," *Russkaya mysl'* (Paris), July 7, 1977, p. 2. He argued that the "linkage' of rights with duties (Art. 39), combined with the caveat of Art. 50, effectively "canceled" his rights as a citizen. Snigerev is a writer and documentary film maker who had been active in Ukrainian dissident circles since 1966. In 1974, he was expelled from membership in the Communist party and the professional organization necessary for him to work in films apparently for refusing to renounce publicly his friendship with the dissident writer Viktor Nekrasov, now an émigré. For information on dissidents' reactions to the Soviet Draft Constitution, I am indebted to Dr. Gene Sosin, Radio Free Europe/Radio Liberty, New York, New York. For postratification émigré dissident criticism of the new Soviet Constitution in general and its civil rights clauses in particular, see Vladimir Bukovsky, "An Appeal to the Heads of State and Government of the Thirty-five Countries that Signed the Helsinki Agreements," *New York Review of Books*, October 13, 1977, p. 44; and Valery Chalidze, "Human Rights in the New Soviet Constitution," *A Chronicle of Human Rights in the USSR*, no. 28 (October–December 1977).

[91]Article 52 reads in part: "The incitement of hostility and hatred in connection with religious beliefs is prohibited."

[92]Information on the religious appeal is from RFE/RL. For the party rule referred to in the religious petition, see John N. Hazard, *The Soviet System of Government*, 4th ed. (Chicago: University of Chicago Press, 1968), Appendix, p. 244. In contrast to the religious dissidents, a colonel in the military law office of the Soviet Army urged a far more restrictive religious freedom clause (Art. 52). See *Krasnaya zvezda*, July 31, 1977, p. 2. See also, *Pravda*, September 1, 1977, p. 3.

[93]*Bakinskiy rabochiy*, July 2, 1977, p. 2; and *Literaturnaya gazeta*, No. 29, July 20, 1977, p. 2. See also *Izvestiya*, August 17, 1977, p. 2.

[94]Article 155 specifies that both "Judges and people's assessors are independent and subordinate only to the law."

[95]Doctor of Jurisprudence G. Z. Anashkin is former Chairman of the Criminal

Division of the USSR Supreme Court. His article appeared in *Pravda*, July 11, 1977, p. 3. Also see *Izvestiya*, July 3, 1977, p. 2; *Pravda*, July 8, 1977, p. 3; and the joint letter from two well-known jurists urging reinforcement of the independence of the procurator from the local soviet in his jurisdiction, as a safeguard for ensuring the observance of legality, *Izvestiya*, August 3, 1977, p. 2. Earlier, in *samizdat*, Roy Medvedev had advanced similar proposals. He, too, suggested broadening the court's jurisdiction so that citizens could seek judicial remedies against administrative abuses. See his *On Socialist Democracy* (New York: Knopf, 1975), esp. pp. 162–163. On the policy and law of pardon, see Zigurds L. Zile, "Amnesty and Pardon in the Soviet Union," *Soviet Union*, vol. 3, part 1 (1976), pp. 37–49.

[96]*Pravda*, July 6, 1977, p. 3.

[97]Deputy Procurator Gusev was far less persuasive in his previous "exchange" with Sakharov and Chalidze on the Op-Ed Page of *The New York Times*. See *The New York Times*, February 23, 1977, p. A23; Valery Chalidze's rebuttal, March 5, 1977, p. 19; and Sakharov's reply, March 29, 1977, p. 27.

[98]*Pravda*, July 11, 1977, p. 3; *Izvestiya*, July 3, 1977, p. 2; and Snigerev, "Open Letter." Snigerev was referring to the conviction of two Ukrainian dissidents in June 1977 for their leadership of an unofficial "watch group" in Kiev whose purpose was to monitor Soviet compliance with the Helsinki accords. The trial had taken place in an out-of-the-way small town instead of in Kiev, thus making it very difficult for the defendants' relatives and supporters to attend and in effect rendering it de facto a "closed trial." A few months later, in September 1977, Snigerev was arrested in Kiev. See *A Chronicle of Human Rights in the USSR*, no. 27 (July–September 1977), p. 21.

[99]*Izvestiya*, July 3, 1977, p. 2; *ibid.*, June 26, 1977, p. 2; and *Pravda*, August 3, 1977, p. 3. On the earlier debates over the right to counsel and the presumption of innocence, see Gorgone, "Soviet Jurists in the Legislative Arena: The Reform of Criminal Procedure, 1956–1958," *loc. cit.*; and Kazimierz Grzybowski, "Soviet Criminal Law," *Problems of Communism* (March–April 1965), especially pp. 60–62.

[100]While everyone may be "for" science, this does not preclude possibly serious disputes over the allocation of science-targeted funds. In particular, those who would tighten the "link with production" by directing a still larger share of the science budget into "applied research" will no doubt come into conflict with the interests supporting "basic research."

[101]For a sample of such letters, see *Pravda*, June 27, 1977, p. 3; *ibid.*, July 20, 1977, p. 3; *ibid.*, August 3, 1977, p. 3; *ibid.*, August 14, 1977, p. 3; *Izvestiya*, July 1, 1977, p. 2; *ibid.*, August 3, 1977, p. 2; *Vechernyaya Moskva*, July 7, 1977, p. 2; and *Bakinskiy rabochiy*, July 1, 1977, p. 2. See also, *Pravda*, September 14, 1977, p. 3.

[102]*Pravda*, July 10, 1977, p. 3; *Izvestiya*, July 8, 1977, p. 2; *Pravda*, July 21, 1977, p. 3; and *Vechernyaya Moskva*, June 27, 1977, p. 2. The enactment in June 1977 by the USSR Supreme Soviet of the all-union Fundamental Principles of Forest Legislation, which was accompanied by a number of proenvironmentalist speeches by various deputies, gave additional impetus, no doubt, to the ad hoc lobby on environmentalism. See *Izvestiya*, June 18, 1977, pp. 1–7. For other letters on the general issue, see, for example, *Bakinskiy Rabochiy*, July 1, 1977, p. 2; *Ekonomicheskaya gazeta*, no. 27 (July 1977), p. 8; *ibid.*, no. 30 (July 1977), p. 6; *Izvestiya*, July 24, 1977, p. 2; *Krasnaya zvezda*, July 30, 1977, p. 2; *Pravda*, August 22, 1977, p. 3; and *ibid.*, September 11, 1977, p. 3.

[103]See *CDSP*, October 26, 1977, p. 4. According to well-informed sources with whom the author has had discussions, the enlarged Secretariat numbered approximately 500 people and the two articles that drew the most communications were reportedly the housing clause (Art. 44) and the clause on "individual labor activity" (Art. 17). Apparently, thousands of people took advantage of the public discussion on the new right of housing to write to higher authorities complaining about and seeking improvements in their housing arrangements.

[104]For a translation of Brezhnev's fall report on the proposed constitutional revisions, see *CDSP*, October 26, 1977, pp. 1–7 and 13, esp. pp. 1 and 5. The final text of the 1977 Constitution was published in *Pravda* and other major newspapers on October 8, 1977. For an English translation, see *CDSP*, November 9, 1977, pp. 1–13.

[105]See *CDSP*, *ibid.*, p. 2.

[106]Otto Kirchheimer, "The *Rechtsstaat* as Magic Wall," in *The Critical Spirit: Essays in Honor of Herbert Marcuse*, eds. Kurt H. Wolff and Barrington Moore, Jr. (Boston: Beacon Press, 1967), p. 312.

11 KONSTANTIN M. SIMIS

USSR: The Corrupt Society*

In Place of An Introduction For the reader to understand the place occupied by corruption in the Soviet state and Soviet society and the way in which the machinery of that corruption functions, he must have at least a general idea about the laws that govern that state and that society and under which its people live. For people born and raised in Western countries, that knowledge is not easy to acquire, even for the few who know Russian, read Soviet newspapers, and have an acquaintance with Soviet law. Even they, not having had the experience of living in the Soviet Union as ordinary citizens (perhaps only as diplomats or journalists), find it hard to understand that the newspapers constantly and deliberately paint a distorted picture of events in the country. That is because all the newspapers are in the hands of the single party—the Communist party of the Soviet Union—which exercises monopoly rule over the country; they are carrying out the propagandistic tasks assigned them by that party.

But for the person who has grown up in a democratic country, the most difficult thing to grasp is the fact that ways and means of governing the huge superpower and the rights and duties of its citizens are defined not by a constitution or any other written laws but by a whole body of unwritten laws, which, although not published anywhere, are perfectly well known to all Soviet citizens and are obeyed by them.

*Reprinted by permission of the author and publisher from *USSR: The Corrupt Society*, trans. Jacqueline Edwards and Mitchell Schneider (New York: Simon and Schuster, 1982), pp. 23–24, 26–28, 33–34, 39–40, 43–47, 51–54, 64, 68, 72–77, 83, 85–86, 94–95, 248–249, 252–254, 258–259, 261, 266–268, 297–300. Copyright 1981 by Konstantin M. Simis. English language translation copyright 1982 by Simon and Schuster. For elaboration of the central themes of the present chapter, together with numerous specific examples, see Simis's book.

The present Soviet constitution states that the power belongs to the people, who exercise it through elected soviets—councils—and the government of the country is carried out by the Council of Ministers and other administrative bodies. The fact is, however, that true power in the Soviet Union belongs to the *apparat* of the Communist party, and it is the members of that apparat who are the true leaders of the country.

Thus, the real power in the Soviet Union is in the hands of the country's only legal political party, whose apparat is not even mentioned in the constitution or other laws of the land and whose functionaries are not elected but appointed by higher party organs. That power encompasses all spheres of public and private life; it is just as absolute on the national level as it is within each district, each region, and each Union Republic.

The party apparat's power is the more nearly complete since it extends beyond administrative matters to the entire economy of the country. All the country's resources—land, water, factories, banks, transport systems, trade, and services; educational and scientific establishments; even entertainment—belong to the state, which is to say that they are under the control of the party apparat. That strengthens the party's control over society as a whole and over each citizen individually, since it turns the party into a monopoly employer, able to prevent the employment in any job of anyone who fails to observe the unwritten rules on which the party's power is based.

Not only does the party apparat wield supreme power in the country but it also governs the daily life of the country, from the activities of the Council of Ministers to those of a small factory or collective farm. Each of the nation's districts is administered by the apparat of the District Committee (Raikom) of the Communist party; each region by the apparat of the Regional Committee (Obkom); and each Union Republic by the apparat of the Republic Central Committee. The entire state, finally, is ruled by the apparat of the Central Committee of the Communist party of the Soviet Union.

That structure is completely parallel to that of the government; every government department, dealing with every sphere of life—economic, administrative, ideological—has its own corresponding department in the apparat of the party Central Committee. Each of these departments—which in 1977 numbered 17, not counting the Administrative Department, and which control the broad sectors of industry, agriculture, the army, the courts, the media, and so forth—is divided into sections, and the problems of each section are divided up among various supervisors.

The Central Committee's apparat is managed by Central Committee secretaries (formally elected at the Central Committee plenum, delegates to which are chosen at the party congress), but the organ with genuine supreme power is the Politburo of the Central Committee, which consists of 13 to 15 members elected and dismissed by the Central Committee plenum. In each of the links of the chain of the party apparat—Raikom, Obkom, Republic Central Committee, and Central Committee of the CPSU—power is personified in the First Secretary of the committee (known nowadays in the CPSU Central Committee as General Secretary). Within his link, the First Secretary's power is limited by no principles of legality or public opinion or a free press (nonexistent in the Soviet Union) but only by the next-highest party organ to which he is completely subordinate. It is those organs that appoint and depose officials of both the party and state apparats.

Formally, these secretaryships are elective offices. In reality, however, the delegates to district, regional, and Central Committee plenums, whose right it is to elect them, always vote unanimously in favor of the election of a candidate proposed by the higher party body, whose name they hear for the first time on their arrival at the meeting; they vote unanimously in favor of the dismissal of a secretary with whom they may have worked for many years and whom they respect. (There are *never* any exceptions to this unanimity.)

The power of the First Secretary, on whatever stratum, as demonstrated throughout the 63 years of the existence of the Soviet state, is absolute and is not subject to the restraints of the law or of public scrutiny. It is this that forms the fertile ground on which corruption in the Soviet Union has flourished so luxuriantly.

Yet—apart from the stillborn constitution—there are a multitude of laws and codes that really do operate in the Soviet Union. It is on the basis of these that the courts decide on disputes between citizens, try crimes, resolve labor disputes, and so forth. Nevertheless, the principle of legality does not operate in the Soviet Union. Since the regime does not consider itself to be bound by the law, any organ within the system, from a district council to the Supreme Soviet, and any court, from a people's court to the USSR Supreme Court can—indeed, must—violate the law on orders from its opposite number in the party apparat.

The functionaries in the intermeshed party and state apparats are arranged in a huge hierarchical pyramid. At its base, there are the thousands of Raikom secretaries and the chairmen of the district executive committees (the executives of local government), the heads of district offices of the KGB, the police, and certain other institutions. All have the opportunity to take bribes and receive illegal gifts.

Above them stand the secretaries of the regional committees (obkoms) of the Communist party, the chairmen of the regional executive committees, and higher officials in the apparats of the regional party committees, and certain regional state organs. Together they make up the middle level of the ruling party–state apparat.

Finally, at the summit of the pyramid (apart from Politburo members and secretaries of the Central Committee of the CPSU) are the top functionaries in the apparat of the Central Committee, the chairmen of the Council of Ministers and the Presidium of the Supreme Soviet of the USSR (who are nearly always Politburo members), their deputies, members of the government of the USSR, secretaries of the central committees, and chairmen of the councils of ministers and presidiums of the supreme soviets of the 15 Union republics.

There are very significant differences among these three levels in terms of the limits of their power and official position. What is particularly important for our topic is the even greater gap to be seen in their lifestyles. That is important, because it is precisely those differences that determine the features of the corruption inherent in each of the three layers of the ruling party–state apparat.

Despite the differences, however, the corruption of the Central Committee secretary, living in his government house and provided free of charge from special government stores with all the food he needs to keep his family, and the corruption of the secretary of a remote provincial Raikom, who has none of those legalized perquisites, have a common foundation. That common foundation is power, a power unbridled by the principle of subordination to the law, or by a free press, or by the voice of public opinion. It is the power of the party apparat that has turned the Soviet Union, in the 53 years of its existence, into a country eaten away to the very core by corruption.

The Ruling Elite: Legalized Corruption

The main privilege of the ruling elite is not really the high salaries paid to its members (which, by the way, amount to 4 to 10 times those of ordinary white- and blue-collar workers); it is the existence of a whole network of special stores, hospitals, sanitoriums, and service establishments that provide them—and no one else—with goods and services. None of these benefits or privileges are paid for by the members of the ruling caste out of their own pockets; it is the state budget or the party treasury that pays for it all.

Among the privileges that come with membership in the highest levels of the ruling caste, the most important of all is a secure private supply of food, clothing, and other items needed for daily life. Since the forced collectivization of the peasants in the late 1920s and early 1930s, the entire country has constantly suffered from a shortage of food. The ruling elite, however—which is concentrated mainly in Moscow—gets its food supplies through the *Kremlyovskaya stolovaya* (the "Kremlin canteen"), which can be used only by people with special passes—the members of the elite, their families, and their servants.

I do not know the official name of that institution, but everyone who uses it—or has even heard of it—calls it the *Kremlyovka*.

The *Kremlyovka* system includes the dining room, a few food stores, and snack bars scattered through the buildings of the Central Committee of the CPSU, the Council of Ministers, and the Supreme Soviet of the USSR. All these facilities sell foods of particularly high quality, the like of which is never seen in ordinary stores: sausages, fish delicacies, cheeses, bread, vodka, cakes and pastries (baked to specifications in special bakeries); and dairy products, fruits, and vegetables produced and grown on state farms that supply the *Kremlyovka* system exclusively. In addition, the Kremlin stores and snack bars sell imported goods that cannot be bought in normal stores: American cigarettes, Scotch whisky, and English gin.

Not only does the ruling elite have its own stores, it has its own theater-ticket agency, its own bookstore, in which its members can buy scarce volumes, and its own pharmacy, which sells imported drugs unobtainable in ordinary drugstores.

All this makes it possible for the ruling elite to enjoy material advantages that are inaccessible to ordinary citizens. In fact, everything to do with the country's rulers is exclusive and separate. They are serviced by a special network of medical establishments, including sanatoriums, clinics, and hospitals in and around Moscow, as well as many sanatoriums throughout the country, all of them responsible to the Fourth Department of the Ministry of Health.

Housing for the ruling elite is also special and unlike that for ordinary people. Buildings for the privileged are built to special designs and are finished with particular luxury. The families of the ruling elite get—free of charge of course—apartments that are enormous by Soviet standards—four to five times the size of any apartment obtainable by even the most fortunate of ordinary mortals.

The ruling elite even has its own special cemeteries: the Kremlin Wall on Red Square for the most important members and a cemetery on the grounds of what was once the Devichy Monastery for those of somewhat lower rank. And provision has also been made for a possible nuclear war: there is a special shelter designed to house the key members of the elite for months.

All these benefits enjoyed by the ruling elite are doled out in strict accordance with rank within the ruling class. While the range of benefits is very great, the nuances of the way in which they are rationed are very delicate. For about 11 years, I followed the career of a Central Committee official of my acquaintance, and I was able to observe how, as he moved up the official ladder, the spectrum of privileges he received subtly and gradually changed. When he arrived in the apparat of the Central Committee as a lowly *instruktor*, or agent, he was given 80 rubles' worth of Kremlin vouchers per month and had the use of a Central Committee car only for himself personally when on official business. He was given the use of a state *dacha* outside Moscow, but only for the summer and with no maid service. When he and his wife visited the government sanatorium (a resort with medical facilities), they had only one room and took their meals in the communal dining room; liquor was free only in strictly limited quantities.

But the years went by and my acquaintance rose to the lofty rank of deputy head of one of the most important and prestigious departments within the Central Committee. When he reached that rung on the ladder, he could buy food in the *Kremlyovka* without any limits and in even more privileged and tightly closed shops in the system. He could order cars from the Central Committee garage at any time of the day or night and in any number—and for any reason, including that of sending his friends home after an evening of boozing at his *dacha*, 30 kilometers from Moscow. And that *dacha*, which now was his all year round, was serviced by a maid and a cook. Now when he visited a government sanatorium, he was given a suite of rooms, where, if he preferred, he could also take his meals. There were no limits to the liquor he was permitted—and, again, it was free of charge.

Yet, even having won all the perquisites I have mentioned, my acquaintance spoke to me with thinly disguised envy of the benefits accruing to those even higher up on the official ladder. These people had not only maids and cooks in their *dachas* but gardeners as well. They arrived at the sanatoriums with their own personal cooks; special paths on the sanatorium grounds were set aside for their walks, from which other members of the vacationing elite were excluded.

There is also an elite in the Soviet Union that stands beyond all these categories: the members of the Politburo, those 13 to 15 people who make up the highest body in the party apparat, the body that in reality governs the state. Without restrictions and completely free of charge, they get anything they want in any quantity. A special office exists in the Kremlin for the purpose of providing this sector of the elite with their benefits; that office has limitless possibilities and resources.

Illegal Corruption in the Central Government

Even though the members of the ruling elite have arrogated to themselves all those perquisites and privileges, they have not failed to take part in the universal corruption that reigns in the Soviet Union. It is difficult to imagine and even more difficult to understand their psychology. Consider, for example, an official in one of the highest posts in the party or state apparat. He is invested with enormous power; he is provided with all the good things of life (indeed, to excess), but still he contemplates committing crimes for the sake of money. However hard it may be to imagine, corruption, even in the highest stratum of the Soviet ruling elite, has become a fact, and not even a rare fact.

It is not only the precariousness of any official position (and thus of the perquisites that go with it) that acts as catalyst for corruption in the highest reaches of the ruling elite. Even high officials are mortal, and neither a job nor its benefits can be inherited. So there is a natural temptation to ensure not only one's own well-being (in case of loss of one's elite status) but also the future of the family in case of death.

Of course, we cannot discount normal human greed, either; the blind, often irrational greed that has been, is, and ever shall be found in all strata of society, in all epochs, and under all political systems, totalitarian and democratic alike.

Then there is another, purely psychological, factor—after years of working on the lower levels of the party–state apparat and clambering up the official ladder, the future ruler of the country psychologically adapts to a situation in which bribes and gifts are a daily routine for himself and his colleagues, who in no way consider themselves to be criminals. Then, having reached the summits of power, the official retains the same psychological model of his relationship to corruption, which is now ingrained in his attitude.

To the four factors I have enumerated I must add one more: the lack of fear of punishment and a feeling of impunity. High-ranking bribe-takers are very infrequently exposed in the Soviet Union, and it may be said that cases of their being truly punished are extremely rare. The reason for this is certainly not that high-level corruption is such a dark secret; on the contrary, the members of the Soviet ruling elite live under a bell jar. Every step they (and their families) take is known by the KGB officers who are responsible for guarding them; they are accompanied everywhere—to the theater, on visits, and at home. These agents are not responsible only for guarding the members of the ruling elite; they are also engaged in secret surveillance of them.

But even though the KGB has full knowledge of the fact that the ruling elite is infected with corruption, the members of that elite remain inviolate. The fact is that, since its inception, the Soviet regime has been tolerant of the ruling elite's improbity.

The exposure of the ruling clique of Georgia is a case in point. The dubious dealings of the Georgian elite (headed by one Vasili Mzhava-nadze, First Secretary of the republic's Central Committee and a Candidate Member of the Politburo) were exposed as a result of the efforts of its Minister for Internal Affairs, Edward Shevarnadze. He was at least, in part, motivated by ambition, but he apparently did feel genuine hatred for corruption and was truly pained by the decadence he witnessed. "Once, the Georgians were known throughout the world as a nation of warriors and poets; now they are known as swindlers," he commented bitterly at a closed meeting. (This information comes from notes taken by one of the participants in that meeting.)

For several years, agents of Shevarnadze's Ministry for Internal Affairs shadowed all the leading functionaries in the party and state apparats of Georgia, as well as their families, gathering much compromising evidence. This was not a particularly difficult task since a reckless orgy of corruption was raging almost openly in Georgia.

There was a trade in the highest posts in the party and state apparats, which had become so blatant that the underground millionaire Babunashvili was able to order for himself the post of Minister of Light Industry. Babunashvili headed a highly ramified illegal company that produced and marketed fabrics, but his ambition was not satisfied either by his multimillion-ruble income or by his business activities, and he decided that he wanted to cap his career by combining in a single person (himself) both sides of Soviet organized crime: the corrupter (underground business) and the corrupted (government).

Why are the authorities so tolerant of a corruption that has penetrated their own ranks? This tolerance—in a regime that is so forthright and ruthless in punishing all other crimes—is due first and foremost to the fact that too high a proportion of the members of the ruling elite is itself involved in the corruption. The proportion is so great that not even the all-powerful Politburo wants to risk a general purge of the ruling elite or the open confrontation with this elite that would result.

Another reason is the regime's fear of destroying a legend that has been built up over 60 years by the propaganda machinery of the Soviet Union and the foreign Communist parties—the legend of the infallibility of the Communist party of the Soviet Union and its leadership, made up of chastely honest "servants of the people" whose personal needs are few and modest.

The District Mafia

Because of the limitations on the state budget and party funds, the ruling elite of the country is incapable of providing the lower levels of the gigantic ruling apparat with the same privileges they have secured for themselves. All the secretaries of district committees, chairmen of district executive committees, directors of district offices, and other such officials have to look after their own interests by themselves. Their official salaries are not large (e.g., a district committee secretary may earn 250 rubles a month), but, on the other hand, they wield great power in the life of their districts, and they can make up for what they do not get from the state and party by using this power to extort payments in goods and services from people who are dependent on them. This lower stratum is composed of tens of thousands of party and state functionaries, who represent power in the provinces and who are the backbone of the ruling class. They are the main buttress of central power, of which they are the representatives. Consequently, the supreme authorities have to accept the fact that the local authorities compensate for their lack of official perquisites by accepting payments in money and in kind.

In remote parts of the country, the system of tribute has become a characteristic and generally accepted form of corruption on the lower rungs of the ladder of the ruling class. Its salient feature is that, besides accepting bribes for performing some definite action, the members of the district elite receive gifts in kind and in the form of services from everyone dependent on them. And since all institutions and enterprises in the district are in such a position of dependence, the range of goods and services that may be offered is limited only by the possibilities of the district itself. A fairly coherent and nearly complete picture of the way the system of tributes operates in remote areas can be formed on the basis of court case documents, articles in the Soviet press, eyewitness accounts, and my own observations.

A list of tributes in the form of services can be continued ad infinitum: food, free automobile use and repairs in the garages of state enterprises; household repairs at no cost made by the district construction offices; workers from local state enterprises sent during working hours to construct private residences for the local ruling elite and to tend gardens of the officials, and so on.

The circle of people who belong to the elite of a district and who enjoy the fruits of the tribute system cannot of course be precisely delineated. But each member of this circle receives personal tributes in accordance with his position in the district hierarchy and with how much power he wields and the areas over which it extends. Accordingly, a First Secretary of a District Committee of the Communist party is at the apex of this hierarchy, followed by a Chairman of the District Executive Committee, for their power is universal and extends to everything in the district. Therefore, each is able to make use of the services of any institution or enterprise in the district and to receive gifts from all the state and collective farms. These officials accept all this not in return for any specific service but just for a generally favorable attitude and for their patronage. They are given tributes simply because power over the whole district is concentrated in their hands; they are offered services to make sure that they do not use their power against the giver, to forestall any possible trouble, and to ensure that if one of their tributaries was threatened by prosecution, they would exercise their authority to defend him or her.

This type of relationship between district rulers and the managers of enterprises and institutions who are subordinate to them is based on the total power of the party–state apparat and the fact that it is not subject to the law or checked by public opinion and the press. Another major factor is that in the Soviet Union, there exists not one single manager— even the most unshakably, incorruptibly honest of them—who is capable of running his enterprise or institution effectively without breaking the law. Because of that, a manager's happiness and peace of mind hinge on the people who wield the power in the district, on whether or not they will look favorably on his exaggerated reports on fulfillment of planned targets, and on his breaches of the law, and of their own instructions on financial and material expenditures.

But few managers exploit their official positions merely in order to get things done in their respective institutions or enterprises. There are a number of other reasons as well—not the least of which is the need to find the money to pay for all the tributes they have to distribute!—that impel them to misconduct in their own mercenary interests. It is in this way that opportunities for payoffs are opened up to district public prosecutors and police chiefs.

In large cities, too, such as regional centers, capitals of republics, and Moscow itself, the local ruling elite takes advantage of its position to obtain tributes. In these places, however, the tribute system takes on a somewhat different form and operates much less blatantly than its rural counterpart. But despite the fact that the regional or central administration may be in close proximity, the system is still unchanging and ubiquitous in large cities.

Information about this urban version of the tribute system never leaks out into the Soviet press, and I know of no case of a top employee of the party–state apparat being prosecuted for having taken advantage of it. Nevertheless, I was able to collect information about tribute accepted by the district elite in the large cities from my own experience as a lawyer as well as from court files and by questioning members of the elite and food-store employees.

In cases of this kind, it is only the employees of shops, restaurants, and cafés who are ever indicted; their privileged clients never appear in court, even as witnesses. Managers of stores and restaurants, sales-clerks, and refreshment-bar waiters are most often accused of pilfering or of cheating customers.

As in the provinces, the district elite in the large cities have free use of automobiles belonging to the various district institutions and enterprises and of garage services to repair their own cars. Lacking in the large cities are the collective and state farms to provide the elite with produce, but this function is performed by the state stores and restaurants.

In each district of a major city, there are two or three food shops especially set aside for the local elite. Neither their outward aspect, the range of goods on the shelves, nor the mass of customers crowded into them distinguishes them from dozens of other shops. However, behind the scenes—in the managers' offices and in the stockrooms—everything is different: the privileged social status of the customers, the assortment of goods, and even the prices.

The district mafia in the Soviet Union is invulnerable to attack from within the district itself. Its power could be destroyed only by the higher apparat of the Obkom on the regional level of the party if the Obkom were to replace the district leaders and fire or transfer the major figures of the district's criminal world. But in the Soviet Union, that is a rare and extraordinary occurrence, and, considering the way in which the Soviet organized-crime system normally operates, the likelihood of its happening is extremely slight and may on the whole be discounted. For in normal circumstances, the upper levels in the ruling apparat are perfectly well informed about what is going on in the districts but prefer to accept it.

It is quite easy to find evidence of this fact in articles that have appeared n the Soviet press. In columns entitled "Following Our Action" or "After Criticism," which appear in all the central papers published in Moscow (e.g., *Pravda*, *Izvestia*, *Literaturnaia Gazeta*), hundreds of articles are published each year informing us that the bureau of a certain Obkom or Raikom has disciplined a district official or the manager of an institution or enterprise for actions that are in fact violations of the criminal code, such as misuse of office for mercenary purposes, overstating the amount of work actually done in order to obtain illegal bonuses (tantamount to embezzlement of state funds), falsification of accounts, and so forth. These articles almost never say that the offenders have been indicted and tried in courts of law.

Thus, the regional apparat does nothing to combat corruption at the district level, and the central authorities can achieve success in this struggle only with great difficulty, by sabotaging the regional party organs. But even the central authorities do not devote much attention to fighting district corruption and make only extremely rare use of their unlimited law-enforcement powers to deal with the district mafias.

What are the reasons for this tolerance? First, the district elite is linked to the ruling apparat by a chain of corruption, and a portion of the never-ending tributes and bribes flows in a constant stream from the district centers to the regional centers. But the second, and principal, reason for the district mafia's impunity is that virtually all districts of the country are afflicted with corruption, and to struggle against it effectively would require total and constant purging of the ruling apparat in all the districts of all the regions of the country. The ruling clique of the Soviet Union is not prepared to destabilize the government apparat in that way.

Even if the district mafia could be dealt some blows, albeit not fatal ones, from above, it still remains absolutely invulnerable to any attempt to combat its activities from within the district itself. Furthermore, it is always able to strike a counterblow and give short shrift to anyone who encroaches upon its power.

Massive and ubiquitous corruption at the district level of the party–state apparat has forged such close ties between it and the criminal world that there is every justification for saying that a system of organized crime has come into existence in the Soviet Union, a system that has permeated the political power centers of the districts as well as the administrative apparat, the legal system, and key economic positions. Although not conceived as such by its creators, this Soviet variety of organized crime naturally is derived from and has become an organic part of the dictatorship of the apparat of the only political party in the country, the Communist party of the Soviet Union. Organized crime in the Soviet Union bears the stamp of the Soviet political system, the Soviet economy, and, in general, everything that may be lumped together as the Soviet regime. Its paradoxical nature is shown by precisely those factors.

The paradox lies first of all in the fact that the district underworld is not made up of gangsters, drug peddlers, or white slavers. The criminal world of the districts includes store and restaurant managers and directors of state enterprises, institutions, and collective and state farms. They are all members of this ruling monopoly—the Communist party—and their principal professional activities are absolutely legal and aboveboard. But there is another, secondary—and inevitable—side to their activities, which, although inseparable from the operation of their institutions or enterprises, is nevertheless criminal. Therefore, all these upstanding Communists who regularly pay their party membership dues, these members of the raikoms and raiispolkoms, these pillars of the regime, still make up one of the two components of the system of organized crime that pervades the districts of the nation.

The second component in this system is also made up not of gangsters or mafia families but of members of the lowest ranks of the ruling party–state apparat, and this is also highly typical of the system of organized crime in the Soviet Union.

The final characteristic of the system is that the ruling district elite acts in the name of the party as racketeers and extortionists of tribute, and that it is the criminal world per se who must pay through the nose to the district apparat.

Thus it happens that the system of organized regional crime combines with the political regime and the economic system of the country and becomes an inseparable component of them.

The Corrupted People

We are approaching the end of our tale of the land of kleptocracy, in which corruption is rife among the country's rulers at all levels from the very lowest to the very highest.

But how do things stand with those they govern, the people who do not occupy the positions of power that make it possible for them to obtain bribes and gifts? How do things stand with what they call "the people"—ordinary Soviet citizens?

The corruption that has rotted the ruling apparat of the country has had the terrible effect of eating away the morals not only of the people who give or receive bribes but also of the innocent, those who have not been party to corruption but who have merely been living in an atmosphere of corruption and have been forced to breathe its tainted air.

The atmosphere of corruption has bred the conviction in the minds of the people that everything can be attained by bribery: a good job, a university diploma, or an undeserved judicial verdict. And although that conviction is far from justified in all cases, it has led to the climate of tolerance toward corruption that holds sway in Soviet society.

Apart from these moral preconditions for corruption, there is an absolutely fundamental material precondition as well: the need to find additional means to ensure a minimum living standard for one's family. The majority of Soviet people are faced by that need since they are wage slaves, hired by the country's one monopoly employer, the state, which does not even provide them with the barest of living wages.

On-the-Job Stealing. I think I am right in stating that among the illegal ways of supplementing the Soviet family budget the most common is to steal from one's workplace. Over the 63 years of its existence, the Soviet economic system has failed to meet the needs of the population for food and good clothing, both of which are constantly in short supply. It is natural, then, that these are the most popular items to steal from wherever they are produced, processed, or stored.

I have every justification for asserting that food and alcoholic beverages are stolen from all such enterprises without exception. This rule is unfailingly observed, for example, in the small provincial dairy plant, whose employees would never dream of buying butter or sour cream in a shop or at the marketplace when they can simply carry it home without charge. And the same rule operates just as unswervingly in a place such as the gigantic Mikoyan meat-packing plant in Moscow; the workers never buy sausage or meat in the stores but simply take the factory produce home with them.

It is amazing how widespread this phenomenon is. Millions of workers have been caught on their way out of a tobacco factory or a meat-packing plant with a couple of packs of cigarettes or a few pounds of sausage and have been let off with a reprimand from their bosses or a "public censure" from the trade union organization. However, it is not because of any humane considerations that the Soviet state shows such leniency. The present Soviet leaders simply cannot afford to send millions of citizens to the camps, thereby removing them from their jobs.

A reader unfamiliar with Soviet society may deduce from this that the Soviet people are dishonest and immoral, that they are a people for whom thievery has become a way of life. Such a deduction would be misleading; it is simply that the mass of the population does not look upon theft from the state as real theft, as stealing someone else's property.

Of the tens of millions of people who do not think twice about lifting nails, light bulbs, and equipment from their factories, construction sites, or offices, the overwhelming majority would never steal a kopeck from another person. They would, indeed, consider such a theft immoral and would roundly condemn anyone committing the most paltry pilfering of that kind—but only if the victim of the theft is an individual and not some state enterprise. Such are the paradoxical ethics of a Soviet citizen. This demonstrates the complete alienation of the Soviet citizen from the state, his total indifference and even hostility toward it. Without such feelings, factory thefts on such a scale would be impossible.

Shabashniki. Another source of income for Soviet citizens that is not controlled by the state is "freelance" work, referred to in Russia by the strange word *shabashnichestvo. Shabashniki* are people who, having completed their main jobs on schedule (or indeed having walked away from their jobs at a state institution or on a farm), engage in freelance work. The Soviet regime is based on its monopoly power over its people, a monopoly that is composed of all spheres of life—political, economic, and ideological. The *shabashniki*—people who earn their living from sources that are not controlled by the state—infringe on this monopoly power (and not only in the economic sphere) and also undermine the very principle of state monopoly.

Clients are attracted to *shabashniki* because of their diligence and the high quality of their work, and it is these same characteristics that bolster their reputations and win new jobs for them. Of late, it is true, more and more teams of *shabashniki* have appeared on the scene who attract clients not only by the quality and intensiveness of their work but also because of their ability to get hold of scarce building materials. In these cases, "clean" *shabashnichestvo* is complicated by indictable offenses.

Left-Hand Work. It is difficult to draw a clear-cut distinction between *shabashnichestvo* and what in the Soviet Union they call "left-hand" work. As a general rule, *shabashnichestvo* is work done by people outside of their working hours or by people who have no full-time jobs at all; in short, it is work done on the *shabashnik's* own time and with his own equipment. "Left-hand" work, on the other hand, is usually done during working hours, using state tools, equipment, and means of transport.

It is difficult to name a profession whose members have not engaged in left-hand work. It would not be an exaggeration to say that an enormous part of the population of the country, from manual workers to famous actors, was involved in such work.

There are many other professions in the Soviet Union whose members regularly engage in left-hand work about whom I am unable to write. But I cannot pass in silence the left-hand work of transport workers: taxi, bus, and trolleybus drivers in the cities.

Private Commerce. What is commerce?

Since the day that first saw the appearance of the commercial middleman, whose aim it was to supply people with what they needed, buying something and reselling it at a profit has been known as commerce. For many thousands of years, mankind has considered that making a commercial profit is legitimate and natural.

However, in the Soviet Union, buying merchandise and reselling it to make a profit is called commerce only if it is engaged in by the state. When this activity is carried out by a private individual, it is called "speculation" and is a criminal offense. From the very first years of its existence, the Soviet state has concerned itself with the fight against speculators. This fight has been waged through punishment— sometimes even the death penalty—and propaganda.

Newspaper and magazine articles, novels and short stories, movies and plays sang paeans of praise to the glorious Cheka officers who mercilessly annihilated enemies of the Revolution and were full of bombastic scorn for "petty entrepreneurs" and "speculators." In a memoir written in the 1920s, I happened upon an accurate but sad observation: The author expressed surprise at how quickly the Soviet regime had inculcated in its citizens the notion that executing people is an honorable thing, whereas engaging in commerce is ignominious.

But this, while reflecting exactly the feeling of the 1920s, did not turn out to be prophetic. Illegal private commerce in the Soviet Union never disappeared; indeed, during—and especially after—the Second World War, it became a huge, everyday, and all-pervasive phenomenon. There is, in essence, a second market operating in the country parallel to the legal state market. The second market deals in goods that the state is not able to supply the consumer because of permanent nationwide and local shortages.

The distribution of goods throughout the country does not occur spontaneously or according to the laws that govern a free market but is the result of an administrative directive from the state authorities. In the Soviet Union, there are cities, such as Moscow and Leningrad, that enjoy a special supply status. Then there are towns, such as the capitals of the Union republics and the famous resorts, that are allocated goods as Category I localities, and, finally, there are all the remaining towns, which are supplied under Category II.

Naturally, people do everything possible to make this uneven distribution more equitable, and goods available in some towns and not in others tend, like water seeking its own level, to trickle from well-supplied to poorly supplied places. In part, this process occurs spontaneously: People visiting towns other than their own buy things there for themselves and their families and friends which they are unable to acquire at home. However, an important role in the process of the redistribution of goods is played by professional middlemen, who buy up goods wherever they are available and try to sell them in localities where they are scarce. Or, alternatively, they sell them in the very same places they buy them, to people who do not have the time, the inclination, or the strength to spend many hours on line.

These professional retailers spend their own money on transportation as well as their own time and effort in traveling and in acquiring the goods; therefore, it is absolutely normal for them to try to make a profit by selling the goods for higher prices than they paid for them. In the Soviet Union, these retailers are called speculators and are hauled into courts of law.

But as long as there are items that are in demand and that cannot easily be bought in stores, speculation will be ineradicable. Therefore, notwithstanding persecution by the police and the threat of heavy prison sentences of up to 7 years, speculation is so much a part of Soviet life that it is inseparable from it. It is difficult to name any sector of the population that does not have recourse to speculators, whether in the country or in the urban areas.

Conclusion

Thus, the Soviet Union is infected from top to bottom with corruption—from the worker, who gives the foreman a bottle of vodka to get the best job, to Politburo candidate Mzhavanadze, who takes hundreds of thousands of rubles for protecting underground millionaires; from the street prostitute, who pays the policeman 10 rubles so that he will not prevent her from soliciting clients, to the former member of the Politburo, Minister of Culture Ekaterina Furtseva, who built a luxurious suburban villa at the government's expense—each and every one is afflicted with corruption.

I was born in that country and lived there for almost 60 years. Year after year since childhood and throughout my whole conscious life, I watched as corruption ate more deeply into society until it turned the Soviet regime in the 1960s and 1970s into a land of corrupt rulers, ruling over a corrupted people.

Corruption has become a national phenomenon in the Soviet Union. But this does not mean that the average Soviet citizen is immoral and inclines toward deceit. I lived my life with this people, and I can attest that this is not so. The Soviet people are no better and no worse than others. *Homo sovieticus* is not immoral, he simply has two separate systems of morality.

Entering into relations with representatives of the government, dealing with industry, commerce, and services, the Soviet citizen, readily and without thinking about it, uses corruption to get what is necessary for him—most often what is vitally necessary. In the same automatic way, the average Soviet citizen gives a ruble to a salesman in a store to get a piece of meat, 300 rubles to an official of the Ministry of Communications to have a telephone installed in his apartment, or 3000 rubles to an official of the District Executive Committee to get a government apartment. If he does not pay these bribes, his family will not have meat; he will be forced to wait 5 or 6 years before a telephone is installed; he will remain for years with his large family in a single room in a communal apartment.

The Soviet citizen gives all these bribes without thinking about the moral aspect of his actions, without any burden on his conscience. Usually, he understands perfectly well that he is breaking the law, but he does not consider his actions immoral.

Such are the Soviet citizen's relations with the government. But in private dealings, this same citizen will conduct himself in accord with the precepts of common human morality. He will lie to a representative of the government administration but be truthful and honest in relations with friends and neighbors; he is happy to steal 20 packs of cigarettes from a tobacco factory where he works but will not steal a penny from another person.

This double standard results from the complete alienation of the Soviet individual from governmental power. The Soviet citizen rarely comprehends the totalitarian character of the Soviet regime, rarely recognizes his negative relationship to it. He instinctively responds to material deprivations, to lack of freedom, to the complete corruption of those who rule him, to the immorality of the regime by excluding everything connected with the state and the economics of the state from the sphere of moral values.

"They"—who rule over us—take bribes; "their trade," "their services" are corrupt through and through, so in dealing with "them," the norms of human morality do not apply. Thus I may formulate the creed of dual morality.

The virus of corruption, which infects the ruling apparatus of the Soviet Union from top to bottom, is inevitably, by a natural law, spreading to the whole society, to all spheres of its life. To cure the country of this virus appears to be impossible. The powers that be try to fight against the corruption of both the ruling apparatus and the people. However, they do not do this energetically or consistently enough, partly because those who possess ultimate power are themselves predisposed to this or that degree of corruption (in any event, to legalized corruption). But the main reason is that all the remaining links of the ruling apparatus are completely infected by corruption. And that is why it is possible to destroy corruption in the party–government apparatus only by destroying the apparatus itself, which of course is unrealistic. After all, the apparatus ruling over regions, districts, and republics is the body that supports the whole regime.

But even if the ruling elite undertook a decisive battle against corruption, such an attempt would be doomed to failure, since at the root of the general corruption of the Soviet Union lies the totalitarian rule of the Communist party, single-handedly ruling the country. This power is checked neither by law nor by a free press. And the nature of any unrestricted power is such that it inevitably corrupts those who wield it and constantly generates the phenomenon of corruption. So it is that corruption has become the organic and unchangeable essence of the Soviet regime and can be eliminated only by a root-and-branch change in the means of government.

More than 4 years have passed since I was forced to leave my country. It is unlikely that its rulers will ever give me a chance to see once again the places where I passed my life, where people dear to me live, where the grave of my mother is. But they cannot take away my love for my country and for my people.

This is a chapter in which I describe only the dark side of my country's life, only those people who found themselves drawn into corruption. I have not mentioned the many beautiful things about that country that the totalitarian regime could not destroy. I have not mentioned the many wonderful people with whom I lived in that country. I have written about corruption, not about the upright.

And now I ask myself: What next? What is the future of the country?

And I answer my own question with bitterness: The Soviet government, Soviet society, cannot rid itself of corruption as long as it remains Soviet. It is as simple as that.

AMY W. KNIGHT

*The Powers of the Soviet KGB**

During the past decade or so, increasing numbers of Western scholars have rejected the so-called "totalitarian model" of the Soviet Union as simplistic and inaccurate. They claim that the Soviet system has changed significantly since the Stalin era and has become a pluralistic, bureaucratic, authoritarian state that formulates policy rationally, on the basis of input from various interest groups and advice from experts. The main reason cited for this "revisionist" interpretation of the Soviet system is that the power of the Soviet secret police has allegedly been greatly curbed. As the Sovietologist, Jerry Hough, expressed it in a recent book: "Nikita Khrushchev's limitations on the arbitrary power of the secret police eliminated one of the main features of totalitarianism as we have seen it."[1] Another Kremlin expert, Seweryn Bialer, writes that "the still massive Soviet police state was reduced to the political functions of a traditional authoritarian polity."[2]

The revisionist approach to the Soviet Union is undoubtedly appealing to Western policymakers, for it is far less difficult to deal with an adversary who runs his affairs on a rational basis, however unenlightened, than with an unstable totalitarian government operating by means of police terror. In other words, it is comforting to assume that our enemy, particularly in a nuclear age, is to some extent like us. To think of someone like Stalin in control of the Russian's vast nuclear arsenal is indeed disquieting. But what grounds do we have for claiming that the power of the Soviet police, the KGB in particular, has diminished so significantly? How certain can we be that it will not turn into the instrument of terror and oppression that it was under Stalin?

Partly as a result of the unpopularity of the totalitarian model of the USSR, Western scholars have devoted scant attention to the KGB in recent years. As far back as 1973, Robert Slusser noted that "the secret

*Reprinted in revised form by permission of the author and publisher from *Survey* 25, 3 (Summer, 1980), pp. 138–155. Copyright 1980 by *Survey*.

police continues to be the neglected stepchild of Soviet studies" and stressed the need for a full-scale examination of the subject.[3] Since then, despite considerable interest in the KGB's foreign espionage and para-military activities, there have been no serious attempts to assess its impact on the Soviet political process or to examine its role in society.[4] This is a significant omission on the part of Western Sovietology, for in a system such as the Soviet one, the power and influence of the police in relation to other institutions is not necessarily static but rather is subject to change over time. It has been said before, but it is worth repeating, that there are no institutional guarantees against a reversion to the kind of police terror that prevailed under Stalin. As long as the pattern of decision making is unstable, we cannot assume that the Soviet system has changed so fundamentally that this could not occur, however unlikely it may seem. Furthermore, as this chapter will point out, recent trends and developments raise the possibility that the role of the police in the Soviet regime may actually be expanding.

It is well known that, after their almost total dominance over all aspects of society (including the party) during the Stalin era, the security police suffered considerable setbacks under Khrushchev's leadership. He discredited their image of infallibility by openly criticizing their previous excesses; he ousted top police officials, and he greatly circum-scribed their vast powers. In his efforts to bring the police back under party control, Khrushchev appears to have had the support of most of his colleagues, who were as anxious as he to eliminate a threat to the party and to their own security. Yet Khrushchev was careful not to do permanent damage to the prestige and morale of the police. For, as with all those who govern without popular mandate, he depended on the police to ensure the stability of the regime.

Few Western analysts have noted the significance of the fact that, even before Khrushchev's removal, a gradual effort to improve the image of the KGB had begun (accompanied, not coincidentally, by a partial rehabilitation of Stalin and his place in history). This effort was even more noticeable after Khrushchev left the scene, perhaps because, as some have speculated, the KGB had a role in his ousting.[5]

The Soviet leadership launched a vast publicity campaign designed to raise the prestige of the KGB and the militia. In contrast to their low profile in the early post-Stalin years, the *Chekisty*, as KGB personnel are called, were given increased attention in the press. The fiftieth an-niversary of the Cheka was celebrated in 1967 throughout the USSR with the police hailed as one of the pillars of the state. A flood of literature glorifying them and their exploits began to appear in the form of memoirs, biographies, documentaries, and semifictional adventure stor-ies. In 1972, the Soviets published a bibliography of over 50 pages devoted entirely to literature on the *Chekisty*,[6] and in 1976, a special commission of the RSFSR Union of Writers was created for the purpose of promoting the police adventure story as a fully-fledged genre.

The image of the police that this literature and publicity conveyed was one of respectability and legitimacy. As if to dispel the picture of brutality and terror that most citizens had, the *Chekisty* were presented as honest, high-minded people with humane qualities. Thus, in one book, entitled *Chekists about Their Work*, the proceedings of a round-table discussion between journalists and KGB employees were reported. The KGB men stressed how much their organization had changed since the Stalin era and how they were operating completely legally. They portrayed themselves as very ordinary men, who played sports, chess, and even engaged in creative writing.[7] A Soviet film director who emigrated to the West in the early 1970s told of his experience directing a full-length documentary about the struggle against foreign spies in Russia. An officer from the KGB had the final say over all details of the film. According to the director, "his chief concern was to see that the main character—a *Chekist*—was presented in a positive and sympathetic light."[8]

The campaign to rehabilitate the security police has continued unabated to this day, with the active participation of top party leaders, particularly Brezhnev, who has bestowed numerous awards and honors upon KGB personnel in unexpected circumstances. In 1977, two of Andropov's deputies, S. K. Tsvigun and G. K. Tsinev, were awarded the title "Hero of Socialist Labour" on the occasion of their sixtieth and seventieth birthdays, respectively. These honors were unprecedented, since they are rarely given to non-Politburo members, and these officials were not even at the ministerial level. In December 1978, these same deputies, Tsvigun and Tsinev, were promoted to the rank of army general, along with KGB Border Guards Chief, V. A. Matrosov. (Before this, Andropov was the only KGB official to hold this rank.) More recently, in August 1979, G. A. Aliev, a former KGB chief in Azerbaidzhan, was awarded the title "Hero of Socialist Labour," even though it was not his birthday and he is only a candidate member of the Politburo. That same month, Brezhnev presented Andropov with the award of Order of the October Revolution at a ceremony in the Kremlin. In making the presentation, Brezhnev gave an exceptionally warm speech, citing Andropov's weighty contributions to the communist cause and ending by saying "we love and value you."[9]

What are the reasons for this campaign to glorify the security police in the eyes of the public? To the extent that it is designed to boost police morale and give them more credibility so that they can function effectively, it is understandable. But clearly the current efforts go beyond this. They seem to be aimed, first of all, at making society forget about past police crimes. The publication of historical writings on the security police has been very selective, carefully excluding any mention of how they became an instrument of terror against the party itself, and instead idealizing their history. (It is significant that Andropov did not mention past police excesses under Stalin in his speech marking the sixtieth anniversary of the Cheka in 1977, though he did in his 1967 speech.) This "cover-up," as it were, removes what may be an effective barrier to any recurrence of police terror—public acknowledgment of the potential dangers of the powers of the police. Furthermore, the fact that this campaign appears to be inspired, or at least condoned, by Brezhnev, raises the possibility that he is attempting to strengthen the police in order to enhance his own position.

Another development that is just as significant and yet equally unheeded by Western scholars is the KGB's growing representation on party and state organizations. While Khrushchev removed KGB officials from party bureaux at all levels and kept the KGB chief from full membership in the Central Committee, Brezhnev has given the police growing numbers of positions in both the party and government apparatus. In 1973, for the first time since the Stalin era, the security chief, Andropov, was given full membership on the Politburo. At that time, a former KGB chief, Aleksander Shelepin, was still a full member as well (he was not dismissed until 1975). In 1976, Azerbaidzhan party Chief, G. A. Aliev, who had served with the security police from 1941 to 1969, was made a Politburo candidate member.

KGB representation in the Central Committee has increased steadily since 1961, whereas that of the military has shown a slight decline in terms of percentage weight (see Table 1). Though its membership is still small in comparison to the military, the KGB has gone from one candidate member in 1961 to four full members in 1981. (If we include the Ministry of Internal Affairs, the police have five full and one candidate member today, as compared with two candidate members in 1961.) Since 1961, the percentage weight of KGB full membership in the Central Committee has risen by 1.2% and that of the military full membership has declined by 0.8%. Because representation on the Central Committee is thought to be apportioned to institutions rather than to individuals, most scholars consider membership to be an indicator of the relative importance of the institution in question.[10] It may thus be inferred from these trends that the KGB's political influence is increasing relative to other groups. This inference is supported by the fact that the KGB has made considerable gains in representation on republic party bureaux. As the table shows, the number of KGB chairmen serving as full or candidate members on these bureaux, which are the highest policymaking bodies at the republic level, has doubled since 1961. As of 1981, the KGB was represented on party bureaux in all republics, while the military had officers serving on bureaux in only 6 of the 14 republics.

Turning to the government, Table 2 reveals that the number of KGB delegates to both the USSR and RSFSR Supreme Soviets has increased markedly since the Khrushchev era. By contrast, the military's membership has remained almost the same in the USSR Supreme Soviet and has declined in the RSFSR Supreme Soviet. Although the Supreme Soviet has no real decision-making power and is basically a "rubber-stamp" organization, its elections and activities are highly publicized, and

TABLE 1. *Representation of KGB and Military in Leading Party Organs*[11]

Central Committee

	1961		1966		1971		1976		1981	
	Full	Candidate	Full	Candidate	Full	Candidate	Full	Candidate	Full	Candidate
KGB members	0	1	1	0	1	2	1	3	4	0
Percentage of total members	0	0.6	0.5	0	0.4	1.3	0.3	2.2	1.3	0
Military	14	17	14	18	20	13	20	10	23	12
Percentage of total members	8.0	11.0	7.2	10.9	8.3	8.4	7.0	7.2	7.2	7.9

Union Republic Party Bureaux (14)

	1961		1971		1976		1981	
	KGB	Military	KGB	Military	KGB	Military	KGB	Military
Full members	4	4	3	7	5	5	7	6
Candidates	2	3	3	1	7	1	7	0
Total	6	7	6	8	12	6	14	6

Amy W. Knight

TABLE 2. *Representation of KGB and Military on Supreme Soviet*[12]

	USSR Supreme Soviet Deputies			
	1962	1970	1974	1979
KGB deputies	8	10	13	15
Percentage of total	0.7	0.7	0.9	1.0
Military	55	58	56	56
Percentage of total	3.8	3.8	3.7	3.7
	RSFSR Supreme Soviet Deputies			
	1963		1975	1980
KGB deputies	5		6	9
Percentage of total	0.6		0.7	0.9
Military	18		20	18
Percentage of total	2.0		2.2	1.8

considerable prestige is accorded to the deputies. Moreover, it is believed that the deputies are decided upon before the elections by a higher party body, with representation from various interest groups and posts within the party, government, and army carefully allocated, as it is with the Central Committee. Thus, this significant increase in KGB deputies is probably a result of a deliberate policy on the part of the Soviet leadership.

Another development that appears to have strengthened the KGB's position within the government may also be mentioned. This was the change in its status effected in July 1978. Whereas formerly it was the Committee of State Security (KGB) attached to (*pri*) the USSR Council of Ministers, it has been renamed the KGB of the USSR. This seemingly insignificant change had the effect of upgrading the KGB: According to the 1977 constitution, chairmen of state committees attached to the Council of Ministers are not necessarily included in this body, whereas chairmen of state committees of the USSR are automatically members of the Council of Ministers.

The political influence of the KGB is probably enhanced by the close personal and career ties that Brezhnev appears to have with members of the police apparatus. The First Deputy Chairman of the KGB, S. K. Tsinev, who is rumored to be married to Brezhnev's sister, was a top official in the security organs of Moldavia when Brezhnev was serving as First Secretary there (1951–1952). G. K. Tsinev, a Deputy KGB Chairman, was a fellow student of Brezhnev at the Dnepropetrovsk Metallurgical Institute in the early 1930s. Another KGB Deputy Chairman, V. M. Chebrikov, also attended the Dnepropetrovsk Metallurgical Institute, though much later than Brezhnev. He did not begin his party career in Dnepropetrovsk until the late 1950s but might have had indirect connections with Brezhnev. Chebrikov served in the party apparatus in Dnepropetrovsk until 1967, when he was suddenly transferred to Moscow to become head of the KGB Department of Cadres—a powerful position indeed for someone who had had no previous work in the security services.[13] Though Brezhnev has no past career ties with Andropov, the relationship between the two men appears warm, and Andropov is frequently pictured standing close to Brezhnev on official occasions. Some Western observers have even speculated that Andropov is a candidate to succeed Brezhnev.

The two top men in the Ministry of Internal Affairs (MVD) are also closely connected with Brezhnev. Shchekolov, the Minister of Internal Affairs, was another classmate of Brezhnev at the Dnepropetrovsk Metallurgical Institute and worked under him both in Dnepropetrovsk (in the late 1930s) and in Moldavia (in the early 1950s).[14] In 1966, when Brezhnev's ascendancy in the leadership was well established, Shchekolov was brought to Moscow to head the Ministry of Preservation of Public Order (MOOP), later called the MVD. The New First Deputy of the MVD, appointed after the death of V. S. Paputin in December 1979, is Brezhnev's son-in-law, Yu. M. Churbanov. Churbanov was promoted over the heads of other deputy ministers more senior to him.[15]

These close personal and career connections have created a potentially powerful network at the top. On the one hand, the special relationship that the police have with the General Secretary probably places them in a position to exert considerable influence on decision making. On the other hand, the presence of protégés in the top police organs is a source of strength Brezhnev can depend upon to counter opposition from within the leadership. The fact that several of these senior police officials came to Moscow in 1966–1967, a time when he had emerged as *primus inter pares* in the Politburo, is an indication that they were selected by Brezhnev personally, in order to ensure the loyalty of the police organs. In addition, it appears as if Brezhnev's close ally, Chernenko, might have some responsibility for KGB activities in his job as Central Committee Secretary—a situation that further reinforces the ties between the General Secretary and the police.[16]

According to most sources, the KGB is an elite, privileged organization, whose personnel have a strong esprit de corps. Its recruitment process is apparently highly selective, stressing ideological credentials as well as education. The *Komsomol* is said to be one of the main KGB suppliers. Prospective employees are sent to one of the many special training institutes run by the KGB, where they undergo a rigorous program of preparation for their work. The pay for KGB personnel is reportedly much higher than it is in other institutions, and they apparently enjoy a variety of special privileges. According to the late

Andrei Amalrik, whose impression is confirmed by others, their "caste-like seclusion from society is powerful. It breeds not only a feeling of superiority, but also a more subconscious feeling of alienation and resentment."[17]

The relationship between the KGB and the MVD is not altogether clear. Though their functions are generally thought of as separate (the MVD deals with ordinary domestic crimes, while the KGB concentrates on "crimes against the state" and foreign espionage) there appears to be some overlap. Soviet dissidents mention MVD assistance to the KGB in prosecuting citizens, and there is also evidence of MVD involvement in KGB ventures abroad.[18] MVD and KGB officials often appear together at meetings and ceremonies, and obituaries are usually signed by representatives of both organizations. Nevertheless, it would be a mistake to assume that there is a formal connection between these organizations, or to speak of a "KGB/MVD axis," as one recent article does.[19] Since the early 1960s career patterns of leading KGB and MVD officials have followed markedly different tracks, and examples of cadres moving from one police apparatus to the other are rare. The MVD and KGB were made separate and distinct institutions almost 30 years ago for the specific purpose of curtailing the vast powers of the police. As Frederick Barghoorn once expressed it: "Particularly significant is the fact that the MVD–MOOP, or internal public order agency has always been available to counterbalance the Cheka–MGB–KGB, or political police."[20] If this situation were to change, which is of course possible, and the functions of these organizations were to merge, this would make the police a considerably more powerful institution.

What kind of people are the men who run the KGB? Biographical and career information on 14 officials currently holding the top positions in this organization reveal some interesting facts about their backgrounds (see Table 3).

Unlike the early Chekisty, who generally had peasant origins and low educational levels, all but one of the top 14 KGB officials in 1981 have higher education. What is most striking about their backgrounds is the long time that most of them have worked for the state security agencies. Though their average age (62) is considerably less than that of Politburo members (70), 10 out of the 14 KGB officials began their careers in the security organs during the Stalin era. Their long periods of service have undoubtedly fostered a strong identification with the police as well as a sense of cohesiveness among them. More important, these men started out at a time when the police were dominating the whole society, including the party, by means of terror. Since these were the formative and most impressionable years of their careers, it may be expected that they were, to some extent at least, inculcated with the values and mores of this era of violence.

This may be the case with some lower-ranking officials as well. Though Khrushchev dismantled the top ranks of the police after Beria

TABLE 3. Profiles of Top KGB Officials[21]

Name	Position	Date of Birth	Education	Nationality	Career Background
Yu. Andropov	Chm., USSR KGB	1914	Higher	Russian	Komsomol, party, security police since 1967
S. K. Tsvigun	First Dep. Chm., USSR KGB	1917	Higher	Ukrainian	Security police since 1939
G. K. Tsinev	Dep. Chm., USSR KGB	1907	Higher	Ukrainian	Party, military, police since 1953
V. M. Chebrikov	Dep. Chm., USSR KGB	1923	Higher	Russian	Party, security police since 1967
A. S. Boiko	Chm., Turkmen KGB	1925	Higher	Russian	Security police since 1943
V. V. Fedorchuk	Chm., Ukrainian KGB	1918	Higher	Ukrainian	Security police since 1939
A. N. Inauri	Chm., Georgian KGB	1908	Higher	Georgian	Security police since 1953
A. Yuzbashian	Chm., Armenian KGB	1924	Higher	Armenian	Security police since 1943
N. P. Lomov	Chm., Kirghiz KGB	1925	Higher	Russian	Komsomol, party, since 1964 security police
L. N. Melkumov	Chm., Uzbek KGB	1924	Higher	Armenian	Komsomol, security police since 1950
E. I. Perventsev	Chm., Tadzhik KGB	1926	Higher	Russian	Komsomol, security police since 1950
Yu. Yu. Petkiavichius	Chm., Lithuanian KGB	1924	Higher	Lithuanian	Komsomol, party, security police since 1960
A. P. Pork	Chm., Estonian KGB	1917	Middle	Estonian	Security police since 1948
V. T. Shevchenko	Chm., Kazakh KGB	1921	Higher	Ukrainian	Security police since 1943

was shot in 1953 and reduced the overall number of police personnel, he, presumably for practical reasons, left the middle and lower ranks partially intact. There is also evidence that some police who were forced out with Beria were later reinstated. The dissident, Anatolii Marchenko, tells in his book, *My Testimony*, of police officials running the camps under Stalin who were dismissed in 1953–1954, "bided their time," and were eventually rehired.[22]

The current Soviet leadership may consider police personnel who began their careers under Stalin to be more effective in dealing with internal problems. Interestingly, the former Chairman of the KGB in Ukraine, V. F. Nikitchenko, who did not join the police until 1954, was replaced in 1970 by V. V. Fedorchuk, a police official since the 1930s. Nikitchenko was allegedly too mild in his treatment of dissidents, and the regime wanted a harder line. His successor promptly replaced all provincial KGB heads in Ukraine with his own men.[23]

This brings us to the question of the domestic tactics of the KGB and how much they have changed since the days of Stalin. Has the KGB accepted for itself a lesser internal role, circumscribed by the rules of "socialist legality?" Or are its personnel striving to regain some of the powers they enjoyed in the past? It is certainly true that the police's ability to investigate and prosecute Soviet citizens was curtailed considerably under Khrushchev. In particular, the new RSFSR Code of Criminal Procedure, adopted in 1960, set down specific rules according to which the KGB was to conduct its cases. Certain procedures, such as night interrogations, were prohibited, and investigators were placed under the general supervision of the Soviet Procuracy. Yet, despite these legal changes and the fact that there was a brief liberalizing trend in the early 1960s, the police have managed to wield considerable control over society. They have accomplished this largely by the use of "extrajudicial" repression, which can be carried out without adhering to legal formalities—forced exile, various forms of harassment, and, most important, confinement of dissidents in psychiatric hospitals. As was the case recently with worker-rights advocate, Alexei Nikitin, hospital authorities often inject their dissident patients with harmful drugs.[24]

Along with the increasing use of psychiatric hospitals, "psychological persuasion" is being adopted by KGB interrogators. Much of the recent dissident literature mentions how sophisticated the KGB has become in the use of psychological tactics with those under arrest. The Ukrainian dissident, Mikhailo Osadchy, for example, writes of "seasoned police officials who expertly applied . . . the classical Pavlovian approach of alternating humiliation and decency."[25] In his *Prison Diary*, Eduard Kuznetsov describes a carefully co-ordinated campaign of psychological torture employed against him by the KGB.[26] These impressions are supported by Soviet legal writings on the use of psychological techniques during the investigatory process. The sheer volume of such legal literature that has appeared in the past few years is significant in itself. Numerous handbooks and textbooks for investigators (often designated for KGB use) stress the necessity of using strong psychological pressure in order to get "correct" testimony. A book entitled *Forensic Psychology for Investigators*, for example, recommends that the interrogator give the suspect false information and act in a purposely irrational manner in order to confuse him. Another book suggests setting psychological traps in order to obtain confessions.[27]

Equally ominous are the claims by several Soviet dissidents that KGB interrogators have begun to resort to physical violence. The writer, Vladimir Voinovich, for example, stated that in 1975 the KGB tried to kill him with poison in a Moscow hotel.[28] General Pyotr Grigorenko has told of a special KGB decree sanctioning physical coercion of those being questioned in certain cases and has asked whether "the rebirth of Stalinism in the propaganda of the newspapers and in other propaganda" may be a "signal for the rebirth of Stalinist methods in interrogations as well."[29]

As leading Soviet human rights activists have pointed out, the KGB is successfully continuing its repressions under the guise of legality. Andrei Amalrik summed up the situation:

> Back in 1970 Boris Shragin remarked that to the extent that the Soviet civil rights movement began to emerge from the underground and openly declare itself, so into the underground began to retreat the KGB, and its methods started to assume an ever more criminal character, even from the point of view of that state whose security it was called upon to protect.[30]

The effectiveness of KGB methods and the extent of their control over society is attested to by the fact that, toward the end of 1980, Western observers were pronouncing the dissident movement in the USSR crushed and demoralized.

When discussing Soviet interest groups that contribute to foreign policy, Western analysts often place the security forces together with the regular military on the assumption that both represent a "hard-line" element. The paramilitary status of the KGB—and the MVD as well—reinforces this assumption. Not only do security officials have military designations, but also, for purposes of the twice yearly call-up of military forces, the regular army, KGB border troops, and MVD internal troops are lumped together in the Ministry of Defence announcements. It should be stressed, however, that both the KGB and the MVD have chains of command that are entirely separate from that of the regular armed forces. Moreover, the KGB and the military have been played off against one another by party leaders in the past. Stalin used the police to prevent military leaders from coalescing into a group that might challenge his authority, while Khrushchev, in his initial bid for power, relied on the military to curb the strength of the police and bring it back under party control. Today, the party ensures the loyalty of the military through an extensive system of KGB surveillance. By means of its Armed Forces Directorate, which has departments for all branches of the services, the KGB places its officers at every echelon of the armed forces. This arrangement undoubtedly creates friction and rivalry between the military and the KGB.[31]

In addition to internal competition, it appears that the KGB and the military may have differences over foreign policy. There is evidence that the KGB does not always go along with those elements in the armed forces that advocate military instead of political means of achieving Soviet global objectives. A consideration of Andropov's speeches during the 1970s, for example, shows that his attitude toward foreign policy and relations with the West appears considerably more moderate than those of some Politburo colleagues. Thus, in a March 1976 speech to KGB party activitsts, Andropov voiced strong enthusiasm for détente and hailed the relaxation of international tensions. A month later, in a speech celebrating the 106th anniversary of Lenin's birth, Andropov affirmed his strong support for peaceful coexistence and was optimistic about prospects for a long and durable peace.[32] Meanwhile, Ustinov, who had recently been appointed Minister of Defence, was much more cautious about détente, noting that its success was limited and continuing to talk about the threat of war.[33]

Andropov's foreign policy views have also differed from those of Ukrainian party chief Shcherbitsky. In a July 1978 speech in Kiev, Shcherbitsky warned that détente was not irreversible and criticized Western striving for military superiority and attempts to distort the Helsinki accords. Less than a month later, Andropov gave a speech in Petrozavodsk, where his tone was markedly different. He was optimistic about the future of relations with the West and positive about the results of the Helsinki accords, noting that "the road ahead is clear"—a road of "patient, constructive settlement of conflicts and divergencies; of new steps toward containment of the arms race; of the expansion and intensification of relations between countries with differing social systems, between all states."[34]

Andropov has continued to manifest a positive attitude toward relations with the West, showing himself to be a strong supporter of Brezhnev's détente policies. His remarks in his 1980 Supreme Soviet election speech indicate that he may even have disagreed with the Soviet decision to send a large-scale military force into Afghanistan or at least was unhappy with the outcome. He was the only Politburo member to be pessimistic about the world situation after the invasion, noting that "it must be said frankly that anxiety for the future and the destiny of détente and peace has real foundations."[35] By contrast,

Ponomarev stated explicitly that "Soviet people have no grounds for alarm or uncertainty."[36] Ustinov, too, was much more positive than Andropov and noted: "imperialism's opportunities for disposing of people's destinies as it sees fit have shrunk considerably . . . the relaxation of tension has become the determining trend of world development."[37]

This raises the question of why the KGB chief would have a moderate outlook and oppose "military solutions" to Soviet foreign policy problems. It has been suggested that Andropov may not be so liberal as he pretends to be, but that he adopts this stance in order to overcome his "policeman image" so that he may be considered a viable candidate for the succession.[38] This hypothesis is consistent with the view expressed by others that the KGB has resisted extensive ties with the West, since, being responsible for the internal security of the Soviet state, the KGB sees contacts between Soviet citizens and foreigners as a considerable political danger not outweighed by the concommitant economic and technological benefits.[39] Clearly, the economic, technological, and cultural ties between the Soviet Union and the West present problems for the security police, and though their statements have been toned down considerably since the early 1970s, KGB officials still discuss the grave dangers of ideological subversion.

It does not necessarily follow, however, that the KGB opposes détente per se and that it would prefer the USSR to pursue a hard-line stance toward the West, especially if this line is accompanied by military interventionism and a stepped-up arms race. Such policies also present problems for the KGB. Increased defence spending not only enhances the domestic influence of the military, it also places greater strains on the economy, draining more resources away from the already weak consumer sector. In view of what has occurred in Poland, the security police may have good reason to be nervous about the possibility of food shortages and other failures to meet consumer needs. Moreover, as the police may see it, interventionist Soviet military moves, such as the Afghanistan invasion, have the potential of creating political dissatisfaction among the Soviet population.

If one considers how the KGB appears to perceive its own international role, it is possible to see how the application of military power to Soviet foreign policy may be viewed as a threat to the KGB's own interests. According to their statements, KGB officials see their primary function as an ideological one—the promotion of the interests of the Soviet state by means of the class struggle. This struggle does not focus on military forces but rather on ideas and social systems. It is a form of "ideological competition" that takes place even under conditions of peaceful coexistence. As KGB First Deputy Tsvigun has pointed out, "however great the positive changes in international relations may be, the current development stage is characterized by the intensified class struggle in the world arena."[40] The struggle is portrayed as both a defensive and offensive one. Thus, KGB officials speak of the need to protect the Soviet Union from "subversive activity by imperialist forces," and "ideological sabotage." KGB border troops play an important role in this regard by preventing unwanted foreigners from entering the Soviet Union. At the same time, the KGB is on the offensive when it "lends support" to the national liberation movements and "revolutions of oppressed peoples" in all parts of the world.

There is a definite theoretical basis for this type of KGB activity. In a recent article on Soviet global policy, Vernon Aspaturian explained how the Soviets distinguish between the concepts of "correlation of forces" and "balance of power." As Aspaturian pointed out, the Soviets define "correlation of forces" as a conglomeration of "various 'exotic' nonmilitary elements"—social, economic, political and revolutionary processes that give one social system an advantage over another, whereas the "balance of power" refers primarily to the state of the military balance. These nonmilitary elements are important factors in the international power equation:

> Soviet leaders, in short, have long recognized that social conflicts, tensions, frustrations and resentments, particularly between classes, conceal tremendous reserves of pent-up social power, which can be detected by dialectical analysis and then tapped, mobilized and transmuted into concrete political power subject to the manipulation of Soviet policy.[41]

It is in this realm of the international arena that the KGB operates, striving for a more favorable "correlation of forces," by means of a wide range of covert activities, including propaganda and disinformation, subversion, and sabotage.

Of course, as Aspaturian makes clear, the dichotomy between "balance of power" and "correlation of forces" is in some sense a false one, since the two are very much interrelated. Furthermore, it is difficult to accept the Soviet insistence that its class struggle against imperialism has no relation to the sphere of interstate relations and is compatible with peaceful coexistence. But the point here is that the Soviets do differentiate, in theory at least, between military and "ideological" struggles, and the KGB's activity lies in the latter area.

This is not to say that the KGB engages in no military activities. Its border guards force, which numbers around 200,000 men, is trained and equipped for combat and has in fact engaged in fighting along the Sino–Soviet border in recent years. The KGB also has other forces subordinate to its control, such as the troops of the Ninth Directorate, which guard party and state leaders, and the signal troops. In a wartime situation, these troops, particularly the Border Guards, would be called upon to assist the military as they were in the Second World War. But these military functions are secondary to the KGB's political role.[42]

It thus seems reasonable to assume that the security police would prefer nonmilitary solutions in situations where there are opportunities for exploiting social and political factors to the benefit of the Soviet Union. This enables them to have a greater influence over Soviet global strategy. Furthermore, overt military moves on the part of the Soviet Union probably make the ideological struggle more difficult. When the Soviet Union has the image of an aggressor, it is not easy for the KGB to exploit social and political upheavals (such as in Iran) and influence the course of "liberation movements." Of course, when political stability in Eastern European countries is threatened, the KGB doubtless favors military intervention, since the "correlation of non-military elements" is to their disadvantage and a possible threat to Soviet internal stability. But in general, the KGB probably advocates a more cautious stance, and Afghanistan is a case in point.

Before its military intervention in December 1979, the Soviet Union had been "lending support" to Afghanistan's national liberation movement and "encouraging positive political and social processes" that were taking place in Afghanistan. Though they had military personnel there, the type of activities the Soviets were engaged in was mainly in the realm of the KGB and apparently the MVD, whose involvement in Afghanistan is attested to by the death of MVD First Deputy Paputin there in December 1979, right after the Soviet invasion began. Allegations that Paputin committed suicide because he was blamed for the unplanned death of Amin raise the possibility that Paputin may have been a victim of lack of coordination between the security forces and the military in Afghanistan. In any case, the arrival of large-scale Soviet forces there must have put an end to most of the political activity of the KGB and MVD and changed significantly any plans they might have had for nonmilitary solutions to political problems in Afghanistan.[43]

Despite the blatant Soviet aggression in Afghanistan, many experts argue that the development of thermonuclear weapons has led the Soviet Union to modify its approach to foreign policy during the past decade or so. Although they have by no means excluded the possibility of war with the United States or its allies and continue to prepare for it, the Soviets do appear anxious to avoid confrontational military moves that may increase the danger of nuclear war. As a result, they seem to favour nonconfrontational tactics to achieve their global objectives: the use of surrogate military forces and various clandestine operations, including the support of international terrorism, that subvert and destabilize governments. Since these covert activities, which are arousing increasing concern in the noncommunist world, are directly in the realm of the KGB, it may be expected that its role in formulating and executing Soviet foreign policy will continue to grow.

Most Western observers place their strongest hopes for long-term peace with the USSR on a gradual change within the Soviet system—a slow process of internal liberalization that would eventually lead Soviet leaders to abandon their expansionist and destabilizing policies abroad. These hopes have rested, to a certain extent at least, on the assumption that the role of the police in the Soviet system was diminishing. Yet, as this chapter points out, there are signs that just the opposite may be happening. The honors and publicity the KGB has received, the steady increase in KGB representation on party and government bodies, the success it has enjoyed in repressing internal dissent, and the growing use of KGB clandestine strategies abroad all support this conclusion. The possibility that the MVD may be drawing closer to the KGB offers additional grounds for concern, since the institutions were separated as a means of ensuring that neither becomes too powerful.

What is perhaps most significant about the expansion of the KGB's influence is that it appears to have been furthered by Brezhnev himself with the possible cooperation of some close allies, such as Chernenko. By filling the top police positions with his own protégés, Brezhnev may be attempting to reinforce his personnel power base. Control over a powerful police organization would give him the potential to eliminate opposition among the party leadership and also to counter attempts by the military to challenge party authority.[44]

If history serves as a precedent, the KGB will not stand idly by during the future succession crisis but will actively attempt to ensure that Brezhnev's successor is favorable to its interests. Though it is possible that the KGB's influence will diminish after Brezhnev goes, just the opposite may happen if its powers are employed to determine the outcome of the succession. Of course, a return to the police terror of the 1930s would probably require another Stalin to emerge in the leadership, which is unlikely. But until the party ceases to draw a curtain over the past and openly discusses the way in which the police under Stalin became an instrument against the party, the possibility will always be there. In the meantime, Western scholars should focus closer attention on the role of the KGB, with a view to reinstating the discredited totalitarian model of the Soviet Union.

Postscript
(February 1983)   Developments that have occurred since this chapter first appeared—in particular, the death of Brezhnev and Andropov's successful bid for the post of General Secretary—indicate that the political importance of the KGB has continued to grow. It seems clear that the security police played a key role in the succession struggle by providing Andropov with the power base necessary to defeat his main rival and Brezhnev's heir apparent, Konstantin Chernenko. Though Brezhnev had placed several allies in the KGB in an effort to ensure control over this organization,

Andropov seems to have built up his own network of loyal KGB supporters by making substantial changes in the top KGB apparatus over the past few years. Eleven out of the 14 republic KGB chairmen have been replaced since 1978, and in 1982 alone, three new republic KGB chiefs were appointed. Also, among the delegates to the Twenty-Sixth Party Congress in 1981, the names of three new USSR KGB deputy chairmen were listed.[45] These personnel changes probably benefited Andropov politically, as did the sudden death in January 1982 of Brezhnev's most powerful ally in the KGB, Semyon Tsvigun. (Tsvigun's death, along with the death of Suslov a week later, was followed by a marked rise in Andropov's political prominence.)

Changes in the leadership that have taken place since Andropov came to power have served to increase further the political role of the KGB. Geidar Aliev, a former KGB official and since 1969 First Secretary of the Azerbaidzhan Communist party, was made a full Politburo member and First Deputy Premier. The leadership of both the KGB and the MVD—traditionally reserved for loyal party *apparatchiks* to ensure party control over the police—is now in the hands of two trusted KGB officials, V. M. Chebrikov and V. V. Fedorchuk. This could give the KGB effective control over the regular police and increase its powers substantially. Thus, it seems that several of the safeguards instituted by the party after the fall of Beria in 1953 to protect the party from police domination have now been discarded. Whatever these developments portend, they do not bode well for those who hope for internal liberalization in the Soviet system in the near future.

Notes

[1] Jerry F. Hough, *Soviet Leadership in Transition* (Washington D.C., 1980), p. 4.

[2] Seweryn Bialer, *Stalin's Successors: Leadership, Stability and Change in the Soviet Union* (Cambridge University Press, 1980), p. 51.

[3] Robert Slusser, review article in the *Slavic Review* (December 1973), p. 825.

[4] The most comprehensive study of the KGB in recent years, John Barron's *The KGB, The Secret Work of Soviet Secret Agents* (Readers Digest Press, 1974) concentrates primarily on the activities of KGB agents abroad.

[5] This speculation was aroused by important police promotions at the November 1964 plenum, following Khrushchev's ousting: Semichastny, KGB chief, was coopted into full membership of the Central Committee, while the former KGB chief, Shelepin, climbed straight to full membership in the Presidium. See M. Tatu, *Power in the Kremlin* (New York, 1967), p. 420.

[6] N. S. Aksenov and M. V. Vasil'ev, *Soldaty Dzerzhinskogo soyuza beregut. Rekomendatel'nyi ukazatel' literatury o chekistakh.* (The Soldiers of Dzerzhinsky's Union are Guarding. A list of Recommended Literature on the Chekists) (Moscow, 1972).

[7] *Chekisti o svoem trude* (Moscow, 1965).

[8] The film was entitled *Nezvanye gosti* (Uninvited Guests). See M. Dewhirst and R. Farrel, eds., *The Soviet Censorship* (Metuchen, N. J., 1973), pp. 111–113.

[9]See *FBIS Daily Report, Soviet Union,* August 31, 1979.

[10]For example, according to J. Hough and M. Fainsod, *How the Soviet Union Is Governed* (Harvard University Press, 1979): "The principle of representation of institutions rather than individuals has been observed with sufficient rigor in recent decades that western scholars have normally been able to rely upon Central Committee membership or nonmembership for an institution's or region's top official as an indicator of the relative importance of the institution or region" (p. 458).

[11]*XXII s"ezd kommunisticheskoi partii sovetskogo soyuza, stenograficheskii otchet* (Moscow, 1961) etc; Grey Hodnett and Val Ogareff, *Leaders of the Soviet Republics 1955–72* (Canberra, Australia, 1973); *C.I.A. Directory of Soviet Officials, Vol. I: National Organizations* (March 1979); and, for 1981, *Pravda,* March 4, 1981, and the party republic newspapers such as *Sovetskaya Belorussiya,* January 30, 1981, etc.

[12]*Deputaty verkhovnogo soveta SSSR.* Shestoi sozyv, 1962; Sedmoi sozyv, 1966; vosmoi sozyv, 1970; devyatyi sozyv, 1974; desyatyi sozyv, 1979; *Izvestiya,* March 7, 1963; *C.I.A. Directory of Soviet Officials, Vol. II: RSFSR Organizations;* and *Izvestiya,* February 28, 1980.

[13]Biographies of these officials appear in *Deputaty verkhovnogo soveta SSSR, desyatyi sozyv* and *Ezhegodnik* (Yearbook) of the *Bol'shaya sovetskaya entsiklopediya* (Moscow, 1976).

[14]This network of personnel ties extends to other Politburo members. The careers of Shcherbitsky and Tikhonov also include work in Dnepropetrovsk when these police officials were there.

[15]Churbanov recently had a book published about the militia and the *Komsomol,* with a dedication by Brezhnev: *Tovarishch militsiya* (Comrade Militia) (Moscow, 1980).

[16]Chernenko oversees the work of the Central Committee's General Department, which, according to Leonard Schapiro, has close contact with the KGB on security matters. [See L. Schapiro, "The General Department of the CC of the CPSU," *Survey,* no. 96 (Summer 1975), pp. 53–65.] Moreover, it is possible that Chernenko also oversees the Administrative Organs Department, which has direct responsibility for the KGB. The secretary in charge of this department has never been openly mentioned, and by process of elimination, a good case can be made that it is Chernenko.

[17]Andrei Amalrik, "The KGB in Asia," *Far Eastern Economic Review,* December 31, 1976, pp. 20–21. See also a book by a former KGB official, Aleksei Myagkov, *Inside the KGB* (New Rochelle, N.T., 1976).

[18]Among this evidence is the report that MVD First Deputy Paputin was killed in Afghanistan at the time of the Russian invasion in December 1979. See the *Washington Post,* March 14, 1980.

[19]See John J. Dziak, "Soviet Intelligence and Security Services in the Eighties: The Paramilitary Dimension," *Orbis* (Winter 1981), p. 776.

[20]F. Barghoorn, "The Security Police," in *Interest Groups in Soviet Politics,* eds. G. Skilling and F. Griffiths (Princeton, New Jersey, 1971), pp. 116–117.

[21]Sources for these profiles are cited in Note 13.

[22]Anatolii Marchenko, *My Testimony,* trans. Michael Scammell (New York, 1969), pp. 265–266. Marchenko was arrested in March 1981 for the sixth time.

[23]See Mikhailo Osadchy, *Cataract,* trans. and ed. Marco Carynnyk (New York and London, 1976), p. 204.

[24]See the *Washington Post,* April 22, 1981.

[25]Osadchy, *Cataract*, introduction.

[26]Eduard Kuznetsov, *Prison Diaries*, trans. Howard Spier (London, 1975).

[27]A. R. Ratinov, *Sudebnaya psikhologiya dlya sledovatelei* (Moscow, 1967); A. V. Dulov, *Osnovy psikhologicheskogo analiza na predvaritel'nom sledstvii* (Principles of Psychological Analysis During Preliminary Investigation) (Moscow, 1973). See also A. N. Vasil'ev *Sledstvennaya taktika* (Investigatory Tactics) (Moscow, 1976).

[28]Vladimir Voinovich, "Proisshestvie v 'Metropole'," (Incident in the Metropol), *Kontinent*, no. 5 (1975), pp. 51–97.

[29]*Radio Liberty Research Bulletin*, no. 269/77 (1977), p. 3.

[30]Andrei Amalrik, "Arrest On Suspicion of Courage," *Harpers* (November 1976), p. 56.

[31]See John Barron, *The KGB*, pp. 19–21, for a more detailed discussion of KGB surveillance of the military.

[32]Andropov's speeches have recently been published: Yu. V. Andropov, *Izbrannye rechi i stat'i* (Moscow, 1979).

[33]See D. F. Ustinov, *Izbrannye rechi i stat'i* (Moscow, 1979), pp. 280–291.

[34]See Andropov, *Izbrannye rechi*, pp. 277–287 and *FBIS Daily Report, Soviet Union*, Vol. III, no. 146 (July 28, 1978).

[35]*Pravda*, February 12, 1980.

[36]*Ibid.*, February 5, 1980.

[37]*Ibid.*, February 14, 1980. It is noteworthy that Andropov suddenly disappeared from public view right after his speech and did not reemerge until early April. It is doubtful that he was ill, since the press reported that he voted from his constituency in the RSFSR Supreme Soviet elections on February 25. Usually such unexplained absences are an indication of internal policy disagreements. Right after Andropov reemerged, Ustinov disappeared from view for over 2½ months.

[38]*Radio Liberty Research Bulletin*, no. 187/77 (August 1977).

[39]Bruce Parrott, "Technological Progress and Soviet Politics," *Survey*, no. 103 (Spring 1977–78), pp. 39–60.

[40]*Znamya*, no. 12 (1977), p. 205.

[41]Vernon Aspaturian, "Soviet Global Power and the Correlation of Forces," *Problems of Communism* (May–June 1980), p. 7.

[42]It was suggested in a recent article by John Dziak (see Note 19) that the KGB engages in quasi-military missions of a highly specialized nature. Dziak claims that the KGB has large numbers of troops at its disposal for such missions, including 260,000 MVD troops that fall under the control of the KGB for operational purposes.

[43]Paputin has been mistakenly labelled a close "crony" of Brezhnev and a member of the "Dnepropetrovsk mafia" (see Dziak, p. 781). In fact, he has no career ties with Brezhnev and, judging from the scant attention given to his death in the Soviet press, he died in disgrace. Indeed, his death was fortuitous for Brezhnev, since it enabled him to give his son-in-law, Churbanov, Paputin's post. (See Paputin's obituary in *Pravda*, January 3, 1980.)

[44]The sudden deaths of two party colleagues in puzzling circumstances makes one wonder whether Brezhnev has not already employed the KGB to eliminate opposition. F. Kulakov, thought to be a prime contender for Brezhnev's post, suffered some clear setbacks right before his unexpected death on July 17, 1978: He stood last in the leadership line-up on May Day and was absent from a crucial CC Plenum on agriculture in early July, though he was party

secretary responsible for this sector and seen at other functions. Surprisingly, Brezhnev, Kosygin, and Suslov were all absent from his funeral. P. Masherov, Belorussian party leader and candidate Politburo member, was reported to have died in a car crash in the countryside on October 6, 1980. Just a month before, while Masherov was away from Minsk, the KGB chairman in Belorussia was replaced after 10 years in that post, and other personnel shakeups followed. No Politburo members attended Masherov's funeral—an unprecedented slight— but K. Mazurov, the former Politburo member ousted by Brezhnev in 1978 and a close ally of Masherov, emerged from obscurity to attend.

[45]These officials are S. N. Antonov, G. F. Grigorenko, and V. A. Kryuchkov. Kryuchkov and Grigorenko were identified at the Twenty-Fifth Party Congress in 1976 as heads of Main Administrations of the USSR KGB.

13   PAUL COCKS

Rethinking the Organizational Weapon: The Soviet System in a Systems Age*

As Kremlin leaders climb the learning curve of what is officially called the "contemporary scientific and technological revolution" (STR), they are becoming increasingly aware of the changing conditions and new demands associated with this phenomenon. Above all, there seems to be growing realization, at least in some elite circles, that the STR is as much a managerial and even a cultural revolution as it is a scientific and industrial revolution. The key task of the times is to develop not only modern technical hardware, but also an effective and distinctive software that is appropriate to Soviet conditions as well as capable of accelerating technological change and of managing the innovation process. Indeed, that is the essence of Brezhnev's call, articulated at the 1971 CPSU Congress and reiterated at the 1976 Congress, for "combining organically the achievements of the revolution in science and technology with the advantages of the socialist economic system, to unfold more broadly our own, intrinsically socialist forms of fusing science with production."[1]

Wrestling with the new agenda of problems raised by the STR, Soviet analysts and policymakers have begun to think seriously, for the first time, about *organization* in the broadest sense. Studies involving important "cognitive reorientation and conceptual search," to borrow Erik Hoffmann's terminology, have been sanctioned and are underway.[2] Basic ideas about organization and the structural requirements of tech-

*Reprinted by permission of the author and publisher from *World Politics* 32, no. 2 (January 1980), pp. 228–257. Copyright 1980 by The Trustees of Princeton University.

nical progress are being reexamined. A relatively static view of organizational structure as an immutable given is being replaced by a more dynamic conception of organization as a set of complex variables about which some choice can be exercised. In short, the notion of "the organizational weapon," which is deeply rooted in Leninist doctrine and Soviet experience, has been rediscovered and given new life and meaning by the STR. It needs only to be retooled to the changed requirements of a different developmental stage and technological era.

Soviet Development, Technical Progress, and Organizational Lag

More and more, science, technology, and organization have moved to the forefront of the Soviet Union's modernization strategy. In 1970, Brezhnev had already observed that "the solution to many of our economic problems should now be sought at the juncture between progress in science and technology and progress in management." At that time, he also made the statement that has since become a slogan of the day: "The science of victory [in building socialism] is, in essence, the science of management."[3] Dzherman Gvishiani, Deputy Chairman of the State Committee for Science and Technology, also noted early that "fusion of the latest achievements in science and technology with the most up-to-date achievements in organization and management is an imperative of the contemporary STR."[4] Increasingly, organization is seen to be the decisive element that links technology and development. As P. M. Masherov, the Belorussian First Party Secretary and candidate member of the Politburo, observed shortly before the Twenty-Fifth Congress, "The deepest roots of our successes, of our failures, and of our capabilities are to be found precisely in the organizational factor."[5]

Underlying these ideas is enhanced awareness of a direct correlation between technology and structure and the realization that technological innovation rests on and requires administrative adaptation as well. As Masherov told the 1971 Party Congress, "It is impossible to 'squeeze' the revolution in science and technology into the framework of old methods and organizational forms of work."[6] Indeed, to attempt to put the research-to-production cycle into traditional forms is, according to some specialists, "like trying to use a steamboiler to harness atomic energy."[7] Accordingly, qualitative changes in organization and management are said to be "becoming a precondition for and a result of progress in science and technology."[8]

Experience has demonstrated the difficulties of applying new techniques of planning and management—including computerized information systems—in established institutions without organizational reform. Indeed, computers can simply "mechanize" deficiencies that are rooted in basic structure and administration. Because of this danger, some members of the elite emphasize: "At the basis for improving the system of management must lie not techniques of information processing but the organization of administration."[9] The troubles encountered in the introduction of computer technology and methods in the USSR exemplify, in fact, an old lesson: institutions may struggle to cope with problems of applying powerful and sophisticated methods and yet fail to improve effectiveness, sometimes even reduce it, and often damage the credibility of the technique in the process, because they have not been able to deal with organizational deficiencies rooted in established administrative arrangements and structural forms. These deficiencies have been exposed by new techniques but cannot be dealt with at the level of technique.

More and more, then, there is movement in the Soviet Union toward the view that "structure follows strategy"—that organizational forms, to be effective and sound, must adapt to changes in technology. A critical organizational lag and managerial gap is an integral part of the perceived technological gap. At issue, thus, are really two kinds of innovation—technological (hardware) and organizational (software and know-how) in the broad sense or, as some specialists prefer, administrative. The latter type of innovation deals with changes in the methods of running business operations that make more effective use of resources. They may include changes in structure, procedure, policies, or personnel management. However, the prospect of organizational change and administrative restructuring immediately raises a host of complex questions: On what basis? According to what principles? Toward what ends? Significantly, some Soviet analysts are beginning to address these problems and to offer some new responses and solutions.

Organizational Design: A Newly Evolving Field in the Soviet Union

In the course of the 1970s, organization emerged as a subject of intensive theoretical and applied research, along with other modern disciplines in social science, such as management science and systems analysis. Such studies have evolved as explicit aids to Soviet policymakers and change strategists. Organizational design—the systematic and purposive modeling of structures and decision processes to maximize organizational effectiveness—is itself becoming a distinct and important area of expert analysis and management specialization. This newly emerging field is regarded in some Kremlin circles as one of the main keys to building the management superstructure of tomorrow. More effective structuring of organization and decision processes is a way of preparing for—indeed designing—the future and of ultimately mastering the STR.

To be sure, Soviet leaders have long had a penchant for organization-al engineering. Almost by reflex, they have reached for reorganization as an all-purpose cure. Khrushchev in particular was enamored of reorganization as an end in itself, often without organizational studies and consultation. Until well into the 1960s, the political command simply did not see any need to do anything about organization, to think about structure, much less to think through to a new structure. The principles and purposes of organization had become, in effect, frozen. This not only inhibited creative thinking about structure and the de-velopment of new approaches to organizational change; it also contrib-uted to and reflected the growing ossification and bureaucratization of Soviet institutions. The ruling elite became captive to organizational principles and structural forms with which it had grown familiar and that it was fearful of abandoning. The escape into structure and system was psychologically comfortable and politically reassuring.

In general, Leninist elites have long respected the power of organiza-tion and the use of technology in the pursuit of political goals. Political development under Leninist regimes has also mainly consisted of organ-ization building. Basically, however, organization and technology have figured prominently as instruments of policy and agents of change in society during the transformation and consolidation stages of socialist development, to use Ken Jowitt's words.[10] Until relatively recently, they were not accorded a central place in the functioning and management of mature socialist society. On the contrary, the ideological emphasis on the ultimate withering away of the state and on self-administration by the masses, which found renewed support under Khrushchev, led to the neglect and devitalization of state agencies and of public administra-tion. Only with their belated discovery of the contemporary scientific revolution have the ruling elites come to appreciate the role of science, technology, and organization in modern society, and their potential for building and administering developed socialism.[11]

In view of this background, it is not surprising that growth of the Soviet administrative structure has been in many ways a disorganized and disorganizing process. Little thought or analysis has been given to organizational design and development. There has been little con-ceptualization, measurement, or assessment of organizational effective-ness. For the most part, organizations have simply "evolved," largely in an unplanned and unsystematic fashion. The creation of new and the revamping of old structures have "relied more on experience, analogy, conventional schemes, and finally intuition than on any firm scientific methods of organizational design."[12] Formal considerations have dominated design decisions, including criteria such as "no more" or "no less" than in other structures, "prescribed" or "not prescribed" units and subdivisions, "this hasn't been done before" or "nothing of this sort exists elsewhere," and so forth.[13] Frequently, the interests of an entrenched management staff, rather than organizational goals and final results, have determined the extent and shape of structural adaptations.[14] Old managerial forms have been mechanically carried over to new organizational models without eliminating their deficiencies or examining their suitability under changed conditions and objectives. The tendency has been not to transform the basic building blocks but simply to move them around, sometimes almost constantly, to produce different but not qualitatively new configurations. Further, the job of designing management schemes has frequently been entrusted to people who are responsible for supervising staff discipline, reflecting the extent to which conceptions of organization have narrowed to essentially an instrument of control.[15]

Gradually, however, a new attitude is beginning to penetrate and shape Soviet thought. Boris Milner, one of the leading authorities on industrial design and management in the USSR, represents this new style of thinking. The careful design of organizations, he stresses, is just as important a task as the development of new technology or the planning of production. Moreover, to perform this task today, Milner insists, "trained organization specialists are needed, not just reorganizers who are able only by intuition to put together new combinations from old administrative elements."[16] Indicating there is political support for this view, Brezhnev has also accented the need for a more scientific approach to organization building and administrative restructuring. Speaking about these issues in Alma Ata in March 1974, he said, "We must act not by eye, not by intuition, but be led by experience, experiments, and the conclusions of modern management science."[17]

Above all, a change of focus is called for. In the past, those who worked on problems of structural design concentrated on unchanged functions instead of changing tasks. They dealt "in statics, not in dynamics," as Milner puts it. Structures were regarded more or less "as a permanent collection of line and staff services, formed over a period of 30 years, without showing any developmental tendencies or the need to take into account new tasks." "The basic focus," he adds, "was on the differentiation and specialization of functions, not on their integration and joint actions with respect to common goals."[18] In short, Soviet structural design had become locked into an iron law of hierarchy and the traditional administrative pyramid. Monolithic organizational perspectives rather than multi-institutional views dominated management theory and practice, resulting in structural rigidity and low adaptability.

The "new school" of organization theorists, on the other hand, has adopted a systems approach to structural design. Its adherents see structure not as an aggregate of universal functions carried out by separate and distinct units but as a means for achieving organizational goals. Goals, then, are the chief determinant of both structure and process, and the principal means by which tasks are allocated and performance is motivated, rewarded, and controlled. As Milner succinctly puts it, "Thus, in the beginning is the goal; then comes the mechanism for achieving it." Management activities are the guidance and control processes of the organization. The task of management is "to combine, 'to fuse' the various parts of the organization into a single whole." Similarly, the focus of decision making is not on each function performed separately, but rather on the interaction and integration of functions. In addition, the orientation in designing structures must be mostly toward change rather than control and permanency of relationships. "The task is to ensure dynamism, flexibility, and adaptability in the systems of management," writes Milner.[19]

Organizational development has not kept pace with the growing complexity of the situations with which Soviet planners and administrators are faced. Significantly, as conventional approaches to organization have become ineffective in dealing with problems, the "systems" view has emerged as a way of coping with complexity and change. Because it focuses attention on interrelationships, interdependencies, and integration, the systems approach is regarded by many to be a more viable conceptual framework for analyzing and solving issues of structural design and development. Its emphasis on study of organization of the research-to-production cycle as a total system is new and underscores the emerging broader view of organizational structure as a means of facilitating decision making, motivation, and control.

The new systems approach to organizational design distinguishes, in fact, between two separate but interrelated concepts: the *process* and the supporting organizational *structure* for performing that process. Indeed, Soviet organization studies today are generally giving increased attention to the importance of processes in decision making and administration. Alongside their traditional focus on "structural principles" and "administrative methods," textbooks on management now frequently contain chapters on organizational processes dealing with communications, information flows, and policymaking. This new focus reflects an awareness that many problems today cannot be solved by means of improving the formal structures and techniques of management alone. As the Director of the Center for Management Problems at Moscow University explains, "Process is becoming more and more not simply a necessary consequence of structure but something that significantly supplements, corrects, and improves structure."[20] The persistence of "departmental barriers" in blocking both technological and organizational innovations has revealed the constraining role of structure in effecting institutional change. It has been shown all too clearly that structure influences, if not dictates, process.

New Dimensions in Structural Design: Project Management and Matrix Organization

Rising interest in structural design has brought to the fore the problem of what an organization should be rather than simply how to get the best results from an existing organization. The task facing organizational planners and administrative reformers today revolves in large part around how to design structures that will maximize organizational performance for achieving given objectives. In the process of addressing this task, they are beginning to take a new look at traditional organization charts and generally accepted principles of specialization, span of control, responsibility, authority, and accountability in the assignment and allocation of decisions. New definitions of centralization and decentralization are being sought as the search continues for ways to build more flexible and responsive structural forms.

With the growing size and complexity of the Soviet economy, two principles of design in particular are being singled out by the modernists as necessary for achieving organizational flexibility and managerial effectiveness. Both principles address major structural deficiencies of existing institutions. The first is the need *to separate strategic and coordinating functions from operating management and control.* According to Milner, the failure of existing management structures to incorporate and maintain this division of tasks has caused them "to freeze the development of technology and the efficiency of production." In practice, both strategic and operational functions are concentrated at the highest levels of management. Consequently, the command channels become overloaded as problems are constantly referred upward in the hierarchy for resolution. Decisions are delayed and their quality is reduced. Top executives become absorbed in current questions and diverted from strategic and policy concerns that only they have the right and the power to decide.[21]

Second, there is the need *to formalize and expand horizontal patterns of management as well as to combine vertical and horizontal channels of administration.* At the bottom of this principle lies a growing realization of the limitations of organizing strictly by function and by hierarchy. Structures built exclusively along vertical and functional lines are especially inappropriate for solving complex problems where work is fragmented and responsibility for final results is divided among many subdivisions. Under these conditions, Milner notes, *any* question—no matter how trivial—of a complex and crossfunctional nature must almost always go to the highest level. Integration can take place only at the apex of the organizational pyramid. Thus, top management becomes heavily involved in securing horizontal joint actions and in coordinating goal achievement by various functional units at lower levels. Again, the result is the overload situation described earlier and the failure of organizational leaders to conduct strategic planning and decision making for the future. Because the number of complex problems demanding joint efforts is growing daily, numerous attempts have been made by industrial enterprises and associations to create special bodies responsible for coordinating and harmonizing lateral ties at all levels of management. However, they have generally proved to be ineffective, Milner points out, "because they try basically to adapt the traditional line-and-staff structure to solve tasks for which it is not suitable." Such problems can be solved most effectively, he maintains, "within the framework of a special structure, one that cooperates with a line-and-staff structure, supplements it, but is not identical to it."[22]

Interestingly, the recent Soviet structural response to these twin needs has been to follow, by and large, the pattern of organizational adaptation in the United States. During the 1960s, many American business firms found that conventional structural designs and management shapes were inadequate in coping with problems of advancing technology and complexity. They faced many of the same kinds of pressures and design problems that preoccupy the Kremlin today. Similarly, interest in the design of strategic planning systems mushroomed as ways were sought to free top executives from operational worries. Concepts of differentiation and integration were applied to structural design in order to achieve greater organizational flexibility and effectiveness. Additional managerial roles were created to provide coordination on a horizontal basis across functional lines and vertical flows of authority. Among the most important structural innovations to emerge out of the 1960s were project management and matrix organization.[23]

These same two concepts lie at the basis of Soviet structural refinements and managerial reforms in the 1970s. According to Milner, they provide for a more flexible and dynamic system of coordination and subordination of different subsystems in organizing for goal accomplishment. The project approach molds organization around a specific task and makes the project leader the focal point for synchronizing and integrating functional activities from start to finish. The project manager becomes "the integrator of horizontal ties."[24] The use of a project team breaks down intraorganizational fences in the pursuit of common goals and thus avoids the basic weakness of functional structures.[25]

The matrix structure is an extension of the team principle; it seeks to combine both functional and project organizational forms. Basically, it consists of horizontal project groups overlaid on a vertical functional hierarchy. The result is a kind of "compromise" organization that tries to balance conflicting objectives, such as resource utilization and goal

achievement, with conflicting principles of management, such as efficiency and flexibility. Just as it does in the United States, the matrix
structure seems to offer organization designers in the Soviet Union "a
way out of a fix and an answer to some real needs."[26] According to K. I.
Taksir, this "fundamentally new type of structure is distinguished by
flexibility and adaptability, by the ability to adjust to new tasks and to
ensure a high level of specialization with maximum effectiveness of
operations."[27] The main advantage of matrix organization, E. I. Gavrilov
explains, is that it makes possible the transfer of operational management to lower levels and thus permits top organizational leaders to step
out of day-to-day decision making and to concentrate on the development of strategy.[28] In short, "the matrix system of management to a
large extent corresponds to the conditions of decision making dictated
by scientific and technical progress."[29]

It is not surprising, therefore, that these new types of structures have
begun to find application largely in the development and introduction of
new technology. In no area of activity is organizational flexibility so
important as in innovation. In the United States, too, the initial impetus
for new design concepts in organization and management came largely
from the aerospace and other industries pushing the state of the art in
developing technical hardware. The creation of new prototypes, retooling of production, and raising of product quality are all complex problems that are not easily handled within existing functional structures in
the USSR.[30] Indeed, it is in the area of science and technology that the
rigidities of bureaucratic structure are being particularly felt. As
Gvishiani readily admits, "[Soviet] science has, so to speak, an excess of
stability and even of conservatism." Hence, one of the main demands
on science policy today, he stresses, is to make R&D organizations more
flexible and responsive to rapid changes in organizational environment
and purpose.[31]

Suffice it to say that the so-called "science-production associations,"
which have evolved since the late 1960s as special institutional forms for
accelerating the innovation process, have become crucibles for Soviet
experimentation with these new modes of management. Some major
production associations, notably the giant Kama River Truck Complex
and the Urals Electrical Heavy Machine Building Association (*Uralelektrotiazhmash*) in Sverdlovsk have been designed and organized according
to these concepts. In addition, project management and matrix organization are being introduced at higher levels of the administrative ladder
as part of the ongoing process of ministerial restructuring. The radio,
chemical, and electrical equipment industries are on the frontiers of
experimentation in this area.[32]

It is difficult at present to assess the impact and the future of these
new dimensions in structural design. Information is lacking about the
actual practice and results of project and matrix management in the

USSR. Evidence suggests, nonetheless, that these organizational innovations are not easily or rapidly assimilated. They challenge the way organizations are structured and the way people are managed. Fundamentally, the conflict and ambiguity they build into organizational relationships and roles go against the grain of the principles of unity of command and strict superior–subordinate relations that are enshrined in democratic centralism and organizational Leninism.

Indeed, the remarks of a project manager at Uralelektrotiazhmash help put these recent developments into perspective. At the Association, new systems approaches to management have been introduced and exist alongside old administrative forms. "When any serious situation arises, however," he notes, "top management prefers to go by the old ways." Though project management has been established by statute, it has not yet in practice received the "right of full citizenship." Many in the organization regard the project manager as some kind of "geographical novelty." "The main difficulties," we are told, "are neither organizational nor technical, but purely psychological." Over a span of more than 40 years, certain traditions, mutual relations, and simple notions have developed with respect to the duties and behavior of officials and subordinates. Accordingly, a kind of "inertia by style" exists that makes it very difficult to change anything.[33] The conversion to matrix-style management and more complex organizational forms will necessarily be slow and difficult.

Putting Organization Theory into Practice: Institutional Restructuring and the Planning Process

Organizational design and development are of interest not only to theorists and model builders in ivory towers. These issues have become a major concern of the political leadership in its drive to accelerate technological innovation and administrative improvement. Brezhnev has repeatedly and forcefully hammered on this theme throughout the 1970s. He told the Central Committee in December 1973 that of all the ways to improve planning and management, better structuring of administration and decision making was the most important and the most urgent. Obviously with Khrushchev in mind he noted, "In our time we justly condemned the unwarranted tendency for organizational restructuring which took place in the past." "But at the same time," he insisted, "it is impossible to allow the ossification of organizational structures."[34] At the Twenty-Fifth Congress,, the General Secretary again emphasized:

> The Central Committee is against hasty, ill-conceived reorganization of the managerial structure and of established methods of administration. It is necessary, as the saying goes, to measure the cloth not seven times, but

eight or even ten times before cutting. But once we have done the measuring, once we have understood that the existing economic mechanism has become too tight for the developing economy, we must fundamentally improve it.[35]

Additional practical importance is attached to organizational planning because the basic building blocks of Soviet science, technology, and industry are gradually being reshaped into larger structures and more integrated associations. The formation of these new "complex organizations" has indeed become a phenomenon, if not a fad, of the times. "Nowadays, calling a research institute merely an institute or a plant merely an enterprise somehow seems clumsy, an admission of one's backwardness."[36] In the era of the scientific and technological revolution, institutional nameplates must be changed to keep pace with the times. Meanwhile, however, many of the new complexes and associations have failed to take the intended "structural leap." Instead of being unified and integrating "organic systems," they are frequently little more than mechanical aggregations of autonomous units that bear the strong imprint of preexisting organizational forms and manuals of operation.

These unsuccessful efforts at organization building are due in part to the failure of ministries to take a modern systems approach to problems of design. Research and production associations of all kinds have sometimes been put together without any systematic diagnosis of design questions or any criteria for evaluating performance and progress. Little consideration has been given to their place in the context of future directions and the needs of the branch as a whole. In the absence of clear guidelines from the center, ministerial authorities have created associations as they see fit, often obliterating the boundaries between different kinds of research and production complexes. In general, a trial-and-error method and pro forma approach have prevailed, sometimes resulting in an interminable process of reorganization upon reorganization or, in the Soviet vernacular, "administrative troop movements." Sometimes associations have been formed on the assumption that "in time everything will work itself out and fall into place." When this does not happen, even after several years of waiting and unending efforts to get an organization moving, "no one in the ministry wants to admit the mistake, since such an admission would make it necessary to name specific parties responsible for such an unsuccessful experiment."[37]

Clearly, not everyone has yet realized that these new institutional forms are not simply the sum of their parts but represent qualitatively new types of organizations. Indeed, all the difficulties encountered in getting these new structures to work effectively reflect the underdevelopment of organizational design as a distinct form of activity and the impoverishment of creative thinking in this whole sphere. These difficulties also show the extent to which the regime has become captive to a constraining organizational legacy.

Issues of organizational modeling have also acquired special importance because each ministry was obliged during the Tenth Five-Year Plan to draw up a master plan for modernizing and streamlining management for the branch as a whole by 1980. The focus of organizational design and reform has finally moved to the top of the administrative pyramid. From the mid- to late 1960s, the enterprise was the center of attention. As the feeling grew that this was too small and inadequate a unit upon which to base the Soviet Union's technological modernization—in large part due to its traditional separation from the world of scientific research and development—the focus shifted to the new basic building blocks, the research and production complexes and associations, and to the intermediate levels of the administrative ladder, notably the industrial associations that are replacing the former chief administrations or *glavki* in many sectors. Since the mid-1970s, however, there has been growing realization that reorganization of individual links of the system alone cannot give the proper result.[38] One cannot approach and design each level separately and autonomously. The starting point must be an overall conceptualization of the organization and structure of industry as a dynamic hierarchical system. Any other way amounts essentially to a piecemeal approach to structural problem solving and results in much wasted motion, not to mention considerable redesigning exercises, as demonstrated by recent Soviet experience.[39]

Though ministerial offices are busy with reorganization studies, it is difficult at this time to see where all this activity will lead and what results it will have. A. S. Vain, the principal architect of the general management scheme for the Ministry of the Chemical Industry, considers the current master plan only the first step. "The development of [Soviet] economic potential in the 1980s and 1990s requires radical improvement of existing forms and the creation of qualitatively new forms of industrial organization," he writes. Thus, the need arises to think about the shape of management not only today but toward the year 2000 as well.[40]

Meanwhile, it should be emphasized that organizational planning is an entirely new direction in Soviet economic activity. Only recently has it come to be seen as an integral and essential part of the planning of both production and technology. The absence of organizational planning in the past is now believed to have been a serious deficiency of Soviet policy and long-term programs, especially as regards the development and delivery of technology.[41] Yet, very little research has been done on the host of complex and interrelated problems involved in such forecasting and modeling. A methodology for designing internally dynamic organizations still does not exist. Adequate indicators and norms have not yet been devised for evaluating the effectiveness and benefits of the new structures. There are still very few specialists skilled in the analysis of organizational problems and policy, and limited facilities exist for training organization designers.[42] For that matter, management science more broadly, which began to emerge in the USSR over a decade ago, is said to be "still living through its formative period."[43]

Hence, most of these special plans should be seen as experiments in organizational design rather than as mature formulations and viable models. The whole field of organizational design and engineering is new and still evolving; its shape and potentiality are far from settled, and its problems far from solved. As regards the management of giant economic complexes and organizational systems, one high Soviet official admits, "We are essentially only beginning work."[44]

In view of this situation, it is not surprising that increasing attention has been devoted recently to the need to raise the level of organization of administrative rationalization, to organize the reorganization planners and new systems designers. As one observer emphasizes, "It is impossible to do systems analysis of management without a system."[45] Another specialist notes that the improvement of organization and management is fast "becoming a mass movement."[46] Though this formulation seems premature, it is clear that both the volume and the importance of work in this policy sphere have grown appreciably since the decision of March 2, 1973 to reform the Soviet ministerial structure. In some branches of the economy, 5–8% of the funds allocated to scientific research and development are being channeled into R&D on management improvement. According to estimates by *Gosplan*, in 1975 there were nearly 300,000 people engaged in drawing up management modernization programs in various branches and regions of the USSR. The level of effort involved amounted to annual wages totaling not less than 600,000 rubles.[47]

As part of this general movement, centers of organizational analysis and policy planning have been created at different levels of the administrative structure. Some ministries have formed special subdivisions under various names: a Department for Improving the System of Management (ferrous metallurgy); a Department of Organization on Management Systems and Processes (electrical engineering); and an Administration for Computer Technology and Organizational Structures (coal industry). In general, they are to serve as special departments of innovation, handling organizational and structural change at all levels of the branch hierarchy. In the majority of ministries, however, there is still no single group or office in charge of organizational development and innovation-related matters. These activities are found under different departmental jurisdictions. Each unit tends to deal with change in terms of the viewpoint of its own area of influence and interest. Because of the absence, in fact, of any structural subdivision concerned exclusively with these issues, most ministries have had to create special commissions or ad hoc working gourps to develop and draft the management master plans called for by central authorities. Much of this work has, in turn, been subcontracted out to different research facilities. However, many of the institutions engaged in organization and management studies are not scientific organizations and are not really qualified to deal with specific problems.[48]

Though detailed information is lacking about the final shape of the ministerial reorganization in process, evidence suggests that the reform plans fall short of any radical systems change. By the middle of 1977, 36 industrial ministries and departments had worked up drafts of their management master plans. Each had approached administrative restructuring in its own way. Basically, however, two approaches had been taken. One group of ministries developed rather comprehensive plans that projected fundamentally new management modes and major structural transformations throughout the branch. The other group adopted individual and partial measures aimed at improving planning and management, touching on only a few elements of the branch system.[49] In short, diversity of method and multiple approaches have prevailed.

On the national level, too, a systems approach to administrative rationalization is visibly lacking. The three main avenues of activity—research, management training, and the application of research results (including the diffusion of successful organizational experiments and innovations)—are conducted in a fragmented and uncoordinated manner. Different functional agencies with overlapping jurisdictions, incomplete mandates, and conflicting interests participate in various aspects of the total disjointed enterprise. The main arena for working out the general management plans and modernization programs for the ministries has been the Interdepartmental Commission of *Gosplan*. Because of its subordinate status, however, this commission and *Gosplan* in general have not been able to wield decisive influence in these matters and to cut through the heavy crust of bureaucratic politics and ministerial resistance surrounding institutional reform.

Since the late 1960s, several proposals have been made to centralize responsibility for this increasingly important issue area and to create a supraministerial body in charge of administrative rationalization—a kind of blue-ribbon commission on executive reorganization—near the apex of the power structure directly under the Council of Ministers or even the Politburo. Such an organ, it is suggested, could take the form of similar bodies that have been established in recent years in Poland, East Germany, and Hungary. Or, as others point out, a combined party–state agency could be reestablished along the lines of the Central Control Commission and Workers and Peasants Inspection, which served as the main modernizing arm of the Soviet party leadership in this area during the 1920s and early 1930s.[50] Because of the general reluctance of the Brezhnev regime to do major battle with the bureaucracy, however, these recommendations have not found full support among the political high command.

Recently, however, some measures have been taken to strengthen action in this sphere. In July 1978, Premier Kosygin revealed that a permanent "commission on current questions" had been formed under the Presidium of the USSR Council of Ministers. Though the exact powers and purview of this new body are not known, priority issues related to organization, planning, and management—especially with respect to major interbranch problems—presumably fall within its competence.[51] Interestingly, a standing commission has also been newly created under the council of ministers in Estonia (and headed by one of its deputy chairmen) explicitly to oversee and coordinate all administrative rationalization activity in the republic.[52]

Management training has limped along for more than a decade in a very ineffective and fragmented fashion, but here too, important developments have occurred recently at the highest level of both the government and the party structures. In October 1978, the newly established USSR Academy of the National Economy, which functions directly under the Council of Ministers, opened its doors. V. I. Dolgikh, the CPSU Secretary in charge of heavy industry, presided over the official inaugural ceremonies. He noted, "With the formation of the Academy, the whole business of training economic management is raised to a new and higher level."[53] A month before, Politburo member Suslov officiated at the opening of the newly reconstituted Academy of Social Sciences attached to the CPSU Central Committee. The new Academy is an amalgamation of the old Academy of Social Sciences, the Higher Party School, and the Higher Party Correspondence School; it also represents, according to Suslov, "a qualitatively new higher party educational institution," which bears primary responsiblity for training the top party elite in the requisite leadership skills, attitudes, and techniques for meeting the challenges of the STR.[54] Though the words of Dolgikh and Suslov may ultimately ring hollow, these institutional changes point, nonetheless, to the continuing concern of the ruling group about the issue of modern management training and possibly an enhanced determination to do something about it.

For research, a new instrument has also been created to assist Kremlin authorities in measuring and redesigning the administrative machinery. In the summer of 1976, the Institute on Systems Research was established; it reports both to the State Committee for Science and Technology and to the USSR Academy of Sciences. This Institute is the brainchild of Gvishiani, its director, who has long had a keen interest in modern organization and management. The new center is to serve as the principal "think tank" for research and analysis on organizational issues, advising government agencies and ministries on problems of structural design and administrative change. What Georgy Arbatov has done for American studies in the USSR, Gvishiani seems determined to do for organization studies. During the 1970s, Arbatov and his Institute have been instrumental in informing Soviet leaders about the United States and in framing Soviet foreign policy. In the 1980s, Gvishiani and his colleagues may perhaps play a similar role in shaping the Kremlin's perceptions and actions in domestic management and technology policies. The USA Institute has helped the political leadership become aware of and deal more effectively with international complexities; the Institute on Systems Research has a similar mission, it seems, with respect to domestic complexity and change. Like Arbatov a decade ago, Gvishiani in putting together a staff is raiding various institutions—including the USA Institute—for the best experts he can find. Boris Milner, who headed the Department on Systems Management at Arbatov's Institute, has himself moved over to Gvishiani's center. A new and important institution appears to be in the making.

Admittedly, the end results of this still evolving field of policy analysis and planning are not yet apparent. Developments nonetheless seem to reflect the following underlying assumptions and expectations with respect to institutional adaptation in the future: The requirements for innovation and efficiency must be more explicitly and effectively translated into structural terms. Organizations must be deliberately designed for change and for the ability to steer change. If administrative structures are to become and remain effective, they must change; and this change must as much as possible be by design rather than by default.

Innovation and Change: The Complexities of Passage

The scientific and technological revolution has posed the issue of governmental effectiveness in new terms. In the 1970s, the USSR has placed increasing emphasis on the urgency of administrative improvement for national development and on the need to enhance managerial capabilities in coping with problems of advancing technology and complexity.

On the one hand, the old structural forms and administrative ways have become too rigid and cumbersome to be effective. The difficulties of trying to manage with an organizational structure designed for an earlier era have become apparent. Soviet leaders have come to recognize that the problems of economic growth and technical progress must be solved rather than just endured. They have also come to realize that the inadequacies of existing institutional arrangements are so great that—at least in some areas—a major reorganization, involving more complex and flexible structural designs, is needed rather than simply an improvement of conventional forms and methods.

On the other hand, the new institutional configurations and organizational innovations that have emerged in recent years have not yet acquired, for the most part, what in the American terminology of political science is called "enabling effectiveness." They are still largely experimental, untried, and distrusted structures and methods, coexisting with the old—and not always peacefully. Until they gain status and legitimacy, borne of the experience of their usefulness, these new organizational designs will inhibit as much as they enable innovative and effective action. The conversion to complex structural forms, like matrix management, takes time; and change does not come easily. Both old and new structures, then, are "transitional organizations." At present, the whole Soviet architecture of linkage between science and industry is in transition and in motion, even if slow motion.

Through new or at least modified institutional frameworks, it is hoped that organization can be made a force that fosters rather than impedes innovation and change. In view of the heavy stress on organizational issues and approaches, in fact, the key to innovation seems at times to be simply "management by structure." Yet there are important complexities and constraints at work in the system, which necessarily limit the efficacy of structural solutions.

Indeed, all the problems met in creating economic complexes and in disseminating successful organizational experiments serve as a reminder that the effectiveness of an organizational change depends not only on the nature of that change but also on other nonorganizational features of the system.[55] The problems of innovation in the USSR—and elsewhere—are fundamentally human problems. Behind the so-called "departmental obstacles" are invisible psychological barriers. Organizational engineering requires a corresponding behavioral remolding and attitudinal change. Above all, fundamental problems of power and politics constrain institutional adaptation. Many basic problems remain unresolved and incapable of solution by organizational weapons alone.

Solutions to complex problems are themselves usually complex. Although this fact is not always understood or appreciated, some Soviet analysts are fully aware of the difficulties of effecting change. Milner himself has articulated the basic dilemma that the leadership faces today in rethinking the organizational weapon. There is no doubt, he says, that modern systems approaches and more sophisticated techniques make planning and management more difficult. They bring it "into a new class, into a new situation." "But it is not possible by any other way," he maintains, "to solve the new and complex problems of development of the national economy, which have no precedent in our past experience."[56] Appearing in a publication designated "for official use only" and circulated in just 500 copies, these words were not meant simply for foreign consumption.

Generally speaking, the Soviet regime under Brezhnev has moved toward the idea of change as a *process*. The gradual shift from a phase-dominant and disjointed model of technological innovation to a process-and-systems view underpins the drive to create integrated complexes for research and development. These new associational forms are intended to give institutional expression and coherence to the research–to-production cycle. They reflect enhanced awareness that it is necessary to *organize* for innovation. The innovation cycle must be structured and managed as a process, which it has not been in the past. Significantly, in the 1970s, one of the Soviet leadership's major discoveries about innovation has been the importance of the "management connection," together with the realization that action must be negotiated and mediated throughout the activity chain. Some Soviet specialists prefer, in fact, to speak in terms of a "research–managment–production cycle," because it conveys a more adequate image of this complex process. Such phraseology also explicitly identifies and emphasizes the critical management function and linkage.[57]

As regards organizational innovation, too, Brezhnev and his colleagues have repeatedly stressed the notion that administrative improvement is a dynamic and continuing process. Change is not a single action. A situation cannot be radically altered by political fiat or by one structural blow of the organizational cudgel. Consequently, the regime has adopted an essentially experimental and incremental approach to change. Various administrative experiments using new planning and management techniques, incentive systems, and structural arrangements have been organized to effect improvements that would set examples for the rest of the system. The focus of reform strategy has come to center on organizational experiments at the microlevel, as a prelude to and precondition for any broader systems-engineering and macrolevel change.

To be sure, there is an important political rationale for this piecemeal and cautious approach. It is quite appropriate for a ruling oligarchy that is strongly apprehensive about any major and arbitrary assault on the status quo and entrenched bureaucratic interests. Organizational experiments on a "local" and limited basis provide a proving ground for new ideas. They tend to reduce fears of risk and feelings of uncertainty about change and help to convince conservative critics of the correctness and benefits of innovation. Programs of management training and executive development—which form an integral part of this approach— provide opportunities to both party and government cadres for learning and retooling and thus diminish fears while increasing familiarity with modern concepts and techniques. In fact, one may say that, given Soviet conditions, this strategy is the only politically feasible one open to reform-minded authorities, and it has permitted the Brezhnev administration to survive, if not to succeed at raising administrative performance and capacity appreciably.

At the same time, however, one may argue that a kind of general "learning experience," which also contributes to this experimental and incremental perspective, seems to have taken place among the ruling elite. The Khrushchevian legacy made Soviet leaders not only weary but also wary of hasty, ill-conceived, and sweeping reorganizations. Through his frequently uninformed and forced interventions, officially dubbed "adventurist and harebrained schemes," Khrushchev sometimes made things different but not always better. Though his successors still grasp at panaceas and simplistic solutions, a new level of sophistication is evident in their wrestling with the issues of technological progress and management improvement. There is greater awareness of the multiplicity of factors involved in innovation, along with greater appreciation of the importance of effective coupling throughout the process. Steps forward have invariably turned out to be only half-steps. All the official acclaim about and accent on the need for a systems approach notwithstanding, there does seem to be increasing realization that perhaps there are no simple and total solutions, only partial remedies for the problems at hand. The complexity of Soviet society and the difficulty of effecting change in any one issue area have become steadily apparent and seem to defy, if not deny, any rapid and radical systems engineering.

The focus of Soviet politics and policy, therefore, has moved away from "change"—perceived and defined in rather broad and sharp systems terms (and often associated with whole stages of development)—to "adaptation," which captures the idea of within-system change as a dynamic process of gradual steps and adjustments. Adaptation also stresses the relationship between organization and environment and the need for institutions to fit themselves to their complex surroundings.[58] Stated somewhat differently, the emphasis in development strategy and tactics has shifted from "major changes" to "marginal improvements"—to the accumulation of limited changes as the most appropriate means of producing ultimately extensive transformations. In the process, the level of elite expectations (and fears) has been lowered with respect to social engineering. At issue, then, is a kind of evolutionary development that stresses differences of degree rather than of kind. More and more, the dialectic of development assumes the form, *plus ça change, plus c'est la même chose*. Thus, a different kind of drama appears to be at work. Change through adaptation is more subtle, more ambiguous, more difficult to define, detect, and measure than the arbitrary wrenchings of the system and abrupt turnover of institutions, individuals, and policies that marked the movements of the regime in the past.

In light of the foregoing, a change of perspective and of language also seems to be in order with respect to the study of the Soviet Union by Western analysts. We, too, have long tended to think of change in starkly defined terms and simple dichotomies, like "degeneration" or "transformation," "petrification" or "pluralism."[59] Such a perception of the problem can make us insensitive to marginal adjustments, evolving experiments, and creeping innovations within the system. By posing developmental issues in predominantly "either/or" terms, we some-times forget that reality is much more complex and resembles rather a "both/and" condition. Processes working both for and against change are always present, and the balance of forces between them is constantly shifting. A strongly exclusivist approach yields not only essentially static and excessively rigid models of the Soviet system but causes us to lose sight of the very dynamics and dilemmas, the conflicts and choices, that underlie Soviet development and the political process. Just as the new reality, named the era of the STR, is generating adaptation and change in Soviet cognitive processes and attitudes, so it also makes it incumbent upon Western Sovietologists to sharpen their conceptual lenses and tools of analysis. We need, in particular, to become more aware of and to appreciate the growing complexity of Soviet society and the implications of this complexity for policy and change in the 1980s and beyond. Soviet authorities increasingly seem to recognize this dominant condition— even if grudgingly and slowly. It is important that we do so as well.

The Soviet System in a Systems Age   What are we to make of this commotion about the so-called contemporary scientific and technological revolution, which seems to have become the Krem-lin's frame of reference in the 1970s for organizing both domestic and foreign policy? With the "systems approach" fast becoming the last word in Soviet discussions of planning and manage-ment, are we indeed on the threshold of an era of change and a remaking of the Soviet system, if only with a more modern technological lining? Do recent developments portend the displacement of the *appar-atchik* by a new Soviet organization man, the *sistemshchik*? Or, is all this talk mere rhetoric, the new jargon coined for purposes more of image-making than of policymaking?

There are, it seems, at least two ways of approaching these questions and of gaining some perspective on the significance of the current concern with systems. One way is to focus on the battery of new analytical and administrative techniques that are being developed to resolve problems attending the processes and consequences of develop-ment. This task involves examining the "modernization of technique" and assessing the effectiveness of new managerial devices for improving executive performance, such as Soviet-style matrix structures, project management, network planning, cost–benefit analysis, and com-puterized information systems. The basic problem with this approach, however, is that "effectiveness" is not easily measured and evaluated. The trouble lies not only in a lack of information about the actual practice of these innovations; there are also severe conceptual and methodological obstacles. It is exceedingly difficult to disentangle technique from a host of other factors with which it interacts—to "disembody" technology from the larger system of which it is an organic part.

On balance, it appears that the new management approaches and methods—when judiciously applied—do contribute to better performance. The improvements have been only marginal, however. The actual gains are much less comprehensive in scope and uneven in distribution than they are generally said to be. As a rule, innovations in technique tend to be greatly oversold—perhaps a necessary condition for getting attention and approval in the first place. Technique has become a fetish, and exaggerated expectations are the result. In the course of practical application, initial hopes invariably give way to disappointment, to a sobering of estimates, and ultimately to a new line of organizational panaceas and technological fixes upon which everything is supposed to depend. That is the perennial story of all Soviet reforms.

Alternatively, it is possible to look not at the new managerial tool kit in the making but at the underlying problems to which the quest for improved technique is addressed. From that perspective, the significance of the USSR's belated awakening to the modern systems age is the discovery by its rulers that the Soviet system is, in fact, not a system in the sense of a well-integrated assembly of parts pulling together in the same direction. On the contrary, compartmentalization of activity and fragmentation of government stand out as dominant features of contemporary Soviet society. A confusing array of piecemeal approaches, programs, and structures exposes all too clearly the many "holes in the whole" and serious deficiencies in integrative capabilities. The rising stress on systems terminology and technology suggests a unity, coherence, and wholeness that are lacking in reality. Indeed, the systems approach is being used to a large extent as a rhetorical device for advocating comprehensive efforts at redesigning and improving the parts on which the regime relies but which continue to disappoint in their performance.[60]

Similarly, the main theme that implicitly pervades studies of Soviet organization is the "disorganization" of policy and administration. The increasing burden of rigid and unresponsive institutions underlies the attention that is being given in the sphere of organizational design to the creation of dynamic, flexible, and adaptable structures. More and more, it is the bureaucratic features of the Soviet system that have come to the fore and pose the greatest challenges for the future. The Kremlin's real basis of concern, therefore, is growing realization and fear that the USSR lacks not just modern hardware but, more important, the management software for mastering the contemporary STR.

At issue here are fundamental questions of power and leadership. In general, there has been a gradual erosion and diffusion of executive authority throughout the administrative structure since Stalin's death. Integrative capabilities, both analytical and managerial, are particularly lacking for large-scale, multiministerial projects that cut across organizational boundaries. Problems of science and technology as well as the development of regional resources are good examples of such "interbranch" projects. The importance of this class of problem is increasing due to the forces of economic growth and the requirements of technical progress.[61] The crux of the matter is that the scale of these priority problems exceeds the competency of any agency to deal with them. As a result, they tend to fall victim to disaggregated and fragmented solutions. By their nature, such complex problems require close lateral relationships, joint collaboration, and strong coordination. Traditional management approaches, which emphasize hierarchy or informality, are hardly adequate for the task. A major aim, therefore, of the systems movement is to develop managerial devices that will facilitate effective patterns of interaction and integration.

The underlying deficiencies are to a certain extent faults in organizational design or in the adaptability of institutions to meet problems and opportunities. At the same time, however, they also appear to signify, if not the failure of leadership, then the failure of execution somewhere below the top. All the trappings of sophisticated technique aside, the core problems behind the professed need for a modern systems approach to planning and management basically involve issues of the effective distribution of power, responsibility, and accountability. As one prominent Soviet systems enthusiast acknowledges, "In itself, this approach is nothing new. It always appears where there is good management."[62]

It is therefore not accidental, writes M. P. Ring, that methods and forms of project management are at present being expanded, especially in the area of science and technology. Though the USSR Academy of Sciences has long used so-called "problem coordinators" to direct some of its major research programs, these individuals generally have only advisory authority. Similarly, chief designers are appointed in various branches of machine building, as are chief technologists or chief chemists in the chemical industry, to oversee the development of certain kinds of products and equipment. Because of their insufficiently defined powers and juridical status, however, they are frequently unable to carry out their functions. What is needed, according to Ring, are effective forms of project management that explicitly identify leadership roles and responsibilities. The alleged advantage of such administrative innovations is that they "combine the authority of power with the power of scientific authority, official responsibility with personal scientific duty, and the management of projects with direct participation in projects." Ring notes further that "the task is to put under this activity the necessary organizational foundation, to combine in an optimal way executive and advisory authority." The USSR can no longer afford to base planning and management of some of its most important programs on essentially voluntary and informal methods.[63]

The call for modern systems or project management is a demand for greater personalization of power and authority and for the creation of more viable forms of "one-man command" for interbranch projects. More than any other kind of decision problem, these projects are subject to the practices and pathologies of interagency bargaining, committee decision making, and collective leadership. Behind the criticism of existing policies and procedures, one can sense a longing for a strong administrative hand and leadership to break through the labyrinth of bureaucracy.

The notion of "the organizational weapon" embodies the amalgamation and use of power and technology in the pursuit of political goals. The basic predicament confronting the Soviet rulers on the eve of the 1980s is that they appear to lack both the power and the technique for dealing with the complex problems of the present era. The administrative arsenal, built largely for purposes of propelling the Soviet Union into the steel age, is hardly adequate for moving it into the computer age. New organizational weapons are needed to break the new barriers of complexity.

How the leaders respond to these conditions of heightened complexity will be a key factor in the decade ahead. They may learn to live with, and to cope with, complexity and its constraints in a creative way along lines suggested by Boris Milner and other analysts. Such an attitude may lead them to seek not only more flexible organizational models and sophisticated management techniques but new definitions of administrative and political rationality as well. On the other hand, the ruling group may come to feel overwhelmed by change and complexity. Those who remain skeptical of the relevance of advanced management methods to the problems at hand may grow in number and influence. Reorganization planners who, like Milner, press for restraint in the fact of complexity and change strategists who champion an incremental and experimental approach may increasingly be seen as counselors of despair. Growing impatient and dissatisfied with the marginal returns of limited reforms and complex solutions, some members of the ruling establishment may hark back to a more heroic tradition and radical approach to systems engineering—with greater reliance on raw power, rapid changes and strong personal leadership to work the needed improvements in the bureaucracy, economy, and society.

Though it is difficult to foresee the particular mix of power, organization, and technique in the offing, we can reasonably assume that at least the immediate future will not entail an "age of discontinuity." Political dynamics and systemic inertial forces militate against any comprehensive and fundamental systems change. Indeed, the machinery of rule bears the heavy stamp of past reorganizations that have resulted in considerable bureaucratic layering. Administrative echelon has been piled upon administrative echelon in an unremitting quest for coordination and order. The crazy-quilt pattern of Soviet administration with all its crosscutting jurisdictions and interests aggravates the difficulties of making changes in organizational structures, procedures, and policies. Although almost every issue seems to cry out for a systems approach, conditions make comprehensive solutions both impossible and undesirable. Moreover, the growing complexity and interdependency of society impose their own kinds of constraints and require greater differentiation as well as integration in policymaking and execution. Existing deficiencies cannot be easily eradicated—and certainly not by misleading holistic terms and the use of modern systems phraseology by the Kremlin.

The extent to which the Soviet political command is able to bring the perspectives and techniques of space-age management to bear, not just in the military sphere but on its civilian problems and programs, will provide the real test of leadership in the next decade. The dominant issues of today and tomorrow challenge the adaptive capabilities of the administrative system and force attention to the need for more imaginative and effective management approaches and methods. Herein lies the significance of recent Soviet efforts to rethink the organizational weapon.

Notes

[1] *XXIV s"ezd KPSS: Stenograficheskii otchet* [Stenographic report of the Twenty-Fourth Congress of the CPSU] (Moscow: Politizdat, 1971), I, p. 82: *XXV s"ezd KPSS: Stenograficheskii otchet* [Stenographic Report of the Twenty-Fifth Congress of the CPSU] (Moscow: Politizdat, 1976), II, p. 237. All translations from the original Russian are by the author.

[2] Hoffmann, "Soviet Views of 'The Scientific-Technological Revolution,' " *World Politics* 30 (July 1978), pp. 615–645, at 617.

[3] *Pravda*, June 13, 1970.

[4] Gvishiani, *Organization and Management: A Sociological Analysis of Western Theories* (Moscow: Progress Publishers, 1972), p. 172.

[5] *Sovetskaia Belorussiia*, February 5, 1976.

[6] *XXIV s"ezd KPSS* I, pp. 179–180.

[7] P. Danilovtsev and Yu. Kanygin, *Ot laboratorii do zavoda* [From laboratory to Plant] (Novosibirsk: Nauka, 1971), p. 40.

[8] Boris Z. Milner, "Organization of the Management of Production," *Social Sciences*, no. 3 (1976), p. 48. (Moscow). See also Nikolai S. Kalita and German I. Mantsurov, *Sotsialisticheskie proizvodstvennye ob"edineniia* [Socialist production associations] (Moscow: Ekonomika, 1972), pp. 3–4.

[9] Georgy Arbatov, "Proektirovanie organizatsii krupnykh proizvodstvenno-

khoziaistvennykh kompleksov i upravleniia imi," [Designing the organization and mangement of large-scale economic production complexes], *Planovoe khoziaistvo*, no. 5 (May 1975), p. 26. For a discussion of the deficiencies in designing computer information systems, especially the failure to link their introduction to organization and decision processes, see Boris Z. Milner, "Kak sproektirovat, organizatsiiu?" [How should an organization be designed?], *Izvestiia*, May 13, 1973.

[10]Jowitt, "An Organizational Approach to the Study of Political Culture in Marxist–Leninist Systems," *American Political Science Review* 68 (September 1974), pp. 1171–1191; Jowitt, "Inclusion and Mobilization in European Leninist Regimes," *World Politics* 28 (October 1975), pp. 69–96.

[11]For a more general discussion of these issues, see Cocks, "Retooling the Directed Society: Administrative Modernization and Developed Socialism," in Jan F. Triska and Paul M. Cocks, eds., *Political Development in Eastern Europe* (New York: Praeger, 1977), pp. 53–92; also, Fleron's introduction to Frederic J. Fleron, ed., *Technology and Communist Culture: The Socio-Cultural Impact of Technology under Socialism* (New York: Praeger, 1977), pp. 1–67.

[12]Boris Z. Milner, ed., *Organizatsionnye struktury upravleniia proizvodstvom* [Organizational structures for managing production] (Moscow: Ekonomika, 1975), p. 5.

[13]Milner, "Kak sproektirovat' organizatsiiu?"

[14]Boris V. Gubin and Nikolai G. Kalinin, *Organizatsiia upravleniia promyshlennostiu v usloviiakh dvukh- i trekhzvennoi sistemy* [The organization of industrial management in conditions of a two- and three-link system] (Moscow: Ekonomika, 1977), p. 5; E. P. Torkanovskii, "Programmno-tselevoe upravlenie" [Programmed-goals management], *Sovetskoe gosudarstvo i pravo*, no. 3 (March 1978), p. 30.

[15]Milner, *Organizatsionnye*, p. 5.

[16]*Ibid.*, p. 4; see also Arbatov, "Proektirovanie," p. 21.

[17]*Pravda*, March 16, 1974.

[18]Boris Z. Milner, "Formirovanie organizatsionnykh struktur upravleniia" [Forming organizational structures of management], *Ekonomika i organizatsiia promyshlennogo proizvodstva*, no. 6 (November–December 1975), pp. 4–5.

[19]See Milner, *Organizatsionnye*," pp. 5, 6, 16–17, 37.

[20]Gavriil Kh. Popov, ed., *Organizatsiia protsessov upravleniia* [Organization of management processes] (Moscow: Ekonomika, 1975), pp. 31, 44–45.

[21]Milner, "*Formirovanie*," p. 8; Milner, *Organizatsionnye*, p. 7.

[22]*Ibid.*, pp. 7, 8, 16, 108; Milner, "Formirovanie," pp. 8–9. The kind of new structure he has explicitly in mind is the "matrix organization."

[23]For general discussion of the evolution of organizational design in the West, see Derek Newman, *Organization Design: An Analytical Approach to the Structuring of Organizations* (London: E. Arrold, 1973); Jay R. Galbraith, "Matrix Organizational Design: How to Combine Functional and Project Forms," *Business Horizons* 14 (February 1971), pp. 2–40; Peter Lorange and Richard F. Vancil, *Strategic Planning Systems* (Englewood Cliffs, N.J.: Prentice-Hall, 1977); Gene W. Dalton, Paul R. Lawrence, and Jay W. Lorsch, *Organizational Structure and Design* (Homewood, Ill.: R. D. Irwin, 1970); Fremont E. Kast and James E. Rosenzweig, *Organization and Management: A Systems Approach* (New York: McGraw-Hill, 1970); David I. Cleland and William R. King, *Systems Analysis and Project*

Management (New York: McGraw-Hill, 1975); Stanley M. Davis and Paul R. Lawrence, *Matrix* (Reading, Mass.: Addison-Wesley, 1977).

[24]Milner, *Organizatsionnye*, pp. 108, 110.

[25]Kim I. Taksir, *Nauchno-proizvodstvennye ob"edineniia* [Science-production associations] (Moscow: Nauka, 1977), p. 85.

[26]Kenneth Knight, ed., *Matrix Management* (New York: PBI-Petrocelli Books, 1977), p. 1.

[27]Taksir, *Nauchno-proizvodstvennye*, pp. 81–82.

[28]Evgenii I. Gavrilov, *Ekonomika i effektivnost'nauchno-tekhnicheskogo progressa* [Economics and effectiveness of scientific–technical progress] (Minsk: Vyshaia shkola, 1975), p. 280. Also on the advantages of the matrix structure, see Nikolai E. Drogichinskii, ed., *Sovershenstvovanie mekhanizma khoziaistvovaniia v usloviiakh razvitogo sotsializma* [Improving the management mechanism in conditions of developed socialism] (Moscow: Ekonomika, 1975), pp. 169–170.

[29]Mikhail M. Kreisberg, *S Sh A: Sistemnyi podkhod v upravlenii* [The USA: The systems approach to management] (Moscow: Nauka, 1974), p. 192.

[30]Milner, *Organizatsionnye*, pp. 108. 117.

[31]Dzherman M. Gvishiani, "The Scientific and Technological Revolution and Scientific Problems," *Social Sciences* (January-March 1972), pp. 55–56.

[32]See Taksir, *Nauchno-poizvodstvennye*, pp. 80–93; Milner, *Organizatsionnye*, pp. 110–115, 121; Valerii I. Kushlin, *Uskorenie vnedreniia nauchnykh dostizhenii v proizvodstvo* [Accelerating the introduction of scientific achievements into production] (Moscow: Ekonomika, 1977), pp. 133–136; Dzherman M. Gvishiani, ed., *Voprosy teorii i praktiki upravleniia i organizatsii nauki* [Questions of theory and practice in the management and organization of science] (Moscow: Nauka, 1975), pp. 14–17.

[33]See A. G. Vel'sh, "Effektivnost' upravleniia povysilas'," [The effectiveness of management has risen], *Ekonomika i organizatsiia promyshlennogo proizvodstva*, no. 6 (November–December 1975), pp. 36–37. V. S. Rapoport, who favors more extensive study of matrix organization and American experience with these types of management designs, also observes, "Uralelektrotiazhmash shows how difficult is the transition to new management structures, how high are the psychological barriers." See his comments in *EKO*, no. 2 (March–April 1978), p. 165.

[34]Leonid I. Brezhnev, *Ob osnovnykh voprosakh ekonomicheskoi poliiki KPSS na sovremennom etape: rechi i doklady* [On fundamental questions of economic policy of the CPSU at the contemporary stage: speeches and reports] (Moscow: Politizdat, 1975), II, pp. 355–356.

[35]*Pravda*, February 25, 1976.

[36]G. Ivanov and G. Yakovlev, "Pod novoi vyveskoi" [Under a new name-plate], *Pravda*, March 26, 1978.

[37]*Ibid.*

[38]Gubin and Kalinin, *Organizatsiia*, p. 35.

[39]A. S. Vain, "Formy organizatsii promyshlennosti," [Forms of industrial organization], *Izvestiia Akademii nauk SSSR*, seriia ekonomicheskaia, no. 5 (1977), pp. 61–62.

[40]*Ibid.*, pp. 59–60, 62.

[41]See Gavriil Kh. Popov, *Effektivnoe upravlenie* [Effective management] (Moscow: Ekonomika, 1976), p. 35.

[42]See Fedor M. Rusinov, "Organizatsionnye problemy upravleniia sotsiali-

sticheskim proizvodstvom" [Organizational problems of managing socialist production], in *Nauchnoe upravlenie obshchestvom* [Scientific management of society], ed. Viktor G. Afanas'ev, IX (Moscow: Mysl', 1975), pp. 163–175.

[43]Dmitrii Pravdin, "Osobennosti formirovaniia nauki upravleniia sotsialisticheskoi ekonomikoi" [Particular features of forming a science of management for socialist economy], *Voprosy ekonomiki*, no. I (January 1978), p. 59. For background information, see Robert F. Miller, "The New Science of Administration in the USSR," *Administrative Science Quarterly* 18 (September 1971), pp. 247–255.

[44]Vadim A. Trapeznikov, "Upravlenie naukoi kak organizatsionnoi sistemi" [The management of science as on organizational system], in *Osnovnye printsipy i obshchie problemy upravleniia naukoi*, ed. Dzherman M. Gvishiani (Moscow: Nauka, 1973), p. 25.

[45]Ivan Syroezhin, "O kompleksnoi organizatsii sovershenstvonaiia upravleniia proizvodstvom [On the integrated organization of improving management of production], in *Problemy organizatsii sovershenstvovaniia upravleniia sotsialisticheskim proizvodstvom* [Problems of organization in improving the management of socialist production], ed. G. Kh. Popov (Moscow: Izd-vo Moskovskogo Universiteta, 1975), p. 33.

[46]E. N. Bliokov, "Model' sistemy 'nauka-proizvodtsvo' i reshenie zadach planomernoi organizatsii nauchno-tekhnicheskogo i ekonomicheskogo razvitiia" [A model of the "science-production" system and solution to the tasks of the planned organization of scientific, technical and economic development], *Izvestiia Akademii nauk SSSR*, seriia ekonomicheskaia, no. 2 (1978), p. 58.

[47]Popov, *Problemy organizatsii*, pp. 51, 55fn.

[48]See Gubin and Kalinin, *Organizatsiia*, pp. 121–123.

[49]*Ibid.*, pp. 37–38.

[50]See *Ibid.*, pp. 179–180; Mikhail I. Piskotin, *Nauchnye osnovy gosudarstvennogo upravleniia v SSSR* [Scientific principles of state administration in the U.S.S.R.] (Moscow: Nauka, 1968), pp. 134–135; G. Kh. Popov, *Problemy teorii upravleniia* [Problems of management theory] (Moscow: Ekonomika, 1970), p. 173; G. V. Atamanchuk, *Gosudarstvennoe upravlenie: Problemy metodologii pravovogo issledovaniia* [State administration: problems of methodology in legal research] (Moscow: Iuridicheskaia Literatura, 1975), pp. 198–200; Viktor G. Afanas'ev, D. M. Gvishiani, V. N. Lisitsyn, and G. Kh. Popov, eds., *Upravlenie sotsialisticheskim proizvodstvom: Voprosy teorii i praktiki* [Management of socialist production: questions of theory and practice] (Moscow: Ekonomika, 1975), pp. 637–651; Popov *Problemy organizatsii*, p. 10; Popov, *Effektivnoe upravlenie*, pp. 141–142.

[51]Its specific function, Kosygin said, "is to examine and resolve current questions of economic construction and to exercise systematic control over the fulfillment of the state plan and budget." In his report on the new law on the USSR Council of Ministers, Kosygin also noted that questions dealing with interbranch problems and programs were absorbing more and more of the Council's attention. See *Pravda*, July 6, 1978.

[52]Popov, *Problemy organizatsii*, p. 146.

[53]*Pravda*, October 3, 1978.

[54]*Ibid.*, September 2, 1978.

[55]Joseph S. Berliner, *The Innovation Decision in Soviet Industry* (Cambridge, Mass.: M.I.T. Press, 1976), p. 146.

[56]Boris Z. Milner, "Sovershenstvovanie organizatsionnykh struktur uprav-

leniia" [Improving organizational structures of management], in *Sovremennye metody upravleniia narodnym khoziaistvom* [Modern methods of managing the national economy], II (Vilnius: Litovskii Nauchno-Issledovatel'skii Institut Nauchno-Tekhnicheskoi Informatsii i Tekhniko-Ekonomicheskikh Issledovanii, 1974), p. 22.

[57]V. I. Berlozertsev, "Soedinenie nauchno-tekhnicheskoi revoliutsii s preimushchestvami sotsializma" [Combining the scientific and technological revolution with the advantages of socialism], in *Problemy soedineniia dostizhenii nauchnoteckhnicheskoi revoliutsii s preimushchestvami sotsializma* [Problems of combining the achievements of the scientific and technological revolution with the advantages of socialism] (Voronezh: Izd-vo Voronezhkogo Universiteta, 1974), pp. 11–12.

[58]For an insightful discussion of the general problems of adaptation and change, see Herbert Kaufman, *The Limits of Organizational Change* (University, Alabama: University of Alabama Press, 1971). For a look at the Soviet experience from what is predominantly a perspective of adaptation, see Karl W. Ryavec, ed., *Soviet Society and the Communist Party* (Amherst: University of Massachusetts Press, 1978).

[59]See, for example, the seminal articles by Zbigniew Brzezinski, "The Soviet Political System: Transformation or Degeneration?" *Problems of Communism* 15 (January–February 1966), pp. 1–15, and Jerry Hough, "The Soviet System: Petrification or Pluralism?" *Problems of Communism* 21 (March–April 1972), pp. 25–45.

[60]For an excellent discussion of systems concepts and applications, though in a different context, see Ernst B. Haas, "Is There A Hole in the Whole? Knowledge, Technology, Interdependence, and the Construction of International Regimes,"*International Organization* 29 (Summer 1975), pp. 827–876.

[61]Mikhail P. Ring, a leading expert on science policy, writes: "The solution of interbranch, interregional, and national economic, scientific, and engineering problems determines on the whole the development of science and technology in the epoch of the STR." See "Problemnoe upravlenie v nauke: pravovye aspekty" [Problem-oriented management in science: legal aspects], *Vestnik Akademii nauk SSSR*, no. 7 (July 1976), pp. 12–13. Professor Popov, Dean of the economics Faculty at Moscow University, similarly notes, "Today virtually all questions of any importance—above all, the key problems of scientific and technical progress—have become interbranch in nature. That is why improvement of the mechanism of interbranch coordination is one of the core problems of management." See Popov, "Kakova nadezhnost' stykov?" [How reliable are the interfaces?], *Pravda*, July 27, 1976.

[62]G. Pospelov, "Sistemnyi podkhod" [The systems approach], *Izvestiia*, March 21, 1974.

[63]Ring, "Problemnoe upravlnie v nauke" [Problem-oriented management in science], *Vestnik Akademii nauk SSSR*, No. 8 (August 1976), 34–35. In the past, scientific leaders of national priority programs were often powerful individuals who wielded considerable authority: Igor Kurchatov in nuclear industry, S. P. Korolev in the space program, and Trofim Lysenko in agriculture, were all strong "project managers" in their respective areas. As one knowledgeable observer writes, they "were able to force some ministers to resign if they found them inefficient in the management of the 'state-important' scientific programs." See Zhores Medvedev, *Soviet Science* (New York: Norton 1978), 130–31. In general, though, this kind of broad systems-management capability has been lacking in Soviet civilian-oriented research and development programs.

14   DAVID HOLLOWAY

War, Militarism, and the Soviet State*

In the military structure of the world, the Soviet Union and the United States stand in a class by themselves. They mount the two largest military efforts and between them account for one-half of the massive resources that the world devotes to arms and armed forces. There are, it is true, considerable differences between the military forces of the Soviet Union and the United States, but these are insignificant when compared with the differences between them and the forces of other states.

From the armed forces it maintains and the weapons it produces, it is clear that the Soviet military effort is large. It is difficult, however, to say precisely what resources it consumes. The Soviet government publishes a figure for the defense budget each year, but this is of little help in estimating the military burden because it is not clear what the budget covers. In any event, observers outside the Soviet Union agree that the Soviet Armed Forces could not be paid for by the official defense budget without the help of very large hidden subsidies. Western attempts to assess Soviet defense spending must be treated with caution, too, because of the intrinsic difficulties of making such estimates.[1] It is evident, nevertheless, that only a major commitment of resources has enabled the Soviet Union in the last 20 years to attain strategic parity with the United States, maintain large well-equipped forces in Europe and along the frontier with China, extend the deployment of the Soviet Navy throughout the world, and engage in continuous modernization of arms and equipment.

*Reprinted in revised form by permission of the author and publisher from *Alternatives* 6, no. 1 (March 1980), pp. 59–92. Copyright 1980 by Institute for World Order. Prepared for the World Order Models Project group on de-militarization. The author would like to acknowledge the helpful comments received on an earlier draft from Silviu Brucan, Judith Reppy, and William Sweet.

A military effort of this scale necessarily has a far-reaching impact on the Soviet economy. An extensive network of military research and development establishments is required to develop armaments, while a major sector of industry is needed to produce them in quantity. The Soviet Union has amassed military power roughly comparable to that of the United States, even though its Gross National Product is only about one-half as large. Consequently, a higher rate of extraction of resources has been necessary with consequences that will be examined shortly.

The maintenance of standing forces of some 4 million people (primarily men) has not only economic but also social and political consequences.[2] Institutional arrangements exist to draft a substantial proportion of each generation of young men into the armed forces. A considerable effort is made to ensure that reserves are available for mobilization if necessary. Voluntary military societies provide moral support for the armed forces and military training for the population at large. Secondary school children are given preinduction military training from the age of 15 years. In recent years, there has been a growing campaign of military–patriotic education that attempts to instill in the population the values of patriotism and respect for military virtues. Party leaders seemingly believe that obligatory military service can help to foster social discipline and to bring the different nationalities closer together. They also appear to believe that association of the party with the armed forces will strengthen Soviet patriotism and the commitment of the people to the existing political order.[3] At the highest political level, the close relationship between party and army has been underlined by the awarding to General Secretary Brezhnev of various military honors, including the rank of Marshal of the Soviet Union.

All this is a far cry from the vision of socialist society that the founders of Marxism and the makers of the Bolshevik Revolution held. Marxist thought has been marked traditionally by a strong antipathy to militarism, viewing war and armies as the product of the world capitalist system. Before 1917, socialists agreed that standing armies were instruments of aggression abroad and repression at home; the proper form of military organization for a socialist state would be the citizen army that would not degenerate into a military caste or create a military realm separate from other areas of social life. Although he had to lead the young Soviet republic against the White armies and foreign intervention, Lenin never succumbed to the worship of things military or tried to enhance his own authority by the paraphernalia of military command.

Why is it, then, that the country in which the first socialist revolution took place is so highly militarized? Why is Soviet military organization so different from original socialist concepts, with rank and hierarchy distinguished in a very marked way? Why is the defense sector accorded a special place in the economy? Why are the values of military patriotism given so much emphasis? This chapter examines the obstacles to disarmament and demilitarization in the Soviet Union and discusses whether or not there exists in Soviet society the possibility for initiatives in that direction. In order to do this, the internal causes of arms policies and militarization must be examined by attempting to answer the questions raised here.

Methodological Issues

Soviet writers claim that there is nothing intrinsic to Soviet society that would generate arms production or armed forces, and that the military effort has been forced on the Soviet Union by the enmity of the capitalist world. This claim is not usually argued at length and is based on a general statement about the nature of socialism rather than on a specific analysis of the Soviet system. A contrast is drawn with the fundamentally aggressive nature of imperialism and the incentives that the capitalist system offers for arms production. In this view, Soviet military policy is purely a response to external stimuli. (Interestingly, the same writers often claim that Soviet society is, for various reasons, peculiarly suited to building up military power; among the reasons given are the disciplined, hierarchical, military-like organization of the party and the planned economy that enables the party to mobilize resources for military purposes.)[4]

A rather different view is given by those peace researchers who argue that the East–West arms race is now firmly rooted in the domestic structures of the two military superpowers. The military competition between East and West, it is claimed, did have its origins in international conflict but has now become institutionalized in powerful military–industrial–scientific complexes. This is why the settlement of major political disputes in Europe in the early 1970s was not accompanied by any significant moves toward demilitarization. This argument points not to specific features of socialism or Russian history but to characteristics that the Soviet Union shares with the United States.[5]

The Soviet Union has been subjected to this kind of critical analysis primarily since its emergence as a full fledged military superpower. The attainment of strategic parity with the United States has made the Soviet Union seem to share full responsibility for the continuing arms race. Soviet arms policies in the 1970s have proved profoundly disappointing to those who hoped that the SALT I agreements would lead to a slackening of the arms race. They, and others, have come more insistently to ask: What drives Soviet arms policies? What are the domestic roots of those policies?

The problem of militarization is, however, wider than that of disarmament. Andreski has pointed out that the term *militarism* is used in a number of different senses: first, an aggressive foreign policy, based on a readiness to resort to war; second, the preponderance of the military in the state, the extreme case being that of military rule; third, subservience of the whole society to the needs of the army, which may involve a recasting of social life in accordance with the pattern of military organization; fourth, an ideology that propagates military ideals.[6] In this chapter, I use the term *militarization* to refer to the third of these phenomena, specifying the others when necessary. Andreski defines militarism as a compound of these elements, although it remains an interesting question whether they are necessarily related to one another.

In an essay on the militarization of Soviet education, William Odom argues that Soviet militarism is to be explained by two major factors.[7] The first of these is the similarity that exists between socialism and the war system. By this, he means that both socialism and a state at war "sacrifice individuals and their private interests for the state's political objectives."[8] (This is akin to the argument made by Soviet writers who point to the capacity of the Soviet system for creating powerful armed forces.) The second factor is the inheritance by the Soviet state of the military–political tradition of Tsarism. The very process of consolidating Soviet power against external and internal enemies meant that the Bolshevik state "had to accept as its birthright most of the tensions that had made militarization of the old state seem imperative to the imperial leadership."[9] The argument here is not that socialism is inevitably militarist but that the Imperial military tradition combined with the Soviet experience to create a form of socialist militarism. In other words, Odom sees the militarization of Soviet society as primarily a product of Russian history and the Soviet system. This is an important argument, but it needs to expanded by an analysis that relates present militarizing tendencies to current developments in the Soviet Union, and not merely to an inherited tradition.

There are, of course, many who see the militarization of Soviet society as a consequence of both external and internal factors and explain it in terms of the Cold War rather than of the Russian past. Many socialists and liberals in the West, for example, held the view—particularly in the early years of de-Stalinization—that if the tensions of the Cold War could be relaxed, that would facilitate not only a shift of resources away from military purposes but also political change in the direction of freedom and democracy. In other words, many of the distortions of Soviet socialism could be explained in terms of the international pressure under which socialist construction had to be carried out in the Soviet Union.

In the mid-1970s, E. P. Thompson wrote of the policy of nuclear disarmament and positive neutrality that the New Left advocated in Britain in the late 1950s and the 1960s:

> It was a critical part of our advocacy that with each effective movement of detente there would follow a relaxation in military and bureaucratic pres-

sures within the United States and the Soviet Union. Thus the relaxation of Cold War tensions was a precondition for further deStalinization, and a precondition for resuming socialist and democratic advances, East or West.[10]

Thompson goes on to ask whether Soviet policy in the early 1970s—détente with the West allied with sharper repression of dissidents at home—invalidates this argument. He concludes that it does not on two grounds: First, that the détente of the early 1970s amounted only to great power agreement to regulate their interests from above; second, that the repression of dissidents is a sign that even a little détente sharpens internal contradictions in the Soviet Union by threatening to deprive the bureaucracy of its functions and the official ideology of its credibility. Over the long run, he argues, international tension helps to justify repression while détente will help to weaken that justification and increase the possibilities of movement toward democracy.[11]

It is precisely this kind of argument that has been challenged by those peace researchers who claim that the arms race is so deeply rooted in domestic structures that the lessening of international tension will have no effect on it. Some see the arms race and detente coexisting for a long time, while others see détente falling victim to tensions generated by the military–industrial complexes. In either case, the peace research argument is that the resolution of international political disputes may be a necessary condition for disarmament and demilitarization, but that it is by no means a sufficient condition.

This is not a comprehensive, much less an exhaustive, survey of the approaches that have been taken in examining the obstacles to disarmament and demilitarization in the Soviet Union, but it does point to the relationships that have to be analyzed. The first of these is the interaction of internal and external factors. The particular form that socialist construction has taken in the Soviet Union cannot be understood without reference to the international context in which the Bolsheviks undertook the transformation of Russian society. Consequently, the militarization of Soviet society has to be examined in the light of international, as well as of domestic, relationships. Moreover, some attempt must be made to discuss what is specific to militarism in the Soviet Union and what it shares with militarism elsewhere.

Second, it has been seen that different historical perspectives—some rooted in the Russian Empire, some in the Cold War—have been adopted. This raises interesting questions about the way in which patterns of political relationships are reproduced in a given society. Although it is important to provide a historical perspective, there is the danger that the Russian tradition will be presented as monolithic and that militarism will be seen as a genetic inheritance, transmitted from one generation (or even one social formation) to the next. This would be disheartening in its suggestion that no change is possible and also wrong. The Russian political tradition is diverse, embracing not only militarism but also the antimilitarism of Tolstoy and Kropotkin. The Soviet tradition, too, contains various strands, and the diversity is very wide if the views of contemporary dissidents are taken into account. Moreover, the tendency of recent writing on Russian and Soviet history has been to stress not its inevitable but its contingent character and to point to the openness of choices at critical junctures—between 1905 and 1914, in the 1920s, and even in the 1950s, for example. Further, the militarization of Soviet society is a relative, not an absolute, phenomenon—a matter of more or less, not of either/or. Consequently, it would be a mistake to begin this analysis by portraying this militarization as either inevitable or all-embracing.

War and the Soviet State

Analyzing the militarization of Soviet society involves much more than an effort to identify a military–industrial or military–bureaucratic complex, elimination of which would remove the internal dynamic of Soviet military policy and leave the rest of the social system untouched. The history of the Soviet state is intimately bound up with war and the preparation for war. This is true both in the classic sense that armed force has established the territorial limits of the state and secured internal rule and in the sense that war and the preparation for it have profoundly affected the internal structure of the state.

This does not mean that the course of Soviet history is to be explained only in terms of the international environment, but it does mean that the formation of the Soviet state and the enterprise of socialist construction cannot be explained without reference to interstate relations. It is indeed one of the striking features of the history of Tsarist Russia and the Soviet Union that rivalry with other, economically more advanced, states has provided a major stimulus to economic and political change. This was true of Peter the Great's reforms and of the reforms that followed the Crimean and Russo–Japanese wars; it was also a major factor in Soviet industrialization. One consequence of this pattern has been the role of the state as the dominant agency of change; it was through the state that social and economic relationships were altered with the aim of mobilizing resources to increase the power of the state.[12]

When the Bolsheviks seized power, they faced the problem of consolidating their rule in the face of enemies at home and abroad. The early experience of the young Soviet state—civil war, foreign intervention, and internal unrest—had a profound impact on Bolshevik ideas about military organization. The early vision of militia-type forces did not survive the realization that the Bolsheviks faced considerable opposition from inside Soviet society and from foreign powers. The military reform of 1924–1925 created a mixed system, with the main emphasis on standing forces; the territorial–militia element was retained for economic reasons rather than on grounds of principle. Trotsky's project of combining labor with military training was not implemented. Of more immediate practical importance was the view advanced by Frunze, Trotsky's successor as Commissar of War, that under conditions of economic constraints on defense, every civilian activity ought to be examined for the contribution it could make to military preparedness. By the late 1920s, the Red Army did have features that distinguished it from the armies of bourgeois states—its social composition and the commissar system, for example—but it was far from embodying the earlier socialist ideas of military organization.[13]

With the failure of revolution in Europe, the Soviet Union was left largely isolated in a hostile world. This helped to stimulate a great debate about the direction of socialist construction, and in the mid-1920s, the idea of building "socialism in one country" began to gain ground in the Bolshevik party. This idea, as E. H. Carr has noted, marked the marriage of Marxist revolutionary goals and Russian national destiny.[14] The policy of industrialization that was embarked upon toward the end of the decade was the practical offspring of this marriage. In 1931, Stalin, now the dominant leader who had set his own brutal stamp on the industrialization drive, justified the intensity of the policy by referring to the need to overcome Russia's backwardness and thus prevent other powers from beating her.

> Do you want our Socialist fatherland to be beaten and to lose its independence? If you do not want this you must put an end to its backwardness in the shortest possible time and develop genuine Bolshevik tempo in building up its Socialist system of economy. There is no other way. That is why Lenin said during the October Revolution: "Either perish, or overtake and outstrip the advanced capitalist countries."
> We are fifty or a hundred years behind the advanced countries. We must make good this distance in ten years. Either we do it, or they crush us.[15]

Although this justification was not explicitly military, it did provide a clear rationale for the development of the defense industry.

Industrialization was made possible by a massive extraction of resources from the population and their investment in heavy industry. A vast and powerful party–state bureaucracy ensured that resources were forthcoming, enforced the priorities set by the party leaders, and managed the new industrial economy. The defense sector was given high priority in the allocation of investment funds, scarce materials, able managers, and skilled workers. During the 1930s, a powerful defense industry was created that produced large quantities of weapons, some of which were of high quality. The Soviet Union had rejected the idea, which was popular in the West at the time, of building a small, highly mechanized army and sought instead to combine mass and technology—to create a mass army equipped with the best possible armaments. The territorial–militia element of the armed forces was gradually abandoned. Yet, for all that had been done, the Winter War of 1939/1940 with Finland exposed serious weaknesses in the Red Army, some of which resulted from the great purge that Stalin had inflicted on Soviet society in the late 1930s.

The German invasion of June 22, 1941 took Stalin by surprise and found the Red Army in a state of unreadiness. The opening months of the war proved disastrous, with the German forces advancing to the outskirts of Moscow. Only by an enormous effort over the next 4 years was the Soviet Union able to halt the German advance, turn the tide of war and push the German armies back to Berlin. The degree of industrial mobilization was much greater in the Soviet Union than in the other belligerent states, and Soviet losses of people and material goods were immense. The Soviet name for the war with Germany—the Great Patriotic War—symbolizes the appeal that Stalin made to the Soviet people's patriotism. In contrast to the bitter social and political tensions of the 1920s and 1930s, state and people were largely united in the common effort to defeat the Nazi enemy.[16]

Victory brought the Soviet Union gains of territory and influence that had seemed inconceivable in the early months of the war. However, victory also brought political conflicts with the wartime allies, and these soon found their expression in intense military rivalry, which centered on the development of nuclear weapons and their means of delivery. By 1947, the Soviet Union had four major military research and development programs under way: nuclear weapons, rockets, radar, and jet-engine technology. After Stalin's death, the implications of this "military–technical revolution" became more pressing. The existence of nuclear weapons in growing stockpiles raised fundamental questions about the relationship of war to policy and about the appropriate structure for armed forces in the nuclear age—questions that have dominated Soviet military policy ever since.

Khrushchev now put greater stress on peaceful coexistence between East and West and set in motion major changes in military doctrine and military institutions. In the late 1950s and early 1960s, he tried to devise a new military policy based on nuclear-armed missiles that would be militarily and diplomatically effective while freeing resources for civilian purposes. He even floated the idea of restoring the territorial–militia element in the armed forces. But internal opposition, which was strengthened by a succession of international crises (the U-2 incident in 1960, the 1961 Berlin crisis, and the Cuban missile crisis of 1962) and by

the Kennedy Administration's build-up of strategic forces, finally defeated Khrushchev's efforts.[17]

If we can speak of a "Soviet military build-up", then its origins lie in
the defeat of Khrushchev's policy. His successors have devoted considerable attention to the overall strengthening of Soviet military power.
A major increase in strategic forces has brought parity with the United
States. The ground forces have been expanded, in particular, along the
frontier with China, and have received more modern equipment. The air
forces, too, have been modernized. Soviet naval presence has been
extended throughout the world. Arms transfers to Third World countries have grown substantially in this period. Certainly, Soviet policy has
been subject to many rash and alarmist interpretations in the West, but
the evidence does point to a steady and significant increase in Soviet
military power since the early 1960s.[18]

In the first 10 years after the end of the Second World War, a clear
bipolar structure emerged in world politics, with the United States and
the Soviet Union as the dominant powers. Since that time, new forces
have emerged to transform the international system. The creation of the
Third World as a political force was helped by the existence of the Soviet
bloc, which could provide a counterweight to Western power.
Fissiparous tendencies, both East and West, have further complicated
international politics. By the late 1960s, Japan and the E.E.C. had
become major centers of economic power, while the rivalry between the
Soviet Union and China had assumed military form. From the Soviet
point of view, the international environment had become more complex, with the ever-present danger that the various centers of power
would combine in opposition to it. Indeed, elements of such a combination have been evident in the 1970s, motivated in large part by the desire
to offset growing Soviet military power; in its turn, this countervailing
power has provided the Soviet leaders with further reasons for military
forces.

The Soviet Union now possesses large armed forces, an advanced
defense industry, and an extensive military research and development
(R&D) network. In no other area has the Soviet Union come so close to
achieving the goal of "catching up and overtaking the advanced capitalist powers." As a consequence, the law of comparative advantage seems
to operate in Soviet external policies, giving a major role to the military
instrument. The Soviet Union conducts its central relationship with the
NATO powers from a position of military strength but economic weakness. In Eastern Europe, the Soviet Union has suffered political setbacks
but has used military force and the threat of military force to underpin
its dominant position. Soviet relations with China have now acquired an
important military dimension with the build-up of forces along the
Chinese frontier. In the Third World, the Soviet Union has used arms

transfers and military advisors as a major instrument of diplomacy. Thus, despite the fact that the Soviet concept of the "correlation of forces," in terms of which international politics is analyzed, does not place primary emphasis on military force, military power has become a basic instrument of Soviet external policy.

It is not surprising that the present generation of Soviet leaders should see military power as the main guarantee of Soviet security and position in the world. The men now at the top levels of leadership came to positions of some power in the late 1930s, and Brezhnev and Ustinov are only the most prominent members of this generation to have had a direct part in managing the development and production of arms. Victory in the war with Germany, the attainment of strategic parity with the United States, and the long period at peace since 1945 are regarded by this generation as among its greatest achievements. When one considers the course of Soviet history from 1917 to 1945, it is no surprise that this should be so.

It should be clear from this brief outline how important war and the preparation for war have been in the formation of the Soviet state. This is not to say that the course of Soviet development has been determined by forces outside the Soviet Union or that every event in Soviet history is to be explained in terms of external conditions. The rise of Stalin and his system of rule cannot be explained without reference to social, economic, and political conditions in the Soviet Union. Moreover, not everything in the Stalinist period can be seen as a response to external threats. The great purge of 1936–1938 was justified in this way, but the justification was patently false, and the purge greatly weakened the Red Army. But the Stalinist industrialization drive had as its major goal the development of heavy industry as the basis for economic growth and military power, and it was in these terms that it was justified.

This policy involved the extensive mobilization of the resources and energies of Soviet society and the extraction from society of those resources by the state, which then channelled them toward the ends laid down by the party leadership. The process was dominated by the party–state apparatus, which forced changes in social and economic relationships, extracted the resources from an often unwilling population, and managed the new economic system. In order to secure the loyalty of the party–state apparatus, special social and economic privileges and distinctions were introduced. (It was at this time that prerevolutionary ranks began to be reintroduced into the Red Army.) The rate of extraction was very high, leaving the mass of the population with minimal living standards and sometimes (as when famine occurred) not even those. Coercion was an intrinsic part of this policy.

Victory in the war seemed to show that, whatever the "mistakes" of Stalin's policies in the immediate prewar years, the general emphasis on industrialization had been correct. After the war, the high rate of extraction continued as industry was reconstructed and military rivalry with the West pursued. But since Stalin's death, important changes have taken place that have a bearing on the questions of disarmament and demilitarization. First, the rate of economic growth has slowed considerably, provoking intensive debate about economic reform. It has been widely argued inside and outside the Soviet Union that the system of economic planning and administration was suited to the industrialization drive, but it has now become a brake on industrial development, particularly technological innovation. Second, terror has been abandoned as a system of rule, and the party leadership has been searching for new sources of legitimacy for the state. Repression of opposition and dissent still takes place, but greater effort has been made to secure popular support. Among the ways in which this has been done is through the provision of more and better goods and services to the mass of the population and through appeals to nationalist sentiments. Third, as a result of the greater attention that has been paid to the living standards and welfare of the population, the priorities of resource allocation have become more complex than they were under Stalin. In the rest of this chapter, militarizing trends in the Soviet Union will be related to these developments.

The Defense Sector and the Soviet Economy

In the last section, I discussed how the whole structure of the Soviet state had been affected by war and the preparation for war. I argued that the militarization of Soviet society involves far more than the institutions directly concerned with the development, production, and use of armaments. But these institutions, too, must be examined in order to determine their place in the structure of the state.

It was in the 1930s that the basic features of the Soviet system of economic planning and management took shape, and these have been modified rather than transformed by the various reforms of the postwar period. Oskar Lange referred to the Soviet economy as a "war economy."[19] He did so not because preparation for war was given first priority but because the instruments of economic management in the Soviet economy were akin to those employed in capitalist economies in wartime. The point that Lange made was that there was nothing inherently socialist about these instruments, and that to abandon them was not tantamount to abandoning socialism. This characterization underlines the suitability of the Soviet economic system for mobilizing resources in the pursuit of political purposes, including the creation of military power.

The organization of the defense sector is similar to that of the rest of Soviet industry.[20] The enterprises that produce arms and equipment are controlled by a series of ministries that have responsibility for the different branches of the sector. The work of these ministries is, in turn, planned by the central planning agencies (in line with the general policy laid down by the Politburo), since the activities of the defense sector must be coordinated with those of the rest of the economy. There are, however, special institutional arrangements in the defense sector that are designed to ensure that military production has priority claim on scarce resources. In this sense, the defense sector is distinct from the rest of the economy.

Since the war, some important changes have taken place in the defense sector. It has expanded to include new branches of production, in particular nuclear weapons, rockets, and electronics. Along with this expansion has come the creation of an extensive network of R & D establishments to provide the basis for innovations in weapons technologies. These establishments are controlled by the production ministries in the defense sector. The size of the network is impossible to establish with any precision, but the number of establishments must be in the hundreds, while those engaged in military research and development must number in the hundreds of thousands. Research institutes from outside the defense sector, for example, from the Academy of Sciences, are also drawn into military work. In military R & D, as in production, there are special arrangements to ensure that performance is as effective as possible.

Military R & D is more effective than civilian R & D in the Soviet Union. The defense sector is well-suited to the development and production of follow-on systems (e.g., of tanks) where no great shift of mission or technology is required. The Soviet Union has also been able to organize large-scale innovation when the political leaders have deemed it necessary; the R & D system is well-suited to the concentration of resources on specific goals such as the development of the atomic bomb or the development of the intercontinental ballistic missile. It is not so well adapted to the lateral or horizontal transfer of technology across departmental boundaries, unless this is organized as a matter of priority from above.[21]

The defense sector is, nevertheless, part and parcel of the Soviet economy, and the civilian technological base has an important influence on the performance of military R & D. Moreover, the patterns of weapons development and production cannot be understood without reference to the overall system of economic planning and management. Soviet planners have tried to protect the defense sector from failings and shortcomings elsewhere in the economy, and this has resulted in a degree of separation from the rest of the industry. But this separation is relative, and it would be wrong to lay too much stress on it. The defense sector produces civilian goods on a large scale—passenger aircraft, merchant ships, and consumer durables, for example. Further, branches outside the defense sector produce goods for military use, while other ministries—for example, those of Civil Aviation and Communications—appear to be closely tied into the military infrastructure. Special military departments exist in these ministries to ensure that military needs are looked after there. Thus, the requirements of the armed forces extend throughout the economy as do the arrangements for ensuring that these requirements are met.

Soviet military–economic policy is supposed to be guided by three main principles:

1. To maintain a high level of armaments production
2. To ensure the flexibility of the economy (e.g., in shifting from civilian to military production, in raising the rate of arms production, or in introducing new weapons)
3. To secure the viability of the economy in wartime.[22]

These principles were elaborated in the 1930s and are still taken as the most important indicators of the state's economic potential—that is, of its ability to provide for the material needs of society while producing everything necessary for war. Certain features of the defense sector—the protection of plants against bomb damage, preparation of civilian enterprises for conversion to defense production, and the existence of "buffer production" of civilian goods at defense plants—can be seen as attempts to follow these principles. It is, however, more difficult to implement them now than it was in the 1930s, and even then they were not always put into practice.

Despite the flexibility recommended by these principles, the available evidence suggests that there is considerable stability in the defense sector, and that this has a major influence on its mode of operation. The research institutes and design bureaus, where new weapons are created, are funded from the budget, and their finances do not seem to depend directly on orders for specific systems. Coupled with the institutional continuity of the military R & D network, this provides the basis for a steady effort in the design and development of weapons. Consequently, a strong tendency to create follow-on systems can be discerned. Stable production also appears to be a feature of the defense sector, with no major variation in output from year to year. There are exceptions, however, especially, it seems, in the Khrushchev period. Moreover, the avilable data are too crude to register any but the largest fluctuations, so that firm conclusions should not be drawn from them. Theoretically, the existence of buffer production at defense industry plants should create flexibility but, as far as one can see, it does not do so in fact.[23]

Besides the stability of its structure and its operations, the defense sector is marked by the continuity of its leading managers. For example,

D. F. Ustinov, the present Minister of Defense, became People's Commissar (i.e., Minister) of Armament in 1941, and until his appointment to his present position in 1976, he played a major role in weapons development and production. Another example is Ye. P. Slavskii, the Minister of Medium Machine-Building (in charge of nuclear weapons development and production), who has held that position since 1957 and has been involved in the nuclear weapons program since 1946.

The managers of the defense industry form a coherent group with interlocking careers. There is, however, little evidence that they have acted together as a lobby. The one occasion on which they seem to have done so was in the period from 1957 to 1965 when they took part, with some success, in resistance to Khrushchev's decentralization of the system of economic planning and management. In 1963, after some recentralization had taken place, Khrushchev indicated his dissatisfaction with Ustinov and the "metal-eaters" and complained that secrecy made it difficult to criticize the shortcomings of the defense industry.[24] The opposition of the defense industry managers seems to have rested on the grounds that economic reorganization threatened the special position of the defense sector and its ability to perform effectively (although defense spending and specific weapons programs might have been at issue, too). It would be wrong to assume that the defense industry managers will always act as a group or share the same views on military spending or economic reform. The reason for doubting this is that the defense sector depends—perhaps to a growing extent—on the performance of the rest of Soviet industry, and the different branches of the defense sector relate to the rest of the economy in different ways.

This is the only occasion on which the performance of the defense sector emerged into the open as an issue in the arguments about economic reform. In the post-Stalin period, there have been intensive debates about the need to reform the system of economic planning and administration in order to stimulate technological innovation. In the 1960s, it was widely held by Soviet and foreign economists alike that, sooner or later, the Soviet leaders would have to choose between plan and market, and that any significant reform would involve a move toward some form of "market socialism." Such a reform would not be incompatible with a high level of defense expenditure. Even if the Soviet Union now devotes 12–15% of its GNP to defense (and this is the upper range of Western estimates), this level could be maintained in an economy where the market played a significant role; after all, some capitalist countries devote a higher proportion of the GNP to defense without instituting a "war economy."[25] Thus, the present Soviet system of economic planning and management cannot be said to be entailed by the level of defense expenditure. This is not to deny, of course, that the managers who have been used to working in the present system may be fearful of changes on the grounds that their high priority position would be jeopardized.

In any event, the choice of market socialism has not been made in the Soviet Union. The Czechoslovak crisis of 1968 was a major setback for the Soviet advocates of far-reaching reform because political developments in Czechoslovakia were widely seen as the consequence of economic reform. The problems of economic growth and technological progress have not vanished in the Soviet Union, however, and piecemeal reform has been under way. Interestingly, the trend of reform in the 1970s has been to take the defense sector as a model for the rest of the economy. At the Twenty-Fourth Party Congress in 1971, Brezhnev declared that "taking into account the high scientific–technical level of defense industry, the transmission of its experience, inventions and discoveries to all spheres of our economy acquires the highest importance."[26] In the 1970s, certain organizational features and management techniques—especially in the area of technological innovation— have been borrowed from the defense sector and applied in civilian industry.[27] This marks an attempt to use the defense sector as a model or dynamo of technological progress in the economy as a whole. There also may have been an effort to increase the production of nonmilitary goods in the defense sector. For the first time since the 5-year plans were instituted, the ninth plan (1971–1975) called for a more rapid rate of growth for light industry than for heavy industry. About the time of the Twenty-Fourth Congress, a number of articles appeared in the press listing the nonmilitary goods produced in the defense industry.

It is not altogether clear, however, that this direction of reform will prove to be effective. It is true that the defense sector has performed more successfully than civilian industry, especially in bringing new technologies into production. But it may not be possible to reproduce the conditions of success in civilian industry. The effort to boost consumer goods production in the ninth 5-year plan did not achieve the desired results.[28] There are various explanations for this. One is that international crises—especially the Middle East War of October 1973— interfered with the plan. A more interesting reason is that the priority of military production is a matter not only of central decisions but also of the structure of industry and the attitudes of workers and managers. This was clearly illustrated by an article in *Literaturnaya Gazeta* in 1972 and the correspondence it provoked. The author of the article pointed out that in numerous ways—in prestige, in the priority given by other ministries (e.g., in construction projects), in wages, in cultural and housing facilities, in labor turnover—light industry fared worse than heavy industry.[29] One of the correspondents wrote that

the best conditions are given to the so-called "leading" branches. Then we have the remaining enterprises in Group A/heavy industry. Last in line are the Group B enterprises. Naturally the most highly skilled cadres—workers, engineers or technicians—find jobs or try to find them where the pay is highest, so they are concentrated in the "leading" branches of industry.

> What is more, these branches receive the best materials, the most advanced technology, the latest equipment etc. etc. . . . Even at the same machine-building enterprise, in the production of "prestige" output and Group B output, there is no comparison in quality and in the attitude to the categories of output (in terms of technology, design work, management, pay, etc.).[30]

There is little doubt that within heavy industry, the defense sector occupies the position of highest prestige and therefore shows these features to the highest degree.

A further condition for the successful performance of the defense sector has been the existence of a powerful customer in the shape of the armed forces. The Ministry of Defense and the General Staff draw up requirements, issue specifications, supervise weapons development, conduct trials, and exercise quality control during production. In this way, they have considerable control over the weapons acquisition process. Backed by the high priority that the party leaders have given to defense, this managerial role helps the armed forces to get what they want out of the defense industry. Although some features of the defense sector can be transferred to civilian industry, this is one important condition that it would not be easy to reproduce there.

The Soviet system of economic planning and administration has not been altered fundamentally since it was first established. It remains a relatively effective mechanism for extracting resources from the economy and directing them to the goals set by the political leaders, and one of the most important of these goals has been the creation of military power. The defense sector occupies a key—and in some respects, a privileged—position in this system, not only in terms of central priorities but also in terms of the organization of industry and the attitudes of workers and managers. The debates about economic reform have resulted in partial and piecemeal changes rather than in a fundamental transformation of the system. There has been a tendency over the last 10 years to use the defense sector as a model for the rest of industry. In terms of the militarization of the Soviet economy, this is an ambiguous development. On the one hand, it testifies to a political concern about the performance of civilian industry; on the other, it highlights the special position and performance of the defense sector.

The Armed Forces and the Rationales for Military Power

There is little evidence of opposition inside the Soviet Union to Soviet military policy. Since 1965, there have been few, if any, indications of disagreement in the party leadership about the level of military expenditure. This contrasts with the Khrushchev period when military outlays did pro-

vide a focus of political argument. And in the dissident *samizdat* literature, although sharp criticism has been made of many features of Soviet
life, few voices have been raised against the military policy of the Soviet
state. Almost the only exception is the warnings that Andrei Sakharov
has given the West of the growing military power of the Soviet Union;
and Sakharov's background in nuclear weapons development makes
him in this instance a very special case. Thus, the situation is rather
different from that in the United States where militarism and racism
formed the chief targets of protest in the 1960s and 1970s. There are
many reasons for this difference, but the chief one appears to be that
inside the Soviet Union, the Soviet military effort is widely seen as
legitimate and as pursuing legitimate goals. This despite the fact that the
burden of military expenditure is greater than in the NATO countries,
and that there are many competing claims for the resources that are
devoted to defense.

One of the main reasons for the acceptance of Soviet military policy is
no doubt that for the last 30–35 years the Soviet Union has enjoyed a
period of peace and internal stability that stands in sharp contrast to the
wars and upheavals of the first one-half of the century. The Soviet
armed forces have seen very little combat since 1945—certainly nothing
to compare with the military role of the American, British, and French
forces. The Soviet claim that Soviet military strength is conducive to
peace does not, therefore, fly directly in the face of reality. This is one
reason why there has been, in the Soviet view, no contradiction between
the processes of political detente and the growth of Soviet military
power. Soviet military power is regarded as a crucial element in detente
because it makes it impossible for the West to deal with the Soviet Union
from a position of strength or to use its armed forces in an unfettered
way throughout the world.[31]

Although Soviet forces have been engaged in realtively little combat
since 1945, military power is certainly regarded by the Soviet leaders as
contributing to their political purposes. The main object of that policy
has been to prevent the West from conducting offensive actions—
whether military or political—against the Soviet Union and its allies.
Soviet military aid to Third World countries is to be seen in the same
context. Since the 1960s, the Soviet Union has come to use its military
power—in the form of advisors and arms transfers—more frequently as
a way of gaining influence and undermining Western power. (There
may now be an economic element in Soviet arms transfers: Excess
production can be exchanged—in some instances—for hard currency.
But the primary rationale is still political.)[32]

Military power has also been a major factor in Soviet relations with
socialist states. The Soviet Union used military force in Hungary in 1956
and in Czechoslovakia in 1968 in order to maintain its dominant position
in Eastern Europe. That position is underpinned by the ever-present

threat of military force, even though that threat is not voiced openly. In the 1960s, the confrontation with China assumed a military form with the build-up of forces along the Chinese frontier. Thus, apart from deterring offensive policies directed against the Soviet Union and helping to destroy Western domination in different parts of the world, Soviet military power has been used as an instrument to create and sustain Soviet domination over other states. Moreover, as Soviet military strength has grown, new roles have been found for it, particularly in the projection of power far from the Soviet frontiers.[33]

In the late 1960s, the Soviet Union attained strategic parity with the United States, and on that basis, entered into negotiations to limit strategic arms. In the context of Western debates about the nature of Soviet policy, even that statement is controversial because there are those who point to Soviet military doctrine as indicating a striving for overall superiority. This is a rather complex issue, and it does appear that at least some elements in the armed forces have opposed the acceptance of parity; but Brezhnev's recent statements to the effect that parity and equality are the goals of Soviet policy must be taken as authoritative statements of Soviet military doctrine.[34]

Of course, it remains extremely difficult to say what constitutes parity or equality. (Does it mean equality with one particular state, or with all potential enemies combined?), and acceptance of the principle still leaves great scope for disagreement both within and between the negotiating states. Moreover, the principle of parity provides a basis for negotiation between the Soviet Union and the United States only because they have so many more nuclear weapons than other states that even the other nuclear powers can be left largely out of account. But, does every state have the right to parity? Obviously not, since the Non-Proliferation Treaty represents a commitment of a kind to stop the spread of nuclear weapons. Negotiations between the superpowers on the basis of parity goes along with the attempt to prevent other states from attaining that status. Precisely because the Soviet Union and the United States are using arms control negotiations in this double-edged way, they are likely to stimulate other states to acquire nuclear weapons of their own. Consequently, arms control negotiations on the basis of parity are by no means the foundation for a process of radical de-militarization.

Despite of the acceptance of parity as the basis for negotiations to limit strategic arms, it remains true that there are major differences between Soviet and American strategic thought. American thinking has laid particular emphasis on the ability, under all circumstances, to inflict widespread destruction on the enemy's society. Soviet thinking, on the other hand, has been concerned to limit the damage to Soviet society in the event of nuclear war. Even in a relationship of parity, Soviet policy has been directed toward limiting the vulnerability of the Soviet Union to nuclear attack and ensuring the viability of Soviet society in wartime.

Whether this can be achieved seems very doubtful (even though viability is a realtive term), but it does appear to be the rationale behind important elements of Soviet military, military–economic, and civil defense policies, and it does have important implications for the militarization of Soviet society.

The main bulk of the Soviet forces is made up of the five branches of service: the Strategic Rocket Forces, the National Air Defense Forces, the air forces, the ground forces, and the navy. There are also special forces that sometimes engage in civilian work. The Construction Troops carry out construction work for the armed forces and on high priority civilian projects; the Academic City near Novosibirsk, for example, where the Siberian Division of the Academy of Sciences is based, was built by them. The Railroad and Road Troops play an important part in building and maintining the Soviet rail and road communications system. These are quite natural offshoots of the Soviet armed forces. But there are three elements of the Soviet military system that are of greater interest from the point of view of the militarization of Soviet society. These are the civil defense organization, DOSAAF (*Dobrovol'noe obshchestvo sodeistviya armii, aviatsii i flotu* [the Voluntary Society for Cooperation with the Army, Aviation, and the Navy]), and the system of military–patriotic education. All are designed to strengthen the ability of the Soviet Union to defend itself, and all have political functions beyond that goal.

Soviet civil defense has three major objectives: (1) to provide protection for the population against weapons of mass destruction; (2) to ensure stable operation of the economy in wartime; and (3) to eliminate the effects of enemy use of weapons of mass destruction.[35] Civil defense organizations may also take part in disaster relief operations. The effectiveness of the civil defense effort is very difficult to judge because it would greatly depend on the way in which nuclear war was initiated. It could not prevent widespread destruction, although it could reduce its scale. It has been estimated that about 100,000 full-time personnel are engaged in civil defense work at all levels of the government and economic structure.[36] There is an extensive program of education and training that is designed to enable the population to carry out civil defense measures should the need arise.

This may suggest a policy of subordinating all economic and social life to the contingencies of war. But it is not always possible to put such a policy into practice. For example, dispersal of industrial plants is an essential measure for ensuring the viability of the economy in wartime, but there is no evidence that it has been implemented to any degree, presumably because of the costs involved and the need for new plants to be near suppliers, transport networks, labor supply, and so on. Moreover, the civil defense effort does not appear to be met with great enthusiasm on the part of the population, who may not be convinced of its necessity or its effectiveness.[37]

DOSAAF has as its main objective the strengthening of the Soviet

Union's defense capability by training the Soviet people for the defense of the socialist fatherland.[38] DOSAAF is open to all Soviet citizens over the age of 14 and has about 80 million members. Its main activities are: military–patriotic education; training of young people for service in the armed forces; training in technical skills; dissemination of military–technical knowledge; direction of sports that have military–technical significance. DOSAAF has clubs and sports facilities and is organized at factories, farms, educational institutions, and so on. It seems clear that DOSAAF's activities are of substantial help to the Armed Forces in providing recruits with skills that will be useful during military service and also in raising the physical and technical level of the Soviet population. For the same reasons, its work is useful to Soviet industry. Much of what DOSAAF does is done by nonmilitary organizations in the West. It is, nevertheless, significant that in the Soviet Union it is the goals of military preparedness and defense capability that provide the justification and the driving force for activities of this kind. Here, again, the importance of the military factor as a modernizing force in Soviet society is evident.

Both civil defense and DOSAAF contribute to the Soviet Union's ability to defend itself; they also contribute to the more diffuse process of military–patriotic education.

> Military-patriotic education is called upon to instill a readiness to perform military duty, responsibility for strengthening the defense capability of the country, respect for the Soviet Armed Forces, pride in the Motherland, and the ambition to preserve and increase the heroic traditions of the Soviet people. Military–patriotic education is carried out in the teaching process in secondary and higher educational establishments, in the system of political education, by means of propaganda in the press, on radio and television, and with the help of various forms of mass-political work and of artistic and literary works. Of great significance for military–patriotic education is the mastery of basic military and military–technical skills which young people acquire in secondary schools, technical schools, higher educational establishments, in studies at the houses of defense and technical creativity, aero, auto motor and radio clubs, at the young technicians' stations, in military–patriotic schools, defense circles, at points of pre-induction training, in civil defense formations. Physical training with an applied military bent presupposes the development of qualities of will, courage, hardiness, strength, speed of reaction, and helps to raise psychological stability, trains the sight, hearing, etc."[39]

As this quotation makes clear, military–patriotic education is a pervasive feature of Soviet life. It must be of value to Soviet defense capability insofar as it helps to create physically strong, well-trained young people and gives them the basic skills and psychological qualities needed for military service. Indeed, the emphasis on military–patriotic education was strengthened in the late 1960s in association with the 1967 Law on Military Service and is designed to ensure that the armed forces' manpower requirements are met, even with shorter terms of military service.[40]

Military–patriotic education is directed not only toward satisfying the practical needs of the armed forces but also toward increasing support for, and loyalty to, the party and the Soviet state. It represents a fusion of communist, nationalist, and military appeals. The Great patriotic War occupies a key position in the program of military–patriotic education as the source of examples and illustrations of the desired qualities. This, as we have noted, was a time when party and people were most closely united in a common purpose, and military–patriotic education is evidently an effort to recapture and reinforce that bond by tapping a source of strong sentiment in the Soviet people. In this context, it can be seen as a response to the problems of legitimation that the Soviet state has faced in the post-Stalin period.

This military–patriotic education does not amount to a glorification of war and should therefore be distinguished from Fascist militarism. Indeed, the party's peace policy (the effectiveness of which is seen to rest on Soviet military power) is an essential component of the program of education. Moreover, one may wonder just how effective the program is in instilling the desired qualities into a population that seems very far from matching the ideal of the "new Soviet man." But quite clearly, military–patriotic education will help to instill acceptance of the party's military policy and belief in the importance of military power. In this way, it will help to sustain the Soviet military effort and the special position that the defense sector and the armed forces enjoy in Soviet society.

A Military–Industrial State?

As a major instrument of Soviet external policy, the armed forces naturally enjoy an important position in the party–state apparatus. The Ministry of Defense and the General Staff are overwhelmingly staffed by professional officers who have spent all their careers in the armed forces. Since 1945, the post of Minister has, more often than not, been held by a professional soldier, although the present Minister, Ustinov, has spent most of his life in the defense industry. The chief functions of the Ministry and the General Staff are those of similar institutions in other countries: to draw up plans, develop strategy and tactics, gather and evaluate intelligence about potential enemies, educate and train the troops, and administer the whole network of military institutions. The Soviet Union, unlike the United States, does not have an extensive network of civilian institutions conducting research into military operations; operational analysis is done very largely within the armed forces.

The existence of a large military establishment within the state may be thought to pose difficult problems of civil–military relations and to threaten the party's dominant position in Soviet society. It is true that there have been elements of conflict and tension in party-military relations, but the principle of party supremacy has never seriously been threatened. Special mechanisms of control exist in the armed forces, the most important being the Main Political Administration, which is both an administration of the Ministry of Defense and a department of the Central Committee. Some Western observers have seen in this organization an institutionalized party distrust of the military.[41] However, in fact, this view is mistaken, and the Main Political Administration should more properly be seen as a bridge between the party and the armed forces, symbolizing their unity and the assumptions that they share about the importance of military power for the Soviet state.[42]

The Soviet Union embodies the apparent paradox of a militarized social system in which the military, while an important political force, is not the dominant one. This is not to say, however, that the armed forces—or, more particularly, members of the High Command—have played no role in the political crises of the post-Stalin period. In each case of leadership change—Beria's arrest and execution in 1953, Malenkov's defeat by Khrushchev in 1955, the defeat of the "anti-party group" in 1957, and Khrushchev's fall in 1964—members of the High Command played some role. But military support was one factor among others and probably not the decisive one. Moreover, Marshal Zhukov's disgrace in 1957, only months after he had helped Khrushchev to defeat the "anti-party group" in the Central Committee, shows that engaging in leadership politics can be a risky business for soldiers. The specter of Bonapartism was conjured up by Khrushchev as a major justification for Zhukov's removal from office. Even though it appears to have been a contrived justification, it underlines the determination of the party leadership to retain its supremacy over the armed forces.[43] Military involvement has been made possible only by splits in the party leadership and on no occasion has it resulted in a conflict in which party leaders were ranged, on one side, and the military, on the other: the High Command has had its own internal politics and divisions.

The political quiescence of the armed forces is to be explained by reference not so much to the formal mechanisms of party and secret police control as to the way in which military interests have been given priority in party policy. To say this is not to minimize Stalin's brutal treatment of the armed forces or to deny that Khrushchev often pursued policies that were to the distaste of the High Command. But by stressing the importance of international conflict and national solidarity, the party has provided an ideological framework that gives a clear meaning to the armed forces' existence. Party policy has also given the officer corps a privileged material position and a high status in Soviet society. Finally, the professional interests of the officer corps have been generally well served, especially in the allocation of resources to defense and in the opportunities for career advancement; in the matter of political leadership, the armed forces have been less well served although, with some glaring exceptions, this has been cautious and capable, avoiding adventurous policies that would incur the risk of war.[44]

Since Stalin's death in 1953, and more particularly since Khrushchev's fall from power in 1964, officers have been given considerable freedom to discuss questions of military policy and a greater voice in the policymaking process. This has resulted from the general diffusion of power at the center of the Soviet state and has parallels in other areas of Soviet life where vigorous debates have been conducted about matters of policy. The Brezhnev Politburo has placed great emphasis on "scientific" policymaking and on expert and technically competent advice. Although this is a development of considerable importance in Soviet politics, it does not, of course, mean that the Politburo has relinquished its authority over such major decisions as the size of the military effort or the use of military power, or does it mean that requests from the Ministry of Defense or the General Staff will always be granted. In resource allocation, for example, the Politburo has to respond to many pressures, not only to those from the armed forces. Moreover, the policy of ensuring popular support for the State through the provision of goods and services requires investment in light industry and agriculture, while the pursuit of economic growth means that the civilian branches of heavy industry and the production of energy cannot be neglected. Thus, there are important constraints—both economic and political—on Soviet military policy.

Despite these constraints, the armed forces and the defense industry occupy an entrenched position in the party-state apparatus. The high priority that the party leadership has given to military power has thus become institutionalized. The opposition that Khrushchev's policies encountered seems to show that any attempt to effect a drastic shift in priorities away from defense would run into opposition not only from military and industrial circles, but also from within the party, where the commitment to military power has been strong.

The diffusion of power has created what some writers refer to as "institutional pluralism."[45] Like all pluralisms, however, it is imperfect in the sense that some groups and institutions have more power than others. In this respect, the armed forces and the defense industry occupy a special position. The armed forces enjoy wide prestige as the embodiment of national power and integrity—a prestige that is enhanced by the extensive program of military–patriotic education. The Ministry of Defense and General Staff are institutions of undoubted competence, with a monopoly of expertise in military affairs; there are no civilian institutions able to challenge this expertise. The high priority given to the defense sector remains embedded in the system of economic planning and administration. The defense industry has been in the forefront of Soviet technological progress and is seen by the party leaders as something to be emulated rather than restricted in the age of the "scientific–technical revolution." Finally, key aspects of military policy are shrouded in secrecy, and this limits criticism of the priority given to defense in resource allocation and of the way in which those resources are used.

This is not to suggest that the military policy of the Soviet state has been pursued against the wishes of the party leadership. The final decisions on military policy rest with the Politburo and with the Defense Council, which is composed of several leading Politburo members under Brezhnev's chairmanship. All the evidence points to a set of shared assumptions among the leaders about military power and military expenditure. There are differences of view, no doubt, but these appear to be marginal, and the overall policy seems to rest on a broad consensus.[46] It is, however, possible that this state of affairs will change in the post-Brezhnev leadership, and that the level of military effort will become a contentious issue as it was under Khrushchev. The institutional power of the armed forces and the defense industry may then be important in determining the outcome of the argument.

Can we speak, then, of a Soviet "military–industrial complex"? It is true that there is a large military establishment and a large defense industry. But the term itself often carries theoretical connotations that make it inapplicable to the Soviet Union. Sometimes it suggests a degenerate pluralism in which the balanced interplay of interests has been undermined by links between the armed forces and industry; in this sense, it seems not to be appropriate because it implies too great a degree of pluralism—and it implies pluralism as a norm—for the Soviet Union. Sometimes it is implied that the driving force of arms policies is the pursuit of profit by capitalist enterprises; this, too, would be inappropriate, and for this reason, Garaudy has argued that the Soviet Union has a "bureaucratic-military complex"—that is, a military–industrial complex without the economic driving-force.[47] An objection of a different kind is summarized in the statement that the Soviet Union does not *have* a military–industrial complex but *is* such a complex. This is too sweeping a statement, but it does make the point that the history of the Soviet Union is so bound up with military power that it seems wrong to speak of a separate military–industrial complex acting within the state.

Whether or not we say the armed forces and the defense industry constitute a military–industrial complex in the Soviet Union matters less than the fact that they exhibit many features that are identified as a characteristic of such a complex. Because of the way in which the Soviet economic system is organized, it does not exhibit these features in the same way, or to the same degree, as the American defense sector; but it does share them nevertheless. For example, competition is to be found in the weapons development process between offensive and defensive systems, with new technology in one area stimulating innovation in another. This may happen without any direct stimulus from outside. Second, the military R & D system shows considerable inertia in its operations, thus generating strong pressure for follow-on systems. Third, the R & D system does not appear to have a strong innovative dynamic of its own. Intervention by the political leadership is required for major innovations; but because the party leaders have devoted so much attention to this area, such intervention is often forthcoming. Fourth, the military R & D system is not especially conducive to the crossfertilization of technologies to produce new weapons, but this may happen as designers search for ways of meeting new requirements. Finally, the steadiness of Soviet arms policies may be accounted for, in part, by the planning to which weapons development and production are subject.[48]

The Soviet military effort, which was created in the course of international rivalry, is now rooted in the structure of the Soviet state. This is not to say, of course, that the external stimuli have vanished. It is clear that foreign actions do impinge on Soviet arms policies, and this can be seen both in the histories of specific weapons systems and in the direction of overall policy.[49] The advanced capitalist powers have set the pace in making major weapons innovations, and this has served to stimulate Soviet military technology. Of course, it must be borne in mind that military power rests not only on the quality of military technology but also on its quantity and on the way in which the troops are trained to use it. The arms competition between East and West consists of both qualitative and quantitative elements; although the balance of the two may change, the arms race has never been a question of one of these elements to the exclusion of the other. Western military technology has spurred Soviet weapons development but has often been justified in terms of superior Soviet numbers.

It would be wrong, therefore, to deny the effects of foreign actions on Soviet arms policies, but it would be equally mistaken to see Soviet policy as merely a reaction to Western actions. Foreign influences are refracted through the Soviet policymaking process in which Soviet perceptions, military doctrine, foreign policy objectives, and domestic influences and constraints come into play. The effect of foreign actions on Soviet policy is complex and not at all automatic. In many cases, the foreign influences combine with domestic factors to speed up the internal dynamic of Soviet arms policies.[50] The very existence of large armed forces, a powerful defense industry, and an extensive network of military R & D establishments generates internal pressures for weapons development and production. The interplay of demand and invention gives rise to proposals for new and improved weapons. As a system progresses from conception to development, military and design bureau interests become attached to it, building up pressure for production. If it passes into production—and here a decision by the party leadership is required for major systems—enterprise managers are likely to favor long production runs. Of course, not all proposals result in weapons that are deployed. However, the stability of the Soviet military effort suggests that more than enough proposals are forthcoming to keep production at a relatively steady level and to ensure constant modernization of Soviet forces.

Dieter Senghaas has pointed to two principles that are important in understanding military–industrial complexes and that can be applied in the Soviet case.[51] The first of these is the principle of "configurative causality," which states that the overall configuration of the complex can be seen to give rise to pressures for arms production, even though these pressures may vary from case to case and cannot be identified in every specific instance. The second principle is that of "overdetermination" or "redundant causation"; to remove one cause or set of causes is not to eliminate the policies themselves, since other causes remain sufficient. This principle lies behind the argument that it is not enough to tackle the international causes of the East–West arms competition; the domestic roots, too, must be eradicated. These principles are both helpful in understanding Soviet arms policies. Although much of Soviet military policymaking is shrouded in secrecy, enough is known about the structures of the military–industrial–scientific complex to suggest that internal pressures are generated and considerable inertia built up in the military effort. It seems clear, too, that the removal of external stimuli, while it may alter Soviet arms policies in some important respects (e.g., make it less technologically innovative), would not eliminate its driving force entirely because much of that force is derived from domestic sources. (Nor could one say that military power would wither away because it had no role: It has been noted already that as Soviet military power has expanded, it has acquired new roles.) The question then is: how are these domestic sources to be weakened?

Conclusion   This chapter has outlined in general terms the domestic sources of the Soviet military effort and suggested that these sources are deeply embedded in Russian and Soviet history. Disarmament and demilitarization would involve, therefore, more than the surgical removal of some element of the Soviet state; it would have far-reaching effects throughout the whole society. Indeed, complete disarmament and demilitarization could come about only with the destruction of the international state system (and would not necessarily happen then). And although the "withering away of the state" is one of the anticipated consequences of Communist construction, the Soviet Union has one of the most powerful and extensive state apparatuses in the world. Yet, although the sources of Soviet militarism are strong, this chapter has not presented them as absolute, or suggested that there is no scope for initiatives for demilitarization. There are some developments in the Soviet Union today that suggest that a change of direction is possible. It would be a serious error to overestimate their importance or the degree to which they can be influenced from outside the Soviet Union. But it would be an even greater mistake to suppose that no change is possible or that its direction could not be influenced from afar.

Soviet military policy contains several contradictions that may, with time, become more apparent and exert an influence on Soviet politics. Having attained equality of superpower status with the United States, the Soviet Union is now faced with a new set of questions about military power and the direction of its policy. The Soviet leaders have said that they are not striving for superiority, but they have made it clear that they will not fall behind the United States in military power. The Soviet Union has thus locked itself into a relationship of parity with the United States. At one level, the maintenance of parity—along with the arms control negotiations that it underpins—provides the justification for Soviet military policy. At another level, however, the attainment of parity has meant that the Soviet Union has come to share full responsibility for the continuing arms competition. This has had a subtle yet profound effect on the attitude of many people in the West to Soviet military policy. Many of those sympathetic to Soviet policy deemed it legitimate for the leading socialist state to catch up with the leading capitalist power; but sharing responsibility for the arms race is not regarded so favorably, especially in view of the danger of nuclear war. In a similar way, the continuation of a high level of military effort, even after parity has been attained, may help to breed opposition inside the Soviet Union to the amassing of more military power. It is possible, for example, that Soviet militarism may emerge as a more important focus for dissident criticism, though the strength of nationalist sentiment (including dissident Russian nationalism) and the deep roots of legitimation should not be forgotten.

The Soviet Union shares with the United States the contradiction that growing military power does not bring greater security, even for superpowers. The accumulation of military power may only spur other governments to increase their own forces, thus nullifying the original gain. It is true that military power can further foreign policy, but it cannot ensure complete security in the nuclear age. The "Soviet military build-up" of the 1960s and 1970s has brought the Soviet Union political gains, but it has also helped to stimulate countervailing actions, and it is highly doubtful whether, in the last analysis, Soviet security is more assured now than it was 15 years ago. Moreover, the extension of Soviet military power throughout the world increases the risk that the Soviet Union will become embroiled in a military adventure that will arouse opposition at home, just as did the American war in Vietnam or the Russo–Japanese war of 1904–1905. The failure of military power to ensure security should provide, in principle, the opportunity of pressing the importance of pursuing nonmilitary cooperative arrangements for security rather than seeking to provide one's own security at the expense of others'.

These contradictions would be of little importance if there were no possibility of giving them political significance. The last 15 years have been a period of consolidation and conservative reform in the Soviet Union. But beneath the stable surface, changes have been taking place that could result in major shifts of direction in Soviet policy. The rate of economic growth has been declining, thus increasing the prospect that pressure for far-reaching reform will reemerge. Agricultural perform-ance has improved greatly but at a very high cost, again raising the prospect of reform. Other pressures exist for changing the priorities of resource allocation—for example, in order to speed up development of Siberia or to raise living standards. The cumulative effect of such pressures may be to weaken the position of the defense sector or to involve it more deeply in nonmilitary functions. It is not only the economic system that has been the focus of debate; discussion has also been taking place about the Soviet Union's proper relationship to the rest of the world. Some have pressed for as great a degree of autarky and isolation as possible; others have argued for a more outward-looking approach that would recognize that the world faces many problems that can be solved only by common and concerted action.[52] With the im-pending change of leadership, these various factors may combine to create a turning point in Soviet politics. The present leadership, as has been seen, has given immense importance to military power. It is, as yet, unclear how the next generation, which will not have been marked so deeply by the war, will view military power.

In pointing to these developments, one should not forget the militarizing pressures that were analyzed earlier in this chapter, or should one suppose that a change of course undertaken by a Soviet leadership would amount to radical disarmament or demilitarization. But the possibility for some change does exist, and it should be the aim of the peace movement to try to influence that change in the desired direction. There are considerable difficulties in seeking to influence Soviet policy from the outside, for the political system is very imperme-able, both in physical and cultural terms: it is hard to gain access to the policymaking process, and foreign attempts to influence policy will automatically be viewed with suspicion.

There are, nevertheless, two courses to be pursued. The first of these is directed at Western governments and should aim at ensuring that they do not foreclose, through their own policies, the possibility of Soviet moves toward disarmament and demilitarization. This course is a natural concomitant of efforts to press Western governments in that direction, too. But some attempt is needed to take the Soviet dimension consciously into account, and this means that the causes of Soviet militarism and the ways in which pressure on Western governments can also serve to influence the Soviet Union need to be analyzed. Such influence need not necessarily be directed solely at disarmament but could try to draw the Soviet Union into cooperative efforts to solve such problems as the world food supply. This may make it easier subsequently to work out cooperative, nonmilitary security arrangements.

The second course is directed at the Soviet Union and should try to engage people there in a dialogue about the problems of disarmament and demilitarization. Such a dialogue should be as extensive as possible and should not be confined to officials and representatives of officially approved bodies, on the one hand, or to dissidents (whether in the Soviet Union or abroad), on the other. The variety of political views and currents in the Soviet Union is very wide, and dissident and official views overlap and shade into each other; there are, for example, strong nationalist tendencies in both official and dissident thinking, and dissident reformist views find an echo in official circles as well.[53]

The importance of this course is that vigorous debates about Russia's destiny and the proper path of Soviet development are taking place inside the Soviet Union and among Soviet emigrés; in Eastern Europe, too, there is much argument about the future of state socialism. But the issues of disarmament and demilitarization—which are important for everyone's future—scarcely figure at all in these discussions, even though, as this chapter suggests, militarism and the lack of democracy are linked in the Soviet case. If these issues could be injected into the discussions, they would then be subject to a great deal of creative political thinking—and thinking, moreover, that is more attuned to the specific problems and conditions of the Soviet Union. Besides, it has been seen that the military burden in the Soviet Union is very heavy, but that its legitimation is also strong. Debate and discussion about the problems of Soviet militarism may help to weaken that legitimation.

It should not be supposed that everyone will welcome such discussion, and the attempt to generate it may well be regarded as unwarranted interference in the internal affairs of the Soviet Union. In the nuclear age, we are all affected by the military policies of the superpowers and hence, surely, have the right to try to influence them. Besides, the analysis given in this chapter suggests that external factors have had a far-reaching effect on Soviet development, and a reduction in the level of military competition would, in fact, give more latitude for choice in domestic politics. There has been an intensive argument among Soviet dissidents as to whether internal forces or external forces will determine the possibility of greater democracy in the Soviet Union. The analysis in this chapter suggests that internal forces will be more important both for general Soviet development and for Soviet military policy, but it also suggests that external conditions and influences do have a bearing on the domestic choices.

Notes

[1] The figures available on arms production and force levels give only the roughest indication of Soviet military production. They show no very sharp fluctuations since 1950, but they are too crude to register any but the most massive changes. The late 1950s and early 1960s appear to be the period of lowest effort. Western estimates of Soviet defense spending as a proportion of GNP seem to fit this pattern, with the Khrushchev years as the period when the proportion was lowest. Most estimates, derived by whatever means, fall into the range of 8–14%, with the lower estimates for the late 1950s and early 1960s. See, for example, the following: A. S. Becker, *Soviet National Income 1958–64* (Berkeley and Los Angeles, 1969), Chapter 7; F. D. Holzman, *Financial Checks on Soviet Defense Expenditures* (Lexington, Mass., Toronto, and London, 1975); H. Block, in Joint Economic Committee, U.S. Congress, *Soviet Economic Prospects for the Seventies* (Washington D.C., 1973), pp. 175–204; W. T. Lee, *The Estimation of Soviet Defense Expenditures 1955–75* (New York, 1977).

Assessment of the burden in terms of the proportion of GNP devoted to defense may not tell the whole story. An argument can be made that for an economy at a lower level of development—and, in particular, for one striving to catch up with more advanced economies—the same proportion of GNP is a heavier burden than for a highly developed economy because the competing ends to which resources could be devoted are more pressing.

[2] *The Military Balance,* IISS, London, each year gives a figure for the man-power in the Soviet Armed Forces. In 1979, that figure was 3.6 million. (*The Military Balance 1979–80,* p. 9.) This does not include approximately 400,000 KGB and MVD troops. There are also the 700,000 troops who engage in construction, railroad, farm, and medical work. See M. Feshbach and S. Rapawy, in Joint Economic Committee, U.S. Congress, *Soviet Economy in a New Perspective* (Washington D.C., 1976), pp. 144–152.

[3] Defense Minister Ustinov has declared that "service in the Soviet Armed Forces is a wonderful school of labor and martial training, of moral purity and courage, of patriotism and comradeship" (*Pravda,* November 8, 1979, p. 2). See T. Rakowska-Harmstone, "The Soviet Army as the Instrument of National Integration," *Soviet Military Power and Performance,* ed. John Erickson and E. J. Feuchtwanger (London, 1979), pp. 129–154.

[4] See, for example, *Marksizm-Leninizm o voine i armii* (Moscow, 1968), Ch. 5.

[5] See, in particular, Dieter Senghaas, *Rüstung und Militarismus* (Frankfurt am Main, 1972).

[6]J. Gould and W. L. Kolb, eds., *A Dictionary of the Social Sciences* (London, 1964), pp. 429–430.

[7]William E. Odom, "The 'Militarization' of Soviet Society," *Problems of Communism*, no. 5 (1976), pp. 34–51.

[8]Odom, "The 'Militarization' of Soviet Society," p. 51. In a lecture given in 1906, Otto Hintze made a similar point. Writing of Germany, he said: "Militarism still pervades our political system and public life today, generally in a very decisive way. Even Social Democracy, which is in principle against everything connected with militarism, not only owes to it the discipline on which its party organization largely rests, but also in its ideal for the future it has unconsciously adopted a good measure of the coercion of the individual by the community, which comes from the Prussian military state." Otto Hintze, "Military Organization and State Organization," in *The Historical Essays of Otto Hintze*, ed. Felix Gilbert (New York, 1965), p. 211. See also the essay by E. Jahn, "The Role of the Armaments Complex in Soviet Society," *Journal of Peace Research*, no. 3 (1975), pp. 179–194.

[9]Odom, "The 'Militarization' of Soviet Society," p. 51.

[10]E. P. Thompson, "Detente and Dissent," in *Detente and Socialist Democracy*, ed. Ken Coates (Nottingham, 1975), p. 123.

[11]*Ibid.*, pp. 123–5.

[12]See Alexander Gershenkron's "Economic Backwardness in Historical Perspective," (New York, Washington, London, 1965), pp. 5–30; for an interesting general discussion of the relationship between modernization and international relations, see Dennis Smith, "Domination and Containment: An Approach to Modernization," *Comparative Studies in Society and History* (April 1978), pp. 177–213.

[13]On these early debates, see John Erickson, *The Soviet High Command 1918–1941* (London, 1962), pp. 113–213; I. V. Berkhin, *Voennaya reforma v SSSR (1924–25 gg)* (Moscow, 1958).

[14]E. H. Carr, *Socialism in One Country, 1924–1926*, vol. 2 (Harmondsworth, 1970), p. 59.

[15]J. V. Stalin, *Problems of Leninism* (Moscow, 1947), p. 356.

[16]This is not to deny that there was opposition to the Soviet state during the war; but the memory of the war is very potent. See, for example, Ch. 12 of Hedrick Smith, *The Russians* (London, 1976).

[17]On this period of Khrushchev's rule, see especially Michel Tatu, *Power in the Kremlin* (London, 1969).

[18]It is also possible to trace the "Soviet military build-up" to the Central Committee resolution "On the Defense of the Country" in 1929. However, the present phase has its roots in the "revolution in military affairs," which was the subject of much discussion in the early 1960s.

[19]O. Lange, *Papers in Economics and Sociology* (Oxford and Warsaw, 1970), p. 102.

[20]For a discussion of the organization and functioning of the defense sector, see my "Soviet Military R & D: Managing the Research-Production Cycle," in *Soviet Science and Technology*, ed. J. Thomas and U. Kruse-Vaucienne (Washington D.C.: George Washington University for the National Science Foundation, 1977), pp. 179–229; for a more detailed discussion, see my two chapters in *Innovation in Soviet Industry*, ed. R. Amann and J. Cooper, forthcoming.

[21]See my paper "The Soviet Style of Military R & D" in *The Genesis of New Weapons: Decision-Making for Military R & D*, ed. F. A. Long and J. Reppy, forthcoming.

[22]*Marksizm-Leninism o voine i armii* (Moscow, 1968), pp. 258–259.

[23]See Joint Economic Committee, U.S. Congress, *Allocation of Resources in the Soviet Union and China—1978, Part 4—Soviet Union* (Washington D.C.), pp. 12–13, 34–35.

[24]*Pravda*, April 26, 1963; Tatu, *Power in the Kremlin*, pp. 343–344.

[25]Iran and Israel are two examples. See *World Armaments and Disarmament SIPRI Yearbook 1979* (London), p. 43.

[26]*Materialy XXIV s''yezda KPSS* (Moscow, 1971), p. 46.

[27]See especially Julian Cooper, "*Innovation for Innovation in Soviet Industry*" (Centre for Russian and East European Studies, University of Birmingham, Discussion Paper, Series RCB/11 1979), pp. 87–92.

[28]See *Narodnoe Khozyaisvo SSSR v 1977g* (Moscow, 1978), pp. 120–121, where Group B output is shown to have declined as a proportion of total industrial output between 1970 and 1976.

[29]A. Levikov, "'A' i 'B'," in *Literaturnaya Gazeta*, November 15, 1972, p. 11.

[30]*Literaturnaya Gazeta*, February 7, 1973, p. 10.

[31]See, for example, S. Tynshkevich, "Sootnoshenie sil v mire i faktory predotvrashcheniya voiny, *Kommunist vooruzhennykh sil*, no. 10 (1974), p. 16; N. A. Kosolapov, "Sotsialno-psikhologicheskie aspekty razryadki," *Voprosy filosofii*, no. 4 (1974), pp. 36–37; V. M. Kulish, ed., *Voennaya sila i mezhdunarodnye otnosheniya* (Moscow, 1972), Ch. 1.

[32]See *World Armaments and Disarmament. SIPRI Yearbook 1979* (London), pp. 172–173; G. Ofer, "Soviet Military Aid to the Middle East," Joint Economic Committee, U.S. Congress, *Soviet Economy in a New Perspective* (Washington D.C., 1976), pp. 216–239.

[33]This appears to have been the subject of argument and debate in Moscow in the 1970s. See Kulish, *Voennaya*, Ch. 1; and S. G. Gorshkov, *Morskaya Moshch Gosudarstv* (Moscow, 1976). Admiral Gorshkov is Commander-in-Chief of the Soviet Navy.

[34]See, in particular, the article on military doctrine in *Soveskaya Voennaya Entsiklopedia*, vol. 3 (Moscow 1977), pp. 225–229, for the Soviet position.

[35]See the article on civil defense in *Sovetskaya Voennaya Entsiklopedia*, vol. 3 (Moscow 1977), pp. 23–25.

[36]Central Intelligence Agency, *Soviet Civil Defense*, NI 78-10003 (Washington D.C., July 1978), p. 2.

[37]*Ibid*, pp. 3–5.

[38]See Odom, *loc. cit.*, pp. 44–7; *Sovetskaya Voennaya Entsiklopedia*, vol. 3, Moscow 1977, pp. 255–7.

[39]*Sovetskaya Voennaya Entsiklopedia*, vol. 2 (Moscow 1976), p. 245.

[40]Odom, "The 'Militarization' of Soviet Society." p. 44.

[41]This has been a very widespread view, advanced most thoroughly in R. Kolkowicz, *The Soviet Military and the Communist Party* (Princeton, 1967).

[42]T. Colton, *Commanders, Commisars, and Civilian Authority* (Cambridge, Mass., 1979) argues that the Main Political Administration in effect identifies with the military. See also R. Fritsch-Bournazel, "Les Forces Armées et la 'societé socialiste avancée'," *Pouvoirs*, no. 6 (1978), pp. 55–64.

[43]For an analysis that suggests that the charges against Zhukov were unfounded and that the affair should not be interpreted as a party–military conflict, see Colton, *Commanders*, Ch. 8.

[44]*Ibid*, pp. 257–275.

[45]"The Soviet System: Petrification or Pluralism," in *The Soviet Union and Social Science Theory*, ed. J. Hough (Cambridge, Mass., 1977), pp. 19–48.

[46]For a discussion of marginal shifts of resources, see J. Hardt, "Military–Economic Implications of Soviet Regional Policy," prepared for Colloquium at NATO Economic Directorate (Brussels, April, 1979).

[47]R. Garaudy, *The Turning-Point of Socialism* (London, 1970), p. 138.

[48]See my "The Soviet Style of Military R & D."

[49]A very clear example is Soviet atomic bomb development. See my "Entering the Nuclear Arms Race: The Soviet Decision to Build the Atomic Bomb" (Working Paper no. 9, International Security Studies Program, Wilson Center, Washington D.C., 1979).

[50]See my "Research Note: Soviet Thermonuclear Research," *International Security* (Winter 1979/80).

[51]Senghaas, *op. cit.*, pp. 361–364.

[52]For a discussion of the different trends, see W. Clemens Jr., *The USSR and Global Interdependence* (Washington D.C., 1978).

[53]See, for example, the discussion in R. Medvedev, *On Socialist Democracy* (London, 1975), Chs. 3 and 4.

15   TIMOTHY J. COLTON

The Impact of the Military on Soviet Society*

"The Army is a part of Soviet society and is nurtured by it not only materially but spiritually. In the Army are reflected all those socioeconomic and ideological–political processes taking place in society."[1] In these words, a major Soviet text clearly states the first lesson a Western observer grasps about the military—that it must be understood as a part of the whole Soviet social and political system. While it has many of the universal characteristics of military organizations (and of all bureaucracies), its molding by unique and often paradoxical circumstances must never be forgotten. It is the largest peacetime army in history, yet the leader who presided over its founding had opposed standing military forces until weeks before coming to power, and six decades later, his writings are cited to support indefinite accumulation of military "might." The army is subject to strict civilian control (as official pronouncements never tire in declaring), yet the country's foremost civilian recently arranged to acquire, in his seventieth year, the military rank of marshal. The army uses the latest in nuclear and electronic technology, yet the press routinely describes shortages of fresh fruit, footwear, and shower facilities in military garrisons.

The purpose of this chapter is to explore the military's effect on the overall social and political order by which it so obviously has been shaped, and in particular, its effects on those aspects of society that influence foreign policy. This is a question of clear and present significance, both for our overall understanding of Soviet reality and for the formulation of Western foreign policies. The last decade has seen not only a general increase in Western interest in Soviet military affairs but also an introduction into journalistic, academic, and government discus-

*Reprinted by permission of the author and publisher from *The Domestic Context of Soviet Foreign Policy,* ed. Seweryn Bialer (Boulder, Colo.: Westview Press, 1981), pp. 119–138. Copyright 1981 by Westview Press.

sion of themes reminiscent of the notion of "Red militarism" that flourished between the wars.

The Military
and Society:
Western Views

In the past, Western scholars have tended to be more interested in the substance of Soviet military policy than in political and social processes in which the army is involved. Inasmuch as such processes have been analyzed, the dominant concern has been with relations between the military and the ruling Communist party, and the overwhelming consensus has been that these relations are basically adversarial. The military's quest for autonomy is said to clash with party desires for complete hegemony over all potential rivals, thereby resulting in deep-seated and irresolvable conflict. In the words of Roman Kolkowicz, "The relationship between the Communist party and the Soviet military is essentially conflict-prone and thus presents a perennial threat to the political stability of the Soviet state."[2] This antagonism is thought to be resolved in the party's favor principally through bureaucratic control mechanisms (the most important of which is the party's apparatus within the military, the main political administration), but even these controls do not prevent aspects of the conflict from surfacing.

This interpretation has recently been seriously questioned by some scholars. In an ambitious and widely read essay published in 1973, William Odom argued that "value congruence rather than conflict" characterizes army–party relations, and he drew attention to linkages between the two institutions and to symbiotic aspects of their relationship.[3] The present author has found the original model to be particularly misleading when applied to the behavior of the military party apparatus, whose officials have tended, contrary to earlier predictions, to function on most political issues as allies rather than adversaries of military commanders. Rarely does one see sharp lines drawn between an army seeking autonomy and a party wishing to maximize control or between the military command and the political organs tied to the civilian leadership. Rather, consensus and cleavage normally cut across institutional boundaries and involve coalitions primarily based on location and including *both* military commanders and party officials.[4]

Such a pattern of horizontal linkages between party officials and specialized elites, far from being unique, probably applies to many other particularized groups and issue-areas. For example, in the field of industrial management, managers and party workers are in basic agreement on overall goals, and on individual questions most conflicts "arise between one group of industrial and party officials who support one project and another group of industrial and party officials who support another project."[5]

The question that Odom has raised in his more recent work is whether the specific tendency toward civil-military "congruence" and interpretation is found with regard to issues *other* than specialized military ones. In a 1976 article, Odom points to what he calls "the militarization of Soviet society." Concentrating on civil defense, basic military training, and paramilitary programs since 1967, he draws a picture of a society in which military values and institutions increasingly permeate all aspects of life. Odom's views about exactly *who* is managing the militarization process are somewhat unclear. At times, he speaks in general terms of the regime as a whole "organizing the civil society to support the military" and implies that it is soldiers themselves—the professional military establishment, as organized in the Ministry of Defense—who are appropriating an ever greater role.[6]

We have then an approach that—particularly in versions lacking the subtlety of Odom's—conceives of the military's social impact in terms almost diametrically opposed to traditional ones. Kolkowicz's army exerts a sharply limited impact on Soviet society as a whole, its influence being circumscribed by the party's controls and tendency to "regard any increment in the military's prerogatives and authority as its own loss and therefore as a challenge."[7] In Odom's conception, on the other hand, soldiers and their values, with party encouragement, are acquiring more influence.

This chapter will present somewhat of a middle course. It will concur with Odom that military and civilian elites share certain fundamental objectives and interests as well as commitments to major defense programs. However, it will also strive toward greater specificity in identifying issues on which the military affects policy outcomes and the means by which this influence is exerted. The army's impact on society will be examined in terms of three major roles—agent, educator, and claimant—and tentative conclusions will be drawn regarding trends in its overall influence and implications for foreign policy.

The Military as Agent

The most important role Soviet military officers play is that of administrative agents of civilian politicians. This is the dominant image of the military in the rudimentary Soviet theory on civil–military relations. "The Soviet commander," according to the leading text on military strategy, "is the representative of the party and people. He carries out their will and implements party policy in the forces."[8] The line of vertical subordination (extending from party leadership through the successive command and staff layers of the Ministry of Defense) is an obvious and straightforward one.

Perhaps less obvious is what the agent role implies for the military's effect on Soviet society. First, it means that officers exercise a great deal of delegated authority over the lives of a large number of subordinates, including the several million young men (most of them aged 18–20) serving as conscript soldiers and sailors. One-half of all Soviet youths undergo compulsory military service, a proportion that has been considerably higher in the past and will probably increase in the future. For several years, their work, social, and even sleep habits are regulated by officers whose orders are, as military regulations state crisply, law (*zakon*) for their subordinates. Under officers' direction, they operate a vast and intricate system of activity that includes an enormous store of fighting equipment and most of the facilities needed to train, police, clothe, house, feed, transport, heal, clean, counsel, and entertain the men who make the equipment work.[9]

The vast majority of the officers who exercise this authority are members of the party or *Komsomol* (this is especially true in troop command posts and almost universally at ranks of major and above), and the military hierarchy is saturated with a network of appointed and voluntary party agencies. Yet this has never made the army anything other than an organization whose prime purpose is to prepare for, wage, and win armed conflict. Even the military party organs' activity has for most of their history been tailored to military purposes. Soviet officers are soldiers of the party, but they are soldiers nonetheless. They leave their imprint upon their temporary charges as surely as do their counterparts in other armies.

Not only has the party delegated to the military a mission and the authority to perform it, it has also assigned consummate importance to that function. In the belief that defense is, as Stalin said, "the primary task for us,"[10] the regime has created an innovative and productive infrastructure for the military effort—a military–industrial complex, to use the phrase the Soviets often apply to other countries. This system, undoubtedly "the most privileged segment" of the economy,[11] is best seen as registering the impact of military *goals*—as defined by a basically civilian leadership—rather than of the military *establishment*. But the requirements of their administrative mission do bring Soviet officers into contact with numerous other segments of society and of the governmental system.

For instance, military officials, usually in quite specialized agencies, participate as administrators in several areas of mainly civilian jurisdiction into which they have been allowed to extend their efforts to augment military capabilities. Several issue-areas stand out. In the field of construction, the military has long participated in extramilitary projects on a major scale, partly to enhance its own capacity and partly to compensate for civilian deficiencies. Soldiers (usually specially drafted construction troops) build telephone lines, housing, office and other public buildings, and irrigation facilities.[12] In the area of transport, too, construction has been a major activity. Since 1945, specialized railroad troops have laid about 1000 kilometers of track a year and have built hundreds of bridges and other structures; they are currently responsible for the eastern sector of the massive Baikal–Amur Railroad project.[13] All facets of military and civilian transport were tightly integrated during World War II, and even in peacetime, complex arrangements exist to coordinate use of rail lines, airports, canals, harbors, and other facilities.

Officers also seek to secure specific contributions to their delegated mission from a number of civilian organizations, a fact that implies some military participation in realms of decision entrusted primarily to civilians. The ties with the other parts of the military–industrial complex (scientific institutes, defense production ministries, planning bodies) are often mentioned in Western research. There has been rather less heed paid to collaboration concerning civil defense, civil aviation, maritime navigation, and diplomatic representation abroad. Almost nothing has been written about how the army deals at several levels with civilians, providing them with routine goods and services. Its headquarters negotiate agreements with the Ministry of Agriculture (for use of farmland), the Ministry of Oil Refining and Petrochemical Industry (for fuel and lubricants), food-processing ministries, and the Ministry of Trade, Ministry of Light Industry, and other consumer goods producers (for supply of clothing, consumer durables, and other items). At the local level, housing is sometimes leased from civilian authorities, contacts are made with party and government authorities during disaster-relief operations and harvest campaigns, conscription call-ups entail close communication with local health and school officials, and annual contracts are made with republican and local agencies for supply of perishable foods, leisure and supporting equipment, household appliances and chemicals, and a range of other commodities.

The Military as Educator

Implicit in its role as the regime's principal agent in military policy is the army's role as educator. Any peacetime army is essentially an educational organization, teaching citizens how to apply violence in the interests of the state. Yet the role of educator is so important in Soviet military theory and practice and so central to any discussion of the military's impact on society that it merits separate consideration.

Much of the education that occurs within the Soviet military would be familiar to conscripts in other armies: the drill, technical instruction, field exercises, and the like. What is striking about Soviet military training is its deliberate interweaving with a system of ideological and moral upbringing (*vospitanie*). Since the Civil War, Soviet theorists have argued that the training of the good soldier is inseparable from the forming of the good citizen and that wars are won by the side that can field the soldier "who is able in the most difficult of conditions to maintain his high moral spirit and will to victory."[14] To this end, all servicemen are constantly bombarded with political information and exhortation, most of it administered by the political organs. Each man attends 4 hours a week of obligatory political classes and an additional hour of "political information." About 80% of all troops are members of the Komsomol (70% are already members when conscripted), and a much smaller proportion are party members.[15] Cultural and recreational activity (supervised by the political organs) is also laden with ideological content.

It is thus readily understandable that the army is referred to as a "school of Communism," an arena for political socialization as well as specialized military training. Indeed, in the first several decades of Soviet rule, the military was frequently heralded as the country's single most important vehicle for this purpose. Stalin described it as "the sole . . . point of assembly where people from various provinces and regions come together, study, and are schooled in political life."[16] Thousands of servicemen, especially from rural areas, received their first exposure to party ideas (not to mention mass organization and machine technology) in the interwar Red Army. The subsequent growth of the regime's systems of public education and communication has outdated any claim to preeminence, but political training in the military remains an important thread in the overall weave, "continuing the process of Communist education . . . begun in the family, school, and productive process."[17] Because soldiers have already been familiarized with the regime's basic values, the emphasis is now on reinforcing and maintaining the desired attitudes against "nihilism and skepticism."[18]

During the last decade, there has been an upsurge of official interest in military service—in all its aspects—as an inculcator of civic virtue. One now finds statements that the army provides "particularly favorable circumstances for organizing the entire business of upbringing."[19] At the Twenty-Fifth Party Congress in 1976, Leonid Brezhnev's only reference to the military was in precisely this connection:

In speaking about educational work, comrades, it is impossible not to dwell on the enormous role which the Soviet Army plays in this matter. Young men arrive in the soldierly family with no experience in the school of life. But they return from the Army already people who have gone through the school of tenacity and discipline, who have acquired technical and professional knowledge and political training.[20]

Two educational goals are now receiving emphasis. One is the development of such individual lines of character as "tenacity and discipline," which military and party leaders alike often see as lacking in the generation born after 1945. The other reflects what may be an even deeper source of anxiety—the goal of solidarity among the Soviet Union's many nationalities. The army is clearly designed as an integrating and Russianizing institution. Russian is the sole language of instruction and command, and facility in it is a prerequisite for admission to officers' schools. There is an "attempt to reinforce in every soldier the awareness of belonging to a single socialist Motherland, to a great international army."[21] Political officers operate "circles for the study of the Russian language" in some units, and they are urged to combat "elements of national conceit and harmful habits of seeing a national basis for every disagreement or personal insult."[22] This struggle will no doubt become more important as it becomes necessary to conscript larger numbers of non-Russians (particularly Central Asians) in future years.

The development of the last decade that has most caught the eye of foreign observers has been the perceptible increase in military and military-related education *outside* the army. This growth has occurred in three areas.

First, the revised military service law of 1967, while reducing active duty for most conscripts by 1 year, required all predraft-age youths to undergo basic military training (*nachal'naia voennaia podgotovka*) at their places of study or work. Introduced in stages from 1968 to the mid-1970s, the system placed military instructors (*voennye rukovoditeli*)—most of them reserve or retired officers—in secondary and vocational schools and major production enterprises. The 2-year, 140-hour program covers military regulations, use of light weapons, drill, and a technical military specialty (usually operation of a vehicle). Since the early 1970s, many postsecondary students (who normally receive draft deferments) have been required to attend courses in new military faculties. They ultimately are given reserve commissions and are thus liable to later call-up. In addition, the preinduction and other programs of DOSAAF (the Voluntary Society for Assistance of the Army, Air Force, and Navy) have continued to expand, particularly in the area of technical specialties. DOSAAF's capital expenditures increased by almost 60% from 1972 through 1976, and by 1977, it was claiming a membership of 80 million—two-thirds of the entire adult population.[23]

A second area of growth has been the civil defense program, which has acquired greater visibility and perhaps a higher degree of coordination. Civil defense themes have been more prominent in the mass media and in specialized publications, and since 1971, they have been included in curricula for all second- and fifth-grade pupils. The program of instruction in factories and other workplaces was standardized in 1972 (at 20 hours of nonworking time a year for each employee), and both large-scale exercises and specialized courses for officials have become more common.[24]

Third, the regime has placed greater emphasis on the general "military-patriotic education" of the population, particularly the young. The commemoration of past martial exploits, especially the "Great Patriotic War" of 1941–1945, reached a crescendo with the celebration of the 30th anniversary of victory in 1975. In the 5 years 1972–1976, 80 major war monuments were unveiled; from 1974 to 1976, more than 500 books and 300 serialized novels and short stories on the war were published in Russian alone.[25] Perhaps the major innovation has been in terms of participatory and organized forms of inculcation for young people. These various activities include "red pathfinders" clubs, which mount excursions to monuments and battlefields; groups of "young friends" of the army and navy; and military–patriotic "schools" and "universities" (most of them attached to elementary or secondary schools or to DOSAAF clubs). Most ambitious have been the two "military–sports games" organized by the major youth federations— *Zarnitsa* (Summer Lightning) for Young Pioneers (aged 10 to 15), claiming 16 million participants by 1972; and the Komsomol's *Orlenok* (Eaglet), established only in 1972 and, as of 1976, claiming 8 million participants in their later teens.[26]

In terms of sheer ambition and energy, all of these programs warrant further attention from Western scholars. But would such attention establish that Soviet society is being "militarized" and in particular that the power of the military itself is growing? Here a number of cautions are in order.

To begin, one should be careful not to overstate the innovativeness of some of this activity. Preinduction training in the schools does mark a major change (although one accompanied by another change—shorter terms for conscripts—which markedly reduces the exposure of most young men to active military service). Civil defense, on the other hand, dates in its current form from 1961 and, indeed, grew out of a local air defense network established in 1932; the 1972 directive on workplace instruction did not necessarily imply an increased effort, merely a set of minimum standards.[27] DOSAAF, too, has a long history (its predecessors were founded in the 1920s). And military–patriotic propaganda and education are by no means a recent creation. If 80 monuments were built between 1972 and 1976, in 1966 there were already 675 military monuments and memorials in the Ural Military District alone (an area in which no land battles were fought during World War II).[28] The entire military–patriotic program is fundamentally backward-looking, an attempt to foster by deliberate government effort feelings that for earlier generations emerged more spontaneously from experience. Even tributes to the plethora of war novels protest that authors are now more likely to slight martial themes than in the past.

In the second place, it should be realized that many of the measures reviewed here have complex objectives, and that at least some are essentially used to shape civilian society in accordance with the preferences of civilian leaders and in ways that go beyond merely heightening military capability. This is especially true of civilian–patriotic education, in which several kinds of values that have long been important to the civilian elite—discipline, nationalism, and respect for past achievements—are at the very heart of the process. It is certainly significant that the regime has chosen the army and the military idiom as the focus for the effort, but it is true nonetheless that broader civilian purposes prevail. Nationalism is heavily stressed in the program, particularly in non-Russian republics (where it is often referred to as "internationalist" as well as military–patriotic). The appeal to the accomplishments and heroes of the past is an omnipresent theme (to the point that a story can refer to long-dead revolutionaries and soldiers as "standing invisibly" in a Komsomol honor guard at a monument).[29] Here, too, the ideals being promoted far transcend the military realm.

A third pitfall to avoid is confusion of the objectives and exertions of the programs with their actual impact on society. Militarizing government programs do not necessarily mean a militarized society any more than a "war on poverty" in the United States automatically implies greater equality.

Quantitative descriptions of the programs should be treated with great care. It is useful to know that 85,000 young people a year took part in the red pathfinders movement in Turkmenistan in 1971–1972; that 2000 children and teenagers attended summer military–sports camps in Latvia in 1972, and 16,000 were enrolled in military–patriotic schools in Belorussia in 1973; or that in the summer of 1975, 30,000 students from Dnepropetrovsk oblast visited local monuments and another 8000 went on excursions to four "hero cites."[30] What none of these figures indicates (and what Western analysts rarely seek out) is the ratio of participants to eligible populations. The 1970 census makes clear that in these cases the participants amounted, respectively, to 17.6, 0.6, 0.9, 7.5, and 2.0% of the relevant populations (aged 10–19)—proportions that imply far less substantial impact than the absolute numbers might intimate at first glance.

Even where quantitative saturation is indisputably high (as with DOSAAF and the Zarnitsa and Orlenok games, which between them involve half of the 10–19-year-olds), no analysis can refrain from raising questions about program quality and effect. While this is not the place for detailed examination, it should be noted that no serious Soviet discussion of the programs fails to pose such questions.

Basic military training is a partial exception here, at least in the secondary schools; despite construction and other problems, it seems to have produced the desired effect. Nonetheless, even a favorable Soviet overview must conclude that the program "suffices only to acquaint students with the general structure of [a military] machine, with its most important features and basic operating principles. To put it briefly . . . students acquire elementary knowledge and habits concerning only a single military–technical specialty."[31] Soviet evaluations of non-school programs are often much less positive. Reviews of civil defense preparations refer to "formalism and vulgarization" and remark on officials "who 'forget' about civil defense, justifying this by their pre-occupation with production affairs"; reports about both basic training and civil defense mention "indifference" in building and maintaining basic facilities; a speech on war novels scores their "primitiveness" and facile moralizing; and stories tell of participants in military–patriotic projects being assembled from predetermined lists (*po spisku*).[32] The bloated DOSAAF network has been excoriated for similar sins for decades, and this evidence is reinforced by the private testimony of present and former Soviet citizens and the obvious absurdity of some of DOSAAF's self-appraisals.[33] If Zarnitsa and Orlenok seem to be more efficacious, it is probably because they are firmly rooted in the schools; most competitions take place on school grounds (under Pioneer and Komsomol auspices), and only a small proportion of competitors seem to participate in the regional and national games in midsummer.

The fourth and final qualification regarding these programs has to do with their relation to the power of the military itself. Militarizing programs—even a militarizing society—may go hand in hand with greater political power for the professional military, but in the Soviet Union under Brezhnev there is little evidence that they have.

Basic military training, to take the first area, is formally a responsibil-ity of civilian ministries of education, all of which have departments for that purpose. Military instructors are appointed and dismissed by local education departments on recommendation of the school director and with the consent of the local military commissariat. They are paid by the schools and responsible to their directors. In 1972, after receiving letters from several military instructors recommending that they be sub-ordinated to military commissiariats rather than to civilian school au-thorities, the deputy minister of education in charge of the national program dismissed the suggestions as being "so obviously [mistaken] as hardly to warrant comment." The deputy minister went on to observe: "The school must not be transformed into the likeness of a troop subunit. The Soviet school has its own regulations and educational traditions, which the military instructor is obliged to observe."[34]

DOSAAF, which plays a substantial role in several military-related areas, is not under immediate control of the army. It finances its own operations—with considerable difficulty, as many accounts clearly show—from membership dues, lotteries, charges for sports events, and a variety of recreation services. Military officials do not seem to be involved in DOSAAF's perennial campaigns to persuade local authori-ties to implement the vague guidelines on assistance to the organiza-tion's construction efforts.[35]

The fact that civil defense has a uniformed national chief (*nachal'nik*)— currently General of the Army Aleksandr T. Altunin, who has since 1972 also been a deputy defense minister—seems to imply more concerted penetration of civilian society by the military. Yet one should be careful about inferring the "dominant administrative role of the Ministry of Defense"[36] from Altunin's dual appointment (his predecessor had similar status from 1961 to 1964) or on any other grounds. At republican and local levels, the civil defense chief is invariably the civilian chairman of the relevant council of ministers or municipal council. While most administrative responsibility probably lies with their full-time chiefs of staff, who are professional officers, the fact that civilians remain formally in charge is noteworthy and underlines the regime's intention to keep implementation of the program at least partly in nonmilitary hands. Official pronouncements refer to civil defense as being "under the leadership of the [local] party and soviet organs" and describe "constant attention" to it on the part of local party executives.[37] No such statement would ever be made about operations within army jurisdiction, which are essentially outside the purview of local politicians.[38] At the plant level, the chief of civil defense is the enterprise director, and the parttime chief of staff is one of the director's line subordinates, often an engineer and sometimes a man with minor military experience. All formations within the enterprise are created by order of the director, and they are explicitly characterized as nonmilitarized (*nevoenizirovannye*) groups. A number of other civilian organizations participate in civil defense planning and exercises—including the Komsomol, Red Cross, railroads, medical and sanitation services, electrical and gas utilities, sports organizations, and territorial planning agencies—and the evidence suggests that whatever coordination is imposed comes from civilian authorities rather than from the military.[39]

A similar situation applies to military–patriotic education. Active and retired military officers, political organs, and occasionally military units are involved in program implementation, but planning is subject to local party control.[40] The Komsomol is actively involved (all its committees have departments for sport and mass defense work), as are the Pioneers, sports organizations, trade unions, ministries and departments of culture, *Znanie* (the mass information organization), school administrators, and the Academy of Pedagogical Sciences. At best, the military is a partner in a program dominated by civilians and using military values to achieve largely civilian ends.

The Military as Claimant

Besides participating in (and often monopolizing) political decisions within the military establishment, Soviet officers also take part in a variety of decisions together with civilian politicians and administrators. In doing

so, they often put forward claims for recognition and resources in much
the same manner as bureaucratic officials elsewhere in the Soviet
system.

Clearly, their main resource with national leaders is their status as
specialists and experts worthy of consultation. Even Stalin, when confronted by specialized military decisions, "repeatedly asked, 'What does
the General Staff think?' or, 'Has the General Staff examined this
question?' And the General Staff always gave its opinion."[41] Since the
early 1960s, official statements have been much more explicit than
before in referring to consultation as routine: "Before deciding one way
or the other on questions of military development, the Party Central
Committee and Politburo carefully study the state of affairs in the Army
and Navy and consult with the high command and the most important
specialists of the Armed Forces."[42]

Consultation is formalized to some extent through military membership in bodies such as the Council of Ministers, the Defense Council (a
collegium for discussing military policy, currently chaired by General
Secretary Brezhnev), and the Military–Industrial Commission, which
deals with defense production. The military is also represented on the
formal decision-making organs of the party. The 30 military members
and candidates on the 1976 Central Committee (7% of the total) made up
by far the largest contingent from any bureaucratic constituency. At the
peak level, most Politburos prior to 1955 contained one nonprofessional
defense administrator (Trotsky, Frunze, Voroshilov, Bulganin). Since
then, there have been two experiments to seat a defense minister who
was also a professional soldier (Georgii Zhukov in 1956–1957 and Andrei
Grechko in the 3 years before his death in April 1976). Grechko's
successor, Dmitrii F. Ustinov (a civilian Politburo member who has
spent almost his entire career dealing with defense production, most
recently as party secretary), marks at least a temporary reversion to the
pre-1955 pattern and shows that the professional military can in no way
view a Politburo seat as an institutional entitlement. Military officers sit
on lower-level party organs as well. As of the early 1970s, individual
officers belonged to 7 of 14 republican bureaus, an average of 8 sat on
republican central committees, and there was substantial representation
at the local level.

Less formalized channels are probably of equal importance (as is true
for all bureaucratic claimants in Soviet politics). Marshal Grechko, for
example, is said to have attended Politburo discussions on military
matters even before his elevation to that body,[43] and war memoirs
depict similar informal interaction. Some officers seem to have ben-
efitted from personal connections with civilian politicians based on
friendship and common experience (Grechko is said to have had such a
relationship with Brezhnev.) One can also assume the existence of less
personalized linkages with civilians involved in defense research and

production. As in most consultative relationships, there has been no sharp line drawn between advice solicited by civilians and prodding at the military's own initiative. Khrushchev may have grumbled in his memoirs about military "pressure" or even "intimidation" of the party leadership, but there is no evidence he sought to prevent soldiers from speaking their minds on military issues. "I don't reproach the military for that—they're only doing their job."[44]

The Soviet military is denied some of the bargaining resources available to its counterpart in the United States. In particular, the structural primacy of the party executive has precluded the direct appeals to an independent legislature encountered in the United States. Nonetheless, some structural factors clearly work in the Soviet officers' favor. Special weight is lent to their counsel by the fact that their expertise is not widely shared outside the military establishment. Notwithstanding party, KGB, and defense industry involvement in some aspects of military affairs (and the evident growth of military competence in several civilian research institutes over the last decade), the Soviet officer corps does seem to control far more of the information relevant to its mission than do armies in Western societies. The Soviet system does not contain the major nonmilitary sources of military information found in U.S. politics—there is no equivalent to the Central Intelligence Agency or to private consulting firms such as the RAND Corporation.

Officers' status as claimants on the leadership is also reinforced by the high degree of instability and danger that civilians have perceived as inhering in the international milieu, the environment in which military decisions take effect. The tendency of Soviet leaders to resolve uncertainty in foreign policy on the side of safety has clearly made them more receptive to military advice than to that of most other expert groups. Khrushchev's remarks to President Eisenhower in 1959 display this receptivity as well:

> Some people from our military department come and say, "Comrade Khrushchev, look at this! The Americans are developing such and such a system. We could develop the same system, but it would cost such and such." I tell them there's no money; it's all been allotted already. So they say, "If we don't get the money we need and if there's a war, then the enemy will have superiority over us." So we discuss it some more, and I end up giving them the money they ask for.[45]

Such high-level consultations on foreign policy issues are, of course, closed to foreign social scientists (for the period since 1945, at least). So are most of the bureaucratic channels at all levels through which influence on civilians is exerted. Much more readily observable are the public discussions in which army officials participate. Officers are subject to the same constraints as other citizens (for instance, in relation to criticism of Stalin) and to special restrictions in the cause of secrecy. Still, one finds a remarkably wide range of military-related concerns and anxieties aired in public: the status of the army and its mission, specific questions on military policy (such as the relative weight given to different branches of the military), the quality of civilian goods and services, and others. In approaching these public articulations, and less open ones as well, several general points should be kept in mind.

The first is that the military does not claim to be a monolithic or isolated organization. Military participation is specialized according to issue and actor (logistics officers are most concerned with relations with the railroads, political officers with military–patriotic education, and so on). Officers are not necessarily coordinated or unanimous in their preferences and may in fact differ among themselves in major ways. And whatever the range of military opinion, the likelihood is that important aspects of military positions will find support from at least some civilians and not offer a frontal challenge to civilian party leaders or to the interests of the regime as a whole. It is clear, for example, that Khrushchev's force reduction proposals in 1960 were opposed by a wide range of civilian party and state officials as well as by the military high command (and the military party organs).

Precisely such a pattern of ongoing discussion has been visible in this decade of relations with the West regarding the desirability and preferred modes of détente. Most military spokesmen share the ambivalence that infuses almost all official pronouncements about the "relaxation of tensions." While valuing its contribution to Soviet security (they have had virtually nothing to say about the presumed benefits of increased trade and technological exchange), they are anxious about possible Western second thoughts and wary of the long-term effects of relaxation of vigilance on the Soviet population—particularly on the youth.

Undoubtedly, it is the latter train of thought that has been emphasized in public military statements. Soviet soldiers have had to make no apologies for the fact that, as Marshal Grechko said, "For us military men it is impossible to forget" the experience and dangers of war.[46] Military officers have been most forthright in arguing the hazards of failing to extract reciprocal concessions from the West, especially on arms control issues: "A unilateral slackening in the USSR's defense power might call forth sharp changes in the policy of the ruling circles of the imperialist states. . . . Life dictates the necessity of unflagging concern for strenthening . . . the military power of the Soviet Union."[47] It is interesting that some of the most outspoken declarations about the possible pitfalls of détente have come from the Main Political Administration (MPA), a component of the military establishment whose central task is to interpret and enforce party policy in the military realm. MPA chief Aleksei A. Epishev has repeatedly warned against imperialism's "aggressive nature": "In a situation where imperialism, in its efforts to regain its lost initiative, has become even more aggressive and adventuristic, Leinin's words about the need to keep our Army 'fully ready for battle and increase its military potential' are particularly appropriate."[48] Such sentiments have recently been echoed by Ustinov, his civilian background notwithstanding.[49] They are, moreover, sentiments that resonate in many civilian quarters (as is surely the case for corresponding viewpoints in the United States).

In considering the military as a claimant in politics, it is also important to understand that in the majority of cases, the target of military advice and pressure is not the national party leadership at all, but other organizations or groups whose cooperation is necessary for some specific purpose. For instance, the Ministry of Defense and the MPA have repeatedly urged artists and their professional unions to do more work on martial themes. The latest illustration of concerted pressure occurred in April 1977, when General Epishev addressed a hall full of cultural dignitaries (including officials of the Ministry of Culture, the editor of *Literaturnaia gazeta*, and leaders of the writers', composers', filmmakers', and sculptors' unions), demanding more attention to "soldierly labor, which is just as necessary to society as that of the worker or peasant."[50] Quite frequently, at least on routine service issues, it is local officials who are the targets of military efforts. A bottleneck or disagreement may mean that officers will "turn for a decision to the corresponding party and soviet organs."[51] Public criticisms are many and varied, with officers pressing, for instance, for improved housing and nursery facilities for military families, better treatment of reserve officers and veterans (particularly now that many World War II veterans are reaching pension age), more attention to civil defense and paramilitary programs, or more investment priority for local factories producing materials for military construction units.[52]

The final point to be made here is that military claims, for all their complexity, essentially relate to areas of policy in which the army's institutional interests are directly engaged. Soviet leaders have been assiduous in restricting soldiers' participation in administration and politics to questions relating in some way to their professional function and immediate interests. Stalin's conviction that "the military should occupy themselves with their own business and not discuss things that do not concern them"[53] has been retained by his successors. In a way, the list of issues on which the military does not play a major role as agent or claimant—including questions of internal order and rural development, to mention two areas where the Chinese military is much more active—is as impressive as the set of issues in which the army's role is significant. Soviet officers have displayed no tendency to expand their participation into new problem areas, and some have even declined minor opportunities to do so. For instance, the construction of military retail outlets is often not coordinated with that of civilian stores because "military clients and construction agencies do not maintain close working contacts with local executive committees."[54] Some military trade executives "do not meet their local suppliers for years on end" and fail to obtain delivery of goods already contracted for due to the fact that they "do not insist on having their orders filled."[55]

Trends and Implications

The crucial prerequisite for careful examination of the military's impact on Soviet society and politics is the acceptance of the fact that this impact is complex—complex in its determinants, modes, and consequences. It is surely incorrect to reduce the military's role to that of anxious adversary of the party leadership. Yet it would also be dangerous to accept some of the more simplistic notions (particularly those broadcast by Western journalists and Western generals) about pervasive military influence or about a militarizing or militarized Soviet society.

The army's impact has not changed qualitatively during the Brezhnev era. The prospects for qualitative change are not to be dismissed out of hand, yet they will depend essentially on developments outside the military establishment, developments that are extremely difficult to forecast. Any outright disintegration of the political system will inevitably bring the military to center stage, as has happened in other societies. The Brezhnev succession will offer the potential for military involvement in the selection of civilian leaders, but that potential will be realized only if civilians fail to observe the restraint in appealing to military assistance that they have exercised in the past. Short of such dramatic developments, the most likely stimulator of a change in the military impact in the next decade is the emerging labor shortage. This dilemma may force the regime in the 1980s to contemplate ways of fusing military training, civilian education, and economic production that have not been seriously entertained since the 1920s.[56] If past experience is any guide, changes in this or any other area will be incremental and considered. Inroads on civilian authority are likely to come, as Bruce Russett has written of the U.S. military, "not [from] a sudden take-over by . . . soldiers but [from] slow accretions in the scope of military influence in the 'normal' political system."[57]

What do the military's impact and possible changes in it imply for foreign policy? Clearly, the weight of military goals and the availability of military instruments in Soviet policy are major data for consideration in the West. Yet in both cases, these basically reflect the same factor that has been the main determinant of the impact of the military itself on Soviet society—the values and objectives of Soviet *civilians*. The army is an important focus for political socialization, but this is principally due to civilian acceptance of many of the ideals it embodies. The military–industrial complex is a major constituency in Soviet politics but largely because nonsoldiers have made it one. And if the counsel of generals is heard with respect in Moscow, it is primarily because civilian leaders take seriously the goals that officers pursue. In the 1970s, as in the 1920s when Mikhail Frunze summarized this symmetry in perceptions, Soviet soldiers and civilians seem to agree: "The stronger and more powerful [the army] is, and the more it is a threat to our enemies, then the more our interests will be served."[58]

Notes

[1] V. V. Sheliag et al., *Voennaia psikhologiia* (Moscow, 1972), p. 3.

[2] Roman Kolkowicz, *The Soviet Military and the Communist Party* (Princeton, N.J.: Princeton University Press, 1967), p. 11.

[3] William E. Odom, "The Soviet Military: The Party Connection," *Problems of Communism* 22, no. 5 (September–October 1973): 12–26.

[4] Some of my findings are reported in "Military Councils and Military Politics in the Russian Civil War," *Canada Slavonic Papers*, no. 18 (March 1976), pp. 36–57; and "The Zhukov Affair Reconsidered," *Soviet Studies* 29, no. 2 (April 1977): 185–213.

[5] Jerry F. Hough, *The Soviet Prefects: The Local Party Organs in Industrial Decision-Making* (Cambridge, Mass.: Harvard University Press, 1969), p. 265.

[6] William E. Odom, "The 'Militarization' of Soviet Society," *Problems of Communism* 25, no. 5 (September-October 1976): 34–51; quotations on pp. 35, 50. I do not mean to slight the complexity of Odom's argument by making selective reference to it or to equate it with the less sophisticated discussions about Soviet "militarization" that one encounters elsewhere.

[7] Kolkowicz, *The Soviet Military*, p. 105.

[8] V. D. Sokolovskii et al., *Voennaia strategiia* (Moscow, 1968), p. 445.

[9] Most aspects of Soviet military management have been neglected by Western scholars, even though the Soviet military system encompasses huge and costly operations. No serious work has been done, for example, on the expanding system of military state farms (*voennye sovkhozy*), enterprises operated by civilian laborers that "occupy many thousands of hectares of land, contain tens of thousands of cattle and sheep and hundreds of thousands of hogs and fowl, [and produce] tens of thousands of tons of grain, potatoes, and vegetables." *Tyl i snabzhenie Sovetskikh vooruzhennykh sil*, 1973, no. 4, pp. 52–53.

[10] I. V. Stalin, *Sochineniia*, vol. 10 (Moscow, 1949), p. 85.

[11] Karl F. Spielmann, "Defense Industries in the USSR," *Problems of Communism* 25, no. 5 (September–October 1976): 52.

[12] Aggregate statistics are not available, but descriptions of major projects evince substantial effort. See, for example, the report that in Sergeli, a new suburb of Tashkent, troops built 150,000 square meters of housing in only 7 months of 1976, complete with amenities and services (*Krasnaia zvezda*, November 23, 1976, p. 2).

[13]Statistics in *Tyl i snabzhenie Sovetskikh vooruzhennykh sil*, 1968, no. 9, p. 75.

[14]*Izvestiia*, August 9, 1964, p. 3.

[15]The 70% figure for conscript Komsomol membership is in *Krasnaia zvezda*, April 25, 1974, p. 3. The 80% overall figure is inferred from partial data from several sources. Party organizations in the military are dominated, as they have been at almost all other times, by officers.

[16]Stalin, *Sochineniia*, vol. 5, p. 205.

[17]*Krasnaia zvezda*, May 9, 1973, p. 2.

[18]*Morskoi sbornik*, no. 8, p. 6.

[19]*Krasnaia zveda*, December 9, 1976, p. 2.

[20]*XXV s'ezd Kommunisticheskoi Partii Sovetskogo Soiuza: stenograficheskii otchet*, vol. 1 (Moscow, 1976), p. 101.

[21]*Tyl i snabzhenie Sovetskikh vooruzhennykh sil*, 1972, no. 10, p. 13.

[22]Quotation from *Kommunist vooruzhennykh sil*, no. 3 (February 1970), p. 24. For the language circles, see *ibid.*, no. 21 (November 1972), p. 32, and *Bloknot agitatora*, no. 7 (1972), p. 5.

[23]DOSAAF statistics in *Krasnaia zvezda*, January 23, 1977, p. 2, and January 26, 1977, p. 1. Capital expenditures for 1972–1976 totalled 28.2 million rubles. For useful overviews of the three programs being discussed here, see Odom, "The 'Militarization' of Soviet Society," and Herbert Goldhamer, *The Soviet Soldier* (New York: Crane, Russak, 1975), chs. 2–3.

[24]Many civilian officials chafed at having to attend these courses. See, for instance, *Sovetskaia Belorussiia*, October 18, 1972, p. 3, and *Kommunist Tadzhikistana*, August 24, 1973, p. 4.

[25]*Krasnaia zvezda*, April 7, 1977, p. 2.

[26]Statistics in *Sovetskii patriot*, November 29, 1972, p. 2; *Krasnaia zvezda*, August 17, 1976, p. 4.

[27]In Belorussia, for example, the 1971 program required 21 hours, that is, 1 hour *more* than after standardization (*Sovetskaia Belorussiia*, April 2, 1972, p. 3).

[28]*Izvestiia*, May 5, 1966, p. 3.

[29]*Krasnaia zvezda*, August 21, 1976, p. 4.

[30]These numbers are given in *Turkmenskaia iskra*, May 26, 1973, p. 3; *Sovetskaia Latviia*, May 17, 1973, p. 2; *Sovetskaia Belorussia*, November 18, 1973, p. 2; and *Krasnaia zvezda*, February 8, 1976, p. 2.

[31]*Sovetskii patriot*, March 31, 1974, p. 4.

[32]The quotations here are from *Sovetskaia Moldaviia*, August 15, 1972, p. 3; *Krasnaia zvezda*, March 28, 1976, p. 2; *Turkmenskaia iskra*, September 7, 1973, p. 3; *Krasnaia zvezda*, April 7, 1977, p. 2, and May 7, 1976, p. 2.

[33]In 1977, for example, DOSAAF claimed to have "prepared" 2.8 million machine operators for work in agriculture in the previous 5 years (*Krasnaia zvezda*, January 26, 1977, p. 1). Yet the total number of machine operators registered by the 1970 census was only 3.4 million.

[34]*Sovetskii patriot*, August 16, 1972, p. 3.

[35]For a particularly frank discussion of DOSAAF's financial difficulties, see *ibid*, December 3, 1972, p. 2.

[36]Odom, "The 'Militarization' of Soviet Society," p. 47.

[37]These references are common in both civilian and military statements on civil defense. In the first 10 months of 1975, the executive of the Zhdanov raion soviet is said to have discussed civil defense questions on 14 occasions, and the party bureau considered "important questions" a number of times (*Krasnaia*

zvezda, November 16, 1975, p. 1). Other stories report regular discussions in both soviet and party executive organs. The administrative organs departments of local party organs are often reported as being involved in civil defense planning; science and education departments also play some role.

[38]Several dozen local party secretaries sit on the military councils of military districts and fleets, but their participation in decision making seems to be minimal. Soviet sources are quite categorical in denying any legitimate role for local party organs as such in intramilitary affairs.

[39]The Gosplan of the Udmurt autonomous republic has established a commission for overcoming "interdepartmental barriers" on civil defense matters (*Krasnaia zvezda*, March 28, 1976, p. 2). In some areas, civil defense formations are being increasingly used by civilian executives for rescue and recovery work following natural disasters and even "major production accidents" (*Kazakhstanskaia pravda*, July 4, 1973, p. 2). The availability of trained and equipped civil defense groups may actually lessen the likelihood of civilian use of military assistance in such cases.

[40]Local first secretaries are said to confirm (*utverzhdat'*) annual plans for military–patriotic work (*Krasnaia zvezda*, May 6, 1976, p. 1).

[41]S. M. Shtemenko, *General'nyi shtab v gody voiny*, vol. 1 (Moscow, 1968), p. 116.

[42]*Partiino-politicheskaia rabota v Sovetskikh Vooruzhennykh Silakh* (Moscow, 1974). p. 103.

[43]Raymond L. Garthoff, "SALT and the Soviet Military," *Problems of Communism* 24, no. 1 (January-February 1975): 29.

[44]Strobe Talbott, ed., *Khrushchev Remembers: The Last Testament* (New York: Bantam, 1976), p. 540.

[45]*Ibid.*, p. 572.

[46]*Krasnaia zvezda*, January 9, 1976, p. 2.

[47]*Kommunist vooruzhennykh sil*, no. 16 (August 1972), p. 16.

[48]*Pravda*, March 25, 1971, p. 2.

[49]See, for example, Ustinov's article in *Pravda*, February 23, 1977, p. 2, which refers to dangers to Soviet security posed by the governing circles (*praviashchie krugi*), of the Western states. Compare this to Brezhnev's speech in Tula in January (*ibid.*, January 19, 1977, p. 2), which discusses not only "aggressive forces" within the Western countries but "other forces, ones which . . . are capable of taking into account the realities of the contemporary world."

[50]*Krasnaia zvezda*, April 7, 1977, p. 2. Since the late 1960s, the Main Political Administration and the Ministry of Defense have awarded a number of prizes and diplomas designed to induce creative artists to work on military-related themes. They currently award annual prizes for novels, essays, songs, and films.

[51]*Tyl i snabzhenie Sovetskikh vooruzhennykh sil*, 1973, no. 7, p. 63.

[52]Such criticisms are found in a number of sources: individual letters to newspapers, investigative articles in military newspapers and journals, articles by officers in civilian publications, and speeches by commanders and political officers to republican and local party congresses, conferences, and plenums (many of which are printed in republican newspapers).

[53]Quoted in P. I. Iakir and Iu. A. Geller, eds., *Komandarm Iakir* (Moscow, 1963), pp. 111–112.

[54]*Tyl i snabzhenie Sovetskikh vooruzhennykh sil*, 1973, no. 7, p. 62.

[55]*Ibid*.

[56]At current rates of conscription, the military would have to draft almost 85% of all 18-year-olds in 1987 to maintain manpower levels (*New York Times*, April 17, 1977, p. 8).

[57]Bruce M. Russett, *What Price Vigilance? The Burdens of National Defense* (New Haven, Conn.: Yale University Press, 1970), p. 181.

[58]M. V. Frunze, *Sobranie sochinenii*, vol. 1 (Moscow and Leningrad, 1925), p. 365.

III

The Economy and Society

How have the Soviet polity, economy, and society influenced one another? That is, what impact have Soviet political institutions and economic and social policies had on the socioeconomic relationships and quality of life in the USSR? And what effects have economic and social conditions, domestic and international, had on the Soviet policymaking process and on Soviet policy? Did the polity, economy, or society change in significant ways under Khrushchev and Brezhnev? Did the political, economic, and social systems become more responsive to each other and to the changing international environment? If so, how, why, and with what consequences for the 1980s? These are the central questions addressed in Parts III and IV. The information and analysis presented in this section will help the reader to evaluate the different interpretations put forward in the final section.

Most Western analysts maintain that the performance of the Soviet economy is a major, if not *the* major, political issue in the USSR in the 1980s. Westerners generally agree that overly centralized planning and management, together with the increasing shortages of key human and material resources, are the root causes of present-day Soviet economic problems. But Western observers disagree about the seriousness of Soviet problems, the choices open to the Soviet leadership, the problem-solving capabilities of Soviet institutions, and the likely Soviet response to mounting difficulties.

Soviet leaders agree that economic growth and productivity must be enhanced by a shift from "extensive" to "intensive" development. But Soviet officials and analysts disagree about the sources, seriousness, and solutions of economic problems. Although Brezhnev's détente policies of the early 1970s included many reformist components, Brezhnev's leadership thereafter was more conservative than reformist. The critical need for scientific–technical progress, new management methods, and economic ties with the West—key tenets of Soviet "economic modernizers"—influenced conservative thinking. However, conservatives contended that scientific–technical, administrative, and foreign trade initiatives could help to *strengthen* the centralized features of the Soviet economy and polity. In contrast, reformer–modernizers affirmed that innovations in these fields could not be easily stimulated and absorbed without *altering* some of the centralized features of the Soviet economic system and, by implication, of the Soviet political system as well.

How have the structure and performance of the Soviet economy affected the Soviet citizenry? "The view from the bottom"—from the family household—is presented in this section. How have Soviet socio-economic policies influenced demographic trends and particular groups? Social stratification and the emerging problems of a multi-national state are discussed. How have Soviet mass communications and political education programs shaped relations between the leaders

415

and the led? The role of the press and the effectiveness of party propaganda are examined. And how has the Soviet polity coped with public apathy and refusal to assent to official values, attitudes, and beliefs? The increasing pessimism in "civic morale" and the forms and functions of dissent are investigated.

Our contributors discuss many types, sources, and consequences of economic and social change in the Soviet Union. Important types of socioeconomic change include declining industrial growth rates, inflation, shortages of civilian and military manpower, serious lags in labor and technological productivity, a growing demand for consumer goods, decreasing social mobility, and rising death rates for many age groups. Important sources of socioeconomic change include the dramatic scientific and technological advances that have restructured the international system and the global economy since World War II and that have made the USSR more permeable to external influences. And important consequences of socioeconomic change are pressures for *political* change—particularly the need for Soviet leaders to reassess priorities, capabilities, and institutional relationships—a crucial issue raised in Part III and developed at length in Part IV.

16 HENRY ROWEN

Central Intelligence Agency Briefing on the Soviet Economy*

The following report of the Central Intelligence Agency responds to my request† for a balanced assessment of the Soviet economy showing both its capabilities and vulnerabilities. The result is a unique contribution to our understanding of Soviet economics. Its uniqueness lies in the fact that it analyzes the strengths as well as the weaknesses in the Soviet economy.

It is worth highlighting the three principal findings of the study: First, Soviet economic growth has been steadily slowing down. However, there will be continued positive growth for the foreseeable future. Second, economic performance has been poor, and there have been many departures from standards of economic efficiency. But this does not mean the Soviet economy is losing its viability or its dynamism. And third, while there has been a gap between Soviet performance and plans, an economic collapse in the USSR is not considered even a remote possibility.

Analysts in the West have typically focused on Soviet economic problems. The attention to the negative aspects of the Soviet economic system and to the failures of performance is appropriate and necessary. The danger in such an approach is that, by overlooking the positive side, we see an incomplete picture which leads us to form incorrect conclusions.

The Soviet Union is our principal potential adversary, which is all the more reason to have accurate, balanced assessments of the state of its

---

*Reprinted by permission of the author and the United States Central Intelligence Agency. The chaper is not copyrighted.

†Remarks by Senator William Proxmire, Vice Chairman, Subcommittee on International Trade, Finance, and Security Economics, Joint Economic Committee, United States Congress, December 1, 1982.

economy. One of the worst things we can do is to underestimate the economic strength of our principal adversary.

It needs to be understood that while the Soviet Union has been weakened by such harmful developments as the inefficient performance of the farm sector and the heavy burden of defense, it is the world's second largest economy in terms of GNP, has a large and well-trained labor force, is highly industrialized, and possesses enormous reserves of natural resources, including oil, gas, the relatively scarce minerals, and precious metals. It is sobering to reflect on the possibility that Soviet economic trends might improve rather than grow worse.

This chapter should go far to clear up the confusion that exists in Congress and the public as to where the Soviet economy stands. It should also make it obvious that there is at least the same degree of uncertainty in making forecasts about future economic performance in the Soviet Union as there is with respect to our own economy.

United States Congress, Joint Economic Committee Briefing: Introduction	Mr. Chairman, in your request that we brief your subcommittee on Soviet economic prospects, you noted the "unusual amount of confusion in Congress and the general public today as to where the Soviet economy stands." You also suggested that our briefing be built around an assessment of "the capabilities and vulnerabilities of the Soviet economy."

We agree that confusion regarding the Soviet economy abounds. We believe, however, that this confusion results not so much from disagreement over Soviet economic performance as from uncertainty as to how to interpret that performance. Western observers have tended to describe Soviet economic performance as "poor" or "deteriorating" at a time when Soviet defense spending continues to rise, overall Soviet gross national product in real terms continues to increase, and Soviet GNP is second in size only to that of the United States.

These characterizations are not wrong. Given past rates of economic growth, the gap between Soviet performance and plans and expectations, and the marked departure from standards of economic efficiency, the record compiled by the Soviet economy in recent years has indeed been poor. Results that are unsatisfactory when measured by this yardstick, however, do not mean that the Soviet economy is losing its viability as well as its dynamism. In fact, we do not consider an economic "collapse"—a sudden and sustained decline in GNP—even a remote possibility. Our projections indicate that growth in GNP will remain slow but positive. Growth is being retarded by a combination of factors. Some are beyond Soviet control, and some reflect the weaknesses of the Soviet economic system that even the new Andropov regime is not likely to change. Other factors holding down economic growth represent policy choices—for example, the allocation of resources to defense—that could be modified but are unlikely to change much in the near term. Nevertheless, we expect annual growth to average 1–2% for the foreseeable future. Per capita consumption could level off or even fall slightly.

Returning to your initial questions, we will try to give as balanced a picture of the Soviet economy as possible. We will summarize and assess its basic capabilities and vulnerabilities. We will, however, first identify the goals that economic activity is designed to serve in the USSR and then describe Soviet success in meeting these goals. As a final piece of stage-setting, we will discuss how the Eleventh 5-Year Plan is faring, judging by the results of the first 2 years: 1981 and 1982.

Soviet Economic Objectives and Priorities

Turning first to Soviet economic objectives and priorities, we believe that Soviet economic activity has always focused on building military power. But the Soviet leadership has also always placed great stress on rapid economic growth. The good life for the Soviet populace, in the form of a rising standard of living, has been of importance to Moscow, too, for almost 30 years. But improvements in the welfare of Soviet consumers have generally been subordinated to the demands of the military and to the high rate of capital investment necessary to ensure fast GNP growth. It appears, though, that consumer interests are now being treated somewhat less cavalierly. Breaking precedent, the Eleventh 5-Year Plan calls for capital investment to grow more slowly than consumption.

In pursuit of these national objectives, successive regimes have given heavy industry priority status because it is the source of military hardware and investment goods. Meanwhile, despite some experimentation with decentralized forms of economic administration, the Soviet leadership has remained firmly committed to strict central planning and management of most economic activity. The justification has been that rigorous centralization is required for fulfillment of national objectives.

Soviet economic performance in terms of the objectives and priorities established by the leadership has been mixed. The Soviet Union has built an exceedingly powerful military force. Under Khrushchev, the emphasis was on strategic nuclear programs, but Brezhnev presided over an across-the-board expansion and modernization of all Soviet forces. Since the mid-1960s, the USSR has increased its arsenal of intercontinental nuclear delivery vehicles nearly sixfold—overturning United States quantitative superiority—and giving itself an assured nuclear retaliation capability. During the same period, Moscow has more than tripled the size of its battlefield nuclear forces, reducing the credibility of NATO's nuclear weapons as a counterweight to the Warsaw Pact's larger conventional forces. Meanwhile the Soviet Union has more than doubled the artillery firepower of its divisions, increased ninefold the weight of ordnance that tactical air forces can deliver deep in NATO territory, and reduced the West's qualitative lead in such key areas as tank armor. At sea, the USSR has introduced new, heavily armed surface ships, nuclear-powered submarines, and naval aircraft and quadrupled the number of missile launchers on ships and submarines. Meanwhile, under Brezhnev, the USSR has expanded its military activities in the Third World—ranging from arms sales to Soviet forces in defensive roles and support of Cuban forces in combat to intervention in Afghanistan.

While developing its military power, the USSR has, until recently, been able to maintain a rapid rate of economic growth. Soviet GNP, as measured by CIA, grew at an average annual rate of 4.6% from 1950 through 1981. During the same period, U.S. GNP increased by 3.4% per year. Soviet growth, however, has steadily slowed during this period—especially after 1978. The deceleration can be seen in Fig. 1. The average annual rate of increase in GNP was about 6% during the 1950s, 5% during the 1960s, and nearly 4% between 1970 and 1978. In 1979–1981, yearly growth averaged less than 2%. This year, we expect GNP growth to be about 1.5%.

To a remarkable degree, the slowdown in Soviet economic growth has a parallel in OECD countries. During the first 3 years of the 1970s, OECD GNP increased at the rate of 5% per year. The crisis induced by OPEC oil prices brought OECD growth to a halt in 1974–1975. Then, in 1976–1979, the GNP resumed a respectable rate of growth of 4% per year. In 1980–1981, however, GNP growth in the OECD collapsed to 1.2% per year. The slowdown in the USSR in part reflects four consecutive poor or mediocre harvests. But most sectors of the economy have been sluggish, especially industry.

In large measure, industrial performance has been held back by the emergence of serious bottlenecks unconnected with agriculture. Growth in industrial output, which averaged almost 6% a year in 1971–1975, fell abruptly in 1976, and in 1976–1981, it averaged just slightly over 3% annually. The decline in growth has been steady. Industrial production grew by only 2% in 1981 and is expected to rise by 1.5–2% this year.

The higher priority accorded to military strength is suggested by the continued rise in defense spending at the average annual rate of 4% that has prevailed since the mid-1960s. Growth in defense spending has continued despite competition for resources that might have eased strains in the rest of the economy. Defense spending is now about 13–14% of GNP.

At the same time, leadership concern about consumer welfare seems to have somewhat diluted the commitment to growth. The share of Soviet GNP allocated to fixed capital investment—the driving force

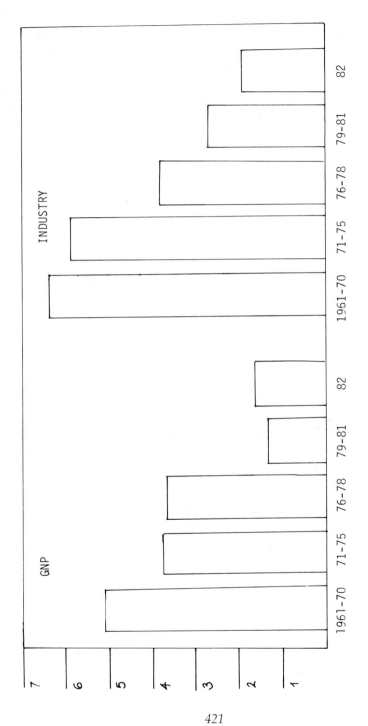

Figure 1. *Growth of GNP and industrial production in the USSR. Data indicate average annual percentage rates of growth, 1961–1982.*

behind Soviet economic growth—has more or less stabilized in the last few years at about 26% (factor cost), compared with about 20% in 1960. Slowing investment growth is explained partly by bottlenecks in sectors providing building materials and machinery. It probably also stems from a political decision to protect Soviet consumers in a time of tightening economic constraints. Nonetheless, as shown in Fig. 2, consumption still accounts for only 55% of Soviet GNP, far below the share in most non-Communist industrialized countries.

The Eleventh 5-Year Plan So Far

Turning to recent developments, the results of the last 2 years must have been most disappointing to Soviet leaders. It is already clear that most of the important goals of the Eleventh 5-Year Plan cannot be met. The plan was excessively ambitious from the start. For example, both industrial production and agricultural output were to grow by about 5% annually, even though production in both sectors had grown at much slower rates in 1976–1980. Performance has been far below plan. The small increase in agricultural output this year will do little more than offset the decline in 1981, while stagnation or falling output in key industrial branches threatens to intensify already serious bottlenecks.

Production of steel and steel products continues to sputter; output this year has changed little from 2 years ago and is below the peaks reached in 1978. Cement production, meanwhile, fell below the 1980 level, and freight car production will decline this year—for the sixth consecutive year. The slump in steel is particularly damaging to machinery production. Along with shortfalls in the output of building materials, it also threatens to curtail growth in construction. Even the moderate 1981–1985 investment targets could be in jeopardy.

From the beginning, the Eleventh 5-Year Plan goals depended on large productivity increases. However, underfulfillment of the productivity plans has been striking. The rise in industrial labor productivity, for instance, averaged only 1.4% a year in 1981–1982, far below the 4.5% per year increase called for by the plan. The unrealistic, almost fantasy-like character of the plan can be illustrated by comparing production goals with investment plans. As our next figure shows (see.Fig. 3), incremental capital output ratios—that is, the amount of additional capital needed to produce an additional unit of output—have been rising steadily and steeply in the USSR for many years, with little prospect that the rise will soon end. Yet, based on little more than admonitions that productivity must rise, capital investment targets in conjunction with output goals imply a decline in these ratios.

Bright spots in economic performance in 1981–1982 are hard to find. However, there have been a few. On the production side, natural gas

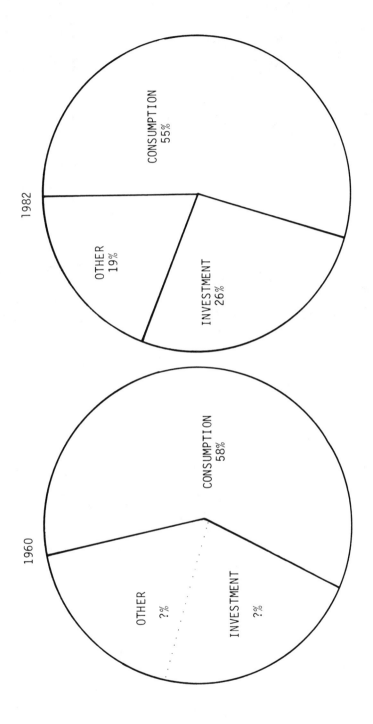

Figure 2. *Percentage shares of GNP by end use in USSR, 1960 and 1982.*

423

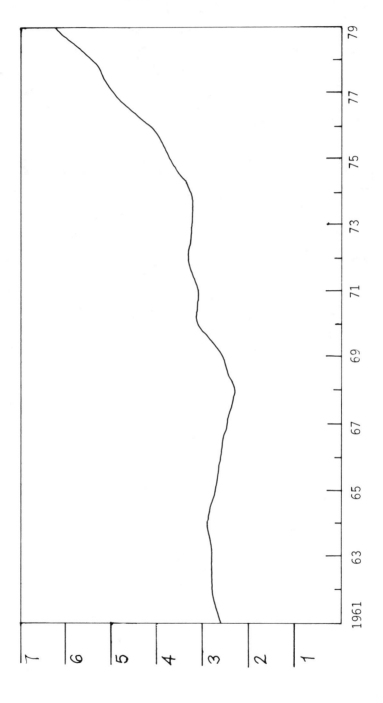

Figure 3. *Incremental capital output ratios in industry in USSR, 1971–1979. Data indicate 3-year moving average.*

continues to rise at a rapid rate—7% in 1981 and nearly 8% this year. Overall energy production may be considered a plus. In 1982, at least, output of all major forms of primary energy rose. Oil production continues to inch ahead—by about 0.9% this year. Coal output, reversing a 3-year decline, evidently will rise by about 2%. At best, however, it will barely exceed the 1980 level.

The USSR has also substantially improved its hard currency balance of trade this year (see Fig. 4). The hard currency trade deficit last year was abut $4 billion, causing some anxiety in Western financial circles. Judging by the results of the first half of 1982, the deficit this year will be reduced to perhaps $2 billion. The central authorities, with their total monopoly of control over foreign trade and the allocation of key resources, sharply raised the volume of oil exports to the West despite softening prices in world markets. At the same time, they held the value of hard currency imports steady. The result was a trade deficit in the first half of 1982 that was almost $4 billion lower than in the same 6 months of 1981. The already relatively small hard currency debt—$11.5 billion at the end of 1981—will rise little, if at all.

The Soviets have paid a price for this success, however. The increase in oil exports to the West came at the expense of deliveries to Eastern Europe and domestic consumption. In holding steady the value of imports, Moscow also accepted a reduction in the volume of hard currency imports. In particular, it scaled back purchases of Western equipment and consumer goods needed to help modernize Soviet industry and meet consumer needs.

Basic Strengths of the Economy   We turn now to our discussion of the strengths and weaknesses of the Soviet economy. We will look first at the USSR's economic strong points, starting with those attributes that shore up the economy as a whole and then move on to identify specific sectors that are performing in a particularly effective fashion.

The sheer size of the economy, reflecting the substantial growth since World War II, is one of its strengths. As Fig. 5 indicates, Soviet GNP in 1982 will equal about $1.6 trillion, roughly 55% of U.S. GNP this year. Per capita GNP is almost $6,000. The population is also large, currently numbering about 270 million. The labor force totals about 147 million and, by world standards, is well-trained and well-educated. Literacy is by now almost universal in the USSR. The educational level of the population has been rising rapidly. Twenty-three percent of those over 16 in 1979 have completed at least a secondary education (tenth grade in the Soviet Union) compared with only 14% in 1970. In 1979, an additional 7.5% also had completed higher education compared with 5% in 1970. A particular effort is being made to expand the education of the indigenous nationality groups in the Central Asian republics. The USSR

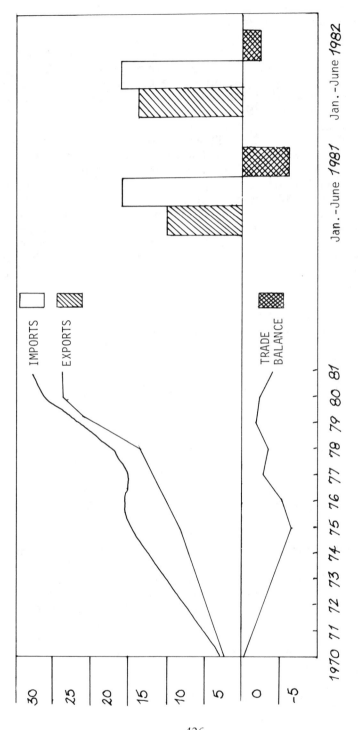

Figure 4. *Hard currency trade (in billion U.S. $) in USSR. 1970–1982.*

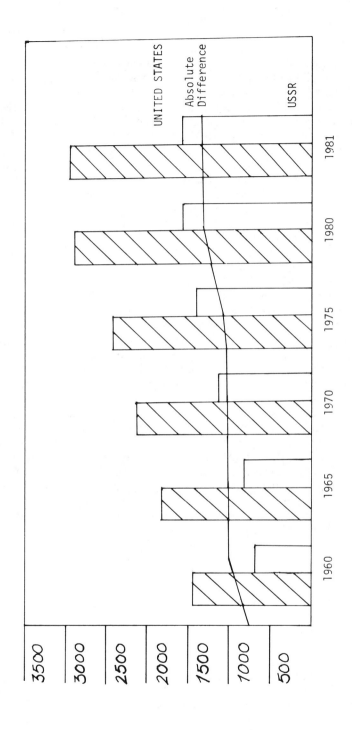

Figure 5. *Comparison of gross national product in the United States and USSR (billion constant 1981 U.S. $), 1960–1981.*

wants to upgrade the skills of the relatively large pool of labor available there and possibly encourage outmigration by assigning these better-educated young people to labor-short areas. Graduates of higher, specialized secondary, and vocational–technical schools receive compulsory work assignments at specific enterprises where, it is hoped, they will continue to work. The emphasis on mathematics, engineering, and science in Soviet schools is also a plus for the technologically oriented Soviet society. About one-third of total instruction time in secondary schools is devoted to mathematics and science. There are serious flaws, however, in Soviet education, including too much rote learning and, at the university level, narrow specialization early on.

Another of the strengths of the Soviet economy is the tremendous accumulation of capital assets that has occurred since World War II. The value of gross fixed capital assets—buildings, machinery, equipment, and the like—amounted to over 1.74 trillion rubles in 1980 according to Soviet published data. The value of Soviet capital assets expressed in constant prices increased almost 11-fold between 1950 and 1980 and about 4.4-fold from 1960 through 1980—long after the USSR had recovered from wartime devastation. This phenomenal expansion reflects the allocation of a large and, until recently, rising share of Soviet resources to capital investment. The rapid growth of capital assets has resulted in a more than 3-fold increase in the amount of capital per worker. The rise was almost 3.5-fold in industry and over 5-fold on state and collective farms.

Two-thirds of the stock of capital assets is concentrated in industry, agriculture, transportation and communications, and construction. Only about 15% of total gross fixed capital consists of housing or is used to provide services to the population such as health care and education. Although the rapid accumulation of capital assets is one of the Soviet Union's strengths, the capital stock includes a disproportionately large share of worn out and technologically obsolete equipment. Soviet policies have kept retirement rates of existing assets artificially low and have prolonged their service lives through repeated capital repairs.

The USSR is exceptionally well endowed with natural resources as the reserve estimates in Table 1 indicate. Beginning with energy, the Soviet Union has about 40% of the world's proven reserves of natural gas—the 30 trillion cubic meters under Soviet control exceed the reserves of all industrialized nations combined. Soviet reserves of coal account for 30% of the world's total recoverable reserves and are sufficient to ensure over 200 years of output at current rates of production. The Soviets do not publish figures for oil reserves as they do for gas and coal. Our estimate is that oil reserves, at least in West Siberia, are substantial though increasingly difficult to exploit.

The USSR is abundantly stocked with other important raw materials. According to Soviet studies, iron ore reserves amount to about 60 billion

TABLE 1. *USSR: Estimated Reserves of Selected Fuels and Nonfuel Minerals*[a]

	Size of reserves	Share of world reserves (%)	Years to exhaustion (at 1980 production)
Gas	30 Trillion m^3	40	65
Coal	165.5 billion tons	27	230
Iron ore	63.3 billion tons	40	250
Manganese	2.5 billion tons	40	250
Chromite	271.2 million tons	10	80
Copper	40.0 million tons	7	28
Nickel	11.3 million tons	18	48
Cobalt	100 million tons	NA	17
Lead	17 million tons	11	28
Zinc	22 million tons	10	24
Gold	200 million troy ounces	35	20
Platinum-group metals	90 million troy ounces	25	25
Tungsten	215 thousand tons	11	24

[a]Corresponding to Western concepts of proven and probable reserves, exploitable at current prices with existing technology.

tons—some 40% of the world's total. With as much as one-fifth of the world's forest resources, the USSR has a virtually inexhaustible source for producing wood and wood products. In addition, the Soviets claim—and may well have—the world's largest reserves of manganese, nickel, lead, molybdenum, mercury, and antimony. They also say that reserves of chromite, gold, platinum-group metals, zinc, and copper are among the largest in the world and sufficient to support Soviet mine production for many decades. The Soviets also have substantial reserves of potash and phosphate rock—raw materials for the production of chemical fertilizers—although a large portion of the newer phosphate deposits consist of poor quality ore.

With its wealth in human, capital, and material resources, the USSR is highly self-sufficient—another of the economy's major strengths (see Fig. 6). The high degree of Soviet self-sufficiency in vital raw materials is shown by its position as a net exporter of a large number of these materials. Net exports of energy—mostly of oil and natural gas—now total about 4 million barrels a day equivalent or about 15% of total energy production. The Soviets are major exporters of precious metals, ferrous and nonferrous ores, metal products, chemicals, and timber. Because of expected gains in output, the Soviets will be able to expand sales of key minerals such as platinum-group metals, nickel, cobalt,

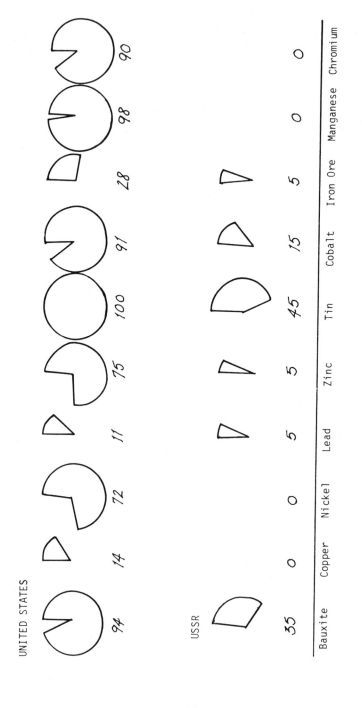

UNITED STATES

	Bauxite	Copper	Nickel	Lead	Zinc	Tin	Cobalt	Iron Ore	Manganese	Chromium
	94	14	72	11	75	100	91	28	98	90

USSR

	Bauxite	Copper	Nickel	Lead	Zinc	Tin	Cobalt	Iron Ore	Manganese	Chromium
	35	0	0	5	5	45	15	5	0	0

Figure 6. *Comparison of imports of minerals and metals as a share of consumption in United States and USSR, 1981. Values in percentages.*

430

manganese, chromite, and gold during the 1980s. We also anticipate major increases in the Soviet exports of ammonia, nitrogen, and potash fertilizer and methanol.

Though highly self-sufficient, the USSR is not autarkic. Indeed, for at least the last decade, trade with the West has been an important element in the USSR's efforts to modernize the Soviet economy and render it more efficient. This point will be developed in detail later, but first it should be mentioned here that the Soviets now must rely on Western imports of capital and technology to increase or maintain production of some of the raw materials in which they are abundantly endowed and self-sufficient. It should also be noted that imports from the West have become critical to Soviet efforts to improve, or simply maintain, the quality of the Soviet diet. In 1981, imports of grain and other agricultural products reached almost $12 billion, or about 40% of the USSR's total hard currency purchases. But despite the large-scale expansion in agricultural imports, the Soviet Union remains basically self-sufficient with respect to food. These imports are intended mainly to prevent a decline in meat consumption and are not essential to maintaining an adequate quantity of food consumption. At 3,300 calories (see Fig. 7 for a comparison of the composition of the United States and Soviet diets), average daily food intake is equivalent to that in developed Western countries. Grain production is more than sufficient to meet consumer demand for bread and other cereal products.

To summarize, when we say the USSR is self-sufficient, we do not mean that the Soviets neither need nor benefit from trade. Imports, particularly form the West, can play an important role in relieving critical shortages, spurring technological progress, and generally improving Soviet economic performance. What we do mean is that the ability of the Soviet economy to remain viable in the absence of imports is much greater than that of most, possibly all, other industrialized economies. Consequently, the susceptibility of the Soviet Union to economic leverage tends to be limited.

In considering fundamental strengths, the highly centralized, rigid system of administering the economy—while perhaps the Soviet Union's major economic millstone—has had its advantages in enabling the leadership to mobilize resources in crash programs to achieve priority objectives. The prime example of this capability has been Moscow's success in building up its military might. This has been achieved through centrally directed mobilization and allocation of the USSR's highest quality human and material resources and a rigorous system of quality control in military production that prevents the shoddiness so characteristic of Soviet civilian output.

Centrally directed concentration of resources does not, of course, work everywhere. Agriculture, which we will discuss in more detail later, is an example. Even though over one-quarter of total investment

Figure 7. *Comparison of diet composition in the United States and USSR, 1980. Calories per day per person, USSR = 3280; U.S. = 3520.*

has been allocated to the farm sector for many years, agricultural output continues to be a disappointment to Soviet leaders. There are many reasons for this, but one overriding reason is that effective central supervision over an activity conducted over so vast a geographical area is virtually impossible. Another is that economic administration by fiat is singularly ill-suited to a sector where incentives to individual producers are so crucial a determinant of output.

We turn now to specific areas where Soviet economic performance has been especially strong. As we mentioned, natural gas has been a major Soviet success story. It will play a pivotal role in meeting the energy needs of the economy in the 1980s, not only as a substitute for crude oil in industry and in home use but also as a potential hard currency earner. The nuclear power industry, although it has not met the full expectations of the leadership, has also done quite well. We estimate that the annual increase in nuclear-generated electricity will increase by about 17% a year during 1981–1985 and supply about 11% of the country's electricity by the end of the period.

Development and production of some Soviet natural resources are proceeding at respectable rates despite the obstacles of remote location and conditions that make extraction exceedingly difficult. The USSR is second only to South Africa in the production of gold. Production in 1981 was about 325 tons. Its stock of gold is about 1900 tons, worth over $25 billion at current prices. Soviet production of platinum-group metals, nickel, and cobalt will jump sharply during the 1980s. Output of these resources will be adequate to meet domestic needs and also to provide increasing quantities for export. Prospects for production of the resources located in more easily accessible regions look even better. Rich new deposits coming on stream in Kazakhstan and Georgia should generate sizable increases in production of both chromite and manganese.

Basic Weaknesses of the Economy

We will now look at the weaknesses or vulnerabilities represented on the Soviet economic ledger. We will focus first on problems stemming from circumstances beyond Soviet control and then turn to the shortcomings and vulnerabilities of the economy that are inherent in the USSR's system of economic planning and administration. We will then consider specific weaknesses.

Soviet economic performance has been hurt in recent years by declining increments to the labor force and by the increasing difficulty of extracting and transporting vital energy and other raw material inputs. Because of lower birth rates in the 1960s, an increase in the number of workers reaching retirement age, and a rising mortality rate among males in the 25–44 age range, increments to the working-age population have been declining since the mid-1970s. The falloff became particularly sharp starting in 1980 and, as Fig. 8 shows, increments will remain very low throughout this decade.

From 1971 to 1981, the working-age population grew by about 23 million. In 1981–1991, it will increase by only about 4 million people. The decline in growth of the labor force—that is, of people actually employed—will be less, largely because of a rise in the share of the population in the 20–39 age group, where labor force participation rates are highest. But the decline in growth will still be substantial. The increment to the labor force in 1981–1991 is expected to be only 9 million, compared with 19 million in 1971–1981. With participation rates in the labor force already very high, there are few unemployed people to draw on to offset adverse demographic conditions.

Other factors will aggravate the labor shortage. Large-scale migration from the countryside to urban areas, formerly a rich source of labor supply to the rest of the economy, has slowed considerably in the past decade. The agricultural sector itself faces shortages of qualified manpower in most areas. This problem is compounded by the fact that rural residents in the Central Asian republics, where increments to the working age population will be highest and where there still is substantial redundant labor, are reluctant to migrate.

As we noted earlier, the Soviet Union is blessed with enormous quantities of a large array of raw materials. But in many instances, these materials are increasingly inaccessible, and thus the cost of exploiting them has been rising sharply. This has been strikingly true of Soviet energy resources.

With the decline in production in the Volga–Urals oil fields in the mid-1970s, growth in Soviet oil production has come from West Siberia, much of it from the giant Samotlor field. However, production in this field probably has peaked, compelling the Soviets to seek oil in even more remote and forbidding regions. In 1981–1985, just to achieve the slowest growth rate planned in oil output since World War II will require greatly expanded drilling and pumping operations.

Decades of mining have depleted the underground coal mines of the European USSR. The Soviets must tunnel deeper shafts and mine thinner seams just to maintain coal output at current levels. During 1976–1980, for example, more than 80% of new mine output was needed to offset depletion at older underground operations.

Even the extraction and distribution of natural gas has grown considerably more expensive. Natural gas deposits in the old producing areas—North Caucasus, Transcaucasus, Ukraine, Volga–Urals, and western Turkmenistan—are severely depleted. More and more gas must be piped from central Asia, and especially Tyumen oblast, to replace exhausted local supplies. Such long-distance transmission of natural gas requires construction of lengthy pipelines and a great many compressor stations—a very expensive operation.

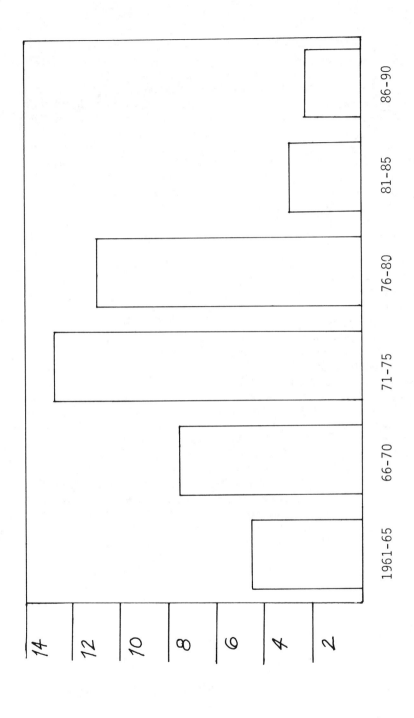

Figure 8. *Increments to working-age population for males (16–59) and females (16–54) by period (in millions of persons), 1961–1990.*

Easily accessible supplies of many nonenergy raw materials have also been exhausted. The Soviets have largely depleted reserves of copper, nickel, and bauxite in the Ural Mountains and are beginning to tap deposits in northern Siberia or, in the case of bauxite, are exploiting non-bauxite ores and boosting imports. Similarly, the richest deposits of phosphate rock in the Kola peninsula have been depleted, forcing the Soviets to move to lower-quality deposits in Siberia. In the case of iron ore, the Soviets have depleted their richest deposits in the Western USSR. To compensate for declining ore grades, increasing amounts of investment must be devoted to ore-enriching facilities, raising both production costs and manpower requirements. The Soviets are also faced with the depletion of forests in the traditional logging areas of the northwestern USSR. Government planners have chosen to overcut these forest tracts beyond the point of natural regeneration so that, at least temporarily, the scale of operations in Siberia could be held down. But when loggers are forced to expand operations in Siberia—and the Far East—recovery costs will be high because of the distances involved, the harsh climate, and the lack of infrastructure.

As Fig. 9 shows, the increase in fixed capital investment has also slowed markedly in recent years. This deceleration can be seen as both forced upon the leadership by shortages of key inputs and—as noted earlier—as a conscious policy choice. Growth was 7% a year in 1971–1975, slowed to about 5% a year in 1976–1978, and fell sharply to an average annual rate of only abut 1.5% in 1979–1980. Growth picked up in 1981—fixed investment rising by 3%—but the Eleventh 5-Year Plan calls for investment in 1981–1985 to rise by less than 2% a year. This is by far the lowest planned rate of increase in the post-World War II period. The rise from 1971–1975 to 1976–1980 was nearly 30%.

Because of tightening demographic, investment, and resource constraints, the traditional Soviet economic growth formula of relying on lavish use of labor, capital, and material inputs is no longer applicable. The Soviets themselves have long recognized the need for a new approach. For at least a decade they have been stressing the necessity of switching from an extensive to an intensive pattern of growth. This means essentially that growth must largely spring from productivity gains—from more efficient use of resources for any given level of technology and from faster technological progress. But the productivity of capital has actually been falling for several years, and labor productivity (see Fig. 10) has been rising at steadily declining rates. For this, shortcomings in the Soviet system seem largely to blame, a matter to which I will now turn.

The Soviet economic system is peculiarly ill-suited to promote efficiency and technological progress. Four features of the system help to explain why.

First, economic planning and management are highly centralized,

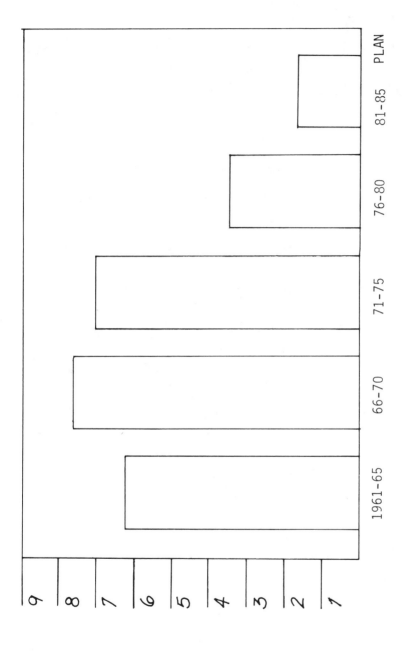

Figure 9. *Growth in gross fixed capital investment in the USSR, 1961–1985. Data in average annual percentage rates of growth.*

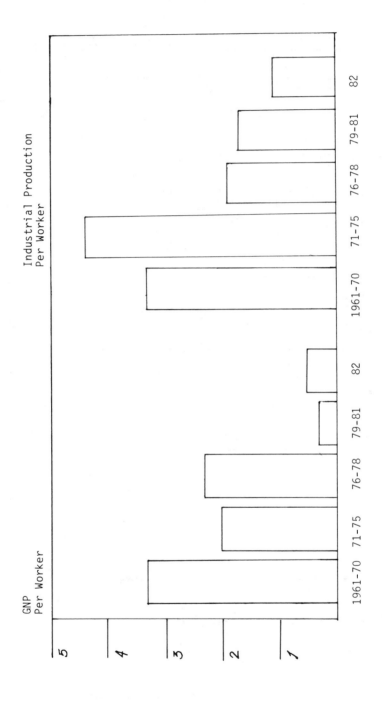

Figure 10. *Productivity trends in the USSR, 1961–1982. Data indicate average annual percentage rates of growth.*

with resources allocated mainly by administative fiat. Reforms aimed at increasing the degree of enterprise autonomy have generally come to naught. Indeed, central control over economic activity has been on the increase for the last several years, as indicated by an increase in the number of commodities that are allocated in physical terms according to central planning decisions. The arbitrary nature of central decisions on allocating inputs and assigning outputs, which is aggravated by the absence of prices that accurately reflect relative scarcities, precludes efficient planning.

Second, along with overcentralization, the goals the central authorities impose on the economy have generally been unrealistic. Faced with a gap between what they want to do and what is possible, Soviet leaders have tended to call for productivity gains and material savings that are beyond the system's capacity. The economy thus chronically operates under conditions of strain and shortage. And, as I indicated earlier, the number and severity of supply bottlenecks have been increasing in recent years. With inputs regularly hard to come by, enterprises have a strong incentive to hoard. This intensifies bottlenecks and leads to more hoarding, in a depressing circle of waste.

Third, overcentralization coupled with unrealistic planning has meant that the behavior of factory directors is largely dictated by the urgency of meeting the plan imposed by higher authorities. Fulfillment, however, is generally measured by multiple and often inconsistent "success indicators" of varying degrees of priority, such as physical volume of output, gross value of output, value added, material savings, and productivity. The principal drawback of this system is that managers often strive to meet the target even at the expense of what is economically rational from the standpoint of the central authorities and society as a whole. For example, if gross value of output is a prime goal, waste is encouraged, as managers seek to make their production as material-intensive as possible. The Soviet Union is currently elevating value added in production to the position of the prime success indicator. Though probably less perverse a target than gross value of output, it, too, is subject to abuse. For example, it could induce managers to increase employment at a time of labor stringency.

Finally, Soviet economic performance has long been impaired by the separation of research, development, and production into different organizations. Each organization operates according to different planning targets. Scientific research institutes do basic research and are paid for successful completion of research projects whatever their practical benefit to the economy. Design bureaus develop the blueprints for new equipment and are largely rewarded for the successful testing of the prototype. Rewards are only loosely linked to successful incorporation of the new product into serial production. Production plants, meanwhile, are rewarded for increasing both physical output and the value of output. The introduction of new products at a plant initially disrupts serial output, jeopardizing plan fulfillment and resulting rewards. The Soviets have no competitive marketplace to force both developer and producer to introduce better products and technologies. Indeed, hostility to technological change at the producer level is characteristic of the Soviet economy—as Yuri Andropov told the Central Committee of the CPSU in late 1982. Because of this division of labor and the system's rewards, Soviet products remain in production for an inordinately long time, new products frequently embody only minimal change, and the fruits of truly advanced research impact on serial production only with great delay. Over the last decade and a half, the Soviets have reorganized development and production establishments to deal with this problem. But the problem persists.

Moving from generalizations to particulars, we will look now at the areas in which the USSR seems particularly weak or vulnerable.

Historically, agriculture has been the economy's leading problem sector. Its performance over the past 4 years has strengthened its claim to that dubious distinction. After peaking in 1978, farm output fell steadily through 1981, when it stood over 10% below the 1978 level. This year, production is expected to rise, but by only about 2%. The grain crop, which reached a record high of 237 million tons in 1978, has not reached 190 million tons in any subsequent year. Last year, the grain harvest was so low that Moscow never announced a figure, although unofficial statements put the crop at 158 million tons. Production of meat—a key commodity in the regime's drive to better the Soviet standard of living—has also fared poorly. It reached 15.5 million tons in 1978 but has been below that level since, ranging from 15 to 15.3 million tons over the last 4 years.

Bad weather has been a major factor in the decline in agricultural production since 1978, but harsh weather and unfavorable geographical conditions constitute a permanent threat and obstacle to agriculture and only partly explain why Soviet efforts over the years to boost farm output have not yielded more dividends. Mishandling of the sector by the Soviet authorities has also had much to do with its disappointing performance. Management and planning processes are much too centralized. Farm efficiency is seriously handicapped by constant intervention of unqualified officials regarding what to plant, when to plant, when to harvest, and the like. Prices of both farm inputs and outputs set by the central authorities are encouraging an assortment of output that is inconsistent with the national plan. At a time when Moscow is striving to expand output of meat, milk, and eggs, relative prices are such that farmers find it more profitable to concentrate on growing crops.

Though investment in agriculture has been heavy—over one-quarter of total investment outlays has gone to the farm sector for many years—much of it has been misdirected. There has been too much emphasis on construction and not enough on equipment. Furthermore, the quality of farm machinery is low, with the incidence of breakdowns high. Deliveries to the agricultural sector of needed material inputs, such as fertilizers, have been insufficient, while the proportion of aged and unskilled workers in the farm labor force—which accounts for about 20% of the total labor force—is high. The regime has also failed to take maximum advantage of the potential of the private sector in agriculture, even in periods such as the present, when it is encouraging expanded output there.

In recognition of the rising popular demand for quality food, Brezhnev told the Central Committee in late 1981 that food was the most important "political and economic problem" of the Eleventh 5-Year Plan. The increase in demand reflects rising consumer expectations and incomes. The inability to satisfy that demand is a function of both stagnant output of most livestock products and the regime's unwillingness—reinforced by Poland's experience—to raise prices in state stores. The leadership has attempted to ease the imbalance between supply and demand by allowing various local rationing schemes under which customers may purchase only limited amounts of certain foods in state stores. But long lines for meat, milk, and milk products remain widespread. To soften the impact of shortages on the work force, the regime has redirected substantial amounts of quality foods from public state retail outlets to special distribution outlets in factories and other economic enterprises.

Against this background, Brezhnev, last May, unveiled his Food Program—in preparation for a year and a half. The objective of the program was to boost Soviet food production and reduce dependence on imports—quickly. The Food Program attacks agriculture's problems from three directions: first, it reorganizes the agricultural administration by creating commissions at all levels of government to coordinate agricultural operations and all related activities, ranging from sectors providing supplies to agriculture to the processing, distribution, and marketing of farm output. Second, without significantly raising previous targets for total expenditures the program seeks to redirect investment to weak links in the food production chain. Investment in sectors producing machinery for agriculture is to rise sharply. To reduce waste, investment in on-farm food processing and storage facilities has been given top priority. More investment in rural housing and roads is scheduled to improve farm-to-market transportation and stem the flow of younger workers to the cities. Upgrading the plant and equipment in food processing is another major target. Third, financial incentives are to be raised. Prices paid by the state to farms for a large variety of agricultural products will increase in 1983. At the same time, prices paid by the farms for equipment, fuel, and fertilizer will be lowered.

For the most part, however, the Food Program represents relatively minor variations of old policies. One exception is the reorganization of agricultural administration, which—by increasing friction and confusion within the bureaucracy—is likely to cause more problems than it solves. The basic defect of the Program lies in its omissions. It does nothing to reduce day-to-day bureaucratic interference in agriculture, and it does not do enough to restructure prices or to change the incentive system so that rewards are directly keyed to performance.

As the recent meetings of the Communist Party Central Committee and the Supreme Soviet made clear, there are very serious problems in other sectors as well. The Soviet steel industry, for example, has become a major bottleneck. Shortages of steel, especially high-quality products, are holding back growth of civilian machine building and other priority sectors of the civilian economy. The appetite of the Soviet economy for steel is probably unparalleled—and a reflection of its relative technological backwardness. Last year, the USSR, with little more than half the GNP of the United States, used 103 million metric tons of rolled steel products compared with United States consumption of 94 million tons. The shortages of steel will not be remedied quickly. Investment requirements to cope with the declining quality of ore are escalating rapidly, and new capacity requires long gestation periods before it can be brought on stream. In addition, supplies of coking coal and iron ore are likely to continue to be tight in the next several years.

Transportation is another sector responsible for recent poor economic performance. Snarls on the railroads—the backbone of the system—have disrupted economic activity across the board but most particularly in the delivery of raw materials such as coal, iron ore, timber, scrapmetal, and chemical fertilizer. The Soviet economy requires a large volume of transport services not only because of its size and complexity but also because the country's resources and people are spread widely over a very large land mass. Compared with North America and Europe, the USSR is poorly served by year-round water transport, and government policy has held back the development of an adequate highway system. The brunt of the transport burden, therefore, has fallen to the railroads. The railroads, however, appear to have reached their capacity ceiling with present technology and facilities. Consequently, the tranport sector will find it difficult to support economic growth through the next several years at least.

In the energy field, the leadership faces rather different problems in the coal and oil industries. Coal production, which dropped during 1979–1981, has been hampered by deteriorating underground mining conditions at larger, established mines, by shortages of labor and declining labor productivity, and by insufficient capital investment. Oil production continues to increase, though slowly. Even the very small growth of the last few years has required an enormous effort.

Finally, shortages of raw materials and depletion of fuel and power supplies have caused a marked slowdown in the production of construction materials. Current output, for example, increased by less than 2% annually during 1976–1980 compared with nearly 5.5% annually in the preceding 5-year period. Shortfalls in the production of cement, roofing materials, construction resources, and wall materials have restricted construction activity throughout the economy.

As we emphasized earlier, the Soviet economy does not depend on trade for survival. Total imports equal about 12 or 13% of GNP; those from the West—only about 5%. But, because of the difficulties just enumerated, the elimination or easing of critical bottlenecks and the achievement of key elements in Soviet development plans are closely tied to imports from the West.

The USSR will have to import a broad range of Western oil and gas equipment if it is to minimize the fall in production in fields where depletion is at an advanced stage, increase output elsewhere, and help locate and develop reserves. Pipelaying equipment capable of handling large-diameter pipe is produced only in the West, and we estimate that the Soviets will need to import 15–20 million tons of steel pipe during the remainder of the 1980s to build the pipelines they have scheduled. They will also continue to need sophisticated exploration equipment, high capacity submersible pumps for the oil fields, and probably high-powered turbines for gas compressor stations.

Soviet requirements for quality steel should result in annual imports of steel other than pipe of about $2 billion (current prices) at least until the mid-1980s. Imports of chemical equipment and technology probably will continue to be large, reflecting the still antiquated character of some parts of the chemical industry and the importance of the industry for agricultural production. Imports of grain and other agricultural commodities have soared in recent years and almost certainly will remain high. Grain purchases in 1979–1982 averaged more than 30 million tons a year.

The USSR's ability to earn the hard currency it needs to pay for its Western imports is, however, already under pressure and may well diminish in the future. The main reason is the leveling off and possible decline in Soviet oil production. Because domestic consumption will continue to rise and because of ongoing demands from Eastern Europe, we expect oil exports to the West—which account for about half of Soviet hard currency merchandise export earnings—to fall. According to our projections, the rise in hard currency earnings from stepped-up exports of natural gas will only partially offset the anticipated decrease in receipts from oil.

Other factors also have restricted Soviet hard currency earning capacity. Primarily because of the softening of energy prices, Soviet terms of trade, vis-à-vis the West, will be less favorable in the 1980s than they were in the 1970s, when upward spiraling oil and gold prices brought the USSR windfall gains. In addition, demand for Soviet raw materials will be weak if Western economic activity fails to pick up. Soviet manufactured goods, which are generally not competitive in Western markets, are unlikely to take up the slack. Finally, less developed countries, including OPEC countries, probably will be less able to pay cash for Soviet arms.

The Soviet capacity to buy from the West is of course backstopped by the USSR's huge stock of gold. But the USSR is reluctant to undertake massive sales of gold in an uncertain market because of the downward pressure that Soviet sales exert on prices. On balance, the unpromising export outlook suggests that the USSR may have to make do with little if any increase in real imports in the 1980s.

The USSR's relations with Eastern Europe add another dimension of strain. Because it wishes to maintain political and social stability in Eastern Europe, the Soviet Union has given favorable economic treatment to five of the six Warsaw Pact countries—Czechoslovakia, East Germany, Bulgaria, Poland, and Hungary. The exception has been Romania. This special treatment, or "assistance," has taken two basic forms: subsidization and credits.

Subsidies have not been given directly. They have instead been extended through preferential terms of trade. That is, Eastern Europe's terms of trade, vis-à-vis the Soviet Union, are more advantageous than those that would prevail if Eastern Europe conducted that same trade with the non-communist world. In essence, the USSR sells energy, mainly oil and other raw materials to Eastern Europe, for less than world market prices and pays more than world prices for the manufactured goods it buys from Eastern Europe. Estimates of the cost to the Soviet Union of giving preferential terms of trade to Eastern Europe are rough—and controversial. According to the highest Western estimate we know of, these subsidies totaled almost $70 billion in 1960–1980, with about 90% of this amount accumulating after 1974. The huge jump implicit in subsidies reflects the explosion in world oil prices in 1973–1980 and the large rise in opportunity costs to the USSR of its oil exports to Eastern Europe.

The credits come mainly from the trade surpluses the USSR has consistently run vis-à-vis Eastern Europe since the mid-1970s, although the Soviet Union has also given some direct hard currency assistance to Poland. Eastern Europe, battling severe economic problems of its own, continues to depend on Soviet assistance. But economic stringencies in the USSR have increased greatly the cost to the Soviets of aiding Eastern Europe. The USSR apparently has decided to give reduced priority to Eastern Europe's economic needs in the future. Soviet oil exports to Eastern Europe were cut this year, and the USSR's trade surplus with the area apparently declined. Soviet subsidies will probably fall, too. But a drastic cut in exports of raw materials and in trade credits and subsidies is unlikely.

Uncertainties Attached to the Growth Forecast   Before summing up our main points, Mr. Chairman, I would like to note that Andropov's advent to power has not altered our assessment of Soviet economic prospects. The exogenous factors impeding economic growth are not affected by the change in leadership. Moreover, Andropov's comments to the Central Committee in 1982 point to no significant changes in economic policy. He indicated that he will take a cautious approach to economic reform. He further made clear that defense and heavy industry will retain their priority. The smattering of economic targets for 1983 announced at the Supreme Soviet meeting a week ago are overambitious, suggesting that relief of economic strains and bottlenecks from more realistic planning is not to be expected.

Andropov is, however, in an extremely early point in his reign. Thus, major policy changes could lie ahead. For this reason—and for reasons unrelated to leadership changes—our forecast of average annual growth in real GNP of 1–2% could be off the mark. Growth could be *more* rapid; for example: (*a*) if the USSR enjoyed a run of good luck with the weather, leading to a succession of good harvests; (*b*) if the new leadership were willing to undertake a substantial reallocation of resources from defense to investment; (*c*) if the new regime were able somehow, perhaps by diverting resources from defense to consumption, to improve morale and labor productivity; (*d*) above all, if efficiency could be boosted by mitigating some of the most damaging features of the existing system. Productivity may be raised, for example, without a drastic overhaul of the system through more balanced allocation of investment to end the neglect of such vital sectors as transport, and by stopping the proliferation of success indicators and of overlapping lines of authority that has characterized the so–alled "reforms" of past years; (*e*) if Andropov—his rule securely established—undertook basic changes that significantly reduced centralization and gave substantially greater play to market forces, the prospects would be even better. Such a reform, however, would be constrained by the imperatives of maintaining political control in a large multinational society. Furthermore, attempts to implement reform would encounter stubborn noncompliance by party and economic bureaucrats.

Growth could be *less* rapid: for example: (*a*) if the bad weather of the last few years continued, causing a permanent depression in agricultural output. In any case, there is a theory, substantiated by evidence, that the generally favorable weather that prevailed between the early 1960s and mid-1970s was an aberration. Although the weather for crops in the past several years was surely worse than any long-run average, a return to the pre-1975 conditions is unlikely; (b) if the new leadership decided to accelerate the growth in defense spending at the expense of investment; (c) if the ripple effect of current bottlenecks intensified; (d) if public cynicism and apathy deepened markedly or active unrest developed. Of these possibilities, serious widespread unrest—as the Polish experience suggests—is the one most likely to hit aggregate output the hardest. However, we consider such an eventuality unlikely. It would probably require a steep and prolonged drop in living standards in the first instance. Large-scale labor disturbances might also occur if Andropov pursued with excessive zeal his promised campaign to impose greater discipline in the work place.

Concluding Comments

To summarize this presentation, Soviet economic growth has slowed markedly in recent years. The slowdown partly reflects declining increments to the supply of labor and the stock of capital and sharply increased costs in producing and transporting vital energy and raw materials. But it also stems from the inability of the system to offset these constraints by bringing about substantial increases in efficiency and productivity. Indeed, economic growth has sharply decelerated even before the labor and energy shortages have reached their maximum severity.

The consequences of the slowdown are: first, much harder choices for the leadership in allocating resources to consumption, investment, and defense; and second, the further invalidation of the USSR's claim that its economy is an appropriate model for the rest of the world, particularly the Third World.

Despite its disappointing performance, the Soviet economy, however, is not going to collapse. Indeed, we expect GNP to continue to grow, although slowly. Furthermore, so far, defense spending continues to rise.

17

ALEC NOVE

The Soviet Economy: Problems and Prospects*

It has become customary on both right and far left to stress the weaknesses of the Soviet economy. The French book market is well stocked with works such as Emmanuel Todd's *La Chute finale*, picturing the USSR as a land where nothing works and everything disintegrates. Senator Jackson's advisers tell him that it is in a state of crisis so acute that the United States can demand major political concessions in exchange for its grain and technology. A variety of neo-Marxist critics point to extremes of inefficiency and waste. Indeed, a catalogue of blunders and distortions can be assembled without difficulty from the pages of the Soviet press. Shortages, corruption, confusion seem endemic, while growth has slowed. But the West, too, faces acute problems, with zero growth, inflation, unemployment, the prospect of major disruptions through strikes and also in the world trading system. It is legitimate to ask: are they in a worse mess than we are? Have they not some "systemic" advantages as well as weaknesses? Have the latter perhaps been exaggerated? Could they be corrected without major political–social convulsions? Is the Soviet system, relatively speaking, an example of stability in an increasingly unstable world? Finally, what light, if any, can Soviet experience shed on the theory or practice of economics under socialism? These seem to be questions of some importance to readers of *New Left Review*. I am a very irregular reader, who does not share many of its assumptions. But the correct assessment of Soviet strength or weakness does not, or should not, depend on political attitudes. If, as may well be the case, my analysis is erroneous, this would be partly because evidence is mixed or inadequate but also because the answer depends on the *weight* that one attaches to those elements of strength and weakness that we identify. There is also the

*Reprinted by permission of the author and publisher from *New Left Review* 119 (January–February 1980), pp. 3–19. Copyright 1980 by *New Left Review*.

vexed question of political stability: it is probably difficult even for the KGB, let alone an outsider, to assess the intensity of discontent, and we should never forget that there are wide gaps in our information. Thus, if by any chance, there were a strike of metal workers in Krasnoyarsk at this moment, we may be reasonably sure that it would not be reported in either the Moscow or the local press (which does not, of course, mean that there *is* a strike in Krasnoyarsk at this moment!).

Priorities and Planability

Let us now try to define the areas of strength and weakness. In my view, there are two factors involved: the *degree of priority* and what could be called *planability*. Both relate to the basic problem of any centrally planned economy: the unmanageably huge number of interrelated decisions to be taken. With market forces absent or severely limited and with prices unrelated (in theory *and* practice) to demand, scarcity, or need, considerations of profitability can only play a subordinate role in decision making. The center plans quantitatively whenever possible. The task of management at all levels is plan fulfillment. Thousands of enterprises produce millions of products, 12 million if fully disaggregated, according to *Voprosy ekonomiki*.[1] The uninitiated seldom appreciate how many varieties there are: a thousand kinds of ball and roller bearings alone, to cite just one example. Each product relates to some distinct use or user, requires a different input of materials and components. According to the logic of the centralized planning model, the central organs know what society needs and can issue and enforce plan-*orders* to ensure that these needs are effectively and efficiently met. This requires multimillion instructions as to what to produce, to whom deliveries should be made, from whom inputs should be received, and when. All this must be made to cohere with plans for labor, wages, profits, investment financing, material-utilization norms, quality, productivity for each of many thousands of productive units. In practice, this task can never be completed, plans are repeatedly altered in the period of their currency, supplies and output targets fail to match, there are numerous instances of imbalance and incoherence. This is due not to the lack of commitment of officials or to stupidity but to the fact that the magnitude of the task far surpasses the possibility of fulfilling it. The "center" is inevitably divided into ministries and departments, and these, together (or in conflict) with local interest groups, distort or conceal information and compete for limited investment resources.

However, the system is effective in the imposition of centrally determined priorities. When there is shortage (of materials, rail wagons, labor or whatever), the central party–state apparatus ensures that what it regards as most important gets what it needs. Thus, the defense industries appear to be reasonably efficient, as are the steel, oil, and electricity generating industries. Electricity can also serve as a good example of planability. It presents no product-mix problems (KWH are KWH are KWH), power stations on a grid can be centrally controlled from a single control panel, and the information about need, now and in the future, is best assessed at the center (and not only in Soviet-type economies!). In the planning of fuel and energy, the USSR does well. A long view can be taken of this high-priority sector and the necessary investments accordingly determined. Our own market-oriented economies accommodate themselves badly to supply shortages of oil, for instance. The USSR has responded to its own energy problem by massive efforts to develop oil and gas in Siberia, efforts that have achieved marked success in the face of formidable natural obstacles. The USSR's irrational prices matter little when decisions are taken that relate to energy supply in (say) 1990; none of us know what will be the prices and costs in 1990, and we must proceed on best estimates of future demand and supply largely in quantitative terms, which the Soviet central planners can estimate at least as well as, probably better than, any Western capitalist oilman. Furthermore, action can be taken without having to bother with the pressure groups, lobbyists, or the need to win the next election.

Further "pluses" for the Soviet system are the absence of serious unemployment—in fact, labor is frequently short—and the relative stability of wages and prices made possible by a centrally imposed incomes policy (with no independent trade unions), though, as we shall see, there is some partially concealed inflation. These "pluses" are accompanied by formidable deficiencies, which, it is important to appreciate, are also the consequence of the system and so may be regarded as a "cost" of the advantages just listed. This is one reason why reform proposals designed to overcome these deficiencies have met with strong opposition, from the beneficiaries of the existing arrangements.

The first and most obvious point is that priorities, to be effective, must relate only to the relatively small part of the totality. Therefore, most activities are nonpriority, and under conditions of over-full utilization of resources ("taut planning"), they frequently run into trouble: failures in deliveries of materials, long delays in construction of new plants, lack of coordination between output and inputs, poor quality, and so on. The central authorities, of course, desire that output should match requirements, that user demand be studied, that buildings be completed on time, that technical progress be encouraged, and pro-ductivity raised and repeatedly issue decrees to that effect. But, outside of the top-priority sectors, there is great difficulty not merely of enforce-ment but of meaningful definition of these doubtless excellent objec-tives. Let me illustrate. Overworked planners have to aggregate, that is, to issue plans for such categories as "footwear," "spare parts for farm machinery," or "window-glass," not having either the time or the information to enable them to instruct a given factory to make and deliver 200 hundred brown shoes of a given size and quality, or piston-rings, or glass of a particular specification. Plan-instructions are therefore, so to speak, nonspecific, defining an aggregate total that may be in tons, rubles, square meters or whatever. *This* instruction is clear and binding, and so enterprises produce not what the user actually requires but that assortment that adds up to required aggregate quantity. This long-standing disease has been the subject of innumerable critical articles in the Soviet press. One consequence among many is the unintentional stimulation of waste of materials: if the plan is in tons, the heavier the goods the better; if in ruble-value, then the dearer the inputs the better, provided this finds its reflection in the officially approved prices. Conversely, initiatives leading to less heavy or expensive materials threaten plan-fulfillment in tons or rubles.

Bureaucracy Replaces the Market

One reason for the persistence of these distortions is that those who "commit" them are supervised by officials (ministerial or party) who are themselves directly interested in plan fulfillment. So much so that, as numerous reports testify, these officials alter plans upward or downward, adjusting them during the period of their currency to the expected performance of their subordinate managers so as to report that there are no failures. In any case, plan-fulfillment targets are bound to cause distortions howsoever defined, so long as there is a multiplicity of types, designs, and weights of the given product. Thus, when window glass was planned in tons, it was too thick and heavy; so they shifted the plan "indicator" to square meters, whereupon it became too thin. Common sense tells us that glass should be thick or thin according to the circumstances of its use, but such detail is not and *cannot* be within the cognizance of the central planning organs. Aggregation is a "must" if next year's plan is to be drafted before the end of the century.

The greater the multiplicity of possible alternative products and methods, the less the "planability" of the given sector. One sees this in agriculture, where land can be used for many purposes, and there is a wide variety of natural conditions and weather hazards. Agricultural mechanization suffers greatly from poor-quality machines, the notorious lack of spare parts, and what Soviet critics (from Brezhnev down) call *nekomplekstnost'*, that is, lack of essential complementary equipment, which causes bottlenecks. Another example of *nekomplekstnost'* was illustrated in a *Krokodil* cartoon; a passenger in a train points to mountains and asks: "have we reached the Caucasus?" The train conductor replies: "No, these are nitrogenous fertilizers, over there is potash; the Caucasus we get to tomorrow." We see here how achievements in one sector (fertilizer output has risen impressively) are partly negated by failure in a related sector (which is the responsibility of a different ministry); thus, there are insufficient bags, means of transportation, machines for actually getting the fertilizer to the farms and spreading it on the fields, so it piles up at railway sidings.

If management is rewarded primarily for plan-fulfillment (i.e., obeying orders), it is plain that it is interested in easy-to-fulfill plans, and so there is concealment of productive possibilities and also overapplication for inputs and hoarding of materials and labor. There is also an unintentional "built-in" disincentive to innovate. All innovation carries with it some risk and requires changes in plans. But risk is not rewarded, and long before the advantages of the proposed innovation become apparent, the manager may be transferred or demoted because he has not fulfilled the current plan. Emphasis is indeed given to technological innovation, but in practice, its diffusion depends on the initiatives of thousands of managers, and it often suffers the same fate as well-intentioned orders to economize materials, which conflict with the overriding need to fulfill current aggregate plans.

Plans are "taut" because they are designed to stimulate effort, to achieve growth, to combat tendencies to routine and inerita (i.e., to act as a substitute for competition). Planners should, in theory, express in their orders the needs of society. However, experience shows how difficult it is in practice to *define* what is needed and to identify how best to provide it, in operationally meaningful detail. In its functioning, the system is unresponsive to user needs, is wasteful of resources, is not geared to innovation. It is bureaucratic not primarily (as some imagine) because of the self-interest of bureaucrats, but because the overwhelmingly difficult task of coordination, inherent in central planning, requires a complex bureaucratic structure of ministries and departments. Bureaucrats replace the market-mechanism. (This happens also *within* large Western corporations, since their internal interrelationships are *administered*.)

Is Alienation the Problem?

A view held by some on the left is that Soviet planning is not planning at all. How can it be "real" planning when these distortions occur and when the outcome frequently fails to conform with the intentions of the planners themselves? This is more than a matter of terminology, for underlying this view is the belief that there could now exist a "real" socialist democratic planning system which would dispense simultaneously with market, bureaucracy, and hierarchy, based upon some undefined form of mass democracy. Those who hold this view are usually quite unaware of the complexities of the modern industrial structure, with its innumerable complementarities and interdependencies. It is not clear where, in this process, is the place for political democracy as an alternative to both market and bureaucracy. Democratic procedures are indeed essential, but these cannot be meaningfully applied to multiple millions of microeconomic decisions: An elected assembly can vote on broad priorities (e.g., more for primary education, or housing, or developing a region) but hardly on whether three tons of constructional steel should be allocated to this or that building site, or that production of red dyestuffs be increased by 3%.

It is sometimes argued by Marxist "fundamentalists" that the basic problem lies in alienation, in the conflicts of interest between workers, management, and center; all would be well if they all identified with a common interest. These conflicts do indeed exist (and between different branches of the center also). Yet this line of thought contains or implies several fallacies. One is that a more positive or cooperative attitude on the part of those concerned could resolve the essence of the problem. It is doubtless true that human attitudes affect the *quality* with which work of all kinds is done. But this does not of itself even begin the task of coping with multiple millions of complex interrelationships. The essential point is not one of whether workers or managers or planners wish to do the right thing but one of discovering what the right thing to do is and then acquiring or ensuring the means to do it. Action requires the presence of three elements: *information, motivation,* and *means.* If any one of these is absent, decisions cannot be taken or implemented. Motivation alone is, quite evidently, not enough. Many well meaning efforts are frustrated because the required resources are allocated by several remote plan offices. It is also not appreciated that the marketless planning model is of necessity centralized (how can a purely local body decide what *society* needs and how best to provide it?), and it is precisely the vast and complex scale of operation of central planning that is a major cause of this very alienation. "Unless one is prepared to accept that the structure of regulation in interconnected production is objectively hierarchical, then the whole problem of socialist democracy can only be raised in an agitational way," wrote Bahro, without, unfortunately, drawing from this the conclusions that suggest themselves. Finally, it is implied that a society can or could exist in which there would be no conflict between sectors and between sectors and center, not to mention individuals, over the allocation of resources. This essentially utopian part of the Marxist tradition rests, and can only rest, on a vision of abundance. There must surely be plenty for *all* (i.e., when the concept of opportunity–cost, of choice between mutually exclusive alternatives, loses its meaning). Economics would then have withered away, along with the state. Let us leave aside the question of whether it is a valid or useful vision of a remote future. It is clearly not a state of affairs relevant to what was, is, or could have been in the Soviet Union.

May I add that this is *not* to deny that the spread of democracy and the reduction of privilege in the USSR would make a difference to the Soviet economy or to the now somewhat cynically negative attitude of many workers to their work; merely that it is self-delusion to suppose that this would solve the basic problems of micro-economic planning.

Workers' self-management (i.e., some version of the Yugoslav model) is quite another matter. But, of course, this rests squarely on the basis of *market*-orientated enterprise autonomy. Needless to say, this too causes its own difficulties, in terms of both efficiency and doctrine. But the beginning of wisdom in these matters is to appreciate that there *are no* solutions which, along with their positive elements, do not have some negative aspects. It is, therefore, my contention that the Soviet economy *is planned centrally*, and that the defects and distortions that are noted (*and rightly noted*) by its critics are inherent in centralized planning itself.

Balance Sheet of Soviet Economic Performance

So, after this (in my view necessary) detour, let us return to the present state of the Soviet economy. The following points appear to be uncontroversial and probably figure prominently on the agenda of the Politbureau.

1. Statistics clearly show a slowdown in growth, and the current five-year plan will *not* be fulfilled in a number of important sectors and overall. Growth does continue but, when allowance is made for certain kinds of statistical exaggeration, perhaps at 3–3.5% per annum, rather than the claimed 4–4.5% or so.[2]

2. To the heavy cost of armaments (which would rise even if SALT had been ratified by the U.S. Senate) must be added the cost of agriculture. Close to one-third of total investments are now devoted either directly to agriculture or to the sectors of industry that serve it. The rate of return to those investments is small. Far from being a source of revenue, agriculture has become a net burden on the rest of the economy. The subsidy to livestock raising now amounts to 23,000 million rubles annually (say £15,000 million, at the not-too-unrealistic official rate of exchange).

3. It has been (rightly) decided to invest massively in Siberia to ensure essential supplies of fuel and materials. For obvious reasons, it is expensive to invest in these inhospitable and remote regions, and workers must be offered good wages and amenities, otherwise they refuse to go or to stay (forced labor being no longer of economic significance). In the long run, the riches of Siberia will be a major "plus." In the shorter run, Siberia absorbs resources on a huge scale, and there could be a serious energy bottleneck in the next five years. Official sources stress the need to economize fuel.

4. There is a shortage of labor due in part to demographic factors: a low birth rate, except in formerly Moslem areas, has brought the rate of increase in the total labor force close to zero. Virtually all growth must now be based upon higher productivity. But there are also plenty of instances of overmanning and inefficient use of labor (inadequate mechanization, geographical maldistribution, and so on). Agriculture is short of labor at peak periods, requiring mobilization of millions of urban workers and soldiers to help with the harvest. Redeployment of labor, difficult to achieve without compulsion, is a "must." Experiments designed to achieve this (e.g., the so-called Shchekino experiment)[3] have made little difference.

5. Also essential are the more efficient use of investment resources and more rapid diffusion of technical progress. There is a chronic tendency to start too many projects, which then cannot be completed for lack of necessary materials and labor. Orders are then issued to complete only the most important projects, which causes the others to remain unfinished for a decade or so, leading to bottlenecks through the nondelivery of complementary materials, components, etc. Brezhnev declared that this is to be a "quinquennium of effectiveness and quality." Effectiveness in the use of investment resources; quality not only of machinery and technology but also, he insisted, of consumers' goods, with much greater influence of the user and his (or her) requirements on what is produced and distributed. Progress in these respects has been much too slow.

6. Finally, there is a serious problem of poor distribution, of imbalances between demand and supply, affecting both the allocation of inputs to industry *and* the citizen as a purchaser of goods and services. Shortages are endemic. There are queues. Such items as meat, and also many manufactured goods, are unobtainable for long periods. All this gives rise to many negative phenomena commonly associated with a sellers' market: indifference to the customer's requirements, petty and not-so-petty corruption, hoarding, and so on. It is widely believed that shortages have grown worse in recent years. This is *not* due to a reduction in supply; on the contrary, consumption has been rising. But incomes have been rising faster, and there has been a reluctance to increase retail prices. For example, meat prices have remained unaltered for 18 years, while average money wages have risen by close to 70%. No wonder there is a meat shortage! Recent increases in certain prices (coffee and petrol in 1979, restaurant meals, furniture, jewelry, etc., in 1980) will not be sufficient to cope with this chronic "concealed inflation."

7. There are also problems connected with foreign trade. In years of large grain imports, the USSR runs a larger deficit than can be covered by gold sales. Some of her allies (especially Poland) are in a much more vulnerable position, with very large debts to the West. Comecon integration progresses slowly, since both the USSR and the other countries

concerned must increase their exports to the West so as to cover their needs for hard-currency imports.

It seems desirable, indeed necessary, to quote some statistics, but this is less simple than it sounds. For reasons already given, aggregate statistics tend to overstate the growth rate. How misleading can be even some "sectoral" statistics may be illustrated from a *Pravda* article: when a plant making pipe produced cheaper, better-quality pipe weighing 25% less, the statistical "effect" was a reduction in both the "volume" of output and in labor productivity.[4] This explains the reluctance of management to adopt more economical variants but also shows the imperfection of measurement. Perhaps the following table (1), which relates to physical output of some important products, can be used to illustrate both the shortfall in plan-fulfillment *and* the fact that growth continues, albeit at a slower rate.

It is not disputed that the rate of increase in the productivity of labor and the yield on capital investment have been falling, as has the level of profitability. Industrial and construction costs have edged upward, and new machinery in particular is often much dearer, and not much more productive, than the models it replaces.

In agriculture, the record year 1978 has been followed by the much less satisfactory 1979 (the difference is attributable to weather conditions). The much greater degree of mechanization and "chemicalization" lays a greater burden on the planning of industrial supplies, and rising costs are a measure of inadequacies in this direction. At least equally important is labor morale: peasants seem to be unwilling to work harder at the peak harvest periods, and this, as well as incomplete mechanization, cause a massive "import" of labor from the cities (and the army) every autumn. Collective and state farms are too large, and interference with their managements by party officials further complicates their task. The huge investments made in agriculture have had some effect: both output and productivity have been rising, but at a slow rate. Meanwhile, the relative cheapness of foodstuffs (compared with industrial consumers' goods) ensures that demand exceeds supply, resulting in chronic shortages in many parts of the country.

It is instructive to contrast the Brezhnev period with the Khrushchev era. Khrushchev—and the performance of the economy under his rule—contained some very contradictory elements. Some of his actions had positive results. Thus in 1953–1958 his agricultural policies contrasted with Stalin's earlier neglect and led to a quick rise in output, over 50% in 5 years. However, in the next 5 years, growth virtually ceased, and his numerous "campaigns" and reorganizations caused much confusion. In industry, he rightly gave priority to oil, gas, chemicals, all previously neglected, but again his methods led to confusion, resent-

TABLE 1. *Soviet Economic Performance*

	1965	1970	1975 (plan)[a]	1975 (actual)	1978	1980 (plan)[a]	(1980) (est.)[b]
Electricity (mlrd kWh)	507	741	1065	1039	1202	1380	1295
Coal (million tons)	578	624	695	701	724	800	745
Oil (million tons)	243	353	505	491	572	640	606
Gas (mlrd m³)	128	198	320	289	372	435	435
Steel (million tons)	91	116	146	141	151	168	157
Fertilizer (gross)	31	55	90	90	98	143	(120)
Chemical fibers (gross)	0.40	0.62	1.06	0.95	1.10	1.49	(1.35)
Cement (gross)	72	95	125	122	127	144	(134)
Fabrics (mill m²)	7320	8640	11,100	10,100	10,600	12,800	(11,400)

[a]The 5-year plan targets, set 5 years earlier.
[b]Baibakov, *Pravda*, November 29, 1979 (figures in brackets are my estimates).

456

ment, disorganization. Brezhnev brought greater predictability and stability; there have been no "harebrained schemes," no massive reorganizations, more reliance on expert advice. But the ageing leadership has now slipped towards immobility. Instead of Khrushchev's admittedly unsound ideas about introducing communism by instalments at specified dates (after having "overtaken America"), we now have the present state of affairs defined as "mature socialism" (sometimes as "real socialism"—shades of Bahro's *real existierende Sozialismus*!), which surely reflects a greater degree of complacency, not necessarily shared by citizens queuing for sausage! Urgent problems still await solution.

The Scope for Administrative Reform

Does all this constitute a crisis? In one sense, I think we can call it such. A system of centralized planning originally designed under Stalin for ultrarapid industrialization of a backward country is now increasingly an obstacle to efficiency, no longer able to cope with the problems and complexities of a modern industrial economy. But then is the West able to cope with them? What could they learn from us? What paths are there to the reform of their system that will not carry with them dangers of accelerating inflation, instability, unpredictable social–political consequences? Conversely, can the existing system be so improved and streamlined as to eliminate some of the worst inefficiencies and distortions, while preserving the elements of strength? How far is the political leadership committed to resisting major changes? The party–state machine derives very considerable advantages from the present system; it provides them with a function and enhances their power and influence (replacing the invisible hand with the visible hand, *their* hand). Power over allocation is used to divert scarce goods and services for their own use, through a network of special shops, hospitals, villas, etc. These and similar arguments lead some critics to the conclusion that "the party" will block all changes, and that no change is possible without prior political convulsions, which would shake or overthrow the dominance of the party.

There is clearly a strong case to be made along these lines. But it should be recalled that the party leaders want not only privilege, control, and stability; they want results. They may indeed be conservative septuagenarians, but they know and say, with Brezhnev, that the scientific–technical revolution requires fundamental changes in methods of planning and management.[5] It adversely affects Soviet power in the world if grain has to be massively imported from America, if Soviet technology lags behind, if growth rates fall, if plans are unbalanced, and resources wasted. When citizens react angrily to goods shortages, this is bad also for internal security. It worries the leadership that, with the existing system of incentives, waste often "pays," indeed shows up in statistics as increased output and productivity. There is here a theoretical as well as a practical weakness: "The greater the total expenditure of labor and materials, the greater the [apparent] productivity. Use–values are not counted."[6] Corrective action is seen to be essential.

But *what* corrective action? Here opinions differ widely. Brezhnev and his comrades appear to be seeking greater efficiency through a mixture of exhortation, computerization, and reorganization. Industrial enterprises are being merged into associations or corporations (*obyedineniya*), thereby reducing the number of units to be planned and facilitating specialization. There is a drive to form "agroindustrial complexes" in rural areas. Planners are instructed to pay more attention to ensuring coherence of plans, managers are ordered to carry out their delivery obligations, various experiments are undertaken to reduce waste (tighter utilization norms, measurement of plan fulfillment in terms of *net* output, bonus schemes to encourage labor productivity and discourage the hoarding of labor by management, and so on). Efforts are made to reward quality. The Mathematical Economics institute, under Fedorenko, and other research institutes have been seeking to adapt computers and programming techniques to the needs of centralized planning.

On July 29, 1979, *Pravda* published a decree on economic reform. Commentaries referred to many of the weaknesses that were mentioned in this chapter, and that the reform is designed to overcome. The key changes are as follows:

1. Construction enterprises are to be judged in relation to buildings *completed*, not by work done and money spent.
2. Long-term plans are to be more closely integrated with current (annual) plans at the center and in industries.
3. The use of "normed net product," instead of gross value of output or of sales, is to eliminate the inducement to using dear material inputs.
4. More use is to be made of long-term agreements between firms.
5. There will be greater emphasis on the fulfillment of contractual delivery obligations.
6. Obligatory plan-instructions will cover also the introduction of new technology, the size of the labor force, quality indicators, material utilization norms, in some cases also cost reduction, reduction in number of unskilled workers, labor productivity targets, output targets in physical terms, profits, etc.
7. New measures are also intended to ensure a closer link between industrial–sector and territorial–regional planning and between the plans for investments and the material means of implementing them.

It is too soon to judge the effect of these proposals, since they have yet to be worked out in detail, let alone implemented, but I take leave to doubt whether these measures are on the right lines. No doubt some improvements are possible; thus, for instance, it has long been necessary to eliminate the interest of construction organizations in using dear materials and delaying completions. But already one can see two major weaknesses in the "reform." The first and most important is the multiplicity of plan indicators. This not only put an even greater burden on the planning organs, but virtually guarantees inconsistencies and anomalies. One has only to look at the preceding list. Secondly, the "normed net output" indicator is far more complicated than may appear. Let me illustrate with an example. Suppose an industrial association or enterprise makes 15 different products. To calculate the net output of each, one has to subtract material inputs, but some of these will be common overheads. It will also be necessary to allocate to each its share of profit, and this will be done by arbitrarily assuming that each product is equally profitable, which, at the given prices, will not be the case. Consequently, there will be a contradiction between real profitability and the notional "net-product" calculation and probably also between both and the duty of fulfilling *quantitative* plan targets. Millions of extra calculations will have to be made to determine "normed net product." Not only this: In an article commenting on the reform, the authoritative D. Valovoi warns that if the growth in volume of output (and therefore also of labor productivity) were still measured in terms of gross value of output, this would introduce yet another contradiction, so he advocates measuring growth in terms of net output, "as is done in developed capitalist countries."[7] So there is no clarity yet on this point, though the text of the decree[8] does speak of planned growth of *net* product. In addition, the proposals envisage retaining gross value of sales as a plan indicator for ministries. If this is done, the ministries will exert pressure on their subordinates to avoid producing too cheaply, for familiar reasons. Surely the cure may be worse than the disease?

Improvements are doubtless possible. However, if my analysis of the basic causes of inefficiency is correct, these measures will make little difference. The essential problem is the impossible *scale* of centralized microeconomic planning, the fact that subordinate units adjust their action to the plan targets laid down from above and not to the needs of other enterprises or to the revealed preferences of the citizens. Of course, Brezhnev and Kosygin agree, indeed repeatedly assert, that production should be for use, that user demand must be taken fully into account, that resources be used economically. The question is: How can the complex and clumsy bureaucracy—complex and clumsy because of the enormous task it has to perform—achieve the required flexibility? How can it preserve the system of "directive planning" (Kosygin's definition) *and* stimulate initiative and innovation? How can plans be made internally consistent when the task of coordination exceeds the capacity of humans and computers alike? A propos the latter, a wise Hungarian economist, Maria Augustinovics, once remarked that one reason for the limited application of computerized programming is that even the most inflexible and hidebound bureaucrat is infinitely more flexible than any computerized program.

The Market Solution

The alternative *must* be in the direction of decentralization, and (pace Bahro) this can only be based on negotiated contracts between producer and customer (plus trade as an intermediary).[9] The relevant model is that of the Hungarian economic reform of 1968. (Hungarian reality has moved some way from the original model.) Its basis was that enterprises were no longer to be handed compulsory output plans from above; they were to make their own plans in negotiation with customers while being free to purchase the inputs they required. The abandonment of centrally determined current output plans and of administered allocation of inputs are two sides of the same medal: The compulsory output plan is integrally linked to the supply plan; the output of most enterprises is some other enterprises' input, and the first step in making up the annual plan in the USSR is the collection of information about the needs of productive enterprises for materials, components, etc. Central *directive* planning would be confined to major investments, with the "microeconomy" steered largely by economic means (taxes, subsidies, etc.).

However, any reform on these lines is necessarily based on production for exchange and not production for use (i.e., relies to a considerable degree on the market mechanism). This upsets both the "fundamentalists" and the neo-Stalinists. Did not Marx and Engels see socialism and commodity production as incompatible? Did not Stalin in his last work advocate a continued reduction in the area in which commodity exchange and "the law of value" operated? But what is the effective alternative to a reform which, in effect, allows production units to negotiate freely with each other as suppliers and as customers? The Bettelheims and Sweezys seek solutions in slogans, such as "the mass line," or in counterposing monetary calculation to plans based on "socially useful effect" (and this without telling us how it should be measured or whose task it is to do the measuring, or how to ensure that decisions are implemented). Nor do they explain how there can be "control by the direct producers," (i.e., meaningful workers participation in economic decision making) unless decisions about production are taken *at the level of the production unit*; it is this that makes the Yugoslav model rely on the market.

There is a real dilemma here for sincere socialists, a dilemma that must be squarely faced, not evaded. Let us take as an example the fact that a market, if it is to function, requires some degree of competition. For many socialists, this is offensive; they counterpose it to socialist cooperation, and indeed it does appear to contradict the notion of workers' solidarity. However, the total absence of competition implies the tieing of customer to supplier by the plan; this situation exists in the USSR and is a cause of much dissatisfaction, since the customer (e.g., the manager of a state factory or retail store) cannot go elsewhere if the quality of the goods or services provided are poor or another supplier is better. But if one *can* go elsewhere, albeit to another state or cooperative supplier, that already implies competition (i.e., the possibility that one producer can gain from satisfying the customer better than another, which in turn implies that an unsuccessful producer would be penalized. Unless one makes the assumption that under an imaginary "real" socialism productive units will never give cause for dissatisfaction, there must, of course, be some sort of penalty or corrective action. In the USSR this is imposed or taken by bureaucratic superiors in the form of reprimand, transfer, demotion, denial of plan-fulfillment bonuses. But experience strongly suggests that none of these is so effective as the provision of *economic* carrots and sticks, linked with *economic* criteria for success or failure. Market and competition require spare capacity, and this raises the spectre of unemployment, whereas the USSR takes pride in ensuring full utilization of resources. Unemployment must, of course, be minimized, but how are efficiency and flexibility to be achieved without spare capacity?

In conceiving a democratic socialism, one ought surely to envisage groups of people (a local community, say, or a factory or farm) being able freely to decide to acquire various goods for use either in production or consumption. Two methods only are known by which they could do so. They could be *free to buy them* from the supplier that suits their needs best, or they would have *to apply for permission* to obtain them. Assuming that these goods have alternative uses, a hierarchical superior would have to consider wherever *this* use for them should be authorized. The "fundamentalist" escapes from this dilemma by identifying socialism with abundance (i.e., with the existence of ample supplies for all purposes on which any group could draw—and this in a world where over one-half the population is on the margin of subsistence!). The bureaucrat considers that it is his (occasionally her) responsibility to allocate scarce goods in accordance with politically determined priorities. Both are hostile to the market in principle. But at least the bureaucrat's view relates to the real world, as well as being in his/her interest.

The market and competition carry with them certain costs and dangers; few doubt this. It would be necessary to avoid excessive income inequalities (but not at the cost of eliminating incentives), and it would also be essential to keep a major role for central planners in the taking of major investment decisions. It is also important to appreciate that certain areas, such as the energy sector, could and should remain under centralized operational control (who would "decentralize" Electricité de France or the Central Electricity Generating Board? Not even Sir Keith Joseph!). The question of the level at which decision making is best located is a complex question, by no means solely economic, and one that surely calls for a wide variety of different solutions, depending on the sector and the type of decision. It is certainly absurd to imply that decentralization plus the market mechanism represent a panacea and do not give rise to difficulties, both economic and political–social. But it is also hard to avoid the conclusion that no solution can be devised that does not involve the market mechanism in some form.

Be all this as it may, the Soviet leadership has shown every sign of being determined to reject the "market" solution. It is unlikely that Brezhnev's successors will be different in this respect. There is too much at stake: the position and role of petty officialdom at all levels, the priority of the "military–industrial complex," the (understandable) fear of instability and of the unpredictable side-effects of major reform of a mechanism which has, in its principles, changed little over the last 45 years or so. Nor can one discern any pressure from below in this direction. True, the workers would like goods of better quality to be available, not to stand in queues, etc., but the market's logic is usually not understood: as also in this country, people want higher wages *and* lower prices, oppose redundancies even if their skills are urgently wanted elsewhere, and blame the resultant shortages on speculators, bosses, bureaucrats, or whatever. It is a fact that in Eastern Europe, opponents of reform can and do appeal to the workers' residual sense of identifying socialism and justice with *opposition* to market forces. Paradoxically, this has the effect of reinforcing the privileges of high officialdom, in so far as these take the form of privileged allocation of goods unavailable to the ordinary citizen; they arise from the fact that demand and supply do *not* balance. It is surely quite incorrect for Bettelheim to argue that the "new bourgeoisie" favors market-type reforms! The *present* system serves their personal material interests best. As for managers, some do indeed want more income and more power, but some prefer the situation which Hegedus has called "organized irresponsibility" to the disciplines imposed by a market, to which they are not accustomed and where they might fail.

Problems and Prospects

Where is the Soviet economy heading if no major reforms are in fact adopted? To repeat a point made earlier, there is no catastrophe imminent, the system is not in chaos, the quality of its planning and of its production are not in decline. Indeed, quality is actually improving. So, to take another example, is agricultural output, allowing for year-by-year weather variations, though at a very high cost. Exclusive emphasis upon chaos and waste, the image of production of unsaleable rubbish, is misleading, especially if contrasted with the past when the Soviet system was *more* wasteful, *more* inefficient, *less* productive. People have *not* become worse off. What has happened is the persistence of the second-rate and a failure to keep pace with the needs of technical progress, the growing complexity of industry, the rising demands and aspirations of the masses, with incomes (demand) outpacing supply. Resources are still often used wastefully. But even if growth stays at the modest levels of 3% per annum over the next few years (which seems to me a reasonable forecast to make), this may contrast favorably with Western economies, reeling under renewed blows from OPEC and driven to beggar-my-neighbor trade policies (and anxious to sell technology to the USSR on favorable credit terms). Even 3% is better than zero.

Is there then no danger to their system, no crisis? This would be going too far, so let us end by trying to identify what appears to me to be a basic source of potential economic (and therefore social–political instability. This is the increasing gap between *rising expectations* and slowly changing reality. There is also the alarming and growing gap between the cash and savings in the hands of the population and the supply of goods, especially foodstuffs. Given the absence of a (legal) professional trading class and the inefficiency of the official distribution network, shortages can and do cause real hardship in some areas. There is also a wide gap between the complacent optimism of the media and the experience of ordinary citizens, reflected in the following Moscow story: "If you wish to find enough food to fill your refrigerator, plug it into the radio." Most observers concur that ideological commitment, in the name of which earlier generations of young people suffered privations to "build socialism," has long disappeared. Mass terror is no more. Work discipline is weak, with many reports of absenteeism, slackness, drunkenness, pilfering. Stability, the isolation of the few active dissidents, depends on giving people grounds for hope of better material conditions: the huge rise in savings bank deposits is due not only to the gap between purchasing power and the value of goods available in the shops but also to saving up for the much-hoped-for car, cooperative flat, or a color television set. If the gap between hopes and reality becomes too wide (and if in addition the car and television set are out of action for lack of spares and repairs to the flat cannot be made without large bribes), this could cause trouble. This trouble can be exacerbated by the government's obstinate refusal to raise prices to reflect actual supply-and-demand conditions. This not only increases the already strong tendencies toward corruption but inevitably causes grave shortages in some towns, distribution being on a "hierarchical" basis, with Moscow at the top. (This has given rise to a cynical jest: "We are said to have reached the stage of mature socialism. What is the dividing line between mature socialism and the lower kind?" Answer: "the Moscow outer circular highway".) Under these conditions, though there are in fact more goods available, people feel more frustrated than ever in their efforts to find the goods they want. Discontent can be enhanced by travellers' tales; not only the glittering "consumerism" of the West but the much greater choice and apparent abundance of Czechoslovakia and Hungary give rise to irritation and impatience.

Engineers, technologists, teachers, doctors, office staffs of most kinds have another source of discontent. They have lost ground in the "wages league," and many earn less than skilled workers. Much "class analysis" of Soviet society suffers from a strange anti-intellectual bias, from a tendency to counterpose the interests of the workers and the in-tellectuals, treating the latter as if they were allies of the party–state elite. Yet far from being privileged, the mass "intellectual" professions are poorly paid, with none of the privileges of high officialdom. Doctors, teachers, middle-grade qualified engineers, most office staff earn less than bus drivers. It is true, sadly, that there is a wide gulf of mutual incomprehension between them and the workers (and indeed also between the workers and the peasants); the regime can appeal to the antiintellectual prejudices of the masses and in the past has frequently done so. It is odd that some of the regime's "new left" critics should help in this task.

This brings me back to the 3% growth rate. Given the demands of the army and Siberia, given also the urgent claims of the Central Asian republics with their rapidly rising (but immobile) populations, *and* the ever-increasing demands of agriculture, plus the need to improve rural amenities to prevent an exodus of skilled labor, there is little room for maneuver, little to spare for improving living standards of workers or intellectuals—*unless* there is a substantial gain in *efficiency and productiv-ity*. But is *this* possible without the sort of reforms that the party leadership is reluctant to contemplate?

On a recent visit to China, I was asked (in Shanghai), "Would you regard the Soviet system as socialist, and, if not, what *would* you regard as socialist?" A difficult question indeed, especially its second part, and complicated by China's own recent experiences. They are seeking a way that is neither that of the convulsions of "cultural revolution," with its downgrading of efficiency and productivity (surely fatal in a backward and very poor country), nor the continuation of the Soviet centralized model, large elements of which have survived earlier attempts at re-form. They, too, are looking for some new economic structure which will combine plan and market, centralization of basic decisions and the stimulation of local initiative, managerial responsibility with workers' participation, material incentives and an egalitarian ideology. The least we can do is appreciate how difficult is the task, in China or anywhere else, of devising a "working model" of a socialist economy, and how small is the relevance in this connection of the theoretical legacy of Marx.

Notes

[1]*Voprosy ekonomiki,* no. 12 (1977), p. 3.

[2]The exaggeration arises mainly from the tendency to conceal price increases (e.g., managers introducing "new" and dearer products which are allegedly better and are not, while withdrawing cheaper models); this affects the output index through the price index that is used to calculate it. There is also false reporting, but this could also take the form of concealment of output as well as exaggerating it.

[3]The idea was to allow wages economized by reduction of overmanning to be shared by the remaining employees, but the scheme has been watered down.

[4]*Pravda,* September 3, 1979.

[5]In his speech to the Twenty-Fifth Party Congress.

[6]D. Valovoi's three articles in *Pravda,* 11, 12, and 13 November 1978 make this and many other points of a highly critical nature.

[7]*Pravda,* September 3, 1979.

[8]*Ekonomicheskaya gazeta,* no. 32 (1979).

[9]Bahro is an opponent of large-scale units and centralization but unrealistically advocates small units that would be largely self-sufficient (see his *The Alternative in Eastern Europe,* NLB: London, 1978).

18   JOSEPH S. BERLINER

Planning and Management*

Introduction   In July 1979, the party and government of the USSR issued a decree announcing a variety of changes in what is now called the economic mechanism. The decree evoked a flurry of interest at the time, but in short order, public attention turned to other things. There are two lessons in that incident. First, the process of modifying the system of planning and management has become routinized. The public has become used to the periodic announcement, usually in advance of the next 5-year planning period, of a series of changes that had been agreed upon since the last such decree. Second, for the most part, the changes are technical rather than fundamental, involving such matters as new success indicators or revised planning procedures.

The capacity of the system to review its methods of operation periodically and to seek ways of improving them must be regarded as one of its strengths. There is a view abroad, however, that the range of alternatives considered, in the public discussion at least, is too narrow to score a significant advance. If Mr. Brezhnev were immortal, that restriction may continue indefinitely. But as the USSR enters the last decades of the century, there is a strong possibility that the range of discussable alternatives may widen, not only because of human mortality but also because of the growing strains to which the economy will be subject.

The objective of this chapter is to explore that wider range of alternative systems of planning and management that may be considered as the next two decades unfold. It is well to begin, however, with a review of the recent history of economic reforms.

*Reprinted by permission of the author and publisher from *The Soviet Economy: Toward the Year 2000,* eds. Abram Bergson and Herbert S. Levine (Boston: George Allen & Unwin, 1983), pp. 350–390. Copyright 1983 by Abram Bergson and Herbert S. Levine.

Some Reflections Five cases of changes in the economic mech-
on Recent History anism will serve as the specimens in this dissection of the past. The details are familiar to this
audience and have been so well studied elsewhere[1] that they need not
be recounted here. The purpose is rather to review those cases for the
light they can shed on the views held by the governors of the economic
system about that system. Two questions will be asked about each of the
cases. First, what were the governors seeking to accomplish by that
particular change? Second, what does that change reveal about their
conception of how their system works? The first question is designed to
identify the objectives of the leadership and the second to understand
their implicit model of their own economy. That sort of knowledge
about past efforts to change the economy should provide some insight
into the future course of such efforts.

The selection of the five cases examined shortly is somewhat arbitrary. Two of them, the Territorial Reorganization of 1957 and the
Economic Reform of 1965, would appear on everybody's list of the most
important efforts at system change. The others have been chosen not
necessarily because of their prominence but because they deal with
different facets of the planning or management system. Other analysts
would select other cases, covering areas I have omitted, like agriculture.
The five that have been chosen nevertheless represent, I believe, a
reasonable selection of changes from which to seek some instructive
generalizations.

The Territorial Reorganization of 1957 The problem to which the
reform was addressed was the diversion of resources into uses different
from those provided for in the plan. To some extent, the issue was the
deliberate violation of the plan; for example, when ministries instructed
their enterprises to alter their shipping plans in favor of customers
within their own ministries. In other cases, the issue was not violations
of the plans but restrictions on the flow of resources in ways that were
contrary to the intent of the plan. A typical instance was the enterprise
that possessed excess stocks of some scarce commodity while a neighboring enterprise's production plan foundered for lack of that commodity; but the redirection of that commodity from the first enterprise to
the second was inhibited because they belonged to different ministries.

The source of the problem, as seen by the reformers, was captured in
the slogan, *vedomstvennost'* or "departmentalism." That may be interpreted to mean that ministries tended to maximize the indicators of
their own performance, which in system terms is equivalent to suboptimization by the component units at the expense of the performance
of the system as a whole. The solution was thought to be a restructuring
of those components by repartitioning them in such fashion that the
identity of the suboptimizing units—the ministries—was obliterated. If
there were no ministries, there could be no suboptimization by ministries.

It is difficult to imagine, in retrospect, that the reformers did not anticipate what the consequence would be; that only the specific form of the objectionable behavior would be changed but not that behavior in general. There had been ample evidence in the past of *mestnichestvo* (localism) in decision making by regional government and party organizations. The outcome was indeed so predictable that a compelling case can and has been made that the whole purpose of the exercise had nothing to do with economics at all but with politics; namely, that the reform was Khrushchev's gambit for crushing the power base of the Moscow bureaucracy by transferring their power to his supporters in the provincial centers. If that were indeed the history, then we are misled in trying to draw too many lessons out of the economics of the reform. But one can recognize the political element in the reform without having to hold that there was no serious economic purpose behind it. If the reformers failed to anticipate the turn that the economy actually took after the reform, it may be because they expected either that (*a*) *mestnichestvo* could and would be more easily contained than the old *vedomstvennost'*, if only because none of the 110-odd provincial economic leaders could wield the power of a major industrial minister, or (*b*), even if that were not so, the cost of *mestnichestvo* would be less than that of *vedomstvennost'*. We know in retrospect that both of those propositions were wrong, but they could have been honestly held by reasonable men at the time.

The episode offers several insights into the thoughts of the system's governors about their system. It is clear that there was no questioning of the principle of central planning as the basis of the economic mechanism. They recognized that planning was not perfect, but that was not the issue to which this reform was addressed. The problem was that even perfect plans are not self-executing but require persons and organizations to carry them out. The task of government was to create a management structure in which managers would make those decisions that are in closest conformity to the plan. In seeking out the villain, of the several levels of management at which the problem could have been attacked, they chose the level of central management—the ministries. Presumably, they saw enterprise-level management as less at fault or perhaps as more compliant. The effective power of choice lay with the central management, and if the central management could be made to behave correctly, enterprise management could be expected to comply. In any event, even if they were not quite that starry-eyed about enterprise management, it was their judgement that the greater damage was being done where the greater overall decision-making power lay—with the central management.

Finally, the problem was seen not simply as one of incentives but of structure. If it were merely incentives, they might have sought to design new incentives—perhaps new success indicators—to induce ministers to alter their decisions. The fact that they did not take that tack indicates that they did not see that as the source of the problem. They must have felt that it was the branch structure of the management system that induced the unfortunate behavior, and no amount of fiddling with success indicators would eliminate the pressures toward maximizing the performance of the branch.

The Territorial Reorganization was introduced in 1957. It is well to recall that that was a period in which the Soviet economy was still growing very rapidly. The reform was the first major effort to eliminate some of the grosser sources of inefficiency in the rigid system of planning and management inherited from Stalin. The evidence of waste was abundant, but the system was thought to be performing quite satisfactorily at the time. The objective of the reform was to enable it to do even better. The beginnings of the decline in the growth rate date from the late 1950s. By the mid-1960s, it was increasingly evident that the decline was not a short-term aberration but was perhaps something systemic. The next major reform was introduced under new conditions; the economy had seen better days, and its governors wished to find a way of bringing those days back.

The 1965 Economic Reform The problem that motivated this reform was similar to that involved in the Territorial Reorganization: enterprises were making a broad range of decisions that were contrary to the intentions of the plan. And as in the earlier reform, the source of the problem was again held to be the organs of central management; that was the meaning of the slogan, "petty tutelage." But one new source was identified this time. That was the use of poorly designed success indicators that directed enterprises into making incorrect decisions.

The petty-tutelage problem was an issue in organizational theory; the question was, what were the optimal levels at which various types of decisions should be made? One can detect in the solution the primacy of informational concerns. That is, the decision to devolve a wide range of choices from the level of central management to that of enterprise management reflected the view that those were areas in which enterprises had more precise and timely information at their disposal than the central ministries.

The success-indicator problem, in contrast, was an issue in economic theory; it was indeed the first reform in which economists rather than politicians and planners had a hand. By identifying the source of the problem as the notorious *val* (gross value of output), the reformers implicitly acknowledged that they were dealing with a process of maximization under constraints, and that in such a process, it is important to get the objectives function right. That way of thinking about the economic mechanism was a giant step forward from the reasoning of the past, which held that the problem was simply to get managers to "fulfill the plan." It led eventually to the formulation that is currently in wide use: "what is best for the economy should be best for the enterprise."

The choice of sales revenue and profit as the new success indicators was a reasonable first step in the direction of designing an optimal objectives function for enterprise management. Though not usually put into the same category, the introduction of a capital charge may also be regarded as a contribution to the improvement of the success indicators. For when profit is promoted to the level of a major argument in an objectives function, it becomes more important to be sure that the relative costs of the factors of production are properly accounted for.

The change in the success indicators required a corresponding change in the incentive structure, which had formerly been linked primarily to *val*. The new system of incentive payments involved nothing new in principle, however. All the elements were there before, in the form of the Enterprise Fund, although the magnitudes of the contributions to the various incentive funds was changed.

In the course of a few years, several features of the original 1965 reform were modified. Among the major modifications was the gradual increase in the number of indicators for which the enterprise had to account to the ministry. The reason for the retreat is instructive because it bears on a problem that arises in all efforts to reform the system of planning and management. The central allocative instrument is still the national plan. Gosplan must be held responsible for the consistency and optimality of the plan, and someone else must be held responsible for assuring that that plan is executed. As long as the executors are the ministries, they must be given authority equivalent to their responsibility. The Economic Reform was an attempt to permit enterprises, on informational grounds, to make a wide range of decisions that affected plan fulfillment but to hold the ministries responsible for the results. In effect, the ministries were put in the position of being held responsible for decisions that they were forbidden to control. The impossibility of that organizational arrangement led eventually to the reassertion by the ministries of control over those kinds of enterprise decisions for which they had to account to the party and the Council of Ministers.

In that piece of history, there is an important lesson regarding the limits of decentralized decision making under central planning. A governing unit (e.g., a capitalist corporation) can delegate decision-making authority to lower units on grounds of informational efficiency if it determines its own objectives function; it can decentralize purchasing while retaining control over pricing, for example. The test of that organizational arrangement is its own evaluation of whether the results are better in the light of its own profit and other objectives. But if a governing unit (like a Soviet ministry) is not an autonomous organization but is responsible to a higher organization for a very detailed plan of operations, then it cannot be limited in the kinds of controls it may exert over its operating units. Specifically, if the material balances in the national plan are carried out in physical or gross-value units, then the ministerial executors of that plan must be held accountable for the production by their operating units of the specified physical quantities or gross values. They simply cannot be denied the power to telephone their enterprises toward the end of the month to inquire how close they are to fulfilling their gross-output targets. And once the telephone calls are made, the message is fully absorbed.

To be sure, a ministry itself may delegate certain decision-making authority to its enterprises on grounds of informational efficiency. But the range of such decentralized authority is likely to be very limited and to deal with secondary choices for which the ministry itself is not directly accountable. Thus, the lesson of the Economic Reform is that genuine decentralization of authority to enterprises is strictly limited by the directive nature of a detailed national economic plan.

With respect to success indicators, the prospects are brighter. What is involved is the choices that must be made that are not dictated by the terms of the plan. The usual instances are choices among qualities not specified in the plan or choices of output-mixes in excess of the minimal assortment-plan targets (i.e., plan overfulfillment.) Since the goal is to induce those decisions that are most consistent with the objectives of the plan, the shadow prices implicit in the plan could serve that purpose, with profits as the maximand in the objectives function. Nevertheless, if the ministry is still held to account for quantities or for gross value of output, it is those magnitudes that will prevail in enterprise decisions.

The Price Reform of 1966–1967 The primary goal of the Price Reform may be judged from the kind of evidence that was presented as justification of the need for such a reform. What was thought to be the most persuasive evidence was the widely published data on the vast spread of profit rates among products and branches, ranging from highly subsidized branches like coal to highly profitable branches like machinery production. Among the reasons that such diversity of profit rates was regarded as bad, the following predominated: (1) subsidies are bad in general because they encourage inefficiency and neglect of cost by producers who anticipate that the government will subsidize the loss; (2) high profits are generally unearned and represent rental elements in income; they are inequitable, and they also weaken cost discipline; (3) large profit differentials between commodities bias product-mix choices by producers and input-mix choices by purchasers. The goal, therefore, was to reestablish a price structure in which most enterprises earned the normal profit rate and a few of the best and worst earned a bit more or less in proportion as their work diverged from that of the "normally operating enterprise."

What does this concern about profit differentials reveal about the leadership's analysis of the economic system? For one thing, it reveals a certain normative notion of what prices should be. The ideal, presumably, was one in which most enterprises earned the normal rate of profit and a few earned somewhat more or less, the excess or shortfall of profit serving both as a success indicator and as an incentive. However, the basis of pricing was to remain average branch cost plus normal profit. The objective was that prices play not an active but a neutral role in decision making. The trouble with large profit differentials is that they convert price into an active element in decision making, in the sense that managers depart from rational or socially desirable decisions because of the profit-related consequences of wide price variability. In other words, the ideal was not that price should serve as an allocative device; the plan was still the primary allocative instrument. The objective was rather a price-structure in which a profit could serve as a success indicator (which requires *some* degree of variability) without at the same time serving as an allocative device by influencing production choices.

Thus, the Price Reform was a reaffirmation of central planning as the allocative mechanism. Managerial decisions were to be made on the basis of plan assignments whenever those assignments were clear and not on the basis of price and profit. The Price Reform recognized, however, that for a broad range of decisions that had to be made by management, there was no clear indication of which alternative contributed most to the fulfillment of the national plan. The Economic Reform of 1965 had designated profit, along with sales, as a major criterion of performance and therefore implicitly as a proper basis of choice. By eliminating the large profit differentials of the past, the Price Reform was designed to assure that the choices made would be in closer conformity with the objectives of the plan.

There were two exceptions that are noteworthy. One was the pricing of new products. In a separate decree issued in 1965, before the Price Reform, the pricing of new products was reorganized on lines entirely separate from those of established products.[2] That decree introduced certain highly active functions for prices in the case of new technology. Profit rates were deliberately differentiated in order to induce management to choose the higher-profit alternatives. It is significant that this concession was made in order to promote technological innovation. Central planning is at its best with well-known technologies and at its worst with technologies not yet fully developed or even yet unknown. In assigning an active function to prices and profit in this case, the system's governors demonstrated a new awareness that in this major area of economic activity, central planning suffers from certain limitations and that more decentralized decision making can be helpful.

The second exception was the introduction of rent-like fixed charges on commodities like petroleum and timber. The use of such charges was a victory for the marginalists and quasi-marginalists who had finally persuaded the leadership that at least in those cases in which the difference between marginal and average cost is very large, price should be used actively to discourage consumption. In this case, it is not only managerial decision making that is to be influenced but also the plan itself. In deciding whether to use oil or coal in a new power plant, for example, it is the marginal cost of the two fuels that planners must take into account. Hence, the purpose of this new provision is to improve the quality of central planning as well as that of managerial decision making.

Production Associations This reform consists of the merger of groups of enterprises into new superenterprises under a single management. In one class of mergers, the key feature is that a formerly independent R & D institute is a part of the new association and sometimes the dominant member. These are the science-production associations. The other production associations follow the familiar pattern of the vertical integration of enterprises, although there are some cases of horizontal integration.

The problem that motivated the founding of the science-production associations is clear enough. It was the unsatisfactory rate of technological progress. This, in fact, is the first of the reforms under review in which the problem of technological progress lay at the heart of the reform, although it played a role in the others. But if technological progress were the only objective of this reform, one could not explain why the merger movement was extended to encompass virtually all of the nonagricultural economy; for most of the mergers do not involve R & D institutes. One must, therefore, postulate a second objective, which appears to be yet another stab at the problem of enterprise-level decision making. The specific facet of the problem in this case was that enterprises produced outputs that did not take sufficiently into account the requirements of their industrial customers. This second objective is related to the first in that it was not merely the quantities of output but also their qualities that were at issue. That is, the concern was not simply that enterprises produced types of products that did not correspond to the needs of users but also that the quality of outputs did not correspond to the needs of users.

The selection of the production association as the device for getting at these two problems suggests a change in the analysis of the source of the problems by the system's governors. In earlier reforms, it was assumed that enterprise managers were motivated to make correct choices. The problem was that they were misdirected, by the ministries in the case of the Territorial Reorganization and by the success indicators and also the ministries in the case of the Economic Reform. In turning to production associations, it appears that the leadership has given up the view that by creating the appropriate environment (better success indicators, better prices, less misdirection by central management), enterprise management could be counted on to get things right. The production associations have virtually eliminated enterprise management, as it had operated for 40 years, as a significant level of economic decision making.

The former enterprise manager now occupies a position that is rather like a glorified version of what in the past was the position of shop chief. The new approach is to take responsibility out of the hands of the enterprise managers and to relocate it at a level that is very much like the central management of the past. The production associations may be regarded as microministries in the sense that they enjoy powers over the former enterprises similar to those formerly enjoyed by ministries over enterprises. They have also acquired some powers that formerly were lodged with the ministries.

With respect to the ministries, the reform is a measure of decentralization.[3] But with respect to the enterprise, it is a measure of recentralization. It is also a vote of confidence in the superiority of "administrative levers" over "economic levers." Before this reform, the strategy was to find ways of inducing enterprise managers to behave by creating the proper conditions for them to behave. Now they are to behave because they have a new superior authority that tells them what to do; an authority not as remote as the ministry and with a span of control not as wide as a ministry, so that it is in a much stronger position to be informed and to impose compliance.

This interpretation of the analysis that underlay the reform applies both to the general problem of enterprise decision making and to the specific problem of technological progress. With respect to the former, producer enterprise A will produce and deliver precisely the outputs required by user enterprise B because they both have the same boss whose career is on the line and who knows the capacity and needs of both enterprises. With respect to technological progress, producer enterprise A will quickly put into production a new product developed by the R & D Institute because, again, they have the same boss, who might, in fact, have been the former director of the institute when it was an independent ministry organization. Nor will the Institute lose interest in the practical success of the product innovation once it has gone into production, as in the past, because the general director of the association is responsible for both units.

Thus the production-association reform is a break with the past. It reflects the continued concern with the problem that had been the major concern in the past—enterprise-level decision making. But it adds a major new concern—the promotion of technological progress. Moreover, the solution chosen reflects a change in the strategy that guided past reforms. Instead of seeking ways of improving the quality of decentralized decision making, it has withdrawn decision-making authority from enterprise management and relocated it at a more central level.

The Comprehensive Planning Decree of 1979 The reforms in the management system just discussed were widely heralded and have been deemed important enough to have acquired names of their own. It is interesting to note that while other changes in the planning system have proceeded throughout the post-Stalin era, history has judged none of them significant enough to have merited a name of its own. It is possible that the planning decree of 1979[4] will pass on in anonymity like the others. I have given it a name not because I judge it to be of name-deserving proportions but because a review of the past would be incomplete without some notice of the changes in the planning system, and the most recent one is the appropriate candidate.

The decree may be regarded as a continuation and extension of a series of changes in the planning system that have been proceeding for some time rather than as a break with the past or as the opening of a new direction. I suggest the term *comprehensive* because it roughly captures the sense of those changes. First, the planning process now comprehends a longer spread of time; the 5-year plan rather than the annual plan is now officially designated as the fundamental plan, and it is to be based on a 20-year program of scientific–technical development and on a 10-year plan that sets forth the main directions of economic and social development. Second, the planning process now comprehends both branch and regional planning; all USSR ministry plans are to be submitted to review by the republic councils of ministers, and the latter are to present to Gosplan their plans for all their enterprises. Third, the decree mandates a more comprehensive set of balances than in the past; balances are to be employed in the 10-year main-directions plan and in the 5-year plan; interbranch balances are to be used for major products; and regional balances are to be used for the production and distribution of major products.[5]

Two problems can be identified as those with which the system's governors sought to deal in the planning decree. One is the promotion of technological progress. The incorporation of 10-year and 20-year plans into the current planning process is intended to build into current planning a basis of consistency with the long lead times of technological advance; that is, to avoid current decisions that lock the economy into directions that may be inconsistent with the probable direction of future technological advance. The technique adopted is to require that current plan decisions be checked for consistency with longer-run structural choices that have already been made and with the forecasts of future technological developments.

The second problem is, once more, enterprise-level decision making. The reforms in the management system previously discussed were all directed at the problems that arise when managers have to make decisions. The necessity for managers to make decisions arises out of imperfections in the planning process; that is, with perfect planning there would be virtually no need at all for decisions to be made by enterprise managers. The system's governors must assume, however, that there will always be considerable scope for managerial discretion, either because the central plan cannot realistically provide for all possible detail, or because of errors in plans, or because of changes in plans. Accepting the inevitability of managerial discretion, the purpose of the management reforms was to improve the quality of those decisions. But the second string to that bow is the improvement of the planning system. The more comprehensive and detailed the plan, the smaller the volume of planning errors; and the less frequent the changes in the plan, the less the need to rely on managerial decision making.

The implication of this view of the relationship between planning reform and management reform is that planning is thought to be good and management bad. The less the discretion that needs to be given to management, the better. In this interpretation, the move toward increasing comprehensiveness of planning reflects the hope that eventually everything can be balanced in advance so that management can be reduced solely to carrying out preplanned instructions. On the face of it, there can be no quarrel with the notion that in a planned economy, plans should be as specific as possible. But that does not necessarily mean that they must be comprehensive. The alternative view is that there may be some optimal level of comprehensiveness beyond which the marginal benefit of more detailed planning diminishes and that of decentralized managerial solutions increases. It is true that as planning techniques improve, the optimal level may involve greater detail. The extension of comprehensiveness does not, therefore, necessarily mean that the leadership is shifting the balance deliberately. But it appears to me that the push is in that direction. Better planning continues to be thought of as a way of decreasing the inefficiency associated with an obdurate management.

Some Lessons of History I make no claim that mine is the only story that a brief review of recent economic reforms can tell. Had a different list of reforms been selected for examination or had another analyst considered the same reforms with a different eye, the story may be different. I trust, however, that this account is a plausible one and serves as a useful prelude to an inquiry into the possible shapes of the future.

The first conclusion is that the reforms give no evidence of a disposition to doubt the efficacy of the system of central planning as the basis of the economic mechanism. On the contrary, the 1979 Planning Decree affirms the intention to strengthen the planning system by improving the quality of the national plans. In this respect, the efforts of the last several decades have probably been successful. The technical equipment now available to planners, including electronic data-processing equipment and mathematical-modelling techniques for checking the consistency of plans, have no doubt been helpful. We may expect that the plan-making process will continue to improve in the future, although the growing complexity of the economy increases the size of the task from plan to plan. We may also expect that each 5-year plan of the future will, like the most recent, be preceded by a decree incorporating in the forthcoming plan a series of newer techniques that have been in the process of experimentation and are ready for adoption.

The second conclusion is that the problem of management has been less tractable than that of planning, and that there have not been significant advances in improving its quality. In principle, planning and management should be expected to complement each other; planners draw up the plans and managers see to their execution. In fact, the relation appears to be viewed by the system's governors as one of tension. Planning is the friend while management is the enemy. Evidence of inefficiency is most often explained as the consequence of bungling or mismanagement. Brezhnev expressed what is probably the general view of politicians when he laid the blame for a series of excesses at the feet of people who "no matter how much you talk to them, no matter how much you appeal to their conscience and their sense of duty and responsibility, nothing helps."[6]

To see the problem as one of poorly trained or venal people is to close one's eyes to possible defects of the system itself. It obscures the fundamental problem: that central planning, which must inevitably be imperfect, makes extremely difficult demands upon management. The central managers—the ministries—are responsible for the execution of a detailed set of targets, all of which cannot be fulfilled in the normal course of events. There is no "bottom line," although gross output comes close to serving as the ultimate criterion. Their own record of performance depends on that of hundreds of enterprise (or production-association) managers, who must also constantly make a variety of decisions for which there is no clear guide in the plans. Hence, alongside the tension between planners and managers, the system's governors have also to contend with the tension between ministries and enterprises. Most of the reforms have attempted to come to grips with the latter problem. In the Territorial Reorganization, it was decided to solve the problem by abolishing the ministries. In the Production-Association reform, it was decided to abolish the enterprises instead. It is difficult to foresee any clear basis for a more effective distribution of authority between the two levels in the context of central planning.

Finally, the history of the recent reforms reflects the growing appreciation of the importance of technological progress. The reforms of the 1950s and 1960s concentrated on the coordination of management and planning and on the increase in static efficiency. But in the more recent reforms, technological progress has been at the forefront of the objectives. The change in emphasis coincides with the gradual acceptance of the view that the decline in the growth rate reflects a fundamental change in economic conditions, which is reflected in the formulation of a change from "extensive" to "intensive" growth. How to adapt the system of planning and management to the new goal of promoting technological progress is likely to be the central concern of those who bear the responsibility for the economic reforms of the future.

The Conservative Model

The status quo rarely has passionate supporters. The passions are normally on the side of change. Support for the status quo is usually based on a lack of conviction that the untried alternatives will produce a better future than the present. That is likely to be the case if the Conservative Model is chosen as the basis of the future system of planning and management in the USSR. It is doubtful that many people, even among the system's governors, regard the present structure as having great merit in its own right. That was not the case two decades ago. At that time, Soviet economists certainly, and political leaders probably, looked over the world of economic systems and pronounced their own as exceptionally good. Today, the system may still command strong support, but very likely in the Churchillian vein, as a rather bad system, "except for all the others."

The Conservative Model retains all the basic structural features of the present system, but it should not be thought of as unchanging in form. Judging from the recent history of reforms, we should expect repeated efforts in the future to try new ways of dealing with old problems. Certainly, the planning system will be continually changed by the incorporation of new techniques of central planning. What will remain unchanged is the commitment to central planning as the basis of the economic mechanism. Beyond that, each analyst is free to forecast efforts to change whatever is his own favorite source of inefficiency in the economy. My own guess is that many of the production associations will be dismantled after a period of time in favor of a system containing a broader mix of large and small enterprises. The reason for this guess is that the size structure of enterprises in the USSR, even before the production associations, was strongly skewed toward large enterprises compared to the size structure in the technologically advanced capitalist countries.[7] With respect to efficiency and certainly to innovation, there must be some range of activities in which there are diseconomies of scale. There are also likely to be further changes in such perennials as the success indicators of enterprise management. The indicator newly introduced in the July 1979 planning decree—normative net output— may well prove to be exceedingly costly to administer and is likely to bias decisions excessively in favor of labor-intensive choices in a period of tight labor supply. There may be some renewed flirtation with profit as a more general success indicator, but the pathological antagonism to the appropriation by enterprises of unearned economic rents will stand in the way; large profits in particular seem to constitute prima facie evidence that they were unearned, probably as a consequence of favorable price changes. New experiments in the use of contractual relations may be tried and also new Shchekino-type efforts to reallocate labor among enterprises by various incentive devices. The recent sharp increase in the price of gasoline suggests that price policy may be called upon more often to ration scarce commodities. Price revisions every few years will continue to keep relative prices from diverging excessively from average branch costs, and there may be some futher incorporation of scarcity pricing into the price structure. Extrapolating from the past, planning may become more detailed, and with the growth of electronic data-processing capacity, the number of balances is likely to increase; however, there may be a reaction at some point because of the mounting complexity of the plan-making process and a return to more aggregated planning.

Certainly, there will be new measures designed to promote technological progress and the quality of production. Some would attempt to make use of "economic levers" through new forms of incentive payments. But most will consist of "administrative measures"; changing the structure of authority, holding more people responsible for the completion of assigned tasks, penalties for not fulfilling quality assignments.

To accept the Conservative Model is to give up the goal of attaining the technological level of the leading industrial countries. For I take it as fairly well established that whatever the merits of the Soviet economic mechanism, the promotion of technological advance is not one of them. But that is an outcome with which the Soviet leadership ought to be able to live. There is no reason why the USSR cannot maintain a position that lags permanently behind that of the technological leaders in world industry by, say, an average of about 5 years. There would be some loss in productivity because of delayed innovation, but that loss would be offset to some degree by savings in research and development expenditures as well as in the costs of learning-by-doing that the country pioneering in any new development must bear. It would be a reasonable strategy for the Soviets to wait until each new major breakthrough is announced elsewhere and then to proceed to develop their own version on the basis of whatever information can be perused, purchased, or purloined. For it is an axiom in the R&D community that the most valuable piece of information in technological advance is the information that a certain result has been successfully accomplished by somebody. The strategy of waiting until the results have been accomplished elsewhere is not only cost-saving but is also appealing to R&D people operating in a risk-averse bureaucratic structure. Moreover, the Soviets have shown that technological excellence can be maintained in a few priority areas where these are deemed crucial for defense or other national purposes.

Taking the foregoing as the essence of the Conservative Model, the question here is, What are the outcomes that can be expected from the adoption of that model? Since the model involves no significant changes from the past, the past can serve as a guide to the economic outcomes to be expected in the future. There is little reason to expect any discontinuous increase either in static efficiency or in the rate of growth. None of the major reforms of the past has succeeded in doing what their initiators must have devoutly hoped for—attaining a quantum leap in efficiency. Indeed, the term *reform* has disappeared from the public discussion and has been replaced by the expression "improving the operation of the economic mechanism."

The evaporation of the spirit of reform may reflect the view that the system of central planning and management has now reached the practical limit of its perfectability. An economic system is like a technological innovation. When first invented, a steam engine or an internal-combustion machine represents a major advance over its predecessor, but it is a very inefficient mechanism in terms of its own potential. In the course of time, its efficiency increases, very rapidly at first and more slowly thereafter, with successive waves of "reforms" or "improvements." Eventually, it attains a degree of efficiency that can be regarded as the effective maximum that is realistically attainable within the limits of its basic conception; there is only so much one can expect to get out of a machine the basic conception of which is a piston in a cylinder. It is rather like a Kuhnian paradigm in the development of scientific theory; not much more can be expected to happen until someone breaks out of the paradigm with a very different conception of how power may be generated.

That vision may be applied to the invention of central economic planning as an economic mechanism by the Soviet leadership of the 1930s. In the course of time, it became a more efficient mechanism than it was when first introduced. But like all inventions, the possibilities of improvement within the basic paradigm might have been largely exhausted by the 1960s. It should be noted that the economic mechanism was designed in a period in which the strategy of economic progress consisted of what was later described as "extensive growth." It is perhaps still a reasonably successful model for that purpose. The problem is that the conditions within which the economy operates today are not such as to generate high rates of extensive growth. Three percent per year more or less may be the most that can be expected of an economy designed according to that model. It is in that sense that the economy may be doing as well as can be expected under that economic mechanism.

It is entirely possible, of course, that this judgement may be too pessimistic. To assert that there are few opportunities for further improvement is to imply, paradoxically, that the economy is highly efficient, in the sense of operating close to its production-possibilities frontier as defined by the existing economic structure. A future government may yet find ways of extending that frontier. Some such ways have been proposed by Western analysts: the creation of enterprises specializing in production for export, correcting those relative prices that create perverse incentives in agriculture, providing greater autonomy for small-scale production units within the collective farm. Without abandoning the Conservative Model, its limits may be extended by adopting some of the features of the other models discussed shortly. While a bold package of such measures may prove that the Conservative Model contains greater potential than its recent record reveals, the history of the reforms just sketched does not offer great encouragement. Individual changes in prices and organizational structures that make good sense in themselves have not produced the desired results because they clashed with the imperatives imposed by the dominating structures of central planning and management.

Suppose, then, that the Conservative Model does not in fact produce better results than those forecast on the basis of the experience of the recent past. The question is whether the leadership can continue to be satisfied with it; that is, to turn to no alternative model but simply to muddle through with only small variations on old themes. I think they can, on one condition—that the decline in the growth rate decelerate and eventually stabilize. A constant rate of growth, even if very low, would constitute a chronic condition that does not ordinarily lead to disruption. It is the acute problems, such as those encountered with continuous decline, that must ultimately lead to disruption. With a chronically low but stable growth rate, the century could end with a whimper. Otherwise it may end with a bang.

We cannot judge what the minimally sustainable growth rate is—3, or 2, or 1% per capita. However, it is safe to say that it is likely to depend primarily on the consumption level. A threshold level of consumption may be defined, in political terms, as the level below which dissatisfaction would result in outburts of disorder that would strain the authorities' instruments of political control. It would be an error for the leadership to believe, however, that there is no danger so long as consumption levels exceeded that political threshold. For there is another threshold at which the economy would begin to suffer from the erosion of incentives. If that incentives threshold, which must be higher than the political threshold, were not maintained, then it will prove to be impossible to maintain even that low level of stable growth. Output and consumption would decline reciprocally until the political threshold were reached, and then the whimper will turn into a bang. Hence, the key to the question of whether slow growth will turn from chronic to acute will depend on whether the rate of growth can be stabilized at a level sufficiently high to maintain consumption above the incentive threshold.

The Soviet leadership may possibly have some rough notion of the range within which the incentive threshold lies, but outside analysts can do little more than guess. My own guess is about the same as the judgement of Gertrude Schroeder that a steady increase in per capita consumption of 1–2% per year would "provide consumers with a sense of forward motion."[8] Under the baseline projection of SOVMOD, GNP would grow at 3.2% and consumption per capita at 2%.[9] With a bit of luck, that outcome should keep the economy above the incentives threshold. Under the low-productivity scenario, however, GNP grows at 2.3% and consumption per capita at only 0.7%.[10] At that rate, it is conceivable that the erosion of incentives would preclude the stabilization of the growth rate, and consumption may decline to the perilous level of the political threshold.

There is a fair chance that the economy can stabilize at the levels of the baseline projection of Bond and Levine. The long period of declining growth may presage continued decline in the future, but it need not. It may signify, instead, that the economy has been readjusting from the high growth rates of the past to low but stable growth rates in the future. In that case, poor performance in static efficiency or in technological progress need not compel the abandonment of the Conservative Model so long as consumption does not fall below the incentive threshold.

The Reactionary Model

The political characteristics of a neo-Stalinist reaction are not difficult to portray. One thinks first of a restoration of the power of the secret police, perhaps not quite to the level of the Stalinist terror but well beyond the present level. Contacts with capitalist countries would be greatly reduced, the iron curtain reimposed, a xenophobic nationalism reinstituted, and ideological, political, and social discipline generally tightened.

If one asks, however, what changes would have to be made to return to a Stalin-like economic system, the answer is not self-evident. The exercise is a reminder that, however great the changes in Soviet political life since Stalin, the essentials of the economic system have not been that greatly changed. The inclination of the leadership under the Reactionary Model is toward the restoration of discipline and order, and they will view their mission as the reassertion of strong central control. But they will find that the clock has moved so little in the system of planning and management that it hardly needs to be turned back very much.

In the organization of central planning, while the political leaders under the Reactionary Model may harbor a Stalinist contempt for theoretical economics, the practical value of "optimal planning" would overcome the aversion, and it would elicit strong support. For it promises a possibility of centralization of decision making and control far beyond anything dreamed of in Stalin's time. It is, in the words of a close student of the subject, an ideal instrument for an "autocratic political mechanism."[11] However, the possibility of introducing that form of plan making is still too remote to be of use in the near future. Short of that, it is difficult to imagine that the leaders of the Reactionary economy could contrive ways of extending the scope of central planning that are not already contained or implicit in the 1979 planning decree.

With respect to the management system, because the 1965 Economic Reform has been so greatly modified, there are few changes that will be seen as essential for the restoration of central control. No great purpose would be served by eliminating the capital charge or restoring *val* as the dominant success indicator. Those small ways in which the present-day enterprise manager is less accountable to the center than in the past are not likely to be eliminated. What may be changed is the spread of *khozraschet* (financing an organization's expenditures out of its own revenues) to the agencies of central management—ministries and chief administrations. To the extent that centralization is the desideratum, the degree of independence that *khozraschet* would provide for these units would probably be regarded as unacceptable. The inclination would more likely be to proceed with the creation of the superministries that have been discussed from time to time. Similarly, to the extent that contract-financed production has replaced planned production, for example in the financing of R&D organizations, that practice may well be ended.

Another of the post-Stalin moves toward decentralization was the establishment of the wholesale-trade program. That measure started out as the bold idea of offering an alternative to the "material–technical supply" system. The program for a large network of well-stocked stores where enterprises could purchase small quantities of whatever was needed never did materialize. What evolved instead was a system of warehouse supply, differing from the Stalinist system only in that it is managed by the hierarchy of *Gossnab* rather than by the ministries' own supply organizations. It is difficult to imagine that a neo-Stalinist leadership would find it a matter of some importance to abolish *Gossnab* and turn its functions back to the ministries. *Gossnab* may, in fact, be regarded as the more centralized supply system, even though its operating units are territorially based.

The production associations would very likely find favor with the Reactionary leadership, resembling as they do the vast scale of enterprise that was characteristic of Stalin's time. One of the virtues of that organizational form is that it reduces the task of central planning by "internalizing" within the superenterprise a certain number of transactions that were formerly interenterprise transactions and therefore the responsibility of the central planners. The more self-contained the producing unit, the simpler the job of the planners. There has been a growing trend toward self-containment in recent years that merits more attention than it has received. Many enterprises, for example, have begun to develop their own subsidiary farms to provide produce for their own workers.[12] That development is an extension of a very old practice by management of seeking independence of the uncertain supply system by the practice of "universalism," or the in-house production of as much of their inputs as they can manage. That practice has been criticized in the past, and the present Conservative leadership has taken a dim view of it. In the aforementioned speech, Brezhnev was sharply critical of that he described as "a recent widespread practice for local agencies to recruit people from enterprises and to do various kinds of work—help with the harvest, work in procurement organizations, on construction jobs, on beautification projects and so forth." A Reactionary leadership, however, may be less concerned with the contraction in the division of labor and the loss of the economies of specialization that this "new feudalism" entails. It may be inclined to support large universalist enterprises that encompass a variety of activities and that relieve the burden on the central planners.

Thus, planning and management will be somewhat more centralized under the Reactionary Model than under the Conservative, but the difference in that respect cannot be very large. The major differences between the two models will be found not in organizational forms but in policies. High on the list would be a policy of tightening labor discipline. One may envision a return to the severe laws of the late 1930s, making it illegal to leave one's job without authorization and providing criminal penalties for such violations as lateness to work, unauthorized absence from the job, and drunkenness. There may also be a disposition to return to the high-investment growth strategy that was associated with the rapid-growth years of the post-war period, although that would require a disavowal of the intensive-growth views that have prevailed subsequently. The corollary of a high-investment strategy would be a return to a policy of slow growth of consumption, or even possibly a decline. That would very likely be a subject of dispute even among supporters of a Reactionary Model on a variety of grounds. First, the popular hostility it would arouse would challenge even the greatly tightened political controls. Second, there would be serious doubts about the efficacy of that strategy at this time in history. Third, since agriculture is no longer the predominant sector of origin of national income, the growth-rate gains from the suppression of the consumption of the agricultural population would no longer be so great as they were thought to be in the past. However, the recent trend toward the virtual transformation of the collective farms into state farms may be accelerated rather than reversed on the assumption that the collective farm had been an enforced compromise and the state farm is more consistent with a neo-Stalinist structure.

Since a neo-Stalinist model implies the existence of a neo-Stalin, the leadership must be presumed to possess the power to carry through the changes that it finds necessary. One is a strong drive against "speculators" and the second economy. Another is a purge of the managerial elite, both at the central and at the enterprise level. The Stalin period was characterized by rapid upward mobility of managers that, while purchased at some cost, nevertheless conveyed certain clear benefits: in weeding out dead wood, in cementing the loyalty of the new managers, in lowering their average age, and in generating an unusual level of effort (though perhaps at a cost in the form of increased risk aversion). One may guess that the long tenure enjoyed by the present managerial corps has contributed to a decline in its quality. It is interesting to note, in this context, that in present-day China, the virtual lifetime tenure of the party and management elite has come under increasing criticism, and Vice Premier Deng and his supporters seem determined to end that practice. A new and secure Soviet leadership may very likely see things the same way, though perhaps not with respect to themselves.

Finally, we are likely under this model to see a return to a policy of relative autarky in an effort to reduce the volume of contacts with the West. Some level of import of advanced foreign technology would be maintained, but the new regime is likely to place a greater weight on the ideological costs of involvement with the West and to assign less value to its economic benefits than the Khrushchev-Brezhnev governments.

In evaluating the prospective economic performance of the USSR under the Reactionary Model, one tends to regard it as a mere romantic nostalgia for a simpler and in some ways better age that never really was and that could not be successfully restored under present-day conditions. But it would be an error to dismiss it entirely, for it may well bring some benefits of a purely economic kind.

For one thing, it may offer some short-run gains in the form of freeing up of the "hidden reserves" that are so often the object of special campaigns. A few well-publicized trials and convictions may lead to the disgorging of excess inventories and a scaling-down of the diversion of resources from public to private uses. The tempo of production is likely to be sped up and labor discipline tightened generally. It would not be surprising if the change were followed for a time by a significant rise in productivity and output.

If the economy is indeed characterized by a large degree of underemployment in the form of excess numbers of workers whose marginal productivity is very low, as many Soviet economists claim to be the case, the tightening of political controls in a time of labor shortage may make it possible to launch an effective drive to reallocate labor to more productive uses. One can imagine a campaign in which every enterprise would be obliged to deliver a quota of young workers to be relocated to the labor-short areas in the East, much as the collective farms once delivered their quotas for the staffing of new industrial enterprises. Whatever form it finally takes, the neo-Stalinist regime would very likely regard the reallocation of labor as one of its prime objectives, and that may be expected to have a favorable impact on economic performance.

In the longer run, it is possible that the recentralization of economic activity may also produce some economic gains. The view is sometimes expressed that the present-day Soviet economy is the worst of possible worlds. Change has not proceeded far enough to yield the benefits of genuine decentralized markets, yet the central-planning and management system has given up control of a variety of functions in the interest of decentralization. The system, according to this view, is neither fish nor fowl and enjoys neither the advantages of true markets nor of full central planning. Either alternative would be better than the particular mixed economy that has evolved out of the Khrushchev–Brezhnev regimes.[13]

In evaluating this point of view, one may question, as we have, whether the reforms of the post-Stalin years constitute a significant degree of decentralization. Nevertheless, there may be merit in the argument that many of the forms of decentralization have brought little genuine benefit. An instructive case is the conversion of the R&D institutes from budget financing to contract financing, a change that was introduced for the purpose of increasing the client's interest in and power over the work produced by the institutes. The instrument of a contract is crucial to the operation of a market economy, and it may seem that the replacement of administrative orders by contracts in the Soviet economy is a measure of market-like decentralization. However, the contexts are so different that it is an error to associate the word *contract* with any of the real functions played by that instrument in a decentralized economy. For one thing, the client regards the payment for the services as made with "the government's money"; if it is in the enterprise plan, financing is provided for it in the plan. Second, the contractor's income is limited by the conditions of the incentive structure. Regardless of how profitable the innovation is, the size of the reward is stipulated in the statutory incentive schedule, and the balance of profit is simply appropriated by the ministry of Finance as a "free remainder." It would be an exaggeration to say that there is no difference at all between a management system in which the R&D institute operates under a plan and reports to an official in the Ministry and one in which it operates on the basis of contracts entered into with enterprises. But the nature of the dependence of a market-economy firm on its contracts and that of a Soviet firm on its contracts are of different orders of magnitude. In that sense, this act of formal decentralization, like so many others, is more a matter of detail than of critical importance in the decision-making process.

Plan making should proceed under the Reactionary Model in much the same manner as under the Conservative Model. Nor is there any reason why, with intelligent administration, innovation should not proceed as well under a Reactionary Model as it does at present. The same material-incentive system would be employed as at present, and the prestige of science would be undiminished. Presumably, the tightening of political and ideological controls would not extend to the extremes of Stalinist terror nor to Lysenko-like constraints on science. The major loss perhaps would be that which would result from the decreased level of scientific contact with the more advanced countries, including very likely some decrease in the import of advanced technology. But if the leadership should accept realistically the policy of the permanent technological lag, the loss would not be regarded as very large. Only as long as the objective is to overtake and surpass the West in technological attainment would the decrease in scientific contact be of major significance.

The prospects for agricultural performance are probably much poorer under this model. The continued transformation of the collectives into state farms will satisfy some aspirations for ideological purity, but it is not likely to reverse what comes through the literature as the widespread demoralization of the agricultural labor force. Restrictions on private subsidiary agriculture are likely to be tightened, with a further loss in agricultural output. Agriculture may well be the sector in which the Reactionary Model will encounter its major failures.

I conclude that, with the exception of agriculture, the economy may exhibit some sharp short-run gains relative to the recent past. It is also entirely possible that in the longer run it could also outperform the Conservative Model, particularly if it is successful in tightening labor discipline and in massively reallocating labor among jobs. However, a major condition is that it avoid the excesses of Stalin, for Stalin was the worst part of Stalinism. An intelligent Reactionary leadership may well squeeze more out of the economy than the cautious and compromising leadership of the recent decades.

The Radical Model

If the Reactionary extreme is the recentralization of planning and management, the Radical extreme must entail the decentralization of planning and management. The characteristics of the model may be taken from the Hungarian experience. One may think of it simply as central planning without directive targets to enterprises. But that innocent-sounding formulation involves more than a simple modification of the centrally planned economy. For without the power to assign directive targets to enterprises, much of the fabric of central planning unravels. If enterprises cannot be required to produce according to directives, they cannot be held responsible for the delivery of specified intermediate materials and supplies, and the time-honored system of material–technical supply must be largely abandoned. In the absence of directive targets, the criteria for evaluating enterprise performance must be modified, and it is then difficult to imagine any criterion other than some suitably modified form of profit. But if profit is to serve as the dominant criterion of performance, it will become the effective objective function for management, and it is then necessary to assure that the prices and costs in terms of which decisions are made are reasonably reflective of marginal social benefits and costs. That must entail the abandonment of 40 years of centralized administration of average-cost-plus-normal-profit pricing. Similar changes would have to be introduced in the management of the labor market, the financial system, and in other parts of the economy.

Party and government control of the economy would very likely continue to be maintained in several areas. First, most investment, particularly investment in social overhead and in new plant and equipment, would continue to be a central function, and it would become the most powerful instrument for determining both the rate of investment and the direction of growth. Investment would be financed by taxation on profits and personal income and also on the basis of a capital charge and depreciation allowance. That is, the state would continue to own all productive assets and would require a return on them from the collectives that hold them in trust. Incentives would be derived from some profit-sharing plan.

Second, the state would continue to maintain an interest in prices, primarily in order to prevent excessive use of market power to maintain monopoly prices. To the extent that the objective of state policy would be to trade some efficiency for equity or for some other social goal, the option of price regulation would be maintained for that purpose as well. The legitimacy of selective state price control would be based not only on state power in general but on the state ownership of the assets of enterprises. That is, the state continues not only to own the enterprise but to exercise national sovereignty.

Third, it is safe to say that the Soviet leadership will have very little interest in supporting self-management or other forms of worker control. The more delicate problem is the policy to be taken toward the possible increase in involuntary unemployment.

Fourth, income taxation (or perhaps consumption taxation, which would make more sense in an investment-conscious economy) would be relied upon to regulate income distribution. Commodity taxation could be employed for financing public expenditures, but it could not be used to regulate the powerful new entrepreneurial forces that (one would hope) would arise and would tend to widen the income distribution. For if the Radical Model succeeds in generating vigorous entrepreneurship, there will be large incomes to be earned in eliminating disequilibria in the centrally planned economy. The function of eliminating disequilibria has been one of the main economic responsibilities of the party in the past.[14] The income-distribution problems will be particularly pressing during the transition period because of the large disequilibria inherited from the period of central planning that have not yet been diminished by market forces.

Turning to the question of how the Soviet economy may fare under the Radical Model, one must begin with such hard evidence as we have on that type of system operating in another country. The form of radical decentralization that the Soviets are most likely to draw upon is the New Economic Mechanism introduced in Hungary in 1968. One conclusion is clear; Hungary has produced no economic miracle. When the East European countries are ranked by order of their long-term growth rates, Hungary comes at about the center of the group behind such less-developed countries as Romania and Bulgaria, as one would expect.[15] Nor has that relative position changed, for while Hungary's growth rate increased in the years following the 1968 reform, so did that of most of the other countries that retained their central-planning systems.[16] Per capita consumption increased during 1970–1975, but that was also the case in Romania during the same period. It is true, however, that Hungary was particularly hard hit by adverse changes in its markets abroad and suffered from a number of costly policy errors while learning to control the new economic mechanism. Under the circumstances, Portes concludes, Hungary probably did better than it would have done under the old central-planning system.

One suspects that the statistical record may have missed something important. Most knowledgeable observers, including Hungarian economists who tend to be among the most severe critics of their own economy, report that without question there has been a considerable improvement in the quality of goods and services generally. The usual formulation is that the growth-rate performance has not been distinctive, *but* the quality of goods and services has increased greatly. An alternative formulation may be that the quality of goods and services has increased greatly, *but* the growth-rate performance has not been distinctive. If a significant quality change can be attributed to the system change, that is no mean claim. Perhaps the judicious conclusion is that the Hungarian economy performs generally better under the new mechanism but not by an order of magnitude. Certainly one hears no Hungarian pining for the good old days.

Hungary is no Japan. But then again the USSR is no Hungary, and one must entertain the possibility that the new economic mechanism in the USSR may perform better or worse than in Hungary. In one major respect, the USSR is like Hungary. The Hungarian reform has been limited by a set of political considerations, which include a commitment to extensive job security and to strict limitations on income differentiation.[17] Those same considerations are likely to prevail in the USSR and to limit the effectiveness of the reform in the same ways. The USSR has one potential advantage in the size of the domestic market, which could yield some of the benefits of interenterprise competition, but job-security and income-differentiation concerns could spill the wind out of the sails of competition. There is no cogent reason for expecting the USSR to perform better under this type of decentralization than Hungary.

There is one reason, however, why the USSR may be expected to perform worse. Western analysts have been struck by the vigor with which the patterns of the former centrally planned system reasserted themselves under the new Hungarian decentralized system. Hungary, however, had lived under central planning for only two decades. The managers, politicans, and economists who engineered the reform of 1968 had lived the first 30-odd years of their lives in a market economy. They found no mystery in a system in which no one tells the enterprise what it should produce and from whom it is to obtain its supplies. Many, we may also suppose, had conceived a certain fondness for aspects of that kind of economic arrangement, socialists though they are. In the USSR, by contrast, hardly a soul is now alive who remembers such a system. The notion that somehow the "right" amount of coal can be produced even though no one tells the coal mines how much to produce is not an idea that is easily grasped if one has not lived it. I can cite two pieces of evidence for this view. One is a recent study by The International Communications Agency (ICA) on Soviet perceptions of the United States, based on interviews with Americans who have had close associations with Soviet officials at high levels of authority. The study reports that "Soviets who study the U.S. have long assumed that hidden somewhere in the economic system is the key to American success, and that there must be a planning mechanism for the American private sector." Even Soviet experts on American management and industry "seem puzzled that the private sector has no apparent planning center. They know that the system works, but they are puzzled how."[18] The second piece of evidence is the observation by a prominent émigré authority that most Soviet economists sincerely believe the price mechanism to be only a temporary necessity.[19] While there is a sophisticated minority who have learned to comprehend the nature of general-equilibrium decentralized systems, they are not the ones who will be managing the government and economy. The "legacies" of the centrally planned period that Neuberger once identified in the case of Yugoslavia have been found to operate in the Hungarian economy as well.[20] The legacies of a half-century of central planning must be expected to be particularly restrictive. Kenneth Boulding once remarked that the bus from capitalism to socialism runs only during the early stage of capitalism. If a nation misses the bus, capitalism is there to stay. The same may be said of the bus from central planning to socialist markets. The Hungarians caught it in time, but central planning has endured so long in the USSR that the Soviets might have missed the bus.

There are two aspects to the legacies that one structure bequeaths to another. The first may be described as the human-capital aspect. In moving from one technology to another, while new capital is being built up in the form of knowledge and experience in the operation of the new technology, old capital is being lost as knowledge and experience of the old technology disappears. That process applies to social as well as physical technology. There is a vast stock of human capital that supports the operation of a decentralized economy that is lost after a few generations of not having been learned and used.

The second feature of the legacy is the large number of points in the old system that are in disequilibrium with respect to the requirements of the new system. I refer to the structure of productive capacity relative to the structure of the demand for output under the new system and similarly with the structure of wages and prices. Because of supply inelasticities, many of those disequilibria are likely to be large and to endure for relatively long periods of time, making for potentially large rental incomes. It is doubtful that the market processes under the new system could readily close those disequilibria without the emergence of very large inequities. After a half-century of central planning, those disequilibria in the USSR are likely to be of massive dimensions and, therefore, a source of a great deal of social tension and economic strain.

For these reasons, the Radical Model established in the USSR may not secure even that modest improvement in economic performance that it secured in Hungary. And yet there could hardly fail to be some gains in the quality of goods and services, similar to that reported in Hungary. The requirement that a producing unit be obliged to decide what to produce by consulting potential purchasers rather than by instructions from the ministry—which is the heart of the model—cannot fail to discipline management to respond actively to demand, providing that demand is not in excess. To the extent that it is politically difficult in socialist countries (and increasingly in capitalist) to permit the market to determine the penalties for failure, the tightness of that discipline is attenuated, but it is likely to prevail to a greater extent than under the central planning of output. Similarly, the enterprise as purchaser—now both obliged to and permitted to seek out its own sources of supply—is likely to assign a higher place to cost considerations in its calculations. These observations apply also to the quality of innovation. If the decision to introduce a new process or product is genuinely that of the enterprise, it cannot fail to be more resistant than in the past to pressures to adopt inferior work produced by the R&D centers and more inclined to seek out and introduce genuinely superior innovations. Again, to the extent that the politics of distributional equity cut into the rewards for risk taking, the beneficial effect of the Radical Model on innovation will be attenuated.

Perhaps that is as far as speculation should be permitted to range. My judgement is that the USSR under the Radical Model would experience some benefit in the quality of its goods and services and in the rate and quality of technological innovation but to a degree not quite equal to the modest gain experienced by Hungary.

The Liberal Model

I call the Radical Model by that name because it involves the total abandonment of directive target planning. From the present Soviet perspective, it is difficult to get more radical than that without being downright revolutionary. This last model is properly called Liberal because it conserves the traditional planning methods for most of the economy while liberalizing the present restrictions on private initiative.

It may also be called a neo-NEP model. Like that first great reform, it would come as a response to mounting economic difficulties. In the present case, those difficulties are not nearly as critical as they were at that time, but then neither is the scope of this reform as extensive as the earlier one. The heart of this reform, however, is the same as that of the other: the withdrawal of the socialized central-planning sector to the "commanding heights" of the economy. This time, however, the "commanding heights" comprise the overwhelming portion of the whole economy. Its boundaries may be demarcated by whatever limits the leadership finds politically and economically optimal. Within those boundaries, the economy operates as in the past with enterprise-directive targets, material–technical supply, centralized price administration, and the rest.

Outside of those boundaries, however, individuals or small groups would be encouraged to engage in any economic activity for private profit. They would be permitted to employ the labor of other people; wage rates would presumably not fall below the levels in the state sector, which remains an employer of last resort. The size of the private enterprises would be limited by law; initially, the limit would be fairly small, but if the reform were successful, the limit may be raised in the course of time. Enterprises would be permitted to own capital and to rent land from state agencies. They would be required to file periodic reports with the Central Statistical Agency and with the Ministry of Finance, on the basis of which taxes would be levied.

Neo-NEP enterprise would flourish in those activities in which smallness of scale has a comparative advantage. First is the consumer-service sector; food services, home-care services (clothing repair, washing and cleaning, plumbing, carpentry), and appliance repairs. Second is handicrafts and the manufacture of consumer goods in short supply (warm winter clothing) or of higher quality than is produced by state industry. Third is all manner of retailing services; small shops that purchase both state-produced and private-produced goods and compete with the retail services provided by government shops. Fourth is construction work by small *artels* for both private persons, cooperatives, and private and state enterprises. Fifth is special-order and job-lot production work for industry. Sixth is the supply of specialized services to industry, like R&D and technical consulting. The supply of goods and services to industry is particularly important because it would provide the flexibility that state planning is unable to offer. It may serve the function that small-scale enterprise serves in the modern oligopolistic capitalist economy. In Japan, for example, small-scale enterprises take up the slack of the business cycle and serve as valuable supplementary sources of supply for the large corporations. In the United States, the small enterprise is often the vehicle for innovations that, if successful, are subsequently bought up by larger firms. It is very likely, as Dr. Kvasha argued, that the absence of the small enterprise is a significant gap in Soviet organizational structure for the promotion of innovation and for industrial efficiency generally, a gap that must have widened since the Production Association reform.[21]

Several critical decisions would have to be made on how the neo-NEP sector would transact with the state sector. The first is the conditions under which private enterprise may purchase materials and equipment from state enterprises. One possible arrangement is that the physical-output targets of state enterprises be divided into two parts, the quantity to be delivered to other state enterprises and the quantity to be sold to private enterprise. The state deliveries would be handled by the planning agencies on the basis of the standard method of material balances, while the deliveries to private industry would be handled on the basis of market-demand analysis. The deliveries to private industry may thus serve as a useful balancing instrument for the central planners. Suppose, for example, that in the first trial balance of wood nails, the planners find that the state industry's demand for nails exceeds the supply proposed in the draft of the enterprise-production plans. Balance could then be attained simply by reducing the quantities that the planners had originally allocated to private enterprises and increasing the quantities allocated to state enterprises. The consequence could be that in that year, private industry would have to scramble for nails, develop substitutes, or reduce its output; or resort to bribery, to which we will return presently.

Second, a decision would have to be made on the prices of transactions between state and private enterprises (transactions between private enterprises and consumers need not be regulated). One approach would be to employ a purchase tax on sales by state to private enterprises. The former would receive the same price for its product regardless of whether it was sold to a state enterprise or to a private enterprise, but the private purchaser would have to pay the state tax. The purpose of the tax is partly to recapture any subsidies in the enterprise wholesale price and partly for the political purpose of strengthening the competitive position of state industry against private enterprise. That is to say, private enterprise would have to contribute more than a marginal gain to the economy in order to justify the ideological cost of tolerating it.

Third, the private retail network would provide a higher quality and larger range of many consumer goods and services than are available in the state stores. The higher prices may kindle popular hostility if it is felt that the private stores are "crowding out" the distribution of state-supplied goods. It is, therefore, important that the state continue to supply the traditional array of consumer goods and services at conventional prices. They would continue to be rationed by queuing, while those whose incomes or preferences are different could purchase at the private stores.[22] Similarly, the state sector must continue to act as employer of last resort, as it in fact does now. Workers would not, therefore, be at the mercy of their employers as in a capitalist system, for if they are dissatisfied with the pay or working conditions in the private sector, their alternative is not unemployment.

For evidence on how the economy would perform under this model, one may go back to the experience of the original NEP. But the more relevant evidence is that of the present-day second economy. The lesson that is usually drawn from that peculiar institution is that the centrally planned economy tends to spawn corruption. The story may be told differently, however. The lesson of the second economy is that within a socialist system, there is a vast store of initiative that cannot be tapped through the normal institutions of central planning. To benefit from that great productive potential, the economy must provide some institutional arrangement in which it can flourish in a socially responsible way. The introduction of a controlled domain of limited private enterprise would be such an arrangement.

It is possible to supply anecdotes on the kinds of initiative that burst forth even under the present inhibiting conditions. I shall mention only two that I have found particularly instructive. One is the case of the Fakel' firm. It was formed by a small group of engineers and scientists in Novosibirsk for the purpose of providing research, development, and innovation services to industry on a spare-time basis. Operating out of a few dormitory rooms, they solicited contracts from enterprises, drawing upon consultants' services as needed from specialists in the area. In about 4 years, they received 3.5 million rubles from 263 contracts, which they claim to have saved 35 million rubles for the economy, for which they received fees for themselves and their consultants. Their activities sparked an intense controversy, and they were finally forced to close down because of the objections of the State Bank and the Ministry of Finance.[23] The second is the case of the agronomist I. Khudenko, who was given a free hand in farming a tract of unused State Farm land. Operating under the form of an "extended link," Khudenko and a few colleagues ran the operation virtually as a private farm with phenomenal success. The controversy was more bitter in this case and Khudenko was found guilty on criminal charges and died in prison in 1974.[24] The vast store of tales like these testifies to the existence of a powerful innovative and productive potential in the nation that would flourish under the Liberal Model.

Like the Radical Model, the Liberal Model is that of a "mixed economy." There is a critical difference between the two, however. The Radical Model is a mix of central planning and markets, but all enterprises are state enterprises. What is radical about it is the abandonment of directive target-planning of enterprises, which is the heart of Soviet-type central planning. The Liberal Model retains the traditional form of central planning for most of the economy. It is a mix of state enterprises and private enterprises. I would not quarrel with the view that a mix of that kind may be regarded as more radical than the abandonment of directive planning. The main point is that the two models reflect different judgements about the pathology of the Soviet socialist economy. The Radical Model reflects the view of the major body of Western economic theory of socialism deriving from Lange and Lerner. That theory is preoccupied with issues of Pareto-efficiency and looks upon markets as a way of increasing the efficiency of socialist economies. The Liberal Model directs attention not to allocative efficiency but to something like Leibenstein's X-efficiency. It says, in effect, that the problem of centrally planned socialism is not in the central planning but in the socialism, or at least in the monopoly of socialist organizations. Concern with that issue, incidentally, can also be found in Lange in his remarks about the danger of the "bureaucratization" of economic life even in his market model of socialism.[25]

If the evidence on the Radical Model is the experience of Hungary, the relevant evidence on the Liberal Model, I have found to my surprise, is the experience of the GDR. That stern government permitted private craftsmen to operate throughout its history, and while there was some retrenchment in 1972 by the nationalization of the larger private firms, small-scale production continued to be given the "fullest support of the Socialist Unity Party and the state."[26] In their judicious comparison of the performance of the two Germanys, Gregory and Leptin credit the toleration of private enterprise in handicraft, retail trade, and agriculture in the GDR as one of the reasons for the success of the incentives policy of the country.[27] The dismal state of Polish agriculture may be regarded as evidence of the failure of private enterprise in a socialist context, but the stronger argument is that the fault in that case was the gross mismanagement of agriculture policy by the national leadership. For the USSR under the Liberal Model, the prospect for agriculture is not full-scale private farming after the Polish example, but perhaps a full commitment to the "link" as the basic unit of socialized agriculture. Like the "team" in the People's Republic of China, the link can be made sufficiently small to restore one of the central elements of X-efficiency, namely, the direct association of one's income with one's effort. Along with the elevation of the link, the spirit of the Liberal Model requires that the State give full support to private subsidiary agriculture. The link and the private plot would constitute the kind of "wager on the strong" with which an earlier Russian reformer—Peter Stolypin—had sought to release the peasant's initiative from the restraints of the commune.

Two issues that would have to be faced are corruption and income distribution. The first issue is not whether the Liberal Model will produce corruption. It certainly will. The question is rather whether corruption will be larger in scope and more detrimental than that which is presently generated under central planning. The answer is not at all self-evident. The large expansion in lawful opportunities for earning private incomes will increase the gains from the illegal diversion of state property to the private market. On the other hand, to the extent that the private sector succeeds in closing the disequilibrium gaps, the volume of bribes currently demanded by custodians of state-owned goods in short supply will be reduced. Moreover, the Liberal Model would convert into acceptable "red markets" some of the variously colored markets that Katsenelinboigen has detailed,[28] thus reducing the volume of corruption by defining as legal that which was formerly illegal. The principal objective of this model, however, is not simply to distribute already produced goods more efficiently but to stimulate the production of new goods and services that would not otherwise have been produced. Corruption in that kind of activity would have less undesirable social consequences than that which merely redistributes real income in favor of those who have access to goods and services in short supply. Hence, it is quite possible that corruption will be less of a problem under the Liberal Model than under the present system.

More than any of the other models, this one will test the limits of income inequality that the society is willing to tolerate. The period immediately following its adoption will generate the largest individual incomes because of the large disequilibria inherited from the present system. In the course of time, however, as the backlog of unrepaired television sets is worked off and the supply of hand-knitted wool gloves expands, the initial transient windfall incomes will moderate in size. The eventual steady-state income differentiation may still be larger than the political system can tolerate. In that case, it would be perfectly reasonable for the leadership to take measures to rein in the scope of the private sector. A society has the right to decide what combination of income and inequality it prefers. An informed social choice, however, requires that the price of greater equality be known. The experiment with the Liberal Model will provide both the leadership and the population with a clear measure of the price currently being paid, if there is such a price, for the prevailing degree of equality; and of the price that would have to be paid if the Liberal Model is eventually abandoned.

Finally, the Liberal Model has the virtue of administrative and political flexibility. The Radical Model would be difficult to implement in parts: to operate certain sectors without target planning while in other sectors traditional central planning prevails. As in Hungary, it is an all-or-nothing proposition. The Liberal Model, however, is infinitely divisible. Certain types of private production can be declared lawful while others remain unlawful as at present. If either the level of corruption or the degree of income differentiation should exceed the politically acceptable, the boundaries of the private sector can be constricted. The income-distribution problem can be separately controlled by tax policies that can make whatever discriminations are thought to be desirable.

The longer any model endures, the greater are the interests that become vested and the greater the resistance to reversal of policy. But that risk is slight under the conditions of present-day Soviet society. One need only to think back to the original NEP to be convinced of the difference. At that time, NEP was a risk of major proportions because the state-run commanding heights did not command a very large part of the economy. The political fears of the Left were entirely justified; the strengthening of private enterprise in trade and small-scale industry, and particularly in an agriculture that engaged some 80% of the population, could very well have eventually generated a political force to challenge the usurped power of the relatively small Communist party. The Liberal Model poses no such threat in Soviet society today. The ideological awkwardness would be small compared to the economic gain from what may be the most effective model for the Soviet economy of the future.

Political
Issues

When the choice is finally made, the economic prospects under the various models will no doubt enter into consideration. But it is politics and not economics that will dictate the choice in the end. In reviewing the array of political forces, I shall first discuss the political disposition of the major social groups and then consider the political viability of each of the four models.

For the urban working class, there are two primary concerns; job security and the level of consumption. The evidence for the latter comes primarily from the Polish experience, and we may err in transferring the lesson directly to the Russian working class, which may be much more compliant. There is no direct evidence that Soviet workers are prepared to go to the barricades over the price of meat, but the Soviet leadership acts as if they thought that may occur. What is more certain is that a decline in real income would at some point lead to an attenuation in incentives, with possibly worse consequences for productivity and growth.

The centrality of job tenure to the workers is evident in the long-standing inability of the Soviet leadership to find a politically acceptable way of redistributing workers among jobs. The Shchekino experiment, in which part of the wages of dismissed redundant workers was added to the wage fund of the remaining workers, was the boldest move to date in that direction, but it has not had a major impact. Evidently, the prospect of dividing up the wages of their dismissed comrades did not prove to be an incentive sufficient to crack labor's solidarity on this issue. Soviet analysts of innovation regard the difficulty of dismissing technologically redundant workers as a major obstacle to innovation.[29] Nearer at hand is the evidence of the Hungarian reform, much of the potential of which had to be forgone out of a concern to avoid a clash with labor on this issue. The Yugoslav experience, on the other hand, testifies to the capability of at least one socialist government to survive extensive unemployment. But the Soviet leadership is probably correct in its own assessment that it is not an issue on which it would want to be tested.

The key to peasant sentiment is the private plot. That is the institution that is the focus of his potential political involvement, and alterations in the official status of that institution have a major impact on his material and psychic life. By contrast, the steady conversion of collective farms into state farms seems not to have aroused a ripple, suggesting that the difference between those two organizational forms has long since ceased to be salient to the peasants. One has the impression that farm life continues to be highly unattractive to young people who must be restrained from fleeing from it by social and legal pressures. The attachment to the private plot suggests that the peasants would be attracted by the possibility of greater individual autonomy over a larger piece of land. But they have had no experience with the fluctuations of farm prices and incomes that accompany that autonomy in uncontrolled markets, and it is not at all certain that they would gladly pay that price for a larger say over their own land.

The intelligentsia are likely to be the least resistant to change in the economic mechanism since the basis of their social position is least system-specific; there will be jobs for journalists and engineers under any likely economic arrangement, though the stars of some would rise while others fall. The liberal intelligentsia are likely to be disposed toward more decentralized systems that allow greater freedom for individual action. But the technical intelligentsia may well be disposed toward more conservative systems. Sharing with enterprise management the responsibility for trying to keep the trains running on time, and with no practical experience in the operation of decentralized systems, they are likely to see the solution in better planning, organization, and management. Perhaps only among economists has there developed an understanding of decentralized systems and some attraction to them, but close observers regard their number to be rather small. For most economists, Soviet means central planning.[30]

Enterprise managers are second to none in their grumbling about the inefficiencies of the centrally planned economy within which they operate. The general view, however, is that their grumbling is of a highly conservative kind. They want the supply system to work better and the ministry to be less bureaucratic in attending to the needs of their enterprises. All the vibrations suggest that they are quite content in principle with a system in which they are told by someone else what to produce and where someone else has the responsibility for providing them with the inputs they require. It is doubtful that they would see much virtue in a system that required them to take the risks of guessing what unspecified customers would be willing to buy from them and that permitted other enterprises to steal away their customers. Doubtless they believe they merit higher incomes than they earn, but they are aware that the combination of their pay, perks, and prestige places them in the upper echelons of the society. They have achieved as a class a form of job security they never attained under Stalin, when the rapid turnover of managers was a characteristic feature of their lives. Most have held their jobs for very long periods, a state of affairs that disposes them to both managerial and political conservatism. The question of the political power that management can muster in defense of its interests has been the subject of controversy.[31] The most recent test of that power was the introduction of Production Associations, which threatened a substantial number of enterprise directors with the loss of their authority to the general directors of the Associations. The evidence is mixed. Many Associations were indeed formed, and although initially a controversy broke out over the status of the directors of the merged enterprises, that status was eventually largely submerged.[32] On the other hand, the Production Association reform appears to be proceeding very slowly, and one of the reasons is thought to be the intense opposition of managers, as well as of some ministry personnel.[33] The evidence is not conclusive because this reform divided the interests of managers; those who expected to be promoted to the general directorate of the Production Associations had a great deal to gain. Hence, it cannot be thought of as an issue on which management would have a unified interest. Nevertheless, the rearguard action mounted by what must have been a substantial number of managerial officials was evidently successful in retarding the pace of the reform and constricting its scope, perhaps permanently.

With respect to labor relations, the demise of the Shchekino experiment suggests that management has little stomach for the job of taking on labor in a campaign to cut costs by dismissing redundant labor. Nor would they gladly share their power with worker representatives under some form of genuine self-management or democratization of the work place. The system of central planning and management thus makes for a very comfortable position for enterprise management; protecting them from workers' demands for participation that may arise under greater decentralization and relieving them of the responsibility to economize on labor in ways that would threaten workers' job security.

About the interests of the central management—the ministerial bureaucracy—there can be no doubt. They are to central planning as capitalists are to capitalism. Close to the pinnacle of power and prestige, they are as "establishment" as one can get, save perhaps the party. The more centralized the system of planning and management, the larger the power they wield. To be sure, under most conceivable models of socialism, there will still be national economic ministries, for the state will always be obliged to implement national policies and to monitor the activities of enterprises; and for that purpose, national bureaucracies are necessary. But to be a ministerial official under decentralized conditions is to be a much less substantial person.

This group is likely to be the strongest defender of the system of central planning and management against efforts at substantial change. Yet their power would be limited in a conflict with a strongly supported party policy. The classic test was Khrushchev's Territorial Reorganization, which was directed against precisely this stratum of officialdom and virtually dismembered it, with large numbers of ministry officials being sent out to the provinces to staff the new territorial economic councils. Their return to office with the restoration of the ministries after Khrushchev's departure is evidence not of their power per se but of the growing awareness that that reorganization had been a failure and needed to be reversed. More recently, their power has been tested again in what is reported to be extensive ministerial opposition to the Production Associations. That reform has created a class of new association managers presiding over much larger domains than the old enterprise managers and therefore much more substantial people who are less easily intimidated by ministerial power. Here too, however, the opposition was a rearguard action and the reform has been pushed through, although the slowing of its pace may be attributed to continued ministerial as well as managerial resistance.[34]

I take it as self-evident that the party and policy *apparat* must be regarded as conservative in economic matters. The same is probably true of the military officer corps, although it ought not to be surprising if the nature of their responsibilities lay them more open to alternatives. The responsibilities I have in mind are the maintenance of a fighting force equipped with the armaments required to defeat a coalition of countries all of whom are more technically advanced. No other group in Soviet society confronts foreign competition in so stark a form. I know of no evidence on the subject, but it should not be surprising to learn that the military, in the vital quest for technological advance and of necessity knowledgeable about the technological processes and products of its potential antagonists, may prove to be a force for greater autonomy at lower levels of the production system.

About the Politburo itself, three things may be said. First, in the short- or medium-term, the composition of that body will change greatly. Precisely what the political–economic orientation of the new leadership will be is impossible to know, but it is a good bet that it will feel freer to entertain a wider range of alternatives than can be expected of the present leadership. Second, a younger leadership is likely to take a longer-run planning horizon and may, therefore, be more impelled to take action, drastic if it need be, to arrest the decline in growth and to "get the economy moving again." Third, any drastic action must be threatening to some substantial interests in the country. The new leadership will, therefore, have to establish a power base upon whom it can rely for support, as Khrushchev sought to rely on the provincial party *apparat*. For these several reasons, of all the groups we have discussed in this chapter, the top party leadership may be the most likely agent of change in the economic mechanism, carrying it out as a "revolution from above."

Among the national minorities, nationalist sentiments may conflict with class interests. Russified or Sovietized party officials and managers are likely to see their interests in the same way that their Great Russian colleagues do. But where nationalist feelings run deep, centralization means Moscow, which means Russian domination. A significant portion of the party and managerial groups among the minorities are, therefore, likely to support decentralizing measures primarily because they will reduce the power of Moscow over their lives. The Yugoslav experience may appear to suggest the contrary; there, the smaller Southern republics have promoted centralization while the larger Northern ones have pushed hard for a weakening of central government. One of the major factors in the Yugoslav case, however, is the division of the country among the less developed republics and the more developed. It is the poorer republics like Montenegro that have fought for centralization because the more powerful the central government the greater the redistribution of income and investment in their favor. For the same reason, the richer republics like Slovenia have supported increased republic power, as a means of slowing down what they regard as the draining of their resources for the support of the less productive republics to the South. The Soviet case is notably different for at least two reasons. First, republic differences in per capita income and consumption are probably much smaller in the USSR than in Yugoslavia, although I know of no evidence on this question. Second, a number of the national minorities enjoy higher living standards than the Great Russians; particularly the Baltic nations and perhaps Georgia and Armenia as well. Nor are Central Asians notably far behind the Great Russians, if at all. Hence, the special feature that operates in the Yugoslav case is not salient in the Soviet. The nationalist-minded members of the national minorities will see the issue not primarily in income-distribution terms as in Yugoslavia but in political terms. From that perspective, any reform that will reduce the power of Moscow will command support.

If this chapter on the interests of the relevant groups conforms even roughly with political reality, it implies that the Conservative Model is most likely to prevail unless one of two conditions obtains. One condition is that the rate of growth under that model fails to stabilize at a level above what was described earlier as the incentive threshold. If it falls below that level, the erosion of work incentives would trigger off new forces that would make for continued decline. Even if the economy did not yet fall to the political threshold, but certainly if it did, a change to another model would be inevitable. The second condition is that in the succession politics after Brezhnev, a new and younger leader either (a) develops a power base strong enough to force a change over the opposition of major vested interests, or (b) wins the support of a major social group, Mao-like, by forcing a change that is strongly supported by that group.

We are not charged to foretell the future; to forecast, in this case, whether either of these conditions will in fact obtain. The probability is large enough, however, to pursue the question of which of the other models might be adopted if the Conservative Model is abandoned.

The strongest political support, it seems to me, can be marshalled in favor of the Reactionary Model. It is the alternative that does the least violence to the interests of the groups that are most closely tied to the regime—central and enterprise management, the party *apparat,* the military, and so forth. There would be some loss to these groups from the restrictions that are likely to be placed on the second economy. But the organized system of special shops would presumably be continued. The experience of the 1980 Polish workers' strike may lead to a reconsideration of the special shops, the abolition of which was one of the workers' demands. But political wisdom may dictate the retention of those privileges nonetheless, because it is precisely those social groups that would be most counted on to forestall such workers' action.

The Reactionary Model would also command strong ideological support from a variety of sources. There are first those party loyalists for whom strong party leadership and control of the economy are matters of deep conviction and are believed to be the only proper way to run a Marxist–Leninist society. Most observers hold that few people in Soviet society are motivated by Marxist–Leninist ideology today, and I do not dispute it. But the ideology I have in mind is not the grand socialist idealism associated with those revered names, but simply the set of ideas on the right way to manage the Soviet state and society that emerged from World War II. In any case, certainly much larger is that portion of the society that would support the Reactionary Model because it promises a return to a more orderly, less contentious, and perhaps simpler way of life. Though the words ring strange in Western ears, internal observers report a widespread nostalgia for the "blessed" Stalinist times, when "there was rigid discipline in the country, when there were no difficulties, for example with labor power."[35] That this sentiment is also widely held among the elite was corroborated by the ICA survey, which found that while Soviet professionals are attracted to many features of American society, like access to information and freedom of travel, they "believe that similar access by the Soviet *narod* (people) would unbalance the society" and that "widespread freedoms would lead to chaos in society and perhaps undermine their own positions."[36]

How the *narod* would respond is harder to guess. It is likely that a strong law-and-order policy coupled with the usual combination of xenophobia, nationalism, antisemitism, and antiintellectualism will command extensive populist support. The tightening of police controls will affect mostly intellectuals and "speculators," and while there will be some loss in consumption levels from the curtailment of the second economy, it is the producers for those markets and not the consumers who will be dispatched to the camps. If, as I have argued, the economy will perform somewhat better under the Reactionary Model, the extent of that loss may be small.

A critical question is the response to the tightening of labor discipline, which is a major condition for the economic success of the Reactionary model. Certainly, the program would have to be presented as part of a great new national campaign, perhaps even packaged as a program to raise the consumption level of the people. Something of the sort would be necessary to sustain the compulsion that would be required to pull workers away from the "collective" in which they have worked all their lives and assign them to work in other enterprises and in other regions. In the short run, there is a fair possibility that an imaginative political leadership can pull it off. In the longer run, however, it is more problematical.

The Radical Model runs counter to the interests of all the main groups that support the traditional regime. Most of the officials of the central-planning and central-management bureaucracy would be out of jobs. Enterprises would still require directors, but they are not likely to be the same persons who directed the factories in the past. As in Hungary, a effort is likely to be made to mollify the directors by assuring them of their job security under the new system.[37] But the managers whose skills and outlook were cradled in a system of *mat-tekh snabzhenie* (centralized supply of enterprise inputs) are not likely to survive in a genuinely decentralized system; particularly if, unlike the Hungarians, they have never lived in one. They are likely to resist this model as strongly as the central managers.

The workers are likely to perceive a decentralized system, correctly, as a threat to their job security. And as in Hungary, the regime would have to give such strong assurances on that score that one of the major potential benefits of decentralization would be lost. Similar assurances had to be given in Hungary,[38] but because of its older legacies, the cost would be greater in the USSR.

In fact, in surveying the various interest groups, the only ones that are likely to support the Radical Model are the national minorities, a small group of economists, and perhaps a smattering of liberal intelligentsia who would support any weakening of the central bureaucracy as a step toward more personal freedom. Perhaps if the model included some extensive decentralization of agriculture as well, it may also command the support of the peasantry.

If this judgment about the very weak support for the Radical Model is correct, it raises the interesting question of why the USSR is different from Hungary and Czechoslovakia. In the latter case, decentralization had vast support in the country, including eventually large sections of the party. In Hungary, the support was perhaps not so extensive, but one has the impression that decentralization, nevertheless, commanded fairly broad support. The difference, I suspect, is that in Eastern Europe, the system of central planning is identified with rigid party orthodoxy and, ultimately, with Russian domination of their countries. To smash central planning is to strike a blow at a Soviet-like Communist party and symbolically at the USSR. From this perspective, hostility to the USSR was an important political factor in enabling the leadership to marshal support in favor of decentralization. But if a USSR is vital in promoting the Radical Model elsewhere, who will be the USSR's USSR? Perhaps China.

If the Radical Model is to be adopted in the USSR, it will come about only because the small band of liberal economists have somehow gotten the ear of the new leader and persuaded him that it is the best course for both himself and for the country. But that, as we have argued, would be a hard case to make, for the Hungarian performance has not (yet) been so successful that its effectiveness is beyond dispute, particularly for the USSR. If the leader, nevertheless, did decide that the Radical Model was the best course for the USSR, he must then face the prospect of engineering a revolution from above, for he will have no support from the conventionally loyal groups. Nor is he likely to turn like Mao to an unconventional group like the students in order to create a new power base. The military may conceivably be neutral on the technical issue of whether the decentralized model will outperform the centralized, but it will hardly rally around a leader who contemplates a new revolution in favor of decentralization. A revolution from above of this magnitude would require that the new leader first concentrate in his hands the personal power of a Stalin. On the other hand, Stalins do not decentralize.

It should now be evident why the Liberal Model would command much greater support than the Radical. No one loses his job, for the centrally planned sector operates largely as it did before. The party leader who introduces that model will, moreover, have a new basis of support in both the producers in the new private sector and the consumers who will have access to a significantly improved range of goods and services. For if the assessment just presented should prove to be correct, the population will experience a sharp improvement in the quality of life, sharp enough to leave no doubt about the success of the policy and the person who gets the credit for it.

Among the political obstacles, one thinks first of the ideological. But an imaginative leadership should have little difficulty presenting the model in a favorable light, providing that Mr. Suslov has passed from the scene. It is, after all, modelled on the NEP, and what Soviet leader would not wish to be the one to pick up the baton of Lenin? Moreover, the NEP is associated in the public mind with a period of hope and prosperity; I have heard even young people refer to it as the "golden age" of Soviet history. The Liberal Model could also supply the missing part of an ideological puzzle that has been created by the adoption of the notion that the USSR has entered the new historical stage of "mature socialism." It is clear that central planning was the appropriate economic model during the stage of the building of socialism, but now that socialism has entered the stage of maturity, the historical process should be expected to produce a new set of production relations. The dialectician should expect a negation of the negation, producing a social formation similar to the older one but on a new and higher plane. Viewed from that perspective, central planning was the negation of private enterprise. The negation of central planning can reasonably be thought to be a new form of private enterprise but on a higher plane in the sense that it is now socially responsible because it is embedded in a mature socialist society. Moreover, since the transition to mature socialism is accompanied by the scientific–technical revolution, the historically progressive economic system is one that enables the society to reap the fullest benefits of that revolution. Central planning was an appropriate economic model in a period in which the task of socialism was to adopt the advanced technology of the time that was already known and in operation in the capitalist world. The historical task having been completed, a new economic model is required that not simply adopts known technology but also produces yet unknown technological knowledge in the age of the scientific–technical revolution. Central planning is the historically correct form for applying known technology, but planning the yet unknown is a qualitatively different task. Hence, the rise of a new synthesis in which the private initiative of socialist men and women serves to promote technological innovation in the matrix of a centrally planned socialist economy.

I conclude that the prospects for change in the system of planning and management depends on the performance of the economy under the Conservative Model. If the growth rate should stabilize at a level that may be low but that, nevertheless, exceeds the incentive threshold, that model will be retained, and the century will limp quietly to its end. Chronic cases do not normally evoke extreme measures. Only acute attacks, like depressions or rebellions, galvanize a society into such measures. If the Conservative Model cannot stabilize the growth rate even at that low level, the accumulation of social and political pressures will propel the leadership into either the Reactionary or the Liberal Model. Both are likely to improve the performance of the economy, but the greater potential lies with the latter. If the counsels of political prudence prevail, however, the lot will fall to the former.

Notes

[1]Gertrude E. Schroeder, "The Soviet Economy on a Treadmill of 'Reforms'," in Joint Economic Committee, U.S. Congress, *Soviet Economy in a Time of Change* (Washington, D.C.: U.S. Government Printing Office, 1979), pp. 312–340.

[2]Joseph S. Berliner, *The Innovation Decision in Soviet Industry* (Cambridge, Mass.: MIT Press, 1976).

[3]Alice C. Gorlin, "Industrial Reorganization: The Associations," in Joint Economic Committee, U.S. Congress, *Soviet Economy in a New Perspective* (Washington, D.C.: U.S. Government Printing Office, 1976), pp. 162–188.

[4]*Ekonomicheskaia gazeta*, no. 32 (1979).

[5]The decree deals not only with the planning system but with the management system as well. The major new departure with respect to management is the introduction of a new success indicator—normative net value of output. The intent of the new indicator is to eliminate the benefit that enterprises derive from their assortment plans in favor of products with a large proportion of purchased inputs.

[6]*Pravda*, November 28, 1979. Transl. in *Current Digest of the Soviet Press* 31, no. 48 (December 26, 1979): 8.

[7]Ia. Kvasha, "Kontsentratsiia proizvodstva i mel'kaia promyshlennost'," *Voprosy ekonomiki*, no. 5 (1967).

[8]Gertrude E. Schroeder, in *The Soviet Economy: Toward the Year 2000*, eds. Abram Bergson and Herbert S. Levine (Boston: George Allen & Unwin, 1983), pp. 311–349.

[9]Bond and Levine, in *The Soviet Economy*, p. 13.

[10]Bond and Levine, in *The Soviet Economy*, p. 18.

[11]Aron Katsenelinboigen, *Studies in Soviet Economic Planning* (White Plains: M. E. Sharpe, 1978), p. 41.

[12]Boris Rumer, "The 'Second' Agriculture in the USSR," mimeographed (Russian Research Center, Harvard University, 1980).

[13]Janusz G. Zielinski, *Economic Reforms in Polish Industry* (London: Oxford Univ. Press, 1973), pp. 312–321.

[14]Gregory Grossman, "The Party as Entrepreneur" (forthcoming in 1982).

[15]Paul Marer, "Economic Performance, Strategy, and Prospects in Eastern Europe," in U.S. Congress, Joint Economic Committee, *East European Economies Post-Helsinki* (Washington, D.C.: U.S. Government Printing Office, 1977), pp. 523–566.

[16]Richard Portes, "Hungary: Economic Performance. Policy and Prospects," in U.S. Congress, Joint Economic Committee, *East European Economies Post-Helsinki* (Washington, D.C.: U.S. Government Printing Office, 1977), pp. 766–815.

[17]David Granick, "The Hungarian Economic Reform," *World Politics* 25, no. 4 (1973), 414–429. See also Portes, "Hungary," 1977.

[18]Gregory Guroff, "Soviet Perceptions of the US: Results of a Surrogate Interview Project" (Washington, D.C.: International Communications Agency, 27 June 1980).

[19]Katsenelinboigen, *Studies in Soviet Economic Planning*, p. 15.

[20]Edward A. Hewett, "The Hungarian Economy: Lessons of the 1970s and Prospects for the 1980s," in U.S. Congress, *East European Economic Assessment* (Washington, D.C.: U.S. Government Printing Office, 1981). See also Egon Neuberger, "Central Planning and Its Legacies: Implications for Foreign Trade," in *International Trade and Central Planning*, ed. Alan A. Brown and E. Neuberger (Berkeley: Univ. of California Press, 1968).

[21]Kvasha, "Kontsentratsiia."

[22]It may not be possible to mollify populist egalitarian hostility to the two types of stores. One of the demands of the Polish workers in the 1980 strike was the abolition of the "special shops" open only to the elite. The private-enterprise shops would be open to all purchasers, but they may kindle resentment nonetheless.

[23]John Löwenhardt, "The Tale of the Torch—Scientists–Engineers in the Soviet Union," *Survey* 20, 4 (93) (Autumn 1974): 113–121.

[24]Katsenelinboigen, *Studies in Soviet Economic Planning*, p. 66.

[25]Oskar Lange, "On the Economic Theory of Socialism." Rept. in *On the Economic Theory of Socialism*, ed. B. Lippincott (Minneapolis: Univ. of Minnesota Press, 1938).

There is a third position, which may be taken as the Yugoslav interpretation. This interpretation shares the Radical view that markets are superior to central planning, and it shares the Liberal view that enterprises should not be state-owned. It parts company with the Liberal view, however, in holding that the best alternative to state-owned enterprise is not private enterprise but self-managed enterprise. The notion of worker self-management is so far out of the bounds of the thinkable in the USSR that I have not explored that model here.

[26]Hilda Scott, *Does Socialism Liberate Women? Experiences from Eastern Europe* (Boston: Beacon Press, 1974), p. 196.

[27]Paul Gregory and Gert Leptin, "Similar Societies under Differing Economic Systems: The Case of the Two Germanys," *Soviet Studies* 29 (October 1977), 519–542.

[28]Katsenelinboigen, *Studies in Soviet Economic Planning*.

[29]Berliner, *The Innovation Decision in Soviet Industry*, chapter 5.

[30]Katsenelinboigen, *Studies in Soviet Economic Planning*.

[31]Jeremy R. Azrael, *Managerial Power and Soviet Politics* (Cambridge, Mass: Harvard Univ. Press, 1966).

[32]Berliner, *The Innovation Decision in Soviet Industry*, pp. 136–143.

[33]Gorlin, "Industrial Reorganization," 1976.
[34]*Ibid.*
[35]Katsenelinboigen, *Studies in Soviet Economic Planning,* p. 57.
[36]Guroff, "Soviet Perceptions," p. 16.
[37]Granick, "The Hungarian Economic Reform."
[38]*Ibid.*

19   THANE GUSTAFSON

*Lessons of the Brezhnev Policies on Land and Water and the Future of Reform**

Prior to the 1970s, there was not a decade in the turbulent history of the Soviet Union that did not put the political system to the test. By comparison, the last 10 years were a period of calm; consequently, we must bear in mind that policies were formed and carried out in an unusually benign atmosphere. But beginning in the 1980s, the Soviet political system faces two further tests, one political and one economic. The first is a sweeping change in political leadership. Within the next few years, power will pass to a new generation of rulers, not only in the Politburo but also in the top several hundred positions of the party and government. Incredible as it may seem, this will be the first true succession in the Soviet elite since the Great Purge of 1938–1939.[1] One may say without much exaggeration that nearly two-thirds of a century after the 1917 Revolution, the Soviet political system is just beginning its third generation. The second test is economic. The country will face shortages of several key resources, particularly energy, manpower, and capital, each of which has the potential to create a crisis as serious as the one in agriculture in the 1960s.[2] Together, these two impending challenges may create a climate with more possibilities for changing the traditional structure and rules of Soviet politics than at any time since the 1920s.[3]

As they react to this grim and complex picture, Brezhnev's would-be successors are bound to be influenced by their perception of the success

*Reprinted by permission of the author and publisher from *Reform in Soviet Politics: Lessons of Recent Policies on Land and Water* (New York: Cambridge University Press, 1981), pp. 149–161, 207–210. Copyright 1981 by Cambridge University Press.

511

or failure of his agricultural and natural-resource programs, not only because these have grown into one of the largest segments of the Kremlin's budget but also because they are the only instance in their recent experience of a high-priority, country-wide innovation in policy. Accordingly, in this chapter, we evaluate the lessons of the Brezhnev policies and attempt to draw from them the implications for the future of policy reform in the next two decades.

A Preliminary Balance Sheet How does the record of the last 15 years of agricultural and related reforms appear from Moscow? The results can be measured by three different standards. The most basic one is whether, thanks to the Brezhnev program, the Soviet leaders have successfully countered the clear and immediate threats that created an agricultural crisis in the first place. In particular: After 15 years of the Brezhnev policy is the country now safe from the humiliation of periodic crop failure, with all its consequences?

The answer so far is no. Year-to-year variations in farm output remain as dizzying as a generation ago, mainly because of weather; the difference in grain output between 1975 and 1976, for example, was 84 million tons. Soviet farmers are once again resorting to some of the risky practices of the Khrushchev years, planting in marginal lands and reducing clean fallow in arid areas.[4] Soviet grain reserves provide a buffer but only a partial one.[5] In bad years, such as 1972, 1975, and 1979, Soviet agriculture has seemed more vulnerable and more dependent upon the outside world than ever. Though in the last 15 years Soviet farm output (as measured by a 3-year moving average) has increased by half,[6] the leadership expected to do better than that, and on the basis of that expectation, pursued a rapid expansion of animal husbandry. Demand for fodder has far outrun supply,[7] and neither the tripling of agricultural capital stock that has taken place in the last 15 years nor the greatly expanded output of fertilizer and farm machinery has closed the gap.

However, the gap exists not simply because agricultural output failed to increase as fast as was expected but also because the leadership evidently made a deliberate choice, once the gap appeared, not to allow it to interfere with their plans for livestock expansion; they relied instead on imports to cover the shortfall as much as possible.[8] This represented a very substantial change in traditional Soviet behavior. In the 1950s and 1960s, the Soviet leaders' first goal was autarky, as it had been more or less continuously since the end of the First 5-Year Plan. When the harvest was bad, they slaughtered livestock to economize on feed, but until 1963, they had never imported more than 1 million tons of grain in any year. In 1975, in contrast, the Soviets imported 26 million tons of foreign grain from the United States and limited the slaughter of livestock as much as possible.[9] For the next 4 years, the Soviet Union imported considerably more than 10 million tons of grain each year, spending billions in foreign exchange to maintain livestock, apparently reconciled to the idea of depending on foreign suppliers in one of the world's most unstable markets.

This apparently deliberate policy means that massive imports by themselves should not be interpreted as a failure of Brezhnev's policy but simply that foreign suppliers were being used to provide a buffer that an overextended Soviet agriculture as yet could not. This was a very different situation from the pathetic agricultural failures of the 1950s and 1960s. Soviet leaders may worry about the opportunity costs of so much imported grain and about the future availability of oil to pay for it,[10] but they are no longer on the brink of disaster as they once were. In this sense, then, the Brezhnev program by the end of the 1970s had succeeded in moving the country well away from the nadir of 1963.

Then came the American grain embargo of 1980. At this writing, the embargo has failed to cause the Soviets major or lasting hardship. From July 1979 to June 1980, they managed to import, by one path or another, 31.5 million tons of grain, compared to their original target of 34 million tons. Though they had to pay as much as 25% more than the American selling price, the extra hard currency was easily available at a time of record gold and oil prices.[11]

More interesting, however, are the possible effects of the embargo on the attitudes of the Soviet leadership. These men, who were reared on Stalinist autarky and for whom it was a large step to allow themselves to depend on world markets for a major and vital commodity, have been given a stunning reminder of the risks. What lesson will they draw from it? They may well conclude that it was unwise, in retrospect, to have allowed themselves to slip into a situation in which the centerpiece of their agricultural policy became a *pièce en prise*, hostage to the goodwill of the American adversary. If they do, then it will not be hard to explain to the Soviet people who is responsible for the lack of meat on their plates. The net effect of the embargo may simply be to hand the Soviet leadership a ready way to liquidate a gap that, in view of the foreign exchange it ate up, might have been dimly viewed within a part of the Soviet elite to begin with.[12] On the other hand, the failure of the attempted embargo may encourage the Soviet leaders to persevere in the present course, as they may reason that they have too much invested in the livestock program to turn back.

A second and stiffer standard by which to evaluate the Brezhnev program is whether Soviet agriculture can soon reach a sustained takeoff. What such a takeoff means in economic or agronomic terms may be difficult to define, but in political terms it is quite clear: The infrastructural transformation currently under way must reach a point soon at which the heaviest part of the job is done and the need for further massive investment declines, before the political coalition behind the Brezhnev program weakens and agriculture's bloated share of the capital investment budget comes under attack. How soon? The grace period may be no longer than Brezhnev's dwindling lifetime, for capital is now so short that agriculture is certain to be cut as soon as he is gone, or maybe even before.

Read in terms of this looming deadline, the latest statistics must make discouraging reading in the Kremlin. The major indexes of productivity and return on capital say that, far from producing a takeoff, agricultural investment is yielding rapidly diminishing marginal returns.[13] Of course, to a degree, that is just what one would expect. The Brezhnev program involved nothing less than a wholesale transformation of the countryside, and it will not produce a fast return. Whole industries have been launched, millions of people trained or retrained, and so forth. Until the enormous input has been assimilated, returns are bound to be very low, but in time they are also bound to improve.

Presumably, this is also the argument of the program's supporters, but it is bound to weaken politically as time goes on for two reasons. First, the requirements for investment in agricultural infrastructure seem to have no end, and filling one need only exposes another. For example, the latest of many Soviet concerns is rural roads. Only 40% of all collective and state farms have any hard-surface roads at all, and only 17% have 10 km or more. What exists is poorly built and maintained. Now that Soviet farms are increasingly mechanized and interdependent, their inaccessibility in bad weather (which traditionally includes much of the late winter and spring, the infamous *rasputitsia*) has become intolerable. Yet the job of building an all-weather network of rural roads has hardly begun, and it promises to cost further billions.[14] Other tasks that are still at their beginning include construction of service buildings and rural housing, supply of spare parts and maintenance services for agricultural machinery, transportation, storage, processing and preservation facilities for produce—the list goes on and on, seemingly endless.

Second, looming in the 1980s are serious shortages of manpower, water, fuel, and foreign exchange. We shall consider their larger implications in a moment, but as far as agriculture is concerned, they raise the very unpleasant prospect that to make good on what has already been invested, the leaders may be required to invest even more. Consider manpower first: Despite major efforts to raise farm incomes and increase the amenities of rural life, Moscow has failed to dissuade the young and the skilled from leaving the farm. From 1971 to 1974, 2.6 million tractor drivers and combine and machine operators were trained in what must rank as one of the world's most ambitious rural education programs. Yet during that period, the net number of rural workers in those categories rose by little more than a quarter million;[15] in fact, for the entire period from 1965 to 1979, it has increased by only 1.3 million (from 3.1 million to 4.4 million).[16] Some vital agricultural regions are especially affected, such as the non-black-earth zone, the Volga basin, and Kazakhstan. But people with employable skills will undoubtedly continue to leave these areas, for the major Russian cities do not reproduce their own numbers, warmer climates and better living conditions beckon, and Soviet industry adds to urban demand for labor by hoarding reserve workers just as it does raw materials. The one great exception to the overall shortage, Central Asia, does not help the rest of the country because most Central Asians do not wish to move.[17] The result is a seller's market for labor in which agriculture is in most places the loser.

To stem the flight from the farms, the government is working in four directions at once, by raising incentives to stay, mechanizing farm operations, favoring private farming, and even, in some places, moving in contract workers from other regions. The overall statistics are impressive: the real income of *kolkhoz* farm workers more than doubled between 1965 and 1979; the power available per agricultural worker passed from 7.7 horsepower to 22; and rural electricity consumption quadrupled.[18] Some recent straws in the wind indicate the lengths to which the government may be prepared to go, either toward liberalization or coercion: Since 1978, both in speeches and in his official autobiography, Brezhnev has advocated a greater role for private plots, the acre-size allotments that peasant families are allowed to cultivate for their own profit and which still provide an important share of Soviet fare.[19] Another straw is that in certain provinces of the non-black-earth zone, Central Asian reclamation workers are so numerous that the road signs are written in both Russian and Uzbek.[20] But these are partial measures that do not offset the fact that many farm operations are still performed by hand, that most Central Asians are reluctant to leave their home villages, and that private plots account for a steadily declining share of total agricultural output.[21] Only more investment, more time, and the availability of more amenities in the countryside will make a dent in the rural manpower problem. The situation will get worse before it gets better.

The second problem is fuel and its connection with foreign exchange. If current forecasts that Soviet oil production will peak in the early 1980s are accurate,[22] Soviet agriculture will be affected in two ways. First, because mechanization and modernization are transforming it into a major consumer of petroleum and petrochemicals for fertilizer and pesticides, rural electricity, farm machinery, food processing, and so on, agricultural modernization becomes more difficult and expensive if oil runs short. Second, if Soviet oil exports decline, then Brezhnev's successors may not be able to afford the foreign exchange to import from 10 million to 35 million tons of grain each year to support the country's livestock, even if (in the wake of the American embargo) they should be inclined to do so.

The third key shortage of the 1980s is water. Shortages of water are tied to the other two, and none can be addressed separately from the others. Farms overuse irrigation water, for example, partly because they lack manpower to control the water, maintain the ditches, and repair the pumps and sprinklers. In Central Asia, on the other hand, it is the excess of rural manpower and its reluctance to leave the region that is causing Moscow to consider bringing in water from Siberia. Interbasin diversions would require energy to pump water uphill, and the resulting loss of hydropower to other uses may have to be covered by fossil fuels. One may well speak, then, not of individual shortages but of a massive triple squeeze that must somehow be gotten through before the Brezhnev agricultural program can reach takeoff. The prospect is for even greater investment, not less, and therefore by our second standard also, the Brezhnev program is in trouble.

The last and most demanding standard is whether Soviet agriculture is moving toward eventual self-sufficiency in its day-to-day operations. Will it always be the sick man of the Soviet economy? Will there ever come a day when it will not require the pure oxygen of high-priority political support, the daily intravenous feeding of subsidies, or periodic emergency rescue through massive foreign imports? This was Brezhnev's own ultimate vision, but can it be attained through the agricultural program as it is presently being conducted?

To judge from the experience of other industrial countries, a self-sufficient modern agriculture can be achieved only if the following three elements are present: specialized and vigorous industrial support oriented toward the needs of the farms; a prestigious and high-quality agricultural science closely tied to local operations through extension services and experimental stations; and an agricultural labor force consisting not of peasants but of educated agricultural technicians and entrepreneurs. All three elements must be responsive to local conditions, changes in demand, requirements of different groups, the availability of different inputs—in short, to both local needs and national demand.

Soviet progress in these respects has been uncertain. Much of the industrial support for agriculture comes from ministries whose main jobs are anything but agricultural. Brezhnev has committed the defense-related ministries to support the agricultural program, and they bring to it their high priority and abundant skills and resources.[23] But because their main business lies elsewhere, they cannot be expected to make special efforts in agriculture unless they are continually prodded. This means that if the commitment of the Politburo to agriculture should weaken even slightly, much of this industrial support could vanish as it did in 1966–1967. Yet so long as constant political attention is required to maintain full industrial involvement in agriculture, we can safely say that the third standard is not being met.

The same is true of scientific support. The growth of the agricultural sciences has been among the slowest of all the scientific specialties in the last quarter century, and there is no sign of a change in that respect. The Lenin Academy of Agricultural Sciences (VASKhNIL) does not compare in prestige or in quality with the USSR Academy of Sciences, and within the Academy of Sciences itself, most agricultural research is performed by the republican academies, which have much lower prestige and funding than their Union-level counterpart. Despite the revival of genetics in the Soviet Union since 1964, plant breeding and seed selection are weak areas, especially when judged by their actual contributions to farming.[24] For example, according to the CIA, Soviet wheat growers largely use only one spring variety and two winter varieties for strong wheat, and for durum wheat, they rely almost totally on one older variety. These were developed before the Brezhnev program began and are considered inadequate for mechanized, irrigated farming.[25] Similarly, Soviet chemical engineering for the production of modern fertilizers has not improved enough in the last two decades to give the Soviets an independent and modern industry, and for the production of compound and nitrogenous fertilizers, the Soviets have chosen to rely instead on foreign suppliers of production equipment.[26]

Some of the main problems in securing industrial and scientific support for agriculture are similar to those encountered elsewhere in the economy. Only very gradually is Soviet industry beginning to think of its products as packages that must include maintenance and spare parts, training for users, and arrangements for responding to the users' needs and to their suggestions for further innovations.[27] Similarly, the classic weakness of Soviet research and development lies not so much in the quality of its science as in its separation from the users' needs and its relative neglect of field experimentation and diffusion of successful innovations. These well-known Soviet problems have especially serious consequences in agriculture. For example, though Soviet agricultural geneticists have a network of some 1500 stations through which they test some 12,000 new plant varieties annually, only a few of the stations actually have their own land and equipment. Nearly all of them rely on contracts with local farms, but because the farms have pressing production targets of their own, experimental plots have the last claim. Meanwhile, in Moscow, seed selection is in the hands of a minor and relatively powerless State Commission in the Ministry of Agriculture.[28] In other words, agricultural technology suffers from the same problem of *vnedrenie* (i.e., introduction of new developments into production) as the rest of Soviet technology.

As for the growth of a modern agricultural labor force, important changes are taking place, but slowly. Alongside the traditional work force is appearing a rural but nonfarm working class, employed in service functions related to agriculture. In agriculture management, educational levels are rising. Between 1965 and 1978, the proportion of agricultural personnel with higher or specialized secondary education increased from 20 to 61 per 1000.[29] These people include farm managers, agronomists, and assorted specialists, who altogether make up about 7% of total farm personnel.[30] Eventually, these trends will transform local agricultural management, but how soon?

The kinds of changes involved here require more than high-priority investment; they require time, the redirection of incentives, and the disappearance of a tenacious bias in favor of cities and heavy industry. And because problems of industrial support, technological innovation, and skilled manpower affect not merely agriculture but the entire economy, one should not expect them to disappear in agriculture ahead of other sectors. Success by the third standard may be a generation away.

To sum up: After 15 years of sustained, high-priority effort and the investment of more than 600 billion rubles[31] in agriculture and related programs, the Brezhnev policies have produced some progress toward meeting the first, and politically most urgent, standard; they may meet the second if given sufficient further investment and time; but they are not yet even close to meeting the third. Put another way, the Brezhnev reform has succeeded in improving and stabilizing Soviet diets and diminishing the danger of massive crop failure and has begun to reverse the consequences of long neglect of the countryside. But even if the present effort continues for another decade at its present level (which is unlikely), it will not free the country from periodic reliance on foreign imports, heavy infrastructural investment, and constant intervention and subsidy. This is both a great failure, and yet, all the same, no small achievement. It is a failure in terms of the goals the Brezhnev coalition set for itself and the resources it expended to pursue them (and, therefore, we may expect the future of the agricultural program to be one of the major issues of the coming succession). The figure that best captures this partial success is that in 1978, one Soviet farm worker still fed only 9.7 people compared to 7.3 people in 1965.[32] But at the same time we should not overlook the fact that, faced with a crisis that would soon have threatened its legitimacy and stability, the Kremlin reacted decisively and with considerable effect. We should not underestimate the vitality and power of a political system that can act to ensure its survival by diverting hundreds of billions into a previously neglected—in fact, despised—sector of the economy. Those who ask themselves whether the Soviet regime will survive beyond 1984 should look elsewhere than to agriculture as the source of the regime's fatal weakness, for with their gigantic investment, the Soviet leaders have bought themselves at least a measure of security. But they aimed higher, and when we appraise their efforts in that light, we can only wonder at the relative modesty of the results gained at such cost.

The causes are obviously complex. Two generations of deliberate neglect of agriculture (and many generations of rural backwardness before that) did not leave merely a physical legacy of damaged soils and primitive infrastructure but also a social and cultural legacy of contempt for the countryside and a system of administration and political power biased toward industry and cities. No crash program could erase that in a mere 15 years. We argue that the basic weakness of the Brezhnev program is more fundamental: In its genesis, development, and implementation, it is not a third-generation reform at all but the last of the great industrializing campaigns. It is, therefore, limited to what such campaigns can achieve; and it is attended by the same problems that have always bedeviled such campaigns in the past: excess, overoptimism, subversion, and waste.

Does that mean that the present political system is incapable of producing reforms appropriate to the requirements of a third-generation economy? To judge that question, we must look beyond the performance record of the Brezhnev policies to the political lessons they contain.

Political Lessons of the Brezhnev Programs

The first and most important lesson of the Brezhnev conservation and agricultural programs is that even a leadership as conservative and as fearful of change as the Brezhnev coalition was able to perform successfully a major shift in its priorities, reorient investment funds and resources against the bias of tradition and established lines of priority and prestige, rethink long-established assumptions and approaches, develop new programs and new agencies, and pursue this new course systematically, consistently, and energetically.

What is most striking about the rise of the new agricultural policy, however, is how long it took to establish it securely, especially if one bears in mind that it entailed no change in the Kremlin's most basic objectives (economic development and so on) nor any alteration of the system's basic structures or rules. Therefore, while giving appropriate credit to the evident energy of the Soviet political system, we may wonder whether the changes it produces in the future will always be so slow and so conservative.

Not necessarily. True, we stress the theme of an increasingly constrained leadership, but we should remember that those constraints are largely economic, technological, and social rather than directly political. Compared with their predecessors of the 1960s, the leaders of the 1980s may actually be *less* constrained in waging the intraelite politics that lead to new coalitions and new policies. In the 1960s, there were several unique circumstances at work that combined to make the process slower: First, the post-Khrushchev succession was not a true replacement of the ins by the outs. Second, the political elite's strong reaction against Khrushchev's freewheeling ways produced unprecedented constraints on his successors' ability to use the traditional instruments of power and contributed to the selection of a leader who, whether by necessity or by temperament (or both), ruled by slow concertation. Third, in the 1960s, there was still widespread optimism in Moscow about the effectiveness of traditional economic methods and remedies, and this, in turn, undoubtedly produced a strong bias in favor of the kind of industrializing agricultural policy that Brezhnev advocated. None of those circumstances will necessarily hold in the 1980s. In short, when the next succession comes, the new occupants of the Kremlin may find themselves freer to seize and wield the instruments of intraelite power to develop new policies and to do it more quickly.

Indeed, behind the scenes, the basis for consensus on new and bolder policies may already be taking shape just as it did in agriculture in the 5 years or so before Khrushchev's fall. As we look back a decade or two from now, we may see that a similarly slow process of change in elite attitudes was taking place in the apparently inconclusive discussions of the 1970s about different management arrangements, price and incentive systems, energy policy, and so on. Through such debates (or, rather, the discussions behind the scenes of which they are the imperfect shadow), Soviet minds are perhaps even now being prepared for changes that we cannot yet see, even though they may require a change of leadership to emerge.[33]

The second important lesson of the Brezhnev programs is that the Soviet political leadership was able to draw upon new thinking in several fields long frozen and to expand its horizons and incorporate new ideas into policy while channeling innovations in conservative and safe directions and keeping control of issues with radical potential. The leaders' treatment of agricultural specialists during this period was very different from the contempt, exploitation, and harassment to which agronomists, geneticists, soil scientists, and others had been subjected in the past; and specialists in those fields responded energetically to the new opportunities, creating or recreating with astonishing speed established professions where there had been only barren ruins or undeveloped sites a few short years before.

I argue that despite this change of atmosphere and the strong response it evoked, the essential features of the traditional relationship between Soviet political leaders and their sources of ideas and advice appear unchanged. One is almost equally tempted to argue the exact opposite because the relaxation of negative controls and the resulting vigor of public debate have been so striking in so many "technical" fields. To be sure, negative controls unrestrained by countervailing power may be reimposed at any time (as the case of IKSI eloquently demonstrates). But is it not clearly in the interest of the leaders *not* to reimpose them? And does not power, even absolute power, rest ultimately on the values, habits, and expectations of leaders and led alike, so that power long unused decays? Would not an attempt to reimpose ideological controls on, say, cybernetics seem illegitimate and absurd, not least to the leaders themselves? One is tempted to say that compared to a generation ago, something in the Soviet political culture has changed and the relationship of knowledge to power along with it.

Nevertheless, as far as the participation and influence of technical specialists in actual policymaking are concerned, I do not think one can go quite so far. The position of Soviet specialists, in the end, remains entirely dependent upon the goodwill and needs of political authorities; their participation is governed by the authorities' pleasure; the advice given is largely secret; the portion of it that is subject to public debate is for the most part a weak echo of what is really being discussed behind the scenes; and there is no appeal—none, that is, that the leaders are obliged to take account of. The Soviet expert, at least in the areas of policy as we have discussed here, is clearly on tap, not on top, however much he may be useful or necessary.

What are the consequences for policymaking? The cases we have discussed suggest that barriers (both vertical and horizontal) to the flow of information might have aggravated the tendency of the leadership to proceed too fast and too far in their new policies because of a lack of open, expert, countervailing criticism. In the future, as technical issues grow ever more complex and interconnected, the usefulness to the leaders of having them thrashed out publicly will increase, for only a wide airing will preserve the leaders from the biased information "interested" ministries may provide or from the one-sided advocacy of specialist–entrepreneurs and regional "patriots." In policy formation, as in implementation, an increase in effective power may require continued relaxation of traditional powers.

The third lesson suggested by the Brezhnev programs is that the apparent influence of institutional groups derives not from resources and instruments of power of their own but from constraints that the political leadership tacitly accepts, largely because they arise from the leaders' own objectives, the complexity and interrelatedness of tasks in a modern economy, and the growing scarcity of resources, including manpower. Therefore, if we see evidence of argument and conflict, it is not the precursor of political pluralism but the playing out of delegated powers of state agencies, that, as we have seen, can be granted or withdrawn on short notice. The playing out is neither fast nor smooth; state agencies can use their delegated powers (for a time) to obstruct and divert but not to oppose official policy openly or impose an alternative (though they may propose one). The most carefully drafted initiative from specialists or agencies below, painstakingly threaded through the bureaucracy to gain the approvals of all the agencies concerned, and earnestly argued for years through the consultants of the Central Committee or the *referentura* of the Council of Ministers, may be reversed at a moment's notice by the leadership's sudden decision, without possibility of public appeal or countervailing action. Thus, to take a recent example, the gradual development of a balanced energy policy in response to concern about declining oil reserves, which one can trace through Soviet journals in the 1970s, was abruptly pushed aside at the November 1977 plenum of the Central Committee in favor of a massive return to a strategy based on western Siberian oil, even in the face of mounting evidence from the experts that such a policy was extremely risky.

This means that the Soviet leaders retain awesome power, but, it is power of the wrong kind. The genie produced by the command economy is ham-handed, capable of flooding the countryside with half-finished irrigation projects and agroindustrial livestock combines, but not of producing stable harvests or substantial increases in meat output. *Krokodil* captures the absurdity neatly with a standard cartoon that comes straight from Gogol: A tractor roars across the fields of Russia, drawn by a flying *troika* of plowhorses.

It follows that the Soviet leaders will not soon be able to afford another such "reform," and, consequently, it will not do as a model for meeting third-generation economic problems across the board, not even as a stopgap, because it is simply too expensive and too slow. Brezhnev's successors will not be able to deal simultaneously with energy, transportation, industrial modernization, housing, and so on by the same methods that were used in the Brezhnev agricultural program. In energy policy, for example, the balance to be struck is between conservation and further development of new sources. Naturally, the Soviet economy will need plenty of both; but the point is that if the Soviet energy policy of the 1980s ends up being channeled in the same lopsidedly "extensive" directions as the Brezhnev agricultural policies of the 1960s and 1970s, that is, toward production rather than conservation, one may safely predict that the country will be in trouble. The Soviet Union is already the least efficient producer and user of energy of any modern industrial power (despite some zones, it should be said, of outstanding efficiency); and its energy intensiveness, instead of declining as in most advanced economies, is rising.[34] A policy that stresses development of new sources of energy without dealing with the organizational structures and economic incentives that produce overconsumption will not solve the Soviet Union's energy problems. And although a second-generation approach, though inadequate, still has some rele-

vance when applied to a problem like energy or Central Asian development or transportation, it has almost none when applied to some of the
other problems rising up in the 1980s, such as geographically unbalanced birthrates, labor shortages and low labor productivity, slow or
inappropriate technological innovation, low-quality output, hidden inflation, or the spread of the underground "second economy." In short,
second-generation reform is not enough to enable the Soviet political
system to deal with the problems of a third-generation economy.

How the Soviet leaders react to this problem depends mainly, of
course, on how severe the 1980s turn out to be. If the decade proves to
be relatively benign, the Kremlin may be able to pursue further the
partial evolution it has already undergone in the last 15 years. One may
reasonably expect further experimentation with new schemes to promote technological innovation (such as profit-making associations
geared toward export markets), greater reliance on material incentives
and even local enterprise (such as a further elaboration of the present
trend toward specialized "brigades" in the factory and on the farm), a
gradual acceptance of the need for the "hidden hand" of meaningful
prices but also (as Joseph Berliner puts it) for the "hidden foot" of
possible unemployment—one can go on. The Brezhnev period has not
been a treadmill of meaningless reform;[35] there has been slow, but
definite, learning. But what is needed is the right mixture of stress and
leisure for the political elite to accustom itself to the meaning of governing by fingers instead of thumbs and to reconcile itself to the political
price that will have to be paid by abandoning some degree of formal
control. The danger is that they will not have that leisure.[36] If oil output
falls to 9 million barrels a day or less by 1990, if during the decade of the
1980s the weather is bad, if perceived international pressures (or opportunities) incline the leaders toward even higher levels of military spending, if migration patterns and labor turnover worsen—all of which are
quite conceivable—then there will be neither time nor patience for slow
experimentation. Soviet leaders will be forced to use what power they
have, which may mean Draconian measures to enforce labor discipline,
curtail the second economy, limit fuel use, cut back consumption,
reallocate manpower, and so on. Such stopgap devices could get the
country through the rapids of the 1980s and into the calmer waters of the
1990s. For example, by accepting a partial cutback in the objectives for
meat production, the Soviet Union could use some of the foreign
exchange now being spent for foreign grain to buy foreign energy
technology instead.

The government can also free investment resources by cutting back
the entire agricultural sector, which many Soviets now openly view as
the most bloated sector in the Soviet investment budget. This can be
done by cutting back selectively on the least successful programs, such
as the non-black-earth zone, and postponing programs that are not

immediately needed, such as the major interbasin diversions. A second measure immediately available to free capital and lessen energy consumption is to concentrate resources on the large number of unfinished investment projects now dotting the countryside.[37] In sum, if the 1980s prove to be harsh, the Soviet leadership has a range of stopgap measures available, which in order to see them through the decade need not do more than help out in the short run and at the margin. As for the prospect of calmer waters by the 1990s, it would not take much optimism to reason as follows: the labor shortage will be relieved slightly in the 1990s; the energy problem will abate, for it is due in the first place to the decline of European sources and the premature peaking of west Siberian oil; but natural gas will take up the slack, followed, in the longer term, by other sources of energy from the resources of Siberia. As for agriculture, the front-end investment already made is bound to yield results, especially in fodder production. Consequently, the 1980s will not necessarily be a decade of crisis and Draconian reaction in the Soviet Union. On the contrary, the combination of political succession and policy pressures may be just the combination required to shake the political elite out of its immobilism.

But in what direction will it choose to move? We ask whether the Soviet political elite is capable of responding to the social and economic problems gathering before it in the third generation of Soviet rule to promote greater balance, quality, longer horizons, and efficiency. After observing the response of the Brezhnev leadership to the agricultural problem in its many ramifications, we cannot doubt the energy of this political system. But whether it has the ability to develop the instruments of power appropriate to modern reform cannot yet be judged. The success of the next generation of Soviet leaders in matching the evolution of their increasingly modern society and economy with modern political instruments will depend less on their ability to launch new programs and reorganizations, incentive systems and indexes, than on their capacity to rethink the inherited relations between knowledge and power, between control and autonomy, and between a safe conservatism and progress.

Notes

[1]See Seweryn Bialer, *Stalin's Successors* (Cambridge: Cambridge University Press, 1980).

[2]On upcoming energy problems, see Central Intelligence Agency, National Foreign Assessment Center, *The World Oil Market in the Years Ahead*, ER 79-10327 (Washington, D.C.: U.S. Government Printing Office, 1979); and J. Richard Lee and James R. Lecky, "Soviet Oil Developments," in U.S. Congress, Joint

Economic Committee, *The Soviet Economy in a Time of Change,* 2 vols. (Washington, D.C.: U.S. Government Printing Office, 1979) 1:587–599; hereafter cited as *Time of Change.* On manpower, see Murray Feshbach and Stephen Rapawy, "Soviet Population and Manpower Trends and Policies," in U.S., Congress, Joint Economic Committee, *The Soviet Economy in a New Perspective* (Washington, D.C.: U.S. Government Printing Office, 1976), pp. 113–154.

[3]Seweryn Bialer, "The Politics of Stringency in the USSR," *Problems of Communism* 29 (May–June 1980):19–33.

[4]Roy D. Laird and Betty A. Laird, "The Widening Soviet Grain Gap and Prospects for 1980 and 1990," in Roy D. Laird, Joseph Hajda, and Betty A. Laird, eds., *The Future of Agriculture in the Soviet Union and Eastern Europe: The 1976–1980 Five-Year Plan* (Boulder, Colo.: Westview Press, 1977), pp. 27–48. For recent comments on continuing controversy over clean fallow in the Virgin Lands, see A. Baraev, "Vazhnyi rezerv," *Pravda,* August 19, 1980.

[5]See Padma Desai, "Estimating Soviet Grain Imports in 1980–85: Alternative Approaches" (Occasional Paper of the Russian Research Center, Harvard University, Cambridge, Mass., revised 1980). The Soviet Union drew 16 million tons of grain out of its reserve in 1977, restored 19 million tons in 1978, and drew down 17 million tons in 1979 (Robert L. Paarlberg, "Lessons of the Grain Embargo," *Foreign Affairs* 59, no. 1 [Fall 1980]:156–157). The U.S. Department of Agriculture's figures are 14, 19, and 16 million tons, respectively. See U.S. Department of Agriculture, Foreign Agriculture Service, *World Grain Situation: Outlook for 1980/81* (Washington, D.C., 1980), p. 18.

[6]David W. Carey and Joseph F. Havelka, "Soviet Agriculture: Progress and Problems," in *Time of Change,* 2:55–86. A valuable Soviet source is A. M. Emel'ianov, ed., *Kompleksnaia programma razvitiia sel'skogo khoziaistva v deistvii,* 2nd ed. (Moscow: Ekonomika, 1980), p. 42.

[7]See Michael D. Zahn, "Soviet Livestock Feed in Perspective," in *Time of Change,* 2:165–87.

[8]Carey and Havelka, "Soviet Agriculture," p. 66.

[9]David M. Schoonover, "Soviet Agricultural Policies," in *Time of Change,* 2:105. See also Judith G. Goldich, "USSR Grain and Oilseed Trade in the Seventies," in the same collection, pp. 133–164.

[10]Daniel L. Bond and Herbert S. Levine, "Energy and Grain in Soviet Hard Currency Trade," in *Time of Change,* 2:244–290.

[11]Paarlberg, "Lessons of the Grain Embargo." The U.S. Department of Agriculture takes a slightly different view, based on a belief that the Soviets intended to import 37.5 million tons and that the real shortfall has consequently been 6 million tons, which was concentrated primarily in the spring months of 1980. The USDA reports declines in Soviet animal weights and in milk and meat production, and it points to the possibility that some distress slaughtering may take place. Paarlberg believes the USDA has exaggerated the extent of the Soviet import shortfall. See U.S. Department of Agriculture, "Impact of Agricultural Trade Restrictions on the Soviet Union,"Foreign Agricultural Economic Report No. 158 (Washington, D.C., April 1980), and same, "Update: Impact of Agricultural Trade Restrictions on the Soviet Union," Foreign Agricultural Economic Report No. 160 (Washington, D.C., July 1980).

[12]This conclusion is shared by Paarlberg, "Lessons of the Grain Embargo," p. 159.

[13]For recent statistics, see Emel'ianov, *Kompleksnaia*, pp. 78–81, 89.

[14]I. Ivannikov, "Kapital'nym vlozheniiam v sel'skoe khoziaistvo—effektivnoe napravlenie," *Planovoe Khoziaistvo* 10 (1978): 65–66.

[15]Address by Professor Gale Johnson of the University of Chicago at the Faculty Club, Harvard University, February 5, 1979. A summary is available under the title "Economic Results in 1978: Is There a Slow-Down in the Soviet and East European Economies?" (Occasional Paper of the Russian Research Center, Harvard University, Cambridge, Mass., February 1979).

[16]Emel'ianov, *Kompleksnaia*, p. 209.

[17]S. Enders Wimbush and Dmitry Ponomareff, *Alternatives for Mobilizing Soviet Central Asian Labor: Outmigration and Regional Development*, R-2476-AF (Santa Monica, Calif.: Rand Corporation, 1979).

[18]Emel'ianov, *Kompleksnaia*, pp. 68, 208.

[19]See, for example, the comments by Brezhnev in the chapter of his auto-biography devoted to the Virgin Lands ("Tselina," *Novyi Mir*, no. 10[1978]:3–55).

[20]Wimbush and Ponomareff, *Alternatives*.

[21]Emel'ianov, *Kompleksnaia*, p. 251. The share of private activity in the total income of collective-farm families has declined from 36.5% in 1965 to 25.2% in 1978.

[22]See Note 2.

[23]See George Breslauer, *Dilemmas of Leadership in the Soviet Union since Stalin: 1953–1976* (Berkeley: University of California Press, forthcoming).

[24]M. Fedin, "Ot delianki do polia," *Pravda*, June 20, 1979.

[25]Central Intelligence Agency, National Foreign Assessment Center, "Biological and Environmental Factors Affecting Soviet Grain Quality" (Washington, D.C.: December 1978).

[26]Philip Hanson, "Soviet Strategies and Policy Implementation in the Import of Chemical Technology from the West, 1958–1978" (California Seminar on Arms Control, Pasadena, Calif., 1980).

[27]The Western scholar who has made the most of this concept is Seymour Goodman in his brilliant work on Soviet computers. See N. C. Davis and S. E. Goodman, "The Soviet Bloc's Unified System of Computers," *ACM Computing Surveys* 10, no. 2 (June 1978): 93–122.

[28]Fedin, "Ot delianki."

[29]Emel'ianov, *Kompleksnaia*, p. 75.

[30]P. I. Simush, "Social Changes in the Countryside," *Kommunist* 16 (1976):61–73. Abstracted in *Current Digest of the Soviet Press* 28, no. 49 (January 5, 1977):1.

[31]Emel'ianov, *Kompleksnaia*, p. 172, gives a total of 466 billion rubles invested between 1966 and 1977 in the entire "agro-industrial complex."

[32]*Ibid.*, p. 75.

[33]This idea is developed further in a forthcoming analysis by Nancy Nimitz of the Rand Corporation on the implications of the July 1979 decree and the future of Soviet economic reform.

[34]Industry in the USSR consumes a larger amount of energy than in the United States, even though Soviet industrial output is some 20% smaller than that of the United States. See Robert W. Campbell, *Soviet Fuel and Energy Balances*, R-2257 (Santa Monica, Calif.: Rand Corporation, 1978). The best overall account of Soviet energy problems is that of Leslie Dienes and Theodore Shabad, *The Soviet Energy System* (Washington, D.C.: Winston, 1979).

[35]Gertrude E. Schroeder, "The Soviet Economy on a Treadmill of 'Reforms,' " in *Time of Change*, 1:312–340.

[36]George Breslauer, *Five Images of the Soviet Future: A Critical Review and Synthesis* (Berkeley: Institute of International Studies, University of California, 1978), writes about the possiblity of "changes in regime-type that come largely from above or through political forces within the Establishment that are strengthened by crisis situations" (p. 4). Included as a factor in Breslauer's analysis are the domestic conditions that may facilitate the realization of one or another scenario.

[37]F. Douglas Whitehouse, "Soviet Resource Allocation in the 1980's: Some Speculation" (Paper prepared for the Council on Foreign Relations' Study Group on Domestic Sources of Soviet Foreign Policy, November 1979).

20

JAMES R. MILLAR

The Household Sector:
*The View from the Bottom**

Introduction: A Methodological Note
   Most western economists assume that the purpose of economic activity is to satisfy individual members of society, and Soviet economists are no exception to this rule. N. Ia Petrakov, a well-known Soviet economist, defined the aim recently as "maximization of the average level of satisfaction of the needs of all members of society." Placement of the individual consumer at the center of the economic universe represents a prescriptive rather than a descriptive judgment, and I concur in the desirability of this view. From a descriptive standpoint, however, several other possible ways of construing ends and means in an economic system exist, and each approach presents certain advantages and disadvantages for analysis.

   If we assume that satisfaction of the wants of the individual is the sole and proper end of all economic activity, then we shall find it difficult to justify certain kinds of government expenditures that we all take for granted, such as defense expenditures, welfare outlays, and the like, where benefits and costs are not distributed according to the individual's evaluations. Moreover, our analysis cannot deal satisfactorily with a situation in which one individual's satisfaction depends upon another's fortune or misfortune. We must assume away both envy and saintliness.

   Karl Marx assumed that all-round physical and intellectual fulfillment of the individual would become the goal of economic activity under socialism, at which time the creation of economic plenty would have undermined self-interest as motive to economic activity and thus the rationale for both envy and saintliness. He assumed that profit would be

*Reprinted by permission of the author and publisher from *The ABCs of Soviet Socialism* (Urbana, Il.: Illinois University Press, 1981), pp. 83–120. Copyright 1981 by The University of Illinois Press.

the goal of economic activity while capitalism prevailed, and he accordingly described the capitalist economy as based upon the exploitation of the many by the few in the quest for profits. The consumer is not, therefore, the end for capitalist economies in Marx's analysis. Similar assumptions have been, and are still, often made by non-Marxists too, particularly by certain social reformers such as consumer advocates or environmental protectionists who see a conflict between the interests of ordinary people and those of giant corporations in quest of profits. Although this assumption often offers an interesting construction for thinking about the economy, it also presents problems from an analytic standpoint. Marx, for example, never did explain why capitalists were devoted to the maximization of profits nor how they could remain blind to a growing conflict of their interests with those of workers and consumers that would, in his view, ultimately eject capitalists from the system. Marx also failed to explain what kinds of motives would ensure satisfactory production of goods and services for use rather than for profits in a system in which distribution would be according to need.

Thorstein Veblen drew a different distinction—between productive and pecuniary employments by which he attempted to divide economic activities into those that serve matter of fact—*real* human needs and those that serve meretricious needs derived from ignorance, gullibility, or propaganda. Hence, he adopted the assumption that individual consumers *ought* to be the goal of economic activity but tried to constrain their needs to a rational, scientifically based set of requirements. Veblen would have restricted economic activities to those that involve providing socially acceptable goods or services. In this respect, he sought to combine the best features of both the neoclassical and Marxian approaches. The problem remains, of course, in distinguishing unambiguously between the good and the bad products. Veblen thought that this distinction would be resolved by a natural process of scientific enlightenment, but it is clear some 60 years later that this was too optimistic a view.

I have reviewed these various assumptions about what the goal of economic activity ought to be in order to emphasize the evaluative and thus the relative nature of any such assumption. Many western students of the Soviet economy have sought to describe it as an economy in which planners' preferences prevail. That is, they assume that the purpose of economic activity is to satisfy those who plan the economic system. The term *planner* is used here in what is ultimately a political and not at all an operational sense. The Politburo, not Gosplan, represents the planners in question. This assumption, like the others I have mentioned, has certain advantages when it comes to describing central planning, especially where it is conceived as command planning. There are other advantages that make it attractive when describing the Soviet economy, where economic goals are at once also high political issues. Even so, as with any such assumption, it is not a purely descriptive concept. It was derived as the obverse of a system of consumer preferences, and no analyst has ever put it forward anywhere as a *desirable long-term basis* for organizing economic activity. It is a pejorative standard instead, and for good reason. Although never fully worked out, it would appear that an economy organized strictly according to the principal of planners' preferences would ultimately have to be an economy in which everyone who is not a planner would be a slave—or perhaps a mindless contributor to economic activity like a worker bee or ant.

We shall have recourse to all of the standards I have described in considering the place of the household in the Soviet economy. We shall see that there is more than a grain of truth in the claim of contemporary Soviet economists that individual satisfaction is the aim of economic activity, and it is useful, in any case, to assess the discrepancies between such a standard and Soviet reality. Similarly, it will be informative to see to what extent the Soviet economy departs from the standard of planners' preferences and to try to understand how consumer and planner preferences are in fact mediated. We shall also find the standards erected by Veblen and by Marx useful alternative measures. As everywhere, it is not always easy to distinguish "goods" from "bads" when it comes to the products of the Soviet or any other economy, and the contrast that Marx drew between capitalism and socialism is helpful because it raises two fundamental and as yet unresolved problems in the economics of distribution and the ethics of human conduct. If distribution of the products of economic activity is to be set according to need, how can this be reconciled with the demand that any incentive system, to be effective, must reward individuals according to their contributions? But if individuals are instead to be rewarded strictly according to their contributions to the economy, what do we do with the helpless? Moreover, do we not thereby also reinforce "lower" rather than "higher" forms of human conduct, thereby sacrificing saintliness and enhancing invidious comparison, envy, and unabashed self-interest? Are self-regard and greed the only workable bases of economic activity?

The View from the Bottom   By describing households as the bottom of the Soviet economy, I mean to contrast the perspective of a single household with that of an agency such as the Council of Ministers or Gosplan, not to indicate the ranking of the household. Individual households look out upon the economy from narrow and highly differentiated windows. The view from the bottom is a collection of views, and we shall build up a reasonably comprehensive and representative general view from the separate standpoints of various households. Although no one household has so broad a view as members of an agency such as the Council of Ministers, there are aspects of household experience that are not visible from the top. The view from the top is not better nor more complex than the view from the bottom. It is merely different.

Over 55% of the Soviet population now lives in regions classified as urban, but this is a recent development, and a large proportion of the urban population of the USSR is first-generation urban. Approximately 25% of the labor force is still directly engaged in agricultural pursuits in the Soviet Union as opposed to less than 4% in the United States. The exodus from the rural community has been exceedingly rapid during the last decade, averaging about 2 million persons per year. This rapid outflow from the rural sector reflects the great differential that exists between standards of living in rural and in urban areas of the USSR, and the outflow is impoverishing the rural community because the young, the energetic, the educated, and the ambitious are the ones who are leaving.

By comparison with the United States or the countries of Western Europe such as France, Italy, or Germany, the USSR is still highly rural in character and is experiencing rapid demographic change. Moreover, the gap between living conditions and professional prospects in rural and urban areas is much greater than in the West. The USSR occupies a very large area, equal to about one-sixth of the surface of the earth. By world standards, it is still lightly populated. Population tends to be concentrated in European Russia, but even this is a large region, and population density is low by comparison with most developed economies. The transportation network is huge when measured in total kilometers. Densities remain relatively low, however, especially in the vast reaches of Siberia and Central Asia. Consequently, the isolation of rural communities is far greater than in the West, and the absence of any significant number of private automobiles or trucks in rural areas is a contributing factor to their isolation. There is no equivalent in the USSR to the pickup truck of the American farm to take the family into town on weekends. There are some regions so remote, in fact, that there is virtually no exit for months at a time during the winter. Television reaches most of these communities, but its message is the superiority of urban life, especially urban life in the choice cities of the USSR: Moscow, Leningrad, Kiev.

Not just anyone may decide to live in a city. In order to obtain an apartment or room in a Soviet city, the individual must ordinarily be employed in the city, but it is hard to find employment unless one already lives in the city. If an individual wishes to live in Moscow, for example, he could sign up with the labor exchange and take his chances on being assigned to Moscow. No one in his right mind would expect so far-fetched a hope to come true. Moscow is the most difficult city of all to move to permanently. Successful provincial administrators and party officials often are assigned to Moscow in the twilight years of their careers as a special sign of preferment and as a reward for faithful service, but ordinary folk are assigned to the regions and cities that are slated for net growth, not to Moscow. Restrictions on movement to desirable cities such as Moscow can be circumvented but essentially only by exceptional professional success, subterfuge, or *blat*. *Blat* is probably the most important. *Blat* is used by Russians to refer to pull, connections, or string-pulling that is used to advance one's own or one's family's interests. (The polite word for *blat* is *protektsiia* [protection].)

There is a hierarchy of living conditions in the Soviet Union with Moscow at the pinnacle and the remote villages of Siberia and Central Asia at the bottom. The upward slope measures more than access to cultural events such as the Bolshoi Ballet or the Mayakovsky Theater. Moscovites live at the center of political power, which acts as a magnet for all of the good things in Soviet life. Food supplies are more reliable and abundant in Moscow than elsewhere. Industrial commodities designed for consumers gravitate to Moscow. Housing is superior; the provision of child-care centers is more adequate; and so it goes.

Since Moscow is the political hub of a highly centralized bureaucracy, it is the best place to get things done. Moscow is the city of *blat*, an artificial city reflecting the best and the worst in the USSR. People who live elsewhere in the USSR must make periodic trips to this political and economic Mecca of the Soviet system to have petitions heard, to meet with superiors, to buy commodities available nowhere else, and to vacation richly. Peasants come to Moscow from the outlying regions with their bags packed with fruit, vegetables, honey, and anything else that can be sold on the *rynok* (private market). After selling everything, they go to see Lenin's remains in Red Square. Next, they spend in Moscow everything they earned at the *rynok*, buying things for themselves and their friends; and they return home with their bags packed with clothing, toys, rugs, china, meat, and phonograph records. Although the details differ, a similar pattern obtains for everyone who lives outside the gates of Moscow and the other major urban centers of the USSR.

We shall begin our examination of the household sector in Moscow and work our way back along the slope down to the muddy lanes of a Siberian village. Along the way, we shall need to consider differentiating factors other than urban location. National and ethnic differences, the place of women, and other factors need to be evaluated as well. Moscow is unique in many such respects, and we must bear this in mind in considering the view from the Moscovite window.

Private Enterprise and Property

The institution of private property exists in the Soviet Union, but it is circumscribed by state (public) ownership of the "means of production," which are defined to include all land, mineral wealth, and most of the reproducible capital. Private individuals may own, and are free to sell privately or to sell through state stores that sell on commission, a wide range of items of personal property. These include not only articles of clothing, television sets, refrigerators, and other personal effects but also certain types of capital equipment such as hand tools, typewriters, gardening supplies, and the like, plus such large items of nonproductive capital as automobiles, apartments, and houses. Moreover, certain attributes of private property adhere to some forms of state property in that the right to use the property can in fact be alienated and transferred to another private party for personal gain. Families may, for example, trade state-owned apartments with each other for mutual benefit. A newly formed family, for example, where wife and husband are legally entitled to and already hold two separate one-room apartments, may trade these for a two- or three-room apartment that houses two families. Similarly a state-owned apartment located in a desirable city such as Moscow may be traded for an apartment in a less desirable city, plus "considerations."

Buying, selling, and trading of personal property is a perfectly legal and open activity either through state "commission" outlets or directly. Certain locations in each city have become trading centers where advertisements are posted and meetings are arranged for purposes of direct trading. The owner of the property, or the property right, is free to charge what the market will bear, without government interference. Legal marketing, of course, shades imperceptibly into illegal trading. Certain types of transactions are proscribed, such as the exchange of rubles for foreign currency. It is also illegal to serve as a middleman in private transactions. That is, one may not legally purchase goods for the purpose of reselling them for personal gain. The deciding factor is intent because a large number of such private transactions do in fact take place at a profit to the seller. It is also illegal to purchase an apartment or an automobile for the purpose of leasing it or otherwise using it as a source of income.

Although no private individual may own land in the Soviet Union, every citizen who is in good legal standing is provided with access through one avenue or another to land for private use. Collective-farm workers receive a plot of land on which to build a home and to maintain a kitchen garden as a function of satisfactory work on the collective farm. The legal situation for state-farm workers is different, but actual arrangements are essentially the same as for collective-farm workers. The great bulk of privately produced and privately marketed food products derives from these two types of private-plot agriculture. Rural households not engaged directly in agricultural employments, such as the local schoolteacher or a clerk in a consumer-cooperative (rural) outlet, are provided access to plots of land on which to build homes, to keep animals, and to tend gardens. Urban dwellers are also provided access to small plots of land on the outskirts of town, where they may build a *dacha* and keep a garden. Because the location is not ordinarily convenient, city dwellers rarely build substantial dwellings on the plots. They are used instead to build *dachas* as summer and/or winter retreats, and most of them are primitive and have few modern conveniences. Ownership of free-standing homes is, therefore, primarily a rural and primitive phenomenon. Similarly, few urban dwellers use their plots to raise substantial gardens.

The ways in which urban dwellers gain access to plots of land are complex and varied, and the size of the plot to which individuals are entitled varies by type of access. A worker may obtain a plot of land through the enterprise for which he or she works. A military officer ordinarily receives a plot through the military bureaucracy. Individuals not otherwise covered may obtain plots of land through the city administration or through a cooperative arrangement and so forth. Over one-half of the privately held plots of land in the Soviet Union today are held by members of the nonagricultural population.

It has become increasingly popular for individuals to build or purchase apartments under cooperative arrangements. Many cooperatives are organized by a place of work, such as the Academy of Sciences, Moscow State University, and Gosplan; and employees sign up to purchase from their employer. The usual arrangements call for 20% down payment and the remainder in installments, frequently without interest. Apartments purchased in this way are expensive, but they offer the roomiest and most comfortable living quarters available in the major cities. A group of private individuals may also arrange to build a condominium and borrow a portion of the cost from the Gosbank. In this instance, an interest charge is involved, normally 2% per annum. Apartment ownership affords the individual in the Soviet Union the largest and probably the most lucrative investment available for private ownership and potential gain. Individuals who purchase an apartment do not pay anything for the land on which the building sits, which is a considerable private benefit in any major city.

In addition to apartments, automobiles, and other consumer durables, individuals may purchase jewelry, paintings, rare books, and similar items as forms of private savings. Private individuals may also own financial assets, which include hand-to-hand currency, savings accounts with the state bank, and state 3% lottery bonds. A type of checking account is now available to certain Soviet citizens, but it is of little domestic use in an economy in which almost all payments are made in cash. Apart from interest receipts on savings accounts and winnings on state-lottery bonds, income from property is illegal in the Soviet Union. One may lend money to a friend, but charging interest would violate the law. Under certain circumstances, one may receive something in consideration for subletting one's apartment or for renting a room (a "corner") to a student, but it is not legal to go into the business of taking in boarders or renting out apartments.

All private wealth may be legally inherited in the Soviet Union. Survivors ordinarily have first claim on the family apartment or *dacha* and, in this respect, certain aspects of private ownership attach to such publicly owned items.

All other property, with the sole exception of collective farms, whose members are supposed to have indivisible (that is, inalienable) rights in the farms' capital stock, is publicly owned in the Soviet Union. Therefore, the profits of state enterprises and rental payments of the population residing in state housing are paid into the various governmental budgets. The state claims all property income in the name of the people and uses income from it to finance investment in state enterprises and to finance construction of new housing and other outlays.

Private enterprise is not actually prohibited, but it is severely limited by prohibitions on hiring others for personal profit, on middleman activities, and on private ownership of the means of production. What private enterprise does exist is necessarily small-scale. The line between legal and illegal private enterprise is not an easy one to draw. Individuals may sell newly produced items that they or their families have produced—for example, on private plots; and they may sell "secondhand" items too. A writer may hire a typist to type his manuscripts; families may hire housekeepers and babysitters; and anyone may hire work to be done or repairs to be made around the house, even though such hiring may contribute to personal income by making the hirer more efficient or by freeing him or her to earn more money elsewhere. True private enterprise is restricted in the Soviet Union to the sale of products of private agricultural plots and to one-man enterprises for home repairs or to such sideline activities as taking patients or clients after work. A large proportion of the latter two categories is conducted in the penumbra of the legal. Nevertheless, private enterprise is ubiquitous and significant in almost everyone's economic life.

Most Soviet citizens work for the state in one way or another for wages or salaries, and most older members of Soviet society receive pensions from the state. Although at one time, an attempt was made to maximize the share of earnings that the worker received in direct nonmonetary benefits, this is no longer the case. Education is free, including higher education in which success in entrance examinations assures all successful applicants free access plus a stipend. Medical care is free, too. Prescription drugs are highly subsidized, as are public transport and even the apartments that most urban dwellers rent from the state. Meals are served very cheaply both in schools and at places of work, and childcare facilities (when available) are provided essentially free. Even so, the bulk of the typical Soviet household's income is received in money, which necessarily implies the existence of retail outlets in which households may choose the ways that their incomes are distributed among the various goods, services, and financial assets that are available. Hence, we see the importance of urban retail markets in the USSR.

Urban Retail Markets

Urban consumers are served by four different types of retail markets. All urban areas are served by state retail outlets. The great bulk of urban household income is expended in these shops. Soviet marketing follows the general European pattern, and most state retail outlets specialize in particular types of products, such as fish, meat and dairy products, bread and confectionary items, clothing, drugs, paper supplies, and so forth. The supermarket and the discount house are found rarely in Moscow and a few other large cities. Most families shop everyday in the assortment of stores in their neighborhoods, purchasing bread in one, milk and dairy products in another, meat in a third, and beer in a fourth. Before American-style retail marketing could become widespread even in Moscow, the average household would have to buy a larger refrigerator, and automobile ownership would have to quadruple. What supermarkets do exist in Moscow work poorly because crowds are too great. One must queue to enter various departments of the store, which defeats a main function of supermarketing. Household members would also have to become accustomed to eating food that is several days old, which would require both a revolution in Soviet packaging and a deterioration in the average citizen's tastes.

Prices are fixed for state retail outlets and are not subject to bargaining. Restaurants and hotels are all state retail enterprises in the Soviet Union, too, and uniform pricing frequently causes anomalies. For example, most meat markets do not grade the meat that they sell by cut. Butchers (who work only with meat axes) divide the meat into portions that are equally composed of good and poor sections of the animal. The flat two-ruble charge per kilo is "justified" in this way. If one knows the butcher, the effective price for "good" cuts may be very low. Similarly, prices on similar dishes are exactly the same in good restaurants as well as bad. Consequently, a meal in a good restaurant is a great bargain, and the same meal in a poor restaurant may be indigestible.

Two kinds of subsidies obtain from many state retail outlets, therefore. Many food products are substantially underpriced and are directly subsidized by the state budget. Most meat products, especially beef, are instances. Underpricing tends to cause queuing for the products affected, not because people go hungry or do without adequate protein, but because at state-quoted prices, which retail outlets cannot vary, these goods are a great bargain. Uniform pricing and the restricted mobility of the typical Soviet customer causes customers of poorly run shops and restaurants to subsidize the well run. Because the better managed shops cannot expand and compete with the poorly run, these differences tend to be self-perpetuating.

An experienced and energetic Soviet shopper learns where to shop for particular items in order to take advantage of peculiarities caused by uniform prices and variations in quality. The system rewards specialized knowledge, friendship, and reciprocity. Goods do not get distributed evenly, and as we have seen, the farther one lives from a major city the less likely that any desirable commodities will ever appear. Meat, including beef, is usually relatively plentiful in Moscow; but 200 km away probably none is to be found most of the time. Moreover, goods are not distributed evenly within the confines of a city such as Moscow. For complex and little understood reasons, certain shops tend to get better and more reliable supplies than others. A certain buffet in a dormitory, for example, may almost always have beer in stock, while regular retail outlets run dry for days at a time. State retail outlets run dry for days at a time. State retail outlets also operate "casual" stands and kiosks for "surplus" items at irregular intervals as well as their regular outlets. An alert shopper learns that certain corners frequently have temporary outlets where particularly desirable goods (such as oranges and apples in winter) are sold when available. By keeping an eye on these locations, remembering which stores nearly always have milk or beer or better meat, and by staying alert to the formation of a queue anywhere, a smart shopper can maximize his opportunities to procure what Soviets call "deficit commodities." The term is used to refer to goods or services that are in short supply all or most of the time. Although there are exceptions, deficit commodities are underpriced items in the state retail network, which causes excess demand to exist for them most of the time.

It pays to make friends with sellers in the USSR, for nearly all the desirable goods that are sold in Soviet state retail outlets are in deficit supply and require the exercise of purchasemanship, the technical equivalent of salesmanship in an economy such as that of the United States. A judicious gift may get deficit commodities set aside for you. Tickets to the Bolshoi Theater ballet performances, for example, ordinarily are impossible to obtain in any normal way from a ticket window in Moscow. They are all either specially ordered for tourists, high officials, and special purposes, or they are distributed under the counter. Soviet shoppers worth their salt develop networks of contacts among those who sell or distribute state retail products and services that allow them to jump the queue for deficit commodities. Frequently, the recipient of such a favor is not required to pay extra for it, but he or she incurs a reciprocal obligation for the future.

Most deficit commodities and services are goods and services provided through state retail outlets, and the individuals who market them can collect what economists call the monopoly rents on these scarce and underpriced items. That is, the employee is in a position to capture a part, or all, of the difference between the actual price established by the state committee in retail prices and the (higher) price that would be required to clear the market (i.e., exactly match the number of buyers with the number of items available). For all intents and purposes, this is a property right individuals acquire by default from the state and are able to exchange for the other deficit commodities they desire.

The second type of retail outlet is the *rynok* (also called the collective farm market). About one-third of the value of all retail food sales in the USSR flows through the *rynok*, which is a completely unfettered market where farmers and others who have grown or produced their own products may hire a stall (and refrigeration if necessary) to sell them. Collective farms may ship their surplus produce to the *rynok*, too. Every city has one or more such markets. Many are enclosed for operation during the winter. Typical products available are carrots, potatoes, pickled cucumbers, tomatoes, peppers, apples, pickled cabbage, honey, cheese and fermented dairy products, dried mushrooms, flowers, spices, seed, and fresh meat in winter time; and the list includes more fruits and vegetables in summer. Prices are generally much higher on the *rynok* than in state retail stores, and one is free to haggle about price. Many Soviet shoppers visit the *rynok* at least once a week, even though it is more expensive than state outlets. Quality tends to be higher, and some items sold there are unavailable in other retail outlets. Anyone planning a dinner party would be certain to visit the *rynok* to buy a delicacy or two. The role of the *rynok* is probably less significant in Moscow than it is elsewhere as a source of staples such as potatoes, milk products, meat, and vegetables because these items are more readily available in state outlets in Moscow. Even so, Moscovites are relatively wealthy and able to afford the higher prices charged on the *rynok*. As a general proposition, it is fair to say that the *rynok* plays a pervasive role in the supply of food products to the Soviet household, and all would be poorer without it. Thus, strange as it seems, most Soviet households deal regularly in a perfectly legal free market for day-to-day needs.

The third type of retail market available to urban dwellers is a private, informal, and legal market in homemade and in secondhand commodities, in apartments and in certain personal services, such as television repair and hairdressing. The state operates secondhand stores on a commission basis. In addition, certain corners have become customary trading sites, and individuals meet there at customary times privately to trade apartments and to sell used automobiles, clothing, records, and the like. Much of this trade is barter, and some of the items that are traded, such as state-owned apartments, are not in fact the property of those trading them. Newspapers take advertisements for certain types of goods, and both formal and informal bulletin boards are used to place advertisements. In addition, certain individuals sell their labor services informally. Any person with a skill, such as repairing electrical equipment, may work on the side on his own time. Whether or not the activity is legal depends upon the nature of the service, the source of spare parts used, and the social implications. Unskilled women frequently do laundry for busy single men, and they may help in shopping, child care, and cooking on a strictly private basis.

This third category of legal informal marketing is difficult to identify uniquely, for it shades off into illegal economic activities on the one side and into legal state-organized secondhand markets on the other. It is worth attempting to isolate this category because of the private and legal character of these transactions. It is important to grasp the volume and diversity of private economic transactions that take place in the USSR on a perfectly legal basis. These transactions are also absolutely unavoidable if the institution of private property in personal possessions is to have operational significance. Open exchange of private property is also important as a means for redistributing durable property from those who no longer require it to those who need it. As with garage sales in the United States, in the process, everyone is made better off without anyone being harmed.

Illegal market transactions comprise the fourth and final type of retail market in the Soviet Union. This market is very complex and ranges from misdemeanors to very sinister economic dealings. Because these transactions are illegal, the outside observer can obtain only a very sketchy impression of them. The evidence suggests, however, that illegal trading at the level of misdemeanor is widespread. A large proportion of the Soviet urban population is implicated—at least on a petty level. Illegal transactions are described variously by Soviet citizens. Soviets talk of obtaining goods *nalevo* (on the left), *po znakomstvu* (through a contact), *na chernom rynke* (on the black market), and *po blatu* (through pull). Each describes an important aspect of this market. Buying *po znakomstvu* is perhaps the most common and least criminal of all. In many circumstances, it is more improper than illegal. Normally in this type of purchase, no direct pecuniary gain is involved for the friend, who instead merely earns a reciprocal claim upon the purchaser. Purchases on the black market are ordinarily from private entrepreneurs who operate for a profit. *Blat,* on the other hand, can be accrued either by bribing someone or by being someone important with whom others seek to curry favor. The most colorful phrase, buying *nalevo,* is the most general: Its meaning encompasses the entire range of illegal and semi-legal activities, both in markets and outside of them, that are encouraged by the institutional and legal structure of the Soviet economy. (Although it may offend the ears of native speakers of Russian, for convenience I shall henceforward use *nalevo* as an adjective as well as an adverb.)

The most desirable consumer goods and services are in deficit supply most of the time in the Soviet economy, and yet prices on these deficit commodities are kept constant. Consequently, queues always develop when these commodities become available, and those who deal in them for the state cannot but be tempted to take advantage of their strategic monopolistic positions to increase their own incomes, to curry favor with superiors, or to benefit their friends. Oddly enough, then, the institutional structure of the Soviet economy actually fosters a large volume of petty trading, petty middleman activities, and petty private enterprise. Today, the Soviet Union is an acquisitive society, a nation of marketeers; and an enormous amount of time is absorbed in shopping, selling, trading, scouting, and queuing for deficit commodities.

Consumption and Living Standards

By the most careful Western estimates, consumption per capita has almost doubled since Stalin's death in 1953. The fact that deficit commodities remain numerous reflects both the incredibly low standard of living at the end of postwar reconstruction and the continuation of official policies that tend to perpetuate such deficits. In planning the volume of consumer goods and services to be made available, Gosplan must consider two aspects. First, it is obvious that the total value of consumer goods and services provided by the state must have *some* relationship to the quantity of labor the state intends to employ and the average earnings of these workers. Second, and more important, the more developed the society is, the proportions in which the different consumer goods are produced (i.e., how many automobiles, refrigerators, and sewing machines, and how much meat, milk, and wool cloth to produce) must bear a definite relationship to the way in which consumers wish to distribute their incomes among them. The output of consumer goods has increased very sharply in the USSR over the last 25 years, but changes in the composition of output have not kept pace, perpetuating the existence of deficit commodities.

Prices in state retail outlets are set by a state committee of the Council of Ministers, and they reflect many factors other than supply and demand. Prices on many items of food, such as bread, meat, and milk, have been set below cost, whereas prices on certain scarce luxury goods are set relatively high, approximating supply–demand conditions. Therefore, willingness to stand in line becomes a factor in the distribution of many goods, and the final result is a distribution of goods and services that is probably more equal than the distribution of money income. To some extent, this is deliberate policy, but it also reflects a policy of stability in retail prices that Soviet leaders have promised the population ever since Stalin died. Accordingly, apart from surreptitious price changes mainly on nonessentials, retail prices have increased only marginally in more than two decades. The Soviet population clearly appreciates this policy, for it prevents the erosion of their savings by inflation; and this is particularly important in an economy in which installment payments and other forms of credit buying are not available to consumers.

The policy of price stability has had adverse effects, however. For many food products, notably meats and products of animal husbandry, retail price stability has led to massive subsidies by the state, for the real cost of producing agricultural products has been rising rapidly since 1953. Relative prices for industrial commodities and for agricultural products are completely unrealistic, therefore, and an adjustment is long overdue. Thus far, however, the political leaders have apparently felt that trading *nalevo* (i.e., under the counter) and all that it implies is more acceptable than the adverse reaction they expect to increased prices. Eventually, however, an adjustment will have to be made between agricultural products and industrial products and among individual food products as well.

In addition to a policy that fosters the persistence of deficit commodities, the system of state retail sales outlets is inadequate to the task of supplying the Soviet consumer. Space for retail sales is inadequate. Poor service has no effect upon the incomes of retail service workers, and inventories that cannot be sold do not have a serious impact upon incomes or incentives of those who work in retail outlets. There is little incentive to provide good service, therefore; and that many commodities remain in deficit supply makes service workers surly more often than not. Retail outlets cannot respond to their customers' preferences in any case but must retail what they receive. The only room for maneuver they have is on an individual basis, which means *nalevo*.

The scarcity of the more desirable consumer goods and services has become institutionalized officially as well as privately. Whereas the private response has been to expand activities *nalevo*, the official response has been to create special shops that permit selected people to avoid queuing for deficit commodities. These special groups include foreign tourists, correspondents, and diplomats, which is understandable in a country anxious to earn foreign exchange. But these groups include individuals in Soviet society who are rewarded through special access to stores that are well stocked and do not have queues. The temptation posed by the existence of deficit commodities, which produces trading *nalevo* privately, yields special stores with curtained windows to screen out unwelcome eyes for high-placed party and government officials and for other successful people as well. The right to purchase deficit commodities in special stores or by special order is clearly a powerful incentive in the Soviet economy, and it certainly makes sense to exempt hard-working highly placed officials from queuing with the population. Yet the persistence of deficit commodities is having a negative effect upon the fabric of Soviet life. The closest analogy in American history is perhaps Prohibition, when keeping the right hand from knowing what the left hand was doing became a national pastime, encouraged general contempt for the law, and facilitated the widespread development of organized crime. The great expansion of trading *nalevo* and of special stores in the Soviet Union during the last decade or so is undoubtedly contributing not only to similar developments but to widespread cynicism regarding the idealistic goals the regime so often and loudly proclaims.

As I already indicated, Moscow is an artificial city in many respects, particularly when it comes to retail trade. Moscow's retail network is larger and better supplied than elsewhere in the USSR. The state also operates a large number of special stores, most of them known as *berëozki*, where foreigners and Soviets who somehow acquire foreign currency or are given special privileges for some official reason may purchase goods not available elsewhere or may jump the queue on generally scarce items. Naturally, there is a good deal of leakage from these special stores into private markets, and foreign visitors and dwellers offer many additional opportunities to purchase foreign-made items, such as blue jeans, Persian coats, and the like, as well as for exchanging currency. *Nalevo* markets in Moscow are, therefore, also better stocked than elsewhere.

Because of these exceptional opportunities and because of the relative wealth of the city's population, Moscovites are better dressed, better housed, better fed, better entertained, and more sophisticated than Russians in other cities, although Leningraders would be reluctant to agree on all points. Moscovites are also probably more alienated than any comparable population in the USSR, too. Certainly, it is a hotbed of dissidence. Nonetheless, what is true of Moscow is true in one degree or another for other parts of the USSR. The Soviet retail distribution system is sluggish and works only in fits and starts. The farther one gets from Moscow, the less effective it is, and the smaller the community to be served, the worse the service.

Even in Moscow, for example, oranges will suddenly flood the city in the middle of winter. Oranges will be seen being vended everywhere: in regular retail outlets, in dining halls, and on street corners by state retail clerks; and for 2 weeks, there will be an orgy of orange sales and consumption. Just as suddenly as the sale began, it will end because the entire boatload from Egypt or Sicily will have been exhausted. Wise customers, knowing that sales will soon end, will have bought as many oranges as possible. A few weeks later, a similar scene will involve lemons, which will have been unavailable for a month or so previously.

Moscow and other large Soviet cities are "black holes" in the Soviet system of retail distribution, which is why smaller communities rarely see deficit commodities in their stores or on their streets. That such commodities appear first in the major cities encourages villagers to visit periodically to exploit their availability, and city folks always buy extra for their relations in less favored retailing regions. In this sense, Moscow is the supermarket of the USSR, for the Soviet retail distribution system relies heavily upon private cash-and-carry distribution of deficit commodities beyond the confines of Moscow. An examination of the personal cargoes of individuals returning to Novosibirsk, Omsk, Tomsk, or Irkutsk will provide astounding confirmation of the actual volume of private distribution of deficit commodities. All major cities serve similar roles.

Rural areas are officially served by what is known as consumer cooperatives, but this network only had a true separate existence years ago. Today, these outlets are indistinguishable from state retail stores (except, perhaps, in being more poorly stocked), and its employees are state workers. The consumer cooperative network is, if anything, less efficient and effective than the state network, primarily for the reasons just given. In 1974, the total turnover in trade carried on in this system was less than one-half that of state retail outlets, despite the fact that it serves almost as large a population. Consequently, those people who live in the thousands and thousands of villages that compose the state and collective farms of the USSR must rely much more heavily than urban dwellers upon their own productive efforts and upon the rural *rynok*, which is a more informal market than its urban counterpart. Rural dwellers in warm agricultural regions fare quite well when it comes to certain kinds of food products such as tomatoes, cucumbers, and fruits, which are deficit items in northern cities. Opportunities to trade these products in urban markets can offer substantial profits, too. Even so, a drawback for all who live in places distant from major cities is the need both to transport their own products to market and to carry back industrial products at their own expense. Having a relative or two in a major city is an essential condition for reasonable living in most rural regions. In a similar way, although cultural opportunities are provided by the state agencies in remote cities and even in villages of the USSR, such appearances are sporadic and rarely include leading performers.

The difference between retail distribution systems in most Western capitalist countries and that of the USSR resembles the difference between a gravity-flow and a forced-air central heating system for a building. The latter tends to distribute heat more or less uniformly throughout the building, with only minor losses of efficiency in extreme wings. A gravity system must be properly designed to avoid uneven heating problems. The Soviet retail distribution system resembles a malfunctioning gravity-flow system, with Moscow located in such a way that deficit commodities gravitate to it at the expense of all other regions. Leningrad, Kiev, and Novosibirsk, for example, do better than Novgorod, Alma-Ata, or Irkutsk; and a hierarchy exists in the supply system that stretches all the way to the village. Moreover, the state retail system operates primarily on the basis of the tastes and cultural preferences of the great majority of the population that lives in European Russia. There are villages in Siberia and in Central Asia, for example, that are so remote culturally as well as geographically that the state retail system does not penetrate at all. The weakness of the state retail distribution system is, therefore, a powerful contributor to maintenance of the already large discrepancies that exist in the USSR today between urban and rural standards of living.

According to western estimates, the Soviet over-all standard of living has almost doubled since 1953; but this seems difficult to believe when one examines Soviet life firsthand today. It seems unreasonable, in the first place, that the standard of living in 1953 could have been low as is implied. Our evidence indicates that the standard of living in 1953 was not materially different, over-all from what it had been in 1928; and 1928 was probably not much better than 1913. For 40 years, then, Soviet living standards remained at, or below, the prerevolutionary level. In the second place, it is not immediately apparent to a contemporary observer what the improvements have been.

The most striking advances in living conditions for anyone who has watched these improvements over the years are in clothing, including shoes; the supply of food, particularly in animal husbandry products, fruits, and vegetables; housing; and in ownership of consumer durables and automobiles. Ten or 15 years ago, any foreigner in Moscow stood out like a sore thumb because of the quality and cut of his clothing, and his shoes were a dead giveaway, too. When women dressed their best in those years, they looked inferior to women in ordinary street clothing in Moscow today, and the same holds for men's suits, overcoats, and shoes. Vegetables and fruits were simply never available in the wintertime, and the amount of meat regularly available today is striking by comparison. Housing construction has continued at a high rate for two decades now, and renovation of older dwellings has also been carried out on a large scale. The number of square feet per urban dweller has increased despite a rapid increase in the size of the urban population, and the quality of new apartments has improved because they are self-contained, not communal. Actual construction quality has probably declined, however. Some consumer durables that are commonplace today were rarities only 15 years ago. Even the peasants have refrigerators today, although many complain that they stay empty most of the time. Sewing machines are widely owned, as are, of course, radios, television sets, and stereo systems. Finally, anyone who visited the Soviet Union in the early 1960s and returned for the first time today would be amazed by the number of private automobiles on the streets of Moscow. In the 1960s, even Moscow looked like a huge construction site or a giant factory, for the streets carried mainly trucks and buses. The few automobiles were official cars or taxis.

I believe that it is possible to credit a large increase in the Soviet standard of living over the last 25 years, but this increase has not been evenly distributed geographically. A visit even to a large city in Siberia, for example, takes one back to the way Moscow looked 10 or so years ago. Queues have diminished everywhere, and they exist in the major cities mainly for luxuries—for the best meat, for premium butter, for cucumbers or lemons in March, and so forth. The population has money, and it has the habit of queuing, and it will be a long time before queuing is eliminated from Soviet shopping habits. Scarcity-mindedness causes individuals to buy large quantities of scarce items when they appear. They buy for the future, for their relatives, and for their friends. Thus, as a hedge against doing without, individuals provide the storage space for many items that are not actually scarce. Psychologically, the Soviet shopper has been traumatized by shortages and has organized her or his life in such a way that queuing, taking advantage of un-expected appearances of deficit commodities, and sharing with friends are integral aspects of everyday life. The long years of sacrifice will take an even longer time to be compensated and forgotten. Meanwhile, everyone shops with determination, a pocketful of rubles, and surpris-ing generosity.

Labor Markets and Private Entrepreneurship

Gosplan and the various ministries plan the allocation of labor in the same way that they do other resources. Labor balances are worked out for each region and republic and compared with enterprise requirements. The allocation of labor involves markedly different problems and methods. Marxist theory, of course, distin-guishes sharply between labor and commodities under socialism, for labor represents a very special kind of resource and one for which economic activity is largely intended, according to Marxian assump-tions. In addition, the labor market is open. That is, although it is a regulated market in the sense that a state committee of the Council of Ministers sets wage rates, safety standards, and other conditions of work for all public employment, individual workers exercise primary discretion concerning their own participation in the economy.

Labor markets may be separated into five different categories: state, collective-farm, private-plot, and legal and illegal private labor service. This division emphasizes the significance of private markets. I am not suggesting that these markets operate separately. On the contrary, these various markets are intertwined in complex ways, and to an unknown degree, private markets actually help to explain why the Soviet economy functions as well as it does concerning the satisfaction of consumer preferences. Products and services that would not otherwise be avail-able are produced privately in the USSR, and private trade helps to distribute and redistribute commodities and services that would otherwise never reach those who want them most. In addition, and of particular importance, private markets tend to convert public property into private property for private gain. One result is a different distribution of final consumer goods and services from that which would take place in the absence of private enterprise and trade, and this means in all likelihood a distribution of goods and services that benefits higher income classes more than the state intends. Another result is to convert what are intended as investment and government expenditures into private consumption, which tends to benefit all current consumers taken together at the expense of state nonconsumption projects. In other words, private markets, particularly illegal private markets in this instance, tend to undermine the percentage shares given in the plan for investment and for government outlays. It may, of course, be argued that current consumers are gaining at the expense of future consumption or the future military safety of the population rather than at the expense of the state; but few citizens would be deterred by such an argument after long years of sacrificing for a future that never seems to arrive.

Immediately prior to, during, and for some years following World War II, strict controls were applied in the allocation of labor and to minimize labor shirking; and civilian labor was even at times conscripted along with military. Soviet citizens today, however, exercise considerable freedom of calling in that they may decide whether or not to work, allocate themselves among jobs, and, to a lesser extent, among locations of work; and they may determine the intensity with which they will work as well. Freedom of calling is further bolstered by the availability of employments in occupations not controlled by the state, both legal and illegal.

Most Soviet able-bodied citizens work for the state in one capacity or another. Most work for a state industrial or agricultural enterprise, but no small number is employed in the various state bureaucracies. The largest exception to state employment is the collective farm, but employment on collective farms today is not significantly different in terms and conditions from employment on state farms. For the present, therefore, we shall lump together collective- and state-farm workers. Both in the countryside and in urban areas, the rate of female participation is very high in the Soviet Union, higher than anywhere else in the world. The high rate of female participation reflects at least two factors: liberation of women by the Bolshevik philosophy and the necessity of two incomes for maintaining a satisfactory standard of living.

All able-bodied citizens are under considerable social pressure to contribute gainfully to the economy. Legal measures are also possible and have been invoked against those persons who are designated *social parasites*. The charge of social parasitism is more common these days, however, as a weapon against political dissidents than it is as a source of labor. Recently, able-bodied individuals, including those who are alien-ated from Soviet society, have been allowed to remain outside of regular gainful employment so long as some family member is prepared to guarantee support. If the person in question is an able-bodied woman with young children, she may withdraw from employment voluntarily to care for them and her husband with little notice. The wives and children of well-to-do successful members of Soviet society are not troubled by antiparasite laws either. There are many other Soviets, most of whom are beyond the age for retirement (60 for males and 55 for females), who have the choice of supplementing their incomes by working as cloakroom clerks, doormen, watchmen, and so forth. A large proportion of the existing Soviet labor force is completely free to work or to withdraw from employment as it sees fit. As a result, the Soviet labor force must be regarded as a function of individual evaluation of real wages as it is in labor markets in capitalist countries. Thus, we shall describe the labor market as open, and this has an essential bearing, as we shall see, upon the central planning and management of the Soviet economy.

The labor market comprises a complex collection of markets—some public, others private; and it is a huge market because it touches the life of every Soviet household and every enterprise and organization. Be-cause it is an open market in which individuals exercise freedom of vocation within broad limits, it is more accurate to conceive of labor as being centrally managed rather than planned, for planning under such circumstances can mean little more than extrapolation of current trends. Direct central allocation applies only to the military service, to the penal system, and to available educational slots in the USSR today. The remainder of the labor force is self-allocated by incentives provided in public and private employments, and the intensity with which in-dividuals work in any given employment is also self-determined.

The largest and most important single labor market is employment in state and industrial enterprises. Most able-bodied men and women in the Soviet Union work with one of these economic enterprises or with the administrative, military, or police bureaucracies of the state. A large number of retired persons are also employed by state enterprises and agencies on a full- or part-time basis. Pensions are low, and not every-one of pensionable age today is entitled to a pension. Thus, many old persons work to make ends meet. A pensioner is entitled to earn up to a fixed amount per month before his pension is docked, which is a powerful incentive to work because the upper limit is relatively high.

Employment with state enterprises and agencies is, superficially at least, not noticeably different from employment in similar occupations elsewhere in the developed world. Although there was some disagree-ment during the 1920s about adopting the factory system that the Bolsheviks inherited from Tsarist Russia and Europe, the system was adopted in all important respects. State employees work a fixed time now averaging close to 40 hours per week, are expected to appear regularly and punctually, and to work under the supervision of foremen, who are themselves directed by a single manager and his staff. In general, a casual observer from the West would see nothing peculiar about the way work goes forward on the shop floor in a Soviet enterprise.

There are, however, some distinctive features of this labor market. No Soviet enterprise or official endeavor lacks a corresponding branch of the Soviet trade-union system, known as the *profsoiuz*. But, as was pointed out earlier, trade unions have no say in the management of state enterprises or agencies. Neither do they have the legal right to strike or to order any organized withdrawal of efficiency or to protest about wages, hours of work, and so forth. Agreements are worked out periodically between the *profsoiuz* and enterprise, trust, or other administrative level, which spell out conditions of work, safety provisions, welfare benefits, and so forth, but they do not specify wage benefits. Local *profsoiuz* representatives serve as grievance boards to settle petty disputes among workers and between workers and management, and they also serve as "cheerleaders" in support of fulfilling plan targets. The Soviet *profsoiuz* is little more than an ineffectual company union with all that implies in the way of serving the interests primarily of the bosses. Recent efforts to create independent, worker-controlled, nationally affiliated unions in Poland have no visible counterparts in the USSR, but success in Poland may very well set a powerful example for Soviet workers. Hence the Soviet government's watchful concern.

Salary and wage scales are determined for all state enterprises including state farms and organizations, according to schedules that are developed and maintained by the State Committee on Labor and Wages. Wage differentials are determined by considering a number of factors—such as unpleasant or dangerous conditions at work, remoteness of the region in which employment is offered, the degree of skill or educational preparation required, and seniority. Many of these factors reflect, of course, the evaluations that many individuals would make concerning the desirability of these various jobs, and to this extent, centralized wage-setting reflects supply conditions indirectly. The ultimate test of a wage rate is whether too few or too many workers apply for the jobs that it governs, and in this respect, the State Committee on Labor and Wages is ultimately influenced by general conditions of supply and demand as well as by the formal criteria elaborated for wage determination. The government has been trying to persuade workers to move permanently to Siberia, for example, to take part in the exploitation of the vast, almost untouched resources of the region, and wage differentials are set to make working in Siberia attractive. The differential has attracted workers, but it has not been sufficient to induce them to bring their families.

Consequently, workers return home to warmer, more hospitable climes after several years of concentrated saving. Given the priority that development of Siberia has had for more than two decades, this example illustrates the limits that freedom of calling places on the State Committee on Labor and Wages.

Moreover enterprise managers compete with each other for skilled reliable workers, which has reinforced the impact of specific shortages upon effective wages. Although managers cannot change wage-rates, they can promote desirable individuals into higher pay-categories in order to retain them. Or the managers can let their employees hold more than one position—so that they earn two, three, or even four salaries. In general, then, supply and demand do influence the allocation of labor in the Soviet Union both between state employment and employment in the private sector (or leisure) and among employments in the socialized sector of the Soviet economy. Wage differentials in the state sector have, however, been diminished substantially in recent years by relatively high minimum wages and by the difficulty that managers face in attempting to eliminate redundant labor. Incompetent or otherwise unsatisfactory workers are almost impossible to fire; and wage differentials are often too weak to prevent the oversupply of some kinds of labor at the cost of undersupply for others.

Collective farms employ a large but diminishing number of individuals in the Soviet economy, and the conditions under which collective-farm workers (*kolkhozniks*) work are not substantially different today from those under which state-farm workers (*sovkhozniks*) work. *Kolkhozniks* are eligible for pensions; they receive the bulk of their pay in money wages rather than in kind; and they receive regular wages based upon a minimum guaranteed annual wage. *Kolkhoz* workers normally are given access to a larger private plot than the state-farm worker, and children of *kolkhozniks* have a right to become a member of the *kolkhoz*, a right the children of *sovkhozniks* do not have. More important today is the fact that members of wealthy collective farms, which usually means those that specialize in the production of certain labor-intensive and highly valuable commodities such as tea leaves, silk, or tobacco, do better on the average than state-farm workers. Most collective-farm workers do worse, however, although the difference has narrowed recently as a result of converting poor collectives into state farms.

The income that peasants earn from both state and collective farms has increased substantially over the last 25 years. Although the rate of increase has reduced the gap between industrial–urban occupations and rural employments, it has not prevented the continued migration of the most ambitious and highly skilled young people from rural occupations. Cultivation of private plots by *kolkhozniks*, *sovkhozniks*, and other rural dwellers is the third largest source of employment in the Soviet Union today, and it is the largest single private sector. At one time, Soviet economists believed that private-plot agriculture competed with collective-farm agriculture for workers, and it might once have been so. Today, however, Soviet economists are persuaded that few able-bodied workers are engaged in private-plot agriculture, and the few who are able-bodied are nearly always women with young children to care for, who would not offer extensive employment to the collective in any case. Even so, the presence of the private plot serves as a powerful incentive to have one member of any rural family qualify as a full-time worker on a state or collective farm. Earnings from the plot provide an important source of consumption and of additional money income for rural families, and labor is utilized that would not otherwise be available to the farm, particularly that of the very young and the old. Private-plot agriculture supplies most of the products that flow through the urban *rynok* and plays an important supplemental role in both the income of farm workers and the diets of urban dwellers.

There is a fourth legal labor market in the USSR of indeterminant size. It is not possible to distinguish unambiguously between the legal market in private labor services and the illegal, but the distinction is important. Many individuals participate in both legal and illegal aspects of private employment, and some activities take place in the penumbra between the legal and illegal where the distinction is one for the courts to resolve. Among the legal occupations are those that involve a direct personal service for someone, such as caring for children, housekeeping, typing manuscripts, doing laundry, and gardening. In addition, anyone may sell the products of his own (or of his family's) labor in the *rynok* or personally. It is also legal for a group of individuals, such as carpenters, bricklayers, or other craftsmen to band together in a collective to build homes, do repairs, and the like on a private, but cooperative, basis. Just how important such collectives are is not an available statistic, but they have always been more important in rural areas than in urban because there are many more private homes and *dachas* in the countryside. In general, an individual may exercise a skill that he has acquired in order to earn, or to supplement, his income; but here we move into an obscure territory. A person who knows how to repair electrical equipment may freely repair his own or his friend's television set. He may also repair a set belonging to a "friend of a friend" without charge but with the clear intention of collecting a reciprocal favor at a future time from the friend or the set's owner. It may even be legal for the repairer to receive a cash payment for his service, although this is not patently clear. The situation, however, is rarely so neatly defined. Any of these instances would be illegal if the repairman used spare parts taken from his official place of work, used stolen tools, or did the repairs on working time in the state shop without billing the customer for it.

Plumbers, carpenters, repairmen of all sorts, handymen, individuals who own private cars or who chauffeur for the state, and so forth can periodically earn a personal profit on the basis of their skills or their access to state property. Although it is technically illegal to do so, chauffeurs for state officials frequently use time that they know will otherwise be spent sitting in wait to taxi individuals for private gain, and the state pays for the gasoline. Some individuals specialize in approaching foreign tourists in hopes of buying or begging some prize item for subsequent (illegal) resale or in the expectation of obtaining foreign currency in exchange for rubles. Many individuals manufacture *samogon* (illegal drinking alcohol) in their kitchens, and those who make it well and in large quantity can exchange or sell it as a sideline. Drivers of state-owned taxis frequently take advantage of late-night fares to earn something over and above the standard fare, to sell liquor after hours, and to refer clients to ladies of the night.

In a similar vein, *blat* can get one out of a difficult spot, it can help one jump a queue, and it can be used for personal advancement. For deficit commodities or services, rubles are frequently useless unless mixed with *blat*, friendship, or a contact in the black market. Where legality ends and illegality begins in these instances is hard to determine, and anyone who is involved in these kinds of transactions takes a certain risk in doing so. Interestingly enough, this implicates almost every household in the major cities of the USSR and no small number of rural folk, where producing *samogon* is the most frequently cited crime. The exceptions are likely to be officials so highly placed that *blat* works silently and unbidden for them anyway. There was a time when it was said that "*blat* is higher than Stalin." Today, it is accurate to say that *blat* is the only hard Soviet currency.

To exaggerate the volume of illegal and quasi-legal economic transactions in the USSR today would be wrong. No figures and no official estimates are available about them as there are for the collective-farm markets and private-plot agriculture, but no one doubts that private trading, both legal and illegal, is extremely pervasive. Whether total turnover on this market is 10 or 15% of total real Soviet national product, no one can say with confidence; but that it touches every household on at least a weekly basis no one could doubt. The apparent sharp increase in *nalevo* markets in recent years may serve as a measure of a growing disparity between planners' and consumers' preferences in the USSR. The lesson seems to be that planners cannot enforce their own preferences in the face of an open labor market. This would require, in all likelihood, a return to strict labor controls, a resumption of forced labor, and much more extensive policing of economic activities. No current leader has indicated willingness to pursue so drastic a solution, although one does hear nostalgic references to the public "order" that Stalin maintained.

Labor-Force Participation, Mobility, and Productivity Given existing legal restraints on working age, existing wages, and work conditions, and the social and legal pressures on the individual to contribute to economic activity, the available labor force in the USSR is determined essentially by the rate at which the overall population grows and by the way this increase is distributed geographically. The Soviet population as a whole has been growing relatively slowly over the past two decades. The rate for both the USSR and the USA has been in the neighborhood of 1.4% per annum, and it is declining. Like the United States, the USSR experienced a postwar baby boom. Now that this bulge in the population has been absorbed into the labor force, available labor will increase at a much slower pace than previously, and the miniscule growth of the labor force in the 1980s will adversely effect the growth of Soviet national income. Because labor-participation rates of both men and women are high, little additional labor can be obtained by trying to increase participation rates. The Soviet labor-participation rate for women is so high that it is much more likely to fall than to rise, and the same may be true for males, too, unless purchasing power increases steadily.

The main source of possible growth of the labor force for the industrial sectors of the economy would be by the diminishing of the labor force required by the agricultural sector. As we have seen, the proportion of labor that is currently devoted to agricultural production is large by comparison with other developed countries—about 25% of total employment. It is doubtful, however, that this potential pool of industrial labor can be realized in the near future because productivity is increasing very slowly and because of the priority that expansion of agricultural output occupies at present.

The distribution of the rural population poses an additional problem for Soviet planners. Population-growth rates are generally lower in the cities than in rural regions; and, more important, growth rates are highest in both urban and rural regions where certain minority ethnic groups live. The populations of Central Asia, for example, are growing rapidly, especially in rural areas. Growth of the Soviet industrial-labor force will require the absorption of the net increase in these populations. There are two ways to go about it. One is to encourage non-Russian nationals to move to the industrial cities outside their traditional cultural regions by creating appropriate wage differentials. Thus far, Soviet planners have been reluctant to encourage members of minority groups such as those of Central Asia to move to the cities of European Russia, and it would appear also that the campaign to induce workers to move permanently to Siberia has been conducted mainly among the various European populations of the USSR. In any event, Soviet planners have not looked with favor upon the creation of ethnic outposts in the main industrial centers of the USSR. Great Russians go out to the various non-Russian republics to fill high administrative posts and skilled occupations, but no significant reverse flow of the unskilled to European Russia has taken place. Many Soviet and western students of Soviet ethnic groups claim that these ethnic groups do not wish to move and cannot be induced to move in any case, but the argument is undermined by the presence of similar cultural and ethnic minorities—that is, Turks, Pakistanis, Indians, and Persians, in the cities of Western Europe and England, which are further removed from the centers of their native culture than are the cities of European Russia or Central Siberia.

The alternative is to distribute investment preferentially to these minority republics and regions in order to utilize the relatively rapid natural increase in their populations; but this procedure tends to reinforce "undesirable" centrifugal ethnic and national forces already under way in the USSR. Soviet planners, therefore, face a difficult dilemma, neither horn of which can be completely evaded. This is just one component of the problem that the Soviet Union's restless national minorities pose for Soviet planners and political leaders in the near future, and the underlying economic problem of labor scarcity cannot be resolved independently of official nationality policy. It is useless for Soviet leadership to proclaim, as Brezhnev has said repeatedly, that the nationality problem has been solved. The problem is yet to be addressed as a living fact, but labor scarcity and rising ethnic-consciousness ensure that it will be posed, probably in dramatic fashion, in the near future.

If little industrial labor is likely to result from a diminution in the agricultural labor force during the next 5 years, the main source of growth must lie in the productivity of labor already in the industrial sector. When measured on an average annual basis, Soviet industry has a good record regarding increases in labor productivity since the early 1950s. The increase has, however, been erratic; and a more serious problem is an apparent downward trend over the last decade. This trend may be spurious, of course; but the evidence for stagnation in the rate of growth of labor productivity seems firm. The decline that has taken place probably reflects the fact that the largest gains from borrowing new technology from the West and from training the illiterate have already been assimilated. The decline no doubt also reflects the shift of a much larger share of investment resources to the agricultural sector in the last decade or two, for agriculture has not yielded the kind of gains in productivity that were registered in the industrial sector earlier. There is another problem that may be more fundamental—the intensity with which Soviet labor works. Increased productivity in industry and in agriculture as well will require the elimination of redundant labor and a renewed willingness of Soviet workers to work harder and to learn new skills.

A good deal of evidence suggests that Soviet workers could readily increase the efficiency and intensity with which they work. The problem for central planners, however, is overcoming the institutional barriers that encourage and protect redundancy and low productivity. Even casual observation reveals several different types of redundancy in the Soviet economy. In the first place, a large number of jobs exist that appears to signify little economically. For example, every public building has a doorman or woman, several coatchecks, a number of janitors, and various repairmen. Moreover, every separate institute or administrative division within the building has a watchman or woman who controls access to the floor or wing that the office or institute occupies. University dormitories and many apartment buildings have similar persons who ensure against unauthorized entry and therefore against theft or encroachment. Similarly, almost every office, institute, factory, and store has a fleet of automobiles and vans that are used to transport authorized people on business; and many people have chauffeured cars assigned for their exclusive use. These drivers sit idle much of the time, waiting to take someone to or from an assignment. Many of these functions are either necessary or useful, such as the ubiquitous coatchecks in a country where one wears heavy clothing over half the year, and many are sinecures that provide small incomes to retired or invalided persons. Other positions, however, such as personally assigned chauffeurs and KGB guards, are held by the able-bodied and afford good incomes.

The second type of redundancy that casual observation reveals in the USSR is in staffing services, particularly in certain types of retail sales and in offices. Oddly, this may not be true redundancy on a global basis because retail sales, for example, are understaffed in aggregate. Existing workers are badly distributed among outlets. Some hardly have enough people to serve all the customers, while others have few products to sell and nothing for half the staff to do most of the time. Judging by comments in Soviet professional magazines and newspapers, this kind of maldistribution of the existing labor force is characteristic of industrial and agricultural enterprises as well. The institutional basis for the persistence of an inefficient allocation of the labor force lies, first, in the legal difficulties that managers face in removing individuals from the work force and, second, in the fact that there is little incentive for managers to trim redundant labor. On the contrary, it is often convenient to have a certain amount of redundancy (the Soviet terminology is *reserves*) to handle peak demand, for managerial bonuses result primarily from fulfilling annual output-targets, not in minimizing costs.

A third source of the inefficiency that characterizes the Soviet labor force taken as a whole is the ineffectiveness of the material incentive system. Much emphasis has always been placed in Soviet industry upon moral incentives. Moral incentives refer to nonmaterial kinds of gratification workers and managers may obtain from doing good work. They include the receiving of medals, winning competitions, having one's name or factory written up in the newspaper, and the like. Moral incentives were important sources of productivity gains in the 1930s, during World War II, and afterward; but they have apparently lost much of their effectiveness today. Unfortunately, the system of material incentives has never been thoroughly overhauled to reflect its increased significance as the prime mover in inducing efficiency and con-scientiousness. Moreover, persistent shortages in retail outlets tend to undermine the effectiveness of material incentives, particularly where the individual cannot be fired for laziness or have his salary docked for lacking ambition. Obviously, a society in which acquisition of the most desirable commodities requires either queuing or *nalevo* involvement in the economy is one in which a clever worker may find advancement to a more responsible or otherwise demanding position no advantage what-ever. The move up may reduce the time that he or she has available for queuing, or it may remove the individual from the strategic position he or she occupies with respect to deficit commodities or *blat*.

Increased productivity is an inviting path toward increased output in the Soviet economy, but it can only be attained in the long run by changing the institutional structure within which Soviet workers and managers operate. That the great bulk of all Soviet employed persons work for the state in one capacity or another makes the problem of eliminating redundancy and increasing productivity a political issue in the same way that the pricing of products in state retail outlets is a political problem. As an economic problem, neither issue presents any conceptual or behavioral difficulties. Socialization of the means of pro-duction has politicized economic decision making in the USSR as it has elsewhere following widespread nationalization. Some important prob-lems are solved, of course, by taking them out of the economic realm; but others that are very intractable for political decision making are often created at the same time. Although the balance depends upon one's objectives, wholesale nationalization has become less attractive to many contemporary socialists owing to this realization.

One problem that wholesale nationalization did solve in the USSR, however, involved periodic layoffs resulting from business fluctuations. The fact that Soviet enterprises do not lay off workers when sales or profits lag is, of course, the obverse side of the job-security problem that managers face in trying to use labor forces efficiently. Soviet national income and industrial and agricultural output do fluctuate but for reasons distinct from those that bring about business cycles in capitalist countries. Employment does not fluctuate systematically with output because the two are severed by job security and by the commitment of the government to provide jobs for all who seek to work. Redundancy in Soviet economic enterprises reflects these factors.

The Soviet Union has unemployment, however; but it tends to be one of three noncyclical types. Individuals who are in the process of voluntarily seeking different or better-located employment as well as those who have just joined the labor force through graduation from school contribute to frictional unemployment. Structural unemployment also presents problems in the Soviet Union. That is, as the economy changes under the impact of new technology and changing tastes of the population or the government (military demand, for example), certain jobs are eliminated, causing skills of established workers to become obsolete. Because the USSR does not pay unemployment benefits, individuals who suffer from structural or frictional unemployment may be obliged to take much inferior jobs—or to do without work until something suitable opens up. The third type of unemployment that individuals suffer in the USSR is seasonal, which affects primarily the rural population.

Education has always been an important means for upward mobility in the USSR, and the Soviet Union adopted the American open-enrollment educational system at its inception to maximize opportunities for individuals to become educated and to learn skills. Education remains today a very important basis for successful advancement on the job, but the USSR is running into the problem of overqualified workers that afflicts many advanced countries today. Individuals who find that they must accept employment in positions that are inferior to the positions for which they prepared themselves are likely to become alienated, and they are *underemployed* members of society. This should perhaps be listed as a fourth type of unemployment in the Soviet Union.

In the USSR, women are heavily represented in the category *overqualified workers*. Over one-half of the total Soviet labor force is female. Official doctrine calls for equal educational opportunities, equal pay for equal work, the provision of child-care services, and support for the desirability of female participation in the labor force on a full-time basis. Even so, several factors militate against the attainment of true equality with men when it comes to economic opportunities and achievements. Soviet data reveal, for example, that occupations in which women form the majority of employees, regardless of the status of these occupations outside the USSR, tend to be low-prestige, poorly paid occupations. The most flagrant example is medicine, in which women dominate the ranks of MDs. Yet, even in occupations such as medicine or primary education, men dominate both the higher administrative and most specialized categories and thus the higher-paid employments. Most enterprise managers and collective-farm chairmen are men, and most high officials in the party are male.

There are many reasons why women have not been able to take full advantage of the Bolsheviks' ideological commitment to equal opportunity for women. Soviet statistics make it clear that women do take advantage of early educational opportunities, but they are less likely than men to continue education to the highest levels. Accordingly, few women are surgeons, although many earn MDs. Second, although child-care centers exist, the spaces available are inadequate to provide care for the children of all women who wish to work, and the deficiency increases the farther one moves away from major urban areas. Third, although it seems very unlikely that there is any official support for a secondary role for women in the Soviet system, the state conducts no affirmative-action programs to reverse longstanding patriarchal attitudes. These attitudes are particularly strong in certain ethnic regions such as Central Asia, where they take the form of social prohibitions on participation by women in factory employment or the appearance of women in certain public situations. Even in European Russia, familial expectations and cultural patterns seriously handicap women. Most women do work full-time throughout the USSR, but fewer put their careers ahead of other considerations than do men.

A woman who desires to compete with men for success in a career can probably do so in the USSR more easily and with less criticism than in Europe or in the United States, but she still runs counter to cultural expectations, and this takes its toll. Women in European Russia, for example, are expected to work full-time and yet do the shopping, prepare meals, keep house, and care for the children. According to reports, husbands are more willing today than in the past to assist in all of these activities, but primary responsibility remains with the woman. Should a child be ill, for example, it would almost certainly be the mother rather than the father who would stay home. Job advancement involving a change of cities would be more likely to follow the husband's opportunities than the wife's. Many women do not object, of course, to the pattern in which they, like their husbands and parents, have been inculcated. But for those women who do object, the situation is no less fraught with contradictions and emotional tensions than in the West. Women comprise, therefore, the largest proportion of those who are overskilled for the positions they occupy in the Soviet labor force.

No discussion of labor in the Soviet Union would be complete that failed to take forced labor into account. Although forced labor is apparently no longer a significant source of labor in the USSR, at one time, forced labor contributed significantly to national income. The total number of individuals so impressed remains secret and is thus disputed among western scholars, and the matter will not be resolved in the near future. Everyone agrees, however, that the total was great, that it reached a peak in the years immediately following World War II, and that it began to be reduced systematically under Khrushchev, especially following his secret anti-Stalin speech in 1956. Economists generally believe that forced labor is inferior to paid labor in efficiency, and maintaining large forced-labor camps is expensive. In any event, forced labor was used in the Soviet Union to perform very dangerous or particularly arduous tasks, such as construction and mining in the Arctic Circle.

The Household Sector

The typical Soviet urban household contributes labor to the economic process and receives pecuniary and non-pecuniary benefits in return primarily for its contributions. Nonpecuniary benefits have been declining as a share of total family income, and thus most of the family's time is spent earning and spending money income. From the family's standpoint, it does not matter whether its transactions involve the private or the public sector, but when things go wrong in the public sector, the state is blamed. Most households in the USSR have more than one primary wage-earner, and most also receive some direct payment from a state agency. A grandparent may live with the family and draw a pension. He or she may also work at a part-time job, and in any event, the grand-parent would be fully occupied helping in queuing for deficit commodit-ies, walking the baby, sitting with the children, gardening, and helping with the housework. The family may have a child in the university or in a technical school, in which case he or she would receive a stipend that would be contributed to the family's weekly income.

Spending the family income is also a collective affair, involving state retail markets, the *rynok*, private trading, and *nalevo* markets, without anyone paying much attention to the breakdown among them. Family members old enough to be responsible would normally carry a sub-stantial sum of cash with them at all times against finding unexpected deficit commodities. Everyone in the family knows what these are and what a reasonable price would be for them. What the family does not spend is set aside for purchasing large durable goods such as auto-mobiles, stereo sets, and so forth. Some western observers claim that Soviet families are unable to spend as much as they like in Soviet markets and that they are therefore accumulating savings unwillingly. This is a most unlikely conclusion for the simple reason that households do not have to earn more income than they wish. The amount of income that a family earns is not determined by the state but by collective decision of the members of the household. Because queuing is so important a function in the acquisition of deficit commodities in the Soviet Union, it will always pay for one member of the family to increase his or her free time for queuing rather than to work at a job from which the income would be of little or no use.

So long as individuals are free to make their own purchases in the market and so long as individual households may elect the total number of hours that they wish to be employed, planners are not able to determine unilaterally either the total volume of labor forthcoming in the economy or the total amount and composition of consumer goods and services that it will make available, and this constraint is enhanced by the presence of private employment and private retail markets. It is further enhanced by the opportunities that individuals have to convert public property into private means to personal gain.

If the state wishes households to contribute more to economic activity, it must provide something in exchange, and that has increasingly come to mean commodities and services rather than promises of a better future or assurance against an aggressive external force. In this respect, the member of a Soviet household does not experience a different economic world from his counterpart in the West. A Soviet who is suddenly transposed into a capitalist economic environment is not disoriented by the difference, although the plethora of goods and of choices available may be overwhelming at first. Neither is a Western shopper disoriented in Soviet markets. The difficulties involved are irritating, but not completely strange, for there are still queues in the West for certain kinds of sporting and cultural events, and queues for gasoline have reeducated an entire generation. The Soviet system of central planning and management has not yet, however, learned to accommodate independent-minded workers and equally independent-minded consumers.

The term *second economy* has become popular among certain Western specialists on the Soviet economy to describe various aspects of what I have called open markets and trading *nalevo*. The term *second economy* is potentially misleading because it may be taken to imply a greater degree of distinctness between the "first" economy and the "second" than exists. The concept of a dual economy was first developed in the study of developing economies to describe the difference between the advanced sector of the economy and the traditional predevelopment economy. Since the advanced sector in a primitive economy may be an exclave of Western or Soviet technology, the notion of a dual economic system is not remote for many countries, but the concept has proved troublesome even in the development literature because there are usually connections and therefore interactions between the two parts of the dual economy that are important to the functioning of each. Such is the case regarding economic transactions that take place *nalevo* in the USSR. As a matter of fact, neither the "first" nor the "second" economy would work so well in the absence of the other, although there are, of course, contradictions between them, too.

The second drawback with the notion of a "second" economy is the fact that no investigator has yet advanced a definition that everyone finds satisfactory. Every adult Soviet citizen knows the difference between the *nalevo* economy, the legal private markets, and the public economy; and it seems preferable to stick with common usage. Some Western scholars define the second economy to consist of all free-market transactions, legal and illegal. Others define the concept as composed of all illegal economic transactions, but this bunches general criminal activities with market transactions and loses altogether the distinction between private- and public-sector transactions. Enterprise managers, for example, know how to use the *nalevo* economy to achieve state enterprise targets as well as their own creature comforts. Finally, still other Western specialists define the second economy to include only private economic activity and use it to contrast private enterprise with state planning and management. Each aspect involved in the various definitions is as important as the other in gaining an understanding of the way that Soviet planning and management of the economy interacts with the interests and behavior of the private individuals and households that comprise the system. Soviet households are involved simultaneously in planned and unplanned economic transactions, in market and nonmarket economic relationships, and in private and public economic institutions. They form an undifferentiated whole in the experience of a household member, and each is an essential component of the way the Soviet economy functions for the people who live and work in the system.

| 21 | DAVID LANE |

Social Stratification

*and Class**

Many radicals seek, in one way or another, to make society more egalitarian, to reduce the distance between social strata: to give the powerless more power, the poor more riches, the social outcasts more status. The study of social stratification is concerned with these and related problems. In the first place, a student of society is interested to know the forms social inequality may take. Second, he seeks to describe the extent of this inequality in specific societies. Third, he is anxious to know why it is that inequality exists in society: is it a necessary condition to maintain the equilibrium of a social order? Is it a functional requirement necessary "to ensure that the most important positions are conscientiously filled by the most qualified persons"?[1] Or is it a process by which the privileged have seized an unfair share of the desirable things in life and, thereafter, by force and fraud (of which the ideology of inequality is a part), maintain a *status quo* that is mainly in their own interests? The case of the USSR may be used to illustrate these problems and to answer some of them.

Let us first attempt a definition of social stratification. It means the division of society into a hierarchy of strata, each having an unequal share of society's power, wealth, property, or income and each enjoying an unequal evaluation in terms of prestige, or honor, or social esteem. There are two aspects of stratification that must be distinguished: the *objective* inequality between groups and the *subjective* ranking of individual group members by others. Marxist writers tend to emphasize objective inequality between classes based on the ownership or nonownership of property, even if this does not give rise to a subjective

*Reprinted by permission of the author and publisher from David Lane, *Politics and Society in the USSR*, 2nd ed. (London: Martin Robertson & Co., 1978), pp. 382–422 (reprinted with corrections 1982). Copyright 1982 by Martin Robertson & Co.

feeling of class identification on this "objective" basis. Non-Marxist sociologists tend to define strata in subjective terms of status or honor.

Subjective inequality involves interpersonal evaluations of honor or status. Talcott Parsons defines stratification as "the differential ranking of the human individuals who compose a given social system and their treatment as superior and inferior relative to one another in certain socially important aspects."[2] Not all persons, of course, bestow honor on the same criteria. Some may rank highly professional footballers, others cabinet ministers. Thus, the kind of evaluations, the degree of consensus or disagreement among the members of a society as to what determines "honor," the ranking of individuals' status, and the groups of persons who enjoy common evaluation as equals, all vary between societies and the ways sociologists classify them. There is no unique configuration of grades of social evaluation, though we shall see later that there are similarities between major societies.

Studies of stratification attempt to delineate the "socially important" groups, to determine the relationship between political privilege, economic inequality, and social rank. In this chapter, we shall consider first Marx's attitude to class; second, the policies adopted by the communists after the revolution; third, the profile of the main social groups today (intelligentsia, workers, and peasants); and finally, we shall discuss the implications of Soviet experience for social restructuring.

The Dictatorship of the Proletariat

Marx and Engels made ownership the fundamental determinant of class position. The owners of the means of production constitute the ruling class over the nonowners. Originally, the division of labor in society gave rise to economic classes. Associated with class position and dependent on it are social status and political power. In capitalist society, the industrial *bourgeoisie* owns the means of production and employs labor; its superior financial and organizational resources give control over the state; its wealth gives access to culture and education and gives rise to a style of life. The *proletariat* is distinguished by the fact that it sells its labor power on the market (where it has a bargaining disadvantage); it has little participation (power) in the affairs of the state; it is deprived educationally and culturally. For Marx, class, power, and honor in society are inextricably related and are highly correlated.

Capitalist society is characterized by the contradiction between the bourgeoisie and proletariat; only with its resolution and the subsequent creation of socialist society can classes be eliminated. In the *Communist Manifesto*, Marx wrote: "When in the course of development class distinctions have disappeared and all production has been concentrated in the hands of a vast association of the whole nation, then public power will lose its political character." As social and political inequality was sustained by economic class inequality, the abolition of private property and of the capitalist class based on it would entail the elimination of political and social inequality. Only in communist society would "all the springs of co-operative wealth flow more abundantly—only then can . . . society inscribe on its banners: From each according to his ability, to each according to his needs!" Under communism, there would be no division of labor and therefore no antithesis between mental and manual labor.[3] From the point of view of social stratification, the October Revolution was to create conditions for a truly equal and classless society. In place of a system of stratification determined by class relations and by the forces of the market, it was thought that social relations would be determined by the ideology and goals of the Communist party.

After the revolution, the Bolsheviks' main concern was to abolish the ownership relations on which capitalism rested. Nationalization of property and the seizure of land and factories helped destroy the old possessing classes and the middle strata associated with them. But before and during the New Economic Policy, private ownership and private trade continued. In market terms, separate classes still existed: the proletariat and a property owning class (particularly among the peasantry).

The proletariat was, in theory, the political base of the new order. To safeguard the revolution, the Bolsheviks thought it necessary that the proletariat act initially as the *ruling class*. During the period up to 1936, the official definition of Soviet society was that of "the dictatorship of the proletariat." From the communist viewpoint, the proletariat consisted of three strata—workers, landless peasants, and employees. The strata hostile to the proletariat were made up (during the New Economic Policy) of private traders (*nepmen*), rich peasants (*kulaks*), and the technical intelligentsia having sympathy for a bourgeois order. These "hostile" groups had restricted political rights: They were barred from official positions, they had no vote, and could not join the Communist party.[4]

In terms of social esteem, a most complex situation existed: the values of the old regime still lingered on in people's consciousness, while the communists attempted to assert the mores of a new order. Official policy was egalitarian, an attempt was made to give higher status to skilled and unskilled factory workers. In April 1917, Lenin had said that the pay of officials must not exceed that of "competent workmen." The status of the old managerial and executive groups was undermined: For example, in 1917, the Council of People's Commissars fixed salaries at 500 rubles basic for Commissars. Soviet policy was to reduce high salaries to the earnings of the average worker.[5] Wage differentials were reduced, giving government employees of the lowest category of office worker 350 rubles a month.[6] This, however, should not be taken as the "introduction of communism"; wage equalization and the rationing that went with it were temporary measures intended to distribute the scarce resources available under "War Communism." In January 1919, a wage scale approved by the Second Trade Union Congress laid down wages of the highest grades of workers and employees at only 1.75 times those of the lowest paid grade in each category—a drastic reduction of the differentials pertaining before the revolution.[7] In practice, however, it was difficult to enforce these trade union statutes, and the wages of "scarce" workers went above the ceiling. In 1921, when Lenin introduced the New Economic Policy, a wage structure with 17 divisions covered all grades of workers and employees. The differential was widened; highly skilled workers received 3.5 times the wage of the lowest category, and the ratio of the highest salary to the lowest was eight to one.[8] It is interesting to note that in the 1920s, the differentials between workers followed a ranking similar to the prerevolutionary pattern: printers, tanners, and workers in the food industry receiving more than miners, metallurgists, and engineers.[9] Here is an example of the way forces of tradition were stronger than Bolshevik policy at this time. In 1926, the law was again changed and differentials were reduced to much below the prewar levels. This was part of a policy by the communists to ameliorate the position of the most deprived strata. Even so, as Bergson has pointed out, income inequality among Soviet industrial workers in 1928 "was closely proximate to that among American industrial workers in 1904."[10]

But this egalitarian policy was cut short and replaced under Stalin by a system of greater wage differentiation. Only under full communism, Stalin argued, would individuals receive according to need; under socialism, wages must be paid according to work performed. The "Marxist formula of socialism" stated: "From each according to his ability, to each according to his work."[11]

In 1932, in an interview with Emil Ludwig, Stalin made clear his views on equalitarianism.

> The kind of socialism under which everybody would get the same pay, an equal quantity of meat and an equal quantity of bread, would wear the same clothes and receive the same goods in the same quantities—such a socialism is unknown to Marxism. . . . Equalitarianism owes its origin to the individual peasant type of mentality, the psychology of share and share alike, the psychology of primitive "communism." Equalitarianism has nothing in common with Marxist socialism. Only people who are unacquainted with Marxism can have the primitive notion that the Russian Bolsheviks want to pool all wealth and then share it out equally. That is the notion of people who have nothing in common with Marxism.[12]

Accordingly, a steeper gradation between skills and occupations was introduced, and wage ratios increased between the lowest and highest paid.[13] Stalin's immediate justification for the change was the need to reduce labor mobility and to introduce incentives for the unskilled to become skilled—a policy substantiated, at least in part, by the most authoritative Western writer on this subject.[14]

Postrevolutionary experience, therefore, saw, after an initial egalitarian phase, the assertion of wage inequality. The Russian communists, in this sphere of social life as in others, found themselves faced with introducing socialism in a backward underdeveloped country. Without the economic basis provided by an advanced industrial economy, a system of differentiation based on egalitarianism could not come to fruition, especially when introduced after a revolution, a civil war, a general famine, and economic collapse. In practice, the inequality between occupational strata of other industrial societies became also a characteristic of Soviet Russia. As Robert Hodge and others have suggested, economic development depends upon the recruitment and training of men in skilled clerical and administrative positions, and a system of differential social evaluation is therefore a necessary condition of rapid industrialization.[15]

To attract workers to the industries essential for the industrialization effort, wages in them were increased. In 1934, the highest wages were paid in engineering, followed by the power industry, ferrous metallurgy, oil, coking, iron ore, and coal industries.[16] While it is sometimes thought that Stalin personally created a system of severe social inequality, it is more accurate to view the changes in social stratification of the early 1930s as determined by the demands of industrialization and the forces to which they gave rise. The centrally *administered* economy recognized these demands. In doing so, a system of wage payment was introduced in which "the principles of relative wages in the Soviet Union are also capitalist principles."[17]

The USSR as a Socialist State

In 1936, the USSR was proclaimed a "socialist society." In Soviet Marxist terms, this implied that no contradictory class relationships existed. The owners of the means of production had finally been expropriated, but inequality persisted. Under socialism, men were paid according to their work. The 1936 USSR Constitution defined three friendly cooperative groups each with full civil rights: the workers, the intelligentsia (sometimes defined as employees or nonmanual workers), and the collective farm peasantry. The first two groups are the main subdivisions of the working class, which is seen in a firm friendly union with the collective farm peasantry. Two social (but not antagonistic) "classes" therefore exist, differentiated by their relationship to the means of production. Though the means of production (the land) on collective farms is owned by the state, the products of collective farms belong to collective farmers, they are sold to the state, and the proceeds of sales are shared. Manual and nonmanual workers, including farmers on state farms, directly employed by the state which owns their produce, are paid wages.

The social structure of Soviet state *socialism* (not communism) involving social inequality is not as contradictory as is sometimes supposed. In Soviet terms, property relations have been changed: private ownership has been abolished. But this does not imply that inequality has been eliminated. Unequal incomes giving rise to privileges in consumption and status differences have been officially admitted, with differential access to power position or political stratification. To understand adequately the process of social stratification, much more than a crude mechanical relationship between ownership relations, on the one hand, and honor and political power, on the other, is required. We must bear in mind that in the USSR, "socialism" is defined in terms of Marxist property relations. In Western social–democratic theory, socialism is *defined* in terms of egalitarianism. As Roy Jenkins pointed out in 1952: "The desire for greater equality has been part of the inspiration of all socialist thinkers and of all socialist movements. The absence of this desire indeed, provides the most useful of all exclusive definitions of socialism."[18]

In Marxist theory, under capitalism, wealth is dependent on the ownership of the means of production; under socialism, income is determined according to one's work, and only in a communist society does one receive according to need. The introduction of graded wage scales in place of the more egalitarian early postrevolutionary policy has important social implications, for it shows that wage incentive was used to reward workers for greater effort and for gaining higher qualifications. As Stalin wrote:

> The consequence of wage equalization is that the unskilled worker lacks the incentive to become a skilled worker and is thus deprived of the prospect of advancement; as a result he feels himself a "visitor" in the factory, working only temporarily so as to "earn a little" and then go off to "seek his fortune" elsewhere. . . .
>
> Hence, the "general" drift from factory to factory; hence the heavy turnover of labor power.
>
> In order to put an end to this evil we must abolish equalization and discard the old wage rates. In order to put an end to this evil we must draw up wage scales that will take into account the difference between skilled and unskilled labor, between heavy and light work. We cannot tolerate a situation where a rolling-mill hand in a steel mill earns no more than a sweeper.[19]

Though the lack of skilled manpower may be partly accounted for by the rapidity of industrialization, Stalin's statement should not be derided by egalitarians. (Nor should it be inferred, on the other hand, that egalitarianism is impracticable.) The significance of Soviet experience is that to achieve a rapid rate of industrial growth from a relatively low level of industrial development, income differentials seem to be necessary, or at least useful, levers of labor recruitment; they also help sustain labor stability.

Social Stratification in Modern Russia

We have seen that in a state socialist society, there can be no *class conflict*, in the sense that Soviet sociologists use the term. This does not mean, even in theory, that there is complete harmony or that no system of social stratification prevails. An authoritative article in *Kommunist*[20] emphasizes the conflict inherent in present Soviet society. Glezerman quotes Lenin's description of social classes as

> large groups of people differing from each other by the place they occupy in the historically determined system of social production, by their relation (in some cases fixed and formulated in law) to the means of production, by their role in the social organization of labor, and, consequently, by the dimensions and mode of acquiring the share of social wealth of which they dispose.[21]

This definition of class is much wider than Stalin's interpretation of Marx defined previously in strict terms of ownership. The place one occupies in "the social organization of labor" and by "the dimensions and mode of acquiring the share of social wealth" of which one disposes may be independent of one's ownership relations. Here the division of labor could be a basis for differentiation.

Glezerman continues by defining four main kinds of social distinction under socialism: (1) a class division proper between workers and peasants; (2) distinctions between rural and urban populations; (3) those between manual and mental labor; (4) those between "people of different trades, skills and incomes within the working class, peasantry, intelligentsia and office workers." Before considering these distinctions, we may begin by turning to the empirical composition of Soviet social strata. First, we may describe the broad groupings as defined by Soviet sociologists in official classifications. Second, we shall consider the significance of social stratification in the USSR as seen by Western sociologists. Finally, we shall turn to social mobility.

Manual and nonmanual workers (*sluzhashchie*) include all engaged in state and cooperative institutions and members of collective farms regularly employed in industry, building, transport (etc.), and only part or not at all employed on the collective farm. Collective farmers include members of the *kolkhoz* and their families engaged in agricultural production.[22] A collective farmer is in a different *class* because he is not employed by an enterprise for a wage, he is a member of the collective that owns the seeds and their produce. The 1978 handbook of the Soviet economy[23] defines manual and nonmanual workers as comprising 84.9% of the population and collective farmers and cooperative handicraftsmen 15.1%. By 1970, none were self-employed peasants or craftsmen. These crude divisions do not preclude further subclassification, which may first be most conveniently analyzed in terms used by Soviet writers.

The Soviet "Intelligentsia," Nonmanual Workers

Under socialism, the existence of separate "mental" and "manual" strata is determined "above all else by the different role of these groups in the social organization of labor."[24] A Soviet theorist notes that under socialism, the division of labor gives rise to a "qualitative difference" between nonmanual and manual labor[25] which is abolished only under communism.

Such a definition of "mental labor" includes a very wide range of employees—from storemen to cabinet ministers. Sometimes, the term *intelligentsia* is restricted to an exclusive group of specialists possessing higher educational qualifications, and the word *sluzhashchie* is used to describe unqualified or junior white-collar workers.

Another Soviet writer divides nonmanual workers into eight main social groups; the first four being *intelligentsia*, executives in government administration and public organizations, the technical and economic intelligentsia, the scientific cultural intelligentsia; the last four being *sluzhashchie*, including counting-house employees, transport employees, those in communications, and subordinate employees in local and municipal utilities (watchmen, porters).[26] The literature on the subject is, therefore, highly ambiguous. In the widest sense, the *intelligentsia* and *sluzhashchie* are synonymous—"nonmanual workers." But the more specific use of intelligentsia is to define a highly qualified creative executive and technical stratum.

If we consider the number of employeed specialists with higher and specialist secondary education, the total size of the intelligentsia was 24 million in December 1976: 10 million with higher and 14 million with secondary specialist education.

The Soviet *intelligentsia* cannot be considered a homogeneous social group. Rutkevitch distinguishes between "mental labor" as a general category and those of this stratum engaged in a leading or directing capacity. This group he estimates to be some 1.8 million strong. To the chiefs of government administration and factory directors (352,000) he adds head doctors and other health chiefs (44,000), heads of educational institutions (114,000), directors of wholesale and leading retail organizations (334,800).[27] In Table 1, I have shown all groups of men and women defined in the 1970 Census as having some leadership role. This is a total of some 3.5 million. Mervyn Matthews has narrowed down these groups to an occupational elite of about a quarter of a million. These are men and women who have responsible posts and earn at least an estimated 450 rubles per month—about four times the average wage. These include party officials (95,000), government, trade union and Komsomol officials (60,000), intellectuals (43,000), factory managers (22,000), military, police, and diplomatic service (30,000).[28]

Many writers point out that the level of income, culture, and education varies between the subgroups. Teachers in primary schools, those in inspection and control are not very much different (in their way of life) from manual workers, whereas the heads of state administration, higher scientific workers, and those in art, literature, and publishing are significantly differentiated in their way of life from workers, collective farmers, and other nonmanual workers. This kind of analysis of *intra-class* differences has occupied Soviet attention only from the late 1950s and reveals the existence of status gradations between strata within a given Soviet-defined *class*. We shall turn to consider hierarchy again after defining the other major social groups in Soviet society.[29]

TABLE 1 *Groupings of Persons Having Positions of Responsibility and Leadership*[a]

Chiefs of organs of government administration and their structural subdivisions	210.8
Chiefs of party, Komsomol, trade unions, other social organizations, and their structural subdivisions	194.9
Chiefs of enterprises, collective farms, and their structural subdivisions	1570.1
Chiefs in research and teaching institutions (excluding primary schools)	633.2
Chiefs and their assistants in publishing	39.2
Directors in culture and art	20.7
Directors and chiefs in trade and catering	463.3
Heads of planning, finance, and economic institutions	85.8
Chief doctors and other leaders in medicine	57.7
Leading specialists among engineering–technical employees	282.2
	3547.9

[a]*Source: Itogi vsesoyuznoy perepisi naseleniya*, vol. 6, (1970) table 2.

The Manual   The working class as shown in Soviet statistics
Working Class   may be divided into those occupied in agriculture
                   (on state farms) and those employed in industry.
In 1958, a sixth of those defined as "workers" were employed on state
farms.[30] In 1978, of an employed "working class" of 75.8 million, 10.4
million were in agriculture (state farms and related enterprises). (There
were 11.8 million collective farmers at work.[31])

Workers are divided for purposes of pay into strata according to skill.
Such divisions vary from one industry to another.[32] A Soviet sociologist
has distinguished between three main strata or divisions of workers:
first, those with physical skills (stevedores, dockers, draymen, laborers);
second, those whose jobs require physical labor and knowledge (turn-
ers, lathe operators, milling machine operators, polishers, etc.); third,
those whose work requires mainly knowledge (laboratory assistants,
furnacemen, electricians). Soviet labor theorists contend that, with the
development of the economy, the first division will die out, and that
eventually all workers will be in the third category. In support of this
view, it is pointed out that in the Ukraine between 1959 and 1962, the
first group declined by 10%, the second increased by 30%, and the third
increased by 50%.[33]

There are, therefore, clear divisions of pay and education between
unskilled, semiskilled, and skilled workers. In Soviet theory, the development to communism will see the merging of these three groups.

The Peasantry   The factors that generally distinguish the peasan-
                   try as a socioeconomic group are: residence in a
rural habitat, labor on the land with the family being the fundamental
unit, an ideology of attachment to the soil, to the family, and to the local
community. The peasantry as a social group has a certain self-sufficiency
and isolation from the social world but is, nevertheless, part of a wider
society and is to a greater or lesser extent influenced by urban areas.
Unlike an agricultural worker, the peasant is largely sustained by the
produce from the land he works. Though he may not own it, he
determines to a large degree the inputs (both in terms of hours worked
and kinds of crops to be produced) and has control over the distribution
of products.

Soviet classification of social classes is dependent on the individual's
relationship to the means of production. To understand the Soviet
concept of *state* and *collective* farmer, one must examine the chief
characteristics of the two forms of agricultural production: *state* and
collective farms. On state farms, workers are paid a wage, and all
proceeds accrue to the state. The farm director is appointed by the state.
Such men (*sovkhozniki*) are defined as part of the working class—not the
peasantry. On the collective farm, the land is collectively tilled. The

produce is, in theory, owned by the collective. The means of production belong to the state, the products of production belong to the individual collective farms, as their own property (as is labor and seeds)."[34] Their *class* position, therefore, is not that of hired labor; collective farmers (*kolkhozniki*) are in cooperative production and, in Soviet theory, form a separate class. But as ownership of the land is vested in the state, the collective farmers do not form a class with antagonistic interests to the workers, they are a "nonantagonistic" class forming a "friendly union" with, although under the leadership of, the working class.

The extent to which collective farmers constitute a "proper" peasantry has been disputed by non-Soviet writers on the peasantry. Basile Kerblay, for instance, has argued that in the collectivized sector, the control over labor input by the peasant has been vitiated: "his work has become subject to the same direction as in industry, except that its remuneration is still a residual income and not a fixed wage," and a collective farmer, in this respect, therefore "cannot be considered a peasant."[35] While it is true that crucial input–output decisions are taken out of the collective farmers' hands by the Soviet planning agencies, it should not be forgotten that all peasants are subject to urban pressures and especially to market forces; therefore, the difference is not so sharp as Kerblay suggests. It must be conceded, then, that the Soviet collective farm peasantry, in so far as it works on the *collective's lands*, is neither a family work unit nor has it control over decisions concerning planting. But in other respects, it has some of the characteristics of a more traditional "peasantry." The collective farmer decides the amount of time he spends and the kind of crops he will produce on his own plot. His mode of work is manual, and much of his labor is expended in the traditional peasant fashion. Yet Soviet power has changed traditional attitudes: mass education is widespread, and popular aspirations are for mass consumption goods—washing machines and refrigerators. In this context, it is doubtful whether the term *peasant* should be applied to them.[36]

To analyze the social strata of the Soviet peasantry, Soviet sociologists use a number of criteria: the character of work and the qualifications, culture, income level, and class consciousness of the farmers. On these criteria, not all members of collective farms are simply "peasants." One Soviet writer suggests a threefold grouping of strata. Group 1 is engineering/technical and administrative personnel—the farm chairman and his subordinates, economists, agronomists, veterinarians, engineering mechanics, bookkeepers, and others with middle and higher education. In the mid 1960s, these men made up from 6–9% of *kolkhozniks*. Group 2 is constituted of those utilizing farm machinery (*mekhanizatory*)—tractor and machine-harvester drivers and operators. These totalled from 10–13% of the collective farm labor force. Group 3 are collective farmers having no trade or speciality, being occupied only in physical labor,[37] and form the "peasantry" proper. The first two groups by occupation and culture form separate, as it were, "nonpeasant" strata, for they have no particular attachment to traditional forms of land working and have been influenced through training and education by urban values and skills. While about three-quarters of collective farmers are of the unskilled manual worker or "peasant" category, the relative proportion of state farmers is only 41%—showing their higher technical and cultural level.[38]

While workers and peasants live "in harmony," the working class is the leading social force; it is politically, economically, and socially superior to the peasantry and acts as a model for it. Gradually, argue Soviet theorists, with the building of communism, the peasantry will wither away, and the differences between town and country will be obliterated. The countryside will be "pulled up" to the level of the town. It is said that there are three ways in which this leveling will take place.

First, the "growing together" of the urban working class and the collective farm peasantry is related to the mechanization of agriculture that will increase the number of machine workers and operators in the countryside (Group 2). By virtue of their trade, such men are "brought near to the working class."[39] The point Soviet theorists are trying to make here is that a highly mechanized and capital-intensive agriculture undermines the traditional "peasant" mentality, and that on this basis, an agricultural working class rather than a peasantry will grow.

On what Soviet writers call the "development of intracollective relations" rests the second main way to change the character of the collective farms. By this, it is meant that conditions of production and consumption will move closer to the practice in the towns: that wages will be paid on guaranteed monthly rates and that social services (pensions, provision of schools and medical care) will be provided on the same basis as in the town.

Third, the structure of the collective farm alters through migration of people from the country to the town and the consequent reduction in the rural population. At the same time, the level of skill in the countryside will rise, labor productivity will increase, and thus the living standards of the peasant will be brought into line with workers in the towns.[40]

Having described some of the features of the Soviet system of social classes, we may now turn to discuss the inequality that exists between them.

Social Inequalities

The liberal ideology of Western societies accepts inequality, and many claim that it is not only inevitable but necessary in modern societies. For example, it is argued that unequal power is essential for the organization of production, and unequal rewards are desirable to encourage the development of scarce skills. Rather than the abolition of inequality, many progressive social–democratic thinkers emphasize *equality of opportunity*:[41] that is, the opportunity for the deprived to ameliorate their existing position so as to give all persons an equal chance of becoming unequal. American and, to a lesser extent, British sociology has been preoccupied with measuring social inequality between strata and with the degree to which individuals may better or worsen their status (or class) position.

In Soviet society, status or power ranking is not part of the official ideology. The classes of peasantry and workers live in "friendly collaboration," only distinguished by the leading role of the working class in building communism. As Ossowski has pointed out, the Soviet image of contemporary Russia "is of a society without class stratification . . . nor are there upper classes and lower classes in the sense in which we encounter them in the American scheme of gradation. . . . In the Soviet Union economic privileges and discriminations have, in accordance with Soviet doctrine, nothing in common with class divisions."[42] The grading or ranking of individuals into groups of superior or inferior status is alien to the Soviet concept of socialism. Sociological work investigating such grading, therefore, is not carried out—or is done only indirectly. Unlike in the United States, where a plethora of empirical work has been carried out into status differences, in the USSR, very little is known about such stratification.

Soviet official ideology impels sociological research to describe inequalities between town and country, between worker and peasant. Such research illustrates the gulf between these strata, which we may describe before considering other forms of stratification.

The level of education of collective farmers is considerably lower than that of the working class as shown in Table 2; we see that nearly twice as many workers have a higher and middle education compared to collective farmers. Collective farm women are also shown to be underprivileged. While it is true that the age structure of the village influences the figures—the larger number of older relatively uneducated women to some extent explains the very low number of women with the highest qualifications—it is striking that only 19 collective farm women per 1000 of the employed have higher education compared to 34 per 1000 of the working class.

The differences in social structure between town and country may be illustrated by the educational standards of workers in a collective farm, a state farm, a settlement, and a suburb of Sverdlovsk. The figures are divided between manual and "specialist" nonmanual workers and are shown in Table 3.

A clear pattern emerges from the table. If we study those with middle and higher education, the numbers increase as we read across the page

TABLE 2 *Educational Level of Workers and Collective Farmers in Employment (1979)[a,b]*

Social group	Higher, incompleted higher, and middle specialist	Middle education
Workers		
Both sexes	37	165
Men	40	169
Women	34	159
Collective farmers		
Both sexes	28	75
Men	37	91
Women	19	61

[a]*Source:* Census of 1979. *Vestnik statistiki,* no. 2 (1981), p. 63.
[b]*Per 1000 persons of a given social group having the indicated education.*

from *kolkhoz* to the town suburb. For example, under "manual workers," we see that only 1% of *kolkhoz* manual workers have a middle general education, the figure rises to 2.6 in the *sovkhoz*, 5.2 in the settlement, and 16.3 in the town; under "specialists," those with higher education are 15.8% of the *kolkhoz* nonmanual staff, but 23.5%, 31.7%, and 37.3% for the *sovkhoz*, settlement, and town, respectively. On the other hand, if we study the distribution of the lowly educated, we see that they are clustered at the bottom left-hand corner of the table—as we move from collective farm to town, the numbers decline. For example, under "manual workers," 27.6% of *kolkhoz* manual workers had under 4 years of schooling, whereas the proportion was 25.3% in the *sovkhoz*, 19.8% in the settlement, and 8.6% in the town.

The provision of services is also very much more rudimentary in the village than in the town, as shown in the tabulation below:

	Number of persons occupied in service trades in town and village	
	Per 10,000 of the population[a]	
	Town	Village
All persons engaged in service trades	1507	716
Education	260	186
Health services	230	90

[a]*Source:* E. Manevich, *Problemy obshchestvennogo truda v SSSR* (Moscow, 1966), p. 40.

TABLE 3 *Distribution of Manual Workers and Specialists by Education Level between Collective Farm, State Farm, Settlement, and Town (in Percentage)[a]*

	Kolkhoz (Collective farm)	Sovkhoz (State farm)	Settlement	Town (Sverdlovsk suburb)
Manual Workers				
N	507	994	1026	318
Education				
Middle specialist	0	0.2	0.4	2.5
Middle general	1.0	2.6	5.2	16.3
8–9 classes	5.3	4.8	7.9	17.3
7 classes	16.6	16.0	26.6	27.8
5–6 classes	21.9	19.5	20.7	16.8
4 classes	27.6	31.6	19.4	10.6
Under 4 classes	27.6	25.3	19.8	8.6
Specialists				
N	38	86	111	206
Education				
Higher	15.8	23.3	31.7	37.3
Middle specialist	29.0	32.5	53.0	38.5
Middle general	29.0	24.4	7.2	15.5
8–9 classes	2.6	4.7	—	3.4
7 classes	7.9	13.9	3.6	1.4
5-6 classes	5.2	—	0.9	3.4
4 classes	7.9	1.2	0.9	0.4
Under 4 classes	2.6	—	2.7	—

[a]*Source: Klassy, sotsial'nye sloi i gruppy v SSSR* (Moscow, 1968), p. 130.

Obviously, the collective farm community is underprivileged. It has less than its proportional share of scarce educational and medical facilities. The figures show that the urban areas have two times more workers (doctors, nurses, radiographers, etc.) and 40% more teachers per head than the villages. Some of this difference may be accounted for by the location of regional hospitals and educational institutions in the towns, but as the population is widely scattered in the countryside, one should not expect such a large difference. Similarly, the provision of retail services (shops, cinemas) is much worse in the village than the town.

The general cultural level is also lower in the village than the town. The distribution of television sets and radios is uneven: in the Moldavian Republic in 1967, per 100 inhabitants, in the towns, 13.5 had televisions and 22.3 radios, while in the villages, the numbers were 3.3 and 7.2, respectively.[43] In the survey of Siberia previously cited, it was found that in no household either in the *kolkhoz* or *sovkhoz* was there a television set, whereas 22% of households had one in the settlement and

59% in the Sverdlovsk suburb. The number of radios was lower in the countryside (34.8% of households in the *kolkhoz* and 78.1% in Sverdlovsk), but radio relay points were much more frequent—in 48% of peasant households and only 20.7% of those in Sverdlovsk suburb. The number of books in the house and the frequency of subscription to journals was significantly lower in the rural than in the urban communities.[44] Even so, one must not ignore the fact that life in the villages has changed enormously. Now a "majority of rural inhabitants regularly read newspapers and listen to radio. . . ." The cultural impact is particularly important on the young: "high proportions of young men in particular visit their club cinema two or three times a week and cannot but be influenced by the steady bombardment of urban values and life-styles."[45]

Income

An important kind of inequality is that of income. Soviet theorists regard income as generating differentiation rather than a status hierarchy. A high income may differentiate groups of workers, but it may not lead to the creation of strata with a definite ranking on a scale of social worth—some being "superior" to others.[46] In the USSR, it is denied by some sociologists that there is a definite "style of life" associated with income differentials.

While we have no adequate survey data to test whether *social* status by income exists, we may describe the form income differentials take. Earlier in this chapter, we saw that rewards were related to skill and output, and that differentials were sharpened under Stalin. Since the early 1950s, a reversal of this inegalitarian trend has occurred. Among workers, for example, the ratio of highest paid to the lowest paid has fallen from 3.6:1 to 2.6:1 in the ferrous metals industry, in light industry from 2.6:1 to 1.8:1, and in machine-building from 2.5:1 to 2:1.[47] Here, again, we see an example of the way the economic and social structure influences wage differentials. In 1956, Mikoyan, envisaging the elimination of the "excessive gap" between the highest and lowest paid, said:

> During the period when we were carrying out industrialization in a peasant country, this gap was natural, since it stimulated the rapid formation of cadres of highly skilled workers of whom the country was in dire need. Now, when there exists a working class which is highly skilled and has a high cultural level, and which is annually replenished by people graduating from seven and ten-year schools, the difference, though necessarily preserved, must be reduced. This proceeds from the new level of our development and signifies a new step forward in the advance towards Communism.[48]

Wages are regarded as an important "lever" to influence the workers' choice of occupation and place of work. Differential wage rates attempt to attract workers to the more needed occupations and to reward them for improving their skill. The harsher climate and lack of amenities in some parts of the USSR have induced the Soviet authorities to relate pay to various "zones" of the country. Pay is from 10 to 20% higher in the Urals, Kazakhstan, and Central Asia and up to 70% greater in the extreme north. Extra earnings are also derived from higher qualifications: Doctors of Science receive an extra 100 rubles per month while Candidates (a lower postgraduate degree) receive 50 rubles.[49] (At the official rate of exchange, 1 ruble is equivalent to $1.34; £1 is exchanged for 1.28 rubles).

As to actual earnings, a minimum wage of 40–45 rubles per month (the lower figure is for rural, the upper for urban areas) was decreed in 1965 and raised to 70 rubles in 1975.[50] Average monthly money wages for manual and nonmanual workers in 1981 were 172 rubles (over double the minimum wage), an estimated real income of 235 rubles including services in kind.[51] Figures are also published showing averages for many different sectors of the economy: In "industry" in 1980, the average monthly money wage was 185.4 rubles, in building it was 202.3 rubles, on state farms and in agricultural enterprises 149 rubles, in transport 200 rubles (railways 187 rubles, on water 232 rubles, road haulage, including chauffeurs and town transport, 202 rubles), communications 145 rubles, trade, catering, supplies 138 rubles, housework and service (zhilishchnokommunalinoe khozyaystvo) 133 rubles, health and social services 127 rubles, education 136 rubles, science 179.5 rubles, credit and insurance 162.2 rubles, public administration 144 rubles.[52] Though these figures are only averages, the occupational composition of different industries indicates a hierarchy with sailors and scientists at the top and post-office workers and those in household service and agriculture at the bottom. Figures have also been published showing average earnings of manual workers, "engineering and technical" personnel, and white collar employees in different industries. In 1980, the average wages of these groups in industry were: 184 rubles, 212 rubles, and 146 rubles, respectively.[53] In 1980, the highest paid workers were in coal mining (298.9 rubles per month) and the lowest in the sewing industry (136 rubles). In 1981, it was decreed that coal miners wages be raised by up to 27%.

These broad "industrial" categories obviously mask differences between occupations. Matthews has collected data (mainly from émigrés) on the earnings of party officials: he cites a figure of 600 rubles per month for the secretary of a Union Republic. Of the military elite, a Marshal of the USSR might receive "up to 2000 rubles" per month; top academics, such as a director of a research institute, earn a maximum of 700 rubles per month; the editor of a Republican newspaper, 500 rubles. The "basic salary" of a collective farm chairman would be about 180 rubles. No hard data are available for elite jobs. It is said that a government minister might earn 1500 rubles and a top party secretary (Brezhnev) 900 rubles. A composer in a good year might receive 8000 rubles a month. In addition to ruble money income, there are other payments for certain elites. These include foreign currency payments available for purchase of superior quality goods in foreign currency shops; other special shops and restaurants are provided for senior officials; special holidays and medical facilities are available to certain elitist groups. Occupational groups have access to housing which favor the academic, political, and industrial elites; access to cars is also given to men and women in high-level posts.[54] These groups undoubtedly have a higher standard of living than the masses, and these "grey" markets provide them with extra privileges. At the other end of the scale, a secondary school teacher may earn 140 rubles per month, a fork-lift operator 110 rubles, a taxi-driver 140 rubles, a doctor 100–130 rubles.[55]

The money income of agricultural workers is generally below that of industrial workers. In 1975, the average monthly income of a state farmer was 125 rubles.[56] To this, of course, must be added income from private plots—both produce consumed and sold—which is something of an unknown quantity, but it may increase income by 20 rubles, which brings up the wage near to the average of workers and employees: 146 rubles in 1975.[57] Though collective farm incomes have risen by 13.6% per annum between 1951 and 1975 (collective farmwork only, excluding other income),[58] the earnings of collective farmers are probably still below the average of all workers and employees. By 1975, it has been estimated by Western specialists that kolkhoz family income was the same as that of a sovkhoz family.[59] Since July 1966, collective farmers have been paid at similar rates to state farmers, though this has not resulted in equal "take-home" pay because the collective farmer is only employed for about 185 days per year, whereas the state farmer is in paid employment all the year round. The collective farmer's income is made up by employment outside the farm and by the sale of his own produce, which has been estimated at 27% of his income.[60] Whereas in 1964 the state farmer had a wage of 70.6 rubles, the collective farmer received from the collective 31 rubles.[61] Schroeder and Severin[62] argue that by 1973, nearly all the collective farmers' wages were paid in money, and they calculate that the average farm incomes were 86% of nonfarm ones. A social survey carried out in a village in the Caucasus showed that three-quarters of the income of the collective farmers was made up from collective farm earnings. Average total *family* income here ranged from 150 rubles to 208 rubles per month; the richest families received as much as 333 rubles a month.[63]

Another form of discrimination is that between the sexes. Women enjoy legal equality, they predominate in some professions, such as medicine and teaching, but they still bear the burden of household chores. Even in the occupational sphere, at the highest levels, women are relatively underprivileged; while in 1975 there were 22,900 Academicians, corresponding Members of the Academy and Professors, women accounted for only 2400—10.4% of the total; similarly, they constituted just over one-fifth of the university teachers.[64] Women are mainly occupied in health (84% of the labor force), education (73%), banking and insurance (82%) and trade, catering, procurement, and supply (76%). While the average money wage in 1978 was 160 rubles, it is interesting to note that *all* these branches of the economy were below it: the figures are health (116 rubles), education (132.4 rubles), banking and insurance (148.4 rubles), and trade, etc. (124 rubles).[65]

In a survey of sex differentiation in a number of Urals factories, it was found that women still made up a large proportion of the unskilled workers and clerical staff. For instance, at one factory, women accounted for 44% of the work force, but 92.7% of the white-collar workers and 91.9% of the junior ancillary staff and their share of the skilled technical engineering jobs was only 26.8%. Of men employed in the factory, 68.7% wanted to continue to study, but only 45.5% of the women did; those actually studying came to 30.1% of the men and only 14.8% of the women. Perhaps a more telling statistic is that of earnings: whereas the average wage of men and women was 122 rubles 80 kopeks that of the women was only 98 rubles—the differential between men and women, therefore, must have been considerably greater than this.[66]

The prevalence of discrimination by sex shows that, despite the genuine attempts of the authorities to emancipate women, the attitudes engendered by centuries of male domination cannot be eradicated by the passing of laws or by giving access to previously male occupations, though these measures help. Let us now turn to wage differentials between other groups.

The differentials between technically qualified personnel ("engineering–technical personnel") and other manual workers and between "nonmanual" and "physical" labor have declined considerably since the 1930s. This is shown in Table 4, which refers to earnings (not rates). Figures released since Yanowitch's article was published confirm the trend. The average monthly wages in ratios of mannual workers, technical personnel, and white-color staff are shown below in Table 5.

As in the advanced West, the Soviet income structure shows how wage and salary rates are similarly related to the forces of demand and supply. With the growing maturity of the Soviet economy, differentials between manual and white-collar workers have shown a similar tendency as in the West—a growing equalization, an improvement in the income of unskilled manual workers at the expense of clerical and similar strata. The growing level of literacy has made less scarce the

TABLE 4 *Wage Ratios Between Nonmanual and Manual Workers (in Percentage of Average Earnings of Workers)[a]*

Year	Average earnings of engineering-technical personnel	Average earnings of nonmanuals
1932	263	150
1935	236	126
1940	210	109
1950	175	93
1955	165	88
1960	150	n/a[a]

[a]*Source:* Yanowitch, "The Soviet Income Revolution," *Slavonic Review*, no. 22 (1963), p. 688.

[b]Yanowitch says that where data are available on an industry basis the trend is in the same direction.

skills of clerks, and the rising output of engineers and technicans has also increased their supply in relation to demand.

Transfer payments in the form of pensions and welfare benefits have also increased from 19 rubles *per capita* in 1950 to 123 rubles in 1975;[67] this again has had the effect of equalizing incomes. There can be no doubt that the general tendencies in Soviet society are for differentials to decline: In the last two decades, such narrowing has been described as "enormous." In 1946, the ratio between the top 10% of earners and the bottom 10% was 7:1; by 1970, it had fallen to 3:1.[68]

Intersociety comparisons are extremely difficult to make. The official ratio of 13 to 1 is much below the equivalent in Great Britain. If we take

TABLE 5 *Wages between Groups of Workers[a]*

Year	Workers	Engineering/technical workers	White-collar workers
1960	100	151	82
1972	100	130	83
1978[b]	100	118	80

[a]*Source:* P. Wiles, "Recent Data on Soviet Income Distribution," *Survey* (1975), p. 31.

[b]In industry. *Narkhoz v 1978g.* (1979), p. 372.

into consideration individual *unearned* income in capitalist states, the income differentiation in Soviet society is certainly less than in most western states. Comparative figures collected by Lenski indicate that in the United States the maximum income is 11,000 times the minimum and 7000 times the average, whereas the comparative Soviet figures are only 300 times and 100 times respectively.[69] The ideology of "building communism" together with collective ownership probably accounts for the much lower Soviet differential. As Wiles and Markowski have concluded, "capitalism produces extremely rich people with a great deal of capital, and this is the most striking difference between [income distribution under communism and capitalism]."[70]

The changes just described in Soviet policy since the revolution indicate that the political elite in the USSR has been constrained by economic and social laws that operate in a similar way as in Western society. The history of the changes in wage differentials illustrates that the system of wage differentiation could only be changed within limits. The inequality demanded by a quickly industrializing social structure overcame the leaders' early egalitarian aims and induced a change in the belief system to justify it. As Margaret Dewar has concluded:

> The organisational structure of the Soviet labour force up to the time of Stalin's death displayed no essentially novel or advanced methods of disciplining labour and increasing productivity which had not been employed in the West. By and large, the industrialisation of the USSR showed features also inherent in the periods of industrialisation of other countries, modified, of course, by contemporary methods of production and labour incentives . . . .[71]

While such income differences give rise to privilege in consumption, we must bear in mind that many goods and services are excluded from the market, and therefore, *income* inequality may not be so significant as in Western societies. Let us now turn from the study of income inequality to other forms of social hierarchy.

Hierarchy
in Soviet
Society

Inkeles has used a combination of measures to determine stratum membership: occupation, income, power, and authority being the main elements.[72] Though he does not explain precisely how he measures group cohesion, he defines 10 "major social–class groups" as follows. The intelligentsia he divides into four main units:

1. *Ruling elite:* a small group consisting of high party, government, economic, and military officials, prominent scientists, and selected artists and writers

2. *Superior intelligentsia*: composed of the intermediary ranks of the categories, mentioned under "ruling elites," plus certain important technical specialists.
3. *General intelligentsia*: incorporating most of the professional groups, the middle ranks of the bureaucracy, managers of small enterprises, junior military officers, technicians, etc.
4. *White collar group*: largely synonymous with the Soviet term for employees, which ranges from petty bureaucrats through accountants and bookkeepers down to the level of ordinary clerks and office workers.

Inkeles groups the working class into three main strata:

1. *Working class "aristocracy"*: the most highly skilled and productive workers, in particular large numbers of the so-called Stakhanovites (i.e., highly paid "rate busters").
2. *Rank-and-file workers*: those in one of the lesser skilled grades slightly above or below the average wage for all workers.
3. *Disadvantaged workers*: estimated to include as many as one-fourth of the labor force, whose low level of skill and lack of productivity or initiative kept them close to the minimum wage level.

The peasantry had two main subgroups:

1. *Well-to-do peasants*: consisting of those particularly advantaged by virtue of the location, fertility, or crop raised by their collective farms (i.e., those living on the so-called "millionaire" farms) and those whose trade, skill, or productivity pushes them into the higher income brackets even on the less prosperous farms.
2. *Average peasant*: shading off into the least productive or poor peasant groups.

Finally, a separate group of those in forced labor camps who, according to Inkeles, was "outside the formal class structure" and had its own social structure derived from the structure of the society as a whole.

While the ranks within each main stratum are shown in the lists, they do not coincide with the ranking of each subgroup within the society as a whole, which Inkeles says was as follows:[73]

1.   Ruling elite
2.   Superior intelligentsia
3.   General intelligentsia
4.   Working class aristocracy
5.5. White collar
5.5. Well-to-do peasants

7.   Average workers
8.5. Average peasants
8.5. Disadvantaged workers
10.   Forced labor

The main drawback to Inkeles's classification is that the subjects were drawn from a group living in Russia before the Second World War. Another estimate is that of Wädekin who, on the basis of the 1959 census, has attempted to define and quantify the social strata. His hierarchy has four main divisions: upper, upper-middle, lower-middle, and lower.[74] In fact, it is very similar to Inkeles's, save that the latter's final two categories are ignored. While Inkeles's top three groups follow quite closely the economic stratification, there are some examples of an economic subgroup being ranked in a different order in the status hierarchy (i.e., the working class aristocracy coming above the white collar worker, and the well-to-do peasants are ranked above the average workers). Inkeles asserts that these groups "had begun to develop fairly definitive styles of life, to elaborate differential patterns of association and to manifest varying degrees of group-consciousness."[75] Such a pattern of stratification, including occupational prestige, level of income, and political authority, brings the social structure of Soviet society closer in kind to that of other modern industrial societies than Stalin's view of the USSR as a morally and politically unique society.

The relative honor or status of different occupations may be shown quantitatively by data from the Harvard project reported in *Sociometry*. Table 6 lists 13 different occupations ranked by "general desirability," "material position," "personal satisfaction," "safety," and "popular regard."[76] Even if the nature of the sample and the conditions in Europe at the time of the survey lead to caution in accepting the findings as typical for the USSR as a whole, by considering the differences in the four columns, we may make at least three fairly safe inferences. Party secretaries are ranked highly in both material position (1) and personal satisfaction (1), while low in terms of "desirability" (11) and popular regard (13); we may infer that political stratification and status stratification are not highly correlated. A second important implication of the table is that material position is not highly correlated with social esteem. The top four in the popular regard column are not in the top four of the material means. A third characteristic, to which I shall return later, is the similarity of the high social status groups (i.e., general desirability) with their counterparts in capitalist countries.

The intercorrelation matrix shown in Table 6 brings out more clearly the relationship between the variables. Row 2 shows the very high positive correlation between material position and personal satisfaction (0.92); and row 1 the high correlation again between desirability and personal satisfaction (0.898). The negative association (-0.818) between

TABLE 6 *Ranking of Soviet Occupations*[a,b]

Occupation	General desirability	Material position	Personal satisfaction	Safety (from arrest)	Popular regard
Doctor	1	7	3	2.5	1
Scientific worker	2.5	5	4	9	2
Engineer	2.5	6	5	12	3
Factory manager	4.5	2	2	13	10
Foreman	4.5	9	7.5	7	6
Accountant	6	8	7.5	5.5	8
Officer in armed forces	7	3	6	10.5	9
Teacher	8	11	10	4	4
Rank and file worker	9	12	12	1	5
Farm brigade leader	10	10	11	5.5	11
Party secretary	11	1	1	8	13
Collective farm chairman	12	4	9	10.5	12
Rank and file collective farmer	13	13	13	2.5	7

Intercorrelations among ratings

	Desirability (1)	Material position (2)	Personal satisfaction (3)	Safety (4)	Popular regard (5)
Desirability (1)	—	+0.67	+0.898	−0.401	+0.525
Material position (2)	+0.67	—	+0.920	−0.818	−0.180
Personal satisfaction (3)	+0.898	+0.92	—	−0.644	+0.167
Safety (4)	−0.401	−0.818	−0.644	—	+0.301
Popular regard (5)	+0.525	−0.180	+0.167	+0.301	—

[a]*Source:* P. H. Rossi and A. Inkeles, "Multidimensional Ratings of Occupations," *Sociometry* no. 3 (1957), p. 247.

[b]Based on written questionnaires completed by 2146 former Soviet citizens, who were in displaced persons' camps in Germany (1505) or who had emigrated to the USA (1950–1951).

material position and personal safety indicates a feeling of "high risk" for the higher occupational positions—particularly for the factory manager. It may be inferred from this that social mobility was hindered by the terror of the Stalin era; more competent men preferring a safe but modest occupation rather than the risky highly paid. The authors of the study conclude that "the *personal satisfaction* which inheres in the job is the prime determinant of its rated *desirability*."[77] The "popular regard" (row 5) associations do not show highly positive correlations on all scores, and with material position (column 2), there is even a negative association. The data here suggest rather a differentiated social system, with values being allocated separately on criteria—such as power, safety, popular regard, and material position—rather than a highly stratified society with such indexes showing a positive correlation throughout. This result is what one perhaps should expect when a society is in flux and characterized by rapid social and political change.

The Rossi and Inkeles survey is now rather dated, and unfortunately, we have no recent comparable survey from Soviet sources. Research in Leningrad illustrates how earnings are related to other factors—education, party membership) and voluntary participation in social work. Some of the results of the survey are shown in Table 7. The wage differential shows that managerial personnel receive on average just under double the income of unqualified workers. This does not exclude, of course, a greater range between the factory director and laborers as bonus payments, and other nonmonetary rewards might not have been counted in the survey.[78] Highly qualified production workers are the second most highly paid in the factory, Clerical workers, despite their relatively higher education, are the lowest paid, receiving even less than the unqualified manual workers.

The striking conclusion to be drawn from the table is the high positive correlation between the four factors: education, wages, party membership and social work. This is shown on the intercorrelation matrix in the tabulation below.

| | Spearman rank correlation matrix | | | |
	Education	Wages	Party membership	Social work
Education	—	.52	.71	.76
Wages	.52	—	.67	.79
Party membership	.71	.67	—	.81
Social work	.76	.79	.81	—

From the data presented we may make some inference about stratification. At the top the table, we see a group that is highly educated, has high income, very high Party/Komsomol membership (60.8%) and good participation in voluntary work. At the bottom of the table, the unqualified manual workers seem to constitute a relatively deprived group having low incomes, with a very short education (only

TABLE 7 *Some Aspects of the Social Structure of Leningrad Engineering Workers*[a]

Groups of workers	Education (years)	Wages (in rubles, monthly)	Party/Komsomol membership (%)	Participation in social work (%)
Management (factory directors, shop superintendents)	13.6	172.9	60.8	84.2
Workers in highly qualified technical–scientific jobs (designers)	14.0	127.0	40.2	70.4
Qualified nonmanual workers (technologists, bookkeepers)	12.5	109.8	42.8	82.4
Highly qualified workers in jobs with mental and manual functions (tool setters)	8.8	129.0	37.6	79.2
Qualified workers of superior manual work (fitters, welders)	8.3	120.0	37.4	60.7
Qualified manual workers (machine–tool operators, press operators)	8.2	107.5	39.5	54.3
Nonmanual workers of medium qualifications (inspection and office workers)	9.1	83.6	27.1	54.5
Unqualified manual workers	6.5	97.5	13.8	35.1

[a]*Source:* Adapted from O. I. Shkaratan, "Sotsial'naya struktura sovetskogo rabochego klassa," *Voprosy filosofi*, no. 1 (1967), p. 36.

6.5 years), a small proportion of party members (only 13.8%) and their participation in voluntary work (35.1%) is also minimal. Unlike the Rossi and Inkeles survey, this work, with the positively correlated factors of education, wages, party membership and voluntary work, suggests a "consistent" system of stratification.

While Soviet research is deficient on the status of particular social groups, studies conducted in the West on the prestige given to different occupations show a high correlation between their ranking in the USSR and other industrial countries. The correlation of matched occupations between the Soviet Union and other countries is highly positive: with Japan it was 0.74, Great Britain, 0.83, New Zealand, 0.83, United States, 0.9, and Germany, 0.9.[79] Some notable differences, however, show up in Inkeles's and Rossi's research. The "worker" was given a relatively higher ranking in the USSR than in the United States, Great Britain, and New Zealand; and engineers were also given a higher rating in the Soviet Union than in the United States. At the other extreme, farmers were all rated lower in the USSR than in the United States, Great Britain, and New Zealand, and scientists have less prestige than in the United States. Further data on the desirability of occupations are available from the study of aspirations of Soviet schoolchildren. Such studies show conclusively that at the top of children's preferred jobs are those requiring higher educational qualifications—mathematicians, physicists, physicians; at the bottom are unskilled jobs in agriculture and service industries.[80]

Social relations between groups do involve assumptions about statuses. Solzhenitsyn illustrates a party official discussing his son's marriage:

> He was such a naïve boy, he might be led up the garden path by some ordinary weaver girl from the textile factory. Well, perhaps not a weaver, there'd be nowhere for them to meet, they wouldn't frequent the same places. . . . Look at Shendyapin's daughter, how she'd very nearly married a student in her year at teachers' training college. He was only a boy from the country and his mother was an ordinary collective farmer. Just imagine the Shendyapin's flat, their furniture and the influential people they had as guests and suddenly there's this old woman in a white headscarf sitting at their table, their daughter's mother-in-law, and she didn't even have a passport. Whatever next? Thank goodness they'd managed to discredit the fiancé politically and save their daughter.[81]

While the data available to us do not allow very firm conclusions to be drawn, it does seem likely that despite the ways in which Soviet society is structurally different from Western industrial systems, "there is a relatively invariable hierarchy of prestige associated with the industrial system, even when it is placed in the context of larger social systems which are otherwise differentiated in important respects."[82] The relatively lower rank given to "farmers" in the USSR is partly a reflection of the different structure of agriculture and coincides not only with their lower political standing in the USSR but also with the relatively unskilled work of the collective farmer. The higher status given to "workers" in the USSR is quite important and shows the influence of political ideology in the social sphere.[83] What is particularly interesting to note in the Soviet case are not only the high status given to the worker, a value engendered by Marxist ideology, but also the high evaluation of the professional employees—a factor shared with the West.

Social Mobility

The hierarchical arrangement of Soviet social strata raises the question of social mobility between them. How far are there distinct self-recruiting strata, and how far are the top positions equally accessible to different social groups lower down the hierarchy?

During the Stalin era, not only were wage differentials increased but other privileges also accrued to the rich. During the Second World War, access to higher education (and the top three classes of secondary schools) was made conditional, in most cases, on the payment of fees. The rationing system and shops restricted to higher strata strengthened status differentials as did inheritance being taxed at lower rates[84] and the highest decorations in the armed forces being restricted only to the top ranks. In addition, after the Second World War, the family as a unit was strengthened. These factors tended to reduce mobility.

Other factors worked in an opposite direction. Very rapid industrialization, particularly between 1928 and 1939, provided a large number of skilled and executive jobs associated with the factory system. The changes in the social structure are illustrated by the official figures cited below (Table 8). The proportion of manual and nonmanual workers rose from 17.6% to 50.2% of the employed population, though these figures included, of course, workers on state farms.

Between 1928 and 1937, the numbers employed in industrial production increased by 268% and between 1931 and 1961, the number of manual workers increased threefold, that of engineers fivefold and other nonmanual employees by 33%.[85] In addition to the effects of industrialization, the purges depleted the higher ranks of the bureaucracy and provided extra opportunity for upward mobility, and the war, with the terrific loss of older experienced manpower, also created greater possibilities for rapid social mobility.

The tables cited illustrate the changes in the general composition of Soviet society since the revolution. They imply considerable upward social mobility, for the increase in the size of the intelligentsia and working class presumes recruitment from the peasantry (in at least one of the categories), though this does not preclude a high rate of internal recruitment from the intelligentsia itself. The results of the survey of Russian émigrés reported by Inkeles and Bauer show that access to higher education and, therefore, to high status occupations was differentially related to social background. Inkeles has generalized this tendency by saying that "as stratification has become institutionalized

TABLE 8 *Official Figures of Soviet Social Change (Total Population)*[a]

Groups of workers	1913	1928	1939	1959	1979
Manual and nonmanual workers	17.0	17.6	50.2	68.3	85.1
Collective farmers and cooperative handicraftsmen	—	2.9	47.2	31.4	14.9
Independent peasants and handicraftsmen	66.7	74.9	2.6	0.3	0.0
Bourgeoisie	16.3	4.6	—	—	—
	100.0	100.0	100.0	100.0	100.0

[a]*Source: Narkhoz v 1978g.* (1979), p. 9. In the 1979 census, the percentages were manual workers, 60; nonmanuals, 25.1; collective farmers, 14.9.

there has been a noticeable tendency for social mobility to decline and for the system to become less an open class structure."[86]

However, it certainly would not be correct to think that the social horizons of lower social strata have been lowered. Aspiration for higher social position is widespread. Of 2518 parents surveyed in Sverdlovsk, 64% wanted a higher education for their children. The aspirations were greatest among the "specialists" (workers with professional qualifications) of whom 89% wanted higher education for their children; the figure fell to 64.9% for workers and 36.2% for collective farmers.[87] These figures show a terrific demand for higher education and, indirectly, high social position. The "institutionalization" of status position referred to by Inkeles, therefore, must take place in the process of educational selection.

It is likely, as Inkeles points out, that those who have legitimately acquired privilege in the system will seek to preserve it and pass it on to their children. In 1938, for instance, 47% of the student body was made up of children with intelligentsia background.[88] Again, we have no comprehensive statistics for recent Soviet developments. Soviet sociologists tend to emphasize the opportunities for upward mobility. For example, a study by Rutkevitch of full-time students in the Sverdlovsk Mining Institute illustrates the changing composition of its full-time students, shown in Table 9.

The table shows the increasing number of children of working class origin entering the institute: a rise of 28.3% between 1940 and 1963. The increase in numbers of students with a working class "social position" (from 4.6 to 61.9%) reflects the practice of selecting students from men who had already had production experience after school. Of course, one may expect such a large proletarian intake in a technological institute, and Rutkevitch goes on to cite other statistics. In 1963, children from working class families accounted for 51% of full-time students at the Urals university and 42% at the Sverdlovsk medical institute. At a teacher's training college in 1962–1963, children from working class families constituted 66.8% of the intake.[89]

Rather greater inequality has been found among evening and correspondence course students. Of students at various institutes of higher education in Sverdlovsk, 47.1% of the evening students and 63.5% of the correspondence students were either nonmanual workers or the children of this stratum. It is clear that nonmanual workers predominate among the students to a far greater extent than in the population as a whole. The lack of opportunity for peasants is also noteworthy: of evening students, they accounted for 0.4% and 0.9% of the correspondence group. The working class students tend to be clustered in the polytechnic, the railway and mining institute, and the economics institute, whereas in teaching and law, at the conservatory and university, nonmanual workers or their children are predominant.[90]

Advancement to positions of authority in industry would probably be more open to children of manual workers than to other strata. In Shkaratan's survey of Leningrad workers, 54.2% of factory chiefs were of manual worker and collective farm family background.[91] Most seem to have worked their way up through the factory. This evidence is corroborated by S. T. Guryanov, who found that of 1000 workers in Moscow electrical engineering factory who started work as semiskilled operators, 14 were promoted after 10 years experience to engineer or technical status.[92] E. C. Brown, on a visit to 19 factories, found that at least 14 of the factory directors had begun as manual workers. "In their family origin and in part their work experience most of these directors and their chief engineers and other technical and administrative people had a common bond with workers and union officers."[93]

A survey of staff and workers at two factories in the Urals shows that a large proportion of the "directing personnel" are of worker and peasant background. Some of the data in this survey are given in Table 10.

Here we see that 48% of the top management at GPZ-6 and over 27%

TABLE 9 Social Structure of Full-time Students in Sverdlovsk Mining Institute 1940, 1955, 1961, 1963[a]

Year	Social origins (%)[b]			Social position (%)[c]			
	Worker	Employee	Peasant	Worker	Employee	Peasant	Student
1940	33.4	30.2	36.4	4.6	5.9	—	85.5
1955	27.7	57.3	15.0	5.1	9.6	—	84.3
1961	59.8	25.0	15.2	62.8	20.2	3.0	14.0
1963	61.7	25.0	13.3	61.9	25.0	—	13.1

[a]Source: M. N. Rutkevitch, "Izmenenie sotsial'noy struktury sovetskogo obschestva i intelligentsiya," Sotsiologiya v SSSR, vol. 1 (Moscow, 1965), p. 412.
[b]Social origin denotes occupation of father.
[c]Social position is first or current occupation of person.

TABLE 10 *Composition and Social Origin of Directing Personnel in Factories GPZ-6 and UKZ (in Percentage)*[a]

Category of worker	Social origin			Began work as				Party membership
	Worker	Peasant	Nonmanual worker	Worker	Peasant	White-collar	Specialist	
Directors of work on a factory scale								
GPZ-6	28	48	24	52	12	16	20	76
UKZ	27	27	46	23	12	11	54	73
Shop Managers								
GPZ-6	46	38	16	77	—	—	23	61
UKZ	67	33	—	67	—	—	33	83

Source: Protsessy izmeneniya sotsial'noy struktury v Sovetskom obshchestve (Sverdlovsk, 1967), p. 194.

at UKZ were of peasant social origin. Note also the high proportion who began work as manual workers: at GPZ-6, 52% of the directors and 77% of the shop managers. These men worked their way up and many were able to study in their spare time.

A second index of the degree to which the "middle class" is passing on its privilege is another study by Rutkevitch of scientists employed at the Eastern Coal–Chemical (Research) Institute. Here, 56.6% of the scientists were from nonmanual families, which make up 25% of the total population. Of scientists under 30 years of age, 23.4% were of parents from the higher intelligentsia and 46.8% from other middle class strata. While of the scientists aged over 50 years, 17.5% were of peasant origin; only 4.3% of the young scientists (under 30) were of such stock.[94]

Opportunities would seem to be more generally available for upward social mobility in industrial production than in research where the superior cultural background of the nonmanual worker gives his children a great advantage. This tendency seems to have been strengthened in recent years in the USSR. It gives rise to privileged social and political elites, which have been described by journalists such as Hedrick Smith.

These figures confirm what was said earlier about the ways family background influenced fulfillment of children's educational aspirations. There can be no doubt that in the USSR, the social position of parents plays a most important role in determining the education and, therefore, the subsequent social standing of children.

It is not wished to imply that the Soviet regime intentionally restricts mobility. After 1956, tuition fees were abolished in education, and in recent years, children of lower educational strata (manual workers and collective farm peasantry) were given special consideration for admission to *vuzy*.[95] For instance, in Lvov Polytechnic, admission standardds are related to the social position of candidates—the children of workers, peasants, and lower employees having to fulfill lower requirements than those of the intelligentsia.[96] In 1969, arrangements were announced for setting-up special preparatory departments in universities to prepare workers and peasants lacking formal requirements.[97] The regulations demanding practical work experience also tended to work in favor of lower strata children. Other acts have been passed intended to reduce social distance between strata: wage differentials have been reduced, minimum wages raised, old age pensions increased, salaries of managerial and technical staffs have been frozen in the 1970s.

Nevertheless, despite the attempts of the Soviet government to reduce inequality, the operation of general social laws has inhibited exchange mobility in the USSR as they have in Western societies. Social position, based on the division of labor, is a common characteristic of all modern urban industrial societies. Perfect social mobility is prevented because those with scarce skills and specialist training are able within their family sphere to perpetuate the advantages which these skills and training give them. The strengthening of the Soviet family has encouraged this tendency, though the family's right to transmit a claim on the appropriation of the social product does not pertain as in the West. On the other hand, upward social mobility has probably been greater in Soviet Russia than in contemporary Western societies. This upward mobility may only partially be accounted for by "communist" values. Forces engendered by the rapid industrialization process entailed the recruitment, training, and upward mobility of previous lower strata.

Socialism and Egalitarianism

What, then, are the implications of Soviet experience for the more general questions raised in this book?

First, the evidence shows that Soviet society is not and has never been at any time in its history "classless": Social inequality is a universal social phenomenon.

Second, the forms of social stratification in the USSR differ from those of Western liberal societies. There is no property-owning class; large-scale industrial societies, therefore, can function without the *private* accumulation of property and the inequalities to which it gives rise. This is now an obvious, though most important, conclusion to be drawn from the Soviet experience.

Third, the functionalists' view that inequality is necessary (*a*) to induce individuals into positions requiring special skills and abilities and (*b*) to reward them differentially so that their tasks may be efficiently carried out has been substantiated in Soviet conditions. It is sometimes said, by radicals and egalitarians, that if one could change the values or socialization pattern of a society, then inferiority could be abolished. In other words, if people do not believe in inequality, they do not take cognizance of income, power, or occupational differentials in their social relationships. The trouble with this argument is that it does not explain the conditions under which such a value pattern or socialization process can take place. Both the process of the division of labor and the maintenance and socialization functions of the family preclude such a development in modern society. Occupations differentiate the roles of individuals, and as long as these are specific, intellectual or creative occupations will always be more highly valued by members of society because they are inherently more agreeable; they also promote a way of life culturally distinct from those occupied in routine, manual jobs. A necessary condition of a truly classless society is, as Marx long ago pointed out, the absence of the division of labor. The family, even if its legal rights over property are abolished, differentially socializes children; by doing so, it makes the inculcation of universal social mores difficult; it also makes some children more capable of benefitting from education than others. Thereby, inequality is perpetuated. Under the conditions of industrial production known to us both in state socialist and capitalist societies, the division of labor is more specialized and the family is as persistent as it ever has been. As far as Marxist theory is concerned, the existence of social inequality *under the industrial conditions inherited by the Soviet communists* has never been in doubt. The main dispute in the USSR has been over the ratio between the richest and the poorest, and in practice, this ratio is now very much lower than in Western societies.

Fourth, political elites play an important role in *defining* the inequalities or the system of positions in which one is rewarded more than in another. In the USSR, engineers, Academicians, and coal miners get higher pay than doctors. The recruitment of doctors does not depend on a high reward "commensurate with the sacrifice" necessary to undertake medical studies.[98] This reflects the political priorities of a society, which become embodied in an ideology that justifies a certain income inequality.

Fifth, while the political authorities may influence certain kinds of privilege, particularly income and education, they are subject to external social constraints. Some elements of a subjective status hierarchy transcend societies: here, control over life itself, exercised by doctors, gives honor; those with technical qualifications in industrial societies and those who transmit knowledge similarly have a high status ranking.

Sixth, political values may affect the status of occupations: "The worker" in Soviet society is more highly rated than in liberal–democratic ones; and perhaps more important, the ideology of "building communism" has minimized the range of inequality between the richest and poorest and between men and women.

The last general conclusion to be drawn is that social inequality of one kind or another seems to be inevitable as long as societies are characterized by a division of labor and as long as the family plays an important role in the maintenance of children.

Having discussed stratification, the economy, and the political system, we may now make some general conclusions about the more sociological aspects of Soviet society.

Some Conclusions about the Soviet Social System   In analyzing the class structure of any society, we need to distinguish between three class models: antagonistic class society, unitary class society, and classless society. These classifications are derived from the Marxist notion of the basis of a society. Capitalism is an antagonistic class society because rights to ownership (and disposal) of property inhere in the bourgeoisie which is able through the market to extract a surplus from the working class. Theoretically, a postcapitalist *classless* society is predicated on an economically advanced technological economy in which the means of production are collectively owned and controlled and in which major forms of inequality and the state as an instrument of oppression have been abolished. Here the superstructure is congruent with the basis. State socialist societies are not classless, but they are not antagonistic class societies either. They are single class societies or workers' states.

The party acts for the working class, and the extraction of surplus by the state is to maintain a high level of investment to ensure all-round industrialization; while this process has kept down living standards, it is quite different from extracting surplus as a factor source of profit. But the contemporary economy of the USSR is not at an economic level equal to, or in advance of, the leading capitalist states, and shortages entail an uneven and unequal distribution of commodities. In addition, the cultural formation and the political arrangements characteristic of the superstructure of society are not yet at the socialist level. Elements of the superstructure may be determined by presocialist culture (the "style" of administration) and may also be an integral part of the system of distribution of commodities affecting one's general life chances in terms of education and style of life.

Unlike the official theory of these societies, however, we do not conceive of such forms of inequality as epiphenomena but as contradictions built into the system for as long as the level of production leaves some socially determined wants unfulfilled. And only at very high levels of industrial production is equal political participation by citizens possible, for only then will citizens have sufficient time to attend to the affairs of the state; and only under these circumstances will the working class rule directly. The relatively unsophisticated cultural heritage and the low level of productive forces allow other inequalities to persist. The inequalities and conflicts between various groupings reflect differences of interest which are important elements in the analysis of state socialist society, and such differences are either ignored or minimized in the official ideology. Contrary to Giddens' analysis, however, it is my assertion that a class*less* society is by definition less exploitative than a class society, for it has no ruling and no exploited class.[99] The differences between an antagonistic class society and a homogeneous (or single) class society are less great, but nevertheless, a major distinction must be made between the capitalist and socialist relations of production.

Giddens and other critics, such as Churchward,[100] of crude Marxism are correct in pointing to the inadequacies of its conceptual armory for distinguishing between different types of capitalist and state socialist societies and to developments within these modes of production. Also one of the most general criticisms of convergence and postindustrial theories is that they are insensitive to variations between and within capitalism and state socialism. Here we propose to typologize different societies in terms of (*a*) Marxist categories of class relations and (*b*) forms of consumption, ideology, cultural values, and type of government.

In Figure 1, we typologize six types of society. Three are capitalist: socialist–utopian as desired, for instance, by Christian social–democrats favoring highly egalitarian forms of consumption and a property-owning class; capitalistic social–democracy, having in practice a more modest form of inequality characteristic of states such as Denmark; and free enterprise capitalism such as the United States, having very high income differentials. Three are socialist: In communist society (not yet attained) there is a very high degree of egalitarianism; under state socialism (USSR), differentials remain considerable; and in "market" workers' states (Yugoslavia), they are in theory much greater than in more centrally planned workers' states but less than under free enterprise capitalism. This figure brings out the achievements of countries such as Denmark and Sweden in redistributing income through social services and taxation, giving rise to egalitarian forms of consumption. State socialist societies share many features of the distributive ("bourgeois") characteristics of capitalism, and the most typical form of distribution is akin to Western welfare states. Only at the advanced economic level of communist society is a significant move to egalitarianism possible.

The particular pattern of industrialization followed by Soviet society is derived from the overriding value system of Marxism–Leninism and cannot be understood independently of ideas of historical materialism that legitimate the forms of development pursued. But to argue, as do Giddens and some developmental sociologists,[101] that capitalism and state socialism are merely variants of an industrializing mode, is a gross oversimplification and ignores the different dominant *values* that distinguish these forms of society. Bell[102] has suggested that the dynamic of state socialist societies is a form of ideological activism. This should be considered as a form of elective affinity in which the goals of the political elites become wedded to Marxism–Leninism.[103] Those writers who deny the role of Marxist ideology and postulate a "great retreat" by communist leaders[104] ignore the adaptation and subordination of policy (on the family, on economic incentives, etc.) to the pursuit of the goal of industrial development, itself derived from Marxism–Leninism. The developmental ideology of state socialist societies is also much wider in scope and is projected much further in time than the "instrumental activism" of capitalist-type societies;[105] the level of productive forces, however, distinguishes different types of both capitalist and state socialist society.

The cultural context also has an important and *relatively* independent role in determining the individual orientations and various forms of

	Class Relations to Means of Production	
	Single Class *Public Ownership*	*Antagonistic Classes* *Private Ownership*
Forms of Consumption *Degree of Egalitarianism*		
High	Classless Society (Communism)	Socialist–Utopian
Medium	State Socialism	Capitalistic Social–Democracy
Low	"Market" Workers' States	Free Enterprise Capitalism

Figure 1. *Types of capitalist and socialist society.*

inequality. The cultural context, in a Marxist sense, may be interpreted in the light of the movement from previous modes of production. The leadership of a country such as Stalin's Russia, inheriting a deep-seated autocratic social ethos, is faced with ingrained attitudes that are quite alien to socialist ideology. Western societies, where liberal-democracy has been more advanced (such as Britain), have a more congruent belief system on which to build. Marx, of course, believed that only socialism could ensure the human rights aspired to by bourgeois liberalism.

The ways in which culture influences the class structure may be illustrated by reference to women as a minority group. In partial agreement with women's liberation writers such as Millet,[106] cultural values are seen as having an important determining influence on the roles of women. In addition, however, the class structure acts as an equally important determinant. Changes in cultural values under capitalism certainly improve the position of women in relation to men. In countries such as Denmark and Sweden, women have many positive rights, and such states may be defined as democratic patriarchies. These rights are in terms of legal status and citizenship and give women control of their bodies (e.g., by rights to abortion and contraception). Such countries remain patriarchies because of the domination of men in politics, industry, and many fields of employment. There is, however, a great difference between them and other forms of authoritarian patriarchy where women are denied equality as citizens, having no rights to own property, no right to vote, and exclusion from positions in certain institutions such as the Church, the stock exchange, and universities.

Unitary class societies, as we know them in existing workers' states, do not ensure the equality of all social groups, and women is one of them. In the early history of such states, forms of discrimination continue, despite the early enactment of laws by the political elites promoting equality.[107] With the development of the industrial base, state socialist societies normally quickly procure many advances for women, particularly in education and in occupational opportunity. Such societies, though socialist, remain patriarchal, for authority relations (particularly leading political roles) are dominated by men, and women have greater responsibility for the upbringing of children.

The fact that state socialist society is a unitary class society does not mean that political conflict ceases: politics is endemic to workers' states. The formal political apparatus is responsible to a much wider extent in determining, to use Lasswell's terms, "who gets what, when and how": the political process decides the distribution of resources between various social groups and interests, though this is limited by the economic basis.

To conclude, we may say that state ownership of the means of production, the dominance of working class values, and the absence of an antagonistic ascendant class in state socialist society ensure its basic character as a workers' state; its chief forms of *production* are socialist. Western capitalist societies have quite a different basis and dynamic: they are characterized by social classes that have rights over the disposal of property and of income from property; the capital market and the making of profit in the context of a more or less regulated economy are essential dynamics of modern capitalism. Hence, convergence theories that are concerned with a single type of *modern* society and Marxist-type theories postulating convergence to a single form of *capitalist* society are to this extent incorrect. But workers' states do not have a superstructure congruent with the socialist basis: They are not class*less* societies. Following Mandel,[108] they are considered to be transitionary. They do not fall under the capitalist mode of production, but neither are they complete socialist societies. They have a dominant ruling class defining the structure of the socialist state while at the same time they have an essentially inegalitarian or "bourgeois" system of unequal distribution of commodities—expressed through the price and wage system and in other forms of market relationships. These include the political: a workers' state is ruled for the workers rather than there being direct forms of worker management. The pattern of distribution of various types of commodities (including education) is similar to that of bourgeois societies and entails status differentiation and inequality of political power; such distribution involves ranking and hierarchy rather than social polarization.

Notes

[1] Kingsley Davis, *Human Society* (New York, 1948), p. 367.

[2] Talcott Parsons, "An Analytical Approach to the Theory of Social Stratification," *Essays in Sociological Theory, Pure and Applied* (Glencoe, Ill., 1949), p. 166.

[3] "Critique of Gotha Program," in Marx and Engels, *Selected Works*, vol. 2 (1950), p. 23.

[4] In addition, the clergy and members of the royal family had restricted political rights.

[5] V. I. Lenin, "The Immediate Tasks of the Soviet Government," *Collected Works*, vol. 27 (1965), pp. 249, 581n.

[6] See A. Bergson, *The Structure of Soviet Wages* (Cambridge, Mass. 1954), p. 190.

[7] Bergson, *Soviet Wages*, p. 182.

[8] *Ibid.*, p. 185. See also *Trud i zarabotnaya plata v SSSR* (Moscow, 1968), p. 323.

[9] L. Kostin, *Wages in the USSR* (Moscow, 1960), p. 16.

[10] Bergson, *Soviet Wages*, p. 92. In the sphere of education, workers and peasants were given preference for admission to higher educational institutions. At the same time, laws weakening the family were passed.

[11] J. V. Stalin, "Talk With Emil Ludwig," *Collected Works*, vol. 13, p. 120.

[12] Stalin, "Talk with Emil Ludwig," pp. 120–121.

[13] See comparison computed by Bergson, *Soviet Wages*, pp. 101, 118.

[14] *Ibid.*, pp. 200–201, 203–204.

[15] Robert W. Hodge *et al.*, "A Comparative Study of Occupational Prestige," in *Class, Status and Power*, ed. R. Bendix and S. M. Lipset (1967), p. 320.

[16] Kostin, *Wages in the USSR*, p. 16.

[17] Bergson, *Soviet Wages*, p. 208.

[18] Roy Jenkins, "Equality," in *New Fabian Essays* (1952), p. 69.

[19] J. Stalin, "New Conditions—New Tasks in Economic Construction," in *Problems of Leninism* (Moscow, 1952), pp. 463–464.

[20] G. Glezerman, "Sotsial'naya struktura sotsialisticheskogo obshchestva," no. 13, 1968. See also *Soviet News*, November 12, 1968.

[21] Marx and Engels, *Selected Works*, vol. 3, p. 248.

[22] P. G. Pod'yachich, *Naselemie SSSR* (Moscow, 1961), p. 154.

[23] *Narodnoe khozyaystvo SSSR v 1978g.* (Moscow, 1979), p. 9.

[24] M. N. Rutkevitch, "Izmenenie sotsial'noy struktury sovetskogo obshchestva i intelligentsiya," *Sotsiologiya v SSSR*, vol. 1 (Moscow, 1965), p. 401.

[25] F. Konstantinov, "Sovetskaya intelligentsiya," *Kommunist*, no. 15 (1959), p. 50.

[26] V. S. Semenov, "Ob izmenenii intelligentsii i sluzhashchikh v protsesse razvernutogo stroitel'stva kommunizma," *Sotsiologiya v SSSR*, vol. 1 (Moscow, 1963), p. 418.

[27] Rutkevitch, "Izmenenie sotsial'noy," p. 412.

[28] M. Matthews, "Top Incomes in the USSR," *Survey*, no. 3 (Summer 1975), p. 13.

[29] See section in this chapter, *"Hierarchy in Soviet Society."*

[30] G. Smirnov, "Rabochi klass SSSR," *Kommunist*, no. 4 (March, 1960), p. 43.

[31] *Narkhoz v 1978g.* (Moscow, 1979), pp. 364, 368.

[32]In 1965, 72% of workers were employed in industries with six basic wage divisions. See *Trud v SSSR*, pp. 150–151.

[33]The workers are now divided between the three groups in these proportions: 29.3%, 43.7%, and 27%. "Sotsialisticheskoe proizvodstvo i razvitie rabochego klassa," *Klassy, sotsial'nye sloi i gruppy v SSSR* (Moscow, 1968), pp. 52–54.

[34]J. Stalin, "Ekonomicheskie problemy sotsializma" (1952), *Sochineniya*, vol. 16 (Stanford, 1967), p. 205.

[35]Basile Kerblay, "The Russian Peasant," *St. Antony's Papers*, no. 19 (1966), p. 15. Also, many collective farmers are now paid regular wages at the same rates as *sovkhozniki*.

[36]See I. Hill, "The End of the Russian Peasantry?" *Soviet Studies* 27 (January 1975) pp. 109–127.

[37]"Kolkhoznoe krest'yanstvo i sovetskaya derevnya na puti k kommunizmu," *Klassy, sotsial'nye sloi i gruppy v SSSR* (Moscow, 1968), pp. 85–86.

[38]"Kolkhoznoe krest'yanstvo," p. 92.

[39]I. I. Bodyul, *Preodolenie sushchestvennykh razlichiy mezhdu gorodom i derevney v usloviyakh Moldavskoy SSR* (Kishinev, 1967), p. 86.

[40]One Soviet estimate is that the productivity of labor will rise from five to six times between 1960 and 1980 resulting in a 20–30% reduction of the labor force. "Strukturnye izmeneniya v krest'yanstve," *Klassy sotsial'nye sloi i gruppy v SSSR*, p. 119.

[41]C. A. R. Crosland, *The Future of Socialism* (1956).

[42]S. Ossowski, *Class Structure in the Social Consciousness* (1963), pp. 112–113.

[43]Bodyul, *Preodolenie sushchestvennykh*, p. 80.

[44]"Pod'em kultury kolkhoznogo sela," *Klassy, sotsial'nye sloi i gruppy v SSSR* (Moscow, 1968), p. 127.

[45]I. Hill, "The End of the Russian Peasantry?" p. 120.

[46]See M. Tumin, "On Inequality," *American Sociological Review* 28, 1963.

[47]Figures cited in *Klassy, sotsial'nye sloi i gruppy v SSSR* (Moscow, 1968), p. 53.

[48]*XX S"ezd KPSS*, vol. 1, p. 307, cited by Robert Conquest, *Industrial Workers in the USSR* (1967), p. 50.

[49]For details see G. Mustinov, *Raschety po zarabotnoy plate rabochikh i sluzhashchikh* (Moscow, 1965), pp. 11–12.

[50]*Pravda*, September 27, 1967. *Narkhoz 1975g.* (1976), p. 548. In 1976, the average money wage rose to 151 rubles.

[51]*Vestnik statistiki*, no. 5 (1981), *Soviet News*, August 18, 1981.

[52]*Vestnik statistiki*, no. 8 (1981), pp. 78–79.

[53]*Ibid.*

[54]Matthews, "Top Incomes." Hedrick Smith, *The Russians* (1976), chapter 1.

[55]Figures from émigré reports.

[56]*Narodnoe khozyaystvo v 1975g.* (Moscow, 1976), p. 546.

[57]*Ibid.*, p. 545.

[58]G. E. Schroeder and B. Severin, "Soviet Consumption and Income Policies in Perspective," in U.S. Congress Joint Economic Committee, *Soviet Economy in a New Perspective* (Washington, D.C.: U.S. Government Printing Office, 1976), p. 628.

[59]K. E. Wädekin, "Income Distribution in Soviet Agriculture," *Soviet Studies* 27, no. 1 (1975), p. 11.

[60]*Ibid.*, p. 6.

[61]J. F. Karcz, "Seven Years on the Farm: Retrospect and Prospects," *New Directions in the Soviet Economy* (Washington, 1966), pp. 359–6.

[62]Schroeder and Severin," Soviet Consumption," p. 629.

[63]*Sovremennoe Abkhazskoe selo* (Tbilisi, 1967), pp. 22–23.

[64]*Narodnoe khozyaystvo SSSR v 1975g.* (1976), p. 165.

[65]*Narkhoz v 1978g.* (1979), p. 372–73.

[66]E. P. Ovchinnikova and S. V. Brova, "O likvidatsii ostatkov sotsial'nogo neravenstva rabochikh i rabotnits na promyshlennykh predpriyatiyakh," in *Protsessy izmeneniya sotsial'noy struktury v sovetskom obshchestve* (Sverdlovsk, 1967), pp. 37–40.

[67]Schroeder and Severin, "Soviet Consumption," p. 630.

[68]D. W. Bronson and B. S. Severin, "Soviet Consumer Welfare: The Brezhnev Era," in U.S. Congress, Joint Economic Committee, *Soviet Economic Prospects for the Seventies* (Washington, D.C.: U.S. Government Printing Office, 1973), p. 379.

[69]Gerhard E. Lenski, *Power and Privilege* (New York, 1966), 312–313.

[70]P. Wiles and S. Markowski, "Income Distribution under Communism and Capitalism," *Soviet Studies* 22 (1971), p. 344. See also, A. McAuley, "The Distribution of Earnings and Incomes in the Soviet Union," *Soviet Studies* 29 (1977), p. 234.

[71]M. Dewar, "Labour and Wage Reforms in the USSR," *Studies on the Soviet Union* 3, no. 3 (Munich, 1962), p. 80. See also for a similar view E. C. Brown, *Soviet Trade Unions and Labour Relations* (Cambridge, Mass., 1966), p. 44.

[72]A. Inkeles, "Social Stratification and Mobility in the Soviet Union 1940–1950," *American Sociological Review* 15 (1950), reprinted in A. Inkeles and K. Geiger, *Soviet Society* (1961).

[73]Inkeles, "Social Stratification," p. 560.

[74]See Karl-Eugen Wädekin, *Ost Europa*, no. 5 (1965).

[75]Inkeles, "Social Stratification," p. 561.

[76]Based on data given in P. H. Rossi and A. Inkeles, "Multidimensional Ratings of Occupation," *Sociometry* 20, no. 3 (1957).

[77]*Ibid.*, pp. 250–251.

[78]Also, the factory director is included in these statistics with other managerial personnel.

[79]Soviet data were derived from interviews with emigres. A. Inkeles and P. H. Rossi, "National Comparisons of Occupational Prestige," *American Journal of Sociology* (January 1956), no. 61 (4), p. 333.

[80]See D. Lane and F. O'Dell, *Soviet Industrial Workers* (1978), chapter 5.

[81]Solzhenitsyn, *Cancer Ward*, pp. 212–213. Internal passports were not generally issued to peasants, thereby their occupational and geographical mobility was restricted.

[82]Inkeles, "Social Stratification," p. 339. See also the extension of this work by Hodge *et al.*, "A Comparative Study of Occupational Prestige."

[83]It is relevant here to point out that a recent study in Poland explicitly using the methods of Inkeles and Rossi shows a positive correlation of the rankings of occupational prestige hierarchies between Warsaw and the United States to be 0.884, Warsaw/England 0.862, Warsaw/West Germany 0.879. Adam Sarapata,

"Stratification and Social Mobility," in *Empirical Sociology in Poland* (Warsaw, 1966), p. 41. Skilled workers are rated higher and white collar workers lower in Poland than in western advanced societies (*ibid.*, p. 42).

[84]For details see Inkeles, "Social Stratification."

[85]See V. S. Semenov, "Ob izmenenii intelligentsii," p. 422. A. G. Rashin, "Dinamika promyshlennykh kadrov SSSR az 1917–58gg.," *Izmeneniya v chislennostii i sostave sovetskogo rabochego klassa* (Moscow, 1961), p. 29.

[86]Inkeles, "Social Stratification," p. 571.

[87]Ya M. Tkach, "Roditeli o sud'bakh svoikh detey," *Protesessy izmeneniya sotsial'noy struktury v Sovetskom obshchestve* (Sverdlovsk, 1967), p. 145.

[88]*Kul'turnoe stroitel'stvo SSSR* (Moscow, 1940), p. 114. Cited by Inkeles, "Social Stratification," p. 572.

[89]Rutkevitch, "Izmenie sotsial'noy," pp. 412–413.

[90]See Tkach, "Roditeti o sud'bakh," pp. 133, 139.

[91]Shkaratan, "Sotsial'naya struktura," p. 39.

[92]"Vertical mobility of employees in an enterprise," in G. V. Osipov, *Industry and Labour . . .* , p. 126.

[93]E. C. Brown, *Soviet Trade Unions and Labor Relations* (Cambridge, Mass., 1966), p. 175.

[94]*Klassy, sotsial'nye sloi i gruppy v SSSR* (Moscow, 1968), p. 160.

[95]Higher Educational Institutions.

[96]K. Tidmarsh, *The Times*, November 20, 1968.

[97]See *Soviet News*, October 28, 1969, p. 46.

[98]Davis, *Human Society*, p. 369.

[99]A. Giddens, *The Class Structure of the Advanced Societies* (London, 1973), p. 138.

[100]Lloyd Churchward, "Theories of Totalitarianism," *Arena* 12 (Australia, 1967), p. 43.

[101]See particularly: Giddens, *Class Structure*; J. Kautsky, *Communism and the Politics of Development* (New York, 1968); D. Lane, "Leninism as an Ideology of Soviet Development," in *Sociology and Development*," ed. E. de Kadt and G. Williams (London, 1974).

[102]Daniel Bell, *The End of Ideology: On the Exhaustion of Political Ideas in the Fifties* (New York, 1961) and Daniel Bell, "*The End of Ideology in the Soviet Union?*" in *Marxist Ideology in the Contemporary World—Its Appeals and Paradoxes*, ed. M. M. Drachkovitch (New York, 1966).

[103]See Lane, "Leninism."

[104]N. S. Timasheff, *The Great Retreat* (New York, 1946), p. 358.

[105]Talcott Parsons, "Characteristics of Industrial Societies," in *Structure and Process in Modern Societies*, (Glencoe, Ill., 1960), pp. 172–173.

[106]Kate Millett, *Sexual Politics* (London, 1969).

[107]J. W. Salaff and J. Merkle, "Women and Revolution: The Lessons of the Soviet Union and China," in *Women in China*, ed. M. B. Young (Ann Arbor: Center for Chinese Studies, 1973).

[108]Ernest Mandel, *Marxist Economic Theory* (London, 1968); *The Inconsistencies of State Capitalism* (London, 1969).

22

JEREMY R. AZRAEL

*Emergent Nationality Problems in the USSR**

This chapter examines some of the policy problems that will confront the Soviet leadership in the 1980s and 1990s as a result of the rapidly changing ethnodemographic composition and ethnopolitical orientation of the Soviet population. Unlike some recent commentaries, the chapter does not contend that these problems foreshadow a breakdown of the Soviet system, or even that they are likely to reach crisis proportions.[1] Contrary to the view that still prevails in many quarters, however, it *does* contend that these problems are neither adventitious nor recessive and could significantly influence the future development of the Soviet system.[2]

Ethnodemographic Trends

The most elemental of the ethnodemographic problems confronting the regime is the large and persistent disparity in the growth rates of the country's "European" (Slavic and Baltic) nationalities and its "non-European" (Caucasian and Central Asian) nationalities.[3] As can be seen in Fig. 1, of the major "European" nationalities, which constitute about 80% of the country's total population and therefore dominate its overall demographic performance, only the Moldavians have increased by more than 1.2% per annum in recent years, and some of them have scarcely increased at all. (See Appendix for fuller detail.) Of the major "non-European" nationalities, on the other hand, only the Georgians and Tatars have fallen below a 2% increase per annum; and the Central Asian nationalities have achieved annual increases of close to 4%. As a

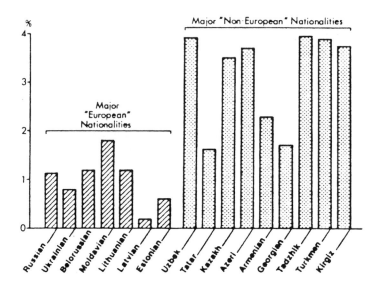

Figure 1. *Average annual population growth rates of major "European" and "non-European" nationalities, 1959–1970.*

result, "non-Europeans" have increased their share in the country's total population from 11.5% in 1959 to a conservatively estimated 17% in 1977.[4]

This disparity (the size and persistence of which the regime apparently had underestimated prior to the 1970 census) has become a source of mounting official concern. There is little doubt, for example, that it was instrumental in the regime's decision to create a special high-level Scientific Council on Nationality Problems under the Presidium of the Academy of Sciences.[5] In addition, it almost certainly was a factor in Brezhnev's recent call for the formulation of an official demographic policy that would take account of "a number of population problems which have lately become exacerbated."[6] For the immediate future, however, there is little that the regime can do to stimulate the growth rate among "European" nationalities; and no conceivable combination of pro- and antinatalist policies can avoid a lengthy continuation of the overall trends displayed in Table I. In consequence, by the end of the century, between 20 and 25% of the country's total population and almost 40% of its teenagers and young adults will be "non-Europeans," of whom the vast majority will be Central Asians.[7]

That this prospect has aroused deep-seated psychological and political anxieties among members of the ruling elite is indicated, among

TABLE 1 *Changing Composition of USSR Population, 1959–1970*

Nationality	Percentage of total population		Percentage change
	1959	1970	
Major "European"	79.6	77.2	− 2.4
Russian	54.6	53.4	− 1.2
Ukrainian	17.8	16.9	− 0.9
Belorussian	3.8	3.7	− 0.1
Moldavian	1.1	1.1	0.0
Latvian	0.7	0.6	− 0.1
Lithuanian	1.1	1.1	0.0
Estonian	0.4	0.4	0.0
Major "non-European"	12.6	15.2	+ 2.6
Uzbek	2.9	3.8	+ 0.9
Tatar	2.4	2.4	0.0
Kazakh	1.7	2.2	+ 0.5
Azeri	1.4	1.8	+ 0.4
Armenian	1.3	1.5	+ 0.2
Georgian	1.3	1.3	0.0
Tadzhik	0.7	0.9	+ 0.2
Turkmen	0.5	0.6	+ 0.1
Kirghiz	0.5	0.6	+ 0.1
Others	7.8	7.6	− 0.2
Selected national groups			
Slavs[a]	76.3	74.0	− 2.3
Non-Slavic "Europeans"[b]	3.3	3.2	− 0.1
"Non-European"	2.6	2.8	+ 0.2
Christians[c]		12.4	
"Non-European" Muslims[d]	10.0	7.6	+ 2.4
All other	7.8		− 0.2

[a]Slavs are defined as the total of the Russian, Ukrainian, and Belorussian populations.

[b]Non-Slavic "Europeans" are defined as the total of the Moldavian, Lithuanian, Latvian, and Estonian populations.

[c]"Non-European" Christians are defined as the total of the Georgian and Armenian populations.

[d]"Non-European" Muslims are defined as the total of the Uzbek, Tatar, Kazakh, Azeri, Tadzhik, Turkmen, and Kirghiz populations.

other things, by the epithet "yellowing" (*ozheltenie*) that is applied to it in the private conversations of many Soviet officials. These anxieties, in turn, are strongly reinforced by the "jokes" that have gained currency in certain Central Asian circles about the impending restoration of the Tatar yoke, the forthcoming confirmation of the proposition that "when you scratch a Russian you find a Tatar," and the fate that will befall the Russians when the Chinese "liberate" Turkestan.[8] Nonetheless, the current ruling elite is not discernibly racist in its outlook or composition, and it is doubtful that it feels immediately threatened by an erosion of "white supremacy" or the emergence of a Chinese "fifth column." The fact that it has chosen to treble the number of Turkic representatives on the Politburo (from one to three, with the addition of an Azeri, G. A. Aliev, and a Kazakh or Uighur, K. A. Kunaev, to the Uzbek incumbent, Sh. R. Rashidov) on the eve of a potential succession crisis suggests a relative indifference on the first count; and there is no evidence to suggest that the Central Asians, who are, of course, not yellow but brown, have any real (as against rhetorical) sympathy for the Chinese. Although Chinese propaganda against the domination of Central Asia by "new tsars" undoubtedly strikes responsive chords, its pro-Chinese content is filtered through an almost primordial Sinophobia and a widespread awareness (cultivated by the Soviet regime) of the unhappy fate of the Turkic minorities in the People's Republic of China.[9]

At a minimum, the Kremlin's concern on both these counts is almost certainly less urgent than its concern over the implications of the "yellowing" process for the national economy. In this connection, moreover, what is most troubling is not the shift in the ethnic balance per se but the low "European" (and, hence, all-union) growth rates and the fact that the Central Asian nationalities have remained outside the mainstream of the country's economic development and contain a heavy preponderance of undereducated peasants with a weak-to-nonexistent knowledge of Russian and a tenacious aversion to interregional or even intraregional migration.[10]

Economic Dilemmas

What the shortfall in the country's "European" population means for the economy is that the latter will no longer be able to provide large-scale reinforcements for the industrial work force. By the late 1980s, the number of "Europeans" reaching working age will decline from the present average of about 4 million per annum to only slightly over 2 million per annum, and the regime will be extremely hard pressed to find enough "European" workers to replace those whose retirement (even if extended beyond the current norms of 60 for men and 55 for women) can no longer be delayed.[11] What makes this prospect particularly unsettling is the fact that the vast bulk of the increase in industrial output that has occurred in the postwar Soviet Union is attributable to increases in the "European" work force rather than to increases in per capita labor productivity, which has grown only modestly despite the regime's frantic efforts to raise it.[12] Even if it manages to replenish its "European" work force—by reducing draft terms and/or draft quotas, curtailing full-time secondary education, or accelerating the already rapid flight of young "Europeans" from the countryside—the only way the regime can hope to staff the many new enterprises on which it has staked so much of its prestige and credibility is either to locate the bulk of them in Central Asia or to mobilize large numbers of Central Asians for work in other regions.[13] Unfortunately for the regime, however, these policies could exact a very heavy price.

Whatever its ultimate benefits, a rapid buildup of Central Asia's industrial capacity obviously would require the diversion of a great deal of scarce capital and equipment both from the already industrialized regions of the country and from underdeveloped regions such as Siberia and the Far North, which are far richer than Central Asia in essential (and hard-currency-convertible) natural resources. In addition to capital and equipment, moreover, such a buildup could easily have the ironic but historically familiar effect of drawing scarce manpower away from other regions into Central Asia. Despite rising educational levels and urbanization rates, the number of native engineers, technicians, and skilled workers is still extremely limited; and local plant and factory directors have good reason to favor the long-distance recruitment of experienced "European" workers over the employment of ready-to-hand but inexperienced Central Asians, who are perceived as undependable and are actually far more likely to miss work and change jobs than their "European" counterparts.[14] Finally, resources (including human resources) that are transferred to Central Asia (or are retained there when they could be productively relocated) and that do not directly contribute to Soviet area-defense capabilities could be exposed to Chinese weapons when they might otherwise be largely out of range.

Moreover, in contrast with the situation that may have existed in the 1950s or 1960s, it can no longer be assumed that the mere fact of their location in Central Asia will make strategic objectives significantly less accessible or less vulnerable to U.S. forces. In consequence, those who advocate the rapid industrialization of the one region of the country with a large natural surplus of otherwise scarce labor are likely to encounter strong resistance from military planners as well as from those party and managerial cadres and foreign-trade officials who are eager to increase Soviet exports and prevent a sharp deterioration in the country's balance of hard-currency payments.[15] As these advocates undoubtedly will point out, however, it may be no less difficult and risky to move the industrial mountain to Mohammed than to attempt the process in reverse.

The chances that large numbers of Central Asians will spontaneously migrate into the labor-deficit regions of the country are virtually nil. To be sure, in the absence of accelerated industrialization of their own region, hundreds of thousands, if not millions, of natives will be unable to find full-time employment in the public sector (industrial or agricultural) of the local economy.[16] In addition, thanks to the tenacity of early marriage and prolific childbearing practices, many of those concerned undoubtedly will have a large number of dependents to support. As is the case today, however, the very existence of large families will serve as a constraint on migration to cities in general and to overcrowded "European" cities in particular; and these constraints will be further reinforced by the nexus of tradition of which early marriage and high fertility are a part.[17] Moreover, in the absence of strong counteractions by the regime, many natives who cannot find jobs in the public sector will still be able not only to survive but also to prosper on the proceeds of the individual or familial cottage industries and private household plots that already account for a sizable share of Central Asian personal income.[18]

These earnings undoubtedly could be curtailed if the regime were willing to pursue the necessary restrictive policies. Such policies, however, would be not only intrinsically difficult and costly to enforce but also potentially dangerous. At a minimum, they would create serious local shortages of at least temporarily irreplaceable foodstuffs, consumer goods, and personal services. In addition, they might well lead to a slowdown in centrally planned cotton and silk production by the disgruntled native collective farmers who would be the principal victims. Furthermore, they could touch off violent protests and terrorist outbursts similar to those that accompanied a recent official crackdown on private entrepreneurship in Georgia.[19] Even if these policies accomplished their immediate purpose, moreover, both the time-tested welfare practices of the still-prevalent extended family system and the legally mandatory income-sharing procedures of the collective farms system would significantly reduce their efficacy as spurs to out-migration.[20]

A search for other, potentially more effective policies that the regime might use to increase the supply of Central Asian *gastarbeiter* yields two basic alternatives: administrative mobilization and economic stimulation. In administrative mobilization, the already existing requirement that graduates of institutions of higher and specialized secondary education work for 2 to 3 years at state-assigned jobs could be focused to generate a steady westward flow of younger Central Asian cadres. In addition, the regime could make more extensive use of the already common practice of conscripting militarily "superfluous" or "marginal" Central Asians into the armed forces and posting them to units that perform essentially civilian economic tasks.[21] Going further in the same direction, it could reintroduce a compulsory labor draft of the sort that existed under Stalin, with the sole difference that Central Asian draftees could no longer expect job assignments in their home regions. This last measure would almost certainly have to be accompanied by the reimposition of a large number of highly counterproductive Stalinist controls, however, and even the more moderate variants seem likely to entail political and social costs that would be hard to "recapture" from the output of transient and disgruntled Central Asian workers who accurately viewed themselves as victims of a system of involuntary and discriminatory servitude.

The problems associated with reliance on "Eurocentric" relocation bonuses or pay incentives to attract Central Asian *gastarbeiter* are substantially different from those just mentioned but are in no way less problematical. At the very least, such incentives would be extremely difficult to design and administer and would powerfully reinforce the already strong inflationary pressures within the all-union economy. In addition, it is likely that the native respondents would include a disproportionate number of skilled workers and technical cadres whose contribution to the all-union economy would be equally great (or greater) on their home ground and whose enticement away from home would be strongly resented by local party and government leaders with an interest in the economic performance and progress of Central Asia. Finally, a "Eurocentric" wage or bonus policy could easily precipitate a mass exodus of Central Asia's "European" settlers, whose departure would not only leave key sectors of the regional economy (including the agricultural economy) at least temporarily crippled but would also deprive the regime of some of its most reliable agents of central control.[22] Over the long run, the regime may lose most of these agents anyway, since the combined demands of Central Asian workers for local jobs and of "European" employers for "European" employees will generate strong pressure for their "repatriation." Even if the regime had no reason to resist this pressure, it undoubtedly would prefer to accommodate it incrementally in order to prevent repatriation from becoming an unregulated and headlong process.

The prospect of choosing among such unpalatable alternatives would give any leader pause, and it would not be surprising if Brezhnev continued to substitute further study for decisive action. Moreover, it is not unlikely that his successors also will try to "muddle through." Over the longer run, however, the only way in which they can reasonably hope to maintain anything like current growth rates without recourse to measures of the kind just discussed is to secure substantial technology transfers from the West and to implement administrative and managerial reforms that will curb their own day-to-day power and weaken the overall framework of central control. Given the resistance that these prospective outcomes are certain to engender and the difficulties in acquiring and using Western technology, the chances for a successful nullification of the ethnodemographic constraints on the Soviet economy of the 1980s and 1990s seem rather dim. In consequence, it would not be surprising if industrial growth rates declined substantially and if the regime found it increasingly difficult to satisfy both its own appetite for international power and the rising economic expectations of its citizens.

Military Consequences

Unless there is a rise in international tensions or wider reliance on military conscription as a form of de facto labor draft, the size of the Soviet armed forces is likely to decrease in the 1980s (it is now estimated to be 4–5 million men).[23] Even if the reduction in the draft term from 3 to 2 years were rescinded, it would be exceedingly difficult and costly to secure the requisite number of conscripts (currently estimated to number about 1.5–1.6 million per year) from a country in which the entire cohort of 18-year-old males will be only slightly over 2 million (as against 2.6 million today) and in which, because of the age structure of the general population and the virtually complete (except in Central Asia) "emancipation" of women, there cannot possibly be an increase in the size of the overall civilian work force except at the military's expense.[24] In addition to facing a prospective cutback, moreover, the armed forces seem almost certain to undergo a very extensive "yellowing." This outcome is foreshadowed, if not foreordained, by the fact that the proportion of "non-Europeans" among prime draft-age males will rise from a low of 20–25% in the late 1980s to almost 40% by the turn of the century.

Indeed, if the regime were to follow the dictates of economic rationality alone, the military would become an almost entirely "non-European" institution. In this way, it would be possible not only to avoid the inordinately high civilian opportunity costs of "European" soldiers but also to realize disproportionately high civilian returns on its investments in in-service training programs. Although these programs are often redundant for European trainees, they frequently provide Central Asians with new and readily transferable skills as well as with a career orientation that could make them somewhat less averse to postservice outmigration. For reasons that by now are familiar, however, an economically rational conscription policy would significantly exacerbate the already serious military and military–political problems that the natural "yellowing" of the armed forces is sure to pose.

Even if the regime were to flout economic logic and overconscript "Europeans," it would have to abandon what seems, by nearly all refugee accounts, to be its current practice of assigning only a few atypical Central Asians to high-priority military units, including not only units of the strategic rocket forces and anti-aircraft defense but also of the air force, the armored corps, the artillery, and even the front-line motorized infantry. Although these units could be kept preponderantly "European," their ranks would still have to be filled with typical Central Asians, who now are assigned mostly to construction, supply, and rear service functions. By the late 1980s and 1990s, it is true, typical Central Asian conscripts probably will be somewhat better-educated than their contemporary counterparts, who average less than ten years of formal schooling.[25] Barring a massive educational breakthrough, however, the vast majority of them will almost certainly still be graduates of second- and third-rate rural schools, which will continue to offer rudimentary versions of the military training courses that are becoming standard features of the senior high school curriculum.[26] In consequence, there is little prospect that any impending decline in the quantity of Soviet military manpower could be counterbalanced by a significant increase in its quality, let alone by an increase that would keep pace with the accelerating "scientific–technological revolution in military affairs."

The difficulties created by the low educational attainments and technical skills of typical Central Asian conscripts will be exacerbated and compounded by their rudimentary command of Russian, which is the only authorized medium of communication within the armed forces, and will almost certainly remain the only language spoken by the majority of senior officers.[27] If there is a significant increase in the percentage of Central Asians who are urbanized, the proportion of Central Asians who speak Russian with some fluency may rise above the current 16%.[28] However, there is little prospect that it will rise sharply, and present trends suggest that it actually may decline as the proportion of "Europeans" in Central Asia becomes progressively smaller.[29] In any event, the language-related command, control, and communication problems that have heretofore been largely confined to relatively low-priority units are likely to become prevalent in other units as well, with corresponding degrading effects on the country's military capabilities.[30] Judging by what is reported to have occurred in various enterprises and offices in Central Asia, there is good reason to believe that units in which Central Asian natives become a substantial minority will be particularly prone to demoralizing ethnic tensions and open ethnic conflict.[31]

Many of these difficulties could be at least partially alleviated by the reinstitution of national military formations of the sort that were the norm until 1936 and were selectively rehabilitated during World War II.[32] Assuming that this was not accompanied by a politically provocative and military counterproductive injunction against "home-basing," such a measure could yield a number of other benefits. For one, it would chasten critics of the spurious character of the "sovereignty" of the Soviet Union's constituent republics, including several outspoken dissidents who have placed the absence of national military formations high on their list of grievances.[33] In addition, it could foster a closer identity between national pride and Soviet patriotism, two sentiments that the regime has long sought to reconcile and fuse and that in fact can both coexist and be mutually reinforcing. Finally, the existence of national military formations could lead to more efficient and effective civil–military cooperation at the local level in the event of an all-out mobilization, civil defense emergency, or resort to martial rule.

In view of these considerable advantages of a return to "military federalism," it would not be surprising if the possibility of such a return has been deliberated in official circles. That it has in fact been done is at least indirectly suggested by the expanded treatment of the interrelationship between national policy and military policy that differentiates the otherwise only slightly modified first (1974) and second (1975) editions of the late Marshal A. A. Grechko's highly authoritative *The Armed Forces of the Soviet State*.[34] Furthermore, an extremely reliable and unusually well-informed refugee source has reported that in the early 1970s, the Kazakh and Estonian party leaderships both submitted official requests that conscripts from their republics be assigned predominantly to local garrisons rather than intentionally dispersed, and that the Kazakh request was granted.[35]

Whatever discussions or experiments may be occurring, however, the regime is unlikely to sanction a return to full-fledged military federalism or to permit the "indigenization" of local bases and garrisons to become a general policy. Rather, the fact that the constitution, ratified in 1977 to replace the so-called Stalin Constitution of 1936, drops both the latter's references (in Articles 14-g and 18-b) to republic-level military formations suggests that the regime is eager to stifle all hopes and expectations to the contrary.[36] Like the late Marshal Grechko, official commentators probably will continue to dwell on "the difficulty of preparing training manuals in different national languages" and the importance of reinforcing internationalist sentiments.[37] The underlying motive, though, will almost certainly be a fear that indigenous units may provide tacit or open military support for nationalist challenges to central authority.

That such fear can be a significant factor in official thinking is indicated, for example, by Nikita Khrushchev's conduct during the riot opposing de-Stalinization that broke out in Tbilisi, Georgia, in March 1956. Although this riot clearly was beyond the control of the civil authorities, Khrushchev canceled the marching orders of a nearby military unit that happened (by a rare anomaly) to be predominantly Georgian, and allowed the rioters to rampage for 12 hours while more typical, ethnically heterogeneous troops were dispatched from outlying bases.[38] Some years later, it is true, Khrushchev proposed creation of a territorial militia to compensate for the troop reductions that he was introducing, partially in response to mounting demographic pressures.[39] Moreover, there is no doubt these pressures (which stemmed from a sharp but temporary drop in the country's supply of teenagers) were mild compared with those that are now emerging.[40] Before drawing any hasty inferences from these facts, however, it is worth recalling that Khrushchev's militia proposal was never implemented and that any future analogues, let alone cognate proposals affecting the regular army, will be evaluated in the light of recent ethnopolitical developments that make it clear (as it was not clear in 1960) that the Tbilisi riot was not the last such event and that even greater disturbances may be in the offing.

Political Currents

When Brezhnev alleged in 1972 that the past 50 years had witnessed the formation of a new "Soviet nation" or "Soviet people" (*sovetskii narod*) that was now sufficiently robust to survive any ethnopolitical crisis and eventually would encompass the entire population of the USSR, he may or may not have been engaged in wishful thinking.[41] At a minimum, he could point to indisputable and massive demonstrations of all-union loyalty during World War II and to a steady, albeit slow and by no means universal, postwar growth in bilingualism, ethnic intermarriage, and interregional mobility. However, when he went on to assure his audience that the Soviet Union definitely had solved its "historical nationality problem"— the problem of national deviationism and centrifugal nationalism—he was clearly and knowingly overstating what was at best a dubious, if not a completely indefensible, case.[42] Indeed, the countervailing evidence is so well known that a detailed exposition seems gratuitous. A summary rundown will serve to remind the reader.

1. Many members of the country's major diaspora nationalities, including not only the Jews but also the Volga Germans, the Greeks, and the Meskhetian Turks, have become so embittered at the continued denial of their communal rights that they have renounced their Soviet citizenship and have demanded to be "repatriated" to their quite foreign "homelands."[43]

2. Nearly all of the country's "European" and Caucasian nationalities and at least one Turkic nationality (the Crimean Tatars) have produced outspoken critics of official nationality policies and practices. These critics have managed not only to replenish their own ranks in the face of hundreds, if not thousands, of arrests, but also to establish dynamic and resilient dissident organizations, ranging from clandestine parties, through editorial boards for the preparation of regular *samizdat* or underground journals, to networks for the public circulation of programs, petitions, and letters of protest, including one 1972 petition (to U.N. Secretary–General Kurt Waldheim) that was signed by more than 17,000 Lithuanians.[44]

3. A number of nationalistically inspired acts of violence have included a 2-day riot in Kaunas, Lithuania, in 1972 and several recent protest bombings and reported assassination attempts in Georgia.[45]

4. There have been numerous organized protest demonstrations against centrally imposed curbs on national self-expression, including several mass gatherings by Crimean Tatars and a 1965 street vigil in Erevan that reportedly was attended by 100,000 Armenians.[46]

5. There has been an extremely rapid increase in the membership of republic and local ethnographic societies and so-called societies for the preservation of architectural and historical monuments that were established in the 1960s to provide outlets for environmentalist and conservationist concerns. There is no doubt that the mushroom growth of these societies and their exceptional popularity reflect a more than merely antiquarian or folkloristic interest in national history and culture. In fact, there is every reason to suspect—as some Soviet security officials clearly do—that many of their members are no less nationalistic than the members of the not-so-remotely analogous Matica Hrvatska and Matica Srpska organizations that provided key recruitment bases for the massive national protest movements that have rocked Yugoslavia.[47]

6. There have been numerous cases in which native party and state officials, including a Georgian, V. P. Mzhavandze, and a Ukrainian, P. Ye. Shelest have pursued the "parochial" interests of their fellow nationals at the expense of their all-union responsibilities.[48] These cases have been widely publicized in the Soviet press, and there is no reason to doubt that most of the officials concerned are at least partially "guilty" as charged and have in fact encouraged (or failed to discourage) the retention of local resources for local use, the curtailment of immigration by ethnic "aliens," the preferential treatment of native cadres, the publication of "nationally pretentious" books and articles, the "tendentious" designation of historical monuments, the perpetuation of "archaic" traditions and retrograde survivals of the past, and even the lenient treatment of dissident nationalist intellectuals.[49]

Although these manifestations of national self-affirmation and self-assertiveness are a far cry from the explosive international or center–periphery confrontations that took place in earlier periods of Soviet history (during the Revolution and Civil War and the early wartime and postwar years) or that have recently occurred in a number of other multinational polities (Yugoslavia, Canada, Belgium, the United Kingdom), they are more than sufficient to demonstrate that the USSR has neither transcended its own history nor become immune to worldwide trends.[50] Unless the regime undergoes an improbable re-Stalinization or an even more improbable liberal-democratic transformation, such manifestations are likely to become more frequent and more insistent over time.[51] Although piecemeal reforms and partial crackdowns undoubtedly could have a tranquilizing effect, they would at best produce a temporary and deceptive calm; and there is a strong possibility that they would merely further agitate an already turbulent situation. Summarily stated, this seems to be the "lesson" of both the Khrushchev and Brezhnev–Kosygin eras; and it is a lesson that is likely to retain its validity for the foreseeable future.[52]

One reason for anticipating an escalation in national self-affirmation and self-assertiveness is the accelerating "modernization" of the Central Asian nationalities, who have been conspicuously passive since their great uprising in the early 1920s, but who are almost certain to become more militant as, in one way or another, they are drawn into the mainstream of the country's economic development.[53] At the same time, moreover, the "European" nationalities are likely to become increasingly restive as they are subjected either to an "onslaught" of Central Asian *gastarbeiter* or to an "expropriation" of "their" resources to speed the industrialization of distant Central Asia. In this connection, a particularly strong reaction probably can be expected from the Russians, among whom are numerous spokesmen who contend that the regime has sacrificed Russia's economic welfare and cultural integrity for the sake of an illegitimate "internationalism" and who will soon undergo the psychological distress of losing their majority status within the country's total population.[54] Also, increasing education and urbanization and improved communications will make it much harder for the regime to isolate the masses from dissident nationalist spokesmen or from the demonstration effects of nationalist protests within the Soviet Union or in the outside world. Finally, an increasing number of actual and potential nationalist protesters are likely to possess weapons and explosives as a result of the diffusion of scientific and technical know-how, the multiplication of laboratories and workshops (including those in homes), and the proliferation of local civil defense and preinduction training arsenals.[55]

Barring a breakdown of central control that might accompany a major war or the political degeneration that might accompany a prolonged and unfettered succession struggle, there is little likelihood that national protest will rise to unmanageable levels.[56] Under more normal circumstances, centrally manipulated sanctions and incentives will almost certainly suffice to prevent large communal uprisings or national insurgencies. This seems all the more certain because, as examples of the United States during the Cold War and of China today suggest, even the most hostile foreign powers are unlikely to risk the retaliation that might follow efforts to provide would-be insurrectionaries with significant external support. The most that can be readily conceived, therefore, is "merely" more of the same—that is, more numerous acts of individual and small-group terrorism, more frequent episodes of collective violence, more massive protest demonstrations, and more extensive public or semipublic dissent. Even such manageable outcomes, however, would impose serious constraints on the regime.

At a minimum, the regime would be forced to increase its police budget and to introduce security procedures that not only would be eonomically counterproductive but also would demoralize and even disaffect citizens on whose loyalty and commitment it otherwise could rely. In the second place, the regime would find it increasingly difficult to persuade even strongly détente-oriented Western governments to sponsor or authorize the volume of technology transfers, grain sales, and development credits that could significantly brighten its somewhat gloomy economic prospects. Try as they may, such governments will be harder put to ignore Soviet violations of communal rights as the victims of these violations escalate their protests, especially if the latter come, as they almost certainly will, from groups such as the Jews, Germans, Lithuanians, and Ukrainians whose foreign conationals (in the United States, West Germany, Canada, and Australia) constitute important domestic political constituencies. In the same vein, moreover, the regime could find it difficult to maintain or consolidate profitable political and economic relations with a range of non-Western countries whose native populations have strong ethnic affinities with restive nationalities in the USSR—a category of countries that includes Romania (Moldavians), Iran, (Tadzhiks and Azeri), Afghanistan (Azeri and Turkmen), and Turkey (Meskhetian Turks and the entire Soviet Turkic population), and that could, by extension, include all of the countries of the Muslim world. Finally—at least for present purposes—escalating national protest would further discredit the Soviet "model" of international integration everywhere in the Third World and would undermine the regime's credibility as a spokesman for the oppressed nationalities in non-Communist countries.

Implications for the West   Despite the ethnodemographic and ethnopolitical pressures that it faces, the Soviet regime probably will remain an imperialistic and potentially expansionistic dictatorship. As already indicated, these pressures are more likely to lead to increased domestic coercion and repression than to a liberal-democratic transformation of the regime. In addition, they are likely to strengthen the regime's determination to retain its East European empire. If these pressures became sufficiently intense, the regime may be tempted to try to dissipate them by initiating political–military confrontations of a sort that could activate an otherwise recessive or inoperative "Soviet patriotism." Unless they happen to be "gratuitously" relieved by Western actions, however, these pressures also seem likely to offer some favorable opportunities for the containment and redirection of Soviet power.

For one thing, the Soviet Union could become more amenable to balanced force reduction agreements of the sort it has hitherto refused seriously to entertain. In addition, it might become more sensitive to the danger that its continued support of "national liberation movements" in other countries could lead to a retaliatory campaign on behalf of the oppressed nationalities of the USSR. At the moment, the People's Republic of China is the only major power pursuing such a campaign in earnest, but the West's relative forbearance (as illustrated by United States actions to downplay Captive Nations Week, to semi-recognize Soviet incorporation of the Baltic states, to modulate the tone of official propaganda broadcasts, and to stress individual rather than communal rights in its diplomatic exertions) is at least a potentially reversible decision that the Soviet Union may be more than ordinarily eager to keep in force. Finally, the Soviet Union is likely to become substantially more dependent on Western economic cooperation and assistance, which will thereby acquire greater potential as negotiating instruments and sources of diplomatic leverage.

Whether these opportunities can be utilized to the West's advantage will depend importantly on the ability of the United States to act in concert with its allies in a purposeful and timely fashion. Unfortunately, this capability is far easier to invoke than to attain, and by no means all currently observable signs are auspicious. Furthermore, policies designed to capitalize on these opportunities are likely to provoke strong normative, strategic, and tactical disagreements within the United States. Although some of these disagreements probably could be avoided by a more systematic assessment of past experiences and a more rigorous formulation of analytical guidelines, others seem certain to persist. How these disagreements will be resolved is intrinsically unpredictable, and this chapter is not the place for even a preliminary consideration of the potentially contentious issues. Given the continuing competition between the Soviet Union and the West, however, it seems appropriate to suggest that opportunities to induce a less expansive Soviet "globalism" and a lower Soviet profile in international affairs should not be rejected a priori or dismissed as chimerical before they have been prudently but seriously tested in practice.

Notes

[1]See the remarks of Richard Pipes in "Reflections of a Nationality Expert," in *Nationalities and Nationalism in the USSR: A Soviet Dilemma*, ed. Carl A. Linden and Dimitri K. Simes (Washington, D.C.: Center for Strategic and International Studies, Georgetown University, 1977), pp. 9–11, esp. p. 10. For a somewhat more qualified statement by Pipes, see his "Reflections on the Nationality Problem in the Soviet Union," in *Ethnicity*, ed. Nathan Glazer and Daniel P. Moynihan (Cambridge, Mass.: Harvard University Press, 1975), pp. 453–465, esp. pp. 464–465. Compare also the prediction of President Mu'amaar al-Qadhaffi of Libya in his political treatise *The Third Theory*, that, as a result of "the nationalist movement," "a day will come when it [the Soviet Union] will split." (Mu'ammar al-Qadhaffi, *Fi-al-nazerayah al-thalithah* [Benghazi, 1974], p. 28.) According to Zbigniew Brzezinski, "the national question . . . creates a major block to gradual evolution" in the USSR and "could prove itself to be the fatal

contradiction of Soviet political evolution." (Brzezinski, *Soviet Politics: From the Future to the Past?* [New York: Research Institute on International Change, Columbia University, 1975], p. 31.)

[2]For a sophisticated and well-informed defense of the proposition that the Soviet Union has become essentially "denationalized" and that the evidence to the contrary derives from a brief and anomalous flare-up of interethnic tensions in the period 1965–1970, see David Zil'berman, "Ethnography in Soviet Russia," *Dialectic Anthropology* no. 1 (1976): 135–153, esp. 149.

[3]The reader will, of course, recognize that the categories "European" and "non-European" are synthetic, and that each includes nationalities that differ from one another in important respects. In the case of the "non-Europeans," the crucial internal distinction is probably between Christians (Georgians and Armenians) and Muslims (Azeri, Uzbeks, Turkmen, Tadzhiks, Kirghiz, and Kazakhs). Except for the Tadzhiks, all of the Muslim nationalities speak mutually comprehensible languages and share a common Turkic background that may be more important to them than their Soviet-sponsored national identities. A striking bit of evidence to this effect is the statement by the Kirghiz novelist, Chingiz Aitmatov, that recent literary output in Central Asia filled him with "Turkic national pride." (N. Khudaiberganov, "Vdokhnovennaia ispoved'," *Pravda vostoka*, December 10, 1976, p. 3.) That such a statement presently could be made about "Slavic" or "Baltic" national pride seems doubtful. On the mutual comprehensibility of Soviet Turkic languages, see G. K. Dulling's review of a major Soviet study of Turkic languages in *Central Asian Review* 15, no. 2 (1967): 160.

[4]S. I. Bruk and M. N. Guboglo, "Development and Interaction of Ethnodemographic and Ethnolinguistic Processes in Soviet Society," *Istoriia SSSR*, no. 4 (July/August 1974): 26–45, in *Translations on USSR Political and Sociological Affairs* no. 556, JPRS 62984 (September 17, 1974): 90–123, esp. 93.

[5]This council was created in late 1969 or early 1970 but apparently was moribund until 1974–1975, when it went into high-gear operation. For an account of its work, see M. N. Guboglo, "V sektsii obshchestvennykh nauk Prezidiuma AN SSSR—v nauchnom sovete po natsional'nym problemam," *Voprosy istorii*, no. 4 (1976): 148–150.

[6]Translated in *Current Digest of the Soviet Press* 28, no. 8 (March 24, 1976): 27. Even prior to Brezhnev's statement, the legal implications of possible official demographic policy were discussed at a "roundtable" convened by the editors of the journal *Soviet State and Law* and attended not only by jurists but also by representatives of the Central Statistical Administration and the Lenin Military–Political Academy. See "Legal Aspects of Demographic Policy," *Sovetskoe gosudarstvo i pravo*, no. 1 (1975): 25–28, in *Translations on USSR Political and Sociological Affairs* no. 621, JPRS 64573 (April 18, 1975): 1–14, esp. 5.

[7]See Appendix. The lowest U.S. government projections, which are based on assumptions that almost certainly understate probabilities on the Muslim side and probably overstate them on the European side, envision a 21.3% Muslim component (65 million) in a 307 million population. Compare J. F. Besemeres, "Population Politics in the U.S.S.R.," *Soviet Union/Union soviétique*, no. 2, pt. 1 (1975): 69, who, after citing these figures, concludes that they "are so cautious (as regards Muslim growth rates) as to be almost foolhardy."

[8]As reported by numerous Soviet émigrés and Western visitors to the USSR.

See Igor Shafarevich, "Separation or Reconciliation," in *From under the Rubble,* ed. Alexandr Solzhenitsyn, Michael Agursky *et al.* (New York: Bantam Books, 1976), p. 87, where the author affirms that "in our Central Asian cities I and many others have often heard the cry, 'Just wait til the Chinese come, they'll show you what's what!'"

[9]For representative Chinese attacks on Soviet nationality policy, see Hung Chuan-yu, "The New Tsars—Common Enemy of the People of All Nationalities in the Soviet Union," *Peking Review* (July 4, 1969), no. 27: 25–27; and an unsigned article, "Soviet Social-Imperialism Pursues a Policy of National Oppression," *Peking Review* (May 28, 1976), no. 22: 19–23. Although these and other Chinese statements deal with the "plight" of all non-Russian nationalities, the focus is on the nationalities of Central Asia and on the Ukrainians, who constitute a significant proportion of the "European" population in Kirghizia and Kazakhstan. For a typical Soviet commentary on China's maltreatment of its Turkic minorities, see V. A. Bogoslovskii, A. M. Kuz'mina *et al.*, *Velikoderzhavnaia politika maoistov v natsional'nykh raionakh KNR* (Moscow: Izdatel'stvo Politicheskoi Literatury, 1975). See also the speech of the Kazakh Party first secretary, D. A. Kunaev, to the Twenty-Fifth Party Congress, *Current Digest of the Soviet Press* 28, no. 9 (March 31, 1976): 42; the speech of the Kirghiz Party first secretary, T. U. Usubaliyev, to the Twenty-Fifth Party Congress, *Current Digest of the Soviet Press*, 28, no. 11 (14 April 1976): 15–16; and the review of a new Uighur-language book by M. K. Khamraev in *Kazakhstanskaia pravda*, August 23, 1973, p. 3, which is synopsized in ABSEES, January 1974, p. 31. For a description of a Soviet newspaper published for the tens of thousands of Turkic refugees from China, see Christopher S. Wren, "Kazakhstan Beckons Refugees from China," *New York Times*, April 24, 1976, p. 8. See also Rasma Silde-Karklins, "The Uighurs between China and the USSR," *Canadian Slavonic Papers* 17, nos. 2 and 3 (1975): 341–365.

[10]On the extremely low rates of interregional mobility among Central Asians, see V. N. Korovaeva, "Population Migration in the USSR," in *Vsesoiuznaia perepis' naseleniia 1970 goda*, ed. G. M. Maksimov (Moscow: Statistika, 1976), esp. p. 259. The proportion of Central Asian natives who claim fluency in Russian is under 20% among all nationalities except the Kazakhs, where it is almost 42%. See *Sovetskaia pedogogika*, no. 11 (November 1971): 65.

[11]Derived from Murray Feshbach and Stephen Rapawy, "Soviet Population and Manpower Trends and Policies," in U.S. Congress, Joint Economic Committee, *Soviet Economy in a New Perspective* (Washington, D.C.: U.S. Government Printing Office, 1976), p. 150, table 16.

[12]See TsSU SSSR, *Narodnoe khoziaistvo SSSR v 1974 godu* (Moscow: Statistika, 1975), p. 85. According to this official Soviet source, the annual percentage growth of labor productivity in Soviet industry rose from 3.7 in 1964 to 6.3 in 1974. 1974 was a peak year, however, and the annual growth rate figures during the intervening decade were substantially lower. In the 1976–1980 Five-Year Plan, the planned average annual growth in industrial labor productivity is 5.7%. See *Izvestiia*, March 7, 1969, p. 5.

[13]It is also possible, of course, that the Soviet Union could recruit large numbers of foreign workers, thereby emulating not only the labor-deficit countries of Western Europe but also some of its East European neighbors (see Malcolm W. Browne, "Czechoslovakia Is Importing Vietnamese Workers," *New*

York Times, April 25, 1976, p. 10). That such a policy is thinkable for the Soviet Union is indicated by the extensive importation of Chinese workers during the mid-1950s and by the current employment of some East European and Scandinavian workers on special projects. Nevertheless, a systematic mass recruitment policy would be almost impossible to sustain without drastically changing current economic and political premises and practices.

[14] According to *Narodnoe khoziaistvo Kazakhstana*, no. 10 (1971): 76–80, translated in *ABSEES*, April 1972, p. 12, the "deficit" of Central Asian engineers and technicians is indicated by the fact that Kazakhs make up only 17% of the specialists in their republic's nonferrous metallurgy, 13% in light industry, and only 10–24% of the students in technical institutes. In Tadzhikistan, Tadzhiks constituted less than one-third of all specialists with secondary education in 1966. See L. M. Drobizheve, "O sblizhenii urovnei kul'turnogo razvitiia soiuznykh respublick," *Istoriia SSSR*, no. 3 (1969): 61–79. On the preferences of local factory directors and the reasons for them, see V. Perevedentsev, "Shagni za okolitsu," *Komsomol'skaia pravda*, January 28, 1976, p. 2; and L. Chizhova, "Regional'nye aspeckty izpol'zovaniia trudovykh resursov," in *Naselenie ekonomika*, ed. D. Valenti (Moscow, 1973), p. 25, where the author reports that "practice has shown that some of them (i.e., Central Asians) still adapt badly to industrial labor."

[15] The military undoubtedly will continue to favor a transportation buildup in Central Asia to facilitate its logistical operations on the Sino–Soviet "front."

[16] Agricultural underemployment, as measured by the average number of "labor days" worked by individual collective farmers, is already high in parts of Central Asia and can be expected to grow rapidly as a result of ongoing and accelerating mechanization. See V. Litvinov in *Pravda vostoka*, November 3, 1974, p. 2, summarized in *ABSEES*, July 1974, p. 55.

[17] The average size of rural Uzbek families grew from 4.8 to 5.8 persons between 1959 and 1970, and the "ideal" family envisioned by younger Central Asian women is larger than the current average Central Asian family. See E. K. Vasil'eva, *Sem'ia i ee funkstsii* (Moscow: Statistika, 1975), p. 42; T. N. Roganova, "Number and Composition of Families in the USSR," in *Vsesoiuznaia perepis' naseleniia 1970 goda, sbornik stat'ei*, ed. G. M. Maksimov (Moscow: Statistika, 1976), pp. 260–275; Izaslaw Frenkel, "Attitudes toward Family Size in Some Eastern European Countries," *Population Studies* 30, no. 1 (March 1976): 56.

[18] The earned income of Central Asian collective farm families, as of 1970, was significantly higher than that of their European counterparts; and the Central Asian cost of living index is lower than that in central Russia. See Gertrude Schroeder, "Soviet Wage and Income Policies in Regional Perspectives," *ACES Bulletin*, Fall 1974, pp. 3–19, and *Ekonomicheskie nauki*, no. 1 (January 1971): 52. See also O. Latiffi, "Problems of the Rational Utilization of Labor Resources in Tadzhikhistan," *Pravda*, June 1, 1975, p. 2, translated in *Current Digest of the Soviet Press* 27, no. 12 (June 25, 1975): 1: "If we place a house and a personal plot of ground on one side . . . and a city apartment on the other . . . there is no doubt that for the time being the scales will tip toward the first alternative—*out of economic advisability* and from the standpoint of social psychology." (Emphasis added.)

[19] According to informed reports, a great deal of the recent unrest in Georgia stems from the regime's pressure on the republic's flourishing "second econ-

omy" rather than from directly political sources. See *Soviet Analyst* 2, no. 12 (June 7, 1973): 3.

[20]Although collective farms can legally expel members, superfluity or redundancy is not an authorized ground for doing so.

[21]Representative Les Aspin has calculated that the Soviet armed forces include some 250,000 men who are kept in uniform to do civilian construction work. The Defense Intelligence Agency allegedly has confirmed the basic accuracy of this figure (see John W. Finney, "U.S. Statistics on Soviet Question Extent of Threat," *New York Times*, April 24, 1976). Representative Aspin also contends that 75,000 troops are permanently assigned to "military farms," a claim that the DIA denies, while acknowledging that large numbers of Soviet soldiers are assigned to farm details on an intermittent basis. Soviet refugees uniformly report that construction units contain a highly disproportionate number of Central Asians.

[22]"European" outmigration from the Caucasus, Kazakhstan, and Kirghizia has been increasing (see Bruk and Guboglo, "Development and Interaction," p. 106), and the regime has raised wages in Central Asia in a clear effort to stem the tide. See *Izvestiia*, December 28, 1976, p. 1. One source of this outmigration has been the repatriation (to the RSFSR) of Volga German collective farmers in Kazakhstan. The number of German repatriates has reached 10,000 per annum and is likely to remain at this level for some time to come. J. A. Newth, "The 1970 Soviet Census," *Soviet Studies* 24, no. 2 (October 1972): 204.

[23]Some informed Western analysts estimate Soviet military manpower to be only slightly more than 4 million, whereas others consider 5 million a likely figure. 4.5 million is the low estimate of General Daniel Graham, head of the DIA, for 1975. See U.S., Congress, Joint Economic Committee, *Allocation of Resources in the Soviet Union and China—1975* (Washington, D.C.: U.S. Government Printing Office, 1975), pp. 73, 121.

[24]See Feshbach and Rapawy, "Soviet Population," p. 147, for current conscription estimates, and p. 150, table 16, for supply of 18-year-old males in the 1980s and 1990s. This supply, which is currently more than 2.6 million, will fall to 2.01 million during the 1980s and will not begin to rise until 1989, at which point it will rise only slowly and remain below current levels throughout the 1990s. See also, and more generally, Z. Perevedentsev, "Each of Us and All of Us," *Literaturnaia gazeta*, no. 33 (August 13, 1975): 22; and "The Family: Yesterday, Today, and Tomorrow," *Nash sovremennik*, no. 6 (June 1975): 118–31, in *Translations on USSR Political and Sociological Affairs*, no. 682, JPRS 65850 (October 6, 1975) and no. 645, JPRS 65142 (July 3, 1975), respectively.

[25]Although 10 years of education is compulsory in the Soviet Union and the numbers of rural residents who have completed the tenth grade are higher in Central Asia than in the USSR as a whole, Soviet sources leave no doubt that the quality of rural education is far lower than its urban counterpart; and the vast majority of Central Asians live in rural areas, whereas most "Europeans" are city dwellers. Furthermore, there is reason to believe that official data on Soviet educational attainments in general and Central Asian educational attainments in particular are substantially inflated (see Jeremy Azrael, "Bringing up the Soviet Man: Dilemmas and Progress," *Problems of Communism* 17, no. 3 [May/June 1968]: 23–31.)

[26]On the introduction and spread of military training programs in the schools,

see H. Goldhamer, *The Soviet Soldier* (New York: Crane, Russak, 1975), pp. 47–67.

[27]*Ibid.*, pp. 188–189.

[28]On the other hand, the very fact that the cities in question will be undergoing substantial "indigenization" may reduce their role as centers of russianization.

[29]Thus, according to a verbal communication from Murray Feshbach, the results of the 1970 census suggest a slight decline in the proportion of younger Central Asians who claim fluency in Russian. See also *Radio Liberty Research*, RL 287/76 (June 2, 1976): 1, for the report of a Soviet demographic conference—described in *Voprosy ekonomiki* (1975), no. 8: 149–152—at which one speaker contended that "the number of people of non-Russian nationality who do not speak Russian is increasing." Also see S. I. Bruk and M. N. Guboglo, "Bilingualism and the Drawing Together of Nations in the U.S.S.R (from 1970 Census Data)," *Sovetskaia etnografiia*, no. 4 (July/August 1975): 18–32, in *Translations on USSR Political and Sociological Affairs*, no. 693, JPRS 66078 (November 5, 1975): 10–29, esp. p. 26, for the lower percentage of Russian-speaking bilinguals among 11–19-year-old Georgians, Azeris, Armenians, Lithuanians, and Estonians than among 30–49-year-olds in these national groups. For a report on a recent official meeting on the problems of teaching Russian to non-Russians, see *Narodnoe obrazovanie*, no. 3 (March 1974): 7–10, in *Translations on USSR Political and Sociological Affairs*, no. 517, JPRS 61706 (April 9, 1974): 37–47. According to this report, there is a serious shortage of Russian–language teachers in the Central Asian and Caucasus republics "as a result [of which] the question about teaching the Russian language in the elementary grades of many schools, particularly the rural schools, has become a very acute one" (p. 39). See also O. Chelpanov and S. Matevosyan, "Time for Examinations, and Still . . . ," *Uchitel'skaia gazeta*, 28 June 1973, p. 3, in *Translations on USSR Political and Sociological Affairs*, no. 457, JPRS 60524 (November 1973): 23–28, esp. pp. 23–24, where it is reported that in an Armenian senior high school in Erevan, "senior grade pupils cannot answer in Russian the most simple questions . . ." and that the best high school graduates in rural Armenian high schools "do not even satisfy the requirements [in Russian] stipulated in the elementary program"; and the recent article by Uzbek SSR Minister of Education S. Shermukhamedov, who reports:

> The Russian language was not taught at all in some schools and in other schools was only partially taught in individual classes . . . because of the lack of Russian language teachers. . . . The subject was not taught in 191 schools during the 1971–72 school year. Russian language instruction in the elementary grades has been conducted and is still being conducted [not] only by non-specialists but by teachers who have a poor command of the Russian language. *Translations on USSR Political and Sociological Affairs*, no. 689, JPRS 65986 (October 22, 1975): 2, from "Unremitting Attention to Russian Language Study," *Narodnoe obrazovanie*, no. 9 (September 1975): 6–10.

[30]The nature of these problems is indicated by the materials cited in Goldhamer, *The Soviet Soldier*, pp. 188–189. Refugee reports are far more eloquent.

[31]These reports come from both Western observers and Soviet refugees. In this connection, the Soviet shipboard mutiny in the Baltic is rumored to have been at least partially sparked by ethnic frictions. See John K. Cooley, "Mutinied

Soviet Destroyer Dispatched on Long Voyage," *Christian Science Monitor*, June 29, 1976, p. 6. It's worth noting the report of Soviet ethnographers that 9.3% of a 1970 sample of Tatar workers who did not know Russian resented being directed by persons "of another nationality" (overwhelmingly Russian), while only 2.8% of those who know Russian expressed such resentment. See I. Arutiunian, *Sotsialnaia struktura sel'skogo naseleniia SSSR* (Moscow: Izdatel'stvo Mysl', 1971), p. 195, table 2. Concern on these accounts might well have been one of the factors responsible for the inauguration in the late 1960 of a major Soviet research program in military sociology and the sociology of the armed forces. See Ilya Zemtsov, *IKSI: The Moscow Institute of Applied Social Research* (in Russian), Soviet Institution series, no. 6 (Jerusalem: Soviet and East European Research Center, Hebrew University, 1976), pp. 26–29.

[32]For a brief but authoratative outline of the history of national military formations, see A.A. Grechko, *Vooruzhennye sily sovetskogo gosudarstva*, 2nd ed. (Moscow: Voennoe Izdatel'stvo, 1975), pp. 133–157. See also M. I. Kulichenko, *Natsional'nye otnosheniia v SSSR* (Moscow: Izdatel'stvo Mysl'; 1972), pp. 324–325.

[33]See, for example, the protest letter of 17 Soviet political prisoners, first published in Sweden in August 1974 and translated from the Swedish in *USSR National Affairs—Political and Social Developments* 3 (August 16, 1974): R12.

[34]See Grechko, *Vooruzhennye*, 2nd ed. and Grechko, *Vooruzhennye sily sovets-kogo gosudarstva*, 1st ed. (Moscow: Voennoe Izdatel'stvo, 1974), pp. 125–143.

[35]Personal communication to the author and to Murray Feshbach.

[36]Article 14-g of the 1936 Constitution grants the central government the right to establish "guiding principles" for "the organization of the military formation of the union republics." Article 18-b affirms that "each union republic has its own military formations." The draft of the new constitution makes no mention of republic formations and states that the central government is responsible for "the organization of defense and leadership of the armed forces" (*Izvestiia*, June 4, 1977, p. 3).

[37]Grechko, *Vooruzhennye*, 2nd ed., p. 150.

[38]See Paul K. Cook, "The Soviet Union in the Year 2000" (Seminar notes, Russian Research Center, Harvard University, December 19, 1974), p. 15. The Tbilisi riot took place on March 9, 1956, and according to an untitled and unsigned Georgian samizdat report in the present author's possession, resulted in the death of around 500 rioters, some of whom were machine-gunned by tank units.

[39]See N. S. Khrushchev, "Disarmament Is the Path towards Strengthening Peace and Ensuring Friendship among Peoples" (Report to a session of the USSR Supreme Soviet, *Pravda* and *Izvestiia*, January 15, 1960, pp. 1–5, translated in *Current Digest of the Soviet Press* 12, no. 2 [February 10, 1960]: 3–16, 23.

[40]The scarcity of teenagers in the late 1950s and early 1960s was, of course, a consequence of sharply falling wartime birth rates.

[41]L. I. Brezhnev, *O piatidesiatileti SSSR* (Moscow, 1973), p. 19.

[42]*Ibid.*, p. 24.

[43]The Jewish exodus movement is too well-known to require any further commentary. The Greek exodus, which has been reported in various sources, apparently has not been seriously impeded by the regime and therefore has not been accompanied by any overt protest. For the German exodus movement, see Robert C. Toth, "Germans in Russia," *Los Angeles Times*, April 24, 1976, pp. 1, 25; David K. Shipler, "Soviet Germans Rally in Red Square," *New York Times*

March 9, 1977, p. A12. On the Meskhetian Turks, see S. Enders Wimbush and Ronald Wixman, "The Meskhetian Turks: A New Voice in Soviet Central Asia," *Canadian Slavonic Papers* 17, nos. 2–3 (1975): 320–340; Ann Sheehy, *The Crimean Tartars, Volga Germans, and Meskhetians*, Minority Rights Group, no. 6 (London, 1973).

[44]For a good survey of Soviet national dissidence and national protest up to 1972, see *Conflict Studies*, no. 30 (December 1972): 1–27. For the Ukraine, See Michael Browne, ed., *Ferment in the Ukraine* (New York: Macmillan, 1971). For the trial of members of a separatist party in Armenia, see Christopher S. Wren, "Separatist Group Tried in Armenia," *New York Times*, November 17, 1974, p. 9. For the Baltic states, see V. S. Vardys, "Modernization and Baltic Nationalism," *Problems of Communism*, September/October 1975, p. 47. On samizdat especially and dissident activity more generally, see Gayle Durham Hollander, "Political Communication and Dissent in the Soviet Union," in *Dissent in the USSR*, ed. Rudolf L. Tokes (Baltimore and London: Johns Hopkins University Press, 1976), pp. 233–275.

[45]See Theodore Shabad, "Lithuanian Trial of Eight Starts," New York *Times*, September 26, 1972, p. 15; *Soviet Analyst* 2, no. 12 (June 7, 1973): 3.

[46]On the Crimean demonstrations in Tashkent and Chirchick, Uzbekistan, see Sheehy, "The Crimean Tartars, Volga Germans, and Meskhetians," p. 17. In 1966, the Tatars also presented the Kremlin a protest letter, demanding repatriation to their Crimean homeland, with over 130,000 signatures—the greater part of the adult Crimean Tatar population. See Roy Medvedev, *On Socialist Democracy* (New York: W. W. Norton, 1975), p. 35, n. 4. On the Erevan demonstration, see Wren, "Separatist Group Tried in Armenia," p. 9.

[47]For secret policy concern about these societies, see *Soviet Analyst* 3, no. 19 (19 September 1974): 1–2. More generally, see "Preservation of Historical Cultural Monuments," *Soviet Union*, no. 10 (1972), and S. T. Palmer, "The Restoration of Ancient Monuments in the USSR," *Survey*, no. 74/75 (Spring/Summer 1970): 163–174. The first of these articles quotes a Soviet source (p. 4) that claims these societies have more than 7 million individual and 41,000 collective members.

[48]In addition to the Ukraine and Georgia, Armenia has suffered a particularly extensive "renewal" of leading cadres as a result of the regime's vigilance campaign against "local nationalism."

[49]For charges to these effects, see the articles translated in *Current Digest of the Soviet Press* 25, no. 11 (April 11, 1973): 12–16, and 25; no. 16 (1973): 5–10, 36. See also the article by Armenian Party first secretary Shevarnadze translated in *Current Digest of the Soviet Press* 24, no. 14 (November 29, 1972): 15, and in *Translations on USSR Political and Sociological Affairs*, no. 386, JPRS 59134 (May 25, 1973): 25 ff., esp. 29–30. See also I. I. Groshev, *Bor'ba partii protiv natsionalizma* (Moscow: Politizdat, 1974), esp. pp. 113–114.

[50]For a good treatment of nationality conflicts during the Revolution and Civil War, see Richard Pipes, *The Formation of the Soviet Union* (Cambridge, Mass.: Harvard University Press, 1954). For the war and immediate postwar periods, see John Armstrong, *The Politics of Totalitarianism* (New York: Random House, 1961), esp. pp. 144–157.

[51]See Zbigniew Brzezinski, ed., *Dilemmas of Change in Soviet Politics* (New York: Columbia University Press, 1969).

[52]See Jeremy R. Azrael, "Communal Protests and Communal Rights in the USSR," Paper delivered to the Council on Foreign Relations, New York, 1976.

[53]There were, however, reports on a riot in Tashkent in 1969, during which many demonstrators shouted "Russians out of Uzbekhistan"; see *Chronicle of Current Events*, no. 8 (June 30, 1969); *Soviet Uzbekistan* (June 10, 1969). In addition, there apparently was some sort of nationality-related disturbance in the Narab region of Tadzhikistan in September 1970. See Barbara Wolfe Jancar, "Religious Dissent in the Soviet Union," in Tokes, *Dissent in the USSR*, p. 219.

[54]On the "revival" of Russian nationalism, see the following articles in *Slavic Review* 32, no. 1 (March 1973): Jack V. Haney, "The Revival of Interest in the Russian Past," pp. 1–16; Thomas E. Bird, "New Interest in Old Russian Things," pp. 17–28; and George L. Kline, "Religion, National Character, and the 'Rediscovery of Russian Roots'," pp. 29–40. Also see Sergei Vikulov, ed., *Nash sovremennik: Izbrannaia proza zhurnala, 1964–74* (Moscow: Sovremennik, 1975). For an officially published, though publicly criticized, pseudoscientific genetic "theory" of Russian racial superiority, see the articles of L. N. Gumilev, cited in V. I. Kozlov, "On the Biological–Geographical Conception of Ethnic History," *Voprosy istorii*, no. 12 (December 1974): 72–85, abstracted in *Current Digest of the Soviet Press* 27, no. 20 (June 11, 1975): 1–5. According to Kozlov, Gumilev's ideas lead to the conclusion that virtually all of the non-Slavic peoples of the USSR are "illegitimate" and could not survive without the aid of the genetically better-endowed Slavs, who are able to preserve this superior endowment only by resisting intermarriage. On dissent manifestations of Russian integral nationalism and xenophobia, see Dmitri Pospielovsky, "The Samizdat Journal *Veche*: Russian Patriotic Thought Today," *Radio Liberty Research Papers*, no. 45 (1971). For an interesting Ukrainian émigré criticism of the views of Russian dissidents on the nationality problem, see the editorial in *Ukrainian Quarterly* 31, no. 4 (Winter 1975): 350–357.

[55]For a very unusual Soviet article on the need for stricter gun control and on legislation to implement such control, see Yu. Feofanov, "Reflections on a Well-know Truth," *Izvestiia*, June 12, 1976, p. 5, translated in *Current Digest of the Soviet Press* 28, no. 24 (July 14, 1976): 13. See also the even more interesting article by Colonel General D. Molashvili, chief of staff of the Georgian Republic Ministry of Internal Affairs, "Who Has Explosives?" *Zaria vostoka*, April 1, 1976, p. 4, translated in *Current Digest of the Soviet Press* 28, no. 19 (June 9, 1976): 13. This article, which clearly was inspired by the contemporaneous outbreak of terrorist bombings in Tbilisi, calls for the creation of "a single organization to conduct all work with explosives in the republic," since the control exercised by the 23 ministries that "do a significant amount of work with explosives" is often lax and "the evidence indicates that it isn't very difficult" to steal explosives from their stockpiles, storage facilities, work sites, and other places.

[56]As is well known, several prominent Soviet dissidents have predicted that the outbreak of a major war, especially a war with China, would lead to violent national uprisings and international pogroms. See John P. Dunlop, "Solzhenitsyn in Exile," *Survey* 21, no. 96 (Summer 1975): 136; Peter Dornan, "Andrei Sakharov," in *Dissent in the USSR*, ed. Tokes, pp. 360–371; Andrei Amalrik, *Will the Soviet Union Survive Until 1984?* (New York: Harper and Row, 1970), pp. 62–64.

APPENDIX

Nationality	National population (thousands)		Annual growth rate[a] (percentage)	Straight-line projection of population[b]				"Eurocentric" projection of population[c]	
				(thousands)		(percentage of total)		(thousands)	(percentage of total)
	1959	1970		1985	2000	1985	2000	2000	2000
"European"									
Russian	114,114	129,015	1.12	153,427	180,305	51.2	47.9	183,483	50.2
Ukrainian	37,253	40,753	0.82	46,061	52,062	15.4	13.8	55,084	15.1
Belorussian	7,913	9,052	1.23	10,874	13,063	3.6	3.5	13,063	3.6
Moldavian	2,214	2,698	1.81	3,533	4,626	1.2	1.2	4,626	1.3
Lithuanian	2,326	2,665	1.24	3,208	3,862	1.1	1.0	3,862	1.1
Latvian	1,400	1,430	0.19	1,472	1,515	0.5	0.4	1,760	0.5
Estonian	939	1,007	0.63	1,118	1,219	0.4	0.3	1,337	0.4
Total "European"	166,159	186,620	1.06	219,693	256,652	73.2	68.1	263,215	71.9
"Non-European"									
Uzbek	6,015	9,159	3.90	16,250	28,832	5.4	7.7	21,871	6.0
Tatar	4,968	5,931	1.62	7,552	9,616	2.5	2.6	9,442	2.6
Kazakh	3,622	5,299	3.52	8,904	14,958	3.0	4.0	11,984	3.3
Azeri	2,940	4,380	3.69	7,543	12,991	2.5	3.5	10,152	2.8
Armenian	2,787	3,559	2.25	4,967	6,933	1.7	1.8	6,567	1.8
Georgian	2,692	3,245	1.71	4,187	5,401	1.4	1.4	5,235	1.4
Tadzhik	1,397	2,136	3.94	3,811	6,800	1.3	1.8	5,129	1.4

	1,002	1,525	3.89	2,704	0.9	4,794	1.3	3,639	1.0
Turkmen	1,002	1,525	3.89	2,704	0.9	4,794	1.3	3,639	1.0
Kirghiz	969	1,452	3.75	2,520	0.8	4,375	1.2	3,392	0.9
Total "non-European"	26,392	36,686	3.03	58,438	19.5	94,700	25.1	77,411	21.2
All other | 16,135 | 18,334 | 1.16 | 21,823 | 7.3 | 25,411 | 6.7 | 25,411 | 6.9 |
Total population | 208,686 | 241,640 | 1.34 | 299,954 | 100.0 | 376,763 | 100.0 | 366,037 | 100.0 |

[a] Annual growth rates were obtained by solving the following equation: $(1 + r') = P_{70}/P_{59}$ for r, where $t = 11$.

[b] Straight-line projections for 1985 and 2000 were obtained by using the formula $P_{70}(1 + r)^t$, where $t = 15$ for 1985 and $t = 30$ for 2000.

[c] "Eurocentric" projections for 2000 were obtained by using the formula $P_{85}(1 + r)^t$, where P_{85} is the straight-line projection of population in 1985 and altering the annual rates of growth (r) in the following manner: For Russians, Ukrainians, Latvians, and Estonians, the annual rate of growth was increased to 1.2%; for Moldavians, Belorussians, and Lithuanians, the annual rate of growth for 1959–1979 was continued; for Armenians, Georgians, and Tatars, the annual rate of growth was decreased to 1.5%; for Uzbeks, Kazakhs, Azeri, Tadzhiks, Turkmen, and Kirghiz, the annual rate of growth was decreased to 2%.

23

HEDRICK SMITH

*Information: White Tass and Letters to the Editor**

> A censored press only serves to demoralize. The greatest of vices, hypocrisy, is inseparable from it. . . .The government hears only its own voice while all the time deceiving itself, affecting to hear the voice of the people while demanding that they also support the pretense. And on their side, the people either partly succumb to political skepticism or completely turn away from public life and become a crowd of individuals, each living only his own private existence.
>
> Karl Marx, 1842

In early August 1972, Moscow was enveloped for days in a mysterious blue haze. It hung motionless over the city. The big domestic airport at Domodyedovo, south of Moscow, had to divert flights because of poor visibility. From our eight-floor apartment some mornings, we could see no more than 300 yards. Muscovites were coughing terribly, wiping tears from their eyes. Streetcars and automobiles were forced to use headlights. People were alarmed by rumors that fires in the fields around Moscow were menacing populated areas. Yet for nearly a week, the press said nothing. Finally, one skimpy back-page article mentioned a peat-bog fire near Shatura, about 60 miles east of Moscow. Two days later, another newspaper added the obvious fact that "smoke had reached Moscow" but did not say whether the city was in danger. The smoke seemed too dense and stable to have been blown 60 miles.

*Reprinted by permission of the author and Julian Bach Literary Agency, Inc., from *The Russians* (New York: Quadrangle/The New York Times Book Co., 1976), pp. 344–374. Copyright 1976 by Hedrick Smith.

I knew a middle-aged scientist, anxious to learn more, who tried to bluff some information out of the Central Moscow Fire Station. Posing as the doctor for the prestigious Writers' Union, he telephoned the fire station claiming that he had patients sick with pneumonia and in danger from inhaling the smoke. He demanded to know whether they should be evacuated from the city.

"The chief is out at the fire," the dispatcher told him.

"Then give me the deputy," the scientist said.

"He's out at the fire, too."

"Then, let me talk to someone in charge."

"They're all out at the fire," the dispatcher insisted. "I'm the only one left."

"Then you tell me how serious it is and how long you think it will last," the scientist said. "I need to know if it's under control."

"I don't know," the dispatcher said. "They're all out at the fire and they still can't do anything about it."

My friend hung up feeling more uneasy than when he began. In a few days, however, the smoke abated. Another article appeared, blaming the bad summer drought for fires in the peat-bogs but also announcing regulations against camping, picnicking, and lighting fires in a large, tinder-dry region around Moscow. Obviously, a lot was being left unsaid. Much later, some fire officials were cited for heroism, and an obituary of one youth was printed, discretely placed on the inside pages. Ultimately, in bits and pieces, it came out that fires had broken out in early July, fully a month before the press mentioned them, and had raged over thousands of acres. More than 1000 firefighters including planes, paratroopers, and entire military units had joined the battle. It turned out that some fires were extinguished no more than 15–20 miles from the Kremlin, very close to populated suburbs of Moscow. Yet most of the press printed practically nothing, and *Pravda*, the party's flagship newspaper, ran not a word.

The absence of such routine and obviously necessary information is typical. Russians take it as a fact of life that much of the information they need to know just to get along day by day does not appear in their press. I was talking one evening about this problem with the scientist who had called the fire station. We had gone out for a walk. "Going for a walk" has a special meaning for Russians because it is the standard precaution for talking frankly about some sensitive aspect of Soviet life safely out of earshot of telephone taps or room-bugs. We were taking our walk not far from the Foreign Ministry in the Old Arbat, a warren of peeling eighteenth- and nineteenth-century homes with fussy stucco moldings and faded Victorian facades, the former homes of nobility or intellectuals like Gogol, Herzen, and Scriabin, now museums or communal apartments with laundry hung incongruously behind lace curtains. That evening, a mid-October rain had left a penetrating London dampness and deserted streets. I asked my scientist friend what impact the restrictions on information had on people's personal lives.

He told the tragic story of a young woman from Central Asia who had flown the year before from Karaganda to Moscow to take entrance examinations for Moscow State University. She was scheduled to spend a week in Moscow. Her parents waited 10 days and became concerned at hearing nothing from her or from friends in Moscow. After 2 weeks, the father himself flew to Moscow to try to find her. When he got to the University, he was told that his daughter had never appeared for the exams, and people knew nothing about her. He called on family friends with whom she had thought of staying, but they had not seen her. He went to the police. At one precinct station, an officer suggested trying the airport police detachment. There, as everywhere, he appealed for help in locating his daughter. Only then was he informed confidentially—and instructed to keep the information confidential— that her plane from Karaganda to Moscow had crashed, and she had been killed with other passengers. He was stunned: it was the first he or his friends had heard of the plane crash.

The Soviet press does not report such catastrophes except in the rare cases where foreigners or Soviet VIP's are involved, and then only briefly and cryptically. This means that ordinary people are not alerted by the press to the possibility that someone dear to them may have died in an airplane crash. What is more, my scientist friend explained, Aeroflot often does not take down the addresses of passengers or their next of kin. So when a plane goes down, Aeroflot does not know whom to notify. That is why this poor man had to go hunt for his missing daughter and dig out the sad news for himself.

This silence technique of the Soviet press undermines its credibility. In October 1974, a Jack-the-Ripper murderer was stalking Moscow's streets. Enough women were killed on the sidewalks for Muscovites to suffer a bad case of nerves over street crime and to worry that things had gotten "as bad as New York," as one plump matron said to me. During that period, I heard more real personal stories from Russians about robbings, burglaries, purse-snatchings, and car thefts than I had ever imagined took place. When our office called the Moscow police about the reported murderer, we got the brush-off. But Soviet women told me they were being officially warned at work not to go out at night and were being cautioned by apartment watchmen not to open their doors to strangers. "My husband is more gallant than he has been in years," one gray-haired Russian lady told me, half-jokingly. "He's never worried about me before. But now he insists on meeting me at the bus stop and walking me home after dark." Auxiliary police, called in to expand the manhunt, were given a portrait of a handsome, friendly, muscular young blond with a weakness for women who wore red.

The press printed nothing, though I learned that at one newspaper office, the staff was told that seven women had been stabbed to death by a psychopath. From that and other similar briefings, rumors spread. There were said to be not one killer but two, then a gang. For days we heard that a train transferring a large load of young psychopaths from one prison to another had derailed and 200 convicts had escaped and were loose in Moscow. Later, the figure rose to 500. Ultimately, on October 28, police officials who had previously shied away from admitting a problem to the Western press, privately told Reuters, the British news agency, that they had arrested a young man believed responsible for 11 women's deaths—three in the previous 24 hours—and had him put under psychiatric observation. This report was confirmed elsewhere. Yet that same day, in an apparent attempt to reassure Moscow's jittery populace, the newspaper, *Evening Moscow*, quoted Viktor Pashkovsky, deputy chief of the Moscow police, as saying, "No dangerous crimes have been committed in the city in the last ten days."

My Russian friends reacted with total skepticism, so great had the credibility gap become. They scoffed at Pashkovsky's ludicrous denial that there had been any killings. They knew better than that from what they had been told privately at work and from comments of individual police officers. But they felt so deceived that they also disbelieved the Western press version that the killer had now been caught and the danger was really over.

"They may have caught one," said one middle-aged mother whose response was fairly typical, "but there is a second killer. They still have not caught the main one."

It takes a great leap of imagination for Westerners, especially Americans, who are literally blitzed by information, to picture the poverty of information in Russia. In the past decade, Americans have been inundated by news cascading over them simultaneously with events—by the Vietnam war exploding on television screens or a Watergate Presidency crumbling before their eyes. They are submerged by a Niagara of information that Russians are routinely denied—not only inside information like the Pentagon Papers or background information leaked by a Henry Kissinger but economic information on the latest wiggle of the consumer price index or the unemployment rate, sociological information on crime, smoking, or sex habits, opinion polls on politicians or race relations, census information about divorce rates, migration, education, or unsolicited advertising information on fads and bargains.

Russia by comparison is an information vacuum. Strictly speaking, of course, it is not a perfect vacuum because the world of science has its own body of information and because the Soviet press and libraries teem with cheerful official statistics that limn what one Soviet pamphlet immodestly termed "the story of the unprecedented growth and allround development" of the socialist homeland and trace "a path unparalleled in history." But hard, down-to-earth useful information is rationed out in dribs and drabs. It is restricted, as the Marquis de Custine, a French nobleman, observed on a trip to tsarist Russia, by the legendary Russian obsession with secrecy ("In Russia secrecy presides over everything: secrecy—administrative, political, social," Custine wrote in 1839, and it still holds). Like their tsarist predecessors, Soviet officials find it distasteful to admit anything has gone wrong or has gotten out of hand, as with airplane crashes or the summer fires around Moscow. They are obsessively insecure about admitting failure. Perhaps they restrict information about the Jack-the-Ripper murderer in order not to panic people or to deny criminals dramatic publicity that would encourage more crime. But I suspect that this, too, is more of the same—covering up awkward facts that suggest something is amiss and reveal that the weeds of crime have somehow grown in the healthy garden of Soviet socialism. Sometimes, too, information is bottled up through sheer bureaucratic clumsiness. More often, it is withheld because the powers-that-be (and this can be mere petty bureaucrats) reckon that the ordinary man or woman simply has no real need to know.

The first visit to Moscow of President Nixon in May 1972 stands out in my mind as an example of keeping the public unnecessarily in the dark, not just about the high politics but the simple mechanics of the occasion. In advance, the Western press was full of stories about the trip, whereas the Soviet press carried only a single advance story (though Muscovites were amply forewarned by the thorough face-lifting given their city and were joking about "the big *kniksen*," a play on the Russian word for curtsy). On the day Nixon was due to arrive, *The New York Times* ran a map of his motorcade route from the VIP airport at Vnukovo to the Kremlin. But no route was shown in Soviet newspapers. Even the timing of his arrival was undisclosed except to those discerning enough to decipher the real meaning of an item innocuously labeled "4 P.M.—International Program" in the daily television diary.

Thousands profited from that little tip and played hookey from work to try to see the first American president ever to visit their capital. But many of them miscalculated because their information was insufficient. I came across one crowd of about 2000 still standing eight rows deep at Manezh Square, not far from the Kremlin, fully half an hour after Nixon had been deposited inside the fortress by a motorcade that had used another entrance, blocks away and out of sight.

"Why are you waiting?" I asked several people.

"To see," replied a shirt-sleeved student with a briefcase.

"Why didn't you wait at the other end of the Kremlin where he was supposed to go?" I inquired.

"Because this is better—a better view," he asserted in ignorance.

"But Nixon has already gone into the Kremlin—at the other end," I said, "I saw him go in. It's all over."

"Oh," said the young man, frozen to his spot. I walked away, but the crowd remained, patient, hopeful, and unknowing.

That first Nixon visit to Moscow was a striking illustration of how effectively the Soviet leadership can insulate its own public from political reality. The entire event took place for Russians in a different dimension from that for the Western public. Ordinary Russians were too ill-informed to fathom either the trial or the triumph of that summit.

No Soviet citizen outside a narrow slice of the political elite had been given any reason to expect important accords to be signed on limiting the strategic arms race. The acronymic stepchildren of the nuclear balance of terror—SALT, ICBM, MIRV, ABM—never had a chance to become household words because they had rarely been mentioned to the Soviet public. Soviet news coverage of arms negotiations over the previous 2.5 years had been limited to the bland, unrevealing arrival-and-departure statements of chief negotiators. So much in the dark was everyone but those at the pinnacle of power that one thoroughly trusted and experienced Soviet journalist foolishly bet me a bottle of cognac that there would be—and could be—no major arms agreement until the Vietnam war was settled. And the bet was made before the crisis over Nixon's mining of Haiphong harbor. The journalist simply knew nothing about the progress already made in the arms talks, which had been quite evident in the Western press.

On Haiphong, too, the Soviet public was spared the agony of being informed. In Washington, the sense of confrontation over the mining of Haiphong harbor was palpable. The world press blossomed with comparisons to the Cuban missile crisis of 1962 and speculation about Soviet minesweepers trying to break the mine blockade. Nixon was accused by Democrats of risky brinksmanship, and the White House seemed to encourage the interpretation that it wanted to force a showdown with Moscow.

Given that picture, intelligent Soviets would undoubtedly have found it hard to understand how the Kremlin could stomach such humiliation and go through with the Nixon visit at the price of disagreement with allies in Hanoi who were burning mad over the mining. Pyotr Shelest, the Ukrainian Communist party boss, reportedly lost his job for urging the Politburo to call off the visit. But because the Brezhnev-led majority chose to slide around Nixon's challenge rather than meet it head-on, the Soviet press kept its citizenry in the dark. For 20 days before, during, and after the summit, the controlled press did not mention the mining except for one brief aside buried in one news item. Moreover, it ignored the return to Moscow during the summit talks of a plane carrying two dead and 20 wounded Soviet seamen back from North Vietnam, casualties of American air raids against port areas. Normally an item for blistering attacks on America, this news was inconvenient to the Kremlin. So it was suppressed.

The result, not surprisingly, was that ordinary Russians took Soviet press denunciations of American air raids against North Vietnam as routine. They knew too little of the dangerous situation to share the real frustration of the Soviet elite—just as after the summit, the Soviet public understood too little to share the leadership's sense of triumph at the agreements reached. For months afterward, I was asked privately to explain the accords to Soviet scientists, writers, and other intellectuals. No one had bothered to read the texts of the agreements that were printed by the press verbatim without the explanation necessary to make them intelligible. Moreover, the most important document—the protocol that specified the precise number of land missiles and missile submarines for each side—was never printed by Soviet newspapers. To have revealed to ordinary Russians that the two sides had agreed on such a precise calibration of their forces, one scientist told me, would have undermined the party's campaign to maintain Cold War vigilance among the population and would have made it very difficult to continue to insist that Soviet scientists swear, as they must, that in publishing any innocent, totally nondefense-related academic paper, that they are not disclosing anything secret. In other words, the rationale for an entire system of secrecy would unravel if the extent of the arms agreements was really understood by the Soviet intelligentsia.

The Nixon visit ended pretty much as it had begun. At the Kremlin the day before Nixon's departure, an American reporter traveling with the President noticed a Russian couple approach the plainclothes security man at the Borovitsky Gate to ask when the Kremlin would be open again to the general public.

"I don't know," the security man said curtly.

"We've come from Leningrad," the Russians explained. "We want to rearrange our plans in Moscow to be sure we have time later to see the Kremlin. Can you say when the American delegation is leaving."

An impassive, unyielding "No" was all they got.

At this point, the American reporter who had been standing nearby, went up to the Russian couple and explained what was general knowledge to readers of the Western press—that the Nixon party was leaving the next day. "Perhaps the Kremlin will open after that," he said.

It was a typical, revealing little episode. For often when Soviet officialdom restricts information available to ordinary Russians—whether street maps, telephone books, advertisements, when the Kremlin will reopen, or other seeming trivia of daily life that Westerners take for granted—it has no deep political motivation. Officials act out of sheer bloody-mindedness or an ingrained, habitual, arrogant Soviet disdain for "the little man."

Intourist, for example, would give out train and aircraft schedules by phone but steadfastly refused to disclose whether there were any seats available. Only in person could that be learned (*after* a hassle about travel permissions). Russians told me that if this frustrated us, they suffered much ruder treatment at railroad stations, ticket offices, and stores. "I never bother to phone a store to ask what they have," one housewife advised. "It's hopeless." The only recourse is to go stand in line. Aeroflot seemed to have an unwritten commandment, or perhaps it was actually in writing somewhere, not to reveal whether its planes were departing or arriving late, a matter of some consequence since its service was so erratic that the chances of delay seemed better than 50–50. Yet its divisions of blue-uniformed ground clerks, whether bossy middle-aged matrons or busty young blondes, refused to give anything other than scheduled departure time. The nationwide loss of time over this policy of noncommunication must have been monumental. I personally spent many hours, up to 17 hours at one clip, and I knew other people who spent as many as 24 or 36 hours pinned to the air terminal waiting for planes. Practically everywhere I traveled, Soviet airports were littered with people, draped like wilted flowers over all available furniture, unable to stray from their tedious vigils because Aeroflot refused to inform them of a likely departure time.

With good reason, Americans groan about the continual bombardment of their senses by ads and commercials on television and in their press. But they might half reconsider if exposed for awhile to the consumer blackout in Russia. Lack of the most basic consumer information is one of the most enervating and crippling facets of Russian life. It is the main reason why Russian sidewalks are so constantly populated by shoppers earnestly plodding from store to store with their string bags and briefcases, engaged in an unending hit-or-miss lottery, hoping to stumble onto a find or to bump into some strange woman on the street and ask her where she got those good-looking oranges.

Soviet advertising is no help to them because it is still so primitive. With the exception of housing exchanges where good detailed information is available, the Soviet consumer depends on expending shoe leather or on the informal grapevine. Soviet advertisements are typically institutional in style ("Watches make the best presents" or "If you want to live to ripe old age and be beautiful, modest, thorough and truthful, drink tea.") Most newspapers publish without ads, though more popular ones like *Evening Moscow* run weekly ad supplements that are mostly personals and a few vaguely worded store ads. Television commercials, bunched together for short bursts on secondary channels at random hours, are amateurish and almost universally ignored. Rarely, if ever, do they tell listeners where to buy the products advertised, a basic flaw with much Soviet advertising.

The shopper looking for choice meat or a stylish dress has no handy yellow pages to let her "fingers do the walking" or the kind of specific daily newspaper supermarket or department store ads that in the West would tip her off where to shop. The closest approach is a 15-minute blurb of commercials on Moscow Radio at 1:45 P.M. (which many of my Soviet friends did not even know existed), where Ready-Made Clothing Store No. 142 offers "a large selection of men's suits, Soviet-made, all wool, half-wool with synthetics, or pure synthetic, from 70 to 150 rubles [$95–200]," or where Electrical Goods Store No. 7 offers a 12-ruble ($16) trade-in for used washing machines on new ones. When I asked a mother of two about these ads, she brushed them aside with a disgusted grunt.

"Listen," she said, "there are basically two kinds of products: those which no one really wants and which sometimes get advertised, and the good items which are in short supply and which stores don't need to advertise." This terse judgment was echoed by others.

In other words, Russians either get inside tips from well-placed friends or else do without. One tall, slender linguist with a face like Andy Gump, chortled smugly as he recalled a life-saving telephone call from a friend in December 1971. The friend had a tip that the next day Moscow's only new car outlet would let people sign up for the first 25,000 Zhiguli cars—the city's entire quota for 2 years. "The guy told me he could hold me a place in line during the night—in spite of the cold they were already lining up out there to spend the night," said the linguist. "But I had to be there by dawn. My friend said it would be a mob scene the next day and he was right. After that, there were no more sign-ups. I had to wait about a year for my car, but I got it. Without that call, I would have been out of luck." No one bothered to advertise that crucial event. Finding out was a matter of luck or the right connections.

Something as ordinary as a map is also a problem, though perhaps for more sinister reasons. Russians do not seem to miss street maps. Not having cars, they just ask each other general directions and take the bus or subway. But Ann and I liked maps for walking tours. In Moscow, some city newsstands sometimes carried subway and street maps. But almost everywhere else we traveled, it was impossible to get a street map, no matter how crude. When we would ask for them, Intourist guides would flood us with folders enticing us to travel to Yalta or some other distant point, or with brochures showing the local fountains, the university, and the main statute of Lenin. But maps were not part of the kit. We scoured bookstores. No maps. Clerks looked at us as if it were a stupid question. "Military secret," said a Soviet journalist opaquely. Another friend, laughing sympathetically at our map frustrations, confided that on the few available Moscow maps, the angles of the streets were purposely just a bit askew to foil Western intelligence. I could not tell by looking at them, but he said he was not joking.

Another common reference tool that Westerners take absolutely for granted—the telephone book—is an item of almost priceless rarity. One of the momentous events during our 3 years in Moscow was the publication of a new phone book. Until that moment—and even afterward—Moscow must have ranked as the largest metropolis in the world without a readily available phone directory. Unlike Western telephone companies, the Soviet Ministry of Communications does not automatically provide phone books to subscribers. Nor are they available at pay phones or in other public places. But then, except for calling friends, Russians seem to use the phone a lot less than Westerners do.

The phone book that went on sale in 1973 was the first directory of personal telephone listings to be published in Moscow in 15 years (though a separate book on offices, stores, hospitals, and other public institutions is printed at somewhat more frequent intervals). The problem with this phone book, as with so many desirable items in the Soviet Union, is that supply made not even the barest pretense of satisfying demand. For a city of 8 million people, the printers published 50,000 phone books. They sold out within a few days at city newsstands even though the full four-volume set cost a hefty 12 rubles ($16).

Those lucky enough to have a full set of office and personal directories noticed some oddities. The Moscow Province and City Administration occupied 32 pages of the office directory, but the Communist party Central Committee, the nation's most powerful and important body constituting a complete shadow government that matches the entire structure of government ministries, modestly gave only one number (206–25–11). Most ministries provided 15 or more numbers, but the Defense Ministry listed only two. The Soviet space program went completely unlisted. The KGB, or secret police, listed a 24-hour inquiry office (221–07–62). But thousands of foreign diplomats, businessmen, and newsmen living in the Soviet Union were entirely omitted, presumably in keeping with the official Soviet effort to isolate foreign residents from ordinary Soviet citizens as much as possible.

Those not fortunate enough to land one of the precious phone books could dial information (09) or go to one of the many little octagonal information kiosks dotted around Moscow. But that is not always so simple as it sounds. I learned that to get a number from the information operator, you needed the full name (first, last, and middle), and an extremely precise address. Once I was asked the year of birth of the person I was trying to reach and was so startled by the question that I apologized and hung up in confusion. I did not want to get the people in trouble, and I was fearful that she might be checking extra closely because I spoke Russian with an accent. But Soviet friends later explained that these were routine questions from operators. Because people live in such massive apartment blocks (often several with the same street number but different building numbers) and because so many Russians have similar names and because there are so many communal telephones, the operators need very specific data to sort out one Ivan Ivanovich Ivanov from another.

Getting someone's address can be equally, if not more, trying as I noticed one day passing Moscow Information Service Booth #57 at

Petrovka Street and the Boulevard Ring Road. Over the window on the booth was a sign that read: "For obtaining information about the address of a Moscow resident, it is necessary to know: first, middle and last name; age; place of birth (city, province, district or village)." I could hardly believe my eyes. "If I were looking for my mother," wisecracked a young Moscow friend, "I could do it. But not for anyone else." Muscovites, he said, did not use the booths much; they were mostly for out-of-towners. And indeed near Red Square, they line up for hours at the information kiosk, fresh off the train or plane from the hinterlands.

Knowing the various shortcuts in Soviet life, I was curious to see whether the system at Booth #57 actually operated according to the stated rules, so I hung around studying the schedule of charges while the gray-haired lady inside handled a customer. A man in a flat cap and brown padded coat approached. He fished out some change, pushed a coin through the window, and asked for the address of some friend who had moved. I could actually hear him rattling off full name, age, and birthplace of the other man. A pause. Then the lady slipped him a scrap of paper through the window. He pocketed the information which had cost him 5 kopecks—as much as a subway ride—and strode off. The schedule of prices showed what other information the lady had: suburban train information (2 kopecks), long distance train or plane information (5 kopecks), information on out-of-town rest homes and sanatoria (8 kopecks), travel information for trips on mixed means of transport—a combination of train, ship, or riverboat—(10 kopecks), unspecified information of a legal character (5 kopecks), information on lost documents (10 kopecks), inquiries requiring a long time to fulfill (30 kopecks).

Like the rest of Soviet life, information is not a matter of money but connections. The better his connections, the better informed a Soviet can be because information, like consumer goods, is rationed out according to rank. Party and government bigwigs, important ministry officials, and propagandists for the main central newspapers, for example, receive both special briefings and a special daily news report from Tass. The ordinary service published for everyone, known as blue or green Tass, is the sanitized and censored version of reports from around the country and abroad that has been tailored to fit the party line and pruned of objectionable disclosures about the Soviet Union itself. Tass headquarters on Moscow's Boulevard Ring Road also acts as a filtering point for newspapers and magazines from all over the world. A Tass man once disclosed to me that 12 editors worked in the American section of Tass in Moscow in addition to the full complement of reporters in Washington and New York.

"What in the world do they all do?" I asked. "There aren't but a few hundred words of Tass reports on America in the Soviet press every day. One man could handle that."

Most of them, he confessed, work on "service Tass"—meaning the special, secret Tass reports running 100 pages or more daily, which circulate to government ministries, party headquarters, and key newspaper offices. Often when I visited senior commentators for *Pravda* or *Izvestia*, I would see stacks of this special "White Tass" service on their desks. It is a far richer and more detailed selection of foreign news and comment (including digests of dispatches sent out from Moscow by Western correspondents) than ordinary Tass. I was also told that White Tass includes accurate and revealing information on Soviet domestic affairs, such as reports of air and train accidents, statistics on crime, word of health epidemics, serious production deficiencies, crop reports, and similar material that the regime would find embarrasing to print openly. Finally, I learned there is an even more rarefied edition of Tass, called "Red Tass" because its covering summary is—or was—printed on red paper. It supposedly goes only to chief editors, the highest government officials and Communist party bigshots. Despite this restricted handling, Soviet newsmen told me that the contents were not based on spy reports or special intelligence. Most of it would be ordinary news to a Western newspaper.

The gradations of Tass are but a part of an entire hierarchy of special publications for Soviet insiders with various degrees of trust and responsibility. For its mass propagandists, the party puts out a weekly, *Atlas*, which contains a bit more detail on current events than most Soviet newspapers. Other organizations do the same, but they are very skittish about acknowledging the existence of such special publications. John Shaw of *Time* magazine told me that just before Nixon's visit to Moscow in June 1974, he was at a public lecture in Moscow and noticed the young woman next to him, evidently a trade union activist, reading an article entitled "What Is Impeachment?" This suprised him because up to then the Soviet press had not carried anything so explicit. He asked her for a look at the magazine. It turned out to be a translation of an East German article, simply explaining the mechanics of impeachment. But it went further than any normal Soviet publication in implying the weakness of Nixon's position. Shaw jotted down the title and phone number of the publication, an internal trade union organ, and noticed that it had a small circulation of about 2000—obviously intended for the central leadership and activists. The next day, he had his translator call to ask for a copy of the publication. But the editors insisted that not only were copies unavailable but that no such publication existed, even though Shaw said he had read it himself.

A parallel phenomenon, vital to the functioning of the Soviet system, is the hierarchy of closed lectures. They are held for party groups, officials in government ministries, newspaper staffs, scientific institutes, and for all kinds of specialized groups. One former party lecturer, an intense young man who had become disillusioned by the privileges and cynicism of party higher-ups, told me the lectures were used to provide more than usually candid explanations of party policy, to start whisper campaigns against dissidents like Solzhenitsyn and Sakharov if the regime did not want to arouse the West by attacking them publicly, to discuss or explain away awkward developments like bad harvests, industrial accidents, or personnel shifts within the party or government, or even to warn people about problems such as the Jack-the-Ripper murderer in Moscow in late 1974. The candor and the amount of information disclosed, this man said, is strictly geared to the importance and political reliability of the audience. At closed party meetings, he said, "if they asked the right questions, we were obliged to answer them. The kinds of information that we could give out, for instance, were what kind of harvest we had, how many tons of grain we bought abroad, and how much gold we paid for it, or things like how much our aid to Vietnam cost—it was costing us two million rubles [$2.67 million] a day. But there were some questions we never answered no matter who asked them. If someone asked what happened to that man who shot at Brezhnev, we did not answer such a question. Or if people asked when would the government lift the temporary price increases introduced under Khrushchev in 1962, we did not answer that question." Before he left on lecture tours, he said, he was given instructions on what he could reveal to different categories of people—the most to top party provincial and district officials; the least to ordinary office workers. But he noticed one general effect at all levels: Closed lectures made everyone feel like an insider, trusted and therefore committed.

Beyond these closed lectures, the *Znaniye*, or Knowledge Society runs innumerable public lectures, much blander than the closed ones but still more revealing than the Soviet press because they allow for question-and-answer periods. At these, I heard Russians asking about grain purchases from America, the treatment of Sakharov, the expulsion of Soviet military advisors from Egypt, or elements of the confrontation with America over trade and Jewish emigration. After the end of Soviet jamming of Voice of America and some other Western stations in September 1973, the questions seemed generally sharper than before, reflecting the fact that in big cities like Moscow and Leningrad, some people not only listened to Western radios but tried to use Western information in an attempt to pry more out of their own authorities. This practice, however, ebbed and flowed with news developments that interested Russians. As Western radio stations became more concerned with Western economic problems, the trend eased.

One idiosyncrasy of the Soviet system, aimed at keeping higher circles well informed without contaminating the minds of ordinary citizens, is the production of "special editions" of significant and politically sensitive foreign books. Plenty of selected Western fiction, from Hemingway, Dreiser, and Galsworthy to Arthur Haley and Kurt Vonnegut is translated into Russian and sold commercially, especially if it gives an unflattering image of Western life or morals. But important nonfiction of interest to the political elite and deemed too provocative for the Soviet public is translated and published in very limited special editions. Mikhail Agursky, a specialist in automated control systems and a dissident Jew who eventually emigrated, told me that during his establishment years, he had seen special editions of books like John Kenneth Galbraith's *Modern Industrial State* or Bertrand Russell's *History of Western Philosophy*. From others, I learned of German linguists who had translated Hitler's *Mein Kampf* for Stalin's edification or William L. Shirer's *The Third Reich* for the contemporary leadership, not to mention English language experts who had translated all kinds of books on American strategic thinking.

These special editions, Agursky said, are marked "only for service libraries," meaning that only high-level party officials or party researchers have access to them. They are easily distinguished from normal Soviet books because they do not carry a fixed price impressed right into their back cover as normal books do. Moreover, Agursky said, they are numbered individually, like highly classified documents in the West, so that no one can get away with a copy without a record of where it is and who is responsible for it.

Not only books but foreign periodicals are also distributed by rank in the Soviet system. Top-level editors, administrators, scientists, and other VIP's are sometimes allowed the special privilege of receiving personal subscriptions to Western publications (including the U.S.I.A. propaganda magazine, *Amerika*). One scientist told me that Pyotr Kapitsa, head of the Institute of Physical Problems in Moscow, received his own copies of specialized publications in his field as well as *Science, Scientific American*, or a general magazine like *Newsweek*, though at politically sensitive times, Kapitsa's subscriptions were cut off. All such publications must, of course, be vetted by international mail censors or a central clearing house for foreign scientific publications. In Soviet technical libraries, I have seen Western magazines that have been through this vetting process. The copies of *Scientific American* that I saw in one Moscow institute had odd white spaces in the table of contents and gaps elsewhere for articles that had been removed, evidently because they dealt with touchy issues like arms technology or made critical evaluations of Soviet science or policy. A science writer I knew told me of the awkward efforts of Soviet officials to cover up their excisions of embarrassing political articles in foreign publications. On a visit to the scientific institute in Moscow, which receives incoming Western publications and photo-reproduces them, he had seen the originals and sanitized Soviet reproductions side by side. "In one magazine," he recalled, "they ran the same advertisement for five pages in a row to try to fill up the space where they cut out an article they didn't like."

With wry amusement, Zhores Medvedev, the dissident biologist, described the operation of this mail censorship apparatus in his book, *The Medvedev Papers*. Painstakingly, he documented that Soviet censors had become so inefficient that it now took twice as long for a letter to reach him from Western Europe than it used to take Lenin's mail from Western Europe to reach his family in Siberia under tsarist censorship. He also told me that in 1972, Solzhenitsyn had sent two letters to Karl Gierow of the Swedish Academy in Stockholm and to his lawyer, Fritz Heeb in Zurich, with a note enclosed to the Soviet mail censors: "You may read this letter, photocopy it, subject it to chemical analysis. But it is your duty to deliver it. If you do not, I will publish a protest against you and it will not bring honor to the postal service." Both letters arrived at their destinations—minus the slips.

What interested Medvedev more was the system for processing his own academic mail and scientific publications from the West. He carefully noted the various markings that censors put on the material sent in from abroad. After reading his book, I kept an eye out for those markings and before long had noticed a copy of the *International Herald Tribune* in an office at *Pravda* bearing the censor's mark ⟨185⟩ which Medvedev said meant very restricted distribution. (Theoretically, the *Tribune* is on sale in the Soviet Union. But in practice, I found it was only occasionally available at hotels for foreign tourists, usually kept under the counter, produced only for foreigners, and almost always out of date if not out of stock.) Later, in Novosibirsk at the Academic City's technical library, the director proudly displayed to me file copies of *The New York Times*. These, too, bore the same telltale restrictive marks of the censor which meant that only someone with special permission could read them, though the library director tried to pass the *Times* off as a publication in general use. The copies he showed me looked untouched.

Perhaps no institution more than the Lenin Library, the Soviet equivalent of the Library of Congress, embodies the carefully stratified Soviet hierarchy of information. Outwardly, it has the imposing, columned facade of august public buildings around the world. Inside, it functions by a web of rules out of Kafka. At the *Leninka*, as it is affectionately known among Muscovites, it is clear that the Soviet state regards knowledge as power and controls it accordingly. To begin with, it is almost impossible for an ordinary citizen without higher education to get a library card, mostly because of the crush of people. Those with cards gain access to general reading rooms, but specialists with advanced degrees (Soviet Ph.D's) get into special reading rooms stocked with more material, especially scientific and technical publications, and occasionally new fiction from the West.

Finally, there are the *spetskhrany*, literally the special holdings, or more accurately, the secret stacks. "The general alphabetical index is secret," said Mikhail Agursky, tugging on his magnificient, ginger-colored side-whiskers as we toured the library one afternoon. What he meant was that the *Leninka* is probably the only great library in the world with two entire sets of catalogues, each occupying huge rooms: one of them a limited censored catalogue open to general readers and the other, the full catalogue of the library's holdings, including the secret stacks, open only to the security-cleared staff.

"It's a problem, for example, to get religious or philosophical literature," Agursky intoned softly, not to be overheard. "It's not forbidden. But you can't find it in the catalogue so you can order it [from the special holdings] through a librarian. And even if I happen to have the catalogue number, the librarian will ask me why I need such a book. It hapened to me several years ago. I was trying to obtain some old religious book and the librarian asked me, 'Why do you need this book? You are a technical specialist. You have very strange interests.'"

"And it was not said with a sense of humor," Agursky said, eyeing me sternly. "She refused to get it."

This kind of problem drives foreign scholars wild. An Indian historian fumed to me over lunch one day, explaining his frustration at having to deal totally through some intermediary who checked the secret catalogue and then the secret stacks. "I am completely at the mercy of this young woman who may be competent or no good at all," he said. A British scholar took some small comfort that foreigners were usually allowed to read more things than most Russians until he angrily remembered that he could not get certain historical materials "until some Russian researcher has gone through to check them first." An American professor was exasperated by the Lenin Library's refusal to xerox some articles by Freud from the closed stacks. "We are forbidden to recopy Freud," the librarian told her. "He has those sexual theories."

Far more than Freud or theological literature is consigned to the secret stacks, to be produced only for those with special permission. By the account of Agursky and others, the secret stacks include any foreign literature and periodicals that take issue with the current Communist party line (in other words, most of it); non-Communist newspapers and magazines and even some Communist ones (during the invasion of Czechoslovakia, I was told, all the foreign Communist press that is normally in open stacks disappeared into the *spetskhrany*); Maoist writings; Communist classics written by proscribed authors like Trotsky and Bukharin as well as lesser-known Soviet works published in earlier periods when the party line differed from today's (for example, works by Stalin, or works praising him too slavishly, or on the other hand, works from the Khrushchev era that are now considered too disparaging of Stalin); and Russian literature generally, either pre- or post-Revolutionary if it is unfavorable to the Communist cause or the current Kremlin rulers—unless it is so illustrious (Dostoyevsky or Tolstoy) that the Soviets would be embarrassed before world opinion to conceal it.

Like any system of censorship, this one has its imperfections, its slip-ups, and amusing little inconsistencies. For example, books by or about Trotsky are banned, but it is possible to read Communist newspapers of the 1920s quoting Trotsky's speeches. But generally, the library controls work effectively enough to frustrate any Soviet who is intellectually curious and lacks the rank to command the access he wants.

Indeed, the degree of compartmentalization of information in the Soviet Union is hard for Westerners to fathom. American arms negotiators were stunned, for example, to discover in the strategic arms talks that Vladimir Semenov, the Deputy Foreign Minister who nominally headed the Soviet delegation, and his civilian aides knew practically nothing about the Soviet strategic arsenal. In other words, they were in no real position to negotiate since the Soviet Defense Ministry had not made them privy even to the most basic information on Soviet weaponry. American officials admitted later that they had had to spend the first months educating the Soviet civilians on the nuclear facts of life before the talks could move ahead.

On a much less exalted level, I met a young Soviet researcher who had been given special access to *The New York Times* as part of a research project to which he was assigned at his institute. It was his first exposure to a big Western newspaper, and he was amazed at the volume of information that piqued his curiosity for more. One day, killing time near the librarian who handed out foreign publications from the restricted stacks at the institute, this young man found himself absentmindedly pawing through a copy of *Life* magazine that had been left sitting on the counter. He was talking with the librarian as he glanced at *Life* and suddenly realized that she had become quite nervous and was looking at him disapprovingly.

"What's wrong?" he asked. "Did I say something wrong?"

"No," she said. "It's just that with you, *The New York Times* is permitted, but not *Life* magazine."

Before going to Moscow, I had assumed that Soviet science, because of its prestige and importance to the state, might be spared such problems over information. But later I met Soviet scientists who maintained they had trouble keeping abreast of developments abroad and an even worse time keeping up with new work among their Soviet colleagues because of restrictions on the flow of information or because of the way the party controls channels of scientific contact with the West. Zhores Medvedev, who specialized in problems of aging, told me while he was still in Russia, he found it impossible to obtain full Soviet mortality statistics with a breakdown on the causes of death, even though such data were essential to his work. "Mortality statistics are treated like state secrets," he protested. A biomedical engineer at Moscow's top surgical institute said doctors there could not obtain cumulative figures on patients who died or otherwise suffered from complications after surgery. A French doctor related to me the tragic case of a West German diplomat who had died of spinal meningitis in Moscow because his illness was not quickly enough diagnosed, largely because Soviet health authorities had suppressed information about other recent cases of spinal meningitis in Moscow. More broadly, outspoken nonconformist intellectuals like Andrei Sakharov, the physicist, and Roy Medvedev, the Marxist historian, have charged that Soviet science suffers from what Medvedev called "the authoritarian atmosphere and lack of intellectual freedom, the dominating role of the censor."[1]

As an objective branch of knowledge beyond ideology and as a field that enjoys enormous prestige, science has long posed a problem for the Communist party. The Academy of Sciences, established in 1726, has been almost unique as an institution that has preserved a modicum of independence from party overseers. It has repeatedly rebuffed efforts to push ranking party officials like Sergei Trapeznikov, the head of the Central Committee's Science Department, into its membership, and it has balked at expelling such iconoclasts as Sakharov and Ben Levich, the electrochemist who applied to emigrate to Israel. Lenin himself is supposed to have proposed an amendment to the Academy's statutes exempting all of its publications from censorship, though this has been systematically disregarded.

In years past, Soviet science has paid a heavy price for political interference. The most infamous example was the quarter of a century during which genetics was suppressed while Trofim Lysenko reigned over biology. It was his theory, sold to Stalin and Khrushchev, that characteristics acquired from the environment could be transmitted in the evolutionary process. Mendelian genetics became anathema; its advocates were dismissed and persecuted, and their leader, the brilliant biologist, Nikolai Vavilov, died in a Stalinist camp in 1942. At other times, dogmatic Marxists opposed the theory of relativity, obstructing Soviet advances in nuclear physics, and fought against the science of cybernetics.

One ranking Soviet scientist told me he felt that it was only as the Kremlin came to see military applications for various fields of modern science that these fields flourished. "Before the war, science was some kind of plaything for intellectuals," he said, "but then Stalin understood the importance of atomic weapons and this gave a great boost to physics"—the nuclear physics, particle physics, accelerators, atom-smashers, and the whole paraphernalia for which the Russians are now internationally well known. In 1950, he added, cybernetics was so mistrusted that a leading Stalinist theoretician, Boris Agapov, attacked it in an article, "Cybernetics: A Bourgeois Pseudo-Science." But it was kept alive within the military establishment and under Khrushchev, in about 1956, the scientist said, cybernetics was recognized by the Kremlin for its importance in developing computers and ultimately missiles with their complex guidance systems. The official line did a 180-degree turn, and the same Boris Agapov wrote a new article, "Cybernetics: The New Science." The next beneficiary, he said, was theoretical mathematics, which got a lift from missile research as did chemistry, especially the chemistry of polymers, vital for heat-resistant nose cones in rockets. Biology got a push from the post-Khrushchev leaders, the scientist said, because of applications in both agriculture and biological warfare. "Where the state sees a military benefit," this man asserted to me, "scientists have won considerable freedom in their work."

Internationally, Soviet science has a reputation for some of the world's most brilliant theoreticians in physics and mathematics but only spotty strengths elsewhere and general weakness in experimental work. Privately, top scientists blame this on bad management, rigid bureaucracy, political interference, and second-rate equipment. These problems hamper experimenters more than theorists. "We can read about experiments in American scientific journals that we cannot even repeat because we do not have the equipment, the computers," a dejected Soviet physicist told an American friend of mine. Others say Soviet science inevitably lags behind America despite talented individual scientists because information on new developments in world science or Soviet science circulates so slowly.

I have heard several scientists assert that the West overestimates Soviet science. Andrei Sakharov, who gained distinction as a theoretical physicist who helped create the Soviet H-bomb, was once asked by Murray Seeger of the *Los Angeles Times* how Soviet scientists had been able to make breakthroughs despite political controls, and he shot back: "What breakthroughs? Since the Second World War there have been no significant breakthroughs in Soviet science. For every important scientific paper published by a Soviet, there are 30 published in America." He blamed the stifling intellectual and political climate. Later, in his essay, *My Country and the World*, Sakharov said the diversion of resources to the military and the elite had held back Soviet science and asserted that early Soviet space age achievements "and certain successes in military technology are the result of a monstrous concentration of resources in that sphere."[2] I knew other scientists, while less categorically self-critical than Sakharov, who privately shared his complaint that the general climate of controls—though eased from Stalin's time—still inhibit science, especially in the fastest developing fields.

Soviet science is hurt, they said, by poor communications among Soviet scientists who are terribly compartmentalized. Normally it takes a year or two for new findings to get into scholarly journals, a process that in the West can be cut to weeks or days for important breakthroughs and thus speed scientific progress. The ferment and fast moving exchange of ideas prevalent in Western science, I was told, is largely absent in Soviet science. A rising young physicist complained that even at Novosibirsk's *Akademgorodok* (Academic City), set up in the early 1960s to promote cross-fertilization of ideas among scientists in different fields, this did not go on any more. Nor do Soviet researchers share ideas informally by phone the way Westerners do. "No one talks about technical matters on the phone," a Moscow science writer told me. "People have the habit of not talking about anything that relates to secrecy." And Russians treat most science as falling in that category, for scientific papers require a special security clearance (known as the *akt ekspertisa*) to be published.

The Russians make a tremendous effort to cull all Western scientific publications for every scrap of useful information through the All-Union Institute for Scientific and Technical Information. While this represents a much more systematic effort to tap Western science than the West makes to monitor what the Soviets are doing, the centralized approach is often slow and cumbersome.

Soviet scientists pointed out to me that at times of experimental discoveries, modern science can move with great speed. Theorists compete to explain any new phenomenon. In this race, Soviet specialists complained that they are at a competitive disadvantage because of the information-lag, among other things. An able mathematician–physicist cited to me the discovery in mid-November 1974, by American scientists at the Stanford Linear Accelerator and Brookhaven National Laboratories, of the new psi-meson particle as an illustration of the short-comings of Soviet science. The Americans, this Russian said, had done better experimental work to achieve the breakthrough. With the fast flow of scientific information in the West, the discovery was confirmed by West German and Italian scientists within a couple of days. Although the Americans had also informed Soviet experimental nuclear centers at Dubna, Novosibirsk, and Serpukhov of their discovery, it was nearly 6 months before the Russian confirmation came through. My Russian scientist friend attributed this delay largely to Soviet equipment that was less precise than American or other Western equipment—atomic particle accelerators at Dubna and Novosibirsk, for example, that could not achieve the same particle-beam intensity as American accelerators be-cause of lower-grade electronic and magnetic technology. And because of restrictions on the flow of information and compartmentalization of Soviet science, he said, Soviet theoretical physicists were left in the dark and could not compete with Western rivals in explaining the new phenomenon.

Pravda had run four paragraphs on the American discovery initially, but only by chance, he said, did theoretical physicists at Moscow's prestigious Lebedev Institute learn the technical details they needed. A young Soviet physicist happened to be on academic exchange in Switzerland and sent a report by mail to his mentor, the theoretical physicist, Lev Okun, at the Lebedev Institute. Otherwise, my friend said, it would have been months before the technical report came into print and filtered through the Soviet bureaucracy to scientists who needed it. So frustrated was Professor Okun that when he briefed a closed meeting of important scientists in Moscow on the American discovery, my friend said, he pleaded for reforms "to speed up the exchange of information with the West and to solve the difficulties with experimental equipment or otherwise we will simply lag behind completely."

If science as an objective field of knowledge has to bend to political realities, then politics is presented to the Soviet public in cut-and-dried fashion to make it seem immutable and scientific. The front pages of the big dailies are so similar that they look as if they were laid out by one Managing Editor. (Indeed, I was told that Tass does circulate instructions on how to play stories.) And to the Western eye, the formula that he uses seems fated to kill readership—no scoops, no crime or sensations, no inside dope stories or background leaks, no social gossip columns on beautiful people, no bad news, stock market finals, comics, or race results. As one government worker remarked to me, "Reading our press is like eating dry noodles—no flavor." The staple of a paper like *Pravda* is an ample serving of what Lenin called "production propaganda" framed by smiling workers with blowtorches; windy, turgid, repetitive editorials; and political commentaries that cast the world in terms of irreconcilable class conflicts and malignant conspiracies against the Communist cause or the Soviet homeland. It represents advocacy journalism carried to the extreme, with little pretense at objectivity.

But *Pravda* claims the largest circulation in the world for any daily paper—more than 10 million—and gives every evidence of prospering even though it runs no ads and only charges 3 kopecks for a six-page paper. And for all the grumbling that I heard from intellectuals (some of whom made a point of boasting that they never read the Soviet press), it struck me that *Pravda* and other Soviet papers were serving their system rather effectively by their own lights, for they left no room for nagging doubts among their readers about the legitimacy of the system.

They do, however, make astonishing reading. Soviet history is treated as an unimpeded and uplifting march toward a more plentiful and joyous collective existence. Clichés reach a crescendo at Revolutionary holidays when commentaries embroider the party's rousing slogans: "Working people of the Soviet Union! Struggle for a Communist attitude toward labor. Hold public property sacred and multiply it. Strive for savings of raw materials, fuel, electric power, metals, and other materials. Workers in the national economy! Persistently master economic knowledge and up-to-date methods of economic management and administration. More widely introduce in production the scientific organization of labor, advanced experience, and the latest achievements of science and technology."

The average 30-minute nightly television newscast consists of a long feature on grain harvesting by "our outstanding collective farmers" at the Dawn of Communism Collective Farm in the Ukraine; a report that the shockworkers at the Magnitogorsk Metallurgical Combine have pledged to fulfill this year's economic plan 3 weeks ahead of time; and an interview with a Lebanese Communist who manages to answer one question with a nonstop, 5-minute recitation that varies only minutely from the latest *Pravda* commentary on the Middle East. These anchor items lead into riot pictures from Ireland, demonstrations outside the American Embassy in Greece, miscellaneous Soviet sports news, and weather reports. Accompaniment for the main items consists of stock newsreel shots of grain pouring into railroad cars, harvest combines in carefully staggered phalanxes rolling across fields, and steelworkers pouring molten steel into troughs, or white-hot ingots sliding toward the camera. The themes and pictures are unvaried day in and day out and seem to have very little connection to the date on which they are shown.

Dull as it strikes the Westerner, this kind of propaganda has a long-term subliminal effect on Russians. It plays to the deep-seated Russian instinct of national pride and collective identification with "our" national achievements. Individuals may privately scoff, but cumulatively this type of "news coverage" compensates for the obvious shortcomings that people see in their own lives.

Another objective, clearly, is to avoid any sense of excitement. The bigger the news, the smaller the story. When a Soviet airliner crashed in Moscow in October 1972, killing 176 persons (at that date, the largest civil aviation single-plane crash in history), it merited only two paragraphs from Tass. When the Soviet TU-144 supersonic transport split up in midair at the Paris Air Show on June 3, 1973, *Pravda* tucked 40 words away on the back page. But the epitome of Soviet news management during my tour came when Khrushchev died on September 11, 1971. The next morning, *The New York Times* ran a 10,000 word obituary and a roundup of Communist press reaction from around the world— excluding Moscow. The night he died, I went out on the streets to gather comment from ordinary Russians, but people were incredulous about the news and suspicious of me.

"Too bad, he was a sick old man," said a woman at a sidewalk vegetable stand, anxious to get rid of me.

"How do you know that?" skeptically inquired a movie cashier.

"I haven't seen anything in the press," parried an elderly man sliding away from me into a phone booth.

It was true. When the man who had ruled Russia for most of a decade died, the Soviet press was struck dumb. For 36 hours, we waited for a word about Khrushchev. Finally, there appeared a tiny item at the very bottom right-hand corner of the front page of *Pravda* and *Izvestia* (no other papers ran it)—one solitary sentence announcing the death of "pensioner Nikita Sergeyevich Khrushchev," squashed beneath a fat harvest report and a profile of the visiting King of Afghanistan.

The main reason for the delay, of course, was that the Kremlin leaders needed time to figure out how to handle Khrushchev, and 7 years after his ouster, they found him still too hot to handle. But the delay was also typical of the unhurried pace of Soviet journalism. Whenever I visited *Pravda* or *Izvestia*, there was none of the deadline frenzy of the Western press, the rush to beat competition into print. Senior journalists worked in roomy offices rather like American boardrooms done in Spartan furnishings and decorated with inspiring portraits of Lenin; and their pace was leisurely. The reason was obvious: news in our sense was not their primary business. At *Pravda*, editors told me that less than 20% of their paper was devoted to breaking news—unless Brezhnev or some other leader delivered a major speech, in which case it was simply printed verbatim. Visiting *Pravda* in late morning, I have frequently seen the next day's paper all ready except for a few blank holes. The page proofs were laid out, meaning that the stories had been put into type 2 or 3 days before and gone over with a fine tooth comb. *Pravda*'s 17-member editorial board meets at 11 A.M. to approve tomorrow's paper and put together the day after's. Such advance work enables *Pravda* and other Soviet papers to achieve a typographical perfection that would be the envy of any Western editor or reader. But even if a slip-up does occur, there would be no printed correction because *Pravda* does not admit mistakes (though occasionally other papers do).

The idiosyncrasies of the Soviet press produce special habits among Soviet readers. They usually pass up blockbuster commentaries and look for the little items with the real news—the 40 words on the TU-44 crash in Paris or the one-sentence obit on Khrushchev. Most announcements of big foreign trips by Brezhnev or Kosygin break the same way: in two-line items at the bottom of massive columns of type on the front page. This leads, of course, to reading from the bottom up.

People also told me they prefer to read *Pravda* from back to front, and the few newspaper polls about which I heard confirm that this generally reflects reader tastes (high on human interest, sports, and articles dealing with social mores, and low on ideology). People know, for example, that in 1957, word of Marshal Georgi Zhukov's ouster as Defense Minister ran in a back-page item labeled "Chronicle," and that the tip-off for Nixon's arrival time in 1972 was buried in *Pravda*'s back-page television diary. The expulsion of Aleksandr Solzhenitsyn in February 1974 was also a back-page short. But *Pravda*'s back page has other attractions—sports, chess, and cultural news, occasional human interest features or satirical exposés. Page five is the newiest of all in the Western sense because it runs breaking foreign news. Farther forward the going gets heavier.

Soviet readers become expert, too, at culling the kernel of news from the chaff of propaganda. Some intellectuals I knew got the message in 1973 that Egyptian President Anwar Sadat had expelled Soviet military advisers when the Soviet press ran a little item from Cairo saying that the Egyptians had thanked the Soviet advisers for completing their mission (though many other readers missed the point). Others divined the bad harvests of 1972 and 1974 by the failure of the press to run its usual glowing crop reports. One couple I knew figured out there had been a big airplane crash (near Sochi) after noticing five unusual husband and wife obituaries regretting their "untimely deaths"—a circumlocution often used for accidental deaths. Yet another technique is to work backward from the penchant of Soviet propagandists to project Soviet problems onto other countries.

"If you read in our press about a big airplane crash in America, it means there's been a crash in the Soviet Union," said a woman from a children's publishing house.

"That's not quite true," her husband, a journalist, corrected her. "What happens is this: if in Russia there was an airplane crash, then for the next month, the Soviet press will run stories about airplane crashes in America, West Germany, Formosa—anywhere. That's how you can tell we had one." The same logic applies, he said, to health epidemics, price increases, crime waves, harvest setbacks, water shortages, jailing of political prisoners, and so on. Western problems are reported as object lessons in the miseries of life under capitalism and to distract people from similar difficulties at home. "It's very effective propaganda: 'Life is bad under capitalism; it was terrible under the tsars,'" a young scientist remarked. "People may not yet be convinced that life here is as perfect as the press pretends. But the masses do believe that it is worse elsewhere."

Despite the similarity of Soviet front pages, the Western image of absolute uniformity throughout the Soviet press is inaccurate. The spectrum may be narrow, but there are some variations—from the conservative Cold-War right of *Red Star*, the Armed Forces newspaper; stodgy *October* magazine; and the neo-Stalinist, *Young Guard*, monthly to the more modern-minded youth newspaper, *Komsomolskaya Pravda*; and the mildly liberal, *New World*, magazine. By far the most interesting newspaper in recent years, however, has been *Literary Gazette*, the Writers' Union weekly that has been an important outlet for the tenuous budding of sociology in the Soviet Union. No other newspaper has gone so far in trying to deal realistically with some contemporary Soviet social problems, within the limits prescribed by censors. On occasion, *Literaturka*, as it is known among devotees, nibbles at the fringes of policy. It took a lead in the battle against industrial pollution of Lake Baikal in Siberia and has delved into the issues of traffic congestion, pollution, urban transportation, inadequate service and supply of spare parts raised by the belated and uncoordinated Soviet plunge into the auto age. One series, quite impressive to me, documented the sharp disadvantages in pay, housing, and other benefits to workers in consumer industries compared to those in heavy industry. The implication, though nothing was directly stated, was that the Kremlin was not living up to its pledge to give consumers a better deal. *Literaturka* has also run articles probing the causes for the high Soviet divorce rate, decrying the pressures of the university entrance examination system, humorously mocking the disastrous inadequacies of consumer services, and once—albeit gingerly and with a protective citation from a Brezhnev speech—even suggesting that the Soviet Union experiment with privately run cooperative service shops to improve the situation.

Nor is *Literaturka* unique in pointing up problems in Soviet life. Criticism of shortcomings is obligatory for the Soviet press. Soviet editors I knew used to brag that they were "watchdogs for the people," and "we have our investigative reporters like you." The analogy is beguiling but misleading.

The Soviet press does have a watchdog role, and Soviet officialdom does genuinely fear exposés in its own press. "Journalists are very dangerous people," a Soviet sports official once remarked to me. "You talk to them. They write something down. And if it comes out in ways that other people do not like, you have to answer for it." He made clear he meant not only foreign journalists but Soviet ones as well. Later, a Moscow journalist showed me a case of choice *Gorilka*, Ukrainian pepper vodka, that he had brought home from Kiev, "a gift" from Ukrainian officials to persuade him to cover up some malfeasance he had found.

Pravda does its own special kind of muckraking week in and week out. In one month, I noticed for example, that it scolded brewery, tannery, and automotive enterprises in the Siberian city of Chita for building factories without providing housing for their workers; it castigated Yuri Shikhaliyev, head of the Karadag Carbon Black Plant in Baku, for the soot and pollution that his plant was spewing out over the city; it chastised A. Pokrovskaya, forewoman at the Novograd-Volynsky Meat Combine, for letting her workers steal hoards of huge salami sausages from work; it upbraided the Ministry of the Paper Industry for failing to provide enough paper for books and magazines; and it ran a revealing report that "many [Soviet] villages are still without water, gas, and the entire array of consumer services."

These "self-criticisms," as they are known in Soviet parlance, have two common elements. First of all, with the exception of the rural article, they are focused on individual plants, directors, foremen, or ministries. They fit the motto quoted to me by one Soviet journalist, "Criticize But Don't Generalize." In other words, it's all right to find fault in a particular situation, but do not write general conclusions because that is politically dangerous. This is precisely the point of Soviet "muckraking"—find flaws to touch up the overall masterpiece. Nonetheless, there is an inherent paradox in major criticisms that appear in papers like *Pravda*. Each case of corruption or mismanagement in some distant city or province is treated in print as an isolated shortcoming, and yet by giving it prominence in the national press, the party bosses are signaling their nationwide apparatus that this is a general problem to be dealt with forthwith.

The second common element is that the criticisms that I cited—and the bulk of those that appear in the press—are made from top downward, on behalf of the leadership, pointing out errors of executions by middle-level management or petty bureaucrats. The infallible wisdom of the party—of Brezhnev, the Politburo, the Party Central Committee, the party as a corporate body, and party policy—is always protected. The very vocabulary of Soviet "self-criticism" is designed to avoid making, or inviting, moral or policy judgments. Soviet "muckrakers" expose "shortcomings" or "mistakes," but they do not spotlight outright failures. This has the effect of appeasing the masses by conveying the impression that problems are recognized on high without ever letting on that some policy may be wrong, that different elements of society have conflicting interests, or that something is fundamentally amiss with Soviet life.

"It may sound strange to you," one Soviet journalist commented to me privately, "but the kind of criticism that we print in our press has the effect of increasing popular acceptance of the idea that the Soviet system is sound, and that it is only a few officials who are bad." A persuasive observation, I found, one echoed by people I knew who had close contact with ordinary working people—Gennadi, the state farm accountant, and Yuri, the young metal worker. Soviets privately grouse about their living conditions, complain about corruption, mock the pretenses of their ideology, and privately joke about their leaders, but they accept the system as fundamentally sound, as paradoxical as that may seem. It never seems to strike more than a mere handful of dissidents and perhaps some hidden loyal oppositionists within the establishment that anything major is on the wrong track.

Moreover, contrary to what many people think in the West, the Soviet press does offer a safety valve for minor grass roots dissatisfaction—letters to the editors. I was surprised to discover that it is big business. *Pravda* gets close to 40,000 letters a month and has 45 people in its letters department. *Liberary Gazette* gets 7000 letters a month, and one of the reform efforts in which its chief editor, Aleksandr Chakovsky, takes the greatest pride was prompted by reader letters several years ago. After so many readers had complained about bad mail service, *Literaturka* decided to experiment for itself. It sent out test batches of mail, found it took nearly 5 days for a letter to reach Leningrad (comparable in distance from New York to Chicago), 6 days to Tbilisi, and nearly 8 to Novosibirsk. *Literaturka* ran several articles chastising the Communications Ministry and now claims credit for helping to establish the Soviet postal code to speed the sorting of mail (though more recent articles suggest that mail service is not much faster now).

"We're not afraid of criticism," Chakovsky rumbled at several American reporters one afternoon in his office. Chakovsky is a large, portly man with an ego to match his girth, a fondness for smoking cigars down to the nub and then spraying ash over the table as he lisps in quite competent but heavily accented English, affecting confidentiality about Soviet life with comments like, "I'll tell you candidly," or "Let me give you a sophisticated answer." As a ranking party man, he invites ideological combat and kiddingly calls himself "a shark of socialism" (for all its liberalism on some domestic issues, his paper has spearheaded vitriolic attacks on Sakharov, Solzhenitsyn, emigrating Jews, and Western journalists).

"*The New York Times* thinks its task is over after a reader's letter is printed," Chakovsky puffed at me. "But we think the task begins with printing letters. After that, we expect an immediate reply from the responsible agency, and this reply is also printed in our newspaper. If the reply does not satisfy us or seems too formal, we write an editor's note that we consider the reply of this particular ministry or agency unsatisfactory and demand a more detailed and thorough answer." Sometimes it does work out that way (if the party wants) but Chakovsky made it sound considerably more fearless and independent-minded than his own staff later described it to me in private. They cited cases where reporting had been stopped or articles killed because they ran afoul of some party official, even at a pretty low level. One writer recalled repeated efforts merely to expose a party-backed scholar guilty of fraudulent work that had ended in the wastebasket. This was not to mention all the topics, like frictions among Soviet nationalities or the privileges of the Soviet elite, which editors and reporters know are taboo from the outset.

But the regime generally finds letters useful. They give ordinary Soviets a chance to vent their frustrations at the notoriously inefficient bureaucracy, to sound off about poor consumer goods, and to let off steam generally. In the process, they give the party an excellent means for monitoring the behavior of officialdom as well as the morals and attitudes of the general citizenry. In effect, letters trigger the press in its watchdog role. And for editors, they sometimes provide some sauce to season the dry ideological noodles.

Nor is there any great risk taken. Most letters that get into print are fairly innocuous: the woman in Dnepropetrovsk who is angry because her apartment walls are like iron and she cannot drive in a nail or a hook to hang pictures and curtains; the Moscow teacher irked by the long hair and rumpled outfits of Soviet soccer players; the workers at Bratsk supposedly irate to discover that their factory is supporting a bunch of professional athletes who theoretically work at the factory but actually play soccer—and poorly; the mother in Odessa disturbed by her teenage daughter's acquisitive instincts; women complaining about drunken husbands.

Sometimes, as two writers for *Literary Gazette* told me, newspapers deliberately stir up readers with "provocative articles" intended to generate letters. Then they manipulate the responses to keep debates sputtering on uselessly for years. One perennial topic is alcoholism; another is whether husbands should help working wives more with the housework and shopping. A third dead-ender, flogged during my 3 years by *Literary Gazette,* was whether more flunking grades should be given in Soviet schools. This is not to mention the inspired letters that staffers told me were actually written by the newspapers themselves or by Communist party activists and then foisted on ordinary workers or big-name intellectuals to sign in order to make it appear as though the party line was riding a groundswell of popular support. "We used to have lists of people to call—some of them very important writers—and we would simply tell them what the party expected them to say," said one former *Literary Gazette* staffer.

Suicidal as it sounds, people also send letters that oppose the party line. "I know for sure that during the campaign against Solzhenitsyn and Sakharov (1973), *Literaturka* got some letters supporting these two men and other letters saying that it was wrong for people to denounce them without even knowing what they have said or without printing what they have written," one staff writer told me. "But of course these letters are not printed. Once a month, a KGB official comes to our office and goes through our letters. Always he takes some away with him, usually the *anonymkas* [anonymous ones]." Other letter writers are sometimes publicly denounced for wayward views. *Leningradskaya Pravda* once scolded four readers by name for their letters—one for abusive language, a second for opposing the policy of détente with the United States, a third for declaring that it was "our duty to help Israel in its defensive war against Arab extremists and nationalists," and a fourth for saying that Soviet society was divided into rich and poor classes.

Occasionally, editors themselves seem to veer mistakenly toward touchy topics and are steered back on course by some higher authority. The newspaper, *Soviet Russia*, once opened a new column on "The Female Problem" with a letter from a distraught lady economist who complained bitterly about the double burden of women and proposed that women get more pay, shorter hours, and be given more time to raise their children. The newspaper invited reader responses, but no follow-up column ever appeared. Obviously, the party had no intention of reducing women's working hours because they are too essential to the economy to be let off with part-time jobs.

Some who have worked with readers' mail on the inside told me they regarded the show of debate on social issues a charade because it is so thoroughly manipulated behind the scenes. There are exceptions, one writer said, when some leadership faction wants to use reader complaints to advance a viewpoint or to put pressure on other officials for its own purposes. On rare occasions, other letters slip by censors and raise important issues. But the entire process is crippled by the dictum, "Criticize But Don't Generalize," and it is here, perhaps, that Soviet censorship is playing its most vital function.

In the West, Soviet censorship has a reputation for suppressing bad news like airplane crashes or political purges, or for turning Trotsky, Khrushchev, and other foes of the regime into nonpersons. But what is more important is that on behalf of the Soviet elite, the system of censorship suppresses the facts of life in many areas that seem to have no obvious connection with national security or the political secrets of Soviet rulers—and this cripples independent public discussion of almost any serious issue.

I was once given five pages of typed notes summarizing the basic censor's list. It was a tiny fragment from the huge looseleaf notebooks used by *Glavlit*, the Soviet censorship organization left over, curiously enough, from tsarist times. It contained the expected prohibitions against printing certain material about the military, the operations of the secret police, the system of correctional labor camps, about censorship itself, about foreign aid doled out by the Soviet Union and foreign credits received by it, or about putting out advance word on the movement and whereabouts of Soviet leaders.

But what intrigued me far more were the bans on more innocent sounding things: data on the amount of crime and numbers of arrests; the number of uncared-for children; the number of people engaged in vagrancy or begging; the number of drug addicts; about illness in the population from cholera, the plague, and other diseases including chronic alcoholism; about industrial poisonings and vocational illness; about occupational injuries; about human victims of accidents, wrecks, and fires; about the consequences of earthquakes, tidal waves, floods, and other natural calamities; about the duration of training camps for athletes, "their rates of pay, the money prizes paid to them for good performances," and the financing, upkeep, and staff of sports teams.

Anyone who has followed the Soviet press for any length of time can expand that list from simple observation. The information gaps in the press are enormous—nationwide statistics on the number of people still living in communal apartments; on the amount of labor turnover; on how successful women really are in their careers; on who gets to go abroad; on the social breakdown of those who get into universities; on the real earning power of members of the Soviet elite (including pay, bonuses, prizes, and other perquisites); on the relative costs and standards of living in various parts of the country (which a Siberian journalist admitted to me were deliberately suppressed "because it might bring pressure from people who feel at a disadvantage"); on the relative availability of social services in rural areas compared to cities; on just what percentage of the applicants for hospital beds, rooms in sanatoria, subsidized vacations, or other welfare benefits, get satisfaction; on class attitudes of various strata of Soviet society or the attitudes of various minority nationalities toward Russians and each other.

What is striking about such a list is that the Soviet people are being denied an accurate general picture of their own life and their own society, let alone a chance to compare it with other societies. Censorship prevents that. Some articles, often based on localized sociological studies, do appear from time to time touching on some of the important social issues that I have mentioned. But by and large, the party's monopoly of the means of communication makes it not only exceedingly difficult for divergent viewpoints to find public expression but also for independent public opinion to form on any issue. In consequence, as the young Karl Marx observed, censorship breeds public hypocrisy, political skepticism, and people "become a crowd of individuals, each living only his own private existence." I have heard that sad cry from Soviet intellectuals.

"We are an atomized society," a bearded writer lamented to me from his daybed one afternoon. "We do not know what is really happening in our own society and what other people really think. I know what my own small circle thinks, and a bit about other intellectuals in Moscow maybe. But I do not know what workers really think or much about their lives, or what collective farmers really think or much about their lives. We live in separate worlds and we have no common world except the one the party gives us to read about. The only time I mix with people of other classes is when my old military unit holds its annual reunion and we all get drunk together remembering the war. Otherwise we are strangers to one another."

Notes

[1] In his book, *On Socialist Democracy* (Knopf, New York, 1975), Medvedev has an excellent chapter on how the entire censorship mentality has constricted Soviet intellectual activity in literature, the arts, and science. His brother, Zhores Medvedev, in *The Medvedev Papers* (MacMillan, London, 1971) has a long section on problems of Soviet scientists.

[2] Andrei Sakharov, *My Country and the World* (Knopf, New York, 1975).

24

STEPHEN WHITE

The Effectiveness of
Political Propaganda in the USSR*

Both Western and Soviet commentators have normally agreed that among the most distinctive features of the Soviet political system is the central importance it attaches to ideology. The theorists of totalitarianism, among the former, held that all totalitarian states, such as the USSR, were characterized by six essential traits or features, the first of which was an "elaborate ideology consisting of an official body of doctrine covering all vital aspects of man's existence to which everyone in that society is supposed to adhere, at least passively." Evolve though it might, they wrote, it would be "impossible to write a meaningful history of the USSR without giving sustained attention to ideological issues"; matters of this kind were "decisively important" in the leadership thinking, mass politics, and constitutions and laws of the USSR and the societies it resembled.[1] More recent Western scholarship has not normally followed Friedrich and Brzezinski closely. It has, however, generally agreed that among the features distinguishing Communist-ruled from other states is the fact that the "official ideology of all these states is Marxism–Leninism,"[2] and that it is this ideology that legitimates the leading role of the party and functions as the system's "secular religion."[3] Soviet spokesmen show similarly little diffidence in claiming that the Soviet political system is a "qualitatively new type of political system . . . the ideological basis of which is Marxism–Leninism,"[4] an ideology which "has conquered the consciousness of the absolute majority of the Soviet people [and] has become the inspiration of their socio-political and labour activism."[5]

*Reprinted in revised form by permission of the author and publisher from *Soviet Studies* 32, no. 3 (July 1980), pp. 323–348. Copyright 1980 by University of Glasgow Press.

The attempt to develop a mass political consciousness of this kind has been the object of a lengthy and intensive process of political education and propaganda whose origins go back to the foundation of the regime in 1917 and even (for party members at least) beyond it.[6] The present structure and dimensions of this system are set out in Tables 1 and 2. The numbers engaged at all levels of this system have been increasing steadily since its reconstitution in its present form in the mid-1960s. The total number of students enrolled in the system of political and eco-

TABLE 1. *The System of Political and Economic Education*[a]

Level	Form and period of study	Students (millions) 1976–1977	1980–1981	Subjects of study
Primary	Talks and discussion; 5–6 year period of study	2.4	10.2	Biography of Lenin, fundamentals of political and economic knowledge, current party policy
Intermediate	Lectures and discussion; 6-8 year period of study	8.0		History of the CPSU political economy, Marxist–Leninist philosophy, fundamentals of scientific communism
Advanced	Mainly independent study and practical work; period of study depends upon form concerned	10.4	12.4	Various; depends upon form of advanced study concerned
Komsomol	Talks and discussion	7.1	8.7	Komsomol history, biography of Lenin, fundamentals of Marxism–Leninism, current party policy
Economic	Talks and discussion	31.0	38.0	Economic and production questions and current party policy

[a]Sources: *Partiinaya zhizn'*, no. 21 (1977), p. 42; N. A. Petrovichev *et al.*, eds., *Partiinoe stroitel'stvo. Uchebnoe posobie*, 5th ed. (Moscow, 1978), pp. 310–315; *Spravochnik partiinogo rabotnika*, vyp. 21 (Moscow, 1981), p. 502.

TABLE 2. *The Mass Agitation System*[a]

Conducted by	Numbers (millions)		Typical method of work
	1976–1977	1980–1981	
Agitators	3.7	4.1	15–20 minute talk or discussion (*beseda*) usually on production theme; normally conducted weekly
Political instructors (*politinformatory*)	1.8	2.1	20–30 minute lecture (*politinformatsiya*) on economic, political, cultural, or international theme; conducted three or four times a month.
Lecturers (*dokladchiki*)	0.3	0.3	1–2 hour lecture (*lektsiya*) on major questions of foreign or domestic policy; conducted on important occasions, anniversaries, etc.
Znanie (Knowledge) Society lecturers	3.0	3.2	Lectures on philosophy, party history, popular science, etc.; varying frequency

[a]Sources: *Partiinaya zhizn'*, no. 10, (1976), p. 23; M. P. Gabdulin *et al.*, *Agitator, politinformator, dokladchik* (Moscow, 1978), pp. 14–19; *Spravochnik partiinogo rabotnika*, vyp. 21 (Moscow, 1981), p. 502.

nomic education, for instance, has increased from 11.1 million in 1965/66 to over 22 million at present, or more than 70 million if the Komsomol and economic education systems are included;[7] and at the level of talks and lectures delivered to the mass of the population, a level described as "mass-political work" or *Agitprop*, an even more impressive rate of growth has been recorded.[8] Taken together with other aspects of the "ideological work of the party," such as education, literature, the arts, and the mass media, a system of political instruction and persuasion has come into being that is probably unprecedented in its scope and intensity.

The practical effect of this vast effort is less easy to determine. The regime itself certainly claims, as the Central Committee resolution on the sixtieth anniversary of the October Revolution put it, that over the six decades of Soviet rule, a new "Soviet man" has come into existence whose labor achievements, bravery in war, and class solidarity have shown his "deep commitment to the ideals of communism, fiery patriotism and internationalism"; a man who "combines in himself ideological conviction and enormous vital energy, a constant striving for the heights of knowledge and culture [and] a feeling of collectivism and comradely mutual assistance," the "content of whose life has become inspired labor for the sake of communism."[9] Western scholars have generally been sceptical of such claims. Alfred Meyer, however, has argued that "Soviet citizenship training has succeeded and the main tenets of the ideology have been internalized," and Samuel Huntington and Jorge I. Dominguez more recently have argued that "the most dramatically successful case of planned political cultural change is probably the Soviet Union."[10] None of these authors deploys a body of evidence in support of his conclusions, however, and in its absence the sceptics have, not surprisingly, persisted.[11]

It is not the purpose of this chapter to suggest that a definitive verdict can even now be reached upon such matters. The development of sociological inquiry into a number of aspects of party work in the USSR, however, and into the effectiveness of ideological work in particular, does permit at least a closer approximation to such a verdict than has previously been possible. The role of sociology in party work was first authoritatively endorsed in the mid-1960s,[12] since when fairly active sociological groups or commissions, normally on an unpaid basis, have come into existence under the auspices of the Moscow, Leningrad, Chelyabinsk, Tomsk, Sverdlovsk, and other party organizations.[13] Sociological research into various aspects of party work has also been conducted at a number of other institutions, among them the Academy of Social Sciences attached to the Central Committee of the CPSU, whose Department of Ideological Work has sponsored investigations into the system of political and economic education since about 1972 and into mass-agitational work since about 1974.[14] It is upon such sources that this chapter in the main is based.

It must immediately be conceded that much sociological work of this kind is subject to a variety of shortcomings, a number of which Soviet scholars have themselves identified. The samples employed, for instance, may be unduly small, the formulation of questions may leave a lot to be desired, respondents may be given only a limited number of "approved" responses from which to choose, and even elementary arithmetical errors and inconsistencies are not unknown.[15] Party committees have complained in addition that many such inquiries have simply told them what they already knew,[16] that research of this kind may become the "latest craze" and be engaged in for its own sake,[17] and that many of the recommendations that are made for the improvement of party work are impracticable and banal.[18] The technical level of Soviet sociological inquiry is steadily rising, however, and in the investigation of ideological matters as in other areas, the repetition of a finding from one investigation to another, however doubtful the investigation considered individually, does tend to suggest that it rests upon something more substantial than a biased sample or other methodological deficiency.[19] The discussion that follows sets out the main findings that have been reached under a variety of headings; a final section considers what overall conclusions may be drawn from them.

Political Propaganda: Some Indicators of Effectiveness

The *motives for attendance* at political lectures and classes, in the first place, vary considerably in character, with a distinct and sometimes substantial minority explaining their attendance simply in terms of external pressure of some sort. A study conducted by sociologists attached to the Chelyabinsk party organization, for instance, found that of the more than 3000 workers who were polled 72.2% attended political information sessions "with enthusiasm"; 64.6% considered that such sessions "widened their horizons"; 55.7% noted that they obtained answers to the questions that most concerned them; and 45% believed that political information sessions developed their "independence of judgment and conviction of opinions." Some 15.8% of those polled, at the same time, replied that they attended political information sessions unwillingly, and a further 12% declined to answer the question.[20] Inquiries elsewhere have found still lower levels of support and interest. In Taganrog and Saransk, for instance, 35% of those polled reported that the main reason for their attendance at such sessions was "party discipline," "administrative pressure," or a "feeling of duty and obligation,"[21] and in investigations in Moscow, Taganrog, and the town of Mukachevo, 27.3% of those polled expressed little or no interest in the political information sessions they attended.[22]

Political information sessions, moreover, are consistently the most popular form of mass-agitational work,[23] and the evidence suggests that agitational *besedy* and political *lektsii* are regarded with a good deal less enthusiasm. In a poll at a tire factory in Dnepropetrovsk, for instance, 86.2% of those polled expressed an interest in political information sessions compared with only 61.8% who expressed an interest in political lectures (*lektsii*) and 61.2% who expressed in interest in agitational *besedy* (38.8% said frankly that they had no interest whatsoever in such sessions, compared with 13.8% who expressed no interest in political information sessions, and 12.9% who expressed no interest in political lectures (*lektsii*)).[24] Party spokesmen have acknowledged that many *besedy* and *politinformatsii* are "superficial and lacking in content" and that they are "held irregularly and attended unwillingly";[25] so far, however, no solution appears to have been found.

Political education classes should be attended more willingly, directed as they are for the most part toward a smaller and largely self-selected group of activists. A number of investigations have indeed found that between 70 and 90% of those who attended such classes report that they do so willingly and are satisfied with them;[26] and some studies have found that those who attend their classes with enthusiasm have been increasing somewhat in recent years as a proportion of the total enrolment.[27] Investigations in other areas, however, have found a less gratifying picture. In the industrial town of Kamensk in Rostov *oblast*, for instance, 39% of those polled said that they attended their political education classes "because they were obliged to do so";[28] in a poll in the Komi ASSR, a similar proportion replied that they attended their political education classes unwillingly because they saw no necessity for them or found them boring;[29] and in a somewhat earlier investigation at a number of enterprises in Moscow, Chita, and Polotsk, as many as 50.8% replied that they attended their political education classes "reluctantly" (*bez zhelaniya*).[30] Those with higher education appear more likely to manifest a lack of enthusiasm about political education classes than their less well-educated colleagues;[31] but lack of enthusiasm is by no means a monopoly of the better educated. In a poll in a Leningrad factory, for instance, no fewer than 75% of respondents declared that they attended political education classes because they were obliged to do so by party or administrative pressure, and a further 5% reported that they attended simply because they "didn't want to offend the lecturer." This interesting finding, not surprisingly, was omitted from the published version of this study.[32]

The *interest* shown in political lectures and education classes has also been the subject of investigation. In political lectures, for instance, it appears that current topics are consistently more popular than theoretical ones, that foreign topics are more popular than domestic ones, and that sociocultural topics are more popular than philosophical or economic ones. In an investigation in the town of Taganrog, for instance, respondents were asked what kind of information they most liked to receive at political lectures. Some 61% of those polled replied that they were most interested in current affairs; 36% were attracted equally toward current affairs and toward theory; only 1%, however, expressed a preference for more lectures of a purely theoretical character.[33] The subjects in which respondents expressed most interest were international affairs, current national and local affairs (96, 95, and 94%, respectively, of all respondents); there was less interest in the history of the CPSU, with just 50% of respondents expressing an interest in this theme, and Marxist–Leninist philosophy, political economy, and scientific communism attracted the least support of all (37, 40, and 37%, respectively, expressed an interest in these areas, or only 17, 22, and 19%, respectively, of those who did not normally attend lectures).[34]

About 42% of those who attended lectures sponsored by the *Znanie* Society in Chelyabinsk similarly expressed a preference for more lectures on international affairs, compared with only 1.3% who expressed an interest in more lectures on Marxist–Leninist philosophy and 1.8% who wanted more lectures on scientific communism.[35]

The results obtained in a detailed survey of preferences on this question at three factories in Stavropol' *krai* and Moscow *oblast* are set out in Table 3; and similar results have been reported elsewhere. In the Mordovian ASSR, for instance, 79% of the workers who were polled expressed a "consistent and predominant interest" in international affairs and 47% in sport, compared with only 22%, who were mainly interested in economic matters and 17% who were more interested in questions of national politics and culture;[36] and in a series of surveys conducted by the Academy of Social Sciences attached to the Central Committee of the CPSU, some 98% of those polled expressed an interest in current national and international affairs, compared with only 30% who were interested in economic matters.[37] The general preference reported in these and other studies for a greater number of lectures on current and international affairs rather than on Marxist philosophy and economics is remarkably consistent and appears to vary little by education, occupation, nationality, or age group.[38]

There have been fewer investigations into the relative popularity of the various subjects studied within the framework of the political education system.[39] Levels of interest in political study more generally have, however, been recorded, and the conclusions that emerge are scarcely ones that party activists could regard with gratification. A study conducted in Dnepropetrovsk, for instance, found that 62.4% of those polled expressed some interest in their studies, but that 22.5% had little interest in their studies and that 15.1% had no interest at all.[40] A more detailed investigation conducted in the Tomsk and Mogilev *oblasts* found that levels of interest varied considerably depending upon the level of political education concerned (Table 4). At no level, however, was there a degree of interest in political study which could be described as overwhelming, and at three of the four levels considered, fewer than one-half of the students had an interest in their studies that the propagandists responsible for them could describe as "deep and stable." In Tomsk alone, 38% of propagandists described the interest of their students in political study as deep and stable, 60% described it as superficial and unstable, and 2% thought it was nonexistent.[41]

Perhaps not surprisingly, the *content* of political lectures and classes has also been giving rise to some concern. Investigations at a number of industrial enterprises in Moscow, for instance, found that many respondents identified a "whole series of shortcomings" in the political information session they attended. About 20% of those polled complained of the lack of attention given in the sessions they attended to the affairs

TABLE 3. *Preferences in Political Lectures*[a,b]

	Nevinnomyssk chemical combine		*"Elektroavtomatika"* factory, Stavropol'		*"Elektrostal"* factory, *oblast* Moscow	
Subject	Per-centage	Rank order	Per-centage	Rank order	Per-centage	Rank order
International af-fairs	34.4	1	33.4	1	57.3	1
Problems of family and life	31.1	2	26.2	2	18.4	5=
Problems of morality and law	25.5	3	20.2	3	35.9	2
Pedagogy, up-bringing of children	25.3	4	17.8	4	18.4	5=
Literature and art	23.2	5	17.3	5	19.4	4
Industrial af-fairs of col-lective	10.8	6	11.9	6	24.3	3
Philosophy	3.7	7=	1.7	9	11.0	7
Political economy	3.7	7=	1.4	10	4.0	9=
Economic and social policy of the CPSU	2.4	9	2.5	8	4.0	9=
History of the CPSU	2.0	10	4.2	7	5.8	8
Scientific com-munism	1.2	11	1.3	11	3.0	11

[a]Source: G. T. Zhuravlev, ed., *Ideologicheskaya rabota i formirovanie obshchestven-nogo mneniya v trudovom kollektive* (Moscow,1978), pp. 47–48.
[b]Data in percentages and rank order.

of the local enterprise and area; about 17% criticized the superficial level of discussion; 14% found such sessions boring; and 9.5% complained that they were not given convincing replies to the questions they raised.[42] An investigation into *Znanie* Society lectures in Lithuania found similarly that as many as 80% of those who were polled complained of their "insufficiently convincing argumentation" and more than 13% of

TABLE 4. *Interest in Political Education*[a,b]

| | Proportion of all students | Level of interest in studies | | |
Level		Deep and stable	Superficial and unstable	None
Primary	11	56	44	0
Intermediate	53	40	60	0
Advanced	25	47	51	2
Komsomol	11	9	80	11

[a]Source: V. G. Baikova, ed., *Politicheskoe obrazovanie: sistema, metodika, metodologiya* (Moscow, 1976), p. 224.
[b]Assessed by propagandists concerned. Data in percentages.

the lecturer's boring or inexpressive delivery.[43] We've been here forty-five minutes," remarked a member of the audience at one such session; "Isn't that enough?" And nobody, including the lecturer, had objected to concluding the proceedings at that point.[44] Surveys have found a consistent preference for a "prompt response to events," "depth of argumentation," and "clear replies to questions" in such sessions and for more active forms of discussion such as "evenings of questions and answers," round table discussions, and "thematic evenings";[45] no more than 1.1% in an investigation of this subject said that they would listen with more attention to a lecturer who simply read out the text in front of him.[46] It is sessions of this kind, however, that appear generally to predominate.

Not all political talks and lectures, admittedly, seem to suffer from these shortcomings. Sometimes, to judge from newspaper reports, the proceedings may be given over to matters of universal appeal such as sports results or the funny stories from newspaper humor columns.[47] More seriously, perhaps, a number of Soviet émigrés now resident in Israel have told the present author that political information sessions in academic and other institutions might occasionally, if the participants were willing, be directed toward more interesting and relatively unorthodox subjects.[48] Political information sessions appear also to be used to put forward a point of view with which the regime has so far found it inexpedient to associate itself publicly, such as relatively crude anti-Semitism,[49] or to explore public reactions to policy alternatives that cannot yet be discussed in the official press.[50] Sessions of this kind appear to be the exception rather than the rule, however, and criticisms of the lecturer's "superficiality," "avoidance of awkward questions," and "lack of novelty" are much more frequently encountered.[51] From the point of view of the party authorities, moreover, it must be particularly disturbing to find that those with a higher education— an increasing proportion of the total population—are both more demanding of the standard of political lectures and more critical of those that they themselves receive.[52]

The content of political education classes has given rise to complaints of a similar nature. There are repeated criticisms, for instance, of the "low ideological and theoretical level" of many classes, of the propagandist's "oversimplified approach" to many problems, and of his failure to link the subject under discussion with the practical tasks facing the local workgroup in question.[53] Some propagandists conduct classes which are frequently cancelled, badly attended, and in which the lectures are simply a "dry recapitulation of various chapters of the textbook";[54] others conduct no classes at all but nonetheless announce that they have taken place.[55] The composition of many study groups is far from uniform in its educational and occupational make-up,[56] and the amount of preparation that is done for classes is often embarrassingly low.[57] Levels of activism in classes appear to vary a good deal depending upon the level of the political education system that is considered (Table 5), but in general there appears to be less active participation in classes at the higher levels at which an increasing proportion of all students are enrolled.[58] In this and a number of other surveys, it has also been found that the higher the level of study, the less preparation for classes appears to be done,[59] and the higher the level of education, the more dissatisfied the student tends to feel with his classes and the less he feels his knowledge of the subjects concerned has been advanced.[60]

The impact of political lectures and education classes upon *political knowledge* is less easy to determine. Those who attend such lectures and classes regularly do, at least, appear to be better informed about a

TABLE 5. *Levels of Activism of Students in Political Education Classes*[a,b]

Level of party study	Take part in every class	Rarely take part	Do not take part	Prepare synopsis once a year	Do so two or three times a year	Do not do so
Primary	41.6	19.4	2.7	19.4	38.8	2.7
Intermediate	29.2	27.6	3.7	9.2	38.4	3.7
Advanced	5.4	18.9	2.7	27.2	29.7	16.2

[a]Source: G. T. Zhuravlev, ed., *Ideologicheskaya rabota i formirovanie obshchestvennogo mneniya v trudovom kollektive* (Moscow, 1977), p. 39. (Based on an investigation carried out at industrial enterprises in Chernovsty, Ukrainian SSR, and the town of Stavropol'.)

[b]Data in percentages.

variety of political matters than their counterparts who attend such sessions less regularly or not at all. The results that were obtained in an investigation into this question at a factory in Gorky, for instance, are set out in Table 6. Regular attenders of political information sessions and agitational *besedy* emerge up to twice as well informed as nonattenders, with political information sessions in particular markedly increasing most respondents' ability to deal with major aspects of Soviet foreign and domestic policy.[61] Those who attend political information sessions and lectures regularly are also, according to other surveys, more likely to read a daily newspaper, to listen to the radio, and to watch informational and sociopolitical programs on television.[62]

Those who attend political lectures and information sessions most regularly, however, do not necessarily appear to be better informed because of their attendance at such sessions. On the contrary, it is acknowledged in many sources that it is the better informed and educated who are in the first place more likely to attend, with the talks and lectures themselves making little difference to their levels of political knowledge and information.[63] At a number of industrial enterprises in central Russia, for instance, it was found that the proportion of workers

TABLE 6. *Political Knowledge and Attendance at Political Information Sessions and Agitational* Besedy[a,b]

		Political information sessions		Agitational *besedy*	
		Attend regularly	Do not attend	Attend regularly	Do not attend
Knowledge of reasons for relaxation in international tensions	Good	43.4	24.6	47.2	36.5
	Satisfactory	41.2	35.1	36.1	29.6
	Unsatisfactory	15.4	40.3	16.7	23.9
Knowledge of main events in development of relaxation of international tensions	Good	49.6	29.8	57.1	37.2
	Satisfactory	38.1	31.6	34.3	35.1
	Unsatisfactory	12.3	38.6	8.6	27.7
Knowledge of means for improving effectiveness of national economy	Good	51.9	24.6	43.4	33.9
	Satisfactory	32.3	42.1	36.3	43.2
	Unsatisfactory	15.8	33.3	20.3	22.9

[a]Source: V. G. Baikova, *Ideologicheskaya rabota KPSS v usloviyakh razvitogo sotsializma* (Moscow, 1977), p. 150.
[b]Data in percentages.

who reported that agitational *besedy* were among their principal sources of information varied between 2 and 6%; at two factories in Stavropol' *krai* the proportion of workers who learned about factory news from agitators and political informers varied between 4.2 and 9.2%; and at a collective farm in the same area no more than 3–7% learned about such matters from agitators and political instructors.[64] In investigations elsewhere, less than one-quarter of respondents were able to remember the subjects of the last *politinformatsiya* they had attended and the name of the lecturer;[65] more than one-third were unable to name the agitator attached to their local work group;[66] and no more than one-third of those polled came regularly into contact with him.[67]

A broadly similar picture emerges from the investigations that have been made of the impact of political education classes upon the levels of political knowledge of those who attend them. Regular attenders at political education classes, for instance, appear to be consistently better informed about a number of national and international issues than their nonattending counterparts (the results obtained in a series of inquiries on this subject conducted by the Academy of Social Sciences attached to the Central Committee of the CPSU are set out in Table 7). An investigation in Tomsk *oblast* found similarly that some 60% of students enrolled at the primary level of political study were considered by the propagandists concerned to have a "good" or "satisfactory" level of knowledge; 49% of those enrolled at the intermediate level of study were considered to have a level of knowledge that was satisfactory or better, and at the advanced level of knowledge as many as 70% of students could be classified in this way.[68] A further poll of propagandists in Dnepropetrovsk found that 62% thought their students had attained a good level of political knowledge, and that 34% thought their students had reached a satisfactory level of knowledge, and that only 4% thought their students had a level of knowledge that fell below this.[69]

Propagandists have been found to exaggerate the attainment of those for whom they are responsible, however,[70] and in these circumstances, the deficiencies revealed by such surveys are perhaps more striking. In the study in Tomsk *oblast* which has already been mentioned, for instance, 40% of students enrolled at the primary level of study were regarded by the propagandists concerned as having an "unsatisfactory" level of political knowledge; nearly half (46%) of those at the intermediate level were placed in the same category, as well as more than one-quarter (27%) of those at the advanced level. Within the Komsomol education system, similarly, 44% of students were regarded as having a "good" or "satisfactory" level of political knowledge, but nearly one-half (49%) had a level of political knowledge that was described as unsatisfactory and a further 4% could not be categorized.[71] A poll of 600 propagandists in one of the districts of Moscow found that 53% believed that the knowledge their students had acquired had been absorbed, not

TABLE 7. Political Knowledge and Attendance at Political Education Classes[a,b]

Knowledge of	Level of knowledge	Moscow a	Moscow b	Kimry a	Kimry b	Kalinin a	Kalinin b	Gorky a	Gorky b	Bor a	Bor b
Major factors accounting for relaxation of international relations	Good	43.9	27.9	59.7	38.5	57.4	25.0	51.9	27.9	52.9	38.2
	Satisfactory	46.5	53.7	36.9	42.7	33.5	40.7	34.8	35.8	36.2	41.6
	Unsatisfactory	9.5	14.0	4.3	18.8	9.1	34.3	14.2	37.2	10.8	20.2
Major differences between socialist and capitalist ways of life	Good	42.7	30.6	52.2	33.0	57.9	30.4	54.1	28.1	60.5	43.2
	Satisfactory	44.0	51.1	42.8	56.8	35.4	50.9	31.8	47.7	33.4	49.7
	Unsatisfactory	12.1	15.7	5.1	10.2	6.7	18.7	14.0	24.2	6.1	7.1
Means of improving effectiveness of economic production	Good	42.7	29.7	56.9	31.3	53.4	25.1	54.6	28.1	56.6	37.2
	Satisfactory	45.9	48.5	39.6	50.7	36.5	52.7	34.2	41.6	37.3	50.6
	Unsatisfactory	7.7	18.3	4.5	18.1	10.1	22.2	11.2	30.3	6.1	12.2

[a]V. G. Baikova, Ideologicheskaya rabota KPSS v usloviyakh razvitogo sotsializma (Moscow, 1977), p. 148.
[b]Note: a: attenders; b: nonattenders. Data in percentages.

simply memorized; but 43% took the opposite view, and no more than 8.9% thought that the knowledge their students had acquired had been converted into firm personal convictions.[72] In a further poll, no more than 14.5% of propagandists in Moscow and Tomsk thought their students had acquired a capacity for logical thought in relation to the material they had studied.[73]

Objective tests of the knowledge acquired by students of the political education system tend largely to bear out these impressions. The ability of students to define a number of political terms, for instance, was shown in investigations in Moscow and Tomsk to have increased considerably between the first assessment of such knowledge and the second, at the end of the year of study concerned (Table 8). Even by this stage, however, more than one-quarter of the students polled were unable to define "proletariat" or "productive forces"; almost half were unable to define "dictatorship of the proletariat"; and more than 60% were unable to define "reformism." Even lower scores were obtained by students enrolled at the intermediate level of study, whose curriculum includes the history of the CPSU and Marxist–Leninist philosophy. Three quarters of those polled were unable to distinguish between confiscation of the estates and nationalization; only 16% were able to distinguish between "essence" and "appearance"; and as far as 4% were able to apply this distinction to the New Economic Policy period of the 1920s.[74] Even on a more straightforward topic, détente (or the "relaxation of international tensions"), students were generally little better informed. Nearly 80% of those polled in an investigation in Saransk, for instance, were unable to provide an acceptable explanation as to why détente had become possible, and more than half were unaware that it

TABLE 8. *Knowledge of Political Terminology and Attendance at Political Education Classes*[a,b]

	Percentage of correct answers	
Term	First test	Second test
Productive forces	66.6	73.4
National income	53.3	60.0
Proletariat	26.4	70.6
Dictatorship of the proletariat	32.3	58.9
Imperialism	64.1	94.0
Reformism	9.0	39.6

[a]Source: M. T. Iovchuk *et al.*, eds., *Sotsialisticheskii rabochii kollektiv. Problemy dukhovnoi zhizni* (Moscow, 1978), p. 100.
[b]Data in percentages.

would not lead to a relaxation in the ideological as in other fields.[75] This is, of course, a mistake as basic as it is possible to make in this connection.

Of more importance, perhaps, is the impact of political lectures and classes upon *political behavior*. The Soviet authorities themselves have certainly always taken the view that this must be the main object of the program of political education they sponsor. Lenin, for instance, in a quotation much repeated in Soviet texts on this subject, asked: "On what basis can one reach conclusions about the *real* 'thoughts and feelings' of *real* people? Clearly there can be only one such basis: the *actions* of such people."[76] Brezhnev, more recently, has argued that the "measure of the success of the political upbringing of the masses is concrete action. Communist consciousness is a combination of knowledge, convictions, and practical activity." The most advanced ideology, as he has put it, "becomes a real force only when, having conquered the masses, it inspires them to practical action, defines the norms of their daily behaviour."[77] The impact of attendance at political lectures and classes upon political behavior has accordingly received a good deal of attention in the empirical investigations that have been made into the "effectiveness of communist propaganda."[78] What do the results now available suggest?

So far as political lectures are concerned, first of all, it is clear that substantial proportions of those who attend them find that they have little connection with everyday life and are little influenced by them. An investigation at three factories and two academic institutions in Moscow, for instance, found that relatively few of those who attended political information sessions subsequently felt a wish to read something further on the subject discussed, with members of the academic audiences particularly unlikely to wish to do so (Table 9). Relatively low proportions, similarly, feel that the information they receive can be made use of in their daily life. In a poll in Saransk, for instance, no more than 23% thought that they would be able to make practical use of the information they had received;[79] in Stavropol' *krai*, the significance of the achievements or problems raised in political lectures was often not entirely clear; and in some (perhaps untypical) cases, the political lecture might not even be understood.[80]

The most detailed investigation of the impact of mass-agitational work upon political behavior so far to have been conducted was carried out at an aluminum plant in Irkutsk *oblast*. More than 1900 workers at the plant were asked what effect their involvement in mass-political work had had upon the "development of their political and cultural horizons." Their answers were distributed as follows: 22.5% reported listening more frequently to political broadcasts on the radio and television; 21.8% replied that they read more fiction; 17% wished to know more and to be useful to society; 11.2% wanted to raise their educational

TABLE 9. *Replies to Question "Do You Wish to Read Something on the Subject Concerned After Hearing a Political Information Lecture?"*[a,b]

Question	All	Industrial enterprises	Academic institutes
"Yes, I always want to learn more"	25.3	32.1	12.5
"Yes, I have such a wish, but not always"	46.6	46.8	46.1
"No, I have no such wish"	30.3	21.2	41.4

[a]Source: P. V. Pozdnyakov, ed., *Politicheskaya informatsiya. Nekotorye voprosy teorii i praktiki* (Moscow, 1974), p. 22.
[b]Data in percentages.

and political levels; 11.1% took a more critical view of their colleagues' behavior and 9.1% of television and the cinema; 8.6% took a more active part in sociopolitical life; 5% reported that they felt better equipped to take part in mass-political work; and 4.7% read more sociopolitical literature. As many as 16.6%, however, replied that their involvement in mass-political work had had no influence at all upon their subsequent behavior, and about 30% refrained from answering the question altogether.[81] From the party's point of view, these can scarcely be satisfactory findings.

In political education classes, similarly, there are repeated complaints that discussion is too little connected with daily life, and that students are unable to make practical use of the knowledge they have acquired. No more than 21% of those polled in an investigation into the political and economic education system in Chelyabinsk, for instance, said that they were able to put the knowledge they had acquired into practical effect; 40% were able to make only occasional use of such knowledge, and 32% were unable to make any use of it at all.[82] No more than 31% of those polled, in an analogous investigation in Saransk, reported that they were able to make use of the knowledge they had acquired in their daily life and work;[83] and at a state farm in Stavropol' *krai*, the impact of political education classes upon political activism and farm work was found to be "insignificant."[84] Philosophical subjects, perhaps not surprisingly, appear to be among the most difficult to apply in real life. "There is nothing I can apply it to," as a student of the political education system in Kazakhstan put it. "Philosophy is up in the clouds, but we have to try to apply it on earth," remarked another.[85] Many would appear to agree with the views of the recent Soviet émigré, Boris Shragin, that the basic tenets of Marxism–Leninism have simply "nothing in common with contemporary Soviet political reality."[86]

Other studies have found that only a minority of students in fact take a more active part in economic and sociopolitical life, their declared greater willingness to do so notwithstanding. More than two-thirds of those who were polled at a number of political schools in Moscow, for instance, reported that their studies had widened their political horizons, and more than half reported taking a greater interest in political questions. Fewer than one-third of those polled, however, had begun to take a more active part in political life as a result, and no more than one-quarter reported speaking more regularly at the meetings they attended.[87] A further inquiry in Tomsk *oblast* found that 47% of those polled felt they had a better understanding of national and international affairs as a result of their attendance at political education classes, and 37% felt they had a better grasp of the economic and production tasks facing the factory in which they worked. Only 19%, however, thought that political study encouraged them to take a more active part in sociopolitical life, only 9% took a regular part in propaganda work at their place of employment, and only 7% felt they had been stimulated to take a greater interest in political literature.[88]

These, moreover, are the results achieved with those who do attend political lectures and education classes; and despite the increasing size of the total enrolment, there is at present some concern that relatively large numbers of people may lie outside the ambit of the system altogether. In Vitebsk and Taganrog, for instance, it was found that about one-third of those surveyed "hardly ever attend lectures."[89] In an investigation at a number of industrial enterprises in Moscow it was found, similarly, that only 20% of those polled attended agitational *besedy* on a regular basis (once a week);[90] and at a cellulose and paper mill in Gor'ky *oblast*, only 20.8% did so.[91] An investigation conducted in a more rural area, Stavropol' *krai*, found that as many as 44% of those polled "hardly ever" attended political information sessions, and 37% did not normally attend agitational *besedy* (a related set of data are presented in Table 10.)[92] Antireligious lectures appear to suffer particularly from this kind of differential turnout. "The lecturers work with the atheists in the clubs, and we work with the believers in the church," as a priest from Sverdlovsk is reported to have put it; "the atheists do not come to us, and the believers do not go to the club. We do not interfere with each other."[93] Particular problems are also acknowledged to exist with night shifts, in enterprises with low proportions of party members, with young workers resident in dormitories, and in the more remote parts of the country.[94]

The problem of differential *saturation* arises most acutely of all, however, with those who live at home and are for one reason or another not members of the regular labor force. In Chelyabinsk *oblast*, for instance, it was found that children in the later school years and pensioners were effectively outside the reach of the mass-agitational system, and that women (who can retire at 50) were consistently less likely to be covered by the education and lecturing network than their

TABLE 10. *Regularity of Attendance at Political Lectures*[a,b]

Attendance	*Nevinnomyssk* chemical combine	*"Elektroavtomatika"* factory, Stavropol'
Once a week	0.8	7.6
Once a month	21.9	29.9
Once every 6 months	21.2	17.3
From time to time	50.0	32.7
Do not attend	6.1	12.5

[a]Source: G. T. Zhuravlev, ed., *Ideologicheskaya rabota i formirovanie obshchestven-nogo mneniya v trudovom kollektive* (Moscow, 1977), p. 53.
[b]Data in percentages.

male counterparts.[95] It was to overcome problems of this kind that mass-political work on a residential basis has been developed, particularly since the introduction of the 5-day week in 1967.[96] The evidence suggests, however, that residential work may be no more successful in achieving its objectives than agitational work in other areas. A relatively small proportion of the local population appears to be engaged by such measures; they tend to be those who are already engaged in mass-political activities elsewhere; work in this field appears to be given a low priority among all forms of ideological work and to be carried out irregularly or not at all; and it is apparently not very popular with the local population, the vast majority (from 91.3 to 98.2% in various investigations) preferring political agitation and propaganda to be carried out somewhere other than at their place of residence.[97]

The country population are also less likely to be covered by the oral propaganda system than their urban counterparts. In an investigation in Chelyabinsk, for instance, it was found that rural residents attended less than half as many lectures as their urban counterparts, and that collective and state farmers attended only one-fifth or one-quarter as many lectures as a comparable group of industrial workers.[98] In a number of less populated areas and districts, it appears, agitational collectives may not exist at all, or may spring briefly into existence when national campaigns are in progress and then disappear again; and even in the major urban areas, there are marked disparities in the provision of political lectures from one local neighborhood to another.[99] The problem of differential saturation has received some attention in the party press, and a deputy head of the Central Committee Propaganda Department has warned that the party at present may simply be "informing the informed and agitating the agitated."[100] So far, however, no effective solution appears to have been found.

The Effectiveness of Political Propaganda: An Assessment It would clearly be unwise to conclude, on the basis of these investigations alone, that the Soviet political education and lecturing system has in some sense been "a failure."[101] Reliable though most of the individual studies quoted in this chapter appear to be, it is nonetheless impossible to tell from them alone to what extent the shortcomings identified are typical of the "ideological work of the party" more generally. It has normally been assumed—and perhaps rightly—that because of the predisposition throughout the Soviet system to exaggerate successes and understate failure, the real situation must always be much worse than that reported in official sources. These, after all, go through a lengthy filtering process: individual citizens, given the sanctions available, are not less likely than citizens elsewhere to tell the interviewer what they think he wants to hear; interviewers, writing up their reports, are likely to present their findings in a manner calculated to cause the minimum of offense to their superiors; and their reports in their turn, before they can be published, must be approved by the official censor, who is required to delete all mention of certain matters and whose instincts and career aspirations normally incline him toward a conservative view of the limits of the permissible. Given all these biases, it might at first sight seem reasonable to subscribe to what might be called the "tip of the iceberg" convention in analyzing the relevant Soviet publications: that the defects and shortcomings reported in official sources, however numerous, must always be fewer than those that actually exist.

The degree of understatement involved, however, is impossible to determine precisely and is likely to vary from place to place and from time to time; and it must also be borne in mind that a number of biases operate in the reverse direction, toward the overstatement rather than the understatement of real or imaginary shortcomings. The first of these is the "campaign" quality of much reporting in the area. In ideology, as in other areas of Soviet life, investigations are often launched when a particular abuse has reached intolerable proportions, when a change in policy has been decided on and needs some retrospective justification, or simply when the leaders think it is time they had something to say upon the subject. The investigations are then shut off again when the abuse in question has been reduced to more acceptable proportions, when the new policy is thought to have been justified, or when more pressing matters obtrude. Soviet political and economic life since at least the beginning of the first 5-Year Plan has revolved around a series of mass mobilizations designed to reach objectives set out by the central leadership that it has become customary to achieve, or overachieve, somewhat ahead of time in a lather of last-minute "storming." Soviet policymaking in the ideological field, not perhaps surprisingly, has come to share a number of these general characteristics, with more attention being given to quantitative than to qualitative success indicators,[102] to the making of plans rather than to their execution,[103] and to short-lived campaigns against the particular abuses of the moment rather than steady but less spectacular improvement.[104] The "failures" that are reported in the ideological field, considered in this light, may be exemplary rather than representative, intended to highlight and, if necessary, exaggerate the particular problems of the moment so that party activists can be more effectively mobilized toward their resolution.

A further source of bias arises from the possibility, noted particularly by American writers whose exposure to large-scale bureaucratic lobbying is perhaps greater than most, that much of the apparent concern about "failures" or "shortcomings" in the ideological field may be a form of bureaucratic special pleading. The USSR has now a considerable investment of men and resources in the ideological field, and it would hardly be surprising if the officials concerned sought, like their counterparts elsewhere, to defend and even extend their position by drawing attention to the problems that still exist in their area and to the need to devote additional resources to their resolution. "Those who view the complaints of *Agitprop* and ideological specialists as the tip of an iceberg whose submerged mass contains widespread, smouldering resentment," as Walter Connor has put it, "forget that, like any bureaucratic organization, *Agitprop* must justify its continued existence, expenditures and personnel demands. The line that, in spite of great progress to date, there is 'more to be done' is a conventional way of doing this."[105] Most of the evidence considered in this chapter is in fact the work of academic researchers, rather than of *Agitprop* officials or ideological spokesmen; but academics, too, have their vested interests, and few who have devoted their time and effort over perhaps a number of years to a subject of this kind will wish to see its importance—and with it their self-esteem and career prospects—decline. Academic researchers as well as *Agitprop* officials, in other words, are groups of people with shared interests as well as dedicated searchers after truth, and it would be surprising if those interests did not incline them—consciously or not—toward the overstatement rather than the understatement of the "problems" and "unresolved tasks" that confront official policymakers in this field.

Above all, perhaps, what do we really mean by "success" or "failure" in this context? The Soviet authorities, on the evidence presented in this chapter, would certainly seem to have fallen rather short of their professed objective, the universal creation of a "new Soviet man" to inhabit the communist society of the future. The achievement of a fully communist society, however, is nowadays acknowledged to be a matter for the distant, not the immediate future (Brezhnev has suggested it may take half a century or more),[106] and the party leadership may well be content in practice that the political lecturing and educational systems should serve a number of less far-reaching but not negligible purposes.

These would include, for instance, giving party members something to do (not a point that should be lightly disregarded); providing a regular check upon the party's ability to mobilize its forces for the achievement of a variety of centrally determined objectives; involving many nonmembers in various aspects of propaganda work, thus possibly strengthening their commitment or at least exposing their reservations more clearly;[107] and finally, perhaps, making a marginal improvement to the level of economic performance throughout the country. There is not in fact a great deal of evidence that the Soviet people are actively hostile to the main features of the system within which they live, whatever their grumbling about a number of its individual features, and in these circumstances, the party leadership may well be reasonably satisfied with these more limited achievements, though they fall short of the universal conversion of the Soviet population to the norms of Marxism–Leninism.

As against this, it could be argued that the tasks the political education and lecturing systems are required to perform are becoming more complicated, and that the increasing degree of attention they are receiving from the party leadership reflects a growing consciousness of this fact. Policy questions in the USSR, for instance, are becoming more complex and less obviously "political" than they used to be; objectives are more diffuse and less easy to reconcile with one another; and the Soviet mass public is much better educated and less accessible at its place of work than in the past with the introduction of the 5-day week and greater geographical mobility. Above all, the Soviet public has now a much greater degree of access to external sources of information, and in particular to foreign radio broadcasts, than arguably at any period since the revolution.[108] It does not, of course, follow that the more the Soviet public learns about Western capitalist societies, with their inlation, unemployment, and industrial disruption, the more they will wish to imitate them. But a better and more independently informed Soviet public is certainly among the difficulties of which official propagandists have recently been complaining.[109] A nice example of what this can mean in practice is provided by Simon Leys in his book, *Chinese Shadows*. An elderly Chinese émigré, interviewed in the 1960s in Hong Kong, was asked what he thought of Yugoslavia. "It is a pseudo-socialist country run by revisionist hyenas in the pay of American capitalism," he replied. He was then asked where he would ideally like to live. "Well, in Yugoslavia, for instance," he replied. Why? "It seems that in pseudo-socialist countries run by revisionist hyenas in the pay of American capitalism, oil and cotton cloth are not rationed."[110] If Chinese propagandists, separated by a continent, can do no better than this, it is not surprising that their Soviet counterparts have been having difficulties.

The Soviet authorities themselves, moreover, do appear—rightly or wrongly—to be rather concerned about the state of affairs in this field. A series of major resolutions since the early 1970s has acknowledged with more than conventional urgency the shortcomings that exist in ideological work and the importance of eliminating them;[111] a special Politbureau commission was set up in November 1978 to consider measures for the improvement of the party's work in this area;[112] and a comprehensive resolution "On the further improvement of ideological and political educational work," adopted in May 1979, warned that there was a whole series of "shortcomings and inadequacies, some of them extremely serious," in this field, and went on to list a large number of measures designed to bring about a radical improvement.[113] There have, of course, been resolutions on ideological work before, and none of them should necessarily be taken at face value. The resolution of May 1979, however, was followed by meetings at all levels of the party and in other bodies; it is the first on whose fulfilment party and other bodies have specifically been required to report back in December 1979 and December 1980; and more to the point, words have been followed by actions and at least four republican party officials responsible for ideology have lost their jobs in the course of this review.[114] Justifiably or not, there does at present seem to be a measure of genuine concern at the level of the political leadership about the ideological work of the party, its effectiveness and rationale, and on the evidence presented in this chapter, their anxiety could scarcely be said to be without foundation.

Finally, it might be argued that the Soviet authorities are concerned about the relative lack of success of their ideological offensive because it is upon the ideology that their role ultimately depends for its legitimation. Unlike Western governments, whose claim to be obeyed derives— in theory, at least—from their elected or representative character, the Soviet authorities have little on which to base their authority other than the ideology to which they subscribe and their performance in government (what has been described as "rational legitimacy").[115] It would be too much to say that their claim to rule upon the former basis is altogether ineffective; a variety of surveys of Soviet émigrés, for instance, have established that an extensive degree of public ownership, a comprehensive health and education service, and an actively interventionist government are supported by an overwhelming majority even of those who have chosen to leave the Soviet system and live elsewhere. There appears to be no comparable degree of support for the institutions of single-party rule, however, most respondents seeing them as neither good nor bad in themselves but as justified or legitimated in terms of the ends toward which they are directed and the results to which they lead; and there appears to be little identification with either the political leadership as such or with the procedures by which they are selected.[116]

And here, perhaps, there is more genuine cause for concern; for while the rate of Soviet economic advance from the late 1920s until the late 1950s was remarkable in comparison with that of her major Western neighbors, there has since been a steady deterioration, and on present projections, the Soviet economic growth rate may actually drop below that of the major capitalist counties in the early 1980s and beyond.[117] A falling rate of economic growth in turn implies a reduction in social mobility and in the career opportunities that are associated with it, and the inevitable disappointment of the expectation generated by the rapid expansion of past decades. It would be too much to suggest that a slowdown of this kind will place insupportable pressures upon the political system (although it would be surprising if it did not lead at least to some social tensions); and there are further bases of legitimacy toward which the regime may turn, such as (as appears to have been happening since the early 1970s) a form of mildly disguised Russian nationalism.[118] It does appear, however, that the more modest Soviet economic performance that is in prospect will place more weight than has hitherto been the case upon the other main base upon which the Soviet authorities claim to exercise authority, their ideology; and if this occurs, the failures in ideological work reported in this chapter may have to be taken very seriously indeed.

Notes

[1]Carl J. Friedrich and Zbigniew K. Brzezinski, *Totalitarian Dictatorship and Autocracy*, 2nd ed. (Cambridge, Mass., 1965), pp. 22–23 and 107–108.

[2]A. H. Brown, *Soviet Politics and Political Science* (London, 1974), p. 103.

[3]Teresa Rakowska-Harmstone, ed., *Perspectives for Change in Communist Societies* (Boulder, Col., 1979), p. 16.

[4]E. M. Chekharin, *Sovetskaya politicheskaya sistema v usloviyakh razvitogo sotsializma* (Moscow, 1975), pp. 3–4.

[5]K. F. Zugaparov in *Partiya i gosudarstvo v period stroitel'stva kommunizma* (Moscow, 1973), p. 372.

[6]The development of this system is briefly reviewed in Frederick C. Barghoorn, *Politics in the USSR,* 2nd ed. (Boston, 1972), pp. 116–135, and in Stephen White, *Political Culture and Soviet Politics* (London, 1979), pp. 66–74.

[7]*Partiinaya zhizn'*, no. 16 (1979), pp. 63–67.

[8]The number of lectures given by the *Znanie* Society, for instance, has increased from 926,000 in 1950 to 15,103,000 in 1965 and to more than 26 million in 1978 (*Narodnoe obrazovanie, nauka i kul'tura v SSSR. Statisticheskii sbornik* (Moscow, 1977), p. 345; *Ezhegodnik Bol'shoi Sovetskoi Entsiklopedii 1979g.* (Moscow, 1979), p.21.

[9]"O 60-oi godovshchine Velikoi Oktyabr'skoi sotsialisticheskoi revolyutsii. Postanovlenie TsK KPSS ot 31 yanvarya 1977 goda," *Kommunist*, no. 2 (1979), p. 8.

[10]Alfred Meyer, "The USSR Incorporated," in *The Development of the USSR,* ed. Donald W. Treadgold (Seattle, 1964), p. 24; Samuel Huntington and Jorge I. Dominguez, "Political Development," in *Handbook of Political Science*, vol. 3, eds. Fred I. Greenstein and Nelson W. Polsby (Reading, Penn., 1975), p. 31.

[11]See for instance Barghoorn, *Politics in the USSR*, p. 139, and Darrell P. Hammer, *USSR: The Politics of Oligarchy* (Hinsdale, Ill., 1974), pp. 87–88.

[12]*Sotsiologicheskie issledovaniya v ideologicheskoi rabote*, vyp. 2 (Moscow, 1976), p. 7.

[13]*Ibid.*, pp. 13–14; a more detailed list in *Voprosy istorii KPSS*, no. 8 (1977), reports that sociological investigations into party work have been carried out in the Moscow, Leningrad, Ukrainian, Belorussian, Uzbek, Latvian, Moldavian, Estonian, Krasnodar, Stavropol', Gor'ky, Novosibirsk, Chelyabinsk, and other party organizations (p. 41).

[14]G. T. Zhuravlev, ed., *Ideologicheskaya rabota i formirovanie obshchestvennogo mneniya v trudovom kollektive* (Moscow, 1977), p. 93. The Academy, a party higher-educational institution, was founded in 1946; it offers courses in a variety of party-relevant specialisms and sponsors a number of periodical publications including *Voprosy effektivnosti partiinoi propagandy i politicheskoi informatsii* (vyp. 1-, Moscow 1973-) and *Voprosy teorii i metodov ideologicheskoi raboty* (vyp 1-, Moscow 1972-). The publication *Sotsiologicheskie issledovaniya v ideologicheskoi rabote* (vyp. 1-, Moscow 1974-) is jointly sponsored by the Department for the Study of the Effectiveness of Party Propaganda and Political Information of the Academy and by the Section for Sociological Research into Party Work of the Institute of Sociological Research of the USSR Academy of Sciences.

[15]See for instance A. G. Zdravomyslov and V. G. Borisov in *Nauchnye osnovy politicheskoi raboty v massakh* (Leningrad, 1972), pp. 55 and 84.

[16]M. I. Khaldeev and G. I. Krivoshein, comps., *Gorkom, raikom partii: opyt, formy i metody raboty* (Moscow, 1977), p. 255.

[17]*Pravda*, April 23, 1980, p. 2.

[18]*Sotsiologicheskie issledovaniya*, no. 4 (1978), p. 108.

[19]The term *triangulation* has been employed in this context to refer to a cross-check upon the validity of a particular finding (Raymond L. Gorden, *Interviewing: Strategy, Technique and Tactics*, rev. ed. [Homewood, Ill., 1975], p. 40). On the reliability of Soviet social science data see also more generally Ellen Mickiewicz *et al.*, *Handbook of Soviet Social Science Data* (New York, 1973), Elizabeth Ann Weinberg, *The Development of Sociology in the Soviet Union* (London, 1974), and Alec Nove, *The Soviet Economic System* (London, 1979), ch. 13.

[20]*Voprosy teorii i metodov ideologicheskoi raboty*, vyp. 6 (1976), pp. 107 and 116. A number of findings reported in this section were first presented in Stephen White, "Political socialization in the USSR: A study in failure?," *Studies in Comparative Communism*, vol. 10 (1977), pp. 328–342, and in Stephen White, *Political Culture and Soviet Politics*, ch. 6.

[21]N. S. Afonin, *Effektivnost' lektsionnoi propagandy* (Moscow, 1975), pp. 95–96.

[22]V. I. Brovikov and I. V. Popovich, *Sovremennye problemy politicheskoi informatsii i agitatsii* (Moscow, 1969), p. 36.

[23]In a poll in the "VEF" factory in Riga, for instance, 68% of respondents favored more political lectures and information sessions and 60% favored more workplace meetings, but only 15% wanted more "visual propaganda" (posters and the like) and only 6% wanted more agitational *besedy* (*Kommunist Sovetskoi Latvii*, no. 6 [1972], p. 37).

[24]*Voprosy teorii i metodov ideologicheskoi raboty*, vyp. 4 (Moscow, 1975), p. 151.

[25]*Pravda*, May 23, 1977, p. 2.

[26]*Sotsiologicheskie issledovaniya v ideologicheskoi rabote*, vpy. 2, p. 65.

[27]See, for instance, G. I. Balkhanov, *Ustnaya propaganda i ee effektivnost'* (Ulan-Ude, 1974), p. 60; and *Effektivnost' partiinoi ucheby. Iz opyta raboty shkol partiinoi i komsomol'skoi ucheby* (Syktyvkar, 1972), p. 7.

[28]I. I. Kamynin and A. A. Merkulov, eds., *Usloviya povysheniya sotsial'noi aktivnosti rabochego klassa v period stroitel'stva kommunizma. Sbornik statei* (Rostov on Don, 1974), p. 88.

[29]*Effektivnost' partiinoi ucheby,* p. 7.

[30]A. G. Efimov and P. V. Pozdnyakov, *Nauchnye osnovy partiinoi propagandy* (Moscow, 1966), p. 101.

[31]See, for instance, I. S. Soltan, *Politicheskaya ucheba i razvitie obshchestvenno-politicheskoi aktivnosti rabotnikov promyshlennogo predpriyatiya,* avtoreferat kand. diss. (Kishinev, 1973), pp. 18–19.

[32]N. S. Afonin, *Sotsial'no-politicheskie aspekty povysheniya effektivnosti partiinoi propagandy,* avtoreferat kand. diss. (Moscow, 1973), p. 20 (but not in N. S. Afonin, *Lektor i auditoriya,* Saransk, 1973).

[33]V. S. Korobeinikov, ed., *Sotsiologicheskie problemy obshchestvennogo mneniya i sredstv massovoi informatsii* (Moscow, 1975), pp. 101–102.

[34]*Ibid.,* p. 103.

[35]N. I. Mekhontsev *et al., Lektor i slushatel'* (Moscow, 1975), p. 65.

[36]*Voprosy teorii i metodov ideologicheskoi raboty,* vyp. 7 (Moscow, 1977), p. 161–162.

[37]M. M. Rakhmankulov *et al., Ustnaya politicheskaya agitatsiya: teoriya, organizatsiya, metodika* (Moscow, 1977), p. 211.

[38]See, for instance, *Za vysokuyu effektivnost' lektsionnoi propagandy* (Moscow, 1975), p. 137; Afonin, *Effektivnost' lektsionnoi propagandy,* p. 87; *Sotsiologicheskie issledovaniya,* no. 2 (1975), p. 120; *Voprosy teorii i metodov ideologicheskoi raboty,* vyp. 9 (Moscow, 1978), p. 158n.

[39]In the studies that have been conducted, international and topical matters again emerge as the most popular: V. G. Baikova *et al., Politicheskoe obrazovanie: sistema, metodika, metodologiya* (Moscow, 1976), p. 29; and V. G. Baikova, *Ideologicheskaya rabota KPSS v usloviyakh razvitogo sotsializma* (Moscow, 1977), p. 147.

[40]*Voprosy teorii i metodov ideologicheskoi raboty,* vyp. 4, p. 151.

[41]*Sotsiologicheskie issledovaniya v ideologicheskoi rabote,* vyp. 1 (Moscow, 1974), p. 108.

[42]P. V. Pozdnyakov, ed., *Politicheskaya informatsiya. Nekotorye voprosy teorii i praktiki* (Moscow, 1974), p. 87.

[43]*Sotsiologicheskie issledovaniya,* no. 4 (1975), p. 115.

[44]*Pravda,* November 29, 1977, p. 2.

[45]See, for instance, Pozdnyakov, ed., *Politicheskaya informatsiya,* p. 87; *Voprosy teorii i metodov ideologicheskoi raboty,* vyp. 7, p. 162.

[46]N. I. Mekhontsev *et al., Lektsiya v otsenke slushatelei* (Moscow, 1973), p. 69.

[47]Some examples of this kind are reported in White, *Political Culture,* p. 118.

[48]The interviews were conducted in the Jerusalem area in the autumn of 1976; for a full report of findings, see Stephen White, "Continuity and change in Soviet political culture: An émigré study," *Comparative Political Studies,* vol. 11 (1978), pp. 381–395.

[49]See the letter from a recent Soviet émigré in the *New Statesman,* January 12, 1979, p. 48.

[50]John Prosland, personal communication.

[51]See, for instance, Pozdnyakov, ed., *Politicheskaya informatsiya*, pp. 24 and 87; *Voprosy teorii i metodov ideologicheskoi raboty*, vyp. 7, p. 163; Zhuravlev, ed., *Ideologicheskaya robota*, p. 17; *Pravda*, February 20, 1979, p.1.

[52]Afonin, *Lektor i auditoriya*, p. 48; Afonin, *Effektivnost' lektsionnoi propagandy*, p. 14; S. G. Novruzov, *Voprosy sovershenstvovaniya politicheskogo informirovaniya trudyashchikhsya*, avtoreferat kand. diss. (Moscow, 1974), p. 14; N. I. Mekhontsev and M. E. Nenashev, *Effektivnost' politicheskoi informatsii* (Chelyabinsk, 1972), p. 27.

[53]See, for instance, N. N. Bokarev, ed., *Sotsiologicheskie issledovaniya v partiinoi rabote* (Moscow, 1973), pp. 31 and 58; L. M. Molodtsov *et al.*, *Deistvennost' politicheskoi ucheby* (Moscow, 1973), p. 41; *Kommunist Belorussii*, no. 9, (1977), p. 8; *Pravda*, 7 May 1978, p.2.

[54]L. Ya. Zile, ed., *Formy i metody ideologicheskoi raboty partii* (Riga,1974), p. 169; *Partiinaya zhizn'*, no. 20 (1975), p. 42; Baikova *et al.*, *Politicheskoe obrazovanie*, p. 82.

[55]*Pravda*, February 2, 1978, p. 1.

[56]G. T. Zhuravlev, ed., *Sotsial'nye issledovaniya dukhovnoi zhizni sovetskogo obshchestva. Opyt i problemy* (Moscow, 1977), p. 98; *Sotsiologicheskie issledovaniya v ideologicheskoi raboty*, vyp. 1, pp.100–101.

[57]In a number of enterprises in Moscow, Chita, and Polotsk, for instance, it was found that about one-quarter of the students of political education who were polled "in fact did not prepare for their classes"; in another poll in Rostov on Don, more than one-third of the students polled had read none of the works of Marx, Engels, and Lenin despite the requirements of their program (Kamynin and Merkulov, eds., *Usloviya povysheniya sotsial'noi aktivnosii*, pp. 88 and 101). Similar findings have been reported elsewhere (see for instance *Voprosy teorii i metodov ideologicheskoi raboty*, vyp. 9, p. 43; *Partiinaya zhizn' Kazakhstana*, no. 9 (1976), p. 82, and no. 5 (1978), p. 82; and *Sotsiologicheskie issledovaniya v ideologicheskoi rabote*, vyp. 1, p. 108).

[58]Zhuravlev, ed., *Ideologicheskaya rabota*, p. 39.

[59]*Ibid.*, pp. 37–38.

[60]*Voprosy effektivnosti partiinoi propagandy i politicheskoi informatsii*, vyp. 3 (Moscow, 1975), p. 197, *Sotsiologicheskie issledovaniya v ideologicheskoi rabote*, vyp. 1, p. 131; Baikova *et al.*, *Politicheskoe obrazovanie*, p. 204.

[61]Baikova, *Ideologicheskaya rabota KPSS*, p. 150.

[62]Korobeinikov, ed., *Sotsiologicheskie problemy obshchestvennogo mneniya*, p. 107; M. P. Gabdulin *et al.*, comps., *Agitator, politinformator, dokladchik* (Moscow, 1978), p. 83.

[63]See, for instance, Zhuravlev, ed., *Sotsial'nye issledovaniya*, pp. 114–116; *Kommunist Sovetskoi Latvii*, no. 4 (1977), pp. 78–79.

[64]Zhuravlev, ed., *Ideologicheskaya rabota*, pp. 15–16 and 27.

[65]N. S. Afonin, comp., *Politicheskaya agitatsiya v trudovom kollektiv* (Saransk, 1976), p. 28.

[66]*Pravda*, September 6, 1978, p.2

[67]Baikova, *Ideologicheskaya rabota KPSS*, p. 138.

[68]Baikova *et al.*, *Politicheskoe obrazovanie*, p. 223.

[69]*Voprosy teorii i metodov ideologicheskoi raboty*, vyp. 4, p. 150.

[70]See, for instance, D. Gilyazitdinov *et al.*, *Effektivnost' partiinoi propagandy* (Tashkent, 1971), p. 94.

[71]Baikova *et al.*, *Politicheskoe obrazovanie*, p. 223.

[72]*Sotsiologicheskie issledovaniya v ideologicheskoi rabote*, vyp. 1, pp. 141–142.

[73]Pozdnyakov *et al.*, *Effektivnost' ideino-vospitatel'noi raboty* Moscow, 1975), p. 151.

[74]*Ibid.*, pp. 106 and 110.

[75]Afonin, comp., *Politicheskaya agitatsiya*, p. 27.

[76]V. I. Lenin, *Polnoe sobranie sochinenii*, vol. 1 (Moscow, 1958), pp. 423–424.

[77]L. I. Brezhnev, *Leninskim kursom. Rechi i stat'i*, vol. 5 (Moscow, 1976, p. 535, and vol. 3 (Moscow, 1972), p. 287.

[78]To borrow the title of P. V. Pozdnyakov, *Effektivnost' kommunisticheskoi propagandy* (Moscow, 1975).

[79]Afonin, *Lektor i auditoriya*, p. 73.

[80]Zhuravlev, ed., *Ideologicheskaya rabota*, p. 17: Andrei Amalrik, *Nezhelannoe puteshestvie v Sibir'* (New York, 1970), p. 267.

[81]G. I. Mel'nikov, ed., *Kollektiv i lichnost* (Irkutsk, 1973), pp. 133–134.

[82]M. V. Gramov, ed., *Kompleksnyi podkhod v ideologicheskoi rabote. Stil' i metody* (Moscow, 1976), pp. 92–93.

[83]Afonin, *Lektor i auditoriya*, p. 73.

[84]*Pravda*, October 18, 1976, p. 2.

[85]A. I. Zhukova, "Effektivnost ideino-vospitatel'nogo vospitaniya," *Izvestiya Akademii Nauk Kazakhskoi SSR*, no. 2 (1977), p. 63.

[86]Quoted in Donald D. Barry and Carol Barner-Barry, *Contemporary Soviet Politics. An Introduction* (Englewood Cliffs, N.J., 1978), p. 34.

[87]Yu. M. Khrustalev, *Formirovanie politicheskogo soznaniya lichnosti v usloviyakh razvitogo sotsializma*, avtoreferat kand. diss. (Moscow, 1974), p. 33.

[88]*Sotsiologicheskie issledovaniya v ideologicheskoi rabote*, vyp. 1, p. 111.

[89]*Lektsionnaya propaganda: problemy effektivnosti i kachestva* (Moscow, 1978), p. 40.

[90]Pozdnyakov, ed., *Politicheskaya informatsiya*, p. 84.

[91]Zhuravlev, ed., *Sotsial'nye issledovaniya dukhovnoi zhizni*, p. 115.

[92]*Pravda*, September 6, 1978, p. 2.

[93]David Powell, *Antireligious Propaganda in the Soviet Union: a Sudy of Mass Persuasion* (Cambridge, Mass., 1975), pp. 117–118.

[94]See for instance the Central Committee resolutions "O povyshenii roli ustnoi politicheskoi agitatsii v vypolnenii reshenii XXV s"ezda KPSS," *Pravda*, 25 February 1977, p. 1, and "O dal'neishem uluchshenii ideologicheskoi, politiko-vospitatel'noi raboty," *Pravda*, May 6, 1979, pp. 1–2.

[95]Mekhontsev *et al.*, *Lektsiya v otsenke slushatelei*, p. 27.

[96]See Aryeh L. Unger, "Soviet mass-political work in residential areas," *Soviet Studies*, vol. 22, no. 4 (April 1971), pp. 556–561.

[97]*Voprosy teorii i metodov ideologicheskoi raboty*, vyp. 1 (Moscow, 1972), pp. 282–299; Pozdnyakov, ed., *Politicheskaya informatsiya*, p. 85; Zhuravlev, ed., *Ideologicheskaya rabota* p. 51.

[98]Mekhontsev *et al.*, *Lektsiya v otsenke slushatelei*, p. 28.

[99]*Pravda*, March 2, 1977, p. 1, and June 29, 1979, p. 2; Zile, ed., *Formy i metody*, p. 169; B. A. Grinev, ed., *Kul'tura rabochei molodezhi yuzhnogo Urala* (Chelyabinsk, 1973), p. 112.

[100]M. F. Nenashev in *Kommunist*, no. 4, 1977, p. 33.

[101]Cf. White, "Political socialization in the USSR."

[102]For criticisms of the quantitative (*valovoi*) approach, see for instance V. Z.

Serdyuk, "O nekotorykh voprosakh organizatsii partiinoi propagandy," *Problemy nauchnogo kommunizma,* vyp. 6 (Moscow, 1972), p. 235, and E. M. Kuznetsov, *Politicheskaya agitatsiya: nauchnye osnovy i praktika* (Moscow, 1974), pp. 8–9.

[103]The sin of "formalism"; see, for instance, *Pravda,* November 22, 1976, p. 2, and September 7, 1977, p. 1.

[104]For attacks upon the episodic character of some attempts to improve the quality of ideological work (*kampaneishchina*) see, for instance, *Pravda,* September 7, 1977, p. 1; November 29, 1977, p. 2; and June 18, 1978, p. 2.

[105]Walter Connor, "Generations and politics in the USSR," *Problems of Communism,* vol. 24, no. 5 (September–October 1975), p. 23.

[106]Quoted in John A. Armstrong, *Ideology, Politics and Government in the Soviet Union,* 4th ed. (New York, 1978), p. 46.

[107]A point that is emphasized by Aryeh L. Unger, *The Totalitarian Party. Party and People in Nazi Germany and Soviet Russia* (Cambridge, 1974), pp. 164–165.

[108]About 2% of the Soviet population could receive foreign radio broadcasts in 1940, for instance, and about 8% could do so in 1970; but about 50% were estimated to be able to do so by the 1970s. East–West movements of tourists, students, businessmen, and diplomats have also become more considerable. See Stephen White, *Political Culture and Soviet Politics,* pp. 182–83.

[109]See, for instance, *Partiinaya zhizn',* no. 18 (1978), p. 14, and Brezhnev's speech to the November 1978 Central Committee plenum, reported in *Pravda,* November 28, 1978, p. 2.

[110]Simon Leys, *Chinese Shadows* (London: Harmondsworth, 1978), p. 52.

[111]The major resolutions on this subject up to 1976 are reprinted in *Ob ideologicheskoi rabote KPSS. Sbornik dokumentov* (Moscow, 1977). See also the resolution on oral agitation (*Pravda,* February 25, 1977, p. 1), on Orsk *gorkom* (*Pravda,* August 24, 1977, p. 1), and on economic education in Bashkiria (*Pravda,* August 8, 1978, p.1).

[112]*Pravda,* November 28, 1978, p. 2.

[113]*Pravda,* May 6, 1979, pp. 1–2.

[114]*Zarya vostoka,* 20 and 22 December 1978, and *Kommunist Tadzhikistana,* 14 and 15 December 1978, as quoted in Radio Free Europe/Radio Liberty *Current Abstracts and Annotations,* no. 1 (1979), pp. 16–17; Radio Kiev, April 27, 1979, as quoted in *ibid.,* no. 9 (1979), p. 22; and *Bakinskii rabochii,* July 21, 1978, as quoted in Radio Free Europe/Radio Liberty *Research Bulletin,* no. 32 (1978), RL 176/78.

[115]See Robert Rogowski, *Rational Legitimacy* (Princeton, N.J., 1974). There is a more extended discussion of legitimacy in the context of Soviet politics in Jerome M. Gilison, *British and Soviet Politics. A Study of Legitimacy and Convergence* (Baltimore, Md. and London, 1972), ch. 1.

[116]See Stephen White, *Political Culture and Soviet Politics,* ch. 5.

[117]NATO Directorate of Economic Affairs, *The USSR in the 1980s* (Brussels, 1978), esp. pp. 231–238; Alec Nove, "The Soviet economy: Problems and prospects," *New Left Review,* no. 119 (January–February 1980), pp. 3–19.

[118]See on this point, Archie Brown and Michael Kaser, eds., *The Soviet Union since the Fall of Khrushchev,* 2nd ed. (London, 1978), pp. 142–146; John B. Dunlop, "The many faces of contemporary Russian nationalism," *Survey,* 24, no. 3 (Summer 1979), pp. 18–35; and S. Enders Wimbush, "The Russian nationalist backlash," *ibid.,* pp. 36–50.

25 GAIL WARSHOFSKY LAPIDUS

Society under Strain*

As the new Soviet leadership inaugurates the post-Brezhnev era, it faces
an array of economic, political, and social problems whose scope,
complexity, and cumulative impact are unprecedented in the postwar
period. At a minimum they portend a widening gap between the
expectations of the Soviet population and the capacity of the system to
meet them and also growing strains over the conduct of economic
policy, the management of political affairs, and the allocation of status
and rewards among different social and ethnic groups. At a maximum
they could result in real manifestations of sociopolitical instability.

In comparison with the situation likely to prevail in the years ahead,
the decades following Stalin's death were characterized by a high degree
of social and politcal stability. The relaxation of terror diminished what
had been a major source of popular alienation from the regime, while
the combination of rapid economic growth and expanding educational
and occupational opportunities helped strengthen the system's popular
support and legitimacy and eased the task of allocating wealth, status,
and power among rival social claimants. By meeting the population's
modest expectations for improved living standards, by ensuring security
of employment and price stability for basic commodities, and by enhancing the power and status of the Soviet Union on the global scene, the
post-Stalin leadership was able to tap substantial reservoirs of popular
approval and support. It was thus in a position to reduce the role of
coercion and terror as instruments of social control in favor of greater
reliance on normative and material incentives. All these factors contributed, in turn, to the stability and perceived legitimacy of the Soviet

*Reprinted by permission of the author and publisher from *Washington Quar-
terly* 6, No. 2 (Spring, 1983), pp. 29–47. Copyright 1983 by The Center for
Strategic and International Studies, Georgetown University, Soviet project.

regime and help explain its ability to deal successfully with significant challenges to its rule, including an unprecedented level of intelligentsia dissent.

In contrast to the opportunities presented by Stalin's death, the post-Brezhnev leadership confronts a considerably bleaker economic and social environment. Declining economic prospects are compounded by diminishing opportunities for upward social mobility, creating intensified competition over shrinking increments of material goods and social opportunities. Growing tensions among social and ethnic groups, social malaise, and increasing manifestations of social strain are the likely result. In the absence of an overriding external threat, these internal problems are far more likely to divide than to unite the Soviet population. They are also more likely to constrain than to propel the Soviet leadership in its pursuit of expanded influence abroad.

Constraints on Performance

A number of factors will diminish the capacity of the Soviet leadership to meet societal demands and expectations in the 1980s. First and foremost among the potential constraints on regime performance are declining rates of economic growth. Where high rates of growth permitted the leadership to satisfy the demands of key interest groups, bureaucracies, and regional elites, a slowdown in growth will intensify the competition among rival claimants and reduce the resources available for managing conflicts. Where high rates of growth permitted the leadership the luxury of increasing allocations to guns and butter and investment simultaneously, low growth is forcing sharp choices among priorities and is severely constraining the leadership's ability to sustain steady improvements in consumer welfare as well as investment. Moreover, to the extent that current economic problems compel new initiatives in economic policy, they are likely to entail relatively high social costs. Thus, measures that might alleviate current economic difficulties, such as freeing the labor market at the expense of job security or reforming the price structure to reduce the state subsidy of basic commodities, would jeopardize key elements of a tacit social compact between regime and population and generate serious working-class discontent. On the other hand, intensified labor discipline would be unlikely to elicit the motivation and enthusiasm vital to increased labor productivity.

Unfavorable demographic trends constitute a second source of constraints demanding the Soviet leadership's attention. Declining birth rates among the Slavic and Baltic populations, coupled with high rates of reproduction among the Muslim populations of Soviet Central Asia, will intensify competition for resources among different regions and republics and for access to higher education and valued jobs within them. Moreover, differential birth rates will also compound the problems posed by a labor shortage, by an economically irrational distribution of labor resources among the major regions of the country, and by rising ethnonationalism among Russians and non-Russians alike.

The process of political succession now under way is likely to complicate further the management of current problems. The Brezhnev era was characterized by elite consensus around the rules of the political game and a tacit understading to confine conflicts within a circumscribed milieu; the new era offers the likelihood of intensified political competition. The immobilism of the Brezhnev leadership increased the pressures for new initiatives after his departure, while massive turnover of an entire political generation brings a high degree of unpredictability of the political landscape.

Major conflicts over policy and power, articulation of alternative programs, and even appeals to domestic constituencies are possible, given the considerable temptations to would-be contenders for high position to seek a broader social and political base. Thus, we may well see significant shifts in orientations of the political elite, which could affect such major social issues as the relative priority of consumer welfare, the scope and limits of egalitarianism in economic and social policy, the role of private economic activity, and the balance between the claims of Russian nationalism and the demands of the non-Russian nationalities.

Finally, the Soviet leadership faces a less benign international environment than has prevailed during much of the post-Stalin era. The demise of Soviet-American detente and the confrontational foreign policy stance of the Reagan administration in its dealings with the USSR will necessarily impinge on domestic priorities, concerns, and policy debates. Pressures for increased military outlays, greater economic autarchy, heightened internal vigilance, and reduced exposure of the Soviet population to foreign influences are more easily sustained in an atmosphere of siege and confrontation than in the more benign environment associated with detente. A few examples of the tightening of internal controls that has accompanied the deterioration of Soviet-American relations are increased repression of dissidents, renewed jamming of foreign radio broadcasts after a 7-year lull, major cutbacks in telephone communications between the USSR and the West, the decline in the number of exit visas to Israel granted by Soviet authorities (51,000 in 1979, 10,000 in 1981, to under 2,700 in 1982), and renewed attacks on Western lifestyles and on contacts between Soviet citizens and foreigners.

Political legitimacy can be eroded by unfavorable changes in objective social and economic conditions or by subjective changes in expectations and demands, which alter the terms of the implicit social compact between leaders and led. The potential for such a development is greater at this point than at any earlier time in postwar Soviet history, for reasons to be examined at greater length in the following sections.

Stagnation   Possibly the most critical social problem for the Soviet
in Living   leadership of the 1980s, and the one with the greatest
Standards   potential for causing instability, is the likelihood that
               resource constraints will sharply diminish the lead-
ership's ability to improve living conditions to any appreciable degree.
For the first time in the last 30 years, economic performance will be
insufficient to provide more than a marginal increase in per capita
consumption without improved productivity or without the reallocation
of resources away from investment or military spending. In the absence
of resource reallocation or improved productivity the standard of living
could stagnate or even begin to decline.

From the late 1920s until 1953, the Soviet population was the victim of
a strategy of economic growth that accelerated the development of
heavy industrial and military capabilities at the expense of mass welfare.
At the time of Stalin's death, the Soviet living standard was only slightly
above that of 1928; the Soviet people were "ill-fed, ill-housed, and
ill-clothed by any modern standard."[1] The scarcity of consumer goods
and personal services reflected the low priority Stalin's investment
strategy assigned to consumer needs. Only education and health care,
treated as investment in human capital, experienced substantial advances.

The quarter-century that followed Stalin's death saw a major reorder-
ing of priorities to redress the gross imbalance of the Stalinist strategy;
the Soviet consumer benefited from the allocation to consumption of a
higher share of annual increments from the rising gross national product
(GNP). Rising living standards, reflected in improved diet, housing,
supplies of consumer durables, and clothing, resulted from an increase
in per capita consumption averaging roughly 4% annually from 1951 to
1975. The greatest gains were made in the 1950s and in the late 1960s;
during the 1970s growth in per capita consumption slowed to roughly
2.5% per year and fell below 2% in 1981.

Declining allocations to consumption are compounding existing
shortcomings in the provision of consumer goods and services and
intensifying the imbalance between the supply of desired goods and
services and effective demand. Acute shortages of food products and
other prized consumer goods develop alongside rising inventories of
unsellable products. With rising incomes outstripping the production of
wanted goods and services, a thriving private "second economy" has
developed to bridge the gap. Mounting cash deposits in savings banks
exceeded half of total disposable money incomes in 1979, while Soviet
and Western economists alike could only guess at the size of cash hoards
in private hands. The economic and sociopolitical consequences of this
combination of declining growth in material welfare and an enormous
overhang of purchasing power are far-reaching, while available remedies carry high social costs.

The food supply has become an especially serious economic and political problem in the last few years. Longstanding shortcomings in agriculture, compounded by a succession of poor harvests in the past few years, have created near stagnation in agricultural output and widespread shortages of meat, dairy products, fruits, and vegetables, especially in smaller cities. The government has imposed rationing of a number of food products, and has relied increasingly on special distribution channels to supplement distribution through retail trade outlets and to direct scarce supplies to priority sectors. The widening gap in prices between state stores and collective farm markets reflect these growing shortages; official Soviet writings confirm unofficial reports of price differentials ranging from 1.5 to 4 times higher.

The willingness of the Soviet leadership to import large quantities of grain to maintain livestock testifies to its concern about the food supply. One-third of all hard-currency imports are now food products, and these have accounted for virtually all the increased availability of farm products since 1976. Brezhnev himself called for improving the food situation as "not only a paramount economic task but also an urgent social and political task" and convened a special session of the Central Committee in 1982 to address it.

Although the food supply has taken on special urgency, the limited availability and poor quality of consumer goods and services are another important source of dissatisfaction. Rising incomes and living standards have raised the demands and expectations of consumers, who fill Soviet publications with complaints about the poor quality, durability, and style of Soviet products. According to one source, the proportion of goods either rejected or lowered in grade when received by trade organizations has increased in recent years to the point that "trade refuses to accept one of every 10 garments, one of every 8 pairs of shoes, and one of every 10 meters of fabric."[2] Repairs were needed on 227,000 refrigerators from enterprises of one ministry alone and on over 1.5 million television sets of another. Greater consumer leverage has also resulted in growing accumulations of unsaleable goods. In 1978 alone some 4.6 billion rubles worth of goods had accumulated in unsold inventories, and the state budget allocated about $1 billion annually to cover losses on such goods.

The underdevelopment of the retail trade network and the inadequate development of consumer and personal services place heavy burdens on the time and energy of the Soviet consumer. In the mid-1960s housework consumed close to 1 billion man- and woman-hours, and the average Soviet woman walked 12–13 km per day in the course of 4 hours of domestic chores. Shopping was a major preoccupation, described by the term *dostat'* (to procure), a form of "hunting and gathering," with a broad spectrum of connotations: locating desired goods at suitable prices, queuing, bartering, bribing, and exchanging favors. Indeed, a recent Soviet article devoted entirely to the problem of scarcity lamented that "a large part of the population is preoccupied with the search for scarce goods."[3]

The social consequences of declining rates of economic growth will depend both on the severity of the slowdown itself and on the policy choices that the leadership makes in attempting to cope with it. If productivity remains flat in the 1980s, if the share of defense spending remains more or less constant, and if investment continues to rise at 3.5% per year, a growth rate of GNP of roughly 3% per year would permit per capita consumption to rise approximately 2% per year, a level that would allow a slow but nonetheless continuing improvement in living conditions. Under more pessimistic, and likely, assumptions of growth rates at or below 2% per year, or of rising defense expenditures, the growth of consumption would fall below 1% per year, bringing the improvement of mass welfare to a virtual standstill.

While initial economies are likely to touch those categories of socially marginal expenditures least visible in the short run, such as health and education, a severe slowdown over a protracted period would force retrenchment in higher-priority and more visible areas. How the Soviet population would react to severe belt-tightening at this stage of Soviet development is highly uncertain. Past promises and experiences have generated expectations that affect popular reactions to current and prospective trends. While these expectations remain modest by Western standards, the passivity and acquiescence characteristic of an older generation in an earlier era will not necessarily serve as a reliable guide to future behavior.

Because economic performance has been so central to sociopolitical stability, the consequences of this stagnation for Soviet economic, political, and social stability could well be significant. First, a slowdown in the rate of improvement of living standards risks a loss of popular support. While Khrushchev's promise that by 1980 the Soviet population would enjoy "the highest living standard in the world" has long been discounted, the Soviet leadership has repeatedly declared raising the level of material welfare to be its major goal. The large investments of recent years in agriculture, including grain imports, housing, consumer goods, and automobiles offer evidence of the degree to which it bases its own sense of legitimacy on improvements in mass welfare. Stagnation or erosion in living standards will thus impinge on perceived legitimacy at both elite and mass levels.

Second, these problems erode the effectiveness of material incentives critical to efforts to improve labor productivity and to maximize labor force participation. An increasingly educated and sophisticated labor force cannot be coerced into increased efficiency; only a developed and flexible incentive system is likely to elicit desired results. If income cannot purchase desired goods and services, its contribution to worker motivation is undercut. Third, shortcomings in the supply and distribution of goods and services divert increasing shares of time and energy into procurement. The imbalance between effective demand and the supply of goods and services provides a powerful impetus to development of the "second economy," which in turn leads to an unofficial and uncontrollable redistribution of income. Finally, reduced availability of resources for material incentives and the growing difficulties of controlling and directing their use may compel greater reliance on coercive instruments for dealing with labor problems, however counterproductive these might prove to be.

While there are a number of possible remedies to this situation, each of them carries high costs. A price reform that would attempt to bring supply and demand into balance, possibly combined with a campaign against corruption and a currency revaluation to capture large cash hoards, would require sharp increases in the prices of basic commodities, particularly food. While this would make possible a substantial reduction in government subsidies as well, now covering virtually half the cost of meat, to take one example, the Soviet leadership has thus far been reluctant to consider such a step because of its potential for causing social unrest. The risks must appear especially high in light of developments in Poland in recent years.

A second option would attempt to increase labor productivity and make more efficient use of labor resources by encouraging the dismissal and transfer of redundant workers. While such an approach has been attempted in small-scale experiments, its benefits are offset by what are perceived to be a number of problematic consequences. First and foremost, it would threaten the security of employment, which is so central both to the tacit social compact between the regime and the population and to the ideological campaign that contrasts socialist job security with capitalist unemployment.

A third option would allot an increased role to the private sector for providing not only food supplies but other consumer goods and services. Some steps in this direction have already been taken in agriculture, both by expanding private plots and by encouraging industrial enterprises to develop auxiliary agricultural activities, but both ideological and practical constraints place limits on such developments. Finally, the leadership could contemplate a more radical expansion of the private sector, a reform along the lines of the New Economic Policy of the 1920s, which would encourage small-scale private entrepreneurship in retail trade and the services while maintaining central control over the "commanding heights" of the economy. A major reform of the economic system, however, in the direction of decentralization would be so far-reaching in its consequences for vitually every aspect of economic, political, and social life and so threatening to the party apparatus that its prospects are dim. Consequently, a continuing but unofficial expansion of private economic activity and a continuing growth of the second economy—along with sporadic campaigns against corruption in high places—are the most likely responses to the declining prospects of the state sector.

Slowing Upward Mobility Another of the Soviet system's major political assets has been its association with greatly expanded opportunities for educational and professional advancement. The Stalin regime enjoyed immense success in persuading the population that it provided significantly greater chances for upward social mobility than had a tsarism few remembered or a capitalism none had experienced. The rhetorical exaltation of workers as the "leading" social class and of collectivized peasants as their close ally combined, paradoxically, with periodic reminders that Soviet conditions made it easy for the talented to ascend from these classes and become members of the intelligentsia. Membership in the "leading class" and upward mobility out of it were taken, simultaneously, as evidence of the justice of the new social order. In a period of slowing growth and growing crystallization of the social structure, this particular political asset is nearly spent.

Moreover, it is the conjunction of diminishing economic growth with slowing social mobility that creates a distinctively new set of problems. An economy in straitened circumstances can moderate public dissatisfaction if it can nonetheless offer large numbers the prospect of improving their individual positions by some combination of effort, acquisition of credentials, and expertise. Career success, the ability to claim a larger share of a stable or shrinking economic pie, and enhanced social status can serve to offset or compensate for a slowdown in mass consumption. However, the Soviet economy and bureaucracy are no longer expanding in ways that hold out that prospect, and the comparatively fluid social structure of earlier times has frozen in ways that tend to maintain existing social groups in their places.

The drama of transition from a rural to urban, from peasant to industrial society is a tale once told. But the desires it fostered and the aspirations for mobility with which it suffused many sectors of society remain and will continue to create a major problem for the Soviet leadership in the years ahead. The problems became visible in the early 1960s, when the Soviet social system reflected many features associated with modern industrial societies everywhere. It was a hierarchical social system composed of five major groups. At the bottom of the social ladder were the collective farm peasants, disadvantaged on virtually all social indicators and excluded until the mid-1960s from state pensions and other welfare benefits. Next in the hierarchy stood workers, varying in their educational level, skills, and incomes, depending on whether they worked in favored branches of heavy industry or in lower-paid light and consumer industries. The white-collar stratum, largely female in composition, ranked somewhere in the middle in terms of education, income, and prestige. At the apex of the social pyramid stood the intelligentsia and the *nachalniki*, or governing political elite, sharing comparable life styles and incomes but differentiated by the fact that the power of the ruling elite derived from its positions, while that of the intelligentsia stemmed from the authority and prestige inherent in the functions it performed.

These broad social groups differed significantly not only in such objective indicators as education, income, prestige, political participation, and access to scarce goods and services, but also in attitudes, life styles, and behavior, as a proliferation of Soviet sociological studies have made abundantly clear.

Because the distribution of rewards reflects political regulation to a more significant degree than market forces, the policy choices of different groups of leaders have considerable influence on both individual incomes and the position of social groups. To the extent that the party consciously attempted to prevent social strata from consolidating and transmitting their privileges, as was the case under Khrushchev, the system preserved elements of its earlier social fluidity. In more recent years, however, the combination of enhanced personal security, reduced political turnover, and consolidation of elite prerogatives has promoted the emergence of a privileged stratum that enjoys not merely high incomes but access to goods and services not available on the market or accessible to the ordinary Soviet citizen: high-quality housing, restricted stores carrying deficit or imported goods at nominal prices, special medical and vacation facilities, and travel abroad.

The crystallization of a new social hierarchy was also accompanied by the growing ability of new elites to transmit their advantaged position to offspring. Here the development of the Soviet educational system played a crucial role. While a "sorting" process still occurs at the transition from 8- to 10-year education (with the social profile of those who continue for the ninth and tenth year more "elite"), a growing share of the age cohort, or statistical group, completes the 10 years of education necessary for subsequent admission to a higher educational institution. However, admissions to such institutions are restricted, and their rate of growth slowed from 10% between 1961 and 1965 to 2.5% between 1966 and 1970 to only 1.2% between 1971 and 1975. In short, a progressively smaller share of a growing cohort of secondary school graduates could continue to higher education: from over 50% in the early 1950s to under 14% today. A growing gap between the aspirations of young people for higher education and the possibilities of their realization was the result. Khrushchev's ill-fated educational reforms of 1958, though largely prompted by a growing labor shortage, reflected a concern with just these issues: a society increasingly overeducated for its occupational structure, a generation of young people aspiring to be engineers and disdainful of manual jobs, and a privileged elite attempting to use the educational system to pass its advantaged position to its offspring.

By the 1960s a lack of fit between the educational and career aspirations of young people and the possibilities open to them was evident in a succession of Soviet sociological studies. They revealed that over three-quarters of the graduating secondary school students hoped to continue their studies, while far fewer were actually able to do so. In the heightened competition for access, different social strata differed markedly in their success ratios: 9 out of 10 of the children of urban non-manual workers who desired to continue their education full-time were able to do so, while only 1 out of 10 peasant offspring were so able.

In the view of many Soviet sociologists, the combination of excessively high aspirations, on the one hand, and disdain for blue-collar jobs, on the other, has resulted in serious demoralization when expectations were disappointed. The "shattering" of career plans contributes to "attitudes of skepticism" and "a weakening of belief in ideals," according to one leading Soviet sociologist.[4] High labor turnover reflects the unhealthy tendency for young people to roam from one low-level and unsatisfying job to another, jobs they view as temporary evils until they succeed in gaining admission to a higher educational institution, which usually fails to happen.

Some Soviet scholars maintain that the problem has begun to ease in the last few years as students lower their aspirations to correspond with a realistic assessment of their chances. Supporting his contention that "the career plans of graduating students are moving into greater conformity with the objective requirements of Soviet society," one well-known Soviet sociologist, F. R. Filippov, maintains that 80–90% of secondary school students in the mid-1960s were inclined to continue their studies, but that the figure had dropped to about 46% in 1973–1975.[5] Fragmentary evidence of a decline in applications to higher educational institutions, from 269 per 100 vacancies in 1970 to 245 per 100 in 1977, would support his view. Children of workers and collective farmers, however, are more likely to scale down their aspirations than are the offspring of employees and specialists. Consequently, the increasing competitiveness of access in the past 2 decades has tended to strengthen the position of children from advantaged families.

Numerous studies conducted by Soviet sociologists since the early 1960s document that children from higher status families tend to begin formal schooling with better preparation, achieve higher levels of academic performance, have higher educational aspirations, and experience greater success in fulfilling those aspirations than their less advantaged counterparts. They dominate the specialized secondary schools for talented children, which offer advanced training in the sciences, mathematics, and foreign languages. Moreover, not only do they make up a disproportionate share of the applicant pool at higher educational institutions, but they are more successful in winning admission.

Family position affects educational opportunities in more direct and material ways as well. Children of higher status families are more successful in passing the entrance examinations because of their ability to utilize private tutoring. The rector of Moscow University himself explained in 1969 that 85% of the students admitted to the Faculty of Mechanics and Mathematics that year had received private instruction prior to taking the entrance examinations.

Financial circumstances also affect the ability of young people to defer employment in order to continue their studies. Although the state heavily subsidizes higher education, providing stipends for almost three-fourths of the full-time students and subsidized dormitory accommodations for roughly one-half, students still depend in varying degrees upon family support.

Finally, the meritocratic features of educational access are tempered by informal practices that discriminate against or offer preferential treatment to particular individuals or members of social groups. Mounting evidence suggests that examination procedures are manipulated to exclude Jewish applications or to promote "affirmative action" on behalf of non-Russian nationalities and that well-placed or well-endowed parents are frequently in a position to influence the selection process on behalf of their offspring. Although the resort to influence or bribery by elite families has come under attack in recent years, the selection process itself virtually invites corruption.

As a consequence, higher educational institutions have taken on an increasingly elitist profile, with the most prestigious institutions drawing a larger share of students from families of the intelligentsia, while those of lower quality or offering training in less prestigious fields attract higher proportions of students of working class or peasant background. The emergence of a hierarchically stratified system of higher educational institutions thus corresponds to the crystallization of status within the population more broadly and to the decline in opportunities for upward social mobility for worker and particularly for peasant youth.

The Soviet leadership has attempted to defuse the frustration of aspirations inherent in this situation in a number of ways. Not wishing to expand enrollments in higher education, and thereby create an even greater imbalance between educational enrollments and occupational needs, it has sought simultaneously to expand opportunities for lower social strata and to lower social strata and to lower aspirations.

First, it established highly visible, if limited, opportunities for more disadvantaged young people to enter higher educational institutions. In 1969, it created preparatory divisions, reminiscent of the *rabfaki* of an earlier era, to alter the social composition of higher educational institutions by offering college preparatory programs to young people employed as workers or collective farmers for at least a year. At the same time, the leadership has vocational-technical schools to attract larger numbers of young people into programs training skilled workers. Third, it has sought to increase the attractiveness of blue-collar occupations by increasing their rewards. The narrowing of wage differentials between blue-collar, white-collar, and engineering occupations during the past two decades represents just such an effort, although it appears to have reached its limit. Finally, the leadership has launched a highly visible, if selective, attack on bribery and other forms of corruption in the competition for educational access. Indeed, Aliev specifically alluded in a *Literaturnaia Gazeta* article (November 18, 1981, #47, p. 10) to a decree that went so far as to forbid family members of the Azerbaijan political elite from even applying for admission to medical schools, an implicit admission that only the most Draconian measures could forestall corrupt practices.

It is too early to evaluate the success of the efforts. Yet even if aspirations expressed by application to higher education are moderating, this does not resolve the problem; an expressed willingness to settle for a career less than that of intelligentsia may mask serious disgruntlement. If this were not the case, young men and women would surely make more use of specialized secondary or vocational-technical trade schools. While enrollment in the latter increased in the 1970s for those deciding not to complete academic secondary school (from 6.4% of those completing eighth year in schools in the Russian Republic in 1973 to 14.0% in 1977), so also did the percentage increase of eighth graders moving on to complete academic secondary education (54% in 1973 to 61% in 1977).

Moreover, even if a larger cohort moves from secondary education directly into employment, the gap between aspirations and job content will not necessarily diminish. Rising educational attainments tend to increase the demand for more satisfying and nonroutine jobs, but a number of studies indicate that educational attainment in the USSR is outrunning the growth in the proportion of such jobs. Indeed, many Soviet analysts are concerned that job dissatisfaction will be a growing rather than a diminishing problem in the years ahead.

Thus, Soviet social policy faces in the 1980s and 1990s a situation that calls for considerable finesse. Ideally, in the face of labor and capital shortage, the state should divert teenagers from academic training and instead provide specialized secondary or vocational-technical education, which would bring them jobs as skilled and more productive workers. Psychologically, this outcome should eliminate the morale problems of the sort noted among young workers who have completed secondary education without adding skills and who are discontented with jobs whose average demand is for 7 or perhaps 8, but not 10, years of general education. Morale should rise, productivity should increase, and this generation of new workers should, in turn, raise a generation of offspring ready in large numbers to duplicate their parental status, in line with a realistic appreciation of the economy's needs in the years to come.

This is not likely to happen. As the prospects for significant further improvement of living standards grow distant in a low-growth economy, the stakes in the mobility competition increase. Except in the unlikely event of diversion of resources from investment and defense to consumption, the relative costs of being a worker and the advantages of being a professional will increase. A highly stratified Soviet society may be able to block from higher education those who desire to rise through it to higher status, but not to eliminate or even diminish those desires. A time of stable or declining living standards in a society far from affluent by its own citizens' calculations is unlikely to make people ready to remember their place. If Soviet citizens are like their counterparts elsewhere in this respect and material rewards and social status motivate them to seek to rise, then as both the rewards and the titles grow relatively more scarce, the level of dissatisfaction and frustration is likely to rise.

The Decline of Civic Morale

Possibly the most dramatic change of recent years, and one with profound implications for the legitimacy and stability of the Soviet system, has been a shift in attitudes among the Soviet population, especially in the adult middle generation, during the past 2 decades: growing pessimism about the Soviet future, increasing disillusionment with official values, and an accompanying decline in civic morale. While this judgment necessarily rests on fragmentary data from Soviet opinion surveys, the press, and Soviet fiction, on familiarity with Soviet society, and on emigré sources, these diverse sources all reinforce the view that this shift is far-reaching in scope and profound in its implications.

In order to fully comprehend the nature and implications of this change, it will be useful to look backward briefly to the most extensive body of evidence concerning popular attitudes and expectations and their bearing on Soviet political culture: that of the Harvard Project on the Soviet Social System, conducted in 1950–1954 and based on a survey of almost 2500 refugees. The findings of this survey, which Alex Inkeles and Raymond Bauer summarized in *The Soviet Citizen* (Cambridge: Harvard University Press, 1959), were extraordinarily revealing, for they called into question beliefs then widely held about the fragility of the Soviet system. On the contrary, the project found that the regime had acquired a high degree of legitimacy in the eyes of its people and conformed in such important respects to their fundamental expectations and values that even refugees not favorably disposed to many specific features of the system nonetheless expressed a high degree of attachment to many core values and institutions. This study did not anticipate the emergence of serious dissent by the intelligentsia or nationalist disaffection in subsequent years, for a number of reasons. But its findings with respect to the core political culture were reinforced some 25 years later when a new wave of Soviet emigration enabled scholars to compare the attitudes of a new Soviet generation with those of their predecessors. The continuity of the two proved striking.

Both surveys demonstrated a substantial degree of consensus around basic elements of Soviet political culture. Respondents in both groups attached high value to order, discipline, and strong leadership. While they saluted the principle of civil liberties, they were willing to tolerate a high degree of governmental intervention as long as it was exercised benevolently. Tolerance for extensive government paternalism was reinforced by strong support for the welfare-oriented features of the system. The refugees placed considerable value on free public education, socialized health care, job security, and other social benefits and considered them the most attractive features of the Soviet system. Its basic political and economic arrangements were also widely accepted, except for the terror, which all resented. Public ownership of heavy industry was more solidly supported than of light industry and the services, but on the whole respondents were proud of Soviet accomplishments and criticized regime performance rather than institutional arrangements. There was little evidence that they saw any alternatives to the system, or that they viewed "capitalism" as preferable. Political freedom had attractions, but they associated it with anarchy, lack of control, and insecurity.

Moreover, the study carried potential implications for future social trends. While all respondents were relatively modest in their material and political aspirations, a positive correlation emerged between social status and approval of the system. Workers and collective farmers, the two groups experiencing the greatest degree of material deprivation, tended to express greater dissatisfaction and alienation, while those with higher levels of education and social status expressed greater approval. Thus, although higher educational level was also associated with greater "liberalism," economic and social opportunity had greater impact on political attitudes than did political conditions in and of themselves. Finally, acceptance of the Soviet system appeared to increase with each successive generation, with younger cohorts expressing more favorable views than their parents or grandparents.

Had the Khrushchev leadership read *The Soviet Citizen*, it could not have responded more directly and astutely to the sources of alienation the study identified. By reducing the terror, identifying improved material welfare—particularly among workers and collective farmers—as a high priority for the regime, and promising the Soviet population a standard of living that would overtake that of the West within a short period of time, Khrushchev's reforms tapped substantial reservoirs of popular approval and support. They also created an atmosphere of optimism and heightened expectations about the future. Despite economic difficulties in the mid-1960s that provoked working-class demonstrations and compelled the leadership's partial retreat from unrealistic promises, that optimism persisted. If anything, the sobriety of the Kosygin-Brezhnev leadership offered greater assurances that the future was in good hands. Opinion surveys not only within the USSR but also among emigrés who had recently left testify to the widespread view that the people believed the regime had their interests at heart, and that conditions were likely to continue to improve.

The intellectuals were among the first to experience a shift in attitude. The partial rehabilitation of Stalin that began in the mid-1960s, the trials of dissident writers, the invasion of Czechoslovakia, and the general tightening of political controls played a major role in their increased malaise. But not until prospects of an economic slowdown reinforced political concerns did its mood spread to the middle class more widely and to the working class as well. The 1975 crop failure provided the final shock; growing food shortages and disruptions of supply in subsequent years simply compounded the growing conviction that the economy was unable to deliver further improvements in living standards and that the economic system itself was at fault. Shortcomings, which were viewed in the early 1960s as deviations from the overall upward movement, had by the 1970s come to be viewed as the norm.

The decline in optimism was strikingly captured by two Soviet opinion surveys, the first taken in 1971 to ascertain the social expectations of working people in Leningrad and the second, taken 4 years later, to determine whether anticipated improvements had occurred. In the case of both earnings and education, improvements had exceeded expectations. In other categories, however, including living conditions, service industries, and medical services, achievements fell short of what had been anticipated by respondents. Moreover, the expectations themselves appeared quite modest: while 57% of those surveyed expected improvements in the quantity and quality of manufactured goods during the Tenth 5-Year Plan, only 45% were convinced their incomes would rise during this period and only 35% expected their housing conditions to improve.[6]

Rising pessimism reflected a shift in the standards by which many social citizens evaluated regime performance. The traditional explanations of failure—the survival of capitalist remnants, growing pains, the aftermath of war, the machinations of unseen enemies—were no longer compelling to a generation raised to expect that the USSR was on the verge of overtaking the West. The distant past no longer formed the standard against which to measure present achievements; it was rather the recent past and expectations of the future. Moreover, the comparative reference was no longer the peasant or worker household of the 1930s but the living standard of the Soviet or, increasingly, foreign elite.

The growing exposure of the Soviet population to the world outside its borders, one of the major consequences of the changes after Stalin and of détente, had an incalculable impact on the evolution of Soviet society. Increasing imports of Western scientific and technical equipment for Soviet laboratories, factories, mines, and oil wells and of consumer goods from Eastern and Western Europe, exposed millions of Soviet citizens to the qualities of Western products. Scientific and cultural exchanges as well as expanded tourism provided growing opportunities for Soviet citizens to travel abroad, to encounter foreign visitors in the USSR, or to hear of the experiences and impressions of acquaintances who enjoyed such opportunities and who flaunted the products of their privileged travel. Western books, films, and radio broadcasts supplemented direct personal experience in providing information about, and whetting appetites for, the accoutrements of a Western lifestyle. The emigration during the 1970s of over 300,000 Soviet citizens, many of whom maintained close communication with friends and relatives back home, added to the flow of information about Western goods and prices. The variety, quality, and sheer quantity of Western goods seen and described established new standards for evaluating Soviet products and services, and invited increasingly negative evaluations of Soviet economic performance.

Even comparisons with an Eastern Europe more accessible and less ideologically suspect to the average Soviet citizen had subversive implications. From 1960 to 1976, roughly 11 million Soviet tourists visited Eastern Europe, perhaps one-half of them for the first time, and 2.5 million soldiers and a large number of East Europeans visited the USSR. The legendary acquisitiveness of Soviet travelers abroad offers ample testimony to both the scarcity and the poor quality of Soviet goods.

The growing tide of criticism gradually extended beyond the realm of consumer goods and services to include even features of the Soviet system once quite highly regarded. Health care is a case in point. Widespread criticism of this institution, once hailed as one of the system's great achievements, is now commonplace in Soviet writings. The 1976 survey of attitudes toward living standards and prospects for improvements discussed earlier revealed the greatest disappointment in the area of medical services. Whether the system has actually deteriorated in recent years is the subject of some controversy, but it is clear that medical care, like many other social services, has failed to keep pace with new needs, or with the expectations placed upon it by an increasingly educated and demanding population less tolerant of shortcomings and failures than at earlier stages of Soviet development.

The implications of this growing pessimism are far-reaching. George

Feifer, a veteran observer of the Soviet scene, returning to Moscow in 1981 after an absence of some 10 years, offers especially graphic testimony on a whole array of social changes that countless Western observers, emigrés, and Soviet sources have reported.[7] Food shortages and disruptions in the supply of other goods and services have generated a preoccupation with procurement that extends from manual workers to senior engineers and that feeds a rapidly growing second economy. Energy is increasingly diverted from work, and from other civic activities, into moonlighting, blackmarket activities, and the pursuit of desired goods: "It is private enterprise running wild, although the enterprise goes almost entirely into obtaining, rather than into producing, goods and services." The loss of confidence in public distribution and the surge in cheating and bribery have led to disintegration of old restraints and widespread demoralization. As one friend of Feifer's recounted, "The scorn [for official values] has led to the moral emptiness—as demonstrated by mass apathy, lying and cheating—in which we live."

This decline in civic morale has three distinct though interrelated elements: loss of optimism, loss of purpose, and disintegration of internal controls of self-discipline. The loss of optimism is associated with a growing sense that the system cannot live up to expectations and that problems associated with a new stage of development have outrun the capacity of existing institutions. A growing feeling is developing within the elite that the problem may be systemic, but there is little sense of viable alternatives and no belief that the United States, or any other capitalist system, offers a preferable model.

The loss of a sense of purpose is connected with the declining relevance and vitality of official ideology. Khrushchev's effort to revive the utopian, egalitarian, and populist features of Marxism-Leninism as a way of rekindling mass enthusiasm and dedication represented a last gasp of a tradition well on the way to extinction. There is increasing recognition that the values and policies of an earlier era are inadequate to contemporary challenges and require serious rethinking.

Finally, the erosion of social control and individual self-discipline, evident in significant increases in the entire gamut of "antisocial" behavior, from alcoholism to corruption and violations of labor discipline to theft of state property, reflects the limited success at internalizing new social norms and their breakdown under conditions of greater social relaxation and reduced reliance on coercion. At an earlier period of Soviet history the leadership could attribute such behavior to capitalist remnants or to strains associated with urbanization and the subjection of a peasant population to the discipline of factory life. Two generations later, without a great national crisis to bind the social fabric, traditional explanations ring hollow.

The loss of optimism associated with declining performance has been accompanied by a shift of expectations to the private realm. The decline in the relevance and vitality of ideology has awakened a quest for alternative sources of values and a revival of religious activity, and the breakdown in social controls has fueled a nostalgia for greater order and discipline and a growing social conservatism.

The shift in expectations and concerns to the private realm is nowhere more powerfully illustrated than in the virtual revolution in Soviet attitudes toward the family that has occurred in recent years. It suffices to evoke the image of Bolshevik feminist Alexandra Kollontai to recall the critical attitude of revolutionary Marxism-Leninism toward the bourgeois family and the expectation that in the socialist society of the future the traditional economic and social functions of the family, from cooking and housework to childcare, would be taken over by communal facilities. While the Stalin period inaugurated a shift away from these expectations, only in recent years has a family-centered value system emerged full-blown. The economic and social policies of the Brezhnev regime supported this trend by assigning the family a central social role, enhancing the resources of income, privacy, and leisure available to it, and strengthening its role in transmitting social status.

Official policy is paralleled and supplemented by a growing body of literature that virtually glorifies the family as the basis of social stability, the decisive factor in the education, socialization, and moral upbringing of children, and the indispensable provider of necessary social services the state either cannot or should not supplant. In a striking inversion of revolutionary values, leading Soviet sociologists now maintain that communal arrangements would not permit satisfaction of increasingly diverse and individual needs, tastes, and lifestyles and that, even if society were in a position to assume the burdens of housework and childcare, it should refrain from doing so in order to maintain, even artificially, the cohesion of the family as a social unit.

An analogous shift in values is evident in recent discussions of the balance to be struck between public and private consumption. Specialists are now questioning the traditional reliance on social consumption funds as an instrument of income equalization and a symbol of social solidarity. Arguing that the Soviet system need no longer retain social arrangements that originated in the different historical conditions of the 1920s and 1930s, some urge that, although a safety net should still extend to low-income families, the state should reduce or end its subsidizations of housing, medical care, vacations, and other goods and services and should allow and indeed encourage the use of private incomes for their purchase.

These two examples, even though limited to relatively specialized scholarly publications, illustrate the emergence in recent years of an intellectual and moral rationale for the increasing privatization of Soviet life and legitimization of the greater social inequality as well as diversity it is bound to generate.

The decline in a sense of purpose—and with it the disappearance of the enthusiasm and zeal that accompanied, in varying degree, such great campaigns of earlier times as the First 5-Year Plan, the Great Fatherland War, and even the Virgin Lands program—and the spread of cynicism and political apathy have also prompted a relatively wide-spread quest, largely by the intelligentsia, for alternative values and sources of meaning. Heightened interest in religion among younger people, evident in increased church attendance, growing use of religious symbolism, and the affirmation of moral and spiritual values are manifestations of this quest. It is associated as well with a revival of interest in national traditions and nostalgia for the past. Moreover, this revival is not confined to the Russian past; from the Baltic to central Asia it has parallels and counterparts among the non-Russian nationalities.

While much of this interest focuses on culture and is illustrated by the rapid rise in massive membership (reportedly 12 million) of the Society for the Preservation of Historical and Cultural Monuments, the first grass-roots organization to emerge in the USSR, it has political im-plications as well. To the extent that this quest embodies a critical attitude toward, or even rejection of, the scientific positivism and materialistic world view associated with official ideology and the "scientific-technological revolution" that it so repetitiously extols, it also contains elements of an anti-urban, anti-industrial set of values. The emergence of a Soviet-style environmental movement, the first more or less spontaneous large-scale phenomenon of its kind in the USSR, represents both a concern for the preservation of the natural environ-ment against the ravages of unbridled industrialism and an effort to exert pressure on behalf of a balanced weighing of costs and benefits. Finally, there is the impulse of sheer escapism, whether to other countries in the form of travelogues, to the more intimate universe of personal relations, to the realms of parapsychology, or the unexplored universe of science fiction.

Widespread anxiety over the erosion of traditional social norms and growing evidence of indiscipline and social disorder, and corruption extending to the highest levels of the political hierarchy have evoked a growing impulse for restoration of law and order, a reassertion of authority. This finds expression in a variety of ways, from nostalgia for Stalin, the *krepki khozyain* (strong boss), to the inchoate yearning ex-pressed in the "village prose" movement for a return to an idealized patriarchal rural society where male and female roles were more sharply differentiated and "women knew their place and things were in order." The selection of Andropov as Brezhnev's successor might well be a response to this widespread yearning for strong and decisive leadership after the immobilism of the late Brezhnev period.

Anxiety over the erosion of civic morale is also a factor in the extraordinary importance of World War II as a cultural symbol. This search for sources of pride and satisfaction and for heroic causes with which to identify leads backward rather than forward, to a renewed emphasis on patriotism, the focus on World War II, and widespread praise of military virtues. World War II offers the single, most potent, unifying symbol for positive identification; it epitomizes the optimism, clarity of goals, righteousness of purpose, and extremes of self-discipline that the nation had once sustained and that are now felt to be lacking, especially among a younger generation viewed as preoccupied with consumerism and self-gratification and tainted by pacifism. It is, however, far more a focus of nostalgia and comfort than a premonition of future intent; few foreign policy objectives, short of a conflict with China, could generate comparable intensity.

The political consequences of this erosion of civic morale are therefore ambiguous. These trends reflect a growing retreat from rather than a direct challenge to the political domain, a diversion of energies and ambitions into more rewarding private concerns. They ease the tasks of ruling even as they reject the mobilization ethos. At the same time, they are a source of serious concern to a political elite already worried about declining labor productivity, social discontent, and diminishing respect for authority, and fearful that its own legitimacy will be eroded by the revival of many elements of traditional values and behavior.

Implications for Domestic Stability

What are the likely political consequences of these broad social trends? These developments point to a widening gap between the leadership's aspirations to shape and channel the direction of social change and its diminishing capacity to do so, the result of a progressive weakening of the three mechanisms of social control traditionally available: the coercive, material, and normative mechanisms.

A diminished reliance on terror, increased predictability in the definition and punishment of violations of Soviet law, and greater use of material and normative incentives to elicit desired social behavior have characterized the period since Stalin. While this shift reflected an assessment that the benefits of such an approach would outweigh the costs, particularly in view of the new challenges and opportunities presented by the emergence of an increasingly complex modern society and educated population, the shift also created dilemmas for the system. At an earlier time one could speak of a "revolution from above," with connotations of state domination of a largely passive society. Today the image no longer corresponds to reality. Social forces have not only achieved a certain degree of autonomy, but actively impinge on the political system in unprecedented ways. The erosion of political control over important sectors of economic life is clearly demonstrated by the evolution of the second economy, which by its existence subverts centrally established priorities and challenges centralized control over prices, income distribution, and the allocation of resources of manpower as well as capital. The spread of corruption, particularly within the political elite, threatens the organizational integrity and political legitimacy of the party, and feeds both the resentment of those excluded from patronage and the hostility of those critical of its existence.

A parallel development is visible in the escape of important dimensions of social behavior from regime control. Families marry, reproduce, and divorce without reference to demographic policy; populations migrate from north and east to south and west, rather than vice versa; labor absenteeism and turnover defy repeated calls for strengthening labor discipline; and religious practices continue despite efforts to invigorate atheistic propaganda. A whole spectrum of social pathologies, from rising alcoholism and crime to declining civic morale dramatize the limits of regime control. While the diminution of terror reduces the costs of such behavior, it remains unclear to what extent reimposition of tighter social controls would in fact resolve these problems. In a complex modern society successful social policies require a high degree of fine tuning, a strategy of the scalpel rather than of the hammer. While a more authoritarian pattern of political rule might produce greater compliance, it would hardly elicit the initiative, creativity, and motivation that current problems demand.

Having increased its reliance on material incentives and social advancement to elicit greater individual initiative and productivity, the Soviet leadership now faces a situation in which the combination of economic slowdown and diminished social mobility erodes the availability of these incentives as a mechanism of social control. The ties between the political elite and the working class are especially vulnerable. The precarious balance of the existing social compact is threatened by the possibility that the elite may not match declining mass consumption by equivalent sacrifices but will adopt a more energetic defense of established privileges. Unless the new leadership acts decisively to forestall such developments, the combination of deteriorating welfare and growing inequalities could enhance the potential for social unrest.

Finally, the weakening of the normative underpinnings of the system of social control is visible in the decline of civic morale. Throughout its history, the Soviet system has successfully mobilized its population on behalf of a succession of political and economic goals, defining a series of large purposes in heroic terms and invoking external and internal enemies to elicit the popular zeal and national unity necessary. This "heroic" period of Soviet history is past. Neither official ideology nor current economic and social policies are capable of eliciting the popular enthusiasm and unity of purpose that characterized an earlier epoch now remembered with nostalgia, and it is not clear that pride in superpower status will continue to offer a sufficiently powerful compensation.

Thus, the cumulative nature of current social difficulties exacerbating the erosion of traditional mechanisms of social control presents the Soviet leadership with unprecedented problems. During the 1980s a new and less experienced leadership will have to address simultaneously economic stagnation, declining prospects for social mobility, unfavorable demographic trends, and the rise of both Russian and non-Russian nationalism, at a time of eroding civic morale within the Soviet Union, a major systemic crisis in Poland, and a less benign international environment.

While these problems are serious and not easily managed, only a very particular and somewhat remote conjunction of circumstances could endow them with crisis proportions. First, although the gap between expectations and possibilities may be widening, the demands of the Soviet population for material goods, social opportunities, and political freedoms remain modest, not only by comparison with Western societies but even with much of Eastern Europe. Moreover, unlike the situation in Poland, patriotism strengthens support for the Soviet regime rather than working against it. Given the likelihood that economic difficulties will cause a slowdown in improvements but not an absolute decline in mass welfare, the regime will still have at its disposal resources with which to moderate discontent.

Even if social frustrations were to reach considerable proportions, the Soviet system imposes severe constraints on their political expression. The paucity of institutionalized channels for making demands on the system and the numerous barriers to the formation of groups and articulation of interests make the mobilization of social protest difficult. Moreover, deep cleavages divide Soviet social strata and ethnic groups from each other, preventing the formation of broad social coalitions, which might sustain alternative political programs. By contrast with Czechoslovakia in 1968 and Poland in 1980, there have been few efforts in the USSR thus far to link dissent by the intelligentsia with working class demands. While the force of nationalism might bridge the gap in some non-Russian areas, such as the Baltic republics, the relative success of the regime in co-opting local elites reduces the likelihood of such developments. Thus, while the decades ahead could well see increased working-class unrest, and more frequent though still sporadic outbreaks of strikes and demonstrations, these are likely to be local rather than nationwide, focusing on specific economic grievances and submitting to a combination of repression and redress.

The Soviet leadership has, moreover, demonstrated considerable skill at conflict-management. It has successfully isolated and managed cultural and political dissent by a combination of repression, bribery, and emigration. At the same time, it has recognized the need for more and better information about social attitudes, trends, and behavior, and has sponsored an increasingly broad and sophisticated program of social research. Virtually every major party organization and industrial complex has its resident, or consulting, sociologist, and the call for greater party reliance on opinion surveys as a guide to popular attitudes has come from leading figures within the Politburo itself, including K. U. Chernenko, a leading candidate for the succession. The party has not only sought to keep in touch with social trends, but it has also committed considerable resources to policies aimed at improving food supplies, raising living standards, and heading off working class unrest, all with the spectacle of developments in Poland very much in mind. Moreover, it has attempted to co-opt both social and national elites by offering a substantial stake in the system and considerable rewards in exchange for loyalty, exploiting both social and ethnic cleavages to undermine the foundations of hostile coalitions.

While the Soviet system may well evolve in more authoritarian directions in the years ahead and rely on a greater degree of repression to contain growing social tensions and conflict, it is difficult to imagine circumstances under which current social trends will become unmanageable or provoke a serious political crisis. Indeed, the power and the resolution the leadership has consistently shown—and the respect and fear the security police and the other forms of repression still command—constitute a convincing demonstration that the regime will not tolerate the expression of serious discontent and will crush any efforts to give it organized form.

Foreign Policy Implications

How will these internal problems affect Soviet objectives and capabilities in the international environment in the years ahead? Will these accumulating domestic problems have a restraining effect on Soviet behavior abroad, or are they likely on the contrary to evoke a more assertive and expansionist pattern of behavior to compensate for domestic failures?

There is no way to predict confidently the impact of domestic factors on Soviet foreign policy for several reasons. First, social trends will affect foreign policy only indirectly, as they are mediated through the filter of leadership perceptions and perceived reactions. Our uncertainty concerning the composition of the future Soviet elite, our lack of knowledge of its major concerns and priorities, and the difficulty in anticipating the international environment it is likely to encounter make our efforts to anticipate its behavior highly speculative.

Moreover, the feature of Soviet foreign policymaking that most distinguishes it from that of the United States is its insulation from domestic social pressures. Control over information and access to the policymaking process are even more tightly circumscribed in the case of foreign policy than they are with respect to domestic issues, even within the ruling group. Soviet citizens are notoriously ignorant about the outside world, and they have virtually no exposure to competing points of view about foreign policy. The tradition of rallying around the state against a foreign enemy, especially in circumstances when knowledge of the nature and character of the enemy is limited and gravely distorted, assures the Soviet leadership considerable freedom in formulating and executing its policies toward other states.

Some observers have argued, therefore, that the Soviet leadership is likely to compensate for domestic failures by pursuing a more aggressively expansionist foreign policy and by calling upon reserves of patriotism, if not outright chauvinism, in support. Such an effort could forge increased national unity in the face of growing social divisiveness, rekindle a fading sense of national purpose, and revive public morale. Its domestic consequences would be a strengthened Russian nationalism, an appeal to patriotic and military virtues, increased reliance on the military as a symbol of national power and a potent source of legitimation, and repression of domestic dissent.

While such a scenario cannot be excluded, it suffers from several flaws. First, it tends mechanistically to project outward from domestic conditions without adequate consideration of the international environment itself and the kinds of opportunities or challenges it will present to the Soviet leadership in the years ahead. Moreover, there is no historical precedent for the view that the Soviet Union has used external adventures to compensate for domestic dificulties, and much evidence to suggest the contrary. Periods of domestic crisis have usually been accompanied by a partial withdrawal from international involvement. While the achievement of strategic parity may reduce the relevance of historical precedents in predicting future behavior, it is significant that Soviet press treatment of the Soviet involvement in Afghanistan has, if anything, sought to minimize its military dimension and to focus on the cultural and administrative support rendered by Soviet troops. Similarly, the Soviet press has played down Soviet involvement in Ethiopia and Angola and the massive Soviet economic assistance to Cuba, seeking less to exploit its role publicly than to head off possible domestic criticism of the diversion of resources from internal needs. China aside, it is difficult to imagine a foreign policy scenario that would serve as the functional equivalent of World War II in mobilizing the Soviet population on behalf of a popular and unifying national cause.

This does not preclude the possibility that Soviet imperial arrogance will exacerbate the succession of regional problems and crises, which are likely in the years ahead, and that competitive demagogy and greater risk-taking will contribute to increase international instability. While many factors, and above all the international environment itself, will shape Soviet foreign policy behavior in the 1980s and while it is as difficult to anticipate the many opportunities and challenges that will arise as it is to predict the outcomes, the Soviet leadership will undoubtedly have accumulating domestic problems and vulnerabilities very much in mind as it weighs the costs and benefits of alternative foreign policies.

Notes

[1]Gertrude Schroeder Greenslade, "Consumption and Income Distribution," in *The Soviet Economy to the Year 2000*, eds. Abram Bergson and Herbert Levine (London: Allen and Unwin, 1982), p. 2. See also her article "Soviet Living Standards: Achievement and Prospects," in U.S. Congress, Joint Economic Committee, *The Soviet Economy in the 1980s: Problems and Prospects* (Washington, D.C., USGPO, 1982).

[2]*Voprosy Ekonomiki* [Questions of Economics], 1978, no. 7, p. 60.

[3]V. I. Zorkaltsev, "Anatomiia defitsita: voprosy bez otveta" ["Anatomy of a Deficit: Questions without Answers"], *Ekonomika i organizatsia promyshlennogo proisvodstva* [*Economics and Organization of Industrial Production*], 1982, no. 2.

[4]*Zhiznennye plany molodezhi* [*Life Plans of Youth*], ed. M. N. Rutkevich (Sverdlovsk: 1966), p. 35.

[5]F. R. Filippov, "The Role of the Higher School in Changing the Social Structure of Soviet Society," *Sotsiologicheskie issledovaniia* [Sociological Research], 1977, no. 2, p. 48.

[6]V. K. Alekseev, B. Z. Doktorov, and B. M. Firsov, "Izuchenie obshchestvennogo mneniia: opyt i problemy" ["Study of Public Opinion: Experience and Problems"], *Sotsiologicheskie issledovaniia*, 1979, no. 4, pp. 23–32.

[7]George Feifer, "Russian Disorders," *Harper's*, February 1981, pp. 41–55.

26   ALEXANDER SHTROMAS

*Dissent and Political Change in the Soviet Union**

The term *dissent* is used here to mean the refusal to assent to an established or imposed set of values, goals, and ideas.[1] In this sense, dissent does not necessarily imply resistance to or the refusal to comply with the policies, rules, or decisions of a governing body. Dissent may express itself simply in the fact that the values, goals, and ideas in question are not "internalized" by people whose routine social behavior is therefore motivated by a different (and mainly contrary) set of values, goals, and ideas.

Consideration of the phenomenon of Soviet dissent should not, therefore, be limited to the manifest expressions of opposition to government or current policies, be this opposition factional, sectoral, or subversive.[2] The whole spectrum of activities of the Soviet people, insofar as their refusal to assent to official Soviet aims, values, and ideas is reflected in these activities, should be taken into account in discussion of dissent in the USSR.

Political change is a very broad concept. It has become common to divide it into "within-system" and "system-rejective" categories.[3] I believe that the Soviet political system has no room for substantial "within-system" change. Its basic feature is the unlimited power of the highly centralized party apparatus, the party's absolute control over all socially relevant activities and developments in the country, be they economic or social, in education, in culture and the arts, in the circulation of information, or in the exercise of justice and governmental

*Reprinted in revised form by permission of the author and publisher from *Studies in Comparative Communism* 12, nos. 2 and 3 (Summer/Autumn, 1979), pp. 212–244. Copyright 1979 by School of International Relations, University of Southern California. This chapter is a shortened version of a paper presented to the Communist Politics Group (Convener: A. H. Brown) of the Political Studies Association of the United Kingdom at its annual conference held at the University of Liverpool in April, 1977.

functions. If that "leading role of the party" were to be affected by any change, it would mean that the change was "system-rejective." Only if the leading role of the party is being strengthened or at least left intact may the appropriate change be listed as a "within-system" one. But in this case, one would be dealing merely with administrative change rather than with political change in the fullest sense.

It would be wrong to divide the views of Soviet dissidents into those advocating "within-system" and those advocating "system-rejective" change, either according to what they say about the matter or to the reaction of officialdom to such views. There is here an absolutely objective criterion: Those who advocate a "socialist market economy," a system of strict "socialist legality," creative freedom, or any other kind of genuine autonomy of social function or of an organizational unit from the total control of the party are objectively striving for a "system-rejective" change, although they might think (or pretend to think) that they are only seeking to improve the structure or the performance of the present political system (i.e., asking for a "within-system" change). The stagnant pattern of the Soviet regime during the last 14 post-Khrushchevian years (and Khrushchev was ousted from his position in 1964 because the rest of the leadership regarded his involvement in constant reorganization as dangerous to the system) is the best proof of the narrow limits for "within-system" political change.[4] Thus, the term *political change* is used here in the sense of "system-rejective" change.

Historic
Stages

Mass dissent was a natural consequence of the Bolshevik seizure of power. This is not to suggest that the Russian people were so conservative as to be drastically opposed to any political and social modernization of their country. On the contrary, the revolution of March 1917 clearly demonstrated that Russia as a nation was already ripe to part from its *"ancien régime"* without regret and to accept radically new vistas for its sociopolitical development. But the Bolsheviks wanted to make out of the revolution much more than the Russian people were willingly able to accept. The Bolshevik concept of *socialism*, which derived from a radical interpretation of Marxist dogma rather than from the need to solve the country's actual problems, was entirely alien to the Russian nation as a whole and to all its larger social groups in particular. The Bolsheviks did not initially bother to adjust their stance on socialism to what could be acceptable in it to the people at large, even after they captured power in November 1917. On the contrary, they tried to adjust the nation to their theoretical stance, ruthlessly imposing their sectarian values, ideas, and goals upon Russian society, thus driving a majority of the people of that society into a dissident position. It was not so much the nation's resistance to the Bolsheviks (which was also considerable) as the attitudes of the Bolsheviks to the nation that produced in the USSR the phenomenon of mass dissent—dissent of which the Bolsheviks were probably more clearly aware than the dissenters in the masses.

The whole history of the Soviet regime can be seen as a continuous fight against dissent. The outcome of this struggle will shape the social and political future of Russia and therefore profoundly affect international order in the decades to come.

In order to achieve at least an imposed assent of the Russian nation to their aims, values, and ideas, the Bolsheviks had to resort to stronger measures. The merciless terror in which they kept the country for decades provides an adequate measurement of the scale of dissent in the Soviet Union during those decades. But the struggle of the Soviet regime against dissent was not entirely straightforward; it went through different stages, knew its ups and downs, its advances and retreats.

During the first stage of this fight, the Bolsheviks were facing a sporadic resistance, which later developed into the Civil War (1918–1920), won by the Bolsheviks despite their lack of majority support. F. C. Barghoorn rightly pointed out that although the Bolsheviks in this Civil War "succeeded in the holding on to power, they found themselves ruling a hostile or at least indifferent population. . . ."[5]

The uprisings in Tambov and Kronstadt, the strikes in Petrograd and other cities (the so-called *volynki*) in 1921 showed not only how universal was people's hostility to the new regime but also how fragile was the regime's grip on the country. To stop the development of further resistance and to be able to hold on to power without excessive risk, the Bolsheviks were forced to proclaim a New Economic Policy (NEP), which marked the second stage in the development of their fight against dissent. This policy was a straightforward concession to the dissident spirit of private enterprise and consumerism. Accompanied by measures that substantially reduced the scale of terror, introduced a kind of legal system, and so on, NEP was meant to present the Soviet regime as a normal government that responded to people's requests and merited their confidence. By so doing, the regime managed to achieve a reconciliation with the people, exhausted by wars and disruptions, and was able to remove many of the threats to its survival. In fact, the Bolsheviks used the NEP, which was the price they paid for being allowed to hold on to power, as a necessary respite before launching a new attack against dissent. In the years of NEP, they managed to strengthen immensely their apparatus of power by organizing it on a really totalitarian basis. They also were busy during this time liquidating all the remaining non-Bolshevik political organizations and groups, destroying other potentially oppositional forces (like the Russian Orthodox church), and eliminating their leaders and activists. Though terror was substantially reduced and conducted in a more discriminating manner, it persisted in a way that was discreet enough not to attract too much attention from the masses, who were beginning to enjoy their newly acquired prosperity.[6] NEP appeared to be a trap. As soon as the Bolsheviks were sure that the reins of power were firmly in their hands and that the people could no longer effectively resist them (the goal of totalitarian power is completely to eliminate the possibility that the people will establish independent "horizontal" links among themselves), they simply abolished NEP by nationalizing or closing down all small private businesses and by forcefully "collectivizing" agriculture.

Collectivization started the third (and the most important) stage in the development of the Soviet regime's fight against dissent. The year 1929 was really, as Stalin called it, "the year of great change," and from that time until 1941 Nazi aggression against the USSR, active mass terror was relentlessly employed by the Soviet authorities in "consolidating" the new Soviet socialist society on the basis "of the moral-political unity of the Soviet people."

The war that marks the fourth stage of the Soviet regime's fight against dissent again forced the Bolsheviks to make some concessions. Russian national and religious sentiments were rehabilitated to make people feel more comfortable in opposing foreign aggression. The Bolsheviks used this device very successfully in uniting the people against Hitler. Although many Russians at first regarded Hitler's forces as liberators, their hopes were shortly dashed as Hitler proceeded to treat the Russians even worse than they were treated by the Bolsheviks.

The Bolsheviks also exploited Great Russian nationalist sentiment to attract popular assent to their rule after the war. The newly acquired "national–imperial form" of Bolshevik rule did not mean, however, that the Bolsheviks were starting to play the role of a genuinely national government of Russia. On the contrary, they were now using the "national–imperial" legitimation in addition to the "Marxist–Communist" one as a reason for being even more insistent on popular adherence to Bolshevik sectarian values and aims. All aspirations to see the situation developing the other way round were mercilessly crushed by the Bolsheviks in a new wave of terror, which started immediately after the war in 1945, reached a peak in 1947–1948, and crescendoed in 1952–1953. The fifth stage in the development of the Soviet regime's struggle against dissent lasted until Stalin's death in 1953.

The turning point here was April 4, 1953 when the doctors who had been arrested a few months before as "plotters" and "murderers" were suddenly rehabilitated. But a new "moderate" policy in the regime's dealings with dissent was established in a more or less comprehensive shape only in 1956 after Khrushchev's formal denunciation of Stalin at the Twentieth Congress of the CPSU. This act brought the Bolshevik struggle against dissent into the beginning of the sixth (and latest) stage of its development.

Soviet Assent: The Soviet regime's continuous struggle against
Current dissent has not as yet given a decisive victory to
either side. Although the Communists would
Relations appear to be winning, none of their victories has
between the been either complete or final, despite the fact that
Regime and on the surface they have always totally dominated
the People the political scene and have reorganized Russian
society in accordance with their theoretical plans
about the construction of socialism. What they have completely failed to
achieve is the "internalization" of their aims, values, and ideas by the
people whom they officially rule. This does not mean that the systematic
Communist fight against dissent has left the traditional values of the
Russian people intact. The Communists have managed to destroy those
values quite substantially (though not completely), but they have been
unable to replace them with another set of moral and social values of
their own choosing. People learned to adjust to the conditions of life
created by the Communist zeal for forceful social change but not to
identify it with their own moral and social ideals and values.

The main Communist instruments to achieve, at least superficially,
popular assent have been terror and corruption. In a totalitarian situation, personal moral values and convictions that contradict the official
ones become socially irrelevant anyway, but active terror makes them
incompatible with physical survival. On the other hand, even artificial
subservience to the rulers' requirements is rewarded by an increase in
physical security, material well-being, and social status. Under such
circumstances, people learn—some faster, some more slowly—either to
dismiss their moral values as unrealistic prejudices or to hide them as
much as possible from other people, in both cases adjusting their
behavior to official requirements and concentrating on gratifying drives
and needs that can be satisfied. The value of physical survival (and, for
some, indeed, of a survival in the nicest possible way) thus becomes a
leading, if not the sole, value of people constantly threatened with terror
and tempted by corruption. After several decades of this treatment, it is
no wonder that the new Soviet man, the standard loyal Soviet citizen,
should have turned out not to be an idealistically minded believer in
Communism or Marxism–Leninism but an opportunistic, cynically selfish personality with a minimized "superego" and a hypertrophied
"ego."[7]

The ascent of this *homo sovieticus*[8] was the greatest achievement of the
Communists in their long and bloody fight for people's assent to their
aims, values, and ideas, and they had no choice but to see in that new
Soviet man the main bulwark of their regime. In fact, this meant that the
real winner in the fight against dissent was the dissident spirit of NEP,
which not only survived in that fight but matured so that it could fit

perfectly into the framework of the totalitarian Communist regime, becoming in time its real moving spirit.

The ultimate victory of that essentially dissident spirit was registered in 1956 at the Twentieth Congress of the CPSU, when the typical representatives of *homo sovieticus* in the Communist hierarchy, led by Khrushchev, firmly assumed party leadership; this victory was consummated in 1957 by ousting from the Politburo the last remainders of the Bolshevik old guard (such as Molotov and Kaganovich) and their supporters (the other members of the so-called anti-party group), who represented the radical spirit or traditional Bolshevism and were insisting on the continuation of a radically intolerant, ideologically based policy.

The new Soviet leadership was essentially pragmatic. Its primary, if not sole, interest lay in solidifying its power. And it saw the way to strengthen that security by establishing a pattern of reconciliation with the populace by reducing the traditional ideological zeal of the regime. People were no longer asked to believe in Communism or to "internalize" its values but simply to behave according to its rules and customs. It was no longer necessary for people to accept Communism as an ideal so long as they accepted it as the sociopolitical framework of reality within which to further their personal interests and goals. The pursuit of these personal interests and goals was thus tacitly, if partially, recognized by the authorities as a valid basis for socially approved behavior.

Formal (though largely meaningless) adherence to the official Communist ideology, as expressed, for instance, in a person's observance of all necessary rites and other public performances, was considered to be the best proof of his or her readiness to pursue personal goals in recognized and approved ways. Thus, adherence to the official ideology became the way to demonstrate one's practical political loyalty to the regime and one's readiness to cooperate unconditionally with the authorities. Ideology thus acquired in the Soviet political structure a very essential pragmatic function but was completely abandoned as a set of genuine values, ideas, and aims as well as a criterion for assent or dissent. In other words, instead of being "internalized," the Communist ideology was entirely "externalized"; it was transformed into a mere device of the new Soviet leadership's effective exercise of power and control over the population.

Practically all unofficial Soviet authors bear witness that the Communist ideology is now dead in the USSR. "Throw away the *dead* ideology . . . ,"[9] appeals Solzhenitsyn to the Soviet leaders, asking them to concentrate on the vital national political issues. Sakharov notes that present Soviet society is marked by a total "ideological indifference," with the ideology being "pragmatically used" by the authorities "as a convenient 'façade' . . . replacing in our present conditions the oath of faithfulness."[10] Similar conclusions could be drawn even from a careful study of some results of official sociological research in the Soviet Union. Z. Katz, who has analyzed these results, states, for instance, that they "have shown present-day Soviet youth to be lacking in some if not all of the qualities that they should supposedly have acquired."[11] Another analyst of Soviet sociological research data rightly refers to "discontinuity" and "inconsistency" in Soviet socialization.[12]

This "discontinuity" and "inconsistency" in the internalization of values only indicates that Soviet socialization is really based on values very different from those officially claimed as being essential for a "good" member of the Soviet socialist society. Blatant consumerism amounting to predatory selfish cynicism is, for instance, a perfectly valid basis for socialization in the Soviet Union, provided that it is expressed in "pragmatically realistic" terms (i.e., in terms of complete submission to the regime and in hypocritical claims to share its officially proclaimed values). In order to reconcile that hypocrisy with the remains of the person's superego and thus to strengthen the argument for such socialization, "patriotic" references are invoked, such as: "Whatever one thinks of this particular government it is the government of Russia, to which every Russian owes loyalty." (For the non-Russian, a "patriotic" argument for support of the regime would be formulated in entirely different terms but still would remain as valid as for a Russian.) "Dissident" ideologies of Great Russian chauvinism and materialistically selfish consumerism in the disguise of full commitment, or at least of complete loyalty, to Communism are today approved by the authorities not simply as a concession given to dissent in order to fill the gap between the regime and the people (thus providing the latter with an acceptable basis for socialization and the former with more vistas for a "peaceful and stable reign") but as a genuine ideology that the contemporary rulers do not mind sharing with their subjects.[13]

All this indicates a substantial shift of the whole Soviet "regime–dissent" relationship in the present (sixth) stage of its development. This shift is marked by a *consensus between the regime and the people,* reminding one very much of the old formula of "live and let live." Under this consensus, the government promises the individual minimally reliable assurance of physical security and a tolerant (even encouraging) attitude to his efforts to satisfy his consumer and other selfish demands in exchange for the individual's absolute political loyalty and noninterference in governmental business. In accordance with this consensus, some of the dissident values and ideologies (referred to previously) have been accommodated into the framework of the official system and, though very much restricted by the system's inherent rigidity, have become its only living spirit.

The absolutely unnatural symbiosis of the regime, which still possesses all the essential Bolshevik features, with the partial institutionalization of dissent does not make the dissidents nor those very few supporters of original pure Bolshevism very content. To almost everybody, the maintenance of the regime in its present shape makes no sense whatsoever, *except* as the only possible way of keeping Soviet society together as a crippled, but still somehow functioning, whole. Everyone in Soviet society today finds political change desirable and yet, at the same time, feels himself an impotent prisoner of the inertia imposed by the existing political system. One way or another, every Soviet citizen nowadays feels like a dissident and to a certain extent is a dissident in real terms. As V. Bukovsky put it in answering a correspondent's question about the number of political prisoners in the Soviet Union: "There are at the present time 250 million political prisoners in the USSR."[14] The only questions concern how well one has adjusted to that sort of imprisonment and whether or not one has a vested interest in its continuance.

A consensus based on such schizophrenic grounds is inevitably precarious and needs constant thoughtful balancing. This consensus has produced a clear shift of the borderline between assent and dissent, thereby creating an artificial compromise between elements incompatible in principle. This cannot last for long. In my view, the only genuine borderline between assent and dissent, as long as the Communist regime retains power, is the original one of ideological purity. All attempts at accommodating within it non-Communist (and, hence, anti-Communist) attitudes can only be provisional: they will in the course of time either bring down the authoritative system of Communist values (together with the regime) or be suppressed by the regime in a new development of its struggle against dissent, bringing it probably to a next (seventh) stage. One way or other, the Communist struggle against dissent, already six decades old, is continuing though in new forms and gradually moves toward the fatal question: "Who beats whom?" ("*Kto kogo?*")

Soviet Dissent: Forms and Structure

The historical analysis of the stages of the regime's struggle against dissent leads to the analysis of different types of contemporary Soviet dissent and its structure.

Potential Dissent. For the time being, the consensus between the Soviet regime and the population is viable and fruitful. On the surface, there is not much political unrest, and the internal political situation is more peaceful than in the past. Dissent, as overwhelming as it is psychologically and even behaviorally, rarely expresses itself in political terms and remains mainly *potential*. But there are at least three reasons why Soviet potential dissent should be considered as both politically relevant and extremely important.

First, since the Soviet regime has hardly any genuine supporters (in terms of the ideology it is based on) and persists only by its own oppressive inertia, it has little "immunity" to change. The slightest destabilization of its precarious balance of power could start a chain of events leading to a complete disintegration of the whole "monolithic" Soviet system. (Events in Hungary in 1956, in Czechoslovakia in 1968, and in Portugal in 1974 illustrate this point.)

Second, the fear that potential dissent will become rebellious dissent strongly reinforces the consensus between the regime and the people and makes the authorities no longer able to exercise absolute power. The strikes and riots during the late 1950s and early 1960s in Temir-Tau, Novocherkassk, Krasnodar, Minsk, and some other Soviet towns, which were provoked by the carelessness of Khrushchev's administration in honoring this consensus, taught the present government a lesson about how to keep political peace in the Soviet Union. Potential dissent thus became a constant and very serious variable to be reckoned with in political decision-making.[15]

Third, people's genuine motives and aims, even if carefully disguised, are inevitably somehow reflected in behavior. Potential (in a political sense) dissent thus expresses itself in a variety of daily activities within the officially endorsed framework, although it is not always easily detectable. People's dissident motives and aims, as expressed in "normal," officially endorsed activities or in activities under the disguise of officially endorsed ones, are forming Soviet *"intrastructural"* dissent—the main and the most important body of Soviet dissent.

Intrastructural Dissent (Negative). The most massive display of "intrastructural" dissent is of a negative nature, mainly connected with people's use of their public positions to achieve personal goals. One could call it also *egoistic dissent*. Communist concessions to consumerism have almost legitimized the view that the position a person holds in the official Soviet system (and everybody holds one position or other) is given to him not so much for the fulfillment of a public service as for gratification of his material and psychological needs. Every office thus becomes to a certain extent an official ground for collective unofficial and, in many instances, illegal activities of the people holding positions there. The state office is thus a vehicle for the pursuit of selfish interests to the detriment of the interests of the state. In this respect, as the saying in the Soviet Union goes, the office replaces the motherland as the focus of people's loyalties and solidarity. One could even say (and it is quite a widespread view among the Russian intelligentsia) that the ruling stratum has changed its ideology from the Bolshevik to the "office–patrimonial" one (*"votchinno-vedomstvennaya ideologiya"*). The result is the deterioration of the pattern of social integration as represented by the regime. Among the aspects of "office activity" for the office's own advantage are self-promotion to impress superior authorities and attempts to put pressure on them.

Many Western observers of this phenomenon conclude that Soviet society has lost its totalitarian structure and works today already according to a pluralistic model compatible (and comparable) with the Western one.[16] They have somehow forgotten that in contradistinction to Western systems, the Soviet system is formed not only of particular "group bureaucracies" but also possesses a supreme, unifying "super-bureaucracy"—the party apparatus—which holds the whole totalitarian structure together. (Almost all of these authors, incidentally, wrongly see the party apparatus as only one of the many "group bureaucracies.") Moreover, they fail to realize that offices as such seldom act as distinctive groups whose interests compete with those of the party apparatus.[17] They only compete among themselves before the party apparatus, using the latter's values as arguments to win their particular case. The so-called pluralistic pattern in Soviet conditions either does not represent dissent at all or expresses a purely negative dissent that does not advance social goals or group interests but works for the egoistic interest of bureaucrats and office staff to the detriment of the integrative social interests as represented by the state.

The advantages that offices thereby obtain from superior authorities under false pretenses (additional supplies, finances, bonuses) are not the most important aspect of negative "intrastructural" dissent. The crucial element in it is social sabotage and economic delinquency. They are closely linked to each other since sabotage is either a device for asking for illegal incentives (as exemplified by the work of all the service industries[18]) or a response to measures to curtail illegal activities by tightening the grip of authoritative control over offices or even by reforming some of the official structures in which they operate. Similarly, economic delinquency is closely related to sabotage since it diverts so much effort, attention, time, and materials from the officially assigned job. Economic delinquency in the Soviet Union is rampant. Vast numbers of Soviet citizens are involved either as a delinquent or as a customer of that delinquent and in most cases in both capacities.[19] Delinquency ranges from straightforward theft of "state and social" property[20] to highly organized private enterprise activities masked as activities of state or social enterprises.[21] Wholesale theft, embezzlement, and speculation[22] lead to wholesale corruption, reaching, in some instances, the highest echelons of power,[23] since without that it could not survive for so long and be as viable as it is.

The regime is entirely unable to cope with this problem. On the one hand, by rehabilitating consumerism and accepting egoism as a viable basis for a modus vivendi with the people, the regime encourages predatory attitudes toward state property. On the other hand, the only way to eliminate economic delinquency without changing the system would be to launch mass terror on Stalin's scale, which the present authorities for many reasons are unable to do. (They are afraid to jeopardize their security and the consensus with the people.) Thus, the government deals with the problems on a case-by-case basis, taking to court only certain careless groups of economic delinquents (who either failed to observe the minimal rules of secrecy, or denounced each other, or neglected to bribe the necessary individuals). In essence, the regime is forced to tolerate economic delinquency.[24] Under these circumstances, economic delinquency has acquired such a prominent and stable position that some authors call it the "parallel market"[25] and others the "counter-economy."[26] The latter term seems the most apt because it shows that this economy is not simply supplementing the official social and economic order but is gradually undermining it, jeopardizing its very survival. Marx and Engels, when defining crime as "a revolt of an individual against the dominant social relationships,"[27] could not foresee the Soviet situation in which crime would become an expression of mass revolt against the dominant social relationships. Stalin was not far off the mark when he equated those plundering socialist property with "spies and traitors";[28] in objective terms, their activities are politically subversive: they gradually let the whole Soviet system down.

Intrastructural Dissent (Positive). The positive, socially minded "intrastructural" dissent, which consists of pursuit of constructive (but officially controversial) political, social, economic, or cultural goals is less visible than negative "intrastructural" dissent but is a much more functional vehicle of political change. It expresses itself mainly in the activities of individuals or informal groups, who try to use their official positions and contacts for dissident purposes, although such individuals or groups rarely have the backing of their entire office.[29] I know of only three cases where whole offices tried to advance positive dissident ideas and aims: the magazine *Novy mir* under Simonov (1954–1958) and Tvardovsky (1958–1970), which still exists but no longer plays such a role; the Institute of Applied Social Research (IKSI) under the academician Rumyantsev (1968–1973) before it was dismantled and replaced by the new Sociological Institute under Professor N. M. Rutkevich,[30] and the Academy of Sciences' Council on Forecasting, which also was dismantled in 1971, with its Chairman Tardov arrested.

Because offices are ruled by bureaucrats whose power, as B. Meissner rightly pointed out, "rests in the position they hold,"[31] they are, as a rule, much more responsive, if at all, to negative than to positive dissidence. But the real work in the offices is done by professionals whose power "is rooted in the authority and the prestige of the function"[32] they perform and not in the position they hold. The natural interest of such people (if the Soviet reality has not eradicated it) consists in enhancing the status of those functions and the conditions for their performance. That is the motivation for positive "intrastructural" dissident activities.

Professional motives are the first to drive people to positive dissent since the whole system not only submits them to the dictates of nonprofessional, arbitrary, "partocratic"[33] leadership but undermines the realization of their full potential by depriving them of any initiative and by restricting the proper use of their skills, talents, and knowledge. Insofar as a professional person cares about his performance and some social issues implicit in his function, he automatically becomes in the Soviet Union a positive socially minded dissident. In this sense, the term *professional* embraces the whole of the intelligentsia (including the technical one) and all skilled workers and farmers. These people (one should call them the technocrats) are spontaneously, on purely professional grounds, looking for a change that will enable them in the end to free themselves from the detrimental control of the partocratic bureaucracy over their professional activities, as well as from its irrational, ideologically and politically motivated management of the economy, society, and state. And it is of secondary importance whether these technocrats realize that their aim of "change for rationality" is incompatible with the present political system.

The technocrats are as pragmatic as the present partocrats, but their pragmatism is based on a professionally assessed rationality, whereas the partocrats seek to maintain the outdated and therefore irrational Communist system of power and management. This system implies the totalitarian rule of a purportedly ideologically minded partocratic clique claiming to possess special ability for fulfilling an extraordinary task—the construction of a Communist society. The persistence of this irrational system is the sole viable basis not only of the partocracy's power and privileges but of its very social survival; thus to maintain the system is its most pragmatic task.

This different basis of pragmatism also engenders different ideologies. The technocratic ideology (leaving aside all possible varieties and differences and stressing only the points of general agreement) could be expressed in four maxims:

1. Efficiency, quality, and productivity should be the leading principles on which the economy of the country is based, even if this conflicts with the concept of the socialist economy or with other political and/or ideological dictates.

2. All social and political issues should be subordinated to rational national interests as opposed to those related to Communist ideology and the interests of the ruling group.

3. Professional jobs should be carried out on the basis of responsibility (which implies personal initiative and independent decision making) rather than on the basis of mechanical execution of initiatives taken and decisions made by authoritative bodies from outside.

4. All positions in all fields should be filled according to people's qualifications and skills as opposed to their political suitability and trustworthiness from the standpoint of the ruling partocracy.

This ideology is anti-Communist and objectively incompatible with the Soviet regime and is, therefore, obviously dissident. Technocrats who spontaneously adhere to it cannot help but advance its aims in their officially endorsed social activities, thus engaging in "intrastructural" positive dissent.

"Intrastructural" dissidence takes the form of either theoretical proposals (explicit or implicit in the theoretical idea) accompanied by efforts to bring about appropriate reforms or practical initiatives and experiments.

Under the category of theoretical proposals are the activities of *Novy mir*, IKSI, Council on Forecasting, or the strong movement among Soviet economists to introduce elements of a market economy into the Soviet industrial production and trade. The start of this movement is usually identified with the famous 1962 article of Professor Y. G. Liberman in *Pravda*;[34] it reached its peak in 1965 with such prominent people as academicians Nemchinov and Aganbegyan and professors Belkin and Birman taking a lead in it. Despite initial party approval, this movement did not achieve much since its 1965 proposal for economic reform was never implemented. Nevertheless, these reform activities represented a practical step forward since from then on the real mechanisms of economic life became a legitimate object of study when dealing both theoretically and practically with the problems of the economy and its management. This "rational" trend in Soviet economic science and practice, despite the practical failure of its first step, continues, enjoys official recognition,[35] and is likely to have an important effect on the future development of the Soviet economy. The most recent manifestation of this trend was the April 1973 decision to establish new economic units in industry—the so-called productive associations (*proizvodstvennyye obyedineniya*) long advocated by Aganbegyan. The implementation of that decision involves risks, however, and has therefore proceeded sluggishly.

The second category would include, for instance, the attempts of collective farms to initiate industrial activities. Suppression was the first reaction of the authorities to such "malevolent" practices. Many trials have taken place condemning those involved in such practices for committing serious economic crimes. These repressive measures did not, however, achieve their aim. Pressure on the authorities was growing, risks were still taken, and in 1973–1974, it became legal for collective farms to engage in industrial activities.

One "intrastructural" dissident venture manifested both theoretical and practical characteristics in the attempts to reorganize production on collective and state farms by replacing the faceless brigade as the main work unit with a family-based productive link (*zveno*). A campaign in favor of this change, led by agricultural economists and journalists, provided a theoretical proposal (and even a motion), and Ivan Khudenko, the director of the state farm Akshi in Kazakhstan, provided the experimental base. His experiment was enormously successful economically. (Despite the disastrous 1972 harvest, Khudenko collected a record crop; in general, the productivity of his farm was 20 times higher than that of the neighboring ones, and the wages that he paid his workers were almost as many times higher.) But because it challenged the whole basis of Soviet agriculture, it could not be tolerated by the authorities. Khudenko was accused of trying to restore capitalist agriculture, and a decree was issued in 1973 closing down his farm. Khudenko was soon arrested, charged with economic crimes, and sentenced to 6 years in a corrective labor colony where he died in 1974[36]—a prime example of how the authorities treat a pragmatic professional "instrastructural" dissident when they think that his dissident activities have gone too far or become too radical. Though Khudenko's experiment was destroyed, other experiments with "productive links" continue, though on a much more modest scale and, of course, without attempts to liquidate the "sacred" brigade.

The same professional motivations drive many writers and artists to create works which, while controversial from the official point of view, express their technical skills, images, ideas, visions, and inspirations. That is why so much "intrastructural" dissent occurs in cultural activities and why so much good artistic work is still being produced, despite the enormous difficulties inherent in the official Soviet cultural framework.

Much as Soviet authorities would like to crush positive "intrastructural" dissent, they are forced to tolerate it at least to a certain extent. They are very much aware of the creeping paralysis of their economy and of the slow disintegration of the Soviet social order. They also know that if they want to survive in a position of power, they have to be able to hold the society together and to keep things going. Being unprepared to change the system—the most natural way to attempt to solve these problems—the authorities are looking for positive economic and social ventures that would be compatible with the system's persistence. And "intrastructural" dissent alone offers them something viable in that respect. The authorities hope that by controlling and manipulating this dissent they will be able to reduce and reprocess its ideas and ventures so as to protect themselves and to assure the survival of the system. In this way, the authorities expect to improve the social situation without altering anything essential in the Soviet political structure. What they really want is to exploit "intrastructural" dissent and to take advantage of innovations in science and technology, which they regard as the only acceptable panaceas for social ills. They also need innovations in the arts in order to acquire more cultural prestige abroad. In this, they have had some success. But "intrastructural" dissidents also successfully exploit the partocracy's immense greed for "socially cheap" innovations by increasing their influence in the decision-making process and becoming more and more insistent on promoting real change. This is how a pattern of a relatively peaceful coexistence between the regime and "intrastructural" dissent has been established in the USSR. For the time being, the one is not yet able to do without the other. But only for the time being. In principle, the technocrats can readily do without the partocracy, and they become more and more aware of it.

The situation described reflects the constant struggle for power between the "upper" class (partocrats) and the "middle" class (technocrats),[37] but in addition to the technocrats, the category of positive "intrastructural" dissent also includes people motivated by more general moral, philosophical, political, and cultural ideals and commitments. If the pure professionals are mainly "apolitical," "aphilosophical," and even perhaps "amoral," those joining them for mainly moral reasons are rather "aprofessional" (i.e., any professional motivation is subordinated to more fundamental values). I would divide these moral dissenters into three main categories: civic (or social) dissenters, national dissenters, religious dissenters. The emphasis in this classification is not so much on ideologies as on the areas of major concern for change.

Civic dissenters are mainly concerned with general social or political problems affecting both Soviet society and the world: the political and economic system, cultural development and freedom of information, the rights of the individual in society, ideology, world order and the Soviet place in it, and so on. Different ideological–philosophical perceptions exist in this group, with each faction trying to advance its own vision of desirable change, though all factions share the conviction that the present regime represents no one and must be changed. The evidence points to the existence of a very strong liberal faction, which is a natural ally of the technocratic dissenters, sharing their aspirations for economic pluralism, personal initiative, and responsibility, and their longing for the end of the society's compulsory ideology. Although the liberals would stress the character of the social order first and professional autonomy second, they would also share the natural ideology of the Soviet technocracy, as defined previously.

The liberal faction is backed by the Soviet Union's few remaining

socialists and "critical Communists."[38] They object to the oppressive-
ness of the Soviet regime and its betrayal of libertarian socialist (Communist) ideals and aspire to replace it with a "genuinely" socialist
(Communist) order based on freedom and democracy; thus objectively
they are striving for a liberal change of the present order. On the other
hand, the civic dissent category also includes a tiny neo-Stalinist
faction[39] as well as a much more powerful faction representing fascist
views.[40] Because the latter is not very well articulated, it has not seemed
very important, but this impression could prove misleading.

National dissenters are mainly concerned with the problems affecting
one particular Soviet nationality and not the whole of the Soviet society.
Their current "defensive" aims are to preserve their nation's identity
and to assure its numerical prevalence within the national territory.
Their current "offensive" aims are to strive for more autonomy from the
central government along with more advantages, privileged treatment,
and improved financial and other conditions for their nation. Thus, in its
accent on advancing egoistic goals of a particular nation at the expense
of the state and society as a whole, national dissent resembles negative
dissent. But, for national dissenters in terms of social interests, there is
no such thing as the Soviet state or Soviet society. They regard their own
nation as a self-sufficient social whole, which for reasons independent of
their choice was included in the larger and inorganic framework of the
USSR. The main strategic aim of national dissenters is to acquire
national independence or at least a genuine national autonomy. Their
current aims are a temporary tactic to allow their nation to survive in the
most favorable conditions until the hour of national freedom arrives. As
soon as there is a realistic possibility of achieving national freedom, they
will put as much effort into achieving it as they do today in advancing
their more narrowly conceived national interests.

A distinction must be made between non-Russian and Russian
national dissenters in the USSR. Every nationally conscious non-Russian
is by definition at least potentially a national dissident. He is perfectly
aware of the fact that Soviet authorities are seeking to assimilate his
nation[41] ("Sovietizing" it in the context of Russification) and is eager to
resist this policy by all means in his power. For him the Soviet regime is
a foreign, specifically a Russian, power under whose imposed colonial
rule he has to live but with which he is unable to identify his national
statehood. His long-term aim is thus a single national and state identity.
For a non-Russian national dissenter this is, indeed, the main problem.
He assumes that his nation, if left on its own, could more easily solve the
problems of civic dissent on which it currently has no appreciable effect
at an "All-Union level." Thus, problems of civic dissent are for him of
secondary importance; he is concerned with how to improve his nation's
lot under the given "civic" circumstances.

The situation is very different with the Russians. For many of them, the Soviet regime, good or bad, is still their national government. But for quite a lot of Russians, national dissenters, the acquisition of an adequate national statehood means the ending of the Soviet regime and the establishment of a true Russian national government. This brings their problems much closer to those of civic dissent. Russian national dissent is characterized by two different sentiments: one is nostalgia for the cultural tradition based on Orthodox Christianity and other genuinely Russian national values, which the Bolsheviks have sought to censure or destroy; the other is anxiety that the Soviet regime may sacrifice Russian national interests in order to protect the sectarian Communist ideological interests. Briefly, Russian national dissenters are those Russians who are aware of the "anational" sectarian nature of Communism, who rightly regard it as a basically anti-Russian force, and want a non-Bolshevik national government whose first commitment would be to the Russian nation and its genuine interests. In the last few years, Russian national dissent has been increasing and gradually merging into the pattern of non-Russian national dissent. In that merging pattern, national dissent, despite its inherently partial nature, is acquiring a universal shape which exposes the regime to one of the most serious challenges it has ever experienced.

Religious dissent is similar to national dissent in its concern for the survival and status of a particular denomination and not for the whole of Soviet society. The religious believers are, in the USSR, as automatically dissident as nationally conscious non-Russians. Their views are incompatible with Communism, and as long as the Communists are in power, their communities are threatened by extinction. On the other hand, religious dissent is less universal than national dissent since not everybody in the USSR is a member of a religious community, whereas everybody is a member of a national community. In many instances, religious dissent overlaps with national dissent (as in Russia, Georgia, Lithuania), but in some cases, it is a completely separate issue (the Evangelical Baptists, the Pentecostal sect, and so on). Even if religious dissent is not universal,[42] it does represent a critical challenge to the regime, mainly because religion is the most powerful source of an alternative ideology that the authorities have to tolerate within the official framework of society. Although politically the Communists are in control of almost all churches (except those outlawed), they have seemed unable to stem the growing and independent impact of religion on the people.[43]

Extrastructural Dissent. These types of Soviet dissent express themselves not only in "intrastructural" but also in "extrastructural" forms (i.e., in the independent activities of individuals and groups outside the framework controllable by the authorities). "Extrastructural" dissent activities directly undermining, challenging, or criticizing the regime and its current and long-term policies, and aiming at political change, take two main forms:

1. *Overt dissent*—expressing itself in (*a*) conscious, planned action, such as open protests (petitions and demonstrations) over specific issues of policy, public criticism of the official ideology or of the regime and its performance, direct presentation of demands and alternative policy projects; (*b*) spontaneous outbursts of protest activities, such as strikes, riots, and the like.

2. *Concealed dissent*—secret political societies and other conspiratorial activities, including anonymous political acts of individuals and groups.

Some dissident activities are almost exclusively either "intrastructural" or "extrastructural." For instance, egoistic dissent is predominantly "intrastructural," though in some cases it extends into the "extrastructural" domain, whereas the spokesmen for national and religious groups, which lack official territorial or community status in Soviet society, engage exclusively in "extrastructural" forms of overt dissidence. So the Crimean Tartars who do not have a recognized national status or a territory assigned to them have no choice but to fight for their rights in "extrastructural" ways. By openly demonstrating and publicly protesting, they attempt to advance their demands. Similarly, the Uniates, Evangelical Baptists, Pentecostal sect, Adventists, and other officially unrecognized denominations are struggling for the rights of their communities to exist and worship God in their own way. The national minorities whose specific dissident aims consist in emigration to their "historic homelands" (Jews, Volga Germans, Meskhs) are also committed to "extrastructural" forms of struggle for their rights. But in most other cases, "extrastructural" dissent is either the logical continuation or the extreme manifestation of appropriate activities normally pursued in "intrastructural" forms.

Generally speaking, Soviet dissenters of all kinds prefer to remain "intrastructural" and further their causes by using their official positions within the system, the support of other like-minded people in related official positions within the system, as well as official channels of communication, including media. Sometimes the dissident impulse impels them to engage in some additional "extrastructural" activities, but usually not at the risk of their "intrastructural" position. A classical example of the extension of "intrastructural" dissent to concealed "extrastructural" dissent is the famous case of Sinyavsky and Daniel. Both were typically "intrastructural" dissidents. Sinyavsky was a reputable literary critic whose numerous officially published articles and books aimed either at advancing controversial authors (Pasternak) or at propagating innovative and libertarian ideas on literature, insofar, of course, as such works could get through the censorship. Daniel, a well-known translator of foreign poetry into Russian, had chosen poems that he thought would help develop the consciousness and awareness of his Russian readers. In addition, both men were secretly writing novels and short stories which were sent abroad to be published under the mysterious pen names of Abram Tertz and Nikolai Arzhak. The secret of such "double activities" lasted for 10 years until the KGB established the identity of the two authors and took them to court for anti-Soviet propaganda.

A more recent case is that of the clandestine group of L. Karpinsky and O. Latsis, both former high officials and quite famous journalists and scholars. Until the KGB disclosed it in 1975, this group was working on a program for introducing political change in the USSR. Probably the model example of combined "intra" and "extra" structural activities is Khrushchev's removal from office. An "extrastructural" conspiracy of "intrastructural" officials (leading members of the party's Central Committee) culminated in October 1964 in an "intrastructural" act, whereby a plenary session of the Central Committee carried out an institutionalized coup d'état. This time the conservative partocrats staged the action and brought it to a successful conclusion. No one can gauge the potential strength of a future conspiracy of this kind, but the technocratic elements of the leadership are the most likely to play such a role. Concealed "extrastructural" dissent is not only compatible with positive "intrastructural" dissent but is a logical extension of it.[44] In my view, only a proper combination of "intrastructural" and concealed "extrastructural" dissident activities could bring about a major political change in the Soviet Union.

What then about overt "extrastructural" dissent which attracts so much attention in the outside world and is regarded by so many here as the only real dissent in the USSR? Although overt dissent is neither complementary to, nor compatible with, "intrastructural" dissident activities, it is in a way also only an extension of "intrastructural" dissent. An overt dissident is usually a former "intrastructural" dissident whose activities have crossed the threshold of official tolerance and who has therefore been removed from any official position from which he could continue such activities. The typical overt dissident is in most cases a person who has been pushed into the tight corner of overt dissent against his will.

The most classical cases here are those of Solzhenitsyn and Sakharov—people whose names have become symbols of overt dissent. Solzhenitsyn did everything in his power to remain an official member of the prestigious Writers' Union. He saw in this position his only opportunity for publication in the Soviet Union and for communication with the Soviet readership. Solzhenitsyn very much wanted to continue his dissident activities from an "intrastructural" position, but his expulsion from the Writers' Union (1969) and his foreclosure from every means of publication in the USSR forced this "intrastructural" dissenter to become an "extrastructural" one. Had he not been officially silenced, Solzhenitsyn would never have moved from "intrastructural" to overt dissent.[45]

Sakharov was another "intrastructural" dissident who tried to use his scientific authority and his official links with those in power to influence political decision making. The regime had long tolerated Sakharov's interference, but his famous 1968 Memorandum to Soviet leaders on "Progress, Peaceful Coexistence, and Intellectual Freedom" was too much for them to bear, even though Sakharov wrote it with no intention of publication. In the aftermath, he was dismissed from his high position in the institution dealing with nuclear energy. (The authorities probably even arranged for publication of the Memorandum in the West so as to have an excuse for dismissing Sakharov and for classifying him as a dissenter.)[46] An analysis of the biographies of many overt dissenters shows that their route to overt dissent was very much like that of Sakharov and Solzhenitsyn.

Of course, once it had arisen, overt dissent attracted new people, especially young ones, who joined its ranks voluntarily. It challenged them to express themselves in the most direct way, to display their courage, and to prove the strength of their moral commitments. A few found it simply an outlet for their frustration. The core of overt dissent emerged in response to official intolerance for "intrastructural" dissent. This applies even to many young people with no official status who would have preferred the role of "intrastructural" dissidents but were pushed into overt dissent by the repressive measures of the authorities. The biography of V. Bukovsky provides a good illustration of this point.[47]

Overt dissent is thus an outburst of repressed "intrastructural" dissent. Such an outburst was not possible in Stalin's time, when the disclosure of "intrastructural" dissidence was tantamount to a death sentence or life imprisonment in the *gulag*. It became possible after Stalin's death when such measures began to be applied with more discrimination. So long as the Soviet regime is reluctant to reinstitute mass terror, overt dissent will pierce the surface of Soviet society in the same way as the tip of an iceberg rises above the ocean. Repressive measures on a lesser scale can reduce overt dissent, but they are unable to crush it. V. Bukovsky has rightly pointed out that overt dissent "reached its peak in 1968. After 1968 it declined . . . and its minimal level was reached in 1972."[48] To many, its demise then seemed imminent. After the trial of Yakir and Krasin, the 1972 suppression of the "Chronicle of Current Events," and the expulsion from the country or arrest of many of the most active members of the movement, one could hardly believe that overt dissent could ever recover. But the reappearance of the "Chronicle of Current Events" in 1974 and the organization of the Watchdog Committee on Helsinki Agreements (Orlov's Committee) in 1976 show that Soviet overt dissent "is beginning to rise again."[49]

Two sets of views underrate the role of overt dissent in Soviet sociopolitical development. The first is expressed by some Western scholars who assume that Soviet society is basically monolithic and lacks internal dissent other than that of overt dissenters. The prospects of such dissenters are therefore grim. "Political culture links the bureaucratic elite and the masses more closely than it links the dissidents to either. . . . The dissidents often show courage, idealism and ability to challenge the bureaucracy; yet the bureaucracy still commands the forces of coercion."[50] In this view, the overt dissidents are an isolated powerless group unable to have an influence on the country's social and political life. This view ignores the fact that overt dissent is just a tiny fraction of Soviet dissent that has come into the open and that it represents the positive "intrastructural" dissent which, though inconspicuous, is really a mass phenomenon.

The other set of views is expressed by a number of Soviet "intrastructural" dissidents who rightly see themselves as the real viable force making for political change in the Soviet Union. They tend to dismiss the overt dissenters as a group that is basically irrelevant to such change and sometimes even an obstacle to it. "Making a symbol—or spectacle—of oneself . . . would alter nothing except in their own [the overt dissident's] lives. No benefit to the country would accompany their destruction; no constructive impression or piquing of conscience would be produced on the People any more than on their Leaders"[51]— that is how George Feifer rightly describes a typical attitude toward overt dissent of some "intrastructural" dissenters.

It is probably true, as both views suggest, that Soviet overt dissent—civic, national, or religious—is not the most important pressure for political change. Such change will come not from without but from within the official system; "intrastructural," rather than "extrastructural," dissent will bring it about. Yet it would be wrong to deny that overt dissent is an enormous asset to the whole of the Soviet dissident movement. It is essential to dissidence in at least the following respects:

1. *Ideology.* The overt dissidents publicly express what all other Soviet people merely think. Because their ideologies represent the genuine views of the people, they help the Soviet people to sort out their political positions, values, and aims, and to formulate them in logical rather than emotional terms.

2. *Communication.* The ideas and actions of overt dissenters publicized through *samizdat, tamizdat,*[52] and broadcasts in Russian and other

Soviet languages from abroad are becoming subjects of common public knowledge and discussion. This helps people to establish among themselves associations and differentiations on politically relevant lines and to raise their level of political awareness. Moreover, the publicity surrounding overt dissent stimulates people to think about positive dissent and increases the number of such dissenters.

3. *Moral force.* The activities of overt dissidents represent a moral example to the rest of the people. The fact that they have overcome the widespread fear of the regime shames others and challenges them to do likewise. The dissidents also suggest that it is possible to transcend the limits of personal safety set up by the regime, thereby encouraging people to be more active and radical in their "intrastructural" dissident activities. The people learn through the example of overt dissidents "not to live by lying" (Solzhenitsyn). In this way, overt dissent has played (and continues to play) an important role in cleansing the moral climate of the country.

4. *Representation.* The outside world has been able to learn about Soviet dissent only through its overt manifestations; the overt dissenters also enlist world public support for the Soviet dissident cause, which strengthens it enormously and creates links between the Soviet people and the peoples of the rest of the world.

Concluding Notes on Political Change

My views on the problems of political change accord with the concept developed by the Soviet samizdat author mentioned, F. Znakov. According to him, political change always arises out of "intrastructural" activities. Analyzing the experience of the revolutions in England (seventeenth century), France (eighteenth century), and Russia (March 1917), he came to the conclusion that the process of political change always starts "by the establishment on the legal surface of the society of an institution, independent of the existing political system, and able to be set of against it."[53] He called such an institution "the second pivot (*vtoroy sterzhen'*) of social integration"[54] and pointed out that usually it had once constituted an element of the system it was challenging. By separating itself from and challenging the system, it first splits it into "two pivots" and then tries to establish a new political system around a "sole pivot"—its own supreme authority. In seventeenth-century England, the role of the "second pivot" was played by the Long Parliament; in eighteenth-century France, by the National Assembly, which evolved from the Estates General; and in Russia of March 1917, by the State Duma. In the Hungarian Revolution of 1956, Znakov says that the role of the "second pivot" was played by the Petöfi Circle.

Analyzing the Soviet situation as it was 10 years ago, Znakov foresaw that, in seeking a solution of the inevitable next crisis, the party could either establish a new institution of state economic management with large autonomous powers or could increase the autonomy and power of the State Planning Committee or of another similar institution within the system. Any such institution could assume the role of "second pivot" and end the partocratic rule. If the party chose instead to deal with the crisis within the existing institutional framework, its efforts would inevitably fail, and the resultant social chaos could induce the army (the natural partisan of order) to intervene and to assume the role of the "second pivot."[55] One way or the other, the "second pivot," according to Znakov, will inevitably emerge in the Soviet Union and replace the party apparatus in the position of supreme authority. As he sees it, dissent will finally win its struggle with the regime. According to Znakov, those who participate in positive dissent in the USSR, whatever their specific aims, are working for the victory of the "middle class" over the present "upper class"—the ruling partocrats. Znakov (and he is not alone) thinks that this "middle class" is represented by the Soviet technocrats who are already sufficiently mature to replace the parto-crats, as the "upper class" in Soviet society.[56] That is why he and others who think like him regard the professionally motivated positive "in-trastructural" dissent as the real core of the Soviet dissident movement.

"Intrastructural" dissent ventures of the technocrats referred to in the previous section cannot produce any substantial changes so long as the partocracy rules. These ventures, under the present circumstances, will always be only partial successes and overall failures. But such ventures do produce a real awareness of the directions that the technocrats as a social group would like to see the country take and a consciousness of the impossibility of initiating and carrying out such change under partocratic rule.

Even now, the technocrats are not a powerless group. In the age of the "scientific–technological revolution," their share of influence and power in society is rapidly increasing though the partocrats remain supreme. As F. Fleron has shown in his analysis of the composition of the Party's Central Committee, the proportion of specialists in that supreme body of power grew from 25.6% in 1952 to 44% in 1961, a trend that has continued unabated.[57] Similarly, the role of professionals in Soviet society is rapidly increasing,[58] making them one of the most important interest groups in the country. Also, as some Soviet scholars are publicly stating, experts are taking a much more important part than before in the process of political decision making.[59] Their near-to-power position inevitably tempts the technocrats to grasp the whole of it, especially when they have been unable to determine policy on con-troversial issues. The transition from one generation of rulers to the next could offer a tempting opportunity to seize power. The aging of senior party figures and their imminent replacement by a younger generation (almost totally composed of professionals, i.e., technocrats) may also coincide with political change.

Many Western scholars have pointed out that the professionalization (or technocratization) of the Soviet elite is not necessarily linked with political change.[60] The technocrats are not democrats, and "the masses do not demand legality, representative institutions, freedom. . . . The interest in freedom and the rule of law is not broad enough, is not sufficiently a 'mass' interest, to make its accommodation critical."[61] The point about the technocrats and the masses is true, but political change in the USSR does not necessarily imply the establishment of "legality, representative institutions, freedom." Political change in the Soviet Union is less likely to involve the establishment of democratic rule than to establish a *rational* and nationally minded government as opposed to the present *irrational*, single-ideology-based, and "clique"-minded regime. In fact, while the new rational regime that emerges from political change in the USSR will have the full support of the technocrats, it may also be authoritarian for a significant period of time.

But authoritarianism is not totalitarianism, because authoritarian rule does not necessarily encompass in a rigid framework all spheres of human life and activity. Any new political regime in the USSR, authoritarian or not, will not only be compatible with a pluralistic economic pattern and with considerable autonomy for the economic system vis-à-vis the state but, if it is to command the support of the technocrats, must be explicitly based on these principles. Such a regime, authoritarian or not, will do away with the sole official ideology (in a framework of national ideology quite a few political, social, and religious ideologies can coexist) and thus provide conditions for the emergence of a pluralistic ideological pattern in social life. Ideological pluralism, in its turn, implies more freedom for creative work and for expression of different interests, including those now represented by civic, national, and partially religious dissent (partially because ideological tolerance will automatically solve the problems of most religious groups). Under such a regime, the necessary preconditions for creating a democratic system of government could evolve in due course, too, but the establishment of a democracy is not the most immediate and the most realizable task in the struggle to bring about political change in the USSR.

The main problem to be solved in bringing about political change in the Soviet Union is that of separating the civil society from the state— that is to say, creating a legal system that would provide the necessary conditions for the functioning of social and economic institutions not under the discretionary rule of party and state but under the rule of law (i.e., in an independent and self-sufficient way).

The next problem is to sort out the complex network of intranational relations within the Soviet Union as well as in Soviet-dominated Eastern Europe. The third problem is to end 60 years of artificial, ideologically motivated confrontation in East–West relationships and to establish, in accordance with national interests, a pattern of genuine cooperation with the Western world. In comparison with those problems, the problem of what precise form a genuinely national government will take seems to be of secondary importance indeed.

Notes

[1] For elaboration of the central themes of the chapter, see Alexander Shtromas, *Political Change and Social Development: The Case of the Soviet Union* (Frankfort: Verlag Peter Lang, 1981). "Dissent, v.i., refuse to assent." *The Concise Oxford Dictionary of Current English*, 5th ed. (Oxford: Oxford University Press) p. 354.

[2] F. C. Barghoorn, "Factional, Sectoral, and Subversive Opposition in Soviet Politics," in *Regimes and Oppositions*, ed. R. A. Dahl (New Haven: Yale University Press, 1973), pp. 39–40, proposes and substantiates this classification of Soviet opposition.

[3] See S. A. Kochanek, "Perspectives in the Study of Revolution and Social Change," *Comparative Politics* 5, no. 3 (April 1975), esp. pp. 313 ff.

[4] For an illuminating study of the flexibility of the Soviet regime and of the narrow limits of its "within-system" political change (and of the political meaning of Khrushchev's sacking in 1964), see the Soviet samizdat author F. Znakov (pseudonym), "Pamyatnaya zapiska," in Radio Liberty "Arkhiv Samizdata," no. 374 (1966). For a detailed account of sociopolitical developments in the USSR after the fall of Khrushchev, see A. Brown and M. Kaser, eds., *The Soviet Union since the Fall of Khrushchev* (London: Macmillan, 1975).

[5] F. C. Barghoorn, "Factional, Sectoral, and Subversive Opposition," p. 34.

[6] A good and fairly comprehensive account of the development of Bolshevik terror during 1918–1956 is given by A. Solzhenitsyn in *Gulag Archipelago*, vol. 1, chap. 2.

[7] "The superego, for all practical purposes, is the individual's conscience"; "the ego is charged with maximizing the individual's gratification while simultaneously protecting him from self-destruction through the unbridled pursuit of his needs" (M. Palmer, L. Stern, and C. Gaile, *The Interdisciplinary Study of Politics* [New York: Harper & Row, 1974], p. 141). For a more detailed explanation of the concepts of *ego* and *superego*, see W. C. Menninger, *Psychiatry: Its Evolution and Present Status* (Ithaca: Cornell University Press, 1948), pp. 73–75.

[8] The term *homo sovieticus* was introduced in E. Lyons, *Our Secret Allies: The Peoples of Russia* (Boston: Little, Brown, 1953), pp. 369–376.

[9] A. Solzhenitsyn, *Letter to Soviet Leaders* (London: Fontana Books, 1974), pp. 28, 46–49.

[10] A. Sakharov, *O pis'me Aleksandra Solzhenitsyna "Vozhdyam Sovetskogo Soyuza"* (New York: Khronika, 1974), pp. 6–7. The alleged differences between Sakharov's and Solzhenitsyn's views on the role of ideology in Soviet society are partly imaginary. Both recognize that Communist ideology is completely dead in the country. But where Solzhenitsyn rightly sees ideology as the main instrument of Communist power and therefore insists on its official denunciation, Sakharov views it as a ritual device with no essential role in the pragmatic policy of the

regime. Sakharov is, of course, absolutely right in stating that the Soviet process of political decision making is completely dominated by the pragmatic interests of "preservation of power and of the main features of the regime" (*ibid.*, p. 6), but he does not take into account the fact that the preservation of ideology is a decisive factor in the preservation of power and of the regime itself.

[11]Z. Katz, "Sociology in the Soviet Union," *Problems of Communism* 20, no.3 (May–June 1971), pp. 22–40.

[12]G. D. Hollander, *Soviet Political Indoctrination: Developments in Mass Media and Propaganda since Stalin* (New York: Praeger, 1972), pp. 20, 168. I would take issue with those Western students of Soviet political socialization who are more than ready to acknowledge the regime's successes in that field. On the one hand, they confuse the support for the present regime with the genuine acceptance of the regime's ideology taken at its face value; on the other hand, they wrongly assume that the huge system of indoctrination in the Soviet Union does imbue the Soviet people with "superordinate goals" codified in "Communist morality" as U. Bronfenbrenner puts it in his *Two Worlds of Childhood* (New York: Russell Sage Foundation, 1970), pp. 37–49. Probably Bronfenbrenner and J. M. Gillison in his *British and Soviet Politics* (Baltimore: Johns Hopkins University Press, 1972) are the most representative exponents of such views.

[13]A very illuminating discussion of the essential anti-Communism of the present Soviet leaders, who are bound to the Bolshevik legacy but try to apply within its framework what he calls "lumpen-bureaucratic" politics, is N. Korzhavin, "Psikhologiya sovremennogo entuziazma," *Kontinent*, no. 8, and esp. no. 9 (1976), pp. 146–150.

[14]*Le Monde*, October 22, 1976, p. 4.

[15]This point is elaborated in many studies of Soviet politics; see, for instance, F. C. Barghoorn, "Factional, Sectoral, and Subversive Opposition"; A. H. Brown, "Policy-making in the Soviet Union," *Soviet Studies* 23, no. 1 (July 1971); A. Brown and M. Kaser, eds., *The Soviet Union*; H. L. Biddulph, "Protest Strategies of the Soviet Intellectual Opposition," in *Dissent in the U.S.S.R.: Politics, Ideology and People*, ed. R. Tökés (Baltimore: Johns Hopkins University Press, 1976), esp. pp. 101–103; and works referred to in Note 16.

[16]See, for instance: H. G. Skilling and F. Griffiths, eds., *Interest Groups in Soviet Politics* (Princeton: Princeton University Press, 1971); P. H. Juviler and H. W. Morton, eds., *Soviet Policy-Making: Studies of Communism in Transition* (London: Pall Mall, 1967). Although I am critical of particular conclusions of some of these authors, I appreciate very much their differentiated approach to Soviet politics. Of particular interest is the "bureaucratic model" of Soviet decision making presented by G. T. Allison in his *Essence of Decision: Explaining the Cuban Missile Crisis* (Boston: Little, Brown, 1971). The basic premise of Allison's model—officials are conditioned to promote bureaucratic rather than functional interests ("where you stand depends on where you sit")—is very helpful in explaining the "office–patrimonial" ideology behind the initiatives taken and the positions held by Soviet officials (*ibid.*, p. 176). But the trend to ignore the "superbureaucratic" role of the party apparatus and to identify the practices of the Soviet bureaucracy with those of the American one leads Allison to miss very crucial points.

[17]According to M. C. Lodge, self-consciousness is a sociological requisite for a group; he points out that a group must "conceive of themselves as a group

distinct from the party apparatchiki" (quoted in A. H. Brown, "Policy-Making in the Soviet Union," p. 135).

[18]The most impressive analysis of organized sabotage in the service industries is Ustin Malapagin, "Dogovorilis'?" *Izvestiya*, October 9, 1974. The article says that service workers refuse to do their job properly and on time without getting extra cash. Service managers and clerks are kept busy explaining to customers why the service they ask for either cannot be provided or cannot be performed at a convenient time; they suggest that the customer ask the worker to do the job on his own time. The customer then arranges the matter with the worker, pays him and the office, and gets the job done well and quickly. This situation is typical of other branches of the economy, too.

[19] An adequate account of economic delinquency in the USSR is H. Smith, *The Russians* (London: Times Books, 1976), esp. chap. 3, "Corruption: Living 'Na Levo'," pp. 81–101. See also: D. K. Simes, "The Soviet Parallel Market," *Survey*, no. 3(96) (Summer 1975); as well as such occasional reports in the British press as P. Godfrey, "Graft and Grand Masters in Russia," *The Sunday Telegraph*, April 18, 1976; P. Osnos, "Soviet Crime and Punishment (2): Official Figures Mask Web of Graft," *The Guardian*, August 31, 1976. But probably the best source of information on Soviet economic delinquency and on the psychology of people involved in it is, astonishingly enough, the Soviet press.

[20]To quote only the best publicized examples: More than one-third of private car owners in 1972–1973 used gasoline stolen and sold to them by the drivers of state-owned cars (see *Izvestiya*, January 1, 1975). According to the *Literaturnaya Gazeta*, construction workers systematically steal building materials for their private enterprise, making "additional improvements" to people's new apartments; in Moscow alone, people annually pay more than 10 million rubles for such services. (See the digest of this article in *Radio Liberty Research Bulletin*, no. 34 [August 21, 1974].)

[21]One of the best-known examples, though an extreme one, is that of O. Lazeishvili, boss of a humble synthetics laboratory, who produced fashionable clothes and other goods in short supply in a huge private factory with several separate local branches (see H. Smith, *The Russians*, pp. 98–99; P. Godfrey, "Graft and Grand Masters"). More typical are cases of so-called parallel production within officially functioning factories. Such factories exceed the production of planned goods (usually by "economizing" on raw materials supplied for their production—one of the causes of the notorious low quality of Soviet goods), and the factory managers privately sell the surplus to accomplices in wholesale shops; the wholesalers then sell the goods to the retailers, who sell them to the people. Each level of the transaction extracts some profit.

[22]A well-publicized example is speculation in books. Bookstore managers sell books in short supply to blackmarket operators at several times the official price, and these operators charge the public prices several times higher than they have paid. Some books are sold on the black market at prices more than 100 times higher than the nominal price. (See, for detail, F. Crepeau, "The Black Market Sales of Books Is Flourishing in Moscow," *The International Herald Tribune*, October 8, 1974.) The quoted example emphasizes the last step in the process of speculation. The main difficulty is to get the goods in short supply to the right retailers' shops to pass them to the black market. Special private agents linking producers, wholesalers, and retailers engage in the most complicated activities

to provide the stock for speculation. A representative case was that of a certain Khikhinashvili, who, for the purpose of getting stuff in short supply to certain retail shops in Georgia, established a huge "criminal" network consisting of managers of textile factories all over the Soviet Union, of wholesale institutions of several All-union ministries, and of many other organizations (see A. Sukontsev, "Manufaktur-Sovetniki," *Pravda*, November 13, 1973.)

[23]There is no available information on corruption above the level of the highest authorities of the union republics and administrative districts, except perhaps for the case of Mrs. Furtseva, the late Soviet Minister of Culture. But one of the corrupt republic leaders, former First Secretary of the Georgian Party Central Committee V. P. Mzhavanadze, was a candidate member of the Politburo (see H. Smith, *The Russians* pp. 97–99). In the early 1960s, several hundred leading figures of Leningrad's retail trade (including the head of the Trade Department of the Leningrad City Council) were tried on charges of plundering many millions of rubles. The case went to court immediately after the First Secretary of the Leningrad Party Committee and full Politburo member F. R. Kozlov was transferred to Moscow and made a secretary of the party Central Committee. There were strong allegations that before moving to Moscow, he had been the patron of the network of plunderers with a big share in its profits, and that it was therefore impossible to arrest these people. In another case of the late 1950s, the economy of Kirghizia was turned into a huge semiprivate enterprise under the alleged protection of the then First Secretary of the republic party's Central Committee, I. Razzakov, who supposedly had a great share in it. Other well-known cases of similar regional networks under the highest party patronage are those of the Voroshilovgrad Party District Committee's First Secretary, V. Shevchenko (see H. Smith, *The Russians*, p. 99) and of former First Secretary of the Azerbaijan Party Central Committee, I. Akhundov (see I. Zemtsov, *Partiya ili mafiya. Razvorovannaya respublika* [Paris: Les Editeurs Réunis, 1976]).

[24]A similar conclusion is drawn by D. K. Simes: "Generally speaking during recent years some degree of tolerance, if not approval, has developed in the Soviet Union towards certain kinds of parallel market activities" (D. K. Simes, "The Soviet Parallel Market," p. 52).

[25]*Ibid.*, P. Osnos, "Soviet Crime and Punishment."

[26]H. Smith, *The Russians*, p. 86.

[27]K. Marx and F. Engels, *The German Ideology*; quoted from K. Marx, F. Engels, *Sochineniya*, 2nd ed. Vol. 3 (Moscow: GIPL, 1955), p. 323.

[28]Josef Stalin, *On the Economic Situation of the U.S.S.R.* (1937), quoted in *Ugolovnoye pravo. Osobennaya chast'*, 2nd ed. (Moscow: Yuridicheskoye Izdatelstvo NKYuSSSR, 1939), p. 100.

[29]As is rightly observed by some students of Soviet politics in the West, many interest groups are united on both institutional and functional (i.e., interinstitutional or even extrainstitutional) lines. See, for instance, J. Schwartz and W. Keech, "Group Influence on the Policy Process in the Soviet Union," *American Political Science Review* 62, no. 3 (September 1968).

[30]For more details, see I. Zemtsov, "I.K.S.I.: The Moscow Institute of Applied Social Research" (Research Paper of the Soviet and East European Research Centre of the Hebrew University of Jerusalem, Jerusalem, 1976; text in Russian).

[31]B. M. Meissner, "Totalitarian Rule and Social Change," in *Dilemmas of*

Change in Soviet Policy, ed. Z. Brzezinski (New York: Columbia University Press, 1969), p. 77.

[32]*Ibid.*

[33]I draw the reader's attention to my use of the word *partocrats* where *party* might have been expected. In my conception, the ideas conveyed by the two terms do not coincide. The party is an apparatus, a definite structure inside the Soviet political system, whereas partocrats represent a specific group of the Soviet elite whose members work not only within the party system but also in other organizations such as the government, the trade unions, the Young Communist League, and even the Red Cross. The rule of this group over all sections of the Soviet society and state I call partocracy (the rule of the partocrats), including in this notion also the leading role of the party and its apparatus.

[34]*Pravda*, September 9, 1962.

[35]Academician A. Aganbegyan is the director of the influential Institute of Economics in Novosibirsk. In the late 1960s, after the failure to get the economic reform implemented, Acad. V. Nemchinov created the influential Central Economic-Mathematical Institute of the USSR's Academy of Sciences; he remained its director until his death. This institute, which became a stronghold of "progressive" economists—almost a "dissident" institution—not only survived but still carries much weight in economic decision making. When Nemchinov died, a hardliner, Acad. N. Fedorenko, was appointed director. He adjusted to the Institute, rather than the other way around, and increased the Institute's influence with the power holders.

[36]For more details, see H. Smith, *The Russians*, pp. 213–214.

[37]The concept that the struggle for power between the partocratic "upper class" and the technocratic "middle class" is the decisive factor for political change in the USSR was developed by the samizdat author, F. Znakov (see Note 4). He attributes the concept to George Orwell's *1984*, simply applying it to the present situation in the Soviet Union. After Znakov formulated the idea in 1966, it became quite popular among the theoretically minded Soviet samizdat and émigré writers. It is developed, for instance, by A. Amalrik in *Will the Soviet Union Survive until 1984?* and A. Yanov, "Detente and the Soviet Managerial Class," *The New York Times*, August 21, 1975. Western scholars are rather skeptical about the idea in general and especially about the political potential of the Soviet managers. See, for instance, W. D. Connor, "Differentiation, Integration, and Political Dissent in the U.S.S.R.," in Tökés, *Dissent in the U.S.S.R.*, especially the comprehensive analysis of Western scholars' views on pp. 153–154.

[38]Here I have in mind the late Aleksey Kosterin, Ivan Yakhimovich, General Pyotr Grigorenko in his early dissident days, the Krasnopevtsev-Rendel group of 1956, and the anonymous group of people who have published in the late 1960s the samizdat periodical *Prestupleniye i nakazaniye*.

[39]A neo-Stalinist dissident group led by Fetisov was arrested in the spring of 1968, and its members were put in a special psychiatric asylum (*Khronika tekushchikh sobytiy*, no. 7, in *Posev*, special issue, no. 2, p. 13).

[40]Typical expressions of fascist ideology in samizdat documents are: Valeriy Skurlatov's "A Code of Morals" (the whole text of this essay dating from 1965 is published in A. Yanov, *The Russian New Right* [Berkeley: Institute of In-

ternational Studies, University of California, 1978], pp. 170–172) and the notorious *Slovo natsii* published by an anonymous group (Document no. 590 in Radio Liberty's *Arkhiv Samizdata*). A theocratic version of Russian fascism is represented in Gennadiy Shimanov's samizdat books: *Pis'ma o Rossii* and *Protiv techeniya* (both available in the Keston College Archives).

[41]For more details on the official Soviet policy toward assimilation of non-Russian nations, its poor results, and the growing resistance to this policy, see R. Pipes, "Reflections on the Nationality Problems in the Soviet Union," in *Ethnicity: Theory and Experience*, N. Glazer and D. P. Moynihan, eds. (Cambridge, Mass.: Harvard University Press, 1975), pp. 453–465, esp. pp. 459–465; M. Agursky, "Natsionalnyy vopros v SSSR," *Kontinent*, no. 10 (1976).

[42]According to Barbara Jancar, there are 50 million Russian Orthodox, 5 million Catholics, 30 million Muslims, and 500,000 Baptists (B. Wolfe Jancar, "Religious Dissent in the Soviet Union," in *Dissent in the U.S.S.R.*, ed. Tökés, p. 197). M. Bourdeaux estimates the Russian Orthodox Church at "30 or even 50 million strong" and the Muslim community in Central Asia at about 40–45 million members (see M. Bourdeaux, "Religion," in *The Soviet Union*, ed. Brown and Kaser, p. 64). He adds that the Muslims "may already surpass the Russian Orthodox Church numerically and therefore be the largest of all" (*ibid.*, p. 171).

[43]A major article in *Pravda* illuminates the whole "regime versus religion" situation. It shows that the regime is extremely worried about the growing influence of religion, especially among young people, and strongly blames shortcomings in official antireligious work. It clearly states that religion has become the central issue in the party's ideological work because religion is the main obstacle confronting the party's chief task: "forming in all Soviet people a monolithic, dialectical-materialistic Weltanschauung." The article bewails the inefficiency of antireligious education and cries out for new and more numerous kinds of antireligious work as the core of the "whole process of educating the new man" (A. Belov, N. Tarasenko, "S aktivnykh pozitsiy," *Pravda*, December 1, 1976).

[44]There are also instances of concealed "extrastructural" dissident activities that have no links with "intrastructural" dissent as, for instance, in the case of VSKhSON)Vserossiyskiy Sotsial'no-Khristianskiy Soyuz Osvobozhdeniya Naroda). All members of this highly secret organization, which aimed to overthrow the Soviet regime by force, behaved inconspicuously in their official life. Their "safety rule" was to play the role of obedient Soviet citizens, enthusiastically supporting all new party ventures, and never engaging in controversial enterprises or conversations in their official life. This is a rather untypical case since very few people in the USSR would believe it possible to resist the regime efficiently by working purely through a secret political society. Of course, such secret societies do emerge from time to time; the NTS (Narodno-Trudovoy Soyuz), too, has a number of clandestine cells that managed to operate for quite long periods of time. Such organizations play a minor role in the overall context of Soviet dissent, however.

[45]Solzhenitsyn's efforts to impede his expulsion from the Writers' Union, his keenness to get the Lenin Prize, etc., prove this point. He tells about these efforts in *Bodalsya telyonok s dubom* (Paris: Y.M.C.A. Press, 1975).

[46]For details on Sakharov's life see *Sakharov about Himself* (New York: Knopf, 1974).

[47]While in school, Bukovsky started to publish an unauthorized magazine of schoolboy jokes; and "intrastructural" activity for which he was expelled. This background barred him from further education and impeded his career. All his attempts to change his fate failed. He managed to enter the university surreptitiously but was expelled from it, too. The constant repression of each step practically forced Bukosvsky to become an overt dissenter on an almost professional scale. For more details on his life see N. Bethel's interview with him in *The Sunday Times*, January 9, 1977.

[48]See Michel Tatu's interview with Bukovsky in *Le Monde*, January 5, 1977, pp. 1–2.

[49]*Ibid.*

[50]W. D. Connor, "Differentiation," pp. 155–156.

[51]G. Feifer, "No Protest: The Case of the Passive Minority," in *Dissent in the U.S.S.R.*, ed. Tökés p. 423.

[52]*Samizdat*—literally "self-publishing"—the system of multiplication and distribution of manuscripts produced by the dissidents. *Tamizdat*—literally "there-publishing"—books and journals in Russian and other Soviet languages published abroad.

[53]Znakov, "Pamyatnaya zapiska," p. 21.

[54]*Ibid.*, p. 22.

[55]*Ibid.*, p. 23.

[56]*Ibid.*, pp. 6–12. A similar theory was developed by M. Djilas after he had written his *New Class*. He first called this "middle-class" the "new new class" but then settled for the straightforward term *middle class*. In his *Unperfect Society*, Djilas writes: ". . . in the whole of the East European Communist world . . . *ground has already been covered for the creation of a new social stratum*—a special middle class. . . . The sum and substance of this new stratum of society are *specialists* of all kinds. . . . The very fact that the growing strength of this class cannot now be restrained . . . means that this is the class of the future. . . . I feel that I am in a sense its spokesman because I can at least envisage the inevitability of its progress" (London: Unwin Books, 1972, pp. 146–147). The German political scientist H. F. Achminov, writing before Znakov and Djilas, stated simply that "the technical intelligentsia are the gravediggers of Communism" (*Die Totengräber des Kommunismus* [Stuttgart: Steinbrüben Verlag, 1964], p. 150). See also the works of A. Amalrik and A. Yanov referred to in Note 37.

[57]F. J. Fleron, Jr., "Cooptation as a Mechanism of Adaptation to Change: The Soviet Political Leadership System," in *The Behavioral Revolution and Communist Studies*, ed. R. E. Kanet (New York: Free Press, 1971), p. 138.

[58]The average annual increase of "scientific workers" amounts to 12.3%, that of industrial workers only to 3.5%; the number of scientific workers doubled between 1956 and 1960 and doubled again between 1960 and 1966. (See: S. A. Kugel, "Izmeneniye sotsialnoy struktury sotsialisticheskogo obshchestva pod vozdeystviyem nauchno-tekhnicheskoy revolyutsii," in *Voprosy filosofii*, no. 3 [1969], pp. 18–19).

[59]See, for instance, F. M. Burlatsky, "Notion of Ideological Regime" (paper presented to the Tenth World Congress of the International Political Science Association, Edinburgh, August 1976).

[60]See, for instance, W. D. Connor, "Differentiation," pp. 139–157.

[61]*Ibid.*, p. 155.

IV
Continuity and Change

Have the fundamental characteristics of the Soviet polity fostered or fettered scientific and technological progress? Conversely, has scientific and technological progress spurred or impeded fundamental change in the Soviet polity? One's responses to these questions depend heavily on a subjective identification of the essential elements of the Soviet political system. Western commentators affirm that if there is to be systemic transformation in the USSR, it must come through changes in key areas such as: one-party rule; the proscription of factions in the Communist party; the proscription of associational interest groups; the CPSU's job assignment procedures (*nomenklatura*); restrictions on freedom of expression; a judiciary that is subject to party domination in political cases; and a secret police with enormous powers (see John Hazard's chapter below).

But some Western analysts underscore the political, economic, and social changes that have taken place at different stages in Soviet history. Other analysts underscore political, economic, and social stability. And still others underscore political stability and social and economic change. For example, Robert V. Daniels affirms that

> The confluence of socioeconomic modernization and political–administrative immobilism has given a distinctive, if not always neatly categorizable, form to the evolving Soviet system. It is neither despotic nor free, neither totalitarian nor pluralistic, but a curious amalgam of functional interests and technical imperatives embedded in a commitment to monopoly of power.[1]

Western specialists agree, however, that pressures for political change are intensifying in the Soviet Union. New scientific–technical and socioeconomic conditions, domestic and international, are thought to be reducing the effectiveness of traditional Soviet policies and policy-making procedures. Factors such as the increasing need for scientific and technological innovation, the declining rates of economic growth and productivity, the high per capita expenditures for defense, the proliferation of the Moslem population in Central Asia, the possibility of greater cohesiveness among professional groups and social strata, and the imminent rise to power of a whole new generation of party and state leaders have been cited as "sources of tension and potential sources of tension which are capable, in due course, of producing fundamental political change."[2]

The Soviet polity did not change fundamentally in the Brezhnev years, according to most Western observers. To be sure, adjustments took place in the attitudes and beliefs of scientific–technical, managerial, and educational elites and among segments of the general population. Some of these new perspectives were reformist and others were conservative. Both were responses to changes in the Soviet social structure and world economy and to the increasing inertia and ineffectiveness of Brezhnev's collective leadership. But Soviet attitudes and beliefs changed much more than Soviet policies and policymaking procedures, especially in the 1970s and 1980s. The traditional political and socioeconomic institutions remained intact, decisions were postponed, choices became circumscribed, and problems mounted. Although Soviet leaders increasingly recognized the seriousness of the USSR's economic and social problems, the Brezhnev administration was reluctant to initiate major economic or social reforms, most likely because they would dilute the concentration of power at the highest levels of the CPSU and weaken party control over society.

Whether fundamental Soviet values and institutions will change and whether scientific–technical and socioeconomic pressures will induce fundamental changes in Soviet elite and mass behavior and attitudes are among the critical questions addressed in our final chapters. The editors and most of the contributors conclude that politicized judgments and perspectives, not the inexorable "demands" of scientific–technical and demographic forces, will decisively shape Soviet domestic and international politics for the foreseeable future. Scientific and technological progress and social and economic change can influence, but cannot dictate, political choices.

Notes

[1] Robert V. Daniels, "Political Change in the USSR: Moving the Immovable?" *Problems of Communism* 30, no. 6 (November–December, 1981), p. 49.

[2] Archie Brown, "Political Developments: Some Conclusions and an Interpretation," in Archie Brown and Michael Kaser, eds., *The Soviet Union since the Fall of Khrushchev* (London: Macmillan, 1975), pp. 255–256.

27   ALFRED G. MEYER

*The Soviet Political System**

A. C. H. C. de Tocqueville had it easier than we. Like us, he represented a political tradition that had been challenged by a revolutionary new order established half a century before. Like us, he wished to study this new political system and assess its strengths and weaknesses, its achievements and failures. Unlike us, however, he had infinitely greater opportunities for using his eyes and ears for the extensive survey he wished to make. Moreover, there was no cold war raging then to inflame the passions and blind the eyes. To be sure, democracy was as frightening a bogey in 1831 as communism is in 1967; and there was an ideological barrier, a modicum of reserve if not suspicion putting the young aristocrat on guard against the revolutionary experiment in the New World. Yet this latent hostility pales in comparison with the antagonism between the Western de Tocquevilles of today and the more recent revolutionary experiment in the USSR. After all, his own country had made its experiments with revolutionary democracy at the same time as the New World and was soon to make others, whereas the Western world today, facing the communist world, still has its *ancien régime.* For this reason alone, the ideological gulf appears deeper.

This gulf opens at the very moment we begin to assess the development and achievements of the Soviet political system in the first half-century of its existence. Our first impulse may be to go back to the birth of the system and examine the expectations with which it came into life. Already at this point, ideological differences appear because different people expressed divergent expectations. In the Western world, and

*Reprinted by permission of the author and publisher from *The USSR after 50 Years: Promise and Reality,* ed. Samuel Hendel and Randolph L. Braham (New York: Alfred A. Knopf, Inc., 1967), pp. 39–60. Copyright 1967 by Samuel Hendel and Randolph L. Braham.

among Russian counterrevolutionaries, the political leaders were nearly unanimous at first in predicting the early collapse of the Bolshevik regime. They did not credit the Bolshevik leadership with sufficient political skill to maintain themselves in power or to create any orderly governmental machinery; nor did they believe a socialist or communist social order capable of functioning. The pervasiveness and strength of these views in the first years after the October Revolution deserve to be remembered. Indeed, 30 years after the Bolshevik seizure of power, assumptions of this sort still formed the basis for the judgment of George Kennan and others, who argued that the Soviet regime was by its nature incapable of satisfying a sufficient number of citizens, hence unable to acquire stability or legitimacy.

Only seemingly in contrast with such pessimistic (or, from the point of view of Western observers, optimistic) appraisals of the system's staying power are views that prevailed among Western scholars in the first 10 years after World War II, the formative years of American Sovietology. During that period, most writers seemed to take it for granted that the Soviet political system was innately incapable of changing. More specifically, those of its features deemed most obnoxious (individual dictatorship, terror, total indoctrination and thought control, as well as economic austerity) were regarded as essential elements of "totalitarianism" without which the entire system would disintegrate. Indeed, the basic lack of legitimacy, stability, and viability of the regime, it was argued, made "totalitarianism" and its syndrome of negative features inevitable. Thus, the two seemingly opposite hypotheses— instability and inability to change—were linked to each other.

Prognoses of this kind are now being reviewed by our Western de Tocquevilles, who today tend to smile at the earlier expectations engendered by the October Revolution. They do have the satisfaction to know that the people on the other side were equally hasty in predicting the results of communist rule. What the Bolshevik leaders expected at the time of the October Revolution is well known. Lenin and his party comrades predicted the immediate establishment of a socialist society managed in democratic fashion by the masses of the citizens themselves. It would be a society of equals, without classes or a strict division of labor, and without exploitation. Such a polity would no longer require institutions of coercion or a complex administrative machinery; they would disappear together with oppressive kinship rules, moral codes, false ideologies, internecine competition between individuals, and other concomitants of class-torn societies. The speedy development of this new society, the Bolsheviks argued, was guaranteed by the impending spread of communism over all or most of the civilized world.

Obviously, this extension of communist rule has not taken place; and, equally clearly, the Soviet political system of 1967 corresponds to the expectations of its founders as little as it does to the prognoses of their enemies. The task remains of defining what in fact it has been and now is, and in what fields of endeavor it has succeeded or failed.

Let me begin by challenging the reader with an exaggeration: To define the Soviet system as it has existed in the past five decades is impossible because it has changed so often and so thoroughly. In other words, there is no such thing as The Soviet Political System; there is only a succession of systems sharply differing from each other in purpose, structure, and functioning.

Having overstated my case, I hasten to point to a number of continuities in the entire history of the Soviet Union. Except in periods of total revolutionary change, there are some elements of political systems that are fundamentally "given," that change slowly or not at all—the geographic and demographic base, the social structure, the political culture. Still, one might argue that one of the persistent traits of Soviet politics is the attempt of the rulers to wreak change in this very substructure. Some scholars think of communist rule as self-perpetuating revolution. The very factors we see as given, factors underlying not only the entire Soviet history but also linking the Soviet system to its tsarist predecessor, are among the factors that communism seeks to change. Communist political systems would thus come close to the dialectical model combining perpetual self-destruction with self-perpetuation or, more aptly, perpetual self-renewal, with stress on the newness.

There are, however, continuities of a less substructural kind, perpetual traits present in all phases of the Soviet regime. To support my claim that there has been a succession of different political systems since the October Revolution, I would have to convince my readers that these are merely *formal*, hence illusory, continuities, which obscure the succession of several different systems.

One could argue, for instance, that the Soviet political system from its beginning to our day has been governed by the same party. Therefore, the political leadership that came to power in 1917 has managed to perpetuate itself more successfully than most other contemporary elites. Moreover, the position their party has occupied within the political structure of the country, the functions it has served within the system, the methods it has applied, the goals that have guided it, the world outlook its leaders have professed—all these central features, one might claim, have remained constant. My view is that the external forms have remained relatively constant, but the actual political relationships have been extremely variable. The self-perpetuation of the Communist party as the sovereign elite conceals the fundamental transformations that have occurred in the party—the several shifts in the character of its membership; the repeated and thorough turnover of leaders, obscured though it is by the longevity and staying power of selected personalities; the subtle but by no means negligible changes in its relation to the political system as a whole. The continuity in ideological heritage can be dismissed as purely formal, because, despite the perennial use of identical words, both the content and the functions of "Marxism–Leninism" within the Soviet political system have changed repeatedly and thoroughly. Robert V. Daniels has aptly referred to these shifts as ideological vector changes. Again, the persistence of dictatorship and paternalism, the perennial readiness of Soviet rulers to use violence, their ever-present fear of spontaneous activity—in short, the persistent authoritarianism of Soviet government—should not prevent us from seeing the countervailing tendencies that have made themselves felt, with varying strength, in different periods. I have in mind the pre-occupation of the communist leadership with methods of rational man-agement, with the establishment of stable structures and orderly routines, and, indeed, the rule of law. Dictatorship may have persisted, but it has been exercised with varying degrees of arbitrariness. Similarly, the social base of the dictatorship has been in flux, as the class structure of Soviet society was subjected to violent shocks and revolutionary changes, only to show recurrent tendencies to settle in a fixed mold. There have been significant changes in the degree and manner of citizens' participation in government, in the material benefits the system granted them, in popular attitudes toward the entire system, and many other crucial variables. In short, by concentrating on the persistence of dictatorship, we neglect the changing nature, intensity, aims, and effects of this dictatorship and of the entire system. Perhaps many of us tend to forget how prevalent dictatorship is among political systems, and how rare and vulnerable are the polities that have managed to dispense with it. Because of this prevalence of authoritarianism, it is necessary to differentiate between its many forms.

The reason for the changeability of the Soviet system (or for its succession of stages) may be presented in several ways. Earlier, I alluded to the built-in urge for perpetual revolution. This urge can be explained as a function of an interplay between the various "input" forces impinging on Soviet politics—changing elite goals, conflicting priorities among such goals, changes in the political culture of the masses, challenges coming in from the outside world—or one can show that in the first half-century of the Soviet system, these and other inputs have never been in a stable equilibrium. Another explanation (possibly no more than a rephrasing of what was just said) could be sought in the technological revolution of our century, which has a tendency to impose permanent instability on the entire society and thus to make any political system obsolete as soon as it has established itself, precisely because technological change upsets the balance of societal forces of which the political system is a function.

One can, of course, conceive of political systems that restructure themselves in response to such substructural changes, in the manner of self-regulating automatic machines. Karl Deutsch, in his *The Nerves of Government*, has made this one of the salient features in his model of a well-functioning political system. But 120 years earlier, Karl Marx already argued that the ideal democratic constitution would be such a self-regulator; and his self-professed adherents in the USSR argue that their political order is in fact such a self-adjusting democracy. Were this correct, my assertion that since 1917 we have witnessed a succession of political systems would have to be rejected. Instead, we would have observed one marvelously designed system changing itself in response to changes in circumstances.

I do not mean to get bogged down in scholastic arguments. But I do wish to make clear why I am not ready to accept such a view. The reason is that, in my opinion, it gives a false image of spontaneous, smooth, and effective self-adjustment; it presents a picture of a political machinery so finely devised that it does in fact regulate itself. In reality, the Soviet system has shown little talent for smooth self-regulation. On the contrary, it has manifested recurrent tendencies toward institutional, procedural, and ideological rigidity and conservatism, in short, toward self-entrenchment. To use another Marxian concept: The superstructure has again and again assumed a dynamic of its own; it has lagged behind substructural developments and become dysfunctional to the social system. Major adjustments therefore had to be made in near-revolutionary (or near-counterrevolutionary) fashion. They have usually been violent, and they could be accomplished only because at the top of the system a powerful dictatorship or oligarchy was operating with few restraints. Today, the checks on arbitrariness, hence on permanent revolution, are getting stronger; and perhaps the Soviet political system is entering a phase during which self-regulating adjustments or grand restructuring by dictatorial fiat become more difficult. In any event, neither the past nor the present Soviet political system can be described as the marvelous self-regulating machinery that it proclaims to be. Instead, every readjustment has been a major crisis.

One final explanation of the instability of the system is a reference to its revolutionary origins. As Crane Brinton has shown, the process of great revolutions takes on a morphology incorporating a number of typical phases. One need not accept the pattern he has outlined in order to apply this insight to the Russian Revolution of 1917; and one then discerns distinct stages of Soviet political development. At each stage, the society faced challenges specific to that stage and responded to them with an equally specific political system. At the same time, each of these successive political systems had to deal with ever recurrent problems— challenges to which every Russian ruler, or every modern state, or any political system whatever, must respond. In order to justify my viewpoint about a succession of political systems, I would have to show that each of the Soviet regimes tackled these persistent tasks in its own specific fashion. Within the space allotted here, I will probably not be able to give more than hints and scattered examples.

Let me begin with a brief description of the successive political systems. The first, in existence from 1917 to the end of 1920, is aptly called War Communism. Its chief problem, undoubtedly, was to maintain the newly established communist rule against seemingly overwhelming challenges and, by destroying the challengers, to institutionalize itself. Its principal methods of government were destructive: military operations against foreign and domestic troops; the destruction of all rival political parties; the abolition of established property relations; and serious attempts to do away with the entire framework of entrenched institutions, including the family, the churches, laws and courts, money, and moral codes. From the ruins of the old order, the communists assumed, a new system would rise at once, conforming to the more utopian hopes of Marx and his Bolshevik followers. We have sketched the outlines of this utopia in the beginnings of this chapter. In retrospect, one must point out that the new rulers had totally inadequate notions about how to implement such a program or about the difficulties standing in the way of its spontaneous emergence. The communist leadership at the time was so constituted, however, that it could not sufficiently become aware of this inadequacy. And when the masses of the citizens wanted to act out their own utopian expectations, the regime restrained them forcibly.

As a result, War Communism was characterized by the sharpest possible tension between intentions and capabilities, between expectations and potentialities, from the points of view of both the elite and the masses. Such tension is not conducive to the formation of a viable political system, because effective and reasonably stable institutions can develop only where the ruling elite and the people have a fairly realistic conception of the resources at their disposal and, on that basis, work out policies, programs, aspirations, and expectations.

At the same time, in the years 1917–1921, there were no resources for orderly government of any kind in Russia, nor was there any elite or counterelite that could have found or created them. The old system had disintegrated. The economy was ruined. The population was bitterly divided, so that civil war was inevitable; the people were in a destructive mood. The mass of the citizens, moreover, was illiterate and lacked almost all traditions of self-government. To the extent self-government operated, it had a divisive, anarchic effect. In short, it would have been impossible to create a stable political system. Hence, the only elite that could have managed to impose any semblance of order was one out of tune with reality. Only utopians and fanatics could have had the recklessness or courage to go on governing. Realists would have despaired. Precisely because the Bolsheviks had expectations ludicrously out of tune with reality did they hold the system together.

If, indeed, one can speak of a system at all. Even though some basic institutions were established, Soviet politics during the civil war was primarily chaos, improvisation, and a succession of dire emergencies. It was rule by sheer force—government by pointing the loaded pistol. Such a nonsystem could maintain itself only because of the war and the resulting militarization of all politics. Once the civil war was over, it was scrapped just before it was threatening to collapse entirely.

The second Soviet political system (1921–1927) was in many essentials the reverse of the first. I am tempted to sum it up by stating that it sought to make do with the society that had emerged from the civil war. This society included the numerically overwhelming class of economically independent peasants owning small plots of land; these peasants the regime sought to use by making it profitable for them to farm their plots. The regime furthermore endeavored to make use of all members of the prerevolutionary professional elite still remaining in the country. It even utilized institutions copied from the capitalist world. Such institutions as civil law and a stable currency, to mention only two, had to be reintroduced, having been abolished or left to disappear by the first Soviet political system. The entire policy of making do with social and cultural forces available was symbolized by the slogan of "peaceful coexistence." Although it was meant to express the aims of Soviet foreign policy, it can be applied to domestic policies just as well.

The first system had lived on dreams. In the second, the dreams were shelved for the time being. The first had been revolutionary; the second was one of retreat and retrenchment. The first had been destructive; the second was interested in reconstruction of what had existed before. Beyond this, it sought to improve these residues of the past: to make the economy more efficient, to make the peasants literate, to teach former professional revolutionaries how to function as effective administrators. Socialism was to be achieved, according to party doctrine at the time, by the wise utilization and improvement of the things tsarism and capitalism had left.

For the Communist party, the second Soviet political system was an interregnum during which neither leadership nor long-range policy was well defined. Hence, both were the subject of controversy. Lenin, who had created both the first and the second Soviet system, did not survive the formation of the second one for very long. His illness and death plunged the USSR into a succession crisis lasting until the end of the second phase. At the same time, his passing became the occasion for a significant transformation of the party membership through the admission of large numbers of new applicants.

The leadership was divided in groping for definitions of problems and policies. In the administration of virtually all social endeavors, it collaborated with the intellectual holdovers from tsarism. It showed grudging toleration for heterogeneity and noncommunist subcultures in its policies toward the peasants, toward trade unions, toward national minorities, private traders, and foreign capitalist concessionaires. The party showed this tolerance probably because the system as a whole was too weak to fight these undesired elements. The entire political system was a holding action—an attempt to maintain party supremacy within an unfavorable political culture, so as to preserve the power conferred on the party by the Revolution and the civil war. The entire functioning of the system was related to this uneasy balance between the party and the hostile society it sought to contain. While engaged in this holding action, however, the party repaired its unity and built up its political strength. Hence, a remade party emerged at the end of this second Soviet political system.

Once it had gathered strength and unity, the Communist party destroyed the second political system it had created. It launched a new revolution designed to eliminate the various subcultures the previous system had tolerated and integrated, and on whose participation and cooperation it had depended. Again, therefore, the new order was in some crucial aspects a reversal of the preceding one. This is true not only of the underlying social structure but also of the functioning of the system. The second Soviet political system had been founded on an attitude of compromise, retrenchment, and grudging compromise. The third was militant in its outlook and violent in its methods. It resembled the first phase more than the second.

It did so not only in its destructiveness and violence but also in its constructive efforts. Whereas the second system had sought to improve existing resources, the third attempted to construct an entirely new economy and polity, one that, this time, would surely transform the country into a socialist one. The methods it employed for this, too, were similar to those of the first phase: industrialization took the form of a reckless crash program. It was undertaken with sovereign disregard for the difficulties, hence quite irrationally, and was carried out in a euphoric spirit of storming the heavens, quite in contrast to the sense of boredom, futility, if not despair, prevalent in the party during the preceding system.

System No. 2 had begun modestly and almost inadvertently: a single concession to the peasants had necessitated, as if on afterthought, a thorough restructuring of the social and political order. Similarly, the crash program of industrialization led to a restructuring of Soviet politics so thorough that an entire new system emerged in the late 1930s. Because this system was created and operated by Joseph Stalin, it may appropriately be called the Stalinist political system.

The Stalinist system was built around industrialization as a long-range undertaking, to which all the resources of the society should be devoted. It may, therefore, be defined as the institutionalization of the crash program. A crash program is an effort in which the style is determined by impatience and a sense of dire urgency. It operates by commandeering resources and deploying them by command, emphasizing rapid expansion rather than balance, quantity rather than quality, quick results rather than smooth operations.

The difference between a crash program and a more deliberate or "rational" effort can be symbolized by an example from engineering. Before building a dam across a river, those in charge of the construction project, ideally, should study the geomorphology of the dam site, together with pertinent data about such things as water flow, annual rainfall, ice formation, maximum and minimum temperatures, soils, rocks, and other geological facts. By complicated calculations, the engineer can then determine the necessary strength, curvature, height, and other features of the dam. But he can also dispense with such calculations, either in impatience or because of lack of skilled personnel, and simply start to pour concrete as high and as thick as his budget will allow. If the budget is skimpy, as it is likely to be in an economy where scarcity reigns, he will sacrifice all refinements for the purpose of sinking the biggest and strongest possible slab of rock into the river gorge. The method is crude, but it works. And the USSR under Stalin not only built dams in this fashion but, figuratively speaking, its entire economy.

The third Soviet political system (1928 to the mid-1930s), in mobilizing the citizens for the construction effort, had relied primarily on command, violence, and revolutionary enthusiasm. Under Stalinism, much of the enthusiasm had waned. Violence and command, meanwhile, had lost their sporadic character and turned into routines and institutions. They were supplemented by a system of positive incentives, through managed inequality, and a concerted effort of education and indoctrination. The Stalinist regime endeavored not only to create a new technical–managerial elite; it also sought to reeducate the entire population for life in the machine age and for accepting the Stalinist system as legitimate.

Stalinism, then, was a period of system-building on a grand scale. All previous Soviet systems either were oriented to destructive tasks or appear, in retrospect, to have been false starts, interregnums, or breathers between revolutions. The system emerging under Stalin had greater permanency. Or so it seemed to Western social scientists, who until recently tended to assume that under Stalin the Soviet political system emerged in its permanent form.

The beginnings of the Stalinist system took on the character of yet another bloody revolution—the Great Purge of the late 1930s, which almost completely destroyed the previous political elite. This removal of Lenin's comrades-in-arms was accompanied by a redefinition of the ruling ideology so thorough that we must see it as a radical change in contents. Furthermore, the basic institutional structure of the country underwent significant change: the sovereignty of the Communist party gave way to the sovereignty of Stalin and his personal secretariat. The party, in declining, became merely one of the dictator's instruments of rule, on an equal footing, so to speak, with the police. Rapid sociological change, typical of industrialization and urbanization processes everywhere, resulted from the economic growth the system promoted. This change included the emergence of a new pattern of social stratification, or class structure, together with an ideology designed both to conceal and to justify it. It was accompanied by changes in family life, religious habits, and the ethnic distribution of the population, as well as by deep changes in the educational profile of the population. In short, Stalinism created Soviet society as we know it today. It did so, again, by command, formulated at times by whim or by rule of thumb, backed up by a harsh system of sanctions and sharply differentiated rewards, and complemented by indoctrination designed to restructure the citizens' personalities. In seeking to educate a "new Soviet man," the Stalinist system attempted to create a civic culture of obedience, collectivism, and statism. The people were to endure hardships cheerfully while denying their existence, toil joyously for the common good, and heartily agree with every pronouncement of the dictator.

Let me exaggerate once again. Every Soviet political system destroyed itself by its success. Each rendered itself superfluous and jeopardized its own existence by solving some major problem or problems confronting it; precisely for the solution of those problems it functioned and structured itself.

The first system successfully utilized the utopian anarchism of workers, poor peasants, and national minorities for destructive tasks and almost succumbed to this destructiveness.

The second system successfully utilized classes and cultures antagonistic to communism to such an extent that it perceived these classes and cultures as a threat. At the same time, one may argue that their usefulness had been exhausted toward the end of the second system.

The third system once again made use of revolutionary urges in the party and the population, only to perceive them as dangers once the drive for industrialization was well under way and the classes deemed hostile had been destroyed. Hence, the revolutionary ideology was changed to an ideology of collective entrepreneurship, and the sovereign party, with its old personnel, was superseded by a ruthless, single-minded entrepreneur who fashioned a primitive command system for the task of building the industrial society.

This crude, primitive, but effective Stalinist system, once again, became obsolete because of its success. Having built an industrial society, it was poorly equipped by its own structure and operating methods to maintain, manage, and improve this society. Erected around a crash program of system-building, the political machinery of the Soviet

Union was unsuited for the orderly routines necessary for system-management.

Soviet society has become complex and heterogeneous. Its components have become increasingly interdependent. Hence, it is a society in need of ever more sensitive, sophisticated, and difficult coordination. A congeries of interests has developed, which must be balanced and aggregated to ensure the continued functioning of the system. This need for balance and smooth functioning has tended to overshadow the urge for rapid growth.

In short, the Soviet political system must find structures and methods designed to accommodate it to heterogeneity and interest conflict. This means that terror has become dysfunctional, and so has the overwhelming emphasis Stalinism gave to command and centralized control. The society simply has become too complex to be run from one central control post or by one strongman. Similarly, the ideological dogma can no longer reign sovereign over all thought processes. Total indoctrination has become a hindrance to the smooth functioning of a modern industrial society. And if some of the functions that the indoctrination process served must still be served, then indoctrination has to be replaced by other processes, just as an increase in rewards may be a substitute for, indeed an improvement over, the use of terror—an improvement, that is, from the point of view of the political elite: when available, rewards may be more effective than terror in strengthening a system's legitimacy and authority.

The political developments that have been going on in the Soviet Union since Stalin's death (1953) are, in my opinion, attempts of the system thus to restructure itself. In recent years, I have compared this process to analogous transformations in American corporations, namely, to the shift from centralized authoritarian companies run on command by single-minded, unsophisticated entrepreneurs like John D. Rockefeller or Henry Ford (the Stalins of American industry) to streamlined, decentralized organizations managed by smooth, rational, urbane manipulators like Alfred Sloan or Robert McNamara. If we wanted to use the language of Pareto, we could also describe this process as the replacement of lions by foxes.

When foxes oust the lions or merely supersede them, far more is involved, of course, than merely a subtle change in the character of the elite. Even if we stay within the conceptual framework of Paretan elitism, it would be clear that foxes require different structures from lions, and that their method of government will be different. However gradual it be, the replacement of lions by foxes is a systemic change; it implies the replacement of an entire political system by another. That, too, can be a gradual process, of course. One might add to this that, perhaps, lions (at least human ones) are apt to coalesce into tighter oligarchies, whereas foxes split up into smaller packs. Hence the victory of the latter over the former is likely also to promote the emergence of counterelites.

The systemic change we are witnessing at the present time seems to include some of the following transformations. First, there may be a subtle shift from personal dictatorship to institutional or bureaucratic authority. The indications of this are weak and inconclusive; and built-in urges toward personal dictatorship may reassert themselves repeatedly, or even win out. Since the precise flow of authority at the very tip of the Soviet power pyramid is unknown to us, we can do little more than remain alert to the possibility.

A broader restructuring of authority concerns the function of the top leadership within the entire political system, regardless of whether we see this leadership embodied in a single person, a small group, or the entire top personnel of the Communist party. Under Stalin, the top leadership was in full command. It ruled as sovereignly as an absolute prince. Stalin, his lieutenants, and his party, were the architects of the system and indeed of the entire social structure. They created and abolished institutions as if at will. Today, such sovereign rule has become more difficult, though not entirely impossible. Strongly entrenched social forces have been created by the Stalinist system, with which his successors have to reckon, and which no longer are subject to such easy tinkering. Hence, the relationship between the society and the political leadership is changing. Instead of being able to create and undo, political authority may be shifting to the role of interest aggregator, of arbiter between conflicting groups in society. It will have to respond to pressures from below rather than putting society under pressure. Society is beginning to "determine" the state. The base is beginning to assert an influence over the superstructure.

In order to bring out another facet of this development, let me point out that this growing influence of society over the state must bring with it the institutionalization of conflict within the political system. Previous Soviet political systems, with the exception of the second, made no allowance for conflict. Where it did arise, it was either open class warfare or disagreement among the top leadership, the legitimacy of which was not acknowledged. Both kinds of conflict arose over the most fundamental questions; the very nature of the system depended on how these conflicts would be resolved. In other words, from the point of view of the system, they were life-or-death conflicts. Hence, they decided over life and death also for the individuals participating and the classes involved.

The post-Stalinist system now developing, however, may be able to routinize and institutionalize conflict precisely because it is now over managerial problems rather than problems of system-building. It is likely, therefore, also to be less deadly for the losers. The succession crises since the execution of Beria and his police chiefs have demonstrated this. Indeed, deadly conflict would endanger the system now emerging far more than its predecessors: While heterogeneity induces conflicts, the heterogeneous society is more vulnerable to basic and violent conflicts. We may have here something on the societal level analogous to a phenomenon Freud observed in the individual: The higher the civilization, the greater the need for sublimation.

Incidentally, the growing freedom of discussion (which is not identical with freedom of speech) fits in with this increasing assertion of the divergent forces present in the society Stalin created. Here, too, the political system is likely to be forced in the direction of greater openness and accommodation, that is, toward the institutionalization of debate, dissent, toward the discussion of topics hitherto protected by taboos, and a growing readiness to learn techniques and concepts from Western societies.

The Soviet political system, in its various stages of development, is worth studying carefully, not so much because the USSR is a major world power, although that should not be disregarded, but because it has contributed novel institutions and patterns of government of considerable influence in the contemporary world of politics.

Many Western scholars have dwelled on the novelty of the Soviet system. Most have symbolized it by asserting that the total political experience of the Russian Revolution has led to the development of an entirely new form of government called *totalitarianism*. That term has been defined in various ways, but most writers may agree that it had best be regarded as a syndrome of institutions and operating characteristics. We shall discuss some of these shortly, but also dwell on novel features not usually included in the "totalitarian" syndrome.

First, however, I should like to return to the novelty of the entire Soviet political experience. I prefer to express it by a definition of the Soviet political system so broad that it subsumes most of this experience. This, then, is my definition: The Soviet Union is a political system governed by communists, that is, by an elite that feels the need to legitimize all its activities by referring to the writings of Marx and Lenin. This elite is preoccupied with the task of industrialization and modernization and seeks to solve it by applying bureaucratic methods of management to the entire social system. It has, on the whole, been successful in this task, having transformed the Soviet Union into a major industrial power. With this success, the Soviet political system has established itself as a successful alternative to the social and political systems of western Europe and North America.

Several features of this successful alternative must be considered important contributions to modern political experience. One of them is the attempt to plan and manage an entire economy on a national scale. Even the inefficiencies, mistakes, and failures accompanying this effort have been instructive, and mankind may benefit from the lessons that can be learned by studying it.

Of equal interest has been the development of a political system operating with only one party. One may well argue that the one-party system was invented or pioneered by the Soviet Union, although political scientists from Alabama, Vermont, or Kansas may claim this honor for their own home state. In any event, it has been an exceedingly important invention: Even though the one-party system may be on the decline in the Deep South and the Yankee North, it seems to be very much in the ascendancy in many parts of the globe today. The number of functions served by the party in such systems is great and varied. Single parties, therefore, have been forced to become vast, complex, and highly differentiated political machines—governments within the government. Fifty years of experience with single-party government in a succession of divergent systems have provided students of modern politics important material for the comparative study of one-party systems that has not yet been analyzed sufficiently.

Another major contribution Soviet rule has made consists in its several attempts, some successful, others unsuccessful, to draw the masses of the citizens into active participation in public affairs, to mobilize them for productive work as well as civic activities. The need for this attempt is implicit in Lenin's views concerning the organization of the single party. In its organization and functioning, it was to combine leaders and masses, authority and democracy, discipline and freedom. Consequently, every Soviet system has experimented with institutions designed to promote mass participation in many fields of endeavor. The nature of such institutions and their relation to the total system has varied greatly from one phase of Soviet rule to the other.

This change in nature and function can be seen when studying Soviet labor unions, for instance. But it is best illustrated, perhaps, by the institution that has lent its name to the USSR—the soviet. In 1917, as in 1905, socialists hailed soviets as a novel form of democracy, more direct, more representative, more responsive to public opinion than any previous democratic institution. And, 50 years ago, the creators of the Bolshevik state similarly claimed that a republic of soviets was a novel form of democracy preferable to any previous ones.

Soviets, indeed, originated as institutions of self-government created by the people in times of revolutionary anarchy. In the brief periods during which they functioned more or less spontaneously, they faithfully expressed the rebellious spirit of the poor, for whom they spoke. They enabled people from among the lowest classes to participate in political activity, people who as a rule had not taken part in public life before. The hostility of the soviets, as institutions, to restrictive organization and procedures, their deliberately undefined structure and resistance to institutionalization—these features made the soviets sensitive to the moods of the masses and effective indicators of the anarchic spirit that always accompanies the overthrow of a tyrannical regime. Soviets are institutions of the revolution. More specifically, they symbolize the socialist revolution, because they express the yearning not only for freedom and self-government but also the spirit of collectivism.

But the same qualities make them unstable and disorderly. Hence, to function within a reasonably settled political system (as, for instance, the second Soviet political system), they had to be drained of the anarchic spirit that had created them in the first place. One might describe the process accomplishing this as the taming of the soviets by the Communist party. In subtle fashion, the party managed to transform them into administrative organs responsive to the party leaders rather than to the masses. The soviets lost the sovereignty within the political system that they had possessed for but a fleeting moment (and still have, on paper); they turned into executive agencies. Their representative function was severely diluted. Their decisions were now dictated by the party; their role within the political system became perfunctory.

Still, in the last decade, we have witnessed a certain reversal of this trend. Since Stalin's death, the leaders of the USSR have made persistent efforts to draw larger and larger numbers of citizens into participation in public affairs and in this to widen somewhat the range of discretion that the citizens may wield in such matters. The benefits accruing to the system from wider and more autonomous participation are the mobilization of talent, the tapping of citizens' initiative in matters that may otherwise bog down in bureaucratic routines; they include the ability to spot potential leaders and to give civic-minded activists a sense of participation, hence a stake in the system. They also may include an improvement in the party's ability to supervise and control the lives of the citizens. In general, citizens' participation forges needed links between the government and the people.

I said previously that the Soviet system may be defined as an application of bureaucratic methods of management to a crash program of modernization. Mass participation, at first glance, seems to contradict the emphasis on command, hierarchy, and manipulation, implied by the use of the term *bureaucracy*. Participation fits in, however, when we see it as managed participation. Using soviets, trade unions, many other "mass organization" and peer groups to make a thoroughly bureaucratic system function is a technique that the Soviet political system at the moment is in the process of perfecting. I am tempted to assert that the ideal toward which the system seems to be striving deserves the label *participative bureaucracy*. I am inclined to define this as bureaucracy tempered, and made more tolerable, by extensive participation on the part of the administered. Or, in a rather more cynical mood (after attending yet another futile committee meeting), I may be tempted to define it as a system that adds the burdens of participation to the curse of authoritarianism. Whatever the mood participative bureaucracy engenders in us, it may well become a predominant type of political system in our century.

Consequently, we must acknowledge the pioneering nature of the Soviet system in developing a nationwide system of participative bureaucracy. And we must continue to observe the specific manner in which such a system provides for continued social mobility, for a rise in the general welfare, and for a host of other tokens of effectiveness.

At the same time, we must realize that there are problems that the Soviet political systems of the past have not managed to solve. Put more strongly: The Soviet political experience includes a number of conspicuous failures.

One such failure is the inability of all Soviet systems, so far, to establish orderly routines for replacing the top-ranking leader when his place becomes vacant. Hence, every such vacancy leads to a crisis. The reason for this recurrence of succession crises is the discrepancy between the formal structure and the actual authority relations in the USSR. Formally, the system clings to the fiction of collective authority derived from the people or the party members. It does not provide for the institution of a chief executive or party leader. In actual fact, there has almost always been one man recognized as the nation's political leader and top authority. Since neither the constitution nor the Communist party bylaws recognizes such a position, it must be filled by informal political maneuvers that may vary from one crisis to the next.

Another shortcoming of the political system, through all its transformation, has been the difficulty involved in finding a permanent structure suitable for it. To express this differently: The Soviet government has continually organized and reorganized itself. Its leaders have developed some basic principles for such an organizing effort, but some of these principles are in conflict with each other; and the system has not come up with any way out of the resulting dilemmas. Thus, there is a nagging urge to find an overall structure (writers in the eighteenth century would have said, a constitution) ideally suited for a system trying to cope with a wide variety of specific problems; there is the perpetual urge to improve on the organization of the system; and no amount of tinkering ever satisfies for long.

The Soviet system shares this worrisome preoccupation with organizational forms and principles with all modern bureaucracies. It shares with them also a number of recurrent pathological features, which are so familiar to all students of bureaucratic management that I need not discuss them in detail.[1]

Further, Soviet political systems, especially the more recent ones, have had difficulty in living with the ideological heritage of Marxism–Leninism, on which nonetheless they depend for a variety of reasons. In other words, Soviet political systems live under an ideological tension resulting from the strain between the need for flexible, realistic self-orientation in a changing world, on the one hand, and a deep psychological and political commitment to a rather rigidly formulated dogma, on the other.[2] It would, of course, be an error to assume that similar strains do not beset other contemporary political systems as well.

In a large number of problems, the Soviet political record is spotty or inconclusive, despite 50 years of experimentation. One such problem is that of forging the many varied national cultures of the USSR into one homogeneous Soviet nation without lapsing into colonialism or other oppressive patterns. So far, no policy pursued in this field has been entirely successful, and even Soviet spokesmen today concede that national differences will continue to strain the political system for some time to come. Similarly, the Soviet system has not yet found a satisfactory method of integrating the peasantry into the fabric of Soviet society. The image of modernization prevalent in the Communist party includes a strong urban and industrial bias. In the *ideal* communist society, there is no room for peasants. Soviet ideology expresses this by saying that communism will wipe out the difference between city and country. Yet almost half of the Soviet population still lives on the land. The peasant way of life—traditional, anarchic, in some sense antisocial or at least antisocialist—still is strong. Mere destructiveness or violence, if applied too long, would be self-defeating. Without going into detail, I think I can assert that all the measures the party has taken to integrate the peasants into the Soviet economic and political systems have been compromises satisfying neither the peasants nor the communist leadership.

Perennial strain has been present also in the relationship between the political elite and the professional elite of engineers, managers, scientists, and other experts in many fields. The strain reflects the mutual dependence of these elites on each other and their mutual antagonism and suspicion. Again, this ambivalent relationship is reflected in the institutions set up to regulate it. Here, too, none of the interests concerned is fully satisfied with the existing structures and practices.

Of course, if there were no unsolved problems, there would be no need for a political system at all.

The study of the Soviet political system is as old as the Russian Revolution itself. Our ability to understand and analyze this New World of the twentieth century has improved considerably since 1917, even though we may not yet be able to do for the USSR what de Tocqueville did for our own polity. On the fiftieth anniversary of the October Revolution, it may be proper to express the hope that the Soviet Union become as accessible to counterrevolutionary scholars as the United States was to the French aristocrat, and that the observers we will send to the shores of that new New World have the wisdom, the compassion, and the methodological sophistication of our predecessor. We all may still have a long way to go.

Notes

[1]For elaboration, see my book, *The Soviet Political System* (New York: Random House, 1965), esp. pp. 205–243.

[2]I have tried to elaborate on this problem in "The Functions of Ideology in the Soviet Political System," *Soviet Studies* 17, no. 3 (January 1966), 273–285. See also the various comments on my article in subsequent issues of the same journal.

28

JOHN N. HAZARD

*The Peril-Points**

Democratic forms do not assure democratic government. History has proved that there are places at which counterweights can be placed to prevent democratic functioning of the forms. Modern dictators have shown that it is possible to combine democratic forms with counterweights. This has sometimes been done so cleverly at the early stages of a dictator's bid for power that the general public does not see the peril. It does not realize that it is losing the possibility of influencing policy and choosing leaders.

The blending of popular and dictatorial institutions in a fashion that fools the public may be said to be one of the characteristics of the modern totalitarian state. It is here that the totalitarians have been able to improve upon the system of the authoritarians, typified by the tsars of Russia. The totalitarians have found a way to please the majority of the people, for a time at least, by giving them a parliament, an electoral procedure, trade unions, cooperative associations, local autonomy, a bill of rights, and codes of law. At the same time, they have been able to preserve power by the use of controls over the forms that they have established or inherited. The totalitarians have shown that a people can no longer feel safe from the loss of freedom merely because its system of government incorporates democratic forms.

Soviet experience provides an example of the points at which a dictator has been able to prevent the democratic functioning of democratic forms, and this example has importance because it shows the extremes to which it is possible to go. It is obvious that in those countries that have long enjoyed democracy, the public would not easily be

*Reprinted by permission of the author and publisher from *The Soviet System of Government*, 5th ed. (Chicago: University of Chicago Press, 1980), pp. 228–243. Copyright 1980 by The University of Chicago.

misled into thinking that its system was democratic if the forms were counterweighted as they are in the USSR. Yet, even well-informed leaders of established democratic states have realized that there are points at which democracy can be counterweighted and eventually destroyed. These points may be called the *peril-points*, because they are the places at which restriction of democratic functions imperils the future of a democratic state.

Abraham Lincoln worried about such peril during the crisis of the war between the states, when he wrestled with the necessity of suspending the historic writ of habeas corpus. The Supreme Court of the United States worried about such peril when it had to pass upon the constitutionality of restraints on freedom of speech and of the press enacted by state legislatures during the First World War. During the Second World War and into the subsequent decade, the issue has been faced in many lands. In the United States, first in connection with the problem of protecting society against potentially dangerous individuals of German and Japanese stock living within the United States, and later in connection with the problem of removing communists from positions in which they could cause harm, the Supreme Court has again been testing these restraints to determine whether they go beyond the point of necessity and permanently endanger constitutional freedoms.

It is appropriate at the end of this book to review the principal lessons of the Soviet dictatorship. It bears repeating that the major danger to be avoided is the adoption of the underlying philosophy of the Soviet leaders. The danger lies not in the acceptance of Marxist ideology, for few thinking people in the established democracies have been prepared to accept the limited Marxist explanation of historical phenomena. The danger lies in something deeper than the specifics of Marxism. It lies in the philosophy of its high priests, namely, that one man or one group of men can be infallible in their determination of political policy.

A Sense of Infallibility

In contrast to the leaders of the democratic states, Soviet leaders have professed since the days of their Revolution confidence in their understanding of the forces of history. They believe that Marx and Engels developed a method of analyzing history that is unquestionably correct. They believe that only a small number of thoroughly trained people can understand the method and apply it. They do not imagine that the general public can be taught to understand the method for many years. They conclude for this reason that the public will require leadership for the foreseeable future, and that the leaders must be selected from the narrow circle of people who have been reared in the Marxist method and who have the skill to apply it to an ever changing economic and political situation.

In contrast to the attitude of Soviet leaders, the men and women of the democratic states of the West who work their way to a position of leadership have no such purpose. They do not believe that a theory of history can be deduced with certainty from the events of past centuries, although they enjoy speculating on the plausibility of one or another theory as it is developed by men such as Arnold Toynbee. Having risen from the ranks themselves, whether it be from a farm, a haberdashery shop, or the rough and tumble of a British trade union, they do not believe that any group of men has a monopoly on wisdom or on leadership qualities. They believe that wise ideas may come from many sources, often quite unexpected, and that these sources cannot under any circumstances be limited to a certain school of thought.

Although Western democratic leaders sometimes express the wish that they be let alone for long enough to apply their own schemes for national prosperity, they are prepared to bow, as did Winston Churchill during the Potsdam Conference at what seemed to be the very pinnacle of his career, to the will of the majority and to step down for political opponents with quite different backgrounds, education, and aims. To men such as these, a major purpose of democratic government is to maintain a route through which new views may be aired and new men chosen to give them a trial.

Discipline for Party Members

The Soviet leaders, with their belief in the special wisdom granted to them by their mastery of the Marxist method, have constructed a matrix of government that assures their retention of power. Its core is an apparatus called a *political party* within which there is preserved a discipline like that within an army. Yet, to win and maintain the adherence of the rank and file members of this apparatus, the leaders have had to devise a procedure that can be thought to give the membership an opportunity to shape policy and to choose party leaders. Counterweights have been developed at the peril-points, namely, the selection of delegates to the higher echelons within the party and the manner in which minorities may express their views and organize their supporters within party meetings.

The counterweights to democratic elections within the party have been the establishment of the one-candidate ballot and the indirect election of delegates to the higher levels of the party apparatus. The counterweight to complete freedom of expression guaranteed by Communist party rules is the prohibition against the formation of voting blocs or "factions."

Western democratic parties usually provide that party members may vote for delegates to the national party conventions directly, in primaries, rather than indirectly. Further, Western political parties place no restriction upon the organization of voting blocs within a party, with the result that the world is often startled by such notorious party splits as that between the Clement Attlee and Aneurin Bevan factions in the British Labour Party, that between the Dixiecrats and the Truman leadership within the Democratic party of the United States, and the schism over Pierre Mendès-France in the Radical Socialist party of France.

When one moves beyond the political party to the representative bodies of the state, the contrast between the Soviet system and that familiar in Western democracies is even more noticeable. The principal feature of the contrast is the Soviet denial of the right to form a political party other than the Communist party to function within the representative bodies. The right of association in political parties is specifically limited by the Constitution itself. In Western democracies, the multiplicity of parties is fundamental. It is appreciated by students of politics that influence upon choice of leaders or determination of policy can be had only by association with like-minded persons, and this means, in political terminology, a political party. The right of association means, therefore, the right to form political parties without hindrance.

Yet, even in democratic countries, there are occasions when a single political party in fact exists for a long period of time for some historical reason. While the right to form other parties continues, the right has little practical value because of the traditional situation. Thus, in India, the Congress party gained such prestige in its battle with the British prior to liberation that for a considerable period of time it remained the dominant factor in Indian politics, although smaller parties won some important local victories. Yet, no one questioned the fact of Indian democracy before 1975 because the Congress party permitted its members to influence the choice of leaders and even to split the party. Faith in the democratic process was shattered when the stronger faction of the Congress party silenced all other parties in 1975 by arresting their leaders on charges of conspiracy. Still, the dictatorship was not to last, for the Prime Minister herself called new elections in 1977 (thinking, perhaps, to legitimate her power), freed opposition leaders, and was defeated.

The same possibility of change not only in personalities but even in party domination is true in those regions of other countries in which one or another political party holds power for many years. The important factors are the freedom given small parties to organize and seek votes and the establishment by law of the duty to select candidates for office through primaries permitting party members to choose their own candidates. Voters tend to move from faction to faction and even from party to party as sympathies change. The Supreme Court of the United States has recognized that a one-party system can be democratic in practice if the party that has an effective monopoly of power preserves a democratic structure within itself. The Soviet system provides no such safeguard.

Having eliminated any possibility of effective challenge to their authority from a second political party, or from a faction within the Communist party, the Soviet leaders have turned their attention to other possible sources of pressure upon their determination of policy. One gains the impression that Soviet leaders have sought to find the points at which they are unable, because of public opinion either at home or abroad or, sometimes both at home and abroad, to eliminate a source of power and hence of pressure. They have then made arrangements that have neutralized the actual or political pressure groups, and sometimes they have been successful in bringing a group within their own orbit to exert pressure upon segments of the population or upon workmen throughout the world for the benefit of the Communist party leadership.

Limitations on Potential Pressure Groups

Organized religions have presented a real challenge to the Soviet leadership's monopoly of power, both because of the tenacity with which many Soviet citizens hold to worship of their God and also because foreign pressures have been great. The Soviet leaders have sought to dissuade those nearest to them from religious attitudes by expelling them from party membership if they practice religion. They have sought to win others away from religion through a vigorous campaign against religious belief on the ground that the natural sciences disprove the existence of God. They have sought to restrict the influence of those who will not be frightened away from their beliefs or propagandized out of them by limiting religious education and denying legal status to church communities. Only during World War II, when the Russian Orthodox Church gave its support to Stalin, was a respite granted. It is likely that if the church should become again, as it was in the early days after the Revolution, a strong pressure group against the government, it would find its activities circumscribed as before. By intensifying atheistic propaganda since 1956, the Communist party is losing no opportunity to weaken the church.

The trade unions have also presented a grave problem to Communist party leaders. The trade unions could not be abolished as they were by Hitler, for their strengthening had been one of the slogans of the Revolution, and their vigor was looked upon by many workmen outside Russia as evidence of the healthy policies of the Soviet government. Yet, they could not be permitted to function as a force capable of challenging the policies set by the Communist party. When they appeared to be moving in that direction in 1928, their leaders were purged. They were

provided with new leaders and directed to support governmental policies calling for increased production.

The cooperative associations have also been a potential political
threat. For economic reasons, the communist leaders have had to
expand the cooperatives in the agricultural field and in the artisan field
also to fill the gaps in state-organized production. Such expansion has
created a source of pressure. Yet the cooperatives have been prevented
from becoming a national pressure group. The agricultural cooperatives
have been subordinated to the Ministry of Agriculture and have been
controlled by dictation of the choice of officers whenever the members'
choice was undesirable to the Communist party. They were further
controlled until 1958 by a system of machine tractor stations to which
was transferred maintenance of the mechanical agricultural implements
used by these cooperatives. Since abolition of machine tractor station
control, the party has relied on intensification of party activity within
farms amalgamated to create large agricultural enterprises. The artisan
cooperatives were controlled by limiting their sources of supply and by
regulating the services they performed, and finally they were abolished
except in service trades.

Any pressure that might have been exerted upon leaders by an
industrial lobby, a chamber of commerce, or a real estate lobby has been
eliminated by the expedient of abolishing private ownership of industrial establishments, of land, and also of merchandising enterprises.
Those who manage the public corporations that operate state industry,
sell its produce, and use that part of the land not allocated to the
cooperative societies are permitted to form no independent associations
such as the National Association of Manufacturers or the United States
Chamber of Commerce.

No associations in other fields, even for ostensibly cultural purposes
such as the propagation of literature or music, are permitted to organize
without state authorization, nor can meetings of any group concerned
with members in an area larger than a county be held without a license
on each occasion.

Leaders of Western democracies have had a very different philosophy
as to the value of pressure groups. They have believed that the functioning of the democratic process requires the existence of equally balanced
pressure groups. When the balance has been unfavorable, efforts have
been made to redress it; for example, the Wagner Act was adopted by
the United States Congress to encourage the organization of trade
unions, only to be superseded by the Taft–Hartley Act when the
Congress thought it necessary to restore the balance between management and labor. When industry became so centralized as to threaten the
development of monopolies, the Congress adopted antitrust laws to
preserve competition and to fragment economic power. In the interests
of fostering democratic practices, efforts were made by American ex-

perts in rebuilding Germany and Japan after World War II to limit the concentration of industry in a few hands and to prevent a return to the cartel system of prewar Europe.

Restrictions on Avenues of Expression

Having abolished the base for certain groups, such as those interested in the protection of productive property, and having severely limited the independence of other groups, such as the trade unions and cooperative associations, the Soviet leaders have taken great care to forestall the pressures that may be exerted by a free press. They have had to move carefully at this point, for one of the most obvious yardsticks of a democratic system of government is a free press. To satisfy their own people and win friends abroad, Soviet leaders have found it necessary to guarantee freedom of the press in the Soviet Constitution.

Having established the guarantee of a free press, Communist party leaders have provided counterweights to the guarantee. They have forbidden private citizens to operate even a mimeograph machine, much less a great modern newspaper press. They have created a state printing monopoly and a state censor for all potential publications. Further, they have provided that freedom of the press may be exercised only to the advantage of their system of government, and they have drafted a criminal code that permits prosecution of those who attempt to use press or speech to damage that system.

In sharp contrast to Soviet attitudes toward the press, citizens at all levels of Western democratic governments will fight to maintain a free press. No legal limitations are created in Western democracies on ownership by private persons or corporations of the essentials to publish newspapers, magazines, handbills, and books. No censorship prior to publication is permitted by law, although civil servants who have accepted secrecy as a condition of employment may be silenced, and editors may be asked to keep secrets. Although censorship subsequent to publication has been permitted, by means of confiscation of the offending issue, and although in very unusual cases further publication of a newspaper that has been consistently endangering the security of the state has been prohibited, the administration of censorship is carefully controlled by the courts. It has usually been necessary for the executive to prove to a court that the danger to the democratic regime is obvious and that it is immediate.

The Soviet regime has not silenced its public completely. It has found it advanageous to permit citizens to write letters to the editors of the Soviet press in complaint against mismanagement of Soviet institutions. Such letters have value not only in suggesting to the people that its leaders permit free expression but also because they provide an important source of information for the leaders on the faults of subordinate administrators and on the temper of the people. Yet such letters to the editor do not meet the requirements of a free press, for they need not be published, and the pattern established in them over the years suggests that the writers have created for themselves a code of criticism that limits the subject matter that they will discuss and the personages whom they will subject to abuse.

No Independence for the Judiciary

The courts of the USSR are avowedly an arm of Communist party policy. Soviet jurists accept no doctrine of separation of powers. While lower courts are insulated by law from interference by local party tyrants, the Supreme Court is always subject to control by the highest policy body in the state apparatus, the Supreme Soviet, in which almost 75% of the deputies are members of the Communist party and, therefore, subject to strict political discipline. The courts do much to protect the citizen from mistaken application of state policy and in so doing win the respect of many citizens for the fairness of the regime in matters affecting the employment relationship, family quarrels, and housing disputes, but they cannot be a bulwark against tyranny if the leaders of the party decide that some tyrannical measure is necessary in the interest of security.

The courts of Western democracies are not always considered an independent branch of government beyond the reach of the executive, for there is not always separation of powers in the West. Yet in countries such as England, in which the Lord Chancellor as head of the judiciary is at the same time a member of the government and the presiding officer of the House of Lords, there is a tradition of noninterference with the affairs of the judiciary by the Parliament and its government of the day. The courts of the West have indicated their willingness to enforce human rights, whether guaranteed in a written constitution or by tradition alone, against encroachment by the executive in the name of security.

Legal procedures in the USSR exhibit many of the measures accepted by Western lawyers as constituting procedural due process of law and as helping to assure the defendant an opportunity to present his case. Yet, when the charge is one of attempting to unseat the regime, these very measures of protection had been withdrawn until the reform of 1956 by exceptions written into the procedural codes. It is at this point that procedural protections are needed most if democracy is to be preserved, and the West has always held to this view.

Again, the position of the Western democracies is not an absolute. There have been times when some of the elements of procedural due process of law have been withdrawn, as when the writ of habeas corpus has been suspended during wartime. The very torture of mind through which Abraham Lincoln went in deciding whether to suspend it during the war between the states and the hesitation of the English prime minister when the Battle of Britain was at its height suggest that the difference between the Western and the Soviet approaches is a matter of degree. Yet, in that difference of degree there is an element of difference of quality. In the USSR, procedural due process has been waived even in peacetime. The decision seems to have been made with little reluctance in 1934, at the moment when one of Stalin's aides was assassinated. In the Western democracies, the writ has been waived only in wartime, and after the passing of the emergency, it has been quickly restored.

Few Limitations on the Security Police

Both the USSR and the Western democracies have found it necessary to establish a security police. Both systems of government seem to have approached the institution with caution. The Soviet security police, established in 1918 as the *Cheka,* was limited at the start in its authority, and there were many Communist party members who disliked the idea of having such an agency at all. Yet, it was established. It soon expanded its authority to such an extent that it aroused the anger of the Soviet Ministry of Justice and the Congress of Soviets. It was abolished in 1922 and replaced by an institution with more limited powers and subjected to great control by the cabinet. The new security police then expanded its power, until the leadership found it advisable to abolish it in 1934 to create a still more limited instrument. Yet, this in turn expanded its authority. Since Stalin's death, the security police has been under attack, and measures have been taken to control it through a strengthened Prosecutor-General of the USSR.

While recognizing that real danger, even to the regime itself, lurks in a security police over which there is no line of supervision through an official in close touch with the highest policymakers, the security problem of the Soviet leadership has been seemingly so great that the security police was permitted under Lenin and Stalin to make arrests and to try those whom it had arrested in its own tribunals without reference to the courts. Only the Prosecutor-General of the USSR has had the right to interfere, and even he and his subordinates, through whom he must operate in the daily situation, have been reluctant to intervene because of the prestige developed by the security police in leadership circles. Since Stalin's death, the Prosecutor-General has shown himself to be much more courageous. His office has published accounts showing the servile practice of the Prosecutor-General under Stalin, and the implication is clear that this servility will not occur again. It remains to be seen whether this post-Stalin approach can be maintained in the event of serious political crisis.

The Western democracies have been alert at all times to the danger that a security police may get out of hand. There have been efforts to provide checks upon assumption of authority greater than intended by the legislature by making the security police a subordinate part of a Ministry of Justice or responsible to an attorney-general rather than an independent ministry, as it has been in the USSR. There have been efforts in the West to limit the powers of the security police by permitting it to make arrests only in wartime, rather than in peace and war as is the case in the USSR. There have been other efforts to check its activities—by making it deliver all arrested persons to the judiciary for trial within a fixed period of time or by denying to it the right to pass sentence of any kind against any person. This has been a sharp contrast to the broad rights granted the security police in the USSR until 1953.

Perhaps the surest protection against unlawful assumption of authority by the security police in the Western democracies is the multiparty system. If the security police exceeds its authority to the point that it enrages the citizens, there is the opportunity in a democracy to vote out of power the party whose responsibility it has been to curb the police. This ultimate method of dealing with the problem through the ballot box is not available to the citizens of the USSR, as it was not available to the citizens of Hitler's Germany and of Mussolini's Italy, in both of which the excesses of the security police became symbolic of the character of the regimes.

Finally, among the agencies on which the Soviet regime rests for security when all else fails, there is the army. For the Soviet leaders, the army has been a necessary evil. Its existence is required to protect the regime at home and from foreign powers. It must be strong, yet in its strength lies latent danger to the political leadership, for it could unseat the regime if it were not controlled. The whole history of the relationship between the Communist party and the army has been dotted with experiments in control by the former over the latter so as to assure loyalty without reducing military efficiency. In contrast with the citizens' armies of Western democracies, the Soviet army seems to be under more formal and rigid political controls, although from Stalin's death in 1953 to Marshal Zhukov's ouster in 1957, its leaders appeared to be gaining more influence in policy-making circles.

The army was one of the two major forces that seemed after Stalin's death to be pressing for recognition in the formulation of policy and the selection of leaders. The other force was the managerial and technical class. It was necessary for the Communist party leadership to expand this class, as it was necessary to expand the army. The managers and technicians were essential to the productive functioning of a modern industrial and agricultural plant. To encourage maximum effort, more was found necessary than exhortation on the basis of traditional political goals. It was necessary to give to the managers and technicians preferred status, not only in terms of greater monetary rewards but also in terms of medals, personal praise, and prestige.

Pressures for Change

Following Stalin's death, it became evident that there was pressure for a lessening of the severity with which he had ruled and that this pressure was strong even within the Communist party. Statistics showed that this party had become under his regime a party predominantly of specialists, meriting classification as intellectuals. Most notable within this group were the senior officers in the armed forces, the managers of industrial enterprises, the agronomist–chairmen of collective and state farms, and the professional party functionaries.

As Marxist-trained individuals, these intellectuals probably respected the doctrine that only the enlightened few were yet qualified to rule. It is unlikely that their dreams of the future contained thought of mass participation in the policy-making function. All evidence suggests that the new intellectuals held firmly to the necessity of maintaining the system of state ownership of production and monopoly political direction and rejected any thought of private enterprise or the multiparty system.

The new intellectuals exerted influence upon some of the senior members of the Communist party, if the outsider can judge by results. Khrushchev appears to have been frightened, for in 1957, he began to take a series of steps designed to reduce their power and reshape their thinking and the thinking of their children. The armed forces were returned to their completely subordinate position with the dismissal of Marshal Zhukov and the strengthening of political education. The industrial managers were subjected to audit by production conferences established by the trade unions and by supervisory commissions created within the factories by the Communist party.

A campaign was conducted within the Communist party to proletarianize its membership. Two-thirds of those admitted between 1956 and 1959 were bench workmen and dirt farmers. Within the Presidium of the Central Committee of the party, Khrushchev reestablished at least the semblance of Stalin's authority to forestall the active resistance of dissenters tending to think in terms of factions.

Reshaping of the thinking of the intellectuals took the form of extensive revision of the education law with the professed aim of bringing the next generation into close familiarity with the shop and the field. All but the students needing uninterrupted study to master complex disciplines were required to undergo a period of schooling, including bench labor and dirt farming, before entering upon specialized study in the universities and technical institutes.

While moving to close the gates on potential dissension, Khrushchev continued to denounce Stalin's dictatorial rule as the "cult of the individual," although in less comprehensive form than his denunciation before the party in 1956. He and his colleagues within the Presidium found it desirable, if not necessary, to assure the intellectuals on whom they relied that personal safety could be expected. This assurance took the form of redefining criminal law in the interest of precision and expanding the procedural code to facilitate, in some measure, defense of the innocent.

With its 1961 program, the Communist party made a dramatic move to gain support from the forces brought into being by the needs of a modern industrial society. It declared that antagonistic classes no longer remained, and that the state had become representative of the entire people. It need no longer, and could not longer, be a dictatorship of the proletariat or of the toiling people over other classes.

To this position, the Chinese communists took vigorous exception in a letter of July 1963, but the Soviet communists refused to retreat. To strengthen their newly declared doctrine, they reaffirmed their intention to include large numbers of citizens in the activities of the government in all its functions—legislative, executive, and judicial. They revised the Communist party rules, with the declared intention of popularizing its leadership through a system of rotation of most of the members of the governing bodies of the party.

Khrushchev's ouster in 1964 was used to reinstitute some of the features characterizing the Soviet system of government before he became its chief soon after Stalin's death. Even before his ouster, while his power was waning, the educational system was restored to its earlier form with elimination of the enforced experience in agriculture or industrial production that Khrushchev thought necessary to avoid emergence of a managerial class lacking in knowledge of and sympathy for the working man. Doctrine still called for an experience in production, but it was to be entered into on a voluntary basis and without massive organization of opportunities. Also, the Communist party, while continuing to emphasize the importance of admission of large numbers of workmen and collective farmers, expanded its rolls primarily with the new intellectuals trained as experts in disciplines as well as party leadership. The party also showed itself willing to increase its reliance upon the expert advice of civil servants in the state apparatus and university specialists, rather than to create within its ranks a very large apparatus of specialists with the task of providing a political counterweight to what was being submitted by the technicians.

Restoration of the party to its Leninist structure in 1965, with revocation of the Central Committee decisions of 1962 inspired by Khrushchev, tended also to increase reliance on experts outside the party hierarchy for management of industry and agriculture. There was to be no bifurcation of party organs into agricultural and industrial for the very reason that the experiment had caused overlapping of party and state functions to the detriment of action. The party was to return to its status as the corps of generalists Lenin had created, albeit with a novel feature introduced without benefit of party orders: Its leaders, though generalists, were, by virtue of the fact that education had spread widely among party members, possessors of broad knowledge of techniques as well as of politics. They were both "red" and "expert" as they had not been in the 1920s.

All of these features tended to bring to the foreground the intellectuals' influence as a stabilizing factor. Flexibility and dynamism of policy which had characterized the revolutionary period gave way to stability in production and personal relationships. The Chinese communists were quick to seize upon this fact to charge that the spirit of the Revolution had been lost in a bourgeoisification of Soviet society, and Mao Tse-tung saw the same tendency within his own country, necessitating a revival of revolutionary enthusiasm and dynamism. The reaction of the Soviet communists typified the new thinking in the USSR. To them, the Chinese leader had instituted chaos from which no good could come. They denounced also his espousal of asceticism in personal living, which they felt undesirable as Soviet society increased its resources to the point where it could undertake a plan of consumers' goods production, notably in providing more adequate housing for a population long deprived of this basic asset.

The changes introduced since Stalin's death have obvious importance. They have required a reevaluation of the potential power of the men who defend the frontiers and manage the economy and the lower levels within the Communist party, but they do not suggest an impending change in the Soviet system of government. The system remains, as it has been since 1936, the embodiment of some of the most publicized forms of democracy, but these are counterweighted to prevent their use to unseat the inner circle of the Communist party.

If one looks to the future, it can be predicted that the ranks of the educated will swell within the USSR as elsewhere. Even given the Marxist formulation of Soviet instruction, this expansion of education cannot but have an effect upon the system. It is hard to imagine that the new intellectuals will be content for very long with a position as executives outside the circle that makes policy. Still, it is unlikely that the present system will be threatened in its essentials. At most, there will be an expansion of the circle of the ruling elite.

There is as yet no hint that those who are moving to positions of responsibility as executives are coming to believe that the public generally can be trusted to choose leaders wisely or to formulate policy. There is no reason to think that Stalin's heirs intend to institute a democratic system of government.

29   RICHARD LOWENTHAL

On "Established" Communist Party Regimes*

Communist parties ruling industrial societies sooner or later have to adapt to a new, postrevolutionary role. If they have come to power by indigenous revolution in underdeveloped countries, the characteristic dual effort to promote politically forced modernization and to transform the social structure in the direction of an utopian goal by repeated revolutions from above tends to come to an end as the main tasks of modernization are solved and as further revolutionary upheavals come to be regarded as too costly for the continuous economic growth of a mature industrial society.[1] (This seems to have happened in the Soviet Union at about the time of the adoption of Khrushchev's "revisionist" new party program in 1961.) If they had reached industrial maturity before a communist takeover was forced on them by the expansion of Soviet power, like East Germany or Czechoslovakia, the phase of violent social transformation tends to run out once a structure has been achieved that is reasonably analogous to that of the leading power of the bloc. In special cases, the revolutionary process may be stopped before the achievement of either full industrial maturity or a Soviet-type structure. Thus, in Yugoslavia, the break with Stalin produced the need for a reconciliation with the peasantry, which by 1953 proved incompat-

*Reprinted by permission of the author and publisher from *Studies in Comparative Communism* 7, no. 4 (Winter, 1974), pp. 335–358. Copyright 1974 by School of International Relations, University of Southern California. This chapter is a condensed and updated version of a paper on "The Ruling Party in a Mature Society," contributed by the author to the Salzburg Symposium on "The Social Consequences of Modernization in Socialist Countries," sponsored by the American Council of Learned Societies. The full paper appears in *Social Consequences of Modernization in Communist Societies,* ed. Mark G. Field (Baltimore: Johns Hopkins University Press, 1976), pp. 81–118.

ible with pursuit of the original collectivization program, and in Poland the de-Stalinization crisis of 1956 had a similar effect.

In all these communist-ruled countries, the characteristic problems of forced modernization as a revolutionary process—the problems of "Development versus Utopia"—have come to be replaced by the new problems of a postrevolutionary, "established" single-party regime in a more or less mature industrial society. These new problems seem to be of three main kinds. First, how far and on what conditions can a communist, single-party regime meet the requirements of efficiency and rationality of a modern industrial society that has to compete with noncommunist industrial societies? Second, how far and in what forms can it respond to the shifting interests of the various groups in an increasingly differentiated society, permit their articulation, yet maintain a monopoly of their arbitration? Third, how far can it meet the conditions resulting from the first two sets of problems and at the same time develop a credible form of legitimation reconciling its ideological traditions with its new role? Finally, there arises the speculative but ultimately decisive question of the unforeseen and unintended consequences of the required adjustments in party structure, governing methods, and ideology—the question of the extent to which these adjustments may be liable in the long run to undermine the very system they were intended to stabilize.

Most scholarly discussion of these problems has so far tended to deal with one or another of them in comparative isolation. Thus George Fischer, in his book *The Soviet System and Modern Society*,[2] has concentrated on the problems of technical rationality and economic efficiency, advancing the thesis that the pressure for greater autonomy of the economic subsystem that arises from these problems may be successfully contained, short of the granting of pluralistic political institutions, by a party conceiving its "monistic" monopoly of decision as a "tutelage" over society and its groups—provided that the party succeeds in filling the leading positions increasingly by "dual executives" enabled by their training and career to combine the skills of political leadership with the expert knowledge required for economic and technical decisions. He has added detailed evidence that the share of such "dual executives" among the Soviet communist leaders is indeed increasing. The same set of problems forms the focus of the model of successive stages of bureaucratic enlightenment, advanced with slight variations by Alfred G. Meyer[3] and Peter C. Ludz[4] and based on the results of the sociology of Western industrial organizations. Starting from Meyer's view that the Soviet Union may best be understood on the analogy of a giant corporation embracing the whole national economy, both authors conclude that under the imperatives of efficiency and rationality, communist-ruled industrial societies must evolve along the same lines as Western industrial corporations—that is from "exploitative authoritative" (corresponding in politics to "totalitarian") through "benevolent authoritative" and "consultative" (corresponding to the present political stage) toward "participatory" forms of organization in descending order of the role of coercion and fear and ascending order of cooperation and trust, of a variety of interaction and communication, and of the scope for delegating decisions. But just as Fischer does not discuss the relation between that party and the interest groups implied in his term of *tutelage,* so Meyer and Ludz do not develop their views of the political form of the future "participatory" stage, though according to their sociological authority, that stage requires interaction between groups as well as individuals; all three confine themselves to our first set of problems.

By contrast, Gordon Skilling, the pioneer of the systematic analysis of the role of interest groups in communist-ruled societies, provides a typology of the various degrees of pluralism that have in fact occurred in such societies but no hypothesis about an evolutionary trend.[5] Grouping at one end of his scale "quasi-totalitarianism" of the Stalinist type, where group formation is illegitimate in theory and severely limited in practice, and at the opposite end the "anarchic authoritarianism" of the Chinese Cultural Revolution with its temporary breakdown of the party institution and its open and even violent group conflict limited only by Mao's personal authority, he distinguishes three other categories of direct relevance to our second set of problems. In the first category, for which he adopts Meyer's and Ludz's term of *consultative authoritarianism,* the party leadership's monopoly of decision is intact, and spontaneous group activity is not tolerated; but groups within the bureaucracy are licensed to articulate the interests of the sector for which they feel responsible before a decision, and both individual experts and professional groups may be consulted. This is the system adopted in the Soviet Union since the fall of Khrushchev and in the more sedate East European states since the 1960s. Skilling sees a looser type of "quasi-pluralistic authoritarianism" in Hungary and Poland from Stalin's death to the October crisis of 1956, in the Soviet Union under Khrushchev, and again in Czechoslovakia and Poland in the years preceding the "Prague spring." In these phases, spontaneous and in part critical groups actively exerted influence on sections of the leadership and were temporarily encouraged, though they were not granted institutional legality, and decisions were still made at the top. Clearly, such situations are liable to provoke a coercive backlash and thus are inherently unstable. Finally, Skilling sees Yugoslavia since the early 1950s and Czechoslovakia under the reform leadership of 1968 as two variants of a "democratizing and pluralistic authoritarianism"; here, independent groups are institutionalized and play a recognized role in the political process, though the regime remains authoritarian in maintaining strict party control of the levers of power and excluding political alternatives to its rule. On the basis of this typology, Skilling neither predicts nor excludes a form of communist rule that may evolve, along Czechoslovak lines, even further toward democracy; nor does he link his types of communist rule either with economic trends or with problems of legitimation.

The most comprehensive attempt to deal with the problems of "established one-party systems" has been made by Samuel P. Huntington.[6] It offers an interpretation of the postrevolutionary experience of both communist and noncommunist one-party systems (including among the latter the case of Mexico), irrespective of the particular nature of the revolution and the ideology concerned. Huntington's analysis includes all three sets of problems listed here, but his argument centers around the issue of legitimation. Starting from the recognition that in a postrevolutionary period, both the ideology and the dynamic, "charismatic" leader lose their function of guiding the transformation of society and tend to give way to bureaucratic institutionalization under oligarchic leadership, he goes on to suggest that because of the broad, pragmatic consensus that follows the completion of a revolutionary process, ideology is no longer needed for legitimating the established one-party system either—rather it becomes a potentially harmful, divisive force in a system whose social structure and political procedures have by then come to be accepted by the bulk of the nonbelievers. Once the leaders recognize that ideology is no longer needed to legitimate a rule based in fact on a postrevolutionary consensus, they will also be increasingly able, in Huntington's view, to meet the needs of a mature society by adaptive reforms within the system. In particular, they will accept economic reforms and grant increasing functional autonomy to experts within "depoliticized" subsystems for the sake of efficiency, and they will be ready to institutionalize interest groups in "corporate" forms while preserving the party's monopoly of arbitration between them. Huntington regards even the creation of inner-party channels for policy disagreements and for electoral career competition between individuals as possible within such a system, while political group formation continues to be prevented and intellectual critics questioning the basis of the consensus remain effectively isolated.

My own approach, as sketched on the following pages, is distinct from most of the treatments mentioned in that it insists on the interrelation of the three sets of problems—efficiency, interest articulation, and legitimation. It differs from Huntington's view by insisting that the problems affect communist-ruled societies in a specific way, in particular by giving reasons why they cannot dispense with the legitimating function of ideology and by consequently arriving at a more sceptical verdict on the limits of their adaptability.

Technical
Rationality and
Economic
Efficiency
Among the problems caused to a communist single-party system by the requirements of technical rationality and economic efficiency, I include the need for liberating scientific research from dogma; the need for a free flow of technical and economic information and practical criticism; the need for forms of planning, administration, and training that give scope to managerial initiative and technical innovation; the need for the selection, training, and consultation of competent elites; and the need for elite security under the rule of law.

On the first point, I argue that attempts at dogmatic interference with research in the natural sciences have by now ceased in all advanced countries under communist rule, so that damaging developments like Lysenko's rule in biology or the initial rejection of cybernetics for doctrinaire reasons are unlikely to be repeated. In these fields, the doctrinaires are now safely confined to the philosophical interpretation of scientific results after the event. In the social sciences, too, considerable progress has been made in the empirical study of political developments outside and unforeseen social developments inside the communist countries, as well as in the realistic discussion of their economic problems; but here the insistence on preserving a monopoly of theoretical generalization for the exponents of Marxist–Leninist doctrine continues to lead to recurrent conflicts with independent-minded scholars in the Soviet Union, in the bloc countries, and even in Yugoslavia. These conflicts are bound to impair the development of the social sciences so long as Marxist–Leninist dogma retains its importance for the cohesion and legitimation of the ruling parties.

On the second point, the influx of technical and economic information from abroad has much improved and could well continue to improve in the framework of international détente. The notorious sluggishness of the flow of information between research institutions and production units and among the latter, notably in Russia, appears to be due partly to cultural factors or to an accidental institutional structure and could in principle be remedied within the system. More serious is the structural weakness of the flow of practical criticism from bottom to top and from periphery to center, owing to a rigidly hierarchic and authoritarian climate deeply rooted in the traditions of Russian bureaucracy and management and transferred to the bloc countries in the Stalinist period. A change, recognized as necessary in principle, appears to depend on a combination of decentralizing planning reform and reorientation of training and education with conscious efforts to develop more consultative or "participatory" patterns of management in the sense of the Meyer–Ludz model cited. But those patterns have been evolved in countries where workers enjoy the protection of independent trade unions, civil servants have job security with a high probability of automatic promotion, and managers may change to competing firms in case of conflict with their superiors—and the question arises whether the growth of similar patterns in communist countries is not prevented by the necessary absence of similar props for the independence of critics in their system.

The third point leads to the heart of the controversy on economic planning reforms intended to improve the market indicators available to the managers and to increase their need and scope for responding to them. Scholarly analysis of the controversy has resulted in a broad distinction between a limited and a radical type of reform.[7] The limited type, as undertaken in the Soviet Union and approved by it in a number of variants within the bloc, seeks to correct the officially fixed prices so as to make them better indicators of real cost (including interest on capital), to delegate a number of planning decisions to subordinate branch authorities, and to reduce the number of physical indicators prescribed to the managers while making their "profits" an important monetary indicator for rewarding success. But it rejects free price formation on the market and retains considerable central planning for physical quantities, thus continuing to limit the managers' autonomy. Such limited reforms are clearly compatible with an essentially un-changed system of single-party rule, having been specially designed for that purpose. At the same time, they are likely to improve cost calcula-tion to some extent, and they may overcome some obstacles to technical innovation; but they will neither surmount such hurdles to progress as the absence of a market for producer goods nor provide a competitive market for the consumer remotely matching the performance of capital-ist industry in quality and variety.

The radical type of reform, as instituted by Yugoslavia, planned by the Czechoslovak reform leadership, and cautiously approached by Hungary in different variants, accepts the principle of free price forma-tion on the market and of competitive independence for managers of socialist enterprises. The central authorities seek to determine the level and direction of economic activity by credit policies and direct in-vestments but do not attempt to give the managers detailed orders on what goods to produce, what materials to procure, or how much labor to employ, and leave the managers considerable scope for following cal-culations of profit and risk. Clearly, a radical reform of this kind will create incentives for rational cost calculation, for technical innovation, and for improving the quality and variety of consumer goods similar to those of a capitalist market economy because it permits a similar degree of autonomy to the "economic subsystem"—though its actual success in meeting the requirements of technical rationality and economic efficiency will also depend on such factors as the ability of the monetary authorities and the political forces producing inflationary pressures. But such a radical reform is bound to hurt the massive vested interests not only of the central and regional economic bureaucracy but also of those members of the regional and local party machine that under the centralist system are largely occupied in dealing with deadlocks between different branches of that bureaucracy. The strength of their resistance not only accounts for the rejection of radical reform in the Soviet Union and most bloc countries to date, it also explains why even a leadership determined on reform is unlikely to overcome it without appealing to other social groups and according them institutional rights. Thus, Tito's creation of "workers' councils" preceded his first major steps toward "market socialism"; and the Czechoslovak economic reform, adopted on paper before 1968, only began to be implemented under the new leadership that aimed at a "new political model" as well as an economic one. Hence a radical economic reform meeting the requirements of technical rationality and economic efficiency appears possible only at the price of political changes that, by creating institutional forms for interest articulation, also raise the problem of redefining the role of the party itself.

Concerning the fourth point, the efficiency of the interlocking hierarchies of party and state clearly depends on a high level of specialized competence in the various branches of the state administration and on adequate general education and broad technical and economic understanding in the higher party organs that make the policy decisions and select the administrative personnel. It follows that communist parties ruling industrial societies must be capable of training and selecting elites who combine the required degree of competence with a political–ideological commitment to the party's goals—cadres that are both "red and expert" in the Chinese phrase, or "dual executives" in George Fischer's. In actual fact, all ruling communist parties seem sooner or later to have become aware of that need; obstacles to complying with it in practice have been due less to causes inherent in the system than to the competing claims of deserving veterans of the party's struggle for power—a factor that diminishes in importance with the lapse of time. In the Soviet Union, the share of cadres with higher education, and more particularly with technical training, rose drastically after Stalin's Great Purge and the subsequent 1939 change in the party's rules of admission; that it has continued to rise later is suggested both by Fischer's study and by Frederic Fleron's independent investigation, which moreover shows a growing share of people "coopted" into the party hierarchy after considerable professional experience in industry or agriculture. The one persistent weakness in the quality of Soviet managerial cadres appears to be the low importance attributed to properly economic, as distinct from technical, training—a fact that, by making such managers afraid of independent responsibility, has also become a further factor of resistance to economic reform. The privileged position of uneducated veterans lasted much longer in Yugoslavia but largely ended after the fall of Ranković in 1966. Among the bloc countries of Eastern Europe, the share of such veterans appears to have remained highest where the party was strongest before the seizure of power, notably in Czechoslovakia; it also remained high in East Germany so long as trained technicians could easily take refuge in the West, but there the situation changed drastically after the building of the Berlin Wall in 1961. By contrast, in Rumania and Hungary, where party veterans were extremely few, the regimes have long opened the doors of the administration to young non-party technicians, with the difference that the Rumanians have generally insisted on pulling them into the party on appointment.

No leadership of an industrial society, however, can rely on the advice of its bureaucratic subordinates alone; it needs to get not only a representative reaction from groups likely to be affected by impending decisions but also the opinions of experts outside the bureaucratic hierarchy immediately concerned, be they scientists or outstanding practitioners in the field. In fact, the Soviet Union has increasingly developed such methods of consultation since Khrushchev's time—not only in form of the mass meetings of the Central Committee with people from the industrial, agricultural, or literary "front line" that were discontinued in recent years but also in the less publicized and probably more effective consultations with individuals and small expert groups by the party secretariat and by opening the press to licensed discussion of particular issues for limited periods. In fact, the verdict on the capacity of Communist one-party regimes to consult qualified experts on decisions recognized not to involve questions of political principle must thus be as favorable as that on their capacity to train and select technically qualified office-holders.

On the last point, I do not maintain that an efficient industrial society is only possible under the rule of law in the full sense of the term, but that it requires both the absence of mass terrorism against entire social categories and the immunity of administrative and managerial elites from the charge of "sabotage" if they commit honest mistakes or tender unsuccessful advice. The distinction is important, because no single-party system, communist or noncommunist, seems capable of practicing the rule of law without exceptions. Each reserves the right suddenly to change the limits of permitted political criticism and to impose them on the judiciary with retroactive effect; but this constitutes a risk only to real critics of the regime, not to apolitical executives performing their duties. By contrast, the "restoration of socialist legality" in the course of de-Stalinization has meant the end both of mass terrorism and of prosecutions of officials for honest failures—the two key points that matter for functional elite security—in Russia and the bloc. That kind of security has existed in Yugoslavia for many years. I conclude that elite security in the advanced countries under communist rule is sufficient for the needs of economic and technical progress.

Interest Articulation Under One-Party Tutelage

No political system, however despotic, can do without some form of interest articulation. Even a totalitarian system determined on the annihilation of entire social groups needs to know which particular groups each of its measures is going to hurt, for it does not wish to antagonize all the people all the time. What distinguishes such a system is not that the interests of social groups are ignored but that they have no recognized place in the political process and no autonomous organizations. Thus, in Stalin's time, important conflicts of interest could find expression only in the contest of some of his immediate subordinates for the ear of the Vozhd, and any attempt at political group formation was considered illegitimate and correspondingly dangerous.

The authoritarian one-party regimes in Russia and the bloc today, which have developed from the recognition that at the level of the industrial society the cost of further "revolutions from above" has become prohibitive, are distinct from the Stalinist past by no longer claiming the need to fight hostile classes within their own society; therefore, they must regard the interests of all existing social groups as legitimate in principle. They consequently admit the possibility of conflicts between them, insisting only that these conflicts are "nonantagonistic"—that is, limited enough to be reconciled by the higher wisdom of the party. The party's monopoly of decision becomes from this angle a monopoly of interest arbitration—a kind of tutelage over the plurality of social groups. Of the possible institutional forms of this tutelage listed by Skilling, only two have proved viable for any length of time.

The first, described by Skilling as "consultative authoritarianism," requires only minimal visible change in the party's organization and method of operation. It consists in encouraging the various sections of the bureaucracy and the leaders of the party-controlled mass organizations to speak up, in the inner councils of party and government, for those sectors of society for which they are held responsible—be it heavy industry, agriculture, labor, the armed forces, or security. Such informal and bureaucratic interest articulation is distinguished from the practice of Stalin's time mainly by the fact that quasi-representative forms of consultation cease to be risky and become established as legitimate routine, including the fact that the top spokesmen for the various interests concert their views with a circle of their responsible collaborators or subordinates, thus acting as informal groups. The advantage of this minimum type of legitimate interest articulation is, from the party's point of view, that the line against the risks of open political pluralism remains sharply drawn—hence, it is the only type likely to be adopted by a Communist party regime without the pressure of a major political crisis. Its weakness is that interest articulation remains so indirect and selective that the risk of major misjudgments of the political and social situation cannot be excluded. The problem of the flow of information, discussed previously from the angle of economic efficiency, reappears here from the angle of effective political leadership. The failure of Wladyslaw Gomulka to foresee the effect of the price increases that led to the Polish workers' riots of December 1970 provides a classic example of too indirect "interest articulation" leading through poor political feedback to the crisis of a Communist party regime.

The alternative type of "democratizing and pluralistic authoritarianism," characterized by the formation of representative institutions for group interests in the framework of the party's political monopoly, has been approached spontaneously by the creation of Polish workers' councils in the de-Stalinization crisis of 1956 and again after the December riots of 1970, and also, of course, in the democratic revival of the trade unions and other interest groups in Czechoslovakia in 1968. But only in Yugoslavia, where the representative forms were created from above, on the initiative of the party leadership following the break with Stalin, have they developed into a stable network of institutions representing the interests of groups of producers, local communes, and national republics. Of course, this system of "socialist self-management" has always been threatened by the twin dangers of suffering Soviet-like atrophy if the party members in the representative organs were bound by centralized discipline or escaping the party's control if they were not; on the whole, the solution has been to permit party members to act autonomously on routine issues and to demand discipline only on issues of national importance. In effect, this system has permitted a much fuller articulation of the interests of the main sections of the population than the bureaucratic "minimum system" in force in the Soviet Union; as a price, it has made for recurrent conflicts between the organs of self-management and the central authorities as well as for recurrent inflationary pressures arising from below. Ultimately, a pluralistic system of interest representation of the Yugoslav type exposes the authoritarian top leadership to the risk of situations where undesirable developments at the "participatory" basis can be controlled only by the use of a few reserved levers of power—such as the army, the mass media, and the central banking system.

With either form of permitted interest articulation, the stability of the party's monopoly of arbitration depends on two conditions. The first is that the top leadership must be sufficiently cohesive to assure that no effective coalitions of interests may be formed within it—for a ruling party in which coalitions of interest fight for control is no longer the independent, authoritative arbiter between all groups of society but the object of a quasi-democratic process. The simplest reinsurance against such a development is, of course, the presence of an uncontested leader. Thus, in the Soviet Union, varying coalitions within the leadership appear to have been formed during the succession crisis that followed Stalin's death, but they disappeared for a time when Khrushchev's leadership became assured after the defeat of the "Anti-Party-Group" and the removal of Marshal Zhukov in the course of 1957. Again, as Khrushchev successively alienated various sectional interests in his final years—the secret police by his zeal for de-Stalinization, the army by his Cuban adventure and his one-sided reliance on rocketry, and his own party machine by his experiments with the party structure and his tendency to appeal to public opinion over the heads of the leading party organs—his leadership ceased to be uncontested, and the coalition that formed for his overthrow was no longer as risky as it would have been under Stalin. Similarly, the uncontested authority of Marshal Tito long guaranteed the stability of the Yugoslav system of institutionalized interest representation with party arbitration; but as Tito's authority waned in the late 1960s, a coalition of strongly autonomous-minded leaders of national republics won temporary control and achieved measures potentially dangerous to the stability of the system, as the developments in Croatia eventually showed—until Tito decided to restore at least outward cohesion by the ruthless use of his reserved powers. But in a postrevolutionary society under communist control, uncontested one-man leadership appears not to be the only method to ensure leadership cohesion. The history of the Soviet Union under the post-Khrushchev oligarchy suggests that a voluntary collective discipline under strict ground rules that are binding also on the General Secretary as the common spokesman may be equally effective. At any rate, that oligarchy has successfully avoided the succession struggles that followed the deaths of Lenin and Stalin, and its composition has undergone remarkably few changes in the course of 10 years and two party congresses. One of the successful ground rules appears to be that no member of the Politburo should speak out on controversial issues before they have been decided, so that none should publicly appear to be identified with any particular interest or coalition of interests.

The second condition of stability for a tutelary one-party system is that the articulation of interests, while permitted in principle, must never be allowed to take the form of a mobilization of the masses on behalf of them. Whether in licensed press discussions as in Russia, or in resolutions of autonomous organizations or parliamentary debates as in Yugoslavia, the case for a controversial proposal must be argued in restrained and responsible tones—not in emotional language calculated to produce mass pressure. The party leadership wants to be made aware of the existence of various interests and their arguments, but it wants to remain free to judge, not to have its hands forced by an aroused public opinion. Thus, the Soviet reproach that the Czechoslovak reform leaders had "abandoned the leading role of the party" was directed not merely at the growth of autonomous interest and opinion groups as such but at the crucial fact that, owing to the origin of that new freedom in a political crisis, the outcome of the clash of opinions and the direction that the movement was taking appeared no longer to depend solely on the will of the reform leadership itself. Again, the most serious charge belatedly raised by Tito and his Executive Bureau against the erstwhile Croatian leaders during the recent crisis concerned not the content of their autonomous demands but their toleration and encouragement of a nonparty cultural mass organization and mass circulation paper that mobilized popular pressure for these demands, thus creating a movement that they could no longer control.

Altogether, the problems created by interest articulation in a Communist single-party state ruling an industrial society raise more fundamental dilemmas than does the task of ensuring economic and technical progress. If the ruling party clings to a minimal type of consultative authoritarianism, permitting only informal and bureaucratic interest articulation, it will remain without an effective counterweight to its own bureaucracy and unable to break its inertial resistance to major economic reform. It will also run the risk, sooner or later, of a major political crisis caused by poor political feedback. If, on the other hand, the party chooses a bolder form of pluralistic or participatory authoritarianism, it may avoid those dangers but will find itself perpetually trying to balance the highly heterogeneous elements of a potentially unstable system that combines the existence of quasi-democratic institutions with the authoritarian nature of ultimate power. Though the conditions of stability for such a system—strict leadership solidarity "above the battle" and renunciation of mass mobilization by all groups—may be clearly defined, they are difficult to preserve in the political climate created by pluralistic and participatory institutions. For the changing needs and moods of a dynamic society breed ever-new temptations for both party leaders and group exponents to offend against these conditions; once that happens, a political crisis confronting the authoritarian and the "democratizing" elements of the regime is at hand.

Legitimation and Ideology

The changes in the function of a Communist party governing a postrevolutionary mature society also require adjustments in the legitimation of the regime and the ideology of the party, presenting it both with new opportunities and with new immediate and long-term problems. The new opportunities are inherent in the end of the "revolution from above" with its recurrent waves of mass terrorism. The regime now has a chance to make peace with society—to become, in the words of Khrushchev's new party program of 1961, "a state of the whole people," or to acquire, in the language of sociology, an authority based on a consensus of values.[8] The new, immediate problems arise from the need to find an ideological definition for the party's new role that is convincing to its own members and particularly to its core, the apparatus. The new long-term problem consists in justifying to the various groups of an increasingly mature society why just this party, in this composition and with this ideology, should be the ultimate arbiter of their conflicts— why, even given a broad consensus of values, it should be entitled to a specific role above society and a permanent monopoly of ultimate power.

It is a common historical experience that most regimes created by revolutionary violence acquire effective legitimacy simply by the lapse of time; people grow up with them and get accustomed to regarding them as normal, provided only that revolutionary violence has come to an end. While Stalin conducted recurrent war against important social groups, his regime could hardly expect to benefit from such acceptance; but Khrushchev's proclamation of the end of the domestic class struggle, based as it was on the dual recognition that further revolutionary upheavals were neither economically practicable nor politically needed to preserve the fundamental socialist achievements, finally opened the way for it. As economic development continues in a secure framework of public and collective ownership, without serious fear of capitalist relapses or serious need for further violent transformation, "socialism" in the sense of that framework has become almost universally accepted by the Soviet population, including even most of the bitter political critics of the regime. Its acceptance appears almost equally universal in the bloc countries of Eastern Europe and in Yugoslavia, as far as public ownership of industry is concerned; and this seems to apply not only to countries where industry was largely developed by the state but even in an old industrial country like Czechoslovakia, where the 1968 period of free expression of opinions brought no significant demands for a return to capitalism. More surprisingly, even the agricultural collectives, from which the peasants fled en masse once they got a chance in the 1950s in Yugoslavia and Poland (and temporarily in Hungary), no longer appear to be seriously controversial.

If the peoples of Russia and Eastern Europe have largely accepted the forms of public ownership and planning which distinguish a "socialist" from a capitalist industrial society, they seem to have just as effectively adopted the values that both modern systems have in common in contrast to traditional societies: the belief in the central importance of material progress, measured in technical productivity and the standard of living, for the good life; in advancement according to merit and reward according to performance; in the development of the sciences; and in rational choice of means for given ends. Of course, conflicts occur—just as in the West—between this outlook and remaining traditional religious values as well as between the officially proclaimed and accepted values and social reality—but this does not diminish the importance of the broad consensus of values now existing in these fields.

True, there are important exceptions to this consensus. Perhaps the most general exception is the widespread lack of interest and belief among the peoples in the ultimate communist goal of the classless society, which means that communism has not been accepted in its original meaning as a secular religion; but this creates no immediate problems, since the utopian goal has lost its relevance for the practice of the ruling parties as well. Of much greater political virulence, but over a rather more limited area, is the continued belief of sections of the communist-ruled peoples in liberal individualist values which, while in themselves compatible with the socialist values of public control and the general modern values of efficiency and rationality, are in basic conflict with the needs of self-preservation of an authoritarian single-party regime. The explosive nature of this conflict has been demonstrated in Czechoslovakia, the bloc country where the hold of these "Western" values is strongest. They may be presumed to be of substantial, if less universal, importance in several other East European countries and among some of the nationalities of the Soviet Union; whereas in Russia proper, they have a live tradition chiefly among sections of the intelligentsia and are the source of their dissent.

Finally, it is most difficult to strike a balance between the benefits and dangers of the values of nationalism for Communist party regimes. The integrative value both of "Soviet patriotism" and of Great Russian pride among the Russian people is obvious, while among the non-Russian peoples of the Soviet Union, the effects have been more mixed, as the recurrent troubles between the all-union authorities and the intelligentsia (and sometimes sections of the party elite) of a number of nationalities indicate. National discontent is most obvious among the groups with developed prerevolutionary cultural traditions; with a number of others, and even with the less educated sections of the former, the policy of integration by the expansion of literacy and the widening of career prospects might have been rather more successful.

In Soviet-dominated Eastern Europe, where nationalism was at first the most virulent single source of broad popular rejection of many new regimes, the change has been substantial since the mid-1950s. Greater autonomy, first granted to the national leaderships in the course of de-Stalinization and later expanded by their exploitation of Sino–Soviet rivalry between its beginning in 1958–1959 and the open break of 1963–1964, has enabled them both to broaden their domestic support by material improvements and to appear increasingly as spokesmen of national interests even in relation to the Soviet Union. At the same time, Soviet intervention in Hungary and later in Czechoslovakia has provided arguments for tempering independence with realistic caution in the national interest, thus permitting the growth of a national consensus between rulers and ruled on national interests in most of these countries, only excepting Czechoslovakia. Even the East German leadership that has to legitimate a state artificially dividing a nation, and that still suffers from recurrent ideological difficulties on that account, has at least gained an increased measure of state loyalty on the basis of improving autonomy, rising economic performance, and growing weight within the bloc.

Yugoslavia is probably unique in that value consensus about national unity on a federal basis was one of the strongest assets of the regime at the beginning, when the memory of the wartime massacres and the pride of national liberation were fresh, but has been gravely weakened in the course of time. It was first slowly eroded by economic policy differences between the party and government leaderships of the more advanced and the less developed republics, then undermined by growing cultural conflicts following a generation change, and finally put in jeopardy—following the major extension of the autonomy of the republican parties beginning in 1966—by the open conflict between the Croatian and federal leaderships that ended in a purge of the former and large numbers of arrests. No doubt both the party leadership and the bulk of the people continue to stand for Yugoslav unity and independence, but confidence in the leadership's ability to act wisely in defense of these values appears seriously shaken, at least for the moment.

The overall picture of the growth of value consensus in advanced societies under communist rule is thus far from simple. Yet on the whole, and with allowance for important exceptions, I incline to the view that the lapse of time favors the solution of this aspect of the problem of legitimation, provided that the leadership avoids major mistakes. But the situation seems more difficult with regard to other aspects.

One such difficult aspect concerns the justification of the continued monopoly of a ruling party that no longer describes its rule as a "dictatorship of the proletariat" needed to hold down and even destroy hostile classes. The broad social groups are indeed hardly in a position to raise such fundamental questions: It is the party members themselves, and above all the party officials, who insist on new arguments for the party's "leading role" after its change of function. In the Soviet Union, where the problem was dimly perceived after adoption of the new party program in 1961, a first attempt at an answer was offered within a year when Khrushchev reorganized the party into separate industrial and agricultural sectors. The principal task of the party thereafter was to raise production and productivity, for this was now the high road to the higher stage of communism. But this system made the party officials more directly responsible for economic results than they cared to be, involved them in awkward conflicts of competence with the regular economic administration, and reduced the party ideologues and propagandists to a marginal role; nor could any sound theoretical reason be given why single-party rule should be the best way to achieve a continuous growth of production. Unpopular with the party machine and unconvincing as an argument, Khrushchev's party reorganization of 1962 was the first of his measures to be immediately revoked after his fall.

The subsequent renewed stress on the party's ideological role did not provide a convincing solution either, until by the spring of 1968, Khrushchev's successors hit on the decisive point: The alternative to the party's monopoly was a free play of pluralistic social forces, and that constituted an intolerable danger to the socialist foundations because conflicts between these forces could be exploited by the imperialist enemy. In short, the new role of the party was to guarantee the unity of a complex socialist society in the face of unceasing subversive efforts from abroad. The fundamental Leninist belief in the danger of leaving society to its spontaneous laws of development thus reappeared in a new form. The fear of a spontaneous rebirth of capitalism was replaced by the fear of routine conflicts of interest taking a destructive turn with prompting by the enemy. Only one thing remained inconceivable—that a mature society could find ways to solve its problems without a guardian; for then the monopolistic party would be superfluous.

The fundamental character of this ideological need for an enemy in Communist party regimes is confirmed by the fact that all communist leaderships fall back on it at moments of stress—even if they have pluralistic institutions like Yugoslavia, even if acute conflict with the Soviet Union temporarily makes the latter assume the role of the enemy. It follows from this need for an ideology of tutelage that such regimes have to fall back again and again on essential elements of "Marxist–Leninist" dogma as codified by Stalin; a more flexible and open form of Marxism would not supply the arguments for retaining the party's authoritarian role. This also explains the limits for the liberation of the social sciences from dogma, which we noticed before.

Yet such a dogmatic ideology of tutelage, while indispensable for the confidence and cohesion of the ruling party, is clearly unattractive to the intellectual elite of any modern country. Hence, while communist regimes have no difficulty recruiting gifted technicians for constructive work and making them eventually join the party in the interest of their promotion, it is now chiefly opportunists of limited ability who choose the classical political career through the youth organization into the party machine; the creative intellectuals either keep strenuously out of politics or turn to systematic criticism of the regime.

Moreover, while the rank and file of the parties had an active role in mobilization, agitation, and intimidation during the period of revolutionary transformation, in a postrevolutionary regime the party units in an enterprise or administrative institution have no clearly defined tasks. Hence, in Russia and the bloc, the leaders keep wavering between relying on the performance of administrative and managerial hierarchies, which leads to atrophy and discouragement of the basic party units, and reactivating the latter as organs for "stimulating" the bureaucrats and reporting on them, at the risk of administrative disorganization. As the party seems to need its "basis" only in times of crisis, it is not easy for the ordinary member to preserve a belief in his own function nor for the party organization to recruit members who genuinely believe in the cause. From Russia to Hungary, from Poland to Yugoslavia, the complaints are repeated about self-seekers without conviction flooding the party. The party's self-legitimation by an ideology of tutelage may convince the *apparatchiki* but hardly anybody else—it neither attracts the intellectual elite nor inspires the party's own rank and file.

That leads us to the final aspect of the problem of legitimation—the need to convince society at large that, given a consensus of basic values, the people who rise to the top in the system will normally feel obliged and be qualified to promote these values effectively. In the short run, such a conviction can only rest on successful performance, such as economic progress or the increase of national power. But as no political system can ever guarantee continuously successful performance, long-run legitimacy can be based only on confidence that the institutional procedures by which rulers are selected and decisions are reached offer a reasonable chance of such performance.

In fact, for modern societies, there is no long-run alternative to legitimacy based on institutional procedures. Of the two other types of legitimacy listed by Max Weber—traditional and charismatic legitimacy—the first does not apply to modern conditions and the second does not apply to the long run. There remains Weber's "rational–legal" type of legitimacy; while that does not necessarily require a pluralistic democracy under the rule of law, it does require a system justified in procedural terms. For communist one-party rule, this means that it must make plausible that the party's monopoly will normally bring well-qualified people to the top and produce decisions that correspond to the broad interests of the community and strike a fair balance between its main sections. In other words, the system must produce not merely competent economic or administrative experts but a true *political* elite of leaders able to act as guardians of the national interest and arbiters between group interests. Yet we have seen that the chance of the postrevolutionary single-party system producing such a political elite, either in fact or in the eyes of its subjects, tends to decline with the deterioration in the character and talents of those who take up a political, as distinct from a technical or administrative, career—hence, the characteristic distrust of the older leaders for their opportunist would-be successors. At the same time, the decline in the dedication of party members at large tends to lower the party's prestige among the people.

Of course, the decline of party authority due to such developments is no more than a long-run tendency. In the East European bloc countries, it may even be argued that legitimacy has increased—after all, the fundamentals of the system were less questioned in the Czechoslovak and Polish crises of 1968 and 1970 than in the East German and Hungarian crises of 1953 and 1956. But this is clearly due to the special situation of countries where communist rule was imposed from outside and where it could gain national roots only slowly. In Russia and Yugoslavia, on the other hand, indications of a long-term decline in legitimacy are visible without similar dramatic crises. In both countries, the fiction that the party knows best is openly challenged by an intellectual elite—in Yugoslavia, until recently, in legal periodicals, in Russia in signed underground documents. While the numbers of these dissenters are still small, they do pose a problem to the leadership, causing division on how to handle them and even tempting some leaders to protect them as potential allies. Their critique, by gradually filtering into the minds of parts of the younger generation, may prepare the ground for more powerful challenges, if specific failures of the regimes should one day lead to a crisis situation.

I conclude that while the development of a value consensus between rulers and ruled has appeared relatively favorable to postrevolutionary communist regimes, and while the ideology of tutelage adopted for the party's self-legitimation satisfies the *apparatchiki* only at the price of a hardening of dogma, a persistent need for outside "enemies," and increasing friction with the intellectual elite, and offers no satisfactory role to the rank and file, the third and decisive aspect—the legitimation of the party's tutelary role before the people at large by the plausibility of the institutional procedures of the one-party regime—appears to have deteriorating prospects in the long run. With the party professionals increasingly recruited among ambitious opportunists, the ideology increasingly marked by antiquated dogmatism or patent insincerity, and the rank and file showing growing evidence of cynicism and corruption, the aptitude of the one-party regime to produce a true political elite and a successful policy in the national interest is bound to become less rather than more plausible, and the legitimacy of its monopoly of power to be increasingly challenged first by the intellectual elite and later by wider strata.

Conclusions   Our examination suggests that the problems of assur-
              ing technical rationality and economic efficiency in an
industrial society under Communist party rule are not by themselves so
decisive as is frequently assumed. But while many of those problems
can be solved by a Communist party regime with comparatively minor
adjustments, some of the more difficult ones can only be overcome by a
drastic reduction in the power of both the economic and the party
bureaucracy, which requires the granting of greater autonomy to
pluralistic social forces as a counterweight, or a liberation from
"Marxist–Leninist" dogma, which is bound to raise doubts about the
legitimacy of the party's power.

It follows that theoretical approaches that undertake to judge the
prospects of postrevolutionary Communist party regimes wholly or
chiefly in terms of rationality and efficiency are unsatisfactory. Thus,
while Fischer's observation of the growing role of "dual executives"
seems perfectly convincing for the Soviet Union and highly plausible for
other communist-ruled modern countries, his broader theoretical concept that the requirements of technical rationality are sufficient for
defining the "correct" path of economic and social development for such
a regime is by no means equally convincing. It ignores the persistent
conflict of group interests about priorities at which the real problem of
decision begins, and therefore the need of new *political* qualifications for
the ruling elite as distinct from a mere improvement in expert knowledge.

A similarly one-sided preoccupation with "rationality" also underlies
the thesis of the successive stages of bureaucratic enlightenment put
forward by Meyer and Ludz, as is shown in Meyer's analogy between
the Soviet Union and a giant corporation. *Rationality* is an unambiguous
concept only when it refers to the choice of means for a given end; when
that end is profit, as in a corporation, the rational solution to any
particular problem may thus be defined precisely. But politics is always
(not least in communist regimes) concerned with the choice of priorities
between different ends, and here one solution may not be demonstrably
more rational than the other. More specifically, the evolutionary trend
that both authors extrapolate from the sociology of management in
Western industry refers to a situation in which the major conflicts of
interest between management and labor are settled *outside* the particular
corporation between organizations of employers and labor or by legislative or executive political action. Moreover, as we have seen, the
advantages of consultation in Western capitalist management pre-
suppose the degree of job security for workers and of competitive
alternatives for managerial personnel that are assured by strong trade
unions and a competitive industrial structure. To transfer an evolutionary pattern based on such conditions to a state-managed economy under

communist one-party rule—without independent trade unions or free mobility of managers, and where the problems facing "USSR, Inc." include major policy decisions between nationwide interest groups—must be regarded as an unconvincing analogy.

Turning to the consequences of the plurality of interests in an industrial society, we found that at least an informal and indirect, if not an institutionalized, pluralism of more or less autonomous interest groups under the party's tutelage is indispensable to the survival of Communist party rule in such conditions. At the same time, any step toward the practical, ideological, or institutional admission of a plurality of social forces proved to raise serious dilemmas, both for the cohesion of the party's leadership and for the doctrinaire interpretation and legitimation of its new role to its own cadres.

In our examination of these dilemmas, Skilling's analysis of the different degrees of pluralism under authoritarian communist rule proved a most valuable starting point. I have tried to go further in distinguishing between forms of pluralism that occur only in transitional periods of leadership conflict or a general crisis of authority and forms that have proved capable of developing a minimum of institutional stability. I have concluded that only two of Skilling's five variants—the informal and bureaucratic interest articulation now practiced in the Soviet Union and described by him as "consultative authoritarianism" and the institutionalized form developed in Yugoslavia and characterized by him as "democratizing and consultative authoritarianism"—pass that test. Moreover, while Skilling recognizes no evolutionary trend from one form to another and no inherent link with the stages of economic development, I have tried to show that each form of interest articulation under single-party rule produces its characteristic economic and political dilemmas; that the minimum form leaves the bureaucracy strong enough to prevent radical economic reform, which the institutional form permits; and that the minimum form carries the risk of political crises arising from poor feedback, while the institutional form creates a dangerous tug-of-war between autonomous groups and the central authorities and a recurrent temptation to offend against the conditions of leadership cohesion and avoidance of mass mobilization that this "advanced" system requires for its stability.

We thus remain with the evidence of an unsolved dilemma between the requirements of the one-party system's full adaptation to the pluralistic needs of a mature industrial society and the requirements of legitimating its continued monopoly. All the problems that we have discussed thus seem to converge into the question of the chance of such regimes to acquire a long-term legitimacy, based not only on a value consensus between rulers and ruled and a doctrinaire self-legitimation of the party that satisfies its own cadres but on the plausibility of the claim that its procedures of leadership selection and policy decision are likely to meet the needs of a modern society. But we had to conclude that this plausibility, and with it the institutional legitimacy of the party regime, is bound to decline in the long run, because the limits and conditions within which such a regime can solve the problems of efficient development and pluralistic representation of a modern society are beset with too many dilemmas and therefore are ultimately too cramping—both for the society and for the ruling party itself.

This statement is in sharp contrast to the views of the one author who treats the issue of legitimation as central—Huntington, with his thesis of the growth of a nonideological legitimacy arising from postrevolutionary consensus. My objection to that thesis concerns not the growth of such a value consensus in itself but the assumption that it will eventually enable such regimes to dispense with the remnants of their ideological doctrine. This has not happened so far in any country under communist rule, and Huntington bases his prediction on an analogy between communist and noncommunist one-party regimes that have reached the "institutionalized" stage, in general, and on the case of Mexico, in particular. Mexico's ruling Party of Revolutionary Institutions (P.R.I.) has indeed developed an apparently stable monopoly of arbitration between interest groups organized in corporate form, while allowing the role of ideology to be reduced to symbolic reassurance offered by ritualized repetition of certain standard phrases. Yet Mexico's ruling party was created not to conquer power by revolution but to regularize the procedures of a victorious revolution both for deciding on the presidential succession and the nomination of other office-holders and for arbitrating between interest groups. It has never established a formal single-party state, always tolerating minor outside parties; it has never outlawed the competition of organized groups within the party; and its ideology of national independence, enlightenment, and social progress has never proclaimed utopian and worldwide goals but has confined itself to objectives vaguely defined but clearly limited in space and time. Its leaders have from an early date normally risen by their skill in balancing organized interests, and they have never had to justify pragmatic actions in terms of a utopian doctrine. Hence, the Mexican P.R.I. has never had to face the problem of self-legitimation following a postrevolutionary role change, and it has been geared from its foundation to the creation of a postrevolutionary, procedural legitimacy that is proving so troublesome to the communists. All this suggests that while a further evolution of communist regimes ruling mature societies toward an acceptance of ideological erosion may be conceivable, it would also be an evolution leading away from the monopoly of the party—a step on the road toward democracy.

I conclude by stating my fundamental agreement with an hypothesis put forward by a nonspecialist in our field—the view of the irreplaceable role of pluralistic democracy for mediating consensus in modern conditions, advanced by Talcott Parsons in his famous essay on "Evolutionary Universals."[9] His key formulation with regard to our problem is that

> no institutional form basically different from the democratic association can . . . mediate consensus in its exercise by particular persons and groups and in the formation of particular binding policy decisions. At high levels of structural differentiation in the society itself and in its governmental system, generalized legitimation cannot fill this gap adequately.

To state my agreement with the manner in which Parsons, advancing from considerations of general social theory, has formulated the central point that I here described as the dependence of long-term legitimacy in modern conditions on institutional procedures does not mean that I believe in the "inevitability of democracy" or in the inevitable convergence of communist-ruled and Western democratic systems on the political basis of the latter. It merely means that I share his conviction that modern societies that cannot adopt the basic institutions of pluralistic democracy but that persist under the control of an authoritarian single-party regime will be likely both to stay below the potential of economic achievement that they could otherwise reach and to fall victim to recurrent political crises owing to a long-term decline in legitimacy. Such crises may end in brutal oppression and reaction, in an overthrow of the party regime by another type of authoritarian rule or in limited or far-reaching democratic reform. Nothing that has been stated here enables us to predict a particular outcome to particular crises or to believe in a "logical" process of democratic reform by stages. Societies at any stage of development may fail to solve the problems of transition to the next stage or may fall back, depending on many contingent historical or cultural factors. All we can assert on the basis of our examination of modern communist-ruled societies is that those that do not evolve in the direction of pluralistic democracy will in fact fail to solve some of the crucial problems facing them—and will have to pay the cost of such failure in one form or another.

Notes

[1]For this interpretation of the phase of "posttotalitarian" maturity, see my "Development vs. Utopia in Communist Policy," in *Change in Communist Systems*, ed. Chalmers Johnson (Stanford: Stanford University Press, 1970), which was extensively reviewed in the Spring/Summer 1973 issue of *Studies in Com*

parative Communism. This chapter continues the comparative analysis undertaken in my earlier paper.

[2]George Fischer, *The Soviet System and Modern Society* (New York: Atherton Press, 1968).

[3]Alfred G. Meyer, *The Soviet Political System* (New York: Random House, 1965); also "Theories of Convergence," in *Change in Communist Systems.*

[4]Peter C. Ludz, *Parteielite im Wandel* (Köln: 1968).

[5]H. Gordon Skilling and Franklyn Griffiths, *Interest Groups in Soviet Politics* (Princeton, N.J.: Princeton University Press, 1971); also H. Gordon Skilling, "Group Conflict and Political Change," in *Change in Communist Systems.*

[6]Samuel P. Huntington and Clement H. Moore (eds.), *Authoritarian Politics in Modern Society: The Dynamics of Established One-Party Systems* (New York: Basic Books, 1970), particularly ch. 1, "The Institutional Dynamics of One-Party Systems," by Huntington and ch. 17, "Conclusions: Authoritarianism, Democracy and One-Party Politics," by Huntington and Moore.

[7]See R. V. Burks, "Technology and Political Change," in *Change in Communist Systems* for this and other aspects of our problem.

[8]On postrevolutionary value consensus, see Chalmers Johnson, *Revolutionary Change* (Boston: Little, Brown, 1966) and the same author's introductory essay, "Comparing Communist Nations," in *Change in Communist Systems.* Also Zvi Gitelman, "Power and Authority in Eastern Europe," *ibid.*

[9]Talcott Parsons, "Evolutionary Universals in Society," *American Sociological Review* 29, no. 3 (June 1964), pp. 338–357.

30

CYRIL E. BLACK

The Soviet Union as an Advanced Society*

Much is being written these days about advanced modernization—referred to sometimes as "the postindustrial society," "the third wave," "advanced industrial society," and in the Soviet Union as "developed socialism," according to the differing ideologies and perspectives of the authors. Although there is considerable agreement as to the characteristics of advanced modernization and the ways in which it differs from the preceding period of societal transformation, it is a relatively new phenomenon, the evidence is still incomplete, and there are numerous unresolved problems. Since Soviet theorists live and think in a rather isolated world, it is important to consider the extent to which their conception of "developed" corresponds to the views current in the West—and, more important, how the levels of achievement of the Soviet Union compare with those of other societies insofar as the available indicators permit one to make appropriate comparisons.

The Soviet Perspective   Soviet theorists today see their country's achievement of a "developed" status as a third stage in its development. The first was that of the establishment of the basic institutions of socialism in the years between the Revolution and the adoption of the 1936 Constitution. This was followed by the period from 1936 to 1967 in which the basic structure of socialism was further consolidated. They see the current stage, since 1967, not coincidentally the fiftieth anniversary of their Revolution, as one

*This is a revised and expanded version of a paper on "Characteristics of Advanced Modernization Relative to the U.S.S.R.," presented at the annual meeting of the American Political Science Association in Washington on August 28, 1980.

which Soviet society is taking advantage of the opportunities offered by the scientific and technological revolution to improve its economic productivity and political and social efficiency. The fourth stage will be the classless and stateless society predicted by Marx.

The characteristics attributed to this current stage of "developed socialism" are in many ways similar to those discussed by students of the advanced industrial societies in Western Europe, Japan, and the New World. These include the application of science and technology to the productive processes, leading to higher productivity and the potential for increasing material prosperity, as well as high levels of education, urbanization, and social welfare. Other characteristics discussed in the Soviet literature are more difficult to compare with those of democratic societies. Much is made, for example, of the new role of the Communist party as embodying the general interest of society now that antagonistic classes and interests allegedly no longer exist, and as aggregating the various nonantagonistic interest groups that compete for influence in decision making. Likewise, the Soviet state is seen as becoming more efficient and also more democratic in the sense of providing for greater public participation in administration.[1]

This conception of *developed socialism*, based on the scientific and technological revolution, evolved in the Soviet Union in the 1950s and 1960s under the influence of developments in Eastern Europe. In these years, a thoroughgoing effort was made in Poland, Czechoslovakia, Hungary, and East Germany to introduce the contemporary Western theory and practice of economics, sociology, and management into the realm of research and policy, which for some two decades had been dominated by a dogmatic Marxism–Leninism. The underlying motivation of this new ideological trend was a desire to reconcile the Marxist–Leninist doctrinal heritage with the realities of the postwar world. These realities included not only achievements in economic growth and social change but more fundamentally the advances in science and technology—most obviously nuclear power, computers, and automation—that were transforming the advanced industrial societies. This rapid advancement of knowledge was now recognized as underlying modern societal transformation, and the new outlook soon came to be known as "the scientific–technological revolution" (*nauchno–tekhnicheskaia revoliutsiia* in Russian) or STR.[2]

This recognition of the fundamental importance of knowledge ran counter to the accepted Marxist–Leninist teaching that science and technology, including the social sciences, were part of the superstructure of society which was in the final analysis determined by the economic structure which formed its base.[3] This relationship has now been reversed, and in effect, science (which in Slavic languages means *knowledge* generally, not just the natural sciences) and technology (or perhaps more narrowly *technique*) are acknowledged in the final analysis as the base that determines the superstructure of political development, economic growth, and social integration. The closest that commentators seem to have come to an authoritative justification of this fundamental change is a statement by Marx himself, more an aside than a formal assertion, that as societies develop, production will change "from a simple labor process to a scientific process."[4]

As developed by writers in Eastern Europe, the advances in science and technology were seen as representing a revolutionary change in the possibilities for transforming the human condition. These advances lead to radical changes in the process of production, require a large number of highly trained technicians, and will permit a reduction in the differences between mental and manual labor and between urban and rural life. Their effects also include a great increase in the availability of data for use by the social sciences in the solution of complex problems.

One of the early indications of Soviet receptivity to the new trend was the appearance in 1969 of a Russian translation of Jan Szczepanski's *Elementary Principles of Sociology*, originally published in Warsaw in 1965. This was, in effect, a primer of contemporary sociology, predominantly American and West European, which also drew extensively on Polish work since the 1950s. It contained few references to Marx and none to Lenin. Of more general relevance was *Civilization at the Crossroads: Social and Human Implications of the Scientific and Technological Revolution*, published in Prague in 1966 (with an English edition in 1969), by Radovan Richta and his colleagues at the Institute of Philosophy and Sociology of the Czechoslovak Academy of Sciences. This volume cites primarily Western works dating from the 1940s and places no particular emphasis on Marxism–Leninism. It played, incidentally, an important role in the Czechoslovak events of 1968. Although the Prague reform movement was suppressed by the Soviet Union for reasons of national security, the Soviet and Czechoslovak academies of science collaborated 5 years later in publishing *Man–Science–Technology: A Marxist Analysis of the Scientific–Technological Revolution* (1973). This was a revised and extended version of *Civilization at the Crossroads*, which placed more emphasis on relating the new trends to the Marxist–Leninist tradition.

In the meantime, Soviet theorists had since the 1950s been devoting increasing attention to the economic and social significance of the new developments in nuclear power, automation, and computers and a brief reference to this subject appeared in the Communist Party Program of 1961. The STR finally became a dominant official theme when Brezhnev, in his report to the Twenty-Fourth Congress of the CPSU in 1971, stated that "the task we face, comrades, is one of historical importance: *organically to combine the achievements of the scientific-technological revolution with the advantages of the socialist economic system*, to develop our own, inherently socialist, forms of combining science with production."[5]

In the course of the 1970s, a wide range of views has been expressed in Soviet publications regarding the STR, and there are few areas of activity that have not been challenged to demonstrate that they are achieving the efficiency and productivity made possible by modern techniques.[6] American management and public administration are among the subjects that have attracted most interest, both in the Soviet Union and in the countries of Eastern Europe. Despite the existence of massive central and enterprise bureaucracies in these countries, little systematic attention was devoted before the 1960s to the theory and practice of management. Some specialists were now sent to American business schools for training and research, and in due course, institutions with curricula adapted from American models were established in these countries. A particular problem has been the inefficiency of the highly centralized planning systems and the separation of research and development organizations from the enterprises concerned with production. American business practice has become an important model in the search for more efficient organizational forms.[7] Similarly, in the construction of computers and the adaptation of software to the needs of the users, American technology has been transferred wholesale.[8]

Advanced Modernization: A Comparative Approach

Advanced modernization is the phase in a country's development in which the level of knowledge and of political capacity leads to the application of high technology to a wide range of economic and social processes. A type of society emerges in which specialized education is at a premium, services absorb a larger share of the labor force and of the domestic product than manufacturing and agriculture, and societies become more integrated in a whole series of dimensions. The United States may be said to have entered this phase in the 1930s, the countries of western and central Europe in the 1950s, and Japan and the Soviet Union in the 1960s.

During the preceding period of transformation from relatively nonmodernized to relatively modernized societies, these countries have been concerned with two basic problems. One is the conversion of premodern capabilities to modern uses, and the other is the introduction of new techniques and institutions. These latter may either be developed indigenously, in the case of the early modernizers, or borrowed and adopted, in the case of latecomers. This process of transformation involves vast changes in social relationships. Modern knowledge must be accepted as superseding earlier conceptions of the human environment, and in varying degrees of specialization, large segments of the population become involved in the production and distribution of knowledge. This transformation requires a political leadership capable of guiding the development of an economy and society from a predominantly agrarian and rural to a predominantly industrial and urban way of life.

In seeking criteria by which to define and assess levels of "advancement," it is important to recognize that modernization should not be equated with progress. The engine of change in historical times has been the advancement of knowledge resulting from the interaction of human minds—central nervous systems—with each other and with everything else. Modernization results from the enhancement of the human capacity to understand and make use of the environment, and this enhanced capacity can be used for any purpose. It can be used to promote human betterment in terms of health, education, and welfare, or it can be used to destroy all humankind. World wars and holocausts are as characteristic of modernity as are industrialization, urbanization, and high levels of consumption. In this context, we seek here to evaluate levels of adancement in terms of selected intellectual, political, economic, and social indicators.

Intellectual Aspects. One of the main attributes of advanced modernization is the critical importance of theoretical knowledge—in the broad sense that includes the social sciences and humanities as well as the natural sciences—and the application of knowledge to the many areas of technology and public policy that affect human welfare. Whether one associates this development more narrowly, as Marxist–Leninists tend to do, with the scientific–technological revolution since 1945 or more broadly with the rapid advancement of knowledge that can be traced back to the Renaissance, these approaches have a common theme in the importance of applying the new knowledge to human affairs.[9]

One way of assessing the value that a society places on the advancement of knowledge is to measure the resources allocated to research and development. It has been estimated that in the 1970s, the Soviet Union expended an annual average of about 3.5% of its gross national product (GNP) on research and development. This compares with some 2.3% expended by the United States and the Federal Republic of Germany and somewhat less by France and Japan.[10] These are only rough orders of magnitude and do not measure the quality of research, but they indicate that Soviet performance in this area is at least equivalent to that in the developed Western countries and Japan.

Training for professional and technical occupations is a matter of special emphasis in advanced societies, and levels of educational development can be measured by the enrollments at different levels of education. Enrollments in higher education per 1000 of population are reported to range from about 20 to 50 in advanced societies. Available estimates suggest ratios of 52 in the United States, 20 in Japan and 19 in the Soviet Union. This compares with ratios of 10 in Switzerland, 5 in India, and 1 in many developing countries including China.[11] In this case, it should be noted, the high United States ratio would appear to reflect the tendency of the American educational system to delay serious education for many students until after the secondary school level. Many students in American colleges and universities are being taught skills that are learned in secondary schools in many other countries. It would probably be more accurate to reduce the American ratio by one-half. Apart from this correction, these estimates illustrate the wide gap in the resources devoted to higher education that separates the advanced from the less-developed societies.

Comparative indicators are not available to estimate the economic role of knowledge in advanced societies, but it has been estimated that the share in the United States GNP of the production and distribution of knowledge, very broadly defined, was 29% in 1958. The share of the knowledge-producing occupations in the American labor force tripled between 1900 and 1959, reaching some 30% of the labor force in the latter year.[12] Later estimates suggest that these ratios probably reached the 50% level in the 1970s.[13] Although these estimates are only suggestive, it is apparent that advanced societies are knowledge-intensive, in contrast to the capital-intensive nature of societies in the process of transformation and the labor-intensive premodern societies.

Political Aspects. Political development in advanced societies is characterized by an integrated mobilization of skills and resources by central decision-making bodies, whether public or private, and by increasingly complex patterns of interest representation in the formation of policy. In contrast to the earlier phase of societal transformation, which requires a high allocation of resources to investment and is for most citizens an exercise in the postponement of gratification, advanced modernization is characterized by an emphasis on distribution. In the course of societal transformation, the divisive issues concerning the mobilization and allocation of resources are predominantly regional and class-oriented. In advanced societies, politics becomes more concerned with issues facing society as a whole—the industrial, educational, urban, welfare, and other consequences of the scientific and technological revolution. This change in orientation has led to the growth of the public sector. In the United States, for example, the federal, state, and local government expenditures as a share of GNP have risen from 2.5% in 1900 to 21% in 1970 and about 35% today. Federal expenditures account for about one-half this total.[14] The corresponding role of the public sector in other advanced societies ranges from 40% (Canada) to 63% (Sweden).[15] There are regrettably no comparable estimates for the Soviet Union.

Advanced societies are also characterized by a growth in the proportion of the population that is able to influence political decisions. The question of how social strata, classes, or interest groups and their changing relations should be defined and interpreted is one of continuing controversy. Most forms of interest representation that influence the formation of public policy are organizational in character, defining organizations broadly to include bureaucracies, legislatures, and political parties, as well as voluntary associations, interest groups, educational, religious, and other social institutions, business and research enterprises, and other corporate bodies.

The role of individuals in policy formation should be viewed in a predominantly organizational context. It is not a question of contrasting individual and organizational participation, since individuals are the only participants in policymaking whether they act alone or through organizations. It is a question rather of making the relevant distinctions between the influence of individuals acting alone and through organizations. The forms taken by political participation depend on the political culture and ideology of a society. In democratic societies, interest representation by organizations interacts with autonomous forms of individual participation, especially the election of representatives to legislative bodies on the basis of universal suffrage under conditions in which freedom of speech, press, and association are guaranteed. In authoritarian societies, interests are represented predominantly through organizations, and individuals exert influence only as members of organizations.

The extent to which organizations may foster or obstruct equity in the representation of interests in advanced societies varies with the nature of the organization and the political culture of the society in which it operates. More often than not, organizations tend to reflect the interests of elites or of selected sectors of a society at the expense of the general interest. Corporate forms of organization such as those currently gaining influence in Western Europe tend in particular to provide a privileged status for selected interests. For this reason, there is greater social equity in democratic than in authoritarian societies. At the same time, members of a society whose interests have been poorly represented during the period of societal transformation more often than not find that the best way to redress their grievances is by organizing. The effectiveness of organizations in representing interests also depends on the extent to which organizations are structured in such a way as to provide an equitable representation of the concerns of its members.[16]

Bureaucratic politics may be considered as a special case of organizational participation and is a form of interest representation by elements of a bureaucracy and their leaders in the intragovernmental decision-making procedures by virtue of the information and administrative skills that they command. In the broadest sense, these decisions involve allocations of resources and responsibility. In most governments, such decisions are taken at least once a year at a general level when national budgets are drawn up and usually more frequently as decisions on specific issues are made. These decisions may affect the size or even the existence of a bureau or department; the influence, programs, and the political future of leading officials; and indirectly the fate of powerful private interests affected by government decisions (e.g., taxpayers, farmers, the armament industry).[17]

How can one assess political participation in the Soviet Union in the context of this general characterization based on the Western experience? One may start by noting that the Soviet administrative vocabulary includes such terms as *interested organizations, interested institutions*, and *interested individuals*. These terms refer to organizations, institutions, and individuals that are represented on the collegial bodies that play an important role at all levels of the Soviet government. Some collegia are decision-making bodies, ranging from the presidium of the Council of Ministers to local executive committees, which are responsible for policy in the areas under their jurisdiction. Others are advisory bodies attached to executive offices, whose role is to monitor the activities of the relevant policy area. In both cases, the role of the collegial bodies is to represent the varied interests relating to a given branch of the administrative system, and the members of these collegia have explicit rights regarding the determination of the agenda of their meetings.[18]

It is not easy to distinguish in the Soviet system between the bureaucracy strictly speaking, together with the interrelated bureaucracy of the Communist party, and the considerable range of institutions that may have sufficient autonomy to be considered as corporatist organizations. Soviet society, like others that are relatively advanced, is made up of a considerable range of organizations with varying strengths and degrees of autonomy that seek to play a role in the mobilization and allocation of skills and resources. The role of these corporatist organizations in the political system is mediated by the Communist party agencies, which are concerned with representing these organizations in dealing with the central authorities as well as with the implementation of the directives that issue from the center. There is a considerable literature documenting the range and nature of this interest group activity as a feature of Soviet politics.[19]

Recent studies of Soviet decision making in such areas as agriculture, education, economic reform, and civil–military relations give evidence of extensive public debates among representatives of the relevant interests. No doubt the degree of autonomy of these organized interests varies considerably, and it is a matter of controversy as to how many of them share the characteristics of the corporatist organizations in Western Europe. The Academy of Sciences is perhaps the best example of a public organization possessing a strong bargaining power with the central authorities. Another type of autonomous organization is the

All-Russian Society for the Preservation of Monuments of History and Culture, which has extensive responsibilities in the realm of its special interest and is supported by the dues from its over 10 million members. Coalitions are formed both among autonomous organizations and between them and branches of the party and the bureaucracy, and the role of the central authorities appears to be as much one of forming a consensus out of conflicting views as of dictating policy.[20] There is also evidence that in the case of some controversial issues, such as environmental policy, ad hoc groups of interested individuals may play a significant role. Similarly, individual specialists can participate actively in decision making when they are called in as consultants.[21]

In evaluating the scope of organizational participation in the Soviet Union, it is important to distinguish between the procedures for selecting leaders and the range of organized interests that make an input into policy. The monopoly of political power exercised by the Communist party and the single-candidate electoral system under conditions of severely restricted civil liberties stand out in sharp contrast to democratic multiparty parliamentary systems. There are at the same time significant similarities between the two systems in the extent of organizational participation in policymaking, and these similarities provide an important basis for comparing Soviet politics with that in other political systems.

Economic Aspects. The change from development to distribution involves a basic structural transformation of the economy in the course of which investments and labor force, along with numerous other concurrent trends, are shifted from producer to consumer goods and from manufacturing to services.

Employment of the economically active population is usually classified as primary (agriculture, hunting, fishing, forestry), secondary (mining and quarrying; manufacturing; electricity, gas, water; construction; transportation, storage, communication), and tertiary (wholesale and retail trade, restaurants, and hotels; financing, insurance, real estate, and business services; community, social, and personal services). In the course of societal transformation, the primary sector declines from 80% to 2–3% and the tertiary grows from some 5–60%.

Typical proportions for the three sectors in advanced societies in the 1970s are: United States—3.7,35.4,57.9; Sweden—6.1,41.5,52.4; France—10.8,42.1,47.1; Japan—12.0,41.5,46.6; United Kingdom—2.5,54.6,45.4; and the USSR—21.7,47.2,31.1. One may characterize societies as advanced that have 20% or less of the economically active population in the primary sector and 30% or more in the tertiary sector.[22] In China, by contrast, the comparable proportions were 85,6,9 in 1957 and 77,11,12 in 1975.[23]

Like other aspects of advanced modernization, this decline of the primary sector and growth of the tertiary represents an irreversible completion of trends characteristic of societal transformation.

A similar but less clearly defined and verified change takes place in income distribution. Income distribution generally becomes more equal as societies develop, but this trend is affected by social policy as well as by increases in per capita income, and the evidence is by no means clear. It has been estimated that in the course of economic growth, the share of GNP of the lowest 40% of the economically active population is U-shaped (i.e., in the early stages it declines in proportion to other shares and later rises again); and that of the top 20% is ∩-shaped (i.e., first rises proportionately and then declines). The share of the middle 40% rises from 20 to 40%.

The rapidly increasing GNP in advanced societies is allocated more to an increase in income of all groups than to redistribution. Inequality of distribution between the lowest 40%, the middle 40%, and the top 20% in advanced societies ranges from 10,36,52 (France) to 14,42,44 (Sweden) and 20,40,40 (Japan, United States, Canada, Australia, United Kingdom). The conclusion is suggested that the currently advanced societies have not yet confronted the problem of greater inequality and continue to stress equality of opportunity rather than equality of income. The promise of opportunity has taken the form of an increase in all incomes under a stable pattern of distribution. Some Marxist–Leninist countries claim greater equality of distribution than the advanced societies— 27,40,33 (Bulgaria, Czechoslovakia)—but the evidence is inconclusive.[24] No adequate comparative figures appear to be available for the Soviet Union.

Social Aspects. Similarly in the social sphere, fundamental changes characteristic of societal transformation appear to approach completion. The best example of such a trend and the most carefully studied is the demographic transition. This transition is completed when societies evolve from high fertility and high mortality before the modern era, through an extended period of high fertility and low mortality— resulting in rapid population growth—to a phase of low fertility and low mortality. The rate of natural increase per 1000 in societies that have completed the demographic transition ranges from −4.1 in the Netherlands, −2.4 in the German Democratic Republic, 0.1 in the United Kingdom, and 0.9 in Sweden, to 3.1 in France, 5.8 in the United States, 9.0 in the USSR, and 10.0 in Japan. The rate of natural increase per 1000 in societies at an earlier stage in the demographic transition ranges from 16.6 in China, 20.0 in India, to 25.0 in Turkey, 29.7 in Iran, and 40.6 in Syria.[25]

Likewise in the case of urbanization, the resettlement from countryside to cities appears to be moving in the direction of an almost entirely urbanized society. The percentage of the population in cities of over 100,000 in advanced societies in the 1970s ranged from 29 (Italy) and 36 (USSR) to 58 (Japan) and 72 (United States). The percentage for less-developed countries ranges from 3 (Tanzania) to 10 (India).[26]

As regards the structure of consumption, in advanced societies the share of expenditures devoted to food and clothing tends to decline in comparison with expenditures for durable goods and services. In the 1970s, the share of consumption devoted to food and clothing was 27% in the United States, 35% in West Germany, 37% in the United Kingdom, and 40% in France, but it was 64.7% in the USSR.[27]

In the realm of health, the USSR has had a record until recently of mortality and life expectancy comparable to that of the Western countries and Japan. It is unique among developed countries, however, in the rise of its death rate in the 1970s. This rise has been particularly high among infants and males aged 20–44. At the end of the 1970s, infant mortality was estimated at 39% as compared with 12.9% in the United States. In the ages 20–44, the level of male deaths was 3 to 3.5 times that of females in the same age group. These trends have led to a decline in life expectancy at birth since 1964 of 5 years for males and 2 for females. In this period, the gap between life expectancy for males and females has grown from 4 to 11.6 years. This rise in mortality is due to a variety of causes, among which a decline in health care and a rise in alcoholism loom large. Better reporting is also responsible in part for the higher rates of infant mortality.[28]

How Advanced Is the Soviet Union?

It is no easy task to compare societies at a given level of development, and on the basis of the foregoing discussion, only a partial answer can be given to the question addressed in this section.

So far as the production and distribution of knowledge is concerned, the Soviet Union is not surpassed by many countries, and the share of GNP allocated to research and development in the Soviet Union is among the highest. In the realm of basic research in the natural sciences, American scientists are inclined to regard their Soviet counterparts as among the most competitive in many areas. In terms of enrollments in higher education per 1000 population, the Soviet Union ranks among the top 10 or 15 countries.

It is an awesome task to evaluate levels of political development, but several statements can be made with some assurance. In terms of the "output" of the political system, the Soviet Union has as specialized and developed a bureaucracy as one could wish. Since we are equating modernity with complexity rather than with progress, one should doubtless accord the Soviet Union a high ranking in the sphere of bureaucratic development.

Comparisons of "inputs" into political systems—the extent to which individuals and groups participate in decision making—depend a great deal on one's point of view. If one uses progress toward democracy as the measure, the Soviet Union as a one-party authoritarian system ranks of course very low. If one evaluates polities in terms of the extent to which organized interests are consulted in decision making, the Soviet Union ranks much higher. The task of the staff of the Central Committee is not only to transmit orders to the multitude of organizations and enterprises that make up Soviet society but also to receive and aggregate their demands. There is much evidence of debate and formation of coalitions among organized interests in their efforts to influence the allocation of skills and resources. Ranking is not possible in this sphere, but in this respect, the differences between authoritarian and democratic political systems are much narrower than is normally assumed in the West.

Comparisons become easier in the economic sphere, where the statistics give at least an appearance of accuracy, and here the Soviet record presents a mixed picture. The course of economic growth as reflected in the shift in the employment of the labor force from agriculture to manufacturing and services has been relatively slow, and the proportion of the labor force in nonagricultural employment is lower by a considerable margin than that of the United States, Sweden, France, Japan, or the United Kingdom. Similarly, in GNP per capita—not discussed in the preceding section—the Soviet Union ranked only thirty-first in 1975 among 131 countries for which information was available.[29]

The information regarding income distribution is most inconclusive. While income distribution tends to become more equal as societies develop, the idiosyncrasies of definition and allocation vary so much among societies that a clear pattern is difficult to discern. In view of the continuing emphasis in the Soviet Union on investment for growth rather than distribution, one is inclined to suspect that income distribution is less equal than in other countries at the same level of economic development.

The indicators of social change are somewhat more serviceable than those relating to the economy, since human beings rather than abstract concepts are being measured, and the Soviet Union comes out rather well in this sphere. The share of the population in cities over 100,000 is above that of Italy and Sweden but considerably below that of Japan and the United States. In the trend of the demographic transition toward low birth and death rates, the Soviet Union ranks between Japan and the United States although behind many West European countries. At the same time, in the late 1970s, there was a significant decline in life expectancy at birth, especially among males, and a marked increase in mortality among infants and among males aged 20–44.

Efforts to aggregate a wide range of economic and social indicators are fraught with problems, but a recent attempt to elaborate an index of development provides a further perspective on the extent to which the USSR may be considered to be advanced. This estimate ranks 43 countries independent since 1869 at 5-year intervals on the basis of an index that aggregates 10 variables. The variables are (1) urbanization per capita, (2) revenue and expenditure per capita, (3) imports and exports per capita, (4) rail mileage per square mile, (5) mail per capita, (6) telephones per capita (since 1889), (7) percentage of work force in agriculture, (8) steel production per capita (since 1930), (9) cement production per capita, and (10) GNP per capita. The fourth variable would seem to place Russia/USSR at a disadvantage due to its vast territory and unevenly distributed population. Apart from this qualification and the caution with which all indicators should be approached, this seems to be a fair basis for comparison. On the basis of this index the USSR is ranked seventeenth in 1973, sixteenth in 1963, seventeenth in 1953, twentieth in 1937, and thirty-fifth in 1927; while the Russian empire ranked twenty-seventh in 1911, twenty-fifth in 1901, thirty-second in 1891, and twenty-fourth in 1871.[30]

In conclusion, insofar as a clear pattern of an "advanced" society can be discerned, the Soviet Union appears to qualify for ranking among the top 20 societies of the world. Whether or not it is "advanced" depends on where one wishes to draw the line in this ranking. Due to distortions in the Soviet development resulting from policies directed toward rapid economic growth with particular emphasis on producer goods and armaments, its pattern of development differs somewhat from that of other advanced societies. Since all aspects of development are in the long run interrelated, however, these differences are in degree rather than in kind.

Notes

[1]Recent general treatments of "developed socialism" include *Razvitoi sotsialisticheskoe obshchestvo: Sushchnost, kriterii zrelosti, kritika revizionistskikh kontseptsii*, 2nd ed. (1975); "Razvitoi sotsialisticheskoe obshchestvo," in *Nauchnyi kommunizm: slovar*, A. M. Rumiantsev, ed. (1975), pp. 285–289 (It is interesting to note that there is no article on this subject in the 1969 edition of this handbook); Pyotr Fedoseyev, "Developed Socialism: Theoretical Problems," *Social Sciences* (Moscow), 8 (Summer 1977), pp. 8–23; Iu. A. Tikhomirov, *Mekhanizm upravleniia v razvitom sotsialisticheskom obshchestve* (1978); Ts. A. Stepanian and A. S. Frish, eds., *Razvitoi sotsializm i aktualnye problemy nauchnogo kommunizma* (1979); and Erik P. Hoffmann and Robbin F. Laird, *The Politics of Economic Modernization in the Soviet Union* (1982).

[2]These paragraphs draw on the author's "Changing Mutual Social Science Perceptions: The U.S. and the U.S.S.R. and Eastern Europe," *A Balance Sheet for East-West Exchanges* (1980), pp. 9–36. An authoritative Soviet account of the NTR is D. M. Gvishiani and S. R. Mikulinskii, "Nauchno–tekhnicheskaia revoliut-siia," *Bolshaia sovetskaia entsiklopediia*, 3rd ed., vol. 17 (1974), pp. 341–343. For a general introduction, see Julian M. Cooper, "The Scientific and Technological Revolution in Soviet Theory," *Technology and Communist Culture*, ed. by Frederic J. Fleron, Jr. (1977), pp. 146–179; and N. V. Markov, *Nauchno–tekhnicheskaia revoliutsiia: Analiz, perspektivy, posledstviia* (1973).

[3]See the statement of this proposition cited in A. I. Paskov, "Observations Concerning the Social Sciences in the USSR," *Social Sciences in the USSR*, 2 (1965).

[4]Cited in Gvishiani and Mikulinskii, "Nauchno–tekhnicheskaia revoliutsiia," p. 341, from Marx's *Grundrisse der Kritik der politischen Ökonomie*, published for the first time in 1939, in Marx and Engels, *Sochineniia*, 2nd ed., vol. 46, pt. 2, p. 208.

[5]*Twenty-fourth Congress of the Communist Party of the Soviet Union, March 30–April 9, 1971* (1971), p. 69, emphasis in original.

[6]Erik P. Hoffmann, "Soviet Views of the 'Scientific–Technological Revolution,'" *World Politics* 30 (July 1978), pp. 615–644, reviews some of the principal Soviet treatises on this subject.

[7]V. G. Afanasyev, *The Scientific and Technological Revolution–Its Impact on Management and Education* (1975); Robert F. Miller, "The Scientific–Technical Revolution and the Soviet Administrative Debate," *The Dynamics of Soviet Politics*, ed. by Paul Cocks, Robert V. Daniels, and Nancy Whittier Heer (1976), pp. 137–155; D. M. Gvishiani, S. R. Mikulinskii, and S. A. Kugel, eds., *The Scientific Intelligentsia in the USSR: Structure and Dynamics of Personnel* (1976); Paul Cocks, "Rethinking the Organizational Weapon: The Soviet System in a Systems Age," *World Politics* 32 (January 1980), pp. 228–257; and Boris Milner, "Application of Scientific Methods to Management in the Soviet Union," *Academy of Management Review* 2 (October 1977), pp. 554–560.

[8]Seymour E. Goodman, "Soviet Computing and Technology Transfer: An Overview," *World Politics* 31 (July 1979), pp. 539–570.

[9]Daniel Bell, *The Coming of Post-Industrial Society* (1973), esp. pp. 3–45.

[10]National Science Board, *Science Indicators 1980* (Washington, D.C.: National Science Foundation, 1981), p. 210.

[11]C. L. Taylor and D. A. Jodice, *World Handbook of Political and Social Indicators*, 3rd ed., 2 vols. (New Haven: Yale University Press, 1983), I, pp. 166–167. The ratio for higher education in China is for 1978, computed from the June 27, 1979 communique of the P.R.C. State Statistical Bureau.

[12]Fritz Machlup, *The Production and Distribution of Knowledge in the United States* (1962), chaps. 9 and 10.

[13]Fritz Machlup, *Knowledge: Its Creation, Distribution, and Economic Significance*, vol. 1 (1980), pp. xxvi–xxvii.

[14]Edward R. Fried *et al.*, *Setting National Priorities* (1973), pp. 8–9.

[15]Bank for International Settlements, *Fifty-first Annual Report* (June 1981), p. 24.

[16]Cyril E. Black and John P. Burke, "Organizational Participation and Public Policy," *World Politics* 35 (April 1983), pp. 393–425.

[17]Mark V. Nadel and Francis E. Rourke, "Bureaucracies," *Handbook of Political*

Science, 8 vols. (1975), 5, pp. 373–429; and Graham T. Allison and Morton H. Halperin, "Bureaucratic Politics: A Paradigm and Some Policy Implications," in *Theory and Policy in International Relations*, ed. R. Tanter and R. H. Ullman (1971), pp. 40–79.

[18]Ellen Jones, "Committee Decision Making in the Soviet Union," *World Politics* 36 (January 1984), pp. 165–188.

[19]The best general treatments of interest group participation in the Soviet Union are H. Gordon Skilling and Franklyn Griffiths, eds., *Interest Groups in Soviet Politics* (Princeton: Princeton University Press, 1971); Tatjana Kirstein, *Die Konsultation von "Aussenstehenden" durch den Partei und Staatsapparat sowie den Obersten Sowjet der UdSSR als stabilisierender Faktor des sowjetischen Herrschaftssystems* (Berlin: Harrassowitz, 1972); Boris Meissner and George Brunner, eds., *Gruppeninteressen und Entscheidungsprozess in der Sowjetunion* (Cologne: Wissenschaft und Politik, 1975); Gerd Meyer, *Bürokratischer Sozialismus: Eine Analyse des sowjetischen Herrschaftsystems* (Stuttgart: Frommann-Holzboog, 1977); and Jerry F. Hough and Merle Fainsod, *How the Soviet Union Is Governed* (Cambridge: Harvard University Press, 1979), pp. 518–555.

[20]Representative studies include Sidney Ploss, *Conflict and Decision Making in Soviet Russia: A Case Study of Agricultural Policy, 1953–1963* (Princeton: Princeton University Press, 1965); Joel J. Schwartz and William R. Keech, "Group Influence and the Policy Process in the Soviet Union," *American Political Science Review* 62 (September 1968), pp. 840–851; Philip H. Stewart, "Soviet Interest Groups and the Policy Process: The Repeal of Production Education," *World Politics* 22 (October 1969), pp. 29–50; Abraham Katz, *The Politics of Economic Reform in the Soviet Union* (New York: Praeger, 1972); Theodore H. Friedgut, "Interest Groups in Soviet Policy Making: The MTS Reform," *Soviet Studies* 28 (October 1976), pp. 524–527; Edward L. Warner, III, *The Military in Contemporary Soviet Politics: An Institutional Analysis* (New York: Praeger, 1977); Timothy J. Colton, *Commissars, Commanders, and Civilian Authority: The Structure of Soviet Military Politics* (Cambridge: Harvard University Press, 1979); Erik P. Hoffmann and Robbin F. Laird, *The Politics of Economic Modernization in the Soviet Union* (Ithaca: Cornell University Press, 1982); and Dennis Ross, "Coalition Maintenance in the Soviet Union," *World Politics* 32 (January 1980), pp. 258–280. For a critique of this approach, see William E. Odom, "A Dissenting View on the Group Approach to Soviet Politics," *World Politics* 29 (July 1976), pp. 542–567.

[21]Donald R. Kelley, "Environmental Policy Making in the USSR: The Role of Industrial and Environmental Interest Groups," *Soviet Studies* 28 (October 1976), pp. 570–589; Richard B. Remnek, *Soviet Scholars and Foreign Policy: A Case Study in Soviet Policy Toward India* (Durham, N.C.: Duke University Press, 1975); and Peter H. Solomon, Jr., *Soviet Criminologists and Criminal Policy: Specialists in Policy Making* (New York: Columbia University Press, 1978).

[22]International Labour Office, *Year Book of Labour Statistics, 1977* (1977), pp. 52–167.

[23]Thomas G. Rawski, *Economic Growth and Employment in China* (1979), pp. 37–39.

[24]Hollis Chenery et al., *Redistribution with Growth* (1974), pp. 27–30.

[25]United Nations, *Statistical Yearbook 1977* (1978), pp. 80–85.

[26]Taylor and Jodice, *World Handbook*, I, pp. 200–202.

[27]Gertrude E. Schroeder and Imogene Edwards, *Consumption in the USSR: An*

International Comparison (Washington, D.C.: U.S. Congress, Joint Economic Committee, 1981), p. 23.

[28]Murray Feshbach, "The Soviet Union: Population Trends and Dilemmas," *Population Bulletin* 37 (August 1982), pp. 30–36.

[29]Taylor and Jodice, *World Handbook*, I, p. 110.

[30]Arthur S. Banks, "An Index of Socio-Economic Development, 1869–1975," *Journal of Politics* 43 (May 1981), pp. 390–411, and especially pp. 402–407. An evaluation for the 1960s in Cyril E. Black, "Soviet Society: A Comparative View," in *Prospects for Soviet Society*, ed. Allen Kassof (1968), pp. 14–53, reached a similar conclusion.

31

ROBBIN F. LAIRD
ERIK P. HOFFMANN

The Competition between Soviet Conservatives and Modernizers: Domestic and International Aspects*

Soviet political leaders and social theorists clearly recognize that portentous scientific and technical changes have taken place since World War II and are continuing rapidly worldwide. Foremost among these developments are remarkable scientific discoveries of new sources of energy and materials and technological innovations in transportation, telecommunications, information processing, manufacturing, agriculture, weaponry, consumer goods, and many other fields. Also, Soviet analysts contend that the social structure of an industrializing nation undergoes transformations. For example, urbanization and the growth of a highly educated technical and managerial strata are thought to be having multifaceted consequences in all types of societies. Furthermore, Soviet commentators maintain that the relations among socialist, capitalist, and Third World countries are changing continuously. For example, the specialization and concentration of industrial production are perceived to be creating an international division of labor that is restructuring the world economy and hence is reshaping world politics.

Soviet officials and theorists affirm that such changes are being decisively influenced by the contemporary "scientific–technological revolution" (STR) and by the political and social contexts in which it unfolds.[1] Soviet spokesmen argue that the STR is a global phenomenon

*Reprinted in revised form by permission of the authors and publishers from *The Politics of Economic Modernization in the Soviet Union* (Ithaca, N.Y.: Cornell University Press, 1982), pp. 15–17, 74–81, 176–189, 195, 208–209: copyright 1982 by Cornell University Press; and from *"The Scientific–Technological Revolution" and Soviet Foreign Policy* (Elmsford, N.Y.: Pergamon Press, 1982), pp. x and 181: copyright 1982 by Pergamon Press.

that shapes and is shaped by the distinctive values and behavior of various peoples. That is, scientific–technical and industrial development are thought to be profoundly affecting—and to be profoundly affected by—the political elites and citizens of different nations, the socioeconomic relationships within nations, and the balance of power among nations.

Significantly, Stalin's successors have linked domestic modernization—especially economic growth and productivity—with improved East–West and North–South relations as the global STR takes its course. First under Nikita Khrushchev in the late 1950s, and especially under Leonid Brezhnev in the early 1970s, Soviet leaders have viewed the STR and the internationalization of economic life as "objective" forces that can and must strengthen ties between socialist and nonsocialist systems. Many Soviet policymakers and administrators have argued that the domestic development of the USSR is increasingly dependent upon contributing to and benefiting from the world division of labor. Hence, foreign economic relations are perceived to play a major role in meeting what Brezhnev has identified as the central challenge of the current epoch: *"organically to combine the achievements of the scientific–technological revolution with the advantages of the socialist economic system,* and to develop more broadly our own, inherently socialist, forms of combining science with production."[2]

Soviet analysts see a negative challenge as well. Western nations—some more than others—remain serious military, ideological, and economic rivals. Even the most ardent Soviet proponents of detente emphasize that there are important "limits" to East–West ties. These limits include: the divergent forms of property ownership in communist and capitalist states; the superpowers' perceived need to modernize their military capabilities; Soviet concern that the USSR's growing foreign economic activities could produce excessive dependencies or undue exposure to the instability of the world economy; and the increasing significance of the East–West geopolitical and ideological struggle in the context of the internationalization of economic relations.

The tension between international economic, technological, and scientific *cooperation,* on the one hand, and the multifaceted *conflict* among socialist and capitalist states, on the other, is having a major impact on Soviet thinking about economic progress. Should the USSR pursue a strategy of development that emphasizes foreign trade with industrialized capitalist countries; tighter integration of the Comecon economies and expanded commercial ties with Third World nations; or relatively autarkic patterns of development? Leading Soviet officials in the post-Stalin era have offered a variety of answers to this question. Consequently, the preconditions of economic development are an important political issue. The potential for change and the changes already unleashed by industrialization and urbanization in the USSR lend further support to Soviet arguments that new institutional relationships and new models of development are needed.

Six Needed Changes

In our judgment, and in the judgment of many Western and Soviet analysts as well, there are at least six basic dimensions of transition associated with the contemporary modernization process in the USSR.

First, *there is the need to participate in the worldwide STR.* The advanced forms of scientific and technological development and the increased significance of science and technology for economic growth and productivity are highly correlated with the expansion of the USSR's foreign economic ties. New forms of economic interdependence, however, conflict with the Soviet legacy of insularity. Hence, modernization depends heavily upon the modification of the traditional autarkic nature of the Soviet system. Certain types of interdependence may well be a prerequisite for Soviet economic development, especially economic competitiveness vis-à-vis the highly industrialized Western nations.

Second, *there is the need for increased participation by specialists in decision making,* which conflicts with the Soviet tradition of highly centralized leadership. Historically, the power to initiate and to adjust policies has been concentrated at the pinnacle of the Communist party or in the hands of Stalin, a personal dictator from the mid-1930s to his death in 1953. "Democratic centralism" in theory has meant autocratic or oligarchic centralism in practice.

One of the Soviet polity's oldest and most important sources of legitimacy is the claim that its leaders possess a special understanding of the socioeconomic "laws" of development. The knowledge to act and the power and responsibility to carry out decisions are to be conjoined in a purposeful and disciplined party leadership. But this claim to rule on the basis of knowledge and this relationship between the "conscious" party leaders and the "spontaneous" masses are seriously undermined by advanced modernization, with its increasingly well-educated knowledge elites and its complex and interconnected problems and decisions.

Technical and managerial elites in the USSR have been increasingly involved in the implementation of decisions. Nevertheless, more and better expert participation is necessary to reassess, readjust, and, if necessary, reformulate decisions *after* they have been made. Only by viewing decision making as an ongoing and systemic process can national, regional, and local leaders obtain the information needed to interpret the multifaceted consequences of past policies and to conceptualize and choose among alternative courses of action in the future.

Third, *there is the need to shift from extensive to intensive factors of economic growth,* a transition that is blocked by the centralized planning and management characteristic of the Stalinist industrialization model.

Soviet economic reformers and Western commentators underscore the importance of intensive factors of development. Among the most salient aspects of this new growth model are:

1. A shift from labor-intensive to technology-intensive industries
2. The rise in importance of science-based industrial complexes for economic growth
3. The increased significance of the world economy for domestic economic growth and productivity
4. The development of new administrative skills
5. Broader use of knowledge elites and new technology in comprehensive economic and social planning
6. Greater incentives for managerial initiatives throughout the economy
7. A change from the command-style of planning to optimal planning systems and to a more optimally functioning economy

Fourth, *there is the need to manage an increasingly structurally differentiated society,* a trend that is sharply at odds with the Soviet Union's long-standing official emphasis on ideological homogeneity and on equal socioeconomic opportunities for all citizens. Greater social differentiation makes it necessary for the party to manage a growing number of diverse perceived needs and interests. The CPSU must confront the emerging differences among social groups and must reconcile them from the perspective of the basic long-range interests and developmental capabilities of the society as a whole.

G. Kh. Shakhnazarov, in a lucid and authoritative study of "socialist democracy," elaborates:

> The fact that the basic interests of all social groups and social cells of socialist society are common to all of them does not exclude the existence of specific group and personal interests. . . . Various strata or groups existing within the framework of the actual classes . . . may be more or less clearly defined and highly vocal or only "make themselves heard" occasionally, but they cannot be ignored. . . . A situation may well occur where strata within the same class differ more from one another than strata belonging to different classes.[3]

Significantly, Shakhnazarov declares that the "nonantagonistic contradictions" generated by different interests "may on occasion become *extremely sharp* unless prompt and sensible steps are taken to resolve them." He adds:

Such adjustment is naturally not automatic and requires a carefully devised social policy based on scientific analyses of all the social processes under way, taking into account not only national and class interests but also the specific interests of all sections of society. Thus, it is a question, first of determining what social interests there are and, second, of harmonizing them. *Both of these tasks are exceptionally difficult.*[4]

Fifth, *there is a need to meet consumer needs more effectively,* a need that contradicts the traditional priorities of the Soviet economic system—for example, the long-standing emphasis on heavy industry and deferred personal gratification. Today, if labor productivity is to be increased, there must be more and better consumer goods available to reward hard work. In a society committed to full employment and lacking a clear and overriding sense of national purpose, why should one work energetically and innovatively if there are few attractive consumer goods to purchase with the wages and bonuses one may earn? The shift from extensive to intensive factors of development means that human labor must become more skilled and more efficient *and* that there be greater material, as well as psychological, rewards to develop such new skills and efficiency. As one Western analyst puts it:

> The relative mood of the Soviet consumer is not inconsequential to the leadership. If the Soviet worker cannot see a potential for improving his lot, he will not respond with alacrity to increased incentives at the farm or factory. Yet a substantial boost in labor productivity is essential if the economy's sliding growth rates are to be reversed.[5]

Sixth, *there is a need to develop a modern information system,* a need that is at odds with the traditional instrumental use of the Soviet media. The communication and information systems of the USSR were built to express and to create unity during the industrialization of a relatively primitive society. But, in a developed socialist society, unity is not generated or sustained merely by molding new industrial laborers. Rather, conflict and differences of opinion among an increasingly well-educated and differentiated labor force must be articulated and aggregated. The central leadership's use of the media to control society conflicts with the need for the media to provide a forum for the expression of different opinions and interests and to provide information for decision making and management.

V. G. Afanas'ev, the editor-in-chief of *Pravda* and a prominent social theorist, states:

> The means of mass communication play an important role in introducing and solving the most important economic, sociopolitical, scientific–technical, and ideological problems. . . . [The media under contemporary conditions] do not simply record events . . . but actually intervene in events, guiding developments in conformity with the social interest.[6]

The legitimacy of such a role for the media is underscored by the growing significance of specialization in decision making. The number of bureaucratic, professional, and social groups advocating their interests increases in direct proportion to the stages and levels of decision making and to the range and interconnections among specific "problem situations" that have arisen. Moreover, official policy emerges from organizational conflict and cooperation. Soviet elites use the press to mobilize support for desired policies in many issue areas. In their efforts to redefine and resolve problems, Soviet officials continuously debate the efficiency, effectiveness, and sometimes the wisdom of policy through public, as well as private, communication channels.

Old and New
Models of
Development

The six needed changes identified above can be reduced to four highly significant *tensions* in the transition from the Stalinist to a post-Stalinist model of development. First, there is a tension between autarky and interdependence. Second, there is a tension between an autocratic system of decision making and management and an authoritarian system that is capable of decentralizing decisions of secondary importance and of utilizing the knowledge and skills of well-trained specialized elites at all stages and levels of decision making and administration. Third, there is a tension between a command planning system and a flexible planning system that is responsive to domestic and foreign market forces. Fourth, there is a tension between national priorities that emphasize military and heavy industrial development and priorities that seek to balance military and overall economic development, utilizing recent scientific discoveries and advanced technologies in both the military and civilian sectors.

Each of these tensions highlights a conflict between the old and the new models of Soviet development (see chart that follows below).

The conflict between "conservatives" and "modernizers" in the contemporary USSR is a conflict between defenders of the traditional industrialization model and advocates of an advanced modernization model. This conflict has political, ideological, economic, military, and

Soviet industrialization model	Soviet advanced modernization model
Autarky	Selective interdependencies with the global community
Autocratic centralism	Authoritarian centralism, with high degrees of participation by specialized elites in decision making and administration
Command planning	Optimal planning; optimally functioning systems that are responsive to market forces
Military and heavy industrial priorities	Balance between military and overall economic development; science-based high technology for military and civilian industries

scientific–technological dimensions, and professionals from all of these fields participate in the competition. Soviet "economic modernizers" are those economists, ministerial officials, and production executives who support all or most of the elements of an advanced modernization model for the USSR, especially in the predominantly economic sphere.

Soviet economic modernizers maintain that the present state of the USSR's economy, and especially its shortcomings, provide abundant reasons to justify change. Economic growth and productivity are measurable, and economic competition and cooperation with the West invite macro- and microeconomic comparisons between socialist and capitalist economies. Indeed, one cannot overemphasize the extent to which Soviet economic performance provides an objective basis for the emergence, growth, and political significance of various economic modernization tendencies.

The economic modernization tendency can be subdivided into "conservative," "liberal," and "radical" tendencies.

For the conservative modernizer, the concern is to improve the functioning of the Soviet economy through the introduction of new techniques, such as mathematical economic methods; new technologies, such as computerization and automatic control systems; new organizational and legal practices, such as the clear stipulation of rights and responsibilities; new planning methods, such as optimal planning; and new incentives, such as centrally prescribed "success criteria" that reward quality workmanship and productivity. The conservative modernizer wants to increase the involvement of the USSR in the global economy by perfecting centralized planning, decision making, and management in the foreign trade sphere. Conservative modernizers stress the need to streamline but not to weaken the dominant role of *Gosplan* (the State Planning Committee) and the Ministry of Foreign Trade in international economic activities.

For the liberal modernizer, the critical objective is to alter the operative mechanisms of the Soviet economy so that the economy becomes capable of continuous and "self-generated" innovation. Liberal modernizers are concerned with structural decentralization, the establishment of a more adequate pricing system, the broad-scale introduction of managerial incentives, and the creation of an optimally functioning economy capable of comprehensive and effective long-range economic and social planning. Liberal modernizers want to increase the involvement of the USSR in the global economy by decentralizing planning, decision making, and management in the foreign trade sphere. Liberal modernizers emphasize the need to empower individual production and industrial associations and enterprises to participate directly in foreign trade, relatively independent of centralized control.

Radical modernizers stress the importance of market forces, domestic and international, and the liabilities of centralized economic planning and management, especially in pricing and distributing goods and services and in spurring technological innovation. Radical modernizers advocate the establishment of an economic system akin to NEP's, with a "socialist market," a reduced role for Gosplan and the Ministry of Foreign Trade, and the abandonment—in theory and practice—of "the state monopoly of foreign trade."

In short, Soviet political leaders and policy analysts in the post-Stalin era have developed a variety of perspectives on the modernization of the USSR and on the role that East–West relations play in that process. A classic expression of the conservative Soviet orientation emphasizes the autarkic elements of the traditional Soviet industrialization model.

> Can our country do without scientific and technical cooperation with the United States? Of course it can. And successfully! It is enough to mention the most complex contemporary scientific and technical spheres—the development of nuclear, space, and laser technology in the USSR was done without any help whatever from the United States or any other countries of the world.

An equally classic statement of the Soviet modernizers' view provides a striking contrast.

Exchanges in the sphere of science and technology and the further development of international trade would undoubtedly promote the acceleration of scientific and technical progress throughout the world, an increase in employment, and economic progress. . . . With cooperative effort, the United States could obtain the types of raw materials, semimanufactured products, and finished goods it needs from the USSR by supplying the USSR with equipment for the extraction and manufacture of these types of production, and the USSR could prepare and accelerate the assimilation of new economic regions and raw material resources, including those needed by the United States. . . . [The importation of] foreign experience and technical capability on a reciprocal basis, on the basis of long-term agreements [would also promote] *the strengthening of trust and the growth of economic incentive for the preservation of peace.* Long-term agreements would give these changes a stable instead of a chance character.[7]

The tension or conflict between the Soviet conservative and modernizing orientations is illuminated by the fact that these contrasting statements were made by the president of the USSR Academy of Sciences, A. P. Aleksandrov, in the very same interview in 1976.

Modernizers versus Conservatives in the 1980s

The Soviet political leadership of the 1980s must express and respond to a multiplicity of domestic interests, deal with countless international opportunities, dilemmas, pressures, and contingencies, and make some very difficult choices.[8] On major internal and external policy issues, Soviet conservatives and modernizers advocate different courses of action. Moreover, since specialized elites are playing a greater role in the formulation and administration of policy, the competition between traditional and reformist orientations will continue for the foreseeable future and, under circumstances such as a protracted succession struggle or an economic crisis, will probably intensify. This scenario is made even more likely by the growing impact of international developments upon domestic priorities. Moreover, a recent U.S. Congressional Research Service study concludes:

Elements of a new constituency whose power is knowledge and expertise have taken shape outside the strict formal confines of the party. Within the party itself, as well as in the government, the criterion has been shifting from one of strict political professionalism to the professionalism of the specialist in science, technology, and in the running of a complex national economy.[9]

Soviet economic modernizers, as we have seen, call for substantial changes in planning and management. Modernizers have increasingly viewed the highly centralized Soviet planning and managerial systems as a source of weakness and a barrier to their country's emergence as an economic superpower. In contrast, they have stressed that American economic and administrative capabilities are vital to the exercise of American influence in international politics.

Soviet economic modernizers view greater involvement in the world economy and more know-how from the West as elements critical to the transformation of the USSR into a global economic power. Modernizers underscore the feasibility of incorporating American technical and managerial innovations into the Soviet economy, in order to compensate for Soviet weaknesses. Modernizers take quite seriously the Western economic challenge to the USSR, and they are anxious about the technological level of Soviet industry and about the continuing—and, in some fields, increasing—differences in the quality and marketability of Soviet and Western products and processes. These gaps are attributed in large part to the competitive pressures of the global STR and to the need for more effective Soviet responses to these opportunities and problems.

Soviet economic modernizers stress the growing importance of economic capabilities in the contemporary international system. Soviet military might can be transformed into influence in some areas of the world, they acknowledge, but the USSR must broaden and deepen foreign economic ties in order to maximize the influence at the nation's disposal.

Economic modernizers favor competitive coexistence with the West as part of a strategy of enhancing technological innovation within the Soviet economy. Modernizers look to technology trade with the West as part of an ongoing process of technological development, not as a one-time infusion of advanced technology to revive Soviet economic performance. One Western analyst observes: "The traditional Stalinist strategy is yielding to a new policy of technological interdependence with the West. The new policy implies an acceptance of the need continuously to import technology, in order to maintain the pace of technological progress which exists in the rest of the industrial world."[10]

Soviet policymakers and economic modernizers have not reached a consensus concerning the priority of technological exchange with the United States. In the early 1970s, the Brezhnev collective leadership, despite differences among the top leaders, emphasized the technological preeminence of the United States. But by the mid-1970s there was an increasing division of opinion about whether the USSR should pursue a United States- or a Europe-oriented strategy or a more balanced program of technology trade with the United States, Western Europe, and Japan.[11] One impact of the American economic boycott of the USSR after the occupation of Afghanistan was to strengthen the hand of those conservative and other modernizers who favor economic ties primarily with Western Europe, regardless of the possible advantages of trade with the United States.[12]

During this same period, Soviet leaders began to pay greater attention to the instability of the world economy. Because the USSR was hurt by the recession in the mid-1970s, Soviet officials and analysts became much more cognizant of the advantages of insulating the USSR's economy from oil embargoes and other disturbances on international markets. To be sure, the USSR benefited considerably from the inflated prices of oil and gold in the late 1970s, but the disadvantages of fluctuating world prices and markets, to say nothing of the political vagaries of East–West trade, were of increasing concern to the Brezhnev administration. In a word, the optimism that characterized Soviet modernizers in the early 1970s was tempered by a more conservative assessment of the costs and benefits of extensive participation in an unstable and unpredictable global economy.

Some of the modernizers who have been the most vocal advocates of East–West trade have been closely associated with Soviet–East European trade. Eastern Europe's favorable experience in commercial dealings with Western Europe has encouraged Soviet economic modernizers to think that the USSR can have similar dealings, thereby maintaining or enhancing Soviet national security and Soviet economic competitiveness vis-à-vis their own allies. Hence, East European trade with the West reinforces Soviet modernizers' proclivities toward interdependence rather than autarky.

The disruptions associated with the American economic boycott of the USSR and Poland in the early 1980s strengthened the hand of Soviet conservatives who have opposed East–West cooperation in general and trade with the United States in particular. Also, the boycotts—and perhaps especially the United States' inability to induce other major Western powers (e.g., West Germany) to follow its lead in imposing substantial economic sanctions on the USSR and Poland—fortified the position of Soviet modernizers who have advocated close ties with Western Europe as the chief component of the USSR's technology trade policy.

Moreover, there is an ongoing conflict between Soviet modernizers and conservatives over the primacy of military expenditures and the preconditions for economic modernization.[13] The command style of planning is closely tied to the perceived need to provide the defense sector with its priorities at any, or all, costs. Movement away from the legitimacy of the command style of planning carries with it a shift in emphasis to a broader set of priorities and a recognition of interests other than those of the military–industrial complex. These changes are resisted per se by traditionalist military elites, because such changes imply that there is an objective limit to the level of their needs.[14] This conflict has two critical dimensions.

First, a few Soviet modernizers have publicly raised the delicate question of the inadequacy of technological "spin-offs" from military to nonmilitary sectors. For example, V. G. Afanas'ev states:

> Frequently it is in military agencies that the newest scientific developments and technical and technological innovations are first applied. They are then classified, and this is quite natural. However, innovations age quickly and it is therefore important to declassify them in time and to channel them into the economy. This provides an important source for increasing the rate of the progress of science and technology in civilian sectors.[15]

The spin-off issue is not just a narrow technical problem but involves significant questions regarding the allocation of resources between the military and civilian sectors. Because the military sector is largely isolated from the civilian sector, any effort to increase the linkages between the two is a pressure to increase the nonmilitary payoff from military expenditures. In other words, Soviet modernizers are pressing to have military expenditures justified in part by their contribution to the civilian economy, not just by their contribution to the military's national defense priorities and programs.

Second, greater Soviet involvement in the world economy carries with it the need to increase the level of specialization of the domestic economy, which in turn supports the modernizers' contention that the USSR's industries must become competitive in exporting manufactured goods. At the Twenty-Fifth CPSU Congress in 1976, Kosygin called for the development of a special sector of export-oriented production. "Since foreign trade has become a major branch of the national economy, the problem arises of setting up a number of export-oriented industries to meet the specific requirements of foreign markets."[16] This appeal is highly significant, because it is based on the idea of creating a sector of the economy that would compete with the military for high technology resources. As John Hardt and George Holliday comment, "Such attention to the requirements of the export market might be a step toward establishing export branches of Soviet industry that might even rival the Ministry of Defense as a claimant for high quality inputs."[17] But even more significant than Kosygin's proposal is the fact that there has been virtually no public discussion of the idea since, let alone implementation of the idea.

There are other important trade-offs between military and economic approaches to the strengthening of Soviet national security. For example, the search for and extraction of raw materials can proceed either by the economic development of Siberia, aided by an infusion of Western and Japanese capital and technology (a modernizing strategy), or by military intervention in the critical raw material areas of the Third World (a conservative strategy).[18] These approaches are clearly at odds with one another, because, to the extent that the second strategy is pursued, the first strategy will almost surely be undermined.

Also, the recovery and utilization of raw materials from the oceans must be founded upon a strategy of economic interdependence.[19] To the extent that the United States–Soviet naval rivalry goes unchecked, the development of the ocean's abundant resources becomes exceedingly difficult. Underwater mining operations are extremely vulnerable to military threat or sabotage, for instance. Without military stabilization, economic investments will not flow to and natural resources will not flow from the vast untapped reaches of the world's oceans.

Furthermore, the industrialization of outer space, which many serious Western and Soviet analysts deem to be critical within the next two decades, is considerably undercut by the absence of comprehensive Soviet–American space treaties. Space platforms, for example, are highly vulnerable to military attack, and without effective controls on the arms race in outer space, industrialization will not proceed at the pace that advanced technology has made possible.[20]

Briefly stated, Soviet modernizers forcefully advocate the strengthening of the economic as well as the military capabilities of the USSR. Modernizers contend that greater East–West commercial ties and collaborative development of land-based, oceanic, and nonterrestrial resources would be highly beneficial to the USSR. Modernizers' perceptions of Soviet national security interests differ considerably from those of Soviet conservatives, who continue to emphasize the preeminence of military power and the advantages of self-sufficient economic development.

Even more succinctly put, Soviet spokesmen view East–West relations as a dynamic mix of conflict and cooperation and of centrifugal and centripetal tendencies. But conservatives emphasize East–West conflict and West–West cooperation; modernizers emphasize East–West cooperation and West–West conflict; and both conservatives and modernizers emphasize the competitive aspects of cooperation as well as of conflict.

Conclusion

The ongoing competition between Soviet conservatives and modernizers has enormous domestic and international political implications. Economic and social change far outstripped political change in the last decade of the Brezhnev administration. But Soviet attitudes evolved much more than Soviet institutions. The considerable attitudinal adjustments among the Soviet

bureaucratic elites, technical specialists, and citizenry, and the mounting external and internal pressures for change, *could* significantly alter
traditional Soviet institutional relationships and patterns of political and
organizational behavior. The chief obstacle to modernization, however,
is the distinct possibility that economic reforms would substantially
reduce the powers and privileges of the uppermost echelons of the
Communist party and undermine the predominant role of the party in
Soviet society. As an editor of *The Wall Street Journal* puts it, "Since the
party cannot admit that the system that serves its members so well
serves everyone else so badly, it continues to offer the same old excuses
for failures."[21]

Yet the STR and its socioeconomic consequences pose a serious
challenge to the Soviet political system. Politically influential *Soviet*
critics of the Soviet economy are questioning both its structure and
performance. Furthermore, in the increasingly multipolar world of the
1980s, the components, distribution, uses, and effectiveness of political
resources are not easily or objectively discernible. Political leaders'
perceptions of national challenges and of the linkages between domestic
and foreign policy are becoming more and more salient elements of
international relations. The perspectives of the Soviet bureaucratic and
technical elites have become important factors in world politics. Hence,
Soviet policy groups' contrasting and changing assessments of the
needs, capabilities, and vulnerabilities of their country and others and of
the evolving structure and functioning of the international system must
be analyzed closely for eminently practical reasons.[22]

Because of Brezhnev's death and the imminent transfer of power to a
new generation of party leaders, competing Soviet views on policy and
policymaking are likely to play an especially important role in the
politics of the USSR in the near future. Brezhnev worked diligently to
establish stable and effective decision-making procedures, but an even
more important part of his legacy may be his legitimation of politicized
theoretical and practical discourse about the guidance and management
of an industrialized socialist society in a domestic and international
environment characterized by complex interdependence and by increasing uncertainties and scarcities.

Like the distinctive policy processes under Lenin, Stalin, and Khrushchev, Brezhnev's broadening and deepening of elite participation in
policymaking are having an impact on his successors' views of power
and authority and on future Soviet strategies for socioeconomic modernization and East–West relations. But the nature, magnitude, and
duration of Brezhnev's influence are difficult to gauge. The evolving
perspectives of the increasingly well-educated Soviet bureaucratic elites
and citizenry, intertwined with the struggle for position and influence
after Brezhnev's demise, with some hard choices between real policy
alternatives, and with the serious need for organizational rationalization

posed by the STR, could stimulate a policy dispute over fundamental issues comparable to "the great industrialization debate" of the 1920s. And from this highly politicized and fluid environment could emerge significant changes of either a conservative or modernizing nature in the basic policies and policy-making procedures of the Soviet polity.

Notes

[1] For elaboration of these and related themes, see Erik P. Hoffmann and Robbin F. Laird, *The Politics of Economic Modernization in the Soviet Union* (Ithaca, N.Y.: Cornell University Press, 1982); Erik P. Hoffmann and Robbin F. Laird, *"The Scientific–Technological Revolution" and Soviet Foreign Policy* (Elmsford, N.Y.: Pergamon Press, 1982); and Erik P. Hoffmann and Robbin F. Laird, *In Quest of Progress: Soviet Perspectives on Politics, Society, and Technology under Brezhnev* (forthcoming).

[2] From Brezhnev's address to the Twenty-Fourth Party Congress in 1971, in *Materialy XXIV s'ezda KPSS* (Moscow: Politizdat, 1971), p. 57 (emphasis in original).

[3] G. Kh. Shakhnazarov, *Sotsialisticheskaia demokratiia: nekotorye voprosy teorii*, 2nd ed. (Moscow: Politizdat, 1974), pp. 56–57.

[4] *Ibid.*, p. 68 (emphasis added).

[5] M. Elizabeth Denton, "Soviet Consumer Policy: Trends and Prospects," in *Soviet Economy in a Time of Change*, Vol. 2 (Washington, D.C.: U.S. Government Printing Office, 1979), p. 760.

[6] V. G. Afanas'ev, *Sotsial'naia informatsiia i upravlenie obshchestvom* (Moscow: Politizdat, 1975), p. 383.

[7] A. P. Aleksandrov, interview in *Literaturnaia gazeta*, 18 February 1976; translated in *Daily Report: Soviet Union* (Washington: FBIS, 17 February 1976), pp. A5–A6 (emphasis added).

[8] See, for example, Seweryn Bialer, *Stalin's Successors: Leadership, Stability, and Change in the Soviet Union* (New York: Cambridge University Press, 1980); Jerry Hough, *Soviet Leadership in Transition* (Washington, D.C.: The Brookings Institution, 1980).

[9] *Soviet Diplomacy and Negotiating Behavior: Emerging New Context for U.S. Diplomacy* (Washington, D.C.: U.S. Government Printing Office, 1979), p. 526.

[10] George Holliday, *Technology Transfer to the USSR, 1928–1937 and 1966–1975* (Boulder, Colo.: Westview, 1979), p. 184.

[11] See Rensselaer Lee, *Soviet Perceptions of Western Technology* (Bethesda, Md.: Mathtech, Inc., 1978); and Bruce Parrott, *Soviet Technological Progress and Western Technology Transfer to the USSR: An Analysis of Soviet Attitudes* (Washington, D.C.: U.S. Department of State, 1978).

[12] For a Soviet reaction, see V. F. Petrovskii, "Material'nyi potentsial vo vneshnepoliticheskoi doktrine SShA," *SShA*, 1 (1980), pp. 10–21.

[13] See, for example, Hoffmann and Laird, *"The Scientific–Technological Revolution" and Soviet Foreign Policy*, chapter 4; and Joseph Berliner, "Economic Prospects," in *The Soviet Union: Looking to the 1980s*, ed. Robert Wesson (Stanford: Hoover Institution Press, 1980), pp. 89–110.

[14]For two Western discussions of this theme, see John Hardt, "The Military–Economic Implications of Soviet Regional Policy," in NATO Directorate of Economic Affairs, ed., *Regional Development in the USSR: Trends and Prospects* (Newtonville, Mass.: Oriental Research Partners, 1979), pp. 235–250; and Daniel Gallik, "The Military Burden and Arms Control," in *The Future of the Soviet Economy: 1978–1985,* ed. Holland Hunter (Boulder, Colo.: Westview, 1978), pp. 133–141.

[15]Afanas'ev, *Sotsial'naia informatsiia,* p. 198.

[16]*XXV Congress of the CPSU: Documents and Resolutions* (Moscow: Novosti, 1976), p. 142.

[17]John Hardt and George Holliday, "Technology Transfer and Change in the Soviet Economic System," in *Issues in East–West Commercial Relations* (Washington, D.C.: U.S. Government Printing Office, 1979), p. 86.

[18]On strategies for the development of Siberia, see, for example, Theodore Shabad, "Siberia and the Soviet Far East," in NATO Directorate, ed., *Regional Development in the USSR,* pp. 141–160.

[19]See, for example, P. G. Bunich, *Ekonomika mirnovogo okeana* (Moscow: Nauka, 1977).

[20]See, for example, V. A. Skachkov, *Kosmos i problemy mirovoi ekonomiki* (Moscow: Mezhdunarodnye otnosheniia, 1978); and A. D. Ursul, *Chelovechestvo, zemlia, vselennaia* (Moscow: Mysl', 1977).

[21]George Melloan, "Soviet Productivity Unwinds," *The Wall Street Journal,* 10 July 1981, p. 26.

[22]For diverse Western interpretations, see Erik P. Hoffmann and Frederic J. Fleron, Jr., eds., *The Conduct of Soviet Foreign Policy,* 2nd ed. (Elmsford, N.Y.: Aldine Publishing Co., 1980).

32

SEWERYN BIALER

The Harsh Decade:
*Soviet Policies in the 1980s**

The Brezhnev era is coming to an end. In all probability, the Twenty-Sixth Party Congress (February–March 1981) will prove to have been the last one at which Leonid Il'ich and his aged cronies successfully defended their positions of power. Of course, memories of similar predictions made after the Twenty-Fifth Party Congress alert us to the need for caution in anticipating the current leadership's departure. Yet we base our expectations of the approaching end of the Brezhnev era not only on the passing of the Brezhnev generation, which must ultimately occur. Equally significant is the rapid changing of the domestic and international conditions and circumstances that have shaped the character of the past decade and a half. Thus, even if Brezhnev and his contemporaries were to remain in power for another year or two, dramatic alterations of the international and internal environment of the Soviet Union from the time when Brezhnev was at the height of his rule will profoundly influence the perceptions, behavior, and policies of the Soviet regime. While the Twenty-Sixth Party Congress showed some recognition of the changing international and domestic environment, its attempts to grapple with the resulting issues and problems have been minimal. The CPSU cannot enjoy this luxury much longer.

The Brezhnev era, particularly from 1965 to approximately 1976, will probably go down in history as the most successful period of Soviet international and domestic development. Internationally, it was a period when the Soviet Union fulfilled its major postwar dream: to achieve strategic parity with the United States and become a truly global power. Soviet rule over its empire was legitimized internationally, and the

*Reprinted by permission of the author and publisher from *Foreign Affairs* 59, no. 5 (Summer, 1981), pp. 999–1020. Copyright 1981 by Council on Foreign Relations, Inc.

so-called Brezhnev Doctrine—implying the right and obligation of the Soviet Union to intervene in any communist state to maintain the communist system intact—was developed to secure continuation of that empire by any means. Although the Soviet Union was unable to regulate its relations with the other communist giant, China was torn by cataclysmic internal strife, and Soviet leaders were able to deploy strategic tactical and conventional forces on their eastern border, thus changing the military geography of the area and ensuring against any surprises from the Chinese side.

It was a period when the Soviets increased their influence in the international arena and, at the same time, witnessed the economic and political decline of their chief adversary, the United States. The Soviet Union was able to translate its newly won power and recognition into a new relationship with the Western alliance (particularly the United States), which was called détente and which constituted a promising cornerstone of Soviet long-range strategy. Détente promised economic benefits and, most important, an expansion of Soviet global influence without the danger of confrontation with the United States and its allies. It also promised a further swing in the balance of global influence and power in favor of the Soviet Union.

Domestically, it was a period of great stability of leadership and politics in the Soviet Union, when a system based on elite accommodation, compromise, and bargaining fostered a tranquil political climate. The Soviet leadership dealt successfully with unprecedented dissent movements among the intelligentsia and assured a relatively high degree of political and social stability in the country. On the economic front, for the first time in its history, the Soviet leadership was able to pursue successfully and simultaneously a policy of guns and butter as well as growth. It was a period when the Soviet regime was able to avoid any significant degree of systemic crisis within its social and political system.

During the mid-1970s, however, these domestic and international trends were reversed. By the end of the decade, the previously favorable situation had begun to unravel. The Twenty-Sixth Party Congress convened in a new situation marked by the clear short- and medium-range potential for dangerous and unfavorable developments. The new situation illustrated the adage coined by a European statesman in the interwar period: "Russia is never as strong as she looks, Russia is never as weak as she looks." Today, Soviet developments are riddled with paradox. The Soviet Union exhibits both strengths and weaknesses, assets and liabilities:

- Today, more powerful than ever, the Soviet Union is nonetheless more insecure than it has been during the last 10–15 years. It faces a more assertive United States, as well as a potential alliance between China and the West, and a change in the trend of the balance of military spending which places in jeopardy its attainment of parity. This curious mixture of power and insecurity places a special imprint on Soviet foreign policy and international behavior.

• The Soviet Union has become a global power, feared by friend and foe alike. Its model of rule and development, however, is increasingly considered irrelevant by both Marxists and non-Marxists, and the Soviet socioeconomic and political system is held in greater contempt than ever.

• If Soviet expansion has reached a temporary peak, Soviet leaders see in Poland, their own imperial backyard, the greatest challenge of their postwar history as a national Polish revolution threatens to undermine the centralist Leninist state. The Soviet Union retains control over an extensive internal and external empire in which its political and military dominance is still strongly pronounced. Yet it has ceased to draw economic benefits from that empire and must even support it economically. A curious situation has developed in which the East European standard of living is and will continue to be higher than that in the Soviet Union and in which the Uzbek peasant lives far better than his Russian counterpart. The economic viability of the East European empire, moreover, depends to a large extent on economic help from an interchange with Western adversaries of the Soviet Union.

• Soviet foreign policy in the Brezhnev era has realized significant gains in international influence and major achievements in global expansion. At the same time, however, the Soviet Union has suffered major failures and significant reverses, most notably in the Middle East, where it lost its pivotal influence in Egypt. Such an ambiguous balance of gains and losses leaves the Soviets not only with undiminished appetites but also with a sense of deep frustration.

• During the 1960s and 1970s, the Soviet Union built its foreign policy on the cornerstone of competitive accommodation with the West, particularly the United States. But as it enters the 1980s, this cornerstone has begun to erode. The Soviet Union faces a situation marked not by competitive accommodation but rather by the greatest challenge to its global ambitions of the last 20 years. If the Soviet Union expanded in the 1970s through low-risk and low-cost adventures without a major danger of confrontation with the United States, the risks and costs of expansion in the 1980s will be much higher and the danger of confronting the United States significantly greater. In the 1980s, there is likely to be no Soviet expansion without confrontation.

• During the past 2 decades, the Soviet Union experienced the finest economic, political, and social period in its history. Growth rates remained high; accommodation and compromise defined relations among the elites; mass terror disappeared; the population enjoyed the most rapid growth ever in its standard of living. But in the 1980s, the Soviet Union may well pass through the worst period it has seen since the death of Stalin. Growth rates will be the lowest ever; factionalism and tension will probably disrupt relations among the elites; more coercive policies may return; and the population can expect a stagnating or even declining standard of living. The very stability of the social system may be in question.

The Twenty-Sixth Party Congress convened, then, in a context shaped by these paradoxes. The Soviet Union enters the 1980s at least partly conscious of such paradoxes and the resulting dilemmas. It lacks, however, any long-range vision regarding the means to resolve them.

On what major premises was Soviet foreign policy of the 1970s constructed? First, that détente with the United States would remain irreversible despite zigzags in American policy, and that America's pre-Vietnam assertiveness could not be restored. It was further assumed that Soviet competition with the United States would remain controlled and elements of cooperation retained, given the pressures of the changing military balance, the inward-directed mood of American public opinion, and the demands from America's European allies, particularly West Germany.

Second, that the tilt toward the Soviet Union in the military balance, established in the 1970s, would continue. The Soviets expected that while the West might attempt to make adjustments in the military balance, there would be no new effort by the United States to regain strategic superiority, and that attempts to redress significantly the European theater balance would be successfully resisted by America's allies.

Third, that the Soviet Union would be able to translate its newly won military status into power and influence in those areas of the world that are outside of the great powers' recognized spheres of influence, without risking confrontation with the United States or its allies.

Fourth, that the Soviet Union would continue to exploit targets of opportunity presented by the turmoil in the less developed countries. No area of the world was viewed as being outside the possible spread of its influence.

Fifth, that the basic balance in Europe would be frozen on both sides and that, while no major changes in Soviet influence in Western Europe could be expected, no major dangers to the stability of the East European empire would develop.

Sixth, that the Soviet Union would be able to carry indefinitely the burden of both its expanding role as a global power and its empire without inducing severe economic constraints at home, without violating the existing economic system of planning and management, and without endangering the social and political stability of its home base and empire.

Seventh, that Soviet expansionist policies and the quest for global influence would preclude neither the expansion of economic cooperation with the West nor the influx of advanced foreign technology and credits to the Soviet Eastern bloc and the Soviet homeland itself.

Today, the Soviet Union faces a United States that has for the most part left behind its post-Vietnam and post-Watergate doubts and uncertainties. It faces a new Administration whose policies toward the Soviet Union and the world may constitute a major departure from those of its predecessors in assertiveness in the international arena and willingness to steer a collision course with the Soviet Union where vital interests are concerned. Change in the direction of the balance of military power from that which prevailed in the 1970s is very probable, and the Soviet Union may even be compelled to undertake a new large-scale arms race with the West at a time when it can ill afford the necessary increased expenditures. Meanwhile, it confronts a China which is no longer pursuing a self-destructive course of permanent revolution but is concentrating on modernization and the pursuit of virtual alliance with the United States, Japan, and NATO. These problems are complicated by a situation in Afghanistan that is more troublesome than the leadership expected. Even more dangerous is the situation in Poland, the pivotal country in the Soviet empire, a situation with incalculable implications for the future of both the Soviet empire and the Soviet Union itself, regardless of what course of action the leadership adopts.

The shape of Soviet politics and policies changes very slowly. One must always count on the built-in tendency of the Soviet political system to retain the characteristics and directions typical of the 1970s. Yet in the 1980s, the Soviet Union will be facing issues and events which may make for incremental changes—conceivably even fundamental changes, though this seems less likely—in the nature of politics and the direction of policies. We have discussed some of the foreign policy issues that face Soviet policymakers in the 1980s. We will now discuss some of the key domestic issues.

Perhaps no more portentous problems will exist for Soviet leaders in this decade than those that concern the economy. The impact of these problems on the political system and on the relationship of that system with the society will be extremely significant, probably greater than was the case in the 1970s.

1. In the 1980s, the Soviet Union will face a secular decline in the growth rates of its economy in almost all sectors. It can no longer sustain the high growth rates of the past that were based on the established

practice of injecting ever-larger quantities of investment capital and labor resources into the economy (i.e., a policy of extensive growth). Even without other negative factors and assuming no decline in the quality of the traditional Soviet leadership of the economy, the growth of the Soviet gross national product (GNP) in the 1980s will only be approximately 2.5% per year.

2. The Soviet economic–political system of management, pricing, and incentives is ill prepared to maximize the possibilities for growth from increased productivity of both capital and labor (i.e., intensive growth). The conditions for a relatively rapid change to such intensive growth would require fundamental changes in the economic–political system, changes which are unlikely to be accomplished in the foreseeable future. Among the steps already undertaken by the Soviet government to counteract the trend of declining growth, none will have any major impact on the Soviet economy.

3. The Soviet Union in the 1980s will also face unfavorable demographic trends, such as the very rapid projected decline in the availability of new labor resources. The situation will be further complicated by changes in the composition of the new labor force, which will be overwhelmingly non-Russian.

4. The Soviet Union will face an energy balance that will affect its economic growth unfavorably, particularly with regard to oil. Although the CIA no longer estimates that the USSR will be a net oil importer by the mid-1980s and other economists dispute the extent of the projected decline, they agree that Soviet oil production will decline. Even if one rejects the worst-case scenarios, which predict oil production capacity at 8 million barrels a day, the decrease will be sufficient, it seems, to impose major constraints on the Soviet economy and to limit the Soviets' ability to utilize fully their existing economic capacities.

5. The enormous agricultural investments of the Brezhnev era have produced limited and at best uncertain results. Soviet agriculture in the 1980s will remain a highly volatile sector of the Soviet economy. Moreover, because of the decline in long-term growth in other sectors, the unavoidable agricultural fluctuations will have increasing influence on the size of the Soviet GNP.

There can be little doubt that the Soviet Union will face a difficult economic situation in the 1980s. How difficult it will be is a matter of conjecture. According to the worst-case scenarios, it will be a period of low growth combined with economic stagnation. But even according to the more optimistic scenarios, the Soviet Union will face an economic crunch far more severe than anything it encountered in the 1960s and 1970s.

I must reiterate that the differences between the optimistic and pessimistic scenarios are a matter of great importance; they signify the difference between a difficult situation and a deep crisis. Moreover, choosing the most likely scenario does not depend on a belief in more or less precise and complex computations (or, for a political scientist, on his faith in the skills of one or another group of economic forecasters). It must take into account unpredictable elements, such as vagaries of nature or, equally important, the severity and the effectiveness of the policies adopted by the Soviet leadership to counteract adverse trends. Even assuming that the more optimistic scenario better reflects the reality of the 1980s, what will be the effects of the growing economic difficulties on the Soviet political scene? (Needless to say, those effects will be magnified many times if one of the worst-case scenarios becomes a reality.) The two most important consequences will be a sharply intensified competition for scarce resources among sectors and an equally intense competition among regions.

Historically, the Soviet political system, in both its micro- and its macroeconomic decision-making levels, has been used to scarcities, shortages, and stringencies; dealing with such problems has been its normal modus operandi. Yet it must be remembered that these scarcities, shortages, and stringencies have gone hand in hand with a process of highly uneven development, a concomitant of rapid overall economic growth. Moreover, during the time of extreme stringencies and particularly sharp one-sided development, the system was guarded by a mass terror apparatus introduced by Stalin and dismantled by his successors. In the post-Stalin period, the Soviet economy grew at about 6% a year. Relatively high rates of growth, while still sustaining an uneven development, assured the flow of new resources to all sectors of the economy, including those totally neglected during the Stalin era. While accustomed to scarcities, shortages, and stringencies, the Soviet political system is not accustomed to dealing with prolonged periods of low overall economic growth.

With regard to the question of how to stimulate higher growth rates and how to overcome critical bottlenecks, the Soviet system is ill prepared to deal with these problems for exactly the same reason that growth has decreased: the decline in the effectiveness—or the exhaustion—of the extensive factors of growth. Its past experience in responding to economic difficulties was based on a mass mobilization of capital and labor—a policy of the hammer-blow, not the scalpel.

On the distributive side of the equation, the Soviet political system, on both the mass and the elite levels, will have difficulty in dealing with prolonged low overall rates of growth. This difficulty arises from three sources: (1) the absence of a paralyzing mass terror that would make all sacrifices and demands palatable; (2) the existence of powerful organizational and pressure groups in the decision-making apparatus, complicating the implementation of cutbacks and restraints; and (3) the emergence of new social constraints against such cutbacks.

The sharply increased sectoral competition for resources and the dilemmas that it will create are not difficult to envisage. The policy of guns, butter, and growth that was the political cornerstone of the Brezhnev era is no longer possible. To maintain the rate of growth in military spending at the level of the last decade (around 4%) would necessitate a redirection of resources from other sectors. Yet a number of factors—past Soviet behavior; growing insecurity in the presence of what is perceived as the formation of an alliance of the United States, NATO, and China, creating a new specter of encirclement; the growing determination of the United States to change the existing balance of military power; and finally the breakdown of SALT talks—make it highly unlikely that any configuration of Soviet leaders will decide to slow down the growth in military expenditures, let alone cut actual arms spending, without either a major breakthrough in arms talks or a major disavowal of Soviet global ambitions. If arms spending continues at the same pace as in the past decade, the burden of keeping the Soviet military juggernaut in shape will be felt to a much greater extent than at any time in the Brezhnev era. It will constitute one of the key contentious issues of internal politics.

Another contentious issue, with an even greater potential for divisiveness, concerns the entire complex of questions connected with the rate of growth and the direction of Soviet nonmilitary investment resources. Throughout their history, the Soviets have persisted in holding the share of investment in the national economy and the levels of investment growth very high. How difficult it is to maintain such high rates of investment under the present circumstances is demonstrated by their recent decline. Yet if ever there was a period when the Soviet Union needed substantial large-scale investment in the national economy, it is now. It is difficult to envisage how the Soviet leadership can reduce the difficulties brought about by the limitations of the existing pattern of extensive growth without keeping the percentage of investment in the economy, and even the growth rate of investments, at high levels.

Intensive growth, given Soviet conditions, requires a thorough modernization of the industrial plant and major investments in new technology. Without a very substantial, persistent, and creditable effort in this direction, there is little chance that any increased productivity of Soviet labor will overcome the downward pull of the exhaustion of the extensive factors of growth.

The energy problem facing the Soviets in the 1980s will demand mammoth and prolonged investments, beyond those that have already begun to be made. The development of the Siberian oil and gas reserves

will constitute a new, major—and increasing—burden on Soviet investment resources. Yet it is a burden that the Soviets cannot avoid and can
neglect only at their own peril.

The achievements of Soviet agriculture under Brezhnev—the growth
in grain production and especially the stress on meat production—were
accomplished by an extraordinarily large expenditure of capital. Yet
even with these large-scale expenditures, Soviet agricultural productivity has varied from year to year, and the agricultural sector continues to
be highly volatile. The Soviets have not yet devised a way to assure even
the present inadequate levels of agricultural production without in-
fusions of long-range massive investments. In the coming decade, when
the Soviet economy slows down, the divisive pull of conflicting claims
concerning investment resources will increase to a level unknown
during the Brezhnev era.

One of the most significant accomplishments of the Brezhnev era was
the prolonged and substantial growth of Soviet mass consumption. The
last 15 years have seen a growth in the standard of living of the Soviet
people that was rapid by any—but especially by the Soviet—measure,
particularly in the area of durable consumer goods. Especially notable in
this achievement was the fact that it occurred simultaneously with the
rapid growth of Soviet military power. In other words, the Brezhnev
leadership pursued fully both a guns *and* butter policy. The stability of
the Brezhnev period in the absence of terror can be explained to a large
degree by the leadership's basic ability to satisfy more fully the demands
of the Soviet consumer. The Soviet citizen—worker, peasant, and
professional—has become accustomed in the Brezhnev period to an
uninterrupted upward trend in his well-being and more demanding in
what he expects from the government in terms of goods and services. In
view of the major claims on Soviet resources by other sectors in a period
of declining growth, it will be extremely difficult for the Soviet leadership to continue its policy of consumption growth, even at the lower
rates of the most recent 5-year Plan announced in February, 1981.

It is probable that even without major agricultural disasters or a
particularly severe energy crisis, Soviet consumption may stagnate in
the 1980s. The consequences of such stagnation are difficult to assess,
but they will undeniably be negative. In the first place, it is difficult to
see how the crucial goal of spurring Soviet productivity can be attained
without an increase in wages and other incentives for the labor force.
Second, the stagnation of the standard of living will be felt by the
working population at a time when the other basic avenue of betterment, upward mobility, will also show a downward tendency because
of a relative decline in expenditures on the educational system. Third
and most important, neither the Soviet leaders nor we know how the
Soviet industrial working class will react to such changing circum-

stances. The post-Stalin experience of a society without terror was at the same time the experience of a society with a steadily rising standard of living.

The desire of the Soviet population for a better life has never to our knowledge become unmanageable, has never assumed the form of a revolution or a vicious spiral of rising expectations. The key to Soviet systemic stability was the leadership's successful management of the population's expectations. Yet one should not forget that it was a "management of expectations" that went hand in hand with a sometimes rapidly and steadily growing rate of consumption. This growth in consumption may have been a substitute for, and a damper on, growing political expectations.

To what extent the existing police controls and the management of mass expectations can keep the Soviet working class docile during a prolonged stagnation of its living standards is an open question. One has the impression that the specter of the "Polonization" of the Soviet working class is never far from the minds of the Soviet leadership and the elites.

Of course, not only competition for resources among sectors but also competition for specific priorities within sectors will be much sharper in this decade. Specific elite constituencies represent each of these priorities in the national leadership. At the same time, however, the sharply increased competition for resources among and within sectors will be enmeshed in and complicated by a stronger, more tenacious competition for resources among the various regions of the Soviet Union. Such competition was a normal facet of Soviet politics already in the 1970s. Budgetary squabbles and fights concerning plans of development have been well documented. They are certain to increase in the 1980s.

The difficult political decisions regarding the distribution of available resources are complicated by an underlying economic dilemma: the European part of the Soviet Union has a well-developed infrastructure, and investment there would be relatively cheap and would provide a higher return. But at the same time, the European part of the Soviet Union is on the verge of exhausting new labor resources and is poor in natural resources. The Central Asian region has a limited infrastructure, especially in the technological sector. In addition, the claims of Central Asian elites for new resources would probably be fiercely contested by the dominant Slavic elites. Vast portions of Siberia where the natural resources are located offer virtually no labor resources and lack any infrastructure; investments here will be extremely expensive and difficult to manage.

Complicating the situation is the fact that the regional struggle for resources will be conducted during a period of succession in the Soviet leadership. During such periods, the influence and the political clout of provincial and republican elites traditionally increases, and the potential

for playing good politics instead of good economics is quite considerable. Regional leaders assumed the role of real king-makers during
Khrushchev's rise to power.

The first and foremost response of Soviet authorities to the difficulties
that they face—both the economic difficulties and the volatile political
situation—will be to strengthen the authoritarian character of the Soviet
party–state. The stress on law and order, social discipline, unswerving
loyalty, nationalism, and punitive and restrictive measures against
antisocial behavior may become more pronounced than it was in the
1970s. Not surprisingly, the role of the secret and not-so-secret police
may increase. When the situation becomes difficult, when no prospects
for rapid improvement are in sight, and when a tightening of the belt is
in order, the natural response of Soviet leaders—whether old or new—is
to tighten the screws of political and social control. The capacity, the
potential, and the instruments for such policies already exist.

It is an open question whether such policies will suffice to maintain
order under conditions of new and prolonged economic stringencies. In
my opinion, one may expect an increase in the restlessness of the
industrial labor force and a weakening of the basic stability of the
Brezhnev period and the compact between the elites and the workers.
After the Soviet population realizes that a prolonged decline in the
growth of its living standard is on the way, an increase in labor unrest,
work stoppages, industrial demonstrations, and growing communal
dissatisfaction are clear possibilities. The degree to which they will occur
may have an effect on the allocation policies that the government
adopts.

In the new situation, the nationality problem may also become
aggravated. This may be the case regardless of the kind of policy that the
leadership adopts vis-à-vis the non-Russian regions. The ability of the
Soviet leadership in the 1970s to contain the nationality problem was
partly related to the fact that the nationality areas enjoyed more rapid
growth than the rest of the country, especially in the standard of living
and the conditions of the rural sector. If the party should decide to slow
the growth of those regions under conditions of greater stringency of
resources, the relative peace in Soviet relations among the nationalities
will be strained.

But in this respect, the leadership's manner of responding to the
dilemma posed by the new demographic trend in the growth of Soviet
labor resources will be the most important issue on the Soviet agenda
concerning the nationality question in the 1980s. The need to exploit the
growing non-Slavic—particularly Central Asian—labor resources poses
two options for Soviet policymakers: migration of the non-Slavic labor
force to the industrial areas or a dramatic increase in the industrial
development of Central Asia. Both options carry major destabilizing
potential for nationality relations in the USSR.

In my opinion, the second option is more likely to be adopted. If this is the case, it may produce, in some Central Asian regions, the sort of major social displacement associated with rapid industrialization. It will also involve a rapid and massive influx of Russian bureaucrats into those regions, with all the attendant dissatisfactions and tensions between local, native elites and the newcomers. The non-Russian republics, including those of Central Asia, have only recently developed native administrative and technical cadres that suffice to administer their own affairs without Russian help. Under these conditions, local elites may increasingly assert their own identities and provide difficulties for the central authorities.

The economic realities of the 1980s will sharply strengthen the tendency toward a political climate markedly less benign than that of the 1970s and will contribute immensely to an environment of sharp competition, confrontation, and discord. The virulence of conflict over these economic realities will be intensified to an incalculable degree by the unavoidable onset of yet another unprecedented set of political circumstances—the conjuncture of the replacement of the top leadership and virtually the entire core elite group in the principal hierarchies. Without a doubt, the difficult economic issues will constitute the most important factor in the disputes, conflicts, and realignments that will accompany these successions.

The most important stimulus for political change in the Soviet Union in the 1980s may not be the new policy issues but rather the policy-making process itself. Such change will originate in the impending turnover of the leaders and elites, a turnover that will inject a more pronounced element of unpredictability and uncertainty into the overall Soviet political process than is characteristic of its operation in "normal" times.

The consequences for the political system are profound. The chances for deep personal and policy conflicts within the top leadership structure are increased as are the possibilities for resolving these conflicts in more extreme ways. The tendency toward large-scale personnel changes within the leadership itself and among the top elites and bureaucratic hierarchies is heightened. The period ahead offers a strong potential for destroying the bureaucratic inertia of the departed leaders and for halting the unrelieved drift of their policies. It will be a period ripe for ferment; for greater responsiveness, real and anticipated, to broadening political participation; and for opening the political process. In sum, the succession, aside from its own intrinsic importance, will act as a catalyst for pressures and tendencies that already exist within Soviet society but that previously had only limited opportunity for expression and realization.

The Twenty-Sixth Party Congress was the first one in Soviet history at which no changes in the upper echelons of the leadership took place.

This Congress made abundantly clear that the destabilizing effects of the inevitable succession may be even stronger than had been envisaged. By failing to prepare in even a rudimentary way for change at the top and directly below the top levels of the leadership, the aged Soviet oligarchs are delegitimizing their own rule and increasing the chances of a disorderly struggle for power and of the emergence of alternative policies when they leave the scene.

The approaching succession is in many respects different from those in the past and combines a number of characteristics that make it fraught with very important political implications in the 1980s, for better or for worse from the Western point of view. The most important of these characteristics is the fact that it almost inevitably will combine the replacement of the top leader with the replacement of the core leadership group and a large part of the central elite, as well as with the beginning of generational turnover among the Soviet elites. The age configuration of the Soviet leadership and elites is such that, even if the initial interim leadership comes substantially from the old generation, a massive change in personnel will be needed and will be compressed into a relatively short time span.

The fact that such a succession would have an interim character from the start may, and in all probability will, lead to the destabilization of the central policy-making system; such destabilization, in a highly centralized polity such as the Soviet Union, may have very important consequences. It will involve a breakdown of the consensus among the leadership and the elites, the intensification of factional struggles at the top and middle levels of the bureaucracy, possible realignments of existing alliances, the exploitation of policy issues for the accumulation of power by individual leaders and groups, and sharp twists and turns in central policies. Dislocations in the political arena can only be exacerbated by the nature and depth of the economic problems that the Soviet Union will face in the 1980s.

This scenario for succession is the most probable one, but we cannot exclude the possibility of another in which no interim leader emerges and the new generation replaces the old on a much more massive scale from the outset. This second scenario appears unlikely, since no leadership and elite is ever ready to liquidate itself, especially in a country like the Soviet Union, where retirement is tantamount to political death. Yet one may underestimate the degree of frustration and the extent of dissatisfaction in the Central Committee with the way things are going and with the total grip of the old generation over the affairs of state. If a revolt is brewing among the younger members of the Central Committee and if they succeed in speeding Brezhnev's succession, the push toward changes in the Soviet domestic scene and particularly toward economic experimentation and reform would be much stronger and quicker than that envisaged in the first scenario.

What characteristics will distinguish the new generation of leaders who will make their mark on the Soviet political scene during the 1980s? Given the fragmentary evidence at our disposal, we must at the outset underscore the tentativeness of this profile of the post-Stalin generation. But certainly one of the key traits of this generation is that it entered politics immediately after Stalin's death and therefore did not experience the paralyzing and destructive process of terror which continued to corrode and influence the behavior of earlier generations, despite the renunciation of mass terror as an instrument of rule. Nor does it appreciate from direct involvement—out of its own hide, so to speak— the enormous price paid for Soviet achievement.

Yet one thing seems fairly certain about this new generation. One of its crucial formative political experiences—if not the most crucial—took place during the protracted ferment and shock of Khrushchev's anti-Stalin campaign, a campaign that admitted the monstrosities no one had hitherto dared to name, a campaign that questioned authority and established truths and thereby stimulated critical thought. The post-Stalin generation's entrance into Soviet politics coincided as well with open recognition of the gross inadequacies of Soviet development and the backwardness of Soviet technology and, at the same time, with extravagant predictions of matching Western achievements in the foreseeable future, predictions that collapsed with no little embarrassment.

The new generation is clearly a Soviet generation in its typical and persistent adherence to the cult of the state. One cannot doubt the sincerity of its members' commitment to the basic forms of Soviet political organization or their belief that the system is right and proper for the Soviet Union. At the same time, one is not persuaded that they judge this system suitable or desirable for a developed Western society. If they share with their predecessors a devoted patriotism, they tend to exhibit little of their xenophobia and much less of their fear and deeply rooted suspicion of the outside world. Rather, they display a curiosity that surely reflects intense concern with the patent inadequacies in the working of the Soviet system.

Some traits of the new generation may appear contradictory. On the one hand, one detects a sense of security that contrasts with a sense of insecurity—one may say inferiority—of the old generation; yet at the same time, their attitude toward the Soviet system is defensive. If they seem to feel stronger, more self-confident, they are at the same time more conscious than their predecessors of the failures, shortcomings, and backwardness of the Soviet polity and society and less willing to overlook them. Unlike their predecessors, many of them are more ready to engage outsiders in frank and serious exchanges of opinion.

It is a generation that perceives the inability of the Brezhnev administration in recent years to lay out a direction for Soviet development. It is a generation that deplores the backwardness of Soviet society, the functional deficiencies of the system, and the inability of the present leadership to make progress in rectifying the situation. At the same time, it probably stands confident of its own ability to do so. It is a generation that is less likely to accept actual or potential international achievements as substitutes for internal development. It is a generation that may be willing to pay a higher price in terms of political and social change if it is persuaded that such a price would assure substantial improvement in the growth and efficiency of the productive and distributive processes.

Even if our portrait of the new generation of Soviet officials were less provisional and patchy, it would still be presumptuous and unwise to try to deduce from it any specific kinds of anticipated behavior. The formative political experiences to which these officials were exposed and some of the predilections which they display, and which we have tried to identify, suggest only that they might be different as a group from their predecessors in the older generation.

I should like to make one thing clear. I do not expect from the new generation of Soviet party officials the sort of reformist tendencies advanced by Dubček in Czechoslovakia. Nor do I expect them to favor the highly ideological, frantic, campaign-like reforms associated with Khrushchev. At the same time, I should not be surprised if they were reform-minded within the limits of the Soviet framework or if they were dissatisfied with the thoroughly conservative attitudes toward innovation that pervade the present Brezhnev administration.

Neither do I suggest that they will be easier to deal with in the international arena. It may well be that they will be less cautious, more prone to take risks than the present leadership, precisely because they have no first-hand experience of the costs of building Soviet might and are used to the Soviet Union's great-power status. I am in no way making a judgment here as to whether the new generation of Soviet officials is better or worse from the standpoint of our value system and our interests. I only suggest that the new generation seems to be different from the old.

The West will have to deal in the 1980s, perhaps even in the very near future, with new Soviet leaders who have limited knowledge of international relations and who will have to learn on the job. Their presence in the top Soviet leadership, the entire process of succession, and the confrontational politics that the succession and the difficult economic situation will introduce into elite politics will contribute to increased volatility in international politics and will make the uncertainty we face even more pronounced.

I have no doubt that with the new generation in positions of power, a major effort will be made by the Soviet leadership to reform the antiquated economic system that is no longer able to deal with new priorities and demands. Yet I remain skeptical whether the Soviet Union will succeed in a wholesale revamping of its economic system, even with a new generation of leaders in office. The obstacles to restructuring the Soviet system of management and planning are formidable indeed, and their cumulative effect stultifying with regard to prospects for change.

The interaction of Soviet domestic political and economic developments in the 1980s will yield a number of consequences for Soviet international behavior that might have important international repercussions.

First, clearly contradictory domestic pressures will affect Soviet military policy, especially the growth of military expenditures. On the one hand, certain pressures will work to continue expanding Soviet military might regardless of cost. As achievement in other fields declines, the military might could well become to an even greater extent the showcase of the state's success and glory. Moreover, military power will remain for a long time to come the dominant foreign policy resource of the Soviet Union. High military spending will in all likelihood be assured both by the momentum of the already planned military buildup and by the greater political weight of the military establishment as the potential ally of contending groups in periods of succession and interim leadership.

On the other hand, certain pressures will work to limit military growth and to make the leadership more willing to entertain timely and realistic Western proposals for arms limitations and reductions. As growth declines and resources become increasingly scarce, the costs of a continuing military buildup at the rates of the past decade will burden the Soviet economy and polity more greatly than at any time during the 1970s. Sectors of the leadership and elite groups competing for resources may press to cut the military budget, a decision that has been unacceptable since the early 1960s. The Soviet military–industrial complex does not enjoy the same close ties with the incoming generation of Soviet elites that bound it to elites of the Brezhnev period, for the new men have made their careers for the most part in civilian sectors.

But even if this symbiotic relationship between the political and military leadership threatens to weaken or break down, one should not doubt that a military buildup regardless of cost and sacrifice will meet any perceived danger to the basic security interests of the Soviet Union or to the hard-won parity with the West. This is why those American politicians and analysts who promote regained military superiority over the Soviet Union cannot hope to see their goal realized. Nevertheless, in the difficult and volatile political and economic environment of the 1980s, the new Soviet leaders, unlike their counterparts in the 1970s, may well refuse to accept the demands for a continuous military buildup as an automatic response, indeed almost a conditioned reflex. Of course, much will depend on the conduct of American leaders, who must steer the difficult course between the unquestionable need to safeguard American strengths and interests and the no less important need to appreciate new Soviet dilemmas and avoid belligerent actions.

A second consequence of domestic developments for international policy concerns the new economic ground for Soviet expansionism and international aggressiveness that have hitherto been rooted entirely in political and strategic impulses. Political and strategic motives will almost certainly continue to feed the Soviet quest for greater influence and power in the international arena. In terms of global interests, the Soviet Union is, after all, still a young and expanding power, fighting for its place in the sun. To this already potent challenge to the West in the next decade, however, one must add the disquieting prospect that a new economic rationale may soon join the traditional spurs to Soviet expansion.

Soviet economic and political difficulties suggest two principal motives and targets for expansion. The first and more obvious is the attempt to alleviate domestic oil deficiencies by movement in the Persian Gulf area. I do not at all suggest an inevitable Soviet invasion of Iran, for in the present circumstances, such an adventure seems almost out of the question. Circumstances do change, however, and in the long run, a Soviet effort to secure Iranian oil cannot be excluded. Much will depend on the unpredictable course of Iran's revolution, still only in its initial stages. Should irredentist pressures within Iran lead to a disintegration of the country and its central government, for example, or should leftist forces sympathetic to the Soviet Union assume an important voice in the revolution, then Soviet leaders would be tempted to intervene, their decision reinforced by their own economic and political difficulties.

Of course, Soviet foreign policy may pursue other solutions to its energy problem apart from expansion into oil-rich regions. A much more likely development may involve the negotiation of barter agreements for the purchase of oil by means of overtures to friendly Arab regimes (e.g., Iraq and Libya) and intimidation of conservative regimes (e.g., Saudi Arabia). If successful—and they might well be—such agreements would be clearly political in nature, since any civilian goods involved in the barter would not be competitive on the world market.

The second motive for Soviet expansion is less obvious but may become more important in the 1980s: the desire to secure high technology on favorable terms for the Soviet economy may tempt the Soviet Union to exercise increasing political pressure on Western Europe. The Soviets will in all probability need even more Western technology, know-how, and especially credits in the 1980s. The pattern of recent Soviet–American relations suggests scant likelihood that the United States will serve as a key partner in mutual economic enterprises. The economic role of Western Europe for the Soviet Union, on the other hand, will probably increase substantially, both as a trading partner and a source of credit. Soviet foreign policy in the 1980s will probably try to serve economic as well as political interests by decoupling the détente with the United States from that with its Western allies.

Western Europe's mood today—and it will probably remain so for the next decade—is such that, despite growing signs of Soviet expansionist ambitions, the political classes are determined to have détente with the Soviet Union at almost any price, even without meaningful Soviet concessions on military matters and without a change in the direction of the military balance in Europe itself. This seems to be particularly true for the most influential European country, West Germany. In an effort to improve economic relations with Western Europe and to split further the Western alliance, the Soviets may adopt a tactic of taking a hard position against the United States regarding strategic global military and political matters for which the Europeans have little concern, while at the same time exhibiting a concessionary attitude on European questions.

At the same time, the Soviet policy of offering carrots may not preclude a simultaneous policy of using sticks. The Soviets cannot help but notice that the European attitude toward increasing Soviet military power is rather conciliatory, and that European resistance to Soviet political pressures is weaker than ever before. In any case, one can expect political and economic pressures to be increasingly concentrated on the European theater and on compelling expanded economic relations with Western Europe.

Third, the political and economic situation of the Soviet Union may significantly affect Eastern Europe in the 1980s. While the Soviet Union remains unshakably committed to controlling its East European empire, increasingly it will be forced, owing to economic difficulties, to maintain its domination by intimidation and the threat to use force. Given the projected decline of economic muscle available to hold Eastern Europe, a situation will develop in the next decade where most East European countries will remain *politically* dependent on the Soviet Union but will become *economically* more dependent on the West.

A crucial question here is the degree to which the Soviets will have to cut oil deliveries to Eastern Europe and allow the East European nations to compete for available oil resources on the international market. Ill-prepared for such competition, the East European countries have very limited exportable resources and hard-currency reserves. Even a partial cutoff of Soviet oil deliveries could undercut the already precarious economic situation of many East European countries, particularly Poland. Serious economic difficulties in Eastern Europe have a way of translating into social and political unrest and internal destabilization, to which the Soviets are very sensitive. Until now, fortune has favored the Soviet Union in its dealings with the empire. Revolts, rebellions, unrest, and reform movements have almost always erupted in one satellite country at a time. The coming decade may well bring the coincidence of outbursts among increasingly restive elites and populations in several East European countries at the same time.

A fourth area where domestic developments might influence foreign policy relates to the extension of foreign trade, the infusion of advanced foreign technology, and the attendant questions of credits, foreign indebtedness, and cooperative arrangements. These matters will acquire an importance for the Soviet leadership surpassing even that of the 1970s. Do Soviet leaders regard the infusion of foreign technology and economic cooperation with advanced Western nations as a temporary affair or a long-term commitment? The answer cannot be given a priori, for it depends partly on Soviet ability to arrest the decline in productive growth with domestic resources—a very unlikely prospect even with major economic reforms—and partly on the reliability and cost of Western policies and cooperative arrangements.

The importance of foreign technology for the Soviet leadership goes beyond its intrinsic worth to the largely misguided belief that technological imports will diffuse throughout the economy and significantly stimulate Soviet domestic technological progress without major reforms. The need for foreign technology and know-how, and especially the much greater need for credit arrangements in the difficult decade ahead, are not sufficient or overriding factors in the determination of future Soviet foreign policy. Such needs, however, through the working of the domestic political process, will exert additional pressure to restore détente with the United States and to preserve and enlarge by means of both intimidation and concession the economic relations with American and European allies.

Fifth, foreign adventurism may prove a consequence of the struggle for the top leadership position under conditions of economic stringency and the efforts of the first victorious contender to solidify his position. Contenders for top leadership almost always advance programs on which alliances within the Politburo and among various elite groups can be built. On the road to power, such programs and alliances often prove transitory and tactical in nature. In the long term, no leader can hope to gain and hold power without formulating and implementing major solutions to the country's serious economic difficulties. At a time when few reserves are available for either long-range improvement of the economic situation or for quick and flashy economic fixes, exploitation of a timely opportunity for foreign adventure can rally allies to a leader eager to show his mettle. Such a prospect becomes all the more likely as contenders in the succession struggle compete for the support of one key group, the military establishment.

Sixth, the international climate may well be affected by increased use of coercive means to resolve domestic political and economic problems. As we have seen, in the 1980s, Soviet leaders will need to find ways to counteract the effects of a decline in growth and possible stagnation in the standard of living, to alleviate frictions that develop among elites, to justify greater demands for sacrifice, and to mobilize the population for greater productivity. In all probability, they will resort to coercion in a less restrained manner than their predecessors in the 1970s. It is even highly probable that in the political mood of the 1980s, the Soviet leaders will try to increase persuasive, normative efforts for the purpose of mobilizing the population and promoting sacrifice. One such effort might seek to recreate the atmosphere of a besieged fortress, to rally around the theme of external enemies, and to foster public xenophobia. The harsh conditions and demands that will prevail in the Soviet Union during the next decade are not conducive to the mood of détente. While the need for an "external enemies" syndrome may not prevent the restoration of some sort of détente, given the presence of countervailing pressures, I think it will be an important factor in determining Soviet international behavior, particularly in relations with the United States and China.

Each period of Soviet history and each decade of Soviet development brings before Soviet leaders new dilemmas and choices. The dilemmas and choices of the 1980s are harsher and more difficult than any faced by Soviet leaders since Stalin died. In all areas of domestic, military, and foreign policy, the Soviet Union stands at a crossroads no less significant than that at the end of the New Economic Policy in the late 1920s and at the death of Stalin in 1953. As yet, Soviet policy is moving in accordance with the legacy of inertia of the 1970s. We may expect, however, that this inertia will be interrupted in the 1980s, and that a new Soviet policy will start to emerge.

Soviet Succession:

Issues and Personalities*

Once again, Leonid Brezhnev's[†] health seems to have deteriorated, and speculation about the Soviet succession is rising. This time, however, the situation is substantially different from what it was several years ago. Two of the inner core of the Politburo, Aleksey Kosygin and Mikhail Suslov, have died, and the position of a third, Andrey Kirilenko, appears to have slipped badly. Brezhnev's long-time personal assistant, Konstantin Chernenko,[‡] has continued to gain greater status and now seems to be the number two man in the political system. Most recently, the long-time chairman of the KGB, Yuriy Andropov, has been moved into the Central Committee (CC) Secretariat and into the inner leadership core.

In a recent article in *Problems of Communism*,[1] William Hyland lamented the decline of Kremlinology in the West, and with good reason. There have been only four leaders in Soviet history (five, if one includes Georgiy Malenkov's short interregnum), and each has been associated with major changes in policy and even in the way the political system functions. The succession to Brezhnev will come at a time of critical policy choices. It will probably involve the disappearance of a historic generation from the scene. If not immediately, then over 3 or 4 years, it will almost surely produce substantial change of some kind. Yet, clues about leadership politics have been much scarcer over the last 15 years than in the past.

Despite the uncertainty of the evidence, Hyland is correct in insisting that we give attention to this important subject. This chapter assembles the bits of information that are available about the leading contenders and about the issues that will lie at the heart of the struggle for power.

*Reprinted by permission of the author and publisher from *Problems of Communism* 31, no. 5 (September–October, 1982), pp. 20–40.
[†]This chapter was prepared prior to the death of Leonid Brezhnev.
[‡]Chernenko was selected the General Secretary of the Communist Party, succeeding Yuriy Andropov in February 1984 (see pp. 873–878). Mikhail Gorbachëv was selected General Secretary in March 1985 (see pp. 879–881).

Even if events prove our current thinking wrong, our mistakes may nonetheless indicate where we have to rethink our underlying assumptions about the Soviet political system.

The Issues   Issues have always been important in Soviet successions. In the past, even if the emerging leader rose to power primarily through control of personnel selection, he was careful to identify himself with strong currents of opinion within the party. In this succession, issues will very likely be even more important. There is today no logical successor in the sense of a man of the right age and background serving as the general secretary's chief assistant for personnel selection. Indeed, since personnel turnover in recent years has been slow, it is not clear that anyone has had an opportunity to build a political machine at all. In addition, since the mid-1970s, Brezhnev has steadfastly refused to face up to a growing number of problems, and his successors will not be able to avoid them. The problems are so contentious that there are certain to be leadership differences of opinion about them, and the struggle for power in the succession will surely involve a struggle over issues as well.

The policy issues in this succession will not, however, be simple and clear-cut. Westerners often define the political struggle in the Soviet Union in terms of "reform" or "liberalization" versus "conservativism" or even "neo-Stalinism."[2] There is a strong element of truth in this view, but the situation should not be oversimplified. Issues that are important for most reformers at one time can become unimportant only a short time later. Reforms that are instituted can provide the basis for a new conservative consensus and become in turn the target of a new reform movement. Key values held by reformers (or conservatives) can come into conflict with each other and force difficult choices on specific issues. This last question is particularly crucial now, for the reforms introduced under Khrushchev and Brezhnev have become the essence of the status quo that needs to be attacked if the programs of the contemporary economic reformers are to be realized.

There are many significant issues confronting the Soviet Union. First, the Soviet Union is, of course, a multinational state, with some 20 major peoples with their own language, culture, and territorial base. In particular, the growing number of those with a Muslim background raises new problems. The question of what to do with Central Asians, which has been the center of great, and probably exaggerated, attention in the West, may not be urgent, but it must be faced sometime in the decade. Moreover, the nationality factor is never far beneath the surface on any policy question that arises—for example, the distribution of investment, demographic policy, economic decentralization, or political liberalization.

Second, a series of questions concerning political reform are on the agenda of discussion. Brezhnev has essentially continued Khrushchev's social reforms that favored workers and peasants. But he has moved away from Khrushchev's extreme antibureaucratic tendencies and populist notions of mass participation. The key phrases of the Brezhnev era have been "scientific decision making," "the administration of society," and "the scientific–technical revolution,"all of which connote the flow of influence in decision making to those with specialized knowledge—administrators, scholars, and educated people in general. As a present-day critic, Anatoliy Butenko, has expressed it, "one of the widespread prejudices is that 'power by the workers' is unrealizable and utopian, since the administration of public affairs has become extremely complex and demands deep specialized knowledge, as a result of which the time will never come when 'each cook will rule.' "[3]

Criticism of this Brezhnev policy, however muted, is not difficult to discern in the Soviet media and among Soviet officials and scholars. On the one hand, a number of leading intellectuals inside the party establishment have appealed with increasing frequency for greater democratization. Butenko has published a forceful call for workers' self-management and has suggested—without being specific—substantial changes in the representative institutions as well.[4] Fëdor Burlatskiy, head of the philosophy department of the Institute of Social Sciences of the Central Committee, has made a similar appeal, speaking out for a withering away of the state in the form of a transfer of more functions to the public organs.[5] Together with Georgiy Shakhnazarov, a deputy head of the Central Committee's Socialist Countries Department, he has also called for the establishment of political science and of a political science institute, one of whose purposes would be to work toward the improvement of the political system.[6] Shakhnazarov himself is more cautious in speaking about any withering away of the state but has advocated a democratization of the process by which candidates are nominated as well as a loosening of information policy.[7]

On the other hand, there have been indirect cautions against democratization. No one in the Soviet Union can come out publicly against further democratization. It is quite possible, however, to discuss the importance of professionalization or to hint about the need for continuing repression by speaking of the dictatorship of the proletariat in contemporary conditions.[8] Moreover, there is no reason to doubt the accuracy of Chernenko's report that "at times one hears the question—don't we have too much democracy? Doesn't it lead to a weakening of discipline?"[9]

Third, the relationship of the Soviet Union with the outside world and the level of military spending have become the subjects of intense public debate. The world situation has changed radically in recent years; military parity has been achieved with the West; the relationship with the United States has become confrontational; NATO is under severe strain; the internal changes in China since the death of Mao Zedong raise the possibility of a change in Chinese foreign policy; and the Soviet involvement in the Third World has had little payoff, and none of the major Third World countries has proved revolutionary. Major differences of opinion on how the Soviet Union should respond to each of these changes can be found in Soviet books, journals, and newspapers, and increasingly even on Soviet television.[10]

On the basic question of relations with the West, for example, Vadim Zagladin, the first deputy head of the Central Committee's International Department, has testified that there are two "extreme views":

> There are people who say that the situation is so complex and difficult that there is no way out, that only the worst can be expected, that we are on the very threshold of war. . . . On the other hand, there are some people who say that there have been all kinds of crises, this will pass too. We are strong, we have the strength of the Soviet Union; it will all pass of its own accord.[11]

Although he does not spell out the alternative to these two "mistaken" views, it clearly involves an active diplomatic effort to improve the situation.

Nevertheless, it is the fourth issue—that of economic reform—that will surely be the central issue of the succession, in part because everyone recognizes that the economy is not functioning well. The rate of increase in Soviet industrial growth is declining, and the reduction in the share of GNP allocated to industrial investment in recent years does not bode well for the future. Agriculture is such a concern that three times in the last 4 years Brezhnev has told the Central Committee that the food shortage is a political problem as well as an economic one. The refusal of the leadership even to publish the size of the 1981 harvest is dramatic evidence of the sensitivity of the question. And the poor performance of the service sector is universally conceded. In all these spheres, East European countries have developed a number of reforms, and the question before the Soviet leadership is which, if any, of these innovations to adopt.

Westerners often treat economic reform in the Soviet Union as an obvious good, which has been thwarted only by ideological rigidity and bureaucratic self-interest. Without any question, there are people in the Soviet Union who see the introduction of market mechanisms as an ideological abomination,[12] and many officials in Gosplan, the ministries, and even the provincial apparatus (notably its agricultural components) fear reform as a threat to their power or even to their jobs. Nevertheless, the rigid ideologues are found mainly in the older generation that is passing from the scene. Moreover, Khrushchev was able to scatter the ministerial personnel to new regional economic councils (*sovnarkhozy*) in 1957. If it wanted, the party leadership could hit just as hard at bureaucratic privilege today.

Those with dogmatic ideological views and bureaucratic self-interest certainly oppose reform, but the reasons why reforms have not been instituted so far lie elsewhere. In recent years, the overwhelming obstacle to reform has been Brezhnev himself. As his health has declined, he seems not to have been well enough to run the government on a day-to-day basis, and power in that sense has flowed to others. Although the same can be said of Mao in his last years, it is absolutely clear in retrospect that Mao retained the power to block actions that a majority of the leadership wanted to undertake. Similarly, Brezhnev's ability in the last few years to advance two old cronies, Chernenko and Nikolay Tikhonov, as key men in the political system demonstrates that his position in this respect is not unlike Mao's.

There are also major conceptual and political obstacles to economic reform that will surely outlive Brezhnev. There is no precise blueprint for a successful economic reform in the Soviet Union. The evidence suggests that the various parts of a meaningful reform are interrelated and, therefore, difficult to introduce in a piecemeal manner.[13] While it is easy enough to say that more power should be delegated to local levels, the question of controls is crucial. One of the primary sources of the rapid expansion in inflationary purchasing power in Poland in the 1970s, for example, was a relaxation of centralized controls over managers before strict market controls were introduced.[14] It is also easy to say that the profit criterion should be used to judge managers. But if prices are determined essentially on the basis of costs, managers have an incentive to keep their costs high. Cost-plus contracts are scarcely regarded as the key to efficiency in the United States, and the situation is little different in a socialist system. The logic of using the profit criterion is that prices should be controlled by the market.

On a more theoretical level, it is easy to say that the Soviets should move toward a more market-oriented economy. However, it is no simple matter to establish a system that yields prices close to market prices while maintaining its planned character and avoiding the more serious types of unemployment and inflation found in the West. After all, some prices—particularly commodity prices—fluctuate widely in the West.[15] Is market socialism to have the same fluctuation in prices? Is it to feature the same increases and decreases in production associated with such fluctuation in the West, with marginal producers operating only at times of high prices and eventually closing down?

The task of finding an acceptable model of economic reform is complicated also by the fact that even educated persons in the Soviet

Union often have great difficulty thinking in market or even economic terms.

In the labor sphere, for example, Soviet economists seem torn between the contradictory desires of reducing labor turnover and of giving managers the incentive to economize on labor. The enormous attention devoted by Soviet officials and scholars to the problem of labor turnover comes at a time when Soviet turnover rates are well below those in the West.[16]

Similarly, in Soviet agriculture, a strong case can be made that the long-term secret to agricultural abundance is to turn the terms of trade against the peasant and create structural conditions in which the more productive can mechanize and increase efficiency.[17] Otherwise, marginal producers will never be forced off the farm. Yet the Brezhnev regime has raised the subsidy to agriculture—from about 2 billion rubles in 1965 to 35 billion in 1980—by raising procurement prices paid to the peasants while holding consumer food prices and the prices of industrial goods sold to agriculture essentially steady.[18] Brezhnev has announced that the subsidy will be raised another 16 billion rubles in 1983.[19] Although the consumer price policy can be explained by political considerations, the continual raising of procurement prices seems motivated by a general belief that this is the key to more production.

Even if the Soviet leaders resolve the conceptual problem and decide what kind of reform they want, they still face a political problem. Some of the prerequisites for a thoroughgoing reform are already quite clear and they are politically unpalatable.

First, while the precise point of price equilibrium may be difficult to ascertain, it is absolutely certain that many key prices are now far from that point. As in Poland, the price of meat is politically the most serious problem. The retail price for meat is about one-half the price paid to peasants for it, resulting in continual shortage in the stores, even though per capita meat consumption is not far from the British level.[20] Poland had a per capita meat production well above the British level before the strikes of 1980[21] and nevertheless had severe shortages. The new Soviet food program projects a rise in annual per capita meat consumption to 70 kilograms in 1990—the level the Poles had achieved in the late 1970s. This strongly suggests that even if the Soviet Union fulfills its ambitious plan for meat production, it still will have severe shortages so long as present meat prices are maintained.

Many other politically sensitive prices are also set well below market levels. Some, such as those for mass transportation, pose no problem, for the demand for these items is finite. Where the demand is high, however, the problems can be severe. The price of bread is lower than the procurement price of grain, and it is economically rational for farmers to feed their livestock bread instead of grain. Books are priced so low that a best seller is one that sells out in a single day. Tickets to good plays are unobtainable through regular channels. The number of hospital beds per 100,000 population is double the American level (1249 versus 630 in 1980), and the Soviet figure is still going up, although American health economists consider even the American number excessive.[22]

Second, apart from some rationalization in prices, economic reform also requires some change in policy regarding labor and wages. The existing incentive system tends to reward managers who hoard labor, and the major new performance indicator now being introduced ("normed value-added production"—*normativnaya chistaya produktsiya*) encourages managers to produce more labor-intensive goods than the old gross output target did.[23] As a result, there is an overutilization of labor, and labor productivity has increased more slowly than it should. Moreover, even if a manager wants to get rid of a worker, the existing trade union and legal protection make it difficult for him to do so.

In addition, virtually all Soviet economists contend that wage policy does not provide sufficient incentive to encourage economic growth.[24] During most of the Khrushchev and Brezhnev periods, a marked tendency toward egalitarianism was observable in wage policy.[25] For all wage-earners, the gap between the top tenth and bottom tenth widened a bit in the early 1970s, but those at the bottom of the scale are largely service personnel.[26] In economic terms, the crucial wage differential is that between blue-collar workers and engineering–technical personnel (ITR), for it determines whether workers have the incentive to become foremen and engineers and reflects the extent to which managers are rewarded for performance. Table 1 shows trends in this differential for industry, construction, and agriculture throughout the Brezhnev years. The figures for the second half of the 1970s are little short of astonishing, especially given the countervailing consensus among Soviet economists. In industry, engineering–technical personnel received an average monthly wage increase of 13.3 rubles, while workers received 24.6 rubles. In construction, the respective figures were 5.9 rubles and 27.6 rubles. In agriculture, the wages of the technical personnel rose by only 5.5 rubles (they actually declined between 1977 and 1980) and those of farm workers by 23.7 rubles.

As a result, the fifth issue of the succession must be the nature of Soviet social policy. The policy pursued by Khrushchev and especially Brezhnev has, in a way, represented a gesture toward the Marxist ideal, "To each according to his needs." Everyone has a guarantee to a job—which is secured by giving managers an incentive to retain excess labor force. Everyone can afford the basic necessities (subsidies keep prices low, sometimes below cost), and if only corruption and the black market could be eliminated, these necessities would be rationed by willingness to stand in line rather than by amount of income. Income differentials between managers, on the one hand, and workers and peasants, on the other, have been reduced.[27]

The egalitarian ideal has, of course, not been reached by any stretch

TABLE 1. *Average Monthly Wages in Soviet Industry, Construction, and State Agriculture, 1965–1980 (in Rubles)[a]*

	1965	1970	1975	1980
Industry				
Engineering–technical workers				
(ITR)[b]	148.4	178.0	199.2	212.5
Workers	101.7	130.6	160.9	185.5
Ratio of ITR wages to worker wages	1.46:1.00	1.36:1.00	1.24:1.00	1.15:1.00
Construction				
ITR[b]	160.7	200.0	207.0	212.9
Workers	108.4	148.5	180.3	207.9
Ratio of ITR wages to worker wages	1.48:1.00	1.35:1.00	1.15:1.00	1.02:1.00
State agriculture				
Agricultural–technical personnel[c]	136.3	162.5	180.2	185.7
Workers	72.5	98.8	125.3	149.0
Ratio of agricultural–technical worker wages to worker wages	1.88:1.00	1.64:1.00	1.44:1.00	1.25:1.00

[a]Source: *Narodnoye khozyaystvo SSSR v 1980 g.* [The USSR National Economy in 1980] (Moscow: Finansy i statistika, 1981), pp. 364–365.
[b]This category includes line managers as well as rank-and-file engineers and technicians.
[c]This category includes agricultural specialists (such as agronomists and veterinarians) as well as engineers and technicians involved with equipment and repair.

of the imagination. Many—including many scholars—argue that the policy of egalitarianism should be pushed still further: The minimum wage, the earnings of collective farmers, and pensions should be increased; the income supplements for children of poor families should be raised; more money should be pumped into the countryside to reduce migration to the city; privileges for the well-to-do and powerful should be reduced; more of the country's resources should go into "collective income" (e.g., free day-care centers, subsidized resorts, better free hospital care, and so forth).[28]

Market-oriented reforms, on the other hand, would move away from the egalitarian ideals. If more money were to go to the productive and the innovative, income differentiation would widen. If meat, theater tickets, books, and the like were priced at the supply-and-demand equilibrium point, then low-income people would not be able to afford as much as they can today. If the peasant were unfettered, the old bugaboo of the *kulak* would reappear, for some peasants would be more productive than others and would have to be encouraged to increase their investment and acreage.

Hence, as new Soviet leaders enter the succession period, they will face many dilemmas. Chernenko has called for a "radical (*korennyy*) improvement of the economic mechanism, a removal of class differentiation, and a further widening of participation,"[29] and it is highly likely that the new leadership will enunciate some such program. Ultimately, however, choices will have to be made. In addition to the trade-off between economic growth and social justice as traditionally defined in the Soviet Union, there can be a conflict between workers' self-management or increased trade union power, on the one hand, and economic reform, on the other. A stronger role for the trade union could limit the regime's ability to widen wage differentials. More workers' self-management could affect both the level of workers' wages and the ability of managers to fire unproductive workers or to reduce the work force.

These dilemmas facing the Soviet leaders involve conflicts between central values that all contenders ostensibly hold dear and judgments about the stability of the political system. Throughout the 1970s, the Polish leadership feared—and with good reason—what they knew had to be done. Is there a similar fear among the Soviet leadership? Those major American specialists who privately predict a military dictatorship in the Soviet Union believe that there is. If Soviet leaders were to go ahead with price increases, the resulting political explosion would require martial law in their view.[30] And it is certainly possible that there are Soviet leaders who say or think that, ultimately, martial law is the only way to institute economic reform (or who at least believe that "after me, the deluge"). Otherwise, the inaction to date is inexplicable. There are likely to be other leaders who think that action must be taken soon or the situation will get out of hand.

These dilemmas also involve foreign and defense policy. Economic reform is likely to be expensive in the short run. The artificially low prices are, of course, reflected in subsidies in the state budget. If prices were raised, this money could be saved and transferred to the wage fund. Gross wages could be raised roughly as much as food prices without any other financial consequences. The problem, however, is that those who need the compensatory wage increases are those with lower and middle incomes (or pensioners), not those who can already afford the prices on the collective farm market. If economic reform requires more incentives for the most productive and a widening of the income gap between engineering–technical personnel and workers, the upper-income sector will need to receive even greater increases than will the middle and lower sectors. If the consumer sector is going to function better, it will require some capital expenditures. Moreover, the enormous new budgetary commitments for the food program will be difficult to repudiate. When these various types of expenditures are added together, they do produce a financial strain.

Some of the strain of economic reform could conceivably be relieved by concentrating on price reform, by shifting some of the burden of improving services to an enlarged private sector, and by postponing the increase of rewards to the most productive. Nevertheless, since industrial investment is already being severely restricted and needs to be expanded,[31] the only reasonable source of money to reduce the problems caused by price increases is the defense sphere. While some Soviet leaders do speak about the need both to strengthen defense further and to institute some kind of economic reform—notably, Vladimir Shcherbitskiy, the Ukrainian party leader[32]—significant economic reform is generally dependent on political and military détente, and advocacy of the two tends to go together.

With the politics of internal reform thus intertwined with the politics of foreign and defense policy, the problems for contenders trying to build a winning coalition are complicated even more. It is almost certain that different contenders will choose different trade-offs and therefore will have to base themselves on different social and bureaucratic forces.

The Candidates

Leonid Brezhnev undoubtedly remembers well that when Nikita Khrushchev placed a man of the right age and experience in a post that positioned him to become the successor, that man took advantage of the situation to succeed "prematurely." Determined to prevent anyone from doing to him what he did to Khrushchev, Brezhnev has consistently avoided appointing someone with the proper qualifications to a post that would make him the obvious heir apparent. For this reason, the question of who will succeed Brezhnev has always remained quite difficult to answer, perhaps even for members of the Politiburo itself.

Today, there are at least five men who have or have had at least a reasonable chance to become general secretary and several others with at least an outside chance. The five are Andrey Kirilenko, Konstantin Chernenko, Yuriy Andropov, Viktor Grishin, and Mikhail Gorbachëv.

Andrey Kirilenko. For years, Western Sovietologists have pointed to Kirilenko as the likely heir apparent.[33] They have assumed that he has been de facto second secretary (that is, the secretary providing overall supervision of personnel selection and economic management) of the CPSU Central Committee (CC), and that he therefore has been in a good position to build a winning political machine. In addition, his background is as extensive as that of any of the other candidates, not only because of the breadth of his responsibilities in the Brezhnev period but because of his years of experience as an *obkom* (*oblast* party committee) first secretary both in the Ukraine and in the RSFSR.

One thing is certain—Kirilenko has been associated with Brezhnev for a long time. Born several months before Brezhnev in 1906, Kirilenko actually rose faster then Brezhnev in the wake of the purges of the 1930s. He was named second secretary of the Zaporozh'ye *obkom* in 1939, when Brezhnev was only one of the junior *obkom* secretaries in Dnepropetrovsk. The two men first crossed paths early in the war, when Kirilenko served as the (political) member of the Military Council of the Eighteenth Army of the Southern Front (from November 1941 until April 1942), and Brezhnev was deputy head of the Political Administration of the Southern Front (which supervised the Eighteenth Army) or perhaps head of the Political Department of the Eighteenth Army (a post that would have been subordinate to the member of the Millitary Council).[34]

The two men's association has continued almost uninterrupted since the close of the war. Kirilenko returned to civilian work, resuming his post of *obkom* second secretary in Zaporozh'ye when it was liberated in 1944. In August 1946, Brezhnev became *obkom* first secretary in Zaporozh'ye and, consequently, Kirilenko's boss. In November 1947, Brezhnev was named *obkom* first secretary in Dnepropetrovsk. When he moved on to Moldavia in 1950, Kirilenko succeeded him in Dnepropetrovsk, most likely on Brezhnev's recommendation. From 1955 to 1961, Kirilenko served as *obkom* first secretary in Sverdlovsk, and from 1961 to 1966 as deputy chairman of the Bureau of the Central Committee for the RSFSR. When the Bureau was abolished in 1966, Kirilenko became, together with Suslov, one of the two CC senior secretaries under Brezhnev. In 1976, when Kirilenko received a medal on his 70th birthday, President Nikolay Podgornyy presented the award, but Kirilenko directed his answer primarily to Brezhnev, using the familiar form of "you" (*ty*) to emphasize the closeness of the relationship. Kirilenko is the only Politburo member to have used this form of address in such a public forum.[35]

The exact nature of Kirilenko's responsibilities during the Brezhnev era should be considered more of an open question than it usually is. For most of the Khrushchev period, there was a senior CC secretary— Aleksey Kirichenko from 1957 to 1960, Frol Kozlov from 1960 to 1963, and Brezhnev from 1963 to 1964 —who provided overall supervision of the central state apparatus and personnel selection in at least the non-Russian republics. (It is probable that none of the three had authority over the Bureau of the Central Committee for the RSFSR.) Although it is generally assumed that Kirilenko stepped into this role for Brezhnev, this interpretation should not be accepted without reservations, especially for the period since 1976.

There are, it should be understood, ways of dividing the work of the senior CC secretaries other than the Khrushchev pattern. In the last years of the Stalin period (1950–1953), for example, the responsibility of supervising the lower party apparatus and the central state machinery was split between Khrushchev and Malenkov. It is quite possible that something similar happened in the Brezhnev period, probably at the time of Chernenko's elevation to the Politiburo. At least until very recently, Kirilenko clearly has fulfilled much of the Malenkov role of supervising central governmental policy and economic planning, although he seems not to have Malenkov's responsibility for foreign policy and agriculture.[36] What is lacking is evidence that Kirilenko has continued to have responsibility for the party organs at lower levels.

The crucial question in this respect is the subordination of Ivan Kapitonov, the head of the Organizational Party Work Department of the Central Committee. Kapitonov has direct supervision over personnel selection, and he has placed long-time associates in several posts in this realm. Thus, the first deputy head of the Organizational Party Work Department, Nikolay Petrovichev, worked as head of the propaganda–agitation department of the Moscow *obkom* under Kapitonov in the late 1950s, and the editor of *Partiynaya Zhizn'*, Mikhail Khaldeyev, was Komsomol secretary under Kapitonov in the early 1950s.[37] The assumption has been that Kapitonov, who is not a member of the Politburo, must be subordinate to one of the CC secretaries, namely, Kirilenko. It is, however, within the realm of possibility that Kapitonov always reported to Brezhnev directly, and within the realm of high probability that sometime in recent years—probably in October 1977, when Chernenko became a candidate member of the Politburo— Kapitonov began reporting to Chernenko. Since the mid-1970s, all of Kirilenko's articles have dealt solely with the economy, while Chernenko's have often centered on questions that are the responsibility of the personnel secretary.[38] In 1982, it was Chernenko and Kapitonov who attended the trade union session that removed Aleksey Shibayev as chairman of the Central Council of Trade Unions, while in 1976 it had been Kirilenko and Kapitonov at the session that had installed him.[39]

The height of Kirilenko's power seemed to have come in September 1976, when an apparent protégé, Yakov Ryabov, the first secretary of the Sverdlovsk *obkom*, became the CC secretary in charge of the security forces, the military, and the defense industry. In February 1979, however, Ryabov was removed (he was named first deputy chairman of Gosplan, with responsibilities largely for labor planning). At the same time, a number of signs began suggesting that Kirilenko's status was falling.[40] In 1982, there have been rumors that his health is failing, but his political health is surely worse. (While Suslov's health had been poor for years, his status in the press never fell.)

In the unlikely event that Kirilenko does become general secretary, it is probable that relatively little would change. In his speeches, he comes across as a rather traditional bread-and-butter communist, who emphasizes industrial growth and the increase in living standards that comes from it. He says little about shortcomings and little about changes in the planning process that he has supervised. Some of his articles can be incredibly detailed and narrow in their focus on industrial problems.[41] Except in 1974 when he showed enthusiasm about Soviet–American summit meetings,[42] he manifests relatively little interest in international relations. He certainly expresses more support of détente and less alarm about the Western threat than some of his colleagues, but he seems to take the ebbs and flows of détente for granted, as if on the assumption that relations cannot get too bad.[43] Perhaps he was the target of Zagladin's earlier-mentioned jibe about extreme views in this respect.

Konstantin Chernenko. The great mystery man among the contenders is 71-year-old Chernenko. Most indicators of status place him in the number two position in the Soviet political system, even after Andropov was elected CC secretary in May 1982. It is quite possible that on a day-to-day basis, Chernenko has already been serving as the transitional general secretary.

One can argue that Chernenko has accumulated an extraordinary number of levers of power in his hands. Since 1965, he has been head of the Central Committee's General Department, which handles the flow of classified documents within the party apparatus and until recently supervised the disposition of letters sent by the public to the Central Committee.[44] According to Arkadiy Shevchenko, a former assistant to Foreign Minister Andrey Gromyko, Chernenko has used this role to serve in effect as secretary to the Politburo.[45] In addition, his attendance at recent army and border guard meetings indicates that he, rather than Andropov, supervises the Central Committee's Administrative Organs Department, which in turn oversees the police and the military.[46] And finally, as has just been discussed, Chernenko has by all indications come to oversee the Organizational Party Work Department and personnel selection.

Nevertheless, despite the enormous apparent strength of Chernenko's position, he is difficult to visualize as a general secretary. Since 1960, his main role has been head of Brezhnev's personal secretariat— his Aleksandr Poskrëbyshev—and such people rarely are chosen to succeed their masters in any system. They find it difficult to establish an independent image, and their proximity to power and their service as the leader's "no man" have usually made them many enemies.

Chernenko's background is also most unimpressive. After 3 years in the border guards from 1930 to 1933, Chernenko spent 8 years in low-level ideological work in his native Krasnoyarsk Kray, where, at the age of 31, he became a *kraykom* secretary (presumably the secretary for ideological work).[47] His performance must not have been distinguished, however, for in 1943, at the height of the war, he was sent for 2 years to college—the Higher School of Party Organizers. In 1945, he was again made an *obkom* secretary for ideology, but in a less important *oblast*, Penza.[48] In 1948, he was moved to a still lower job, head of the propaganda–agitation department of the Moldavian Central Committee, although as a Russian outsider he, rather than the Moldavian who held the title, may have been serving as the real ideological secretary.

The major event in Chernenko's life occurred in 1950 when Brezhnev arrived in Kishinëv to become the first secretary of the Moldavian Central Committee. Brezhnev worked in Moldavia only until 1952 and Chernenko until 1956. But when Brezhnev became CC secretary for heavy industry and the defense industry in 1956, Chernenko was named head of the mass political work section of the Central Committee's Propaganda–Agitation Department. (It is fairly common for the associates of one CC secretary to be named as the subordinates of others; the practice seems to serve the functions either of political control or of solidifing alliances among secretaries—in the Chernenko case, the alliance between Brezhnev and Suslov.) When Brezhnev became chairman of the Presidium of the USSR Supreme Soviet in 1960 and again when he became first (and then general) secretary of the CPSU in 1964, he selected Chernenko to head his personal secretariat.

Thus, Chernenko has been exposed to a wide range of decisions as a personal assistant but has no significant experience of his own outside the ideological sphere. He has not run a major economic unit or party organization, he has had almost no direct responsibility in the foreign policy realm, and he has not ever been one of Brezhnev's policy assistants. His education—even if one counts a correspondence degree he received at Kishinëv Pedagogical Institute—is not the sort usually considered appropriate for top posts in the Soviet Union. And, finally, he is not even a good public speaker.

Even today, it is possible that Chernenko's seeming power may be largely illusory. He first came to prominence in 1975 at a time when Brezhnev's health was quite poor, appearing in foreign policy settings (e.g., the Helsinki Conference of Chiefs of State), in which he served largely as an aide-de-camp.[49] The following year, when Brezhnev's health was much improved,[50] Chernenko did not figure as a member of Soviet delegations. But he publicly returned to Brezhnev's side when the latter's health deteriorated once more. Conceivably, Chernenko has been functioning more as Brezhnev's eyes and ears—and even as his memory—than as a real policymaker.[51] If he is serving as personnel secretary, he has not built much of a local machine—only 15 of 71 RSFSR *obkom* first secretaries have been changed in the last 5 years, and some give every apperance of being allied with other contenders.[52]

Chernenko's best chance would seem to be as a transitional leader with relatively little power. But it is dangerous to judge a new leader by his background. Who could have predicted that President Harry Truman, President Anwar Sadat, or Pope John XXIII would turn out to be historic figures?

If Chernenko is purely a transitional leader, his policy preferences might not be very important. Nevertheless, if he does become general secretary, the coalition that he has put together (this will be discussed in the conclusion) and the content of his speeches and articles suggest that he is a strong supporter of détente and of some kinds of reform.[53] When Brezhnev presented Chernenko with awards on his 70th birthday, he praised his assistant for being "restless" in the good sense of the term, a man with "a creative, daring approach." In response, Chernenko acknowledged that he sometimes makes "nonstandard decisions."[54]

Sometimes Chernenko's words seem extraordinarily bold. In his 1980 election speech, he did not speak out in support of the recent invasion of Afghanistan (nor did the slightly abbreviated version published in *Pravda* even mention the subject).[55] In a recent article in *Kommunist*, he explicitly indicated that discussion of the balance between the organizational and ideological roles of the party could indicate the extent to which the party should dominate society (with the revisionist position being that the party should limit itself to ideological work). He then went on to say that, of course, the balance between organizational and ideological work was not fixed once and for all, discussing the issue in a manner that indicated a commitment to a less obtrusive involvement.[56]

Yet, Chernenko's speeches often combine formulations that have been advanced by strong reformers with examples from the past that suggest little change. Hence, they give the impression of skillful efforts to reassure both his boss and a prospective reform coalition. It is not clear who would be disappointed if Chernenko became the new leader.

Judging by his speeches, Chernenko seems to fall more within the Khrushchev tradition than into the camp of economic modernizers. He has written often of the need for "further perfection of the political system"[57] and frequently expresses what sound like antibureaucratic and proparticipatory views. (Indeed, when he spoke at a conference on rural ideological work in 1948, he, unlike the other speakers, is reported to have attacked the Ministry of Agriculture and the Committee for Radio for insufficient installation of radios in the countryside.)[58] He has stated that "some forms and methods of economic administration which arose in preceding stages of socialist construction and which were progressive and effective in their own time cease to be such,"[59] and it is easy to imagine him leading an attack on Gosplan and the ministries. Nevertheless, his language suggests a greater attraction to popular participation than to the use of economic levers, and it is hard to imagine him pushing for a change in social policy in order to provide greater economic rewards to managers.

Yuriy Andropov. If the Central Committee selects the best-qualified major contender as Brezhnev's successor, then it surely will select Andropov. The most urgent problems of the Soviet leadership are handling relations with the United States and China, maintaining control over Eastern Europe, and deciding which, if any, of the East European reforms to adopt in the Soviet Union. Andropov is the only man in the leadership with real expertise on all these questions.

Andropov was born in 1914 and graduated from the Rybinsk Water Transportation Technicum in 1936.[60] (He apparently overlapped for a year in Rybinsk with Kirilenko, who graduated in 1935 from the city's premier institute, the Rybinsk Aviation Institute.) From 1938 until 1951, Andropov served in Komsomol and party posts in Yaroslavl' and the Karelo–Finnish Republic, working under the present Minister of Foreign Trade, Nikolay Patolichev, who was *obkom* first secretary in Yaroslavl'. He worked under (or at least with) Otto Kuusinen, who was chairman of the Presidium of the Supreme Soviet in the Karelo–Finnish Republic. By the time that Andropov was made head of a CC subdepartment (*podotdel*) in 1951, he had accumulated 5 years of college education at Petrozavodsk University and the Higher Party School through part-time study.

Andropov then moved into the foreign policy sphere, in 1953 becoming counselor and chargé d'affaires in Hungary and in 1954 moving up to be ambassador.[61] He was stationed in Budapest both during the evolutionary process that led to the 1956 revolution and during the Soviet invasion itself. In May 1957—just before Khrushchev elevated Kuusinen into the party Secretariat and Presidium (as the Politburo was then called)—Andropov was named head of the newly created Socialist Countries Department of the Central Committee. He retained this position until May 1967. In 1961, he was given the title of CC secretary.

Although little direct evidence is available on Andropov's policy orientation during this period, his personal connections were extremely suggestive. He almost surely was a protégé of Kuusinen, who as CC secretary acted as a progressive counterweight to Suslov in the ideological–foreign policy realm. (Kuusinen's propensities were indicated in his selection of Fëdor Burlatskiy, probably the most vocal proponent of de-Stalinization in the Soviet media between 1954 and 1957, to head his full-time "group of consultants"—his main staff.)[62] When Kuusinen died in 1964, Andropov inherited his group of consultants. He soon chose a new leader for it—Georgiy Arbatov, who had been writing prodétente articles since the mid-1950s.[63]

In May 1967, Andropov was appointed chairman of the KGB. While the KGB is best known for its secret police activities, it also performs foreign intelligence functions, and Andropov was the first secret police head in Soviet history with substantial preparation for these latter responsibilities. The KGB's three major deputy chairmen for internal security—Semën Tsvigun, Georgiy Tsinev, and Viktor Chebrikov—had been associated with Brezhnev in Dnepropetrovsk or Moldavia,[64] and one suspects that Andropov had only partial control over them at best. For both these reasons, it is likely that Andropov gave considerable attention to the foreign policy responsibilities of the KGB. In fact, he was promoted to full membership in the Politburo at a 1973 CC plenary session that ratified détente and simultaneously named the ministers of foreign affairs (Gromyko) and defense (Dmitriy Ustinov) to the Politburo.

In May 1982, only 3 months after the death of Suslov, Andropov was elected a CC secretary.[65] All the evidence suggests that Andropov assumed Suslov's responsibility for supervising two CC secretaries in the ideological–foreign policy realm—Boris Ponomarëv and Mikhail Zimyanin.[66] It is not clear, however, whether Andropov also supervises Konstantin Rusakov, head of the Socialist Countries Department of the Central Committee. In general, he has maintained a fairly low profile. However, in one ceremonial meeting, Andropov did speak for the Politburo, and he was the Central Committee secretary to walk with Brezhnev from the plane when the latter returned from vacation in late August, even though Chernenko was also present both times.[67]

Since 1975, Andropov has been much more urgent in his support for détente than any of the other major contenders. In 1975, when Suslov was expressing worry about ultrareactionary forces in the West and Shcherbitskiy was emphasizing that the nature of imperialism had not changed,[68] Andropov was insisting that the "relaxation of international tension does not occur by itself. . . . It is necessary to actively struggle for it. There cannot be any pause or breathing space since détente is a continuous process which demands constant movement forward."[69] In 1979, he asserted that "it is impossible to underestimate the danger of a course of retarding détente,"[70] and in 1980, he was the only Politburo member to warn that détente was in serious danger.[71] Unlike many other Politburo members, Andropov has coupled his support for peace and détente with a call for negotiations, even in 1980 in the wake of the United States sanction after the Soviet invasion of Afghanistan. As early as 1976, he was quite explicit in stating that "the policy of peaceful coexistence, as is well known, presupposes negotiations and the seeking of mutually acceptable decisions, sometimes of a compromise nature."[72]

Andropov has not expressed his domestic views as clearly as his foreign policy views. As chairman of the KGB, he naturally has spoken out against ideological subversion (although not in his two most recent speeches, one during the 1980 RSFSR Supreme Soviet election and the other on the 1982 anniversary of Lenin's birthday).[73] But he has also alluded repeatedly to "unsolved problems" and, especially in April 1982, to the need to solve them through internal resources.[74] Andropov is likely to favor making the hard choices that economic reform requires (that probably is the meaning of his call to solve problems by internal means). The first ideological decrees issued after he became CC secretary called for a major expansion of economic education and for a fuller discussion in literary journals of contemporary socioeconomic problems.[75] And since he is the Politburo's specialist on Hungary, it is difficult to believe that the Soviet Union would have been as tolerant of Hungarian economic reform—indeed, quite favorable toward it in the last few years—had Andropov not supported it.

Viktor Grishin. Like Andropov born in 1914, Grishin has spent his entire career in Moscow and in Serpukhov, 60 miles to the south. He graduated from two Moscow technicums—one for soil analysis and the other for locomotive service and repair—and worked for several years at a locomotive depot. He then entered party work in Serpukhov, where he became *gorkom* first secretary in 1948.[76] Soon after Khrushchev became Moscow *obkom* first secretary in late 1949, he named Grishin to head the machine-building department (which in large part was apparently also the defense industry department). In 1952, less than 4 years after he had been a mere *gorkom* second secretary in Serpukhov, Grishin was named second secretary of the Moscow *obkom*. In those years, the Moscow *obkom* supervised the city of Moscow in addition to the outlying region (it does not do so now). With Moscow first secretary Khrushchev simultaneously serving as CC secretary in charge of personnel selection, the second secretary was an important figure. Grishin served in this capacity until 1956 when he was named chairman of the Central Council of Trade Unions. In 1967, he became first secretary of the Moscow *gorkom*, by now a post independent of the *obkom*.

From a contemporary perspective, the crucial question about Grishin's early years in Moscow is his relationship with two other men who worked in the city in the early 1950s—Kapitonov and Gorbachëv. Kapitonov preceded Grishin as *obkom* second secretary; and from 1954 to 1956, as *obkom* first secretary, he supervised Grishin directly. Gorbachëv, as Komsomol secretary of Moscow University in 1954–1955, was ultimately subordinated, although at several levels removed, to Grishin's *obkom*. If the two are Grishin supporters, Kapitonov has been in a position to build a political machine for him, and Gorbachëv, to gain support among the younger *obkom* secretaries. The connections could be crucial—if they are friendly.[77]

Because of Grishin's long tenure in Moscow, many in the city claim to have some sense of him as a person. The popular impression seems to be quite uniform. He is usually described as cautious, moderate, and judicious, as a man who is inclined to serve more as a chairman of the board and less as an innovator. Some say that he is of only average intelligence.

Judging by his speeches, Grishin holds rather old-fashioned views.

Indeed, while Kirilenko in 1976 spoke of himself, at age 70, as "middle-aged," Grishin in 1975 spoke of himself, at age 61, as part of the "older generation."[78] To the extent that he ventures beyond discussions of Moscow, he tends to raise traditional themes: the working class, collectivism, and the evils of the private-property psychology. The most striking feature of his speeches is the great emphasis he gives to ideological work, especially in contexts in which it would not necessarily be expected.[79] Unlike many of Chernenko's speeches, Grishin's speeches give no hint that he is speaking about this subject in Aesopian fashion. The foreign policy sections of his election speeches are little more than an endorsement of Brezhnev and his policies, and he supports the existing level of military expenditures.[80] While Grishin may be willing to be a neutral general secretary who presides over change initiated by his colleagues, it is difficult to imagine him leading an attack on Brezhnev's social policy and on the prerogatives of the Moscow ministries. He seems more disposed toward ideological exhortation of the worker than toward radical change in the incentive system, let alone toward a widening of the private sector.

Mikhail Gorbachëv. Gorbachëv is by 8 years the youngest man in the Politburo. Born in 1931, he is part of an important new generation moving toward the top in the Soviet Union. Too young to have fought in World War II and to have its college education disrupted by the war (although not too young to have been affected by it),[81] this "postwar generation" went through Soviet colleges when the standards of admission and instruction were at their highest and went to work as the Stalin period ended.[82] Gorbachëv attended Moscow University, where, as noted, he was Komsomol secretary. He graduated with a law degree in 1955. Although his biographers depict him as a combine operator in his youth, a local newspaper reports that this was a summer job.[83]

Gorbachëv has spent most of his career in his native region of Stavropol'. After graduation, he returned home as a Komsomol official, soon becoming the first secretary of the Komsomol *gorkom*. In 1961, after several years as second secretary of the Komsomol *kraykom*, he was named first secretary. Judging by the local press, he concentrated his attention at this time on such questions as agriculture and rural youth rather than education.[84] In March 1962, he was transferred to party work as party organizer of the *kraykom* in the *kolkhoz-sovkhoz* administration in the district surrounding the city of Stavropol'. In December 1962, when the party apparatus was bifurcated by Khrushchev, Gorbachëv was named head of the party organs department of the rural *kraykom*. From 1960 to 1964, he worked under Fëdor Kulakov, the first secretary of the party *kraykom* and then the rural party *kraykom*, and later to become the CC secretary for agriculture (1965) and a Politburo member

(1971).[85] In 1966, Gorbachëv was named the first secretary of the Stavropol' party *gorkom*. While working in this capacity, he also completed a second college degree—this time through part-time work at the Stavropol' Agricultural Institute. In 1968, he became second secretary of the party *kraykom*, and in 1970, first secretary, a job he held until 1978.

As *kraykom* first secretary, Gorbachëv had a major responsibility for the development of irrigation in the Stavropol' region, historically one of the Soviet Union's major grain producers. The Central Committee and Council of Ministers decided in 1971 to speed construction of the Great Stavropol' Canal and to bring a second link into operation by 1 November 1974. Despite an unexpected encountering of sand instead of clay in the construction of the tunnels, the canal was completed on schedule. The total number of irrigated hectares in the region rose from 192,000 in 1970 to 370,000 in 1977.[86]

When Kulakov died in 1978, Gorbachëv was selected to replace him. In October 1980, he was elected a full member of the Politburo. His current responsibilities seem to extend well beyond agriculture to include the entire agroindustrial complex—a sector of the economy reported to contribute 46% of the country's added value.[87] Since the organization of the CC apparatus links the food industry with light industry, Gorbachëv's supervision of the relevant department also makes him the leading Politburo member for consumer goods.[88] Finally, undoubtedly because of his law degree, Gorbachëv was also elected chairman of the Legislative Proposals Commission of the Council of the Union of the Supreme Soviet. This committee takes part in the drafting of all Supreme Soviet legislation and exercises special oversight over law-and-order questions.

Gorbachëv is young enough and new enough to the leadership that his policy views remain largely unknown. On some questions, such as foreign policy, those views may not even be completely firm. His 1979 election speech expressed fervent support for détente, while his 1981 speech was just as fervent in its support for the Soviet right to intervene in Afghanistan.[89] His published speeches and articles naturally concentrate on agriculture, on which he takes a generally proreform position.[90] If the May 1982 CC decision on agriculture is any indication, he is an extremely timid reformer indeed, but it is likely that that decision reflected the judgment of older colleagues. A man of Gorbachëv's age and responsibilities would almost surely adopt a strong position in favor of economic reform as a way of gaining support from the younger *obkom* secretaries against the central government and of giving himself an excuse to remove old officials and build his own machine.

If the succession takes place quickly, Gorbachëv's youth and relative inexperience with the non-Russian nationalities and with foreign policy will count against him. It should be noted, however, that he has a most striking range of political connections. As already discussed, his patron, Kulakov, was associated with Chernenko in Penza. Kulakov's election as CC secretary in 1965 was quite likely on Chernenko's recommendation. The head of the organizational party work department, and subsequently the organizational secretary of the Stavropol' *kraykom* under Gorbachëv, A. K. Vedernikov, has since served as the head of the section of the Central Committee's Organizational Party Work Department in charge of Moldavia and the western Ukraine.[91] This, too, may have solidified the tie with Chernenko. In addition, Gorbachëv's post as Komsomol secretary in Moscow University placed him under the supervision of Grishin and Kapitonov. His work in Stavropol' was in a *kray* where Suslov had once been first secretary, and at Suslov's funeral, he was the only Politburo member to stop and talk with each member of Suslov's family.[92] Finally, Richard Kosolapov, the chief editor of *Kommunist*, was in Komsomol work with Gorbachëv at Moscow University.[93]

The
Succession
Speculation about the outcome of the struggle for power is fraught with danger. We tend simply to focus on the question of who will be the general secretary, but it should not be forgotten that the real leader—the real strongman—may hold a different post. In the Soviet Union, both Lenin and Malenkov were head of government (rather than head of the party), and in China, Deng Xiaoping chose to rule from a less lofty post. Moreover, the arrangements made immediately after the succession may fall apart quickly. Malenkov was removed as party secretary in a week, the "gang of four" lasted a month, and Lavrentiy Beria was arrested in 4 months. These events, in turn, were only the first steps in a political struggle that lasted for some years.

We also do not know the time of the succession, the health of the various contenders at that time (or even which ones will be alive), the personal relationships among the Politburo members, and their opinions of each other's abilities and judgment. Are, for example, Chernenko and Andropov major adversaries, or have they reached an agreement on the succession? Is Andropov, who looks frail on television, willing to accept the less demanding Suslov portfolio? Is Grishin ill enough that he would be satisfied with Arvid Pel'she's post of chairman of the Party Control Committee (a post for which he would seem well suited by temperament and reputation)? How antagonistic are the Moldavian and Dnepropetrovsk factions of the Brezhnev group? We should not pretend that we have the answers to these and many similar questions.

Events will also affect the succession in ways difficult to foresee. The performance of the economy may absolutely require reform or may permit reform to be postponed. There may be foreign policy crises. The Polish crisis, for example, has no doubt already affected the Soviet succession. It dramatically pointed up the dangers of Soviet pricing policy and of excessive reliance on foreign credits. It surely posed severe dilemmas for Soviet policymakers; some Politburo members probably panicked and counseled invasion, and others advised patience. In the process, the position of some contenders must have been strengthened and the position of others weakened. Even the Middle East crisis might have had an impact.

Besides events, the process of "cabinet-building" may have a major effect on the final outcome. One of the striking facts about this succession is the number of key posts that it is likely to open. If Andropov, Grishin, or Gorbachëv became general secretary, it is highly likely that Tikhonov, Kirilenko, and Chernenko would soon be replaced or moved into more ceremonial positions. Gromyko and Ustinov are also candidates for retirement in the relatively near future, and the new chairman of the KGB, Vitaliy Fedorchuk, could easily be a transitional figure. All these jobs, as well as the former job of the new general secretary, could become open.

Other key posts could be created or strengthened. The post of chairman of the Presidium of the USSR Supreme Soviet could be filled again by a man other than the general secretary. The chairmanship of Gosplan might well be upgraded in a time of economic reform, perhaps even to the level it had under Nikolay Voznesenskiy or Mikhail Saburov. Normally, of course, the post of first deputy chairman of the Council of Ministers has been a highly important one, with several such officials represented on the Politburo. (Today, there is only one first deputy chairman, the 75-year-old Ivan Arkhipov, an old Brezhnev crony who is not even a candidate member of the Politburo and who almost certainly will disappear with Brezhnev.) And the system badly needs a national security adviser to coordinate foreign and defense policy.

A key to the struggle for power, then, will be the ability to distribute these posts to powerful figures within the Central Committee in a way that will build a winning coalition. Any such exercise now is deeply threatening to Brezhnev, unless he has decided to retire, for a coalition in place has little incentive to wait until his death. Unless Brezhnev has permitted Chernenko to build a coalition, the contenders may be avoiding cabinet-building lest Brezhnev get wind of it and move against them. If so, the succession would have to take place in a great hurry under difficult circumstances.

Even if past experience did not point in such a direction,[94] the present situation within the Politburo suggests that the immediate post-Brezhnev leadership will be a collective one. The crucial question, however, is what type of collective leadership will it be? Will it be a status quo collective leadership in which, as has been the case in recent years, the major interests are able to prevent policies that would do them serious harm? Or will it be a collective leadership on the 1953–1957 model—a leadership that, while beset with conflict, permits and even encourages individual members to carry out major policy initiatives in their own spheres of responsibility?

It is easy to make a strong case for either of these options. Even excluding Brezhnev, 7 of the 12 Politiburo voting members are 70 years of age or older. Forty percent of the voting members of the Central Committee will be 65 or older by the end of 1982 (more than half of them 70 or older, and one-fifth 75 or older). Seventy percent of the Council of Ministers members who are voting members of the Central Committee will be 65 or older.[95] Most of these older men must sense that reform means retirement in the relatively near future and would surely prefer a leader such as Grishin (at least if he is described correctly here), who would not challenge the status quo seriously and who might not retire them too quickly.

It seems to me, however, that while this scenario is quite possible, it underestimates the probabilities of near-term reform. Domestically, there is a pressure for change, a frustration at the weakness and indecision of Brezhnev, a desire for a strong leader and some action, and an impatience on the part of younger (really middle-aged) leaders to have their chance. Abroad, there is the threat of an all-out arms race and the disarray in the Western alliance, which give the Soviet leadership an added incentive to go beyond their usual peace offensive and take really meaningful steps toward arms control. Finally, there is the shock over the events in Poland, whose year-and-a-half of turmoil is likely to make the other peoples of Eastern Europe and the Soviet Union more willing to forgo radical action in favor of evolution and more willing to accept price rises in the framework of the promise of reform.[96]

A reformist collective leadership is also politically quite possible. The Politburo has been changed significantly in the last few years through the deaths of Kosygin and Suslov, the decline of Kirilenko, and the selection of a basically nonpolitical transition figure (Tikhonov) as chairman of the Council of Ministers. As a result, the Politburo members who will most likely be the key figures in the brokering—Andropov, Chernenko, Gorbachëv, Grishin, Gromyko, Dinmukhamed Kunayev, Grigoriy Romanov, Shcherbitskiy, and Ustinov—average only 66 years of age, a situation quite different from what it would have been 3 years ago. In the Central Committee, 60% are younger than 65, and a coalition needs only 51% for victory. In addition, at least a few of the older CC members are either anticipating retirement in any case or hoping to be one of those who will benefit from the succession.

If there is to be a reformist collective leadership, it may not matter too much who will occupy precisely which posts. Regardless of his exact position, Gorbachëv would probably concentrate on agriculture and the services sector (that is, on a partial return to the New Economic Policy). Andropov would probably have major responsibility for foreign policy and ideology. Vladimir Dolgikh, the new member of the Politburo, would very likely handle industrial reorganization. Chernenko (if he is included) would concentrate on political reforms.

If one is to speculate about actual posts, I have had the sense that Andropov has the best chance to be general secretary or at least the strongman behind a weak general secretary. As chairman of the KGB, Andropov has been ruthless enough to reassure the conservatives that he would not let reform get out of hand (in fact, he probably would be quite harsh on dissident activity even as he loosened some of the controls on acceptable political activity). That same ruthlessness might reassure the reformers that he has the strength to handle the ministries. I suspect that Andropov has excellent relations with the Army Chief of Staff, Nikolay Ogarkov, who fought on the Karelian front in World War II near the area where Andropov was associated with the partisans.[97] Ogarkov's appointment as minister of defense might complete the needed coalition.

As I read the Soviet media of the last few months, however, my instincts suggest that the coalition may already be in place. In April, the most sophisticated of the Soviet political observers, Fëdor Burlatskiy, wrote about the "interregnum" (*mezhdutsarstviye*) and "time of troubles" (*smutnoye vremya*) in China and included some generalizations that had obvious relevance for the Soviet Union:

In the history of interregnums it often turns out this way: after the death of a sovereign, emperor, or leader who did not leave a successor, a time of trouble ensues, in which different groups compete in a struggle for power until a new leader appears who is capable of ending the political confusion and reestablishing a firm order. Moreover, in the first stage, as a rule, a completely inconspicuous person is advanced. He succeeds in using the favorable situation while the basic rivals have a mortal grip on each other.

Perhaps Mao Zedong calculated on establishing collective leadership after his death? Then he should have stated this and worried about the creation of political mechanisms inside the party and the state which would have made this possible. . . . And, thus, as has often happened in periods of interregnums, the successor at first turned out to be one of the least-known figures—the man on whom no one had turned any attention beforehand, Hua Guofeng.[98]

Whether by coincidence or not, the weeks after this article was published saw a series of events that suggested the major rivals—or perhaps Brezhnev himself—were introducing some order into the situation. In the wake of Kirilenko's 2-month disappearance from public view, Dolgikh was elevated to candidate membership in the Politburo, apparently with Kirilenko's long-time responsibility for the Planning and Financial Organs Department.[99] Kapitonov suffered a significant reduction of status.[100] While this may have been part of a campaign against Kirilenko, it was also a sign that one of Grishin's main hopes was not going to be of any help, and that he, Grishin, was one of the "inconspicuous" candidates who was not likely to make it.

If the immediate succession is more or less in place, and enjoys Brezhnev's approval, then Chernenko must be a big part of it—most likely, either as the general secretary or chairman of the Presidium of the USSR Supreme Soviet (if the two jobs are to be separated). Indeed, if Gorbachëv is linked to Chernenko through Kulakov and if Dolgikh is likewise linked to Chernenko through his long years of work in Chernenko's home region of Krasnoyarsk, it is easy to put together hypothetical "cabinets," with Chernenko as general secretary. If Gorbachëv is politically trustworthy, he would make an excellent personnel secretary, both because of his experience with organizational work and because of his supervision of agriculture. Dolgikh could assume either Kirilenko's post in the CC Secretariat or a high post in the Council of Ministers. Andropov is a natural occupant of the Suslov slot, perhaps even expanded to become "national security adviser." The chairmanship of the Council of Ministers is a problem because the other men are Russians (although Chernenko's name is Ukrainian) and because it usually has had foreign policy responsibilities (if the general secretary has not assumed them). As a Ukrainian, Tikhonov might well be kept on for a while, despite his age; however, non-Russians such as Shcherbitskiy and Eduard Shevardnadze are obvious candidates for promotion.

To repeat, however, the critical question—especially for the outside world—is the basic policy orientation of the majority in any new collective leadership. The Brezhnev regime has lasted for nearly 20 years, and the Brezhnev generation has been near the top for more than 40 years. As a consequence, it has become very difficult for us to judge which features of Soviet politics and policies are inherent in the system and which really reflect more the values of this historic generation. There are enormous differences between communist systems such as North Korea and Yugoslavia—or even Hungary and Romania—and it is at least conceivable that many aspects of the Soviet Union that we have ascribed either to the essence of the system or the Russian national character will turn out to be less permanent than we have assumed.

It seems to me that a new collective leadership is likely to make significant changes—perhaps even quite significant changes—fairly quickly. The Khrushchev–Brezhnev social policy has come to a political dead end. By basing their legitimacy so heavily on egalitarianism, the leaders have set an impossible goal for themselves and will always be judged by their failures rather than their achievements. Indeed, by overrewarding the industrial proletariat, they do not even serve the cause of social justice, for they neglect the truly underprivileged in

Soviet society—the lower white-collar and service personnel. By permitting the gap between prices and the supply-and-demand equilibrium point to widen, they create inexorable pressures for the broadening of a black market that strikes at the moral fiber of the system, and they create a growing privileged group among those willing to function outside the law. The leading theorists who speak out on this subject say that all means should be used to liquidate this problem, and this seems to indicate—and certainly should indicate—price reform and a partial legalization of private activity in trade and the services.[101] For these reasons, the social policy is likely to be modified in the interests of economic growth.

To be sure, policy changes may be halting and uneven, especially if Brezhnev retires with honor rather than dies or is removed. The Soviet Union would certainly not move quickly toward anything approaching Yugoslavia's market socialism, and even movement toward the Hungarian model would be slow. Near-term reforms would conceivably be movement toward meaningful price adjustments, legalization of parts of the second economy, and greater independence for the farms and individual peasants. As in Hungary, a selective importation of key Western consumer goods would symbolize change and absorb excess purchasing power (an importation of 100 million hand calculators would cost only US $500 million—far less than is spent on grain). As in 1953 and 1954, some of the simplest changes are in the foreign and defense policy realms. If there is to be reform, it may come there first. The most severe conflicts between economic growth and social policy are likely to be the center of the second phase of the succession, several years hence.

If, of course, no change takes place in the wake of succession, if the new Soviet leadership pushes forward as blindly as the Polish leadership did in the 1970s, then serious thought has to be given to the question of the stability of the system. Because of the identification of communism with Russian nationalism, one would anticipate that the first riots would be directed against the leadership rather than against the system as a whole. If so, the disturbances could be quieted by reform. However, if troops refuse to fire on rioters—as occurred in March 1917—there will be no threat of outside intervention (as in the Polish case) to save the system. It is precisely the recognition of this fact that is likely to persuade the new Soviet leaders that they cannot wait until later in the decade to begin reform.

Notes

[1]"Kto Kogo in the Kremlin," *Problems of Communism* (January–February 1982), pp. 17–26.

[2]Stephen F. Cohen, "The Friends and Foes of Change: Reformism and Conservatism in the Soviet Union," *Slavic Review* (June 1979), pp. 197–202.

[3]A. P. Butenko, *Politicheskaya organizatsiya obshchestva pri sotsializme* [The political organization of society under socialism] (Moscow: Mysl', 1981), p. 178.

[4]*Ibid.*, esp. pp. 160–190. Butenko is head of the Department of Political and Ideological Problems of the Economy of the World Socialist System Institute (IEMSS)—the leading Soviet institute on Eastern Europe.

[5]F. Burlatskiy, "The Political System of Developed Socialism," *Kommunist*, no. 12 (August 1979), pp. 62–73.

[6]G. Kh. Shakhnazarov and F. M. Burlatskiy, "On the Development of Marxist–Leninist Political Science," *Voprosy Filosofii*, no. 12 (1980), pp. 10–23.

[7]G. Kh. Shakhnazarov, *Sotsialisticheskaya sud'ba chelovechestva* [The socialist fate of mankind] (Moscow: Politizdat, 1978), pp. 187, 191, 196, 212–213.

[8]See, for example, M. I. Baitin, *Sushchnost' i osnovnyye funktsii sotsialisticheskogo gosudarstva* [The essence and basic functions of the socialist state] (Saratov: Izdatel'stvo Saratovskogo universiteta, 1979); and Yu. A. Krasin, "Worker Participation in Management and Professionalism," *Voprosy Filosofii*, no. 4 (1982), pp. 3–14. Krasin is prorector of the Academy of Social Sciences of the CPSU Central Committee.

[9]K. Chernenko, "The Vanguard Role of the Party of Communists: An Important Condition of Growth," *Kommunist*, no. 6 (April 1982), p. 41.

[10]For a survey of the major published debates related to foreign policy, see Jerry F. Hough, "The World as Viewed from Moscow," *International Journal* (Spring 1982), pp. 183–197. For debates related to Latin America, see *idem*, "The Evolving Soviet Debate on Latin America," *Latin American Research Review*, no. 1 (1981), pp. 124–141.

[11]Interview on Prague radio. Translated in Foreign Broadcast Information Service, *Daily Report: Soviet Union* (Washington, D.C.), Aug. 4, 1982, p. CC/11.

[12]Sometimes views of this type can be expressed more easily in discussions about China than in those about the USSR. See, for example, V. I. Lazarev, *Klassovaya bor'ba v KNR* [Class struggle in the PRC] (Moscow: Politizdat, 1981), pp. 12, 20, 311–316; and Ye. A. Konovalov, "On the Evolution of Socioeconomic Structures in the PRC," *Problemy Dal'nego Vostoka*, no. 2 (1980), p. 10.

[13]An East European joke hints at the problem by reporting the result of a dispute over whether to change to the British practice of driving on the left side of the road: They decided to do so incrementally, with the trucks adopting it first and the cars only some months later.

[14]Jerry F. Hough, *The Polish Crisis: American Policy Options* (Washington, D.C., The Brookings Institution, 1982), pp. 13–14.

[15]For example, the January 1 market price of copper rose from $.59 a pound in 1978 to $.69 in 1979 to $1.03 in 1980 and then fell to $.85 in 1981 and $.73 in 1982. These prices are the January futures price for bulk contracts. They are printed in any major newspaper with a major financial section, including *The New York Times*.

[16]The question of labor turnover is discussed in a soon-to-be completed dissertation for the University of Michigan by Peter A. Hauslohner, "Managing the Soviet Labor Market: Policy-making and Political Learning Under Brezhnev." Professor Hauslohner, now at Yale University, emphasizes the conceptual barriers to reform.

[17]See the discussion by James R. Millar in James R. Millar and Alec Nove, "A Debate on Collectivization: Was Stalin Really Necessary?" *Problems of Communism* (July–August 1976), pp. 52–53.

[18]Vladimir G. Treml, "Subsidies in Soviet Agriculture: Record and Pros-

pects," prepared for the forthcoming compendium of the U.S. Congress, Joint Economic Committee, *Soviet Economy in the 1980s: Problems and Prospects.*

[19]*Pravda*, May 25, 1982, p. 2.

[20]In 1980, the annual per capita consumption of meat in the USSR was stated to be 58 kilograms. The per capita British meat consumption was 46.2 kilograms in 1975, down from 50.4 kilograms in 1970. (*Ibid.*, p. 2; and P. G. Hare and P. T. Wanless, "Polish and Hungarian Economic Reforms—A Comparison," *Soviet Studies* [October 1981], p. 492.) The precise Soviet statistics need to be treated with great caution, but the exaggerations are surely not enough to drop Soviet consumption significantly below the 1975 British level.

There are several reasons why such a level of consumption is not inconsistent with shortages in the state stores. First, of course, some meat is sold through the collective farm markets. Second, if goods are priced too low, they may sell out very quickly, but the actual quantity sold in a brief period may be quite substantial—even more so than if prices are so high that the goods do not move and remain on the shelves. Third, Soviet citizens eat their main meal (*obed*) in the middle of the day. Hence they eat most of their meat at the cafeterias at work. In recent years, when I have often observed an absence of meat in Moscow stores, I have always found it in street cafeterias as well as at those in the Lenin Library and the Academy of Sciences institutes, and it has been priced very reasonably. (On one day a week, fish is offered instead of meat.) In light of other preferences given to industrial workers, the same situation must prevail in factory cateterias.

[21]Polish per capita consumption of meat rose from 49.2 kilograms in 1965 to 53.0 kilograms in 1970, to 70.3 kilograms in 1975, and remained roughly at the last level through 1979. See Hare and Wanless, "Polish and Hungarian Economic Reforms," p. 492. The authors state that the British and Polish definitions of meat and meat products are identical.

[22]*The World Almanac and Book of Facts 1982* (New York: Newspaper Enterprise Association, 1981), p. 592; and *Narodnoye khozyaystvo SSSR v 1980 g.* [National economy of the USSR in 1980] (Moscow: Finansy i statistika, 1981), p. 499. To be sure, the problem is not all one of demand unrestrained by cost. For example, the figure for the United Kingdom, which has a comprehensive state medical program, was 894 in 1977 (*World Almanac,* p. 588). In the Soviet Union, the hospital bed figure is the basis for budget decisions, and the Ministry of Health deliberately prolongs hospital stays in order to increase its budget. For example, a woman giving birth without complications is forced to stay in the hospital for 13 days before returning home, even though the possibility of contagion there probably increases the dangers for the newborn and may even be a factor in Soviet infant mortality figures.

[23]The validity of this charge is acknowledged by A. Bachurin, deputy chairman of Gosplan in charge of labor questions. *Pravda,* July 16, 1982, p. 3.

[24]See the discussion in Jerry F. Hough, "Policy-Making and the Worker," in *Industrial Labor in the U.S.S.R.,* ed. Arcadius Kahan and Blair Ruble (New York: Pergamon Press, 1979), pp. 380, 390–391.

[25]Janet G. Chapman, "Recent Trends in the Soviet Industrial Wage Structure," in *ibid.*, pp. 151–183; Alistair McAuley, *Economic Welfare in the Soviet Union* (London: George Allen & Unwin, 1979); and David Lane, *The End of Social Inequality: Class, Status, and Power Under State Socialism* (London: George Allen & Unwin, 1982), pp. 54–66.

[26]Michael Ellman, "A Note on the Distribution of Earnings in the USSR under

Brezhnev," *Slavic Review* (December 1980), pp. 669–671. Professor Ellman concludes that the trend toward egalitarianism ended in 1968. But his evidence does not go beyond 1974. Moreover, the particular indicator used is very sensitive to changes in the minimum wage, and the introduction of a large increase in the minimum wage in 1968 makes that a very atypical year for comparison.

[27]As Hedrick Smith has documented in *The Russians* (New York: Quadrangle, 1976), the topmost elite has been given a number of nonmonetary privileges, but these are provided only to a very narrow sector of the managerial elite. Moreover, even the scale of the privileges to the high officials can be exaggerated in comparative terms. For a case in which one of the country's top 25 publishing officials was unable, despite the support of two Central Committee members, to get his three-room apartment enlarged to four, see Vladimir Voinovich, *The Ivankiad or The Tale of the Writer Voinovich's Installation in His New Apartment* (New York: Farrar, Straus, and Giroux, 1976).

[28]Given the finite amount of funds available, every appeal for a collective good, income supplements, increases in pensions and minimum wages, etc.—and such appeals are innumerable—is, in practice, an appeal that funds be diverted from other goals. In addition, many scholars write articles and books that advocate movement to greater egalitarianism in more general terms. For example, see A. A. Amvrosov, *Ot klassovoy differentsiatsii k sotsial'noy odnorodnosti obshchestva* [From class differentiation to social homogeneity] 2nd ed. (Moscow: Mysl', 1978); and A. P. Butenko, *Sotsialisticheskiy obraz zhizni: problemy i suzhdeniya* [The socialist way of life: problems and judgments] (Moscow: Nauka, 1978).

[29]Chernenko, "The Vanguard Role of the Party," p. 29.

[30]For a surfacing of this argument in print, see L. H. Gann and M. S. Bernstam, "Soviet Vulnerabilities," *National Review* (Aug. 20, 1982), p. 1021.

[31]Seweryn Bialer, *Stalin's Successors*, (New York: Cambridge University Press, 1980), p. 300. See Boris Rumer, "Soviet Investment Policy: Unresolved Problems," *Problems of Communism* (September–October 1982), pp. 53–68, for a fuller discussion of this problem.

[32]For example, see his speech in *Pravda*, June 7, 1975, p. 2. See also Christian Duevel, "Similarities and Differences in the Soviet Leaders' Recent Approach to Some Issues of Foreign Policy," *Radio Liberty Research Reports*, RL 211/78 (Sept. 28, 1978), which compares Andropov and Shcherbitskiy.

[33]See, for example, Richard Coffman and Michael Klecheski, "The 26th Party Congress: The Soviet Union in a Time of Uncertainty," in *Russia at the Crossroads: The 26th Congress of the CPSU*, ed. Seweryn Bialer and Thane Gustafson (London: George Allen & Unwin, 1982), pp. 200–201.

[34]*Sovetskaya voyennaya entsiklopediya* [Soviet military encyclopedia], 8 vols., (Moscow: Voyenizdat, 1976–80), vol. 4, p. 182. This source provides a good comprehensive biography of Kirilenko. Brezhnev's biographies do not make clear when Brezhnev moved from the Southern Front to the Eighteenth Army, but since he held the latter post for "more than two years," it is likely to have been after Kirilenko left. *Ibid.*, vol. 1, p. 586, and vol. 2, p. 367. The first post also was lower in status than Kirilenko's.

[35]*Pravda*, Oct. 15, 1976, p. 1. Even men as close to Brezhnev as Suslov and Chernenko, both of whom Brezhnev addressed in public as "*ty*" spoke to him in the polite form "*vy*." (*Ibid.*, Sept. 25, 1982, p. 1; and Dec. 20, 1981, p. 1.)

[36]In practical terms, Kirilenko supervised Boris Gostev, head of the Planning

and Financial Organs Department of the Central Committee (and himself was almost certainly head of the department until September 1975) as well as the heads of the various industrial, construction, transportation, and trade departments of the Central Committee (some indirectly, through Vladimir Dolgikh and Yakov Ryabov). However, Dolgikh's election to candidate membership in the Politburo in May 1982 seems to have been accompanied by his assumption of responsibility for the Planning and Financial Organs Department. On July 2, 1982, *Pravda* reported two July 1 meetings: a perfunctory one honoring the day of the rural cooperative workers and a CC conference on economic planning. Kirilenko attended the former but not the latter (although both Gostev and a high Gosplan official were there). Mikhail Gorbachёv and Dolgikh represented the Politburo.

[37]U.S. Department of State, *Directory of Soviet Officials* (Washington, D.C.: U.S. Government Printing Office, August 1960), vol. 1, p. 154; 1981 *Yezhegodnik bol'shoy sovetskoy entsiklopedii* [Yearbook of the great Soviet encyclopedia] (Moscow: Sovetskaya entsiklopediya, 1981), pp. 594, 607.

[38]For example, see A. Kirilenko, "The CPSU's Economic Policy in Action," *Kommunist*, no. 4 (April 1975), pp. 15–32; *idem*, "Comprehensive Program of Planning and Management Improvement," *Partiynaya Zhizn'* (Moscow), no. 18 (September 1979), pp. 6–16; and K. Chernenko, "The Great Unity of Party and Nation," *Kommunist*, no. 17 (November 1980), pp. 10–26.

[39]*Pravda*, Mar. 5, 1982, p. 2, and Nov. 24, 1976, p. 2. Moreover, Shibayev was a man out of the Kirilenko mold—an aviation industry engineer who had become a plant manager before becoming an *obkom* first secretary in the RSFSR; the new trade union chief, Stepan Shalayev, despite a managerial background, also had worked for 17 years in the central trade unions (1981 *Yezhegodnik*, pp. 609–610).

[40]In May 1979, Kirilenko was cut out of a Politburo picture in a Moscow newspaper, and even if the omission were accidental, the editor was not removed. In October, East German Communist party leader Erich Honecker called Chernenko Brezhnev's nearest comrade-in-arms. Through 1981, Kirilenko received a number of slights in comparison with Chernenko. In January 1982, he suffered the most remarkable snub of all. In the listing of the members of Suslov's funeral commission, Kirilenko was listed out of alphabetical order behind two other Politburo members. *The New York Times*, May 28, 1979, p. 2; Terry McNeill, "The Brezhnev Succession: Taking Stock of the Candidates," *Radio Liberty Research Reports*, RL 323/79 (Oct. 29, 1974); Boris Meissner, "The 26th Party Congress and Soviet Domestic Politics," *Problems of Communism* (May–June 1981), p. 5; Elizabeth Teague, "Kirilenko at 75, Chernenko at 70: What Chances Does Either Have of Succeeding Brezhnev?" *Radio Liberty Research Reports*, RL 356/81 (Sept. 9, 1981); *Pravda*, Jan. 27, 1982, p. 1.

[41]See, for example, A. Kirilenko, "An Important Factor in Raising the Effectiveness of the Economy," *Kommunist*, no. 7 (May 1978), pp. 23–37.

[42]*Pravda*, June 12, 1974, p. 3.

[43]For example, in 1975 he treated détente as something that the changing correlation of forces required the West to adopt. *Leningradskaya Pravda* (Leningrad), June 11, 1975, p. 2. This line was not included in the shortened version in *Pravda*.

[44]In the past, the department was called the *spetsotdel* (Special Department).

For a discussion of its work, see Leonard Schapiro, "The General Department of the CC of the CPSU," *Survey* (Summer 1975), pp. 53–65.

[45]*The Washington Post,* June 6, 1982, p. 29.

[46]*Pravda,* May 12, 1982, p. 2, and May 28, 1982, p. 2. In January, the obituary of Semën Tsvigun, the first deputy chairman of the KGB, was signed by only two Politburo members—Chernenko and Gorbachëv. Since Chernenko worked with Tsvigun in Moldavia, Gorbachëv's name would seem to imply his responsibility for the Administrative Organs Department at that time. (*Ibid.,* Jan. 21, 1982, p. 2.)

[47]Most of Chernenko's biographies give little information about his early career. It is described, however, in *Sovetskaya voennaya entsiklopediya,* vol. 8, pp. 452–453.

[48]*Kul'tura i Zhizn',* Mar. 11, 1948, p. 1. While Chernenko was in Penza, the head of the agriculture department of the *obkom* and later the head of the agriculture administration of the *oblast* government executive committee was Fëdor Kulakov, the CC secretary for agriculture during most of the Brezhnev era. Kulakov in turn was Gorbachëv's patron in Stavropol'. It would be fascinating to know whether this combination of circumstances created a political link between Chernenko and Gorbachëv.

[49]For Brezhnev's health, see *The New York Times,* June 14, 1975, p. 1; July 31, 1975, p. 2; Aug. 1, 1975, p. 2; and Jan. 25, 1976, p. 1. For Chernenko, see *Pravda,* June 11, 1975, p. 1, and July 29, 1975, p. 1.

[50]*The New York Times,* Jan. 25, 1976, p.1, and Sept. 23, 1976, p. 7.

[51]Arkadiy Shevchenko, the former Soviet diplomat, says that when he attended meetings in 1977 at which Brezhnev was present, the latter's memory functioned very badly. *The Washington Post,* 6 June 1982, p. 28.

[52]For example, P. A. Leonov, shifted from Sakhalin to Kalinin, had been head of the party organs department under Grishin and Kapitonov; B. F. Murav'yëv, the new first secretary in Kuibyshev, graduated in 1952 from Karelo-Finnish University (i.e., an institution in an area where Andropov had been active from 1940 to 1951).

[53]See Hyland, *loc. cit.,* p. 23.

[54]*Pravda,* Sept. 25, 1981, p. 1.

[55]*Moskovskaya Pravda* (Moscow), Feb. 16, 1980, p. 2, and *Pravda,* Feb. 16, 1980, p. 2.

[56]Chernenko, "Vanguard Role of the Party," p. 26.

[57]See, for example, *Pravda,* Feb. 27, 1979, p. 3.

[58]*Kul'tura i Zhizn',* Mar. 11, 1948, p. 1.

[59]K. U. Chernenko, *Voprosy raboty partiynogo i gosudarstvennogo apparata* [Questions of the work of the party and state apparatus] (Moscow, Politizdat, 1980), p. 317.

[60]Andropov's biography can be found in *Bol'shaya sovetskaya entsiklopediya* [Great Soviet encyclopedia], 3rd ed. (Moscow: Sovetskaya entsiklopediya), vol. 2, p. 23.

[61]This assumes that he was not already in this sphere in the CC apparatus from 1951 to 1953. His post is an extremely unusual one. I have seen only several references to a *podotdel* (subdepartment). One turned out to be the group of consultants under Kuusinen in the early 1960s (*Pravda,* Mar. 3, 1964, p. 2). Another was headed by V. M. Churayev in the early 1950s and apparently was

in the Party Organs Department (*ibid.*, Mar. 2, 1982, p. 6). Andropov is likely to have been in the same department.

[62]For a description of Burlatskiy's meeting with Kuusinen, see F. M. Burlatskiy, "O. V. Kuusinen—Marxist–Leninist Scholar and Theorist," *Rabochiy klass i sovremennyy mir*, no. 6 (1979), pp. 99–104.

[63]For Arbatov's relationship to Kuusinen, see Georgiy Arbatov, "Otto Kuusinen: Marxist Theoretician," *New Times*, no. 42 (October 1981), pp. 18–20.

[64]Their biographies can be found in the 1981 *Yezhegodnik*, p. 608.

[65]*Pravda*, May 25, 1982, p. 1.

[66]He has attended many sessions with visiting foreign communists from the communist world (but not the noncommunist world), and he has signed the one obituary of a cultural figure where the ideological secretary's signature was appropriate. (Ibid., June 29, 1982, p. 6.)

[67]*Ibid.*, June 25, 1982, p. 2; FBIS, *Daily Report: Soviet Union*, Sept. 1, 1982, p. R/1.

[68]*Pravda*, June 7, 1975, p. 2, and June 10, 1975, p.2.

[69]*Ibid.*, June 10, 1975, p. 2.

[70]*Ibid.*, Feb. 23, 1979, p. 2.

[71]*Ibid.*, Feb. 18, 1980, p. 2.

[72]*Ibid.*, Apr. 23, 1976, p. 2. For further analysis of Andropov's earlier pro-détente speeches, see Christian Duevel, "Andropov's Lenin Anniversary Speech," *Radio Liberty Research Reports*, RL 262/76 (May 19, 1976); *idem*, "Some Aspects and Implications of Honecker's Revision of 'The Dictatorship of the Proletariat,'" *ibid.*, RL 295/76 (June 4, 1976); and *idem*, "Similarities and Differences in the Soviet Leaders' Recent Approach to Some Issues of Foreign Policy," *ibid.*, RL 211/78 (Sept. 28, 1978).

[73]*Pravda*, Feb. 12, 1980, p. 2, and Apr. 23, 1982, pp. 1–2.

[74]*Ibid.*, June 10, 1975, p. 2, and Apr. 23, 1982, p. 2.

[75]*Ibid.*, June 27, 1982, p. 1, and July 30, 1982, p.1.

[76]The exact date is not known. He was not first secretary in November 1947 but was in the post as of February 1949. He probably assumed the job in December 1948, when the former first secretary was named deputy chairman of the Moscow *oblast* trade union organization. See *Moskovskiy Bol'shevik* (Moscow), Nov. 28, 1947, p. 2, Dec. 28, 1948, p. 1, Feb. 2, 1949, p. 1, and Aug. 3, 1949, p. 2. For further biographical information about Grishin, see *Sovetskaya voyennaya entsiklopediya*, vol. 3, pp. 53–54.

[77]One should never forget that familiarity sometimes breeds contempt and enmity instead of friendship, and the Moscow party organization clearly has had fissures. Kapitonov himself was demoted as Moscow *obkom* first secretary in 1959 and sent to Ivanovo, reportedly because he could not get along with the chairman of the *oblast* government executive committee, Nikolay Ignatov. See "To Educate Cadres in the Spirit of Excellence," *Partiynaya Zhizn'*, no. 8 (April 1979), pp. 10–11. From the late 1950s to the mid-1960s, three *obkom* and *gorkom* first secretaries—G. G. Abramov, N. G. Yegorichev, and V. I. Ustinov—quickly fell into disrepute.

[78]*Pravda*, Oct. 15, 1976, p. 1, and June 7, 1975, p. 2.

[79]See V. V. Grishin, *Izbrannyye rechi i stat'i* [Selected speeches and writings] (Moscow: Politizdat, 1979), pp. 488, 590, and 641.

[80]*Pravda*, June 7, 1975, p. 2, Feb. 15, 1979, p. 2, and Feb. 6, 1980, p. 2.

[81]For example, Stavropol' Kray, where Gorbachëv grew up, was occupied by the Germans. Suslov served as head of the partisans there.

[82]For a discussion of this generation, see Jerry F. Hough, "The Generation Gap and the Brezhnev Succession," *Problems of Communism* (July–August 1979), pp. 1–16; and *idem, Soviet Leadership in Transition* (Washington, D.C., The Brookings Institution, 1980).

[83]*Stavropol'skaya Pravda* (Stavropol'), Feb. 6, 1979, p. 1. For further biographical information on Gorbachëv, see *Deputaty Verkhovnogo Soveta SSSR: Desyatyy sozyv* [Deputies of the USSR Supreme Soviet: tenth convocation] (Moscow: Izdatel'stvo sovetov narodnykh deputatov, 1979), p. 119.

[84]*Stavropol'skaya Pravda*, May 12, 1961, p. 1, June 24, 1961, p. 2, Sept. 26, 1961, p. 2, and Jan. 19, 1962, p. 2.

[85]The association was quite close, for Gorbachëv was a candidate member of the *kray* party committee's bureau while Komsomol first secretary and subsequently a full member of the bureau of the rural *kraykom. Ibid.,* Sept. 26, 1961, p. 1, and Dec. 28, 1962, p. 1.)

[86]*Stavropol'skaya Pravda*, Mar. 26, 1971, p. 1, Jan. 22, 1972, p. 2, Oct. 7, 1972, p. 1, Oct. 10, 1972, p. 2, Dec. 31, 1973, p. 1, Nov. 1, 1974, p. 1, and Jan. 27, 1978, p. 3. The number of hectares of mechanized irrigation, which is reported in the statistical handbooks, is much less but also showed considerable growth.

[87]*Pravda*, June 17, 1982, p. 2.

[88]For example, he has been the Politburo member who attends light industry meetings. *Ibid.,* June 13, 1981, p. 1, and July 3, 1981, p. 2).

[89]*Stavropol'skaya Pravda*, Feb. 3, 1979, p. 2; and *Altayskaya Pravda* (Barnaul'), February 1, 1980, p. 2. These long foreign policy discussions were not included in the versions of the speeches printed in *Pravda*.

[90]For example, M. Gorbachëv, "Current Questions of Agriculture and Its Effectiveness," *Kommunist*, no. 11 (July 1980), pp. 10–26.

[91]*Stavropol'skaya Pravda*, Feb. 21, 1971, p. 1, and Feb. 23, 1974, p. 1; *Sovetskaya Moldaviya* (Kishinëv), Jan. 30, 1976, p. 1; and *L'vovskaya Pravda* (L'vov), Dec. 23, 1978, p. 1.

[92]I am indebted to Mark Zlotnik for this point.

[93]Kosolapov's biography states only that he entered Komsomol work immediately after graduation in 1955 (1981 *Yezhegodnik,* p. 584). That would not have occurred, however, if he had not been active in it in the university (1981 *Yezhegodnik,* p. 584).

[94]For the argument that successions tend to follow the same pattern, including early collective leadership, see George W. Breslauer, "Political Succession and the Soviet Policy Agenda," *Problems of Communism* (May–June 1980), pp. 34–52.

[95]These and later statistics on Soviet officials are drawn from the biographies of Central Committee members, all of which were published at the end of the 1981 *Yezhegodnik.*

[96]For the opposite case, see Seweryn Bialer, "The International and Internal Contexts of the 26th Party Congress," in *Russia at the Crossroads,* ed. Bialer and Gustafson, esp. pp. 33–38.

[97]In a 1942 article that Andropov chose to have republished in his 1979 selected works, he emphasized the closeness to the front and the help that the Komsomol was giving it through the making and collecting of supplies. Yu. V.

Andropov, *Izbrannyye rechi i stat'i* [Selected speeches and writings] (Moscow: Politizdat, 1979), pp. 24–25. For a discussion of Andropov's work at this time, see *Za liniyey Karel'skogo fronta* [Behind the lines of the Karelian front], 2nd ed. (Petrozavodsk: Kareliya, 1979), pp. 62, 78–79, 214, and 289.

[98]Fëdor Burlatskiy, "Interregnum, or Chronicle of the Years of Deng Xiaoping," *Novyyi Mir*, no. 4 (1982), pp. 210–11.

[99]See Note 36.

[100]In recent years, Kapitonov always signed obituaries out of alphabetical order as the first of the CC secretaries not on the Politburo. That is, he signed in front of Dolgikh and Mikhail Zimyanin ("Z" comes before "K" in the Russian alphabet). In addition, he almost always signed minor cultural obituaries with Zimyanin in cases where only the latter seemed appropriate. However, beginning with an obituary published in *Pravda*, Apr. 28, 1982, p. 6, Kapitonov no longer signed the obituaries of minor cultural figures; and beginning with an obituary printed in *ibid.*, June 9, 1982, p. 3, Kapitonov's name was listed in alphabetical order after Zimyanin. (Cf. *ibid.*, June 1,1982, p. 3, the last obituary signed in the old way.)

[101]R. Kosolapov, "Contribution of the 24th, 25th, and 26th CPSU Congresses toward the Solution of Theoretical and Political Problems of Developed Socialism and the Transition to Communism," *Kommunist*, no. 5 (March 1982), pp. 66–67; and V. Pechenov, "On the Firm Ground of Socioeconomic Policy," *ibid.*, no. 11 (July 1982), pp. 41–42.

34   MURRAY FESHBACH

*A Different Crisis**

During the next two decades, the Soviet Union will face special problems that have never before afflicted a major industrialized nation during peacetime. Simply stated, the European part of the population is not replacing itself, while the non-Russian, non-Slavic, non-European people of the Soviet Union—most of whom are of Muslim origin—are experiencing a strong growth in numbers (see Fig. 1). By the year 2000, ethnic Russians will be a clear minority in the country that most Americans still call "Russia."

From this simple fact flow consequences that may, over the next two decades, lead the Soviet Union into peculiar economic, military, and political difficulties.

The USSR's annual rate of economic growth now stands at a low 2%; shortages of skilled labor caused by the slowdown in the ethnic Russian rate of increase could trim that to 0 or even induce a decline. Barring some unforeseen change in the Kremlin's world view, the Soviet military will continue to require hundreds of thousands of conscripts each year through the 1980s and 1990s—but in 15 years, the Red Army may well find itself with large numbers of soldiers who turn toward Mecca at sunset. In short, between now and the end of the century, the ethnic Russian primacy long taken for granted by both tsars and Bolsheviks will be challenged—not by individuals but by inescapable demographic trends.

Single-Sex   The Soviet Union, of course, will have other headaches in
Cities   the years ahead. The question of who will succeed Leonid
Brezhnev, for instance, looms larger with each passing

*Reprinted by permission of the author and publisher from *The Wilson Quarterly* 5, no. 1 (Winter, 1981), pp. 117–125. Copyright 1981 by Woodrow Wilson International Center for Scholars.

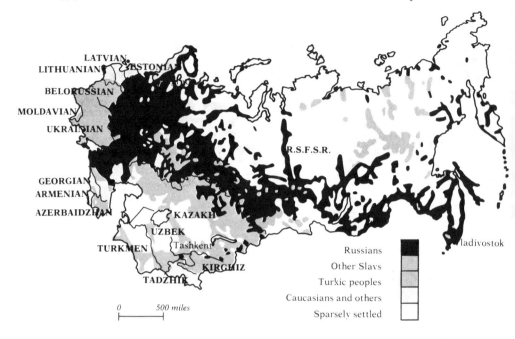

Figure 1. *The USSR: Political and ethnic divisions. In 1980, out of a total Soviet population of 265 million, the eight southern republics accounted for 57 million and the RSFSR, 138 million. Like most Central Asians, Turkic peoples are traditionally Muslim. (Names of Soviet republics are in capital letters.) (Source: U.S. Central Intelligence Agency.)*

day. The Soviet economy is beset by low worker morale, a leveling-off of oil production, sluggish technological progress, and the drain of massive military spending. To Soviet leaders, such ailments are painful, chronic, and familiar, like arthritis. The coming demographic shift is an altogether different type of crisis, one unprecedented in Soviet history.

The demographic shift will magnify the effects of a general demographic *slump*. Overall, death rates are up, and birth rates are down. Since 1964, the Soviet death rate has jumped by 40%; by the end of the century, it is expected to hit 10.6 annually per 1000 population, nearly the same rate as China's is now. Meanwhile, the national birth rate has fallen by 30% since 1950; two decades from now, the rate likely will be down to 16.1 per 1000. Labor is already short, and the available supply will tighten further over the next few years as the annual net increase in the size of the working-age population sags from its 1976 high of 2.7 million to a projected 1986 low of 285,000 (see Fig. 2). For a variety of reasons, the 1980s should also bring a long-term decline in Soviet capital

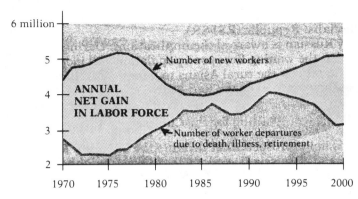

Figure 2. *The Soviet labor squeeze. Declining from a 1976 peak of 5.2 million, the number of 16-year-olds annually entering the Soviet labor force will hit a low of 3.9 million in 1985. Departures add to the squeeze: Soviet workers will retire or die in increasingly high numbers until 1993. (Source: Murray Feshbach.)*

formation—just when more investment in machinery will be needed to help offset labor shortages by boosting productivity.

How did the Soviet Union get caught in this bind?

The past is partly to blame. Stalin's purges of the 1930s took many millions of lives. Battlefield losses during World War II claimed another 15 million Soviet *males* alone. The Soviet Union is still feeling the "demographic echo" of both events. To policymakers in the Kremlin, the phrase "generation gap" has a special gruesome reality.

But the continuing climb in the Soviet death rate indicates that whatever the other problems of the past were, many of them are still around. Indeed, during the last few years, the mortality rate for 20- to 44-year-olds has shot up so fast that male life expectancy has dropped from 66 to 63 years, a full decade less than the life span for females. (The only nation with a larger gap is Gabon.) The chief villain here is, in two words, rampant alcoholism. Among its well-known effects are ill health, malnutrition, and accidental death.

Short-sighted government planning has played a part, creating scores of "single-sex cities" across the Soviet Union. Many an undiversified metropolis such as Bratsk and Abakan was built around a "hot, heavy, and hazardous" industry (e.g., steel, coal, oil-drilling) with almost no jobs for females. Men are correspondingly scarce in textile towns, including Orekhovo-Zuevo and Ivanova, known in the USSR as the "cities of brides."

Soviet babies are also dying in shockingly large numbers. During the past decade, the USSR became the first industrialized nation to experience a long-term rise in infant mortality, which grew, according to the

Soviet definition, from 22.9 per 1000 live births in 1971 to 31.1 per 1000 in 1976. (The Soviets consider infant losses within a week of delivery as miscarriages, not deaths. If calculated by American methods, the 1976 figure would be 35.6 per 1000, more than twice the United States rate.)

One reason for the rise in infant mortality is that abortion has apparently become the USSR's principal means of "contraception," with a present average of six abortions per woman per lifetime, 12 times the United States rate. When used repeatedly, abortion may induce premature delivery in subsequent pregnancies, and premature infants are 25 times more likely to die during their first year than full-term infants. Another baby-killer is female alcoholism, which weakens the fetus.

40 Million Muslims   But the prime culprit may well be the USSR's prenatal and postnatal health-care system, in which the flaws of Soviet medicine and social planning seem to converge. Fed inferior artificial milk, placed in overcrowded day-care centers when only 3 months old (owing in part to the labor shortage, most Soviet women must work full-time), and left there for 8–12 hours a day, hundreds of thousands of Soviet babies have become easy prey to epidemic diseases, particularly influenza.

The labor shortage and its economic implications would, by themselves, be enough to worry the Kremlin. Yet the problem is worsened by regional differences: It is the USSR's Russians and other Slavs who are not producing so many children as they once did. Soviet Central Asians, by contrast, are flourishing. Relatively unaffected both by Stalin's purges and World War II, traditionally shunning both alcohol and abortion, and keeping their birth rate high even as their death rate declines, the Soviet Union's 40 million ethnic Muslims have enjoyed a rate of population increase about five times that of the Russian Soviet Federated Socialist Republic (RSFSR) (see Fig. 3).

Every Russian is aware of the implications: During the next two decades, the waning European population will increasingly be forced to rely on the rural Asians to man the machines of industry and the outposts of the Red Army.

Waiting for the Chinese?   This is not a prospect that delights the Kremlin. Relations between ethnic Russians and their Muslim neighbors have never been smooth. It was the Russian Bolsheviks who, in 1920 and 1921, used the Red Army to put the old tsarist empire back together. In 1924, partly in reaction to Muslim guerrilla groups (the *Basmachi*), the Bolshevik regime divided the vast Central Asian region of Turkestan into five "nations." Kazakhstan, the largest, stretches more than 1500 miles from the Caspian Sea to the

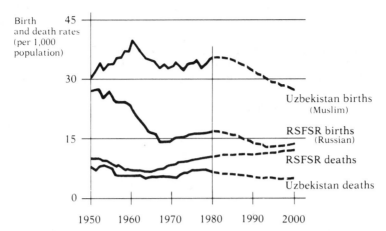

Birth and death rates (per 1,000 population)

Uzbekistan births (Muslim)

RSFSR births (Russian)

RSFSR deaths

Uzbekistan deaths

1950   1960   1970   1980   1990   2000

Figure 3. *Ethnic Russian and Muslim trends: 1950–2000. A comparison of vital statistics. In Uzbekistan, births have so exceeded deaths that the population of the republic (figured as a proportion of the Soviet total) will more than double between 1950 and 2000, from 3.5 to 8.6%. (Source: Murray Feshbach.)*

Chinese border. The others—Kirghizistan, Tadzhikistan, Turkmenistan, and Uzbekistan—lie in the arid southeastern corner of the Soviet Union, where they nestle up against China, Afghanistan, and Iran.

After a half-century of communist rule, Central Asian resentment of the European "elder brothers" still flares up: In 1969, Uzbeks rioted in their capital of Tashkent, beating up all those who looked Russian. On the other side, Europeans living in the southeastern republics seem almost colonial in their habit of deriding the natives as *chernye*—that is, "blacks" (which they are not). While Brezhnev has proclaimed the Red Army "the living embodiment of socialist internationalism," its senior command remains exclusively Slav, and mainly Russian.

Small wonder, then, that the Muslims of the borderlands reportedly taunt the Russians with the warning: "Wait until the Chinese come."

The Chinese may never come, but the year 2000 will, and it might bring a Muslim "victory in the bedroom." At century's end, the population of the Central Asian republics will have grown by one-half, from 40 to 60 million. These five republics, populated mainly by ethnic Turks sharing a common religion and culture, will then account for more than 20% of the entire Soviet population. If one adds the three Transcaucasion republics of Armenia, Azerbaijan, and Georgia, then the turn-of-the-century total for the "Soviet sunbelt" climbs to almost 30%. In 1970, only 1 out of 7 persons in the Soviet Union was of Muslim origin. By the turn of the century, the ratio will be at least 1 out of 5, and perhaps 1 out of 4. Of the Soviet population as a whole, ethnic Russians will be a minority—48%.

While high Muslim fertility seems, at first glance, a partial solution to the USSR's overall manpower shortage, in fact it merely adds a cruel twist. As a practical matter, the Soviet leadership cannot simply replace each Russian worker with a Muslim. There is the problem of location: 60% of the Soviet gross industrial product originates in the RSFSR, and to this day, Soviet Muslims are reluctant to emigrate from the "House of Islam" (*Dar ul-Islam*), their native lands far to the southeast.

There are, of course, Soviet precedents for the coerced movement of large populations. In 1944, for example, 6 days after the liberation of the Crimea from the Nazis, all 200,000 of the local Tatars were condemned by Stalin as a "collaborator nation" and sent to Siberia, the Urals, and Uzbekistan. But slave labor is anachronistic in a technological world; it is better suited to the building of earthen dams than to the manufacture of silicon semiconductors.

The alternative is even more unwieldy: shifting the Soviet Union's industrial plant to the labor-rich southern tier. Again, there are precedents, as when in 1942–1943, up to 50% of European Russia's factories were moved east from the combat zone to the safer Urals. But heavy postwar industrialization in European Russia has now made such an exodus prohibitively expensive. It would probably be vetoed on political grounds anyway, for fear of a Russian "backlash." Housing and food are already scarcer in the RSFSR than in Central Asia, and ethnic Russians would be less than happy to see their industries and resources siphoned off by people they consider inferior ingrates.[1]

Hence the government's present compromise: Whenever possible, it locates *new* plants for labor-intensive industries in the south, a move that recognizes the improbability of Muslim migration. This may help in the long term, but it will do little to dampen the labor squeeze coming in the 1980s.

Coping with   The manpower problem will be exacerbated by the
Demography   demands of the armed forces. If the Communist party
              is the father of Soviet society, the military is its privi-
leged eldest son. Come labor shortage or labor surplus, the Kremlin annually calls up about 1.7 million 18-year-olds to replenish the 4.8-million-man armed forces. But if it takes its usual quota, the Army will conscript enough manpower in 1986 to equal six times that year's net increase in the labor force.

This smaller pool will also include a higher percentage of the country's least educated, least "urban" menfolk. In 1970, only one-fifth of all Soviet conscripts came from the eight southern republics; in the year 2000, the proportion will be one-third. The Red Army's truck driver training course now takes a year. (The U.S. Army's takes 5 weeks.) One wonders what place the sophisticated technological army of the twenty-first century will have for unskilled and (perhaps) untrustworthy draftees from the "backward" border regions, many of them probably still unable to speak Russian fluently.[2]

The USSR has, in its short history, been hit by epidemics, invasions, and famines, all of them staggering blows that might have toppled the regime—but did not. The Soviet people seem able to endure and survive almost any misfortune. But the USSR has never experienced simultaneous blows to both economic health and ethnic Russian supremacy.

Some Western analysts predict that life will simply grind on, that present birth and death trends will continue but that the Soviet Union will plod on without much change. Others see the Kremlin turning away from its domestic difficulties and embarking upon risky foreign adventures to divert the citizenry's attention and stir patriotic fervor.

Such forecasts, in my view, are plausible but improbable.

The Soviet Union will not be able to simply do "more of the same" during the crises of the 1980s and 1990s as it did in the past. The Communist party's goal is to retain power. To do so, it will probably be forced to increase production by implementing fundamental economic reforms, to loosen the state bureaucracy's strangle hold on the everyday workings of the economy, even to the point of permitting some autonomy for shopkeepers, farmers, and cottage industries, as in Poland or Yugoslavia.

Should such reforms succeed (and there is no guarantee of that), the USSR's ethnic Russian leaders will be able to deal with the growing numbers of Central Asians from a position of renewed strength, which will make economic and political concessions to the Muslims seem less dangerous.

Continued economic decline, conversely, might lead to an anti-Muslim crackdown by an insecure and embattled party. And the Muslims themselves might get ideas about autonomy. Nothing breeds solidarity so much as repression; as historian Alexandre Bennigsen has noted, the USSR is the only place in the world where Shiite and Sunni Muslims, often bitter foes elsewhere, regularly take part in the same religious rites.

But these are only scenarios, dim visions of what might possibly happen in the years to come. This peculiar problem of *people* introduces a new element of uncertainty. The demographic trends now underway will in the next few decades challenge the regime in ways that simply cannot be foreseen. In discussions by American analysts of the Soviet Union's future—discussions that address, say, the USSR's bigger missiles, growing navy, and poor economic performance—the coming population shift seems amorphous, distant, almost inconceivable. But it could easily become the Kremlin's most pressing problem of all. For better or worse, it will reshape the Soviet Union, producing a country that in the year 2000 will be far different from the one we know today.

Notes

[1]A rather blunt 1971 dissident *samizdat* document complained that "Russia gets all the knocks" and warned that the regime's ideal of a "new Soviet people" would lead, through "random hybridization," to the "biological degeneration" of the Russian people. In Soviet demographic circles, the current euphemism for Russian "ethnic purity" is "*kachestvo* (quality) of the population."

[2]In 1970, only 16% of Central Asians of all ages claimed fluency in Russian.

35

BLAIR A. RUBLE

Muddling Through*

About the time that the first McDonald's fast-food stand started selling hamburgers outside Chicago in 1955, a potential competitor named Hubie's opened in Dobbs Ferry, New York. Hubie's was a fully automated "hamburger machine." At one end, attendants fed in ground beef, rolls, cheese, pickles, and ketchup; at the other end, hot hamburgers emerged to slide onto the plates of waiting stand-up diners.

But even the best-laid plans go awry, and Hubie's plans were flawed: The meat patties were not uniform in size, and so some fell into the fire; slow-ups on the conveyor belt resulted in buns toasted black; bits of melting cheese dripped onto vital cogs and bearings; and ready-to-go burgers slid not onto the customers' plates but onto their shoes. Rather than admitting failure and abandoning their "futuristic" system, Hubie's executives hired extra workers to supervise matters and even put a few cooks in the back room to supplement the defective machine's output. Yet such expedients finally proved futile. The customers stayed away in droves. Hubie's soon went the way not of McDonald's but of another contemporary, the Edsel.

The Soviet economy—rigidly organized, overly complex, and less than a boon to consumers—is not unlike Hubie's hamburger stand. But the USSR is not the United States. If Hubie's had opened in Moscow, it would probably still be in business since it would be a state-run monopoly. Muscovites craving fast food would have no alternative.

In short, there is more than one way to sell hamburgers or organize an economy. The Russians have no word for "efficient," but when their leaders decide to give one goal top priority, they can be *effective*, as

*Reprinted by permission of the author and publisher from *The Wilson Quarterly* 5, no. 1 (Winter, 1981), pp. 126–138. Copyright 1981 by Woodrow Wilson International Center for Scholars.

when, during the early 1960s, the Soviet government decided to achieve strategic parity with the United States.

This distinction is often overlooked. Led astray by the Soviets' decidedly different methods, Western observers of the USSR have repeatedly concluded that a Soviet economic breakdown was at hand. When the First 5-Year Plan was promulgated in 1928, for example, Western specialists warned that the heavy loads of freight and frequent usage stipulated by the plan would bend the tracks and ruin the roadbeds of the Soviet railway network. Yet the system endured. Indeed, the Soviets got along with only one main east–west railway line—the Trans-Siberian Railroad—until 1974, when construction of the Baikal–Amur Mainline, or BAM, resumed after a two-decade hiatus.

Today, Western specialists variously see looming crises in Soviet energy, manpower and productivity, and agriculture. One must treat their forecasts with a certain prudence.

It is easy to poke fun at the Soviets. With a per capita gross national product (GNP) lower than Italy's, the Soviet economic performance is still far from Nikita Khrushchev's old goal of overtaking the United States by 1980 (see Fig. 1). Indeed, Soviet trade patterns—that is, exporting oil and importing technology and food—resemble those of a resource-rich developing nation such as Saudi Arabia more than those of the United States.

The Kremlin's hopes for the Soviet economy are embodied in a 5-year plan, which (officially, at least) is treated with veneration. Billboards, newspapers, and television programs endlessly repeat official incantations such as "Fullfill on time the tasks of the Five-Year Plan." This is the way it works: Before the outset of each planning period, *Gosplan*, the national state planning agency, draws up a schedule of long-term goals and distributes it to every industrial enterprise throughout the USSR. Each manager, from the smallest provincial factory on up, reviews the proposals and passes a response up the administrative ladder to the next highest industry level. There it is coordinated with similar proposals and consolidated into a new united plan. By this process, plans, as they grow in scope, wend their way through the bureaucracy until they finally reach the national planning headquarters in Moscow, where *Gosplan* prepares the ultimate 5-year plan for the nation.

Bitter Cold and Crumbling Coal

A Communist Party Congress and the USSR Supreme Soviet then approve the plan. Thus ratified, the plan puts managers who fail to follow it in violation of national statutes; as journalist Hedrick Smith observed, the plan comes close to being "the fundamental law of the land." The fundamental flaw in the plan is that it is "finalized" in

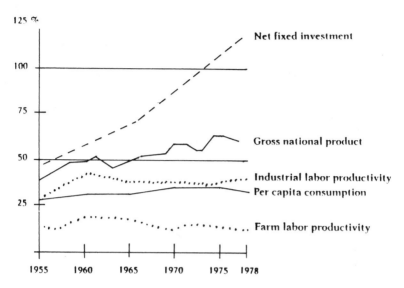

Figure 1. *Soviet economic performance as percentage of United States performance (100%). (Source: CIA; Gertrude Schroeder, Stanley Cohn, Imogene Edwards, Margaret Hughes, and James Noren, "U.S. and U.S.S.R.: Comparisons of GNP," in U.S. Congress Joint Economic Committee,* Soviet Economy in a Time of Change, 1979.)

Moscow but largely implemented at the local level, so the officials who set each factory's targets are not the people who have to meet them.

The new plan that comes before the Twenty-sixth Communist Party Congress, scheduled to convene in February 1981, will have to deal with the usual strains resulting from poor agricultural performance and heavy military spending (which Western analysts estimate to account for at least 8 and perhaps as much as 18% of the GNP, versus United States figures of about 13% in 1954 and 5% in 1979). In effect, the Kremlin has been imposing what strikes many Westerners as a perpetual gray wartime austerity, with top priority given to military needs. But Soviet leaders will also confront difficulties unimagined a decade ago: If Western specialists are correct, the 1980s for the Soviets will be a time of a shifting labor supply, declining productivity, and energy shortages. *Gosplan* will, in one way or another, have to "solve" those problems.

That the Soviet Union could come up short in energy is perhaps the biggest surprise. During the 1970s, the USSR became the world's largest oil producer, pumping 11.7 million barrels a day in 1979 (see Fig. 2). (In second place was Saudi Arabia with a 1979 daily average of about 9 million barrels.) Through sheer volume of production, the USSR man-

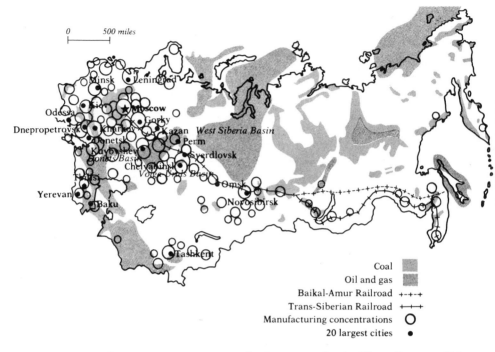

Figure 2. *The USSR: Energy in the East, users in the West. (Sources: CIA; Marshall I. Goldman,* The Enigma of Soviet Petroleum, *[London: Allen & Unwin, 1980].)*

ages to be both the world's second largest oil consumer (after the United States) *and* exporter (after the Saudis). Since 1977, oil exports—to such Western countries as Italy, West Germany, and France—have accounted for more than half of all Soviet hard currency earnings.

Yet throughout the 1970s, Western analysts—most notably those employed by the U.S. Central Intelligence Agency—maintained that the Soviets were facing an energy crunch. Production in the giant Samotlor oil fields in Siberia, which account for one-quarter of the Soviet total, was said to be leveling off. Other energy sources were thought to hold out little hope. The famous coal fields of the Donets Basin in the Ukraine were reportedly petering out after more than a century of mining. The ambitious nuclear power program has fallen well behind schedule, and today, less than 4% of Soviet energy comes from atomic power—among other things, putting it behind firewood as a home heating source.

Moreover, these analysts noted, most of the Soviet Union's fossil fuel reserves lie in Siberia, while some 80% of Soviet energy is consumed in the European part of the USSR (see Fig. 2). With its brief, blazing summers, and prolonged, bitterly cold winters, Siberia is a difficult area to exploit. The expense of laying an oil pipeline across the USSR could far exceed that of constructing the Alaska pipeline, which cost $8 billion and was built with sophisticated technology still unavailable in the USSR. Siberian coal, with its tendency to crumble and self-ignite when exposed to air, is of a far lower quality than that now mined in the European USSR, and coal transportation costs are generally 10 times those of oil. Those who predict a Soviet energy crunch argue that even an advanced Western nation such as France or West Germany would be hard put to conquer such problems, and that the Soviets will be further encumbered by their clumsy planning, lackluster management, and low-grade technology.

A Contrary Argument Yet other Western specialists, most notably Harvard economist Marshall Goldman, have pointed out that at one time CIA experts told us that Soviet petroleum exports would begin tapering off in 1975 (see Fig. 3). When that did not happen, they changed their prediction to 1976, and then 1978, and more recently 1979 and 1980. In 1977, the CIA predicted that Soviet oil production would peak in 1981, with the output for Siberia stabilizing at around 5 million barrels per day. Siberian oil fields are now producing 6 million a day.

Goldman finds little reason to start agreeing with the CIA now. First, he says, the very fact that Soviet prospecting technology is so outmoded means that much of the USSR (unlike the United States) remains unexplored. Second, the CIA has overlooked possible Soviet offshore deposits in the Pacific and Arctic Oceans as well as in the Caspian Sea. Third, the Soviets could benefit from conservation measures: Soviet factories currently use as much energy as their American counterparts but produce only three-quarters the volume of goods. Fourth, the CIA has given short shrift to Soviet natural gas reserves, estimated to be 40% of the world total (see Fig. 2). Gas could soon replace oil at home; the bulk of Soviet energy consumption takes place in stationary boilers and furnaces, thus easing a switchover from oil to gas. Gas could also replace oil as an export, if yet another Soviet–West European pipeline is constructed, as now appears likely. Furthermore, the Soviet commitment to nuclear energy is firm and untroubled by environmentalists' lawsuits and "anti-nuke" demonstrations. The "Atommash" factory at Volgodonsk will soon start turning out 8 to 10 reactors a year. Thus, Soviet energy difficulties are not insurmountable.

In its lagging industrial productivity, the Soviet Union remains in some ways still a "developing nation"—63 years after the Revolution. Here, the system *is* the problem, along with some persistent cultural and psychological hangovers from the past.

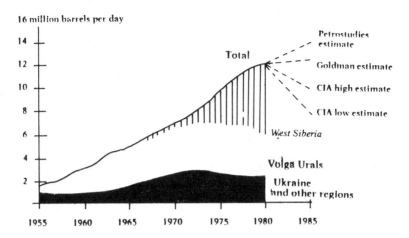

Figure 3. *Soviet Oil: Production and predictions. (Source: CIA; Marshall I. Goldman; Petrostudies, "Soviet Preparations for Major Boost of Oil Exports" [Malmo, Sweden: Petrostudies Co., 1978].)*

Leading the World   To begin with, the Soviets have been notably unsuccessful in transforming peasants into efficient 8-hour-a-day factory workers. With 5 or 6 months of winter and a short growing season, the Russian peasant was long accustomed to vast stretches of idleness followed by frantic bursts of energy. This habit lives on today in the industrial system of "storming" at the end of each month to fulfill the plan. Some factories are said to produce half their total output in the last 10 days of each month; Soviet economist, Leonid Kantorovich, winner of the Nobel Prize in 1975, has estimated that the inefficiency of "storming" reduces national income by 30–50%. Researchers in the USSR discovered that factory hands are idle for as much as half their total worktime. For this and other reasons (poor planning, overmanning, shoddy materials, and outdated technology), the Soviet industrial worker is less than half as productive as his American counterpart.

The problem is not a new one. During the 1930s, Joseph Stalin sought to resolve it by enacting severe criminal penalties; by 1939, 20 minutes tardiness could win a worker a quick ticket to the Gulag (Stalin's "corrective labor" penal system). After Stalin's death, however, criminal sanctions were dropped in favor of economic rewards, first in wage hikes—between 1956 and 1978, the Soviet minimum wage rose by nearly 150%—and then in a system of bonuses for outstanding efforts. The incentives failed for the simple reason that Soviet workers are not enticed by more money, which is of little use when goods are unavailable. As one Soviet wisecrack goes, "We pretend to work, and they pretend to pay us."

Worker dissatisfaction is expressed in high turnover rates, absenteeism, and on-the-job vodka parties. Protected by a labor shortage and by trade union officials, who since the 1950s have been able to discourage and even prevent management from dismissing unproductive workers, the Soviet worker finds that it is almost impossible to lose his job (except for political reasons). In the late 1970s, nearly one-fifth of the USSR's labor force moved on to new jobs each year. And it is difficult to overstate the devastating effect alcohol has had on the Soviet economy—not to mention the health of the population. Per capita sales of alcoholic beverages nearly tripled between 1957 and 1972; during the last decade, the USSR led the world in per capita consumption of distilled spirits.[1] One Soviet economist has calculated that "drying out" the working population would boost industrial productivity by 10%.

Thus, during the 1970s, the Soviets went shopping abroad for new technology with which to sidestep altogether the labor productivity problem. Between 1965 and 1977, annual Soviet machinery imports more than quadrupled, with entire "turn-key" plants, such as the Fiat factory at Togliatti, being purchased from abroad.

One Bad Crop in Three   Yet managers as well as workers have stubbornly resisted "the scientific–technical revolution," as the Kremlin calls it. One might paraphrase Lincoln Steffens: They have seen the past, and *they* think it works better. Under constant pressure from their superiors to meet output quotas every month, Soviet factory managers shy away from the production losses inevitably incurred during any switchover to a new production system. Even when lower-level innovation is welcomed, it leads only to a pat on the back and the same old orders—fulfill the plan. Moreover, turnarounds in American trade policy, most recently with President Carter's post-Afghanistan embargo, have made some top Moscow officials uneasy about industrial policies dependent upon purchases of Western technology. Without such purchases, the task of increasing productivity will be close to impossible; even with them, the system is likely to keep any production gains rather small.

Even so, one might ask, why should the 1980s be so critical? In the past, the Soviets have muddled through; in my view, if the labor shortage squeezes industry too hard, they will (to borrow Sovietologist Seweryn Bialer's phrase) simply start "muddling down." The military will continue to get what the Kremlin decides it needs; the squeeze will be felt by the civilian consumers, who will not challenge the system. Here and there, over the next 20 years, factory workers may protest or strike, but Soviet history suggests that such disturbances will be both rare and brutally suppressed.

The Soviet Union's most intractable failure has been in agriculture. But nature bears part of the blame. Indeed, as Harvard historian, Richard Pipes, has observed, the Soviet Union's poor soil, erratic rainfall, and short growing season (about half that of Western Europe's) explain why, throughout its history, the country has suffered "one bad harvest out of every three."

Early on, farm productivity was further hamstrung by Stalin's policies, which amounted to class warfare. During the late 1920s and early 1930s, Stalin wiped out the well-to-do peasants—the *kulaks*—and collectivized agriculture. The results: famine and the deaths of millions. For the regime, the price was right. For the first time, the party gained total political control of the countryside.

Once implemented, Stalin's brutal policies became a kind of theology; its abandonment would signify an abandonment of socialism itself. Nevertheless, soon after Stalin died in 1953, his successors attempted to eliminate his worst excesses. In agriculture, these efforts became closely connected with the fate of Nikita Khrushchev.

Promoting himself as a farm expert, Khrushchev, an old Ukraine hand, reached for power in the mid-1950s by advocating a liberalization of agriculture policy. From 1956 to 1959, these changes—increased investment, higher rural living standards, and tolerance of private cultivation—coincided with beneficial weather to produce abundant harvests. Khrushchev's policies appeared to be vindicated.

Tomatoes at $5 a Pound   But as Khrushchev consolidated his position, his early pragmatism ebbed. During the early 1960s, he pushed for stricter state control and introduced the "forced crop program." The centerpiece of the program was the conversion of the Ukrainian wheat belt to corn cultivation, an ill-fated policy derived largely from official belief in Soviet agronomist T. D. Lysenko's "Marxist" theory of genetics, which (absurdly) held that plants could be made to adapt to their environment and could then transmit those adaptations to their offspring. According to Lysenko, corn would soon flourish in the Ukraine. It did not, and the spectacular failure of the Soviet European "forced crops" came just as drought hit the Soviet Asian farmlands. The 1963 harvest was a disaster: The USSR decided to import significant amounts of food for the first time since World War II, and in October 1964, Khrushchev was ousted by the Central Committee (see Fig. 4). The Soviet Union, explained his successors, had had enough of Khrushchev's "hare-brained schemes."

Leonid Brezhnev's farm plans, introduced in March 1965, involved an enormous increase in outlays—for machinery, construction, fertilizers, and land reclamation. By 1977, the annual Soviet investment in agriculture ran to nearly $80 billion, more than six times the United States

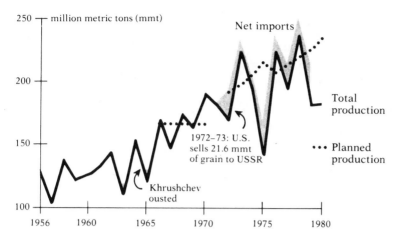

Figure 4. *Soviet grain: Goals, production, imports. (Source: U.S. Department of Agriculture; Alec Nove, "Soviet Agriculture under Brezhnev,"* Slavic Review *[September 1970], p. 406.)*

expenditure. Even so, the Soviets have developed a farming system capable of meeting only the most elementary needs of an industrial society. Grain imports have supplemented the domestic harvest in every year since 1971. Those imports—to feed beef cattle, chickens, and hogs—are perhaps a major cause of the relative stability of Soviet consumption in the Brezhnev era: The impact of agricultural difficulties on the Soviet economy and people has been softened through grain imports paid for by oil exports.

Meanwhile, Soviet farmers supplement official production and imports with their own "private" crops. During the mid-1970s, the private sector occupied 3% of cultivated land; but it is estimated to have produced 59% of the USSR's potatoes, 44% of its fruit, 34% of its vegetables, and 31% of its meat and milk.

It is not only in agriculture that such "hidden" production enables the official state-run system to survive. Throughout the Soviet system, life is made tolerable by what Western academics call the "Soviet second economy." After six decades of socialism, notes University of Virginia economist, Gertrude Schroeder, "nearly everyone seems to have devised ingenious ways to turn its shortcomings to his individual advantage." Indeed, to keep one's job, to meet the plan, to simply operate within Soviet society, it is virtually impossible *not* to participate in the unofficial "gray market" or illegal "black market." Thus, a bureaucrat seeking top quality medical attention will arrange for an appointment in a doctor's home—for a fee—rather than in a government clinic; a

Moscow housewife hungry for tomatoes in mid-winter will find them being sold at $5 a pound by a Georgian farmer who has flown via Aeroflot to the capital with two basketloads; a factory manager, striving to meet his monthly production quota, will use barter or bribes to ensure the timely delivery of needed parts or supplies.

It is, of course, impossible to gauge the true extent of unofficial economic transactions. Workers with access to prized goods tend to be thoroughly corrupt: During 1971, no fewer than one in five Moscow gas station attendants was arrested by the "Department for the Struggle against Plundering of Socialist Property" for profiteering in petrol. One might call the second economy the Soviet "10 percent solution"; overall, Western economists figure its contribution to be between 5 and 15% of the total official GNP. And, to repeat, it provides the kind of lubrication that allows the official system to function as well as it does.

Remembering Papa

Since the early 1970s, United States specialists have held up three alternative visions of the Soviet reaction to an uncertain economic future. The first sees the introduction of a hawkish, repressive neo-Stalinism; the second portrays an enlightened leadership brought to understand that economic production will not increase without liberal reform; and the third simply predicts "more of the same." Neither of the first two possibilities seems plausible.

True, some close observers of the USSR do detect an emerging grassroots neo-Stalinism, and many Soviet citizens, both great and small, seemingly yearn for a romanticized past when Papa Stalin made all decisions, when the Soviet people enjoyed the strange luxury of not having to think. But Stalin's answers do not address today's questions. A neo-Stalinist revival could not bring Siberian oil closer to the factories of Central Russia; it would not make workers of the technological age more productive. Stalin's agricultural policies only barely managed to feed the smaller, less urban population of a half century ago. The possibility of a Stalinist revival persists for no better reason than that it has antecedents in the past. The liberal reformist option, for its part, has no real precedent in Soviet history. It exists more as an exercise in Western logic than as a practical Soviet political choice.

The question to be answered by Brezhnev's successors is not whether to go left or right but whether there is any real alternative to more of the same. "Muddling through" (or "down") is not what will *save* the system—it *is* the system, and, in my opinion, it will absorb the impact of any attempts at neo-Stalinism or liberal reforms just as it has absorbed everything else. And though it is not painless, "muddling through" does possess the great virtue (in Soviet eyes) of predictability. Difficult adjustments by the citizenry may have to be made, but in economic

TABLE 1. *Social Indicators*[a]

	Year	USSR	Italy	United States
Per capita	1951	1,820	1,883	6,157
GNP[b] (in 1979	1961	2,870	3,127	6,802
dollars)	1971	4,260	4,654	8,847
	1977	5,070	5,325	10,224
Per capita	1951	26.0[d]	16.5	74.4
meat con-	1961	39.0	30.7	89.7
sumption[c] (kg)	1971	50.0	56.7	109.1
	1977	56.0	64.7	112.0
Infant mortality	1951	84.0	67.0	28.4
(per 1000 live	1961	32.2	40.7	25.3
births)[e]	1971	22.9	28.3	19.1
	1977	31.5[f]	17.6	14.1

[a]Sources: International Monetary Fund; CIA; U.S. Department of Agriculture; Government of Italy; U.S. Department of Health and Human Services; United Nations; B. R. Mitchell, *European Historical Statistics 1750–1970* (New York, 1975); U.S. Bureau of the Census.

[b]Italian figures are gross domestic product. Italian GDP approximately equals GNP.

[c]In carcass weight.

[d]1950 figure.

[e]Soviet data exclude infant losses within 1 week of delivery.

[f]1976 estimate.

matters, the Soviet threshold of pain is, like the sloth's, far higher than we might expect.

Should stagnation persist, as is likely, the Soviet leadership need not perceive disaster. Decline, after all, is relative. Zero economic growth might in the coming decade seem an outstanding accomplishment when one views the unpromising outlook in the West. Transporting oil from Siberia, no matter how costly, could well turn out to be considerably easier for Moscow than getting it from the Persian Gulf will be for the West.

We should not consider remarkable the fact that Soviet leaders face difficult problems. Rather, what is striking about the economic decisions Moscow will make—or avoid making—is not their difficulty but the fact that they are no more vexing than those that face political and business leaders in Bonn, Paris, London, Tokyo, and Washington. Indeed, the increasing uncertainty of the Soviet economic future may signify nothing more or less than the USSR's slow, stumbling entrance into the ranks of the developed world.

Note

[1]Duke University economist, Vladimir Treml, notes that the alcohol problem places the government in a fiscal dilemma: Although alcoholism damages health and productivity, taxes on alcohol generate about 12% of all government revenues, enough to cover the Soviet Union's officially announced defense budget. (True military expenditures are believed by most Western experts to far exceed the published figure.)

36

WILLIAM E. ODOM

Choice and Change

*in Soviet Politics**

Anticipated for several years, the post-Brezhnev era is at last here. In the West it has been awaited as a turning point, a time when new policy initiatives and new political forces would come into play. Many viewed it optimistically as a chance for positive change in both Soviet foreign and domestic policies. A new generation of younger leaders, it was hoped, might bring a surge of imagination and energy leading to significant reform internally and a new détente with the West—with genuine concessions on arms control and "rules of the game" for regional competition permitting the USSR to draw back from its rather extended commitments, especially in the Third World—in order to give more attention to solving accumulated domestic problems. Others anticipated a rapid turnover of elites, internal reform, but no retreat from an assertive foreign policy.

When Yuriy Andropov speedily succeeded Leonid Brezhnev as party general secretary, it came as a surprise to many, particularly those who expected positive change. How could this happen? How could Andropov, long the head of the secret police (KGB), achieve what his predecessor Lavrentiy Beria apparently tried and failed to achieve after Stalin's death? Surely his accession must be merely the first round in the succession struggle. Surely the younger set among the leadership will not let things settle down until the geriatric Politburo has been repopulated with a youthful membership. To be sure, old age is forcing turnover in elites at an increasing rate; nevertheless, the anticipated breakup of consensus in the Politburo and of the policy-making system has yet to occur and seems unlikely in the near future. The real surprise

*Reprinted by permission of the author and publisher from *Problems of Communism* 32, 3 (May–June, 1983), pp. 1–21.

is that students of Soviet affairs generally did not anticipate what has happened thus far; namely, they did not take the Andropov candidacy seriously and expected a much more erratic transfer of power.

Why Andropov?

Why, indeed, did Andropov win the first round? The answer to this question lies primarily in the organizational and structural features of the Soviet party-state system at its apex. All of Lenin's successors—Stalin, Malenkov, Khrushchev, Brezhnev, and Andropov—held positions in two key institutions: the Politburo and the Secretariat of the Central Committee of the Communist Party of the Soviet Union. As Merle Fainsod, Leonard Schapiro, and others have pointed out, real power in the party-state system depends above all on controlling party cadre assignments, that is, personnel.[1] The institution offering that control is the Secretariat. Lenin depended on Yakov Sverdlov to manage cadres in the early years of the Soviet regime.[2] After Sverdlov's death, Stalin gradually took over this task, using the Organization Bureau and the Secretariat to set up a comprehensive personnel system. Challenges to his grip on cadres failed, and Stalin slowly accumulated enough power to have himself named general secretary in 1922.

The key to cadre control is the *nomenklatura* system, institutionalized early in the Soviet regime. It is a list of positions which can only be filled by persons who have the approval of the higher party apparatus.[3] One of the Secretariat's major roles is looking after the hundreds of thousands of *nomenklatura* posts. They include not just positions in the party apparatus but also thousands of posts judged essential for controlling state and economic institutions. The *nomenklatura* system ensures for the Secretariat a network of reliable agents in all institutions of consequence who are beholden to the Secretariat for the rank, stature, and privileges that accompany these strategic posts. There is no sign that this system has atrophied or weakened significantly since its inception. The Secretariat, therefore, remains key for any aspirant to the top political post in the party. Without it, he could not hope to make the Central Committee and lower party officialdom sing his tune in choosing a new general secretary. It goes without saying, then, that any serious candidate in the post-Brezhnev succession had to be a party secretary. It goes equally without saying that an aspirant for the highest post had also to be a member of the Politburo, the top policy- and decision-making body of the party. There is no precedent in Soviet history of anyone who was not a Politburo member becoming general secretary of the CPSU.

Had Brezhnev died several years ago, Andropov might well have failed to claim the General Secretary's mantle. There were other Politburo members also holding party secretary posts who could have been serious challengers. Mikhail Suslov's position was undoubtedly quite powerful in light of his long tenure in both top party organs. Dmitriy Ustinov held both posts for a time. Andrey Kirilenko was long judged a likely successor precisely because he held both positions. And Konstantin Chernenko's ascendancy as a potential successor derived from the same dual base.

However, in January 1982 Suslov died. Ustinov, who became minister of defense in 1976, had yielded his secretary post in the same year. Kirilenko has been reported to have been in less than robust health during the past few years, a factor that may account for his failure to win the first post-Brezhnev round. Chernenko certainly held the requisite posts, and had to be taken seriously as a competitor, notwithstanding his somewhat mousy character and clerk-like subservience to Brezhnev.

Thus, the key question for a serious Kremlinologist became "who would replace Suslov in the Secretariat?" This would be the critical clue to the nature of the expected succession struggle. There were two dramatically different possibilities. One was unlikely but had to be considered because, had it occurred, the succession dynamics would have been altered fundamentally. This would have been to turn to the Leningrad or Ukrainian party organization, both of which have always played key roles in party factional struggles. Grigoriy Romanov, reportedly a very tough and hard-line younger Politburo member, might well have been brought to Moscow from Leningrad to work as secretary. But Volodymyr Shcherbytskyi, first secretary of the Ukrainian party, was a more likely candidate. Because he is relatively young, he could have brought new energy to the top party apparatus.

Had either of these Politburo members captured Suslov's post as secretary, we would be facing a quite different situation in the post-Brezhnev era. They would have worked rapidly during the last months of Brezhnev's life to shuffle as many party posts as possible in preparation for the succession struggle. They would have brought their own coterie of party *apparatchiki* into the competition. The Moscow center would have been under assault by cadres from a regional center. In that circumstance, a quick and easy transfer of power to a new general secretary would have been virtually impossible. A period of uncertainty would have been inevitable while the regional group fought it out with Andropov, Chernenko, and others who held the important ground in Moscow.

A second possibility is the one that did occur. A new secretary was found in the small circle of those who were already well-entrenched in Moscow. Had the choice been someone who was not also a Politburo member, that would have augured well for Chernenko. Even Viktor Grishin, a Politburo member and head of the Moscow city party organization, might not have posed a serious challenge to Chernenko, since he lacked two trump cards that Andropov brought to the game.

Andropov's first card was obvious: his many years as head of the KGB. This provided him with the power that comes from KGB counter-intelligence work within all state, party, and military organizations. The *internal* counterintelligence role gave Andropov a far stronger position than is generally recognized by Western analysts. It made him very knowledgeable of *nomenklatura* and cadre assignments because clearance for such assignments involves a KGB security check. It also gave Andropov familiarity with the daily institutional activities of all the organizations that his agents watch, that is, virtually the entire state apparatus. In this respect, Andropov had a much closer acquaintance with the operation of the Soviet economy than one might ordinarily suppose. The view occasionally expressed in the West that he has no experience with the economy is factually inaccurate: Andropov has vast experience with the way the economic bureaucrats and factory managers cheat the system, falsify reports, and fulfill their plans in appearance if not in reality. Another little-understood role that Andropov played in the economy as head of the KGB concerns acquisition of Western technology, legally and illegally. The Ministry of Foreign Trade enjoys only a subordinate role in this regard, since the KGB and the Ministry of Defense dominate foreign trade decisions.[4]

Andropov's second card was less obvious. He seems to have been a key figure in the Defense Council. His position on this body may well have been the most significant factor in Andropov's quick gaining of power. To understand the basis for this judgment requires some background on the Defense Council's role and composition. It is the lineal descendant of the Council of Labor and Defense (STO) from the early days of the regime. During World War II, the State Defense Committee (GKO) had a similar role. After the war, the GKO disappeared, at least from public view. The STO and GKO both consisted of a small subset of Politburo members who coordinated manpower, industry, and agriculture, on the one hand, with military requirements, on the other. Both were extremely powerful bodies whose decisions were not challenged by the Politburo as a whole. They could dictate to the economic and industrial planning apparatus. And they were the highest court of appeal on the allocation of resources for the military.[5]

By the early 1970s, and perhaps even earlier, this old organizational device became operative again. The Military Industrial Commission, headed by the deputy chairman of the Council of Ministers, gave the military industries a corporate executive at the highest level. The Military Collegium in the Ministry of Defense provided a parallel corporate executive for the military leadership. The two institutions undoubtedly work in considerable harmony, but issues are bound to arise that transcend that harmony or require a higher policy decision. Such decisions are made in the Defense Council.[6]

When Andrey Gromyko, Andrey Grechko, and Andropov were

elected to the Politburo in 1973, it was not difficult to infer that this old organizational system was reemerging. These men made up the foreign-policy/military/police clique which had formed the STO and GKO in the past.[7] It made sense for Brezhnev to bring them into the Politburo where they could help him carry the vote on his foreign and military policies. In 1974, the Defense Council was mentioned in the Soviet press and its existence has been public knowledge since that time.[8]

We cannot be entirely sure about the make-up of the Defense Council, but it seems logical that Andropov, Gromyko, and—after Grechko's death—Ustinov must have joined Brezhnev to form this body. Possibly Suslov and Aleksey Kosygin were members. In any event, this group includes those who are knowledgeable about military and foreign policy, as well as economic issues, by virtue of their state duties. Every Politburo member does not have time to immerse himself in these areas. The Defense Council subset of the Politburo, therefore, probably has a free hand in foreign policy and military issues since other Politburo members are not in a position to gain adequate information and staff support to challenge the arguments on such matters by the Council members.

Had an outsider like Shcherbytskyi come to the Secretariat, he would have had to abolish the Defense Council or quickly make it subordinate to his wishes. Otherwise, his chances of gaining the top post in the party would have been small. If Chernenko were not a member of the Defense Council, this would have contributed to his political weakness; however, it is probable that Brezhnev had included him.

Speculation has been widespread that Ustinov and the military establishment threw their lot in with Andropov, making his ascendancy possible. Whatever the case, one can assume that Andropov and Ustinov had worked together in considerable harmony for several years. Moreover, if Ustinov did play a key role in Andropov's selection as general secretary, his personal support sufficed; "military" support in the broader sense was not necessary. And unless Ustinov truly detested Andropov, he was unlikely to have backed a regional party chief like Shcherbytskyi or Romanov given the uncertainty and turmoil that the ascendancy of such a leader would bring to the central party apparatus. In fact, one may wonder why Ustinov himself did not bid for the top post, since institutionally he was in a strong position to do so, having served not long ago as a party secretary.

In any event, the uncertainty of the situation was greatly reduced in the spring of 1982 when Andropov became a party secretary. From that point, there was no real possibility of another challenger making a serious bid. Andropov offered a smooth institutional transition, the least turmoil in the succession process. Furthermore, it is improbable that Andropov, Ustinov, and other key figures had not been working out a succession sequence months if not years before Brezhnev died. The succession struggle—to the degree there is one—did not begin with Brezhnev's death; it had been in progress for some time.

However, Andropov himself is not a young man, and the next succession cannot be far off. Will it proceed as smoothly? This depends on who is brought into the Secretariat and the Politburo. If new people can be co-opted in an orderly fashion, the next succession, too, ought to be smooth. Certainly, the organizational structure is such that it can be. A series of deaths among the Politburo members, of course, could force the pace of change, making the co-optation process difficult to manage. But even in that event, the institutional arrangements will remain to define the playing field on which the struggle for the general secretary's position is carried out. The need to organize the society for military-command affairs, for an aggressive foreign policy, and for the continued modernization of Soviet military forces provides strong institutional imperatives that challengers cannot easily dismiss or throw into disarray without consequences they would not desire. The breakup of the central policy-making system, therefore, may not be as likely as some have anticipated.[9]

Brezhnevism: A Legacy

In order to judge prospects for the post-Brezhnev period, it is necessary to define the basic nature of the Brezhnev era. In brief, it combined foreign policy *mobilism* with domesic policy *immobilism*.

In the international arena, Brezhnev scored remarkable gains for the USSR. They were not all of his making, but he certainly took advantage of key opportunities that arose. With the coming to power of the Social Democratic Party (SPD) in West Germany, he reversed Soviet policy toward Bonn and offered small rewards for the SPD's new Ostpolitik. At the same time, he utilized the American opening on strategic arms control to relax tension between the superpowers. In turn, he got a slowing of U.S. strategic programs, acknowledgment that the USSR was a superpower, and a surge of East-West economic interaction financed by the West. At the same time, he brought the West to recognize more formally (at Helsinki) the post-World War II frontiers in Europe, something Khrushchev tried and failed to achieve.[10]

In the Third World, the projection of Soviet power grew unabated. As the United States turned its military attention away from NATO and toward Vietnam, Brezhnev was undoubtedly delighted, not only because it weakened NATO but also because it affected U.S. public attitudes toward an assertive U.S. foreign policy. While appearing to cooperate with the United States on a settlement in Vietnam, Brezhnev kept an abundant supply of military materiel flowing to his North Vietnamese allies.

The major setback for Brezhnev came in 1972 in the Middle East when

Anwar al-Sadat ordered Soviet advisers out of Egypt. Having invested a great deal there as a strategic anchor for Soviet policy in the Middle East, the USSR found itself abruptly expelled from a key position in the region. By the end of the decade, however, with the help of Cuban forces, Brezhnev had reasserted Soviet influence in the region, gaining important positions in Ethiopia and South Yemen while holding on to significant influence in Syria and Iraq. And, of course, the Soviet invasion of Afghanistan created new pressure on the north side of the Persian Gulf region. The Soviet-Cuban venture in Angola made the USSR a larger factor than had been the case previously in southern Africa. After General Anastasio Somoza's fall in Nicaragua in 1979, Brezhnev was able to launch the Soviet-Cuban partnership on a new offensive in the Caribbean region. The U.S. withdrawal from Vietnam gave the USSR, through its client regime in Hanoi, hegemony in Vietnam, Laos, and Kampuchea.

Other than Egypt, the only major negative development from the Soviet viewpoint was the normalization of relations between the United States and China. Brezhnev, of course, inherited the Sino-Soviet split. Apparently accepting it as irreversible in the short run, he set about containing China, establishing a strong position in Southern Asia—in India and Afghanistan—and reducing tensions in Europe while expanding the size of Soviet military forces on the Sino-Soviet border more than threefold.[11]

The backdrop for this foreign policy offensive was the steady Soviet military buildup. In almost all categories of military power the USSR equaled the United States and exceeded it in some.[12] In a real sense, the Soviet military buildup in the 1970s marks a qualitative change in the postwar East-West military balance, no mean achievement for Brezhnev.

The Brezhnev era indeed was a time of great Soviet foreign policy mobilism. Moscow showed astuteness in reading the political climate in the West and in encouraging "realistic" circles there to curb any serious Western attempt to match or check Soviet assertiveness. In the Third World, Moscow not only replaced U.S. influence almost entirely in southeast Asia but also created a major geopolitical challenge to vital Western interests in the Persian Gulf region. Although he lived only long enough to see it begin, Brezhnev threw the USSR into a new offensive for influence in Central America.

On the domestic front Brezhnev left quite another record. The economy certainly enjoyed an infusion of Western technology, but on the whole, economic entropy seems to have been the dominant trend. The "second economy" and massive corruption have grown to proportions that appear to exceed the regime's capacity (or will) to repress them with punitive and "administrative" methods. Two attempts at reform came to nothing. In the 1960s, a number of reforms, associated with the name of

economist Yevsey Liberman, were introduced with little apparent result. In the early 1970s, great press fanfare accompanied the concept of
production associations and the freeing of inefficient labor from economic enterprises. Many officials in the central economic apparatus
were to move closer to production, away from Moscow. In any event,
little of note happened in response to these organizational measures for
economic improvement.[13]

Symptomatic of the decay in the economy was the discussion of the
need to shift from an "extensive" to an "intensive" approach to economic growth. Abram Bergson's estimates of the trends in Soviet factor
productivity cut to the root of the problem.[14] The decline in factor
productivity meant that larger and larger amounts of capital would be
required to sustain growth, and, at best, the rate of growth would
continue to decline unless some significant changes were introduced in
the Soviet growth model. By 1975, matters reached a point where the
leadership, faced with the necessity to cut back in at least one major
sector—investment, consumption, or defense—decided to reduce investment in favor of consumption without touching defense.[15]

This decision tells us a lot about Brezhnevism. The General Secretary
realized that the economy was in serious difficulty. Yet he would not
touch defense allocations. Rather, he reduced investment to save consumption. This was a sign not of aggressive economic leadership but of
resignation, perhaps temporary, in the face of stagnation, lethargy, and
inefficiency. It is also possible that the economic planners had concluded
that the return on larger investment had become too small to make the
pain of sacrifice elsewhere worth it. Defense expenditures, of course,
were paying off abroad, earning money from arms sales and bringing
increased prestige to the USSR as a military superpower.

Added to Brezhnev's economic woes were a number of bad harvest
years and bottlenecks in oil and gas production. Both problems required
foreign currency: to buy grain and to import energy production equipment. The overall energy problem brought sharp shifts in resource
allocations in 1981–82 aimed at relieving bottlenecks, but the result is
meager thus far.[16] The great agricultural program for the non-black
earth region, an attempt to ameliorate the agricultural problem, and
other schemes have accomplished little, compelling the USSR to rely on
imports.[17]

Perhaps the most dramatic sign of domestic policy immobilism is to
be found in the growth of corruption and the so-called second economy.
Konstantin Simis offers an inside account of corruption, its dimensions
and the regime's unwillingness to move against it. The party elite seems
to be the most corrupt and the least punished when caught. Even the
Georgian affair—in which Vasiliy Mzhavanadze, a candidate member of
the CPSU Politburo, was implicated—did not bring indictment or loss of
party membership to the most heavily involved.[18] Ironically, at about

the same time—in 1972—Brezhnev initiated a party "documents exchange" which he described as not simply a "technical" affair but as a
"politically principled inspection of the party's ranks."[19] Traditionally
such exchanges were implemented as purges, designed to reinvigorate
the party apparatus, to bring it back to Leninist norms of self-sacrifice
and revolutionary dedication. The Brezhnev documents exchange drag-
ged on for two years and was still receiving press attention in 1975.[20]
Notwithstanding this "principled inspection" of the party's ranks, few if
any party members were expelled, and corruption continued unabated.
The contrast with the Khrushchev and Stalin shake-ups of the party
could hardly have been greater.

The Soviet dissident movement offers ambiguous evidence about
the Brezhnev regime's inability to prevent internal decay.[21] Judgments
vary on the extent and importance of this movement, but it did test
Soviet repressive capabilities. In the last few years, its vitality has been
sapped by the KGB. In fact, the regime has displayed considerable
ingenuity in breaking it up and, in this regard, the dissidents appear to
have found and exceeded the regime's limits of toleration. Nevertheless,
the mere emergence of the movement indicates a degree of internal
decay.

The Brezhnev period also witnessed serious challenges to Soviet
hegemony in Eastern Europe. Although Brezhnev proved willing to use
force to break resistance in Prague, he had to take the entire Politburo
with him to negotiate with Alexander Dubček on the Czech-Soviet
border in the spring of 1968: clearly he did not have unrestrained power
to act on his own, and he also may have wanted to spread the
responsibility among his colleagues. Problems in Poland, beginning in
the winter of 1970–71, reemerged in far more threatening dimensions in
1980. Political and police "salami tactics" exercised through Polish
authorities have whittled down organized opposition and brought matters in Poland under temporary control, but the mere fact that such
developments could occur indicates the degree of immobilism in bloc
policy that beset Brezhnev's leadership.

Today the Soviet leadership is confronted with both the successes
and failures of Brezhnevism. The successes derived from a highly
flexible and assertive foreign policy accompanied by the largest and
most comprehensive military buildup ever witnessed. The failures
can be attributed to the retention of the Leninist and Stalinist-
party/police/state structure resting on a centrally planned economy
without retention of the system's mechanisms for revitalization, that is,
purges of the party elite and rigid enforcement of labor discipline. This is
not to suggest that the system would have been more successful with
the retention of full-blown Stalinism, but it is to identify the basic change
that permitted domestic policy immobilism and decay to reach their
present dimensions.

Factors of Change and Continuity

The prospects for the Andropov regime and its successors are constrained to a large degree by the objective factors of change that have accompanied Brezhnevism. Western analysis of these factors has not proven very perspicacious. In the 1960s, it became popular among Western specialists on the Soviet Union to take the "group approach" to the political analysis of change in the USSR. De-Stalinization, many agreed, had introduced conditions of significant change in the Soviet system. The task of analysis was to discover what these conditions were and anticipate political development of the system. A review of such endeavors based on the group theory of politics led me to the conclusion that the approach anticipated the results before the evidence was thoroughly examined.[22] Despite the failure of pluralism to develop in the USSR, many analysts still cling to the interest-group approach in analyzing Soviet politics. Some analysts dismiss critiques of the group approach as being an assertion that the system remains "monolithic," an assertion undercut by signs of the diffusion of power.

The important question, however, is not *whether* power is diffused but *how* it is diffusing. Pluralism is only one way for power to be diffused, and it depends on very particular circumstances in a polity whether the pluralist variant of diffusion takes place. Bureaucratic decay is another way for power to be diffused in a monolithic system. Regionalism is yet another way, and when regionalism is reinforced by nationalism, that represents yet another diffusion mechanism not very compatible with the pluralistic model. A review of key institutional, economic, and social factors in the USSR demonstrates that while much has changed and power has diffused within the system, continuity also remains strong and the diffusion of power has hardly followed pluralist patterns.

In assessing the extent to which institutional change has occurred, one must look, above all, at the *centrally planned economy*. While hundreds of small policy changes have been introduced to cope with undesired organizational consequences and behavior, the essential institutional structure remains unaltered. There has been no significant expansion of market pricing, not even in the marginal manner observed in some East European states, most notably Hungary. The USSR State Planning Commission (Gosplan) retains its dominant role in setting prices and allocating resources. Although "economic success indicators" have been modified in many ways in an unending search for more efficiency, the essential character of the system has been carefully preserved.[23] This lack of institutional change, of course, is a reflection of the leadership's strong preference for the kind of political control the system affords for directing the economy, for making its structural development and its output conform to "planner's preferences" as opposed to "consumers' preferences."

The most dramatic change is found in what the unchanged planning institutions are capable of doing. In the 1950s, American graduate students studying the Soviet economy were taught that central planning in the USSR permitted directing a higher investment rate at those sectors that the planners desired to expand.[24] Problem areas such as agriculture and efficiency of capital investment were not ignored, but professors left their students with the impression that the Soviet system could mobilize resources and direct them more or less as the leaders chose, notwithstanding consumer and other demands. That was probably a fairly accurate assessment of the Soviet economic system in its first three or four decades. Today, it no longer adequately describes the system.

The dialectics of growth have brought a major change in the economic system. As the aggregate capital stock has grown, it has required ever larger amounts of new investment to make a proportional change in the structure of the capital stock. In other words, the central planners' ability to shift investment significantly from one sector to another is not as great as it was earlier. The discretion they retain in altering the capital-stock structure declines each year. The extraordinary restructuring of the economy in the 1930s and in the postwar reconstruction period cannot be easily repeated, and is perhaps impossible, today.

This diminution of planners' discretion is not only the result of the size of the economy. It is perhaps equally the result of what economist Fyodor Kushnirsky calls the absence of managerial responsibility.[25] It seems to be beyond the power of Soviet planners to close down inefficient economic activities. They may expand activities and create new ones, but they seldom cause a firm to go bankrupt. The forces against bankruptcy action include not only diffusion of responsibility within the managerial system but also regional party influence and the fear of creating unemployment. Official acknowledgment of the decline of planners' discretion is implicit in the slogan that growth now depends on "intensive" methods rather than traditional "extensive" methods of economic development. The call for greater labor productivity is inspired by keen awareness of the decline in discretionary factor inputs at the disposal of planners.

Yet another change is the expansion of the "second economy" alluded to earlier. Irregular economic activity seems to have taken root at every level in Soviet society.[26] Naturally, this means that resources are diverted from the purposes intended by the central planners. We do not know the size of the second economy; therefore, it is impossible to judge precisely how great a factor it has become in shifting resources away from investment and plan fulfillment. But the impressionistic writings on this subject encourage us to believe that it is not trivial.[27]

The *military economy* is an objective factor of both continuity and change. Probably the greatest failing of Western study of the Soviet Union lies in lack of attention to the military-industrial sector. True, very little information about it is in the public domain, but a great deal of information has long been available about its product: Soviet military forces. They have grown steadily in size, and they are receiving technology in many cases not yet fielded in Western armies.[28] Considerable information is also available about institutional arrangements within the military-industrial sector and its relationship to the rest of the economy.[29]

The striking thing about this growing sector is its structural continuity. The essential structure was developed during World War I and the Civil War. During the ensuing New Economic Policy period, the "military industries" were not demobilized but kept under a single trust. During the First Five-Year Plan, military industry was accorded bureaucratic primacy and priority access to investment allocations. "Military representatives" (*voyenpredy*) formed a vast apparatus that penetrated all industrial activities contributing to the military. They gave the military enormous control over quality, design, and pricing of military goods. They created a supply system of inputs to military industries that ensured priority of allocation. Thus, a siphon system came into being that could pump out of the civilian sector whatever resources the Politburo desired that the military receive.

This system remains essentially unchanged. Without it, the recent Soviet military buildup would have been impossible. And without taking this system into account, no complete understanding of the performance of the economy is possible. At its apex, three institutions give it unchallengeable power. First, the Military Industrial Commission, chaired by the deputy chairman of the Council of Ministers, provides central focus and management for military requirements within the state economic bureaucracy. Second, the General Staff of the Armed Forces generates the military doctrine that dictates military requirements. Through the Ministry of Defense, these requirements are levied on the Military Industrial Commission. Finally, the Defense Council provides guidance over the entire process. The Defense Industries Section of the Secretariat, of course, provides the Politburo and Defense Council with party control over the defense hierarchy. Today, this structural arrangement looks more like the one operative in the late 1920s than the one existing in the 1950s.[30] Continuity, therefore, has reasserted itself.

What has changed is the size and complexity of the military-industrial complex. The military grip on the research and development sector, including the USSR Academy of Sciences, has tightened as modern military technology has increased in diversity and importance. The size of the military-industrial production base, naturally, has grown enormously. This has not been independent of the remainder of the economy. In fact, most Soviet civilian industries have military production lines, active in some cases, on standby in others.[31] The leadership's concern for war mobilization has constrained the profile of Soviet industry perhaps more than any other factor. Military production and mobilization requirements come first. Other production considerations are secondary.

The primacy enjoyed by Soviet military industry goes far in explaining some dysfunctions in other parts of the economy. The leadership, including senior military figures, is not indifferent to the health of the economy as a whole. This should be borne in mind in interpreting recent statements of military leaders about the economy. Marshal Nikolay Ogarkov, the Chief of the General Staff, was quite candid in expressing concern about the Soviet economy.[32] Was he, as some observers have suggested, defending the Soviet military budget? Was he anticipating demands by reformers to shift resources away from military production? Or was he, in fact, articulating a general worry within senior military circles that without reforms and increased labor discipline in the overall economy, the military sector would also suffer? The last interpretation seems the most compelling as one looks more closely into the structure of the system. Marshal Ogarkov and the Minister of Defense, Marshal Ustinov, must be as concerned as other senior leaders about problems in the economy as a whole. Unless institutional reforms are proposed that include the breakup of the Military Industrial Commission and the Ministry of Defense's apparatus of "military representatives" throughout the industrial and the research-and-development sectors, the defense budget is not likely to suffer in ways that military leaders would oppose. Discussions of economic reform to date have not suggested any such radical change; rather, they have been directed toward getting the present system to produce more efficiently. Ustinov and Ogarkov surely would desire that kind of change, and they might even support Politburo decisions that trade off present military production for greater future production. There are precedents for such support by the top military in the 1920s, the late 1940s, and possibly in the late 1950s.[33]

The *new intelligentsia* has been seen by many Western observers as a source of change. Most often this anticipation takes the form of discussions about "generational change," that is, how younger age cohorts, as their members move into positions of power will alter Soviet policy.[34] Analysts who place emphasis on this source of change tend to expect it to have a liberalizing effect on both domestic policy and Soviet relations with the West. Jerry Hough, for example, expects that generational change will have a moderating effect on Soviet foreign policy, although it will certainly not usher in "a period of bliss in Russian-American relations," and will be conducive to significant economic reform on the domestic front. The better-educated younger intelligentsia, particularly in the foreign policy establishment, is not, in Hough's view, as ideological and tough-minded regarding East-West competition as the older generation.[35]

Quite a different interpretation can be placed on the apparent growing sophistication of the younger generation in foreign affairs. John Lenczowski, for example, finds the younger Soviet analysts of Western affairs much abler in understanding and exploiting Western political groups and governments. He finds not so much a decline in the role of Marxism-Leninism as a greater sophistication in the use of its categories for analysis of the "international class struggle."[36] While Hough is encouraged by the pro-détente attitudes he finds among younger Soviet analysts, Lenczowski assesses détente as a major Soviet gain in the East-West competition achieved in part thanks to the more sophisticated insights brought to Soviet policymaking by these younger analysts.

The attempt to anticipate Soviet policy as a function of a generational change is likely to fail. Generations do not make policy. A few individuals in the Soviet system make policy, and even their staffs, although quite large in number, may not be a representative sample of their own generation. Moreover, because of the authoritarian character of the Soviet regime and the lack of competitive interest-articulation by social groups, generational change is less likely to have a direct effect on Soviet policymaking than it has in Western liberal democracies. "Generation" is a useful category for sociological analysis, but for political analysis its utility is distinctly limited.

How are we to deal analytically with the new Soviet intelligentsia? No one disputes that it is different from the older generation of educated elites. Better education, greater exposure to Western influences, less sharp memories of the Stalinist period, a larger proportion growing up in an urban environment, less idealism about the official ideology— these and other factors undoubtedly are causing significant differences between "fathers" and "sons" in the Soviet intelligentsia. Hough suggests that reform on the domestic front—and specifically of the economy—"would tend to benefit the most skilled and the best educated. . . . Since they have every incentive to think of reasons why reform would serve the interests of others and of the economy as a whole, it is difficult to believe that they will not do so. The combination of a demographic problem and an energy crisis will provide them with a golden opportunity to make the case for greater efficiency."[37] This line of reasoning may well occur to many of the new Soviet intelligentsia. Yet, for reasons we shall offer below, such reform is unlikely to occur, notwithstanding the "golden opportunity."

How will the intelligentsia react to frustration and disappointment? This is the critical factor that the leadership must face, and it is the crux of the kind of change that the new generation will bring to the system. While no one knows how they will react, we are not without historical parallels to stimulate our thinking about the possibilities. Throughout the 19th century, the autocracy frustrated the intelligentsia by rejecting reform or by failing to carry through when reform was introduced. In the last several decades of the empire, the intelligentsia had more institutional bases for pursuing reform than is now the case in the USSR or is likely to be the case in the foreseeable future. Nonetheless, it did not unite behind enlightened reform. Rather, the intelligentsia tended to polarize into radical wings. The left wing turned to revolutionary activity. The right wing became more reactionary in defense of autocracy. Nothing as dramatic as the Great Reforms of the 1860s is really to be expected in the 1980s, and even that kind of progress left the 19th-century intelligentsia in despair. Are not the conditions of polarization even greater in the 1980s?

More than a little evidence is available to suggest exactly such a social development in the USSR. The dissident movement reflects the anti-regime wing of the new Soviet intelligentsia,[38] while Lenczowski's analysis of the younger generation of Marxist-Leninist foreign policy analysts identifies the pro-regime wing. Its members have been described by many émigrés. The younger KGB personnel show remarkable sophistication in dealing with dissidents. Soviet diplomatic officials abroad today are a much more sophisticated and no less uncompromising generation of operatives for the regime than were their Stalinist predecessors. One can also detect a new confidence and assertive arrogance in the younger officials, as well as a deep cynicism that is perhaps more vicious than that of imperial officials and secret police.

There is little middle ground for the younger intelligentsia. Either they choose the highly principled path of the dissident movement and sacrifice all hope of the comforts of modern society or they submit to the morally debasing standards of success and upward mobility within the Soviet system. Aleksandr Solzhenitsyn traces the psychological trauma of *Novyy mir* editor Aleksandr Tvardovskiy as he sought to find a middle ground. In the end, Tvardovskiy failed.[39] Where this polarization will eventually lead is difficult to anticipate, but it certainly does not augur well for reform. Instead, at least for a decade or so, it would seem to encourage a heightened struggle between the regime and its loyalists, on the one hand, and periodically emerging dissident groups, on the other. In any event, the appearance of a better-educated intelligentsia is an important factor of change within the system, one which the regime is already devising new means of managing.

It is important to remember that the military intelligentsia is not immune to the general social and political dilemmas that confront the Soviet intelligentsia as a whole. The imperatives of modern military technology have led to a dramatic growth in the system of officer education, not just in size but also in sophistication.[40] Officers probably feel sufficiently secure personally to explore unorthodox ideas more readily than many of their civilian contemporaries. The Riga naval officers' group of dissidents and Major General Petro Grigorenko provide examples, albeit small in number.[41] While most officers are likely to tilt to the pro-regime wing of the intelligentsia, some of them are likely to join the anti-regime wing. It seems most unlikely, however, that this polarization will affect the policy orientation of the senior military leadership. Rather, the anti-regime elements will be expelled from the military as they are discovered, and will lend their support—those who have the courage—to dissident groups in the civilian sector, provided such groups continue to exist either openly or furtively.

Much attention has been given to *demographic change* in the USSR. The expanding Central Asian ethnic groups stand in contrast to the slower-growing Slavic ethnic groups. Employment opportunities are greater in the Slavic area, leading some analysts to anticipate migrations from Central Asia into the European part of the USSR. Such a migration, however, has not occurred at a dramatic level; it is also possible to infer that hidden unemployment exists in the large industrial centers.[42] It does not seem, therefore, that labor migration would necessarily help the Soviet economy. Demography may eventually have a significant impact on Soviet politics, but we are not likely to see this in the 1980s. It is not likely to have much of an impact on Soviet military manpower policy.[43] In fact, the trained reserve manpower pool is sufficiently large for the baby booms and busts to be absorbed without a noticeable effect on force levels or change in military-service policy. Demography may have some effect on policies toward minority nationalities and on regional party politics, but it does not promise to be a large factor in Soviet political development in the Andropov period, and perhaps not even during the rule of his successor.

Alcoholism and a high male death rate have been cited by Vladimir Treml as significant factors in Soviet demography.[44] They definitely indicate social and moral fatigue resulting from low Soviet living standards and impose a resource constraint on the Politburo, but are not likely to cause a policy crisis.

Nationalism ought not to be discounted as a factor for change. Although anti-Russification sentiment is strong in many of the national minority regions, the centrifugal political forces it generates are not likely to create a major crisis of legitimacy for the USSR. (Such a crisis could, however, occur if a war or some similar shock revealed Moscow's instruments of control to be weak.) A more significant effect of nationalism is in instances where it underpins and reinforces deviant behavior, such as corruption and bribery. Konstantin Simis's account of Mzhavanadze's Georgian circle of corruption is a case in point.[45] Ethnic and clan ties provided the social structure for cooperative efforts in corruption and proved surprisingly resilient against party, police, and KGB instruments of control; they were even able to gain a grip on Mzhavanadze, a Politburo candidate member. This form of active ethnic and national sentiment is probably more difficult for the regime to suppress than the separatist sentiments and overt hostility to Russification found in the Baltic republics.

There is a tendency to overlook *religion* as a factor for change and resistance to Soviet authority. Sectarian activities can, of course, be lumped together under the general category of the dissident movement, but they appeal to quite different and broader social strata. The dissident "democratic movement" was composed almost wholly of the intelligentsia. Baptist sects recruit from much less sophisticated social circles. The Orthodox Church also plays a highly complex role, dissident in some regards, more ambiguous in others, especially in its implicit support of Soviet foreign policy through its external relations bureau. It attracts a large number of people from the ranks of the intelligentsia, and not just from those tending toward anti-regime sentiments. A strain of neo-Slavophilism, supportive of the Russian church as well as the regime, has been alleged to exist and to find sympathy among the military and the KGB.[46] To be sure, some of the intelligentsia find in Orthodoxy an alternative to the official ideology, a source of cultural and historical roots, and a haven for "internal immigration." While religion poses no serious threat to the regime's control, it does create a nuisance politically and ideologically. The impressionistic view one gains in the Soviet Union is that religion has grown both in its social and spiritual attraction as well as in institutional size. We may well misjudge both the degree and nature of religious influence. If it is true that Moscow inspired the attempt on the Pope's life, that act reflects the deep concern the leadership feels about the political strength of the Polish Catholic Church and probably about Catholics in the Soviet Union. And, of course, Muslim groups have a model in Iran that does not comfort Moscow, even if an Iranian-style upheaval is most unlikely in Central Asia or the Caucasus.

Finally, *ideology* is thought by many to be changing, that is, declining in influence. Measuring such change is difficult, and most judgments about its decline are based on impressionistic observations. Whatever the case, the language of the Soviet press shows no lack of adherence to the traditional ideological norms. Nor has the time devoted to ideological training in Soviet institutions decreased.

Two realities should be kept in mind before pronouncing Marxism-Leninism dead. First, a multinational empire like the Soviet Union requires a legitimacy principle for maintaining its rule over non-Russian peoples in an age when nationalism is the most prevalent legitimacy principle in the world. Marxist-Leninist "internationalism" provides such a theory. Also critically important for Moscow's power is the Marxist-Leninist view of property. State control of property is the cornerstone of the entire edifice of economic and police instrumentalities. It is difficult to imagine even a marginal retreat from the basic tenets of the official ideology in light of these considerations of its positive role for Soviet power.

Second, Marxism-Leninism offers a sophisticated set of categories and assumptions for political analysis. The same Soviet citizen who confides in private that he is not really a Marxist-Leninist will proceed to discuss international affairs and domestic politics of other countries in Marxist-Leninist categories, apparently having internalized them so fully that he does not recognize them for what they are. Many Soviet officials clearly believe that Marxist-Leninist categories are superior tools of analysis, which provide them with a clear advantage in strategic thinking. Thus, it is too soon to accept the view that the ideology is dead. On the contrary, it may not be dying but rather becoming more fully internalized in Soviet society.

Andropov's Options

Given the heritage of Brezhnevism and the objective factors of change and continuity, what can Andropov do? What must he do? These questions have received no little speculation in the West in recent years, even before Andropov assumed power. The natural tendency has been to focus on the backlog of problems, primarily economic but also social, and to anticipate significant change. Hough has taken a view shared by many that the post-Brezhnev period presents an opportunity for marked improvements, not exactly for a "Prague Spring" but at least for a pragmatic assessment and exploitation of opportunities by a new leader.[47] Trimming back foreign adventures and devising solutions to discrete domestic problems, including cutbacks in the military sector in favor of the civilian sector, seem to be what Hough anticipates. Bialer gives even more emphasis to the enormity of the problems facing the Politburo in the 1980s.[48] While he does not fully share Hough's optimism, he sees the regime at a crossroads. To solve many of the domestic problems, he believes, some factions will press for a reduction in the military sector and for continued access to Western economies for credits, technology, and trade. Yet he does not rule out a continued military buildup and an assertive foreign policy. Bialer's strong implication is that significant change in Soviet politics is bound to occur, although he does not venture to predict its direction.

Andropov's ascendancy, however, has not encouraged us to expect the leadership to make a clear choice between the horns of the many dilemmas. It has not weakened the Defense Council and military-industrial complex as a contending regional party leader might have done in the succession struggle. Nor has it necessarily signaled a larger military role, as is occasionally suggested. Rather, it means that the Brezhnev policy-making system is still intact.

But are the growing problems and forces of change so great that they will soon break up this system? In other words, are the dilemmas so urgent that fundamental choices cannot be avoided? Or can Brezhnevism be sustained for another decade?

The dissident intelligentsia, demographic factors, nationalism, and religion create centrifugal pressures on the regime, but neither singly nor in the aggregate will these pressures prove unmanageable in the coming decade. A major shock to the regime, such as a war, might give these forces such vent that they could become critical for political stability; but short of such a crisis, they have almost no chance of causing major changes.

They cannot, however, be ignored by the regime. They present serious problems and challenges. Co-optation of some of these forces has long been a regime practice, but only if the price were not too high.[49] Coupled with this tactic is repression. As these forces pose more serious problems for the regime, is Andropov likely to abandon the traditional two-tactic policy? Will he merely shift the mix toward more repression as co-optation proves less effective? Does he have an alternative? Genuine concessions to these forces could endanger the system. Is he willing to risk that? Could he bring off an evolutionary systemic change? These forces, if given full expression, are more likely to fragment the system than to take the gradualist road of liberal change. We are compelled, therefore, to expect that Andropov, as well as Andropov's successor, will continue the traditional policy, merely devising new variations on it.

Next, consider ideology. As a source of idealistic fervor, it offers little to the regime. But in a number of other ways its retention remains imperative. There is every reason for Andropov to cling to it. The ideological factor, therefore, works for continuity and against change. It tends to blur the sharp dilemmas Bialer describes, or at least it gives them a unique perspective in Politburo eyes.

Finally, let us consider the economy, including the military sector. Are the economic problems so critical that they demand dramatic changes in policy? Or can the symptoms be treated for another decade while the disease is allowed to persist? In fact, the Soviet economy continues to grow, although at a declining rate. If a real decline— negative growth—occurred, would that bring the regime to dramatic, perhaps systemic, change? It certainly would create enormous domestic political pressures, but what would be the alternative to persevering with the present system? Most Western economic analysts agree that a significant relaxation of central control over resource allocations and prices would carry enormous political risks for the regime. Could the Politburo return to some form of Lenin's New Economic Policy, letting the agricultural sector de-collectivize and allowing small private enterprises to develop in the consumer goods sector? Conceivably that would not topple the regime in the short run, but what dilemmas of power would follow a few years later? Another "scissors crisis," as in 1922–23, when the peasants refused to supply products to the urban areas?[50] Would not the frightened party elite look for another Stalin to reassert central control? Would the West provide a manifold Marshall Plan to rescue the Politburo from its crisis of decentralization? Could the party's legitimacy survive such a dramatic turn of events?

These possibilities would not appeal to Andropov. Nor is it easy to imagine a post-Andropov leadership willing to confront them. A major step in the direction of treating the fundamental ills of the economy would be a step down a very slippery slope. The next step would be difficult to avoid, yet returning up the slope could cause complete loss of footing. Any Politburo will struggle to avoid that course even if it means a lengthy period of economic stagnation and a return to more repressive measures against poor labor discipline, bribery, corruption, and other disorders in the system. Andropov's early moves against corruption, of course, are precisely what should have been expected. The next gambit may be the appearance of "reform," that is, organizational change in the economic apparatus based on new ideas about how to make the old system work. Some shifts in economic policy and organization may provide a moderate arrest of certain economic disorders. Recent investment emphasis on energy and transportation may reduce bottlenecks sufficiently to sustain overall growth, even if only at a declining rate. Measures of this sort may continue for several years before their ultimate failure is demonstrated beyond dispute. In a word, crisis is not as imminent as has sometimes been anticipated.

Agriculture may be an exception. Failure to meet industrial growth plans would not have the immediate social consequences that a crop failure would. The seriousness of the agricultural failures is indicated by Soviet willingness to continue to import large quantities of grain even though Soviet hard-currency reserves are declining. Among reform efforts, we should expect the greatest emphasis in agriculture.

The Soviet military-industrial complex cannot remain unaffected by the overall economic situation. But can it, as is frequently suggested, provide a source of relief for other ailing sectors? The answer is some but not much. Unfortunately, economists have not explored extensively the relationship between defense spending and overall economic performance, not just in the USSR but elsewhere as well. The absence of such scholarly work leaves not only pundits but also many Western specialists on the Soviet Union leaning toward assumptions that what goes to defense is a loss to the rest of the economy; that defense spending is an unambiguous "burden"; and that changing the mix of "guns and butter" is a simple and easy policy choice. Yet, while examples can be found of polities where large defense spending correlates with slower economic growth, examples of the contrary correlation can also be found. Most of the history of the Soviet economy presents a case of rapid economic growth coupled with large military spending. In the last two decades, military spending has increased while growth has slowed, but it is not at all clear that the military sector is the major cause of the decline. It is a contributing cause, however, if one assumes that the centrally planned economic system is essential for the military sector. Such an assumption is compelling. The military product is clearly the preferred choice of the planners. And it is doubtful that military growth could have been sustained at its historical rate had the preferences of Soviet consumers determined resource allocations.

Here we have a bit of a puzzle. Why should we argue that Soviet defense spending has been a "burden" if planners prefer it? Is not the Soviet military buildup a real measure of Soviet economic success? Could one not argue with equal cogency that social costs (environmental, health, etc.) of some sectors of American industry are a "burden"? Of course, but would it follow that the output of those sectors should be considered a "burden" to the gross national product? Certainly not. To understand how the Politburo looks at the Soviet defense "burden," we must keep this analogy in mind. As long as consumers in the United States desire the products of the socially costly industries, these industries are likely to survive. To be sure, interest groups could bring political pressure to bear to reduce those social costs. They would try to make the industries pay for "clean up" or reduction of the social costs. Does not the same thing hold for the Soviet guns and butter relationship?

In part it does, but only in part. First, the Soviet Union does not have, as does the West, institutions for interest articulation that could make the military pay for social costs. Planners can assert their preferences until things become quite bad for the remainder of the economy. Among the elite, those most likely to press the planners for a corrective action are the Defense Council members and military leaders in a position to recognize the danger to future military power arising from too much present neglect of the social costs. Even then, it is not easy in the short run to shift sufficient resources from the military sector to solve problems in another sector. To be sure, there are exceptions. Some military industries could shift production to civilian goods. Tank factories could begin producing more tractors on fairly short notice. When the size and character of Soviet economic problems are considered, however, it is clear that such redirection of production capacity would ameliorate only a few of the problems. For example, radar factories might produce more TV sets, but that would do very little for critical problems of labor discipline and factor productivity in the civilian sector.

Second, military factories are apparently more modern and efficient than other factories. Does it make sense to shift large amounts of capital from the efficient to the inefficient sectors? That would be a bit like selling stocks that are rising in price, to buy ailing stocks in order to force up their price. The analogy is not perfect, but it may reveal something about the dilemmas faced by Soviet planners in making capital allocations.

We can probably expect some shifts of the production mix in the military sector, but such shifts promise only modest relief for the overall economy. A large shift of industrial infrastructure could not take place overnight. It would require years. And, it would not necessarily solve many of the structural problems of the economy. We can also expect that senior military leaders will accept minor shifts, perhaps even large cuts in equipment production. They will do so willingly if they see it as the necessary price for the long-term health of the system that has given them the forces they now have.

On balance, these factors seem less likely to beget major policy changes than to elicit a series of efforts to hold the line in defense of the basic system. In other words, the incentives are strong for Andropov to try to muddle through. Whether he sticks to a "muddle-through" policy, or tries significant initiatives to mitigate or reverse some of the adverse trends within the system, one problem cannot be easily avoided: the declining vitality and responsiveness of the party apparatus.

There are signs that Andropov understands this and intends to deal aggressively with entrenched bureaucrats—party and non-party. Anti-corruption campaigns clearly have the aim of restoring greater administrative efficacy in the state and party apparatus. If they are to achieve notable results, they will have to be sweeping and sustained, and they will create resistance in many party circles. Should they prove ineffective and half-hearted, then "Brezhnevism" will persist under Andropov. Yet, to allow it to persist indefinitely is to risk eventually greater dangers for the system—dangers of a kind that developed for the Polish party.

In Poland, when the party proved no longer able to defeat dissident activity or keep it from large-scale organizational expression, the military had to supply the civilian sector with cadres, that is, with personnel responsive to central party direction. In other words, the Polish leadership turned to its last remaining source of reliable party workers: the officer corps and the police. It remains to be seen if this policy can rebuild a more effective Polish party apparatus.

The Soviet Union does not yet appear to be near the point where such a dramatic move is required. Still, the comparison is instructive in that it tends to sharpen our appreciation of what Andropov is up against. Stalin relied on blood purges to deal with problems of "localism," "careerism," and "drift" in party work. Khrushchev promised the party ranks no more blood purges, but he tried to develop a surrogate through reorganizations and formal requirements for frequent turnover of party and state cadres. Brezhnev was willing to spare the party apparatus even such bloodless purges. Thus, the lower and middle ranks of the party have achieved considerable success in limiting "true Leninist norms" of "democratic centralism"—the principle that made the Bolsheviks a powerful instrument of control and dictatorial policy execution.

Western analysts, by taking the "group approach" to Soviet politics in order to explain the post-Stalin diffusion of power, have tended to miss its key dynamic feature. Conflict is less severe between institutions and incipient groups than it is between higher and lower strata in the hierarchical Soviet system. In the early years of the regime, the narrow top stratum held the initiative. In the Brezhnev years, the middle and lower strata gained significant ground against the party center.[51] The greatest change in Soviet politics has come from this loss of control by the party's Secretariat. It can appoint whom it chooses to *nomenklatura* posts, but soon small face-to-face cliques or "family circles," as the Soviet press calls them, develop to get around the impossible output goals demanded by party direction. These cliques do not aggregate into "groups" in the Western political sense; rather, they thrive within the hierarchical bureaucratic system, reinforcing it.

If Andropov (or his successor) fails to restore party discipline, will he eventually be forced, as were the Poles, to turn to the military and the KGB? We cannot rule out this possibility, although it does not look imminent. If this did occur, it would not be a military takeover in the sense usually meant by a coup. Instead it would be, as in Poland, a shift of party cadres within the system. If this did not lead to an effective purge and rebuilding of the party in a short time, the effects on the military would be severe. The officer corps has a momentous task in simply managing a large and modern military establishment. It does not have cadres to spare. And how long would it be before the officers were trapped in the same "family circles" that they had been sent to eradicate from the party apparatus? This dilemma is so sharp and unpleasant for any Soviet leader that it is difficult to believe he would not use neo-Stalinist methods on the party apparatus before such a crisis arose.

In any event, the central focus for Soviet domestic policy has to be the party cadre problem, that is, the lack of cadre responsiveness to the party center. In the short run, a crisis can be avoided. Andropov can try and fail to reassert effective discipline for a number of years. So can his successor. Yet, unless dealt with, the problem will remain a threat to the very stability of the system.

If that is the outlook for Soviet domestic policy, what must Andropov do in foreign policy? The brief answer is "more of the same," that is, continue Brezhnev's foreign policy "mobilism." Can Andropov do this? Does not domestic stagnation place a drag on Soviet foreign policy? Will not concern with sorting out domestic problems cause the Andropov regime to look for ways to cut back on foreign policy commitments, to reduce costly and dangerous ventures abroad in order to make resources available for dealing with domestic bottlenecks? It is not clear that cutting foreign commitments would create resources that would alleviate some of the domestic resource problems. The sale of Soviet arms, for example, generates hard-currency earnings that would be lost if some commitments were reduced. The fungibility of other foreign policy resources may also not be great. Could hundreds and thousands of military advisers and KGB operatives be easily shifted to industrial problem-solving on the domestic front? The key point here is that there is no way to establish a predictable causal relationship between Moscow's situation at home and its degree of assertiveness abroad.[52] To the extent one were to establish a correlation between the two from Russian and Soviet history, the data are likely to favor the proposition that internal weakness correlates with external assertiveness.

Andropov's views on foreign policy are probably driven less by domestic concerns than by the changing dynamics of Soviet détente policy. That policy should be put in the larger context of the long-standing Soviet concept of "peaceful coexistence," which had its origins in the early 1920s. Finding himself clearly without power to precipitate a revolution in Western Europe—where he had expected it—Lenin designed a new strategy. In dealing with the advanced industrial states, he would seek correct state-to-state relations, trade and aid, and construction of a Soviet industrial base. Stalin, of course, gave this policy the label of "socialism in one country." But peaceful coexistence had another component that is sometimes forgotten: continued revolutionary struggle in what is now called the Third World and what Lenin called the "weak link" in "imperialism, the highest stage of capitalism." That policy was pursued in various forms until the start of World War II.

By the mid-1950s, Moscow returned to the original thrust of the "peaceful coexistence" policy, although initially this policy excluded West Germany. Only after the Czech crisis of 1968 and the coming to power of the SPD in Bonn was Moscow able to reestablish the former broad-based approach to "peaceful coexistence" in Europe. Furthermore, the United States was drawn in as well. For a decade this alternative form of the "international class struggle" (the official definition of "peaceful coexistence") yielded considerable benefits to the USSR. The disenchantment in the United States, however, and the debt problems in East Europe have raised serious questions as to whether the policy can continue to bring Moscow the profits necessary to make it worthwhile.

To date there is no significant evidence of a fundamental Soviet review of the current form of "peaceful coexistence." Andropov is pursuing, although somewhat more aggressively, the Brezhnev policy of trying to split Europe from the United States. The German elections of 1983, bringing a Christian Democratic Union/Christian Social Union coalition to power, were a setback; but the deployment of Intermediate-range Nuclear Forces (INF) in Europe has not yet been accomplished and, to all appearances, Andropov will do what he can to prevent or delay it. If the missiles are deployed, then the Politburo might well begin a basic review. The inclination to do so will be all the greater if economic interaction with the West is stymied or declining, due either to Western trade policies or Soviet lack of credits. The outcome of a basic review of strategy would not be apparent for several months, or even a year or two.

What could it yield? Continuation of détente is not to be discounted. Although détente's "high-yield" years may be past, severe tensions in central Europe would not offer greater yields and modest economic gains at the present level of trade are not to be lightly thrown away. In the Third World, there are no good reasons for Moscow to draw back, except here and there for tactical purposes. The re-arming of Syria and the greater Soviet military involvement there indicate a willingness to run quite high risks of an East-West confrontation. The Iraq-Iran war grinds on, supplied largely by the USSR and its surrogates, creating what Moscow may see as long-term "progressive developments" in Iraq and especially in Iran—the real strategic prize.

In Central America, the Soviets and Cubans seem committed to exploiting the large opening created by the Sandinist victory in Nicaragua. The danger in these two regions—the Middle East and Central America—is that Soviet success might create a backlash in the United States and a policy consensus that Soviet power projection is indeed endangering the Western international order. Thus far, however, Moscow has been able to prevent that, in part by working hard to keep the nuclear weapon and arms control issues at the center of public attention.

On the whole, the Brezhnev variant of "peaceful coexistence" still has much to offer, and its tactical and strategic "mobilism" probably will retain its appeal for Andropov. It has been an offensive strategy, and its gambits are still far from played out. The odds, therefore, seem to be on the side of a continuation of this policy, with many tactical shifts and changes as different situations require. The major worry Andropov must have is the possibility of a re-emergence (in the United States in particular, but also in Europe) of a broad-based public and media reaction against Soviet policy. If the attentive public and the media became convinced that assertive projection of Soviet power, rather than the nuclear issue, is the most pressing danger to peace and stability, then NATO might well be able to offset some of the Soviet conventional military advantage, and the United States would probably allocate much larger resources to competition with the Soviet Union in the Third World. That indeed would prompt a fundamental review of foreign policy in the Kremlin.

In sum, the prospects for the post-Brezhnev era seem to be sound and fury about domestic reform accompanied by little actual change. In external policy, we can expect threats to end détente while Moscow hangs on to its economic access to the industrial West and competes more aggressively in the Third World.

Notes

[1]See, e.g., Merle Fainsod, *How Russia Is Ruled*, Cambridge, MA, Harvard University Press, 1963, pp.180–84; and Leonard Schapiro, *The Communist Party of the Soviet Union*, New York, NY, Random House, 1960, pp. 548, 550–53.

[2]Schapiro, op. cit., pp. 243–50, and William E. Odom, "Sverdlov: Bolshevik Party Organizer," *Slavonic and East European Review* (London), July 1966, pp. 421–43.

[3]See Fainsod, op. cit., pp. 224, 515, 518.

[4]Michael Sadykiewicz, "Soviet Military Politics," *Survey* (London), No. 26, Winter 1982, p. 193, shows the Foreign Trade Ministry's intelligence role and its linkage to the Defense Council.

[5]Ibid., pp. 179–212; Victor Suvorov, *Inside the Soviet Army*, New York, NY, Macmillan, 1983; Sergei Freidzon, "Estimating the Current and Long-run Limitations of the Soviet Defense Burden," prepared for the Office of the Secretary of Defense, Net Assessment, Washington, DC, 1981, pp. 37–57; M. V. Zakharov, et al., *50 let Vooruzhënnykh sil SSSR* (50 Years of the Armed Forces of the USSR), Moscow, Voyenizdat, 1968; Edward L. Warner, III, *The Military in Contemporary Soviet Politics*, New York, NY, Praeger Special Studies, 1977, pp. 272–74. There has been a certain amount of confusion in Western literature on lineal descendency of the Defense Council. Sometimes, as in Warner's case, the STO is seen as the antecedent of the present-day Military Industrial Commission, sometimes of the Military Collegium. Neither is accurate. The Military Industrial Commission traces back through the state economic apparatus, while the Military Collegium is within the Ministry of Defense and traces back to the Revolutionary Military Council. The top-level military/economic/scientific infrastructure is more complex than I have portrayed here. Freidzon gives a good description, especially of the state side including Gosplan, the supply system, and the Council of Ministers. Sadykiewicz gives a particularly interesting analysis of the Defense Council's relationship to the rest of the state and party hierarchy.

[6]Sadykiewicz, loc. cit.

[7]See William E. Odom, "Who Controls Whom in Moscow?" *Foreign Policy* (Washington, DC), Summer 1975, esp., pp. 119–23.

[8]V. G. Kulikov, "The Brain of the Army," *Pravda* (Moscow), Nov. 13, 1974.

[9]See Seweryn Bialer, "The Harsh Decade: Soviet Politics in the 1980s," *Foreign Affairs* (New York, NY), Summer 1981, pp. 1012–15.

[10]See Adam Ulam, *The Rivals: America and Russia since World War II*, New York, NY, The Viking Press, 1971, pp. 299–340, for an account of Khrushchev's scheme to force Western recognition of East Germany.

[11]See Thomas W. Robinson, "The Sino-Soviet Border Conflict," in Stephen Kaplan, ed., *Diplomacy of Power*, Washington, DC, The Brookings Institution, 1981, p. 287.

[12]See *Soviet Military Power*, 2nd ed., Washington, DC, US Government Printing Office, 1983.

[13]See Gertrude Schroeder, "The Soviet Economy on a Treadmill of 'Reforms,'" US Congress, Joint Economic Committee, *Soviet Economy in a Time of Change*, Washington, DC, US Government Printing Office, 1979, Vol. 1, pp. 329–40.

[14]See Bergson, "Toward a New Growth Model," *Problems of Communism* (Washington, DC), March–April 1973, pp. 1–9.

[15]Myron Rush, "Guns over Growth in Soviet Policy," *International Security* (Cambridge, MA), Winter 1982–83, pp. 167–79.

[16]Karl-Eugene Wädekin, "Soviet Agriculture: Dependence on the West," *Foreign Affairs*, No. 60, Spring, 1982, pp. 882–903, provides an analysis of Soviet agrarian problems and performances.

[17]Ibid.

[18]Simis, *USSR: The Corrupt Society*. New York, NY, Simon and Shuster, 1982, pp. 53–60.

[19]See the lead editorials in *Pravda*, June 24, 1972 and *Krasnaya zvezda* (Moscow), June 29, 1972.

[20]See *Pravda*, and *Krasnaya zvezda*, Feb. 7, 1975.

[21]See Andrei Amalrik, *Notes of a Revolutionary*, trans. by Guy Daniels, New York, NY, Knopf, 1982.

[22]See William E. Odom, "A Dissenting View on the Group Approach to Soviet Politics," *World Politics* (Princeton, NJ), July 1976, pp. 542–67.

[23]See Fyodor I. Kushnirsky, *Soviet Economic Planning, 1965–1980*, Boulder, CO, Westview Press, 1982, for an insider's account of the search for efficiency while avoiding fundamental reform.

[24]See, e.g., Maurice Dobbs, *Soviet Economic Development since 1917*, New York, NY, International Publishers,1948; Harry Schwartz, *Russia's Soviet Economy*, Englewood Cliffs, NY. Prentice-Hill, 1950, p. 54; and Abram Bergson, ed., *Soviet Economic Growth*, Evanston, IL, Row, Peterson, 1953.

[25]Kushnirsky, op. cit., pp. 136 ff.

[26]See Dimitri Simes, "The Soviet Parallel Market," *Survey*, Summer 1975.

[27]See, e.g., Gregory Grossman, "The 'Second Economy' of the USSR," *Problems of Communism*, September-October 1977, pp. 25–40; and idem, "Notes on the Illegal Private Economy and Corruption," in US Congress, Joint Economic Committee, op. cit., Vol. 1, pp. 834–55.

[28]See *Soviet Military Power*, op. cit.

[29]See David Holloway, "Innovation in the Defense Sector," in R. Amann and J. Cooper, eds., *Industrial Innovation in the Soviet Union*, New Haven, CT, Yale University Press, 1982, pp. 303–21; and Sergei Freidzon, op. cit. Also Suvorov, op. cit.; and Karl F. Spielmann, "Defense Industrialists in the USSR," *Problems of Communism*, September–October 1976, pp. 52–69.

[30]See N. Suleiman, *Tyl i snabzheniye deyistvuyushchey armii* (Rear Services and Supply for a Combat Army), Moscow, Voyenizdat, 1927, Charts 31, 34; A. Vol'pe, "The Bases for Mobilizing Industry in the USSR," *Voyna i revolutsii* (Moscow), No. 7, November–December 1925, p. 75; M. V. Zakharov, "The Communist Party and the Technical Re-equipment of the Army and Navy during the Prewar Five-Year Plans," *Voyenno-istoricheskiy zhurnal* (Moscow), No. 2, 1971, pp. 3–12. Compare these with Holloway, loc. cit., Freidzon, loc. cit., and Sadykiewicz, loc. cit.

[31]See Holloway, loc. cit., p. 304.

[32]N. Ogarkov, "Defending Peaceful Endeavor," *Kommunist* (Moscow), No. 10, July 1981, pp. 80–91.

[33]I. B. Berkhin, *Voyennaya reforma v SSSR, 1924–26* (Military Reform in the USSR, 1924–26), Moscow, Voyenizdat, 1958, pp. 46–47, details the rationale of

the dramatic demobilization of the Red Army in 1921–23: to redirect resources toward technical modernization for a future larger force. Matthew A. Evangelista, "Stalin's Postwar Army Reappraised," *International Security*, Winter 1982–83, pp. 110–138, discusses the extent of Soviet demobilization in 1947–48. Oleg Penkovskiy, *The Penkovskiy Papers*, Garden City, NY, Doubleday, 1965, pp. 234–43, gives some insight into Khrushchev's manpower reductions in the late 1950s, which it can be inferred, were aimed at cost reductions and higher technical competence in the officer corps.

[34]See, e.g., Bialer, loc. cit.

[35]Jerry Hough, *Soviet Leadership in Transition*, Washington, DC. The Brookings Institution, 1980, pp. 127–30, 144 ff.

[36]John Lenczowski, *Soviet Perceptions of U.S. Foreign Policy*, Ithaca, NY, Cornell University Press, 1982.

[37]Hough, op. cit., p. 138.

[38]See also Rudolf L. Tökes, ed., *Dissent in the USSR*, Baltimore, MD, The Johns Hopkins University Press, 1975, p. 11, for an ideological spectrum of Soviet dissident views.

[39]*The Oak and the Calf*, New York, NY, Harper & Row, 1975.

[40]See William E. Odom, "The 'Militarization' of Soviet Society," *Problems of Communism*, September–October 1976, pp. 34–51.

[41]Peter Reddaway, ed., *Uncensored Russia*, London, Jonathan Cape, 1972, pp. 127 ff, 171 ff.

[42]Murray Feshbach, "Soviet Dynamics in the USSR," paper presented at the conference. "The Soviet Union in the 1980's," January 14, 1983, Washington, DC, sponsored by the US information Agency, with the Center for Strategic and International Studies, Georgetown University, and the Kennan Institute for Advanced Russian Studies, Woodrow Wilson Center for Advanced International Studies.

[43]See Ellen Jones, "Manning the Soviet Military," *International Security*, No. 7, Summer 1982, pp. 105–31.

[44]See his *Alcohol in the USSR: A Statistical Study*, Durham, NC, Duke Press Policy Studies, 1982.

[45]Simis, op. cit.

[46]Hedrick Smith, *The Russians*, New York, NY, Quadrangle, 1976, pp. 429–30; Robert G. Kaiser, *Russia*, New York, NY, Atheneum, 1976, pp. 166–68.

[47]Hough, op. cit.

[48]Bialer, loc. cit.

[49]See Amalrik, op. cit., for an account of the KGB effort to co-opt him that lasted until his final days in the USSR.

[50]Dobbs, op. cit., pp. 149–76.

[51]William E. Odom, *The Soviet Volunteers*, Princeton, NJ, Princeton University Press, 1973, pp. 264–328.

[52]In a larger sense we can establish connections between historically rooted domestic structural dynamics in the USSR and the likelihood of the USSR becoming a nonassertive status quo power. I have outlined the dynamics elsewhere and conclude that without fundamental structural change, the USSR cannot become a status quo power. See "Whither the Soviet Union?" *Washington Quarterly*, No. 4, Spring 1981. It is another question to determine at specific times whether domestic difficulties will temporarily reduce assertiveness in Soviet foreign policy behavior.